Criminal Justice in Action

10e

Larry K. Gaines

California State University, San Bernardino

Roger LeRoy Miller

Institute for University Studies, Arlington, Texas

Australia • Brazil • Mexico • Singapore • United Kingdom • United States

Criminal Justice in Action

10e

Criminal Justice in Action, **Tenth Edition**
Larry K. Gaines
Roger LeRoy Miller

Sr. Vice President, Higher Ed Product, Content, and Market Development: Erin Joyner

Sr. Product Director: Marta Lee-Perriard

Product Team Manager: Carolyn Henderson-Meier

Associate Content Developer: Jessica Alderman

Product Assistant: Megan Nauer

Sr. Marketing Manager: Mark Linton

Marketing Director: Kristen Hurd

Marketing Coordinator: Alexander Rainford

Sr. Content Project Manager: Martha Conway

Digital Content Specialist: Adam Hannah

Production Service: SPi Global

Sr. Designer: Helen Bruno

Text and Cover Designer: Jennifer Wahi

Intellectual Property Analyst: Jennifer Bowes

Intellectual Property Project Manager: Reba Frederics

Cover Images: statue of justice, sebra/Shutterstock.com; corridor of prison with cells, iStock.com/MoreISO; American flag, iStock.com/STILLFX; lights atop police car/emergency vehicle, iStock.com/artolympic; caution tape, iStock.com/TheaDesign; police lights, iStock.com/TheaDesign.

Design Elements: vintage paper texture, LeksusTuss/Shutterstock.com; policemen silhouettes, Darq/Shutterstock.com; justice icons, kuroksta/Shutterstock.com; orange background, Nik Merkulov/Shutterstock.com; crime icons, Rashad Ashurov/Shutterstock.com; distress texture, Miloje/Shutterstock.com; abstract, donatas1205/Shutterstock.com; business icons, rungrote/Shutterstock.com; chevrons, happykanppy/Shutterstock.com; urban texture, Miloje/Shutterstock.com; globe Earth, RedKoala/Shutterstock.com

For product information and technology assistance, contact us at
Cengage Customer & Sales Support, 1-800-354-9706

For permission to use material from this text or product, submit all requests online at **www.cengage.com/permissions**
Further permissions questions can be emailed to
permissionrequest@cengage.com

Library of Congress Control Number: 2017945205

ISBN: 978-1-337-55783-2

Cengage
20 Channel Center Street
Boston, MA 02210
USA

Cengage is a leading provider of customized learning solutions with employees residing in nearly 40 different countries and sales in more than 125 countries around the world. Find your local representative at **www.cengage.com**.

Cengage products are represented in Canada by Nelson Education, Ltd.

To learn more about Cengage platforms and services, register or access your online learning solution, or purchase materials for your course, visit **www.cengage.com**.

Printed at CLDPC, USA, 08-19

Contents in Brief

Preface xv

PART ONE: THE CRIMINAL JUSTICE SYSTEM

1 **Criminal Justice Today** 3
2 **Causes of Crime** 37
3 **The Crime Picture:** Offenders and Victims 69
4 **Inside Criminal Law** 99

PART TWO: THE POLICE AND LAW ENFORCEMENT

5 **Law Enforcement Today** 133
6 **Problems and Solutions in Modern Policing** 171
7 **Police and the Constitution:** The Rules of Law Enforcement 215

PART THREE: CRIMINAL COURTS

8 **Courts and the Quest for Justice** 253
9 **Pretrial Procedures:** The Adversary System in Action 283
10 **The Criminal Trial** 317
11 **Punishment and Sentencing** 351

PART FOUR: CORRECTIONS

12 **Probation, Parole, and Intermediate Sanctions** 391
13 **Prisons and Jails** 423
14 **The Prison Experience and Prisoner Reentry** 455

PART FIVE: SPECIAL ISSUES

15 **The Juvenile Justice System** 491
16 **Today's Challenges:** Cyber Crime, Security vs. Liberty, and White-Collar Crime 525

Appendix A: The Constitution of the United States A-1
Appendix B: Discretion in Action Case Studies B-1
Appendix C: Table of Cases C-1
Glossary G-1
Name Index N-1
Subject Index I-1

Contents

Preface xv

PART ONE: THE CRIMINAL JUSTICE SYSTEM 2

1 Criminal Justice Today 3
What Is Crime? 5
Determining Criminal Behavior 5
An Integrated Definition of Crime 6
Types of Crime 7
The Purpose of the Criminal Justice System 9
Maintaining Justice 10
Protecting Society 10
The Structure of the Criminal Justice System 11
The Importance of Federalism 11
The Criminal Justice Process 15
Discretion and Ethics 17
Informal Decision Making 17
Ethics and Justice 18
Criminal Justice Today 19
Crime and Law Enforcement: The Bottom Line 19
Gun Control Policy 22
The Changing Landscape of American Policing 24
Homeland Security and Domestic Terrorism 25
Prison Population Trends 27
Chapter One Appendix 35
How to Read Case Citations and Find Court Decisions 35

2 Causes of Crime 37
The Role of Theory 39
Correlation and Cause 39
Criminological Theories 39
The Brain and the Body 40
Crime and Free Will: Choice Theories of Crime 40
"Born Criminal": Biological and Psychological Theories of Crime 42

Bad Neighborhoods and Other Economic Disadvantages 46
Sociological Theories of Crime 46
Social Conflict Theories 49
Life Lessons and Criminal Behavior 51
Family, Friends, and the Media: Social Processes of Crime 51
Looking Back to Childhood: Life Course Theories of Crime 53
The Link between Drugs and Crime 56
The Criminology of Drug Use 57
Drug Addiction and Dependency 57
Crime and Health: The Landscape of Drug Abuse 58
Marijuana Law Trends 60
Criminology from Theory to Practice 61
Criminology and the Chronic Offender 61
Risk Assessment in Action 62

3 The Crime Picture: Offenders and Victims 69
Classification of Crimes 71
Civil Law and Criminal Law 71
Felonies and Misdemeanors 72
Mala in Se and *Mala Prohibita* 73
Measuring Crime in the United States 75
The Uniform Crime Report 75
The UCR: A Flawed Method? 77
The National Incident-Based Reporting System 78
Victim Surveys 78
Self-Reported Surveys 79
Victims of Crime 80
Legal Rights of Crime Victims 80
Victim Services 81
The Risks of Victimization 82

Crime Trends in the United States 84
Looking Good: Crime in the 1990s and 2000s 84
Crime, Race, and Poverty 86
Women and Crime 88
Mental Illness and Crime 90

4 Inside Criminal Law 99
The Development of American Criminal Law 101
English Common Law 101
Written Sources of American Criminal Law 101

The Purposes of Criminal Law 104
Protect and Punish: The Legal Function of the Law 104
Maintain and Teach: The Social Function of the Law 105
The Elements of a Crime 106
Criminal Act: *Actus Reus* 107
Mental State: *Mens Rea* 108
Concurrence 112
Causation 112
Attendant Circumstances 112
Harm 113
Defenses under Criminal Law 115
Excuse Defenses 115
Justification Defenses 119
Procedural Safeguards 122
The Bill of Rights 122
Due Process 124

PART TWO: THE POLICE AND LAW ENFORCEMENT 132

5 Law Enforcement Today 133
The Responsibilities of the Police 135
Enforcing Laws 135
Providing Services 136
Preventing Crime 137
Preserving the Peace 137
A Short History of the American Police 138
The Evolution of American Law Enforcement 138
Policing Today 141
Recruitment and Training: Becoming a Police Officer 145
Basic Requirements 146
Training 147
Women and Minorities in Policing Today 148
Antidiscrimination Law 148
Working Women: Gender and Law Enforcement 150
Minority Report: Race and Ethnicity in Law Enforcement 152
Public and Private Law Enforcement 153
Municipal Law Enforcement Agencies 154
Sheriffs and County Law Enforcement 154
State Police and Highway Patrols 155
Limited-Purpose Law Enforcement Agencies 156
Federal Law Enforcement Agencies 156
Private Security 162

6 Problems and Solutions in Modern Policing 171
The Role of Discretion in Policing 173
Justification for Police Discretion 173
Factors of Police Discretion 173
Police Organization and Field Operations 175
The Structure of the Police Department 175
Police on Patrol: The Backbone of the Department 177
Detective Investigations 179
Aggressive Investigation Strategies 179
Clearance Rates and Cold Cases 180
Forensic Investigations and DNA 181
Police Strategies: What Works 184
Calls for Service 185
Patrol Strategies 187
Smart Policing 188
Arrest Strategies 189
Community Policing and Problem Solving 191
"Us versus Them": Issues in Modern Policing 193
Police Subculture 194
The Physical Dangers of Police Work 195
Stress and the Mental Dangers of Police Work 196
Police Use of Force 197
Police Misconduct and Ethics 200
Police Corruption 200
Police Accountability 202
Issues of Bias in Policing 204
Ethics in Law Enforcement 206

7 Police and the Constitution: The Rules of Law Enforcement 215

The Fourth Amendment 217
Reasonableness 217
Probable Cause 217
The Exclusionary Rule 219

Lawful Searches and Seizures 220
The Role of Privacy in Searches 221
Search and Seizure Warrants 222
Searches and Seizures without a Warrant 224
Searches of Automobiles 226
The Plain View Doctrine 228
Electronic Surveillance 229
Cell Phones and the Fourth Amendment 230

Stops and Frisks 232
The Elusive Definition of Reasonable Suspicion 232
A Stop 233
A Frisk 233
Race and Reasonable Suspicion 234

Arrests 235
Elements of an Arrest 235
Arrests with a Warrant 236
Arrests without a Warrant 238

The Interrogation Process and *Miranda* 239
The Legal Basis for *Miranda* 239
When a *Miranda* Warning Is Required 241
When a *Miranda* Warning Is Not Required 241
The Weakening of *Miranda* 243
False Confessions 243

The Identification Process 245
Essential Procedures 245
Nontestimonial Evidence 246

PART THREE: CRIMINAL COURTS 252

8 Courts and the Quest for Justice 253

Functions of the Courts 255
Due Process and Crime Control in the Courts 255
The Rehabilitation Function 256
The Bureaucratic Function 256

The Basic Principles of the American Judicial System 256
Jurisdiction 257
Trial and Appellate Courts 259
The Dual Court System 259

State Court Systems 260
Courts of Limited Jurisdiction 261
Trial Courts of General Jurisdiction 262
State Courts of Appeals 262

The Federal Court System 263
U.S. District Courts 263
U.S. Courts of Appeals 263
The United States Supreme Court 263

Judges in the Court System 267
The Roles and Responsibilities of Trial Judges 267
Appointment of Judges 269
Election of Judges 269
Judicial Decision Making 270
Diversity on the Bench 272

The Courtroom Work Group 274
Members of the Courtroom Work Group 274
Formation of the Courtroom Work Group 275
The Judge in the Courtroom Work Group 275
The Adversary System 276

9 Pretrial Procedures: The Adversary System in Action 283

The Prosecution 285
Prosecutorial Duties 285
The Office of the Prosecutor 285
The Prosecutor as Elected Official 286
The Prosecutor as Crime Fighter 287

The Defense Attorney 288
The Responsibilities of the Defense Attorney 289
Defending the Guilty 289
The Public Defender 289
The Attorney-Client Relationship 292
Attorney-Client Privilege 293

Pretrial Detention 294
The Initial Appearance 294
Bail and Pretrial Release 296
Alternatives to Bail 298

Establishing Probable Cause 299
The Preliminary Hearing 299
The Grand Jury 300

The Prosecutorial Screening Process 301
Case Attrition 301
Prosecutorial Charging and the Defense Attorney 304

Pleading Guilty 305
   Plea Bargaining in the Criminal Justice System **305**
   Motivations for Plea Bargaining **306**
   Plea Bargaining and the Adversary System **307**
   Going to Trial **310**

10 The Criminal Trial 317
Special Features of Criminal Trials 319
   A "Speedy" Trial **319**
   The Role of the Jury **320**
   The Privilege against Self-Incrimination **321**
   The Presumption of Innocence **322**
   A Strict Standard of Proof **322**
Jury Selection 323
   Initial Steps: The Master Jury List and *Venire* **323**
   Voir Dire **325**
   Race and Gender Issues in Jury Selection **327**
   Alternate Jurors **329**
The Trial 329
   Opening Statements **330**
   The Role of Evidence **330**
   The Prosecution's Case **333**
   Cross-Examination **334**
   Motion for a Directed Verdict **336**
   The Defendant's Case **336**
   Rebuttal and Surrebuttal **337**
   Closing Arguments **338**
The Final Steps of the Trial and Postconviction Procedures 339
   Jury Instructions **339**

   Jury Deliberation **339**
   The Verdict **340**
   Appeals **341**
   Wrongful Convictions **342**

11 Punishment and Sentencing 351
The Purpose of Sentencing 353
   Retribution **353**
   Deterrence **353**
   Incapacitation **355**
   Rehabilitation **356**
   Restorative Justice **356**
The Structure of Sentencing 358
   Legislative Sentencing Authority **358**
   Administrative Sentencing Authority **360**
   Judicial Sentencing Authority **360**
   The Sentencing Process **363**
   Factors of Sentencing **364**
Inconsistencies in Sentencing 365
   Sentencing Disparity **366**
   Sentencing Discrimination **366**
Sentencing Reform 369
   Sentencing Guidelines **369**
   Mandatory Sentencing Guidelines **371**
   Victim Impact Evidence **373**
Capital Punishment 374
   Methods of Execution **375**
   The Death Penalty and the Supreme Court **375**
   Death Penalty Sentencing **377**
   Debating the Sentence of Death **380**
   The Future of the Death Penalty **382**

PART FOUR: CORRECTIONS 390

12 Probation, Parole, and Intermediate Sanctions 391
The Justifications for Community Corrections 393
   Reintegration **393**
   Diversion **393**
   The "Low-Cost Alternative" **394**
Probation: Doing Time in the Community 395
   Sentencing and Probation **395**
   Conditions of Probation **397**
   The Supervisory Role of the Probation Officer **398**

   Revocation of Probation **400**
   Does Probation Work? **402**
The Parole Picture 403
   Comparing Probation and Parole **404**
   Discretionary Release **406**
   Parole Guidelines **408**
   Victims' Rights and Parole **408**
Intermediate Sanctions 409
   Judicially Administered Sanctions **409**
   Day Reporting Centers **412**
   Intensive Supervision Probation **412**
   Shock Incarceration **412**
   Home Confinement and Electronic Monitoring **413**
   Widening the Net **415**
The Paradox of Community Corrections 416

13 Prisons and Jails 423

A Short History of American Prisons 425
  English Roots 425
  Walnut Street Prison: The First Penitentiary 425
  The Great Penitentiary Rivalry: Pennsylvania versus New York 426
  The Reformers and the Progressives 427
  The Reassertion of Punishment 427
  The Role of Prisons in Modern Society 428

Prison Organization and Management 429
  Prison Administration 430
  Types of Prisons 432

Inmate Population Trends 437
  Factors in Prison Population Growth 437
  Decarceration 438
  The Consequences of America's High Rates of Incarceration 440

Private Prisons 441
  Why Privatize? 441
  The Argument against Private Prisons 442
  The Future of Private Prisons 443

Jails 444
  The Jail Population 444
  Jail Administration 446
  New-Generation Jails 448

14 The Prison Experience and Prisoner Reentry 455

Prison Culture 457
  Adapting to Prison Society 458
  Who Is in Prison? 458
  Rehabilitation and Prison Programs 460

Prison Violence 462
  Violence in Prison Culture 462
  Riots 463
  Prison Rape 463
  Issues of Race and Ethnicity 464
  Prison Gangs and Security Threat Groups (STGs) 465

Correctional Officers and Discipline 467
  Prison Employment 468
  Discipline 469
  Female Correctional Officers 471
  Protecting Prisoners' Rights 472

Inside a Women's Prison 473
  Characteristics of Female Inmates 474
  The Motherhood Problem 475
  The Culture of Women's Prisons 475

Return to Society 476
  Types of Prison Release 477
  The Challenges of Reentry 477
  The Special Case of Sex Offenders 481

PART FIVE: SPECIAL ISSUES 490

15 The Juvenile Justice System 491

The Evolution of American Juvenile Justice 493
  The Child-Saving Movement 493
  The Illinois Juvenile Court 493
  Status Offending 494
  Juvenile Delinquency 494
  Constitutional Protections and the Juvenile Court 495

Determining Delinquency Today 496
  The Age Question 497
  The Culpability Question 497

Trends in Juvenile Delinquency 499
  Delinquency by the Numbers 499

  School Violence 501
  Bullying 502

Factors in Juvenile Delinquency 503
  The Age-Crime Relationship 504
  Substance Abuse 504
  Child Abuse and Neglect 505
  Gangs 505

First Contact: The Police and Pretrial Procedures 507
  Police Discretion and Juvenile Crime 507
  Intake 509
  Pretrial Diversion 510
  Transfer to Adult Court 510
  Detention 512

Trying and Punishing Juveniles 513
  Adjudication 514
  Disposition 514
  Juvenile Corrections 514

16 Today's Challenges: Cyber Crime, Security vs. Liberty, and White-Collar Crime **525**

Cyber Crime 527
Crime and the Internet **527**
Cyber Trespass **528**
Cyber Deception and Theft **530**
Cyber Violence **533**
Fighting Cyber Crime **535**

Security vs. Liberty 539
National Security and Privacy **539**
Mass Surveillance **542**
National Security and Speech **544**

White-Collar Crime 547
What Is White-Collar Crime? **547**
Regulating and Policing White-Collar Crime **548**

Appendix A: The Constitution of the United States A-1
Appendix B: Discretion in Action Case Studies B-1
Appendix C: Table of Cases C-1
Glossary G-1
Name Index N-1
Subject Index I-1

Special Features

CHAPTER OPENING STORIES

Ch 1   When tweeting is a crime
Trolling Trouble   **4**

Ch 2   The lead-up to an airport shooting
Excess Baggage   **38**

Ch 3   Sexual assault on college campuses
Statistical Proof?   **70**

Ch 4   Are dealers responsible for overdose deaths?
"Death by Dealer"   **100**

Ch 5   Turning back terrorism at Ohio State
Local Hero   **134**

Ch 6   Body-worn cameras and deadly police force
In a Split Second . . .   **172**

Ch 7   The United States Supreme Court overturns a drug bust
Eight Long Minutes   **216**

Ch 8   Is encouraging suicide via social media a crime?
Text Message   **254**

Ch 9   Prosecutors drop the ball in a Miami murder case
Puzzling Evidence   **284**

Ch 10   Can a lone juror deny justice?
The Holdout   **318**

Ch 11   Protesting light sentences for sex crimes
Questionable Judgment   **352**

Ch 12   Probation or prison for smuggling 1.3 pounds of cocaine?
A Significant Departure   **392**

Ch 13   The movement to reduce America's massive inmate population
Downsizing?   **424**

Ch 14   Inmate labor unites
Two Strikes   **456**

Ch 15   Should juvenile murderers spend the rest of their lives behind bars?
Bad Thing. Good Kid?   **492**

Ch 16   Privacy predators online
"Revenge Porn"   **526**

COMPARATIVE CRIMINAL JUSTICE

The German Way Ch 1: **24**

A Clean, Well-Lighted Place (Canada) Ch 2: **60**

The New Zealand Model Ch 3: **74**

Speech Crime (South Africa) Ch 4: **114**

Conflict Avoidance (Scotland) Ch 6: **199**

The PEACE Method (England) Ch 7: **245**

Back to School (France) Ch 8: **272**

Japan's All-Powerful Prosecutors Ch 9: **302**

Presumed Guilty (Mexico) Ch 10: **323**

"Forgotten Human Waste" (The Netherlands) Ch 11: **355**

Swedish Day-Fines Ch 12: **410**

Prison Lite (Norway) Ch 13: **437**

The Great Firewall of China Ch 16: **536**

MYTH VS REALITY

"Black on Black" Violence   Ch 3: **86**

Are Too Many Criminals Found Not Guilty by Reason of Insanity?   Ch 4: **117**

Women Make Bad Cops   Ch 5: **151**

Consent to Search Automobiles   Ch 7: **225**

Rape Shield Laws   Ch 10: **334**

Modern-Day Debtor's Prisons?   Ch 12: **401**

Does Putting Criminals in Prison Reduce Crime?   Ch 13: **440**

Residency Restrictions   Ch 14: **482**

CAREERS IN CJ

F. W. Gill, Gang Investigator   Ch 1: **11**

Robert Agnew, Criminologist   Ch 2: **49**

Anne Seymour, National Victim Advocate   Ch 3: **87**

Diana Tabor, Crime Scene Photographer   Ch 4: **121**

Arnold E. Bell, Federal Bureau of Investigation (FBI) Agent   Ch 5: **160**

Martha Blake, Forensic Scientist   Ch 6: **182**

William Howe, Police Detective   Ch 7: **218**

Shawn Davis, Bailiff   Ch 8: **274**

Annika Carlsten, Public Defender   Ch 9: **292**

Collins E. Ijoma, Trial Court Administrator   Ch 10: **328**

Ellen Kalama Clark, Superior Court Judge   Ch 11: **361**

Peggy McCarthy, Lead Probation Officer   Ch 12: **399**

Berry Larson, Prison Warden   Ch 13: **431**

Julie Howe, Halfway House Program Manager   Ch 14: **480**

Carl McCullough, Sr., Resident Youth Worker   Ch 15: **516**

Paul Morris, Customs and Border Protection Agent   Ch 16: **546**

LANDMARK CASES

Brown v. Entertainment Merchants Association (EMA) Ch 2: **53**

Maryland v. King Ch 6: **185**

Miranda v. Arizona Ch 7: **240**

Roper v. Simmons Ch 11: **379**

Brown v. Plata Ch 14: **460**

In re Gault Ch 15: **496**

MASTERING CONCEPTS

Crime Control Model versus Due Process Model Ch 1: **20**

The Causes of Crime Ch 2: **55**

Civil Law versus Criminal Law Ch 3: **73**

The Elements of a Crime Ch 4: **107**

Affirmative Action in Law Enforcement Ch 5: **149**

The Difference between a Stop and an Arrest Ch 7: **236**

The Selection of State and Federal Judges Ch 8: **271**

Sentencing Philosophies Ch 11: **357**

The Bifurcated Death Penalty Process Ch 11: **377**

Probation versus Parole Ch 12: **405**

The Main Differences between Prisons and Jails Ch 13: **444**

The Juvenile Justice System versus the Criminal Justice System Ch 15: **513**

CJ & TECHNOLOGY

Facial Recognition Software Ch 1: **21**

Neurocriminology Ch 2: **44**

Statewide Automated Victim Information Notification Program (SAVIN) Ch 3: **82**

Unmanned Aerial Vehicles (UAVs) Ch 4: **105**

High-Tech Cops Ch 5: **140**

911 Apps Ch 6: **187**

Tactical Camera Spheres Ch 7: **229**

Lie Detection in Court Ch 8: **268**

Untested Rape Kits Ch 9: **288**

Wireless Devices in the Courtroom Ch 10: **340**

Global Positioning System (GPS) Ch 12: **415**

Video Visits Ch 13: **443**

Contraband Cell Phones Ch 14: **467**

Gunshot Detectors in Schools Ch 15: **502**

Hacking the "Internet of Things" Ch 16: **530**

DISCRETION IN ACTION

The "Sexting" Scandal Ch 1: **18**

Prosecuting Domestic Violence Ch 3: **90**

Murder or Manslaughter? Ch 4: **110**

Handle with Care Ch 5: **136**

Deadly Force Ch 6: **205**

A Valid Pretext? Ch 7: **228**

The Stolen Valor Act Ch 8: **265**

The Repugnant Client Ch 9: **290**

A Battered Woman Ch 9: **304**

Shadow of a Doubt? Ch 10: **337**

Pledge Night Ch 11: **362**

Cause for Compassion? Ch 12: **408**

"Downing a Duck" Ch 14: **470**

Juvenile Drunk Driving Ch 15: **511**

Facebook Fantasy? Ch 16: **534**

POLICY MATTERS

Concealed Carry on Campus Ch 1: **30**

Legalizing Marijuana Ch 2: **63**

Criminalizing Homelessness Ch 3: **92**

"Stand Your Ground" Laws Ch 4: **127**

Local Police and Immigration Law Ch 5: **164**

Releasing Police Videos Ch 6: **208**

Regulating Stops and Frisks Ch 7: **247**

Tribal Jurisdiction Ch 8: **278**

For-Profit Bail Ch 9: **311**

Statutes of Limitations for Sex Crimes Ch 10: **345**

Death Penalty Reform in California Ch 11: **384**

Civil Forfeiture Ch 12: **417**

The Right to Vote Ch 13: **449**

Solitary Confinement Ch 14: **484**

Police in School Ch 15: **518**

Encryption Battles Ch 16: **551**

For the past twenty years, the authors of the best-selling *Criminal Justice in Action* series have engaged students with the dramatic shifts that mark the field. From historic reductions in crime rates to exciting innovations in policing strategies to monumental changes brought about by homeland security concerns—this introductory textbook has used facts, analyses, and real-life examples to energize this most relevant of disciplines.

As we enter our third decade with this Tenth Edition, our coverage of crime and justice continues to expand. Buttressed by the input of the many professors who have adopted this textbook, *Criminal Justice in Action* offers a kaleidoscope of online activities. Along with the widely diverse inventory of critical thinking exercises within the pages of the text, these activities allow students to see criminal justice not merely as a subject to be learned, but as an essential American institution to be contemplated, critiqued, and held to its highest ideals.

Ethics, Discretion, and Public Policy

Criminal Justice in Action provides students not only with the tools to understand how the criminal justice system *does* work, but also the opportunity to express their opinions on how the criminal justice system *should* work. This opportunity presents itself primarily in the following three components, the first of which is original to the Tenth Edition:

- **Policy Matters.** This new chapter-ending feature gives students the opportunity to "dig deeper" into a policy issue introduced earlier in the text. The *Policy Matters* feature includes two parts. First, an in-depth summary of the controversy surrounding the issue. Second, several review questions and a writing assignment that requires online research of a specific aspect of the policy under review. Subjects covered include handguns on college campuses (Chapter 1), the role of local police in enforcing immigration law (Chapter 6), and statutes of limitations for sex crimes (Chapter 10).
- **Ethics Challenges.** Each chapter contains three of these short challenges, placed at the end of a section.

Besides reinforcing an important concept from that section, the challenges allow students to explore their own values in the context of the criminal justice system. Subjects covered include the use of deception during police interrogations (Chapter 7), judicial campaign contributions (Chapter 8), and the ability of juvenile suspects to understand their *Miranda* rights (Chapter 15).

- **Discretion in Action.** As in previous editions, this feature asks students to step into the shoes of a criminal justice professional or other CJ participant and make a difficult decision. Nine new *Discretion in Action* features drive home the pivotal role that discretion plays in the criminal justice system, covering topics such as prosecuting domestic violence (Chapter 3), police use of deadly force (Chapter 6), and the criminal justice system's response to violent threats made online (Chapter 16).

This expanded coverage of ethics, policy, and discretion allows us to present a *panoramic* view of important criminal justice issues. Chapter 6, for example, opens with an account of the role that body-camera videos played in the trial of two Albuquerque, New Mexico, police officers charged with unlawfully killing a homeless man. Throughout the chapter, issues surrounding body-worn cameras are revisited in the context of police use-of-force, police accountability, and ethical decision making in law enforcement. Finally, the chapter-closing *Policy Matters* feature addresses the issue of whether, when, and how law enforcement should release videos that capture police-citizen interactions to the public.

Careers in Criminal Justice

We are well aware that many students using this text are interested in a criminal justice career. Consequently, as in previous editions, each chapter of *Criminal Justice in Action, Tenth Edition*, includes a **Careers in CJ** feature in which a criminal justice practitioner presents a personal account of his or her profession. These features also include a **Social Media Career Tip**, designed to help students succeed in today's difficult labor market by successfully navigating the opportunities and pitfalls of searching for employment online.

To this same end, each chapter of the Tenth Edition also includes a **new** feature entitled **Getting LinkedIn**. These items focus on professions such as computer forensics, victim advocacy, or homeland security, providing students with information on how to best research the profession while visiting the popular business-oriented social networking website.

Further Changes to the Tenth Edition

Each chapter in the Tenth Edition begins with a new "ripped from the headlines" vignette that introduces the themes to be covered in the pages that follow. Furthermore, the text continues to reflect the ever-changing nature of our topic, with hundreds of new references to **research involving crime and criminal behavior** and **real-life examples describing actual crimes.** The Tenth Edition also includes dozens of **new features and figures,** as well as **discussions of every relevant United States Supreme Court decision** that has been handed down since the previous edition.

Concentrated Critical Thinking

As with previous editions, the Tenth Edition of *Criminal Justice in Action* focuses on developing critical thinking. Almost every feature and photo caption in the textbook includes a critical thinking question, and students are provided with five additional such questions at the end of each chapter. Chapter-opening vignettes are followed by three critical analysis questions, which relate back to the vignette and introduce themes important to the upcoming chapter.

At the beginning of each chapter, students are also introduced to up to ten **learning objectives (LOs)** for that chapter. For example, in Chapter 8, "Courts and the Quest for Justice," Learning Objective 3 (LO3) asks students to "Explain the difference between trial and appellate courts." The area of text that furnishes the information is marked with an LO3 graphic, and, finally, the correct answer is found in the chapter-ending materials. This continuous active learning will greatly expand students' understanding of dozens of crucial criminal justice topics.

Chapter-by-Chapter Organization of the Text

This edition's sixteen chapters blend the principles of criminal justice with current research and high-interest examples of what is happening in the world of crime and crime prevention right now. Each chapter is concisely summarized below.

Part 1: The Criminal Justice System

Chapter 1 provides an introduction to the criminal justice system's three major institutions: law enforcement, the courts, and corrections. The chapter also answers conceptual questions such as "what is crime?" and "what are the values of the American criminal justice system?"

Chapter 2 focuses on criminology, giving students insight into why crime occurs before shifting their attention toward how society goes about fighting it. The chapter addresses the most widely accepted and influential criminological hypotheses, including choice theories, trait theories, sociological theories, social process theories, social conflict theories, and life course theories.

Chapter 3 furnishes students with an understanding of two areas fundamental to criminal justice: (1) the practical definitions of crime, such as the difference between felonies and misdemeanors and different degrees of criminal conduct, and (2) the various modes of measuring crime, including the FBI's Uniform Crime Reports and the U.S. Department of Justice's National Crime Victimization Survey.

Chapter 4 lays the foundation of criminal law. It addresses constitutional law, statutory law, and other sources of American criminal law before shifting its focus to the legal framework that allows the criminal justice system to determine and punish criminal guilt.

Part 2: The Police and Law Enforcement

Chapter 5 acts as an introduction to law enforcement in the United States today. This chapter offers a detailed description of the country's numerous local, state, and federal law enforcement agencies and examines the responsibilities and duties that come with a career in law enforcement.

Chapter 6 puts students on the streets and gives them a gritty look at the many challenges of being a law enforcement officer. It starts with a discussion of the importance of discretion in law enforcement and then moves on to policing strategies and issues in modern policing, such as use of force, corruption, and the "thin blue line."

Chapter 7 examines the sometimes uneasy relationship between law enforcement and the U.S. Constitution by explaining the rules of being a police officer. Particular emphasis is placed on the Fourth, Fifth, and Sixth Amendments, giving students an understanding of crucial concepts such as probable cause, reasonableness, and custodial interrogation.

Part 3: Criminal Courts

Chapter 8 takes a big-picture approach in describing the American court system, giving students an overview of the basic principles of our judicial system, the state and federal court systems, and the role of judges in the criminal justice system.

Chapter 9 provides students with a rundown of pretrial procedures and highlights the role that these procedures play in America's adversary system. Thus, pretrial procedures such as establishing bail and plea bargaining are presented as part of the larger "battle" between the prosecution and the defense.

Chapter 10 puts the student in the courtroom and gives her or him a strong understanding of the steps of the criminal trial. The chapter also attempts to answer the fascinating but ultimately frustrating question, "Are criminal trials in this country fair?"

Chapter 11 links the many different punishment options for those who have been convicted of a crime with the theoretical justifications for those punishments. The chapter also examines punishment in the policy context, exploring the consequences of several decades' worth of "get tough" strategies and investigating recent trends in a more lenient direction.

Part 4: Corrections

Chapter 12 makes an important point, and one that is often overlooked in the larger discussion of the American corrections system: not all of those who are punished need to be placed behind bars. This chapter explains the community corrections options, from probation to parole to intermediate sanctions such as intensive supervision and home confinement.

Chapter 13 focuses on prisons and jails. The phenomenon known as "mass incarceration" has pushed these institutions to the forefront of the criminal justice system, and this chapter explores the various issues—such as overcrowding and the emergence of private prisons—that have resulted from a prison population boom that is only now shoing signs of subsiding.

Chapter 14 is another example of our efforts to get students "into the action" of the criminal justice system, this time putting them in the uncomfortable position of being behind bars. It also answers the question, "What happens when the inmate is released back into society?"

Part 5: Special Issues

Chapter 15 examines the juvenile justice system, giving students a comprehensive description of the path taken by delinquents from first contact with police to trial and punishment. The chapter contains a strong criminological component as well, scrutinizing the various theories of why certain juveniles turn to delinquency and what steps society can take to stop them from doing so before it is "too late."

Chapter 16 concludes the text by taking an expanded look at three crucial criminal justice topics:

1. Cyber crime,
2. Privacy in the age of terrorism, and
3. White-collar crime.

Special Features

Supplementing the main text of *Criminal Justice in Action, Tenth Edition*, are more than one hundred eye-catching, instructive, and penetrating special features. These features have been designed to enhance the student's understanding of a particular criminal justice issue.

Careers in CJ: As stated before, many students reading this book are planning a career in criminal justice. We have provided them with an insight into some of these careers by offering first-person accounts of what it is like to work as a criminal justice professional. Each Career in CJ feature also includes a **Social Media Career Tip** to help students succeed in today's competitive labor market for criminal justice professionals.

Mastering Concepts: Some criminal justice topics require additional explanation before they become crystal clear in the minds of students. This feature helps students to master many of the essential concepts in the textbook.

Discretion in Action: This feature puts students in the position of a criminal justice actor in a hypothetical case or situation that is based on a real-life event. The facts of the case or situation are presented with alternative possible outcomes, and the student is asked to take the part of the criminal justice professional or lay participant and make a decision. Students can then consult Appendix B at the end of the text to learn what actually happened in the offered scenario.

CJ & Technology: Advances in technology are constantly transforming the face of criminal justice. In these features, which appear in nearly every chapter, students learn of one such emergent technology and are asked to critically evaluate its effects.

Comparative Criminal Justice: The world offers a dizzying array of different criminal customs and codes, many of which are in stark contrast to those accepted in the United States. This feature provides dramatic and sometimes perplexing examples of foreign criminal justice practices in order to give students a better understanding of our domestic ways.

Landmark Cases: Rulings by the United States Supreme Court have shaped every area of the criminal justice system. In this feature, students learn about and analyze the most influential of these cases.

Myth vs Reality: Nothing endures like a good myth. In this feature, we try to dispel some of the more enduring myths in the criminal justice system while at the same time asking students to think critically about their consequences.

Extensive Study Aids

Criminal Justice in Action, Tenth Edition, includes a number of pedagogical devices designed to complete the student's active learning experience. These devices include the following:

- Concise **chapter outlines** appear at the beginning of each chapter. The outlines give students an idea of what to expect in the pages ahead, as well as a quick source of review when needed.

- Dozens of **key terms** and a **running glossary** focus students' attention on major concepts and help them master the vocabulary of criminal justice. The chosen terms are boldfaced in the text, allowing students to notice their importance without breaking the flow of reading. On the same page that a key term is highlighted, a margin note provides a succinct definition of the term. For further reference, a glossary at the end of the text provides a full list of all the key terms and their definitions. This edition includes **nearly twenty new key terms.**

- Each chapter has at least six **figures**, which include graphs, charts, and other forms of colorful art that reinforce a point made in the text. This edition includes **twenty new figures.**

- Hundreds of **photographs** add to the overall readability and design of the text. Each photo has a caption, and most of these captions include a critical-thinking question dealing with the topic at hand. This edition includes nearly one hundred new photos.

Acknowledgments

Throughout the creation of the ten editions of this text, we have been aided by hundreds of experts in various criminal justice fields and by professors throughout the country, as well as by numerous students who have used the text. We sincerely thank all who participated in the revision of *Criminal Justice in Action*. We believe that the Tenth Edition is even more responsive to the needs of today's criminal justice instructors and students alike because we have taken into account the constructive comments and criticisms of our reviewers and the helpful suggestions of our survey respondents.

We continue to appreciate the extensive research efforts of Shawn G. Miller and the additional legal assistance of William Eric Hollowell. Product Manager Carolyn Henderson-Meier supplied crucial guidance to the project through her suggestions and recommendations. At the production end, we feel fortunate to have enjoyed the services of our content project manager, Martha Conway, who oversaw virtually all aspects of this book. Additionally, we wish to thank the designer of this new edition, Jennifer Wahi, who has created what we believe to be the most dazzling and student-friendly design of any text in the field. We are also thankful for the services of all those at SPi Global who worked on the Tenth Edition, particularly Ann Borman and Alison Kuzmickas. The eagle eyes of Beverly Peavler and Denne Wesolowski, who shared the duties of copyediting and proofreading, were invaluable.

A special word of thanks must also go to those responsible for creating the MindTap that accompanies *Criminal Justice in Action*, including content developer Jessica Alderman. We are also grateful to Jessica for ensuring the timely publication of supplements, along with content vendor services manager Miranda Marshall. A final thanks to all of the great people in marketing who helped to get the word out about the book, including marketing manager Mark Linton, who has been tireless in his attention to this project.

Any criminal justice text has to be considered a work in progress. We know that there are improvements that we can make. Therefore, write us with any suggestions that you may have.

L. K. G.

R. L. M.

This book is dedicated to my good friend and colleague, Lawrence Walsh, of the Lexington, Kentucky Police Department. When I was a rookie, he taught me about policing. When I became a researcher, he taught me about the practical applications of knowledge. He is truly an inspiring professional in our field.

L.K.G.

To Annie Katz,

Thanks for continuing to amaze me with your new work.

R.L.M.

Criminal Justice Today

To target your study and review, look for these numbered Learning Objective icons throughout the chapter.

Chapter Outline		Corresponding Learning Objectives
What Is Crime?	**1**	Describe the two most common models of how society determines which acts are criminal.
	2	Define *crime*.
The Purpose of the Criminal Justice System	**3**	Explain two main purposes of the criminal justice system.
The Structure of the Criminal Justice System	**4**	Outline the three levels of law enforcement.
	5	List the essential elements of the corrections system.
Discretion and Ethics	**6**	Explain the difference between the formal and informal criminal justice processes.
	7	Define *ethics*, and describe the role that it plays in discretionary decision making.
Criminal Justice Today	**8**	Contrast the crime control and due process models.
	9	Explain how background checks, in theory, protect the public from firearm-related violence.
	10	Describe the defining aspects of a terrorist act, and identify one common misperception concerning domestic terrorism.

Trolling Trouble

▲ Although a significant number of violent threats are made on Twitter and other social media platforms, these threats rarely result in criminal charges. PiXXart/Shutterstock.com

On March 17, 2017, law enforcement agents arrested John Rivello for sending a tweet. Several months earlier, journalist Kurt Eichenwald, seeing that someone using the account @jew_goldstein had replied to one of his Twitter posts with a moving image tweet known as a GIF, clicked on the file. The message, "You deserve a seizure for your posts," appeared, along with a blinding strobe light. Eichenwald, who suffers from a brain disorder called epilepsy, immediately fell to the ground and became unresponsive. He lost feeling in his left hand and had trouble speaking for several weeks following the episode.

Searching the suspect's Twitter account, investigators from the Federal Bureau of Investigation found a great deal of evidence that Rivello intended to injure Eichenwald. Rivello had sent numerous messages to other Twitter users about his victim, including one that said, "I know that he has epilepsy" and another expressing the hope that the strobe light GIF "sends [Eichenwald] into a seizure."

Rivello was charged with criminal cyberstalking with intent to kill or cause bodily harm—a rare instance in which an online violent threat triggered a response from the criminal justice system. Millions of such threats are made each year via social media, the difference being that most of these tweets are intended to cause emotional distress rather than the physical damage done to Eichenwald.

Under certain circumstances, however, the practice known as "trolling" can lead to prosecution. Earlier in 2017, Kyler Schmitz, outraged over what he saw as this country's lax attitude toward firearm ownership, sent a number of angry tweets to pro-gun politicians. "I am literally going to buy a gun shoot you in the face I watch your brains splat [sic]," he tweeted at Senator Roy Blount, a Republican from Missouri. Schmitz was eventually charged with making threatening interstate communications and spent two weeks in jail. "I wanted to get a rise," Schmitz said, defending his actions. "I wanted to make a point that I thought was civil disobedience and nonviolent, because I wasn't [planning to hurt anyone]."

FOR CRITICAL ANALYSIS

1. Compare the actions of John Rivello and Kyler Schmitz described above. How are they similar? How are they different? Should Rivello and Schmitz have been punished for their online activity? Explain your answers.

2. Suppose someone tweets to a female politician, "I'm going to rape your ass at 8 P.M. and put the video all over." Given what happened to Schmitz, should the person who sent this message be arrested? Why or why not?

3. Does the fact that Schmitz did not plan to shoot Senator Blount mean he should not have been arrested? In other words, to what extent should the intent of the person who sends a violent threat online matter?

What Is Crime?

Generally speaking, the criminal justice system does not punish Internet speech, no matter how violent, threatening, or distasteful. "People have a right to say what they want. No matter how bad it is and how hurtful it is to other people," says a detective with the Los Angeles Sheriff's Department who investigates bias-related crimes.[1] That right is protected by the First Amendment of the United States Constitution, which gives Americans the freedom to express themselves—even in a hateful or violent manner—without having to worry about being censored by the government.

This right does, however, have a limitation. If speech reasonably causes a person to fear that she or he is in imminent danger from the speaker, that speech is not constitutionally protected.[2] This "true threat" exception allowed law enforcement officials to arrest Kyler Schmitz, whose tweets crossed the line between protected and unprotected speech. As this example shows, a *crime* is not simply an act that seems dishonest or dangerous or taboo. A **crime** is a wrong against society that is *proclaimed by law* and that, if committed under specific circumstances, is punishable by the criminal justice system.

Determining Criminal Behavior

One problem with the definition of crime just provided is that it obscures the complex nature of societies. A society is not static—it evolves and changes, and its concept of criminality evolves and changes as well. Several years ago, for example, the United States Supreme Court ruled that, in "true threat" cases, courts must take into account the motive of the person making the alleged threat.[3] This decision suggests that Kyler Schmitz may not have committed a crime if he could have proven that he never intended to harm the recipients of his tweets.

International examples also show how different societies can have different concepts of criminality. India's Supreme Court recently ordered the country's movie theaters to play the national anthem, accompanied by images of the Indian flag, before films to instill "a sense of committed patriotism and nationalism."[4] Within two weeks of the ruling, Indian authorities had arrested at least twenty moviegoers for failing to stand during the anthem, another requirement of the decision. It is highly unlikely that American courts, bound by our traditions of freedom of speech, would allow any similar police action.

To more fully understand the concept of crime, it will help to examine the two most common models of how society "decides" which acts are criminal: the consensus model and the conflict model.

The Consensus Model The term *consensus* refers to general agreement among the majority of any particular group. Thus, the **consensus model** rests on the assumption that as people gather together to form a society, its members will naturally share similar norms and values. Those individuals whose actions deviate from the established norms and values are considered to pose a threat to the well-being of society as a whole and must be sanctioned (punished). The society passes laws to control and prevent unacceptable behavior, thereby setting the boundaries for acceptable behavior within the group.[5]

The consensus model, to a certain extent, assumes that a diverse group of people can have similar **morals.** In other words, they share an ideal of what is "right" and "wrong." Consequently, as public attitudes toward morality change, so do laws. In seventeenth-century America, a person found guilty of *adultery* (having sexual relations with someone other than one's spouse) could expect to be publicly whipped, branded, or even executed.

Crime An act that violates criminal law and is punishable by criminal sanctions.

Consensus Model A criminal justice model in which the majority of citizens in a society share the same values and beliefs. Criminal acts are acts that conflict with these values and beliefs and that are deemed harmful to society.

Morals Principles of right and wrong behavior, as practiced by individuals or by society.

Learning Objective 1 Describe the two most common models of how society determines which acts are criminal.

Furthermore, a century ago, one could walk into a pharmacy and purchase heroin. Today, social attitudes have shifted to consider adultery a personal issue, beyond the reach of the state, and to consider the sale of heroin a criminal act.

The Conflict Model   Some people reject the consensus model on the ground that moral attitudes are not constant or even consistent. In large, democratic societies such as the United States, different groups of citizens have widely varying opinions on controversial issues of morality and criminality such as abortion, the war on drugs, immigration, and assisted suicide. These groups and their elected representatives are constantly coming into conflict with one another. According to the **conflict model,** then, the most politically powerful segments of society—based on class, income, age, and race—have the most influence on criminal laws and are therefore able to impose their values on the rest of the community.

Consequently, what is deemed criminal activity is determined by whichever group happens to be holding power at any given time. Because certain groups do not have access to political power, their interests are not served by the criminal justice system. For instance, nearly eight of every ten elected prosecutors in the United States are white men, while only 5 percent of these posts are held by members of minority groups.[6] Given the authority of prosecutors to decide which criminal charges will be brought against defendants, this lack of diversity can contribute to the mistrust of law enforcement felt in many minority communities.

An Integrated Definition of Crime

Considering both the consensus and conflict models, we can construct a definition of crime that will be useful throughout this textbook. For our purposes, crime is an action or activity that is:

1.   Punishable under criminal law, as determined by the majority or, in some instances, by a powerful minority.
2.   Considered an *offense against society as a whole* and prosecuted by public officials, not by victims and their relatives or friends.
3.   Punishable by sanctions based on laws that bring about the loss of personal freedom or life.

At this point, it is important to understand the difference between crime and **deviance,** or behavior that does not conform to the norms of a given community or society. Deviance is a subjective concept. For example, some segments of society may think that smoking marijuana or killing animals for clothing and food is deviant behavior. Deviant acts become crimes only when society as a whole, through its legislatures, determines that those acts should be punished—as is the situation today in the United States with using certain drugs but not with eating meat. Furthermore, not all crimes are considered particularly deviant—little social disapproval is attached to those who fail

▼ Forty-one states and the District of Columbia have local laws that ban cigarette smoking in workplaces, restaurants, and/or bars. **Based on the definition in the text, is smoking considered** *deviant* **behavior in our society? Do** *you* **consider it deviant behavior? Explain your answers.**

Ehab Edward/Shutterstock.com

to follow the letter of parking laws. In essence, criminal law reflects those acts that we, as a society, agree are so unacceptable that steps must be taken to prevent them from occurring.

Types of Crime

How crimes are classified depends on their seriousness. Federal, state, and local legislation has provided for the classification and punishment of hundreds of thousands of different criminal acts, ranging from jaywalking to first degree murder. For general purposes, we can group criminal behavior into five categories: violent crime, property crime, public order crime, white-collar crime, and cyber crime.

Violent Crime   Crimes against persons, or *violent crimes*, have come to dominate our perspectives on crime. There are four major categories of violent crime:

- **Murder,** or the unlawful killing of a human being.
- **Sexual assault,** or *rape*, which refers to coerced actions of a sexual nature against an unwilling participant.
- **Assault** and **battery,** two separate acts that cover situations in which one person physically attacks another (battery) or, through threats, intentionally leads another to believe that he or she will be physically harmed (assault).
- **Robbery,** or the taking of funds, personal property, or any other article of value from a person by means of force or fear.

As you will see in Chapter 4, these violent crimes are further classified by *degree*, depending on the circumstances surrounding the criminal act. These circumstances include the intent of the person committing the crime, whether a weapon was used, and (in cases other than murder) the level of pain and suffering experienced by the victim.

Property Crime   The most common form of criminal activity is *property crime*, or those crimes in which the goal of the offender is some form of economic gain or the damaging of property. There are three major forms of property crime:

1. Pocket-picking, shoplifting, and the stealing of any property without the use of force are covered by laws against **larceny,** also known as theft.
2. **Burglary** refers to the unlawful entry of a structure with the intention of committing a serious crime, such as theft.
3. *Motor vehicle theft* describes the theft or attempted theft of a motor vehicle. Motor vehicles include any vehicle commonly used for transportation, such as a motorcycle or motor scooter, but not farm equipment or watercraft.

Arson is also a property crime. It involves the willful and malicious burning of a home, automobile, commercial building, or any other construction.

Murder The unlawful killing of one human being by another.

Sexual Assault Forced or coerced sexual intercourse (or other sexual acts).

Assault A threat or an attempt to do violence to another person that causes that person to fear immediate physical harm.

Battery The act of physically contacting another person with the intent to do harm, even if the resulting injury is insubstantial.

Robbery The act of taking property from another person through force, threat of force, or intimidation.

Larceny The act of taking property from another person without the use of force with the intent of keeping that property.

Burglary The act of breaking into or entering a structure (such as a home or office) without permission for the purpose of committing a felony.

Public Order Crime

The concept of **public order crime** is linked to the consensus model discussed earlier. Historically, societies have always outlawed activities that are considered contrary to public values and morals. Today, the most common public order crimes include public drunkenness, prostitution, gambling, and illicit drug use. These crimes are sometimes referred to as *victimless crimes* because they often harm only the offender. As you will see throughout this textbook, however, that term is rather misleading. Public order crimes may create an environment that gives rise to property and violent crimes.

White-Collar Crime

Business-related crimes are popularly referred to as **white-collar crimes.** The term *white-collar crime* is broadly used to describe an illegal act or series of acts committed by an individual or business entity using some nonviolent means to obtain a personal or business advantage.

As you will see in Chapter 16, where we consider the topic in much greater detail, white-collar crimes involve the use of legal business facilities and legitimate employees to commit illegal acts. For example, a bank teller can't embezzle (steal funds from the bank) unless she or he is an authorized bank employee. This characteristic distinguishes white-collar crime from *organized crime*, which refers to acts by illegal organizations. The traditional preferred illicit markets for organized crime operations include gambling, prostitution, illegal narcotics, and loan sharking (lending funds at higher-than-legal interest rates), along with more recent ventures into counterfeiting and credit-card scams.

Cyber Crime

The newest variation on crime is directly related to the increased presence of computers in everyday life. The Internet, with approximately 3.6 billion users worldwide, is the site of numerous *cyber* crimes—defined simply as crimes that occur in the virtual community of the Internet. The dependence of businesses on computer operations has left corporations especially vulnerable to sabotage, fraud, and embezzlement. Earlier in this decade, two separate incidents of "hacking," or unauthorized access to computer systems, exposed approximately 1.5 billion Yahoo user accounts. The information in these accounts, including names, dates of birth, telephone numbers, and passwords, was eventually offered for sale on the "dark web," a hidden, lawless corner of the Internet that can only be accessed by special software.[7]

Shifting and expanding with each new technological advance, cyber crime poses particular challenges to the criminal justice system. During the past few years, for example, explosive growth in the "Internet of Things" has raised new security concerns. The term refers to the wireless interconnections

▼ In 2017, three executives at the Takata Corporation were criminally charged for fabricating airbag test data, a coverup that has been linked to at least eleven deaths in the United States. **If found guilty of this white-collar crime, should these executives be punished the same as someone who commits a violent crime such as murder or battery? Why or why not?** Joe Raedle/ Getty Images News/Getty Images

FIGURE 1.1 Types of Cyber Crime

CYBER CRIMES AGAINST PERSONS AND PROPERTY	CYBER CRIMES IN THE BUSINESS WORLD	CYBER CRIMES AGAINST THE COMMUNITY
Cyber Fraud: Any misrepresentation knowingly made over the Internet with the intention of deceiving another person.	**Hacking:** The act of employing one computer to gain illegal access to the information stored on another computer.	**Online Child Pornography:** The illegal selling, posting, and distributing of material depicting children engaged in sexually explicit conduct.
Identity Theft: The appropriation of identity information, such as a person's name, driver's license, or Social Security number, to illegally access the victim's financial resources.	**Malware Production:** The creation of programs harmful to computers, such as worms, Trojan horses, and viruses.	**Cyber Terror:** Use of the Internet to further the political goals of individual terrorists or terrorist organizations by, for example, stealing data, disrupting government and corporate computer systems, and spreading propaganda.
Cyberstalking: Use of the Internet, e-mail, or any other form of electronic communication to contact and/or intimidate another person.	**Intellectual Property Theft:** The illegal appropriation of property that results from intellectual creative processes, such as films, video games, and software, without compensating its owners.	

linking tiny computers in automobiles, security cameras, kitchen appliances, and other objects of everyday use via the Internet. These "smart" devices, which number about fifteen billion worldwide, often lack proper security protections and have proved easy prey for hackers. In addition, terrorists increasingly are using "end-to-end" encryption technology available on the Signal, Telegram, and Wickr apps (among others) to hide their communications from authorities.[8] Figure 1.1 describes several of the most common cyber crimes, and we will address this particular criminal activity in much greater detail in Chapter 16.

ETHICS CHALLENGE

Earlier in this section, we used the example of killing animals for clothing and food as behavior that, although deviant to some, is generally accepted by the majority. What is a widespread activity that, although considered "normal" in modern American society, goes against your personal values or morals? What is the likelihood that this activity eventually will become illegal in the United States?

The Purpose of the Criminal Justice System

Defining which actions are to be labeled "crimes" is only the first step in safeguarding society from criminal behavior. Institutions must be created to apprehend alleged wrongdoers, to determine whether these persons have indeed committed crimes, and to punish those who are found guilty according to society's wishes. These institutions combine to form the **criminal justice system.** As we begin our examination of the American criminal justice system in this introductory chapter, it is important to have an idea of its purpose.

Criminal Justice System
The interlocking network of law enforcement agencies, courts, and corrections institutions designed to enforce criminal laws and protect society from criminal behavior.

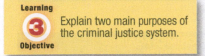

Maintaining Justice

As its name implies, the explicit goal of the criminal justice system is to provide *justice* to all members of society. Because justice is a difficult concept to define, this goal can be challenging, if not impossible, to meet. Broadly stated, justice means that all individuals are equal before the law and that they are free from arbitrary arrest or seizure as defined by the law. In other words, the idea of justice is linked with the idea of fairness. Above all, we want our laws and the means by which they are carried out to be fair.

Justice and fairness are subjective terms, which is to say that people may have different concepts of what is just and fair. If a woman who has been beaten by her husband retaliates by killing him, what is her just punishment? Reasonable persons could disagree. Some might think that the homicide was justified and that she should be treated leniently. Others might insist that she should not have taken the law into her own hands. Police officers, judges, prosecutors, prison administrators, and other employees of the criminal justice system must decide what is "fair." Sometimes, their course of action is obvious, but often, as we shall see, it is not.

Protecting Society

Within the broad mandate of "maintaining justice," Megan Kurlychek of the University at Albany, New York, has identified four specific goals of our criminal justice system:

1. To protect society from potential future crimes of the most dangerous or "risky" offenders.
2. To determine when an offense has been committed and provide the appropriate punishment for that offense.
3. To rehabilitate those offenders who have been punished so that it is safe to return them to the community.
4. To support crime victims and, to the extent possible, return them to their precrime status.[9]

Again, though these goals may seem straightforward, they often are difficult to achieve. After nearly four decades of steady declines, for example, highway fatalities have skyrocketed in recent years.[10] Although no direct link has been proved, many experts blame this trend on the high incidence of *distracted driving*, which occurs when a driver engages in any sort of activity that could distract him or her from safely operating a vehicle. Indeed, a recent poll found that seven out of ten Americans admit to texting, accessing social media, or taking selfies while behind the wheel.[11]

The criminal justice system has fashioned a response to this threat. Fourteen states specifically prohibit the use of hand-held electronic devices by drivers, and forty-six ban texting behind the wheel.[12] Rarely, however, does the punishment for distracted driving rise above a monetary fine, causing one observer to complain that "right now, we have a reed, not a stick" to deter the practice.[13]

Furthermore, it is difficult for law enforcement officers to detect distracted driving or for prosecutors to prove that an accident was caused by a texting driver. Technology does exist that would enable police to determine whether a suspected driver had recently been using a smartphone. Privacy advocates worry, however, that such methods would lead to improper searches of constitutionally protected information, an issue we will address in Chapter 7.[14] Thus, the question of how best to protect society from distracted drivers is, like so many questions relating to criminal justice, complex and difficult to answer.

Justice The quality of fairness that must exist in the processes designed to determine whether individuals are guilty of criminal wrongdoing.

F. W. Gill Gang Investigator

FASTFACTS

Youth intervention specialist/gang investigator

Job description:
- Conducts assessments and refers at-risk youth to appropriate activities, programs, or agencies.
- Serves as a liaison between the police department, schools, other agencies, and the community regarding gang and other youth-related matters.

What kind of training is required?
- A bachelor's degree in counseling, criminal justice, or other social science–related field. Bilingual (English/Spanish) skills are desired.

Annual salary range?
- $70,000–$80,000

The problem, for most of these kids, is that nobody cares. Their parents don't, or can't, get involved in their children's lives. (How many times have I heard parents deny that their son or daughter is a gang banger, even though it's obvious?) Teachers are in the business of teaching and don't, or can't, take the time to get to know their most troubled students. So, when I'm dealing with gang members, the first thing I do is listen. I don't lecture them, I don't tell them that they are throwing away their lives. I just listen. You'd be amazed how effective this can be—these kids, who look so tough on the outside, just want an adult to care.

Not that there is any magic formula for convincing a gang member to go straight. It is very difficult to get someone to change his or her lifestyle. If they don't want to change—really want to change—then nothing I can say or do is going to make much of a difference. Unfortunately, there are many lost causes. I've even had a couple of cases in which a juvenile was afraid to leave the gang because his father was a gang member, and he insisted that the boy stay in the gang. I have had some success in convincing gang members to turn their lives around by joining the military. The military provides discipline and a new outlook on life, things that these kids badly need. The way I look at it, in some cases, war is the best shot these kids have at saving their own lives.

Courtesy of F. W. Gill

SOCIAL MEDIA CAREER TIP When posting on Facebook, assume that your post will be published in your local newspaper and read by a potential employer. If you think the post might reflect poorly on you as a potential employee, keep it offline.

The Structure of the Criminal Justice System

Society places the burden of maintaining justice and protecting our communities on those who work for the three main institutions of the criminal justice system: law enforcement, the courts, and corrections. In this section, we take an introductory look at these institutions and their role in the criminal justice system as a whole.

The Importance of Federalism

To understand the structure of the criminal justice system, you must understand the concept of **federalism,** a form of government in which powers are shared by the national (federal) government and the states. The framers of the U.S. Constitution, fearful of tyranny and a too-powerful central government, chose the system of federalism as a compromise.

Federalism in Action

The appeal of federalism is that it establishes a strong national government capable of handling large-scale problems while allowing for state powers and local traditions. For example, in 2016, California became the fifth state—after Montana, Oregon, Vermont, and Washington—to legalize physician-assisted suicide for certain terminally ill patients. About a decade ago, the federal government challenged the decision made by voters in Oregon and Washington to allow the practice. With its ruling in *Gonzales v. Oregon*

Federalism A form of government in which a written constitution provides for a division of powers between a central government and several regional governments.

(2006), the United States Supreme Court sided with the states, ruling that the principle of federalism supported their freedom to differ from the majority viewpoint in this instance.[15]

Federal Criminal Law The Constitution gave the national government certain express powers, such as the power to coin money, raise an army, and regulate interstate commerce. All other powers were left to the states, including police power, which allows the states to enact whatever laws are necessary to protect the health, morals, safety, and welfare of their citizens. As the American criminal justice system has evolved, the ideals of federalism have ebbed somewhat. Specifically, the powers of the national government have expanded significantly. In the early 1900s, only about one hundred specific activities were illegal under federal criminal law. Today, there are nearly five thousand federal criminal statutes, meaning that Americans are increasingly likely to come in contact with the federal criminal justice system.[16]

Marijuana and the States Today, issues relating to federalism are an important part of the ongoing clash between federal and state marijuana laws. Under federal law, any use of marijuana is illegal. Indeed, the Drug Enforcement Administration (DEA) recently reaffirmed marijuana's status as a Schedule 1 drug—in the same category as heroin—because of its "high potential for abuse."[17] At the same time, the recreational use of small amounts of marijuana is legal in eight states plus Washington, D.C. Twenty-eight states allow marijuana consumption for medicinal purposes, and the drug has been decriminalized in thirteen states, meaning that its use is treated as an infraction similar to a traffic violation rather than as a crime. (See Figure 1.2.)

FIGURE 1.2 Marijuana and Criminal Law

As this map shows, at the beginning of 2017 most states—representing about three-fourths of the population of the United States—allow for the use of marijuana under certain circumstances. Remember that *any* use of the drug is outlawed under federal law.

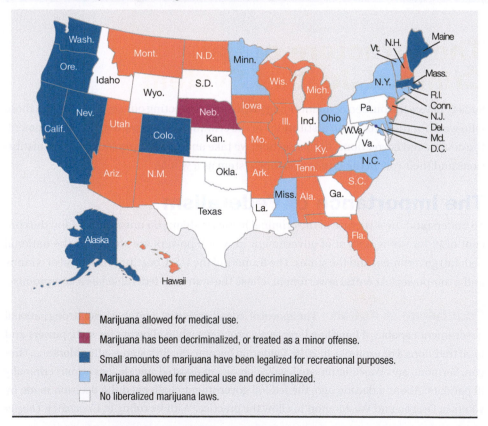

- 🟧 Marijuana allowed for medical use.
- 🟥 Marijuana has been decriminalized, or treated as a minor offense.
- 🟦 Small amounts of marijuana have been legalized for recreational purposes.
- 🔵 Marijuana allowed for medical use and decriminalized.
- ⬜ No liberalized marijuana laws.

In *Gonzales v. Raich* (2005), the United States Supreme Court ruled that, when it comes to marijuana regulation, "if there is any conflict between federal and state law, federal law shall prevail."[18] How, then, have numerous states been able to pass laws that clearly are incompatible with federal marijuana prohibitions? In recent years, based on policy decisions in the administrative branch, the federal government has chosen generally to ignore recreational and medicinal marijuana use in those states with liberalized marijuana laws.[19] The DEA has still conducted raids of large-scale marijuana-growing operations in "pot-friendly" states, however, and recreational marijuana use has remained a crime in federal parks located in those states. Furthermore, depending on the political views of the current administration, the federal government's *laissez-faire* attitude toward marijuana could change in the future.

Law Enforcement   The ideals of federalism can be clearly seen in the local, state, and federal levels of law enforcement. Though agencies from the different levels cooperate if the need arises, they have their own organizational structures and tend to operate independently of one another. We briefly introduce each level of law enforcement here and cover them in more detail in Chapters 5, 6, and 7.

Local Law Enforcement   On the local level, the duties of law enforcement agencies are split between counties and municipalities. The chief law enforcement officer of most counties is the county sheriff. Those who hold the position of sheriff are typically elected, often for a two- or four-year term. In some areas, where city and county governments have merged, there is a county police force, headed by a chief of police. As Figure 1.3 shows, the bulk of all police officers in the United States are employed on a local level. The majority of these work in departments that consist of fewer than 10 officers, but a large city such as New York may have a police force of about 34,500.

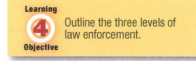

Learning
4 Objective
Outline the three levels of law enforcement.

Local police are responsible for the "nuts and bolts" of law enforcement work. They investigate most crimes and attempt to deter crime through patrol activities. They apprehend criminals and participate in trial proceedings, if necessary. Local police are also charged with "keeping the peace," a broad set of duties that includes crowd and traffic control and the resolution of minor conflicts between citizens. In many areas, local police have the added obligation of providing social services such as dealing with domestic violence and child abuse.

State Law Enforcement   Hawaii is the only state that does not have a state law enforcement agency. Generally, there are two types of state law enforcement agencies,

FIGURE 1.3 Local, State, and Federal Employees in Our Criminal Justice System

Law Enforcement	Judicial and Legal	Corrections	Total
192,354	62,756	37,955	293,065
108,295	175,075	451,512	734,882
882,965	254,148	259,951	1,397,064

■ Federal ■ State ■ Local

Source: Bureau of Justice Statistics, *Justice Expenditure and Employment Extracts, 2012—Preliminary* (Washington, D.C.: U.S. Department of Justice, July 2015), Table 2.

those designated simply as "state police" and those designated as "highway patrols." State highway patrols concern themselves mainly with infractions on public highways and freeways. Other state law enforcers include fire marshals, who investigate suspicious fires and educate the public on fire prevention. State fish, game, and watercraft wardens police a state's natural resources and often oversee its firearms laws. Some states also have alcoholic beverage control officers, as well as agents who investigate welfare and food stamp fraud.

Federal Law Enforcement The enactment of new national laws over the past forty years has led to an expansion in the size and scope of the federal government's participation in the criminal justice system. Among other things, these laws have dealt with terrorism, guns, drugs, and violent crime. The Department of Homeland Security, which we will examine in detail in Chapter 5, combines the police powers of twenty-four federal agencies to protect the United States from terrorist attacks. Other federal agencies with police powers include the Federal Bureau of Investigation (FBI), the Drug Enforcement Administration (DEA), the U.S. Secret Service, and the Bureau of Alcohol, Tobacco, Firearms and Explosives (ATF). In fact, almost every federal agency, including the postal and forest services, has some kind of police power.

Federal law enforcement agencies operate throughout the United States, and often work in cooperation with their local and state counterparts. There can be tension between the different branches of law enforcement, however, when state criminal law and federal criminal law are incompatible. For example, as noted earlier, even though a number of states have legalized the sale and possession of small amounts of marijuana, the drug is still illegal under federal law. Consequently, federal officers are authorized to make marijuana arrests in those states, regardless of the content of those states' criminal codes.

The Courts

The United States has a *dual court system*, which means that we have two independent judicial systems, one at the federal level and one at the state level. In practice, this translates into fifty-two different court systems: one federal court system and fifty different state court systems, plus that of the District of Columbia. In general, defendants charged with violating federal criminal law will face trial in federal court, while defendants charged with violating state law will appear in state court.

The *criminal court* and its work group—the judge, prosecutors, and defense attorneys—are charged with the weighty responsibility of determining the innocence or guilt of criminal suspects. We will cover these important participants, their roles in the criminal trial, and the court system as a whole in Chapters 8, 9, 10, and 11.

Corrections

Once the court system convicts and sentences an offender, she or he is delegated to the corrections system. (Those convicted in a state court will be under the control of that state's corrections system, and those convicted of a federal crime will find themselves under the control of the federal corrections system.) Depending on the seriousness of the crime and their individual needs, offenders are placed on probation, incarcerated, or transferred to community-based correctional facilities.

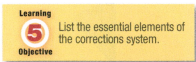

Learning
5
Objective
List the essential elements of the corrections system.

- *Probation*, the most common correctional treatment, allows the offender to return to the community and remain under the supervision of an agent of the court known as a probation officer. While on probation, the offender must follow certain rules of conduct. When probationers fail to follow these rules, they may be incarcerated.
- If the offender's sentence includes a period of *incarceration*, he or she will be remanded to a correctional facility for a certain amount of time. *Jails* hold those convicted of minor crimes with relatively short sentences, as well as those awaiting

trial or involved in certain court proceedings. *Prisons* house those convicted of more serious crimes with longer sentences. Generally speaking, counties and municipalities administer jails, while prisons are the domain of federal and state governments.

- *Community-based corrections* have increased in popularity as jails and prisons have been plagued with problems of funding and overcrowding. Community-based correctional facilities include halfway houses, residential centers, and work-release centers. They operate on the assumption that not all convicts need or benefit from incarceration in jail or prison.

The majority of inmates released from incarceration are not finished with the corrections system. The most frequent type of release from a jail or prison is *parole*, in which an inmate, after serving part of his or her sentence in a correctional facility, is allowed to serve the rest of the term in the community. Like someone on probation, a parolee must conform to certain conditions of freedom, with the same consequences if these conditions are not followed. Issues of probation, incarceration, community-based corrections, and parole will be covered in Chapters 12, 13, and 14.

▲ America's state and federal prisons hold just over 1.5 million inmates, while, on any given day, about 740,000 inmates are locked up in the nation's jails. **What are the basic differences between prisons and jails?** View Apart/Shutterstock .com

The Criminal Justice Process

In its 1967 report, the President's Commission on Law Enforcement and Administration of Justice asserted that the criminal justice system

> is not a hodgepodge of random actions. It is rather a continuum—an orderly progression of events—some of which, like arrest and trial, are highly visible and some of which, though of great importance, occur out of public view.[20]

The commission's assertion that the criminal justice system is a "continuum" is one that many observers would challenge.[21] Some liken the criminal justice system to a sports team, which is the sum of an indeterminable number of decisions, relationships, conflicts, and adjustments.[22] Such a volatile mix is not what we generally associate with a "system." For most, the word **system** indicates a certain degree of order and discipline. That we refer to our law enforcement agencies, courts, and correctional facilities as part of a "system" may reflect our hopes rather than reality. Still, it will be helpful to familiarize yourself with the basic steps of the *criminal justice process*, or the procedures through which the criminal justice system meets the expectations of society. These basic steps are outlined in Figure 1.4.

In his classic study of the criminal justice system, Herbert Packer, a professor at Stanford University, compared the ideal criminal justice process to an assembly line "down which moves an endless stream of cases, never stopping."[23] In Packer's image of assembly-line justice, each step of the **formal criminal justice process** involves a series of "routinized operations" with the end goal of getting the criminal defendant from point A (his or

System A set of interacting parts that, when functioning properly, achieve a desired result.

Formal Criminal Justice Process The model of the criminal justice process in which participants follow formal rules to create a smoothly functioning disposition of cases from arrest to punishment.

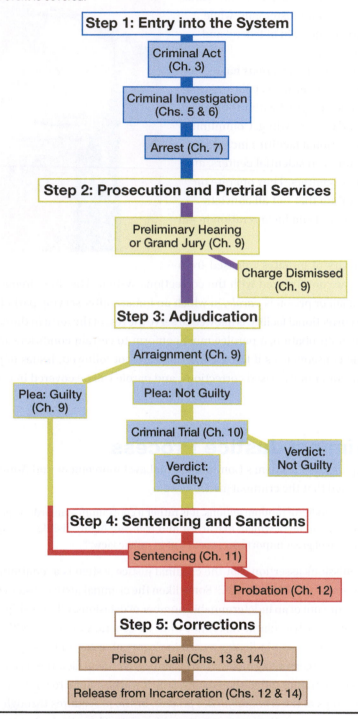

FIGURE 1.4 **The Criminal Justice Process**

This diagram provides a simplified overview of the basic steps of the criminal justice process, from criminal act to release from incarceration. Below each step, you will find the chapter of this textbook in which the event is covered.

her arrest by law enforcement) to point B (the criminal trial) to point C (if guilty, her or his punishment).[24] As Packer himself was wont to point out, the daily operations of criminal justice rarely operate so smoothly. In this textbook, the criminal justice process will be examined as the end product of many different decisions made by many different criminal justice professionals in law enforcement, the courts, and corrections.

Discretion and Ethics

Practically, the formal criminal justice process suffers from a serious drawback: it is unrealistic. Law enforcement agencies do not have the staff or funds to investigate every crime, so they must decide where to direct their limited resources. Increasing caseloads and a limited amount of time in which to dispose of them constrict many of our nation's courts. Overcrowding in prisons and jails affects both law enforcement agencies and the courts—there is simply not enough room for all convicts.

The criminal justice system relies on *discretion* to alleviate these pressures. By **discretion,** we mean the authority to choose between and among alternative courses of action, based on individual judgment and conscience. Collectively, the discretionary decisions made by criminal justice professionals are said to produce an **informal criminal justice process** that does not operate within the rigid confines of formal rules and laws.

Learning Objective 6 Explain the difference between the formal and informal criminal justice processes.

Informal Decision Making

By its nature, the informal criminal justice system relies on the discretion of individuals to offset the rigidity of criminal statutes and procedural rules. For example, even if a prosecutor believes that a suspect is guilty, she or he may decide not to bring charges against the suspect if the case is weak or the police erred during the investigative process. In many instances, prosecutors will not squander the scarce resource of court time on a case they might not win. Some argue that the informal process has made our system more just. Given the immense pressure of limited resources, the argument goes, only rarely will an innocent person end up before a judge and jury.[25]

Interpreting the Law In many instances, criminal justice professionals must use their discretion to interpret laws that are overly broad, vague, or even obsolete. For example, although twenty-one states still ban adultery, such laws are routinely ignored by authorities.[26] Consider, too, an issue mentioned earlier—state distracted-driving legislation. Georgia's law prohibits drivers from engaging in "any actions which shall distract such driver from the safe operation of [her or his] vehicle."[27] This statute could be interpreted to cover a wide range of behavior, from texting or using a smartphone to listening to music while driving. In fact, several years ago an Atlanta police officer came under criticism for using his discretion to ticket a driver who was eating a hamburger while behind the wheel.[28]

In later chapters, we will examine many other circumstances that call for discretionary decision making by law enforcement officers. We will also cover discretion on the part of judges, who must interpret the law when overseeing criminal trials and sentencing guilty defendants, and corrections officials, who have a great deal of discretion in determining how to control prison and jail inmates. (See the feature *Discretion in Action—The "Sexting" Scandal* for insight into how the informal criminal justice process applies to a distinct form of child pornography.)

The Pitfalls of Discretion Unfortunately, the informal criminal justice system does not always benefit from measured, rational decision making. Individual judgment can be tainted by personal bias, erroneous or irrational thinking, and plain ill will. When this occurs, discretion becomes "the power to *get away* with alternative decisions [emphasis added]."[29] Indeed, many of the rules of the formal criminal justice process are designed to keep its employees from substituting their own judgment for that of the general public, as expressed by the law.

Discretion The ability of individuals in the criminal justice system to make operational decisions based on personal judgment instead of formal rules or official information.

Informal Criminal Justice Process A model of the criminal justice system that recognizes the informal authority exercised by individuals at each step of the criminal justice process.

The "Sexting" Scandal

The Situation The first hint of a serious problem came from an anonymous tip on the high school's Safe2Tell hotline. According to the tipster, numerous students were using a photo vault app to share inappropriate images of themselves. Following a lengthy investigation by school officials and local law enforcement, the full extent of the "sexting" activity was revealed: more than one hundred students, both male and female, had contributed photos of themselves posing nude or in their underwear. As far as the investigators could determine, none of these images had been posted on the Internet or shown to adults, and no coercion or bullying was involved.

The Law Under state law, any person who takes, receives, or shares a photo of a "naked body part" of someone under the age of eighteen has committed a Class C felony child pornography offense. Under the law, the fact that such activity is consensual is irrelevant. A conviction for a Class C felony is punishable by four to twelve years in a state prison and a fine of up to $750,000.

What Would You Do? You are the prosecutor responsible for deciding the fate of the students involved in this "sexting" scandal. With nearly unlimited discretion, you have several choices: (1) you can charge the students with committing crimes involving child pornography; (2) you can require that they undergo counseling; or (3) you can do nothing, relying on the students' parents to "straighten them out." Note that any student convicted of child pornography charges would be required to register as a sex offender, making it difficult for her or him to find or keep a job and secure affordable housing in the future. How would you use your discretion in this situation?

To see how a prosecutor in Cañon City, Colorado, reacted in similar circumstances, go to Example 1.1 in Appendix B.

One of the primary arguments for easing marijuana laws, a subject discussed earlier in the chapter, is that those laws are often selectively (and unfairly) enforced. According to a recent Human Rights Watch survey of thirty-nine states, for example, African American adults were four times more likely to be arrested for marijuana possession than white adults, even though usage rates are similar between the two races.[30] In Chapter 7, you will learn more about *racial profiling*, which is the police practice of improperly targeting members of minority groups based on personal characteristics such as race or ethnicity.

Discretion in the courts has also come under criticism. Associate Supreme Court justice Antonin Scalia (1936–2016) believed that discretion in the courts tends to cause discriminatory and disparate criminal sentences, a subject we will discuss in Chapter 11. According to Scalia, the need for fairness and certainty in the criminal justice system outweighs the practical benefits of widespread and unpredictable discretionary decision making.[31]

Ethics and Justice

How can we reconcile the need for some sort of discretion in criminal justice with the ever-present potential for abuse? Part of the answer lies in our initial definition of discretion, which mentions not only individual judgment but also *conscience*. Ideally, actors in the criminal justice system will make moral choices about what is right and wrong based on the norms that have been established by society. In other words, they will behave *ethically*.

Learning Objective 7 Define *ethics*, and describe the role that it plays in discretionary decision making.

Ethics in criminal justice is closely related to the concept of justice. Because criminal justice professionals are representatives of the state, they have the power to determine whether the state is treating its citizens fairly. If some law enforcement officers in fact make the decision to issue a jaywalking citation on the basis of the offender's race, then they are acting not only unethically but also unjustly.

Ethics The moral principles that govern a person's perception of right and wrong.

Ethics and the Law The line between ethics and justice is often difficult to discern, as ethical standards are usually not written into criminal statutes. Consequently, individuals must often "fill in" the ethical blanks. To make this point, ethics expert John Kleinig uses the real-life example of a police officer who refused to arrest a homeless person for sleeping in a private parking garage. A local ordinance clearly prohibited such behavior. The officer, however, felt it would be unethical to arrest a homeless person under those circumstances unless he or she was acting in a disorderly manner. The officer's supervisors were unsympathetic to this ethical stance, and he was suspended from duty without pay.[32]

Ethics and Critical Thinking Did the police officer in the preceding example behave ethically by inserting his own beliefs into the letter of the criminal law? Would an officer who arrested peaceful homeless trespassers be acting unethically? In some cases, the ethical decision will be *intuitive*, reflecting an automatic response determined by a person's background and experiences. In other cases, however, intuition is not enough. *Critical thinking* is needed for an ethical response. Throughout this textbook, we will use the principle of critical thinking—which involves developing analytical skills and reasoning—to address the many ethical challenges inherent in the criminal justice system.

ETHICS CHALLENGE

Refer back to this section's discussion of the police officer who refused to arrest the nonviolent homeless person for ethical reasons. Did the officer act properly in this situation, or should he have carried out the law regardless of his personal beliefs? Explain your answer.

Criminal Justice Today

In describing the general direction of the criminal justice system as a whole, many observers point to two models introduced by Professor Herbert Packer: the *crime control model* and the *due process model*.[33] The underlying value of the **crime control model** is that the most important function of the criminal justice process is to punish and repress criminal conduct. The system must be quick and efficient, placing as few restrictions as possible on the ability of law enforcement officers to make discretionary decisions in apprehending criminals.

Although not in direct conflict with crime control, the underlying values of the **due process model** focus more on protecting the rights of the accused through formal, legal restraints on the police, courts, and corrections. That is, the due process model relies on the courts to make it more difficult to prove guilt. It rests on the belief that it is more desirable for society that ninety-nine guilty suspects go free than that a single innocent person be condemned.[34] (This chapter's *Mastering Concepts* feature provides a further comparison of the two models.)

Learning (8) **Objective** Contrast the crime control and due process models.

Crime and Law Enforcement: The Bottom Line

It is difficult to say which of Packer's two models has the upper hand today. As we will see throughout the textbook, homeland security concerns have brought much of the criminal justice system in line with crime control values. At the same time, decreasing

Crime Control Model A criminal justice model that places primary emphasis on the right of society to be protected from crime and violent criminals.

Due Process Model A criminal justice model that places primacy on the right of the individual to be protected from the power of the government.

trekandshoot/Shutterstock.com

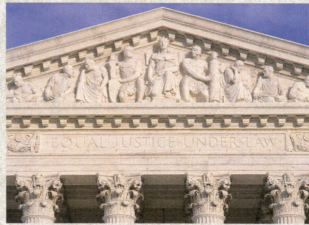

Joseph Sohm/Shutterstock.com

Crime Control Model versus Due Process Model

CRIME CONTROL MODEL	DUE PROCESS MODEL
Goal	**Goal**
• Deter crime by arresting and incarcerating criminals as quickly and efficiently as possible.	• Protect inidividuals charged with crimes against the immense and potentially unjust power of the state.
Methods	**Methods**
• Allow the police to "do their jobs" by limiting the amount of judicial oversight of law enforcement tactics. • Limit the number of rights and protections enjoyed by defendants in court. • Incarcerate criminals for lengthy periods of time by imposing harsh sentences, including the death penalty.	• Assure the constitutional rights of those accused of crimes when they are arrested by law enforcement officers and prosecuted in criminal court. • Whenever possible, allow nonviolent convicts to serve their sentences in the community rather than behind bars. • Protect the civil rights of all inmates, and focus on rehabilitation rather than punishment in prisons and jails.

arrest and imprisonment rates suggest that due process values are strong, as well. Indeed, most measurements of criminal activity are at historically low levels. Federal crime statistics do indicate one worrisome trend, however: in 2015, the murder rate rose by nearly 11 percent, the largest such jump since the 1960s.[35] In Chapter 3, we will discuss some of the reasons for this development, including why violent crime appears to be clustering in the nation's largest cities.

Smarter Policing Just as law enforcement inevitably gets a great deal of the blame when crime rates are high, American police forces have received much credit for the apparent decline in criminality. The consensus is that the police have become smarter and more disciplined over the past several decades, relying, like many other criminal justice institutions, on **evidence-based practices,** or strategies that demonstrably result in positive outcomes.

For example, *predictive policing*, sometimes also known as intelligence-led policing, employs statistical models to anticipate which locations are at the highest risk for criminal activity. Once these high-risk locations, or *hot spots*, are identified, law enforcement agencies can direct resources toward preventing crime in the area. A more controversial

Evidence-Based Practices
Approaches or strategies that have been extensively researched and shown consistently to produce the desired outcomes.

strategy called *proactive policing* promotes rigorous enforcement of minor offenses—such as drunkenness and public disorder—with an eye toward preventing more serious wrongdoing. We will explore these innovative policing strategies, along with many others, more fully in Chapter 6.

Biometrics Methods to identify a person based on unique physical characteristics, such as fingerprints or facial configuration.

Identifying Criminals

Technology has also played a significant role in improving law enforcement efficiency. Police investigators are enjoying the benefits of perhaps the most effective new crime-fighting tool since fingerprint identification: DNA profiling. This technology allows law enforcement agents to identify a suspect from body fluid evidence (such as blood, saliva, or semen) or biological evidence (such as hair strands or fingernail clippings). As we will also see in Chapter 6, by collecting DNA from convicts and storing the information in databases, investigators have been able to reach across hundreds of miles and back in time to catch wrongdoers.

Law enforcement's ability to identify criminal suspects is set to receive another boost with the increased use of **biometrics.** The term refers to the measurement and analysis of a person's unique physical characteristics, especially as a way to establish identity. The use of biometrics gives law enforcement personnel the technological ability to identify whether a person is a criminal suspect.

Perhaps the best-known biometric is the fingerprint, which has been used for decades to establish and authenticate the identity of suspects. Today, police officers in the field can use handheld mobile devices to match a suspect's fingerprints against those stored in state and federal databases. This mobile ID technology enables officers to accomplish a task that used to take hours or even days in as little as forty-five seconds.

Other important forms of biometric identification measure hand geometry, facial features, and the minute details of the human eye. With its $1 billion Next Generation Identification project, the FBI is consolidating all of the organization's biometric information into a single database that will allow local police departments to verify the identities of approximately 125 million criminal suspects.[36]

CJ & TECHNOLOGY

Facial Recognition Software

Recently developed facial recognition software makes even the most technologically advanced fingerprint-matching systems seem sluggish by comparison. This software distinguishes 16,000 points on a person's face—such as the shape of the lips and the distance between the eyes—and conducts point comparisons with photos in law enforcement databases at a rate of more than one million faces a second. Designed by the U.S. military to identify potential terrorists in Iraq and Afghanistan, this technology is linked to surveillance cameras in cities like Chicago and New York for purposes of fighting street crime. It was also used more than 20,000 times from 2011 to 2015 by San Diego patrol officers hoping to establish the identity of suspects in the field.

For all its speed, this technology does have its limitations. The error rate is as high as 20 percent, which suggests the possibility of regular misidentifications. In San Diego, the software succeeded in finding a criminal record match only a quarter of the time, meaning that police officers were, for the most part, photographing non-criminals. Boston recently decided not to link the software to surveillance cameras because, in the words of its police commissioner, "I don't want people to think we're always spying on them."

Thinking about Facial Recognition Software

Suppose a convenience store manager was able to use her smartphone to take a picture of someone robbing the store. How could facial recognition software help solve the crime? What are some of the potential drawbacks of allowing citizens with smartphone cameras to help identify criminal suspects?

Continuing Challenges—The Heroin Epidemic Throughout this textbook, we will discuss the role that the criminal justice system plays in controlling the use of *illegal drugs* in the United States. The broadest definition of a **drug,** which includes alcohol, is any substance that modifies biological, psychological, or social behavior. Although the majority of drug-related arrests in the United States involve marijuana,[37] the most troubling trend in this area is a result of increased *opioid* use by Americans. Opioids are drugs that act on the nervous system to relieve pain. In recent decades, physicians have prescribed large amounts of highly addictive opioids, such as Vicodin, Percocet, and OxyContin, leading to increased black-market demand for such drugs.

The resulting deaths—183,000 fatal opioid overdoses from 1999 to 2015[38]—led governmental agencies to restrict the availability of these painkillers. In response, many addicts switched to heroin, which is actually less expensive and easier to find on the black market. This unintended consequence of the prescription opioid crackdown has led to sharp increases in fatal heroin overdoses and untold social damage to the communities in which the drug is popular. It has also led to violent crime. Law enforcement officials in cities such as Baltimore, Chicago, Philadelphia, and St. Louis attribute their increased homicide rates in part to turf battles among local gangs over control of the heroin trade.[39]

Continuing Challenges—Gun Violence Bloodshed associated with the heroin trade is just one byproduct of the prevalence of guns in America. The vast majority of gun owners are, of course, law-abiding citizens who use firearms for self-protection or recreational activities. Still, about 32,000 people are killed by gunfire in the United States each year, and firearms are used in 71 percent of the nation's murders and 40 percent of its robberies.[40] In 2016, the nation's deadliest city was Chicago. In addition to 762 murders, the city experienced 1,100 more shooting incidents than in the previous year. Local law enforcement officials attribute much of this violence to the actions of **street gangs,** or groups of individuals who band together to engage in violent, unlawful, or criminal activity.[41]

Mass shootings have also focused national attention on gun violence. Definitions vary, but one broad measure defines a mass shooting as "an incident in which four or more people (not including the shooter) are killed or wounded." By this measure, more than one mass shooting a day took place in the United States in 2016.[42] On June 12, 2016, Omar Mateen killed forty-nine people and wounded fifty-three others at an Orlando, Florida, nightclub, the worst mass shooting in the nation's history. Such incidents inevitably lead to difficult questions concerning the nation's approach to both legal and illegal firearms.

Gun Control Policy

For some, much of the blame for mass shootings lies in the easy access to firearms in the United States. According to the Bureau of Alcohol, Tobacco, Firearms and Explosives (ATF), 9 million firearms were manufactured in the United States in 2014, up from 5.4 million in 2010.[43] Based on the ATF's data, the *Washington Post* estimates that there are approximately 357 million firearms in the United States, not counting illegally owned guns and weapons on military bases.[44]

Supporters of stricter *gun control* would like to see this number significantly reduced. **Gun control** refers to the policies that federal and state governments implement to limit access to firearms in this country. Opponents of gun control counter that someone who is planning to commit a crime with a gun is probably going to obtain that firearm illegally. Consequently, stricter gun control "prevents only law abiding citizens from owning handguns."[45]

Drug Any substance that modifies biological, psychological, or social behavior. In particular, an illegal substance with those properties.

Street Gang A group of people, usually three or more, who share a common identity and engage in illegal activities.

Gun Control Efforts by a government to regulate or control the sale of guns.

Regulating Gun Ownership   The Second Amendment to the U.S. Constitution states, "A well regulated Militia, being necessary to the security of a free State, the right of the people to keep and bear Arms, shall not be infringed." Because this language is somewhat archaic and vague, the United States Supreme Court has attempted to clarify the amendment's modern meaning. In two separate rulings, the Court stated that the Second Amendment provides individuals with a constitutional right to bear arms and that this right must be recognized at all levels of government—federal, state, and local.[46]

Background Checks   In both of its Second Amendment cases, the Supreme Court emphasized that, to promote public safety, the government could continue to prohibit certain persons—such as criminals and mentally ill individuals—from legally purchasing firearms. The primary method for doing so involves background checks of individuals who purchase firearms from federally licensed gun dealers. The mechanics of background checks are regulated by the Brady Handgun Violence Prevention Act, enacted in 1993.[47]

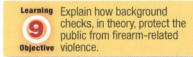

Learning Objective 9   Explain how background checks, in theory, protect the public from firearm-related violence.

Known as the Brady Bill, this legislation requires a person wishing to purchase a gun from a licensed firearms dealer to complete an application. The application process includes a background check by a law enforcement agency, usually the FBI. The applicant can be prohibited from purchasing a firearm if his or her record contains one of a number of "red flags," including a previous felony conviction, evidence of illegal drug addiction, or wrongdoing associated with domestic violence.[48] From the passage of the Brady Bill until the end of 2014, about 2.8 million of 180 million applications for firearms purchases were denied because of federal and state background checks.[49]

Mental Health Issues   Any person who has been involuntarily committed to a "mental institution" or "adjudicated as a mental defective" is barred from purchasing or possessing firearms. A person may be designated "mentally defective" when a court or other legal entity determines one of the following:

1. The person is a danger to herself or himself or others.
2. The person lacks the mental capacity to manage her or his own affairs.
3. The person has been found insane or incompetent to stand trial by a criminal or military court.[50]

In 2007, a student with mental health issues shot and killed thirty-two people on the Virginia Tech campus in Blacksburg. As a result, most states began providing the federal government with the names of residents who had been involuntary committed for psychiatric treatment. About 6,500 firearm purchase applications in this country are denied each year because of the applicant's mental health.[51] (See the feature *Comparative Criminal Justice—The German Way* to learn about a country that has much stricter gun laws than the United States.)

Recent Legislative Gun Control Efforts   Because of federal inaction, it has largely been left to the states to determine the direction of gun control in this country. Following a 2012 mass shooting at an elementary school in Newtown, Connecticut, thirteen states passed measures tightening the background check requirements for firearm purchases within their borders. Seven of these states require such checks for private gun sales, which federal law does not. In addition, sixteen states made it more difficult for mentally ill individuals to buy firearms, and two dozen states passed legislation limiting the ability of domestic abusers to own guns.[52]

At the same time, in 2016 Texas became the fortieth state to permit "open carry"— the popular term for allowing people to carry firearms in plain sight.[53] That same

Background Check An investigation of a person's history to determine whether that person should be, for example, allowed to legally purchase a firearm.

The German Way

Source: Central Intelligence Agency

In Germany, gun ownership is a privilege rather than a right. This distinction does not appear to have had much impact on German acceptance of firearms—the country has the fourth highest number of legal guns per capita in the world. When it comes to gun control, however, Germany imposes constraints on firearm sales and possession that are far more stringent than restrictions in the United States.

TOUGH GUN LAWS

To start, before an adult can purchase a gun in Germany, he or she must obtain an ownership license, or *Waffenbesitzkarte*. This entails a background check to determine whether the applicant has a history of criminal behavior, alcohol or drug abuse, mental illness, or any other attribute that might place her or him at risk for violent behavior. The applicant must also pass a "specialized knowledge test" that proves he or she knows how to handle a gun and ammunition. Any applicant under the age of twenty-five must undergo a further psychological exam to ensure that she or he is fit for gun ownership.

In addition, German authorities emphasize the importance of firearm storage. As part of the licensing process, applicants must prove that they will keep the gun in a safe place where it can be accessed only by its owner. Officers of the state Criminal Office have the authority to carry out random inspections at the homes of gun owners to ensure that they are properly storing their weapons. Supporters of these extreme measures point out that Germany has one of the lowest rates of gun-related deaths in the world, and the country has not experienced a mass shooting since 2009.

FOR CRITICAL ANALYSIS

Before purchasing a gun in Germany, a person must convince authorities that she or he needs the weapon for a specific purpose, such as hunting, competing in shooting competitions, or providing professional security. Self-defense is *not* an acceptable reason for owning a gun in Germany. What is your opinion of this policy?

---

year, Idaho, Mississippi, Oklahoma, and West Virginia enacted legislation that lessened restrictions on gun ownership and use.[54] The United States Supreme Court has declined to hear any new cases involving federal, state, or local firearms regulations since 2008, meaning that the fate of gun control will continue to be decided by the voters and their elected representatives. (To express your own opinion on one aspect of this divisive issue, see the feature *Policy Matters—Concealed Carry on Campus* at the end of the chapter.)

The Changing Landscape of American Policing

Over the course of three tumultuous days in the summer of 2016, American law enforcement found itself under the national spotlight because of three separate, though linked, incidents. On July 5, police officers in Baton Rouge, Louisiana, fatally shot Alton Sterling four times as he was being restrained on the ground. On July 6, a St. Anthony, Minnesota, police officer shot and killed Philando Castile, who was apparently in the process of reaching for his driver's license. Then, on July 7, during a march in Dallas to protest these two deaths, a lone sniper opened fire on the law enforcement officers assembled for the event, killing five and wounding nine others.

The shootings crystallized many of the controversies that plague modern American policing. Both Sterling and Castile were African American, the latest in a series of black men to die at the hands of law enforcement. Their deaths were caught on videotape, and each involved a questionable use of police force. Micah Xavier Johnson, the Dallas sniper, was a black man motivated by "recent police shootings" to "kill white people, especially white [police] officers."[55] According to James Comey, former director of the FBI, it seems clear that "something in policing has changed."[56]

The Camera's Eye

Every year, about 44 million face-to-face contacts between police and civilians take place.[57] The vast majority of these interactions are routine and fail to generate any public interest. On the rare occasions when police-civilian contact does involve force, it has become increasingly likely that the incident will be caught on bystanders' smartphones, surveillance systems, or officers' body cameras. "The video camera has become omnipresent," says Richard Aborn, president of the Citizens Crime Commission of New York City, "and it has become an absolute check on police credibility."[58]

▲ Dallas Police Chief David Brown grieves during a prayer vigil for five police officers killed by a lone sniper on July 8, 2016. **Besides ambushes, which are relatively rare, what dangers do you think police officers face on a daily basis?** Spencer Platt/Getty Images News/Getty Images

Two factors generally command public attention when videos appear to show police misconduct. The first is whether the incident involves a white police officer and a minority suspect. The second is whether the contents of the video contradict the official version of the incident. When these factors are present, the videos "corroborate what African Americans have been saying for years" about rampant police bias, says Paul Butler, a Georgetown University Law School professor.[59]

Pressure on Police

Although videos may shed light on a given incident, law enforcement experts caution that the footage is rarely complete. "Everything happens so quickly and you have just a moment to [think about] living or not getting up tomorrow, or your partner being dead," says one New York City detective.[60] In any case, however, public scrutiny and criticism create pressure. And this pressure has added to the already considerable stresses that come with life as a police officer, a topic we will discuss in Chapter 6.

Increased pressure has led to tension in the law enforcement community. Following the Dallas shootings mentioned above, numerous police departments started requiring officers to patrol in pairs and wear ballistic vests during routine policing activities.[61] Echoing concerns voiced by police administrators across the country, Chicago Police Superintendent Eddie Johnson worries that his officers have become more cautious on the job due to fear of becoming the subject of the next "viral video."[62] In fact, experts have identified a "de-policing" movement—a conscious decision by police organizations or officers to cut back on service. Some observers have proposed that this movement is contributing to rising violent crime rates in Chicago and other large American cities.[63]

Homeland Security and Domestic Terrorism

Without question, the attacks of September 11, 2001—when terrorists hijacked four commercial airlines and used them to kill nearly three thousand people in New York City, northern Virginia, and rural Pennsylvania—were the most significant events of the first

Learning Objective 10 Describe the defining aspects of a terrorist act, and identify one common misperception concerning domestic terrorism.

decade of the 2000s as far as crime fighting is concerned. As we will see throughout this textbook, the resulting **homeland security** movement has touched nearly every aspect of criminal justice. This movement has the ultimate goal of protecting America from **terrorism,** which can be broadly defined as the random use of staged violence to achieve political goals.

Protecting the Homeland

Immediately following 9/11, homeland security in the United States concentrated on preventing large-scale assaults by foreign terrorist operatives. More recently, however, the terrorist threat has shifted to homegrown, self-radicalized individuals who attempt to operate undetected on U.S. soil. Consequently, counterterrorism efforts now focus primarily on **domestic terrorism,** generally defined as acts of terror that are carried out within one's own country and against one's own people.

Despite public perception, domestic terrorism does *not* refer only to extremist acts by radical Muslims in the United States. In fact, a recent survey of local law enforcement agency administrators found that 74 percent identified antigovernment zealots as one of the primary terrorist threats in their jurisdictions, compared with 39 percent who singled out Muslim extremists as a significant danger.[64]

"Crowdsourcing" Terrorism One danger posed by domestic terrorists is that they often behave like ordinary criminals. Compared with preventing traditional large-scale acts of terrorism, stopping them is more like stopping a shooting at a mall or the robbery of a liquor store. These "lone wolves" have little terrorist expertise and little outside support from or contact with known terrorist organizations. Instead of directly managing American-based extremists, Middle East–based groups such as the Islamic State (ISIS) and al Qaeda seek to "crowdsource" their goals with general statements of encouragement. "Determination! Determination!" Abu Mohammed al-Adanani, a senior military leader of ISIS, urged followers before his death in 2016. "The smallest act that you do in [your] lands is more beloved to us than the biggest act done here."[65]

Crowdsourcing efforts take place mostly on social media sites such as Twitter and Instagram, as well as other Internet platforms. ISIS, for example, produces thousands of Internet videos designed to recruit foreign adherents. The terrorist group also maintains a twenty-four-hour online recruiting operation. "By assimilating into the Internet world instead of the real world, I became absorbed in a 'virtual' struggle while disconnecting from what was real," said a Virginia teenager who was arrested several years ago for driving a friend to the airport so the friend could join ISIS in Syria.[66]

Counterterrorism Strategies Counterterrorism investigators monitoring the Internet often struggle to determine which terrorism supporters are mere "talkers" and which are "doers." One common strategy requires an undercover law enforcement officer or informant to work alongside a "doer" so as to apprehend that person in the early stages of his or her plot. Approximately two out of every three prosecutions of people suspected of supporting ISIS involve undercover operations. "We're not going to wait for a person to mobilize on his own time line," says Micheal B. Steinbech, assistant director of the FBI's Counterterrorism Division.[67]

Although this tactic—discussed more fully in Chapter 6—has been responsible for numerous terrorism-related arrests, it does have one major flaw. It is of limited value against potential domestic terrorists who keep their viewpoints and their intentions off the Internet. For example, in 2014 the FBI began an investigation of Ahmad Khan Rahami after receiving a tip from his father. Scouring their databases and Rahami's online activities,

Homeland Security A concerted national effort to prevent terrorist attacks within the United States and reduce the country's vulnerability to terrorism.

Terrorism The use or threat of violence to achieve political objectives.

Domestic Terrorism Acts of terrorism that take place on U.S. soil without direct foreign involvement.

federal agents found nothing to incriminate the suspect and dropped the case. Then, in 2016, Rahami was arrested and accused of setting off a series of homemade bombs in New York and New Jersey. Afterwards, officials found evidence that he had been inspired by extremist propaganda to attack "nonbelievers." The evidence was, however, written in a notebook, apparently seen by nobody except Rahami until it was too late.[68]

▲ In January 2017, Dylann Roof, center, was sentenced to death for fatally shooting nine African American worshippers at a church in Charleston, South Carolina. A self-described white supremacist, Roof chose his victims because they were black and because he felt that, being at church, they would not fight back. **Should Roof be considered a domestic terrorist? Why or why not?**
Pool/Getty Images News/Getty Images

Security versus Privacy

"We've created the world's most powerful terrorism hindsight machine," insists one critic of U.S. counterterrorism efforts.[69] To develop more foresight in this area, homeland security officials have relied on various electronic methods of gathering information on possible terrorist plots. In particular, over the past decade the federal government has conducted surveillance operations in which the phone records of Americans are collected in bulk and analyzed to uncover any links with suspected terrorists. The surveillance does not record the contents of the calls, but rather the metadata, which includes the time of the call, the number of the caller, and the number of the phone that was called.

As we will discuss in Chapter 16, when details of the metadata surveillance program came to light in 2013, it raised the ire not only of American Muslims, who felt they were unfairly targeted, but also of *civil liberties* groups. The term **civil liberties** refers to the personal freedoms guaranteed by the U.S. Constitution, particularly the first ten amendments, called the Bill of Rights. Concerns about balancing personal freedoms and personal safety permeate our criminal justice system. In fact, an entire chapter of this textbook—Chapter 7—is needed to properly examine the rules that law enforcement must follow to protect the civil liberties of crime suspects.

In this instance, critics felt that the government's "snooping" program infringed on the rights of American citizens to keep information about their phone and Internet activity private unless it could be linked to criminal activity. Because of this criticism, in June 2015, Congress passed the USA Freedom Act,[70] which limits the federal government's metadata surveillance abilities. Needless to say, the legislation angered those who feel that metadata collection is a crucial weapon in our homeland security arsenal.

Prison Population Trends

After increasing by 500 percent from 1980 to 2008, the prison population in the United States decreased in five of the six following years.[71] To be sure, these decreases were comparatively modest (an average of about 0.9 percent per year),[72] and the American corrections system remains immense. More than 2.1 million offenders are in prison or jail in this country, and another 4.65 million are under community supervision.[73] Still, the trend reflects a series of crucial changes in the American criminal justice system.

The "Deincarceration" Movement

There is no question that economic considerations have played a role in the nation's shrinking inmate population. Federal, state, and local governments spend $80 billion a year on prisons and jails, and many corrections officials are under pressure to decrease costs.[74] Many state officials have also

Civil Liberties The basic rights and freedoms for American citizens guaranteed by the U.S. Constitution, particularly in the Bill of Rights.

embraced the concept of **justice reinvestment,** an umbrella term for policies that redirect funds saved by lowering a state's prison population into programs aimed at improving community safety. For instance, policymakers in Alabama hope to reduce that state's inmate rolls by nearly five thousand over the next decade, freeing up $26 million to hire additional parole officers and increase behavioral health treatment services for ex-offenders.[75]

In addition to economic concerns, downsizing efforts increasingly reflect "the message that locking up a lot of people doesn't necessarily bring public safety," says Joan Petersilia, co-director of Stanford University's Criminal Justice Center.[76] To reduce prison populations, therefore, federal and state correctional officials are implementing programs designed to curtail the *recidivism* rate of ex-convicts. **Recidivism** refers to the act of committing another crime (and possibly returning to incarceration) after having been punished for previous criminal behavior. To further promote deincarceration, federal and state corrections systems are making efforts (1) to keep nonviolent offenders from being sent to prison or jail and, when possible, (2) to release qualified inmates from prison before their terms end.

Diversion In Milwaukee County, Wisconsin, corrections officials employ evidence-based strategies to determine which nonviolent arrestees are at a low risk of reoffending. These arrestees, rather than being incarcerated, are rerouted to programs that help them with various problems, such as substance abuse and mental health issues. Successful completion of the programs results in dismissal or reduction of the initial charges. This strategy is known as **diversion** because it diverts offenders from incarceration to the community. Over a recent two-year period, Milwaukee County's diversion program kept nearly 42,000 low-level offenders out of prison, with a recidivism rate of only 2.7 percent for participants.[77]

Release and Reentry Under pressure from federal courts to reduce prison overcrowding, California decreased the number of inmates in its state prisons by 51,000—over 30 percent—between 2006 and 2016.[78] Nationwide, similar actions have focused on early release for offenders that Stanford's Joan Petersilia characterizes as "triple-nons": nonserious, nonviolent, and nonsexual. For example, over the past several years, the U.S. Justice Department released more than six thousand nonviolent drug offenders from federal prisons. Indeed, as Figure 1.5 highlights, releases are now consistently surpassing admissions in federal prisons, resulting in an overall decline in the number of federal inmates in the United States.

Some observers feel that this aspect of the deincarceration movement inevitably will lead to increased crime rates as the newly freed prisoners revert to their "old ways." To lessen this possibility, the corrections system has embraced *reentry programs* that provide ex-offenders with treatment for drug and alcohol addictions and mental illness, as well as help in finding housing and employment. We will examine the deincarceration movement, including policies that promote diversion and reentry, in much more detail in Chapters 12, 13, and 14.

Declining Use of the Death Penalty
Another interesting corrections trend involves death row inmates, who are in prison awaiting execution after having been found guilty of committing a **capital crime.** Near the end of 2016, the death row population in American prisons stood at about 2,900, down from 3,653 in 2000.[79] During that same time period, the number of annual executions in this country dropped from 85 to 20, a twenty-five year low. In addition, it seems that judges and juries have become less willing to sentence the "worst of the worst" criminals to death. In 2016, 30 offenders were sentenced to death, down from 49 the year before and 315 in 1996.[80]

Justice Reinvestment A corrections policy that promotes (a) a reduction in spending on prisons and jails and (b) reinvestment of the resulting savings in programs that decrease crime and reduce reoffending.

Recidivism The act of committing a new crime after having been punished for a previous crime by being convicted and sent to jail or prison.

Diversion An effort to keep offenders out of prison or jail by diverting them into programs that promote treatment and rehabilitation rather than punishment.

Capital Crime A criminal act that makes the offender eligible to receive the death penalty.

FIGURE 1.5 Federal Prisons: Admissions and Releases

From 2012 to 2015, the number of inmates released from federal prisons has been greater than the number of inmates admitted to federal prisons, an important factor in the overall reduction of federal inmates in the United States.

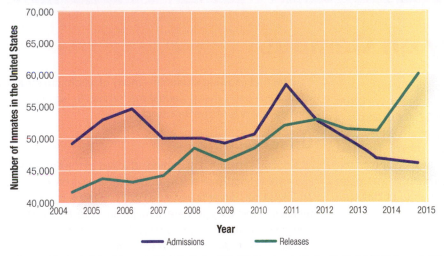

Source: Bureau of Justice Statistics, *Prisoners in 2014* (Washington, D.C.: U.S. Department of Justice, September 2015), Appendix table 2, page 29; and Bureau of Justice Statistics, *Prisoners in 2015* (Washington, D.C.: U.S. Department of Justice, December 2016), Table 7, page 11.

Despite these statistics, according to Gallup, six out of ten Americans still favor the death penalty for persons convicted of murder.[81] Voters in California and Nebraska recently declined to abolish executions in those states. To a certain degree, these attitudes reflect the moral and political strength of *victim's rights* advocates. (For our purposes, a **victim** is any person against whom a crime has been committed or who is directly or indirectly harmed by a criminal act.) Speaking of the death row inmate who murdered her fifteen-year-old daughter in Gering, Nebraska, Irene Guerrero says, "He is still living and breathing and eating . . . and my Heather was taken too early."[82] In Chapter 2, we will take a close look at legislative efforts geared toward making the criminal justice system a safer, and fairer, place for crime victims, and in Chapter 11 we will further explore the controversies surrounding *capital punishment*.

Incarceration and Race   One troublesome aspect of capital punishment is that a black defendant is much more likely to be sentenced to death for killing a white victim than a white defendant is for killing a black victim.[83] Indeed, looking at the general statistics, a bleak picture of minority incarceration emerges. Even though African Americans make up only 13 percent of the general population in the United States, the number of black men in state and federal prisons (523,000) is larger than the number of white men (499,400).[84]

In federal prisons, one in every three inmates is Latino.[85] This ratio has increased dramatically over the past decade as law enforcement and homeland security agencies have focused on immigration law violations, a subject we will consider in Chapter 5. The question of whether these figures reflect purposeful bias on the part of certain members of the criminal justice community will be addressed at various points in this textbook.

Victim Any person who suffers physical, emotional, or financial harm as the result of a criminal act.

ETHICS CHALLENGE

What are some of the ethical issues that arise when a person uses a smartphone to make a video of a police-civilian interaction and then uploads that video to the Internet?

Concealed Carry on Campus

How Things Stand

Over the past decade, a number of mass shootings have taken place on American college campuses. In 2007, for example, a student at Virginia Tech University in Blacksburg fatally shot thirty-three people and injured twenty-three others. The next year, a former student killed six and injured twenty-one on the grounds of Northern Illinois University in DeKalb. In 2015, ten people were killed and nine injured by a gunman at Umpqua Community College in Roseburg, Oregon.

As a Result...

Such incidents inevitably raise a question central to the gun control debate—would allowing guns on campuses make those places more or less safe? All fifty states allow citizens to carry concealed handguns in public, although the conditions for doing so vary. As of 2017, however, only nine states have specific legislation permitting *concealed carry* on college campuses. Twenty-three states leave the decision to ban concealed weapons to individual institutions of higher learning, and eighteen states forbid concealed weapons on college campuses outright.[86]

Supporters of concealed carry on campus argue that students and faculty members with weapons are better able to protect themselves and others from a wide variety of crimes, including mass shootings and sexual assaults. They also wonder why Second Amendment rights should vanish when a person sets foot on a college campus. Opponents counter that allowing students—many of whom are struggling with stress and other potential mental health issues—to arm themselves is a recipe for disaster.

Up for Debate

"It's not that I'm afraid of getting attacked all the time. It's more like a fire extinguisher or a seatbelt. You always have [your gun] and hope you never have to use it. If I call 911, it might be ten minutes before they get here. It might be more. It's nice to know you have ultimate responsibility for your safety."[87]—*Huyler Marsh, student, University of Texas at Austin*

"The Second Amendment allows for a well-regulated militia. What we have is not a well-regulated militia. It's a twenty-one-year-old with a backpack . . . . I'm worried about accidents. Having a weaponized campus is going to make it feel that much less welcoming."[88]—*Lisa Moore, professor, University of Texas at Austin*

What's Your Take?

Review the discussion in this chapter on "Gun Control Policy" before answering the following questions.

1. What are the general arguments for and against allowing adults to carry concealed weapons in public? Are you in favor of concealed carry? Why or why not?
2. Many professors are concerned that students may be afraid to participate in heated discussions on controversial topics when they know guns are present in the classroom. What is your opinion of this issue?

Digging Deeper...

In 2016, a new Texas law went into effect allowing certain students to carry concealed weapons on the campuses of the state's public universities. Search online for the terms **Texas** and **concealed carry on campus** to learn more about this legislation. What are the specifics of the Texas law? That is, who can take advantage of it? Are guns still banned from some parts of campus? What ability do professors have to limit guns in their classrooms and offices? Does this legislation properly balance the rights of gun owners and those who think guns should not be allowed on college campuses? Your written answer to these questions should be at least three paragraphs long.

Gilles Mingasson/Getty Images News/Getty Images

ArtOlympic/Shutterstock.com

SUMMARY

For more information on these concepts, look back to the Learning Objective icons throughout the chapter.

 Describe the two most common models of how society determines which acts are criminal. The consensus model argues that the majority of citizens will agree on which activities should be outlawed and punished as crimes. It rests on the assumption that a diverse group of people can have similar morals. In contrast, the conflict model argues that in a diverse society, the dominant groups exercise power by codifying their value systems into criminal laws.

 Define *crime*. Crime is any action punishable under criminal statutes. Because a crime is considered an offense against society, alleged criminals are prosecuted by the state rather than by victims. Crimes are punishable by sanctions that bring about a loss of personal freedom or, in some cases, life.

 Explain two main purposes of the criminal justice system. The first purpose of the criminal justice system is to provide justice to society by ensuring that all individuals are treated equally under criminal law. The second purpose is to protect society, a far-reaching objective that involves the fair treatment of crime victims and those who may or may not have committed criminal acts.

 Outline the three levels of law enforcement. Because we have a federal system of government, law enforcement occurs (a) at the federal (national) level, (b) at the state level, and (c) at the local level. Because crime is mostly a local concern, most employees in the criminal justice system work for local governments. Agencies at the federal level include the FBI, the DEA, and the U.S. Secret Service, among others.

 List the essential elements of the corrections system. Criminal offenders are placed on probation, incarcerated in a jail or prison, transferred to community-based corrections facilities, or released on parole.

 Explain the difference between the formal and informal criminal justice processes. The formal criminal justice process involves the somewhat mechanical steps that are designed to guide criminal defendants from arrest to possible punishment. For every step in the formal process, though, someone has discretion, and such discretion leads to an informal process. Even when prosecutors believe that a suspect is guilty, they have the discretion not to prosecute, for example.

 Define *ethics*, and describe the role that it plays in discretionary decision making. Ethics consist of the moral principles that guide a person's perception of right and wrong. Most criminal justice professionals have a great deal of discretionary leeway in their day-to-day decision making, and their ethical beliefs can help ensure that they make such decisions in keeping with society's established values.

 Contrast the crime control and due process models. The crime control model assumes that the criminal justice system is designed to protect the public from criminals. Thus, its most important function is to punish and repress criminal conduct. The due process model focuses on protecting the rights of the accused and providing them with the most complete safeguards possible, usually within the court system.

 Explain how background checks, in theory, protect the public from firearm-related violence. Any person who wants to buy a firearm from a federally licensed dealer must go through an application process that includes a background check. This process is designed to keep firearms out of the hands of individuals who are deemed safety risks. Consequently, a person will fail the background check—and have the gun purchase denied—if he or she exhibits any one of a number of dangerous tendencies, including showing signs of mental illness, having a felony conviction, being addicted to illegal drugs, or engaging in domestic violence.

 Describe the defining aspects of a terrorist act, and identify one common misperception concerning domestic terrorism. A terrorist act can be broadly defined as the use or threat of violence to achieve political goals. Domestic terrorism, despite a common public perception, does not include only extremist acts by radical Muslims in the United States.

1. How is it possible to have a consensus about what should or should not be illegal in a country with several hundred million adults from such diverse races, religions, and walks of life?

2. What would be some of the drawbacks of having the victims of a crime, rather than the state (through its public officials), prosecute criminals?

3. Relate the concept of federalism to state laws regarding physician-assisted suicide. What are the benefits of having several states permit a practice that is generally banned throughout the United States? What are the drawbacks? Should the federal government be able to ban the practice in states where it has won the support of voters? Why or why not?

4. Using the Internet or the news media, find three recent examples of domestic terrorism. What factors do these examples have in common? How are they different?

5. As noted earlier in the chapter, corrections officials are reducing prison budgets by releasing nonviolent offenders before their sentences are finished. What is your opinion of this strategy? What might be some of the consequences of large-scale early release programs for drug dealers and those convicted of property crimes?

KEY TERMS

assault 7
background check 23
battery 7
biometrics 21
burglary 7
capital crime 28
civil liberties 27
conflict model 6
consensus model 5
crime 5
crime control model 19
criminal justice system 9
deviance 6

discretion 17
diversion 28
domestic terrorism 26
drug 22
due process model 19
ethics 18
evidence-based practice 20
federalism 11
formal criminal justice process 15
gun control 22
homeland security 26
informal criminal justice process 17
justice 10

justice reinvestment 28
larceny 7
morals 5
murder 7
public order crime 8
recidivism 28
robbery 7
sexual assault 7
street gang 22
system 15
terrorism 26
victim 29
white-collar crime 8

1. James Queally, "The Fine Line for Police between a 'Hate Crime' and a 'Hate Incident.'" *www.latimes.com*. *Los Angeles Times*: January 6, 2017, Web.

2. *Virginia v. Black*, 536 U.S. 343 (2003). Many United States Supreme Court cases will be cited in this book, and it is important to understand these citations. *Virginia v. Black* refers to the parties in the case that the Court is reviewing. "U.S." is the abbreviation for *United States Reports*, the official publication of United States Supreme Court decisions. "536" refers to the volume of the United States Reports in which the case appears, and "343" is the page number. The citation ends with the year the case was decided, in parentheses. Most, though not all, Supreme Court case citations in this book will follow this formula.

3. *Elonis v. United States*, 575 _____ U.S. (2015).

4. Ellen Barry, "Indian Cinemas Must Play the National Anthem, Supreme Court Rules." *www.nytimes.com*. *New York Times*: November 30, 2016, Web.

5. Herman Bianchi, *Justice as Sanctuary: Toward a New System of Crime Control* (Bloomington: Indiana University Press, 1994), 72.

6. "Justice for All?" *www.wholeads.us*. The Reflective Democracy Campaign: July 2015, Web.

7. Vindu Goel and Nicole Perlroth, "For Sale on the Dark Web: Yahoo Users' Stolen Records," *New York Times* (December 16, 2016), B1.

8. David E. Sanger and Nicole Perlroth, "Encrypted Messaging Apps Face New Scrutiny Over Possible Role in Attacks," *New York Times* (November 17, 2015), A12.

9. Megan Kurlychek, "What Is My Left Hand Doing? The Need for Unifying Purpose and Policy in the Criminal Justice System," *Criminology & Public Policy* (November 2011), 909.

10. National Highway Traffic Safety Administration, *Early Estimate of Motor Vehicle Traffic Fatalities for the First Half (Jan–Jun) of 2016* (Washington, D.C.: U.S. Department of Transportation, October 2016), 1.

11. "Smartphone Use While Driving Grows beyond Texting to Social Media, Web Surfing, Selfies, Video Chatting." *www.about.att.com*. AT&T Newsroom: May 19, 2015, Web.

12. "State Laws." *www.distraction.gov*. Disraction.gov: visited January 3, 2017, Web.

13. Jay Winsten, quoted in Matt Richtel, "On Your Phone at the Wheel? Watch Out for the Textalyzer," *New York Times* (April 28, 2016), A1.

14. *Ibid.*

15. *Gonzales v. Oregon*, 546 U.S. 243 (2006).

16. Alison Smith and Richard M. Thompson II, "Criminal Offenses Enacted from 2008–2013," *Congressional Research Service* (June 23, 2014).

17. DEA Public Affairs, "DEA Announces Actions Related to Marijuana and Industrial Hemp." *www.dea.gov*. Drug Enforcement Administration: August 11, 2016, Web.

18. 545 U.S. 1, 15 (2005).

19. John Ingold, "Obama: Feds Won't Arrest Marijuana Users in Colorado, Washington." *www.denverpost.com*. *Denver Post*: December 14, 2012, Web.

20. President's Commission on Law Enforcement and Administration of Justice, *The Challenge of Crime in a Free Society* (Washington, D.C.: Government Printing Office, 1967), 7.

21. John Heinz and Peter Manikas, "Networks among Elites in a Local Criminal Justice System," *Law and Society Review* 26 (1992), 831–861.

22. James Q. Wilson, "What to Do about Crime: Blaming Crime on Root Causes," *Vital Speeches* (April 1, 1995), 373.

23. Herbert Packer, The Limits of the Criminal Sanction (Stanford, Calif.: Stanford University Press, 1968), 154–173.

24. *Ibid.*

25. Daniel Givelber, "Meaningless Acquittals, Meaningful Convictions: Do We Reliably Acquit the Innocent?" *Rutgers Law Review* 49 (Summer 1997), 1317.

26. Deborah L. Rhode, "Why Is Adultery Still a Crime?" *www.latimes.com*. *Los Angeles Times*: May 2, 2016, Web.

27. O.C.G.A. Section 40-6-241 (2010).

28. Alan Blinder, "A Cheeseburger, a Suburban Traffic Stop and a Ticket for Eating While Driving," *New York Times* (January 21, 2015), A10.

29. George P. Fletcher, "Some Unwise Reflections about Discretion," *Law & Contemporary Problems* (Autumn 1984), 279.

30. *Every 25 Seconds: The Human Toll of Criminalizing Drug Use in the United States* (New York: Human Rights Watch, October 2016), 6.

31. Antonin Scalia, "The Rule of Law as a Law of Rules," *University of Chicago Law Review* 56 (1989), 1178–1180.

32. John Kleinig, *Ethics and Criminal Justice: An Introduction* (New York: Cambridge University Press, 2008), 33–35.

33. Packer, *op. cit.*, 154–173.

34. Givelber, *op. cit.*, 1317.

35. Federal Bureau of Investigation, *Crime in the United States, 2015*, Table 1. *www.ucr.fbi.gov*. U.S. Department of Justice: 2016, Web.

36. "Next Generation Identification (NGI)." *www.fbi.gov*. Federal Bureau of Investigation: visited January 5, 2017, Web.

37. Timothy Williams, "Study Finds Disparities in Arrests for Marijuana," *New York Times* (October 13, 2016), A19.

38. "Prescription Opioid Overdose Data." *www.cdc.gov*. Centers for Disease Control and Prevention: visited January 5, 2017, Web.

39. Timothy Williams, "Violence in St. Louis Traced to Cheap Mexican Heroin," *New York Times* (April 3, 2016), A16.

40. *Crime in the United States, 2015, op. cit.*, Expanded Homicide Table 7 and Robbery Table 3.

41. Associated Press, "Chicago Ends Year with 762 Killings, Most in 2 Decades" (January 2, 2017).

42. "Archive 2016." *www.gunviolencearchive.org*. Gun Violence Archive: visited January 5, 2017, Web.

43. Bureau of Alcohol, Tobacco, Firearms and Explosives, *Annual Statistical Update 2016* (Washington, D.C.: U.S. Department of Justice, August 2016), Exhibit 1, page 1.

44. Christopher Ingraham, "There Are Now More Guns than People in the United States." *www.washingtonpost.com*. *Washington Post*: October 5, 2015, Web.

45. Lawrence H. Silberman, quoted in David Nakamura and Robert Barnes, "Appeals Court Rules D.C. Handgun Ban Unconstitutional," *Washington Post* (March 10, 2007), A1.

46. *District of Columbia v. Heller*, 554 U.S. 570 (2008); and *McDonald v. Chicago*, 561 U.S. 3025 (2010).

47. 18 U.S.C. 922(t).

48. Ronald J. Frandsen et al., *Background Checks for Firearm Transfers, 2010—Statistical Tables* (Washington, D.C.: U.S. Department of Justice, February 2013), 1.

49. Jennifer C. Karberg et al., *Background Checks for Firearm Transfers, 2013–2014—Statistical Tables* (Washington, D.C.: U.S. Department of Justice, June 2016), 1.

50. 27 C.F.R. Section 478.11 (2010).

51. Karberg, et al, *op. cit.*, Appendix Table 5, 21.

52. "Gun Laws," *The Economist* (May 3, 2014), 28.

53. "New Laws for Handgun Licensing Program (Formerly Known as Concealed Handgun Licensing): Effective January 1, 2016, *www.dps.texas.gov*. Texas Department of Public Safety: visited January 5, 2017, Web.

54. Campbell Robertson and Timothy Williams, "As States Expand Gun Rights, the Police Object," *New York Times* (May 4, 2016), A10.

55. Matt Zapotosky, Adam Goldman, and Scott Higham, "Police in Dallas: 'He Wanted To Kill White People, Especially White Officers.'" *www.washingtonpost.com*. *Washington Post*: July 8, 2016, Web.

56. Quoted in "Paralysed by YouTube," *The Economist* (October 31, 2015), 28.

57. Bureau of Justice Statistics, *Police Use of Nonfatal Force, 2002–11* (Washington, D.C.: U.S. Department of Justice, November 2015), 1.

58. Quoted in Pervaiz Shallwani, Ana Campoy, and Valerie Bauerlein, "Prevalence of Video Puts Police Under the Lens," *www.wsj.com*. *Wall Street Journal*: April 10, 2015, Web.

59. Quoted in Richard Pérez-Peña and Timothy Williams, "Glare of Video Is Shifting Public's View of Police," *New York Times* (July 31, 2015), A1.

60. Quoted in Michael Wilson and Michael Schwirtz, "Officers Confront Dual Role: Villain and Victim," *New York Times* (July 10, 2016), A1.

61. Jon Kamp, Miriam Jordan, and Douglas Belkin, "After Dallas Shootings, U.S. Police Take Extra Precautions." *www.wsj.com*. *Wall Street Journal*: July 9, 2016, Web.

62. "Chicago Ends Year with 762 Killings, Most in 2 Decades," *op. cit.*

63. Richard Rosenfeld, *Documenting and Explaining the 2015 Homicide Rise: Research Directions* (Washington, D.C.: National Institute of Justice, June 2016), 2–3.

64. Charles Kurzman and David Schanzer, *Law Enforcement Assessment of the Violent Extremism Threats* (Durham, NC: Triangle Center on Terrorism and Homeland Security, June 25, 2015), 3.

65. Quoted in Robin Wright, "After the Islamic State," *New Yorker* (December 12, 2016), 31.

66. Quoted in Scott Shane, Matt Apuzzo, and Eric Schmitt, "Online Embrace from ISIS, a Few Clicks Away," *New York Times* (December 9, 2015), A1.

67. Quoted in Eric Lichtblau, "Once Last Resort, F.B.I. Stings Become Common in ISIS Fight," *New York Times* (June 8, 2016), A1.

68. Devlin Barrett and Pervaiz Shallwani, "N.Y. Bombing Suspect's Notebook Gives First Look at His Motivations." *www.wsj.com. Wall Street Journal*: September 20, 2016, Web.

69. Quoted in Philip Shishkin and Patrick O'Connor, "San Bernardino Shooting Shows How U.S. Terror Defenses Are Tested." *www.wsj.com. Wall Street Journal*: December 6, 2015, Web.

70. H.R. 3361—113th Congress: USA FREEDOM Act, January 11, 2016.

71. Bureau of Justice Statistics, *Prisoners in 2015* (Washington, D.C.: U.S. Department of Justice, December 2016), 1.

72. *Ibid.*, Table 1, page 3.

73. Bureau of Justice Statistics, *Correctional Populations in the United States, 2015* (Washington, D.C.: U.S. Department of Justice, December 2016), Table 1.

74. "One Nation, Behind Bars," *The Economist* (August 17, 2013), 12.

75. *Justice Reinvestment in Alabama: Analysis and Policy Framework* (Washington, D.C.: Bureau of Justice Assistance, March 2015), 1–2.

76. Quoted in Erica Goode, "U.S. Prison Populations Decline Reflecting New Approach to Crime," *New York Times* (July 26, 2013), A11.

77. Erika Parks, et al., *Local Justice Reinvestment: Strategies, Outcomes, and Keys to Success* (Washington, D.C.: Urban Institute, August 2016), 9.

78. "Office of Research: Population Reports." *www.cdcr.ca.gov.* California Department of Corrections and Rehabilitation: visited January 5, 2017, Web.

79. "Death Row Inmates by State and Size of Death Row by Year," *www.deathpenaltyinfo.org.* Death Penalty Information Center: visited January 6, 2017, Web.

80. *The Death Penalty in 2016: Year End Report* (Washington, D.C.: Death Penalty Information Center, 2016), 3.

81. "Death Penalty." *www.gallup.com.* Gallup: October 5–9, 2016, Web.

82. Paul Hammel, "Death Penalty in Nebraska." *www.omaha.com. Omaha World-Herald*: October 30, 2016, Web.

83. "National Statistics on Death Penalty and Race," *www.deathpenaltyinfo.org.* Death Penalty Information Center: December 9, 2016, Web.

84. Prisons in 2015, *op. cit.*, Table 3, page 6.

85. "Inmate Ethnicity." *www.bop.gov.* Federal Bureau of Prisons: November 26, 2016, Web.

86. "Guns on Campus: Overview." *www.ncsl.org.* National Conference of State Legislatures: May 31, 2016, Web.

87. Quoted in Dave Phillips, "Grappling with Guns on Campus," *New York Times* (August 28, 2016), A16.

88. Quoted in *Ibid.*

How to Read Case Citations and Find Court Decisions

Many important court cases are discussed throughout this book. Every time a court case is mentioned, you will be able to check its citation using the endnotes on the final pages of the chapter. Court decisions are recorded and published on paper and on the Internet. When a court case is mentioned, the notation that is used to refer to, or to cite, the case denotes where the published decision can be found.

Decisions of state courts of appeals are usually published in two places, the state reports of that particular state and the more widely used *National Reporter System* published by West Group. Some states no longer publish their own reports. The *National Reporter System* divides the states into the following geographic areas: Atlantic (A. or A.2d), North Eastern (N.E. or N.E.2d), North Western (N.W. or N.W.2d), Pacific (P., P.2d, or P.3d), Southern (So., So.2d, or So.3d), and South Western (S.W., S.W.2d, or S.W.3d). The 2d and 3d in these abbreviations refer to the *Second Series* and *Third Series*, respectively.

Federal trial court decisions are published unofficially in West's *Federal Supplement* (F.Supp. or F.Supp.2d), and opinions from the circuit courts of appeals are reported unofficially in West's *Federal Reporter* (F., F.2d, or F.3d). Opinions from the United States Supreme Court are reported in the *United States Reports* (U.S.), the *Lawyers' Edition of the Supreme Court Reports* (L.Ed.), West's *Supreme Court Reporter* (S.Ct.), and other publications. The *United States Reports* is the official publication of United States Supreme Court decisions. It is published by the federal government. Many early decisions are missing from these volumes. The citations of the early volumes of the United States Reports include the names of the actual reporters, such as Dallas, Cranch, or Wheaton. *McCulloch v. Maryland*, for example, is cited as 17 U.S. (4 Wheat.) 316. Only after 1874 did the present citation system, in which cases are cited based solely on their volume and page numbers in the *United States Reports*, come into being. The *Lawyers' Edition of the Supreme Court Reports* is an unofficial and more complete edition of Supreme Court decisions. West's *Supreme Court Reporter* is an unofficial edition of decisions dating from October 1882. These volumes contain headnotes and numerous brief editorial statements of the law involved in a given case.

Citations to decisions of state courts of appeals give the name of the case; the volume, name, and page number of the state's official report (if the state publishes its own reports); and the volume, unit, and page number of the *National Reporter*. Federal court citations also give the name of the case and the volume, name, and page number of the reports. In addition to the citation, this textbook lists the year of the decision in parentheses. Consider, for example, the case *Miranda v. Arizona*, 384 U.S. 436 (1966). The Supreme Court's decision in this case may be found in volume 384 of the *United States Reports* on page 436. The case was decided in 1966.

Causes of Crime

To target your study and review, look for these numbered Learning Objective icons throughout the chapter.

Chapter Outline		Corresponding Learning Objectives
The Role of Theory	**1**	Discuss the difference between a hypothesis and a theory in the context of criminology.
The Brain and the Body	**2**	Summarize rational choice theory.
	3	Explain how brain-scanning technology is able to help scientists determine if an individual is at risk for criminal offending.
Bad Neighborhoods and Other Economic Disadvantages	**4**	List and describe the three theories of social structure that help explain crime.
	5	Describe the social conflict theory known as the social reality of crime.
Life Lessons and Criminal Behavior	**6**	List and briefly explain the three branches of social process theory.
	7	Describe the importance of early childhood behavior for those who subscribe to self-control theory.
The Link between Drugs and Crime	**8**	Contrast the medical model of addiction with the criminal model of addiction.
Criminology from Theory to Practice	**9**	Explain the theory of the chronic offender and its importance for the criminal justice system.

Excess Baggage

▲ Esteban Santiago is taken to federal court in Broward County, Florida, after being charged with fatally shooting five people at the Fort Lauderdale-Hollywood International Airport.

AP Images/Lynne Sladky

mind was being controlled by a U.S. spy agency. FBI agents eventually turned him over to local authorities, who briefly held him for a psychiatric evaluation. According to his brother, Santiago had become "furious" since serving in Iraq from April 2010 to February 2011 with the Puerto Rico National Guard. He had recently complained about hearing voices and hallucinating.

For the most part, Santiago fit the profile for those who commit random multiple shootings in public places. He was male, single, and had a history of mental illness. Like a number of other mass shooters, he had previously been charged with crimes involving domestic violence. This accumulation of "red flags" does little, however, to answer the basic questions that always arise after outbreaks of seemingly senseless bloodshed. Why did it happen? Can we stop it from happening again? Unfortunately, the evidence suggests that potential killers such as Santiago are unremarkable until, suddenly, they're not. "He was a walk-in complaint," said an FBI spokesperson, defending the agency's handling of the case in Anchorage. "This is something that happens at [our] offices around the country every day."

For his long flight from Anchorage, Alaska, to South Florida, Esteban Santiago checked only a single piece of luggage. When he arrived at the Ft. Lauderdale-Hollywood Airport, at about 1 P.M. on January 6, 2017, Santiago retrieved his bag and went into a bathroom. There, he unpacked and loaded a Walther 9-millimeter handgun. Then, he emerged into the baggage claim area and started shooting. After killing five victims and wounding eight more, Santiago—out of ammunition—lay spread-eagled on the floor, quietly surrendering.

In the days that followed, a number of disturbing details about Santiago's past emerged. A year earlier, he had been arrested and charged with assault for breaking down a bathroom door to get at his girlfriend. In November 2016, Santiago walked into the Federal Bureau of Investigation (FBI) field office in Anchorage to report that his

FOR CRITICAL ANALYSIS

1. Should law enforcement in Alaska have focused more attention on Esteban Santiago because he fit the profile of a mass shooter? What are some of the problems with this crime prevention strategy?

2. Several states have recently enacted laws allowing courts to temporarily take away firearms from people displaying signs of potential dangerousness. What is your opinion of these statutes? How could such a law have been applied in this case?

3. What explanation can you give for the apparent connection in a number of offenders between committing a mass public shooting and having a history of domestic violence?

The Role of Theory

The study of crime, or **criminology,** is rich with different explanations for why people commit crimes. At the same time, *criminologists*, or those who study the causes of crime, warn against using models or profiles to predict violent behavior. To be sure, the risk factors exhibited by a "furious" Esteban Santiago, with his history of mental illness and domestic violence, seem obvious in retrospect. Such characteristics are also found in scores of people who will not become multiple-victim shooters, however. "You can't go out and round up all the alienated angry young men," points out Jeffrey Swanson, a professor of psychiatry and behavioral sciences at the Duke University School of Medicine.[1]

Still, in the case of Santiago, there did seem to be some connection between his characteristics and his violent outburst, particularly when one considers that he had briefly been held in an Anchorage psychiatric hospital unit. That is, there may have been a *correlation* between his behavior and his crimes, a concept that is crucial to criminology.

Correlation and Cause

Correlation between two variables means that they tend to vary together. **Causation,** in contrast, means that one variable is responsible for the change in the other. As we will see later in the chapter, there is a correlation between drug abuse and criminal behavior: statistically, many criminals are also drug abusers. But drug abuse does not cause crime: not everyone who abuses drugs is a criminal.

To give another example, a study led by Scott Wolfe, a criminologist at the University of South Carolina, looked at crime rates in counties where the megastore Walmart added new stores during the 1990s. Wolfe and his co-author found that crime rates in those counties were significantly higher than in those neighboring counties with no Walmart expansion.[2] Despite these results, no criminologist would assert that new Walmart stores *caused* the higher crime rates. Other factors, such as unemployment, poverty, and zoning patterns, must also be taken into account to get a fuller understanding of the crime picture in the studied areas.

So, correlation does not equal cause. Such is the quandary for criminologists. We can say that there is a correlation between many factors and criminal behavior, but it is quite difficult to prove that the factors directly cause criminal behavior. Consequently, the question that is the underpinning of criminology—What causes crime?—has yet to be definitively answered.

Criminological Theories

Criminologists have, however, uncovered a wealth of information concerning a different, and more practically applicable, inquiry: Given a certain set of circumstances, why do individuals commit criminal acts? This information has allowed criminologists to develop a number of *theories* concerning the causes of crime.

The Scientific Method
Many of us tend to think of a *theory* as some sort of guess or a statement that is lacking in credibility. In the academic world, and therefore for our purposes, a **theory** is an explanation of a happening or circumstance that is based on observation, experimentation, and reasoning. Scientific and academic researchers observe facts and their consequences to develop *hypotheses* about what will occur when a similar fact pattern is present in the future. A **hypothesis** is a proposition that can be tested by researchers or observers to determine if it is valid. If enough authorities do find the hypothesis valid, it will be accepted as a theory. See Figure 2.1 for an example of this process, known as the *scientific method*, in action.

Criminology The scientific study of crime and the causes of criminal behavior.

Correlation The relationship between two measurements or behaviors that tend to move in the same direction.

Causation The relationship in which a change in one measurement or behavior creates a recognizable change in another measurement or behavior.

Theory An explanation of a happening or circumstance that is based on observation, experimentation, and reasoning.

Hypothesis A possible explanation for an observed occurrence that can be tested by further investigation.

Learning Objective 1 Discuss the difference between a hypothesis and a theory in the context of criminology.

FIGURE 2.1 **The Scientific Method**

The scientific method is a process through which researchers test the accuracy of a hypothesis. This simple example should provide an idea of how the scientific method works.

 Observation: I left my home at 7:00 this morning, and I was on time for class.

 Hypothesis: If I leave home at 7:00 every morning, then I will never be late for class.
(Hypotheses are often presented in this "If . . . , then . . ." format.)

 Test: For three straight weeks, I left home at 7:00 every morning. Not one time was I late for class.

 Verification: Four of my neighbors have the same morning class. They agree that they are never late if they leave by 7:00 A.M.

 Theory: As long as I leave home at 7:00 A.M., I don't have to worry about being late for class.

 Prediction: Tomorrow morning I'll leave at 7:00, and I will be on time for my class.

Note that even a sound theory supported by the scientific method, such as this one, does not *prove* that the prediction will be correct. Other factors not accounted for in the test and verification stages, such as an unexpected traffic accident, may disprove the theory. Predictions based on complex theories, such as the criminological ones we will be discussing in this chapter, are often challenged in such a manner.

Theory in Action

Criminological theories are primarily concerned with attempting to determine the reasons for criminal behavior. For example, two criminologists from Arizona State University, Matthew Larson and Gary Sweeten, wanted to test their hypothesis that young people involved in romantic breakups are at high risk for destructive behavior. Relying on a survey of high school and college students who were asked about issues in their personal lives, Larson and Sweeten found some support for their hypothesis. According to the data, breakups do indeed correlate with higher rates of criminal offending and substance abuse among young men and higher rates of substance abuse among young women.[3]

The Brain and the Body

As you read this chapter, keep in mind that theories are not the same as facts, and most, if not all, of the criminological theories described in these pages have their detractors. Over the past century, however, a number of theories of crime have gained wide, if not total, acceptance. We now turn our attention to these theories, starting with those that focus on the psychological and physical aspects of criminal behavior.

Crime and Free Will: Choice Theories of Crime

For the purposes of the American criminal justice system, the answer to why a person commits a crime is rather straightforward: because that person chooses to do so. This application of **choice theory** to criminal law is not absolute. If a defendant can prove that she or he lacked the ability to make a rational choice, in certain circumstances the defendant will not be punished as harshly for a crime as would normally be the case. But such allowances are relatively recent. From the early days of this country, the general presumption in criminal law has been that behavior is a consequence of free will.

Theories of Classical Criminology

An emphasis on free will and human rationality in the realm of criminal behavior has its roots in **classical criminology.** Classical theorists believed that crime was an expression of a person's rational decision-making process: before committing a crime, a person would weigh the benefits of the crime against the costs of being apprehended. Therefore, if punishments were stringent enough to outweigh the benefits of crime, they would dissuade people from committing the crime in the first place.

The earliest popular expression of classical theory came in 1764 when the Italian Cesare Beccaria (1738–1794) published his *Essays on Crime and Punishments*. Beccaria criticized existing systems of criminal law as irrational and argued that criminal

Choice Theory A school of criminology based on the belief that individuals have free will to engage in any behavior, including criminal behavior.

Classical Criminology A school of criminology that holds that wrongdoers act as if they weigh the possible benefits of criminal or delinquent activity against the expected costs of being apprehended.

procedures should be more consistent with human behavior. He believed that, to be just, criminal law should reflect three truths:

1. All decisions, including the decision to commit a crime, are the result of rational choice.
2. Fear of punishment can have a deterrent effect on the choice to commit crime.
3. The more swift and certain punishment is, the more effective it will be in controlling crime.[4]

Beccaria believed that any punishment that purported to do anything other than deter crime was cruel and arbitrary.

Positivism and Modern Rational Theory

By the end of the 1800s, the positivist school of criminologists had superseded classical criminology. According to positivism, criminal behavior is determined by biological, psychological, and social forces and is beyond the control of the individual. The Italian physician Cesare Lombroso (1835–1909), an early adherent of positivism who is known as the "Father of Criminology," believed that criminals were throwbacks to the savagery of early humankind and could therefore be identified by certain physical characteristics such as sharp teeth and large jaws. He also theorized that criminality was similar to mental illness and could be genetically passed down from generation to generation in families that had cases of insanity, syphilis, epilepsy, and even deafness. Such individuals, according to Lombroso and his followers, had no free choice when it came to wrongdoing—their criminality had been predetermined at birth.[5]

Positivist theory lost credibility as crime rates began to climb in the 1970s. If crime was caused by external factors, critics asked, why had the proactive social programs of the 1960s not brought about a decrease in criminal activity? An updated version of classical criminology, known as *rational choice theory*, found renewed acceptance. James Q. Wilson (1931–2012), one of the most prominent critics of the positivist school, summed up rational choice theory as follows:

> At any given moment, a person can choose between committing a crime and not committing it. The consequences of committing a crime consist of rewards (what psychologists call "reinforcers") and punishments; the consequences of not committing the crime also entail gains and losses. The larger the ratio of the net rewards of crime to the net rewards of [not committing a crime], the greater the tendency to commit a crime.[6]

In other words, a person, before committing a crime, acts as if she or he is weighing the benefits (which may be money, in the case of a robbery) against the costs (the possibility of being caught and going to prison or jail). If the perceived benefits are greater than the potential costs, the person is more likely to commit the crime.

"Thrill Offenders"

Expanding on rational choice theory, sociologist Jack Katz has stated that the "rewards" of crime may be sensual as well as financial. The inherent danger of criminal activity, according to Katz, increases the "rush" a criminal experiences on successfully committing a crime. Katz labels the rewards of this "rush" the *seduction of crime*.[7]

For example, several years ago Jae Williams was convicted of murdering a classmate at Santa Teresa High School in San Jose, California. "I guess I just finally wanted to kill somebody," Williams told investigators, explaining the motivation behind what prosecutors labeled a "thrill kill."[8] Katz believes that such seemingly "senseless" crimes can be explained by rational choice theory only if the intrinsic (inner) reward of the crime itself is considered.

Positivism A school of the social sciences that sees criminal and delinquent behavior as the result of biological, psychological, and social forces.

Learning Objective 2 Summarize rational choice theory.

Choice Theory and Public Policy

The theory that wrongdoers choose to commit crimes is a cornerstone of the American criminal justice system. Because crime is seen as the end result of a series of rational choices, policymakers have reasoned that severe punishment can deter criminal activity by adding another variable to the decision-making process. Supporters of the death penalty—now used by thirty-one states and the federal government—emphasize its deterrent effects, and legislators have used harsh mandatory sentences to control illegal drug use and trafficking.

"Born Criminal": Biological and Psychological Theories of Crime

As we have seen, Cesare Lombroso believed in the "criminal born" man and woman and was confident that he could distinguish criminals by their apelike physical features. Such far-fetched notions have long been relegated to scientific oblivion. Nevertheless, many criminologists do believe that *trait theories* have validity. These theories suggest that certain *biological* or *psychological* traits in individuals could incline them toward criminal behavior given a certain set of circumstances.

Biology is a very broad term that refers to the scientific study of living organisms, while psychology pertains more specifically to the study of the mind and its processes. "All behavior is biological," pointed out geneticist David C. Rowe. "All behavior is represented in the brain, in its biochemistry, electrical activity, structure, and growth and decline."[9]

Genetics and Crime

Criminologists who study biological theories of crime often focus on the effect that *genes* have on human behavior. Genes are coded sequences of DNA that control every aspect of our biology, from the color of our eyes and hair to the type of emotions we have. Every person's genetic makeup is determined by genes inherited from his or her parents. Consequently, when scientists study ancestral or evolutionary developments, they are engaging in genetics, a branch of biology that deals with traits that are passed from one generation to another through genes.

Twin and Adoption Studies   Genetics is at the heart of criminology's "nurture versus nature" debate. In other words, are traits such as aggressiveness and antisocial behavior, both of which often lead to criminality, a result of a person's environment (nurture) or her or his genes (nature)? To tip the balance toward "nature," a criminologist must be able to prove that, all other things being equal, the offspring of aggressive or antisocial parents are at greater risk to exhibit those traits than are the offspring of parents who are not aggressive or antisocial.

Many criminologists have turned to *twin studies* to determine the relationship between genetics and criminal behavior. If the "nature" argument is correct, then twins should exhibit similar antisocial tendencies. The problem with twin studies is that most twins grow up in the same environment, so it is difficult, if not impossible, to determine whether their behavior is influenced more by their genes or by their surroundings.[10] Because of such problems, some criminologists prefer *adoption studies*, which eliminate the problem of family members sharing the same environment. A number of well-received adoption studies have shown a correlation between rates of criminality among adopted children and antisocial or criminal behavior by their biological parents.[11]

The "Crime Gene"   About twenty-five years ago, Dutch scientists claimed to have determined that males who possessed a mutant copy of the MAOA gene were abnormally aggressive.[12] Dubbed the "warrior gene," MAOA suddenly became the center of a great

Biology The science of living organisms, including their structure, function, growth, and origin.

Psychology The scientific study of mental processes and behavior.

Genetics The study of how certain traits or qualities are transmitted from parents to their offspring.

deal of criminological attention. Additional research, however, proved that this genetic mutation does not, by itself, lead to criminal behavior. Rather, a person with low levels of MAOA, which regulates emotion, exhibits an increased risk for violent behavior only when that person was also abused as a child.[13]

A more recent study of nearly 900 prison inmates in Finland did find that those with a combination of mutated MAOA and another gene called CDH13 were strongly linked to "extremely violent behavior," defined as at least ten murders, attempted murders, or other attacks.[14] Keep in mind, however, that no single gene or trait has been proved to *cause* criminality. The lead author of the just-mentioned Finland study said that combination of the two genes increased only the

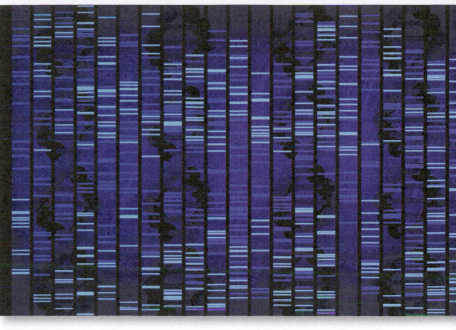

▲ DNA sequences such as the one shown here indicate that we inherit certain genetic traits from our parents. These traits help determine our behavior patterns. **Why might one criminologist insist that all studies of the causes of crime are "polluted" by "hidden genetic effects"?** The Biochemist Artist/Shutterstock.com

"relative" risk of violent behavior. "The absolute risk is still very low," he cautioned.[15] The most that genetics can do, it seems, is raise the possibility for a predisposition toward aggression or violence.

Hormones and Aggression

Chemical messengers known as **hormones** have also been the subject of much criminological study. Criminal activity in males has been linked to elevated levels of hormones—specifically, **testosterone,** which controls secondary sex characteristics and has been associated with traits of aggression. Testing of inmate populations shows that those incarcerated for violent crimes exhibit higher testosterone levels than other prisoners.[16] Elevated testosterone levels have also been used to explain a lessening in criminal behavior with age, as the average testosterone level of men under twenty-eight is double that of men between thirty-one and sixty-six years old.[17]

A very specific form of female violent behavior is believed to stem from hormones. In 2016, a judge sentenced Carol Coronado to three consecutive life terms in prison for fatally stabbing her three young daughters at their home near Carson, California. Coronado's defense attorney had claimed his client was suffering from *postpartum psychosis* at the time of her alleged crime. This temporary illness, thought to be caused partly by the hormonal changes that women experience after childbirth, triggers abnormal behavior in a small percentage of new mothers.[18]

The Brain and Crime

Dr. Margaret Spinelli, a women's health expert at New York City's Columbia University, explains that during pregnancy, a pregnant woman's hormones increase "more than a hundredfold." Then, following birth, hormone levels plummet. This roller coaster of hormonal activity can "disrupt brain chemistry," contributing to postpartum psychosis.[19] The study of how genetics and brain activity influence criminal behavior is called *neurocriminology*. Its practitioners have contributed a great deal to the understanding of what predisposes humans to violent behavior.

Neurocriminology is based on the theory that criminal behavior is often the result of a combination of biological and environmental risk factors. For example, Jessica Wolpaw Reyes, an economist at Amherst College in Massachusetts, focused on the risks posed by

Hormones A chemical substance, produced in tissue and conveyed in the bloodstream, that controls certain cellular and body functions, such as growth and reproduction.

Testosterone The hormone primarily responsible for the production of sperm and the development of male secondary sex characteristics, such as the growth of facial and pubic hair and the change of voice pitch.

lead to help explain the drop in crime rates since the early 1990s, a phenomenon we will address in more detail next chapter.

Numerous studies have shown that exposure to lead damages the brains of children, causing them to have lower IQs, less impulse control, and a propensity for violent behavior. In the late 1970s, the federal government banned lead in gasoline and many types of paint. A generation of lead-free children has reached adulthood since then, and, Reyes believes, its nonviolent tendencies are responsible for half of the recent drop in violent crime rates.[20]

CJ & TECHNOLOGY

Neurocriminology

What can someone's brain activity tell us about her or his potential criminality? Neurocriminology uses brain-scanning technology to help scientists answer that question—at least in part. A technique known as functional magnetic resonance imaging (fMRI) measures the flow of blood in the brain as a subject carries out certain tasks. With the help of fMRI, criminologists have been able to pinpoint areas of the brain that control behavior such as impulsiveness, emotions, and decision making, all of which are associated with antisocial and criminal behavior.

Recently, specialists with the Mind Research Network used a mobile fMRI device to scan the brains of inmates in a New Mexico prison who were soon to be released. The researchers focused on an area of the brain that regulates impulsive behavior, called the anterior cingulate cortex (ACC). These experts predicted, correctly, that inmates with low activity in the ACC were more likely to be rearrested after release than those with normal ACC activity. Another study shows that men with a smaller amygdala—a part of the brain's frontal lobe that controls anger and fear reactions to outside stimuli—are as much as three times more likely to commit violence than those with an average-sized amygdala.

Thinking about Neurocriminology

At present, brain scans cannot come close to predicting future criminal offending. They can only indicate a possibility of future criminal offending. With this limitation in mind, what use should the criminal justice system make of brain-mapping technology, if any?

Learning Objective 3 Explain how brain-scanning technology is able to help scientists determine if an individual is at risk for criminal offending.

Mental Illness and Crime According to the federal government, more than half of all prison and jail inmates in the United States have mental health problems, with smaller percentages suffering from severe brain disorders.[21] In recent years, thanks to several high-profile murders, violent crime has been linked to *schizophrenia*, a chronic brain disorder that can lead to erratic, uncontrollable behavior. Persons suffering from this disease are at an unusually high risk for committing suicide or harming others. Culling data from 160 cases of public mass killings, Grant Duwe, a criminologist with the Minnesota Department of Corrections, found that 61 percent of those responsible showed evidence of mental illness, with the two most common ailments being schizophrenia and depression.[22]

Findings such as these have carried over into the gun control debate. As mentioned in the previous chapter, people who have been involuntarily committed to psychiatric care because of mental illness are prohibited from purchasing firearms. Some criminologists reject this explicit connection between mental illness and violent crime, however. One recent study estimates that eliminating the effects of mental illness would reduce overall gun violence in the United States by only 4 percent.[23] Additional research shows that only about 5 percent of all gun homicides in this country are committed by people who have been diagnosed with a mental illness.[24] Consequently, there may be a correlation between mental conditions such as schizophrenia and violence, but such conditions cannot be said to cause violent behavior.

Psychology and Crime

Like biological theories of crime, psychological theories of crime operate under the assumption that individuals have traits that make them more or less predisposed to criminal activity. To a certain extent, however, psychology rests more heavily on abstract ideas than does biology. Even Sigmund Freud (1856–1939), perhaps the most influential of all psychologists, considered the operations of the mind to be, like an iceberg, mostly hidden.

Freud's Psychoanalytic Theory

For all his accomplishments, Freud rarely turned his attention directly toward the causes of crime. His **psychoanalytic theory,** however, has provided a useful approach for thinking about criminal behavior. According to Freud, most of our thoughts, wishes, and urges originate in the *unconscious* region of the mind, and we have no control—or even awareness—of these processes. Freud believed that, on an unconscious level, all humans have criminal tendencies and that each of us is continually struggling against these tendencies.

To explain this struggle, Freud devised three abstract systems that interact in the brain: the *id*, the *ego*, and the *superego*. The id is driven by a constant desire for pleasure and self-gratification through sexual and aggressive urges. The ego, in contrast, stands for reason and common sense, while the superego "learns" the expectations of family and society and acts as the conscience. When the three systems fall into disorder, the id can take control, causing the individual to act on his or her antisocial urges and, possibly, commit crimes.[25]

Social Psychology and "Evil" Behavior

Another crucial branch of psychology—*social psychology*—focuses on human behavior in the context of how human beings relate to and influence one another. Social psychology rests on the assumption that the way we view ourselves is shaped to a large degree by how we think others view us. Generally, we act in the same manner as those we like or admire because we want them to like or admire us. Thus, to a certain extent, social psychology tries to explain the influence of crowds on individual behavior.

In the early 1970s, psychologist Philip Zimbardo highlighted the power of group behavior in dramatic fashion. Zimbardo randomly selected some Stanford University undergraduate students to act as "guards" and other students to act as "inmates" in an artificial prison environment. Before long, the students began to act as if these designations were real, with the "guards" physically mistreating the "inmates," who rebelled with equal violence. Within six days, Zimbardo was forced to discontinue the experiment out of fear for its participants' safety.[26] One of the basic assumptions of social psychology is that people are able to justify improper or even criminal behavior by convincing themselves that it is actually acceptable behavior. As Zimbardo's experiment showed, they find it much easier to do this when they are acting in groups where others are behaving in the same manner than when they are acting alone.[27]

Psychoanalytic Theory Sigmund Freud's theory that attributes our thoughts and actions to unconscious motives.

▼ On February 1, 2017, a bonfire set by demonstrators burns on the University of California, Berkeley. To protest a speaking appearance by a controversial political figure, the demonstrators also hurled smoke bombs and broke windows, causing $100,000 worth of damage. **How does social psychology explain acts of violence or disorder by large groups of people?** AP Images/Ben Margot

Trait Theory and Public Policy   Whereas choice theory justifies punishing wrongdoers, biological and psychological views of criminality suggest that antisocial behavior should be identified and treated before it manifests itself in criminal activity. Though the focus on treatment diminished somewhat in the 1990s, rehabilitation practices in corrections have made a comeback over the past decade. The primary motivation for this new outlook, as we will see in Chapters 11 through 14, is the pressing need to divert nonviolent offenders from the nation's overburdened prison and jail system.

ETHICS CHALLENGE

Suppose that a woman who harmed or even killed her newborn baby could be proven to be suffering from postpartum psychosis, as described in this section. Would it be ethical to punish her for a criminal act that she may not have had control over? Do you agree with the prosecutor who said, "The mere fact that you have a mental condition is not an excuse for a criminal act"? Explain your answers.

Bad Neighborhoods and Other Economic Disadvantages

From 1995 to 1998, the Chicago Housing Authority demolished a number of buildings in that city's public housing projects because of substandard living conditions. In a recently completed study, Eric Chyn, an economist at the University of Michigan, found that the children of families that moved to other neighborhoods because of this demolition benefited from the forced relocation. Those children were 9 percent more likely to be employed than children who remained in the housing projects and had annual earnings that were 19 percent higher.[28] Such studies are of great interest to criminologists who believe that neighborhood conditions such as poverty and unemployment are perhaps the most important variables in predicting crime patterns.

Sociological Theories of Crime

The importance of sociology in the study of criminal behavior was established by a group of scholars who were associated with the Sociology Department at the University of Chicago in the early 1900s. These sociologists, known collectively as the Chicago School, gathered empirical evidence from the slums of the city that showed a correlation between conditions of poverty, such as inadequate housing and poor sanitation, and high rates of crime. Chicago School members Ernest Burgess (1886–1966) and Robert Ezra Park (1864–1944) argued that neighborhood conditions, be they of wealth or poverty, had a much greater determinant effect on criminal behavior than ethnicity, race, or religion.[29]

The methods and theories of the Chicago School, which stressed that humans are social creatures whose behavior reflects their environment, have had a profound effect on criminology over the past century. Today, the study of crime as correlated with social structure revolves around three specific theories: (1) social disorganization theory, (2) strain theory, and (3) cultural deviance theory.

Learning 4 Objective List and describe the three theories of social structure that help explain crime.

Social Disorganization Theory   Studies have shown that neighborhoods with high concentrations of liquor stores and payday lenders tend to have abnormally high levels of crime.[30] Again, these studies do not suggest that such businesses cause crime.

Rather, the availability of "take-away" alcohol and cash reflects other problems in the neighborhoods that have a more direct relationship to criminality. The theory that crime is largely a product of unfavorable conditions in certain communities was popularized by Clifford Shaw and Henry McKay, contemporaries of the Chicago School mentioned previously.[31] Shaw and McKay's influence is shown in the widespread acceptance of **social disorganization theory** in contemporary criminology.

Social Disorganization Theory
The theory that deviant behavior is more likely in communities where social institutions such as the family, schools, and the criminal justice system fail to exert control over the population.

Disorganized Zones Studying juvenile delinquency in Chicago, Shaw and McKay discovered certain "zones" that exhibited high rates of crime. These zones were characterized by "disorganization," or a breakdown of the traditional institutions of social control such as family, school systems, and local businesses. In contrast, in the city's "organized" communities, residents had developed certain agreements about fundamental values and norms.

Shaw and McKay found that residents in high-crime neighborhoods had to a large degree abandoned these fundamental values and norms. Also, a lack of social controls had led to increased levels of antisocial, or criminal, behavior.[32] According to social disorganization theory, factors that lead to crime in these neighborhoods are:

1. High levels of high school dropouts
2. Chronic unemployment
3. Deteriorating buildings and other infrastructures
4. Concentrations of single-parent families

(See Figure 2.2 to better understand social disorganization theory.)

The Value of Role Models In the late 1990s, sociologist Elijah Anderson of the University of Pennsylvania took Shaw and McKay's theories one step further. According to Anderson, residents in high-crime, African American "disorganized" zones separate

---

FIGURE 2.2 **The Stages of Social Disorganization**

Social disorganization theory holds that crime is related to the environmental pressures that exist in certain communities or neighborhoods. These areas are marked by the desire of many of their inhabitants to "get out" at the first possible opportunity. Consequently, residents tend to ignore the important institutions in the community, such as businesses and education, causing further erosion and an increase in the conditions that lead to crime.

The Problem: Poverty
The Consequences:
Formation of isolated impoverished areas, racial and ethnic discrimination, and lack of legitimate economic opportunities.

 Leads to

The Problem: Social Disorganization
The Consequences:
Breakdown of institutions such as school and the family.

 Leads to

The Problem: Breakdown of Social Controls
The Consequences:
Replacement of family and educators by peer groups as primary influences on youth; formation of gangs.

 Leads to

The Problem: Criminal Careers
The Consequences:
The majority of youths "age out" of crime, start families, and, if they can, leave the neighborhood. Those who remain still adhere to the norms of the impoverished-area culture and may become career criminals.

 Leads to

The Problem: Cultural Transmission
The Consequences:
The younger juveniles follow the model of delinquent behavior set by their older siblings and friends, establishing a deep-rooted impoverished-area culture.

 Leads to

The Problem: Criminal Areas
The Consequences:
Rise of crime in poverty-stricken neighborhoods; social acceptance of delinquent behavior by youths; shunning of area by outside investment and support.

Source: Adapted from Larry J. Siegel, *Criminology*, 10th ed. (Belmont, CA: Thomson/Wadsworth, 2009), 180.

themselves into two types of families: "street" and "decent." "Street" families are characterized by a lack of consideration for others and poorly disciplined children. In contrast, "decent" families are community minded, instill values of hard work and education in their children, and generally have "hope for the future."[33]

Spending time in these disadvantaged areas, Anderson discovered that most "decent" families included an older man who held a steady job, performed his duties as husband and father, and was interested in the community's well-being. When external factors such as racial discrimination and lack of employment opportunities reduce the presence of these traditional role models, Anderson theorizes, "street" codes fill the void and youth violence escalates.[34] In a study released more recently, criminologists Eric A. Stewart and Ronald L. Simons tested Anderson's theories. They observed the behavior of more than seven hundred African American adolescents and found that, indeed, in disorganized neighborhoods where a violent street culture dominates, juveniles are much more likely to commit acts of violent delinquency.[35]

Strain Theory

Another self-perpetuating aspect of disorganized neighborhoods is that once residents gain the financial means to leave a high-crime community, they usually do so. This desire to escape the inner city is related to the second branch of social structure theory: **strain theory.** Most Americans have similar life goals, which include gaining a certain measure of wealth and financial freedom. The means of attaining these goals, however, are not universally available. Many citizens do not have access to the education or training necessary for financial success. This often results in frustration and anger, or *strain*.

Strain theory has its roots in the works of French sociologist Emile Durkheim (1858–1917) and his concept of *anomie* (derived from the Greek word for "without norms"). Durkheim believed that *anomie* resulted when social change threw behavioral norms into a flux, leading to a weakening of social controls and an increase in deviant behavior.[36] Another sociologist, American Robert K. Merton, expanded on Durkheim's ideas in his own theory of strain. Merton believed that *anomie* was caused by a social structure in which all citizens have similar goals without equal means to achieve them.[37] One way to alleviate this strain is to gain wealth by the means that are available to the residents of disorganized communities: drug trafficking, burglary, and other criminal activities.

In the 1990s, Robert Agnew of Emory University in Atlanta, Georgia, updated this line of criminology with his *general strain theory*, or GST.[38] Agnew reasoned that of all "strained" individuals, very few actually turn to crime to relieve the strain. GST tries to determine what factors, when combined with strain, actually lead to criminal activity. By the early 2000s, Agnew and other criminologists settled on the factor of negative emotionality, a term used to cover personality traits of those who are easily frustrated, quick to lose their tempers, and disposed to blame others for their own problems.[39] Thus, GST mixes strain theory with aspects of psychological theories of crime.

Cultural Deviance Theory

Combining elements of social disorganization and strain theories, **cultural deviance theory** asserts that people adapt to the values of the subculture to which they belong. A **subculture** (a subdivision that exists within the dominant culture) has its own standards of behavior, or norms. By definition, a disorganized neighborhood is isolated from society at large, and the strain of this isolation encourages the formation of subcultures within its borders. According to cultural deviance theory, members of low-income subcultures are more likely to conform to value systems that celebrate behavior, such as violence, that directly confronts the value system of society at large and therefore draws criminal sanctions.

Strain Theory The assumption that crime is the result of frustration felt by individuals who cannot reach their financial and personal goals through legitimate means.

Anomie A condition in which the individual feels a disconnect from society due to the breakdown or absence of social norms.

Cultural Deviance Theory A branch of social structure theory based on the assumption that members of certain subcultures reject the values of the dominant culture by exhibiting deviant behavior patterns.

Subculture A group exhibiting certain values and behavior patterns that distinguish it from the dominant culture.

Robert Agnew Criminologist

FASTFACTS

Criminologist

Job description:

● Work for local, state, and federal governments, on policy advisory boards, or for legislative committees. In some cases, a criminologist may work for privately funded think tanks or for a criminal justice or law enforcement agency. Most often, employment as a criminologist will be through a college or university, where both teaching and research will be conducted.

What kind of training is required?

● An advanced degree is required. Specifically, some combination of degrees in criminology, criminal justice, sociology, or psychology is preferable. Graduate level education is a must for any research position.

Annual salary range?

● $73,000–$140,000

When I first became interested in criminology, my research led me to "strain" or *anomie* theories that said when a person stumbles in achieving financial success or middle-class status due to social factors beyond his or her control, he or she may turn to crime. While strain theory made a lot of sense to me, I felt that the theory was incomplete. When I looked around me, it was easy to spot other sources of frustration and anger, such as harassment by peers, conflict with parents or romantic partners, poor grades in school, or poor working conditions.

I outlined sources of strain as the loss of "positively valued stimuli" such as romantic relationships, or the threat of "negatively valued stimuli" such as an insult or physical assault. I also pointed out that monetary success was just one among many "positively valued goals" that might cause strain when not achieved. Furthermore, I noted that people who experience strain may turn to crime for several reasons—crime might allow them to achieve their monetary and status goals, protect positively valued stimuli, escape negative stimuli, achieve revenge against wrongs, or simply deal with the strain (such as taking drugs to forget problems). I drew on these observations and my own experiences to develop a new "general strain theory."

Courtesy of Robert Agnew

SOCIAL MEDIA CAREER TIP Find groups on Facebook and LinkedIn in which people are discussing the criminal justice career or careers that interest you. Participate in the discussions to get information and build contacts.

Social Structure Theory and Public Policy If criminal behavior can be explained by the conditions in which certain groups of people live, then it stands to reason that changing those conditions can prevent crime. Indeed, government programs to decrease unemployment, reduce poverty, and improve educational facilities in low-income neighborhoods have been justified as part of large-scale attempts at crime prevention.

Social Conflict Theories

Strain theory and the concept of *anomie* seem to suggest that the unequal structure of our society is, in part, to blame for criminal behavior. This argument forms the bedrock of social conflict theories of crime. These theories, which entered mainstream criminology in the 1960s, hold capitalism responsible for high levels of violence and crime because of the disparity of income that it encourages.

Marxism versus Capitalism The genesis of social conflict theory can be found in the political philosophy of a German named Karl Marx (1818–1883). Marx believed that capitalist economic systems necessarily produce income inequality and lead to the exploitation of the working classes.[40] Consequently, social conflict theory is often associated with a critique of our capitalist economic system. Capitalism is seen as leading to high levels of violence and crime because of the disparity of income that results. The poor commit

Social Conflict Theories Theories that view criminal behavior as the result of class conflict.

property crimes for reasons of need and because, as members of a capitalist society, they desire the same financial rewards as everybody else. They commit violent crimes because of the frustration and rage they feel when these rewards seem unattainable.

It is important to note that, according to social conflict theory, power is not synonymous with wealth. Women and members of minority groups can be wealthy and yet still be disassociated from the benefits of power in our society. Richard Quinney, one of the most influential social conflict theorists of the past forty years, incorporates issues of race, gender, power, and crime in a theory known as the social reality of crime.[41]

For Quinney, along with many of his peers, criminal law does not reflect a universal moral code, but instead is a set of "rules" through which those who hold power can control and subdue those who do not. Any conflict between the "haves" and the "have-nots," therefore, is bound to be decided in favor of the "haves," who make the law and control the criminal justice system. Following this reasoning, Quinney sees violations of the law not as inherently criminal acts, but rather as political ones—as revolutionary acts against the power of the state.

Patterns of Social Justice

Those who perceive the criminal justice system as an instrument of social control point to a number of historical studies and statistics to support their argument. In the nineteenth century, nearly three-quarters of female inmates had been incarcerated for sexual misconduct. They were sent to institutions such as New York's Western House of Refuge at Albion to be taught the virtues of "true" womanhood.[42] Today, about two-thirds of the approximately 31,000 Americans arrested for prostitution each year are women.[43]

After the Civil War (1861–1865), many African Americans were driven from the South by "Jim Crow laws" designed to keep them from attaining power in the postwar period. Today, the criminal justice system performs a similar function. One out of every ten black men in their thirties is in prison or jail on any given day,[44] and African American males are incarcerated at about 5.6 times the rate of white males.[45]

Racial Threat Theory

After an African American suspect named Freddie Gray died while in Baltimore Police Department custody, the U.S. Department conducted a review of police practices in that city. The federal report, released in 2016, detailed widespread evidence bias in the department. For example, one black man in his mid-fifties had been stopped thirty times in less than four years by police officers without being charged for any wrongdoing. In general, 91 percent of those arrested in Baltimore for discretionary offenses such as "failure to obey" were African American, and paperwork for trespassing arrests had a description of the arrestee automatically filled in: "A Black Male."[46]

For social conflict experts, such behavior is example of *racial threat theory* in action. This theory is based on the hypothesis that, as minority groups increase in population and expand geographically, the majority group employs the criminal justice system to oppress those minority groups.[47] Baltimore is 63 percent black, and a number of other cities recently subjected to Justice Department investigation for civil rights abuses—a topic we will cover in Chapter 6—also have large African American populations.

Racial threat theory is also applied in the context of Latino Americans, the largest minority group in the United States. In 2006, for example, the city of Hazleton, Pennsylvania, passed an ordinance that made it illegal to rent local housing to certain immigrants. City officials justified the ordinance, in part, as a response to rising crime rates caused by an influx of undocumented Mexicans.[48] The ordinance's constitutional flaws doomed it in federal court,[49] but it was also based on faulty criminology. Numerous studies show that high

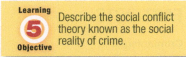

Learning Objective 5 Describe the social conflict theory known as the social reality of crime.

Social Reality of Crime The theory that criminal laws are designed by those in power to help them keep power at the expense of those who do not have power.

concentrations of immigrants result in lower neighborhood crime rates, not higher ones.[50]

Social Conflict Theory and Public Policy

Given its radical nature, social conflict theory has had a limited impact on public policy. Even in the aftermath of situations in which class conflict has had serious and obvious repercussions, few observers feel that enough has been accomplished to improve the conditions that led to the violence. Indeed, many believe that the best hope for a shift in the power structure is the employment of more women and minorities in the criminal justice system itself.

▲ Two law enforcement officers investigate a burglary in Camden, New Jersey—one of the poorest cities in the United States. **How would a criminologist who advocates social conflict theories of criminal behavior explain high crime rates in low-income communities such as Camden?**

Spencer Platt/Getty Images News/Getty Images

Life Lessons and Criminal Behavior

Some criminologists find class theories of crime overly narrow. Surveys that ask people directly about their criminal behavior have shown that the criminal instinct is pervasive in middle- and upper-class communities, even if it is expressed differently. Anybody, these criminologists argue, has the potential to commit crimes, regardless of class, race, or gender.

Family, Friends, and the Media: Social Processes of Crime

Philip Zimbardo conducted a well-known, if rather unscientific, experiment to show the broad potential for misbehavior. The psychologist placed an abandoned automobile with its hood up on the campus of Stanford University. The car remained in place, untouched, for a week. Then, Zimbardo smashed the car's window with a sledgehammer. Within minutes, passersby had joined in the destruction of the automobile, eventually stripping its valuable parts.[51]

Social process theories function on the same basis as Zimbardo's "interdependence of decisions experiment": the potential for criminal behavior exists in everyone and will be realized depending on an individual's interaction with various institutions and processes of society. Social process theory has three main branches: (1) learning theory, (2) control theory, and (3) labeling theory.

Learning 6 Objective List and briefly explain the three branches of social process theory.

Learning Theory

Popularized by Edwin Sutherland in the 1940s, **learning theory** contends that criminal activity is a learned behavior. In other words, a criminal is taught both the practical methods of crime (such as how to pick a lock) and the psychological aspects of crime (how to deal with the guilt of wrongdoing). Sutherland's *theory of differential association* held that individuals are exposed to the values of family and peers such as school friends or co-workers. If the dominant values a person is exposed to favor criminal behavior, then that person is more likely to mimic such behavior.[52] Sutherland's focus on the importance of family relations in this area is underscored by research showing that sons of fathers who have been incarcerated are at an increased risk of delinquency and arrest.[53]

Social Process Theories Theories that consider criminal behavior to be the predictable result of a person's interaction with his or her environment.

Learning Theory The theory that delinquents and criminals must be taught both the practical and the emotional skills necessary to participate in illegal activity.

More recently, learning theory has been expanded to include the growing influence of the media. In the latest in a long series of studies, researchers released data in 2013 showing that children and adolescents who watched "excessive" amounts of violent television content faced an elevated risk of exhibiting antisocial behavior such as criminality in early adulthood.[54] The issue of whether academic and anecdotal evidence can be used to conclusively link youthful entertainment to violent behavior has been addressed by the United States Supreme Court, as shown in the feature *Landmark Cases*—Brown v. EMA.

Control Theory

Criminologist Travis Hirschi focuses on the reasons why individuals do not engage in criminal acts, rather than why they do. According to Hirschi, social bonds promote conformity to social norms. The stronger these social bonds—which include attachment to, commitment to, involvement with, and belief in societal values—the less likely that any individual will commit a crime.[55]

Control theory holds that although we all have the potential to commit crimes, most of us are dissuaded from doing so because we care about the opinions of our family and peers. James Q. Wilson and George Kelling described control theory in terms of the "broken windows" effect. Neighborhoods in poor condition are filled with cues of lack of social control (for example, broken windows) that invite further vandalism and other deviant behavior.[56] If these cues are removed, according to Wilson and Kelling, so is the implied acceptance of crime within a community.

Janet Lauritsen, a criminologist at the University of Missouri–St. Louis, contends that familial control is more important than run-down surroundings in predicting whether crime will occur. Lauritsen found that adolescents residing in two-parent households were victims of crime at similar rates, regardless of the levels of disadvantage in the neighborhoods in which they lived. By contrast, adolescents from single-parent homes who lived in highly disorganized neighborhoods were victimized at much higher rates than their counterparts in more stable locales. In Lauritsen's opinion, the support of a two-parent household offers crucial protection for children, whatever the condition of their neighborhood.[57]

Labeling Theory

A third social process theory, labeling theory, focuses on perceptions of criminal behavior rather than the behavior itself. Labeling theorists study how being labeled a criminal—a "whore" or a "junkie" or a "thief"—affects that person's future behavior. Sociologist Howard Becker contends that deviance is

> a consequence of the application by others of rules and sanctions to an offender. The deviant is one to whom that label has successfully been applied; deviant behavior is behavior that people so label.[58]

Such labeling, some criminologists believe, becomes a self-fulfilling prophecy. Someone labeled a "junkie" will begin to consider himself or herself a deviant and continue the criminal behavior for which he or she has been labeled.

Following this line of reasoning, the criminal justice system is engaged in artificially creating a class of criminals by labeling victimless crimes such as drug use, prostitution, and gambling as "criminal." There are also practical consequences when a person is labeled a criminal, such as difficulty in finding employment.

Social Process Theory and Public Policy

Because adult criminals are seen as too "hardened" to unlearn their criminal behavior, crime prevention policies associated with social process theory focus on juvenile offenders. Many youths, for example, are diverted from the formal juvenile justice process to keep them from being labeled

Control Theory A series of theories that assume that all individuals have the potential for criminal behavior, but are restrained by the damage that such actions would do to their relationships with family, friends, and members of the community.

Labeling Theory The hypothesis that society creates crime and criminals by labeling certain behavior and certain people as deviant.

Brown v. Entertainment Merchants Association (EMA)

In 2006, reacting to studies linking violent video games to violent behavior in children, then–California governor Arnold Schwarzenegger signed a bill prohibiting the sale or rental of games that portray "killing, maiming, dismembering or sexually assaulting an image of a human being" to people younger than eighteen years old. The law imposed a $1,000 fine on violators. Immediately, video game sellers sued the state, saying it had violated their constitutional right to freedom of speech. After two lower courts accepted this argument and invalidated California's law, the issue finally arrived before the United States Supreme Court.

Brown v EMA
United States Supreme Court
559 S.Ct. 1448 (2010)

In the Words of the Court . . .

Justice Scalia, Majority Opinion

Like the protected books, plays, and movies that preceded them, video games communicate ideas—and even social messages—through many familiar literary devices (such as characters, dialogue, plot, and music) and through features distinctive to the medium (such as the player's interaction with the virtual world). That suffices to confer First Amendment protection. Under our Constitution, "esthetic and moral judgments about art and literature * * * are for the individual to make, not for the Government to decree, even with the mandate or approval of a majority."

No doubt a State possesses legitimate power to protect children from harm, but that does not include a free-floating power to restrict the ideas to which children may be exposed.

California relies primarily on * * * research psychologists whose studies purport to show a connection between exposure to violent video games and harmful effects on children. These studies have been rejected by every court to consider them, and with good reason: They do not prove that violent video games *cause* minors to act aggressively (which would at least be a beginning). Instead, "[n]early all of the research is based on correlation, not evidence of causation * * * ." They show at best some correlation between exposure to violent entertainment and minuscule real-world effects, such as children's feeling more aggressive or making louder noises in the few minutes after playing a violent game than after playing a nonviolent game.

Decision

In the absence of any provable negative effects on minors from violent video games, the Court ruled that California's ban was unconstitutional and therefore could not be enforced.

FOR CRITICAL ANALYSIS

If states have the "legitimate power" to "protect children from harm," why did the Court invalidate California's violent video game law? How did Justice Scalia use the concepts of *cause* and *correlation* to support the Court's decision? (You can review those terms from our discussion earlier in the chapter.)

"delinquent." Furthermore, many schools have implemented programs that attempt to steer children away from crime by encouraging them to "just say no" to drugs and stay in school. As we shall see in Chapter 6, implementation of Wilson and Kelling's "broken windows" principles has been credited with lowering the violent crime rate in New York and in a number of other major cities.

Looking Back to Childhood: Life Course Theories of Crime

If crime is indeed learned behavior, some criminologists are asking, shouldn't we be focusing on early childhood—the time when humans do the most learning? Many of the other theories we have studied in this chapter tend to attribute criminal behavior to factors—such as unemployment or poor educational performance—that take place long after an individual's personality has been established. Practitioners of **life course criminology** believe that risk factors that exist in early childhood are the strongest predictors of future criminal behavior and have been seriously undervalued in the examination of why crime occurs. These factors include, for instance, having a difficult temperament, low learning ability, and a disadvantaged family background.[59]

Self-Control Theory

Focusing on childhood behavior raises the question of whether conduct problems established at a young age can be changed over time. Michael Gottfredson and Travis Hirschi, whose 1990 publication *A General Theory of Crime* is one of the foundations of life course criminology, think not.[60] Gottfredson and Hirschi believe that criminal behavior is linked to "low self-control," a personality trait that is formed before a child reaches the age of ten and can usually be attributed to poor parenting.[61]

In general, someone who has low self-control is:

1. Impulsive,
2. Thrill-seeking, and
3. Likely to solve problems with violence rather than intellect.

Learning Objective 7 Describe the importance of early childhood behavior for those who subscribe to self-control theory.

Gottfredson and Hirschi think that once low self-control has been established, it will persist. In other words, childhood behavioral problems are not "solved" by positive developments later in life, such as healthy personal relationships or a good job.[62] Thus, these two criminologists subscribe to what has been called the *continuity theory of crime*, which essentially says that once negative behavior patterns have been established, they cannot be changed.

The Possibility of Change

Not all of those who practice life course criminology follow the continuity theory. Terrie Moffitt, for example, notes that youthful offenders can be divided into two groups. The first group are life-course-persistent offenders: they are biting playmates at age five, skipping school at ten, stealing cars at sixteen, committing violent crimes at twenty, and perpetrating fraud and child abuse at thirty.[63] The second group are adolescent-limited offenders: as the name suggests, their "life of crime" is limited to the teenage years.[64] So, according to Moffitt, change is possible, if not for the life-course-persistent offenders (who are saddled with psychological problems that lead to continued social failure and misconduct), then for the adolescent-limited offenders.

Robert Sampson and John Laub take this line of thinking one step further. While acknowledging that "antisocial behavior is relatively stable" from childhood to old age, Sampson and Laub have gathered a great deal of data showing, in their opinion, that offenders may experience "turning points" when they are able to veer off the road from a life of crime.[65]

A good deal of research in this area has concentrated on the positive impact of getting married, having children, and finding a job,[66] but other turning points are also being explored. John F. Frana of Indiana State University and Ryan D. Schroeder of the University of Louisville argue that military service can act as a "rehabilitative agent."[67] Several researchers have studied the role that religion and spirituality can play as "hooks for change."[68] Furthermore, particularly for drug abusers, the death of a loved one or friend from shared criminal behavior can provide a powerful incentive to discontinue that behavior. (See this chapter's *Mastering Concepts* for a review of theories discussed so far in this chapter.)

Life Course Theories and Public Policy

Life course theories intersect with public policy mainly with regard to two crucial institutions that influence early

The Causes of Crime

Choice Theories

Key Concept: Crime is the result of rational choices made by those who decide to engage in criminal activity for the rewards—financial and otherwise—that it offers.

Example: Over a six-month period, LaTroy Staglin intentionally caused a series of car accidents in Oklahoma City so that he could file false insurance claims for damages worth thousands of dollars. Staglin was sentenced to eighteen years behind bars.

Biological and Psychological Trait Theories

Key Concept: Criminal behavior is explained by the biological and psychological attributes of an individual.

Example: A sixty-three-year-old physician from Southern California who illegally distributed a massive amount of prescription drugs was found to be afflicted with a form of brain damage called frontotemporal dementia (FTLD). Research shows that about one-third of FTLD sufferers exhibit criminal behavior.

Sociological Theories

Key Concept: Crime is not something a person is "born to do." Rather, crime is the result of the social conditions such as poverty, poor schools, unemployment, and discrimination with which a person lives.

Example: Five large cities with significant recent murder rate increases (Chicago, Dallas, Las Vegas, San Diego, and San Jose) have experienced higher-than-average rates of poverty and unemployment since the mid-2000s.

Social Conflict Theories

Key Concept: Through criminal laws, the dominant members of society control the minority members, using institutions such as the police, courts, and prisons as tools of oppression.

Example: Between July 2006 and June 2007, law enforcement officers from the Arizona Department of Public Safety stopped and searched African American and Latino drivers 2.5 times more often than white drivers. These higher search rates were not justified by evidence that African American or Latino drivers were more likely to be carrying illegal contraband.

Social Process Theories

Key Concept: Family, friends, and peers have the greatest impact on an individual's behavior, and it is the interactions with these groups that ultimately determine whether a person will become involved in criminal behavior.

Example: According to the Pittsburgh Youth Study, having a close relative—particularly a father—convicted of a crime significantly increases the chances that a young male subject will eventually be convicted of a crime.

Life Course Theories

Key Concept: Criminal and antisocial behavior is evident at each stage of a person's life. By focusing on such behavior in early childhood, criminologists may be able to better understand and predict offending patterns that emerge as a person grows older.

Example: Children who suffer from issues such as lack of concentration, a tendency to daydream, and restlessness at the age of five are more likely than their peers to engage in delinquency at the age of fourteen.

childhood: parenting and school. In many jurisdictions, parenting-skills classes are available (or mandatory) for mothers and fathers of children with behavioral problems. Often, such problems are first identified by preschool teachers, and public school systems generally offer in-house intervention and counseling services.

FIGURE 2.3 Illegal Drug Use in the United States

In 2015, about 27 million Americans reported using an illegal drug at least once in the previous twelve months. As this graph shows, marijuana is by far the most popular illicit drug in the United States.

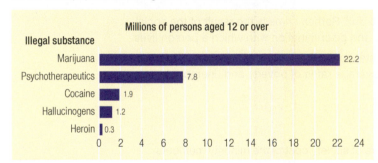

Marijuana: The most popular form of this drug is made using the dried, flowering tops of the cannabis plant, often mixed with tobacco, and smoked in the form of a cigarette. It primarily affects the central nervous system, causing feelings of relaxation, euphoria, and heightened sensory perception.

Psychotherapeutics: This term covers prescription drugs (pain relievers, tranquilizers, stimulants, and sedatives) used for nonmedical purposes. It includes methamphetamine, a highly addictive stimulant that is manufactured using prescription and nonprescription drugs.

Cocaine: Derived from coca leaves, this stimulant is most commonly snorted as a powder, though it can be injected and, in a crystallized form known as "crack," smoked. Use of cocaine produces an instant euphoria, as well as numbness and feelings of increased energy and confidence.

Hallucinogens: A category that includes LSD, mescaline (from the peyote cactus), and PCP ("angel dust"). These drugs are known for their "psychedelic" effects, which cause users to experience reality in a distorted state.

Heroin: Derived from the poppy plant, this opioid is most commonly injected directly into the user's veins, though it can be snorted or smoked. Heroin use creates feelings of sedation and decreased anxiety, as well as a rush of euphoria.

Source: Substance Abuse and Mental Health Services Administration, *Key Substance Use and Mental Health Indicators in the United States: Results from the 2015 National Survey on Drug Use and Health* (Washington, D.C.: U.S. Department of Health and Human Services, September 2016), Figure 1, page 7.

The Link between Drugs and Crime

Earlier in this chapter, we discussed the difference between correlations and causes. As you may recall, criminologists are generally reluctant to declare that any one factor causes a certain result. Richard B. Felson of Penn State University and Keri B. Burchfield of Northern Illinois University, however, believe that alcohol consumption has a causal effect on crime victimization under certain circumstances.[69] Felson and Burchfield found that "frequent and heavy" drinkers are at a great risk of assault when they are drinking, but do not show abnormal rates of victimization when sober. They hypothesize that consuming alcohol leads to aggressive and offensive behavior, particularly in men, which in turn triggers violent reactions from others.

According to the National Survey on Drug Use and Health, only 10.1 percent of those questioned had used an illegal drug in the past month. Even so, this means a significant number of Americans—about 27.1 million—are regularly using illegal drugs. That figure mushrooms when consumers of legal substances such as alcohol (138 million users) and tobacco (64 million users) are included.[70] (See Figure 2.3 for an overview of illegal drug use in the United States.) In this section, we will discuss two questions concerning these habits. First, why do people use drugs? Second, what are the consequences for the criminal justice system?

The Criminology of Drug Use

At first glance, the reason people use drugs, including legal drugs such as alcohol, is obvious: such drugs give users pleasure and provide a temporary escape for those who may feel tension or anxiety. Ultimately, though, such explanations are unsatisfactory because they fail to explain why some people use drugs while others do not.

Theories of Drug Use   Several of the theories we discussed earlier in the chapter have been used by experts to explain drug use. *Social disorganization theory* holds that rapid social change can cause people to become disaffiliated from mainstream society, causing them to turn to drugs. *Control theory* suggests that a lack of social control, as provided by entities such as the family or school, can lead to antisocial behavior such as drug use.

Drugs and the "Learning Process"   Focusing on the question of why first-time drug users become habitual users, sociologist Howard Becker sees three factors in the "learning process." He believes first-time users:

1. Learn the techniques of drug use.
2. Learn to perceive the pleasurable effects of drug use.
3. Learn to enjoy the social experience of drug use.[71]

Becker's assumptions are evident in the widespread belief that positive images of drug use in popular culture "teach" adolescents that such behavior is not only acceptable but desirable. The entertainment industry, in particular, has been criticized for glamorizing various forms of drug use.

Drug Addiction and Dependency

Another theory rests on the assumption that some people possess overly sensitive drug receptors in their brains and are therefore biologically disposed toward drug use.[72] Though there is little conclusive evidence that biological factors can explain initial drug experimentation, scientific research has provided a great deal of insight into patterns of long-term drug use.

Drug Use and Drug Abuse   In particular, science has aided in understanding the difference between drug *use* and drug *abuse*. **Drug abuse** can be defined as the use of any drug—licit or illicit—that causes either psychological or bodily harm to the abuser or to third parties. Just as most people who drink beer or wine avoid abusing alcohol, most users of illegal substances are not abusers. Indeed, more than 90 percent of first-time users do not become dependent on illicit drugs, though the number drops sharply among those who continue to use the drug for more than one year.[73]

   Despite their relatively small numbers, drug abusers have a disparate impact on the drug market. The 20 percent of Americans, for example, who drink the most consume more than 80 percent of all alcoholic beverages sold in the United States. The data are similar for illicit substance abusers, leading to the conclusion that, to a large extent, abusers and addicts sustain the market for illegal drugs.

Addiction Basics   The most extreme abusers are addicted to a drug. That is, they are compulsive users of the substance. To understand the basics of addiction, you must understand the role of *dopamine* in the brain. Dopamine is the neurotransmitter responsible for delivering pleasure signals to brain nerve endings in response to behavior—such as eating delicious food or engaging in sex—that makes us feel good. The bloodstream delivers

Drug Abuse The use of drugs that results in physical or psychological problems for the user, as well as disruption of personal relationships and employment.

drugs to the area of the brain that produces dopamine, thereby triggering the production of a large amount of the substance in the brain.

Over time, the continued use of drugs physically changes the nerve endings, called *receptors*. To continue operating in the presence of large amounts of dopamine, the receptors become less sensitive, meaning that greater amounts of any particular drug are required to create the amount of dopamine needed for the same levels of pleasure. When the supply of the drug is cut off, the brain strongly feels the lack of dopamine stimulation, and the abuser will suffer symptoms of withdrawal until the receptors readjust.[74]

Addiction and *physical dependence* are interrelated, though not exactly the same. Those who are physically dependent on a drug suffer withdrawal symptoms when they stop using it, but after a certain time period, they are generally able to emerge without further craving. Addicts, in contrast, continue to feel a need for the drug long after withdrawal symptoms have passed. For many years, researchers have been striving to determine if some people are more likely than others to become addicts for biological reasons. In 2008, a group of researchers from Peking University in China made significant headway toward doing so by showing that many addicts share a particular set of *enzymes*, or proteins that trigger chemical reactions in the body.[75]

Crime and Health: The Landscape of Drug Abuse

As you will see throughout this textbook, the prosecution of illegal drug users and suppliers has been one of the primary factors in the enormous growth of the American correctional industry. Of course, because many drugs are illegal, anybody who sells, uses, or in any way promotes any of these drugs is, under most circumstances, breaking the law. The drug-crime relationship goes well beyond the language of criminal drug statutes, however.

The Drug-Crime Relationship
Studies that connect drug use to criminality can be problematic, mainly because such activity is likely one risk factor among many in a criminal user's life. Still, drugs and crime are related in three general ways:[76]

1. *Drug-defined offenses*, or violation of laws prohibiting the possession, use, distribution, or manufacture of illegal drugs. Examples include possession of marijuana and methamphetamine production.

2. *Drug-related offenses*, such as crimes motivated by drug abuse or committed to further the illegal drug trade. Examples include gang violence between rival drug dealers and theft to get money to buy illegal drugs.

3. *The drug-using lifestyle*, experienced by many drug abusers who do not participate in the legitimate economy and thus rely on crime for the means of survival. These users often support short-term goals with illegal activities such as prostitution and welfare fraud.

▼ A young woman prepares to use heroin under a bridge in Portland, Maine. **Do you think that drug abusers should be treated as criminals to be punished or as ill people in need of treatment? Explain your answer.**

Cheryl Senter/*New York Times*/Redux

According to the federal government, at least two-thirds of all persons arrested in this country have illegal drugs in their systems when apprehended.[77] Legal drugs also play a role in the crime picture of the United States. About 37 percent of state prisoners and 33 percent of jail inmates incarcerated for a violent crime were under the influence of alcohol at the time of their arrest.[78] Richard Friedman, who studies the effect of drugs on behavior, estimates that abusing alcohol and other drugs increases the likelihood of violence by a factor of seven.[79]

Drugs and the National Health

The laundry list of health problems associated with drug abuse is lengthy and sobering. It includes a weakened immune system, increased susceptibility to infection, heart conditions (including heart attacks), liver damage, brain damage, and nausea, vomiting, and abdominal pain.

As we discussed in Chapter 1, the United States is presently experiencing an opioid crisis. In 2015, approximately 15,000 people died from overdoses involving **prescription drugs,** or those drugs—mostly painkillers—that can legally be obtained only with the permission of a licensed health care professional.[80] In fact, drug overdoses are the driving force behind a surprising trend in this country: death rates for white adults ages twenty-five to thirty-four are rising for the first time since the AIDS epidemic more than twenty years ago. The overdose death rate for this demographic group is five times higher today than it was in 1999, and heroin-related overdose death rates have quadrupled since 2002.[81]

Many of these overdose victims were initially prescribed a painkiller for a legitimate health reason before becoming fatally addicted. Such was probably the case with the performer Prince, who died in April 2016 from an accidental overdose of fentanyl, taken to ease his chronic hip pain. Fentanyl—fifty times stronger than heroin—is an example of a *synthetic* drug, or a drug with a slightly altered chemical structure that makes it much more powerful than previously known narcotics. The potential for harm to society from these drugs is enormous. Over the course of six days in the summer of 2016, 174 overdoses in the Cincinnati region were attributed to carfentanil, a synthetic drug a hundred times more potent that fentanyl.[82]

Models of Addiction

What is the best way for society to deal with addicts? According to the **medical model of addiction,** addicts are not criminals, but mentally or physically ill individuals who are forced into acts of petty crime to "feed their habit." Those who believe in the *enslavement theory of addiction* advocate treating addiction as a disease and hold that society should not punish addicts but rather attempt to rehabilitate them, as would be done for any other unhealthy person.[83] According to federal estimates, only one of every ten Americans addicted to alcohol or drugs is receiving treatment for the problem.[84]

Although a number of organizations, including the American Medical Association, recognize alcoholism and other forms of drug dependence as diseases, the criminal justice system tends to favor the **criminal model of addiction** over the medical model. The criminal model holds that illegal drug abusers and addicts endanger society with their behavior and should be punished the same as persons who commit non-drug-related crimes. (To learn how one European country employs a "harm reduction" model of addiction, which aims to reduce the negative consequences of drug use for addicts and for society, see the feature *Comparative Criminal Justice— A Clean, Well-Lighted Place.*)

Prescription Drugs Medical drugs that require a physician's permission for purchase.

Medical Model of Addiction An approach to drug addiction that treats drug abuse as a mental illness and focuses on treating and rehabilitating offenders rather than punishing them.

Criminal Model of Addiction An approach to drug abuse that holds that drug offenders harm society by their actions to the same extent as other criminals and should face the same punitive sanctions.

Learning Objective 8 Contrast the medical model of addiction with the criminal model of addiction.

Source: Central Intelligence Agency

A Clean, Well-Lighted Place

The banner hanging outside the facility, located in downtown Vancouver, British Columbia, reads, "InSite Saves Lives." Inside, addicts line up to use one of thirteen booths, each featuring mirrors and bright lights like backstage dressing rooms. Between 600 and 900 people visit InSite daily to shoot heroin and consume other illegal drugs such as cocaine or methamphetamine—legally, with the backing of the Canadian government.

GOVERNMENT-FUNDED ADDICTION

Vancouver officials opened InSite about fifteen years ago in response to a wave of heroin-related deaths plaguing the city. The facility provides not only a clean indoor space in which to use drugs, but also sterile equipment such as needles and crack pipes and a well-trained medical staff to intervene when a user overdoses. InSite personnel will help addicts who want to break their habits, but do not push detox services on those who want to continue using.

"You're not risking dying; it's a lot safer," said one frequent InSite visitor. "In the back of your mind, you know

if [you're] going to overdose, those people are there to save your life." Studies show that heroin overdose deaths in downtown Vancouver have decreased significantly since InSite opened, as has the incidence of infectious diseases such as HIV and Hepatitis C that are spread by "dirty" needles. Still, the program is controversial within Canada's health care community. "I understand reaching out and saying [to an addict], 'do you want to get clean? It can happen, you can do it,'" says David Berner, who opened the country's first residential drug treatment center in 1967. "I don't understand, 'here's a needle, go shoot some more.'"

FOR CRITICAL ANALYSIS

Officials in Ithaca, New York, recently proposed opening a "supervised injection center" similar to Vancouver's InSite facility to deal with the city's growing heroin overdose problem. What would be the benefits of such a policy? What would be the drawbacks? Do you support this form of government-supported illegal drug use? Why or why not?

Marijuana Law Trends

How would the link between certain illegal drugs and crime change if those drugs were legalized? That is, what if a particular illegal drug was treated in the same manner as alcohol and tobacco—heavily regulated, but available to persons over the age of twenty-one? While these questions are not being asked with regard to "hard" drugs such as heroin and cocaine, the legalization of marijuana—America's most-used illicit drug—has become an important policy issue. Indeed, as we noted in Chapter 1, in 2016, four states voted to legalize the possession and sale of small amounts of marijuana for recreational use, bringing to eight the total number of states where the once unlawful drug is now part of the legal mainstream.

Popular Support   According to Gallup, in 2005 only 36 percent of American adults favored marijuana legalization. By 2016, that number had grown to 60 percent, a huge factor in trends favoring legalization of the drug.[85] As might be expected, support for marijuana legalization is greatest among young people, with 77 percent of those aged eighteen and thirty-four in favor, compared with only 45 percent of those over the age of fifty-five.[86] Perhaps not surprisingly, marijuana use in the United States doubled between 2001 and 2013,[87] and college students now are more likely to be smoking marijuana than tobacco on a daily basis.[88]

The Legalization Debate   Those in favor of marijuana legalization generally rely on the following arguments to support their position:

1. Nationwide legalization would put the black market for marijuana—estimated at about $41 billion year[89]—out of business, ending violent crime associated with the pot trade and depriving scores of criminals of their livelihood.

Legalization To make a formerly illegal product or action lawful. In the context of marijuana, the process includes strict regulation, including a ban on sale to or use by minors.

2. It would remove the stigma of recreational marijuana use for millions of people who are otherwise unconnected with criminal activity and keep millions of nonviolent offenders out of prison.

3. It would provide a double "peace dividend" by saving our criminal justice system the costs associated with the approximately 640,000 marijuana arrests that occur each year,[90] while at the same time providing governmental agencies with millions of dollars in tax receipts.

Chronic Offender A delinquent or criminal who commits multiple offenses and is considered part of a small group of wrongdoers who are responsible for a majority of the antisocial activity in any given community.

Proponents also insist that casual marijuana use by adults is relatively benign,[91] a claim that the opponents of marijuana legalization argue is only marginally relevant. These detractors point out that, more crucially, in the first year that recreational marijuana use was legal in Washington State, "drugged driving" arrests, marijuana-related fatal car crashes, and hospitalizations for overdoses all increased.[92]

Another foreseeable problem with marijuana legalization is *diversion*. This occurs when marijuana from states where it is legal inevitably begins supplying the black market for the drug in states where it is not legal. Of course, diversion would not exist if marijuana were legal throughout the United States. We address the contentious issue of nationwide legalization of marijuana in the *Policy Matters* feature at the end of the chapter.

ETHICS CHALLENGE

In fiscal year 2015, the Colorado Department of Revenue brought in $70 million in taxes related to the sale of legal marijuana. Do you think there are any ethical issues with collecting taxes on a product that may have harmful health effects for users? Why or why not? (Note that Colorado also collected $42 million in taxes on alcohol that year.)

Criminology from Theory to Practice

You have almost completed the only chapter in this textbook that deals primarily with theory. The chapters that follow will concentrate on the more practical and legal aspects of the criminal justice system: how law enforcement agencies fight crime, how our court systems determine guilt or innocence, and how we punish those who are found guilty.

Criminology can, however, play a crucial role in the criminal justice system. "A lot of my colleagues just want to write scholarly articles for scholarly journals," notes Professor James Alan Fox of Northeastern University in Boston. "But I think if you're in a field with specialized knowledge that can be useful to the community, you should engage the public and policymakers."[93]

Criminology and the Chronic Offender

Perhaps the most useful criminological contribution to crime fighting in the past half century was *Delinquency in a Birth Cohort*, published by the pioneering trio of Marvin Wolfgang, Robert Figlio, and Thorsten Sellin in 1972. This research established the idea of the **chronic offender,** or career criminal, by showing that a small group of juvenile offenders—6 percent—was responsible for a disproportionate amount of the violent crime attributed to a group of nearly 10,000 young males: 71 percent of the murders, 82 percent of the robberies, 69 percent of the aggravated assaults, and 73 percent of the rapes.[94]

Learning Objective 9 Explain the theory of the chronic offender and its importance for the criminal justice system.

Risk Assessment A method for determining the likelihood that an offender will be involved in future wrongdoing.

Further research has supported the idea of a "chronic 6 percent,"[95] and law enforcement agencies and district attorneys' offices have devised specific strategies to apprehend and prosecute repeat offenders, with dozens of local police agencies forming career criminal units to deal with the problem. Legislators have also reacted to this research: habitual offender laws that provide harsher sentences for repeat offenders have become quite popular. We will discuss these statutes, including the controversial "three-strikes-and-you're-out" laws, in Chapter 11.

Risk Assessment in Action

As we have just seen, research shows that a small percentage of offenders pose the greatest risk of future wrongdoing. In the twenty-first century, *risk assessment* aimed at identifying these offenders has become a crucial point of intersection for criminologists and criminal justice practitioners. **Risk assessment** is the process of determining the likelihood that offenders will recidivate. Today, police administrators, prison wardens, sentencing authorities, and probation and parole supervisors are increasingly relying on risk assessment tools to identify the best way to allocate scarce resources and protect the public.

Risk Assessment and Domestic Violence

In 2011, following a string of domestic violence-related murders, authorities in Maine decided to fashion a response that focused on risk. (*Domestic violence* broadly refers to the abuse of a spouse or someone otherwise in a close or intimate relationship with the offender.) Partnering with local law enforcement, they began to use the Ontario Domestic Assault Risk Assessment (ODARA) method. ODARA consists of thirteen "YES/NO" questions covering the offender's history of violence and antisocial behavior and details of the most recent assault. Depending on the number of YES answers to these questions, the ODARA predicts the amount of time until the next assault, how many assaults will occur, and how severe they will be.[96]

The ODARA is designed for simplicity. A trained law enforcement officer can administer it in ten minutes at the scene of the domestic violence incident to determine if the victim is in immediate danger. Afterward, it is used to fashion the criminal justice system's management of the offender. Developed in Canada, ODARA is being used by law enforcement agencies throughout the United States, with some notable results. In Brooklyn Park, Minnesota, for example, the conviction rate for domestic assault and similar crimes increased 240 percent in the four years after local police began implementing ODARA strategies.[97]

Risk Assessment and Sentencing

As you will see in Chapter 11, the process of sentencing is often an inexact science. In an effort to make it more exact, jurisdictions are turning to risk assessment. Wisconsin judges, for instance, rely on a mathematical instrument called Correctional Offender Management Profiling for Alternative Sanctions (COMPAS) to establish risk and severity of punishment. Significantly more detailed than ODARA, COMPAS consists of 137 questions dealing with the offender's criminal history, employment status, social life, education level, drug use, and belief system.[98]

Critics of risk assessment believe that such methods are inherently unfair. First, they argue that risk assessment tools rely on the faulty assumption that group behavior will accurately predict the behavior of any given individual. Second, they point out that such tools are inherently biased against poor defendants.[99] Risk assessment strategies such as COMPAS have, however, been upheld by the courts,[100] and they seem poised to become more common as criminologists understand more about the causes of crime. Indeed, future advances in the fields of biology and genetics, discussed earlier in the chapter, could revolutionize the field of risk assessment and, by extension, the criminal justice system as a whole.

Legalizing Marijuana

How Things Stand

When Karen Strand was pulled over by a U.S. Forest Ranger on a gravel road in Washington's Olympic National Park, she did not worry about the two grams of marijuana she was carrying. After all, state law allows for 28 grams of pot for personal use. The national park is on federal land, however, and she was charged with marijuana possession and faced up to six months behind bars and a $5,000 fine. "It is exceptionally confusing," said Strand.[101] Those words neatly sum up a situation in which marijuana remains illegal under federal law, while about 23 percent of the nation's population live in states where recreational use of the drug has been legalized.

As a Result...

Several years ago, the Ending Federal Marijuana Prohibition Act was introduced before the U.S. Congress.[102] Among other things, this bill, which never passed, would have legalized marijuana under federal law and regulated it in much the same way alcohol is regulated. Proponents of this approach point to Colorado, which legalized the drug in 2012 and in many ways has spearheaded the legalization movement, as proof of the many benefits of legalized marijuana. By 2016, that state was experiencing a thriving marijuana industry that had created about 18,000 full-time jobs and generated $2.4 billion in economic activity.[103] "There are a certain number of folks, like myself, who were pretty reticent about [legalization] to begin with," said one state legislator. "[But] the sky didn't fall."[104]

At the same time, many in the medical community are stressing that, as one health professional puts it, "Marijuana is not good for you."[105] Frequent marijuana use has been linked to mental disorders such as depression and anxiety. It is also associated with respiratory problems, IQ reduction, and immune system weakness.[106] Given that minors can often easily obtain legal but controlled drug products such as cigarettes and alcohol, it seems reasonable to assume that as marijuana is legalized, minors will have greater access to it as well.

Up for Debate

"Legalization will take money and power away from the cartels and the gangs. Murder rates will plummet if gang bangers stop shooting each other and innocent bystanders."[107] —*Anonymous police officer*

"We are teaching our kids more and more that living in an altered state is a societal norm. This is not about a war on drugs—it's a battle to protect the human brain, the mind, our futures, our kids."[108] —*Scott Chipman, chairperson of Citizens Against Legalizing Marijuana, Southern California branch*

What's Your Take?

Review the discussion in this chapter on "Marijuana Law Trends" before answering the following questions.

1. Does the nation's experience with legal and regulated alcohol make you more or less likely to support nationally legalized marijuana? Explain your answer.

2. In 2016, the city of Nashville, Tennessee, passed an ordinance giving local police officers the discretion to either arrest someone caught in possession of marijuana or to issue a civil citation and a $50 fine. What is your opinion of this compromise approach to pot legalization? What are some of its drawbacks and benefits?

Digging Deeper...

One of the unexpected challenges of marijuana legalization has been the rapid growth in *edibles*, or food items containing marijuana. To learn more about this problem, go online and search for the terms **pot edibles, children**, and **new rules**. What forms do pot edibles take? What have been some of the consequences of their popularity for public health and for local law enforcement? Find an example of a local ordinance that has been passed to prevent the harm caused by pot edibles. Will this law have its intended effect? Your written answer to these questions should be at least three paragraphs long.

Gilles Mingasson/Getty Images News/Getty Images

SUMMARY

For more information on these concepts, look back to the Learning Objective icons throughout the chapter.

 Discuss the difference between a hypothesis and a theory in the context of criminology. A hypothesis is a proposition, usually presented in an "If . . ., then . . ." format, that can be tested by researchers. If enough different authorities are able to test and verify a hypothesis, it will usually be accepted as a theory. Because theories can offer explanations for behavior, criminologists often rely on them when trying to determine the causes of criminal behavior.

 Summarize rational choice theory. According to rational choice theory, a person contemplating whether to commit a crime weighs the benefits of doing so against the potential costs of doing so. If the perceived benefits "weigh" more than the perceived costs, it is more likely that the person will commit the crime.

 Explain how brain-scanning technology is able to help scientists determine if an individual is at risk for criminal offending. Brain scanning technologies such as fMRIs provide scientists with detailed depictions of brain structure and brain activity. When these depictions show abnormalities associated with antisocial or violent behavior, the subject is at greater risk of criminal offending.

 List and describe the three theories of social structure that help explain crime. Social disorganization theory states that crime is largely a product of unfavorable conditions in certain communities, or zones of disorganization. Strain theory argues that most people seek increased wealth and financial security and that the strain of not being able to achieve these goals through legal means leads to criminal behavior. Finally, cultural deviance theory asserts that people adapt to the values of the subculture—which has its own standards of behavior—to which they belong.

 Describe the social conflict theory known as the social reality of crime. This theory holds that criminal law, rather than being designed for the common good, is a set of "rules" put in place by those members of society who hold power to control and subdue those who do not.

 List and briefly explain the three branches of social process theory. (a) Learning theory contends that people learn to be criminals from their family and peers. (b) Control theory holds that most of us are dissuaded from a life of crime because we place importance on the opinions of family and peers. (c) Labeling theory holds that a person labeled a "junkie" or a "thief" will respond by becoming or remaining whatever she or he is labeled.

 Describe the importance of early childhood behavior for those who subscribe to self-control theory. Advocates of self-control theory believe that violent and antisocial behavior in adulthood can be predicted, to a large extent, by low levels of self-control in early childhood. Therefore, a child who is impulsive and tends to solve problems with violence is at risk for adult offending.

 Contrast the medical model of addiction with the criminal model of addiction. Those who support the medical model believe that addicts are not criminals, but mentally or physically ill individuals who are forced into acts of petty crime to "feed their habit." Those in favor of the criminal model believe that abusers and addicts endanger society with their behavior and should be treated like any other criminals.

 Explain the theory of the chronic offender and its importance for the criminal justice system. A chronic offender is a juvenile or adult who commits multiple offenses. According to research conducted by Marvin Wolfgang and others in the 1970s, chronic offenders are responsible for a disproportionately large percentage of all crime. In the decades since, law enforcement agencies and public prosecutors have developed strategies to identify and convict chronic offenders with the goal of lessening overall crime rates. In addition, legislators have passed laws that provide longer sentences for chronic offenders in an attempt to keep them off the streets.

1. Research shows that when levels of single-family mortgage foreclosures *rise* in a neighborhood, so do levels of violent crime. Explain the correlation between these two sets of statistics. Why is it false to say that single-family mortgage foreclosures *cause* violent crimes to occur?

2. Why would someone who subscribes to choice theory believe that increasing the harshness of a penalty for a particular crime would necessarily lead to fewer such crimes being committed?

3. Consider the following statement: "The government should protect the public from mentally ill persons who are potentially dangerous, even if that means hospitalizing those persons against their will." Do you agree or disagree? Why?

4. Review the theory of differential association in this chapter. Then, review the definition of white-collar crime in Chapter 1. How could the theory of differential association be used to describe high levels of white-collar crime in any particular business or industry?

5. Suppose you were asked to create a risk assessment tool to determine the likelihood that an offender previously arrested for stealing prescription drugs from a pharmacy would commit a similar crime in the future. List five risk factors that you would consider in predicting this offender's chances for future wrongdoing.

KEY TERMS

anomie 48
biology 42
causation 39
choice theory 40
chronic offender 61
classical criminology 40
control theory 52
correlation 39
criminal model of addiction 59
criminology 39
cultural deviance theory 48
drug abuse 57

genetics 42
hormones 43
hypothesis 39
labeling theory 52
learning theory 51
legalization 60
life course criminology 54
medical model of addiction 59
positivism 41
prescription drug 59
psychoanalytic theory 45
psychology 42

risk assesment 62
social conflict theories 49
social disorganization theory 47
social process theories 51
social reality of crime 50
sociology 46
strain theory 48
subculture 48
testosterone 43
theory 39

1. Quoted in N. R. Kleinfield, et al., "Killers Fit a Profile, but So Do Many Others," *New York Times* (October 4, 2015), A1.

2. Scott E. Wolfe and David C. Pyrooz, "Rolling Back Prices and Raising Crime Rates? The Walmart Effect on Crime in the United States," *British Journal of Criminology* (March 2014), 199–221.

3. Matthew Larson and Gary Sweeten, "Breaking Up Is Hard to Do: Romantic Dissolution, Offending, and Substance Abuse During the Transition to Adulthood," *Criminology* (August 2012), 605–635.

4. James Q. Wilson and Richard J. Hernstein, *Crime and Human Nature: The Definitive Study of the Causes of Crime* (New York: Simon & Schuster, 1985), 515.

5. Cesare Lombroso, *Criminal Man*, ed. Mary Gibson and Nicole Hahn Rafter (Durham, N.C.: Duke University Press, 2006).

6. Wilson and Hernstein, *op. cit.*, 44.

7. Jack Katz, *Seductions of Crime: Moral and Sensual Attractions of Doing Evil* (New York: Basic Books, 1988).

8. "San Jose Man Found Guilty in Brutal 'Thrill Kill' of Classmate." *www.latimes.com. Los Angeles Times*: May 8, 2014, Web.

9. David C. Rowe, *Biology and Crime* (Los Angeles: Roxbury, 2002), 2.

10. Callie H. Burt and Ronald L. Simons, "Pulling Back the Curtain on Heritability Studies: Biosocial Criminology in the Postgenomic Era," *Criminology* (May 2014), 223–262.

11. Raymond R. Crowe, "An Adoption Study of Antisocial Personality," *Archives of General Psychiatry* (1974), 785–791; Sarnoff A. Mednick, William F. Gabrielli, and Barry Hutchings, "Genetic Influences on Criminal Convictions: Evidence from an Adoption Cohort," *Science* (1994), 891–894; and Remi J. Cadoret, "Adoption Studies," *Alcohol Health & Research World* (Summer 1995), 195–201.

12. Hans G. Brunner, et al., "Abnormal Behavior Associated with a Point Mutation in the Structural Gene for Monoamine Oxidase A," *Science* (October 22, 1993), 578–580.

13. Avshalom Caspi, et al., "Role of Genotype in the Cycle of Violence in Maltreated Children," *Science* (August 2, 2002), 851–854.

14. Jari Tiihonen, et al., "Genetic Background of Extreme Violent Behavior," *Molecular Biology* (October 2014), 1–7.

15. Jari Tiihonen, quoted in Melissa Hogenboom, "Two Genes Linked with Violent Crime." *www.bbc.com.* BBC News/Science and Environment: October 28, 2014, Web.

16. L. E. Kreuz and R. M. Rose, "Assessment of Aggressive Behavior and Plasma Testosterone in Young Criminal Population," *Psychosomatic Medicine 34* (1972), 321–332.

17. H. Persky, K. Smith, and G. Basu, "Relation of Psychological Measures of Aggression and Hostility to Testosterone Production in Men," *Psychosomatic Medicine 33* (1971), 265, 276.

18. Cindy-Lee Dennis and Simone N. Vigod, "The Relationship between Postpartum Depression, Domestic Violence, Childhood Violence, and Substance Use: Epidemiologic Study of a Large Community Sample," *Violence against Women* (April 2013), 503–517.

19. Quoted in Pam Belluck, "'Thinking of Ways to Harm Her': New Findings on Timing and Range of Maternal Mental Illness," *New York Times* (June 16, 2014), A1.

20. Jessica Wolpaw Reyes, *Environmental Policy as Social Policy? The Impact of Childhood Lead Exposure on Crime* (Cambridge, Mass.: National Bureau of Economic Research, May 2007).

21. Bureau of Justice Statistics, *Health Problems of Prison and Jail Inmates* (Washington, D.C.: U.S. Department of Justice, September 2006), 1.

22. Kleinfield, et al., *op. cit.*

23. Jeffrey W. Swanson, et al., "Mental Illness and Reduction of Gun Violence and Suicide: Bringing Epidemiologic Research to Policy," *Annals of Epidemiology* (May 2015), 366–376.

24. Jonathan M. Metzl and Kenneth T. MacLeish, "Mental Illness, Mass Shootings, and the Politics of American Firearms," *American Journal of Public Health* (February 2015), 240–249.

25. David G. Myers, *Psychology*, 7th ed. (New York: Worth Publishers, 2004), 576–577.

26. Philip Zimbardo, "Pathology of Imprisonment," *Society* (April 1972), 4–8.

27. Jean Marie McGloin and Kyle J. Thomas, "Incentive for Collective Deviance: Group Size and Changes in Perceived Risk, Cost, and Reward," *Criminology* (August 2016), 459–486.

28. Eric Chyn, "Moved to Opportunity: The Long-Run Effect of Public Housing Demolition on Labor Market Outcomes of Children." *www.ericchyn.com.* Eric Chyn, Department of Economics, University of Virginia: October 12, 2016, Web.

29. Robert Park, Ernest Burgess, and Roderic McKenzie, *The City* (Chicago: University of Chicago Press, 1929).

30. Sam Bieler and John Roman, *Addressing Violence and Disorder around Alcohol Outlets* (Washington, D.C.: District of Columbia Crime Policy Institute, January 2013), 3–5.

31. Clifford R. Shaw, Henry D. McKay, and Leonard S. Cottrell, *Delinquency Areas* (Chicago: University of Chicago Press, 1929).

32. Clifford R. Shaw and Henry D. McKay, *Report on the Causes of Crime, vol. 2: Social Factors in Juvenile Delinquency* (Washington, D.C.: National Commission on Law Observance and Enforcement, 1931).

33. Elijah Anderson, *Code of the Street: Decency, Violence and the Moral Life of the Inner City* (New York: W. W. Norton, 2000), 35–65.

34. *Ibid.*, 180.

35. Eric A. Stewart and Ronald L. Simons, "Race, Code of the Street, and Violent Delinquency: A Multilevel Investigation of Neighborhood Street Culture and Individual Norms of Violence," *Criminology* (May 2010), 569–603.

36. Emile Durkheim, *The Rules of Sociological Method*, trans. Sarah A. Solovay and John H. Mueller (New York: Free Press, 1964).

37. Robert K. Merton, *Social Theory and Social Structure* (New York: Free Press, 1957). See the chapter on "Social Structure and Anomie."

38. Robert Agnew, "Foundation for a General Strain Theory of Crime and Delinquency," *Criminology 30* (1992), 47–87.

39. Robert Agnew, Timothy Brezina, John Paul Wright, and Francis T. Cullen, "Strain, Personality Traits, and Delinquency: Extending General Strain Theory," *Criminology* (February 2002), 43–71.

40. Lawrence L. Shornack, "Conflict Theory and the Family," *International Social Science Review 62* (1987), 154–157.

41. Richard Quinney, *The Social Reality of Crime* (Boston: Little, Brown, 1970).

42. Nicole Hahn Rafter, *Partial Justice: Women, Prisons, and Social Control* (New Brunswick, N.J.: Transaction Publishers, 1990).

43. Federal Bureau of Investigation, *Crime in the United States, 2015*, Table 42. *www.ucr.fbi.gov.* U.S. Department of Justice: 2016, Web.

44. "Racial Disparity." *www.sentencingproject.org.* The Sentencing Project: visited January 9, 2017, Web.

45. Bureau of Justice Statistics, *Prisoners in 2015* (Washington, D.C.: U.S. Department of Justice, December 2016), Table 5, page 8.

46. Civil Rights Division, *Investigation of the Baltimore City Police Department* (Washington, D.C.: U.S. Department of Justice, August 10, 2016), 7, 37.

47. Cindy Brooks Dollar, "Radical Threat Theory: Assessing the Evidence, Requesting Redesign." *www.hindawi.com. Journal of Criminology*: 2014, Web.

48. Muzaffar Chishti and Claire Bergeron, "Hazleton Immigration Ordinance that Began with a Bang Goes Out with a Whimper." *www.migrationpolicy.org.* Migration Policy Institute: March 28, 2014, Web.

49. *Ibid.*

50. John H. MacDonald, John R. Hipp, and Charlotte Gill, "The Effect of Immigrant Concentration on Changes in Neighborhood Crime Rates," *Journal of Quantitative Criminology* (June 2012), 191–215.

51. Philip G. Zimbardo, "The Human Choice: Individuation, Reason, and Order versus Deindividuation, Impulse, and Chaos," in *Nebraska Symposium on Motivation,* ed. William J. Arnold and David Levie (Lincoln, Neb.: University of Nebraska Press, 1969), 287–293.

52. Edwin H. Sutherland, *Criminology*, 4th ed. (Philadelphia: Lippincott, 1947).

53. Michael E. Roettger and Raymond Swisher, "Associations of Fathers' History of Incarceration with Sons' Delinquency and Arrest among Black, White, and Hispanic Males in the United States," *Criminology* (November 2011), 1109–1147.

54. Lindsay A. Robertson, Helena M. McAnally, and Robert J. Hancox, "Childhood and

Adolescent Television Viewing and Antisocial Behavior in Early Adulthood," *Pediatrics* (March 2013), 439–446.

55. Travis Hirschi, *Causes of Delinquency* (Berkeley: University of California Press, 1969).

56. James Q. Wilson and George L. Kelling, "Broken Windows," *Atlantic Monthly* (March 1982), 29.

57. Janet L. Lauritsen, *How Families and Communities Influence Youth Victimization* (Washington, D.C.: Office of Juvenile Justice and Delinquency Prevention, 2003).

58. Howard S. Becker, *Outsiders: Studies in the Sociology of Deviance* (New York: Free Press, 1963).

59. Jeremy Staff, et al., "Early Life Risks, Antisocial Tendencies, and Preteen Delinquency," *Criminology* (November 2015), 677–701.

60. Michael R. Gottfredson and Travis Hirschi, *A General Theory of Crime* (Stanford, Calif.: Stanford University Press, 1990).

61. *Ibid.,* 90.

62. *Ibid.*

63. Terrie Moffitt, "Adolescent-Limited and Life-Course-Persistent Antisocial Behavior: A Developmental Taxonomy," *Psychological Review 100* (1993), 679–680.

64. *Ibid.,* 674.

65. Robert J. Sampson and John H. Laub, *Crime in the Making: Pathways and Turning Points through Life* (Cambridge, Mass.: Harvard University Press, 1993), 11.

66. *Ibid.;* John H. Laub and Robert J. Sampson, *Shared Beginnings, Divergent Lives: Delinquent Boys to Age 70* (Cambridge, Mass.: Harvard University Press, 2003); and Derek A. Kreager, Ross L. Matsueda, and Elena A. Erosheva, "Motherhood and Criminal Desistance in Disadvantaged Neighborhoods," *Criminology* (February 2010), 221–257.

67. John F. Frana and Ryan D. Schroeder, "Alternatives to Incarceration." *www.cjcj.org. Justice Policy Journal:* Fall 2008, Web.

68. Peggy C. Giordano, Monica A. Longmore, Ryan D. Schroeder, and Patrick M. Seffrin, "A Life-Course Perspective on Spirituality and Desistance from Crime," *Criminology* (February 2008), 99–132.

69. Richard B. Felson and Keri B. Burchfield, "Alcohol and the Risk of Physical and Sexual Assault Victimization," *Criminology* (November 1, 2004), 837.

70. Substance Abuse and Mental Health Services Administration, *Key Substance Use and Mental Health Indicators in the United States: Results from the 2015 National Survey on Drug Use and Health* (Washington, D.C.: U.S. Department of Health and Human Services, September 2016), 7, 13, 18.

71. Becker, *op. cit.*

72. Myers, *op. cit.*

73. National Survey on Drug Use and Health, "The NSDUH Report." *www.archive.samhsa. Substance Abuse and Mental Health Services Administration,* March 27, 2008: Web.

74. Anthony A. Grace, "The Tonic/Phasal Model of Dopamine System Regulation," *Drugs and Alcohol 37* (1995), 111.

75. Li Chuan-Yun, Mao Xizeng, and Wei Liping, "Genes and (Common) Pathways Underlying Drug Addiction." *www.journals.plos.org. Public Library of Science:* January 4, 2008, Web.

76. Bureau of Justice Statistics, *Fact Sheet: Drug Related Crimes* (Washington, D.C.: U.S. Department of Justice, September 1994), 1.

77. *ADAM II: 2013 Annual Report* (Washington, D.C.: Office of National Drug Policy, January 2014), xi.

78. Bureau of Justice Statistics, "Alcohol and Crime: Data from 2002 to 2008." *www.bjs. gov.* Bureau of Justice Statistics: September 3, 2010, Web.

79. Richard Friedman, "Why Can't Doctors Identify Killers?" *New York Times* (May 28, 2014), A21.

80. "Prescription Opioid Overdose Data." *www .cdc.gov.* Centers for Disease Control and Prevention: visited January 10, 2017, Web.

81. Gina Kolata and Sarah Cohen, "Drug Overdoses Propel Rise in Mortality Rates of Young Whites," *New York Times* (January 17, 2016), A1; and Katharine Q. Seelye, "Obituaries Shed Euphemisms to Chronicle Toll of Heroin," *New York Times* (July 12, 2015), A16.

82. "Coroner Fears Heroin Dealers Use Area as 'Test Tube,'" *Associated Press* (September 8, 2016).

83. James A. Inciardi, *The War on Drugs: Heroin, Cocaine, and Public Policy* (Palo Alto, Calif.: Mayfield, 1986), 148.

84. "Executive Summary." *www.addiction .surgeongeneral.gov.* U.S. Surgeon General: 2016, Web.

85. Art Swift, "Support for Legal Marijuana Use Up to 60 percent in U.S." *www.gallup.com.* Gallup: October 19, 2016, Web.

86. *Ibid.*

87. Elahe Izadi, "Marijuana Use More than Doubles in Just 12 Years." *www.washingtonpost.com. Washington Post:* October 21, 2015, Web.

88. Lloyd D. Johnston, et al., *Monitoring the Future: National Survey Results on Drug Use, 1975–2014, Vol. 2* (Ann Arbor: University of Michigan Institute for Social Research, July 2015), 86, 91.

89. "The Black Market." *www.havocscope .com. Havocscope:* visited January 10, 2017, Web.

90. *Crime in the United States, 2015, op. cit.,* Persons Arrested and Table 29.

91. Mark J. Pletcher, et al., "Association between Marijuana Exposure and Pulmonary Function over 20 Years," *JAMA* (January 2012, 173–181).

92. "Legalized Marijuana," *The Week* (November 25, 2016), 11.

93. Quoted in Timothy Egan, "After Seven Deaths, Digging for an Explanation," *New York Times* (June 25, 2006), 12.

94. Marvin Wolfgang, Robert Figlio, and Thorsten Sellin, *Delinquency in a Birth Cohort* (Chicago: University of Chicago Press, 1972).

95. Lawrence W. Sherman, "Attacking Crime: Police and Crime Control," in *Modern Policing,* ed. Michael Tonry and Norval Morris (Chicago: University of Chicago Press, 1992), 159.

96. The Ontario Domestic Assault Risk Assessment (ORARA)." *www.waypointcentre.ca.* Waypointe Centre for Mental Health Care: visited on January 11, 2017, Web.

97. Shellie Enright and Mark Bergeron, "Domestic Violence Risk Assessments: Increasing Accountability and Engaging with Victims," *The Police Chief* (September 2015), 23.

98. "COMPAS." *www.ncsc.org.* Pretrial Justice Center for Courts: visited on January 11, 2017, Web.

99. Anna Maria Berry-Jester, et al., "The New Science of Sentencing." *www.themarshall project.com.* The Marshall Project: August 4, 2015, Web.

100. Colin Holloway, "Wisconsin Supreme Court Approves Use of Risk Assessment Test in Sentencing." *www.freeadvice.com.* FreeAdvice Legal: July 15, 2016, Web.

101. Quoted in "Marijuana Busts on Federal Lands Highlight Challenges for Pot-Friendly States," *Associated Press* (September 16, 2013).

102. "S.2237—Ending Federal Marijuana Prohibition Act of 2015." *www.congress.gov.* Congress.gov: November 4, 2015, Web.

103. Miles Light, et al., *The Economic Impact of Marijuana Legalization in Colorado* (Denver, Colo.: Marijuana Policy Group, October 2016), 8.

104. Dickey Lee Hullinghorst, quoted in "Legalizing Marijuana," *op. cit.*

105. Susan Weiss, policy chief for the National Institute on Drug Abuse, quoted in "Is Marijuana Bad for You?" The Week (November 30, 2012), 11.

106. *Fact Sheet: Office of National Drug Control Policy* (Washington, D.C.: Executive Office of the President, October 2010), 2.

107. Quoted in Doug Wyllie, "Legalizing Marijuana: Police Officers Speak Out." *www .policeone.com.* PoliceOne.com: December 16, 2011, Web.

108. Quoted in Thomas Fuller, "Votes in 5 States Are Potential Turning Point for Legal Marijuana," *New York Times* (October 25, 2016), A1.

3

The Crime Picture:
Offenders and Victims

To target your study and review, look for these numbered Learning Objective icons throughout the chapter.

Chapter Outline		Corresponding Learning Objectives
Classification of Crimes	**1**	Discuss the primary goals of civil law and criminal law and explain how these goals are realized.
	2	Explain the differences between crimes *mala in se* and *mala prohibita*.
Measuring Crime in the United States	**3**	Identify the publication in which the FBI reports crime data and list the two main ways in which the data are reported.
	4	Distinguish between the National Crime Victimization Survey (NCVS) and self-reported surveys.
Victims of Crime	**5**	Describe the three ways that victims' rights legislation increases the ability of crime victims to participate in the criminal justice system.
	6	Explain the routine activities theory of victimization.
Crime Trends in the United States	**7**	Identify the three factors most often used by criminologists to explain changes in the nation's crime rate.
	8	Explain why income level appears to be more important than race or ethnicity when it comes to crime trends.
	9	Discuss the prevailing explanation for the rising number of women incarcerated in the United States.

Statistical Proof?

▲ Students protest the high incidence of campus rape during a sexual assault awareness night campout at Occidental College ("Oxy") in Los Angeles. Bloomberg/Getty Images

The headlines were terrifying, particularly for high school seniors about to go to college: "1 in 4 Women Experience Sex Assault on Campus," declared the *New York Times*. "More than 1 in 5 Female Undergrads at Top Schools Suffer Sexual Attacks," stated the *Washington Post*. And, in fact, a survey of more than 150,000 students from twenty-seven universities recently released by the Association of American Universities (AAU) did paint a dire picture. According to the study, 23 percent of female college students reported experiencing some form of unwanted sexual contact on campus.

While the AAU survey highlighted a crucial safety issue for American higher education, it also highlighted the inherent difficulties in accurately measuring unlawful and unacceptable behavior. Immediately following its release, the study's authors cautioned that to conclude that 23 percent of female students had been victims of "sexual attacks" would be "oversimplistic, if not misleading." The study's definition of sexual assault included both unwanted penetrative sex *and* unwanted sexual touching and groping.

Defining sexual assault in a way that is consistent with criminal rape statutes, the survey showed that 11 percent of females had been victimized—a number that, while still high, is not as high as the headlines suggested.

Experts also point out that the AAU survey may suffer from "nonresponse bias." Although 150,000 students participated in the study, 780,000 students had been asked to participate, via e-mail. It is possible that the 19 percent of students who responded were more likely to have experienced unwanted sexual contact than the 81 percent who did not. This could be one reason why the AAU study's results were inconsistent with those released by the federal government just nine months earlier. Using the National Crime Victimization Survey, which we will examine later in the chapter, the federal government found that 6.1 of every 1,000 female college students had suffered a sexual assault. Those numbers, however, are so low as to have generated their own criticism, with many wondering if the government's definition of sexual assault was too narrow or too confusing for survey respondents.

FOR CRITICAL ANALYSIS

1. About a decade ago, the federal government surveyed 4,000 college women about their experience with rape (coerced or unwanted sex) and found that one in four had survived a rape or attempted rape at some point during the previous year. Compared with the AAU survey just discussed, which study is more useful? Why?

2. Explain the reasoning behind "nonresponse bias." Do you think it is a valid criticism of the AAU survey, as described above? Why or why not?

3. Several universities recently considered banning female students from fraternity houses to lessen the risk that these women would be sexually assaulted. What is your opinion of this policy?

Classification of Crimes

Statistical measurements such as the AAU's survey of unwanted sexual contact on college campuses[1] are important because they often spur policy change. For example, reacting to numerous studies detailing the magnitude of this particular problem, in 2013 Congress passed the Campus Sexual Violence Elimination Act. This legislation requires American secondary schools to, among other things, educate incoming students on the risks of dating violence and sexual assault.[2]

Legal definitions of criminal acts also matter. In a course designed to lessen the risk of rape, one first-year university student was surprised to learn that a person who is incapacitated by alcohol cannot legally give consent to sex. Reflecting on a high school sexual incident during which she was drunk, she said, "I no longer felt shame and guilt about it being my fault."[3]

In this chapter, we will examine the crucial role that definitions and statistical research play in answering vast questions such as "How common is crime in United States" and "Who is most at risk of being victimized by crime?" We start our discussion of these topics with a short overview of three concepts crucial to criminal justice: the distinctions between (a) civil law and criminal law, (b) felonies and misdemeanors, and (c) crimes *mala in se* and *mala prohibita.*

Civil Law and Criminal Law

All law can be divided into two categories: civil law and criminal law. These two strands of law are distinguished by their primary goals. The criminal justice system is concerned with protecting society from harm by preventing and prosecuting crimes. A crime is an act so reprehensible that it is considered a wrong against society as a whole, as well as against the individual victim. Therefore, the state prosecutes a person who commits a criminal act. If the state is able to prove that a person is guilty of a crime, the government will punish her or him with imprisonment or fines, or both.

Civil law, which includes all types of law other than criminal law, is concerned with disputes between private individuals and between entities. Proceedings in civil lawsuits are normally initiated by an individual or a corporation (in contrast to criminal proceedings, which are initiated by public prosecutors). Such disputes may involve, for example, the terms of a contract, the ownership of property, or an automobile accident. Under civil law, the government provides a forum for the resolution of *torts*—or private wrongs—in which the injured party, called the **plaintiff,** tries to prove that a wrong has been committed by the accused party, or the **defendant.** (Note that the accused party in both criminal and civil cases is known as the *defendant.*)

Learning Objective 1 Discuss the primary goals of civil law and criminal law and explain how these goals are realized.

Guilt and Responsibility

A criminal court is convened to determine whether the defendant is *guilty*—that is, whether the defendant has, in fact, committed the offense charged. In contrast, civil law is concerned with responsibility, a much more flexible concept. For example, in 2012 Ruth Kurka lost control of the motorized shopping cart she was piloting in a Cleveland area Giant Eagle supermarket and struck seventy-one-year-old Barbara Rieger. The impact caused Rieger to suffer significant neck and head injuries. The incident was certainly an accident, and local authorities never considered charging Kurka with any crime. At the same time, in 2016 a civil jury decided that Giant Eagle was **liable,** or legally responsible, for Rieger's injuries because the corporation failed to properly instruct Kurka how to use the motorized shopping cart.

Most civil cases involve a request for monetary damages to compensate for the wrong that has been committed. Thus, the civil court ordered Giant Eagle to pay Barbara Rieger $1.3 million as compensation for her pain and suffering and as punishment for the corporation's carelessness.

Civil law The branch of law dealing with the definition and enforcement of all private or public rights, as opposed to criminal matters.

Plaintiff The person or institution that initiates a lawsuit in civil court proceedings by filing a complaint.

Defendant In a civil court, the person or institution against whom an action is brought. In a criminal court, the person or entity who has been formally accused of violating a criminal law.

Liable In a civil court, legal responsibility for one's own or another's actions.

Beyond a Reasonable Doubt The degree of proof required to find the defendant in a criminal trial guilty of committing the crime. The defendant's guilt must be the only reasonable explanation for the criminal act before the court.

Preponderance of the Evidence The degree of proof required in a civil case. In general, this requirement is met when a plaintiff proves that a fact more likely than not is true.

Felonies Serious crimes, usually punishable by death or imprisonment for a year or longer.

Misdemeanor A criminal offense that is not a felony; usually punishable by a fine and/or a jail term of less than one year.

The Burden of Proof

Although criminal law proceedings are completely separate from civil law proceedings in the modern legal system, the two systems do have some similarities. Both attempt to control behavior by imposing sanctions on those who violate society's definition of acceptable behavior. Furthermore, criminal and civil law often supplement each other. In certain instances, a victim may file a civil suit against an individual who is also the target of a criminal prosecution by the government.

Because the burden of proof is much greater in criminal trials than civil ones, it is almost always easier to win monetary damages than a criminal conviction. The most famous (or infamous) example of such a situation in recent memory occurred about twenty years ago. After former professional football player O. J. Simpson was acquitted of murder charges in the deaths of his ex-wife, Nicole, and Ronald Goldman, the families of the two victims sued Simpson. In 1997, a civil court jury found Simpson liable for the wrongful deaths of his ex-wife and Goldman, and ordered him to pay their families $33.5 million in damages.

During the criminal trial, the jury did not find enough evidence to prove **beyond a reasonable doubt** (the burden of proof in criminal cases) that Simpson was guilty of any crime. In contrast, the civil trial established by a **preponderance of the evidence** (the burden of proof in civil cases) that Simpson had killed his victims in a fit of jealous rage. (See this chapter's *Mastering Concepts* feature for a comparison of civil and criminal law.)

Felonies and Misdemeanors

Depending on their degree of seriousness, crimes are classified as *felonies* or *misdemeanors*. **Felonies** are crimes punishable by death or by imprisonment in a federal or state prison for one year or longer (though some states, such as North Carolina, consider felonies to be punishable by at least two years' incarceration). There are, in general, four degrees of felony:

1. Capital offenses, for which the maximum penalty is death.
2. First degree felonies, punishable by a maximum penalty of life imprisonment.
3. Second degree felonies, punishable by a maximum of ten years' imprisonment.
4. Third degree felonies, punishable by a maximum of five years' imprisonment.

▼ In most jurisdictions, a first-time DUI (driving under the influence) arrest not involving an injury will be charged as a misdemeanor. Any further DUI arrests will then be charged as felonies. **What is your opinion of this strategy? What would be the benefits and drawbacks of charging first-time DUIs as felonies?**

Paul Biryukov/Shutterstock.com

For the most part, felonies involve crimes of violence, such as armed robbery or sexual assault, or other "serious" crimes, such as stealing a large amount of money or selling illegal drugs.

Types of Misdemeanors

Under federal law and in most states, any crime that is not a felony is considered a **misdemeanor.** Misdemeanors are crimes punishable by a fine or by confinement for up to a year. If imprisoned, the guilty party goes to a local jail instead of a prison. Disorderly conduct and trespassing are common misdemeanors. Most states distinguish between *gross misdemeanors*, which are offenses punishable by thirty days to a year in jail, and *petty misdemeanors*, or offenses punishable by fewer than thirty

MASTERING CONCEPTS

Civil Law versus Criminal Law

ISSUE	CIVIL LAW	CRIMINAL LAW
Area of concern	Rights and duties between individuals	Offenses against society as a whole
Wrongful act	Harm to a person or business entity	Violation of a statute that prohibits some type of activity
Party who brings suit	Person who suffered harm (plaintiff)	The state (prosecutor)
Party who responds	Person who supposedly caused harm (defendant)	Person who allegedly committed a crime (defendant)
Standard of proof	Preponderance of the evidence	Beyond a reasonable doubt
Remedy	Damages to compensate for the harm	Punishment (fine or incarceration)

days in jail. Probation and community service are often imposed on those who commit misdemeanors, especially juveniles. As you will see in Chapter 8, whether a crime is a felony or misdemeanor can also determine in which criminal court the case will be tried.

Infractions   The least serious form of wrongdoing is often called an **infraction** and is punishable only by a fine. Even though infractions such as parking tickets and traffic violations technically represent illegal activity, they generally are not considered "crimes." Therefore, infractions rarely lead to jury trials and are deemed to be so minor that they do not appear on the offender's criminal record.

In some jurisdictions, the terms *infraction* and *petty offense* are interchangeable. In others, however, they are different. Under federal guidelines, for example, an infraction can be punished by up to five days behind bars, while a petty offender is liable only for a fine.[4] Finally, those who string together a series of infractions (or fail to pay the fines that come with such offenses) are in danger of being criminally charged. In Illinois, having three or more speeding violations in one year is considered criminal behavior.[5]

Mala in Se and *Mala Prohibita*

Criminologists often express the social function of criminal law in terms of *mala in se* or *mala prohibita* crimes. A criminal act is referred to as *mala in se* if it would be considered wrong even if there were no law prohibiting it. *Mala in se* crimes are said to go against "natural laws"—that is, against the "natural, moral, and public" principles of a society. Murder, rape, and theft are examples of *mala in se* crimes. These crimes are generally the same from country to country and culture to culture.

In contrast, the term *mala prohibita* refers to acts that are considered crimes only because they have been codified as such through statute—"human-made" laws. A *mala prohibita* crime is considered wrong only because it has been prohibited. It is not inherently wrong, though it may reflect the moral standards of a society at a given time. Thus, the definition of a *mala prohibita* crime can vary from country to country and even from state to state. Bigamy, or the offense of having two legal spouses, could be considered a *mala prohibita* crime.

Making the Distinction   Some observers question the distinction between *mala in se* and *mala prohibita*. In many instances, it is difficult to define a "pure" *mala in se* crime. That is, it is difficult to separate a crime from the culture that has deemed

Learning Objective 2
Explain the differences between crimes *mala in se* and *mala prohibita*.

Infraction In most jurisdictions, a noncriminal offense for which the penalty is a fine rather than incarceration.

Mala in Se A descriptive term for acts that are inherently wrong, regardless of whether they are prohibited by law.

Mala Prohibita A descriptive term for acts that are made illegal by criminal statute and are not necessarily wrong in and of themselves.

it a crime.[6] Even murder, under certain cultural circumstances, is not considered a criminal act. In a number of poor, traditional areas of the Middle East and Asia, the law excuses "honor killings," in which men kill female family members suspected of sexual indiscretion.

Our own legal system excuses homicide in extreme situations, such as self-defense or when a law enforcement agent kills in the course of upholding the law. Therefore, "natural" laws can be seen as culturally specific. Similar difficulties occur in trying to define a "pure" *mala prohibita* crime because different cultures have different ways of looking at similar behavior. More than 150 countries, including most members of the European Union, have legalized prostitution. With the exception of seven rural counties of Nevada, prostitution is illegal in the United States. (To consider whether our legal and moral attitudes toward prostitution should change, see the feature *Comparative Criminal Justice—The New Zealand Model.*)

The Drug Dilemma

The *mala in se/mala prohibita* distinction helps explain a contradiction that we touched on in the previous chapter: Why has society prohibited the use of certain drugs while allowing the use of others? The answer cannot be found in the risk of harm caused by the substances. Just as with illegal drugs, many legal drugs, if abused, can have serious consequences for the health of the user or of others. According to the Centers for Disease Control and Prevention, excessive alcohol use is responsible for nearly 90,000 deaths annually (mostly due to alcohol-related illness and drunk driving fatalities),[7] and cigarette smoking causes about one in every five deaths in this country each year.[8]

COMPARATIVE CRIMINAL JUSTICE

Source: Central Intelligence Agency

The New Zealand Model

Addressing an audience in Los Angeles, Meg Muñoz recalled a time in her early twenties when she had rent and car insurance to pay and was saving funds for college. "I was moving toward a goal, and sex work helped me to do that," Muñoz said, explaining her choice to be a prostitute. She even enjoyed the work, until a domineering boyfriend blackmailed her for a cut of the profits. "Because the work I was doing was illegal, he started to hold it over my head," Muñoz recalled.

EMPOWERMENT OR VICTIMIZATION?

Muñoz believes that prostitution should be legalized in the United States, which would lead to the "empowerment of the sex worker." In 2003, New Zealand set a precedent for such a policy by passing the Prostitution Reform Act. Under this legislation, it is legal to be a sex worker and to operate a brothel in which sex workers provide their services. Additionally, sex workers have the same rights to workplace safety and health care as other employees in New Zealand. (It is, however, against the law to coerce someone to provide sexual services for pay or to aid someone under the age of eighteen in providing them.)

Critics of the New Zealand Model contend that this policy encourages human trafficking. That is, it gives organized criminal gangs an incentive to import vulnerable women from other countries and force them into sex work in New Zealand. Critics also point out that, even when protected by the law, prostitutes are at a high risk for violence, drug abuse, self-harm, and exploitation.

Supporters counter that legalization leads to greater protection of sex workers by police, who are freed to focus on more important tasks than curtailing prostitution. In addition, the policy is geared toward reducing the incidence of sexually transmitted disease—an estimated 99 percent of New Zealand's 6,000 prostitutes now use condoms, in accordance with the government's safe sex requirements.

FOR CRITICAL ANALYSIS

Compare the arguments for the legalization of prostitution with the arguments for the legalization of marijuana that we discussed in the previous chapter. Do you think a similar "legalize prostitution" movement is likely in the United States? Would you support such a movement? Explain your answers.

Nor is illegality linked to the addictive quality of the drug. According to the American Medical Association, nicotine is the most habit-forming substance, with over two-thirds of people who smoke cigarettes becoming "hooked."[9] One professor of preventive medicine has concluded that "there are no scientific . . . or medical bases on which the legal distinctions between various drugs are made."[10]

If drug laws are not based on science or medicine, on what are they based? The answer lies in the concept of *mala prohibita*: certain drugs are characterized as illegal while others are not because of dominant social norms and values. Alcohol and tobacco are legal not because they are considerably different from or safer than illegal drugs, but rather because the law, as supported by society, says so.[11] As we saw in the preceding chapter's discussion of the legalization of marijuana, though, sometimes certain segments of society challenge the status quo, placing pressure on criminal law to adjust accordingly.

Uniform Crime Reports (UCR) An annual report compiled by the FBI to give an indication of criminal activity in the United States.

Measuring Crime in the United States

So far in this textbook, you have been exposed to a number of studies relating to the criminal justice system. For the most part, these analyses have dealt with narrow topics such as the racial makeup of marijuana arrestees, the impact of Walmart expansion on offending, and the possible existence of a "crime gene." The best-known annual survey of criminal behavior, however, tries to answer the broadest of questions: How much crime is there in the United States?

The Uniform Crime Reports

One of the more troubling aspects of sexual assaults on college campuses is how infrequently these offenses are reported to law enforcement. According to the federal study referenced in the opening of this chapter, only 20 percent of student sexual assault victims communicate with the police.[12] Among these students, the most common reason given for keeping silent is, "I did not think [the incident] was serious enough to report."[13]

This trend almost certainly leads to the underreporting of sex crimes in the nation's most far-reaching and oft-cited set of national crime statistics, the **Uniform Crime Reports (UCR).** The UCR is a compilation of data prepared by the Federal Bureau of Investigation (FBI). Since its inception in 1930, the UCR has attempted to measure the overall rate of crime in the United States by collecting data on "offenses known to law enforcement."[14] To produce the UCR, the FBI relies on the voluntary participation of local law enforcement agencies. These agencies—approximately 18,000 in total, covering most of the population—base their information on three measurements:

1. The number of persons arrested.
2. The number of crimes reported by victims, witnesses, or the police themselves.
3. Police employee data.[15]

Once this information has been sent to the FBI, the agency presents the crime data in two important ways:

1. As a *rate* per 100,000 people. For example, suppose the crime rate in a given year is 3,000. This means that, for every 100,000 inhabitants of the United States, 3,000 *Part I offenses* were reported to the FBI by local police departments. The crime rate is often cited by media sources when discussing the level of crime in the United States.

Learning Objective 3 Identify the publication in which the FBI reports crime data and list the two main ways in which the data are reported.

2. As a *percentage* change from the previous year or other time periods. From 2006 to 2015, there was a 22.2 percent decrease in violent crime and a 25 percent decrease in property crime. Thus, according to the UCR, that decade saw a significant reduction in criminal behavior in the United States.[16]

The FBI publishes its data annually in *Crime in the United States*. Along with the basic statistics, this publication offers an exhaustive array of crime information, including breakdowns of crimes committed by city, county, and other geographic designations and by the demographics (gender, race, age) of the individuals who have been arrested for crimes.

Part I Offenses

The UCR divides the criminal offenses it measures into two major categories: Part I and Part II offenses. **Part I offenses** are those crimes that, due to their seriousness and frequency, are recorded by the FBI to give a general idea of the "crime picture" in the United States in any given year. For a description of the seven Part I offenses, see Figure 3.1.

Part I violent offenses are those most likely to be covered by the media and, consequently, most likely to inspire fear in the population. These crimes have come to dominate crime coverage to such an extent that, for most Americans, the first image that comes to mind at the mention of "crime" is one person physically attacking another person or a robbery taking place with the use or threat of force. Furthermore, in the stereotypical crime, the offender and the victim do not know each other.

Given the trauma of violent crimes, this perception is understandable, but it is not accurate. According to UCR statistics, almost half of the homicides in the United States are

---

FIGURE 3.1 Part I Offenses

Every month, local law enforcement agencies voluntarily provide information on serious offenses in their jurisdiction to the FBI. These serious offenses, known as Part I offenses, are defined here. (Arson is not included in the national crime report data, but it is sometimes considered a Part I offense nonetheless, so its definition is included here.) As the graph shows, most Part I offenses reported by local police departments in any given year are property crimes.

Murder. The willful (nonnegligent) killing of one human being by another.

Rape. The penetration, no matter how slight, of the vagina or anus with any body part or object, or oral penetration by a sex organ of another person, without the consent of the victim.

Robbery. The taking or attempting to take of anything of value from the care, custody, or control of a person or persons by force or threat of force or violence and/or by putting the victim in fear.

Aggravated assault. An unlawful attack by one person on another for the purpose of inflicting severe or aggravated bodily injury. This type of assault is usually accompanied by the use of a weapon or by means likely to produce death or great bodily harm.

Burglary—breaking and entering. The unlawful entry of a structure to commit a felony or a theft. Attempted forcible entry is included.

Larceny/theft (except motor vehicle theft). The unlawful taking, carrying, leading, or riding away of property from the possession or constructive possession of another.

Motor vehicle theft. The theft or attempted theft of a motor vehicle.

Arson. Any willful or malicious burning or attempt to burn, with or without intent to defraud, a dwelling house, public building, motor vehicle or aircraft, personal property of another, and the like.

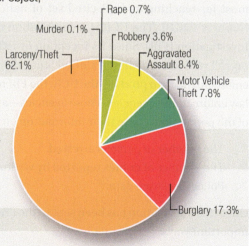

Larceny/Theft 62.1%
Murder 0.1%
Rape 0.7%
Robbery 3.6%
Aggravated Assault 8.4%
Motor Vehicle Theft 7.8%
Burglary 17.3%

Federal Bureau of Investigation, *Crime in the United States, 2015*, Offense Definitions. www.ucr.fbi.gov. U.S. Department of Justice: 2016, Web; and Federal Bureau of Investigation, *Crime in the United States, 2015*, Table 1. www.ucr.fbi.gov. U.S. Department of Justice: 2016, Web.

committed by a relative or other acquaintance of the victim.[17] Furthermore, as is evident from Figure 3.1, the majority of Part I offenses committed are property crimes. Notice that 62 percent of all reported Part I offenses are larceny/thefts, and another 17 percent are burglaries.[18]

Part II Offenses

Not only do violent crimes represent the minority of Part I offenses, but Part I offenses are far outweighed by **Part II offenses,** which include all crimes recorded by the FBI that do not fall into the category of Part I offenses. While Part I offenses are almost always felonies, Part II offenses include crimes that may be classified as misdemeanors. Of the nineteen categories that make up Part II offenses, the most common are drug abuse violations, simple assaults (in which no weapons are used and no serious harm is done to the victim), driving under the influence, and disorderly conduct.[19]

Information gathered on Part I offenses reflects those offenses "known," or reported to the FBI by local agencies. Part II offenses, in contrast, are measured only by arrest data. In 2015, the FBI recorded about 2 million arrests for Part I offenses in the United States. That same year, about 8.8 million arrests for Part II offenses took place.[20] In other words, Part II offenses were four and one-half times more common than Part I offenses. Such statistics have prompted Marcus Felson, a professor at Rutgers University School of Criminal Justice, to comment that "most crime is very ordinary."[21]

The UCR: A Flawed Method?

Even though the UCR is the predominant source of crime data in the country, there are numerous questions about the accuracy of its findings. For one, there is scattered evidence that some local police departments manipulate their crime reports. A recent internal investigation found that a group of New York City police officers downgraded the severity of criminal activity in their precinct, distorting the area's annual crime reports.[22] Furthermore, the UCR most likely suffers from the twin problems of underreporting and inconsistency.

Police Notification

For the UCR to be accurate, citizens must report criminal activity to the police, and the police must then pass this information on to the FBI. Criminologists have long been aware that neither citizens nor police can be expected to perform these roles with consistency.[23] Citizens may not report a crime for any number of reasons, including fear of reprisal, embarrassment, or a personal bias in favor of the offender. Many also feel that police cannot do anything to help them in the aftermath of a crime, so they do not see the point of involving law enforcement agents in their lives.

Surveys of crime victims reveal that only 47 percent of violent crimes and 35 percent of property crimes are reported to the police.[24] In general, people seem more willing to notify police about robberies and aggravated assaults by strangers than about rapes or violence that occurs within the family context.[25]

Problems with Discretion and Definitions

Local police departments have a great deal of discretion in interpreting what constitutes a Part I offense, which can lead to inconsistencies. In Illinois, for example, if one person strikes another person but does not cause any harm, the offender is usually charged with a misdemeanor. If the victim is a police officer or a teacher, however, the misdemeanor becomes felony assault. So, in that state, an incident in which a teacher's finger is scratched and one in which a victim is shot nonfatally could both be reported to the FBI as "aggravated assaults."[26]

Furthermore, the FBI and local law enforcement agencies do not always interpret Part I offenses in the same manner. In Chicago, for example, the police department routinely

Part II Offenses All crimes recorded by the FBI that do not fall into the category of Part I offenses. These crimes include both misdemeanors and felonies.

labels unsolved homicides as "noncriminal death investigations" rather than murders as defined by the UCR. This occurs even when a "willful killing" seems apparent, as was the case with one "noncriminal death" victim whose decomposed body was found with evidence that she had been tied to a chair with telephone wire.[27]

The National Incident-Based Reporting System

In the 1980s, well aware of the various criticisms of the UCR, the Department of Justice began seeking ways to revise its data-collecting system. The result was the National Incident-Based Reporting System (NIBRS). In the NIBRS, local agencies collect data on each single crime occurrence within twenty-three offense categories made up of forty-nine specific crimes called Group A offenses. These data are recorded on computerized record systems provided—though not completely financed—by the federal government.

The NIBRS became available to local agencies in 1989. Twenty-six years later, 36 percent of all law enforcement agencies that participate in the UCR program were submitting data to the NIBRS, and NIBRS is slated to replace the UCR in 2021.[28] Criminologists are responding enthusiastically to the NIBRS because the system provides information about four "data sets"—offenses, victims, offenders, and arrestees—unavailable through the UCR.

The NIBRS also presents a more complete picture of crime by monitoring all criminal "incidents" reported to the police, not just those that lead to an arrest. For example, the 2015 NIBRS, which recorded about 4.9 million criminal incidents, found that sex offenses were most likely to take place between midnight and 12:59 A.M. and that 4 percent of all aggravated assaults resulted from "lover's quarrels."[29] (See Figure 3.2 to get a clearer sense of the differences between the UCR and the NIBRS.)

Victim Surveys

One alternative method of data collecting attempts to avoid the distorting influence of the "intermediary," or the local police agencies. In victim surveys, criminologists or other researchers ask the victims of crime directly about their experiences, using techniques such as interviews or e-mail and phone surveys. The most comprehensive

---

FIGURE 3.2 Comparing the UCR and the NIBRS

As the following scenario shows, the data collection under the NIBRS is much more comprehensive than the reporting system of the UCR.

At approximately 9:30 P.M. on July 26, 2017, two young males approach a thirty-two-year-old African American woman in the parking garage of a movie theater. The first man, who is white, puts a knife to the woman's throat and grabs her purse, which contains $220. The second man, who is Latino, then puts a gun to the woman's temple and rapes her. When he is finished, he shoots her in the chest, a wound that does not prove to be fatal. The two men flee the scene and are not apprehended by law enforcement.

	UCR	NIBRS
Crime reported to FBI	One rape. Under the UCR, when more than one crime is involved in a single incident, only the most serious is reported. Also, attempts are not recorded.	One rape, one robbery, and one attempted murder.
Age, sex, and race of the victim	Not recorded.	Recorded.
Age, sex, and race of the offenders	Not recorded.	Recorded.
Location and time of the attack	Not recorded.	Recorded.
Type and value of lost property	Not recorded.	Recorded.

Source: U.S. Department of Justice.

such project in the United States is the National Crime Victimization Survey (NCVS), which started in 1972. Conducted by the U.S. Bureau of the Census in cooperation with the Bureau of Justice Statistics of the Justice Department, the NCVS conducts an annual survey of approximately 90,000 households with about 169,000 occupants over twelve years of age. Participants are interviewed twice a year concerning their experiences with crimes in the prior six months. As you can see in Figure 3.3, NCVS questions are quite detailed.

Proponents of the NCVS highlight a number of ways in which the victim survey is superior to the UCR:

1. It measures both reported and unreported crime.
2. It is unaffected by police bias and distortions in reporting crime to the FBI.
3. It does not rely on victims directly reporting crime to the police.[30]

Because of these factors, victim surveys such as the NCVS can provide criminologists with a better understanding of the **dark figure of crime,** or the actual—rather than reported—amount of crime that takes places in the United States.

In the past, the NCVS was criticized for the use of confusing, technical jargon in its questions. As is clear from Figure 3.3, efforts have been made to simplify the survey's language so that it is more easily understood. Another potential problem with any victim survey is that the responses cannot be verified. If a participant, for whatever reason, fails to answer truthfully, the faulty response is recorded as fact.[31]

Self-Reported Surveys

Based on many of the same principles as victim surveys, but focusing instead on offenders, **self-reported surveys** are a third source of information for criminologists. In this form of data collection, persons are asked directly—through personal interviews or questionnaires, or over the telephone—about specific criminal activity to which they may have been a party. Self-reported surveys are most useful in situations in which the group to be studied is already gathered in an institutional setting, such as a juvenile facility or a prison. One of the most widespread self-reported surveys in the United States, the Drug Use

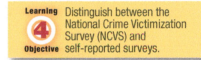

Learning Objective 4 Distinguish between the National Crime Victimization Survey (NCVS) and self-reported surveys.

Dark Figure of Crime A term used to describe the actual amount of crime that takes place. The "figure" is "dark," or impossible to detect, because a great number of crimes are never reported to the police.

Self-Reported Surveys Methods of gathering crime data that rely on participants to reveal and detail their own criminal or delinquent behavior.

FIGURE 3.3 Sample Questions from the NCVS (National Crime Victimization Survey)

36a. **Was something belonging to YOU stolen, such as**
   a. Things that you carry, like luggage, a wallet, purse, briefcase, book
   b. Clothing, jewelry, or cell phone
   c. Bicycle or sports equipment
   d. Things in your home—like a TV, stereo, or tools
   e. Things outside your home, such as a garden hose or lawn furniture
   f. Things belonging to children in the household
   g. Things from a vehicle, such as a package, groceries, camera, or CDs?

41a. **Has anyone attacked or threatened you in any of these ways?**
   a. With any weapon, for instance, a gun or knife
   b. With anything like a baseball bat, frying pan, scissors, or stick
   c. By something thrown, such as a rock or a bottle
   d. Include any grabbing, punching, or choking

   e. Any rape, attempted rape, or other type of sexual attack
   f. Any face to face threats OR
   g. Any attack or threat or use of force by anyone at all? Please mention it even if you are not certain it was a crime.

43a. **Incidents involving forced or unwanted sexual acts are often difficult to talk about. Have you been forced or coerced to engage in unwanted sexual activity by**
   a. Someone you didn't know
   b. A casual acquaintance OR
   c. Someone you know well?

45. **During the last six months, did anything you thought was a crime happen to YOU, but you did NOT report it to the police?**
   a. Yes
   b. No

Source: Adapted from U.S. Department of Justice, *National Crime Victimization Survey 2009* (Washington, D.C.: Bureau of Justice Statistics, 2013).

Forecasting Program, collects information on narcotics use from arrestees who have been brought into booking facilities.

Because there is no penalty for admitting to criminal activity in a self-reported survey, subjects tend to be more forthcoming in discussing their behavior. Researchers often use self-reported studies to get a better idea of the actual amount of sexual assault that takes place in our society. These studies invariably show that many more rapes take place than are reported to the police.[32] Such conclusions underscore the most striking finding of self-reported surveys: the dark figure of crime, referred to earlier as the *actual* amount of crime that takes place, appears to be much larger than the UCR or NCVS would suggest.

ETHICS CHALLENGE

Given the importance placed on crime statistics by the public and the media, the temptation within local police departments to "doctor" these stats, described in this section, is inescapable. What steps could police administrators take to discourage this clearly unethical behavior?

Victims of Crime

It is no coincidence that the U.S. Department of Justice launched the first version of the National Crime Victimization Survey in the 1970s. The previous decade had seen a dramatic increase in the rights afforded to criminal defendants. To offset what they saw as a growing imbalance in the American criminal justice system, advocates had begun to argue that crime victims also needed greater protection under the law. Initially, the victims' rights movement focused on specific areas of crime, such as domestic violence, sexual assault, and, through the efforts of Mothers Against Drunk Driving, vehicular homicide. Today, an emphasis on the rights of all crime victims has a profound impact on the workings of law enforcement, courts, and corrections in the United States.

Legal Rights of Crime Victims

Thirty-five years ago, a presidential task force invited federal and state legislatures to "address the needs of the millions of Americans and their families who are victimized by crime every year and who often carry its scars into the years to come."[33] This call to action was, in large part, a consequence of the rather peculiar position of victims in our criminal justice system. That is, once a crime has occurred, the victim is relegated to a single role: being a witness against the suspect in court. Legally, he or she has no say in the prosecution of the offender, or even whether such a prosecution is to take place. Such powerlessness can be extremely frustrating, particularly in the wake of a traumatic, life-changing event.

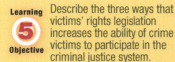

Learning 5 Objective Describe the three ways that victims' rights legislation increases the ability of crime victims to participate in the criminal justice system.

Legislative Action   To remedy this situation, all states have passed legislation creating certain rights for victims. On a federal level, such protections are encoded in the Crime Victims' Rights Act of 2004 (CVRA), which gives victims "the right to participate in the system."[34] This participation primarily focuses on three categories of rights:

1. The right to be *informed*. This includes receiving information about victims' rights in general, as well as specific information such as the dates and times of court proceedings relating to the relevant crime.

2. The right to be *present*. This includes the right to be present at court hearings involving the case at hand, as long as the victim's presence does not interfere with the rights of the accused.

3. The right to be *heard*. This includes the ability to consult with prosecutorial officials before the criminal trial (addressed in Chapter 9), to speak during the sentencing phase of the trial (Chapter 11), and to offer an opinion when the offender is scheduled to be released from incarceration (Chapter 12).[35]

Some jurisdictions also provide victims with the right of law enforcement protection from the offender during the time period before a criminal trial. In addition, most states require *restitution*, or monetary payment, from offenders to help victims repay any costs associated with the crime and rebuild their lives. In 2016, for instance, a circuit court judge ordered Krystal Gonzalez to pay $1.2 million to the residents of an apartment complex in D'Iberville, Mississippi, that she accidentally burned down after intentionally setting fire to her boyfriend's T-shirt.

Enforceability

Although many victims have benefited from victims' rights legislation, advocates still find fault with the manner in which such legislation is applied. The main problem, they say, is that the federal and state laws do not contain sufficient enforcement mechanisms. That is, if a victim's rights are violated in some way, the victim has little recourse. This situation is changing, gradually, thanks to state ballot initiatives, a process we will discuss in the next chapter. In 2008, for example, California voters passed "Marsy's Law," a ballot initiative named after a woman whose murderer was released from prison without state officials notifying that woman's family.

Importantly, the law provides *legal standing* for crime victims. This means that, if a California crime victim believes that his or her rights have been violated, he or she can go to court to have those rights enforced.[36] Several years ago, for example, families of the victims in a series of Los Angeles murders used Marsy's Law to force a trial date for Lonnie Franklin, Jr., known as the "Grim Sleeper." Franklin's defense attorney had been trying to delay the proceedings. In June 2016, Franklin received a death sentence for his crimes. Illinois, Montana, North Dakota, and South Dakota have passed their own versions of Marsy's Law, and several other states are considering similar actions.[37]

Victim Services

The consequences for crime victims go well beyond frustrations with the criminal justice system. Many feel some degree of anxiety, anger, fear, and depression as a result of their experiences.[38] In particular, victims of violent crimes are at a high risk of post-traumatic stress disorder (PTSD), a condition that burdens sufferers with extreme anxiety and flashbacks relating to the traumatic event.

▼ Andrea Volcy addresses a criminal court in Boston during the sentencing of Shabazz Augustine for murdering her niece. **Should crime victims and their families have the "right" to participate in criminal justice proceedings? Why or why not?** *Boston Globe*/Getty Images

Crime victims also experience higher-than-normal levels of depression, drug abuse, and suicidal tendencies.[39]

In addition to the emotional support of family and friends, a number of victim services exist to help with these symptoms of victimization. Hundreds of *crisis intervention centers* operate around the country, providing a wide range of aid. For example, the Donald W. Reynolds Crisis Intervention Center in Fort Smith, Arkansas, offers counseling, shelter, and relocation guidance to victims of domestic violence and sexual assault. These centers also allow for contact with *victim advocates*, or individuals that help victims gain access to public benefits, health care, employment and educational assistance, and numerous other services. The impact of such programs is, however, somewhat limited. Only about 9 percent of victims of violent crimes avail themselves of victim service agencies.[40]

CJ & TECHNOLOGY

Statewide Automated Victim Information Notification Program (SAVIN)

The right of crime victims to be informed about relevant offenders, featured prominently in all victims' rights legislation, could be meaningless without reliable information technology. In 2016, South Dakota became the latest state to offer such technology by inaugurating its Statewide Automated Victim Information and Notification System (SAVIN). At no cost, the South Dakota SAVIN program provides crime victims with instant updates concerning a wide range of information, from arrest warrants issued to the result of court hearings to the release (or escape) of an offender from custody.

The vast majority of nationwide SAVIN notifications are delivered by phone, though participants can also request to receive their alerts via e-mail, regular mail, or text message. Glitches can occur. Several years ago, Oregon's SAVIN system erroneously informed crime victims that 8,000 state inmates had been released, including one prisoner who had been sentenced to life behind bars for murdering two schoolgirls. On the whole, however, SAVIN has been welcomed by victims and criminal justice professionals alike. "It's probably saved lives we don't even know about," says Wilson County (Tennessee) Sheriff Terry Ashe.

Thinking about SAVIN

In South Dakota, SAVIN is only available to those who fit the state's legal definition of a crime "victim." This means that numerous crimes—including vehicular homicide, arson, fraud, and misdemeanor sexual assaults—are not covered. Why do you think the state would exclude this large class of crime victims from the benefits of the service?

The Risks of Victimization

Anybody can be a victim of crime. This does not mean, however, that everybody is at an equal risk of being victimized. (See Figure 3.4 for an overview of how this risk is distributed among different demographic groups.) In the previous chapter, we noted that residents of neighborhoods with heavy concentrations of payday lending businesses are targeted by criminals at unusually high rates.[41] To better explain the circumstances surrounding this type of victimization, criminologists Larry Cohen and Marcus Felson devised the *routine activities theory*. According to Cohen and Felson, most criminal acts require the following:

Learning 6 Objective Explain the routine activities theory of victimization.

1. A likely offender.
2. A suitable target (a person or an object).
3. The absence of a capable guardian—that is, any person (not necessarily a law enforcement agent) whose presence or proximity prevents a crime from happening.[42]

When these three factors are present, the likelihood of crime rises.

Cohen and Felson cite routine activities theory in explaining the link between payday lenders and crime. People who use payday lenders often leave those establishments with large sums of cash, late at night or during weekends when there is less street traffic. Consequently, they act as suitable targets, attracting likely offenders to neighborhoods where the payday lenders are located.[43]

Repeat Victimization   Cohen and Felson also hypothesize that offenders attach "values" to suitable targets. The higher the value, the more likely that target is going to be the subject of a crime.[44] A gold watch, for example, would obviously have a higher value for a thief than a plastic watch and therefore is more likely to be stolen. Similarly, people who are perceived to be weak or unprotected can have high value for criminals. Some research, for example, shows that undocumented Latino immigrants have elevated victimization rates because criminals know that these noncitizens are afraid to report crimes to authorities for fear of being removed from the country.[45]

Resources such as the National Crime Victimization Survey provide criminologists with an important tool for determining which types of people are most valued as potential victims. Statistics clearly show that a relatively small number of victims are involved in a disproportionate number of crimes. These findings support an approach to crime analysis known as **repeat victimization.** This theory is based on the premise that certain populations—mostly low-income residents of urban areas—are more likely to be victims of crimes than others and, therefore, past victimization is a strong predictor of future victimization.[46] Further criminological research shows that factors such as drug and alcohol use and depression also increase the possibility that a crime victim will be revictimized.[47]

The Victim-Offender Connection   Not only does past victimization seem to increase the risk of future victimization, but so does past criminal behavior. Using risk assessment strategies discussed in the preceding chapter, the Chicago Police Department keeps a list of those known offenders who are most likely to be violent offenders or victims of violent crime. A primary factor on the list is a previous arrest on a firearms charge. About 70 percent of those Chicago residents victimized by gun violence are on this list.[48] "The notion that [violent crimes] are random bolts of lightning, which is the commonly held image, is not the reality at all," says David Kennedy, a professor at New York's John Jay College of Criminal Justice.[49]

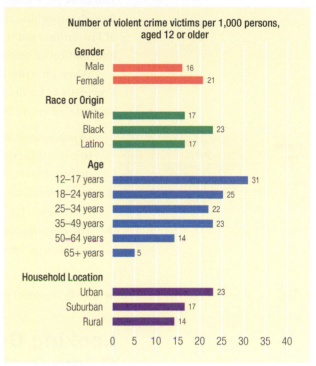

FIGURE 3.4 Crime Victims in the United States

According to the U.S. Department of Justice, minorities, residents of urban areas, and young people are most likely to be victims of violent crime in this country.

Number of violent crime victims per 1,000 persons, aged 12 or older

Gender	Male	16
	Female	21
Race or Origin	White	17
	Black	23
	Latino	17
Age	12–17 years	31
	18–24 years	25
	25–34 years	22
	35–49 years	23
	50–64 years	14
	65+ years	5
Household Location	Urban	23
	Suburban	17
	Rural	14

Source: Bureau of Justice Statistics, *Criminal Victimization, 2015* (Washington, D.C.: U.S. Department of Justice, December 2016), 9, 10.

Repeat Victimization The theory that certain people and places are more likely to be subject to repeated criminal activity and that past victimization is a strong indicator of future victimization.

ETHICS CHALLENGE

Criminal justice professionals have an ethical obligation to be objective and impartial. In most cases, however, victims cannot be expected to be objective or impartial. A victim would never, for example, be allowed to sit on a jury. Indeed, some worry that increasing the legal rights of victims creates an imbalance in our criminal justice system. Do you agree? Do you see any ethical problems with the three categories of victim's rights listed earlier in this section? Explain your answers.

Crime Trends in the United States

The UCR, NCVS, and other statistical measures we have discussed so far in this chapter, though important, represent only the tip of the iceberg of crime data. Thanks to the efforts of law enforcement agencies, educational institutions, and private individuals, more information on crime is available today than at any time in the nation's history.

When interpreting and predicting general crime trends, experts tend to rely on what University of California at Berkeley law professor Franklin Zimring calls the three "usual suspects" of crime fluctuation:

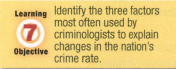

Learning Objective 7 Identify the three factors most often used by criminologists to explain changes in the nation's crime rate.

1. *Imprisonment,* based on the principle that (a) an offender in prison or jail is unable to commit a crime on the street, and (b) a potential offender on the street may be deterred from committing a crime by the fear of winding up behind bars.
2. *Youth populations,* because those under the age of twenty-four commit the majority of crimes in the United States.
3. The *economy,* because when legitimate opportunities to earn income become scarce, some people will turn to illegitimate methods such as crime.[50]

Pure statistics do not always tell the whole story, however, and crime rates often fail to behave in the ways that the experts predict.

Looking Good: Crime in the 1990s and 2000s

In 1995, eminent crime expert James Q. Wilson, noting that the number of young males in the United States was set to increase dramatically over the next decade, predicted that "30,000 more young muggers, killers, and thieves" would be on the streets by 2000. "Get ready," he warned.[51] Other criminologists offered their own dire projections. John DiIulio foresaw a swarm of "juvenile super-predators" on the streets,[52] and James A. Fox prophesied a "blood bath" by 2005.[53] Given previous data, these experts could be fairly confident in their predictions. Fortunately for the country, they were wrong. As is evident from Figure 3.5, starting in 1994 the United States experienced a steep crime decline that, despite a few upticks, we are still enjoying today.

The Great Crime Decline

The crime statistics of the 1990s are startling. Even with the upswing at the beginning of the decade, from 1990 to 2000 the homicide rate dropped 39 percent, the robbery rate 44 percent, the burglary rate 41 percent, and the auto theft rate 37 percent. By most measures, this decline was the longest and deepest of the twentieth century.[54] In retrospect, the 1990s seem to have encompassed a "golden era" for the leading indicators of low crime rates. The economy was robust. The incarceration rate was skyrocketing. Plus, despite the misgivings of James Q. Wilson and many of his colleagues, the percentage of the population in the high-risk age bracket in 1995 was actually lower than it had been in 1980.[55]

Several other factors also seemed to favor lower crime rates. Police tactics, many of which we will discuss in Chapter 6, became more innovative—thanks in no small part to "zero-tolerance" policies inspired by Wilson's writings. Furthermore, many of those most heavily involved in a crack cocaine boom that shook the nation in the late 1980s had been killed or imprisoned, or were no longer offending. Without their criminal activity, the United States became a much safer place.[56]

Continuing Decreases   According to the UCR and the NCVS, the two most extensive measurements of national crime rates, the United States is presently enjoying historically low levels of crime. Since the early 1990s, both the violent crime rate (see Figure 3.5 again) and the property crime rate have declined by about 50 percent.[57] James Alan Fox, a crime expert and law professor at Northeastern University, points to four factors that likely have contributed to this trend:

1. Longer prison terms for offenders since the 1990s, when a sentencing reform movement that we will cover in Chapter 11 took hold in many state legislatures.
2. Continued improvement in law enforcement, including intelligence-based policing techniques that focus crime prevention tactics on "hot spots" of criminal activity and technology that improves the rapidity with which police respond to citizen reports of crime.
3. An aging population, meaning that older Americans—who are statistically less prone to criminal behavior—are having a greater influence on overall crime rates.
4. More lenient marijuana laws in many states (covered in Chapter 2), which reduce the amount of violent and property crime associated with this drug.[58]

Amid this general good news, the 2015 UCR—released in the fall of 2016—delivered something of a shock: the national murder rate rose 11 percent (the largest one-year increase in nearly half a century), and violent crime in general rose about 4 percent.[59] A number of explanations have been given for this violent crime surge, including gang violence, the heroin epidemic, and the economy. As we noted in Chapter 1, some experts have also pointed to a reluctance among police officers to confront criminal suspects for fear of being accused of using excessive force or displaying institutional racism.[60]

On closer inspection, however, the data from 2015 were more ambiguous. Notably, the nation's overall crime rate dropped for the fourteenth consecutive year. The NCVS, which does not record murders, saw no increase in violent crime.[61] Furthermore, only four urban areas—Baltimore, Chicago, Milwaukee, and Washington, D.C.—accounted for about 20 percent of the year's murder increase.[62] According to Richard Berk, a criminology professor at the University of Pennsylvania, "It isn't a national trend, it's a city trend, and it's not even a city trend, but a problem in certain neighborhoods."[63] Thus, most criminologists are taking a "wait and see" attitude toward the possibility of

---

FIGURE 3.5 Violent Crime in the United States, 1990–2015

According to statistics gathered each year by the FBI, American violent crime rates dropped steadily in the second half of the 1990s, leveled off for several years, and then decreased steadily until a slight rise in 2015.

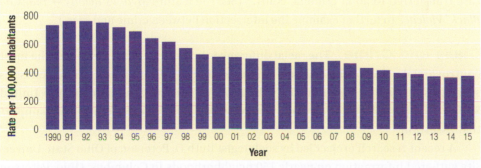

Source: Federal Bureau of Investigation.

"Black on Black" Violence

The Myth According to the latest federal statistics, about 90 percent of African American homicide victims are killed by other African Americans. These data, along with disproportionately high rates of black violent offending and violent victimization, are evidence of a "black on black" crime epidemic that is sweeping the United States.

The Reality The recent focus on the spread of "black on black" crime has several implications. First, the label implies that African Americans are inherently lawless compared with other racial and ethnic groups. Second, it suggests that African American communities have a greater tolerance for criminal and immoral behavior than do other segments of American society.

In fact, the vast majority of all homicides and violent crimes occur within racial and ethnic groups. In 2015, for example, white offenders killed about 81 percent of white homicide victims. The number was 80 percent for Latino offenders and victims. This trend is largely a result of demographics. That is, most criminals commit crimes against victims that live nearby, and most Americans live in racially and ethnically homogeneous neighborhoods. Furthermore, violent crime victims and offenders often shared a prior relationship, and such relationships are more likely to occur within racial and ethic groups.

By focusing on "black on black" crime, the media, politicians, and police officials not only give credence to stereotypes that create fear of African Americans, particularly young black men. They also ignore other causes of criminality, such as disadvantaged neighborhood conditions, which we explored in the previous chapter.

FOR CRITICAL ANALYSIS

What are some of the ways in which "black on black" crime rhetoric might influence policing strategies in African American neighborhoods?

continued rising crime rates, while police chiefs and residents of many major American cities are hoping that 2015 was a "one-year blip."[64]

Crime, Race, and Poverty

Although crime and victimization rates have decreased across racial lines over the past twenty years, the trends have been less positive for African Americans than for whites. For example, blacks are considerably more likely to be both homicide victims and homicide offenders than are whites.[65] African Americans are particularly susceptible to gun violence, with firearm murder rates of 14.6 per 100,000 adults, compared with 1.9 for whites and 4.0 for Latinos.[66] Chicago's West Garfield Park neighborhood, which is 96 percent black, has a homicide rate of 116 per 100,000 people. By comparison, Honduras, the worldwide leader in murders, has a homicide rate of 90 per 100,000.[67]

Race and Crime Homicide rates are not the only area in which there is a divergence in crime trends between the races. Official crime data seem to indicate a strong correlation between minority status and crime: African Americans—who make up 13 percent of the population—constitute 36 percent of those arrested for violent crimes and 28 percent of those arrested for property crimes.[68] Even as overall marijuana arrests plummeted in Colorado and Washington State after the drug was legalized, African Americans were still twice as likely as whites to be arrested for using the drug.[69] Furthermore, a black juvenile in the United States is more than twice as likely as a white juvenile to wind up in delinquency court and 30 percent more likely to have his or her case transferred to adult criminal court.[70] (See the feature *Myth vs Reality—"Black on Black" Violence* to further examine the intersection between crime and race.)

Class and Crime The racial differences in the crime rate are one of the most controversial areas of the criminal justice system. At first glance, crime statistics seem to support the idea that the subculture of African Americans in the United States is disposed toward criminal behavior. Not all of the data, however, support that assertion.

A recent research project led by sociologist Ruth D. Peterson of Ohio State University gathered information on nearly 150 neighborhoods in Columbus, Ohio. Peterson

Anne Seymour National Victim Advocate

The aspect of my job that I enjoy the most is my direct work with crime victims and survivors. These are people who have been severely traumatized by pain and suffering and loss, and I consider it a true honor to be able to assist them. I'll never forget the day I met a young survivor who had been abducted, beaten within an inch of her life, raped, and then left to die in the forest. This young woman became one of my closest friends, and I helped her to speak out in her state and at the national level. Every time she does so, she has a powerful impact on our society. So my help in turning a victim/survivor into a stellar victim advocate/activist began on the day I met her, and it continues.

Courtesy of Anne Seymour

Victim advocacy is one of the most exciting and rewarding careers you could ever embark on, though it is not one that you should get into because of the money. (Few victim advocates become rich doing this work!) Every day is unique and different, reflecting the people I assist and the colleagues with whom I interact. I am never, ever bored and never will be. AND I go to bed every single day knowing that I have done at least one thing—and often many more than one!—to promote social justice and to help someone who is hurting. It's an amazing feeling!

SOCIAL MEDIA CAREER TIP Social media technologies are about connecting and sharing information—which means privacy is an important issue. Make sure you understand who can see the material you post and how you can control it. Facebook has numerous privacy settings, for example, as does Google+.

FASTFACTS

National victim advocate

Job description:
- Provide direct support, advocacy, and short-term crisis counseling to crime victims.

What kind of training is required?
- Bachelor's degree in criminal justice, social work/psychology, or related field.
- A minimum of two years' experience in the criminal justice system, one year of which must have involved direct services with victims.

Annual salary range?
- $26,000–$47,000

and her colleagues separated the neighborhoods based on race and on levels of disadvantage such as poverty, joblessness, lack of college graduates, and high levels of female-headed families. She found that whether the neighborhoods were predominantly white or predominantly black had little impact on violent crime rates. Those neighborhoods with higher levels of disadvantage, however, had uniformly higher violent crime rates.[71]

Learning 8 Objective Explain why income level appears to be more important than race or ethnicity when it comes to crime trends.

Income Level and Crime Peterson's research suggests that, regardless of race, a person is at a much higher risk of being a violent offender or a victim of violence if he or she lives in a disadvantaged neighborhood. Given that African Americans are two times more likely than whites to live in poverty and hold low-wage-earning jobs, they are, as a group, more susceptible to the factors that contribute to criminality.[72]

Indeed, a considerable amount of information suggests that income level is more important than skin color when it comes to crime trends. A 2002 study of nearly 900 African American children (400 boys and 467 girls) from neighborhoods with varying income levels showed that family earning power had the only significant correlation with violent behavior.[73] More recent research conducted by William A. Pridemore of Indiana University found a "positive and significant association" between poverty and homicide.[74] Lack of education, another handicap most often faced by low-income citizens, also seems to correlate with criminal behavior. About one in every ten male high school dropouts winds up in juvenile detention or an adult inmate, compared with about one in thirty-three male high school graduates.[75]

The Class-Crime Relationship The sociological theories of crime you studied in Chapter 2 predict that those without the financial means to acquire the consumer goods and services that dominate our society will turn to illegal methods to "steal" purchasing power. But, logic aside, many criminologists are skeptical of such an obvious class-crime relationship. After all, poverty does not *cause* crime. The majority of residents in low-income neighborhoods are law-abiding.

Furthermore, self-reported surveys indicate that high-income citizens are involved in all sorts of criminal activities[76] and are far more likely than low-income citizens to commit white-collar crimes, which are not included in national crime statistics. These facts tend to support the theory that high crime rates in low-income communities are at least partly the result of a greater willingness of police to arrest poor citizens and of the court system to convict them. (The chapter-ending feature *Policy Matters—Criminalizing Homelessness* explores a trend in criminal law that, according to critics, makes being poor a crime in many American cities.)

Ethnicity and Crime

In the past, crime experts and statisticians have tended to focus on race, which distinguishes groups based on skin color, rather than *ethnicity*, which denotes national or cultural background. Given that Americans of Latino descent are the largest minority group in the United States, however, interest in ethnic crime research is growing. The FBI recently incorporated ethnicity into the UCR, finding, for example, that nearly a fifth of all arrests in this country involve a Latino suspect.[77] Furthermore, even though the firearm victimization rate of Latinos in this country is more than twice that of whites,[78] the NCVS shows that their overall violent victimization rates are somewhat lower.[79]

The research treatment of other minority categories, such as Asian Americans, Native Americans, and Native Hawaiians, is mixed. The UCR has separate offense categories for these groups, with Native Americans arrested at a rate consistent with their population numbers and Asian Americans arrested at a much lower rate than their percentage of the country's overall population.[80] For its part, the NCVS refers to these disparate races and ethnicities collectively as "other" and shows them having greater victimization rates than whites and Latinos.[81] In particular, American Indian and Alaska Native women report experiencing high levels of violent victimization,[82] an issue we address more fully in Chapter 8.

Women and Crime

To put it bluntly, crime is an overwhelmingly male activity. Sixty-three percent of all murders involve a male victim and a male perpetrator, and in only 2.5 percent of

▼ Police question a Latino minor caught tagging a wall with gang graffiti in the Wilshire neighborhood of Los Angeles. **Why is it likely that crime experts will continue to increase their focus on issues of Latino offenders and victims in the United States?**

Robert Nickelsberg/Getty Images News/Getty Images

homicides are both the offender and the victim female.[83] Only about 9 percent of the national prison and jail population are female, and in 2015 only 24 percent of all arrests involved women.[84]

A Growing Presence

The statistics just cited fail to convey the startling rate at which the female presence in the criminal justice system has been increasing. Between 1991 and 2015, the number of men arrested each year declined about 18 percent. Over that time period, annual arrests for women increased by 31 percent.[85] In 1970, there were about 6,000 women in federal and state prisons, but today, there are about 11,500.[86] Two possible explanations have been offered to explain these increases. Either (1) the life circumstances and behavior of women have changed dramatically in the past forty years, or (2) the criminal justice system's attitude toward women has changed over that time period.[87]

In the 1970s, when female crime rates started surging upward, many observers accepted the former explanation. "You can't get involved in a bar fight if you're not allowed in the bar," said feminist theorist Freda Adler in 1975.[88] It has become clear, however, that a significant percentage of women arrested are involved in a narrow band of wrongdoing, mostly drug- and alcohol-related offenses or minor property crimes such as shoplifting.[89] Research shows that as recently as the 1980s, many of the women now in prison would not have been arrested or would have received lighter sentences for their crimes.[90] Consequently, more scholars are convinced that rising female criminality is the result of a criminal justice system that is "more willing to incarcerate women."[91]

Learning Objective 9 Discuss the prevailing explanation for the rising number of women incarcerated in the United States.

Women as Crime Victims

Although males dominate criminal violent offender statistics, women are victims of violent crime at a higher rate than men, as shown in Figure 3.4 earlier in the chapter.[92] The most striking aspect of women as victims of crime is the extent to which such victimization involves a prior relationship. According to the National Crime Victimization Survey, a male is twice as likely as a female to experience violence at the hands of a stranger.[93] With regard to intimate partner violence—involving a spouse, ex-spouse, boyfriend, girlfriend, ex-boyfriend, or ex-girlfriend—the gender difference is even more pronounced. Nearly one in ten women in the United States has been raped by an intimate partner, compared with one in forty-five men, and over their lifetimes, women are at significantly more risk for intimate partner violence than are men (24 percent versus 14 percent).[94]

Statistically, women are also at greater risk of being victims of **domestic violence.** This umbrella term covers a wide variety of maltreatment, including physical violence and psychological abuse, inflicted among family members and others in close relationships. Though data show that women are significantly more likely to be victims of domestic violence than men,[95] these findings are not unquestioned. Men, many observers assume, are less likely to report abuse because of the social stigma surrounding female-on-male violence.[96] Domestic violence presents a number of problems for the criminal justice system, as you can see in the feature *Discretion in Action—Prosecuting Domestic Violence.*

A third crime that appears to mainly involve female victims is **stalking,** or a course of conduct directed at a person that would reasonably cause that person to feel fear. Such behavior includes unwanted phone calls, following or spying, and a wide range of online activity that we will address in Chapter 16. Stalkers target women at about three times the rate they target men, and seven out of ten stalking victims have had some prior relationship with their stalkers.[97]

Domestic Violence An act of willful neglect or physical violence that occurs within a familial or other intimate relationship.

Stalking The criminal act of causing fear in a person by repeatedly subjecting that person to unwanted or threatening attention.

DISCRETION IN ACTION

Prosecuting Domestic Violence

The Situation According to the arrest warrant, during an argument at their home, Greg threw Nicole to the floor and into a bathtub, slammed her against a futon, and "strangled" her. Greg also threatened to kill Nicole "in a manner and under circumstances which would cause a reasonable person to believe that the threat was likely to be carried out." Soon after the alleged assault, however, Nicole told prosecutors that she did not want Greg to be charged with a crime, and she left the state so that she wouldn't have to act as a witness against him in court.

The Law Legally, crime victims are not the clients of public prosecutors. That is, as you will see in Chapter 9, prosecutors have the ultimate authority to decide when to bring a case to court, regardless of the victim's wishes. In practice, domestic violence cases unfold somewhat differently. Because the victim is usually the only witness to the violence, if she or he refuses to participate, such cases can be very difficult to prosecute successfully.

What Would You Do? For a number of reasons, domestic violence victims frequently choose not to side with law enforcement against their abusers. These motivations include fear of retaliation, financial dependence on the offender, issues of custody and child support, and complex emotional ties. Indeed, if a domestic violence victim chooses to cooperate with law enforcement officials, she or he often becomes more vulnerable to retaliatory attacks by the abuser.

At the same time, many observers believe that the public benefits when prosecutors ignore the wishes of domestic violence victims in these instances. Arguably, aggressively prosecuting domestic violence offenses will deter others from committing similar wrongdoing and send the message that domestic violence is a serious crime. Taking both sides of the issue into account, if you were a prosecutor, would you file charges against Greg despite Nicole's opposition? Explain your answer.

To see how a similar case in Mecklenburg County, North Carolina, was resolved, go to Example 3.1 in Appendix B.

Mental Illness and Crime

In the opening of Chapter 2, we detailed the shooting rampage carried out on January 6, 2017, by Esteban Santiago at a South Florida airport that left five people dead and six wounded. As you may recall, Santiago reported "hearing voices" and had been briefly held for psychiatric evaluation in an Anchorage, Alaska, hospital. Such incidents draw national public attention and create the assumption that "not normal" people such as Santiago pose a particular danger to society. The reality concerning mental illness and crime is much more nuanced and complex.

Risk Factors for Violent Crime

In the context of the criminal justice system, the term *mental illness* covers a wide variety of symptoms, ranging from recurring depression and anger to hallucinations and schizophrenia (defined in Chapter 2). It also indicates recent treatment by a mental health care practitioner. Government research shows that, using these descriptions, about 11 percent of Americans over the age of eighteen—some 26 million people—suffer from some form of mental illness.[98] Do all these people pose a high risk for violent behavior?

As noted in Chapter 2, numerous studies show that people with mental illness do not pose a statistically substantial threat to society. To give just one example, a 2006 study published in the *American Journal of Psychiatry* stated that only 4 percent of violent crime in the United States can be attributed to people with a mental illness.[99] Although the possibility of violent behavior increases for those with serious conditions such as schizophrenia or bipolar disorder,[100] the most significant risk factor for the mentally ill is substance abuse. Between 80 and 90 percent of all mentally ill inmates in American prisons and jails are abusers of alcohol or other drugs.[101]

Risk Factors for Victimization

Those who suffer from mental illness are much more likely to be victims of crime than perpetrators. There are several reasons for this high victimization risk:

1. Mental illness often interferes with a person's ability to find and keep employment, and therefore leads to poverty, which, as we have seen, correlates with victimization.

2. The mentally ill are more likely to be homeless, a circumstance that leaves them particularly susceptible to crime.[102]

3. Mental illness can restrict a person's ability to make prudent decisions in potentially dangerous situations, increasing her or his chances of being assaulted.[103]

▲ Nearly every state restricts firearm ownership by the mentally ill and federal law prohibits the sale of firearms to anyone who has been "adjudicated as a mental defective" or "committed to any mental institution." **Are these legal constraints fair? Are they necessary to protect the public from gun violence? Explain your answers.** NEstudio/Shutterstock.com

One review of the subject found that rates of victimization among people with mental illness are as much as 140 percent higher than in the general population.[104]

Mental health advocates insist that increasing services such as treatment and temporary housing for America's mentally ill citizens will reduce the harm they cause themselves and others. The prohibitive costs of such services, however, seem to guarantee that mental illness will continue to be a problem for the criminal justice system and for society at large.

ETHICS CHALLENGE

Under California law, all state colleges and universities must implement an affirmative consent policy. Such policies are designed to ensure that all student sexual activity on campus is the result of "affirmative, conscious, and voluntary agreement," which can be verbal or communicated through actions. Given the reports of sexual assault on college campuses discussed at the opening of this chapter, do you think this policy is a positive development? Why or why not? What might be some of the ethical ramifications of such "yes means yes" requirements?

Criminalizing Homelessness

How Things Stand

A shortage of affordable housing, combined with low vacancy rates for low-rent apartments and a decline in federally-subsidized housing, has led to an increase in homelessness in various American cities. Because of unpleasant conditions in homeless shelters, many people in this difficult situation have chosen to live in encampments on public property in cities such as Denver, Los Angeles, San Francisco, and Seattle. City leaders, neighborhood residents, and business groups often see these campsites as incubators not only of unsanitary living conditions, but also of drug use and crime.

As a Result...

Numerous municipalities have passed ordinances that have the practical effect of criminalizing life on the streets. In a recent survey of 187 cities, the National Law Center on Homelessness and Poverty found that half prohibit camping in certain public places. Other commonly banned activities include sleeping in public, sitting or lying down in public, panhandling, living in vehicles, and "loitering, loafing, and vagrancy."[105] Between January 2012 and November 2015, Dallas law enforcement issued over 11,000 citations for sleeping in public. From 2014 to 2016 authorities in Honolulu, Hawaii, handed out nearly 17,000 warnings and summonses for sitting and lying down in public places.[106]

Critics contend that such methods actually worsen the problem by saddling homeless people with criminal records that make it more difficult for them to find work or housing.[107] They also question the morality of laws that, in practice, punish people for being poor. City authorities argue that the encampments are a health hazard both for those living in them and for members of the surrounding community. Denver officials insist that the city's camping ban is meant to steer homeless people to shelters where they can be fed and receive health care.[108] One homeless man living in a Denver camp echoed the sentiments of others, however, when he pointed out that the local shelters were infested with bedbugs and said, "I don't like being crowded up like that."[109]

Up for Debate

"People should not be living in public. What we're saying is the response should not be to make it a crime. The response should be to ensure that people have a place to live."[110] —*Maria Foscarinis, executive director of National Law Center on Homelessness and Poverty.*

"In my council office, I have zero calls—complaints—about how the city is enforcing the cleanup [of homeless encampments]. I have a hundred calls about how we're not doing enough."[111]—*Denver City Council President Albus Brooks*

What's Your Take?

Review the discussions in this chapter on "Classification of Crimes" and "Crime, Race, and Poverty" before answering the following questions.

1. Do you consider criminal acts such as panhandling, camping or sleeping in public, and sitting or lying down on a sidewalk during business hours to be crimes *mala in se* or crimes *mala prohibita*? Is the distinction useful in resolving this controversy over criminalizing homelessness? Explain your answers.

2. Homeless advocates argue that if a person has nowhere to sleep but on public property, then cities should not able to pass laws that essentially criminalize that person's homelessness. Do you agree that there should be a "right" to sleep in public? Why or why not?

Digging Deeper...

Go online and search for the terms **Portland** and **Safe Sleep Policy**. What was Portland's Safe Sleep policy? What burdens did this strategy place on local law enforcement and the community? Why was "Safe Sleep" ended? If you had to devise an alternative policy to "Safe Sleep" for the city of Portland, Oregon, what would be some of its key components? Would you include ordinances that, in practice, criminalize aspects of being homeless? Your written answer to these questions should be at least three paragraphs long.

Justin Sullivan/Getty Images News/Getty Images

Justin Sullivan/Getty Images News/Getty Images

For more information on these concepts, look back to the Learning Objective icons throughout the chapter.

 Discuss the primary goals of civil law and criminal law and explain how these goals are realized. Civil law is designed to resolve disputes between private individuals and other entities such as corporations. In these disputes, one party, called the plaintiff, tries to gain monetary damages by proving that the accused party, or defendant, is to blame for a tort, or wrongful act. In contrast, criminal law exists to protect society from criminal behavior. To that end, the government prosecutes defendants, or persons who have been charged with committing a crime.

 Explain the differences between crimes *mala in se* and *mala prohibita*. A criminal act is *mala in se* if it is inherently wrong, while a criminal act *mala prohibita* is illegal only because it is prohibited by the laws of a particular society. It is sometimes difficult to distinguish between these two sorts of crimes because it is difficult to define a "pure" *mala in se* crime—that is, it is difficult to separate a crime from the culture that has deemed it a crime.

 Identify the publication in which the FBI reports crime data and list the two main ways in which the data are reported. Every year the FBI releases the Uniform Crime Reports (UCR), in which it presents different crimes as (a) a rate per 100,000 people and (b) a percentage change from the previous year.

 Distinguish between the National Crime Victimization Survey (NCVS) and self-reported surveys. The NCVS involves an annual survey of more than 40,000 households conducted by the Bureau of the Census along with the Bureau of Justice Statistics. The survey queries citizens on crimes that have been committed against them. As such, the NCVS includes crimes not necessarily reported to police. Self-reported surveys, in contrast, involve asking individuals about criminal activity to which they may have been a party.

 Describe the three ways that victims' rights legislation increases the ability of crime victims to participate in the criminal justice system. (a) The right to be informed of victims' rights in general and of specific information relating to the relevant criminal case; (b) the right to be present at court proceedings involving the victim; and (c) the right to be heard on matters involving the prosecution, punishment, and release of the offender.

 Explain the routine activities theory of victimization. The routine activities theory holds that victimization is more likely to occur when the following three factors are present: (a) a likely offender; (b) a suitable target, in the form of either a person or an object to be stolen; and (c) the absence of a person who could prevent the crime, such as a law enforcement agent.

 Identify the three factors most often used by criminologists to explain changes in the nation's crime rate. (a) Levels of incarceration, because an offender behind bars cannot commit any additional crimes and the threat of imprisonment acts as a deterrent to criminal behavior; (b) the size of the youth population, because those under the age of twenty-four commit the majority of crimes in the United States; and (c) the health of the economy, because when income and employment levels fall, those most directly affected may turn to crime for financial gain.

 Explain why income level appears to be more important than race or ethnicity when it comes to crime trends. Criminologists have found that the most consistent indicators of criminal behavior are circumstances such as low family earning power and the absence of a parent. In addition, failure to obtain a high school diploma appears to have a positive correlation with criminal activity, regardless of the race or ethnicity of the individual. Finally, some believe that high arrest rates in low-income minority neighborhoods can be attributed to a willingness of police to arrest residents of these communities and of the court system to convict them.

 Discuss the prevailing explanation for the rising number of women incarcerated in the United States. Experts believe that many women are arrested and given harsh punishment for activity that would not have put them behind bars several decades ago. For the most part, this activity is nonviolent: the majority of female arrestees are involved in drug- and alcohol-related offenses and property crimes.

1. Give an example of how one person could be involved in a civil lawsuit and a criminal lawsuit for the same action.

2. For nearly eight decades until 2013, the federal government defined rape as sex with "a female forcibly and against her will." Compare this definition with the new definition in Figure 3.1. Which do you think is more representative of the crime, and why? What are the consequences of removing "forcibly" and "against her will" from the previous definition?

3. Assume that you are a criminologist who wants to determine the extent to which high school students engage in risky behavior such as abusing alcohol and illegal drugs, carrying weapons, and contemplating suicide. How would you go about gathering these data?

4. Earlier in the chapter, we saw that some criminologists predicted that the violent crime increase of 2015 would turn out to be a "blip" rather than the beginning of a trend. Go online and research our national violent crime rates. Were those predictions correct, or did violent crime rates continue to rise? What is the source of your answer?

5. Research shows that female college students who have been the victim of rape or attempted rape are at an unusually high risk of repeat victimization if they engage in binge alcohol drinking. What victim services should colleges provide to reduce the chances that this group of victims will be revictimized?

beyond a reasonable doubt 72

civil law 71

dark figure of crime 79

defendant 71

domestic violence 89

felonies 72

infraction 73

liable 71

mala in se 73

mala prohibita 73

misdemeanor 72

Part I offenses 76

Part II offenses 77

plaintiff 71

preponderance of the evidence 72

repeat victimization 83

self-reported surveys 79

stalking 89

Uniform Crime Report (UCR) 75

victim surveys 78

1. David Cantor, et al., *Report on the AAU Campus Climate Survey on Sexual Assault and Sexual Misconduct* (Rockville, Md.: Westat, September 21, 2015).

2. "The Campus Sexual Violence Elimination Act of 2013." *www.campussaveact.org.* Campus Save Act: visited January 13, 2017, Web.

3. Quoted in Jan Hoffman, "College Rape Prevention Program Proves a Rare Success," *New York Times* (June 11, 2015), A15.

4. *Federal Criminal Rules Handbook*, Section 2.1 (West 2008).

5. 625 Illinois Compiled Statutes Annotated Section 5/16–104 (West 2002).

6. Johannes Andenaes, "The Moral or Educative Influence of Criminal Law," *Journal of Social Issues 27* (Spring 1971), 17, 26.

7. "Facts Sheets—Alcohol Use and Your Health." *www.cdc.gov.* Centers for Disease Control and Prevention, visited January 13, 2017, Web.

8. "Tobacco-Related Mortality." *www.cdc.gov.* Centers for Disease Control and Prevention, visited January 13, 2017, Web.

9. John Slade, "Health Consequences of Smoking: Nicotine Addiction," *Hearings before the Subcommittee on Health and the Environment of the House Committee on Energy and Commerce* (Washington, D.C.: U.S. Government Printing Office, 1988), 163–164.

10. Steven Jonas, "Solving the Drug Problem: A Public Health Approach to the Reduction of the Use and Abuse of Both Legal and Recreational Drugs," *Hofstra Law Review 18* (1990), 753.

11. Douglas N. Husak, *Drugs and Rights* (New York: Cambridge University Press, 2002), 21.

12. Bureau of Justice Statistics, *Rape and Sexual Assault Victimization Among College-Age Females,* 1995–2013 (Washington, D.C.: U.S. Department of Justice, December 2014), 1.

13. Cantor, et al., *op. cit.,* iv.

14. Federal Bureau of Investigation, *Crime in the United States,* 2015. *www.ucr.fbi.gov.* U.S. Department of Justice: 2016, Web.

15. *Ibid.,* About Crime in the U.S.

16. *Ibid.,* Table 1.

17. *Ibid.,* Expanded Homicide Data Table 10.

18. *Ibid.,* Table 1.

19. *Ibid.,* Offense Definitions.

20. *Ibid.,* Table 29.

21. Marcus Felson, *Crime in Everyday Life* (Thousand Oaks, Calif.: Pine Forge Press, 1994), 3.

22. Pervaiz Shallwani, "NYPD Officers Misrepresented Crime Figures, Commissioner

23. Eric P. Baumer and Janet L. Lauritsen, "Reporting Crime to the Police, 1973–2005: A Multivariate Analysis of Long-Term Trends in the National Crime Survey (NCS) and National Crime Victimization Survey (NCVS)," *Criminology* (February 2010), 132–133.

24. Bureau of Justice Statistics, *Criminal Victimization, 2015* (Washington, D.C.: U.S. Department of Justice, October 2016), Table 4, page 6.

25. Lynn Langton, et al., *Victimizations Not Reported to the Police, 2006–2010* (U.S. Department of Justice, August 2012), 4.

26. Dave Gathman, "Counting Crime in the Smaller Towns," *Courier News* (Elgin, Ill.) (November 14, 2012), 8.

27. David Bernstein and Noah Isackson, "The Truth about Chicago's Crime Rates." *www.chicagomag.com.* Chicago Magazine: April 7, 2014, Web.

28. "FBI Releases 2015 Crime Statistics from the National Incident-Based Reporting System, Encourages Transition." *www.ucr.fbi.gov.* Federal Bureau of Investigation: December 12, 2016.

29. "National Incident-Based Reporting System: Tables with All Offenses." *www.ucr.fbi.gov.* Federal Bureau of Investigation, 2016: Web.

30. Victor E. Kappeler, Mark Blumberg, and Gary W. Potter, *The Mythology of Crime and Criminal Justice*, 2d ed. (Prospect Heights, Ill.: Waveland Press, 1993), 31.

31. Frank A. Hagan, *Introduction to Criminology: Theories, Methods, and Criminal Behavior*, 7th ed. (Thousand Oaks, Calif.: Sage Publications, 2011), 41.

32. David Lisak and Paul M. Miller, "Repeat Rape and Multiple Offending among Undetected Rapists," *Violence & Victims* (2002), 73–84.

33. Lois H. Harrington, et al., *President's Task Force on Victims of Crime: Final Report* (Washington, D.C.: U.S. Department of Justice, December 1982), viii.

34. 18 U.S.C. Section 3771 (2006).

35. Susan Herman, *Parallel Justice for Victims of Crime* (Washington, D.C.: The National Center for Victims of Crime, 2010), 45–48.

36. "Victims' Bill of Rights." *www.oag.ca.gov.* State of California Department of Justice: visited January 16, 2017, Web.

37. "Get Involved in Your State." *https://marsyslaw.us/.* Marsy's Law: visited January 14, 2017, Web.

38. Bureau of Justice Statistics, *Socio-emotional Impact of Violence Crime* (Washington, D.C.: U.S Department of Justice, September 2014), Table 1, page 4.

39. Herman, op. cit., 17–21.

40. Lynn Langton, *Use of Victim Service Agencies by Victims of Serious Violent Crime, 1993–2009* (Washington, D.C.: U.S. Department of Justice, August 2011), 1.

41. Chris E. Kubrin, et al., "Does Fringe Banking Exacerbate Neighborhood Crime Rates?"

42. Larry Cohen and Marcus Felson, "Social Change and Crime Rate Trends: A Routine Activity Approach," *American Sociological Review* (1979), 588–608.

43. Kubrin, et al., *op. cit.,* 441.

44. Cohen and Felson, *op. cit.*

45. Stefano Comino, Giovanni Mastrobuoni, and Antonio Nicolo, *Silence of the Innocents: Illegal Immigrants Underreporting of Crime and their Victimization* (Bonn, Germany: IZA, October 2016).

46. Marre Lammers, et al., "Biting Once, Twice: The Influence of Prior on Subsequent Crime Location Choice," *Criminology* (August 2015), 309–329.

47. R. Barry Ruback, Valerie A. Clark, and Cody Warner, "Why Are Crime Victims at Risk of Being Victimized Again? Substance Use, Depression, and Offending as Mediators of the Victimization-Revictimization Link," *Journal of Interpersonal Violence* (January 2014), 157–185.

48. Monica Davey, "Chicago Police Try to Predict Who May Shoot or Be Shot," *New York Times* (May 24, 2016), A11.

49. Quoted in Kevin Johnson, "Criminals Target Each Other, Trend Shows," *USA Today* (August 31, 2007), 1A.

50. Franklin E. Zimring, *The Great American Crime Decline* (New York: Oxford University Press, 2007), 45–72.

51. James Q. Wilson, "Concluding Essay in Crime," in James Q. Wilson and Joan Petersilia, eds., *Crime* (San Francisco: Institute for Contemporary Studies Press, 1995), 507.

52. John Dilulio, *How to Stop the Coming Crime Wave* (New York: Manhattan Institute, 1996), 4.

53. James Fox, *Trends in Juvenile Violence* (Boston: Northeastern University Press, 1996), 1.

54. Zimring, op. cit., 6.

55. *Ibid.,* 197–198.

56. *Ibid.,* 82.

57. Federal Bureau of Investigation, *Crime in the United States*, 2010, Table 1. *www.ucr.fbi.gov.* U.S. Department of Justice, 2011, Web; and *Crime in the United States, 2015, op. cit.,* Table 1.

58. Quoted in Reid Wilson, "In Major Cities, Murder Rates Drop Precipitously." *www.washingtonpost.com.Washington Post:* January 2, 2015, Web.

59. *Crime in the United States, 2015, op. cit.,* Table 1.

60. Scott Calvert and Pervaiz Shibani, "Homicide Rose in Most Big Cities This Year." *www.wsj.com.Wall Street Journal:* December 22, 2016, Web.

61. *Criminal Victimization, 2015, op. cit.,* 4.

62. Timothy Williams, "Whether Crime Is Up or Down Depends on Data Being Used," *New York Times* (September 28, 2016), A12.

63. Quoted in *ibid.*

64. Zusha Elinson and Pervaiz Shibani, "Cities Grapple with Rising Murder Rates." *www.wsj.com. Wall Street Journal:* March 12, 2016, Web.

65. *Crime in the United States 2015, op. cit.,* Expanded Homicide Data Table 3; and *Crime in the United States, 2015, op. cit.,* Expanded Homicide Table 3.

66. Michael Planty and Jennifer L. Truman, *Firearm Violence, 1993–2011* (Washington, D.C: U.S. Department of Justice, May 2013), 5.

67. Justin Glawe, "America's Mass Shooting Capital Is Chicago." *www.thedailybeast.com. The Daily Beast:* October 8, 2015, Web.

68. *Crime in the United States 2015, op. cit.,* Expanded Homicide Data Table 6.

69. Keith Humphreys, "Pot Legalization Hasn't Done Anything to Shrink the Racial Gap in Drug Arrest." *www.washingtonpost.com. Washington Post:* March 21, 2016, Web.

70. Julie Furdella and Charles Puzzanchera, *Delinquency Cases in Juvenile Court, 2013* (Washington, D.C.: Office of Juvenile Justice and Delinquency Prevention, October 2015), 2.

71. Ruth D. Peterson, "The Central Place of Race in Crime and Justice—The American Society of Criminology's 2011 Sutherland Address," *Criminology* (May 2012), 303–327.

72. Patricia Y. Warren, "Inequality by Design: The Connection between Race, Crime, Victimization, and Social Policy," *Criminology & Public Policy* (November 2010), 715.

73. Eric A. Stewart, Ronald L. Simons, and Rand D. Donger, "Assessing Neighborhood and Social Psychological Influence on Childhood Violence in an African American Sample," *Criminology* (November 2002), 801–829.

74. William Alex Pridemore, "A Methodological Addition to the Cross-National Empirical Literature on Social Structure and Homicide: A First Test of the Poverty-Homicide Thesis," *Criminology* (February 2008), 133.

75. Andrew Sum, Ishwar Khatiwada, and Joseph McLaughlin, *The Consequences of Dropping Out of High School* (Center for Labor Market Studies, October 2009), 10.

76. Charles Tittle and Robert Meier, "Specifying the SES/Delinquency Relationship," *Criminology 28* (1990), 270–301.

77. *Crime in the United States 2014, op. cit.,* Table 43A.

78. *Hispanic Victims of Lethal Firearms Violence in the United States* (Washington D.C.: Violent Policy Center, April 2014), i.

79. *Criminal Victimization, 2015, op. cit.,* Table 7, page 9.

80. *Crime in the United States, 2015, op. cit.,* Table 43A.

81. *Criminal Victimization, 2014, op. cit.,* Table 7, page 9.

82. André B. Rosay, *Violence against American Indian and Alaska Native Women and Men* (Washington, D.C.: National Institute of Justice, 2012).

83. *Crime in the United States, 2015, op. cit,* Expanded Homicide Table 6.

84. Bureau of Justice Statistics, *Correctional Populations in the United States, 2015* (Washington, D.C.: U.S. Department of Justice, December 2016), Appendix table 4,

page 17; and *Crime in the United States, op. cit.,* Table 33.

85. Federal Bureau of Investigation, *Crime in the United States, 2000* (Washington, D.C.: U.S. Department of Justice, 2001), Table 33, page 221; and *Crime in the United States, 2015, op. cit.,* Table 33.

86. Bureau of Justice Statistics, *Prisoners in 2015* (Washington, D.C.: U.S. Department of Justice, December 2016), Table 1, page 3.

87. Jennifer Schwartz and Bryan D. Rookey, "The Narrowing Gender Gap in Arrests: Assessing Competing Explanations Using Self Report, Traffic Fatality, and Official Data on Drunk Driving, 1980–2004," *Criminology* (August 2008), 637–638.

88. Quoted in Barry Yoeman, "Violent Tendencies: Crime by Women Has Skyrocketed in Recent Years," *Chicago Tribune* (March 15, 2000), 3.

89. Elizabeth Swavola, Kristine Riley, and Ram Subramanian, *Overlooked: Women and Jails in an Era of Reform* (New York: Vera Institute of Justice, 2016), 23–24.

90. Schwarz and Rookey, *op. cit.,* 637–671.

91. Meda Chesney-Lind, "Patriarchy, Prisons, and Jails: A Critical Look at Trends in Women's Incarceration," *Prison Journal* (Spring/Summer 1991), 57.

92. *Criminal Victimization, 2015, op. cit.,* Table 7, page 9.

93. Erika Harrell, *Violent Victimization Committed by Strangers, 1993–2010* (Washington, D.C.: U.S. Department of Justice, December 2012), 2.

94. *Intimate Partner Violence in the United States* (Atlanta, Ga.: National Center for Injury Prevention and Control, February 2014), 1–2.

95. "Domestic Violence National Statistics." *www.ncadv.org* National Coalition Against Domestic Violence: visited January 15, 2017, Web.

96. Eve S. Buzawa, "Victims of Domestic Violence," in Robert C. Davis, Arthur Lurigio, and Susan Herman, eds., *Victims of Crime,* 4th ed. (Los Angeles: Sage, 2013), 36–37.

97. Shannan Catalano, *Stalking Victims in the United States–Revised* (Washington, D.C.: U.S. Department of Justice, September 2012), *1,* 5.

98. Doris J. James and Lauren E. Glaze, *Mental Heath Problems of Prison and Jail Inmates* (Washington, D.C.: U.S. Department of Justice, September 2006), 3.

99. Seena Fazel and Martin Grann, "The Population Impact of Severe Mental Illness on Violent Crime," *American Journal of Psychiatry* (August 2006), 1397–1403.

100. Jeffrey W. Swanson, et al., "Violence and Psychiatric Disorder in the Community: Evidence from the Epidemiologic Catchment Area Surveys," *Hospital & Community Psychiatry* (July 1990), 761–770.

101. James and Glaze, *op. cit.,* 6.

102. Arthur J. Lurigio, Kelli E. Canada, and Matthew W. Epperson, "Crime Victimization and Mental Illness" in *Victims of Crime,* op. cit., 216–217.

103. *Ibid.,* 217–218.

104. Roberto Maniglio, "Severe Mental Illness and Criminal Victimization: A Systematic Review," *Acta Psychiactra Scandinavica 119* (2009), 180–191.

105. *Housing Not Handcuffs* (Washington, D.C.: National Law Center on Homelessness and Poverty, 2016), 9–10.

106. *Ibid.,* 28–29.

107. *Ibid.,* 13.

108. Jack Healey, "Where Homelessness Can Be a Crime," *New York Times* (January 10, 2017), A8.

109. Quoted in Associated Press, "Report: Cities Passing More Laws Making Homelessness a Crime" (November 15, 2016).

110. Quoted in Pam Fessler, "Tide Starts to Turn Against the 'Crime' of Being Homeless." *www.npr.org.* National Public Radio: November 3, 2015, Web.

111. Quoted in Jon Murray, "Homeless People and Advocates Denounce 'Sweeps,' Ask Denver City Council to Repeal Camping Ban." *www.denverpost.com.* Denver Post: December 5, 2016, Web.

4

Inside Criminal Law

To target your study and review, look for these numbered Learning Objective icons throughout the chapter.

Chapter Outline		Corresponding Learning Objectives
The Development of American Criminal Law	**1**	List the four written sources of American criminal law.
	2	Explain precedent and the importance of the doctrine of *stare decisis*.
The Purposes of Criminal Law	**3**	Explain the two basic functions of criminal law.
The Elements of a Crime	**4**	Delineate the elements required to establish *mens rea* (a guilty mental state).
	5	Explain how the doctrine of strict liability applies to criminal law.
Defenses under Criminal Law	**6**	List and briefly define the most important excuse defenses for crimes.
	7	Discuss a common misperception concerning the insanity defense in the United States.
	8	Describe the four most important justification criminal defenses.
Procedural Safeguards	**9**	Distinguish between substantive and procedural criminal law.
	10	Explain the importance of the due process clause in the criminal justice system.

"Death by Dealer"

▲ Numerous states and the federal government are enforcing laws designed to punish the person who sells the illegal drugs, such as this heroin confiscated by the Burlington (Vermont) Police Department, that are used in a fatal overdose. Robert Nickelsberg/Archive Photos/Getty Images

dealers for the overdose deaths of their clients. By law, then, the fact that Massena had not meant for Hernandez to die was irrelevant. Prosecutors needed only prove that he had sold Hernandez the fentanyl that led to the overdose.

Such "death by dealer" prosecutions are controversial within the legal community. "Where's the intent to cause death?" asks one former prosecutor. "And how can it be proved that dealer sold the exact drugs that caused someone's death?" Indeed, as you will see later in the chapter, criminal law usually requires *intent* and *causation* to convict someone of a crime, particularly a homicide. Supporters of these laws counter that drug dealers should be held responsible for the damage that results from their illegal activity. Furthermore, Frank Hernandez—Christian's father—is not alone in praising the deterrent impact of harsh sentences for those who contribute to overdoses. "[Drug dealers will] think twice now before they pick this as a career path," he said after Massena's trial.

The night before he died, twenty-three-year-old Christian Hernandez chatted via video from Palm Beach County, Florida, with his former fiancée, who was in Maine. As he took "hit after hit" on-screen of what he thought was heroin, he told her that it "tasted funny." In fact, Hernandez was ingesting fentanyl, which is much more potent than heroin, and it killed him. Following clues on Hernandez's cell phone, law enforcement traced the fentanyl to Christopher Massena, a local dealer. Massena was eventually charged with homicide under a federal law that holds a person who sells drugs criminally responsible if those drugs cause a fatal overdose. In December 2016, a jury convicted Massena, and he was sentenced to thirty years in federal prison.

For the most part, criminal law treats fatal drug overdoses as accidents, not crimes. In response to the opioid epidemic we discussed in Chapters 1 and 2, however, the federal government and a number of states recently have enacted or revised laws designed to punish

FOR CRITICAL ANALYSIS

1. Who deserves the most blame in the aftermath of a fatal overdose: the person who sold the drugs or the person who chose to abuse the drugs? Taking this question into consideration, is it fair that criminal law holds Christopher Massena responsible for Christian Hernandez's death? Why or why not?

2. A person can be convicted of vehicular manslaughter if he or she kills someone while driving drunk. How is "death by dealer" similar to vehicular manslaughter? How are the two legal concepts different?

3. Drug overdose deaths often are not the result of taking a single drug once, but rather of taking many drugs over a long period of time. How might a defense attorney use this fact to defend a client against charges of selling the drugs that caused a fatal overdose?

The Development of American Criminal Law

Given the various functions of *law*, a single definition of this term is difficult to establish. To the Greek philosopher Aristotle (384–322 B.C.E.), law was a "pledge that citizens of a state will do justice to one another." Aristotle's mentor, Plato (427–347 B.C.E.), saw the law as primarily a form of social control. The British jurist Sir William Blackstone (1723–1780) described law as "a rule of civil conduct prescribed by the supreme power in a state, commanding what is right, and prohibiting what is wrong." In the United States, jurist Oliver Wendell Holmes, Jr. (1841–1935), contended that law was a set of rules that allowed one to predict how a court would resolve a particular dispute. Although these definitions vary in their particulars, all are based on the following general observation: Law consists of enforceable rules governing relationships among individuals and between individuals and their society.[1]

English Common Law

American criminal law owes a debt to the English system of law that took shape during the reign of Henry II (1154–1189). Henry sent judges on a specific route throughout the country, known as a circuit. These circuit judges established a **common law** in England. In other words, they solidified a national law in which legal principles applied to all citizens equally, no matter where they lived or what the local customs had dictated in the past. When confusion about any particular law arose, the circuit judges could draw on English traditions, or they could borrow from legal decisions made in other European countries.

Once a circuit judge made a ruling, other circuit judges faced with similar cases generally followed that ruling. Each interpretation became part of the law on the subject and served as a legal **precedent**—a decision that furnished an example or authority for deciding subsequent cases involving similar legal principles or facts. Over time, a body of general rules that prescribed social conduct and that was applied throughout the entire English realm was established, and subsequently it was passed on to British colonies, including those in the New World that would eventually become the thirteen original United States.

What is important about the formation of the common law is that the law developed from the customs of the populace rather than simply the will of a ruler. As such, the common law came to reflect the social, religious, economic, and cultural values of the people. In any society that is, like our own, governed by the **rule of law,** all persons and institutions, including the government itself, must abide by the law. Furthermore, the law must be applied equally and enforced fairly, and must not be altered arbitrarily by any individual or group, no matter how powerful.

Written Sources of American Criminal Law

Originally, common law was *uncodified*. That is, the body of the law was not written down in any single place. Uncodified law, however, presents a number of drawbacks. For one, if the law is not recorded so that citizens have access to it, then it is difficult, if not impossible, for people to know exactly which acts are legal and which acts are illegal. Furthermore, citizens have no way of determining the procedures that must be followed to establish innocence or guilt.

Common Law The body of law developed from custom or judicial decisions in English and U.S. courts and not attributable to a legislature.

Precedent A court decision that furnishes an example or authority for deciding subsequent cases involving similar facts.

Rule of Law The principle that the rules of a legal system apply equally to all persons, institutions, and entities—public or private—that make up a society.

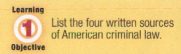
Learning Objective 1 List the four written sources of American criminal law.

FIGURE 4.1 **Sources of American Law**

Constitutional law	**Definition:** The law as expressed in the U.S. Constitution and the various state constitutions.	**Example:** The Sixth Amendment to the U.S. Constitution states that any person accused of a crime has the right "to be informed of the nature and cause of the accusation."
Statutory law	**Definition:** Laws or ordinances created by federal, state, and local legislatures and governing bodies.	**Example:** Illinois state law considers exposing a cat or dog to life-threatening weather a criminal act punishable by up to a year in jail.
Administrative law	**Definition:** The rules, orders, and decisions of federal or state government administrative agencies.	**Example:** Federal U.S. Fish and Wildlife Service regulations make it a crime to kill a wolf in certain protected areas except when necessary for the immediate defense of human life.
Case law	**Definition:** Judge-made law, including judicial interpretations of the other three sources of law.	**Example:** A federal appeals court overturns a Michigan law criminalizing peaceable panhandling in public places on the ground that the statute violates the constitutional right to freedom of speech.

Constitutional Law Law based on the U.S. Constitution and the constitutions of the various states.

Statutory Law The body of law enacted by legislative bodies.

▼ George Washington, standing at right, presided over the constitutional convention of 1787. The convention resulted in the U.S. Constitution, the source of a number of laws that continue to form the basis of our criminal justice system today.
Bettmann/Getty Images

U.S. history has seen the development of several written sources of American criminal law. These sources include:

1. The U.S. Constitution and the constitutions of the various states.
2. Statutes, or laws, passed by Congress and by state legislatures, plus local ordinances.
3. Regulations, created by regulatory agencies, such as the federal Food and Drug Administration.
4. Case law (court decisions).

We describe each of these important written sources of law in the remainder of this section. (For a preview, see Figure 4.1.)

Constitutional Law The federal government and the states have separate written constitutions that set forth the general organization and powers of, and the limits on, their respective governments. **Constitutional law** is the law as expressed in these constitutions.

The U.S. Constitution is the supreme law of the land. As such, it is the basis of all law in the United States. Any law that violates the Constitution, as ultimately determined by the United States Supreme Court, will be declared unconstitutional and will not be enforced. The Tenth Amendment, which defines the powers and limitations of the federal government, reserves to the states all powers not granted to the federal government. Under our system of federalism (see Chapter 1), each state also has its own constitution. Unless they conflict with the U.S. Constitution or a federal law, state constitutions are supreme within their respective borders. (You will learn more about how constitutional law applies to our criminal justice system throughout this textbook.)

Statutory Law Statutes enacted by legislative bodies at any level of government make up another source of law, which is generally referred to as **statutory law.** *Federal statutes* are laws that are enacted by the U.S. Congress. *State statutes* are laws enacted by state legislatures, and statutory law also includes the *ordinances* passed by cities and counties. A federal statute, of course, applies to all states. A state statute, in contrast, applies only within that state's borders. City or county ordinances apply only to those jurisdictions where they are enacted.

Legal Supremacy   It is important to keep in mind that there are essentially fifty-two different criminal codes in this country—one for each state, the District of Columbia, and the federal government. Originally, the federal criminal code was quite small. The U.S. Constitution mentions only three federal crimes: treason, piracy, and counterfeiting. Today, according to a recent study, federal law includes nearly 5,000 offenses that carry criminal penalties.[2] Inevitably, these federal criminal statutes are bound to overlap or even contradict state statutes. In such cases, thanks to the **supremacy clause** of the Constitution, federal law will almost always prevail. Simply put, the supremacy clause holds that federal law is the "supreme law of the land."

So, for example, hundreds of individuals have been charged with violating federal law for possessing or selling medical marijuana in states where such actions are legal under state law.[3] As we discussed earlier in the textbook, marijuana use—for medicinal purposes or otherwise—remains illegal under federal law, and, in the words of one federal judge, "we are all bound by federal law, like it or not."[4] Along the same lines, any statutory law—federal or state—that violates the Constitution will be overturned. Therefore, in the late 1980s, the United States Supreme Court ruled that state laws banning the burning of the American flag were unconstitutional because they impinged on the individual's right to freedom of expression.[5]

Ballot Initiatives   On a state and local level, voters can write or rewrite criminal statutes through the **ballot initiative.** In this process, a group of citizens draft a proposed law and then gather a certain number of signatures to get the proposal on that year's ballot. If a majority of the voters approve the measure, it is enacted into law. Currently, twenty-four states and the District of Columbia accept ballot initiatives, and these special elections have played a crucial role in shaping criminal law in those jurisdictions. Changes in state laws regarding assisted suicide, marijuana legalization, and victims' rights, discussed earlier in this text, resulted from ballot initiatives.

Like other state laws, laws generated by ballot initiatives are not immune from review by state and federal courts. In 2015, for example, a federal judge invalidated the results of a ballot initiative that would have banned the farming of genetically modified crops in Maui County, Hawaii. According to the judge, decisions concerning agricultural policy could be made only at the federal or state level, and thus the county had overstepped the boundaries of its legislative power.[6]

Administrative Law   A third source of American criminal law consists of **administrative law**—the rules, regulations, orders, and decisions of *regulatory agencies*. A regulatory agency is a federal, state, or local government agency established to perform a

Supremacy Clause A clause in the U.S. Constitution establishing that federal law is the "supreme law of the land" and shall prevail when in conflict with state constitutions or statutes.

Ballot Initiative A procedure in which the citizens of a state, by collecting enough signatures, can force a public vote on a proposed change to state law.

Administrative Law The body of law created by administrative agencies (in the form of rules, regulations, orders, and decisions) in order to carry out their duties and responsibilities.

▼ In 2015, voters in Washington State passed a ballot initiative that outlawed sales relating to the trafficking of products made from ten endangered species, including elephants, marine turtles, lions, and tigers. Breaking the new state law could result in a maximum of five years in prison and a $10,000 fine. **What are some of the pros and cons of using ballot initiatives to create criminal law?**

Csehak Szabolcs/Shutterstock.com

specific function. The Occupational Safety and Health Administration (OSHA), for example, oversees the safety and health of American workers. The Environmental Protection Agency (EPA) is concerned with protecting the natural environment, and the Food and Drug Administration (FDA) regulates food and drugs produced in the United States.

Breaking an administrative rule can be a criminal violation. For example, the Food, Drug, and Cosmetic Act authorizes the FDA to enforce regulations to which criminal sanctions are attached. In an ongoing inquiry, the FDA's Office of Criminal Investigations found that ConAgra Grocery Products had caused an outbreak of salmonella poisoning several years ago by shipping contaminated peanut butter to stores around the country. In December 2016, the company agreed to pay an $8 million criminal fine and forfeit $3.2 million in assets—the largest penalty ever paid in a food safety case.[7]

Learning Objective 2 — Explain precedent and the importance of the doctrine of *stare decisis*.

Case Law   As is evident from the earlier discussion of the common law tradition, another basic source of American law consists of the rules of law announced in court decisions, or precedents. These rules of law include interpretations of constitutional provisions, of statutes enacted by legislatures, and of regulations created by administrative agencies. Today, this body of law is referred to variously as the common law, judge-made law, or case law.

Case law is the basis for a doctrine called *stare decisis* ("to stand on decided cases"). Under this doctrine, judges are obligated to follow the precedents established within their jurisdiction. For example, any decision of a particular state's highest court will control the outcome of future cases on that issue brought before all the lower courts within that state. Under the supremacy clause, discussed earlier, all U.S. Supreme Court decisions involving the U.S. Constitution are binding on *all* courts, because the U.S. Constitution is the supreme law of the land.

The doctrine of *stare decisis* does not require the U.S. Supreme Court *always* to follow its own precedent, though the Court often does so. At times, a change in society's values will make an older ruling seem obsolete, at least in the eyes of the Supreme Court justices. In *Bowers v. Hardwick* (1986), for example, the Court upheld a state law that banned certain homosexual acts that were lawful when performed by a man and a woman.[8] Seventeen years later, in *Lawrence v. Texas* (2003), the Court overturned that decision, ruling that the government cannot treat one class of citizens differently from the rest of society when it comes to sexual practices between consenting adults. The original case "was not correct when it was decided, and it is not correct today," wrote Justice Anthony Kennedy.[9]

The Purposes of Criminal Law

Learning Objective 3 — Explain the two basic functions of criminal law.

Why do societies need laws? Many criminologists believe that criminal law has two basic functions: one relates to the legal aspects of a society, and the other pertains to the society's need to maintain and promote social values.

Protect and Punish: The Legal Function of the Law

The primary legal function of the law is to maintain social order by protecting citizens from *criminal harm*. This term refers to a variety of harms that can be generalized to fit into two categories:

1. Harms to individual citizens' physical safety and property, such as the harm caused by murder, theft, or arson.
2. Harms to society's interests collectively, such as the harm caused by unsafe foods or consumer products, a polluted environment, or poorly constructed buildings.[10]

Case Law The rules of law announced in court decisions.

Stare Decisis (pronounced ster-ay dih-*si-ses*). A legal doctrine under which judges are obligated to follow the precedents established in prior decisions.

Because criminal law has the primary goal of protecting people from harm, new criminal laws are often passed in response to specific acts. For example, in 2015, the California Department of Motor Vehicles recorded a number of crashes involving drivers using handheld cell phones, including twelve deadly crashes, five hundred crashes that resulted in injuries, and seven hundred crashes that caused property damage. The next year, state legislators passed a law prohibiting people from using cell phones while driving in California unless they can operate the devices while keeping their hands on the wheel.[11]

CJ & TECHNOLOGY

Unmanned Aerial Vehicles (UAVs)

An estimated one million unmanned aerial vehicles (UAVs), commonly referred to as drones, are operating in the United States. Most of them weigh only a few pounds and are "virtually toys," according to one enthusiast. These "toys" have, however, caused a multitude of problems. They have interfered with firefighters, crashed into buildings, and been used to smuggle contraband into prisons. Most seriously, pilots of passenger planes and other aircraft are reporting about one hundred sightings or close calls with UAVs each month.

The law is now trying to catch up with this emerging technology. The Federal Aviation Administration recently announced that recreational UAV owners must register their drones with the government. Any registered operator who interferes with air traffic will be subject to a fine. In addition, twenty states have passed criminal legislation related to UAVs. For example, New Hampshire prohibits the use of drones for hunting, fishing, or trapping. In Texas, it is, for the most part, a crime to take photographs of people or real estate with the aid of UAVs.

Thinking about UAVs

Should it be against the law to fly a camera-equipped drone onto or over another person's private property? Should the law punish someone who damages a drone that is flying over her or his property without permission or is flying unreasonably close to her or his family? Explain your answers.

Maintain and Teach: The Social Function of the Law

If criminal laws against acts that cause harm or injury to others are almost universally accepted, the same cannot be said for laws that criminalize "morally" wrongful activities that may do no obvious, physical harm outside the families of those involved. Why criminalize gambling or prostitution, for instance, if the participants are consenting?

Expressing Public Morality   The answer lies in the social function of criminal law. Many observers believe that the main purpose of criminal law is to reflect the values and norms of society, or at least of those segments of society that hold power. Legal scholar Henry Hart has stated that the only justification for criminal law and punishment is "the judgment of community condemnation."[12]

Take, for example, the misdemeanor of bigamy, which occurs when someone knowingly marries a second person without terminating her or his first marriage. Apart from moral considerations, there would appear to be no victims in a bigamous relationship, and indeed many societies have allowed and continue to allow bigamy to exist. In the American social tradition, however, as John L. Diamond of the University of California's Hastings College of the Law points out:

> Marriage is an institution encouraged and supported by society. The structural importance of the integrity of the family and a monogamous marriage requires unflinching enforcement of the criminal laws against bigamy. The immorality is not in choosing to do wrong, but in transgressing…a fundamental social boundary that lies at the core of social order.[13]

▲ Several years ago, France passed a law banning "excessively thin" models. To participate in advertising or live events such as Paris Fashion Week, shown above, models now need a doctor's note that their health is "compatible with the practice of the profession." Fashion industry employers whose models break this law could face up to six months in jail and a fine of about $80,000. **What social purpose does this law serve? Do you agree with its goals? Explain your answers.** AP Images/Thibault Camus

Of course, public morals are not uniform across the entire nation, and a state's criminal code often reflects the values of its residents. In Kentucky, for example, someone who uses a reptile as part of a religious service is subject to up to $100 in fines, and New Hampshire prohibits any person or agency from introducing a wolf into the state's wilds.[14] Sometimes, local values and federal law will conflict with one another. Nine states, mostly in the western half of the country, have passed "nullification" laws that seek to void federal gun legislation within their borders. For example, in Idaho, state law enforcement officers can be charged with a misdemeanor and fined up to $1,000 dollars for enforcing a federal gun law.[15] (No state has, as of yet, attempted to enforce this form of "nullification," which probably would violate the supremacy clause, discussed earlier in the chapter.)

Teaching Societal Boundaries   Some scholars believe that criminal laws not only express the expectations of society, but "teach" them as well. Professor Lawrence M. Friedman of Stanford University thinks that just as parents teach children behavioral norms through punishment, criminal justice "'teaches a lesson' to the people it punishes, and to society at large." Making burglary a crime, arresting burglars, putting them in jail—each step in the criminal justice process reinforces the idea that burglary is unacceptable and is deserving of punishment.[16]

This teaching function can also be seen in traffic laws. There is nothing "natural" about most traffic laws: Americans drive on the right side of the street, the British on the left side, with no obvious difference in the results. These laws do, however, lead to a more orderly flow of traffic and fewer accidents—certainly socially desirable goals. The laws can also be updated when needed. As we just noted, for instance, California recently banned the use of handheld cell phones while driving. Various forms of punishment for breaking traffic laws teach drivers the social order of the road.

ETHICS CHALLENGE

For a variety of reasons, many parents in this country are refusing to have their infant children vaccinated against measles and other infectious diseases. By doing so, according to the medical community, these parents are putting not only their own children but also other children at a much greater risk of contracting a wide range of diseases, some of which are fatal. Would it be ethical for the government to pass a law forcing parents to have their children vaccinated for the good of society as whole? Why or why not?

Corpus Delicti The body of circumstances that must exist for a criminal act to have occurred.

The Elements of a Crime

In fictional accounts of police work, the admission of guilt is often portrayed as the crucial element of a criminal investigation. Although an admission is certainly useful to police and prosecutors, it alone cannot establish the innocence or guilt of a suspect. Criminal law normally requires that the *corpus delicti,* a Latin phrase for "the body of the crime," be proved before a person can be convicted of wrongdoing.[17]

Corpus delicti can be defined as "proof that a specific crime has actually been committed by someone."[18] It consists of the following:

Actus Reus (pronounced *ak*-tus *ray*-uhs). A guilty (prohibited) act.

1. The *actus reus*, or guilty act
2. The *mens rea*, or guilty intent
3. Concurrence, or the coming together of the criminal act or the guilty mind
4. A link between the act and the legal definition of the crime
5. Any attendant, or accompanying, circumstances
6. The harm done by the crime.

See this chapter's *Mastering Concepts* for an example showing the three most basic elements of a crime.

Criminal Act: *Actus Reus*

Suppose Mr. Smith walks into a police department and announces that he just killed his wife. In and of itself, the confession is insufficient for conviction unless the police find Mrs. Smith's corpse, for example, with a bullet in her brain and establish through evidence that Mr. Smith fired the gun. (This does not mean that an actual dead body has to be found in every homicide case. Rather, it is the fact of the death that must be established in such cases.)

Most crimes require an act of *commission*, meaning that a person must *do* something in order to be accused of a crime. The prohibited act is referred to as the **actus reus,** or guilty act. Furthermore, the act of commission must be voluntary. For example, if Mr. Smith had an epileptic seizure while holding a hunting rifle and accidentally shot his wife, he normally would not be held criminally liable for her death.

A Legal Duty   In some cases, an act of *omission* can be a crime, but only when a person has a legal duty to perform the omitted act. One such legal duty is assumed to arise in "special relationships" such as those between parents and their children, adult children and their aged parents, and spouses.[19] Certain persons involved in contractual

MASTERING CONCEPTS

The Elements of a Crime

Camilo Torres/ShutterStock.com

Carl Robert Winchell walked into the SunTrust Bank in Volusia County, Florida, and placed a bag containing a box on a counter. Announcing that the box held a bomb, he demanded an unspecified amount of cash. After receiving several thousand dollars in cash, Winchell fled, leaving the box behind. A Volusia County Sheriff's Office bomb squad subsequently determined that the box did not in fact contain any explosive device. Winchell was eventually arrested and charged with robbery.

Winchell's actions were criminal because they satisfy the three basic elements of a crime:

1. *Actus Reus:* Winchell **physically** committed the crime of bank robbery.
2. *Mens Rea:* Winchell **intended** to commit the crime of bank robbery.
3. *Concurrence:* Winchell's intent to rob the bank and his use of the false bomb threat* **came together** to create a criminal act.

*Note that the fact that there was no bomb in the box has no direct bearing on the three elements of the crime. It could, however, lead to Winchell's receiving a lighter punishment than if he had used a real bomb.

relationships with others, such as physicians and lifeguards, must also perform legal duties to avoid criminal penalty. A number of states have even passed "duty to aid" statutes requiring their citizens to report criminal conduct and help victims of such conduct if possible.[20] Another example of a criminal act of omission is failure to file a federal income tax return when required by law to do so.

A Plan or Attempt

The guilty act requirement is based on one of the premises of criminal law—that a person is punished for harm done to society. Planning to kill someone or to steal a car may be wrong, but the thoughts do no harm and are therefore not criminal until they are translated into action. Of course, a person can be punished for *attempting* murder or robbery, but normally only if he or she took substantial steps toward the criminal objective and the prosecution can prove that the desire to commit the crime was present. Furthermore, the punishment for an **attempt** normally is less severe than the punishment for a completed act.

Mental State: *Mens Rea*

A wrongful mental state—*mens rea*—is usually as necessary as a wrongful act in determining guilt. The mental state, or requisite *intent*, required to establish guilt of a crime is indicated in the applicable statute or law. For theft, the wrongful act is the taking of another person's property, and the required mental state involves both the awareness that the property belongs to another and the desire to deprive the owner of it.

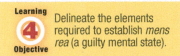

Learning Objective 4 Delineate the elements required to establish *mens rea* (a guilty mental state).

The Elements of *Mens Rea*

A guilty mental state includes elements of purpose, knowledge, negligence, and recklessness.[21] A defendant is said to have *purposefully* committed a criminal act when he or she intended to engage in certain criminal conduct or to cause a certain criminal result. For a defendant to have *knowingly* committed an illegal act, he or she must be aware of the illegality, must believe that the illegality exists, or must correctly suspect that the illegality exists but fail to do anything to dispel (or confirm) his or her belief.

Negligence Criminal **negligence** involves the mental state in which the defendant grossly deviates from the standard of care that a reasonable person would use under the same circumstances. The defendant is accused of taking an unjustified, substantial, and foreseeable risk that resulted in harm.

In 2016, for example, authorities charged Michael Pekarek with negligent homicide as the result of a bow-hunting accident. Pekarek and Jeffrey Cummings were sighting a mule deer near the side of a road in Deschutes County, Oregon. After losing sight of the deer, Pekarek turned with his bow pointed toward Cummings and mistakenly shot an arrow into his friend's stomach. Pekarek obviously had no intention of killing Cummings. At the same time, there is a foreseeable risk in handling a deadly weapon so carelessly.

Recklessness A defendant who commits an act recklessly is more blameworthy than one who is criminally negligent. The standard definition of criminal **recklessness** involves "consciously disregard[ing] a substantial and unjustifiable risk.[22] So, in 2016, a Milwaukee jury convicted Carl Barrett, Jr., of first degree reckless homicide for fatally shooting a five-year-old girl who was sitting on her grandfather's lap inside their home. Barrett mistakenly thought he was firing at the house of a different target, someone against whom he had a grudge. Although Barrett—like Michael Pekarek in the previous

Attempt The act of taking substantial steps toward committing a crime while having the ability and the intent to commit the crime, even if the crime never takes place.

Mens Rea (pronounced mehns ray-uh). Mental state, or intent. A wrongful mental state is usually as necessary as a wrongful act to establish criminal liability.

Negligence A failure to exercise the standard of care that a reasonable person would exercise in similar circumstances.

Recklessness The state of being aware that a risk does or will exist and nevertheless acting in a way that consciously disregards this risk.

example—had no intention of killing his victim, the substantial risk of serious harm to bystanders in carrying out a "revenge shooting" is evident.

Mens Rea and Degrees of Crime

In the previous chapter, you learned that crimes are graded by degree. Generally speaking, the degree of a crime is a reflection of the seriousness of that crime and is used to determine the severity of any subsequent punishment. Degree sometimes depends, at least in part, on *mens rea*, as we discuss here with respect to degrees of homicide.

First Degree Murder

With murder, the degree of the crime is, to a large extent, determined by the mental state of the offender. Murder is generally defined as the willful killing of a human being. It is important to emphasize the word *willful*, which means that murder does not include homicides caused by accident or negligence. A death that results from negligence or accident generally is considered a private wrong and therefore a matter for civil law.

In addition, criminal law punishes those who plan and intend to do harm more harshly than it does those who act wrongfully because of strong emotions or other extreme circumstances. First degree murder—usually punishable by life in prison or the death penalty—occurs under two circumstances:

1. When the crime is premeditated, or contemplated beforehand by the offender, instead of being a spontaneous act of violence.
2. When the crime is deliberate, meaning that it was planned and decided on after a process of decision making. Deliberation does not require a lengthy planning process. A person can be found guilty of first degree murder even if she or he made the decision to kill only seconds before committing the crime.

Second Degree Murder

Usually punishable by a minimum of fifteen to twenty-five years in prison, second degree murder does not involve premeditation or deliberation. It does, however, involve an offender's wanton disregard for the consequences of his or her actions. Both these conditions—the premeditation and deliberation of first degree murder and the wanton disregard of second degree murder—fall under the classification of *malice aforethought*.

The difference between first and second degree murder is illustrated by the case of Thu Hong Nguyen, a Kansas City woman who, several years ago, intentionally set fire to a business that she owned. This alleged act of arson turned deadly when a wall of the burning building collapsed, killing two firefighters who were battling the blaze. Although Nguyen may have intentionally committed arson, there was no evidence that she planned to kill either of the two men. At the same time, she certainly acted with wanton disregard for her victims' safety. Therefore, local authorities charged Nguyen with second degree murder, which carries a maximum penalty of life in prison in Missouri, rather than first degree murder, which is punishable by death.

Types of Manslaughter

A homicide committed without malice toward the victim is known as *manslaughter* and is commonly punishable by up to fifteen years in prison. **Voluntary manslaughter** occurs when the intent to kill may be present, but malice is lacking. Voluntary manslaughter covers crimes of passion, in which the emotion of an argument between two friends leads to homicide. Voluntary manslaughter can also occur when the victim provoked the offender to act violently.

Voluntary Manslaughter A homicide in which the intent to kill was present in the mind of the offender, but malice was lacking.

DISCRETION IN ACTION

Murder or Manslaughter?

The Situation It is after midnight, and George, drunk and angry, decides to pay a visit to Yeardley, his ex-girlfriend. When Yeardley refuses to let George in her apartment, he kicks the door down, grabs Yeardley by the neck, and wrestles her to the floor before leaving. Several hours later, Yeardley's roommate finds her dead, lying face down on a pillow soaked with blood.

The Law George can be charged with one of three possible crimes: (1) first degree murder, which is premeditated and deliberate; (2) second degree murder, which means he acted with wanton disregard for the consequences of his actions; or (3) involuntary manslaughter, which involves extreme carelessness but no intent to kill.

What Would You Do? Further investigation shows that, two years prior to Yeardley's death, a jealous George put her in a chokehold in public. Furthermore, just days before breaking into her apartment, George sent Yeardley an e-mail in which he reacted to news that she was dating someone else by threatening, "I should have killed you." In his defense, George says that although he did have a physical confrontation with Yeardley, she did not seem injured when he left the apartment. George's lawyer claims that Yeardley died from suffocation, not from any wound caused by George.

If it were your decision, would you charge George with first degree murder, second degree murder, or involuntary manslaughter? Why?

[To see how a Charlottesville, Virginia, jury responded to a similar situation, see Example 4.1 in Appendix B.]

Involuntary Manslaughter A homicide in which the offender had no intent to kill the victim.

Strict Liability Crimes Certain crimes, such as traffic violations, in which the defendant is guilty regardless of her or his state of mind at the time of the act.

Involuntary manslaughter covers incidents in which the offender's acts may have been careless, but he or she had no intent to kill. For example, Maria Hyrnenko and three associates knowingly installed illegal gas lines in a building she owned in New York City and conspired to hide the faulty system from inspectors. A malfunction in the gas lines caused an explosion that burned down the building and set fire to several adjoining businesses, killing two people who were eating at a nearby restaurant. In 2016, prosecutors charged Maria Hyrnenko and her co-conspirators with involuntary manslaughter. Although Hyrnenko did not intend to kill anybody, local authorities believed her to be criminally responsible for the two deaths.

Comparing Hyrnenko's case with that of Thu Hong Nguyen on the previous page, you can see that the distinction between malice aforethought and carelessness is not always clear. The feature *Discretion in Action—Murder or Manslaughter?* provides further insight into the differences between various homicide charges, with an emphasis on the importance of ascertaining the offender's intent.

Strict Liability

For certain crimes, criminal law holds the defendant to be guilty even if intent to commit the offense is lacking. These acts are known as **strict liability crimes** and generally involve endangering the public welfare in some way.[23] Drug control statutes, health and safety regulations, and traffic laws are all strict liability laws.

Protecting the Public In some ways, the concept of strict liability is inconsistent with the traditional principles of criminal law, which hold that *mens rea* is required for an act to be criminal. The goal of strict liability laws is to protect the public by eliminating the possibility that wrongdoers could claim ignorance or mistake to absolve themselves of criminal responsibility.[24] Thus, a person caught dumping waste in a protected pond or driving 70 miles per hour in a 55 miles-per-hour zone cannot plead a lack of intent in his or her defense.

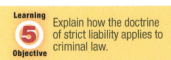

Learning Objective 5 Explain how the doctrine of strict liability applies to criminal law.

The "death by dealer" laws that we discussed in the opening to this chapter are an example of strict liability legislation. These laws hold that people who distribute drugs that lead to fatal overdoses are "strictly liable" for those deaths, regardless of whether there was any intent to kill. Opponents of this type of legislation argue that the *mens rea* requirement is too important to be discarded in homicide prosecutions. "Heroin distributers are not murderers, and they're not murderers when their customers die from an overdose," says Rutgers University professor Douglas Husak.[25]

Protecting Minors One of the most controversial strict liability crimes is statutory rape, in which an adult engages in a sexual encounter with a minor. In most states, even if the minor consents to the sexual act, the crime still exists because, being underage, he or she is considered incapable of making a rational decision on the matter.[26] Therefore, statutory rape has been committed even if the adult was unaware of the minor's age or was misled to believe that the minor was older.

Accomplice Liability

Under certain circumstances, a person can be charged with and convicted of a crime that he or she did not actually commit. This occurs when the suspect has acted as an *accomplice*, helping another person commit the crime. Generally, to be found guilty as an accomplice, a person must have had "dual intent." This level of *mens rea* includes *both*:

1. The intent to aid the person who committed the crime, and
2. The intent that such aid would lead to the commission of the crime.[27]

Assume that Jerry drives Jason to a bank that Jason intends to rob. If Jerry has no knowledge of Jason's criminal plan, he does not fulfill the second prong of the "dual intent" test. As for the *actus reus*, the accomplice must help the primary actor in either a physical sense (for example, by providing the getaway car) or a psychological sense (for example, by encouraging her or him to commit the crime).[28]

In some states, a person can be convicted as an accomplice even without intent if the crime was a "natural and probable consequence" of his or her actions.[29] This principle has led to a proliferation of felony-murder legislation. Felony-murder is a form of first degree murder that applies when a person participates in a serious felony that results in the death of a human being. Under felony-murder law, if two men rob a bank, and the first man intentionally kills a security guard, the second man can be convicted of first degree murder as an accomplice to the bank robbery, even if he had no intent to hurt anyone.

Along these same lines, if a security guard accidentally shoots and kills a customer during a bank robbery, the bank robbers can be charged with first degree murder because they committed the underlying felony. Felony-murder laws have come under criticism because they punish individuals for unintended acts or acts committed by others. Nevertheless, the criminal codes of more than thirty states include some form of the felony-murder rule.

Statutory Rape A strict liability crime in which an adult engages in a sexual act with a minor.

Felony-Murder An unlawful homicide that occurs during the attempted commission of a felony.

▼ New York City Police Department officer Rosa Rodriguez leaves the hospital after recovering from injuries she received responding to a fire in an apartment building. Her partner was killed in the blaze. In 2016, as a result, teenager Marcell Dockery was sentenced to nineteen years to life in prison for felony murder—he started the fire because he was bored and set a mattress alight. **Is this a fair result of the felony murder rule, the felony in this instance being arson? Why or why not?**
Spencer Platt/Getty Images News/Getty Images

Attendant Circumstances The facts surrounding a criminal event that must be proved to convict the defendant of the underlying crime.

Concurrence

According to criminal law, there must be *concurrence* between the guilty act and the guilty intent. In other words, the guilty act and the guilty intent must occur together.[30] Suppose, for example, that a woman intends to murder her husband with poison in order to collect his life insurance. Every evening, this woman drives her husband home from work. On the night she plans to poison him, however, she swerves to avoid a cat crossing the road and runs into a tree. She survives the accident, but her husband is killed. Even though her intent was realized, the incident would be considered an accidental death because she had not planned to kill him by driving the car into a tree.

Causation

Criminal law also requires that the criminal act cause the harm suffered. In 1998, for example, thirteen-year-old Don Collins doused eight-year-old Robbie Middleton with gasoline and set him on fire, allegedly to cover up a sexual assault. Thirteen years later, after years of skin grafts and other surgeries, Middleton died from his burns. A Montgomery County, Texas, judge ruled that, despite the passage of time, Collins could be charged with Middleton's murder. In 2015, he was convicted and sentenced to forty years behind bars.

Attendant Circumstances

In certain crimes, attendant circumstances—also known as accompanying circumstances—are relevant to the *corpus delicti*. Most states, for example, differentiate between simple assault and the more serious offense of aggravated assault depending on the attendant circumstance of whether the defendant used a weapon such as a gun or a knife while committing the crime. Criminal law also classifies degrees of property crimes based on the attendant circumstance of the amount stolen. According to federal statutes, the theft of less than $1,000 from a bank is a misdemeanor, while the theft of any amount over $1,000 is a felony.[31] (To get a better understanding of the role of attendant circumstances in criminal statutes, see Figure 4.2.)

Requirements of Proof and Intent Attendant circumstances must be proved beyond a reasonable doubt, just like any other element of a crime.[32] Furthermore, the *mens rea* of the defendant regarding each attendant circumstance must be proved as well. Consider the two-decades-old case of Gloria Highhawk, who accidentally brought about the death of Steve Wilson by injecting him with heroin. Highhawk was convicted under Pennsylvania's original "drug delivery causing death" law, which included as an attendant circumstance the requirement that the defendant had acted "intentionally or recklessly" in causing the death.

FIGURE 4.2 **Attendant Circumstances in Criminal Law**

Most criminal statutes incorporate three of the elements we have discussed in this section: the act (*actus reus*), the intent (*mens rea*), and attendant circumstances. This diagram of the federal false imprisonment statute should give you an idea of how these elements combine to create the totality of a crime.

Intent	Act	Attendant Circumstances

Whoever intentionally confines, restrains, or detains another against that person's will is guilty of felony false imprisonment.

A state appeals court overturned Highhawk's conviction, ruling that the law was too vague and that prosecutors had failed to prove the defendant's state of mind beyond a reasonable doubt. (In fact, Wilson, a quadriplegic, had requested that Highhawk inject him with the drug.) To close this "loophole," the state legislature quickly passed a new law that removed the *mens rea* attendant circumstances. As a result, in Pennsylvania "drug delivery causing death" is now a strict liability crime.[33]

Hate Crime Laws   In most cases, a person's motive for committing a crime is irrelevant—a court will not try to read the accused's mind. Over the past few decades, however, nearly every state and the federal government have passed *hate crime laws* that make the suspect's motive an important attendant circumstance to his or her criminal act. In general, hate crime laws provide for greater sanctions against those who commit crimes motivated by bias against a person based on race, ethnicity, religion, gender, sexual orientation, disability, or age.

Penalty Enhancements   Hate crime laws are based on the concept of "penalty enhancement." That is, just as someone who robs a convenience store using a gun will face a greater penalty than if he or she had been unarmed, so will someone who commits a crime because of prejudice against the victim or victims. So, for example, under Connecticut law, the punishment for a defendant convicted of a hate crime is enhanced by one level of criminality. In other words, a defendant convicted of committing a Class C felony that is also a hate crime will be sentenced as if he or she had committed a more serious Class B felony.[34]

The Federal Bureau of Investigation recorded almost 7,200 hate crimes in 2015. More than half of those incidents involved the victim's race, ethnicity, or ancestry, with another fifth focused on the victim's sexual orientation.[35]

Punishing Bias   The case for hate crimes law rests on the harm such acts do not only to the individual victim but also to the protected group. If, for example, one American Muslim or transgender person is victimized by a hate crime, then all American Muslims and transgender people may suffer intimidation and fear. Thus, such acts need to be punished more harshly.

Critics of hate crime laws feel that these "penalty enhancements" rest on shaky legal grounds. It is one thing to prove that a robber used a gun, but it is another thing to prove what was in a defendant's mind. Even when an offender's bias is obvious, some legal experts wonder if society wants to send the message that some victims are more worthy of protection than others?[36]

Despite these misgivings, the United States Supreme Court has upheld the constitutionality of hate crime laws as long as the prohibited motive (1) is specifically listed in the legislation as an attendant circumstance and (2) is proved beyond a reasonable doubt during the trial.[37] (As highlighted in the feature *Comparative Criminal Justice— Speech Crime*, many countries have expanded this area of criminal law by punishing hateful words as well as hateful acts.)

Harm

For most crimes to occur, some harm must have been done to a person or to property. A certain number of crimes are actually categorized depending on the harm done to the victim, regardless of the intent behind the criminal act. Consider two offenses, both of which involve one person hitting another on the back of the head with a tire iron. In the first instance, the victim dies, and the offender is charged with murder. In the second, the

Hate Crime Laws Statutes that provide for greater sanctions against those who commit crimes motivated by bias against an individual or a group based on race, ethnicity, religion, gender, sexual orientation, disability, or age.

Speech Crime

The incident, captured on video in Johannesburg, South Africa, is undeniably ugly. A white motorist whose car has just been broken into lashes out angrily at the responding black police officers. "One kaffir is bad enough," the woman says, indicating that she would rather be helped by a white officer. "This happens all the time, all the time. The kaffirs here in Joburg are terrible. I'm so sick of it." Later in the video, she threatens that if she sees a black person, she will "drive him over."

A HISTORY OF RACISM

The word *kaffir* is South Africa's worst racial epithet, rarely spoken in public or reproduced in print. Used by whites to belittle blacks, it is strongly associated with the country's forty-six year period of government-enforced racial segregation, known as *apartheid*, which was not lifted until 1994. Responding to national outrage over the motorist's rant, in late 2016 South African lawmakers introduced new legislation that would make such outbursts a crime. Under the proposed law, any direct or electronic communication that "advocates hatred," causes contempt or ridicule, or incites violence on the basis of race would be punishable by a fine or a maximum of three years in prison. Repeat offenders could be incarcerated for up to ten years.

Critics of the proposed hate speech law warn that it would have a chilling effect on freedom of expression without actually solving the country's social problems. Supporters of the bill counter that any behavior that "perpetuates racism" or "glorifies apartheid" does immeasurable harm to South African society and should be deterred. "In the context of our painful past, racial bigotry and apartheid must be considered serious human rights violations that must be punishable by imprisonment," said a spokesperson for the African National Congress, South Africa's ruling political party.

FOR CRITICAL ANALYSIS

South Africa's proposed law would not break new legal ground. Western democracies such as Britain, Canada, France, and Germany have criminal laws that punish hate speech. Do you think that the United States should criminalize speech that "advocates hatred" against the same groups protected by our hate crime laws? What would be some of the consequences—intended and unintended—of such legislation?

---

victim is only knocked unconscious, and the offender is charged with battery. Because the harm in the second instance is less severe, so is the crime with which the offender is charged, even though the acts are exactly the same. Furthermore, most states have different degrees of battery depending on the extent of the injuries suffered by the victim.

Many acts are deemed criminal even if no harm is done, so long as the harm that could have been done is against the law. Such acts are called **inchoate offenses.** An attempted crime is an inchoate offense. When Jenkins solicits Peterson to murder Jenkins's business partner, Jenkins has committed an inchoate offense, even if Peterson fails to carry out the act. Threats and *conspiracies* also fall into the category of inchoate offenses. Simply stated, a criminal **conspiracy** exists when two or more people agree to engage in an illegal act. The United States Supreme Court has ruled that a person can be convicted of criminal conspiracy even though police intervention made the completion of the illegal plan impossible.[38]

Inchoate Offenses Conduct deemed criminal without actual harm being done, provided that the harm that would have occurred is one the law tries to prevent.

Conspiracy A plot by two or more people to carry out an illegal or harmful act.

ETHICS CHALLENGE

As we stated earlier, some critics contend that hate crime laws are unethical because they seem to indicate that certain victims are more worthy of protection than others. Do you agree with this criticism? Why or why not?

Defenses under Criminal Law

After Robert Conley III was arrested and charged with assault for allegedly attacking Salvador Gomez with a golf club in Saginaw, Michigan, his lawyer argued that Conley could not possibly have committed the crime. The defense attorney produced four witnesses who swore that, at 3:30 A.M. on the morning of June 3, 2016—the time of the incident—Conley was at home.

In other words, the lawyer claimed that Conley had an **alibi,** or evidence that he was elsewhere at the time of the crime, to prove his innocence. Alibis are just one of a number of established defenses for wrongdoing in our criminal courts. These defenses generally rely on one of two arguments: (1) the defendant is not responsible for the crime, or (2) the defendant was justified in committing the crime.

Excuse Defenses

The idea of responsibility plays a significant role in criminal law. In certain circumstances, the law recognizes that even though an act is inherently criminal, society will not punish the actor because he or she does not have the requisite mental condition. In other words, the law "excuses" the person for his or her behavior. Insanity, intoxication, and mistake are the most important excuse defenses today, but we start our discussion of the subject with one of the first such defenses recognized by American law: infancy.

Learning Objective 6 List and briefly define the most important excuse defenses for crimes.

Infancy   The term **infancy,** as used in the law, refers to a person who has not reached the legal age of majority—that is, who is not legally considered to be an adult. Under the earliest state criminal codes of the United States, children younger than seven years of age could never be held legally accountable for crimes. Those between seven and fourteen years old were presumed to lack the capacity for criminal behavior, while anyone over the age of fourteen was tried as an adult. Thus, early American criminal law recognized infancy as a defense in which wrongdoing was excused when the wrongdoers were assumed to be too young to fully understand the consequences of their actions.

With the creation of the juvenile justice system in the early 1900s, the infancy defense became redundant, as youthful delinquents were automatically treated differently than adult offenders. Today, most states either designate an age (typically eighteen) under which wrongdoers are sent to juvenile court or allow judges and prosecutors to decide whether minors will be charged as adults on a case-by-case basis. We will explore the concept of infancy as it applies to the modern American juvenile justice system in much greater detail in Chapter 15.

Insanity   After Jody Kossow fatally stabbed her eight-year-old son Thomas more than fifty times with a kitchen knife, she called 911 and told the dispatcher that police should hurry to the crime scene because "Satan was after" her. In 2017, a Winnebago County, Illinois, judge ruled that Kossow suffered from a severe mental illness that prevented her from knowing that her actions were wrong. As a result, Kossow was sent to a psychiatric hospital rather than prison. Thus, **insanity** may be a defense to a criminal charge when the defendant's state of mind is such that she or he cannot claim legal responsibility for her or his actions.

Alibi Proof that a suspect was somewhere other than the scene of the crime at the time of the crime, typically offered to demonstrate that the suspect was not guilty of the crime.

Infancy The status of a person who is below the legal age of majority. Under early American law, infancy excused young wrongdoers of criminal behavior because presumably they could not understand the consequences of their actions.

Insanity A defense for criminal liability that asserts a lack of criminal responsibility due to mental instability.

Measuring Sanity The general principle of the insanity defense is that a person is excused for his or her criminal wrongdoing if, as a result of a mental disease or defect, he or she

- Does not perceive the physical nature or consequences of his or her conduct;
- Does not know that his or her conduct is wrong or criminal; or
- Is not sufficiently able to control his or her conduct so as to be held accountable for it.[39]

Although criminal law has traditionally accepted the idea that an insane person cannot be held responsible for criminal acts, society has long debated what standards should be used to measure sanity for the purposes of a criminal trial. This lack of consensus is reflected in the diverse tests employed by different American jurisdictions to determine insanity. The tests include the following:

1. *The* M'Naghten *rule.* Derived from an 1843 British murder case, the **M'Naghten** rule states that a person is legally insane and therefore not criminally responsible if, at the time of the offense, he or she was not able to distinguish between right and wrong.[40] As Figure 4.3 shows, half of the states still use a version of the *M'Naghten* rule. One state, New Hampshire, uses a slightly different version of this rule called the "product test." Under this standard, a defendant is not guilty if the unlawful act was the product of a mental disease or defect.

FIGURE 4.3 Insanity Defenses

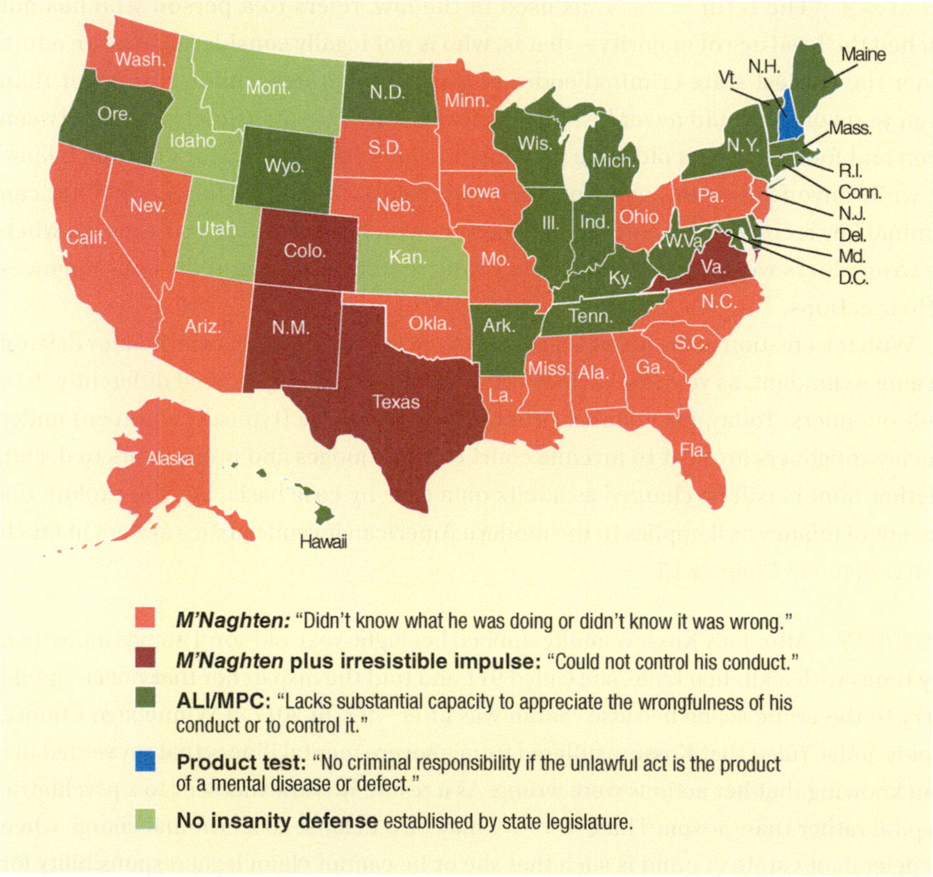

■ **M'Naghten:** "Didn't know what he was doing or didn't know it was wrong."

■ **M'Naghten plus irresistible impulse:** "Could not control his conduct."

■ **ALI/MPC:** "Lacks substantial capacity to appreciate the wrongfulness of his conduct or to control it."

■ **Product test:** "No criminal responsibility if the unlawful act is the product of a mental disease or defect."

■ **No insanity defense** established by state legislature.

Source: Bureau of Justice Statistics, *The Defense of Insanity: Standards and Procedures, State Court Organization, 1998* (Washington, D.C.: U.S. Department of Justice, June 2000).

---

2. *The ALI/MPC test.* In the early 1960s, the American Law Institute (ALI) included an insanity standard in its Model Penal Code (MPC). Also known as the **substantial-capacity test,** the **ALI/MPC test** requires that the defendant lack "substantial capacity" either to "appreciate the wrongfulness" of his or her conduct or to conform that conduct "to the requirements of the law."[41]

3. *The irresistible-impulse test.* Under the **irresistible-impulse test,** a person may be found insane even if he or she was aware that a criminal act was "wrong," provided that some "irresistible impulse" resulting from a mental deficiency drove him or her to commit the crime.[42]

The ALI/MPC test is considered the easiest standard of the three for a defendant to meet because the defendant needs only to show a lack of "substantial capacity" to be released from criminal responsibility. Defense attorneys generally consider it more difficult to prove that the defendant could not distinguish "right" from "wrong" or that he or she was driven by an irresistible impulse.

Determining Competency Whatever the standard, the insanity defense is rarely entered and is even less likely to result in an acquittal, as it is difficult to prove.[43] (See the feature *Myth vs Reality—Are Too Many Criminals Found Not Guilty by Reason of Insanity?*) Psychiatry is far more commonly used in the courtroom to determine the *competency* of a defendant to stand trial. If a judge believes that the defendant is unable to understand the nature of the proceedings or to assist in his or her own defense, the trial will not take place.

When a **competency hearing** (held to determine whether the defendant is competent to stand trial) reveals that the defendant is in fact incompetent, criminal proceedings come to a halt. For example, in August 2016, an El Paso County, Colorado, judge ruled that Robert Dear, Jr., suffered from a delusional disorder and therefore was not fit to stand trial. Dear had been charged with eight counts of first degree murder resulting from a shooting rampage at a Colorado Springs Planned Parenthood clinic eight months earlier. As a result of the judge's decision, Dear will be held indefinitely at a mental institution rather than face further criminal proceedings.

MYTH vs REALITY

Are Too Many Criminals Found Not Guilty by Reason of Insanity?

The Myth Because of the publicity surrounding the insanity defense, many people are under the impression that it is a major loophole in our system, allowing criminals to be "let off" no matter how heinous their crimes.

Learning **7** Objective — Discuss a common misperception concerning the insanity defense in the United States.

The Reality In fact, the insanity defense is raised in only about 1 percent of felony trials, and it is successful only one out of every four times it is raised. The reason: it is extremely difficult to prove insanity under the law. For example, during the 2015 trial of James Holmes, who had killed twelve people and injured seventy others in an Aurora, Colorado, movie theater three years earlier, prosecutors essentially admitted that the defendant was mentally ill. They also argued, successfully, that a heavily armed Holmes knew his actions were wrong when he walked into the showing of a *Batman* movie and began shooting. Holmes was convicted of multiple counts of first degree murder and sentenced to life in prison.

Even if Holmes had succeeded with the insanity defense, he would not have been "let off" in the sense that he would have been set free. Many defendants found not guilty by reason of insanity spend more time in mental hospitals than criminals who are convicted of similar acts spend in prison.

FOR CRITICAL ANALYSIS

Suppose a defense attorney was able to show beyond a reasonable doubt that her or his client was suffering from mental illness at the time of the underlying crime. Do you think that such a showing *should* be sufficient for a successful "not guilty by reason of insanity" defense? Why or why not?

Substantial-Capacity Test (ALI/ MPC Test) A test for the insanity defense that states that a person is not responsible for criminal behavior when he or she "lacks substantial capacity" to understand that the behavior is wrong or to know how to behave properly.

Irresistible-Impulse Test A test for the insanity defense under which a defendant who knew his or her action was wrong may still be found insane if he or she was unable, as a result of a mental deficiency, to control the urge to complete the act.

Competency Hearing A court proceeding to determine mental competence. In the context of criminal law, a hearing may be held before the trial, during the trial, or before sentencing.

Intoxication A defense for criminal liability in which the defendant claims that the taking of intoxicants rendered him or her unable to form the requisite intent to commit a criminal act.

Guilty but Mentally Ill Public backlash against the insanity defense caused six state legislatures to pass "guilty but mentally ill" statutes. Under these laws, a defendant is guilty but mentally ill if

> at the time of the commission of the act constituting the offense, he [or she] had the capacity to distinguish right from wrong . . . but because of mental disease or defect he [or she] lacked sufficient capacity to conform his [or her] conduct to the requirements of the law.[44]

In other words, the laws allow a jury to determine that a defendant is "mentally ill," though not insane, and therefore criminally responsible for her or his actions. Defendants found guilty but mentally ill generally spend the early years of their sentences in a psychiatric hospital and the rest of the time in prison, or they receive treatment while in prison.

Intoxication

The law recognizes two types of **intoxication,** whether from drugs or from alcohol: *voluntary* and *involuntary*.

Involuntary Intoxication Involuntary intoxication occurs when a person is physically forced to ingest or is injected with an intoxicating substance, or is unaware that a substance contains drugs or alcohol. Involuntary intoxication is a viable defense to a crime if the substance leaves the person unable to form the mental state necessary to understand that the act committed while under the influence was wrong.[45]

Several years ago, for instance, the Ramsey County, Minnesota, district attorney's office dropped child assault charges against Jozetta R. Byrd after determining that the defendant's wrongdoing was the result of a negative reaction to her asthma medication. Because the drug rendered Byrd unable to "determine right from wrong," she was not criminally responsible for attacking her two young children.[46]

Voluntary Intoxication Voluntary drug or alcohol intoxication is also used to excuse a defendant's actions, though it is not a defense in itself. Rather, it is used when the defense attorney wants to show that the defendant was so intoxicated that *mens rea* was negated. In other words, the defendant could not possibly have had the state of mind that a crime requires.

Many courts are reluctant to allow voluntary intoxication arguments to be presented to juries. After all, the defendant, by definition, voluntarily chose to enter an intoxicated state. Indeed, thirteen states have eliminated voluntary intoxication as a possible defense, a step that has been criticized by many legal scholars but was upheld by the United States Supreme Court in *Montana v. Egelhoff* (1996).[47]

Mistake

Ordinarily, ignorance of the law or a *mistaken idea* about what the law requires is not a valid defense. Such was the case when retired science teacher Eddie Leroy Anderson and his son dug for arrowheads near their favorite campground site in Idaho, unaware that the land was a federally protected archaeological site. Facing two

▼ Corey Batey, far right, was one of four University of Vanderbilt football players charged with raping an unconscious woman. His defense attorney claimed that Batey was so drunk on the night in question that he was easily manipulated by the others into committing the crime. In 2016, Batey was convicted and a Nashville judge sentenced him to fifteen years in prison. **Why do you think that the intoxication defense was unsuccessful in this instance?** AP images/*The Tennessean*, John Partipilo, Pool

years in prison for this mistake, they pleaded guilty and were given a year's probation and a $1,500 fine each. "Folks need to pay attention to where they are," said U.S. attorney Wendy Olson.[48]

Mistake of Law As the above example suggests, strict liability crimes specifically preclude the *mistake of law* defense, because the offender's intent is irrelevant. For practical reasons, the mistake of law defense is rarely allowed under any circumstances. If "I didn't know" was a valid defense, the courts would be clogged with defendants claiming ignorance of all aspects of criminal law. In some rare instances, however, people who claim that they honestly did not know that they were breaking a law may have a valid defense if (1) the law was not published or reasonably known to the public or (2) the person relied on an official statement of the law that was erroneous.[49]

Mistake of Fact A *mistake of fact*, as opposed to a *mistake of law*, operates as a defense when it negates the mental state necessary to commit a crime. If, for example, Oliver mistakenly walks off with Julie's briefcase because he thinks it is his, there is no theft. Theft requires knowledge that the property belongs to another. In 2016, to use a real-life example, Hamilton County, Ohio, prosecutors declined to prosecute a father who mistook his fourteen-year-old son for an intruder and fatally shot the boy. The mistake-of-fact defense has proved very controversial in rape and sexual assault cases, in which the accused claims a mistaken belief that the sex was consensual, while the victim insists that he or she was coerced.

Justification Defenses

In certain instances, a defendant will accept responsibility for committing an illegal act, but contend that—given the circumstances—the act was justified. In other words, even though the guilty act and the guilty intent may be present, the particulars of the case relieve the defendant of criminal liability. In 2015, for example, there were 770 "justified" killings of persons who were in the process of committing a felony: 442 were killed by law enforcement officers and 328 by private citizens.[50] Four of the most important justification defenses are duress, self-defense, necessity, and entrapment.

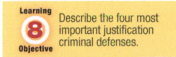

Learning Objective 8 Describe the four most important justification criminal defenses.

Duress Duress exists when the *wrongful* threat of one person induces another person to perform an act that she or he would otherwise not perform. In such a situation, duress is said to negate the *mens rea* necessary to commit a crime. For duress to qualify as a defense, the following requirements must be met:

1. The threat must be of serious bodily harm or death.
2. The harm threatened must be greater than the harm caused by the crime.
3. The threat must be immediate and inescapable.
4. The defendant must have become involved in the situation through no fault of his or her own.[51]

Note that some scholars consider duress to be an excuse defense, because the threat of bodily harm negates any guilty intent on the part of the defendant.[52]

When ruling on the duress defense, courts often examine whether the defendant had the opportunity to avoid the threat in question. Two narcotics cases illustrate this point. In the first, the defendant claimed that an associate threatened to kill him and his wife unless he participated in a marijuana deal. Although this contention was proved true during the course of the trial, the court rejected the duress defense because the defendant made no

Duress Unlawful pressure brought to bear on a person, causing the person to perform an act that he or she would not otherwise perform.

apparent effort to escape, nor did he report his dilemma to the police. In sum, the drug deal was avoidable—the defendant could have made an effort to extricate himself, but he did not, thereby surrendering the protection of the duress defense.[53]

In the second case, a taxi driver in Bogotá, Colombia, was ordered by a passenger to swallow cocaine-filled balloons and take them to the United States. The taxi driver was warned that if he refused, his wife and three-year-old daughter would be killed. After a series of similar threats, the taxi driver agreed to transport the drugs. On arriving at customs at the Los Angeles airport, the defendant consented to have his stomach X-rayed, which led to discovery of the contraband and his arrest. During his trial, the defendant told the court that he was afraid to notify the police in Colombia because he believed them to be corrupt. The court accepted his duress defense, on the grounds that it met the four requirements listed above and the defendant had notified American authorities when given the opportunity to do so.[54]

Justifiable Use of Force—Self-Defense

A person who believes he or she is in danger of being harmed by another is justified in defending himself or herself with the use of force, and any criminal act committed in such circumstances can be justified as **self-defense.** Other situations that also justify the use of force include the defense of another person, the defense of one's dwelling or other property, and the prevention of a crime. In all these situations, it is important to distinguish between *nondeadly* and *deadly* force. As the terms themselves suggest, nondeadly force is unlikely to cause death or great bodily harm, while deadly force is likely to cause death or great bodily harm.

The Amount of Force

Generally speaking, people can use the amount of nondeadly force that seems necessary to protect themselves, their dwellings, or other property or to prevent the commission of a crime. Deadly force can be used in self-defense if there is a *reasonable belief* that imminent death or bodily harm will otherwise result, if the attacker is using unlawful force (an example of lawful force is that exerted by a police officer), if the defender has not initiated or provoked the attack, and if there is no other possible response or alternative way out of the life-threatening situation.[55]

Deadly force normally can be used to defend a dwelling only if an unlawful entry is violent and the person believes deadly force is necessary to prevent imminent death or great bodily harm. In some jurisdictions, it is also a viable defense if the person believes deadly force is necessary to prevent the commission of a felony (such as arson) in the dwelling. Authorities will often take an expansive view of lawful deadly force when it is used to protect another person. So, earlier this decade, a New Orleans man was not charged with any crime after he fatally shot an offender who was sexually assaulting a woman—the first man's companion—at gunpoint.

The Duty to Retreat

When a person is outside his or her home or in a public space, the rules for self-defense change somewhat. Until relatively recently, almost all jurisdictions required someone who is attacked under these circumstances to "retreat to the wall" before fighting back. In other words, under the **duty to retreat,** one who is being assaulted may not resort to deadly force if she or he has a reasonable opportunity to "run away" and thus avoid the conflict. Only when this person has run into a "wall," literally or otherwise, may deadly force be used in self-defense.

Self-Defense The legally recognized privilege to protect one's self or property from injury by another.

Duty to Retreat The requirement that a person claiming self-defense prove that she or he first took reasonable steps to avoid the conflict that resulted in the use of deadly force.

Diana Tabor Crime Scene Photographer

A crime scene photographer's job is invaluable to those who are not present at the scene, yet need to be able to observe the scene as accurately as possible. I like the variety of my work. No two scenes are exactly alike, and the conditions pose different challenges. I have photographed scenes in cramped mobile homes, spacious homes, and out in the woods where we had to hike because there were no roads leading directly to the scene. I've been really hot and sweaty, fogging up the viewfinder. Then I have been so cold that I had to go sit in the van to let my hands and the camera warm up because they had stopped working.

Courtesy of Diana Tabor

I do wonder what the people at the gas stations think when we come in there after we're done to clean up and get something to drink. Fingerprint powder gets everywhere—I have found that nothing less than a shower really gets rid of it completely. It is sometimes difficult to accept that there is nothing to prevent the crime that has already happened, but I take pride in representing the victim when he or she cannot speak.

SOCIAL MEDIA CAREER TIP Don't forget about your phone! Every week, call at least three people from your social media networks and talk with them about your career interests. This kind of personal contact can be far more useful than an exchange of posts.

FASTFACTS

Crime scene photographer

Job description:
- Photograph physical evidence and crime scenes related to criminal investigations.
- Also must be able to compose reports, testify in court, and understand basic computer software and terminology.

What kind of training is required?
- One year in law enforcement or commercial photography OR a degree or certificate in photography and darkroom techniques OR some combination of the above training or experience totaling one year.

Annual salary range?
- $40,000–$75,000

Many states have changed their laws to eliminate the duty to retreat. For example, a Florida law did away with the duty to retreat outside the home, stating that citizens have "the right to stand [their] ground and meet force with force, including deadly force," if they "reasonably" fear for their safety.[56] The Florida law also allows a person to use deadly force against someone who unlawfully intrudes into her or his house (or vehicle), even if that person does not fear for her or his safety.[57]

Proponents of "stand your ground" laws argue that they strengthen the concept of self-defense by making it less likely that persons who are defending themselves will be charged with crimes. Critics counter that by encouraging people to take violent action against their attackers rather than attempting to flee, the laws have created a "nation where disputes are settled by guns instead of gavels, and where suspects are shot by civilians instead of arrested by police."[58] You can make up your own mind about "stand your ground" laws in the *Policy Matters* feature at the end of the chapter.

Necessity The **necessity** defense requires courts to weigh the harm caused by the crime actually committed against the harm that would have been caused by the criminal act avoided. If the avoided harm is greater than the committed harm, then the defense has a chance of succeeding. A Broward County, Florida, jury, for example, recently acquitted a defendant on charges of growing marijuana at his home because

Necessity A defense against criminal liability in which the defendant asserts that circumstances required her or him to commit an illegal act.

the defendant claimed he needed the marijuana to control his severe anorexia. In the eyes of the jurors, the defendant's medical necessity outweighed his alleged crimes.[59] Murder is the one crime for which the necessity defense is not applicable under any circumstances.

Entrapment Entrapment is a justification defense that criminal law allows when a police officer or government agent deceives a defendant into wrongdoing. Although law enforcement agents can legitimately use various forms of subterfuge—such as informants or undercover agents—to gain information or apprehend a suspect in a criminal act, the law places limits on these strategies. Police cannot persuade an innocent person to commit a crime, nor can they coerce a suspect into doing so, even if they are certain she or he is a criminal.

The guidelines for determining entrapment were established in the 1932 case of *Sorrells v. United States.*[60] The case, which took place during Prohibition when the sale of alcoholic beverages was illegal, involved a federal law enforcement agent who repeatedly urged the defendant to sell him bootleg whiskey. The defendant initially rejected the agent's overtures, stating that he "did not fool with whiskey." Eventually, however, he sold the agent a half-gallon of the substance and was summarily convicted of violating the law. The United States Supreme Court held that the agent had improperly induced the defendant to break the law and reversed his conviction.

This case set the precedent for focusing on the defendant's outlook in entrapment cases. In other words, the Court decided that entrapment occurs if a defendant who is not predisposed to commit the crime is convinced to do so by an agent of the government.[61] (For an overview of justification and excuse defenses, see Figure 4.4.)

Procedural Safeguards

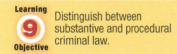

Learning Objective 9 — Distinguish between substantive and procedural criminal law.

To this point, we have focused on substantive criminal law, which defines the acts that the government will punish. We will now turn our attention to procedural criminal law. (The section that follows will provide only a short overview of criminal procedure. In later chapters, many other constitutional issues will be examined in more detail.)

Criminal law brings the force of the state, with all its resources, to bear against the individual. Criminal procedures, drawn from the ideals stated in the Bill of Rights, are designed to protect the constitutional rights of individuals and to prevent the arbitrary use of this power by the government.

The Bill of Rights

For various reasons, proposals related to the rights of individuals, including rights related to criminal procedure, were rejected during the framing of the U.S. Constitution in 1787. In fact, the original constitution contained only three provisions that referred to criminal procedure. Article I, Section 9, Clause 2, states that the "Privilege of the Writ of Habeas Corpus shall not be suspended." As will be discussed in Chapter 10, a writ of *habeas corpus* is an order that requires jailers to bring a person before a court or judge and explain why the person is being held in prison.

Article I, Section 9, Clause 3, holds that no "Bill of Attainder or *ex post facto* Law shall be passed." A bill of attainder is a legislative act that targets a particular person or group for punishment without a trial, while an *ex post facto* law operates retroactively, making an event or action illegal though it took place before the law was passed. Finally, Article III,

Entrapment A defense in which the defendant claims that he or she was induced by a public official—usually an undercover agent or police officer—to commit a crime that he or she would otherwise not have committed.

Substantive Criminal Law Law that defines crimes and punishments.

Procedural Criminal Law Law that governs procedures for investigating and prosecuting crimes.

FIGURE 4.4 Excuse and Justification Defenses

Excuse Defenses: Based on a defendant's admitting that she or he committed the criminal act, but asserting that she or he cannot be held criminally responsible for the act due to lack of criminal intent.

	THE DEFENDANT MUST PROVE THAT:	EXAMPLE
INFANCY	Because he or she was under a statutorily determined age, he or she did not have the maturity to make the decisions necessary to commit a criminal act.	A thirteen-year-old takes a handgun from his backpack at school and begins shooting at fellow students, killing three. (In such cases, the offender is often processed by the juvenile justice system rather than the criminal justice system.)
INSANITY	At the time of the criminal act, he or she did not have the necessary mental capacity to be held responsible for his or her actions.	A man with a history of mental illness pushes a woman in front of an oncoming subway train, which kills her instantly.
INTOXICATION	She or he had diminished control over her or his actions due to the influence of alcohol or drugs.	A woman who had been drinking malt liquor and vodka stabs her boyfriend to death after a domestic argument. She claims to have been so drunk that she does not remember the incident.
MISTAKE	He or she did not know that his or her actions violated a law (this defense is very rarely even attempted), or he or she violated the law believing a relevant fact to be true when, in fact, it was not.	A woman, thinking that her divorce in another state has been finalized when it has not been, marries for a second time, thereby committing bigamy.

Justification Defenses: Based on a defendant's admitting that he or she committed the particular criminal act, but asserting that, under the circumstances, the criminal act was justified.

	THE DEFENDANT MUST PROVE THAT:	EXAMPLE
DURESS	She or he was induced to perform the criminal act by another person who wrongfully threatened him or her with serious bodily harm or death.	A mother assists her boyfriend in committing a burglary after he threatens to kill her children if she refuses to do so.
SELF-DEFENSE	He or she acted to defend himself or herself, others, or property, or to prevent the commission of a crime.	A husband awakes to find his wife standing over him, pointing a shotgun at his chest. In the ensuing struggle, the firearm goes off, killing the wife.
NECESSITY	The criminal act he or she committed was necessary in order to avoid a harm to himself or herself or another that was greater than the harm caused by the act itself.	Four people physically remove a friend from her residence on the property of a religious cult, arguing that the crime of kidnapping was justified in order to remove the victim from the damaging influence of cult leaders.
ENTRAPMENT	She or he was encouraged by agents of the state to engage in a criminal act she or he would not have engaged in otherwise.	The owner of a boat marina agrees to allow three federal drug enforcement agents, posing as drug dealers, to use his dock to unload shipments of marijuana from Colombia.

Section 2, Clause 3, maintains that the "Trial of all Crimes" will be by jury and "such Trial shall be held in the State where the said crimes shall have been committed."

Amending the Constitution

The need for a written declaration of the rights of individuals eventually caused the first Congress to draft twelve amendments to the Constitution and submit them for approval by the states. Ten of these amendments, commonly known as the **Bill of Rights,** were adopted in 1791. Since then, seventeen more amendments have been added.

The Bill of Rights, as interpreted by the United States Supreme Court, has served as the basis for procedural safeguards of the accused in this country. These safeguards include the following:

1. The Fourth Amendment protection from unreasonable searches and seizures.
2. The Fourth Amendment requirement that no warrants for a search or an arrest can be issued without probable cause.

Bill of Rights The first ten amendments to the U.S. Constitution.

3. The Fifth Amendment requirement that no one can be deprived of life, liberty, or property without "due process" of law.

4. The Fifth Amendment prohibition against *double jeopardy* (trying someone twice for the same criminal offense).

5. The Fifth Amendment guarantee that no person can be required to be a witness against (incriminate) himself or herself.

6. The Sixth Amendment guarantees of a speedy trial, a trial by jury, a public trial, the right to confront witnesses, and the right to a lawyer at various stages of criminal proceedings.

7. The Eighth Amendment prohibitions against excessive bails and fines and cruel and unusual punishments. (For the full text of the Bill of Rights, see Appendix A.)

Expanding the Constitution The Bill of Rights initially offered citizens protection only against the federal government. Over the years, however, the procedural safeguards of most of the provisions of the Bill of Rights have been applied to the actions of state governments through the Fourteenth Amendment.[62] Furthermore, the states, under certain circumstances, have the option to grant even more protections than are required by the federal Constitution. As these protections are crucial to criminal justice procedures in the United States, they will be afforded much more attention in Chapter 7, with regard to police action, and in Chapter 10, with regard to the criminal trial.

In 2015, several members of Congress introduced a proposed Victims' Rights Amendment to the U.S. Constitution.[63] This proposed amendment would contain many of the same rights that are present in state victims' rights laws and the federal Victims' Rights Act, as discussed in Chapter 3. The difference, claim its supporters, is that such an amendment would give some "teeth" to protections that are now, as you also learned in Chapter 3, mostly discretionary.[64] Victims' rights supporters have been trying, without success, to amend the Constitution in favor of victims since 1996, showing just how important constitutional protections are in the criminal justice system.

Due Process

Both the Fifth and Fourteenth Amendments provide that no person should be deprived of "life, liberty, or property without due process of law." This **due process clause** basically requires that the government not act unfairly or arbitrarily. In other words, the government cannot rely on individual judgment and impulse when making decisions, but must stay within the boundaries of reason and the law. Not surprisingly, disagreements as to the meaning of these provisions have plagued courts, politicians, and citizens since this nation was founded, and will undoubtedly continue to do so.

To understand due process, it is important to consider its two types: procedural due process and substantive due process.

Procedural Due Process According to **procedural due process,** the law must be carried out according to a *method* that is fair and orderly. It requires that certain procedures be followed in administering and executing a law so that an individual's basic freedoms are not violated. Consider a recent case involving the University of Michigan. The university ruled that a sophomore named Drew Sterrett had engaged in sexual intercourse with another student without her consent. Sterret responded by suing the university in federal court, claiming that it had violated his due process rights

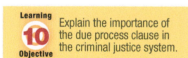

Learning Objective 10 Explain the importance of the due process clause in the criminal justice system.

in coming to a conclusion that would limit his future "education, employment, and career opportunities."

In his lawsuit, Sterrett contended that he had never been provided with the charges against him in writing. In addition, he had not been given a chance to question his accuser or to know the names of the witnesses who had testified against him. These procedural due process rights, as we will see in Chapter 10, are bedrocks of the American criminal justice system. Eventually, following judicial proceedings, the University of Michigan vacated all its findings against Sterrett.[65]

▲ In 2016, a group of sex offenders filed suit claiming that their due process rights were violated by a federal law that proposed to mark the passports of all sex offenders with a "unique identifier" identifying their status. **Would this law violate the substantive due process rights of sex offenders? Why or why not?** alexmillos/Shutterstock.com

Substantive Due Process

Fair procedures would obviously be of little use if they were used to administer unfair laws. For example, suppose a law requires everyone to wear a red shirt on Mondays. You wear a blue shirt on Monday, and you are arrested, convicted, and sentenced to one year in prison. The fact that all proper procedures were followed and your rights were given their proper protections would mean very little because the law that you broke was unfair and arbitrary.

Thus, substantive due process requires that the laws themselves be reasonable. The idea is that if a law is unfair or arbitrary, even if properly passed by a legislature, it must be declared unconstitutional. In the 1930s, for example, Oklahoma instituted the Habitual Criminal Sterilization Act. Under this statute, a person who had been convicted of three felonies could be "rendered sexually sterile" by the state (that is, the person would no longer be able to produce children). The United States Supreme Court held that the law was unconstitutional, as there are "limits to the extent which a legislatively represented majority may conduct biological experiments at the expense of the dignity and personality and natural powers of a minority."[66]

The Judicial System's Role in Due Process

As the last example suggests, the United States Supreme Court often plays the important role of ultimately deciding when due process has been violated and when it has not. (See Figure 4.5 for a list of important Supreme Court due process cases.)

The Court is also called on from time to time to determine whether a due process right exists in the first place. For example, looking back at Figure 4.3 earlier in the chapter, you can see that four states—Idaho, Kansas, Montana, and Utah—do not provide defendants with access to the insanity defense. In 2007, John Delling killed two men in Idaho whom he believed had conspired to steal his soul. Because Idaho does not allow the insanity defense, Delling pleaded guilty to the murders and was sentenced to life in prison. In 2012, his lawyers asked the Supreme Court to rule that the insanity defense was a constitutional right that should be available to all defendants in the United States. The Court refused to do so, allowing individual states to prohibit the insanity defense if they so wish.[67]

Substantive Due Process The constitutional requirement that laws must be fair and reasonable in content and must further a legitimate governmental objective.

FIGURE 4.5 Important United States Supreme Court Due Process Decisions

YEAR	ISSUE	AMENDMENT INVOLVED	COURT CASE
1948	Right to a public trial	VI	*In re Oliver*, 333 U.S. 257
1952	Police searches cannot be so invasive as to "shock the conscience"	IV	*Rochin v. California*, 342 U.S. 165
1961	Exclusionary rule	IV	*Mapp v. Ohio*, 367 U.S. 643
1963	Right to a lawyer in all criminal felony cases	VI	*Gideon v. Wainwright*, 372 U.S. 335
1964	No compulsory self-incrimination	V	*Malloy v. Hogan*, 378 U.S. 1
1964	Right to have counsel when taken into police custody and subjected to questioning	VI	*Escobedo v. Illinois*, 378 U.S. 478
1965	Right to confront and cross-examine witnesses	VI	*Pointer v. Texas*, 380 U.S. 400
1966	Right to an impartial jury	VI	*Parker v. Gladden*, 385 U.S. 363
1966	Confessions of suspects not notified of due process rights ruled invalid	V	*Miranda v. Arizona*, 384 U.S. 436
1967	Right to a speedy trial	VI	*Klopfer v. North Carolina*, 386 U.S. 21
1967	Juveniles have due process rights, too	V	*In re Gault*, 387 U.S. 1
1968	Right to a jury trial ruled a fundamental right	VI	*Duncan v. Louisiana*, 391 U.S. 145
1969	No double jeopardy	V	*Benton v. Maryland*, 395 U.S. 784

Due Process and National Security The due process clause does not automatically doom laws that may infringe on procedural or substantive rights. In certain circumstances, the lawmaking body may be able to prove that its interests are important enough to take priority over the due process rights of the individual, and in those cases the statute may be upheld. For example, the federal Terrorist Screening Database, also known as the "terrorist watch list," contains an unspecified number of names and aliases of persons known—or reasonably suspected—by the federal government to be involved in terrorism. Inclusion on the list can hinder a person's ability to travel internationally, find employment in certain professions, or transfer funds via U.S. banks. Yet the Department of Justice (DOJ) does not inform people that they are on the list, nor does it offer procedures for challenging this inclusion.

Although the DOJ's policy in this matter clearly violates the spirit, if not the letter, of due process law, courts have yet to find that the terrorist watch list violates the Constitution.[68] The need for secrecy can be seen as a crucial part of the counterterrorism strategies that protect Americans from terrorist attacks. This need for secrecy, the courts seem to be saying, is more important than the due process rights of those on the watch list.

ETHICS CHALLENGE

In 2011, an American Predator drone missile attack in the Middle Eastern country of Yemen killed Anwar al-Awlaki, a U.S. citizen and Islamist cleric. Awlaki had been linked to more than a dozen terrorist operations, including a failed plot to blow up cargo airplanes bound for the United States, and his online sermons in English contained numerous threats to Americans. At the time, several legal experts argued that the drone strike was inherently unethical. Awlaki had not been provided with the most basic due process protections. He had not been charged with any crime, and he had not been afforded a trial to prove his innocence. Do you think this assassination of a U.S. citizen was unethical? Why or why not?

"Stand Your Ground" Laws

How Things Stand

On December 18, 2016, an Uber driver named Namique Anderson was on the job in Aventura, Florida, when his car was cut off by a van driven by Kevin Johnson. With a gun in each hand, Johnson got out of the van and walked toward Anderson's stopped car, apparently with the intent to commit robbery. While still in his vehicle, Anderson took out a handgun and fired four times, killing Johnson. Because of Florida's stand your ground (SYG) law, Anderson was not charged with any crime. "He was acting in self-defense," said a police spokesperson.[69]

Generally speaking, SYG laws give a person who is legally in a particular place, be it at home or in public, the right to defend himself or herself with a firearm without retreating as long as that person reasonably believes his or her life to be in danger. Supporters contend that these laws allow people who face serious bodily harm or death to defend themselves without first having to retreat as far as possible. Variations of this basic SYG law now exist in thirty-four states.

As a Result...

SYG laws appear to have led to an increase in the number of justified homicides. In Texas, which passed its SYG law in 2007, the number of justifiable homicides increased from eighteen in 1999 to sixty-two in 2013.[70] In addition, according to a survey conducted the *Tampa Bay Times*, about 70 percent of those defendants who invoke an SYG defense in Florida are able to avoid prosecution for a violent crime.[71]

Further research suggests that states with SYG laws experience an increase in overall homicides[72] and that the laws are applied unequally depending on the race of the offender and the victim involved.[73] These findings are controversial, however, and face numerous challenges on statistical grounds.[74]

Up for Debate

"Imagine a woman being required to flee when attacked in a parking lot, having to turn her back to the attacker, and then likely being run down and raped. Shouldn't she have the option to stand her ground to protect herself?"[75] —*David Simmons, Florida state senator*

"If our aim is to increase criminal justice system costs, increase medical costs, increase racial tension, maintain our high adolescent death rate and put police officers at greater risk, then this is good legislation."[76] —*Dr. Jerry Ratcliffe, Department of Criminal Justice, Temple University*

What's Your Take?

Review the discussion in this chapter on "Justifiable Use of Force—Self-Defense" before answering the following questions.

1. What is your opinion of SYG laws? Do you think they make society safer or more dangerous? Explain your answer.

2. Suppose that, during an argument on a boating dock, Mike tackles Tim, forcing both men into the water. Mike, the larger and stronger of the two, pushes Tim's head under water and nearly drowns him before the fight ends. As Mike is climbing out of the water, Tim fatally shoots him the back of the head. Would Tim be protected from murder charges under Florida's SYG law? Why or why not?

Digging Deeper...

Go online and find an example of a case in which a state **"stand your ground"** law was successfully used as a **defense** against criminal charges. In a short writing assignment, answer the three following questions about the case: (1) Did the defendant have a right to be at the location of the confrontation? (2) Was the defendant engaged in a legal activity? (3) Could the defendant reasonably have been in fear of death or great bodily harm? In light of your answers to these questions, do you think the outcome of the case was legally correct? Was it morally correct? Your answer should be at least three paragraphs long.

For more information on these concepts, look back to the Learning Objective icons throughout the chapter.

List the four written sources of American criminal law. (a) The U.S. Constitution and state constitutions, (b) statutes passed by Congress and state legislatures (plus local ordinances), (c) administrative agency regulations, and (d) case law.

Explain precedent and the importance of the doctrine of *stare decisis*. Precedent is a common law concept in which one decision becomes the example or authority for deciding future cases with similar facts. Under the doctrine of *stare decisis*, judges in a particular jurisdiction are bound to follow precedents of that same jurisdiction. The doctrine of *stare decisis* leads to efficiency in the judicial system.

Explain the two basic functions of criminal law. The primary function of criminal law is to protect citizens from criminal harms (1) to their individual safety and property and (2) to society's interests collectively. The second function is to maintain and teach social values, as well as social boundaries—for example, the boundaries represented by laws against bigamy.

Delineate the elements required to establish *mens rea* (a guilty mental state). (a) Purpose, (b) knowledge, (c) negligence, and (d) recklessness.

Explain how the doctrine of strict liability applies to criminal law. Strict liability crimes do not allow the alleged wrongdoer to claim ignorance or mistake to avoid criminal responsibility. Examples include speed limit violations and statutory rape.

List and briefly define the most important excuse defenses for crimes. Insanity—different tests of insanity can be used, including (a) the *M'Naghten* rule (right-wrong test); (b) the ALI/MPC test, also known as the substantial-capacity test; and (c) the irresistible-impulse test. **Intoxication**—can be voluntary or involuntary, with the latter being a possible criminal defense. **Mistake**—sometimes valid if the law was not published or reasonably known or if the alleged offender relied on an official statement of the law that was erroneous. Also, a mistake of fact may negate the mental state necessary to commit a crime.

Discuss a common misperception concerning the insanity defense in the United States. Contrary to popular opinion, the insanity defense is not an oft-used loophole that allows criminals to avoid responsibility for committing heinous crimes. Insanity defenses are difficult to mount and very rarely succeed. Even when a defendant is found not guilty by reason of insanity, she or he does not "go free." Instead, such defendants are sent to mental health care institutions.

Describe the four most important justification criminal defenses. Duress—requires that (a) the threat is of serious bodily harm or death, (b) the harm is greater than that caused by the crime, (c) the threat is immediate and inescapable, and (d) the defendant became involved in the situation through no fault of his or her own. **Justifiable use of force**—use of force in the defense of one's person, dwelling, or property or the prevention of a crime. **Necessity**—may apply if the harm caused by the crime actually committed is less than the harm that would have been caused by the criminal act avoided. **Entrapment**—can be used when the criminal action was induced by governmental persuasion or trickery.

Distinguish between substantive and procedural criminal law. The former concerns questions about what acts are actually criminal. The latter concerns procedures designed to protect the constitutional rights of individuals and to prevent the arbitrary use of power by the government.

Explain the importance of the due process clause in the criminal justice system. The due process clause acts to limit the power of government. In the criminal justice system, the due process clause requires that certain procedures be followed to ensure that criminal proceedings are fair and that all criminal laws are reasonable and in the interest of the public good.

QUESTIONS FOR CRITICAL ANALYSIS

1. Give an example of a criminal law whose main purpose seems to be teaching societal boundaries rather than protecting citizens from harm. Do you think this behavior should be illegal? Explain your answer.

2. While behind the wheel, Emil suffers an epileptic seizure and passes out. The car careens onto the sidewalk and strikes a group of schoolgirls, badly injuring four of them. Emil knew that he was subject to epileptic attacks that rendered him likely to lose consciousness. What are the arguments for and against charging Emil with committing a crime? Which argument do you feel is stronger? Why?

3. Nine-year-old Savannah lies to her grandmother Jessica about eating candy bars. As punishment, Jessica forces Savannah to run for three hours without a rest. Severely dehydrated, the girl has a seizure and dies. What should be the criminal charge against Jessica, and why?

4. On a dating app, a fourteen-year-old misrepresents herself as being seventeen years old. Based on this information, a nineteen-year-old meets and has sex with her. Is it fair that the nineteen-year-old is found guilty of statutory rape? Why or why not?

5. Suppose that Louisiana's legislature passes a law allowing law enforcement officers to forcibly remove residents from their homes in the face of an imminent hurricane. Why might a court uphold this law even though, in most circumstances, such forcible removal would violate the residents' due process rights? If you were a judge, would you uphold Louisiana's new law?

KEY TERMS

actus reus 107
administrative law 103
alibi 115
attempt 108
attendant circumstances 112
ballot initiative 103
Bill of Rights 123
case law 104
common law 101
competency hearing 117
conspiracy 114
constitutional law 102
corpus delicti 106
due process clause 124
duress 119

duty to retreat 120
entrapment 122
felony-murder 111
hate crime laws 113
inchoate offenses 114
infancy 115
insanity 115
intoxication 118
involuntary manslaughter 110
irresistible-impulse test 117
mens rea 108
M'Naghten rule 116
necessity 121
negligence 108
precedent 101

procedural criminal law 122
procedural due process 124
recklessness 108
rule of law 101
self-defense 120
stare decisis 104
statutory law 102
statutory rape 111
strict liability crimes 110
substantial-capacity test (ALI/MPC test) 117
substantive criminal law 122
substantive due process 125
supremacy clause 103
voluntary manslaughter 109

1. Roger LeRoy Miller and Gaylord A. Jentz, *Business Law Today, Comprehensive Edition*, 7th ed. (Cincinnati, Ohio: South-Western, 2007), 2–3.

2. Alison Smith and Richard M. Thompson II, "Criminal Offenses Enacted from 2008–2013," *Congressional Research Service* (June 23, 2014).

3. Erik Eckholm, "Legal Conflicts on Medical Marijuana Ensnare Hundreds as Courts Debate a New Provision," *New York Times* (April 9, 2015), A14.

4. Quoted in "Judge: Federal Law Trumps Montana's Medical Pot Law," *Associated Press* (January 23, 2012).

5. *Texas v. Johnson*, 491 U.S. 397 (1989).

6. Anita Hofschneider, "Federal Judge Strikes Down Maui County's GMO Moratorium." *www.civilbeat.org. Honolulu Civil Beat:* June 30, 2015, Web.

7. "Conagra Subsidiary Sentenced in Connection with Outbreak of Salmonella Poisoning Related to Peanut Butter." *www.fda.gov.* U.S. Food and Drug Administration: December 13, 2016, Web.

8. 478 U.S. 186 (1986)

9. 539 U.S. 558, 578 (2003).

10. Joel Feinberg, *The Moral Limits of the Criminal Law: Harm to Others* (New York: Oxford University Press, 1984), 221–232.

11. "AB-1785 Vehicles: Use of Wireless Electronic Devices." *http://leginfo.legislature.ca.gov/.* California Legislative Information: 2015–2016, Web.

12. Henry M. Hart, Jr., "The Aims of the Criminal Law," *Law & Contemporary Problems 23* (1958), 405–406.

13. John L. Diamond, "The Myth of Morality and Fault in Criminal Law Doctrine," *American Criminal Law Review 34* (Fall 1996), 111.

14. Kentucky Statutes Section 437.060; and New Hampshire Revised Statutes Section 207:61.

15. "Idaho Senate Bill 1332." *www.legiscan.com. LegiScan:* March 19, 2014, Web.

16. Lawrence M. Friedman, *Crime and Punishments in American History* (New York: Basic Books, 1993), 10.

17. Thomas A. Mullen, "Rule without Reason: Requiring Independent Proof of the Corpus Delicti as a Condition of Admitting Extrajudicial Confession," *University of San Francisco Law Review 27* (1993), 385.

18. *Hawkins v. State*, 219 Ind. 116, 129, 37 N.E.2d 79 (1941).

19. David C. Biggs, "'The Good Samaritan Is Packing': An Overview of the Broadened Duty to Aid Your Fellowman, with the Modern Desire to Possess Concealed Weapons," *University of Dayton Law Review 22* (Winter 1997), 225.

20. Le Trinh, "In Which States Do I Have a Duty to Help?" *http://legalblogs.findlaw.com/.* FindLaw: May 20, 2015, Web.

21. Model Penal Code Section 2.02.

22. Model Penal Code Section 2.02(c).

23. "Strict Liability." *www.law.cornell.edu.* Legal Information Institute: visited January 20, 2017, Web.

24. *United States v. Dotterweich*, 320 U.S. 277 (1943).

25. Quoted in Clarence Walker, "The New War on Drug Dealers: Charging Them with Murder When Their Customers Die of Overdose." *www.alternet.org. Alternet:* May 31, 2015, Web.

26. *State v. Stiffler*, 763 P.2d 308, 311 (Idaho Ct.App. 1988).

27. *State v. Harrison*, 425 A.2d 111 (1979).

28. Richard G. Singer and John Q. LaFond, *Criminal Law: Examples and Explanations* (New York: Aspen Law & Business, 1997), 322.

29. *State v. Linscott*, 520 A.2d 1067 (1987).

30. *Morissette v. United States*, 342 U.S. 246, 251–252 (1952).

31. Federal Bank Robbery Act, 18 U.S.C.A. Section 2113.

32. *In re Winship*, 397 U.S. 358, 364, 368–369 (1970).

33. "Title 18: Chapter 25 Criminal Homicide Sec. 2506." *www.legis.state.pa.us.* Pennsylvania General Assembly: visited January 18, 2017, Web.

34. Conn. Gen. Stat. § 53a-40a (2010).

35. Federal Bureau of Investigation, *Hate Crime Statistics, 2015*, Table 1. *https://ucr.fbi.gov/.* U.S. Department of Justice, 2016, Web.

36. Richard Cohen, "When Thought Becomes a Crime." *www.realclearpolitics.com.* Real Clear Politics: October 19, 2010, Web.

37. *Wisconsin v. Mitchell*, 508 U.S. 476 (1993); and *Apprendi v. New Jersey*, 530 U.S. 466 (2000).

38. *United States v. Jiminez Recio*, 537 U.S. 270 (2003).

39. Paul H. Robinson, *Criminal Law Defenses* (St. Paul, Minn.: West, 2008), Section 173, Ch. 5Bl.

40. *M'Naghten's* Case, 10 Cl.&F. 200, Eng.Rep. 718 (1843). Note that the name is also spelled M'Naughten and McNaughten.

41. Model Penal Code Section 401 (1952).

42. Joshua Dressler, *Cases and Materials on Criminal Law*, 2d ed. (St. Paul, Minn.: West Group, 1999), 599.

43. Danny Cevallos, "Don't Rely on Insanity Defense," *www.cnn.com. CNN:* July 17, 2015, Web.

44. South Carolina Code Annotated Section 17-24-20(A) (Law. Co-op. Supp. 1997).

45. Lawrence P. Tiffany and Mary Tiffany, "Nosologic Objections to the Criminal Defense of Pathological Intoxication: What Do the Doubters Doubt?" *International Journal of Law and Psychiatry* 13 (1990), 49.

46. Paul Walsh, "Rare Defense Wins Dismissal of Child Assault Case, but Jailed Falcon Heights Mom Lost Home, Job." *www.startribune.com. Star Tribune:* July 20, 2015, Web.

47. 518 U.S. 37 (1996).

48. Quoted in Gary Fields and John R. Emshwiller, "As Criminal Laws Proliferate, More Are Ensnared." *www.wsj.com. Wall Street Journal:* July 23, 2011, Web.

49. *Lambert v. California*, 335 U.S. 225 (1957).

50. Federal Bureau of Investigation, *Crime in the United States, 2015*, Expanded Homicide Tables 14 and 15. *https://ucr.fbi.gov/.* U.S. Department of Justice: 2016, Web.

51. Craig L. Carr, "Duress and Criminal Responsibility," *Law and Philosophy 10* (1990), 161.

52. Arnold N. Enker, "In Supporting the Distinction between Justification and Excuse," *Texas Tech Law Review 42* (2009), 277.

53. *United States v. May*, 727 F.2d 764 (1984).

54. *United States v. Contento-Pachon*, 723 F.2d 691 (1984).

55. *People v. Murillo*, 587 N.E.2d 1199, 1204 (Ill. App.Ct. 1992).

56. Florida Statutes Section 776.03 (2005).

57. *Ibid.*

58. Michael Bloomberg, quoted in "A Lethal Right to Self-Defense," *The Week* (May 4, 2012), 13.

59. Ray Downs, "'Medical Necessity' Defense in Marijuana Cases Still a Battle in Florida, but More Victories Possible." *http://www.browardpalmbeach.com/. Broward/Palm Beach New Times:* March 18, 2015, Web.

60. 287 U.S. 435 (1932).

61. Kenneth M. Lord, "Entrapment and Due Process: Moving toward a Dual System of Defenses," *Florida State University Law Review 25* (Spring 1998), 463.

62. Henry J. Abraham, *Freedom and the Court: Civil Liberties in the United States*, 7th ed. (New York: Oxford University Press, 1998), 38–41.

63. "H.J.Res.45—Proposing an Amendment to the Constitution of the United States to Protect the Rights of Crime Victims." *www.congress.gov.* Congress.gov: 2015–2016, Web.

64. Paul G. Cassell, "The Victims' Rights Amendment: A Sympathetic, Clause-by-Clause Analysis," *Phoenix Law Review* (Spring 2012), 301.

65. Emily Yoffe, "A Campus Rape Ruling, Reversed." *www.slate.com. Slate:* September 15, 2015, Web.

66. *Skinner v. Oklahoma*, 316 U.S. 535, 546–547 (1942).

67. Jonathan Stempel, "Supreme Court Declines to Review Insanity Defense Appeal," *Reuters* (November 26, 2012).

68. Jennifer Chambers, "Lawsuits Filed over Muslim Americans on Watch List." *www.detroitnews.com. Detroit News:* April 5, 2016, Web.

69. Charles Rabin, "Uber Driver Fired in 'Self-Defense,' Police Say, as Stand Your Ground Takes Toll." *www.bradenton.com. Bradenton Herald:* December 20, 2016, Web.

70. Kevin Schwaller, "Justifiable Homicides Rise in Texas." *www.kxan.com.* KXAN: January 8, 2015, Web.

71. Kris Hundley, Susan Taylor Martin, and Connie Humburg, "Florida 'Stand Your Ground' Law Yields Some Shocking Outcomes Depending on How Law Is Applied." *www.tampabay.com. Tampa Bay Times:* June 1, 2012, Web.

72. Chandler B. McClellan and Erdal Tekin, "Stand Your Ground Laws, Homicides, and Injuries" (*National Bureau of Economic Research*, Working Paper No. 18187, 2012), 2.

73. John K. Roman, *Race, Justifiable Homicide, and Stand Your Ground Laws: Analysis of FBI Supplementary Homicide Report Data* (Washington, D.C.: Urban Institute, 2013), 4.

74. Cynthia Ward, "'Stand Your Ground' and Self Defense." *http://scholarship.law.wm.edu/.* Faculty Publications: 2015, Web.

75. David Simmons, "Without 'Stand Your Ground,' Attacker Can Have Advantage." *http://www.orlandosentinel.com/. Orlando Sentinel:* April 15, 2012, Web.

76. Quoted in Nadia Prupis, "'Stand Your Ground' Laws Linked to Rise in Homicides, Extreme Racial Bias: Study." *www.commondreams.org.* Common Dreams: August 14, 2014, Web.

5

Law Enforcement Today

To target your study and review, look for these numbered Learning Objective icons throughout the chapter.

Chapter Outline		**Corresponding Learning Objectives**
The Responsibilities of the Police	**1**	List the four basic responsibilities of the police.
A Short History of the American Police	**2**	Tell how the patronage system affected policing.
	3	Explain how intelligence-led policing works and how it benefits modern police departments.
Recruitment and Training: Becoming a Police Officer	**4**	Identify the differences between the police academy and field training as learning tools for recruits.
Women and Minorities in Policing Today	**5**	Describe some of the benefits that female police officers bring to law enforcement.
	6	Identify the main advantage of a racially and ethnically diverse police force.
Public and Private Law Enforcement	**7**	Indicate some of the most important law enforcement agencies under the control of the Department of Homeland Security.
	8	Summarize the duties of the FBI.
	9	Analyze the importance of private security today.

Local Hero

▲ On November 28, 2016, Ohio State University police officer Alan Horujko, who had spent nearly two years at his post, responded to a campus emergency that required the use of deadly force. AP Images/Ohio State University Police

the position, he wrote that it would be an "honor to give something back to the . . . school that has already given so much to me."

On the morning of November 28, 2016, Horujko did just that. While assisting fire fighters responding to a gas leak on campus, the second-year officer watched as a small gray Honda plowed into a nearby crowd of pedestrians. The driver, a student named Abdul Razak Ali Artan, got out of the car and began stabbing bystanders with a butcher knife. (Earlier, Artan had posted online that he was "sick and tired" of seeing Muslims "killed and tortured" by the U.S. military.) Horujko drew his weapon and ordered Artan to drop the knife. The other man refused. After checking that the scene was free of civilians, Horujko fired three times, killing Artan and ending the threat.

In total, eleven people were hospitalized as a result of Artan's attack. Following protocol, Horujko was placed on administrative leave while the Columbus Department of Public Safety investigated the fatal shooting. Certainly, there was little doubt in the community that Horujko's actions were necessary and justified. "We appreciate your service and bravery," wrote one well wisher on the OSU Emergency Management Department's Facebook page. "Thank you for protecting our children," wrote another.

When he first got to Ohio State University (OSU), Alan Horujko planned to be an engineering major. His career path changed, however, when he started volunteering as an unarmed student safety officer with the OSU Police Department. Among other training, this position gave him a chance to patrol areas of the Columbus campus and prepare for active shooter situations. After a taste of law enforcement, "I just couldn't see myself sitting in a cubicle," Horujko said. Three years after his 2012 graduation, Horujko was hired as an OSU police officer. In his application for

FOR CRITICAL ANALYSIS

1. What factors went into Officer Alan Horujko's decision to use deadly force in the situation described above? Was his decision correct? Why or why not?

2. It is standard procedure for a police officer involved in a fatal shooting to be placed on temporary leave while the incident is investigated. What is your opinion of this policy?

3. Describe the law enforcement presence on the campus of your school. Do you feel this presence is sufficient? Explain your answer.

The Responsibilities of the Police

"There has never been a more dangerous or complicated and challenging time to be a police officer," said Columbus Mayor Andrew Ginther of Officer Alan Horujko's timely measures. "We had a dynamic well-trained professional today save the lives of many of our residents and students."[1] Even when they are not engaged in high-profile acts of courage, police officers are the most visible representatives of our criminal justice system. Indeed, they symbolize the system for many Americans who may never see the inside of a courtroom or a prison cell. Still, the general perception of a "cop's life" is often shaped by television dramas and films. In reality, police spend a great deal of time on such mundane tasks as responding to noise complaints, confiscating firecrackers, and poring over paperwork.

Sociologist Egon Bittner warned against the tendency to see the police primarily as agents of law enforcement and crime control. A more inclusive accounting of "what the police do," Bittner believed, would recognize that they provide "situationally justified force in society."[2] In other words, the function of the police is to solve any problem that may *possibly*, though not *necessarily*, require the use of force.

Within Bittner's rather broad definition of "what the police do," we can pinpoint four basic responsibilities of the police:

1. To enforce laws.
2. To provide services.
3. To prevent crime.
4. To preserve the peace.

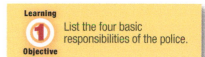

Learning Objective 1 List the four basic responsibilities of the police.

As will become evident over the next two chapters, there is a great deal of debate among legal and other scholars and law enforcement officers over which responsibilities deserve the most police attention and what methods police should employ in meeting those responsibilities.

Enforcing Laws

In the public mind, the primary role of the police is to enforce society's laws—hence, the term *law enforcement officer*. In their role as "crime fighters," police officers have a clear mandate to seek out and apprehend those who have violated the law. The crime-fighting responsibility is so dominant that all police activity—from the purchase of new automobiles to a plan to hire more minority officers—must often be justified in terms of its law enforcement value.[3]

Police officers also see themselves primarily as "crime fighters," a perception that often leads people into what they believe will be an exciting career in law enforcement. Although the job certainly offers challenges unlike any other, police officers normally do not spend the majority of their time in law enforcement duties. After surveying a year's worth of dispatch data from the Wilmington (Delaware) Police Department, researchers Jack Greene and Carl Klockars found that officers spent only about half of their shifts enforcing the law or dealing with crimes. The rest of their time was spent on order maintenance, service provision, traffic patrol, and medical assistance.[4]

Furthermore, information provided by the Uniform Crime Report shows that most arrests are made for "crimes of disorder" or public annoyances rather than violent or property crimes. In 2015, for example, police made about 8.8 million arrests for drunkenness, liquor law violations, disorderly conduct, vagrancy, loitering, and other minor offenses, but only about 505,000 arrests for violent crimes.[5]

Providing Services

The popular emphasis on crime fighting tends to overshadow the fact that a great deal of a police officer's time is spent providing services for the community. The motto "To Serve and Protect" has been adopted by thousands of local police departments, and the *Law Enforcement Code of Ethics* recognizes the duty "to serve the community" in its first sentence.[6] The services that police provide are numerous—a partial list would include directing traffic, performing emergency medical procedures, counseling those involved in domestic disputes, providing directions to tourists, and finding lost children.

As we will see in the next section, many police departments have adopted a strategy called *community policing*. This strategy requires officers to provide assistance of a sort that is not, at first glance, directly related to law enforcement. Often, regardless of official policy, the police are forced into providing certain services. For example, in many instances, law enforcement officers are first on the scene when a person has been seriously injured. As a result, officers increasingly are becoming proficient in emergency medical procedures. Some cities even allow police officers to take injured persons to the hospital in a squad car rather than wait for an ambulance.[7]

In addition, police officers often find themselves on the front lines when it comes to dealing with substance abuse and mental illness. Law enforcement agents in numerous jurisdictions carry naloxone, a drug that can instantly alleviate the effects of an opioid overdose. Over a recent one-year period, local police officers throughout Pennsylvania used naloxone to reverse more than six hundred such overdoses.[8] In cities such as Houston, Los Angeles, and Minneapolis, local police officers are teaming up with mental health specialists to handle emergency calls involving mentally ill persons.[9] (The feature *Discretion in Action—Handle with Care* considers the best course of action for police confronted with a suspect suffering from mental illness.)

DISCRETION IN ACTION

Handle with Care

The Situation Terri lives in a group home for people who suffer from mental illness. After she stops taking her medication, a social worker stops by to check on Terri's well-being. She responds by threatening the social worker, yelling, "Get out of here! I have a knife, and I'll kill you if I have to!" The social worker contacts the police, and Officers Helton and Ramirez take the call. Using a master key to open Terri's locked door, the officers find her holding a five-inch kitchen knife and screaming, "I am going to kill you. I don't need help. Get out." Officers Helton and Ramirez, who do not have their weapons drawn, leave the room and ponder their next move.

The Law Under the Fourth Amendment, as you will see in Chapter 7, law enforcement agents have the right to enter a home or dwelling without permission from a judge in emergency situations. The potential for injury to an occupant of that home or dwelling is one such situation.

What Would You Do? On the one hand, Terri has threatened to kill three people, possesses a deadly weapon, and may harm herself. (Plus, if she escapes from her room, which is on the ground floor and has a window, she could harm others.) On the other hand, police officers should not assume that a person suffering from mental illness necessarily poses a threat to herself or to society. Furthermore, the goal here is not to arrest Teresa, but rather to move her to a mental health facility for involuntary treatment.

Officers Helton and Ramirez have several options. They can reenter Terri's room and try to subdue her themselves. Or they can call for police backup. Or they can request the assistance of mental health experts, thereby lessening the chance that they will need to use force against Terri. Which is the best option? Why?

To see how two police officers in San Francisco reacted in similar circumstances, go to Example 5.1 in Appendix B.

Preventing Crime

Perhaps the most controversial responsibility of the police is to *prevent* crime. According to Jerome Skolnick, co-director of the Center for Research in Crime and Justice at the New York University School of Law, there are two predictable public responses when crime rates begin to rise in a community. The first is to punish convicted criminals with stricter laws and more severe penalties. The second is to demand that the police "do something" to prevent crimes from occurring in the first place. Is it, in fact, possible for the police to "prevent" crimes? The strongest response that Professor Skolnick is willing to give to this question is "maybe."[10]

On a limited basis, police can certainly prevent some crimes. If a rapist is dissuaded from attacking a solitary woman because a patrol car is cruising the area, then the police officer behind the wheel has prevented a crime. Furthermore, exemplary police work can have a measurable effect. "Quite simply, cops count," says William Bratton, who has directed police departments in Boston, Los Angeles, and New York. "[T]he quickest way to impact crime is with a well-led, managed, and appropriately resourced police force."[11] In Chapter 6, we will study a number of policing strategies that have been credited, by some, for decreasing crime rates in the United States.

In general, however, the deterrent effects of police presence are unclear. One study found no relationship between the size of the police presence in a neighborhood and the residents' perceived risk of being arrested for wrongdoing.[12] Furthermore, Carl Klockars has written that the "war on crime" is a war that the police cannot win because they cannot control the factors—such as unemployment, poverty, immorality, inequality, political change, and lack of educational opportunities—that contribute to criminal behavior in the first place.[13]

Preserving the Peace

To a certain extent, the fourth responsibility of the police, that of preserving the peace, is related to preventing crime. Police have the legal authority to use the power of arrest, or even force, in situations in which a crime has not yet occurred but might occur in the immediate future.

In the words of James Q. Wilson, the police's peacekeeping role (which Wilson believed to be the most important role of law enforcement officers) often takes on a pattern of simply "handling the situation."[14] For example, when police officers arrive on the scene of a loud, late-night house party, they may feel the need to disperse the party and even arrest some of the partygoers for disorderly conduct. By their actions, the officers have lessened the chances that serious and violent crimes will take place later in the evening. The same principle is often used in dealing with domestic disputes, which, if they escalate, can lead to homicide. Such situations, to use Wilson's terminology again, need "fixing up," and police can use the power of arrest, or threat, or coercion, or sympathy to do just that.

The basis of Wilson and George Kelling's zero-tolerance theory is similar: street disorder—such as public drunkenness, urination, and loitering—signals to both law-abiding citizens and criminals that the law is not being enforced and therefore leads to more violent crime. Hence, if police preserve the peace and "crack down" on the minor crimes that make up street disorder, they will in fact be preventing serious crimes from occurring in the future.[15]

ETHICS CHALLENGE

Do law enforcement agents have an ethical obligation to provide offenders with medical assistance? What if a police officer's partner has been killed by a suspect during a shootout, and the suspect—also shot—is bleeding profusely nearby? Ethically, must that officer do everything in his or her power to save the suspect's life? Why or why not?

A Short History of the American Police

Although modern society relies on law enforcement officers to control and prevent crime, in the early days of this country police services had little to do with crime control. The policing efforts in the first American cities were directed toward controlling certain groups of people (mostly slaves and Native Americans), delivering goods, regulating activities such as buying and selling in the town market, maintaining health and sanitation, controlling gambling and vice, and managing livestock and other animals.[16]

Furthermore, these police services were for the most part performed by volunteers, as a police force was an expensive proposition. Often, the volunteers were organized using the night watch system, brought over from England by colonists in the seventeenth century. Under this system, all physically fit males were required to offer their services to protect the community on a rotating nightly basis.[17]

The Evolution of American Law Enforcement

The night watch system did not ask much of its volunteers, who were often required to do little more than loudly announce the time and the state of the weather. In addition, many citizens avoided their duties by hiring others to "go on watch" in their place, and those who did serve frequently spent their time on watch sleeping and drinking.[18] Eventually, as the populations of American cities grew in the late eighteenth and early nineteenth centuries, so did the need for public order and the willingness to devote public resources to the establishment of formal police forces. The night watch system was insufficient to meet these new demands, and its demise was inevitable.

Early Police Departments

In 1829, the British home secretary Sir Robert "Bobbie" Peel took a dramatic step to organize law enforcement in London—then as now one of the largest cities in the Western world. He pushed the Metropolitan Police Act through Parliament, forming the London Metropolitan Police. One thousand strong at first, the members of this police force were easily recognizable in their uniforms that featured blue coats and top hats. Under Peel's direction, the "bobbies," as the police were called in honor of their founder, did not carry any firearms and were assigned to specific areas, or "beats," to prevent crime. Peel also believed that the police should be organized along military lines under the control of local elected officials.[19]

London's police operation was so successful that it was soon imitated in smaller towns throughout England and, eventually, in the United States. In 1833, Philadelphia became the first city to employ both day and night watchmen. Five years later, working from Peel's model, Boston formed the first

▼ A horse-drawn police wagon used by the New York City Police Department, circa 1886. **Why might this new form of transportation have represented a "revolution" for early American police forces?** Bettmann/Getty Images

organized police department, consisting of six full-time officers. In 1844, New York City laid the foundation for the modern police department by combining its day and night watches under the control of a single police chief. By the onset of the Civil War in 1861, a number of American cities, including Baltimore, Boston, Chicago, Cincinnati, New Orleans, and Philadelphia, had similarly consolidated police departments, modeled on the Metropolitan Police of London.[20]

The Political Era

Like their modern counterparts, many early police officers were hardworking, honest, and devoted to serving and protecting the public. On the whole, however, in the words of historian Samuel Walker, "The quality of American police service in the nineteenth century could hardly have been worse."[21] This poor quality can be attributed to the fact that the recruitment and promotion of police officers were intricately tied to the politics of the day. Police officers received their jobs as a result of political connections, not because of any particular skills or knowledge. Whichever political party was in power in a given city would hire its own cronies to run the police department. Consequently, the police were often more concerned with serving the interests of the political powers than with protecting the citizens.[22]

Corruption was rampant during this *political era* of policing, which lasted roughly from 1840 to 1930. Police salaries were relatively low, and many police officers saw their positions as opportunities to make extra income through any number of illegal activities. Bribery was common, as police would use their close proximity to the people to request "favors," which went into the police officers' own pockets or into the coffers of the local political party as "contributions."[23] This arrangement was known as the **patronage system,** or the "spoils system," because to the political victors went the spoils.

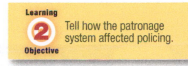

The political era also saw police officers take an active role in providing social services for their bosses' constituents. In many instances, this role even took precedence over law enforcement duties. Politicians realized that they could attract more votes by offering social services to citizens than by arresting them, and they required the police departments under their control to act accordingly.

The Reform Era

The abuses of the political era of policing did not go unnoticed. Nevertheless, it was not until 1929 that President Herbert Hoover appointed the national Commission on Law Observance and Enforcement to assess the American criminal justice system. The Wickersham Commission, named after its chairman, George Wickersham, focused on two areas of American policing that were in need of reform: (1) police brutality and (2) "the corrupting influence of politics."

According to the commission, these reforms should come about through higher personnel standards, centralized police administrations, and the increased use of technology.[24] Reformers of the time took the commission's findings as a call for the professionalization of American police and initiated the progressive (or *reform*) era in American policing.

Professionalism and Administrative Reforms

Many of the Wickersham Commission's recommendations echoed the opinions of one of its contributors—August Vollmer, the police chief of Berkeley, California, from 1905 to 1932.[25] Along with his protégé O. W. Wilson, Vollmer promoted a style of policing known as the **professional model.** Under the professional model, police chiefs, who had been little more than figureheads during the political era, took more control over their departments. A key to these efforts was the reorganization of police departments in many major cities. To improve their

Patronage System A form of corruption in which the political party in power hires and promotes police officers and receives job-related "favors" in return.

Professional Model A style of policing advocated by August Vollmer and O. W. Wilson that emphasizes centralized police organizations, increased use of technology, and the use of regulations and guidelines to limit police discretion.

control over operations, police chiefs began to add mid-level positions to the force. These new officers, known as majors or assistant chiefs, could develop and implement crime-fighting strategies and more closely supervise individual officers. Police chiefs also tried to consolidate their power by bringing large areas of a city under their control so that no local ward, neighborhood, or politician could easily influence a single police department.

The professionalism trend benefited law enforcement agents in a number of ways. Salaries and working conditions improved, and for the first time, women and members of minority groups were given opportunities—albeit limited—to serve.[26] At the same time, police administrators controlled officers much more than in the past, expecting them to meet targets for arrests and other numerical indicators that were seen as barometers of effectiveness. Any contact with citizens that did not explicitly relate to law enforcement was considered "social work" and discouraged.[27] As police expert Chris Braiden puts it, American police officers were expected to "park their brains at the door of the station-house" and simply "follow orders like a robot."[28]

The isolation of officers from the public was made complete by an overreliance on the patrol car, a relatively new technological innovation at the time. In the political era, officers walked their beats, interacting with citizens. In the reform era, they were expected to stay inside their "rolling fortresses," driving from one call to the next without wasting time or resources on public relations.[29]

CJ & TECHNOLOGY

High-Tech Cops

When patrol cars came into common use by police departments in the 1930s, they changed the face of American policing. Nine decades later, the technology associated with patrol cars continues to evolve. The vast majority of police cars in the United States are equipped with mobile data terminals that allow police officers to access information such as calls for service, suspects' outstanding warrants and criminal records, and neighborhood crime data. About two-thirds of police departments also attach video cameras to their patrol automobiles, and many are able to "live-stream" video content from these devices. Another mounted camera commonly found on police autos automatically reads the license plates of nearby vehicles and performs an instant background check on both car and driver.

In addition to their sophisticated transportation, today's police officers enjoy a multitude of other technological advantages. As we saw in Chapter 1, mobile biometric technology provides officers with the ability to immediately identify a suspect using fingerprints or facial features. Advances in through-the-wall sensor devices are increasingly allowing law enforcement agents to track people's movements within buildings. A new generation of handheld translation devices is helping officers in cities where English is not the primary language of many residents. These devices contain hundreds of preset police commands in a variety of dialects, and some even feature voice-activated translation capabilities.

Thinking about Police Technology

Handheld thermography cameras measure changes in body temperature to determine whether a person is in pain or is injured and, if so, to pinpoint which part of the body is affected. How might police officers use such devices to investigate violent crimes and assist victims?

Turmoil in the 1960s and 1970s By the 1950s, America prided itself on having the most modern and professional police force in the world. As efficiency became the goal of the reform-era police chief, however, relations with the community suffered. Instead of being members of the community, police officers were now seen almost as intruders, patrolling the streets in the anonymity of their automobiles. The drawbacks of this perception—and of the professional model in general—became evident in the 1960s, one of the most turbulent decades in American history. The civil rights movement, though not inherently violent, intensified feelings of helplessness and impoverishment in African American communities. These frustrations resulted in civil unrest, and many major American cities experienced race riots in the middle years of the decade. Concurrently, America was experiencing rising crime rates and often violent protests against U.S. involvement in the war in Vietnam (1964–1975).

By the early 1970s, many observers believed that substandard policing was contributing to the national turmoil. The National Advisory Commission on Civil Disorders stated bluntly that poor relations between the police and African American communities were partly to blame for the violence that plagued many of those communities.[30] In striving for professionalism, the police appeared to have lost touch with the citizens they were supposed to be serving. To repair their damaged relations with a large segment of the population, police would have to rediscover their community roots.

The Community Era   The beginning of the *community era* may be traced to several government initiatives that took place in 1968. Of primary importance was the Omnibus Crime Control and Safe Streets Act, which was passed that year.[31] Under this act, the federal government provided state and local police departments with funds to create a wide variety of police-community programs. Most large-city police departments established entire units devoted to community relations, implementing programs that ranged from summer recreation activities for inner-city youths to "officer-friendly" referral operations that encouraged citizens to come to the police with their crime concerns.

In the 1970s, as this vital rethinking of the role of the police was taking place, the country was hit by a crime wave. Thus, police administrators were forced to combine efforts to improve community relations with aggressive and innovative crime-fighting strategies. As we will see in Chapter 6 when we discuss these strategies in more depth, the police began to focus on stopping crimes before they occur, rather than concentrating only on solving crimes that have already been committed. A dedication to such proactive strategies led to widespread acceptance of *community policing* in the 1980s and 1990s.

Community policing is based on the notion that meaningful interaction between officers and citizens will lead to a partnership in preventing and fighting crime.[32] Though the idea of involving members of the community in this manner is hardly new—a similar principle was set forth by Sir Robert Peel in the 1820s—community policing has had a major impact on the culture of American law enforcement by asking the average police officer to be a problem solver as well as a crime fighter.[33] (See Figure 5.1 for an overview of the three eras of policing described in this section.)

Policing Today

Many law enforcement experts believe that the events of September 11, 2001, effectively ended the community era of policing.[34] Though police departments have not, in general, abandoned the idea of partnering with the community, their emphasis has shifted toward developing new areas of expertise, including counterterrorism and surveillance through technology. In particular, the process of collecting, analyzing, and mapping crime data has become a hallmark of law enforcement in the twenty-first century.

Intelligence-Led Policing   Based on hard-earned experience and criminological studies, law enforcement officials know that two strategies are particularly effective in reducing crime: focusing on repeat offenders and focusing on high-crime neighborhoods.

FIGURE 5.1 The Three Eras of American Policing

George L. Kelling and Mark H. Moore have separated the history of policing in the United States from 1840 to 2000 into three distinct periods. Below is a brief summarization of these three eras.

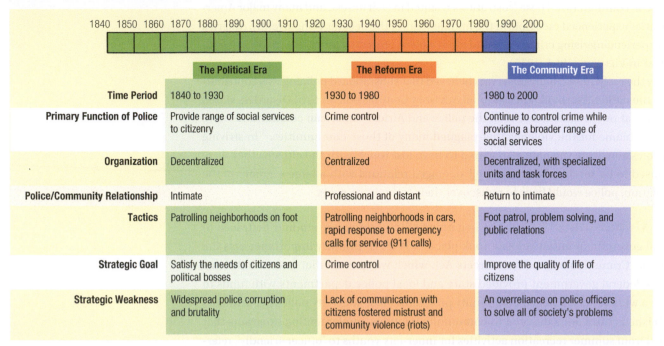

	The Political Era	The Reform Era	The Community Era
Time Period	1840 to 1930	1930 to 1980	1980 to 2000
Primary Function of Police	Provide range of social services to citizenry	Crime control	Continue to control crime while providing a broader range of social services
Organization	Decentralized	Centralized	Decentralized, with specialized units and task forces
Police/Community Relationship	Intimate	Professional and distant	Return to intimate
Tactics	Patrolling neighborhoods on foot	Patrolling neighborhoods in cars, rapid response to emergency calls for service (911 calls)	Foot patrol, problem solving, and public relations
Strategic Goal	Satisfy the needs of citizens and political bosses	Crime control	Improve the quality of life of citizens
Strategic Weakness	Widespread police corruption and brutality	Lack of communication with citizens fostered mistrust and community violence (riots)	An overreliance on police officers to solve all of society's problems

Sources: Adapted from George L. Kelling and Mark H. Moore, "From Political to Reform to Community: The Evolving Strategy of Police," in *Community Policing: Rhetoric or Reality*, eds. Jack R. Greene and Stephen D. Mastrofski (New York: Praeger Publishers, 1991), 14-15, 22–23; plus authors' updates. Reproduced with permission of Greenwood Publishing Group, Inc., Westport, Connecticut.

Police departments across the nation are increasingly relying on technology to put this knowledge to good use.

Thanks to data gathered by its Real-Time Analysis Critical Response Division, for example, the Los Angeles Police Department (LAPD) recently was able to determine that its Newton division was a "hot spot" for drug crime and gang activity. In response, the LAPD launched Operation LASER, which flooded the Newton area with more patrol officers. Over a ten-month period, Operation LASER resulted in a dramatic decrease in gun-related murders and other crimes, including robbery and aggravated assault.[35]

The LAPD's approach to crime in Newton is known as predictive policing, or **intelligence-led policing** (ILP), because it relies on data—or intelligence—concerning past crime patterns to predict future crime patterns. In theory, ILP is relatively simple. Just as commercial fishers are most successful when they concentrate on the areas of the ocean where the fish are, law enforcement does well to focus its scarce resources on the areas where the most crime occurs. With programs such as LASER and other "hot spot" technologies that we will discuss in the next chapter, police administrators are able to deploy small forces to specific locations, rather than blanketing an entire city with random patrols. Doing "more with less" in this manner is a particularly important consideration as police budgets shrink around the country.

"Big Data" If ILP is the crime-fighting strategy of the future, then *real-time crime centers (RTCCs)* are the police departments of the future. Designed to gather data from a wide variety of sources, these centers employ ILP principles to speed up emergency response times and enhance crime-solving capabilities.

Learning Objective 3 Explain how intelligence-led policing works and how it benefits modern police departments.

Intelligence-Led Policing An approach that measures the risk of criminal behavior associated with certain individuals or locations so as to predict when and where such criminal behavior is most likely to occur in the future.

The Houston RTCC's primary function, for example, is to monitor high-priority 911 calls for service and then provide the responding officers with crucial information regarding the suspect.[36] Twenty-two information technology specialists can search through footage from hundreds of surveillance cameras situated throughout the city and multiple drivers'-license and license-plate databases. They can also retrieve open public source data such as property tax records for financial information on homeowners.

The Beware program, utilized by the RTCC in Fresno, California, takes intelligence-gathering possibilities even further. This program scours the Internet for information on a suspect, searching not only for arrest records but also for the suspect's activity on commercial databases, deep Web searches, and social media postings. It then calculates a threat "score" for police officers on the scene to consider before approaching the suspect.[37]

The Warrior-Guardian Split   Some law enforcement veterans are wary of the influence that "Big Data" has gained within the profession. "If it becomes all about the science," says Los Angeles Police Department deputy chief Michael Downing, "I worry we'll lose the important nuances."[38]

The continued importance of the human factor within law enforcement culture is, however, confirmed by what Samuel Walker calls the "war going on for the soul of policing in America."[39] One side of this war promotes protecting law enforcement officers and citizens through aggression and use of force. The other side concentrates on de-escalation and avoidance of conflict.

The Warrior Mentality   In the summer of 2016, a police office named Jeronimo Yanez shot and killed an unarmed African American driver named Philando Castile following a traffic stop in St. Anthony, Minnesota. In the public uproar that followed, some pinpointed a training course entitled "The Bulletproof Warrior" that Yanez had completed two years earlier. The course advocated an aggressive approach to policing while emphasizing the constant dangers of police work. The course booklet, for example, warns that "the will to survive is often trained out of the psyches of" law enforcement agents and rejects the "myth" that "an officer must use the 'least intrusive' option when using force."[40]

This hyperaggressive style of policing is often referred to as **militarism,** as it meshes military training and weaponry with traditional law enforcement strategies. The militarizing of local police departments started with the Los Angeles Police Department's first Special Weapons and Tactics (SWAT) units in the late 1960s. These units, trained and armed like special military forces, were initially designed to deal with extreme circumstances such as riots, hostage situations, and active-shooter scenarios. Today, SWAT teams are used around 50,000 times a year, most often to serve drug-related warrants in private homes.[41]

Militarism The use of military training, tactics, and weaponry in policing.

▲ Members of a police SWAT team search for a suspected terrorist in Watertown, Massachusetts. **What are the arguments for and against providing local police with military training and weaponry? Do you agree that such tactics promote mistrust of law enforcement? Explain your answers.** Spencer Platt/Getty Images News/Getty Images

The Guardian Mentality To counterbalance militarism and the warrior approach, many law enforcement agencies across the country are turning toward a guardian mentality of policing. As the name implies, the guardian approach stresses nonconfrontational tactics to strengthen the bonds between police officers and the communities that they "guard over." In the words of Seth Stoughton, a former police officer who now teaches law at the University of South Carolina, guardians are officers "who treat people humanely, who show them respect, who explain their actions, [and who] can improve the perceptions of officers, or their department, even when they are arresting someone."[42]

The Challenges of Counterterrorism

The trend toward SWAT unit militarization intensified after the terrorist attacks of September 11, 2001, when the federal government began to consider local police the "front lines" of a new kind of war. Since 2001, the Department of Defense (DOD) has donated billions of dollars worth of military equipment to local police departments in all fifty states. In addition, the DOD distributed more than $34 billion in "terrorism grants" to local departments to purchase military gear between 2001 and 2014.[43]

In the period immediately following the 9/11 attacks, local police officers relied on the "ask, tell, make" (ATM) strategy when interacting with terrorist suspects. In other words, an officer started by "asking" the suspect to do something. If this approach did not work, the officer would "tell" the suspect what to do. Finally, the officer "made" the suspect comply with the initial order. As one police trainer admits, many officers would skip "ask" and move directly to "tell" and "make."[44] As the nation moves closer to the twentieth anniversary of 9/11, however, counterterrorism strategies are relying as much on ILP and community outreach as on militarism and the warrior mentality.

Strengths and Limitations On a local level, police departments engage in a variety of antiterrorism tactics. More than one hundred local and state police organizations now operate intelligence units, with at least one in each state. The New York Police Department, in a class by itself, has a permanent counterterrorism force, known as the Critical Response Command, made up of nearly 500 members. This group of experienced officers engages in "hostile surveillance" of suspects, and its arsenal includes special cars mounted with semiautomatic assault rifles.

Most local police departments, however, do not have the resources to make counterterrorism a priority. The Federal Bureau of Investigation (FBI), even with its significant resources, also struggles in this field. FBI agents conduct 10,000 assessments of terrorist suspects each year and are engaged in about 1,000 open investigations of potential "homegrown violent extremists" at any given time.[45] Nonetheless, the agency has been unable to prevent major domestic terrorist attacks in Boston, Orlando, Garland (Texas), and New York City in recent years, despite having previously investigated the suspect in each of these cases.

Fusion Centers Clearly, the best way for local and federal law enforcement agencies to meet the challenges of counterterrorism is through cooperation. With this in mind, the federal government has created seventy-eight **fusion centers** throughout the United States. These centers are designed to enable all levels of law enforcement to share intelligence on homeland security matters. They have also helped federal and local law enforcement team up to prevent crimes involving bomb threats, drug and sex trafficking, and murder.[46]

Fusion Center A collaborative effort between two or more agencies to prevent and respond to criminal and terrorist activities.

Public Relations   As the Department of Homeland Security's "See Something, Say Something" campaign suggests, law enforcement also relies on tips from the public for information about possible terrorist attacks. Beyond this somewhat passive public relations strategy, some police agencies are taking more proactive steps to sow trust and discourage homegrown radicalization.

In Dearborn, Michigan, where a third of the population is of Arab descent, police chief Ron Haddad regularly visits schools and local mosques to ask for help. According to Haddad, on several occasions parents have contacted his department to report suspicious behavior by their sons.[47] Nationally, the FBI has enlisted community leaders to create "Shared Responsibility Committees" in cities with at-risk populations. These committees bring together religious figures, social workers, and school counselors with the goal of "getting to" vulnerable young men before they fall under the influence of extremist ideologies.

Social Media Strategies   Some observers, particularly within American Muslim communities, suspect that the FBI's Shared Responsibility Committees are a smokescreen for intelligence-gathering.[48] To counteract these sorts of suspicions, and to generally build bridges with the public, the FBI operates a Facebook page and an official Twitter account. Indeed, the vast majority of all law enforcement agencies in the United States use social media to interact with the communities they serve.[49]

Law enforcement agencies also use social media to fight crime. It has become commonplace for police agents to create fake profiles online as part of criminal investigations. Federal drug agents, for example, have set up false Facebook pages using the identities of known drug dealers to "friend" their unwitting criminal associates. In New Jersey, authorities operated a fake Instagram account to fool a suspected burglar into sharing photos of stolen cash and jewelry, leading to his arrest. On at least three occasions, the FBI has taken clandestine control of a child pornography website in the hope of uncovering users who would otherwise be protected by anonymity settings.[50]

ETHICS CHALLENGE

The user agreements of both Facebook and Instagram ban law enforcement agents from going "undercover" online by impersonating others or setting up fake accounts. As you just read, this has not stopped police officers from engaging in the practice. Is this an ethical means of conducting a criminal investigation? Why or why not?

Recruitment and Training: Becoming a Police Officer

In 1961, police expert James H. Chenoweth commented that the methods used to hire police officers had changed little since 1829, when the Metropolitan Police of London was created.[51] The past half-century, however, has seen a number of improvements in the way that police administrators handle the task of **recruitment,** or the development of a pool of qualified applicants from which to select new officers.

Efforts have been made to diversify police rolls, and recruits in most police departments undergo a substantial array of tests and screens—discussed next—to determine

Recruitment The process by which law enforcement agencies develop a pool of qualified applicants from which to select new employees.

their aptitude. Furthermore, annual starting salaries that can exceed $70,000, along with the opportunities offered by an interesting profession in the public service field, have attracted a wide variety of applicants to police work.

Basic Requirements

The selection process involves a number of steps, and each police department has a different method of choosing candidates. Most agencies, however, require at a minimum that a police officer:

- Be a U.S. citizen.
- Not have been convicted of a felony.
- Have or be eligible to have a driver's license in the state where the department is located.
- Be at least twenty-one years of age.
- Meet weight and eyesight requirements.

In addition, few departments will accept candidates older than forty-five years of age.

Background Checks and Tests

Beyond these minimum requirements, police departments usually engage in extensive background checks, including drug tests; a review of applicants' educational, military, and driving records; credit checks; interviews with spouses, acquaintances, and previous employers; and a background search to determine whether applicants have been convicted of any criminal acts. Police agencies generally impose physical requirements as well: Normally, applicants must be able to pass a physical agility or fitness test.

In some departments, particularly those that serve large metropolitan areas, applicants must take a psychological screening test to determine if they are suited to law enforcement work. Generally, such tests measure applicants' ability to handle stress, follow rules, use good judgment, and avoid off-duty behavior that would reflect negatively on the department.[52]

Along these same lines, many American police agencies now review an applicant's social media activity on sources such as Facebook, Instagram, and Twitter. "A single posting on Facebook in poor taste won't automatically eliminate someone from our hiring process," explained then Arlington (Texas) Deputy Chief Lauretta Hill. "But if we see a pattern of behavior or something that raises a red flag, it lets us know that we need to dig a little deeper during our background investigation."[53]

Educational Requirements

One of the most dramatic differences between today's police recruits and those of several generations ago is their level of education. In the 1920s, when August Vollmer began promoting the need for higher education in police officers, few had attended college. In the 2010s, 84 percent of all local police departments require at least a high school diploma, and 10 percent require a degree from a two-year college.[54] Although a four-year degree is necessary for certain elite law enforcement positions, such as a Federal Bureau of Investigation special agent, only about 4 percent of large local police departments have such a requirement.[55] Those officers with four-year degrees do, however, generally enjoy an advantage in hiring and promotion, and often receive higher salaries than their less educated co-employees.

Not all police observers believe that education is a necessity for police officers. In the words of one police officer, "Effective street cops learn their skills on the job, not in a classroom."[56] By emphasizing a college degree, say some, police departments discourage those who would make solid officers but lack the necessary education. Indeed, more than half of local police departments that do have a degree requirement will consider military service as an alternative.[57]

Probationary Period A period of time at the beginning of a police officer's career during which she or he may be fired without cause.

Training

If an applicant successfully navigates the application process, he or she will be hired on a *probationary* basis. During this **probationary period,** which can last from six to eighteen months depending on the department, the recruit can be fired without cause if he or she proves inadequate to the challenges of police work. Almost every state requires that police recruits pass through a training period while on probation. During this time, they are taught the basics of police work and are under constant supervision by superiors. The training period usually has two components: the police academy and field training.

Learning Objective 4 Identify the differences between the police academy and field training as learning tools for recruits.

Academy Training

The *police academy,* run by either the state or a police agency, provides recruits with a controlled, militarized environment in which they receive their introduction to the world of the police officer. They are taught the laws of search, seizure, arrest, and interrogation; how and when to use weapons; the procedures for securing a crime scene and interviewing witnesses; first aid; self-defense; and other essentials of police work. About half of all police academies favor a *stress-based* approach to training. This approach relies on a military model that emphasizes intensive physical demands and psychological pressures.[58] (See Figure 5.2 for a breakdown of a standard police academy curriculum.)

FIGURE 5.2 The Main Elements of a Law Enforcement Academy Curriculum

As this figure shows, a typical police academy cadet spends most of her or his time learning about the basic necessities of police work such as defensive tactics, firearms, and patrol procedures.

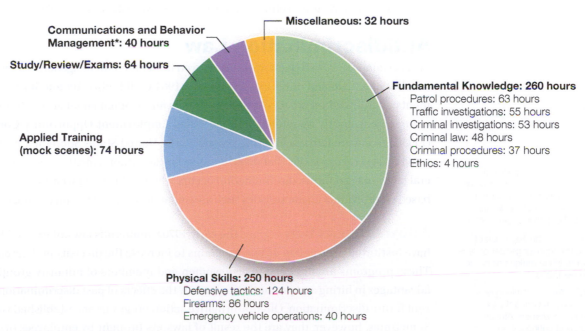

Total Hours: 720

Communications and Behavior Management*: 40 hours

Miscellaneous: 32 hours

Study/Review/Exams: 64 hours

Fundamental Knowledge: 260 hours
Patrol procedures: 63 hours
Traffic investigations: 55 hours
Criminal investigations: 53 hours
Criminal law: 48 hours
Criminal procedures: 37 hours
Ethics: 4 hours

Applied Training (mock scenes): 74 hours

Physical Skills: 250 hours
Defensive tactics: 124 hours
Firearms: 86 hours
Emergency vehicle operations: 40 hours

* This title refers to training in leadership and crisis management skills.

Source: Adapted from Sue Rahr and Stephen K. Rice, *New Perspectives in Policing* (Washington, D.C.: National Institute of Justice, April 2015), Figure 1, page 8.

In the Field Field training takes place outside the confines of the police academy. A recruit is paired with an experienced police officer known as a field training officer (FTO). The goal of field training is to help rookies apply the concepts they have learned in the academy "to the streets," with the FTO playing a supervisory role to make sure that nothing goes awry. According to many, the academy introduces recruits to the formal rules of police work, but field training gives the rookies their first taste of the informal rules. In fact, the initial advice to recruits from some FTOs is often along the lines of "O.K., kid. Forget everything you learned in the classroom. You're in the real world now." Nonetheless, the academy is a critical component in the learning process, as it provides rookies with a road map to the job.

ETHICS CHALLENGE

How much impact do you think ethics training in a police academy will have on the future ethical behavior of recruits? Can ethics be taught, or is each person's concept of "right and wrong" permanently shaped in childhood? Explain your answer.

Women and Minorities in Policing Today

For most of this nation's history, the typical American police officer was white and male. As recently as 1968, African Americans represented only 5 percent of all sworn officers in the United States, and the percentage of "women in blue" was even lower.[59] Only within the past thirty years has this situation been addressed, with many police departments actively trying to recruit women, as well as African Americans, Latinos, Asian Americans, and members of other minority groups. The result, as you will see, has been a steady though not spectacular increase in the diversity of the nation's police forces. When it comes to issues of gender, race, and ethnicity, however, mere statistics rarely tell the entire story.

Antidiscrimination Law

To a certain extent, external forces have driven law enforcement agencies to increase the number of female and minority recruits. The 1964 Civil Rights Act and its 1972 amendments guaranteed members of minority groups and women equal access to jobs in law enforcement, partly by establishing the Equal Employment Opportunity Commission (EEOC) to ensure fairness in hiring practices. The United States Supreme Court has also ruled on several occasions that discrimination by law enforcement agencies violates federal law.[60] In legal terms, discrimination occurs when hiring and promotion decisions are based on individual characteristics such as gender or race, and not on job-related factors.

Affirmative Action Since the early 1970s, numerous law enforcement agencies have instituted affirmative action programs to increase the diversity of their employees. These programs are designed to give women and members of minority groups certain advantages in hiring and promotion to remedy the effects of past discrimination and prevent future discrimination. Often, affirmative action programs are established voluntarily. Sometimes, however, they are the result of lawsuits brought by employees or potential employees who believe that the employer has discriminated against them. (See this chapter's *Mastering Concepts* for an overview of how affirmative action works.)

Field Training The segment of a police recruit's training in which he or she is removed from the classroom and placed on the beat, under the supervision of a senior officer.

Discrimination The illegal use of characteristics such as gender or race by employers when making hiring or promotion decisions.

Affirmative Action A hiring or promotion policy favoring those groups, such as women, African Americans, and Latinos, who have suffered from discrimination in the past or continue to suffer from discrimination.

Affirmative Action in Law Enforcement

When considering the influence of affirmative action on law enforcement hiring practices, it is helpful to understand the following concepts and terms.

- At their core, affirmative action programs are designed as remedies for past discrimination. As such, they must involve an "active effort" to improve the diversity of a law enforcement agency, rather than a "passive effort" to give all candidates an equal opportunity to be hired.

- The first step of any affirmative action is for officials to determine the desired level of female and minority group representation.

- Next, the agency must actively pursue female and minority recruits in advertising job openings. It must also ensure that all tests and educational requirements are designed to be free of discriminatory impact.

- Creating **quotas**, or a fixed number of desired female or minority recruits, can be problematic, as it gives the impression that gender, race, or ethnicity is more important than other qualifications in the hiring process.

- To avoid **reverse discrimination**, or policies that automatically eliminate whites or males from consideration, departments should avoid rigid quotas and consider diversity as only one factor in the hiring process.

- If a court does find that a particular law agency has been discriminating against female and minority applicants, it may implement a **consent decree** to remedy the situation. Under a consent decree, the law enforcement agency agrees to meet certain numerical goals in hiring women and members of minority groups. If it fails to meet these goals, it is punished with a fine or some other sanction.

Source: John S. Dempsey and Linda S. Forst, *An Introduction to Policing, Eighth Edition* (Boston: Cengage Learning, 2016), 200–201.

A great deal of evidence shows that affirmative action programs increase police force diversity. In Pittsburgh, for example, the percentage of female police officers rose from 1 percent to 27 percent after an affirmative action program went into effect, but it began to decline as soon as the program ended.[61] In Chicago, the African American share of new police hires rose from 10 percent to 40 percent in just two years after the implementation of a consent decree.[62] At the same time, a stigma may sometimes be attached to persons believed to have benefited from affirmative action. "I don't want to be in a department where I was hired because of my skin color," said one African American police applicant in Dayton, Ohio. "I want it because I earned it."[63]

Recruiting Challenges   In some instances, legal action spurs changes in recruitment practices. In May 2016, for example, the city of Lubbock, Texas, settled an employment discrimination lawsuit with the federal government by agreeing to update its written examination for police recruits. Between 2010 and 2015, using the old version of the test, 88 percent of white applicants were successful, compared to only 68 percent of Latino applicants.[64] These statistics, federal lawyers concluded, proved that the test had a discriminatory impact.[65]

Regardless of whether legal action is involved, increasing diversity in recruiting is often difficult. According to Delores Brown of the Center on Race, Crime and Justice at the John Jay College of Justice in New York City, two factors work against such efforts. First, mistrust of the police in many minority communities discourages members of those communities from considering law enforcement as a viable career choice. Second, members of minority groups are targeted by police for low-level crimes, leaving them with criminal records that disqualify them from even applying for law enforcement positions.[66]

Such obstacles can, however, be overcome. In Atlanta, African Americans hold more than half of the police department's leadership positions. Former Atlanta police chief

George Turner identifies this evidence of upward mobility as a main reason the city's police force is 60 percent black.[67] Operating under a voluntary consent decree requiring that it increase diversity, the Rochester (New York) Police Department has focused recruiting efforts on local high school seniors and soldiers who are leaving military service. Between 2011 and 2015, 65 percent of the department's new hires were women and members of minority groups.[68]

Working Women: Gender and Law Enforcement

In 1987, about 7.6 percent of all local police officers were women. By 2013, that percentage had risen to 12.2 percent—17.6 percent in departments serving populations of more than one million people.[69] That increase seems less impressive, however, when one considers that women make up more than half of the population of the United States, meaning that they are still severely underrepresented in law enforcement.

Barriers to Entry
There are several reasons for the low levels of women serving as police officers in the United States. First and foremost, our culture generally sees policing as "man's work." For that reason, many qualified women never consider entering the field.

Additionally, generally speaking, female police recruits are more likely to fail physical ability exams than are their male counterparts. In the Lubbock, Texas, lawsuit mentioned earlier, the federal government noted that 62 percent of female applicants failed the city police department's physical fitness test, compared with only 19 percent of male applicants.[70] The lawsuit pointed out, however, that no research has shown a connection between physical strength and success as a police officer. In response, the Lubbock Police Department adjusted its physical exam. To pass, men now have to bench 92 percent of their body weight and run 1.5 miles in 13 minutes, 33 seconds, while women have to bench 49 percent of their body weight and run 1.5 miles in 17 minutes, 15 seconds.[71]

Barriers to Getting Ahead
When women do find employment in law enforcement, their levels of job satisfaction and promotion are often stifled by lack of role models. According to the National Association of Women Law Enforcement Executives, only about 220 women hold top leadership positions in America's approximately 14,000 local police agencies.[72] Consequently, female police officers have few superiors who might be able to mentor them in what can be a hostile work environment.

In addition to the dangers and pressures facing all law enforcement agents, which we will discuss in the next chapter, women must deal with an added layer of scrutiny. Many male police officers feel that their female counterparts are mentally soft, physically weak, and generally unsuited for the rigors of the job. At the same time, male officers often try to protect female officers by keeping them out of hazardous situations, thereby denying the women the opportunity to prove themselves.[73]

Tokenism
Women in law enforcement also face the problem of *tokenism*, or the belief that they have been hired or promoted to fulfill diversity requirements and have not earned their positions. Tokenism creates pressure to prove the stereotypes wrong. When comparing the arrest patterns of male and female officers over a twelve-month period in Cincinnati, Ohio, for example, researchers noted several interesting patterns. Although overall arrest rates were similar, female officers were much more likely than their male

Sexual Harassment A repeated pattern of unwelcome sexual advances and/or obscene remarks. Under certain circumstances, sexual harassment is illegal and can be the basis for a civil lawsuit.

counterparts to arrest suspects who were "non-deferential" or hostile. Also, the presence of a supervisor greatly increased the likelihood that a female officer would make an arrest.

Such patterns, the researchers concluded, show that female officers feel pressure to demonstrate that they are "good cops" who cannot be intimidated because of their gender.[74] One officer said that her female colleagues "go into that physical-arrest mode quicker [because] you want to prove that you can do it."[75] Similarly, women who rise through the law enforcement ranks often face questions concerning their worthiness. According to Tampa (Florida) police chief Jane Castor, "No matter how qualified you are or how much experience you have . . . people will say that you were promoted—in part, if not fully—because you're a woman."[76]

In fact, most of the negative attitudes toward women police officers are based on prejudice rather than actual experience. A number of studies have shown that there is very little difference between the performance of men and women in uniform.[77] (For more on this topic, see the feature *Myth vs Reality— Women Make Bad Cops*.)

Sexual Harassment
According to a female officer interviewed by researcher Teresa Lynn, "The guys can view you as a sex object."[78] Anecdotal evidence suggests that this attitude is commonplace in police departments and often leads to **sexual harassment** of female police officers. Sexual harassment involves a pattern of unwelcome sexual advances or obscene remarks. Such conduct can impact the recipient's career. One victim of sexual comments and physical contact by a superior said that when she rebuffed his advances, "he would retaliate by criticizing my reports or judgment."[79]

Over a nine-month period in 2010, the National Police Misconduct Statistics and Reporting Project confirmed eighty-six incidents of sexual harassment in police departments nationwide.[80] Self-reported surveys, however, suggest that the actual incidence is much higher, with most incidents going unreported.[81]

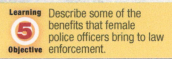

MYTH vs REALITY

Women Make Bad Cops

The Myth The perception that women are not physically strong enough to be effective law enforcement officers prevails both in the public mind and within police forces themselves. Criminologist Susan Martin has found that policewomen are under "constant pressure to demonstrate their competence and effectiveness vis-à-vis their male counterparts." One female police officer describes her experience:

> Learning Objective 5 — Describe some of the benefits that female police officers bring to law enforcement.

> I was the smallest person. . . . [The male officers] didn't feel I could do the job. They tried to get me into fighting situations to see if I would back down. They told me, "You know, if you aren't strong enough or are going to be a coward, we have to find out fast and get you out of here."

The Reality Female police officers are certainly capable of acts of bravery and physical prowess. In fact, a number of studies have shown that policewomen can be as effective as men in most situations, and often are more effective than men. This research indicates that female police officers discharge their firearms and use unnecessary physical force much less often than male police officers do and that they face significantly fewer civilian complaints. In fact, male officers are nine times as likely to be disciplined for excessive force as are female officers. Of seventy-seven law enforcement agents charged with homicide for an on-duty shooting from 2005 to 2016, only three were women.

Studies also show that women in blue are more likely to see their job as a public service than men do, and are more proficient at tension de-escalation, trust building, and communication. Citizens appear to prefer dealing with a female police officer rather than a male during service calls—especially those that involve domestic violence. In general, policewomen are less aggressive and more likely to reduce the potential for a violent situation by relying on verbal skills rather than their authority as law enforcement agents. "All the things people are saying they want in their police forces, women are already naturally good at," said Penny Harrington, a former police chief of Portland, Oregon, and a co-founder of the National Center for Women and Policing.

FOR CRITICAL ANALYSIS

Do you believe that female police officers can be just as effective as men in protecting citizens from criminal behavior? Why or why not?

▲ A female New York City police recruit tries on her bulletproof vest during a training session. Mario Tama/Getty Images News/Getty Images

Despite having to deal with problems such as sexual harassment, outdated stereotypes, and tokenism, female police officers have generally shown that they are capable law enforcement officers, willing to take great risks if necessary to do their job. The names of nearly three hundred women are included on the National Law Enforcement Memorial in Washington, D.C.

Minority Report: Race and Ethnicity in Law Enforcement

As Figure 5.3 shows, like women, members of minority groups have been slowly increasing their presence in local police departments since the late 1980s. A closer look at the statistics shows that the percentage of African American police officers has remained relatively stable since 1993, while the numbers of Latino Americans and Asian Americans on police rolls nearly doubled during that same period.[82]

By most measures, members of minority groups are better represented than women in policing. Cities such as Atlanta and Washington, D.C., have local police departments that closely match their civilian populations in terms of diversity. Furthermore, in 2013, nearly one in three police recruits nationwide were members of an ethnic or racial minority.[83] On other measures, such as promotion, minorities in law enforcement continue to seek parity.[84]

Double Marginality   During a protest outside Fourth Precinct police headquarters in north Minneapolis, a young African American woman turned her attention to a black police officer guarding the station. "[You're] helping them kill us, your own race!" she shouted, calling the officer an Uncle Tom and encouraging him to commit suicide.[85]

FIGURE 5.3 Police Diversity in American Cities

This graph shows that the percentage of members of some minority groups that make up local police department forces in the United States has been steadily growing since the late 1980s.

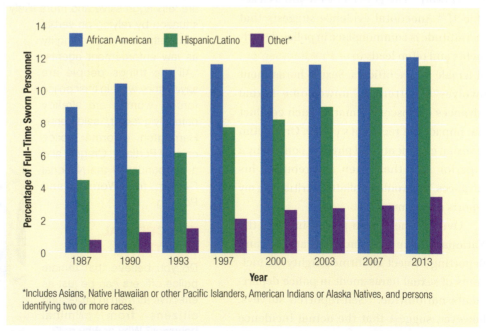

*Includes Asians, Native Hawaiian or other Pacific Islanders, American Indians or Alaska Natives, and persons identifying two or more races.

Source: Bureau of Justice Statistics, *Local Police Departments, 2013: Personnel, Policies, and Practices* (Washington, D.C.: U.S. Department of Justice, May 2015), Figure 5, page 5.

The woman's insults highlight the problem of **double marginality.** This term refers to a situation in which minority officers are viewed with suspicion by both sides:

1. White police officers believe that minority officers will give members of their own race or ethnicity better treatment on the streets.
2. Those same minority officers face hostility from members of their own community who are under the impression that black and Latino officers are traitors to their race or ethnicity.

In response, minority officers may feel the need to act more harshly toward minority offenders to prove that they are not biased in favor of their own racial or ethnic group.[86]

The Benefits of a Diverse Police Force

In 1986, Supreme Court justice John Paul Stevens spoke for many in the criminal justice system when he observed that "an integrated police force could develop a better relationship [with a racially diverse citizenry] and therefore do a more effective job of maintaining law and order than a force composed of white officers."[87] To illustrate, consider that when a mostly white police force in a primarily African American neighborhood uses aggressive law enforcement tactics, such as frequent stops of pedestrians and drivers for minor violations, mistrust can result. Consider, too, that many American cities in which blacks make up at least 35 percent of the population have disproportionately white police forces.[88] These conditions can lead to explosive consequences. In recent years, Baltimore, Cleveland, and Philadelphia have experienced racially charged protests after white officers used force against black citizens that was perceived to be excessive and unfair.

Despite the effects of double marginality, African American officers may have more credibility in a predominantly black neighborhood than white police officers, leading to better community-police relations and a greater ability to solve and prevent crimes. Certainly, in the Mexican American communities typical of border states such as Arizona, Texas, and California, many Latino officers are able to gather information that would be very difficult for non-Spanish-speaking officers to collect. Finally, the best argument for a diverse police force is that members of minority groups represent a broad source of talent in this country, and such talent can only enhance the overall effectiveness of American law enforcement.

Learning Objective 6 Identify the main advantage of a racially and ethnically diverse police force.

Public and Private Law Enforcement

On January 9, 2017, Markeith Loyd killed Orlando police lieutenant Debra Clayton outside a shopping center as she tried to arrest him for murder. Over the next nine days, hundreds of law enforcement agents took part in a manhunt for Loyd, including officers from the Orange County Sheriff's Department, the Orlando Police Department, the Florida Department of Law Enforcement, the Federal Bureau of Investigation, and the U.S. Marshals Service. Loyd was finally captured when several dozen police officers, sheriffs' deputies, and state and federal agents surrounded him in an abandoned house on Orlando's west side.

As the effort to capture Loyd shows, Americans are served by a multitude of police organizations. Overall, there are about 18,000 law enforcement agencies in the United States, employing about 880,000 officers.[89] For the most part, these agencies operate on three different levels: local, state, and federal. Each level has its own set of responsibilities, which we shall discuss starting with local police departments.

Double Marginality The situation in which minority law enforcement officers face suspicion both from their white colleagues and from members of the minority community to which they belong.

Municipal Law Enforcement Agencies

About three-quarters of all *sworn officers*, or officers with arrest powers, work in police departments serving cities with populations of under 1 million residents.[90] While the New York City Police Department employs about 35,000 police personnel, 90 percent of all local police departments have fifty or fewer law enforcement officers.[91]

Of the three levels of law enforcement, municipal agencies have the broadest authority to apprehend criminal suspects, maintain order, and provide services to the community. Whether the local officer is part of a large force or the only law enforcement officer in the community, he or she is usually responsible for a wide spectrum of duties, from responding to noise complaints to investigating homicides.

Larger police departments often assign officers to specialized task forces or units that deal with a particular crime or area of concern. For example, in Washington, D.C., the police department features a Lesbian, Gay, Bisexual, and Transgender (LGBT) Liaison Unit that handles anti-LGBT crimes in the city. The Knoxville (Tennessee) Police Department has a squad devoted to combating Internet crimes against children, while the three hundred officers assigned to the New York City Police Department's Emergency Service Unit are trained in suicide rescue, hostage negotiation, and SCUBA operations.

Sheriffs and County Law Enforcement

The **sheriff** is a very important figure in American law enforcement. Almost every one of the more than three thousand counties in the United States (except those in Alaska and Connecticut) has a sheriff. In every state except Rhode Island and Hawaii, sheriffs are elected by members of the community for two- or four-year terms and are paid a salary set by the state legislature or county board.

As elected officials who do not necessarily need a background in law enforcement, modern sheriffs resemble their counterparts from the political era of policing in many ways. Simply stated, the sheriff is also a politician. When a new sheriff is elected, she or he will sometimes repay political debts by appointing new deputies or promoting those who have given her or him support.

Size and Responsibility of Sheriffs' Departments
Like municipal police forces, sheriffs' departments vary in size. The largest is the Los Angeles County Sheriff's Department, with more than 9,200 deputies. Of the esimated 3,012 sheriffs' departments in the country, sixteen employ more than 1,000 officers, while about 450 employ fewer than ten.[92]

Keep in mind that cities, which are served by municipal police departments, often exist within counties, which are served by sheriffs' departments. Therefore, police officers and sheriffs' deputies often find themselves policing the same geographical areas. Police departments, however, are generally governed by a local political entity, such as a mayor's office, while most sheriffs' departments are assigned their duties by state law. About 80 percent of all sheriffs' departments are responsible for investigating violent crimes in their jurisdictions. Other common responsibilities of a sheriff's department include:

- Investigating drug crimes.
- Maintaining the county jail.
- Carrying out civil and criminal processes within county lines, such as serving eviction notices and court summonses.

- Keeping order in the county courthouse.
- Enforcing orders of the court, such as overseeing the isolation of a jury during a trial.[93]

It is easy to confuse sheriffs' departments and local police departments. Both law enforcement agencies are responsible for many of the same tasks, including crime investigation and routine patrol. There are differences, however. Sheriffs' departments are more likely to be involved in county court and jail operations and to perform certain services such as search and rescue. Local police departments, for their part, are more likely to perform traffic-related functions than are sheriffs' departments.[94]

▲ Local police officer Todd Geist of Medicine Lodge, Kansas, diverts traffic from a road closed by a grass fire. **In what ways are local police departments and sheriffs' departments similar? In what ways do these two law enforcement agencies differ?** AP Photo/Travis Morisse/*The Hutchinson News*

The County Coroner Another elected official on the county level is the  coroner, or medical examiner. Duties vary from county to county, but the coroner has a general mandate to investigate "all sudden, unexplained, unnatural, or suspicious deaths" reported to the office. The coroner is ultimately responsible for determining the cause of death in these cases.

Coroners also perform autopsies and assist other law enforcement agencies in homicide investigations. For example, when fifteen-year-old Andreayah McBain's body was found partially burned outside a vacant mobile home in Stephenson County, Illinois, the local coroner was required to determine the cause of death. By finding that McBain had overdosed on a combination of morphine, Xanax, and amitriptyline, the coroner helped local law enforcement track down another teenage girl and, on May 2, 2016, charge her in connection with McBain's death.

State Police and Highway Patrols

The most visible state law enforcement agency is the state police or highway patrol agency. Historically, state police agencies were created for three reasons:

1. To assist local police agencies, which often did not have adequate resources or training to handle their law enforcement tasks.
2. To investigate criminal activities that crossed jurisdictional boundaries (such as when bank robbers committed a crime in one county and then fled to another part of the state).
3. To provide law enforcement in rural and other areas that did not have local or county police agencies.

Today, there are twenty-three state police agencies and twenty-six highway patrols in the United States. State police agencies have statewide jurisdiction and are authorized to perform a wide variety of law enforcement tasks. Often, they provide the same services as city or county police departments and are restricted only by the boundaries of the state.

In contrast, highway patrols have limited authority. Their duties are generally defined either by their jurisdiction or by the specific types of offenses they have the authority to control. As their name suggests, most highway patrols concentrate primarily on regulating

Coroner The medical examiner of a county, usually elected by popular vote.

traffic. Specifically, they enforce traffic laws and investigate traffic accidents. Furthermore, they usually limit their activity to patrolling state and federal highways.

Limited-Purpose Law Enforcement Agencies

Even with the agencies just discussed, a number of states have found that certain law enforcement areas need more specific attention. As a result, a wide variety of limited-purpose law enforcement agencies have sprung up in the fifty states. For example, most states have an alcoholic beverage control commission (ABC), or a similarly named organization, which oversees the sale and distribution of alcoholic beverages. The ABC monitors alcohol distributors to ensure that all taxes are paid on the beverages and is responsible for revoking or suspending the liquor licenses of establishments that have broken relevant laws.

Many states have fish and game organizations that enforce all laws relating to hunting and fishing. Motor vehicle compliance (MVC) agencies monitor interstate carriers or trucks to make sure that they are in compliance with state and federal laws. MVC officers generally operate the weigh stations commonly found on interstate highways. Other limited-purpose law enforcement agencies deal with white-collar and computer crime, regulate nursing homes, and provide training to local police departments.

Federal Law Enforcement Agencies

Employees of federal agencies do not make up a large proportion of the nation's law enforcement personnel. In fact, the New York City Police Department has about one-fifth as many employees as all of the federal law enforcement agencies combined. Nevertheless, the influence of these federal agencies is substantial.

Unlike local police departments, which must deal with all forms of crime, federal agencies have been authorized, usually by Congress, to enforce specific laws or attend to specific situations. The U.S. Coast Guard, for example, patrols the nation's waterways, while U.S. Postal inspectors investigate and prosecute crimes perpetrated through the use of the U.S. mail. In this section, we discuss the elements and duties of the most important federal law enforcement agencies, which are grouped according to the federal department or bureau to which they report. (See Figure 5.4 for the current federal law enforcement "lineup.")

Learning Objective 7 Indicate some of the most important law enforcement agencies under the control of the Department of Homeland Security.

The Department of Homeland Security Comprising twenty-two federal agencies, the Department of Homeland Security (DHS) coordinates national efforts to protect the United States against international and domestic terrorism. While most of the agencies under DHS control are not specifically linked with the criminal justice system, the department does oversee three agencies that play an important role in counterterrorism and crime fighting: U.S. Customs and Border Protection, U.S. Immigration and Customs Enforcement, and the U.S. Secret Service.

U.S. Customs and Border Protection (CBP) The federal government spends about $20 billion annually to enforce immigration law.[95] A large chunk of these funds go to **U.S. Customs and Border Protection (CBP)**, which polices the flow of goods and people across U.S. international borders. In general terms, this means that the agency has two primary goals:

1. To keep undocumented immigrants, illegal drugs, and drug traffickers from crossing our borders.
2. To facilitate the smooth flow of legal trade and travel.

FIGURE 5.4 Federal Law Enforcement Agencies

A number of federal agencies employ law enforcement officers who are authorized to carry firearms and make arrests. The most prominent ones are under the control of the U.S. Department of Homeland Security, the U.S. Department of Justice, and the U.S. Department of the Treasury.

Department of Homeland Security

DEPARTMENT NAME	APPROXIMATE NUMBER OF OFFICERS	MAIN RESPONSIBILITIES
U.S. Customs and Border Protection (CBP)	44,000	• (1) Prevent the illegal flow of people and goods across America's international borders; (2) facilitate legal trade and travel
U.S. Immigration and Customs Enforcement (ICE)	12,000	• Uphold public safety and homeland security by enforcing the nation's immigration and customs laws
U.S. Secret Service	4,500	• (1) Protect the president, the president's family, former presidents and their families, and other high-ranking politicians; (2) combat currency counterfeiters

Department of Justice

DEPARTMENT NAME	APPROXIMATE NUMBER OF OFFICERS	MAIN RESPONSIBILITIES
Federal Bureau of Investigation (FBI)	14,000	• (1) Protect national security by fighting international and domestic terrorism; (2) enforce federal criminal laws such as those dealing with cyber crime, public corruption, and civil rights violations
Drug Enforcement Administration (DEA)	5,200	• Enforce the nation's laws regulating the sale and use of drugs
Bureau of Alcohol, Tobacco, Firearms and Explosives (ATF)	2,500	• (1) Combat the illegal use and trafficking of firearms and explosives; (2) investigate the illegal diversion of alcohol and tobacco products
U.S. Marshals Service	4,300	• (1) Provide security at federal courts; (2) protect government witnesses; (3) apprehend fugitives from the federal court or corrections system

Department of the Treasury

DEPARTMENT NAME	APPROXIMATE NUMBER OF OFFICERS	MAIN RESPONSIBILITIES
Internal Revenue Service (IRS)	3,200	• Investigate potential criminal violations of the nation's tax code

Consequently, CBP officers are stationed at all 328 ports of entry to the United States. The officers have widespread authority to investigate and search all international passengers, whether they arrive on airplanes, ships, or other forms of transportation. The officers also have the responsibility of inspecting luggage and cargo to ensure compliance with immigration and trade laws.

Visa Issues To ensure that those coming into the United States from abroad have permission to do so, CBP officers check documents such as passports and *visas*. (A visa is a document issued by the U.S. State Department that indicates the conditions under which a holder can enter and travel within the United States.) Under the Office of Biometric Identity Management program, most foreigners entering the United States via airports or seaports on visas are subject to fingerprinting and a facial scan using digital

Visa Official authorization allowing a person to travel to and within the issuing country.

photography. Their names are also checked against criminal records and watch lists for suspected terrorists.

Although the program has been effective in recording the entry of foreigners, it has been less successful in following their movements once they are in the United States. Without the cooperation of the visitor, federal officials are unable to confirm when, or if, a foreign visitor has left the country. In fact, the federal government does not know how many undocumented immigrants living in the United States have overstayed their visas, though the number is certainly in the millions. In February 2016, CBP began testing a program to collect biometric data on visitors entering the country by foot at San Diego's Otay Mesa entry. Without biometric screening of foreigners *leaving* the United States, however, it is unlikely that the federal government will be able to effectively track and count visitors who overstay their visas.[96]

Unregulated Border Entry

The U.S. Border Patrol, a branch of the CBP, has the job of policing the Mexican and Canadian borders between official ports of entry. Every year, hundreds of thousands of non–U.S. citizens, unable to legally obtain visas, attempt to enter the country illegally by crossing these large, underpopulated regions, particularly in the southern part of the country. In 2016, Border Patrol agents apprehended about 415,000 illegal border crossers, down from a high of nearly 1.7 million in 2000.[97]

To a large degree, this decrease reflects the recent economic downturn, which removed some of the monetary incentives for foreign nationals looking for work in the United States. In addition, CBP has "shrunk" the border, focusing the efforts of many of the nation's 21,000 Border Patrol agents on areas where illegal crossings are most likely to occur. Agents working those areas are supported by helicopters, drones, surveillance towers, reconnaissance planes with infrared radar, and highly sensitive cameras.

U.S. Immigration and Customs Enforcement (ICE)

The CBP shares responsibility for locating and apprehending persons in the United States illegally with special agents from **U.S. Immigration and Customs Enforcement (ICE).** While the CBP focuses almost exclusively on the nation's borders, ICE has a broader mandate to investigate and to enforce immigration and customs laws. Simply stated, the CBP covers the borders, and ICE covers everything else. ICE's duties include detaining undocumented aliens and deporting (removing) them from the United States, as well as ensuring that those without permission do not work or gain other benefits in this country. ICE is also responsible for investigating and preventing **human trafficking.** This term broadly describes the crime of coercing a person to go from one country to another for the purpose of performing some form of labor—often prostitution—for the trafficker.

Recently, ICE has been aggressively removing undocumented immigrants from the United States. In 2016, for example, the agency conducted about 240,000 removals, 58 percent of which involved someone who had been convicted of a crime.[98] ICE also

▼ In Roma, Texas, a U.S. Border Patrol agent speaks with undocumented immigrants from Central America who have just crossed into the United States illegally. **What is the main difference in the duties of a U.S. Border Patrol agent and a U.S. Immigration and Customs Enforcement (ICE) agent?** John Moore/Getty Images News/Getty Images

partners with Mexican law enforcement to disrupt drug-smuggling operations along the U.S.-Mexico border. In 2016, as part of Operation Diablo Express, ICE agents helped Mexican authorities apprehend twenty-four members of the Sinaloa Cartel, one of Mexico's largest drug-trafficking organizations. (The *Policy Matters* feature at the end of this chapter focuses on the controversial issue of whether local police officers should be required to aid ICE in enforcing immigration law.)

The U.S. Secret Service   When it was created in 1865, the **U.S. Secret Service** was primarily responsible for combating currency counterfeiters. In 1901, the agency was given the added responsibility of protecting the president of the United States, the president's family, the vice president, the president-elect, and former presidents. These duties have remained the cornerstone of the agency's role, with several expansions. After a number of threats against presidential candidates in the 1960s and early 1970s, including the shootings of Robert Kennedy of New York and Governor George Wallace of Alabama, in 1976 Secret Service agents became responsible for protecting those political figures as well.

In addition to its special plainclothes agents, the agency also directs two uniformed groups of law enforcement officers. The Secret Service Uniformed Division protects the grounds of the White House and its inhabitants, and the Treasury Police Force polices the Treasury Building in Washington, D.C. To aid its battle against counterfeiters and forgers of government bonds, the agency has the use of a laboratory at the Bureau of Engraving and Printing in the nation's capital.

Additional DHS Agencies   In addition to the three already discussed—CBP, ICE, and the U.S. Secret Service—three other DHS agencies play a central role in preventing and responding to crime and terrorist-related activity:

- The *U.S. Coast Guard* defends the nation's coasts, ports, and inland waterways. It also combats illegal drug shipping and enforces immigration law at sea.
- The *Transportation Security Administration* is responsible for the safe operation of our airline, rail, bus, and ferry services. It also operates the Federal Air Marshals program, which places undercover federal agents on commercial flights.
- The *Federal Emergency Management Agency* is the lead federal agency in preparing for and responding to disasters such as hurricanes, floods, terrorist attacks, and *infrastructure* concerns. Our national **infrastructure** includes all of the facilities and systems that provide the daily necessities of modern life, such as electric power, food, water, transportation, and telecommunications.

The Department of Justice   The U.S. Department of Justice, created in 1870, is still the primary federal law enforcement agency in the country. With the responsibility of enforcing criminal law and supervising the federal prisons, the Justice Department plays a leading role in the American criminal justice system. To carry out its responsibilities to prevent and control crime, the department has a number of law enforcement agencies, including the Federal Bureau of Investigation, the Drug Enforcement Administration, the Bureau of Alcohol, Tobacco, Firearms and Explosives, and the U.S. Marshals Service.

The Federal Bureau of Investigation (FBI)   Initially created in 1908 as the Bureau of Investigation, this agency was renamed the **Federal Bureau of Investigation (FBI)** in 1935. One of the primary investigative agencies of the federal government, the FBI has jurisdiction over nearly two hundred federal crimes, including white-collar crimes,

U.S. Secret Service A federal law enforcement organization with the primary responsibility of protecting the president, the president's family, the vice president, and other important political figures.

Infrastructure The services and facilities that support the day-to-day needs of modern life, such as electricity, food, transportation, and water.

Federal Bureau of Investigation (FBI) The branch of the Department of Justice responsible for investigating violations of federal law.

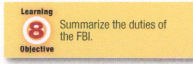

Learning
8 Summarize the duties of the FBI.
Objective

FASTFACTS

FBI agent

Job description:
- Primary role is to oversee intelligence and investigate crimes.
- Special agent careers are divided into five career paths: intelligence, counterintelligence, counterterrorism, criminal, and cyber.

What kind of training is required?
- Bachelor's and/or master's degree, plus three years of work experience. U.S. citizen, 23–36 years old.
- A written and oral examination, medical and physical examinations, a psychological assessment, and an exhaustive background investigation.

Annual salary range?
- $65,000–$75,000

Arnold E. Bell
Federal Bureau of Investigation (FBI) Agent

Courtesy of Arnold E. Bell

I came to the FBI from the U.S. Army, where I worked as a crewman on a UH-1 helicopter and subsequently as a special agent with the U.S. Army Criminal Investigation Command. My work experience in the U.S. Army and degree from St. Leo College (now University) provided the educational foundation that allowed entry into the FBI. After graduating from the FBI Academy in Quantico, Virginia, I was assigned to our Los Angeles division, where I spent the next twelve years. It was a particularly interesting time to be working in Los Angeles, which was experiencing a boom in bank robberies. During the most intense stretches, we were averaging between five and seven bank robberies a day! When I wasn't chasing down a bank robber, I had my hands full with hunting down fugitives, working against organized crime, and dealing with public corruption.

I am currently assigned to the FBI's cyber division as an assistant section chief. The primary mission of my division is to combat cyber-based terrorism and hostile-intelligence operations conducted via the Internet, and to address general cyber crime. Since September 11, 2001, our primary focus has shifted from criminal work to counterterrorism. This has been a difficult transformation for many of us "old-timers" because we grew up in the Bureau doing criminal work. We all recognize, however, the importance of this new challenge, and, despite the difficulties, I believe we have been successful in fulfilling both missions.

SOCIAL MEDIA CAREER TIP Be aware of your e-mail address/screen name/login name and what it represents. Stay away from nicknames. Use a professional and unique name to represent yourself consistently across social media platforms.

---

espionage (spying), kidnapping, extortion, interstate transportation of stolen property, bank robbery, interstate gambling, and civil rights violations.

With its network of agents across the country and the globe, the FBI is also uniquely positioned to combat worldwide criminal activity such as terrorism and drug trafficking. In fact, since 2001, the agency has shifted its focus from traditional crime to national security. Between that year and 2009, the FBI doubled its roster of counterterrorism agents, while reducing its number of criminal investigations. In 2014, the agency even officially changed its primary function from "law enforcement" to "national security."[99]

The FBI and Local Cooperation   The FBI is also committed to providing valuable support for local and state law enforcement agencies. For example, the agency operates Joint Terrorism Task Forces in 104 cities. These units are made up of highly trained analysts, investigators, and weapons specialists from all levels of policing, supported by the FBI's considerable intelligence and technological resources. FBI agents help local police departments in cities with unusually high violent crime rates, such as Baltimore and Oakland, to investigate homicides. Its Identification Division offers assistance in finding missing persons and identifying the victims of fires, airplane crashes, and other disfiguring accidents.

The services of the FBI Laboratory, the largest crime laboratory in the world, are available at no cost to other agencies. In addition, the FBI's Next Generation Identification (NGI) program gathers data such as fingerprints, iris scans, photographs, and information collected through facial recognition software. Eventually, the agency hopes to be able to use NGI to find criminal suspects using drivers' license photos and images from surveillance cameras, and to share this information with local and state law enforcement agencies.

The Drug Enforcement Administration (DEA) The mission of the Drug Enforcement Administration (DEA) is to enforce domestic drug laws and regulations and to assist other federal and foreign agencies in combating illegal drug manufacture and trade on an international level. The agency also enforces the provisions of the Controlled Substances Act (CSA). The CSA specifies five categories of drugs based on the substances' medical use, potential for abuse, and addictive qualities.[100] It also sets penalties for the manufacture, sale, distribution, possession, and consumption of these drugs. (See Figure 5.5 for an overview of the CSA. Notice that, despite the various changes in state law that we discussed earlier in this textbook, the DEA is still legally required to treat marijuana as one of the most dangerous drugs on the black market.)

The DEA operates a network of six regional laboratories used to test and categorize seized drugs. Local law enforcement agencies have access to the DEA labs and often use them to ensure that information about particular drugs that will be presented in court is accurate and up to date. In recent years, Congress has given the FBI more authority to enforce drug laws, and the two agencies now share a number of administrative controls.

The Bureau of Alcohol, Tobacco, Firearms and Explosives (ATF) As its name suggests, the Bureau of Alcohol, Tobacco, Firearms and Explosives (ATF) is primarily concerned with the illegal sale, possession, and use of firearms and the control of untaxed tobacco and liquor products. The Firearms Division of the agency has the responsibility of enforcing the Gun Control Act of 1968, which sets the circumstances under which firearms may be sold and used in this country. The bureau also regulates all gun trade between the United States and foreign nations and collects taxes on all firearm importers,

Drug Enforcement Administration (DEA) The federal agency responsible for enforcing the nation's laws and regulations regarding narcotics and other controlled substances.

FIGURE 5.5 **Schedules of Narcotics as Defined by the Federal Controlled Substances Act**

The Comprehensive Drug Abuse Prevention and Control Act of 1970 continues to be the basis for the regulation of drugs in the United States. Substances named by the act were placed under direct regulation of the Drug Enforcement Administration (DEA). The act "ranks" drugs from I to V, with Schedule I drugs being the most heavily controlled and carrying the most severe penalties for abuse.

	CRITERIA	EXAMPLES
SCHEDULE I	Drugs with high abuse potential that are lacking therapeutic utility or adequate safety for use under medical supervision.	Marijuana, heroin, LSD, peyote, PCP, mescaline
SCHEDULE II	Drugs with high abuse potential that are accepted in current medical practice despite high physical and psychological dependence potential.	Opium, cocaine, morphine, Benzedrine, methadone, methamphetamine
SCHEDULE III	Drugs with moderate abuse potential that are utilized in current medical practice despite dependence potential.	Barbiturates, amphetamine
SCHEDULE IV	Drugs with low abuse potential that are accepted in current medical practice despite limited dependence potential.	Valium, Darvon, phenobarbital
SCHEDULE V	Drugs with minimal abuse potential that are used in current medical practice despite limited dependence potential.	Cough medicine with small amounts of narcotic

Source: The Comprehensive Drug Abuse Prevention and Control Act of 1970.

manufacturers, and dealers. In keeping with these duties, the ATF is also responsible for policing the illegal use and possession of explosives. Furthermore, the ATF is charged with enforcing federal gambling laws.

The U.S. Marshals Service The oldest federal law enforcement agency is the U.S. Marshals Service. In 1789, President George Washington assigned thirteen U.S. Marshals to protect his attorney general. That same year, Congress created the office of the U.S. Marshals and Deputy Marshals. Originally, the U.S. Marshals acted as the main law enforcement officers in the western territories. Following the Civil War (1861–1865), when most of these territories had become states, these agents were assigned to work for the U.S. district courts, where federal crimes are tried.

The relationship between the U.S. Marshals Service and the federal courts continues today and forms the basis for the officers' main duties, which include:

1. Providing security at federal courts for judges, jurors, and other courtroom participants.
2. Controlling property that has been ordered seized by federal courts.
3. Protecting government witnesses who put themselves in danger by testifying against the targets of federal criminal investigations. This protection is sometimes accomplished by relocating the witnesses and providing them with different identities.
4. Transporting federal prisoners to detention institutions.
5. Investigating violations of federal fugitive laws.[101]

The Department of the Treasury

The Department of the Treasury, formed in 1789, is mainly responsible for all financial matters of the federal government. It pays all the federal government's bills, borrows funds, collects taxes, mints coins, and prints paper currency. The largest bureau of the Treasury Department, the Internal Revenue Service (IRS), is concerned with violations of tax laws and regulations. The bureau's criminal investigation division focuses on various forms of tax evasion and tax fraud, as well as prosecuting identity theft and public corruption. Each year, the IRS's criminal investigation division gains about 2,800 convictions in cases involving these types of wrongdoing.[102]

Private Security

Learning Objective 9 Analyze the importance of private security today.

Even with increasing numbers of local, state, and federal law enforcement officers, the police do not have the ability to prevent every crime. Recognizing this, many businesses and citizens have decided to hire private guards for their properties and homes. In fact, according to ASIS International, an industry-research firm, demand for **private security** generates revenues of approximately $377 billion a year.[103] More than 10,000 firms employing around 2 million people provide private security services in this country, compared with about 1.1 million public law enforcement employees.

Privatizing Law Enforcement

As there are no federal regulations regarding private security, each state has its own rules. In several states, including California and Florida, prospective security guards must have at least forty hours of training. Ideally, a security guard—lacking the extensive training of a law enforcement agent—should only observe and report criminal activity unless use of force is needed to prevent a felony.

As a rule, private security is not designed to replace law enforcement. It is intended to deter crime rather than stop it. A uniformed security guard patrolling a shopping mall

Private Security The provision of policing services by private companies or individuals.

parking lot or a bank lobby has one primary function—to convince a potential criminal to search out a shopping mall or bank that does not have private security. For the same reason, many citizens hire security personnel to drive marked cars through their neighborhoods, making them a less attractive target for burglaries, robberies, vandalism, and other crimes.

Secondary Policing

As mentioned, although some states have minimum training requirements for private security officers, such training lags far behind the requirements to be a public officer. Consequently, there is a high demand for secondary policing, an umbrella term that covers the work that off-duty cops do when "moonlighting" for private companies or government agencies.

▲ A private security guard patrols the Manhattan Mall in New York City. **Why is being visible such an important aspect of many private security jobs?** Mario Tama/Getty ImagesNews/Getty Images

Generally speaking, police officers operate under the same rules whether they are off duty or on duty. In addition, 83 percent of local police departments in the United States have written policies for secondary policing.[104] For example, among other restrictions, Seattle police officers cannot work (on duty or off duty) longer than eighteen consecutive hours in a twenty-four-hour period and must clear all private employment with a superior.[105] Off-duty police officers commonly provide traffic control and pedestrian safety at road construction sites, as well as crowd control at large-scale functions such as music festivals and sporting events. They are also often hired to protect private properties and businesses, just like their nonpublic counterparts.

Continued Health of the Industry

Indicators point to continued growth for the private security industry. In general, three factors drive this growth:

1. The problem of crime in the workplace. According to the National Retail Security Survey, American retailers lose about $45 billion a year because of shoplifting and employee theft.[106]
2. Budget cuts in states and municipalities that have forced reductions in the number of public police, thereby raising the demand for private ones.
3. A rising awareness of private security products (such as home burglar alarms) and services as cost-effective protective measures.[107]

Another reason for the industry's continued health is terrorism. Private security is responsible for protecting more than three-fourths of the nation's likely terrorist targets, such as power plants, financial centers, dams, malls, oil refineries, and transportation hubs.

Secondary Policing The situation in which a police officer accepts off-duty employment from a private company or government agency.

Policy Matters

Local Police and Immigration Law

How Things Stand

Enforcement of immigration law is the responsibility of the federal government. Under the federal Secure Communities (S-COMM) program, however, the fingerprints of all individuals arrested at the local level are checked against federal immigration records. If U.S. Immigration and Customs Enforcement (ICE) determines that the suspect (who need not be charged with any crime) has violated immigration law, it can issue a "detainer." Responding to a detainer, the local law enforcement agency will hold the suspect in custody until ICE can determine whether she or he will be removed from the country.

As a Result...

Many local governments willingly participate in S-COMM, helping the federal government identify and remove immigration-law violators. At the same time, more than three hundred jurisdictions across the United States limit their cooperation with the federal government in this matter. These so-called sanctuary cities—including Baltimore, Boston, Chicago, New York, and San Francisco—either refuse to provide ICE with information on undocumented immigrants in their custody or decline to honor ICE's detainer requests.

There are several reasons for these policies. One major consideration is financial. Before California passed a statewide sanctuary law, Los Angeles County was spending $26 million a year to hold undocumented immigrants in jail on ICE's behalf.[108] Furthermore, critics contend that ICE unfairly takes advantage of local cooperation to deport undocumented immigrants who have committed petty crimes or infractions, causing hardship for their families. Finally, many local law enforcement officials believe that, by cooperating with the federal government, they will lose the trust of immigrant communities in their jurisdictions. That is, victims and witnesses of crimes may not contact the police if they believe, rightly or wrongly, that such contact puts them or their family members at risk of being removed from the country.

Up for Debate

"It is my job to investigate crimes. And if I can't do that, I can't get justice for people, because all of a sudden, I'm losing my witnesses or my victims because they're afraid that talking to me is going to lead to them getting deported."[109]—*Detective Brent Hopkins, Los Angeles Police Department*

"Why would any lawmaker want law enforcement to have less rather than more tools to keep our community and citizens and legal residents safe?"[110]—*Bristol County (Massachusetts) sheriff Tom Hodgson*

What's Your Take?

Review the discussion in this chapter on "The Responsibilities of the Police" and "The Department of Homeland Security" before answering the following questions.

1. What would be some of the benefits of giving local police officers the authority to enforce immigration law? What would be some of the drawbacks? Would you favor this policy? Why or why not?

2. A number of sanctuary cities will participate in S-COMM only if the suspect in custody has been convicted of a serious or violent crime. What is your opinion of this compromise?

Digging Deeper...

In November 2016, **President Donald Trump** issued an **executive order** entitled **"Enhancing Public Safety in the Interior of the United States."** After researching this policy statement online, determine (1) how it supports the enforcement of immigration laws by local police and (2) how it punishes local governments that don't comply with federal authorities. What is your opinion of this strategy? Your written answer should be at least three paragraphs long.

AP Images/Richard Drew

SUMMARY

For more information on these concepts, look back to the Learning Objective icons throughout the chapter.

 List the four basic responsibilities of the police. (a) To enforce laws, (b) to provide services, (c) to prevent crime, and (d) to preserve the peace.

 Tell how the patronage system affected policing. During the political era of policing (1840–1930), bribes paid by citizens and business owners often went into the coffers of the local political party. This was known as the patronage system.

 Explain how intelligence-led policing works and how it benefits modern police departments. Intelligence-led policing uses past crime patterns to predict when and where crime will occur in the future. In theory, intelligence-led policing allows police administrators to use fewer resources because it allows them to focus their attention on "hot spots."

 Identify the differences between the police academy and field training as learning tools for recruits. The police academy is a controlled environment where police recruits learn the basics of policing from instructors in classrooms. In contrast, field training takes place in the "real world": the recruit goes on patrol with an experienced police officer.

 Describe some of the benefits that female police officers bring to law enforcement. In addition to possessing bravery and physical prowess, female police officers seem to put citizens at ease and are therefore often more effective during service calls. Policewomen are also more likely to use verbal skills rather than force when placed in situations of potential violence. As a result, they are much less likely than male officers to be disciplined for use of excessive force.

 Identify the main advantage of a racially and ethnically diverse police force. Particularly in communities that are themselves racially and ethnically diverse, police officers who are members of minority groups are often able to communicate more easily with citizens. Their higher credibility enables the officers to do a better job of maintaining order, as well as solving and preventing crimes.

 Indicate some of the most important law enforcement agencies under the control of the Department of Homeland Security. (a) U.S. Customs and Border Protection, which polices the flow of goods and people across U.S. international borders and oversees the U.S. Border Patrol; (b) U.S. Immigration and Customs Enforcement, which investigates and enforces our nation's immigration and customs laws; and (c) the U.S. Secret Service, which protects high-ranking federal government officials and federal property.

 Summarize the duties of the FBI. The FBI has jurisdiction to investigate hundreds of federal crimes, including white-collar crime, kidnapping, bank robbery, and civil rights violations. The FBI is also heavily involved in combating terrorism and drug-trafficking operations in the United States and around the world. Finally, the agency provides support to state and local law enforcement agencies through its crime laboratories and databases.

 Analyze the importance of private security today. In the United States, businesses and citizens spend billions of dollars each year on private security. Increased crime in the workplace, along with concerns about terrorism, have fueled the growth in spending on private security.

1. Which of the four basic responsibilities of the police do you think is most important? Why?

2. Should law enforcement agencies have the same physical agility and fitness requirements for male and female applicants? Explain your answer.

3. Review the discussion of double marginality in this chapter. Why would members of a minority community think that police officers of the same race or ethnicity were "traitors"? What can police departments do to dispel this misperception?

4. One of the major differences between a local police chief and a sheriff is that the sheriff is elected, while the police chief is appointed. What are some of the possible problems with having a law enforcement official who, like any other politician, is responsible to voters? What are some of the possible benefits of this situation?

5. Twenty-nine states do not require any specific training for private security personnel. What are the arguments for and against requiring at least forty hours of training, as is the case in California and Florida?

KEY TERMS

affirmative action 148
coroner 155
discrimination 148
double marginality 153
Drug Enforcement Administration (DEA) 161
Federal Bureau of Investigation (FBI) 159
field training 148
fusion center 144

human trafficking 158
infrastructure 159
intelligence-led policing 142
militarism 143
night watch system 138
patronage system 139
private security 162
probationary period 147
professional model 139
recruitment 145

secondary policing 163
sexual harassment 150
sheriff 154
U.S. Customs and Border Protection (CBP) 156
U.S. Immigration and Customs Enforcement (ICE) 158
U.S. Secret Service 159
visa 157

1. Quoted in Andrew Welsh-Huggins, "Fast-Acting Ohio State Officer Praised for Killing Attacker." *www.bigstory.ap.org*. Associated Press: November 28, 2016, Web.

2. Egon Bittner, *The Functions of Police in a Modern Society*, Public Health Service Publication No. 2059 (Chevy Chase, Md.: National Institute of Mental Health, 1970), 38-44.

3. Carl Klockars, "The Rhetoric of Community Policing," in *Community Policing: Rhetoric or Reality*, eds. Jack Greene and Stephen Mastrofski (New York: Praeger Publishers, 1991), 244.

4. Jack R. Greene and Carl B. Klockars, "What Do Police Do?" in *Thinking about Police*, 2d ed., ed. Carl B. Klockars and Stephen D. Mastrofski (New York: McGraw-Hill, 1991), 273–284.

5. Federal Bureau of Investigation, *Crime in the United States, 2015*, Table 29. *www.ucr.fbi.gov*. U.S. Department of Justice: 2016, Web.

6. Reprinted in *The Police Chief* (January 1990), 18.

7. Jason Busch, "Shots Fired: When a Police Car Becomes an Ambulance," *Law Enforcement Technology* (September 2013), 8-10.

8. Howard Sheppard, "Police Statewide Reverse over 600 Opioid Overdoses with Naloxone." *www.fox43.com. Fox43 News*: March 1, 2016, Web.

9. Libor Jany, "Minneapolis Police to Try Buddy System on Mental Health Calls." *www.startribune.com. Minneapolis Star Tribune*: September 6, 2016, Web.

10. Jerome H. Skolnick, "Police: The New Professionals," *New Society* (September 5, 1986), 9-11.

11. Quoted in Nancy Ritter, ed., "LAPD Chief Bratton Speaks Out: What's Wrong with Criminal Justice Research—and How to Make It Right," *National Institute of Justice Journal* 257 (2007), 29.

12. Gary Kleck and J.C. Barnes, "Do More Police Lead to More Crime Deterrence?" *Crime & Delinquency* (August 2014), 716-738.

13. Klockars, *op. cit.*, 250.

14. James Q. Wilson, *Varieties of Police Behavior: The Management of Law and Order in Eight Communities* (Cambridge, Mass.: Harvard University Press, 1968).

15. James Q. Wilson and George L. Kelling, "Broken Windows," *Atlantic Monthly* (March 1982), 29.

16. M. K. Nalla and G. R. Newman, "Is White-Collar Crime Policing, Policing?" *Policing and Society* 3 (1994), 304.

17. Mitchell P. Roth, *Crime and Punishment: A History of the Criminal Justice System*, 2d ed. (Belmont, Calif.: Wadsworth Cengage Learning, 2011), 65.

18. *Ibid.*

19. Peter K. Manning, *Police Work* (Cambridge, Mass.: MIT Press, 1977), 82.

20. Mark H. Moore and George L. Kelling, "'To Serve and Protect': Learning from Police History," *Public Interest* 70 (1983), 53.

21. Samuel Walker, *The Police in America: An Introduction* (New York: McGraw-Hill, 1983), 7.

22. Moore and Kelling, *op. cit.*, 54.

23. Mark H. Haller, "Chicago Cops, 1890–1925," in *Thinking about Police*, ed. Carl Klockars and Stephen Mastrofski (New York: McGraw-Hill, 1990), 90.

24. William J. Bopp and Donald O. Shultz, *A Short History of American Law Enforcement* (Springfield, Ill.: Charles C Thomas, 1977), 109-110.

25. Roger G. Dunham and Geoffrey P. Alpert, *Critical Issues in Policing: Contemporary Issues* (Prospect Heights, Ill.: Waveland Press, 1989).

26. Ken Peak and Emmanuel P. Barthe, "Community Policing and CompStat: Merged, or Mutually Exclusive?" *The Police Chief* (December 2009), 73.

27. *Ibid.*, 74.

28. Quoted in *ibid*.

29. Peter K. Manning, "The Police: Mandate, Strategies, and Appearances," in *Crime and Justice in American Society*, ed. Jack D. Douglas (Indianapolis, Ind.: Bobbs-Merrill, 1971), 149-163.

30. National Advisory Commission on Civil Disorder, *Report* (Washington, D.C.: U.S. Government Printing Office, 1968), 157-160.

31. 18 U.S.C.A. Sections 2510–2521.

32. Jayne Seagrave, "Defining Community Policing," *American Journal of Police* 1 (1996), 1-22.

33. Peak and Barthe, *op. cit.*, 78.

34. Jason Vaughn Lee, "Policing after 9/11: Community Policing in an Age of Homeland Security," *Police Quarterly* (November 2010), 351-353.

35. Craig D. Uchida and Marc L. Swatt, "Operation LASER and the Effectiveness of Hotspot Patrol: A Panel Analysis," *Police Quarterly* (September 2013), 287–304.

36. Michele Coppola, "Real-Time Crime Center Serves as Force Multiplier." *www.nij.gov. TechBeat*: May 2016, Web.

37. Justin Jouvenal, "The New Way Police Are Surveilling You: Calculating Your Threat 'Score.'" *www.washingtonpost.com. Washington Post*: January 10, 2016, Web.

38. Quoted in Joel Rubin, "Stopping Crime before It Starts," *Los Angeles Times* (August 21, 2010), A17.

39. Quoted in Kimberly Kindy, "Creating Guardians, Calming Warriors." *www.washingtonpost.com. Washington Post*: December 10, 2015, Web.

40. Quoted in Mitch Smith and Timothy Williams, "'Bulletproof Warrior' Course Brings Scrutiny in Minnesota," *New York Times* (July 15, 2016), A17.

41. "Cops or Soldiers?" *The Economist* (March 22, 2014), 27.

42. Quoted in Kindy, *op. cit.*

43. Associated Press, "Militarized Police Forces Come Under Congressional Scrutiny" (September 9, 2014).

44. Quoted in Kindy, *op. cit.*

45. Matt Apuzzo and Eric Lichtblau, "After F.B.I.'s Inquiry, a Focus on What Else Could Be Done," *New York Times* (June 15, 2016), A1.

46. "Fusion Center Success Stories." *www.dhs.gov*. Department of Homeland Security: visited January 22, 2017, Web.

47. "The FBI's Secret Muslim Network," *The Week* (April 8, 2016), 36.

48. Murtaza Hussain and Jenna McLaughlin, "FBI's 'Shared Responsibility Committees' to Identify "'Radicalized' Muslims Raise Alarms," *www.theintercept.com. The Intercept*: April 9, 2016, Web.

49. Bureau of Justice Statistics, *Local Police Departments, 2013: Equipment and Technology* (Washington, D.C.: U.S. Department of Justice, July 2015), 6.

50. Brad Heath, "FBI Ran Website Sharing Thousands of Child Porn Images," *USA Today* (January 22–24, 2016), 1A.

51. James H. Chenoweth, "Situational Tests: A New Attempt at Assessing Police Candidates," *Journal of Criminal Law, Criminology and Police Science* 52 (1961), 232.

52. Yossef S. Ben-Porath et al., "Assessing the Psychological Suitability of Candidates for Law Enforcement Positions," *The Police Chief* (August 2011), 64-70.

53. Quoted in *How Are Innovations in Technology Transforming Policing?* (Washington, D.C.: Police Executive Research Forum, January 2012), 2.

54. Bureau of Justice Statistics, *Local Police Departments, 2013: Personnel, Policies, and Practices* (Washington, D.C.: U.S. Department of Justice, May 2015), 7.

55. *Ibid.*, Table 7, page 7.

56. D. P. Hinkle, "College Degree: An Impractical Prerequisite for Police Work," *Law and Order* (July 1991), 105.

57. *Local Police Departments, 2013: Personnel, Policies, and Practices, op. cit.*, 7.

58. Bureau of Justice Statistics, *State and Local Law Enforcement Training Academies* (Washington, D.C.: U.S. Department of Justice, July 2016), 1.

59. National Advisory Commission on Civil Disorder, *Report* (Washington, D.C.: U.S. Government Printing Office, 1968), Chapter 11.

60. *Griggs v. Duke Power Co.*, 401 U.S. 424 (1971); and *Albemarle Paper Co. v. Moody*, 422 U.S. 405 (1975).

61. Kim Lonsway, et al., "Under Scrutiny: The Effect of Consent Decrees on the Representation of Women in Sworn Law Enforcement." *www.womenandpolicing.com*.

National Center for Women & Policing: Spring 2003, Web.

62. Justin McCrary, "The Effect of Court-Ordered Hiring Quotas on the Composition and Quality of Police." *http://www.nber.org/papers/w12368.pdf*. National Bureau of Economic Research: 2006, Web.

63. Bureau of Justice Statistics, *State and Local Law Enforcement Training Academies* (Washington, D.C.: U.S. Department of Justice, July 2016), 1.

64. *United States v. City of Lubbock, Texas.* United States District Court for the Northern Division of Texas Lubbock Division: December 2, 2015, Web.

65. Justice Department Settles Employment Discrimination Lawsuit against Lubbock, Texas." *www.justice.gov*. U.S. Department of Justice Office of Public Affairs: May 26, 2016, Web.

66. Jen Fifield, "Does Diversifying Police Forces Reduce Tension?" *www.pewtrusts.org*. The Pew Charitable Trusts: August 22, 2016, Web.

67. *Ibid.*

68. Sean Lahman, "Local Police Forces Lack Diversity." *www.democratandchronicle.com*. *Democrat and Chronicle*: January 21, 2015, Web.

69. *Local Police Departments, 2013: Personnel, Policies, and Practices, op. cit.,* Table 4, page 4.

70. *United States v. City of Lubbock, Texas, op. cit.*

71. Lucinda Holt, "Turning Blue: Testing for the Lubbock Police Department." *www.*

lubbockonline.com. Lubbock Avalanche-Journal: July 9, 2016, Web.

72. Kevin Johnson, "Women Move into Law Enforcement's Highest Ranks." *www.usatoday.com. USA Today*: December 2, 2015, Web.

73. Gene L. Scaramella, Steven M. Cox, and William P. McCamey, *Introduction to Policing* (Thousand Oaks, Calif.: Sage Publications, 2011), 318.

74. Kenneth J. Novak, Robert A. Brown, and James Frank, *Women on Patrol: An Analysis of Differences in Officer Arrest Behavior* (Bingley, United Kingdom: Emerald Group Publishing Ltd., 2006), 21–27.

75. Quoted in Robin N. Haarr and Merry Morash, "The Effect of Rank on Police Women Coping with Discrimination and Harassment," *Police Quarterly* (December 2013), 403.

76. Quoted in *Talk of the Nation*, "What Changes As Women Rise Through Law Enforcement's Ranks." *www.npr.org*. National Public Radio: April 2, 2013, Web.

77. Katherine Stuart van Wormer and Clemens Bartollas, *Women and the Criminal Justice System*, 3d ed. (Upper Saddle River, N.J.: Pearson Education, 2011), 318-319.

78. Quoted in Teresa Lynn Wertsch, "Walking the Thin Blue Line: Policewomen and Tokenism Today," *Women and Criminal Justice* (1998), 35-36.

79. Quoted in Kimberly A. Lonsway, Rebecca Paynich, and Jennifer N. Hall, "Sexual Harassment in Law Enforcement:

Incidence, Impact, and Perception," *Police Quarterly* (June 2013), 196.

80. "National Police Misconduct Statistics and Reporting Project: 2010 Quarterly Q3 Report." *www.policemisconduct.net*. The Cato Institute: visited on January 24, 2017, Web.

81. Lonsway, Paynich, and Hall, *op. cit.*, 179-180.

82. *Local Police Departments, 2013: Personnel, Policies, and Practices*, Figure 5, page 5.

83. *State and Local Law Enforcement Training Academies, op. cit.*, 1.

84. David Alan Sklansky, "Not Your Father's Police Department: Making Sense of the New Demographics of Law Enforcement," *Journal of Criminal Law and Criminology* (Spring 2006), 1209-1243.

85. Quoted in Libor Jany, "Minneapolis' Black Police Officers Walk a Cultural Tightrope." *www.startribune.com. Minneapolis Star Tribune*: March 5, 2016, Web.

86. John S. Dempsey and Linda S. Forst, *An Introduction to Policing*, 8th ed. (Boston: Cengage Learning, 2016), 196.

87. *Wygant v. Jackson Board of Education*, 476 U.S. 314 (1986).

88. Matt Apuzzo and Sarah Cohen, "Police Chiefs, Looking to Diversify Forces, Face Structural Hurdles," *New York Times* (November 8, 2015), A14.

89. Bureau of Justice Statistics, *Census of State and Local Law Enforcement Agencies, 2008* (Washington, D.C.: U.S. Department of Justice, July 2011), 1; and Bureau of Justice Statistics, *Federal Law Enforcement Officers,*

2008 (Washington, D.C.: U.S. Department of Justice, June 2012), 1.

90. *Local Police Departments, 2013: Personnel, Policies, and Practices, op. cit.*, Table 3, page 3.

91. *Ibid.*, Table 2, page 3.

92. Bureau of Justice Statistics, *Sheriffs' Office Personnel, 1993–2013* (Washington, D.C.: U.S. Department of Justice, June 2016), Table 2, page 3.

93. Bureau of Justice Statistics, *Sheriffs' Offices, 2003* (Washington, D.C.: U.S. Department of Justice, May 2006), 15-18.

94. Bureau of Justice Statistics, *Sheriffs' Departments, 1997* (Washington, D.C.: U.S. Department of Justice, February 2000), 14.

95. *Budget-in-Brief: Fiscal Year 2017* (Washington, D.C.: U.S. Department of Homeland Security, 2016), 9.

96. Ron Nixon, "U.S. Uncertain of How Many Overstay Visas," *New York Times* (January 2, 2016), A1.

97. "Sector Profile–Fiscal Year 2016 (October 1st through Sept. 30th)." *www.cbp.gov.* United States Border Patrol: 2016, Web.

98. "FY 2016 ICE Immigration Removals." *www.ice.gov.* U.S. Immigrations and Customs Enforcement: visited January 22, 2017, Web.

99. John Hudson, "FBI Drops Law Enforcement as 'Primary' Mission." *www.foreignpolicy.com. Foreign Policy:* January 5, 2014, Web.

100. Uniform Controlled Substances Act (1994), Section 201(h).

101. "Fact Sheet." *www.usmarshals.gov.* United States Marshals Service: March 11, 2016, Web.

102. "Statistical Data for Three Fiscal Years— Criminal Investigation (CI)." *www.irs.gov.* Internal Revenue Service: October 12, 2016, Web.

103. Michael Moran, "Security Market Growth Continues." *https://sm.asisonline.org/Pages/Security-Market-Growth-Continues.aspx.* ASIS International: May 15, 2015, Web.

104. Bureau of Justice Statistics, *Local Police Departments, 2007* (Washington, D.C.: U.S. Department of Justice, December 2010), Table 8, page 13.

105. Seattle Police Department, Seattle Police Manual, "5.120—Secondary Employment."

www.seattle.gov. Seattle Police Department: March 19, 2014, Web.

106. Kelsey Seidler, "2016 National Retail Security Survey Results Released." *www.losspreventionmedia.com.* LPM Insider: August 8, 2016, Web.

107. Kevin Strom, et al., *The Private Security Industry: A Review of the Definitions, Available Data Sources, and Paths Moving Forward* (Research Triangle Park, N.C.: RTI International, December 2010), 4–11—4–15.

108. Judith A. Greene, *The Costs of Responding to Immigration Detainers in California: Preliminary Findings* (Justice Strategies, 2012), 2.

109. Quoted in Cindy Chang, Kate Mather, and Nicole Santa Cruz, "'I'm Not Going to Do It,' Police Aren't Eager to Help Trump Enforce Immigration Laws." *www.latimes.com. Los Angeles Times:* January 30, 2017, Web.

110. Quoted in Shira Schoenberg, "'Trust Act' Revives Debate over Massachusetts Enforcement of Immigration Law." *www.masslive.com.* MassLive: February 4, 2016, Web.

Problems and Solutions
in Modern Policing

To target your study and review, look for these numbered Learning Objective icons throughout the chapter.

Chapter Outline		Corresponding Learning Objectives
The Role of Discretion in Policing	**1**	Explain why police officers are allowed discretionary powers.
Police Organization and Field Operations	**2**	List the three primary purposes of police patrol.
	3	Describe how forensic experts use DNA fingerprinting to solve crimes.
Police Strategies: What Works	**4**	Explain why differential response strategies enable police departments to respond more efficiently to 911 calls.
	5	Explain community policing and its contribution to the concept of problem-oriented policing.
"Us versus Them": Issues in Modern Policing	**6**	Describe the process of socialization in police subculture.
	7	Clarify the concepts of nondeadly force, deadly force, and reasonable force in the context of police use of force.
Police Misconduct and Ethics	**8**	Determine when police officers are justified in using deadly force.
	9	Explain what an ethical dilemma is and name four categories of ethical dilemmas that a police officer typically may face.

In a Split Second . . .

▲ Former Albuquerque police officers Keith Sandy, left, and Dominique Perez, right, confer with legal counsel during their second-degree murder trial for killing a homeless man. AP Images/Juan Labreche

The standoff started with a 911 call to the Albuquerque Police Department (APD) about an illegal campsite at the foot of the Sandia Mountains. When officers arrived on the scene, they found the culprit, James Boyd, to be angry, uncooperative, and armed with two pocketknives. Ordered to drop the knives, he replied, "Don't attempt to give me, the Department of Defense, another directive." As day turned to early evening, APD officers tried to negotiate a resolution. Boyd, who had spent much of his adult life moving between jails and psychiatric hospitals, responded with threats. "I'm bulletproof," he said. "Somebody's dying tonight and it ain't going to be me."

Four hours after the initial call, the APD decided to end the encounter. A K-9 unit moved toward Boyd and attempted to subdue him with a stun grenade. Boyd seemed unfazed by the small explosion and, as APD police officer Dominique Perez testified in court two years

later, possibly moved a hand toward his waistband. Perez, perceiving "an immediate deadly threat" to a K-9 officer who was trying to retrieve his dog nearby, fired at Boyd. Another officer, Keith Sandy, thought Boyd "was going to attack us from a different angle," and also opened fire. Six of the shots from the two officers struck Boyd, killing him.

Ten months later, Perez and Sandy were charged with second degree murder. If convicted, they would face fifteen years in prison. At trial, prosecutors relied heavily on a video from Perez's helmet camera. Shown frame by frame, the video seemed to indicate that Boyd had turned his back to the officers before being shot. Perez countered that, in real time, the situation was not so straightforward. "The way it happened that day, it happened in the blink of an eye, at the speed of life," he testified. After hearing the evidence, jurors could not decide whether Boyd's shooting was justified, and, on October 12, 2016, Judge Alisa Hadfield declared a mistrial. "These are two good men," said one of the officers' defense attorneys following the trial. "Let [them] get on with their lives."

FOR CRITICAL ANALYSIS

1. Generally speaking, a police officer is justified in using deadly force if that officer *reasonably* believes that such force is necessary to save someone from serious harm. Using this standard, do you think the Albuquerque police officers' shooting of James Boyd was justified? Explain your answer.

2. During the trial, prosecutors showed that Boyd, who did not have a firearm, was too far away from the K-9 officer to pose a threat with his knives. Does this fact change your answer to the previous question? Why or why not?

3. Judging from this case, what are some of the pros and cons of having police officers use body-worn cameras to record encounters with suspects?

The Role of Discretion in Policing

One of the ironies of law enforcement is that patrol officers—often the lowest-paid members of an agency, with the least amount of authority—have the greatest amount of discretionary power. Part of the explanation for this is practical. Patrol officers spend most of the day on the streets, beyond the control of their supervisors. Usually, only two people are present when a patrol officer must make a decision: the officer and the possible wrongdoer. As a matter of necessity, the law enforcement officer has a great deal of freedom to take the action that he or she feels the situation requires.

Without this freedom, many police officers might find their duties unrewarding. Indeed, numerous studies have shown that higher levels of officer autonomy are reflected in higher levels of officer job satisfaction.[1] At the same time, discretion can lead to second-guessing on the part of the public, an officer's superiors, and the officer him- or herself. Certainly, the Albuquerque police officers just discussed would have preferred not to have shot and killed James Boyd, regardless of the consequences. Their decisions were made in a split second, under stressful circumstances, and without the benefit of hindsight.

Justification for Police Discretion

Despite the possibility of mistakes, courts generally have upheld the patrol officer's freedom to decide "what law to enforce, how much to enforce it, against whom, and on what occasions."[2] This judicial support of police discretion is based on the following factors:

Learning Objective 1 Explain why police officers are allowed discretionary powers.

- Police officers are considered trustworthy and are therefore assumed to make honest decisions, regardless of contradictory testimony by a suspect.
- Experience and training give officers the ability to determine whether a certain activity poses a threat to society and to take any reasonable action necessary to investigate or prevent such activity.
- Due to the nature of their jobs, police officers are very knowledgeable about human behavior and, by extension, criminal behavior.
- Police officers may find themselves in danger of personal, physical harm and must be allowed to take reasonable and necessary steps to protect themselves.[3]

Dr. Anthony J. Pinizzotto, a psychologist with the Federal Bureau of Investigation (FBI), and Charles E. Miller, an instructor in the bureau's Criminal Justice Information Services Division, take the justification for discretion one step further. These two experts argue that many police officers have a "sixth sense" that helps them handle on-the-job challenges. Pinizzotto and Miller believe that although "intuitive policing" is often difficult to explain to those outside law enforcement, it is a crucial part of policing and should not be discouraged by civilian administrators.[4]

Factors of Police Discretion

There is no doubt that subjective factors influence police discretion. The officer's beliefs, values, personality, and background all enter into his or her decisions. To a large extent, however, a law enforcement agent's actions are determined by the rules of policing set down in the U.S. Constitution and enforced by the courts. These rules are of paramount importance and will be discussed in great detail in Chapter 7.

Elements of Discretion   Assuming that most police officers stay on the right side of the Constitution in most instances, four other factors generally enter the discretion equation in any particular situation.[5] First, and most important, is the nature

of the criminal act. The less serious a crime, the more likely a police officer is to ignore it. A person driving 60 miles per hour in a 55-miles-per-hour zone, for example, is much less likely to be ticketed than someone doing 80 miles per hour.

A second element often considered is the attitude of the wrongdoer toward the officer. A motorist who is belligerent toward a highway patrol officer is much more likely to be ticketed than one who is contrite and apologetic. Third, the relationship between the victim and the offender can influence the outcome. If the parties are in a familial or other close relationship, police officers may see the incident as a personal matter and be hesitant to make an arrest. The fourth factor of the discretion equation is departmental policy.

Would you be in favor of a departmental policy that disallowed all high-speed police pursuits? How about a departmental policy that gave officers discretion to engage a suspect in a high-speed chase "when a reasonable officer would find such pursuit necessary?" What are the benefits and drawbacks of each scenario? Explain your answers. Steve Allen Travel Photography / Alamy Stock Photo

Limiting Police Discretion

Departmental policy can have the effect of limiting police discretion. A **policy** is a set of guiding principles that law enforcement agents must adhere to in stated situations. If a police administrator decides that all motorists who exceed the speed limit by 10 miles per hour will be ticketed, that policy will certainly influence the patrol officer's decisions. Policies must be flexible enough to allow for officer discretion, but at the same time be specific enough to provide the officer with a clear sense of her or his duties and obligations.

High Speed Pursuits Nearly every local police department in the United States has a policy limiting officers' discretion to engage in high-speed automobile chases of suspects, which can place other drivers and pedestrians in grave danger. [6] The impact of such policies can be seen from the results from Milwaukee, which implemented a new set of high-speed pursuit rules in 2010. Under these guidelines, officers may engage in high-speed pursuit only when the suspect "has committed, is committing, or is about to commit a violent felony" or when the danger posed by the fleeing suspect outweighs the danger posed by the chase.[7]

In the first year after Milwaukee's policy went into effect, the number of vehicle chases declined by nearly 75 percent from the high point of the previous decade. In addition, the number of accidents caused by police pursuits dropped by 80 percent from five years earlier, and in 2011 no Milwaukee police officer suffered an injury during a car chase.[8]

Use of Force Following the public outcry that resulted from James Boyd's death, described in the opening of this chapter, the Albuquerque Police Department dramatically changed its use-of-force policy. The revised standards include a section on "de-escalation," requiring that "officers shall use advisements, warnings, verbal persuasion, and other tactics as alternatives to higher levels of force, if feasible."[9]

Many local police departments have implemented use-of-force policies. For instance, a number of police departments forbid using chokeholds or strangleholds, or firing at a moving vehicle unless someone in the vehicle poses a deadly threat. Another common requirement is that officers give a verbal warning before using deadly force.

Policy A set of guiding principles designed to influence the behavior and decision making of police officers.

Such restrictions are not universally popular within the law enforcement community. The Fraternal Order of Police and the International Association of Chiefs of Police have argued that "reasonable use of force in any given situation must be at the discretion of a fully sworn and trained officer."[10] In other words, as long as the use of force is reasonable under the circumstances, there should be no further limitations placed on police discretion in such matters.

Bureaucracy A hierarchically-structured administrative organization that carries out specific functions.

Police Organization and Field Operations

Albuquerque police administrators placed Officers Dominique Perez and Keith Sandy, whose fatal shooting of suspect James Boyd was discussed in the opening of this chapter, on *administrative leave* pending an investigation into the incident. As you might recall from the opening of the preceding chapter, Ohio State University police officials took the same course of action with Officer Alan Horujko after he was involved in a fatal shooting. While on administrative leave, Perez, Sandy, and Horujko were temporarily relieved of their duties. This step does not necessarily imply that the officers were suspected of any wrongdoing. Most law enforcement agencies react similarly when a firearm is fired in the line of duty, both to allow for a full investigation of the event and to give the officer a chance to recover from what can be a traumatic experience.

Administrative leave is a *bureaucratic* response to an officer-involved shooting. In a **bureaucracy,** formal rules govern an individual's actions and relationships with coemployees. The ultimate goal of any bureaucracy is to reach its maximum efficiency—in the case of a police department, to provide the best service for the community within the confines of its limited resources, such as staff and budget. Although some police departments are experimenting with alternative structures based on a partnership between management and the officers in the field, most continue to rely on the hierarchical structure described below.

The Structure of the Police Department

Each police department is organized according to its environment: the size of its jurisdiction, the type of crimes it must deal with, and the demographics of the population it must police. The Metropolitan Police Department of Washington, D.C., operates an Asian Liaison Unit that works within that city's Asian community, while the Evansville, Indiana, Police Department has set up a "No Meth" task force. Geographic location also influences police organization. The San Diego Police Department has a Harbor Patrol Unit, which would be unproductive in Grand Forks, North Dakota—as would be the Grand Forks Police Department's snowmobile patrol in Southern California.

Chain of Command Whatever the size or location of a police department, it needs a clear rank structure and strict accountability to function properly. One of the goals of the police reformers, especially beginning in the 1950s, was to lessen the corrupting influence of politicians. The result was a move toward a militaristic organization of police.[11] As you can see in Figure 6.1, a typical police department is based on a "top-down" chain of command that leads from the police chief down to detectives and patrol officers. In this formalized structure, all persons are aware of their place in the chain of command and of their duties and responsibilities within the organization.

FIGURE 6.1 A Typical Police Department Chain of Command

Most American police departments follow this model of the chain of command, though smaller departments with fewer employees often eliminate several of these categories.

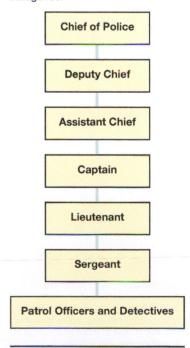

▲ A Tucson (Arizona) police officer questions witnesses following a domestic violence disturbance on the city's south side. **What are some of the benefits of having police officers patrol the same beat or precinct for extended periods of time?** Scott Olson/Getty Images News/Getty Images

Delegation of authority is a critical component of the chain of command, especially in larger departments. The chief of police delegates authority to division chiefs, who delegate authority to commanders, and on down through the organization. This structure creates a situation in which nearly every member of a police department is directly accountable to a superior. As was the original goal of police reformers, these links encourage discipline and control and lessen the possibility that any individual police employee will have the unsupervised freedom to abuse her or his position.[12]

Furthermore, experts suggest that no single supervisor should be responsible for too many employees. The ideal number of subordinates for a police sergeant, for example, is eight to ten patrol officers. This number is often referred to as the *span of control*. If the span of control rises above fifteen, then it is assumed that the superior officer will not be able to effectively manage his or her team.[13]

Organizing by Area and Time

In most metropolitan areas, police responsibilities are divided according to zones known as *beats* and *precincts*. The smallest area, a beat, is the stretch that a police officer or a group of police officers regularly patrol. A precinct—also known as a *district* or a *station*—is a collection of beats. A precinct commander, or captain, is held responsible by his or her superiors at police headquarters for the performance of the officers in that particular precinct.[14]

Police administrators must also organize their personnel by time. Most departments separate each twenty-four-hour day into three eight-hour *shifts*, also called *tours* or *platoons*. The night shift generally lasts from midnight to 8 a.m., the day shift from 8 a.m. to 4 p.m., and the evening shift from 4 p.m. to midnight. Officers either vary their hours by, say, working days one month and nights the next, or they have fixed tours in which they consistently take day, night, or evening shifts.[15] A number of police departments have implemented compressed workweeks, in which officers work longer shifts (ten or twelve hours) and fewer days. Such schedules are believed to improve the officers' quality of life by providing more substantial blocks of time off the job to recover from the stresses of police work.[16]

Law Enforcement in the Field

To a large extent, the main goal of any police department is the most efficient organization of its *field services*. Also known as "operations" or "line services," field services include patrol activities, investigations, and special operations. According to Henry M. Wrobleski and Karen M. Hess, most police officers are "generalists." That is, most officers are assigned to general areas and perform all field service functions within the boundaries of their beats.

Larger departments may be more specialized, with personnel assigned to specific types of crime, such as illegal drugs or white-collar crime, rather than geographic locations. Smaller departments, which make up the bulk of local law enforcement agencies, rely almost exclusively on general patrol.[17]

Delegation of Authority The principles of command on which most police departments are based, in which personnel take orders from and are responsible to those in positions of power directly above them.

Police on Patrol: The Backbone of the Department

Every police department has a patrol unit, and patrol is usually the largest division in the department. More than two-thirds of the sworn officers (officers authorized to make arrests and use force) in local police departments in the United States have patrol duties.[18]

"Life on the street" is not easy. Patrol officers must be able to handle any number of difficult situations, and experience is often the best and, despite training programs, the only teacher. As one patrol officer commented:

> You never stop learning. You never get your street degree. The person who says . . . they've learned it all is the person that's going to wind up dead or in a very compromising position. They've closed their minds.[19]

It may take a patrol officer years to learn when a gang is "false flagging" (trying to trick rival gang members into the open) or what to look for in a suspect's eyes to sense if he or she is concealing a weapon. This learning process is the backdrop to a number of different general functions that a patrol officer must perform on a daily basis.

The Purpose of Patrol As police accountability expert Samuel Walker has noted, the basic purposes of the police patrol have changed very little since 1829, when Sir Robert Peel founded the modern police department. These purposes include:

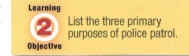

Learning **2** Objective · List the three primary purposes of police patrol.

1. The deterrence of crime by maintaining a visible police presence.
2. The maintenance of public order and a sense of security in the community.
3. The twenty-four-hour provision of certain services that are not crime related.[20]

The first two goals—deterring crime and keeping order—are generally accepted as legitimate police functions. The third, however, has been more controversial.

Community Concerns As noted in Chapter 5, the community era saw a resurgence of the patrol officer as a provider of community services, many of which have little to do with crime. The extent to which noncrime incidents dominate patrol officers' time is evident in the Police Services Study, a survey of 26,000 calls to police in sixty different neighborhoods. The study found that only one out of every five calls involved the report of criminal activity.[21] (See Figure 6.2 for the results of another survey of crime calls.)

There is some debate over whether community services should be allowed to dominate patrol officers' duties. The question, however, remains: If the police do not handle these problems, who will? Few cities have the financial resources to hire public servants to deal specifically with, for example, finding shelter for homeless persons. Furthermore, the police are on call twenty-four hours a day, seven days a week, making them uniquely accessible to citizens.

Law Enforcement and Mental Illness

Of particular concern is the frequency with which police officers on patrol find themselves acting as psychiatric social workers. According to various studies, between 7 percent and 10 percent of all

FIGURE 6.2 Calls for Service

Over a period of fifteen months, researchers at the University of New Mexico gathered information on approximately 700,000 calls for service received by the Albuquerque Police Department (APD). As the data below show, the APD deals with far more calls for service involving nonviolent incidents than violent incidents. Indeed, traffic-related calls occurred almost three times as often as the next most common type of call.

CALL TYPE	PERCENT OF CALLS
Traffic	37
Suspicious persons	13
Public disorder*	13
Property crime	9
Violent crime	5
House alarm	5
Auto theft	2
Hang up call	1
Unknown/other	15

*Examples: drunk, disorderly, begging, prostitution.

Source: Dan Cathey and Paul Guerin, *Analyzing Calls for Service to the Albuquerque Police Department* (Albuquerque, N.M.: Institute for Social Research, University of New Mexico, June 2009), Table 4, page 6.

▲ Given that most patrol shifts end without an officer making a single arrest, what activities take up most of a patrol officer's time?

Rod Lamkey Jr/AFP/Getty Images

police-public contacts involve people with mental illness.[22] If law enforcement officers are not properly trained or otherwise prepared for these encounters, fatalities can result, as in the case described in the opening of this chapter. By one estimate, at least half of the people justifiably killed by the police each year are mentally ill.[23]

To better prepare officers for dealing with such situations, a number of law enforcement agencies have instituted mandatory *crisis intervention team (CIT)* training programs. CIT teaches officers to recognize behavioral cues associated with mental illness and develop strategies of de-escalation, primarily with the goal of preventing the use of force against mentally ill civilians. More than three thousand state and local police departments have established crisis intervention teams, which often include the following elements:

1. Law enforcement officers who have completed the CIT program.
2. Access to mental health professionals who are "on call" to respond to police requests for assistance.
3. Drop-off locations, such as hospitals or mobile crisis vehicles, that provide mental health services beyond the expertise of law enforcement agencies.[24]

On the positive side, it appears that the crisis intervention model is favorably viewed by police officers and can result in reduced arrest rates for mentally ill persons.[25] At the same time, such programs may be beyond the limited financial and personnel resources of small law enforcement agencies in rural areas.

Patrol Activities   To recap, the purposes of police patrols are to prevent and deter crime and also to provide social services. How can the police best accomplish these goals? Of course, each department has its own methods and strategies, but William Gay, Theodore Schell, and Stephen Schack divide routine patrol activity into four general categories:[26]

1. *Preventive patrol.* By maintaining a presence in a community, either in a car or on foot, patrol officers attempt to prevent crime from occurring. This strategy, which O. W. Wilson called "omnipresence," was a cornerstone of early policing philosophy and still takes up roughly 40 percent of patrol time.
2. *Calls for service.* Patrol officers spend nearly a quarter of their time responding to 911 calls for emergency service or other citizen problems and complaints.
3. *Administrative duties.* Paperwork takes up nearly 20 percent of patrol time. In Albuquerque, officers now spend 15 percent to 20 percent of their shifts saving and logging footage from their lapel cameras.[27]
4. *Officer-initiated activities.* Incidents in which the patrol officer initiates contact with citizens, such as stopping motorists and pedestrians and questioning them, account for 15 percent of patrol time.

The category estimates made by Gay, Schell, and Schack are not universally accepted. Professor of law enforcement Gary W. Cordner argues that administrative duties account for the largest percentage of patrol officers' time. According to Cordner, when officers are not consumed with paperwork and meetings, they are either answering calls for service (which takes up 67 percent of the officers' time on the street) or initiating activities themselves (the remaining 33 percent).[28]

Detective Investigations

Investigation is the second main function of police, along with patrol. Whereas patrol is primarily preventive, investigation is reactive. After a crime has been committed and the patrol officer has gathered the preliminary information from the crime scene, the responsibility of finding "who dunnit" is delegated to the investigator, generally known as the detective. The most common way for someone to become a detective is to be promoted from patrol officer. Detectives have not been the focus of nearly as much reform attention as their patrol counterparts, mainly because the scope of the detective's job is limited to law enforcement, with less emphasis given to social services and order maintenance.

The detective's profession is not quite as glamorous as it is sometimes portrayed by the media. Detectives spend much of their time investigating common crimes such as burglaries and are more likely to be tracking down stolen property than a murderer. They must also prepare cases for trial, which involves a great deal of time-consuming paperwork. Furthermore, a landmark Rand Corporation study estimated that more than 97 percent of cases that are "solved" can be attributed to a patrol officer making an arrest at the scene, witnesses or victims identifying the perpetrator, or detectives undertaking routine investigative procedures that could easily be performed by clerical personnel.[29]

Aggressive Investigation Strategies

Detective bureaus also have the option of implementing aggressive strategies. For example, if detectives suspect that a person was involved in the robbery of a Mercedes-Benz parts warehouse, one of them might pose as a "fence"—or purchaser of stolen goods. In what is known as a "sting" operation, the suspect is deceived into thinking that the detective (fence) wants to buy stolen car parts. After the transaction takes place, the suspect can be arrested.

Undercover Operations and Informants

Perhaps the most dangerous and controversial operation a law enforcement agent can undertake is to go *undercover*, or to assume a false identity in order to obtain information concerning illegal activities. Though each department has its own guidelines on when undercover operations are necessary, all that is generally required is the suspicion that illegal activity is taking place. Today, undercover officers are commonly used to infiltrate large-scale narcotics operations or those run by organized crime.

In some situations, a detective bureau may not want to take the risk of exposing an officer to undercover work or may believe that an outsider cannot infiltrate an organized crime network. When the police need access and information, they have the option of turning to a confidential informant (CI). A CI is a person who is involved in criminal activity and gives information about that activity and those who engage in it to the police. As many as 80 percent of all illegal drug cases in the United States involve confidential informants. "They can get us into places we can't go," says one police administrator. "Without them, narcotics cases would practically cease to function."[30]

Detective The primary police investigator of crimes.

Confidential Informant (CI) A human source for police who provides information concerning illegal activity in which he or she is involved.

▲ On September 16, 2016, two FBI agents search the apartment of Ahmad Khan Rahami in Elizabeth, New Jersey. Rahami was wanted in connection with setting off a series of bombs nearby that injured twenty-nine people. **Which method does the FBI favor when identifying potential terrorism suspects? What are some of the pros and cons of this strategy?**

JEWEL SAMAD/AFP/Getty Images

Preventive Policing and Domestic Terrorism Aggressive investigative strategies also play a crucial role in the federal government's efforts to combat domestic terrorism. Because would-be terrorists often need help to procure the weaponry necessary for their schemes, they are natural targets for well-placed informants and undercover agents. "We're not going to wait for the person to mobilize on his own time line," says Michael B. Steinbach, executive director of the FBI's National Security Branch.[31] According to an analysis by the *New York Times*, about two-thirds of all federal prosecutions involving those suspected of supporting the Islamic State terrorist organization have relied on evidence gathered by undercover operatives or informants.[32]

The recent conviction of Emanuel Lutchman provides an example of *preventive policing*, a popular counterterrorism strategy employed by the federal government. FBI agents arrested Lutchman for conspiring with members of the Islamic State to attack a Rochester, New York, restaurant on New Year's Eve, 2015. Prior to the arrest, a paid FBI informant had driven Lutchman to a Walmart to buy a machete, knives, ski masks, and other supplies needed for the planned attack. In January 2017, Lutchman pleaded guilty to providing material support to the Islamic State and was sentenced to twenty years in federal prison.

With preventive policing, then, the goal is not to solve the crime after it has happened. Rather, the goal is to prevent the crime from happening in the first place. Inevitably, such tactics raise the issue of entrapment. As you learned in Chapter 4, entrapment is a possible defense for criminal behavior when a government agent plants the idea of committing a crime in the defendant's mind. In the case just described, Lutchman's family pointed out that the suspect suffered from mental illness and that the FBI informant had to "loan" him $40 to purchase the supplies for the attack. "He didn't have money to buy Pampers for his son," Lutchman's grandmother said. "How would he find money to go buy these [weapons]?"[33]

Although the entrapment defense has been raised often in domestic terrorism cases involving informants and undercover agents, it has yet to succeed. The government has been uniformly successful in proving that these defendants were predisposed to commit the crime regardless of any outside influence.

Clearance Rates and Cold Cases

The ultimate goal of all law enforcement activity is to *clear* a crime, or secure the arrest and prosecution of the offender. Even a cursory glance at **clearance rates,** which show the percentage of reported crimes that have been cleared, reveals that investigations succeed only part of the time. In 2015, just 62 percent of homicides and 46 percent of total violent crimes were solved, while police cleared only 19 percent of property crimes.[34] For the most part, the different clearance rates for different crimes reflect the resources that a law enforcement agency expends on each type of crime. The police generally investigate a murder or a rape more vigorously than the theft of an automobile or a computer.

Clearance Rates A comparison of the number of crimes cleared by arrest and prosecution with the number of crimes reported during any given time period.

As a result of low clearance rates, police departments are saddled with an increasing number of **cold cases,** or criminal investigations that are not cleared after a certain amount of time. (The length of time before a case becomes "cold" varies from department to department. In general, a cold case must be "somewhat old" but not "so old that there can be no hope of ever solving it."[35]) Even using the various technologies we will explore in the next section, cold case investigations rarely succeed. A RAND study found that only about one in twenty cold cases results in an arrest, and only about one in a hundred results in a conviction.[36]

Forensic Investigations and DNA

Although the crime scene typically offers a wealth of evidence, some of it is incomprehensible to a patrol officer or detective without assistance. For that aid, law enforcement officers rely on experts in **forensics,** the practice of using science and technology to investigate crimes. Forensic experts apply their knowledge to items found at the crime scene to determine crucial facts such as:

- The cause of death or injury.
- The time of death or injury.
- The type of weapon or weapons used.
- The identity of the crime victim, if that information is otherwise unavailable.
- The identity of the offender (in the best-case scenario).

To assist forensic experts, many police departments operate or are affiliated with crime laboratories. Indeed, there are approximately four hundred publicly funded crime laboratories in the United States. As we noted in the previous chapter, the FBI also offers the services of its crime lab to agencies with limited resources. The FBI's aid in this area is crucial, given that the nation's crime labs are burdened with a crippling backlog of requests for forensic services.

Crime Scene Forensics
The first law enforcement agent to reach a crime scene has the important task of protecting any **trace evidence** from contamination. Trace evidence is generally very small—often invisible to the naked human eye—and often requires technological aid for detection. Hairs, fibers, blood, fingerprints, broken glass, and footprints are all examples of trace evidence. A study released by the National Institute of Justice confirmed that when police are able to link such evidence to a suspect, the likelihood of a conviction rises dramatically.[37]

Police will also search a crime scene for bullets and spent cartridge casings. These items can provide clues as to how far the shooter was from the target. They can also be compared with information stored in national firearms databases to determine, under some circumstances, the gun used and its most recent owner. The study of firearms and its application to solving crimes goes under the general term **ballistics.** A new generation of ballistics technology allows technicians to create a 3D image of a bullet and match that image to the gun from which the original was fired.

Fingerprint Reliability
For more than a century, the most important piece of trace evidence has been the human fingerprint. Because no two fingerprints are alike, they are considered reliable sources of identification. Forensic scientists compare a fingerprint lifted from a crime scene with that of a suspect and declare a match if there are between eight and sixteen "points of similarity."

This method of identification, though highly reliable, is not infallible.[38] It is often difficult to lift a suitable print from a crime scene, and researchers have uncovered numerous

Cold Case A criminal investigation that has not been solved after a certain amount of time.

Forensics The application of science to establish facts and evidence during the investigation of crimes.

Trace Evidence Evidence such as a fingerprint, blood, or hair found in small amounts at a crime scene.

Ballistics The study of firearms, including the firing of the weapon and the flight of the bullet.

CAREERS IN CJ

Martha Blake Forensic Scientist

Courtesy of Martha Blake

In high school, I was interested in science, but didn't want to end up being a technician doing the same thing every day. I was looking in college catalogues and came across criminalistics at U.C. Berkeley. The coursework included such courses as microscopy, instrumental analysis, trace evidence, criminal law, and statistics, and it sounded fascinating. I decided in my senior year of high school to become a forensic scientist.

As quality assurance manager at the San Francisco Police Department's crime lab, I am often called to criminal court to testify about evidence that has passed through our lab. I am always nervous when I testify, and I think it is healthy to be a little nervous. As an expert witness, the most challenging part of my testimony is describing my findings to a jury of primarily nonscientists in a way that will make my testimony understandable and credible. I've found that juries tend to understand evidence that is part of their lives. Everyone can identify the writing of a family member or spouse, so describing how handwriting is identified is not too hard. Explaining how DNA analysis works is more difficult.

SOCIAL MEDIA CAREER TIP When people search for you online, they won't click past the first page. Check to see where your material appears on a regular basis.

---

cases in which innocent persons were convicted based on evidence obtained through faulty fingerprinting procedures.[39]

As a result, law enforcement agencies are increasingly relying on technological advances to improve fingerprint collection methods. For instance, forensic science specialists are now able to use ultraviolet light to locate fingerprints (and other trace elements, such as bodily fluids and gunshot residue) at a crime scene. Then, instead of "dusting"—or applying chemicals—to treat the fingerprint, the forensic scientist takes a high-resolution digital photograph of the print. Not only does this process preserve the integrity of evidence on which the fingerprint is located, but it also provides investigators with a much more precise print for comparison.[40]

The DNA Revolution

The technique of **DNA fingerprinting,** or using a suspect's DNA to match the suspect to a crime, emerged in the mid-1990s and has now all but replaced fingerprint evidence in many types of criminal investigations. The shift has been a boon to crime fighters: One law enforcement agent likened DNA fingerprinting to "the finger of God pointing down" at a guilty suspect.[41]

DNA, which is the same in each cell of a person's body, provides a "genetic blueprint" or "code" for every living organism. DNA fingerprinting is useful in criminal investigations because no two people, save for identical twins, have the same genetic code. Therefore, lab technicians can compare the DNA sample of a suspect with the evidence found at the

DNA Fingerprinting The identification of a person based on a sample of her or his DNA, the genetic material found in the cells of all living things.

crime scene. The technicians will look for thirteen points on the DNA fingerprint called "markers." If the match is negative, it is certain that the two samples did not come from the same source. If the match is positive for each of the thirteen markers, the lab will determine the odds that the DNA sample could have come from someone other than the suspect. Those odds are so high—sometimes reaching 30 billion to one—that a match is practically conclusive.[42]

The DNA fingerprinting process begins when forensic technicians gather blood, semen, skin, saliva, or hair from the scene of a crime. Blood cells and sperm are rich in DNA, making them particularly useful in murder and rape cases. DNA has also been extracted from sweat on dirty laundry, skin cells on eyeglasses, and saliva on used envelope seals. Once a suspect is identified, her or his DNA can be used to determine whether she or he can be placed at the crime scene. In 2016, for example, investigators in Chicago connected Losardo Lucas to a home invasion that had taken place two years earlier by obtaining DNA from a cigarette butt he was careless enough to leave behind.

DNA in Action   The ability to find genetic information on such a wide variety of evidence, as well as the genetic information's longevity and accuracy, greatly increases the chances that a crime will be solved. Indeed, police no longer need a witness or even a suspect in custody to solve crimes. What they do need is a piece of evidence and a database.

In 1990, for example, eleven-year-old Robin Cornell and thirty-two-year-old Lisa Story were murdered in a Cape Coral, Florida, apartment that Story was sharing with Cornell's mother. For over twenty-five years, local police were unable to establish any meaningful leads on the killer. In August 2016, however, authorities collected a DNA sample from Joseph Zieler, who had been arrested in North Fort Myers, Florida, on a charge of felony aggravated battery for shooting his son with a pellet gun. Zieler's DNA matched a stored DNA sample taken from the Cape Coral crime scene, and he was charged with, among other crimes, double murder.

Databases and Cold Hits   The identification of Joseph Zieler is an example of what police call a **cold hit**, which occurs when law enforcement officers find a suspect "out of nowhere" by comparing DNA evidence from a crime scene against the contents of a database. The largest and most important database is the National Combined DNA Index System (CODIS). Operated by the FBI since 1998, CODIS gives local and state law enforcement agencies access to the DNA profiles of almost 16 million people who have been connected to criminal activity. As of November 2016, the database had produced about 355,000 cold hits nationwide.[43]

New Developments   DNA fingerprinting has been widely available for a relatively short time, and the scope of its investigative uses continues to expand. For example, a new rapid-testing device reduces the time needed to process DNA samples from at least two weeks to ninety minutes. This technology, which the FBI started using in 2016, will aid law enforcement immensely by quickly matching suspects to crimes.[44] Other recent developments involving DNA fingerprinting technology include:

1. *Touch DNA*, which allows investigators to test for the presence of DNA by scraping items such as a piece of food or an article of clothing for microscopic cells left behind by the suspect.
2. *Familial searches*, based on the premise that parents, siblings, and other relatives have DNA similar to that of suspects who might be unavailable for testing.

Learning Objective 3 Describe how forensic experts use DNA fingerprinting to solve crimes.

Cold Hit The establishment of a connection between a suspect and a crime, often through the use of DNA evidence, in the absence of an ongoing criminal investigation.

3. The possible use of DNA as a *genetic witness* that can provide law enforcement with a physical description of a suspect, including age and eye, skin, and hair color. This developing branch of DNA fingerprinting, known as *phenotyping*, could eventually provide forensic scientists with enough genetic information to create a facial image of a criminal suspect.[45]

Because of its cost, DNA fingerprinting has traditionally been used mostly in conjunction with "important" violent crime investigations. The National Institute of Justice has found, however, that using DNA testing in property crimes not only is cost effective, but also dramatically increases the police's ability to identify burglary and theft suspects.[46] Because many property offenders commit violent crimes as well, it seems logical that apprehending "unimportant" burglars and thieves would prevent a significant amount of more serious criminal activity.[47]

DNA Collection Policies   Authorities in all fifty states are required to collect DNA samples from offenders who have been convicted of felonies. In addition, more than half the states authorize the collection of DNA from those who have been arrested for a crime but not yet convicted. Indeed, the FBI's CODIS database contains more than 2.5 million DNA profiles of arrestees. As the earlier example of Joseph Zieler—who had been arrested for battery— shows, this policy provides a valuable tool for cold case investigators. But is it fair to arrestees who may not have committed a crime? We examine how the United States Supreme Court answered that question in the feature *Landmark Cases*—Maryland v. King.

Police Strategies: What Works

Karlton "Bam" McFay had been discovered shot to death in his Oakland, California, home. Phong Trang, a detective with the Oakland Police Department, was searching for clues at the crime scene when a woman walked up to the line of yellow police tape. The killer was a man called "Quacky," the woman whispered. None of Trang's contacts knew of a Quacky, but one did recall a "Cracky." Following this lead, Trang eventually tracked down Cracky, whose real name was James Watson-Dixon. After Watson-Dixon admitted to shooting McFay during an attempted robbery, he was charged with murder.[48]

Studies show that clearance rates are seven times higher when a suspect is identified early in an investigation.[49] Of course, police officers are rarely lucky enough to have a mysterious stranger walk up and provide the actual wrongdoer's name at a crime scene. In this section, we will examine the strategies being used by police departments to reduce and prevent crime in the absence of such a stroke of good luck.

Maryland v. King

After Maryland resident Alonzo King was arrested for threatening a group of people with a shotgun, local police took a swab of DNA from his cheek. The sample matched evidence from an unsolved rape case in the state DNA database, and King was eventually convicted of that crime and sentenced to life in prison. He challenged this outcome, focusing on the unfairness of a Maryland law that allows for DNA fingerprinting of those who have been arrested, but not yet convicted, of violent crimes. King's challenge gave the United States Supreme Court a chance to decide a crucial question: Is taking DNA samples from arrestees (a) merely the equivalent of traditional fingerprinting or (b) an unacceptable invasion of privacy of the potentially innocent?

> *Maryland v. King*
> **United States Supreme Court**
> 569 U.S. ____ (2013)

In the Words of the Court . . .

Justice Kennedy, Majority Opinion

At issue is a standard, expanding technology already in widespread use throughout the Nation.

DNA identification is an advanced technique superior to fingerprinting in many ways, so much so that to insist on fingerprints as the norm would make little sense to either the forensic expert or a layperson. The additional intrusion upon the arrestee's privacy beyond that associated with fingerprinting is not significant . . . and DNA is a markedly more accurate form of identifying arrestees. A suspect who has changed his facial features to evade photographic identification or even one who has undertaken the more arduous task of altering his fingerprints cannot escape the revealing power of his DNA. * * * The only difference between DNA analysis and fingerprint databases is the unparalleled accuracy DNA provides.

The expectations of privacy of an individual taken into police custody "necessarily [are] of a diminished scope. . . ." "[B]oth the person and the property in his immediate possession may be searched at the station house." * * * A suspect's criminal history is a critical part of his identity that officers should know when processing him for detention. It is a common occurrence that "[p]eople detained for minor offenses can turn out to be the most devious and dangerous criminals."

Decision

The Court upheld Maryland's right to take DNA samples from people arrested for serious crimes and, in the process, validated similar laws in twenty-seven other states. The decision was not, however, based on cold case concerns. Instead, the Court justified the practice as necessary to help police identify suspects in custody.

FOR CRITICAL ANALYSIS

In his dissent, Justice Scalia argued, "[B]ecause of today's decision, your DNA can be taken and entered into a national database if you are ever arrested, rightly or wrongly, and for whatever reason." Do you agree with Scalia that the Court erred in upholding arrestee-DNA-testing laws? Why or why not?

Calls for Service

While law enforcement officers do not like to think of themselves as being at the "beck and call" of citizens, that is the operational basis of much police work. All police departments practice **incident-driven policing,** in which calls for service are the primary instigators of action. Ideally, about one-third of a patrol officer's time should be taken with responding to calls for service.[50] In practice, the percentage is often much greater. During a typical eight-hour shift, for example, a Philadelphia patrol police officer will answer eighty 911 calls for service.[51]

Response Time and Efficiency The speed with which the police respond to calls for service has traditionally been seen as a crucial aspect of crime fighting and crime prevention. In incident-driven policing, the ideal scenario is as follows: A citizen

Incident-Driven Policing A reactive approach to policing that emphasizes a speedy response to calls for service.

sees a person committing a crime and calls 911, and the police arrive quickly, catching the perpetrator in the act. Alternatively, a citizen who is the victim of a crime, such as a robbery, calls 911 as soon as possible, and the police arrive to catch the robber before she or he can flee the immediate area of the crime. Although such scenarios are quite rare in real life, **response time,** or the time elapsed between the instant a call for service is received and the instant the police arrive on the scene, has become a benchmark for police efficiency.

Improving Response Time Efficiency

Many police departments have come to realize that overall response time is not as critical as response time for the most important calls. For this reason, a number of metropolitan areas have introduced 311 nonemergency call systems to reduce the strain on 911 operations. The Miami Police Department deploys about fifty "public service aides" to answer nonemergency calls, freeing up sworn officers for more pressing matters. Another popular method of improving performance in this area is a **differential response** strategy, in which the police distinguish among different calls for service so that they can respond more quickly to the most serious incidents.

Suppose, for example, that a police department receives two calls for service at the same time. The first caller reports that a burglar is in her house, and the second says that he has returned home from work to find his automobile missing. If the department employs differential response, the burglary in progress—a "hot" crime—will receive immediate attention. The missing automobile—a "cold" crime that could have been committed several hours earlier—will receive attention "as time permits," and the caller may even be asked to make an appointment to come to the police station to formally report the theft. For example, officers from the Fort Worth (Texas) Police Department take an average of 7:06 minutes to respond to "top-priority calls," compared with an average of 27:53 minutes for all calls.[52] (See Figure 6.3 for more examples.)

Learning Objective 4 Explain why differential response strategies enable police departments to respond more efficiently to 911 calls.

FIGURE 6.3 Putting the Theory of Differential Response into Action

Differential response strategies are based on a simple concept: Treat emergencies like emergencies and nonemergencies like nonemergencies. As you can see below, calls for service that involve "hot crimes" will be dealt with immediately, while those that report "cold crimes" will be dealt with at some point in the future.

"HOT" CALLS FOR SERVICE—IMMEDIATE RESPONSE	
Complaint to 911 Officer	**Rationale**
"I just got home from work, and I can see someone in my bedroom through the window."	Possibility that the intruder is committing a crime.
"My husband has a baseball bat, and he says he's going to kill me."	Crime in progress.
"A woman in a green jacket just grabbed my purse and ran away."	Chances of catching the suspect are increased with immediate action.
"COLD" CALLS FOR SERVICE—ALTERNATIVE RESPONSE	
"I got to my office about two hours ago, but I just noticed that the laser printer was stolen during the night."	The crime occurred at least two hours earlier.
"The guy in the apartment above me has been selling pot for years, and I'm sick and tired of it."	Not an emergency situation.
"My husband came home late two nights ago with a black eye, and I finally got him to admit that he didn't run into a doorknob. Larry Smith smacked him."	Past crime with a known suspect who is unlikely to flee.

Source: Adapted from John S. Dempsey and Linda S. Forst, *An Introduction to Policing*, 8th ed. (Boston: Cengage Learning, 2016), 273–274.

911 Technology Automatic differential response is an integral part of **computer-aided dispatch (CAD)** systems, used by nearly every police department in the country. With CAD, a 911 dispatcher enters the information from a caller into his or her computer, which prioritizes the emergency based on its nature. CAD also verifies the caller's address and phone number, and determines the closest patrol unit to the site of the emergency. In many jurisdictions, the details, including any previous 911 calls from the location, are then sent to a *mobile digital terminal* in the police officer's patrol car.

About 70 percent of 911 calls are made with wireless phones and often cannot be tracked using existing technology.[53] As utility companies increasingly abandon copper landlines for fiber-optic cables, however, more police departments will be able to adopt Next Generation 911. This system makes it possible for CAD to receive text messages, videos, photos, and location data about crime incidents.

Consider just one example of how text-to-911 can work. In Black Hawk County, Iowa, a woman locked herself in her bedroom when someone broke into her home. Afraid that a noise would alert the intruder to her location, she texted 911, and police officers were able to arrest him without further incident.[54]

CJ & TECHNOLOGY

911 Apps

To address some of the problems with existing cellphone 911 service, dozens of 911 enhancement apps have been created over the past few years. Most of these apps claim to connect the user to 911 more quickly and with greater location accuracy. They also provide "extras" not traditionally associated with 911 systems. For example, the 911 Help SMS app calls 911 while simultaneously notifying predetermined family members and friends with texts that include the caller's GPS coordinates.

Personal safety apps can be tailored for specific crime-related circumstances. The bSafe app will privately alert friends that the user has safely reached his or her destination. When bSafe's alarm is triggered, the app immediately notes the user's GPS location and starts broadcasting video taken by the user's cellphone. In addition, several apps are specifically designed to help domestic violence victims by giving them an easy and silent way to send text messages to law enforcement and trusted contacts. Such apps are often disguised as generic news apps to hide their purpose from any potential abuser who may have access to the phone.

Thinking about 911 Apps

Can you think of any class of crime victims besides domestic violence victims that would benefit from a specialized app? If you were to design a 911 app to help this group, what features would you include?

Patrol Strategies

Many experts believe that, in the words of Grand Rapids (Michigan) police chief Kevin Belk, an overreliance on calls for service "tends to make you a reactive department," rather than a police force that prevents crimes from happening in the first place.[55] Similarly, another traditional police strategy, *random patrol*, is increasingly felt to be an inefficient use of law enforcement resources.[56]

Random patrol refers to police officers making the rounds of a specific area with the general goal of detecting and preventing crime. Every police department in the United States randomly patrols its jurisdiction using automobiles. In addition, 53 percent utilize foot patrols, 32 percent bicycle patrols, 16 percent motorcycle patrols, 4 percent boat patrols, and 1 percent horse patrols.[57]

Testing Random Patrol Police researchers have been questioning the effectiveness of random patrols since the influential Kansas City Preventive Patrol Experiment of the early 1970s. As part of this experiment, different neighborhoods in the city were subjected to three different levels of patrol: random patrol by a single police car, random patrol by multiple police cars, and no random patrol whatsoever. The results of the Kansas City experiment were somewhat shocking. Researchers found that increasing or decreasing preventive patrol had little or no impact on crimes, public opinion, the effectiveness of the police, police response time, traffic accidents, or reports of crime to police.[58]

For some, the Kansas City experiment and similar data prove that patrol officers, after a certain threshold, are not effective in preventing crime and that scarce law enforcement resources should therefore be diverted to other areas. "It makes about as much sense to have police patrol routinely in cars to fight crime as it does to have firemen patrol routinely in fire trucks to fight fire," said University of Delaware professor Carl Klockars.[59] Still, random patrols are important for maintaining community relations, and they have been shown to reduce fear of crime in areas where police have an obvious presence.[60]

Directed Patrols In contrast to random patrols, directed patrols target specific areas of a city and often attempt to prevent a specific type of crime. Directed patrols have found favor among law enforcement experts as being a more efficient use of police resources than random patrols, as indicated by the Philadelphia Foot Patrol Experiment.

During this experiment, extra foot patrols were utilized in sixty Philadelphia locations plagued by high levels of violent crime. During three months of directed patrols, arrests increased by 13 percent in the targeted areas, and violent crime decreased by 23 percent. In addition, an estimated fifty-three violent crimes were prevented over the three-month period.[61]

Smart Policing

In the previous chapter, we discussed how predictive, or intelligence-led, policing strategies help law enforcement agencies anticipate patterns of criminal activity, allowing them to respond to, or even prevent, crime more effectively. Predictive policing is increasingly attractive to police administrators because, in theory, it requires fewer resources than traditional policing.

The New Haven (Connecticut) Department of Police Service's (NHPD) response to rising crime rates at the beginning of the 2010s offers a representative example of "smart policing" in action. First, the NHPD Crime Analysis Unit (CAU) determined that the Newhallville neighborhood—home to three major gangs—had the highest violent crime rates of any neighborhood in the city. Going a step further, the CAU identified high-risk areas within Newhallville and then added extra foot patrols in those areas.

The additional officers were tasked not only with preventing crime but also with engaging the community (common civilian complaints included poor street lighting and too many blighted properties). Twenty-six weeks after the NHPD added the extra foot patrols, violent crime in the high-risk areas of Newhallville had dropped 56 percent.[62]

Finding "Hot Spots" Predictive policing strategies like those used in Newhallville are strongly linked with directed patrols, which seek to improve on random patrols by targeting specific high-crime areas already known to law enforcement. The target areas for directed patrols are often called hot spots because they contain greater numbers of criminals and have higher-than-average levels of victimization.

Directed Patrol A patrol strategy designed to focus on a specific type of criminal activity in a specific geographic area.

Hot Spots Concentrated areas of high criminal activity that draw a directed police response.

Hot Spot Technology On one level, focusing on hot spots seems relatively straight-forward. As one police captain puts it, "We pick the areas that have the most shootings, the most robberies, and the most property crimes, and we put additional cops in those areas to bring down crime."[63]

On another level, to be effective, these strategies must be relatively sophisticated. They often rely on complicated algorithms and computer-based **crime mapping** to locate and identify hot spots and "cool" them down. Crime mapping uses geographic information systems (GIS) to track criminal acts as they occur in time and space. Once sufficient information has been gathered, it is analyzed to predict future crime patterns.

The Effect of Timing Why does hot spot policing work? Deterrence seems to play a crucial role. That is, if offenders see police officers constantly patrolling a block or neighborhood, they will be less likely to offend in that location.

Criminologists Lawrence Sherman and David Weisburd enhanced our understanding of the deterrent impact of these strategies more than twenty years ago by focusing on the importance of geography and time. Sherman and Weisburd observed that after a police officer left a certain high-crime area, about fifteen minutes elapsed before criminal activity occurred at that spot.[64] Therefore, a police officer on patrol is most efficient when she or he spends a certain amount of time at a hot spot and then returns after fifteen minutes.

A more recent experiment involving the Sacramento Police Department supports this hypothesis. Over a three-month period, twenty-one crime hot spots in the city received fifteen-minute randomized patrols, while another twenty-one received normal random patrols. Using calls for service as a measuring stick, the hot spots subject to fifteen-minute patrols were found to experience much less criminal activity.[65]

The Rise of CompStat

Computerized crime mapping was popularized when the New York Police Department launched CompStat in the mid-1990s. Still in use, CompStat starts with police officers reporting the exact location of crime and other crime-related information to department officials. These reports are then fed into a computer, which prepares grids of a particular city or neighborhood and highlights areas with a high incidence of serious offenses. (See Figure 6.4 for an example of a GIS crime map.)

In New York and many other cities, the police department holds "Crime Control Strategy Meetings" during which precinct commanders are held accountable for CompStat's data-based reports in their districts. In theory, this system provides the police with accurate information about patterns of crime and gives them the ability to "flood" hot spots with officers at short notice. Police departments in forty-three of the nation's fifty largest cities are using CompStat,[66] and Wesley Skogan, a criminologist at Northwestern University, believes that CompStat and similar technologies were the most likely cause of declines in big-city crime during the first decade of the 2000s.[67]

Arrest Strategies

Like patrol strategies, arrest strategies can be divided into two categories that reflect the intent of police administrators. **Reactive arrests** are arrests made by police officers, usually on general patrol, who observe a criminal act or respond to a call for service. **Proactive arrests** occur when the police take the initiative to target a particular type of criminal or behavior. "The hypothesis," explains Lawrence Sherman, "is that a high certainty of arrest for a narrowly defined set of offenses or offenders will accomplish more than low arrest certainty for a broad range of targets."[68]

Crime Mapping Technology that allows crime analysts to identify trends and patterns of criminal behavior within a given area.

Reactive Arrests Arrests that come about as part of the ordinary routine of police patrol and responses to calls for service.

Proactive Arrests Arrests that occur because of concerted efforts by law enforcement agencies to respond to a particular type of criminal or criminal behavior.

FIGURE 6.4 A GIS Crime Map

This crime map shows the incidence of gang-activity hot spots in Phoenix, Arizona.

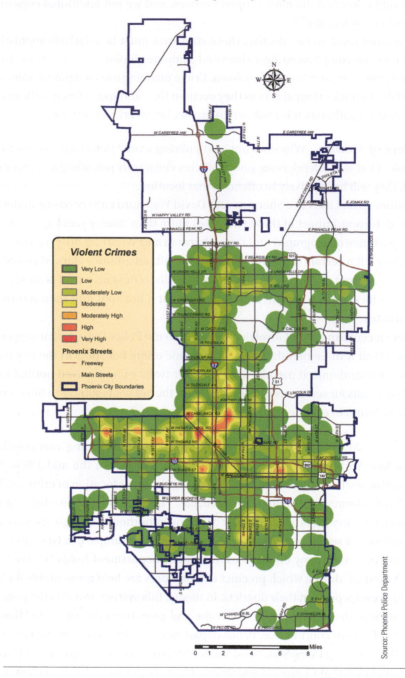

Violent Crimes
- Very Low
- Low
- Moderately Low
- Moderate
- Moderately High
- High
- Very High

Phoenix Streets
- Freeway
- Main Streets
- Phoenix City Boundaries

Miles
0 1 2 4 6 8

Source: Phoenix Police Department

The Broken Windows Effect

To a certain extent, the popularity of proactive theories was solidified by a magazine article that James Q. Wilson and George L. Kelling wrote in 1982.[69] In their piece, entitled "Broken Windows," Wilson and Kelling argued that reform-era policing strategies focused on violent crime to the detriment of the vital police role of promoting the quality of life in neighborhoods. As a result, many communities, particularly in large cities, had fallen into a state of disorder and disrepute, with two very important consequences.

First, these neighborhoods—with their broken windows, dilapidated buildings, and lawless behavior by residents—were sending out "signals" that criminal activity was tolerated. Second, this disorder was spreading fear among law-abiding citizens, dissuading them from leaving their homes or attempting to improve their surroundings. Thus, the **broken windows theory** recommends maintaining order in these neighborhoods by cracking down on "quality-of-life" crimes such as panhandling, public drinking and urinating, loitering, and graffiti painting. Only by encouraging directed arrest strategies with regard to quality-of-life crime, Wilson and Kelling argued, could American cities be rescued from rising crime rates.

A Mixed Evaluation

Along with CompStat, the implementation of Wilson and Kelling's theory has been given a great deal of credit for the crime decreases in the United States (particularly New York) that have occured over the past three decades.[70] It continues to influence police strategy: Several years ago, the Cincinnati Police Department cracked down on traffic accidents in "micro" hot spots of criminal activity such as intersections and street corners. Within twelve months, the impacted areas had experienced a significant decrease in both traffic crashes and crime.[71]

Some experts question how much impact broken windows strategies actually have, pointing out that violent crime rates have also dropped in cities that do not implement this approach.[72] Critics also contend that instituting "zero-tolerance" arrest policies for lesser crimes in low-income neighborhoods not only discriminates against the poor and minority groups but also fosters a strong mistrust of police.[73] Such criticism was behind New York City's Criminal Justice Reform Act, which, in 2016, made quality-of-life crimes such as public urination, public alcohol consumption, and excessive noise civil rather than criminal offenses. The legislation is expected to divert 100,000 cases a year from the city's criminal justice system to civil courts.[74]

Community Policing and Problem Solving

In "Broken Windows," Wilson and Kelling insisted that, to reduce fear and crime in high-risk neighborhoods, police had to rely on the cooperation of citizens. For all its drawbacks, the political era of policing (see Chapter 5) did have characteristics that observers such as Wilson and Kelling have come to see as advantageous. During that period, the police were much more involved in the community than they were after the reforms.

Police officers in the nineteenth century performed many duties that today are associated with social services, such as operating soup kitchens and providing lodging for homeless people. They also played a more direct role in keeping public order by "running in" drunks and intervening in minor disturbances.[75] To a large degree, **community policing** advocates this understanding of the police mission.

Return to the Community

Community policing can be defined as an approach that promotes community-police partnerships, proactive problem solving, and community engagement to address issues such as fear of crime and the causes of such fear in a particular area. Neighborhood watch programs, in which police officers and citizens work together to prevent local crime and disorder, are a popular version of a community policing initiative.

Under community policing, patrol officers have the freedom to improvise. They are expected to develop personal relationships with residents and to encourage those residents to become involved in making the community a safer place. For example, beset by incidents of excessive force and high levels of citizen mistrust, the Albuquerque Police Department recently created six "neighborhood policing teams" to improve community relations. Each of these teams—made up of a sergeant and six patrol officers—works with residents to develop plans addressing specific problems in individual neighborhoods.[76]

Broken Windows Theory Wilson and Kelling's theory that a neighborhood in disrepair signals that criminal activity is tolerated in the area. By cracking down on quality-of-life crimes, police can reclaim the neighborhood and encourage law-abiding citizens to live and work there.

Community Policing A policing philosophy that emphasizes community support for and cooperation with the police in preventing crime.

Learning Objective 5 Explain community policing and its contribution to the concept of problem-oriented policing.

▲ A Grant County (Washington) sheriff's deputy allows local children to sit on his motorcycle during the annual Mattawa Community Days celebration. **How can establishing friendly relations with citizens help law enforcement agencies reduce crime?** Jessica Rinaldi/*Boston Globe*/Getty Images

Collaborative Reform

About two-thirds of all American police departments mention community policing in their mission statements, and a majority of the departments in large cities offer community police training for employees.[77] At the same time, the federal government has shifted local grant funds to fighting terrorism, and many local police departments continue to use aggressive tactics against low-level criminal behavior. The result seems to be a growing lack of trust between law enforcement and the public, particularly in minority communities. One resident of a mixed-race Cleveland, Ohio, neighborhood says that the police "don't make an effort to know us. They're trying to get a bust or a collar."[78]

To improve trust within their communities, a number of police departments have turned to *collaborative reform*. In this offshoot of community policing, law enforcement officials form partnerships with local leaders to address difficult issues such as police use of force and arrest policies. In 2012, in response to unacceptable numbers of police shootings of unarmed civilians, the Las Vegas Metropolitan Police Department (LVMPD) entered into a collaborative reform agreement with the federal government. This accord led to seventy-two LVMPD reforms. Many of them related to improved use-of-force training, as well as increased public involvement in reviews of deadly force incidents. Within two years, the number of officer-involved shootings in Las Vegas had dropped 36 percent.[79]

Problem-Oriented Policing

The city of Glendale, Arizona, was experiencing property crime levels that were 63 percent above the national average. Using crime mapping, the Glendale police found that a disproportionate number of the city's property offenses were taking place at ten Circle K convenience stores. After analyzing the situation, the police determined that Circle K management practices such as inadequate staffing, failure to respond to panhandling, and poor lighting were making the stores breeding grounds of property crime.

By working with Circle K to resolve these issues, as well as putting a proactive arrest strategy into effect in the stores, the Glendale police reduced property crime at the stores by 42 percent in a single year.[80] These efforts are an example of **problem-oriented policing,** a strategy based on the premise that police departments devote too many of their resources to reacting to calls for service and too few to "acting on their own initiative to prevent or reduce community problems."[81]

Long-Term Solutions Problem-oriented policing encourages police officers to stop looking at their work as a day-to-day proposition. Rather, they should try to shift the patterns of criminal behavior in a positive direction. For example, instead of responding to a 911 call concerning illegal drug use by simply arresting the offender—a short-term response—the patrol officers should also look at the long-term implications of the situation. They should analyze the pattern of similar arrests in the area and interview the arrestee to determine the reasons, if any, that the site was selected for drug activity.[82] Then additional police action should be taken to prevent further drug sales at the identified location. (See Figure 6.5 for an example of problem-oriented policing in action.)

Problem-Oriented Policing A policing philosophy that requires police to identify potential criminal activity and develop strategies to prevent or respond to that activity.

FIGURE 6.5 The SARA Model of Problem-Oriented Policing

The reaction of the Boston Police Department (BPD) to a surge in violent crime in the early 2000s gives an example of the four-step SARA (scanning, analysis, response, assessment) model of problem-oriented policing.

Step 1: *Scanning (identifying the problem).* The number of shootings, fatal and non-fatal, in Boston increased 133 percent from 2000 to 2006.

Step 2: *Analysis (researching the problem).* Gun violence "hot spots" covered 5.1 percent of Boston's square mileage and accounted for 53 percent of shooting incidents.

Step 3: *Response (finding a solution to the problem).* The BPD created Safe Street Teams (SSTs) consisting of a sergeant and six patrol officers to work each gun-violence hot spot. These SSTs sought to improve the appearance of the neighborhoods by removing graffiti and trash and repairing lighting systems. They also operated directed patrols and improved social services in the areas.

Step 4: *Assessment (determining whether the solution was effective).* Violent crimes declined by 17.3 percent over a three-year period in the targeted hot spots.

Source: Adapted from Bureau of Justice Assistance, *Boston, Massachusetts Smart Policing Initiative* (Washington, D.C.: U.S. Department of Justice, August 2012).

Focused Deterrence Pioneered in the 1990s as a problem-oriented approach to gang violence, *focused deterrence* has gained a foothold in smart policing tactics. Also known as "pulling levers," this method relies on direct communication with a targeted group of repeat offenders. For example, as part of its Gang Violence Reduction Strategy, the New Orleans Police Department (NOPD) recently called in 158 gang members for meetings with police officers and social service providers.

The message delivered at these meetings was twofold. First, police officers assured the gang members that, from that moment forward, any violent behavior would be met with an immediate and intense law enforcement response. Second, each gang member was offered job training, employment assistance, substance abuse treatment, housing assistance, and a variety of other opportunities. Although relatively few gang members took advantage of the social services, overall homicides in New Orleans declined significantly following the NOPD's implementation of this strategy.[83]

"Us versus Them": Issues in Modern Policing

"Nowadays, we're in a culture where everything's against the police, or at least in the areas I patrol," said Ernie Williams, an officer with the Philadelphia Police Department. "Social media, news outlets, they're really coming down on the police. And we still gotta come to work. I pray nobody's going to get shot or hurt, but the reality is, someone probably is. We still have a job to do. And at times it can be a very difficult job."[84]

Officer Williams was reacting to anti-police publicity that spread throughout the country following a number of high-profile encounters in which unarmed suspects were injured or killed by law enforcement agents. The negative force of these incidents—often captured on smartphone video recordings—was made worse by the fact that, in many cases, the police officer was white and the suspect was a member of a minority group. "Any cop that uses his gun now has to worry about being indicted and losing his job and family," remarked a New York City police officer.[85] This frustration underscores many of the work-related issues that bind police officers together while at the same time potentially alienating them from the society that they are sworn to protect and serve.

Police Subculture

In a national poll of police officers, 86 percent of the nearly eight thousand respondents agreed that the American public does not understand the risks and challenges of police work.[86] This "disconnect" between law enforcement and civilians is one of the hallmarks of **police subculture.** This broad term describes the basic assumptions and values that permeate law enforcement agencies and are taught to new members of a law enforcement agency as the proper way to think, perceive, and act. Every organization has a subculture, with values shaped by the particular aspects and pressures of that organization. In the police subculture, those values are formed in an environment characterized by danger, stress, boredom, and violence.

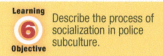

Learning Objective 6 Describe the process of socialization in police subculture.

The Core Values of Police Subculture

From the first day on the job, rookies begin the process of **socialization,** in which they are taught the values and rules of police work. This process is aided by a number of rituals that are common to the law enforcement experience. Police theorist Harry J. Mullins believes that the following rituals are critical to the police officer's acceptance, and even embrace, of police subculture:

- Attending a police academy.
- Working with a senior officer, who passes on the "lessons" of police work and life to the younger officer.
- Making the initial felony arrest.
- Using force to make an arrest for the first time.
- Using or witnessing deadly force for the first time.
- Witnessing major traumatic incidents for the first time.[87]

Each of these rituals makes it clear to the police officer that this is not a "normal" job. The only other people who can understand the stresses of police work are fellow officers, and consequently law enforcement officers tend to insulate themselves from civilians. Eventually, the insulation breeds mistrust, and the police officer develops an "us versus them" outlook toward those outside the force. In turn, this outlook creates what sociologist William Westly called the **blue curtain,** also known as the "blue wall of silence" or simply "the code."[88] This curtain separates the police from the civilians they are meant to protect.

Police Cynicism

A cynic is someone who universally distrusts human motives and expects nothing but the worst from human behavior. *Police cynicism* is characterized by a rejection of the ideals of truth and justice—the very values that an officer is sworn to uphold.[89] As cynical police officers lose respect for the law, they replace legal rules with those learned in the police subculture, which are believed to be more reflective of reality.

Along these lines, policing expert Otwin Marenin of Washington State University suggests that most police place civilians in one of three categories: good citizens, a**holes, and "symbolic assailants." The final category covers people who, through experience, a police officer believes to be capable of violence and therefore deserving of law enforcement attention. "The *good citizen* who walks out the back door of a school at midnight carrying a computer will be dismissed as nothing going on but a *symbolic assailant* will find himself or herself lying on the ground being handcuffed," writes Marenin.[90] Despite all of the laws and policies designed to eradicate this kind of discretionary thinking, it persists.

As suggested earlier, mutual suspicion between law enforcement and the public helps to explain the cynical nature of the police subculture. Two additional factors, discussed next, also strongly contribute to police cynicism:

1. The dangers of police work and
2. The need for police officers to use force.

Police Subculture The values and perceptions that are shared by members of a police department and, to a certain extent, by all law enforcement agents.

Socialization The process through which a police officer is taught the values and expected behavior of the police subculture.

Blue Curtain A metaphorical term used to refer to the value placed on secrecy and the general mistrust of the outside world shared by many police officers.

The Physical Dangers of Police Work

When Houston deputy constable Steve Faulkner leaves the house for work, his ten-year-old daughter gives him a kiss on the forehead and tells him to "be safe." She did not include the cautionary words as part of the ritual until July 7, 2016. On that day, a lone sniper killed five Dallas police officers and wounded seven others who were working a protest march on law enforcement use of force. Deputy Faulkner admits to sharing his daughter's concerns. "[The Dallas shootings change] the way you do patrolling," he says. "Your head's on a swivel now."[91]

Officers Killed and Assaulted

According to the Officer Down Memorial Page, the five Dallas police officers killed during the protest march were among 140 law enforcement officers who died in the line of duty in 2016.[92] The Dallas victims were also among twenty-one law enforcement officers killed in ambush attacks that year, up from eight in 2015 and the largest such figure in two decades.[93] In addition, about 50,000 assaults were committed against police officers in 2015, with 28 percent of these assaults resulting in an injury.[94] These numbers are troubling, but not necessarily surprising. As police experts John S. Dempsey and Linda S. Forst point out, police "deal constantly with what may be the most dangerous species on this planet—the human being."[95]

At the same time, Dempsey and Forst note that according to data compiled by the federal government, citizens and the police come into contact about 44 million times a year.[96] Given this figure, the police have relatively low death and injury rates. The statistical safety of police officers can be attributed to two factors. First, police academies emphasize officer safety, focusing on areas such as self-defense, firearm proficiency, arrest tactics, and nonlethal weapons (which will be addressed later in the chapter).

Second, police officers take extraordinary precautions to protect their physical safety, including wearing protective **body armor** underneath their clothing. The body armor most widely used by American police officers is made of Kevlar, a high-strength fiber discovered in 1964 by chemist Stephanie Kwolek. Low-level Kevlar can stop .357 and 9mm shots, while high-level "tactical armor" can deflect rifle and machine gun bullets. Seventy-one percent of local police departments in the United States require patrol officers to wear body armor at all times while in the field, a policy that has saved thousands of lives.[97]

Accidental Deaths

Despite perceptions to the contrary, a high percentage of deaths and injuries suffered by police officers are not the result of assaults by criminal suspects. Generally speaking, half of all law enforcement officer injuries are due to accidents, and about two-thirds of those injuries occur when officers are doing something other than making an arrest.[98] In particular, from 2006 to 2015, 603 police officers died from traffic-related accidents, compared with 521 who died from gunfire.[99]

▼ Family and colleagues mourn at the funeral of Prince William County (Virginia) police officer Ashley Guindon, who was fatally shot by a suspect in February 2016. **How might violence against police officers contribute to the "blue curtain" between law enforcement and the public?**

AP Photo/Cliff Owen

One reason for the traffic fatalities is that a number of law enforcement officers do not take simple precautions when behind the wheel. A recent study conducted by the National Highway Traffic Safety Administration found that 42 percent of police officers killed in vehicle crashes were not wearing seat belts.[100] Also, as Craig Floyd of the National Law Enforcement Officers Memorial Fund points out, nearly every police officer will be involved in a high-speed automobile response or chase during her or his career, but only 10 percent will be involved in a gunfight. Yet firearms training is common, while driver training is not.

Stress and the Mental Dangers of Police Work

In addition to physical dangers, police work entails considerable mental pressure and stress. Professor John Violanti and his colleagues at the University at Buffalo have determined that police officers experience unusually high levels of *cortisol*, otherwise known as the "stress hormone," which is associated with serious health problems such as diabetes and heart disease.[101] "In general, we train for the conflict itself," says retired police lieutenant Frank Borelli. "We [don't get enough] training on how to manage, long-term, the emotional trauma of the job."[102]

Police Stressors
The conditions that cause stress—such as worries over finances or relationships—are known as **stressors.** Each profession has its own set of stressors, but police are particularly vulnerable to occupational pressures and stress factors such as the following:

- The constant fear of being a victim of violent crime.
- Exposure to violent crime and its victims.
- The need to comply with the law in nearly every job action.
- Lack of community support.
- Negative media coverage.

Police officers may face a number of internal pressures as well, including limited opportunities for career advancement, excessive paperwork, and low wages and benefits.[103]

Both male and female law enforcement agents experience these stressors, as well as others such as lack of sleep and chaotic private lives. Some stressors are, however, unique to female police officers, for reasons we touched on in the last chapter. These challenges include sexism, sexual harassment, the constant demand to prove oneself and lack of acceptance in the male-dominated police subculture.[104]

The Consequences of Police Stress
Police stress can manifest itself in different ways. The University at Buffalo study cited above found that the stresses of law enforcement often lead to high blood pressure and heart problems.[105] Interviewing a random sample of 184 officers from eleven different law enforcement agencies, public health expert Elizabeth Mumford found that over half of both female and male police officers "screened positive for alcohol misuse."[106]

Burnout and PTSD
If stress becomes overwhelming, an officer may suffer from **burnout,** becoming listless and ineffective as a result of mental and physical exhaustion. Another problem related to stress is *post-traumatic stress disorder (PTSD).* Often recognized in war veterans and rape victims, PTSD is an anxiety disorder that develops in

Stressors The aspects of police work and life that lead to feelings of stress.

Burnout A mental state that occurs when a person suffers from exhaustion and has difficulty functioning normally as a result of overwork and stress.

reaction to a traumatic event. For police officers, such events might include the death of a fellow agent or the shooting of a civilian. An officer suffering from PTSD will:

1. Re-experience the traumatic event through nightmares and flashbacks.
2. Become less and less involved in the outside world by withdrawing from others and refusing to participate in normal social interactions.
3. Experience "survival guilt," which may lead to loss of sleep and memory impairment.[107]

Officer Omar Delgado was mentally unable to return to patrol duties after being at the Pulse nightclub in Orlando on June 12, 2016, during a mass shooting in which forty-nine people were killed. Following this incident, Delgado experienced nightmares, depression, and, when he heard a ringing iPhone, panic attacks. The attacks came from Delgado's painful memories of being inside Pulse that night, hearing the constant ringing of cellphones on the dead bodies that surrounded him.[108] John Violanti estimates that between 9 and 19 percent of all police officers will develop PTSD at some point in their careers.[109]

Coping Ability To put it bluntly, many law enforcement officers are exposed to more disturbing images—of violent death, bloody crime scenes, horrible accidents, and human cruelty—in their first few years on the job than most people will see in a lifetime. Though some studies suggest that police officers have higher rates of suicide than the general population, it appears that most develop an extraordinary ability to handle the difficulties of the profession and persevere.[110]

Police Use of Force

Several years ago, a cellphone video caught McKinney, Texas, police officer Eric Casebolt shoving a teenage girl to the ground outside a pool party. Casebolt explained his actions by saying that he was under stress from handling two suicide calls earlier that day.[111] The incident contributed to an ongoing national debate over the use of force by law enforcement agents—a debate that often seems to set the realities of police work against the letter of the law.

It is generally accepted that not only is police use of force inevitable, but that law enforcement agents who are unwilling to use force cannot do their jobs effectively. "The police officer always causes the trouble," stated an appeals court in one well-known use-of-force case. "But it is trouble which the police officer is sworn to cause, which society pays him to cause and which, if kept within constitutional limits, society praises the officer for causing."[112]

Incidence of Force In general, the use of physical force by law enforcement personnel is very rare, occurring in only about 1.6 percent of the 44 million annual police-public encounters mentioned earlier. Still, the Department of Justice estimates that law enforcement officers threaten to use force or use force in encounters with 715,000 civilians a year.[113] Federal researchers have also determined that almost 1,350 potential arrest-related deaths took place in the United States from June 2015 to March 2016.[114]

Of course, police officers are often justified in using force to protect themselves and other citizens. As we noted previously, they are the targets of tens of thousands of assaults each year. Law enforcement agents are also usually justified in using force to make an arrest, to prevent suspects from escaping, to restrain suspects or other individuals for their own safety, or to protect property.[115]

Reasonable Force The degree of force that is appropriate to protect the police officer or other citizens and is not excessive.

Deadly Force Force applied by a police officer that is likely or intended to cause death.

Learning (7) Objective Clarify the concepts of nondeadly force, deadly force, and reasonable force in the context of police use of force.

At the same time, few observers would be naïve enough to believe that the police are *always* justified in the use of force. A survey of emergency room physicians found that 98 percent believed that they had treated patients who were victims of excessive police force.[116] How, then, is "misuse" of force to be defined? To provide guidance for officers in this tricky area, nearly every law enforcement agency designs a *use-of-force matrix*. As the example in Figure 6.6 shows, such a matrix presents officers with the proper force options for different levels of contact with a civilian.

Types of Force To comply with the various, and not always consistent, laws concerning the use of force, a police officer must understand that there are two kinds of force: *nondeadly force* and *deadly force*. The vast majority of force used by law enforcement is nondeadly force—that is, force that is not likely to cause death or great bodily harm. In most states, the use of nondeadly force is regulated by the concept of **reasonable force,** which allows the use of nondeadly force when a reasonable person would assume that such force was necessary for the officer to carry out her or his legal duties.

So, for example, when New York City police officer James Frascatore threw exprofessional tennis player James Blake to the ground several years ago, the officer was not stripped of his badge because he used force on a suspect who was innocent. Frascatore was disciplined because his superiors felt that tackling an unarmed, compliant suspect as part of an investigation into a fraudulent credit card operation was excessive and unreasonable.

In contrast with nondeadly force, **deadly force** is force that an objective police officer realizes will place the subject in direct threat of serious injury or death. A law enforcement agent is justified in using deadly force if she or he reasonably believes that such force is necessary to protect herself, himself, or another person from serious harm.[117] Generally speaking, the key question in use-of-force cases is: Did the officer behave reasonably, under the circumstances? (See the feature *Comparative Criminal Justice—Conflict Avoidance* to learn about a police culture with a dramatically different concept of what constitutes reasonable force.)

FIGURE 6.6 The Orlando (Florida) Police Department's Use-of-Force Matrix

Like most local law enforcement agencies, the Orlando Police Department has a policy to guide its officers' use of force. Such policies instruct an officer on how to react to an escalating series of confrontations with a civilian and are often expressed visually, as shown here.

Source: Michael E. Miller, "Taser Use and the Use-of-Force Continuum," *Police Chief* (September 2010), 72. Photo credit: iStock.com/kali9

The United States Supreme Court and Use of Force The United States Supreme Court set the standards for the use of deadly force by law enforcement officers in *Tennessee v. Garner* (1985).[118] The case involved an incident in which Memphis police officer Elton Hymon shot and killed a suspect who was trying to climb over a fence after stealing ten dollars from a residence. Hymon testified that he had been trained to shoot to keep a suspect

Source: Central Intelligence Agency

COMPARATIVE CRIMINAL JUSTICE

Conflict Avoidance

In Scotland, the average patrol officer carries a baton, handcuffs, and pepper spray—but no gun. In fact, 98 percent of the country's law enforcement agents are unarmed. This policy is in keeping with a primary goal of Scottish policing: the avoidance of injuries to both police officers and suspects. To this end, when confronting a violent suspect, officers rely on a strategy called "tactical withdrawal." Taking its cue from hostage negotiations, this strategy requires that officers keep their distance from suspects while using verbal engagement to de-escalate the situation.

Nonviolence is entrenched in Scotland's police subculture. Deadly force is not considered a viable policing strategy, and retreat from danger is not seen as cowardice. As a result, the last time a law enforcement agent was killed in the country was 1994, and Scottish police have shot civilians only two times in the past decade.

DIFFERENT REALITIES

Several factors contribute to differences in Scottish and American policing. First, police officers in the United States are much more likely to come across an armed suspect than are their counterparts in Scotland, where strict gun control laws limit the number of firearms. Second, Scotland is much less racially and ethnically diverse than the United States and has not experienced the same level of tension between minority groups and law enforcement in recent years. Third, U.S. policing culture does not always accept the premise that law enforcement officers should put their own safety on a par with the safety of suspects. "Simply put," says one police consultant based in California, "the value of our law officers' lives trumps [the value of the lives] of dangerous criminals."

FOR CRITICAL ANALYSIS

To what extent would it be realistic for law enforcement in the United States to borrow from Scotland's tactical withdrawal policies? Would doing so reduce the use of force by and against American police officers? Explain your answers.

---

from escaping, and indeed Tennessee law at the time allowed police officers to apprehend fleeing suspects in this manner.

In reviewing the case, the Supreme Court focused not on Hymon's action but on the Tennessee statute itself, ultimately finding it unconstitutional:

> When the suspect poses no immediate threat to the officer and no threat to others, the use of deadly force is unjustified. . . . It is not better that all felony suspects die than that they escape.[119]

The Court's decision forced twenty-three states to change their fleeing felon rules, but it did not completely eliminate police discretion in such situations. Police officers still may use deadly force if they have probable cause to believe that the fleeing suspect poses a threat of serious injury or death to the officers or others. (We will discuss the concept of probable cause in the next chapter.)

In essence, the Court recognized that police officers must be able to make split-second decisions without worrying about the legal ramifications. Four years after the *Garner* case, the Court tried to clarify this concept in *Graham v. Connor* (1989), stating that the use of any force should be judged by the "reasonableness of the officer on the scene, rather than with the 20/20 vision of hindsight."[120] In 2004, the Court modified this rule by suggesting that an officer's use of force could be "reasonable" even if, by objective measures, the force was not needed to protect the officer or others in the area.[121]

Less Lethal Weapons   Regardless of any legal restrictions, violent confrontations between officers and suspects are inevitable. To decrease the likelihood that such confrontations will result in death or serious injury, many police departments use *less lethal weapons*, which are designed to subdue but not seriously harm suspects. The most common less lethal weapon is Oleoresin Capsicum, or OC pepper spray, which is used by 97 percent of all local police departments.[122] An organic substance that combines ingredients such as resin and cayenne pepper, OC causes a sensation similar to having sand or needles in the eyes when sprayed into a suspect's face. Other common less lethal weapons include tear gas, water cannons, and **conducted energy devices (CEDs),** which rely on an electrical shock to incapacitate uncooperative suspects.

The best-known, and most controversial, CED is the Taser—a handheld electrical stun gun that fires blunt darts up to 21 feet at speeds of 200 to 220 feet per second. The darts deliver 50,000 volts into the target for a span of about five seconds. Nationally, about 80 percent of local law enforcement agencies use CEDs, including Tasers.[123] Those who favor this form of less lethal weaponry maintain that, when properly used, the devices increase the safety of both officers and suspects. According to a study conducted by researchers at Wake Forest University, 99.7 percent of people shocked by Tasers had minor or no injuries.[124] Nevertheless, as claimed by media reports, about one person a week died in the United States in 2015 after being Tasered by police.[125] Often, these deaths occurred because the target had a weakened heart or was in ill health because of drug use.[126]

ETHICS CHALLENGE

Waze, a popular traffic navigation app, has a feature that allows users to pinpoint the location of patrol officers. Some law enforcement trade groups want Waze to disable this function, claiming that it not only encourages law breaking but also acts as a "stalking app" for those who might want to harm an officer. Is Waze acting unethically by providing a police-tracking app? Why or why not?

Police Misconduct and Ethics

If police culture is, as we noted earlier, marked by a certain mistrust of the public, it is only fair to note that the reverse is often true as well. Police are held to a high standard of behavior that can be summarized by the umbrella term **professionalism.** A professional law enforcement agent is expected to be honest, committed to ideals of justice, respectful of the law, and intolerant of misconduct by his or her fellow officers. When police act unprofessionally, or are perceived to have done so, then their relationship with the community will inevitably suffer.

Indeed, Yale University professor Tom Tyler believes that the public's perception of police *legitimacy* is the basis of law enforcement–community relations. That is, if citizens fail to see their moral and social norms reflected in police behavior, then they will be less likely to respect criminal law themselves or aid the police in fighting crime.[127]

Police Corruption

Police *corruption* has been a concern since the first organized American police departments. As you recall from Chapter 5, a desire to eradicate, or at least limit, corruption was one of the motivating factors behind the reform movement of policing. For general purposes, **police corruption** can be defined as the misuse of authority by a law enforcement officer "in a manner designed to produce personal gain."

In the 1970s, a police officer named Frank Serpico went public about corruption in the New York Police Department. City authorities responded by establishing the Knapp

Conducted Energy Devices (CEDs) Less lethal weapons designed to disrupt a target's central nervous system by means of a charge of electrical energy.

Professionalism Adherence to a set of values that show a police officer to be of the highest moral character.

Police Corruption The abuse of authority by a law enforcement officer for personal gain.

Commission to investigate Serpico's claims. The inquiry uncovered widespread institutionalized corruption in the department. In general, the Knapp Commission report divided corrupt police officers into two categories: "grass eaters" and "meat eaters." "Grass eaters" are involved in passive corruption—they simply accept the payoffs and opportunities that police work can provide. As the name implies, "meat eaters" are more aggressive in their quest for personal gain, initiating and going to great lengths to carry out corrupt schemes.[128]

Types of Corruption   Specifically, the Knapp Commission's investigation identified three basic, traditional types of police corruption:

1. *Bribery*, in which the police officer accepts money or other forms of payment in exchange for "favors," which may include allowing a certain criminal activity to continue or misplacing a key piece of evidence before a trial. Related to bribery are *payoffs*, in which an officer demands payment from an individual or a business in return for certain services.
2. *Shakedowns*, in which an officer attempts to coerce money or goods from a citizen or criminal.
3. *Mooching*, in which the police officer accepts free "gifts" such as cigarettes, liquor, or services in return for favorable treatment of the gift giver.[129]

Additionally, corrupt police officers have many opportunities to engage in theft or burglary by taking money or property in the course of their duties. Drug investigations, for example, often uncover temptingly large amounts of illegal drugs and cash. Former FBI agent Scott M. Bowman pleaded guilty in 2016 to improperly "confiscating" $136,000 in cash that had been seized by the agency during drug investigations.

Another scenario involves police misconduct that becomes pervasive, infecting a group of officers. In 2016, federal agents were investigating as many ten officers at the Jersey City (New Jersey) Police Department for running an illegal private security scheme. To evade taxes and circumvent departmental rules, the officers allegedly demanded cash payments from local construction firms for this illicit off-duty work. The officers also allegedly took bribes to escort oversized vehicles on city streets.[130]

Theories of Police Corruption

Not all police corruption is for personal gain. As we will discuss further in Chapter 10, *wrongful convictions* are sometimes the result of officers manipulating evidence or coercing false confessions. "Bad cops give the system what it wants—convictions," says one police corruption expert.[131] In addition, a recent study found a strong correlation between police misconduct and the violent crime rate in the area being policed. Criminologists theorize that officers who patrol high-crime neighborhoods start seeing crime as the norm. Eventually, these officers come to believe, cynically, that residents of such neighborhoods, including crime victims, are less deserving of "good" policing.[132]

▼ In 2016, Chicago Police Superintendent Eddie Johnson, shown here, recommended that seven officers be fired for filing false reports in the shooting of an African American teenager two years earlier. Police union officials criticized Johnson for bowing to public pressure in making this recommendation. **What factors should a police administrator take into account before taking severe disciplinary actions against members of his or her police force?**

AP Images/M. Spencer Green

In general, there is no single reason why police misconduct occurs. Certain types of officers do, however, seem more likely to engage in corruption—those who are young, relatively uneducated (lacking a college degree), have records of prior criminality and citizens' complaints, and are unlikely to be promoted.[133] Criminologists Christopher Donner and Wesley Jennings believe that the roots of police misbehavior are similar to the roots of criminal misbehavior. In Chapter 2, we saw that criminality has been linked to "low self-control," or a predisposition to seek pleasure through deviance. Researching the behavior of nearly two thousand Philadelphia police officers, Donner and Jennings identified low self-control as a "significant predictor" of citizen complaints for physical and verbal abuse and departmental investigations of misconduct.[134]

Police Accountability

Even in a police department with excellent recruiting methods, state-of-the-art ethics and discretionary training programs, and a culturally diverse workforce that nearly matches the makeup of the community, the problems discussed earlier in this chapter are bound to occur. The question then becomes—given the inevitability of excessive force, corruption, and other misconduct—*who shall police the police?*

Internal Disciplinary Measures

Randy Sutton, an ethics expert and former police officer, recognizes three components of accountability within law enforcement agencies:

1. *Self-accountability*. Each officer is responsible for his or her actions, and must be aware that these actions impact the integrity of the agency as a whole.
2. *Supervisory accountability*. Supervisors, such as sergeants, are often in the best position to observe the activities of officers under their command. By being swift and firm with advice or discipline, they can "set the tone" for ethical behavior in a department.
3. *Administrative accountability*. Given the nature of departmental hierarchies, those at the top of the command structure are in a crucial position to implement policies that promote accountability. They must also "walk the walk," ethically, so as to set a good example.[135]

When corruption or misbehavior is uncovered within a department, the first step is generally disciplinary. During this process, the officer being disciplined is generally represented by her or his police union and afforded due process protections.[136]

The mechanism for investigations within a police department is the **internal affairs unit (IAU).** In many smaller police departments, the police chief conducts internal affairs investigations, while midsized and large departments have a team of internal affairs officers. The New York Police Department's IAU has an annual budget of nearly $68 million and consists of about 650 officers.

Self-Surveillance

For thousands of U.S. police departments, body cameras have become the primary technological response to demands for greater accountability. Briefly mentioned earlier, these small video cameras, usually worn on the lapel, chest, or collar, are designed to record police-civilian interactions. In general, body cameras attempt to enhance accountability in several ways:

- Documenting circumstances in which police force is used.
- Documenting daily interactions between police and members of the community.
- Proving or disproving allegations of misconduct against police officers.
- Recording statements made in the field by police officers, suspects, and witnesses.[137]

Internal Affairs Unit (IAU) A division within a police department that receives and investigates complaints of wrongdoing by police officers.

Over the course of a thirty-month test period, the Phoenix Police Department found that officers who had initially been skeptical about body-worn cameras became increasingly comfortable using them. Although the devices did not seem to change the behavior of suspects being filmed, their presence did significantly reduce the number of use-of-force complaints against Phoenix police officers.[138]

Policies regarding the use of body-worn police cameras vary, as law enforcement experts have not yet reached a consensus on how best to implement this new technology. One common suggestion is that officers should be required to turn the cameras on during all traffic stops and arrests, as these often are the situations in which use of force can occur. Indeed, when officers forget to turn on the devices during a use-of-force incident, or a mysterious "malfunction" occurs, police accountability inevitably suffers.[139]

A number of other questions still surround implementation of body cameras. Do they discourage police from engaging with citizens? How long should the recordings be stored? How can the privacy of people being filmed, such as crime victims, be protected? And, as discussed in the *Policy Matters* feature at the end of the chapter, should the recordings be made public?

Citizen Oversight

Many communities rely on an external procedure for handling citizen complaints against the police, known as **citizen oversight.** In this process, citizens—people who are not sworn officers and, by inference, not biased in favor of law enforcement officers—review allegations of police misconduct or brutality. For the most part, citizen review boards can only recommend action to the police chief or other executive. They do not have the power to discipline officers directly.

Police officers sometimes resent this intrusion by civilians, and most studies have shown that civilian review boards are not widely successful in their efforts to convince police chiefs to take action against their subordinate officers.[140] From 2007 to 2016, Chicago's Independent Police Review Authority found officers at fault in only two of four hundred police shootings, and one of the board's investigators was fired after he suggested that several of the shootings were unjustified.[141]

Citizen Surveillance

Where citizen review boards may have proven largely ineffective, citizens with smartphones have had a major influence on police accountability in recent years. To give just one example, on July 6, 2016, Diamond Reynolds used her smartphone to provide a Facebook live stream of the moments after St. Anthony (Minnesota) police officer Jeronimo Yanez fatally shot her boyfriend, Philando Castile, during a traffic stop. The widely seen video stoked public outrage, and in November 2016 Yanez was charged with manslaughter for Castile's death.

As long as they do not interfere with police officers' work or place officers in danger, civilians have a constitutional right to record the actions of law enforcement agents in public places.[142] As one retired sheriff noted, with millions of Americans carrying camera-equipped smartphones, "Officers should conduct themselves as if they are always being recorded."[143]

Police Liability

The American court system also plays a role in policy accountability. To start, police officers can be held criminally liable for misconduct, as we saw at the beginning of this chapter with regard to the two Albuquerque officers charged with second degree murder for allegedly killing a homeless man.

Criminal Charges The fact that those two Albuquerque police officers were not convicted of homicide is instructive. According to data gathered by Philip M. Stinson, an associate professor of criminal justice at Bowling Green State University, between 2005 and

Citizen Oversight The process by which citizens review complaints brought against individual police officers or police departments.

2015 on-duty police officers fatally shot about eleven thousand people. During that time only seventy-five officers were charged with committing a homicide, and only twenty-six were convicted.[144]

The main reason behind this trend is the legal standard for police use of force that we discussed earlier in the chapter. As you may recall, such force is justified if the officer has a *reasonable* belief that is it necessary. Consequently, as the U.S. Justice Department has noted, "Mistake, panic, misperception, or even poor judgment by a police officer does not provide a basis for prosecution."[145]

When a police officer is convicted of improper use of force, the "unreasonableness" of his or her actions is usually obvious and egregious. In 2016, for example, a Portsmouth, Virginia, police officer was found guilty of manslaughter for fatally shooting a shoplifting suspect who had his hands raised when he was shot. (See the feature *Discretion in Action—Deadly Force* to better understand the mechanics of determining whether law enforcement agents are criminally liable for their actions.)

Civil Liability Because prosecutors are reluctant to charge police officers with criminal wrongdoing, many disputes over excessive use of police force wind up in civil court. The results of these civil liability lawsuits can prove costly for local taxpayers. For example, the city of Los Angeles recently agreed to pay the family of an unarmed homeless man fatally shot by police $4 million to settle a wrongful death lawsuit, even though prosecutors had found the killing to be legally justified. Overall, Los Angeles paid more than $57 million to settle civil lawsuits involving its police officers between 2010 and 2014.[146]

Keep in mind that, because of the doctrine of **qualified immunity,** individual police officers generally cannot be sued personally for using poor judgment in their discretionary decisions. Rather, they usually face civil actions only when they were extremely negligent or when they violated another person's legal or constitutional rights. In the words of the United States Supreme Court, qualified immunity gives police officers "breathing room to make reasonable but mistaken judgments."[147]

Issues of Bias in Policing

As noted earlier, in 2016, a police officer named Jeronimo Yanez shot and killed an African American driver named Philando Castile following a traffic stop in St. Anthony, Minnesota. According to his girlfriend, Castile was reaching for his driver's license and registration, as Yanez had requested, when the officer fatally shot him.

Castile's girlfriend recorded his dying moments with her smartphone. After watching the video, Minnesota Governor Mark Dayton said what was on the minds of many, particularly in black communities across the nation. "Would this have happened if the driver were white, if the passengers were white?" Dayton asked. "I don't think so."[148] When polled, African Americans consistently show less confidence in the police than do whites (see Figure 6.7). Consequently, the legitimacy of the police for many minorities is compromised by the specter of bias.

FIGURE 6.7 Racial Attitudes toward the Police

As these polls conducted by the Gallup organization show, members of minority groups are more likely than whites to have negative views of the police.

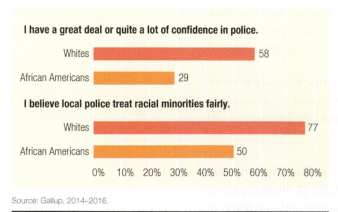

I have a great deal or quite a lot of confidence in police.

Whites — 58
African Americans — 29

I believe local police treat racial minorities fairly.

Whites — 77
African Americans — 50

0% 10% 20% 30% 40% 50% 60% 70% 80%

Source: Gallup, 2014–2016.

Statistical Evidence Two studies released in July 2016 seem to confirm these suspicions. The first, conducted by the Center for Policing Equity, showed that police were

DISCRETION IN ACTION

Deadly Force

The Situation On the day of his death, twelve-year-old Tamir was playing with a pellet gun in a park. Someone called 911 to report Tamir's behavior, saying that the gun was "probably fake" and that the person pointing it at other people was "probably a juvenile." This information was not passed along to Officer Loehmann, who arrived at the park with his partner on the lookout for an armed adult male. Grainy video, taken by a surveillance camera, shows Loehmann stepping out of the police car and immediately firing twice at Tamir, killing the boy. The video also shows that, just before he is shot, Tamir reaches into his waistband and pulls out the pellet gun, possibly either to show the officers that it is not a real gun or to give it to them.

The Law Police officers are authorized to use deadly force when they reasonably believe such force is necessary to protect themselves or third parties from serious bodily harm.

What Would You Do? Officer Loehmann claims that he believed the pellet gun to be real and believed that Tamir— large for his age—was going to shoot him or his partner. Lawyers for Tamir's family counter that Loehmann rushed into the situation and shot Tamir immediately, without first assessing whether the boy actually posed a threat. If you were the district attorney in this jurisdiction, would you recommend to a grand jury (described in Chapter 9) that Loehmann be charged with criminal homicide? Remember, your decision rests on whether you think the officer's actions were reasonable under the circumstances.

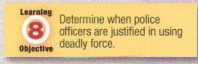

Learning Objective 8 Determine when police officers are justified in using deadly force.

To see how a district attorney in Cleveland, Ohio, decided this case, go to Example 6.1 in Appendix B.

3.6 times as likely to use force against black suspects as against whites.[149] The second, carried out by Harvard economics professor Roland G. Fryer, Jr., found that blacks were 50 percent more likely to be exposed to nonlethal force, such as being handcuffed or pushed to the ground. (Fryer's research did not find any racial differences in the victims of police shootings.)[150] In addition, a recent Justice Department study indicated that, although police pull over white, black, and Latino drivers at similar rates, blacks and Latinos are more than three times more likely to be searched following the stop.[151]

Disparity or Discrimination?

Not all academic studies support the notion that bias is deeply ingrained in American policing. Researchers at the University of Missouri–St. Louis, for example, found that the most important predictor of deadly police shootings in a neighborhood was not that neighborhood's racial makeup or level of economic disadvantage, but rather its violent crime rate.[152]

These findings are in line with a strain of criminology that focuses on disparity in police presence, rather than discrimination in police action, when considering bias in law enforcement. As mentioned earlier in the chapter, the primary operational tactic of all metropolitan police forces is responding to calls for service. According to research by law enforcement experts, the greater police presence in minority communities is mainly the result of calls for service from residents, which, in turn, are caused by higher local crime rates. Indeed, Harvard law professor Randall Kennedy believes that such "selective law enforcement" should be, and for the most part is, welcomed by those who live in high-crime areas and appreciate the added protection.[153]

Civil Rights Violations

In situations where a police officer does act with evident bias, he or she may be subject to federal prosecution or civil actions. A **civil rights violation** involves the denial of the rights afforded to all Americans by the United States Constitution. Such a violation is not protected by qualified immunity, discussed earlier.

Civil Rights Violation Any interference with a citizen's constitutional rights by a civil servant such as a police officer.

Noble Cause Corruption Knowing misconduct by a police officer with the goal of attaining what the officer believes is a "just" result.

Because the Constitution prohibits government officials from discriminating against citizens on the basis of race or ethnicity, many police lawsuits involve members of minority groups.[154]

The U.S. Department of Justice has the power to investigate cities for law enforcement civil rights violations.[155] If, following the investigation, the federal government finds a pervasive pattern of such violations, it can enter into a consent decree (see previous chapter) with the city to improve the situation. In general, under these consent decrees, a local police department agrees to:

1. Implement policies and training that minimize the use of force.

2. Set up tracking systems to identify and discipline the officers most often involved in use-of-force incidents.

3. Improve community relations, particularly by providing effective protocols for responding to citizen complaints.

Since 2009, the Justice Department has opened civil rights investigations in about twenty cities, including Albuquerque, Baltimore, Baton Rouge (Louisiana), Chicago, New Orleans, and Seattle.

Ethics in Law Enforcement

The various forms of police misconduct are intricately connected with the ethics of law enforcement officers. As you saw in Chapter 1, ethics has to do with fundamental questions of the fairness, justice, rightness, or wrongness of any action. Given the significant power that police officers hold, society expects very high standards of ethical behavior from them.

Ethical Dilemmas

Some police actions are obviously unethical, such as the behavior of the FBI agent who stole $136,000, described earlier. Most ethical dilemmas that a police officer will face are not so clear cut. According to criminologists Joycelyn M. Pollock and Ronald F. Becker, any of the following situations can present an ethical dilemma:

- The officer does not know the right course of action.
- The course of action the officer considers right is difficult.
- The wrong choice is very tempting.[156]

Because of the many rules that govern policing—the subject of the next chapter—police officers often find themselves tempted by a phenomenon called **noble cause corruption.** This type of corruption occurs when, in the words of John P. Crank and Michael A. Caldero, "officers do bad things because they believe the outcomes will be good."[157] Examples of noble cause corruption include planting evidence or lying in court to help convict someone the officer knows to be guilty.

Elements of Ethics

Pollock and Becker, both of whom have extensive experience as ethics instructors for police departments, further identify four categories of ethical dilemmas, involving discretion, duty, honesty, and loyalty.[158]

- *Discretion.* The law provides rigid guidelines for how police officers must act and how they cannot act, but it does not offer guidelines for how officers should act in many circumstances. As mentioned at the beginning of this chapter, police officers often use discretion to determine how they should act, and ethics plays an important role in guiding discretionary actions.

Learning Objective 9 Explain what an ethical dilemma is and name four categories of ethical dilemmas that a police officer typically may face.

- *Duty.* The concept of discretion is linked with **duty,** or the obligation to act in a certain manner. Society, by passing laws, can make a police officer's duty clearer and, in the process, help eliminate discretion from the decision-making process. But an officer's duty will not always be obvious, and ethical considerations can often supplement "the rules" of being a law enforcement agent.

- *Honesty.* Of course, honesty is a critical attribute for an ethical police officer. A law enforcement agent must make hundreds of decisions in a day, and most of them require him or her to be honest in order to do the job properly.

- *Loyalty.* What should a police officer do if he or she witnesses a partner using excessive force on a suspect? The choice often sets loyalty against ethics, especially if the officer does not condone the violence.

Duty A police officer's moral sense that she or he should behave in a certain manner.

Although an individual's ethical makeup is determined by a multitude of personal factors, police departments can create an atmosphere that is conducive to professionalism and thus to ethical behavior. Brandon V. Zuidema and H. Wayne Duff, both captains with the Lynchburg (Virginia) Police Department, believe that law enforcement administrators can encourage ethical policing by:

1. Incorporating ethics into the department's mission statement.
2. Conducting internal training sessions in ethics.
3. Accepting "honest mistakes" and helping the officer learn from those mistakes.
4. Adopting a zero-tolerance policy toward unethical decisions when the mistakes are not so honest.[159]

▲ California Governor Jerry Brown presents a Medal of Valor to El Cajon police officer Jarred Slocum, who was shot and wounded by a suspect while entering a burning home. **What role does the concept of duty play in a law enforcement agent's decision, regardless of her or his own safety, to protect the life of another person?** Source: oag.ca.gov

ETHICS CHALLENGE

Beating a suspect to get information that would save the life of a crime victim is an example of noble cause corruption, discussed in this section. Can you think of any circumstances in which such actions are ethically defensible? Explain your answer.

Policy Matters

Releasing Police Videos

How Things Stand

There is no national policy consensus on how, when, and why videos taken by police body cameras and dashboard cameras should be made public. Consequently, law enforcement officials are forced to use their discretion on a case-by-case basis.

As a Result...

Given that each instance of potential police misconduct or misuse of force caught on video is different, police administrators struggle to balance privacy rights against public demands for full disclosure. Some criminal justice professionals believe that body camera footage can be a tool to help communities better understand the challenges of policing while at the same time curbing police abuse. In September 2016, for example, the Tulsa Police Department took only three days to release dashboard and helicopter video of the fatal shooting of Terence Crutcher by one of its officers. "The city will be transparent," said Tulsa mayor Dewey F. Bartlett, Jr. "The city will not cover up."[160]

In contrast, a number of police chiefs and county sheriffs have refused to equip their officers with body cameras so as to avoid the problems that come with public disclosure. "Our view is that we don't want to be part of violating people's privacy for commercial or voyeuristic reasons," explains Steven Strachan, the police chief in Bremerton, Washington.[161] Policymakers also fear that, instead of clarifying what happened, video recordings are often taken out of context and show police officers in the worst possible light. Consequently, at least fifteen states have taken legislative steps to limit the public release of police video footage.[162]

Up for Debate

"If the public doesn't have the opportunity to view the video on their own, they are left with the police version of what happened, and [that] version isn't always what happened."[163]—*Laniece Williams, spokeswoman for the Philadelphia Coalition for Racial, Economic and Legal Justice*

"I know, as a lifelong police officer, that I see people on the worst day of their lives. People shouldn't feel like when the police come to your house that what's happened to you is going to be splashed all over the Internet."[164]—*Los Angeles police chief Charlie Beck*

What's Your Take?

Review the discussion in this chapter on "Police Accountability" before answering the following questions.

1. In North Carolina, a court order is required before police recordings are released to the public. In making this decision, judges consider whether "release is necessary to advance a compelling public interest," as well as whether release "would create a serious threat to the fair, impartial, and orderly administration of justice." What is your opinion of this law? Does it resolve the questions of privacy and transparency raised above? Explain your answers.

2. In an effort to increase transparency, the Seattle Police Department created its own YouTube channel featuring "redacted," or edited, body camera videos. Visit SPD BodyWornVideo on YouTube and look at several of these videos. How do you think this effort will help police-community relations in Seattle?

Digging Deeper...

On September 13, 2016, **police officers in Charlotte, North Carolina, fatally shot suspect Keith Scott**. For two weeks, Charlotte officials refused to release video footage of the incident taken by dashboard and body cameras before finally relenting under extreme pressure from the public. After researching this incident online, summarize the arguments made for and against releasing the footage. Which position do you find to be more compelling? Does this incident bolster Charlotte-Mecklenburg police chief Kerr Putney's assertion that, instead of showing the incontrovertible "truth," police videos can be interpreted a number of different ways and are therefore susceptible to the biases of the viewer? Your written answer should be at least three paragraphs long.

For more information on these concepts, look back to the Learning Objective icons throughout the chapter.

 Explain why police officers are allowed discretionary powers. Police officers are considered trustworthy and able to make honest decisions. They have experience and training. They are knowledgeable in criminal behavior. Finally, they must be able to take reasonable steps to protect themselves.

 List the three primary purposes of police patrol. (a) The deterrence of crime, (b) the maintenance of public order, and (c) the provision of certain services that are not related to crime.

 Describe how forensic experts use DNA fingerprinting to solve crimes. Law enforcement agents gather trace evidence such as blood, semen, skin, and hair from the crime scene. Because these items are rich in DNA, which provides a unique genetic blueprint for every living organism, crime labs can create a DNA profile of the suspect and test it against other such profiles stored in databases. If the profiles match, then law enforcement agents have found a strong suspect for the crime.

 Explain why differential response strategies enable police departments to respond more efficiently to 911 calls. A differential response strategy allows a police department to distinguish among calls for service so that officers can respond to important calls more quickly. A "hot" crime, such as a burglary in progress, will receive more immediate attention than a "cold" crime, such as a missing automobile that disappeared several days earlier.

 Explain community policing and its contribution to the concept of problem-oriented policing. Community policing involves proactive problem solving and a community-police partnership in which the community engages itself along with the police to address crime and the fear of crime in a particular geographic area. By establishing a cooperative presence in a community, police officers are better able to recognize the root causes of criminal behavior there and apply problem-oriented policing methods when necessary.

 Describe the process of socialization in police subculture. This process occurs as inexperienced police officers are taught the values and rules of the police subculture. The officers learn these values and rules by engaging in such rituals as working with senior officers, using force in making an arrest for the first time, and witnessing traumatic on-the-job incidents. Eventually, the socialization process creates a strong bond with other officers and may also lead to mistrust of the civilian population.

 Clarify the concepts of nondeadly force, deadly force, and reasonable force in the context of police use of force. Nondeadly force is force that is not likely to cause death or great bodily harm. Deadly force is force that a police officer is aware will place a subject in direct threat of serious injury or death. In either case, police use of force is legally justified only if it is reasonable—that is, if a reasonable person would find the degree of force necessary under the circumstances.

 Determine when police officers are justified in using deadly force. Police officers must make a reasonable judgment in determining when to use deadly force. That is, given the circumstances, the officer must reasonably assume that the use of such force is necessary to avoid serious injury or death to the officer or someone else.

 Explain what an ethical dilemma is and name four categories of ethical dilemmas that a police officer typically may face. An ethical dilemma is a situation in which police officers (a) do not know the right course of action, (b) have difficulty doing what they consider to be right, and/or (c) find the wrong choice very tempting. The four types of ethical dilemmas involve (a) discretion, (b) duty, (c) honesty, and (d) loyalty.

1. Glenn voluntarily comes to the police station to answer questions about a rape case. When Glenn refuses to provide a DNA sample, police extract his DNA from a tissue he leaves behind on a chair. What arguments could you make to say that this form of DNA collection is unlawful?

2. Criminologists John and Emily Beck suggest that crime reduction strategies should treat crime as if it were a form of pollution. How does this comparison make sense in the context of predictive policing and crime mapping?

3. In many large cities, "hot spots" of crime are located in low-income, minority neighborhoods. Given this reality, how might such data-driven policing contribute to tensions between the police and members of minority groups?

4. In May 2016, Louisiana became the first state to pass legislation that adds police officers to the groups protected by hate crime laws. (See Chapter 4 for a review of hate crime statutes.) What is your opinion of laws that increase the penalties for crimes committed against law enforcement agents?

5. Suppose a police officer is walking up an unlighted stairway. Nervous, he points his gun into the darkness and puts his finger on the trigger, which goes against the training he received as a cadet. The officer accidentally fires his gun, and the bullet, after ricocheting off a wall, kills a man talking to his girlfriend. Apply the concepts of "reasonable force" and "qualified immunity" to this situation. Should the officer be held criminally liable for the shooting? Why or why not?

KEY TERMS

ballistics 181
blue curtain 194
body armor 195
broken windows theory 191
bureaucracy 175
burnout 196
citizen oversight 203
civil liability 204
civil rights violation 205
clearance rates 180
cold cases 181
cold hit 183
community policing 191
computer-aided dispatch (CAD) 187
conducted energy devices (CEDs) 200

confidential informant (CI) 179
crime mapping 189
deadly force 198
delegation of authority 176
detective 179
differential response 186
directed patrol 188
DNA fingerprinting 182
duty 207
forensics 181
hot spots 188
incident-driven policing 185
internal affairs unit (IAU) 202
noble cause corruption 206
police corruption 200

police subculture 194
policy 174
proactive arrests 189
problem-oriented policing 192
professionalism 200
qualified immunity 204
random patrol 187
reactive arrests 189
reasonable force 198
response time 186
socialization 194
stressors 196
trace evidence 181

1. Richard R. Johnson, "Police Officer Job Satisfaction: A Multidimensional Analysis," *Police Quarterly* (June 2012), 158–160.

2. Kenneth Culp David, *Police Discretion* (St. Paul, Minn.: West Publishing Co., 1975).

3. C. E. Pratt, "Police Discretion," *Law and Order* (March 1992), 99–100.

4. "More than a Hunch," *Law Enforcement News* (September 2004), 1.

5. Herbert Jacob, *Urban Justice* (Boston: Little, Brown, 1973), 27.

6. Bureau of Justice Statistics, *Local Police Departments, 2003* (Washington, D.C.: U.S. Department of Justice, May 2006), 24.

7. Kristen Kappelman, *Analysis of March 26, 2010, MPD Vehicle Pursuit Policy Revision* (Milwaukee: Fire and Police Commission, November 15, 2010), 3.

8. Joseph Lawler, *Analysis of 2011 Milwaukee Police Department Vehicle Pursuits* (Milwaukee: Fire and Police Commission, July 1, 2012).

9. Albuquerque Police Department Procedural Orders, *Use of Force* (Albuquerque, N.M.: Albuquerque Police Department, May 1, 2016), 2–14.

10. Chuck Canterbury and Terrence Cunningham, "Statement of the IACP and FOP on Use of Force Standards." *www.iacp.org.* International Association of Chiefs of Police: visited January 26, 2017, Web.

11. Samuel Walker, *The Police in America: An Introduction*, 2d ed. (New York: McGraw-Hill, 1992), 16.

12. George L. Kelling and Mark H. Moore, "From Political to Reform to Community: The Evolving Strategy of Police," in *Community Policing: Rhetoric or Reality*, ed. Jack Greene and Stephen Mastrofski (New York: Praeger Publishers, 1988), 13.

13. Michael White, *Controlling Officer Behavior in the Field* (New York: John Jay College of Criminal Justice, 2011), 19.

14. John S. Dempsey and Linda S. Forst, *An Introduction to Policing*, 8th ed. (Boston: Cengage Learning, 2016), 93.

15. *Ibid.*, 93–95.

16. Karen L. Amendola, "Schedule Matters: The Movement to Compressed Work Weeks," *The Police Chief* (May 2012), 30–35.

17. Henry M. Wrobleski and Karen M. Hess, *Introduction to Law Enforcement and Criminal Justice*, 7th ed. (Belmont, Calif.: Wadsworth/Thomson Learning, 2003), 119.

18. Bureau of Justice Statistics, *Local Police Departments, 2013: Personnel, Policies, and Practices* (Washington, D.C.: U.S. Department of Justice, May 2015), 2.

19. Connie Fletcher, "What Cops Know," *On Patrol* (Summer 1996), 44–45.

20. Walker, *op. cit.*, 103.

21. Eric J. Scott, *Calls for Service: Citizens Demand an Initial Police Response* (Washington, D.C.: National Institute of Justice, 1981), 28–30.

22. Vivian B. Lord, et al., "Factors Influencing the Response of Crisis Intervention Team-Certified Law Enforcement Officers," *Police Quarterly* (December 2011), 388.

23. E. Fuller Torrey, *Justifiable Homicides by Law Enforcement Officers: What Is the Role of Mental Illness?* (Arlington, Va.: Treatment Advocacy Center, September 2013), 3.

24. Lord, et al., *op. cit.*, 390–391.

25. *Ibid.*, 391–392.

26. William G. Gay, Theodore H. Schell, and Stephen Schack, *Routine Patrol: Improving Patrol Productivity*, vol. 1 (Washington, D.C.: National Institute of Justice, 1977), 3–6.

27. Quoted in Ryan Boetel, "APD Chief, IRO Often at Odds over Lapel Video," *Albuquerque Journal* (December 27, 2014), A1.

28. Gary W. Cordner, "The Police on Patrol," in *Police and Policing: Contemporary Issues*, ed. Dennis Jay Kenney (New York: Praeger Publishers, 1989), 60–71.

29. Peter W. Greenwood and Joan Petersilia, *The Criminal Investigation Process: Summary and Policy Implications* (Santa Monica, Calif.: RAND Corporation, 1975).

30. Fletcher, *op. cit.*, 46.

31. Quoted in Eric Lichtblau, "Once Last Resort, F.B.I. Stings Become Common in ISIS Fight," *New York Times* (June 8, 2016), A1.

32. *Ibid.*

33. Quoted in Phil Fairbanks, "Feds Defend Arrest of Rochester Terror Suspect Amid Criticism from Family." *www.buffalonews.com. The Buffalo News:* January 6, 2016, Web.

34. Federal Bureau of Investigation, *Crime in the United States, 2015,* Table 25. *www.ucr.fbi.gov.* U.S. Department of Justice: 2016, Web.

35. James M. Cronin, Gerard R. Murphy, Lisa L. Spahr, Jessica I. Toliver, and Richard E. Weger, *Promoting Effective Homicide Investigations* (Washington, D.C.: Police Executive Research Forum, August 2007), 102–103.

36. Karen Matison Hess, Christine Hess Orthmann, and Henry Lim Cho, *Criminal Investigation*, 11th ed. (Boston: Cengage Learning, 2017), 119.

37. Joseph Peterson, Ira Sommers, Deborah Baskin, and Donald Johnson, *The Role and Impact of Forensic Evidence in the Criminal Justice Process* (Washington, D.C.: National Institute of Justice, September 2010), 8–9.

38. Igor Pacheco, Brian Cerchiai, and Stephanie Stoiloff, *Miami-Dade Research Study for the Reliability of ACE-V Process: Accuracy & Precision in Latent Fingerprint Examinations* (Miami, Fla.: Miami-Dade Police Department Forensic Services Bureau, December 2014), 5–12.

39. Simon A. Cole, "More Than Zero: Accounting for Error in Latent Fingerprinting Identification," *Journal of Criminal Law and Criminology* (Spring 2005), 985–1078.

40. Michele Coppola, "Technology Enhances Capture of Latent Fingerprints and Other Forensic Evidence," *TECHBeat* (January 2016), 11–13.

41. Quoted in "New DNA Database Helps Crack 1979 N.Y. Murder Case," *Miami Herald* (March 14, 2000), 18A.

42. Judith E. Lewter, "The Use of Forensic DNA in Criminal Cases in Kentucky as Compared with Other Selected States," *Kentucky Law Journal* (1997–1998), 223.

43. "CODIS–NDIS Statistics." *www.fbi.gov.* Federal Bureau of Investigation: November 2016, Web.

44. Stephen Mayhew, "NetBio's DNAscan Earns DNIS Approval from the FBI." *www.biometricupdate.com.* Biometric News: April 7, 2016, Web.

45. Jim Dawson, "Defining a Face," *Forensic Magazine* (September 2015), 16–17.

46. Nancy Ritter, "DNA Solves Property Crimes (But Are We Ready for That?)," *NIJ Journal* (October 2008), 2–12.

47. Phil Bulman, "DNA and Property Crimes," *The Police Chief* (April 2013), 16.

48. Zusha Elinson, "FBI Lends Local Police a Hand." *www.wsj.com. Wall Street Journal:* October 26, 2015, Web.

49. Apollo Kowalyk, "Past Predicted: How the Intelligence Paradox Undermines Our Ability to Solve Crimes," *The Police Chief* (September 2015), 26.

50. *Glendale Police Staffing Study* (Glendale, Ariz.: City of Glendale, 2010), 19.

51. Kark Vick, "What It's Like Being a Cop Now," *Time* (August 24, 2015), 35.

52. Dan Cathey and Paul Guerin, *Analyzing Calls for Service to the Albuquerque Police Department* (Albuquerque, N.M.: Institute for Social Research, University of New Mexico, June 2009), Table 2, page 3.

53. "911 Wireless Services." *www.fcc.gov.* Federal Communications Commission: visited January 27, 2017, Web.

54. *Future Trends in Policing* (Washington, D.C.: Police Executive Research Forum, 2014), 31.

55. Quoted in Carl Bialik, "Detroit Police Response Times No Guide to Effectiveness." *www.wsj.com. Wall Street Journal:* August 2, 2013, Web.

56. Cody W. Telep and David Weisburd, "What Is Known about the Effectiveness of Police Practices in Reducing Crime and Disorder?" *Police Quarterly* (December 2012), 344.

57. Bureau of Justice Statistics, *Local Police Departments, 2007* (Washington, D.C.: U.S. Department of Justice, December 2010), Table 12, page 15.

58. George L. Kelling, Tony Pate, Duane Dieckman, and Charles Brown, *The Kansas City Preventive Patrol Experiment: A Summary Report* (Washington, D.C.: The Police Foundation, 1974), 3–4.

59. Carl B. Klockars and Stephen D. Mastrofski, "The Police and Serious Crime," in *Thinking about Police*, ed. Carl B. Klockars and Stephen Mastrofski (New York: McGraw-Hill, 1990), 130.

60. Anthony M. Pate, "Experimenting with Foot Patrol: The Newark Experience," in *Community Crime Prevention: Does It Work?* ed. Dennis P. Rosembaum (Newbury Park, Calif.: Sage, 1986).

61. Jerry H. Ratcliffe, et al., "The Philadelphia Foot Patrol Experiment: A Randomized

Controlled Trial of Police Patrol Effectiveness in Violent Crime Hotspots," *Criminology* (August 2011), 795–830.

62. Christopher M. Sedelmaier and Natalie Kroovand Hipple, *New Haven, Connecticut Smart Policing Initiative* (Washington, D.C.: Bureau of Justice Assistance, August 2016).

63. Quoted in Cory P. Haberman, "A View Inside the 'Black Box' of Hot Spot Policing from a Sample of Police Commanders," *Police Quarterly* (December 2016), 497.

64. Lawrence W. Sherman and David Weisburd, "General Deterrent Effects of Police Patrol in Crime 'Hot Spots': A Randomized Controlled Trial," *Justice Quarterly* (December 1995), 625–648.

65. Renée J. Mitchell, "Hot-Spot Randomized Control Works for Sacramento," *The Police Chief* (February 2013), 12.

66. Oliver Roeder, Lauren Brooke-Eisen, and Julia Bowling, *What Caused the Crime Decline?* (New York: Brennan Center for Justice, 2015), 68.

67. Quoted in "New Model Police," *The Economist* (June 9, 2007), 29.

68. Lawrence W. Sherman, "Policing for Crime Prevention," in *Preventing Crime: What Works, What Doesn't, What's Promising,* ed. Lawrence W. Sherman, Denise C. Gottfredson, and Doris MacKenzie (Washington, D.C.: U.S. Office of Justice Programs, 1977), 229.

69. Lawrence W. Sherman, "Policing for Crime Prevention," in *Contemporary Policing: Controversies, Challenges, and Solutions,* ed. Quint C. Thurman and Jihong Zhao (Los Angeles: Roxbury Publishing Co., 2004), 65.

70. William Sousa and George L. Kelling, "Of 'Broken Windows,' Criminology, and Criminal Justice," in *Police Innovation: Contrasting Perspectives,* ed. David L. Weisburd and Anthony A. Braga (New York: Cambridge University Press, 2006), 77–97.

71. Daniel W. Gerard, "Cincinnati HAZARD: A Place-Based Traffic Enforcement and Violent Crime Strategy," *The Police Chief* (July 2013), 44–46.

72. Richard Rosenfeld, "Crime Decline in Context," *Contexts* (Spring 2002), 25–34.

73. Ralph B. Taylor, "Incivilities Reduction Policing, Zero Tolerance, and the Retreat from Coproduction: Weak Foundations and Strong Pressures," in *Police Innovation: Contrasting Perspectives,* ed. David L. Weisburd and Anthony A. Braga (New York: Cambridge University Press, 2006), 133–153.

74. "Mayor de Blasio Signs the Criminal Justice Reform Act." *www1.nyc.gov.* Official Website of the City of New York: June 13, 2016, Web.

75. Mark H. Moore and George L. Kelling, "'To Serve and Protect': Learning from Police History," *Public Interest* (Winter 1983), 54–57.

76. Dan McKay, "Overhaul at ADP Moves Cops into Neighborhoods," *Albuquerque Journal* (December 15, 2015), A1.

77. *Local Police Departments, 2013: Personnel, Policies, and Practices, op. cit.,* 8, 9.

78. Quoted in Richard A. Oppel, Jr., "National Questions over Police Hit Home in Cleveland," *New York Times* (December 9, 2014), A16.

79. George Fachner and Steven Carter, *Collaborative Reform Model: Final Assessment Report of the Las Vegas Metropolitan Police Department* (Washington, D.C.: Community Oriented Policing Services, May 2014), Table 6, page 26.

80. Michael D. White and Charles M. Katz, "Policing Convenience Store Crime: Lessons from the Glendale, Arizona Smart Policing Initiative," *Police Quarterly* (September 2013), 305–322.

81. Herman Goldstein, "Improving Policing: A Problem-Oriented Approach," *Crime and Delinquency* 25 (1979), 236–258.

82. Bureau of Justice Assistance, *Problem-Oriented Drug Enforcement: A Community-Based Approach for Effective Policing* (Washington, D.C.: Office of Justice Programs, 1993), 5.

83. Nicholas Corsaro and Robin S. Engel, "Most Challenging of Contexts: Assessing the Impact of Focused Deterrence on Serious Violence in New Orleans," *Criminology & Public Policy* (August 2015), 471–505.

84. Quoted in Vick, *op. cit.,* 34.

85. Quoted in Heather MacDonald, "The New Nationwide Crime Wave." *www.wsj.com. Wall Street Journal:* May 29, 2015, Web.

86. Rich Morin, et al., "Behind the Badge." *www. pewsocialtrends.org.* Pew Research Center: January 11, 2017, Web.

87. Harry J. Mullins, "Myth, Tradition, and Ritual," *Law and Order* (September 1995), 197.

88. William Westly, *Violence and the Police: A Sociological Study of Law, Custom, and Morality* (Cambridge, Mass.: MIT Press, 1970).

89. Wallace Graves, "Police Cynicism: Causes and Cures," *FBI Law Enforcement Bulletin* (June 1996), 16–21.

90. Otwin Marenin, "Cheapening Death: Danger, Police Street Culture, and the Use of Deadly Force," *Policy Quarterly* (December 2016), 470.

91. Quoted in "One Shift: Officers Patrol an Anxious America," *New York Times* (July 24, 2016), A1.

92. "Honoring Officers Killed in 2016." *www. odmp.org.* Officer Down Memorial Page: visited January 28, 2017, Web.

93. Tasha Tsiaperas, "2016 Saw Jump in Ambush Attacks on Police, Including

5 Killed in Dallas." *www.dallasnews.com. Dallas Morning News:* January 2, 2017, Web.

94. "FBI Releases 2015 Statistics on Law Enforcement Officers Killed and Assaulted." *www.fbi.gov.* Federal Bureau of Investigation: October 18, 2016, Web.

95. Dempsey and Forst, *op. cit.,* 181.

96. Bureau of Justice Statistics, *Police Use of Nonfatal Force, 2002–11* (Washington, D.C.: U.S. Department of Justice, November 2015), 1.

97. Bureau of Justice Statistics, *Police Departments, 2013: Equipment and Technology* (Washington, D.C.: U.S. Department of Justice, July 2015), 2.

98. Steven G. Brandl and Meghan S. Stroshine, "The Physical Hazards of Police Work Revisited," *Police Quarterly* (September 2012), 263.

99. "Causes of Law Enforcement Deaths." *www. nleomf.org,* National Law Enforcement Officers Memorial Fund: visited January 28, 2017, Web.

100. National Highway Traffic Safety Administration, *Characteristics of Law Enforcement Officers' Fatalities in Motor Vehicle Crashes* (Washington, D.C.: U.S. Department of Transportation, January 2011), Figure 15, page 25.

101. University at Buffalo, "Impact of Stress on Police Officers' Physical and Mental Health." *sciencedaily.com. Science Daily:* September 29, 2008, Web.

102. Frank Borelli, "The Need for Emotional Trauma Training," *Law Enforcement Technology* (December 2015), 9.

103. Gail A. Goolsakian, et al., *Coping with Police Stress* (Washington, D.C.: National Institute of Justice, 1985).

104. Kim S. Ménard and Michael L. Arter, "Stress, Coping, Alcohol Use, and Posttraumatic Stress Disorder among an International Sample of Police Officers: Does Gender Matter?" *Police Quarterly* (December 2014), 309–310.

105. "Impact of Stress on Police Officers' Physical and Mental Health," *op. cit*

106. Elizabeth A. Mumford, Bruce G. Taylor, and Bruce Kubu, "Law Enforcement Officer Safety and Wellness," *Police Quarterly* (June 2015), 122.

107. M. J. Horowitz, N. Wilner, N. B. Kaltreider, and W. Alvarez, "Signs and Symptoms of Post Traumatic Stress Disorder," *Archives of General Psychiatry 37* (1980), 85–92.

108. Frances Robles, "Orlando Officers Grapple with Shooting Trauma," *New York Times* (October 28, 2016), A13.

109. Quoted in Pat Donavan, "Positive Personality Traits May Protect Police at High Risk for PTSD." *www.buffalo.edu.* University of Buffalo News Center: January 6, 2015, Web.

110. Daniel W. Clark, Elizabeth K. White, and John M. Violanti, "Law Enforcement Suicide: Current Knowledge and Future Directions," *The Police Chief* (May 2012), 48.

111. Manny Fernandez, "Texas Officer Was Under Stress When He Arrived at Pool Party, Lawyer Says," *New York Times* (June 11, 2015), A15.

112. *Plakas v. Drinksi*, 19 F.3d 1143, 1150 (7th Cir.) (1994).

113. *Police use of Nonfatal Force, 2002–11, op. cit.*, 1.

114. Bureau of Justice Statistics, *Arrest-Related Deaths Program Redesign Study, 2015–16: Preliminary Findings* (Washington, D.C.: U.S. Department of Justice, December 2016), Figure 1, page 1.

115. David J. Spotts, "Reviewing Use-of-Force Practices," *The Police Chief* (August 2012), 12.

116. H. Range Hutson, Deirdre Anglin, Phillip Rice, Demetrious N. Kyriacou, Michael Guirguis, and Jared Strote, "Excessive Use of Force by Police: A Survey of Academic Emergency Physicians," *Emergency Medicine Journal* (January 2009), 20–22.

117. *Scott v. Harris*, 127 S.Ct. 1779 (2007).

118. 471 U.S. 1 (1985).

119. 471 U.S. 1, 11 (1985).

120. 490 U.S. 386 (1989).

121. *Brosseau v. Haugen*, 543 U.S. 194 (2004).

122. *Police Departments, 2013: Equipment and Technology, op. cit.*, Table 1, page 2.

123. *Ibid.*

124. William P. Bozeman, et al., "Safety and Injury Profile of Conducted Electrical Weapons Used by Law Enforcement Officers against Criminal Suspects," *Annals of Emergency Medicine 53* (2009), 480–489.

125. Cheryl W. Thompson and Mark Berman, "Improper Techniques, Increased Risk." *www.washingtonpost.com.Washington Post:* November 26, 2015, Web.

126. Michael D. White, et al., "An Incident-Level Profile of TASER Device Deployments in Arrest-Related Deaths," *Police Quarterly* (March 2013), 97–98.

127. Tom Tyler, "Legitimacy and Cooperation: Why Do People Help the Police Fight Crime in Their Communities?" *Yale Law School Legal Scholarship Repository* (January 2008), 234–236.

128. Anthony V. Bouza, *The Police Mystique: An Insider's Look at Cops, Crime, and the Criminal Justice System* (New York: Plenum Books, 1990), 72.

129. Knapp Commission, *Report on Police Corruption* (New York: Brazilier, 1973).

130. Jonathan Dienst and Joe Valiquette, "I-Team: FBI Investigates Alleged Corruption in Jersey City Police Department." *www.nbcnewyork.com. NBC New York:* December 22, 2016, Web.

131. Lonnie Soury, quoted in Hella Winston, "Why Do Bad Cops Escape Punishment?" thecrimereport.org. *The Crime Report:* January 26, 2015, Web.

132. David Eitle, Stewart J. D'Alessio, and Lisa Stolzenberg, "The Effect of Organizational and Environmental Factors in Police Misconduct," *Police Quarterly* (June 2014), 103–126.

133. Robert J. Kane and Michael D. White, "Bad Cops: A Study of Career-Ending Misconduct among New York City Police Officers," *Criminology & Public Policy* (November 2009), 764.

134. Christopher M. Donner and Wesley G. Jennings, "Low Self-Control and Police Deviance: Applying Gottfredson and Hirschi's General Theory to Officer Misconduct," *Police Quarterly* (September 2014), 203–225.

135. Randy Sutton, "Policing with Honor." *www.policeone.com. PoliceOne.com:* December 28, 2009, Web.

136. Dempsey and Forst, *op. cit.*, 248.

137. Paul Figueroa, "Body-Worn Cameras: Using the Wealth of Data Effectively," *The Police Chief* (January 2016), 54–55.

138. Charles M. Katz, et al., *Phoenix, Arizona, Smart Policing Initiative: Evaluating the Impact of Police Officer Body-Worn Cameras* (September 2015).

139. Jeremy Gorner, David Heinzmann, and Dan Hinkel, "'I Didn't Know if He Was Armed': Cop Shooting Videos Show Apparent Procedural Errors, Confusion over Who Fired," *Chicago Tribune* (August 6, 2016), 1.

140. Hazel Glenn Beh, "Municipal Liability for Failure to Investigate Citizen Complaints against Police," *Fordham Urban Law Journal 23* (Winter 1998), 209.

141. Mitch Smith, "New Look at Shootings by Police in Chicago," *New York Times* (March 24, 2016), A15.

142. *Glik v. Cunniffe*, 655 F.3d 78 (1st Cir. 2011).

143. Quoted in Russell Contreras and Deepti Hajela, "Citizen Recordings of Police Interactions Growing," *Salt Lake City Tribune* (July 10, 2016), A9.

144. Quoted in Jeff Proctor and Fernanda Santos, "Two Former Albuquerque Officers Are on Trial in the Killing of a Homeless Man," *New York Times* (September 19, 2016), A11.

145. *Department of Justice Report Regarding the Criminal Investigation into the Shooting Death of Michael Brown by Ferguson, Missouri Police Officer Darren Wilson* (Washington, D.C.: U.S. Department of Justice, March 4, 2015), 11.

146. Zusha Elinson and Dan Frosch, "Cost of Police-Misconduct Cases Soar in Big U.S. Cities." *www.wsj.com. Wall Street Journal:* July 15, 2015, Web.

147. *Ashcroft v. al-Kidd*, 563 U.S. 731 (2011).

148. Quoted in Pam Louwagie, "Falcon Heights Police Shooting Reverberates Across the Nation. *www.startribune.com. Minneapolis Star Tribune:* July 8, 2016, Web.

149. Phillip Atiba Goff, et al., *The Science of Justice: Race, Arrests, and Police Use of Force* (New York: Center for Policing Equity, July 2016), 15.

150. Ronald G. Fryer, Jr., "An Empirical Analysis of Racial Differences in Police Use of Force." *www.nber.org.* National Bureau of Economic Research: July 2016, Web.

151. Bureau of Justice Statistics, *Police Behavior during Traffic and Street Stops, 2011* (Washington, D.C.: U.S. Department of Justice, September 2013), Table 5, page 7, and Table 7, page 9.

152. David Klinger, et al., "Race, Crime, and the Micro-Ecology of Deadly Force," *Criminology & Public Policy* (February 2015), 193–222.

153. Randall L. Kennedy, "*McClesky v. Kemp*, Race, Capital Punishment, and the Supreme Court," *Harvard Law Review* 101 (1988), 1436–1438.

154. Dempsey and Forst, *op. cit.*, 252–253.

155. 42 U.S.C. Section 14141 (2006).

156. Jocelyn M. Pollock and Ronald F. Becker, "Ethics Training Using Officers' Dilemmas," *FBI Law Enforcement Bulletin* (November 1996), 20–28.

157. Quoted in Thomas J. Martinelli, "Dodging the Pitfalls of Noble Cause Corruption and the Intelligence Unit," *The Police Chief* (October 2009), 124.

158. Pollock and Becker, *op. cit.*, 20–28.

159. Brandon V. Zuidema and H. Wayne Duff, "Organizational Ethics through Effective Leadership," *Law Enforcement Bulletin* (March 2009), 8–9.

160. Quoted in Liam Stack, "Video Released in Crutcher's Killing by Tulsa Police," *New York Times* (September 20, 2016), A13.

161. Quoted in Timothy Williams, "Downside of Police Body Cameras: Your Arrest Hits YouTube," *New York Times* (April 27, 2015), A1.

162. *Ibid.*

163. Quoted in *Ibid.*

164. Quoted in Kate Mather, James Queally, and Joseph Serra, "Protests Continue after LAPD Release Video Showing Moments before Fatal Police Shooting." *www.latimes.com. Los Angeles Times:* October 4, 2016, Web.

7

Police and the Constitution:
The Rules of Law Enforcement

To target your study and review, look for these numbered Learning Objective icons throughout the chapter.

Chapter Outline		Corresponding Learning Objectives
The Fourth Amendment	**1**	Outline the four major sources that may provide probable cause.
	2	Explain the exclusionary rule and the exceptions to it.
Lawful Searches and Seizures	**3**	List the four categories of items that can be seized by use of a search warrant.
	4	Explain when searches can be made without a warrant.
	5	Describe the plain view doctrine and indicate one of its limitations.
Stops and Frisks	**6**	Distinguish between a stop and a frisk, and indicate the importance of the case *Terry v. Ohio*.
Arrests	**7**	List the four elements that must be present for an arrest to take place.
The Interrogation Process and *Miranda*	**8**	Explain why the U.S. Supreme Court established the *Miranda* warning.
	9	Indicate situations in which a *Miranda* warning is unnecessary.
The Identification Process	**10**	List the three basic types of police identification.

Eight Long Minutes

▲ The United States Supreme Court has ruled that sniff searches of automobiles by police dogs must be done in a reasonable amount of time and a reasonable manner. Aliaksei Smalenski/Shutterstock.com

The use of dogs to find evidence that would otherwise stay hidden is a common and crucial aspect of American law enforcement. As with their human handlers, however, the actions of sniffer dogs are bound by the rules of police procedure. If these rules are not closely followed, a court has the option to undo an otherwise valid arrest. For example, just after midnight on March 27, 2012, police officer Morgan Struble observed a car driven by Dennys Rodriguez veer onto the shoulder of Nebraska State Highway 275. Struble proceeded to perform a routine traffic stop, questioning Rodriguez and running a records check. After issuing Rodriguez a written warning, the police officer asked for permission to walk Floyd, a drug-sniffing dog, around the vehicle. Rodriguez refused.

Struble then had the driver turn off the engine, exit the vehicle, and wait by the patrol car while Struble radioed for backup. When the second police officer arrived, eight minutes later, Struble led Floyd twice around the car.

Midway through the second pass, the dog signaled the presence of drugs. A subsequent search of the vehicle uncovered a large bag of methamphetamine, and Rodriguez was arrested and charged with a drug crime. In court, Rodriguez's lawyers moved to suppress the bag of methamphetamine as evidence. They argued that Struble had no good reason to improperly prolong the traffic stop for the purpose of conducting a sniff search.

Several years ago, in *Rodriguez v. United States*, the United States Supreme Court agreed. According to the Court, Struble erred when he waited eight minutes to search Rodriguez's vehicle without any reasonable suspicion (a concept discussed later in the chapter) that the driver had committed a crime. "A police stop exceeding the time needed to handle the matter for which the stop was made violates the Constitution's shield against unreasonable seizures," explained Justice Ruth Bader Ginsberg. In other words, under the circumstances, the eight-minute interval between Struble's written warning and Floyd's sniff search was eight minutes too long.

FOR CRITICAL ANALYSIS

1. Do you agree with the Supreme Court's reasoning in this case? Why or why not?

2. What steps could Officer Struble have taken that would have allowed Floyd to sniff-search Rodriguez's car without prolonging the traffic stop by eight minutes?

3. When asked by Struble why he was driving so late at night, Rodriguez said that he was returning from Omaha, where he had been looking at a Ford Mustang for sale. Rodriguez also said he had veered to avoid a pothole. In addition, Struble noticed a strong smell of air freshener in the car and thought that the passenger appeared nervous. Taken together, are these factors reason enough to support Struble's "hunch" that drugs were in the vehicle? Explain your answer.

The Fourth Amendment

In *Rodriguez v. United States*, the Supreme Court did not address whether Dennys Rodriguez was guilty or innocent of the charges against him. That was for the trial court to decide. Rather, the Court ruled that the Nebraska police officer had overstepped the boundaries of his authority by using a drug-sniffing dog to discover the bag of methamphetamine in Rodriguez's vehicle.[1] In the previous chapter, we discussed the importance of discretion for police officers. This discretion, as we noted, is not absolute. A law enforcement agent's actions are largely determined by the rules for policing set down in the U.S. Constitution and enforced by the courts.

To understand these rules, law enforcement officers must understand the Fourth Amendment, which reads as follows:

> The right of the people to be secure in their persons, houses, papers, and effects, against unreasonable searches and seizures, shall not be violated, and no Warrants shall issue, but upon probable cause, supported by Oath or affirmation, and particularly describing the place to be searched, and the persons or things to be seized.

This amendment contains two critical legal concepts: a prohibition against *unreasonable searches and seizures* and the requirement of *probable cause* to issue a warrant. (A *warrant* is written permission from a judge to engage in a search or arrest, as will be covered extensively later in the chapter.)

Reasonableness

Law enforcement personnel use searches and seizures to look for and collect the evidence prosecutors need to convict individuals suspected of crimes. As you have just read, when police are conducting a search or seizure, they must be *reasonable*. Though courts have spent innumerable hours scrutinizing the word, no specific meaning for *reasonable* exists. A thesaurus can provide useful synonyms—logical, practical, sensible, intelligent, plausible—but because each case is different, those terms are relative.

In the *Rodriguez* case, the Supreme Court accepted the argument that the search had been so unreasonable as to violate the Fourth Amendment's prohibition against unreasonable searches and seizures. That does not mean that the police officers' actions would have been unreasonable under any circumstances. Indeed, a decade before its *Rodriguez* ruling, the Court accepted a dog sniff search under similar circumstances.

In that case, while an Illinois state trooper was writing a driver a speeding ticket, a K-9 officer walked a police dog around the vehicle. After a signal from the dog, the officer found a large amount of marijuana in the car's trunk. Because the sniff search took place *at the same time* as the "course of a routine traffic stop," the Court upheld the driver's conviction for narcotics trafficking.[2]

Probable Cause

The concept of reasonableness is linked to probable cause. The Supreme Court has ruled, for example, that any arrest or seizure is unreasonable unless it is supported by probable cause.[3] The burden of probable cause requires more than mere suspicion on a police officer's part. The officer must know of facts and circumstances that would reasonably lead to "the belief that an offense has been or is being committed."[4]

Sources of Probable Cause
Probable cause cannot be retroactively applied. It must exist at the moment a police officer takes a certain action. Suppose, for example, a police officer stops a person for jaywalking, finds several ounces of marijuana in

Searches and Seizures A legal term, as found in the Fourth Amendment to the U.S. Constitution, that generally refers to the search for and confiscation of evidence by law enforcement agents.

Probable Cause Reasonable grounds to believe the existence of facts warranting certain actions, such as the search or arrest of a person.

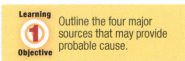
William Howe Police Detective

Each crime scene, each major accident, each time you are called to investigate, you are presented with a puzzle with various pieces missing. When you discover and interpret the interlocking missing pieces together in a successful prosecution, there is no better feeling. The payoff is when you get the opportunity to show off your completed "puzzle" to the jury and they agree that the pieces fit. While I once thrilled at the chase of the bad guy through the alleys and neighborhoods, I now enjoy even more pursuing them with the mental skills I have developed—accident reconstruction, fingerprint identification, and the interpretation of crime scenes. This can be every bit as rewarding as the foot pursuit, not to mention ever so much easier on the body.

Having been in police work for thirty-five years, I have been assaulted only four times on the job (two of which were at gunpoint). This confirmed for me, once and for all, the importance of being able to use your mind rather than your size to, first, talk your way out of trouble and, second, talk the bad guys into going along with your plans for them.

Courtesy of William Howe

SOCIAL MEDIA CAREER TIP For your profile photo, stick with a close-up, business-appropriate photo in which you are smiling and wearing something you would wear as a potential employee. Avoid symbols, party photos, long-distance shots, or baby pictures.

---

the person's pocket, and arrests him for marijuana possession. The arrest will probably be disallowed, even if the officer says the person "looked suspicious." Remember, suspicion does not equal probable cause. If, however, an informant tipped the officer off that the person was a drug dealer, probable cause might exist, and the arrest could be valid.

Several sources that may provide probable cause include:

> **Learning ① Objective** Outline the four major sources that may provide probable cause.

1. *Personal observation.* Police officers may use their personal training, experience, and expertise to infer probable cause from situations that may not be obviously criminal. If, for example, a police officer observes several people in a car slowly circling a certain building in a high-crime area, that officer may assume that the people are "casing" the building in preparation for a burglary. Probable cause could be established for detaining the suspects.

2. *Information.* Law enforcement officers receive information from victims, eyewitnesses, informants, and official sources such as police bulletins or broadcasts. Such information, as long as it is believed to be reliable, is a basis for probable cause.

3. *Evidence.* In certain circumstances, which will be examined later in this chapter, police have probable cause for a search or seizure based on evidence—such as a shotgun—in plain view.

4. *Association.* In some circumstances, if the police see a person with a known criminal background in a place where criminal activity is openly taking place, they have probable cause to stop that person. Generally, however, association is not adequate to establish probable cause.[5]

The Probable Cause Framework   In a sense, the concept of probable cause allows police officers to do their job effectively. Most arrests are made without a warrant, which requires probable cause, because most arrests are the result of quick police reaction to the commission of a crime. Indeed, it would not be practical to expect a police officer to obtain a warrant before making an arrest on the street. Thus, probable cause provides a framework that limits the situations in which police officers can make arrests, but also gives officers the freedom to act within that framework.

In 2003, the Supreme Court reaffirmed this freedom by ruling that Baltimore (Maryland) police officers acted properly when they arrested all three passengers of a car in which cocaine had been hidden in the back seat. "A reasonable officer," wrote Chief Justice William H. Rehnquist, "could conclude that there was probable cause to believe" that the defendant, who had been sitting in the front seat, was in "possession" of the illicit drug despite his protestations to the contrary.[6]

Once an arrest is made, the arresting officer must prove to a judge that probable cause existed. In *County of Riverside v. McLaughlin* (1991),[7] the Supreme Court held that this judicial determination of probable cause must be made within forty-eight hours after the arrest, even if this two-day period includes a weekend or holiday.

The Exclusionary Rule

Historically, the courts have looked to the Fourth Amendment for guidance in regulating the activity of law enforcement officers. The courts' most potent legal tool in this endeavor is the **exclusionary rule,** which prohibits the use of illegally seized evidence. According to this rule, any evidence obtained by an unreasonable search or seizure is inadmissible (may not be used) against a defendant in a criminal trial.[8] Even highly incriminating evidence, such as a knife stained with the victim's blood, usually cannot be introduced at a trial if illegally obtained.

Furthermore, any physical or verbal evidence police acquire by using illegally obtained evidence—known as the **fruit of the poisoned tree**—is also inadmissible. For example, if the police use the existence of the bloodstained knife to get a confession out of a suspect, that confession will be excluded as well.

One of the implications of the exclusionary rule is that it forces police to gather evidence properly. If they follow appropriate procedures, they are more likely to be rewarded with a conviction. If they are careless or abuse the rights of the suspect, they are unlikely to get a conviction. A strict application of the exclusionary rule, therefore, will permit guilty people to go free because of police carelessness or honest errors. In practice, relatively few apparently guilty suspects benefit from the exclusionary rule. Research shows that about 1 percent of felony arrestees avoid incarceration because of improper police searches and seizures.[9]

The "Inevitable Discovery" Exception   Critics of the exclusionary rule maintain that, regardless of statistics, the

Exclusionary Rule A rule under which any evidence that is obtained in violation of the accused's rights, as well as any evidence derived from illegally obtained evidence, will not be admissible in criminal court.

Fruit of the Poisoned Tree Evidence that is acquired through the use of illegally obtained evidence and is therefore inadmissible in court.

▼ Suppose that this gun—used by a defendant to murder a victim—was found as the result of an improper police search. **Why might the exclusionary rule keep evidence of the gun's existence out of court? What is your opinion of the exclusionary rule?**

Orlando Sentinel/Tribune News Service/Getty Images

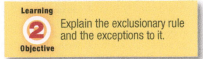

Learning ② **Objective** Explain the exclusionary rule and the exceptions to it.

rule hampers the police's ability to gather evidence and causes prosecutors to release numerous suspects before their cases make it to court. Several Supreme Court decisions have mirrored this view and provided exceptions to the exclusionary rule.

The **"inevitable discovery" exception** was established in the wake of the disappearance of ten-year-old Pamela Powers of Des Moines, Iowa, on Christmas Eve, 1968. The primary suspect in the case, a religious fanatic named Robert Williams, was tricked by a detective into leading police to the site where he had buried Powers. The detective convinced Williams that if he did not lead police to the body, he would soon forget where it was buried. This would deny his victim a "Christian burial."

Initially, in *Brewer v. Williams* (1977),[10] the Court ruled that the evidence (Powers's body) had been obtained illegally because Williams's attorney had not been present during the interrogation that led to his confession. Several years later, in *Nix v. Williams* (1984),[11] the Court reversed itself, ruling that the evidence was admissible because the body would eventually ("inevitably") have been found by lawful means.

The "Good Faith" Exception

The scope of the exclusionary rule has been further diminished by two cases involving faulty warrants. In the first, *United States v. Leon* (1984),[12] the police seized evidence on authority of a search warrant that had been improperly issued by a judge. In the second, *Arizona v. Evans* (1995),[13] due to a computer error, a police officer detained Isaac Evans on the mistaken belief that he was subject to an arrest warrant. As a result, the officer found a marijuana cigarette on Evans's person and, after a search of his car, discovered a bag of marijuana.

In both cases, the Court allowed the evidence to stand under a **"good faith" exception** to the exclusionary rule. Under this exception, evidence acquired by a police officer using a technically invalid warrant is admissible if the officer was unaware of the error. In these two cases, the Court said that the officers acted in "good faith." By the same token, if police officers use a search warrant that they know to be technically incorrect, the good faith exception does not apply, and the evidence can be suppressed.

ETHICS CHALLENGE

Explain the exclusionary rule in terms of its impact on the ethical behavior of law enforcement agents.

Lawful Searches and Seizures

How far can law enforcement agents go in searching and seizing private property? Consider the steps taken by Jenny Stracner, an investigator with the Laguna Beach (California) Police Department. After receiving information that a suspect, Greenwood, was engaged in drug trafficking, Stracner enlisted the aid of the local trash collector in procuring evidence. Instead of taking Greenwood's trash bags to be incinerated, the collector agreed to give them to Stracner. The officer found enough drug paraphernalia in the garbage to obtain a warrant to search the suspect's home. Subsequently, Greenwood was arrested and convicted on narcotics charges.[14]

Remember, the Fourth Amendment is quite specific in forbidding unreasonable searches and seizures. Were Stracner's search of Greenwood's garbage and her seizure

"Inevitable Discovery" Exception The legal principle that illegally obtained evidence can be admissible in court if police using lawful means would inevitably have discovered it.

"Good Faith" Exception The legal principle that evidence obtained with the use of a technically invalid search warrant is admissible during trial if the police acted in good faith.

of its contents "reasonable"? The Supreme Court thought so, holding that Greenwood's garbage was not protected by the Fourth Amendment.[15]

The Role of Privacy in Searches

A crucial concept in understanding search and seizure law is *privacy*. By definition, a search is a governmental intrusion on a citizen's reasonable expectation of privacy. The recognized standard for a "reasonable expectation of privacy" was established in *Katz v. United States* (1967).[16] The case dealt with the question of whether the defendant was justified in his expectation of privacy in the calls he made from a public phone booth. The Supreme Court held that "the Fourth Amendment protects people, not places," and Katz prevailed.

In his concurring opinion, Justice John Harlan, Jr., set a two-pronged test for a person's expectation of privacy:

1. The individual must prove that she or he expected privacy.
2. Society must recognize that expectation as reasonable.[17]

Accordingly, the Court agreed with Katz's claim that he had a reasonable right to privacy in a public phone booth. Even though the phone booth was a public place, accessible to anyone, Katz had taken clear steps to protect his privacy.

A Legitimate Privacy Interest

Despite the *Katz* ruling, simply taking steps to preserve one's privacy is not enough to protect against law enforcement intrusion. The steps must be reasonably certain to ensure privacy. If a person is unreasonable or mistaken in expecting privacy, he or she may forfeit that expectation. For instance, in *California v. Greenwood* (1988),[18] described at the beginning of this section, the Court did not believe that the suspect had a reasonable expectation of privacy when it came to his garbage bags. The Court noted that when we place our trash on a curb, we expose it to any number of intrusions by "animals, children, scavengers, snoops, and other members of the public."[19] In other words, if Greenwood had truly intended for the contents of his garbage bags to remain private, he would not have left them on the side of the road.

Note also that, under the **private search doctrine,** law enforcement officers do not need a warrant to go through personal items that have already been searched by a third-party civilian. The reasoning behind this doctrine is that once a private search has taken place, the owner of the searched items no longer has a reasonable expectation of privacy.[20] So, for example, if an airline employee opens an unclaimed suitcase, finds illegal drugs, and then calls the police, no warrant is required for law enforcement officers to search the baggage and seize the contraband.[21]

Privacy and Satellite Monitoring

As you can see, a number of factors go into determining whether a reasonable expectation of privacy exists. In *United States v. Jones* (2012),[22] the U.S. Supreme Court emphasized

Search The process by which police examine a person or property to find evidence that will be used to prove guilt in a criminal trial.

Private Search Doctrine The legal principle that a private search eliminates an owner's reasonable expectation of privacy regarding the object searched.

▼ Should law enforcement be able to use police helicopters to determine if people are carrying out illegal behavior within fenced-in backyards? Why or why not? Knumina Studios/Shutterstock.com

the important roles that time and technology play in this equation. The Court's ruling invalidated the efforts of federal agents who had placed a GPS tracking device on the car of Antoine Jones, a Washington, D.C., nightclub owner suspected of drug trafficking. Using the device, which relies on satellite transmissions to determine location, the agents were able to follow Jones's movements for a month. This evidence helped bring about Jones's conviction for conspiring to distribute cocaine.

The Court found that the government had "physically occupied" private property—Jones's car—for an unreasonably long time. As a result, all evidence gathered by the GPS device was ruled inadmissible. Several Supreme Court justices also pointed out that most citizens do not expect the police to be monitoring every drive they make over the course of twenty-eight days.[23] As one commentator stated, the ruling seemed to acknowledge that the mere fact that technology now permits greater levels of surveillance "does not mean that society has decided there's no such thing as privacy anymore."[24]

Search and Seizure Warrants

The Supreme Court's ruling in the case of Antoine Jones does not mean that law enforcement officers can *never* track someone for a month using a GPS device or any other technology. Rather, it means that, to do so, they need to obtain a **search warrant,** a step that the federal agents failed to take before beginning their surveillance of Jones. A search warrant is a court order that authorizes police to search a certain area. Before a judge or magistrate will issue a search warrant, law enforcement officers must provide:

- Information showing probable cause that a crime has been or will be committed.
- Specific information on the premises to be searched, the suspects to be found and the illegal activities taking place at those premises, and the items to be seized.

The purpose of a search warrant is to establish, before the search takes place, that a *probable cause to search* justifies infringing on the suspect's reasonable expectation of privacy.

Particularity of Search Warrants

The drafters of the Bill of Rights specifically did not want law enforcement officers to have the freedom to make "general, exploratory" searches through a person's belongings.[25] Consequently, the Fourth Amendment requires that a warrant describe with "particularity" the place to be searched and the things—either people or objects—to be seized.

This "particularity" requirement places a heavy burden on law enforcement officers. Before going to a judge to ask for a search warrant, they must prepare an **affidavit** in which they provide specific, written information on the property that they wish to search and seize. They must know the specific address of any place they wish to search. General addresses of apartment buildings or office complexes are not sufficient. Furthermore, courts generally frown on vague descriptions of goods to be seized. For example, several years ago, a federal court ruled that a warrant permitting police to search a home for "all handguns, shotguns and rifles" and "evidence showing street gang membership" was too broad. As a result, the seizure of a shotgun was disallowed for lack of a valid search warrant.[26]

A **seizure** is the act of taking possession of a person or property by the government because of a (suspected) violation of the law. In general, four categories of items can be seized by use of a search warrant:

1. Items resulting from the crime, such as stolen goods.
2. Items that are inherently illegal for anybody to possess (with certain exceptions), such as narcotics and counterfeit currency.

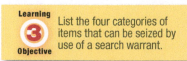

Learning Objective 3 List the four categories of items that can be seized by use of a search warrant.

3. Items that can be called "evidence" of the crime, such as a bloodstained sneaker or a ski mask.

4. Items used in committing the crime, such as an ice pick or a printing press used to make counterfeit bills.[27]

See Figure 7.1 for an example of a search warrant.

Reasonableness during a Search and Seizure
No matter how "particular" a warrant is, it cannot provide for all the conditions that are bound to come up during its service. Consequently, the law gives law enforcement officers the ability to act "reasonably" during a search and seizure in the event of unforeseeable circumstances. For example, if a police officer is searching an apartment for a stolen MacBook Pro laptop computer and notices a vial of crack cocaine sitting on the suspect's bed, that contraband is considered to be in "plain view" and can be seized.

FIGURE 7.1 Example of a Search Warrant

United States District Court
_____DISTRICT OF_____

In the Matter of the Search of
(Name, address or brief description of person or property to be searched)

SEARCH WARRANT

CASE NUMBER:

TO:_____ and any Authorized Officer of the United States

Affidavit(s) having been made before me by_____ who has reason to
                                                    Affiant

believe that ☐ on the person of or ☐ on the premises known as (name, description and/or location)

in the_____ District of_____ there is now
concealed a certain person or property, namely (describe the person or property)

I am satisfied that the affidavit(s) and any recorded testimony establish probable cause to believe that the person or property so described is now concealed on the person or premises above-described and establish grounds for the issuance of this warrant.

YOU ARE HEREBY COMMANDED to search on or before_____
                                                                            Date

(not to exceed 10 days) the person or place named above for the person or property specified, serving this warrant and making the search (in the daytime — 6:00 A.M. to 10:00 P.M.) (at any time in the day or night as I find reasonable cause has been established) and if the person or property be found there to seize same, leaving a copy of this warrant and receipt for the person or property taken, and prepare a written inventory of the person or property seized and promptly return this warrant to_____
                                                                    U.S. Judge or Magistrate
as required by law.

_____ at _____
Date and Time Issued   City and State

_____   _____
Name and Title of Judicial Officer   Signature of Judicial Officer

Note, though, that if law enforcement officers have a search warrant that authorizes them to search for a stolen laptop computer, they are not justified in opening small drawers. Because a computer cannot fit in a small drawer, an officer has no reasonable basis for searching one. Hence, officers are restricted in where they can look by the items they are searching for.

Searches and Seizures without a Warrant

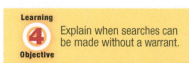

Learning
4 Objective
Explain when searches can be made without a warrant.

Although the Supreme Court has established the principle that searches conducted without warrants are unreasonable *per se* (by definition), it has set "specifically established" exceptions to the rule.[28] In fact, most searches take place in the absence of a judicial order. Warrantless searches and seizures can be lawful when police are in "hot pursuit" of a subject or when they search bags of trash left at the curb for regular collection. Because of the magnitude of smuggling activities in "border areas" such as airports, seaports, and international boundaries, a warrant normally is not needed to search property in those places.

Furthermore, in *Brigham City v. Stuart* (2006),[29] the Court held unanimously that police officers do not need a warrant to enter a private home in an emergency, such as when they reasonably fear for the safety of the inhabitants. The two most important circumstances in which a warrant is not needed, though, are (1) searches incidental to arrests and (2) consent searches.

Searches Incidental to an Arrest

The most frequent exception to the warrant requirement involves **searches incidental to arrests,** so called because nearly every time police officers make an arrest (a procedure discussed in detail later in the chapter), they also search the suspect. As long as the original arrest was based on probable cause, these searches are valid for two reasons, established by the Supreme Court in *United States v. Robinson* (1973):

1. The need for a police officer to find and confiscate any weapons a suspect may be carrying.
2. The need to protect any evidence on the suspect's person from being destroyed.[30]

Law enforcement officers are, however, limited in the searches they may make during an arrest. These limits were established by the Supreme Court in *Chimel v. California* (1969).[31] In that case, police arrived at Chimel's home with an arrest warrant but not a search warrant. Even though Chimel refused their request to "look around," the officers searched the entire three-bedroom house for nearly an hour, finding stolen coins in the process. Chimel was convicted of burglary and appealed, arguing that the evidence of the coins should have been suppressed.

The Supreme Court held that the search was unreasonable. In doing so, the Court established guidelines as to the acceptable extent of searches incidental to arrests. Primarily, the Court ruled that police may search any area within the suspect's "immediate control" to confiscate any weapons or evidence that the suspect could destroy. The Court found, however, that there was no justification

> for routinely searching rooms other than that in which the arrest occurs—or, for that matter, for searching through all desk drawers or other closed or concealed areas in that room itself. Such searches, in the absence of well-recognized exceptions, may be made only under the authority of a search warrant.[32]

The exact interpretation of the "area within immediate control" has been left to individual courts, but in general it has been taken to mean the area within the reach of the arrested person. Thus, the Court is said to have established the "arm's reach doctrine" in its *Chimel* decision.

Searches Incidental to Arrests Searches for weapons and evidence that are conducted on persons who have just been arrested.

Searches with Consent

Consent searches, the second most common type of warrantless searches, take place when individuals voluntarily give law enforcement officers permission to search their persons, homes, or belongings. The most relevant factors in determining whether consent is voluntary are

1. The age, intelligence, and physical condition of the consenting suspect.
2. Any coercive behavior by the police, such as the language used to request consent.
3. The length of the questioning and its location.[33]

If a court finds that a person has been physically threatened or otherwise coerced into giving consent, the search is invalid.[34] Furthermore, the search must be reasonable. In 2007, the North Carolina Supreme Court invalidated a consent search that turned up a packet of cocaine. As part of this search, the police had pulled down the suspect's underwear and shone a flashlight on his groin. The court ruled that a reasonable person in the defendant's position would not consent to such an intrusive examination.[35]

An important standard for consent searches was set in *Schneckcloth v. Bustamonte* (1973),[36] in which, after being asked, the defendant told police officers to "go ahead" and search his car. A packet of stolen checks found in the trunk was ruled valid evidence because the driver consented to the search. As the feature *Myth vs Reality—Consent to Search Automobiles* explains, as a general rule, drivers are not required to agree to such searches.[37]

Numerous court decisions have also supported the "knock and talk" strategy, in which a law enforcement agent simply walks up to the door of a residence, knocks, and asks to come in and talk to the resident.[38] The officer does not need reasonable suspicion or probable cause that a crime has taken place in this situation because the decision to cooperate rests with the civilian.

Recent Developments

Because warrantless searches are relatively commonplace—and crucial for law enforcement—defense attorneys are constantly testing their limits. In recent years, for instance, American courts have determined the constitutionality of warrantless searches of:

1. *Digital devices on the border.* Do the traditional reasons for allowing warrantless searches at entry points—combating smuggling and terrorism—also apply to warrantless searches of laptop computers and cell phones owned by people crossing the border? A federal court has said no, pointing out that a search of a car is not nearly as "comprehensive and intrusive" as a search of the data stored in an electronic device.[39]

2. *Blood used as evidence in drunk driving cases.* In 2016, the United States Supreme Court ruled that—absent suspicious circumstances such as

Consent Searches Searches by police that are made after the subject of the search has agreed to the action. In these situations, consent, if given of free will, validates a warrantless search.

MYTH vs REALITY

Consent to Search Automobiles

The Myth If a police officer pulls over a driver and issues a speeding ticket, and then asks to search the car, the driver must agree to the officer's request and submit to a vehicle search.

The Reality In fact, in this scenario, the driver is well within his or her rights to refuse an officer's request to search his or her car. As long as police officers do not improperly coerce a suspect to cooperate, however, they are not required to inform the person that he or she has a choice in the matter. In *Ohio v. Robinette* (1996), the U.S. Supreme Court held that police officers do not need to notify people that they are "free to go" after an initial stop when no other suspicious activity or an arrest is involved. This lack of notification has significant consequences. In the two years leading up to the *Robinette* case, four hundred Ohio drivers were convicted of narcotics offenses that resulted directly from search requests that could have been denied but were not.

FOR CRITICAL ANALYSIS

Do you think police officers should be required to tell drivers that permission to search a vehicle can be denied? Why or why not?

slurred speech or a strong smell of alcohol—police officers need a warrant to conduct a blood test after an arrest for drunken driving. Officers do not, however, need a warrant to determine driver's blood alcohol content using a breath test. The difference, according to the Court, is that blood tests (requiring a "piercing of the skin") are much more physically intrusive than breath tests and are therefore more deserving of constitutional scrutiny.[40]

3. *Homes over the objection of an absent resident.* Walter Fernandez refused to consent to a warrantless search of his Los Angeles home in connection with a robbery. Police then arrested Fernandez for abusing his domestic partner, who consented to the search while Fernandez was being booked at the local jail. The Supreme Court upheld this strategy, ruling that any occupant's consent is sufficient.[41]

Figure 7.2 provides an overview of the circumstances under which warrantless searches have traditionally been allowed.

Searches of Automobiles

In *Carroll v. United States* (1925),[42] the Supreme Court ruled that the law could distinguish among automobiles, homes, and persons in questions involving police searches. In the years since its *Carroll* decision, the Court has established that the Fourth Amendment does not require police to obtain a warrant to search automobiles or other movable vehicles when they have probable cause to believe that a vehicle contains contraband or evidence of criminal activity.[43]

The reasoning behind such leniency is straightforward: Requiring a warrant to search an automobile places too heavy a burden on police officers. By the time the officers could communicate with a judge and obtain the warrant, the suspects could have driven away and destroyed any evidence. Consequently, the Court has consistently held that someone in a vehicle does not have the same reasonable expectation of privacy as someone at home or even in a phone booth.

Warrantless Searches of Automobiles For nearly three decades, police officers believed that if they lawfully arrested the driver of a car, they could legally make a warrantless search of the car's entire front and back compartments. This understanding

---

FIGURE 7.2 Exceptions to the Search Warrant Requirement

In many instances, it would be impractical for police officers to leave a crime scene, go to a judge, and obtain a search warrant before conducting a search. Therefore, under the following circumstances, a search warrant is not required.

Incident to Lawful Arrest Police officers may search the area within the immediate control of a person after they have arrested him or her.	**Automobile Exception** If police officers have probable cause to believe that an automobile contains evidence of a crime, they may, in most instances, search the vehicle without a warrant.
Consent Police officers may search a person without a warrant if that person voluntarily agrees to be searched and has the legal authority to authorize the search.	**Plain View** If police officers are legally engaged in police work and happen to see evidence of a crime in "plain view," they may seize it without a warrant.
Stop and Frisk Police officers may frisk, or "pat down," a person if they suspect that the person may be involved in criminal activity or poses a danger to those in the immediate area.	**Abandoned Property** Any property, such as a hotel room that has been vacated or contraband that has been discarded, may be searched and seized by police officers without a warrant.
Hot Pursuit If police officers are in "hot pursuit," or chasing a person they have probable cause to believe committed a crime, and that person enters a building, the officers may search the building without a warrant.	**Border Searches** Law enforcement officers on border patrol do not need a warrant to search vehicles crossing the border.

---

was based on the Supreme Court's ruling in *New York v. Benton* (1981),[44] which seemed to allow this expansive interpretation of the "area within immediate control" with regard to automobiles.

In *Arizona v. Gant* (2009), however, the Court announced that its *Benton* decision had been misinterpreted. Such warrantless searches are allowed only in two situations:

1. The person being arrested is close enough to the car to grab or destroy evidence or a weapon inside the car.
2. The arresting officer reasonably believes that the car contains evidence pertinent to the same crime for which the arrest took place.[45]

So, for example, a police officer will no longer be able to search an automobile for contraband if the driver has been arrested for failing to pay previous speeding tickets—unless the officer reasonably believes the suspect has the ability to reach and destroy any such contraband.

Non-Arrest Situations As you can imagine, the law enforcement community reacted negatively to the restrictions outlined in the *Gant* decision.[46] Police officers, however, still can conduct a warrantless search of an automobile based on circumstances other than the incidental-to-an-arrest doctrine. These circumstances include probable cause of criminal activity, consent of the driver, and "protective searches" to look for weapons if police officers have a reasonable suspicion that such weapons exist.[47]

The Supreme Court even allows warrantless searches of automobiles when the law enforcement agent has a mistaken notion of the law. For instance, several years ago a police officer in North Carolina stopped a car for having a broken brake light. The resulting consensual search of the automobile uncovered a sandwich bag of cocaine. North Carolina law only requires a single working brake light, however, meaning that the officer should not have made the traffic stop in the first place. Nonetheless, in 2014, the Court ruled that, because the officer's mistake was objectively reasonable (that is, the type of mistake than any reasonable officer might make), his search was valid.[48]

Pretextual Stops Several years ago, a police officer in Starke, Florida, pulled over professional football player Letroy Guion for "failure to maintain a single lane." While writing a ticket, the officer smelled marijuana, providing him with legal justification to conduct a search. The search uncovered 357 grams of pot, about $190,000 in cash, and an illegally owned firearm in Guion's truck.

It is important to understand that such automobile stops and searches are a valid part of police work. As long as an officer has probable cause to believe that a traffic law has been broken, her or his "true" motivation for making a stop is irrelevant.[49] So, even if the police officer does not have a legally sufficient reason to search for evidence of a crime such as drug trafficking, the officer can use a minor traffic violation to pull over the car and investigate his or her "hunch." (To learn more about such "pretextual stops," see the feature *Discretion in Action—A Valid Pretext?*)

Container Searches
In keeping with the principles of the "movable vehicle" exception, the Supreme Court has also provided law enforcement agents with a great deal of leeway for warrantless searches of containers within a vehicle. In one case, Washington, D.C., detectives received a reliable tip that a man known as the "Bandit" was selling drugs from his car. Without first getting a warrant, the detectives searched the Bandit's trunk and found heroin in a closed paper bag. The Court refused to suppress the evidence, ruling that in such situations police officers can search every part of the vehicle that might

GETTING
Linked in™

In many jurisdictions, only a licensed **phlebotomist** is authorized to draw blood from a person who has been stopped for driving under the influence. You can learn more about the career paths in this field, and how such paths intersect with the criminal justice system, by going to LinkedIn and searching for "**phlebotomist.**"

DISCRETION IN ACTION

A Valid Pretext?

The Situation You are a police officer patrolling an area of Washington, D.C., that is marked by extremely high rates of drug-related crime. You become suspicious of a truck with temporary license plates being driven slowly by a young African American male. Although you do not consider yourself racially biased, you are well aware, from experience, that in this neighborhood many young black men in these types of vehicles with temporary plates are drug dealers. These suspicions do not, however, reach the level of probable cause needed to pull over the truck. Then, the driver fails to signal while making a right turn.

The Law As far as Fourth Amendment law is concerned, any subjective reasons that a police officer might have for stopping a suspect, including any motives based on racial stereotyping or bias, are irrelevant. As long as the officer has objective probable cause to believe a traffic violation or other wrongdoing has occurred, the stop is valid.

What Would You Do? You are convinced that the driver of the truck is selling illegal drugs, and you want to stop and search him. The failure to signal gives you a valid pretext to pull over the truck, even though your real reasons for the stop would be its slow pace, its temporary plates, the race of its driver, and the level of drug crime in the neighborhood. What do you do?

To see how the United States Supreme Court reacted to an officer's decision in a similar situation, go to Example 7.1 in Appendix B.

---

contain the items they are seeking, as long as they have probable cause to believe that the items are somewhere in the car.[50]

Nevertheless, there are limits to what can be searched. As Justice John Paul Stevens stated in his opinion, "[P]robable cause to believe that undocumented aliens are being transported in a van will not justify a warrantless search of a suitcase" in that van.[51] By the same token, if the tipster had told the police specifically that "Bandit has a bag of heroin in his trunk," they would not have been justified in searching the front area of the car without a warrant or probable cause.[52]

The Plain View Doctrine

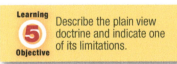

Learning Objective 5 Describe the plain view doctrine and indicate one of its limitations.

As we have already seen several times in this chapter, the Constitution, as interpreted by our courts, provides very little protection to evidence *in plain view*. For example, suppose a traffic officer pulls over a person for speeding, looks in the driver's side window, and clearly sees what appears to be a bag of heroin resting on the passenger seat. In this instance, under the **plain view doctrine,** the officer would be justified in seizing the drugs without a warrant.

The plain view doctrine was first put forward by the Supreme Court in *Coolidge v. New Hampshire* (1971).[53] The Court ruled that law enforcement officers may make a warrantless seizure of an item if four criteria are met:

1. The item is positioned so as to be detected easily by an officer's sight or some other sense.
2. The officer is legally in a position to notice the item in question.
3. The discovery of the item is inadvertent. That is, the officer had not intended to find the item.
4. The officer immediately recognizes the illegal nature of the item.

Plain View Doctrine The legal principle that objects in plain view of a law enforcement agent who has the right to be in a position to have that view may be seized without a warrant and introduced as evidence.

No interrogation or further investigation is allowed under the plain view doctrine.

Advances in technology that allow law enforcement agents to "see" beyond normal human capabilities have raised new issues in regard to plain view principles. *Thermal imagers*, for example, measure otherwise invisible levels of infrared radiation. These devices are particularly effective in detecting marijuana plants grown indoors because of the heat thrown off by the "grow lights" that the plants need to survive.

The question for the courts has been whether a warrantless search of a dwelling through its walls by means of a thermal imager violates Fourth Amendment protections of privacy. According to the Supreme Court, an item is not in plain view if law enforcement agents need the aid of this technology to "see" it.[54] Thus, information from a thermal imager is not by itself justification for a warrantless search.

CJ & TECHNOLOGY

Tactical Camera Spheres

The size and shape of a baseball, with a hard rubber shell and a six-lens camera, the Explorer could be a game changer for police tactical operations. When activated—stationary or in motion—the Explorer's camera snaps images at fifteen frames per second. Software uploads these images to a mobile device, such as a smartphone or tablet, and combines them so that they can be viewed instantaneously as a single, panoramic picture. Various models also have video-streaming capabilities and sensors that can detect hazards such as high carbon monoxide levels.

Law enforcement agents who have used Explorer appreciate the device's simplicity. "You are able to throw it into a room or hallway, somewhere you need to gather immediate tactical intelligence but there's a risk to sending an officer in," says Mark Clevette, Commander of Special Operations for the Maine Department of Corrections. "The safety advantage is obvious."

Thinking about Tactical Camera Spheres

What are some of the circumstances in which Explorer "balls" would be useful to law enforcement? Under what circumstances might law enforcement need to obtain a search warrant before deploying these devices to gather intelligence?

Electronic Surveillance

During the course of a criminal investigation, law enforcement officers may decide to use **electronic surveillance,** or electronic devices such as wiretaps or hidden microphones ("bugs"), to monitor and record conversations, observe movements, and trace or record telephone calls.

Basic Rules: Consent and Probable Cause
Given the invasiveness of electronic surveillance, the Supreme Court has generally held that the practice is prohibited by the Fourth Amendment. In *Burger v. New York* (1967),[55] however, the Court ruled that it is permissible under certain circumstances. That same year, *Katz v. United States* (discussed at the beginning of this section) established that recorded conversations are inadmissible as evidence unless certain procedures are followed.

In general, law enforcement officers can use electronic surveillance only if consent is given by one of the parties to be monitored, or, in the absence of such consent, with a warrant.[56] For the warrant to be valid, it must:

1. Detail with "particularity" the conversations that are to be overheard.
2. Name the suspects and the places that will be under surveillance.
3. Show probable cause to believe that a specific crime has been or will be committed.[57]

Once the specific information has been gathered, the law enforcement officers must end the electronic surveillance immediately.[58] In any case, the surveillance cannot last more than thirty days without a judicial extension.

Electronic Surveillance The use of electronic equipment by law enforcement agents to record private conversations or observe conduct that is meant to be private.

Force Multipliers

A variety of electronic surveillance techniques are allowed under the theory that people who are in public places have no reasonable expectation of privacy.[59] For example, each Fourth of July weekend, the small city of Hollister, California, hosts a bike rally that draws more than 100,000 motorcycle enthusiasts. Included in the throng are numerous members of the Outlaw Motorcycle Gang. With only twenty-eight sworn officers, the Hollister Police Department (HPD) has struggled to control gang activity during the event. Several years ago, however, the city installed more than sixty intelligent video surveillance cameras, providing the police with real-time coverage of almost 100 percent of the downtown area. The city also implemented a location-based monitoring program that searches public social media content during the event.

With these technological aids, the HPD is able to respond to gang threats almost immediately during rally weekend, making the event less prone to outbreaks of violence.[60] In numerous other jurisdictions, computerized infrared surveillance cameras are used to take digital photos of license plates. Usually mounted on police cars or affixed to traffic lights, these automatic license plate recognition (ALPR) devices electronically match all photographed numbers against a national database that contains records of the license plates of stolen cars or other vehicles driven by criminal suspects.

Technological devices such as surveillance cameras, social media monitoring programs, and ALPR are known as force multipliers. That is, they allow law enforcement agencies to expand their capabilities without a significant increase in personnel. Today, more than 75 percent of all local police departments in the United States employ some form of electronic surveillance as a force multiplier.[61]

Constitutional Concerns

Privacy advocates worry that technologically advanced force multipliers are giving the government—through law enforcement—a "way to track all Americans all the time, regardless of whether they're accused of any crime."[62] The Supreme Court's ruling in *United States v. Jones*, the GPS monitoring case discussed earlier in the chapter, did little to clarify this area of the law, as it applies only to lengthy periods of surveillance.

Generally speaking, law enforcement agents do not need a search warrant when using video cameras, ALPR, or other surveillance technologies that record short periods of time in public places. As noted earlier, no reasonable expectation of privacy exists in such situations. American courts have been less consistent in determining the constitutionality of another increasingly common form of police surveillance: tracking a suspect's movements by his or her use of a mobile phone.

Cell Phones and the Fourth Amendment

Given the pervasiveness of cell phones in everyday life and the amount of information stored on these "mobile computers," it should come as no surprise that the devices raise a number of questions about privacy and police searches.

Tracking Cell Phones

State and local Maryland law enforcement agencies have employed StingRay technology to gather evidence used in obtaining as many as two thousand convictions over the past decade. StingRays are *cell site simulators*—small surveillance devices that mimic cell phone towers, providing police with location data on all cell phone use in the area. By tracking the movement of a suspect through her or his cell phone use, this technology can help law enforcement determine the suspect's activities at or around the time of a crime.

The pressing legal question surrounding cell site simulators is whether individuals have a reasonable expectation that their cell phones will not be used as tracking devices. If there is a reasonable expectation of privacy with regard to cell phone tracking, then law enforcement officers must obtain a search warrant before using this technology. If not, then no search warrant is necessary.

The courts are split on this issue. In 2016, Maryland's Court of Appeals ruled that there is an expectation of privacy regarding cell phone tracking. This ruling imperils many of the convictions mentioned above, which were procured by law enforcement agencies that used StingRay without first obtaining a warrant.[63] A year earlier, however, the United States Supreme Court had refused to review a federal appeals court's holding that police do *not* need to secure a warrant before using cell phone records to track a suspect.[64] Absent a Supreme Court ruling or federal statute, each state legislature will have to make its own determination concerning the procedure its police forces must follow when tracking cell phone calls.

▲ The Supreme Court requires police officers to obtain a warrant before searching the contents of a cell phone confiscated during an arrest—except in the event of an emergency. **Name one "emergency" circumstance in which you think a police officer would be justified in searching the contents of an arrestee's cell phone without a warrant and without the owner's consent.**

AP Images/Jose Luis Magana

Searching Cell Phones

In *California v. Riley* (2014),[65] the Supreme Court ruled, unanimously, that police officers need a warrant to search the contents of cell phones belonging to suspects they have just arrested. As we saw earlier in this section, law enforcement agents may, in many instances, carry out a warrantless search of an arrestee following an arrest. Because of the vast amounts of personal information on cell phones, however, the Court decided that these items deserve greater protections than items such as wallets and cigarette packets. Furthermore, once a cell phone has been secured by police, the arrestee will not be able to "delete incriminating data," and the "data on the phone can endanger no one"—the two primary justifications for warrantless searches incidental to an arrest.[66]

In his opinion, Chief Justice John G. Roberts acknowledged that the Court's decision would "have an impact on the ability of law enforcement to combat crime." But, he added, "Privacy comes at a cost."[67] Practically, the ruling does not mean the end of cell phone searches. Rather, it means that police will need to get a warrant before engaging in such searches. Alternatively, they will need the consent of the cell phone owner.

ETHICS CHALLENGE

Suppose a program could provide police agencies with access to real-time social media postings, along with the exact location of the person posting. Under what circumstances would this tool be useful for law enforcement? Would it be ethical to monitor a suspect's social media output without a search warrant? Would it be ethical *with* a search warrant? Explain your answers.

Stops and Frisks

Two experienced Chicago police officers were standing by their patrol car when a woman approached. She told the officers that she had just purchased illegal drugs from a man and provided them with the suspect's physical description and the location of his drug-selling activity. The police officers went to the location—in an area known to both as a hot spot for drug dealing—and saw a man matching the woman's description clasp hands with another man. Believing that they had just witnessed a drug deal, the officers stopped the suspect, patted him down, and, after finding heroin, made an arrest.

Under the circumstances, these two law enforcement agents believed that they had *reasonable suspicion* that the man had committed a crime. When reasonable suspicion exists, police officers may *stop and frisk* a suspect. In a stop and frisk, law enforcement officers (1) briefly detain a person they reasonably believe to be suspicious, and (2) if they believe the person to be armed, proceed to pat down, or "frisk," that person's outer clothing.

The Elusive Definition of Reasonable Suspicion

Like so many elements of police work, the decision of whether to stop a suspect is based on the balancing of conflicting priorities. On the one hand, a police officer feels a sense of urgency to act when he or she believes that criminal activity is occurring or is about to occur. On the other hand, law enforcement agents do not want to harass innocent individuals, especially if doing so runs afoul of the U.S. Constitution. In stop-and-frisk law, this balancing act rests on the fulcrum of reasonable suspicion.

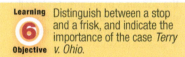

Learning Objective 6 Distinguish between a stop and a frisk, and indicate the importance of the case *Terry v. Ohio*.

Terry v. Ohio The precedent for the ever-elusive definition of a "reasonable" suspicion in stop-and-frisk situations was established in *Terry v. Ohio* (1968).[68] In that case, a detective named McFadden observed two men (one of whom was Terry) acting strangely in downtown Cleveland. The men walked repeatedly past a certain store, peered into the window, and then stopped at a street corner to confer. At one point, while they were talking, another man joined the conversation and then left quickly. Several minutes later, the three men met again at another corner a few blocks away. Detective McFadden believed the trio was planning to break into the store. He approached them, told them who he was, and asked for identification. After receiving a mumbled response, the detective frisked the three men and found handguns on two of them, who were tried and convicted of carrying concealed weapons.

The Supreme Court upheld the conviction, ruling that Detective McFadden had reasonable cause to believe that the men were armed and dangerous and that swift action was necessary to protect himself and other citizens in the area.[69] The Court accepted McFadden's interpretation of the unfolding scene as based on objective facts and practical conclusions. It therefore concluded that his suspicion was reasonable.

The "Totality of the Circumstances" Test
For the most part, the judicial system has refrained from placing restrictions on police officers' ability to make stops. In the *Terry* case, the Supreme Court did say that an officer must have "specific and articulable facts" to support the decision to make a stop, but added that the facts may be "taken together with rational inferences."[70] The Court has consistently ruled that because of their practical experience, law enforcement agents are in a unique position to make such inferences and should be given a good deal of freedom in doing so.

In the years since the *Terry* case was decided, the Court has settled on a "totality of the circumstances" test to determine whether a stop is based on reasonable suspicion.[71] In 2002, for example, the Court ruled that a U.S. Border Patrol agent's stop of a minivan in Arizona was reasonable.[72] On being approached by the Border Patrol car, the driver had stiffened, slowed down his van, and avoided making eye contact with the agent. Furthermore, the children in the van waved at the officer in a mechanical manner, as if ordered to do so. The agent pulled over the van and found 128 pounds of marijuana.

In his opinion, Chief Justice William Rehnquist pointed out that such conduct might have been unremarkable on a busy city highway, but on an unpaved road thirty miles from the Mexican border it was enough to reasonably arouse the agent's suspicion.[73] The justices also made clear that the need to prevent terrorist attacks is part of the "totality of the circumstances." Therefore, law enforcement agents have considerable leeway to make stops near U.S. borders.

A Stop

The terms *stop* and *frisk* are often used in concert, but they describe two separate acts. A **stop** takes place when a law enforcement officer has reasonable suspicion that criminal activity has taken place or is about to take place. Because an investigatory stop is not an arrest, there are limits to how long police can detain someone who has been stopped. For example, in one situation an airline traveler and his luggage were detained for ninety minutes while the police waited for a drug-sniffing dog to arrive. The Supreme Court ruled that the initial stop of the passenger was constitutional, but that the ninety-minute wait was excessive.[74]

In 2004, the Court held that police officers could require suspects to identify themselves during a stop that is otherwise valid under the *Terry* ruling.[75] The case involved a Nevada rancher who was fined $250 for refusing to give his name to a police officer investigating a possible assault. The defendant argued that such requests force citizens to incriminate themselves against their will, which is prohibited, as we shall see later in the chapter, by the Fifth Amendment. Justice Anthony Kennedy wrote, however, that "asking questions is an essential part of police investigations" that would be made much more difficult if officers could not determine the identity of a suspect.[76] The ruling validated "stop-and-identify" laws in twenty states and numerous cities and towns.

A Frisk

The Supreme Court has stated that a **frisk** should be a protective measure. Police officers cannot conduct a frisk as a "fishing expedition" simply to try to find items besides weapons, such as illegal narcotics, on a suspect.[77] A frisk does not necessarily follow a stop and in fact may occur only when the officer is justified in thinking that the safety of police officers or other citizens may be endangered. So, in the case of the two Chicago police officers that opened this

Stop A brief detention of a person by law enforcement agents for questioning.

Frisk A pat-down or minimal search by police to discover weapons.

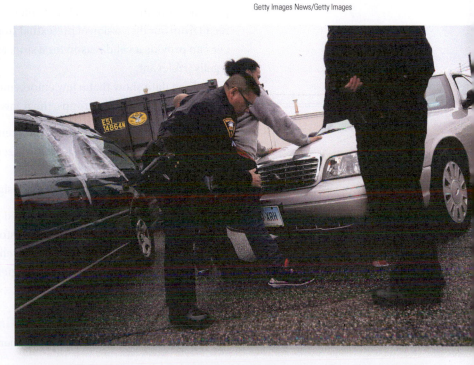

▼ A police officer frisks a suspect in New London, Connecticut. **What is the main purpose behind a frisk? When are police justified in frisking someone?** John Moore/ Getty Images News/Getty Images

section, an Illinois appeals court ruled that while the initial stop was acceptable, the officers had violated the suspect's right by frisking him. The state court was unwilling to accept the contention that the suspect was involved in a drug transaction and "drugs and guns go together" as sufficient grounds for a pat-down.[78]

As with stops, frisks must be supported by reasonable suspicion. The Illinois court rejected the argument that the Chicago police officers had objective reasons to fear for their safety. In the *Terry* case, by contrast, the Supreme Court accepted that Detective McFadden reasonably believed that the three suspects posed a threat. Crucially, the suspects had refused to answer McFadden's questions. Although this refusal was within their rights because they had not been arrested, it provided the officer with sufficient motive for the frisk. In 2009, the Court extended the "stop-and-frisk" authority by ruling that a police officer could order a passenger in a car that had been pulled over for a traffic violation to submit to a pat-down.[79] To do so, the officer must have a reasonable suspicion that the suspect may be armed and dangerous.

Race and Reasonable Suspicion

By the letter of the law, a person's race or ethnicity alone cannot provide reasonable suspicion for stops and frisks.[80] Some statistical measures, however, seem to show that these factors do, at times, play a troubling role in this area of policing. In San Francisco, for example, a review panel found that, over a twelve-month period, African Americans accounted for only 15 percent of police stops but 42 percent of nonconsensual searches. At the same time, San Francisco police found illegal contraband almost 75 percent of the time when they conducted a nonconsensual search of white suspects, compared with 33 percent of the time for black suspects.[81] Furthermore, on a national level, police officers are more than three times as likely to search members of minority groups as whites after a traffic stop.[82]

Racial Profiling   Such statistics are often seen as proof that some police departments or officers use racial profiling in deciding which suspects to stop. Racial profiling occurs when a police action is based on the race, ethnicity, or national origin of the suspect rather than any reasonable suspicion that he or she has broken the law. As you may recall from our discussion of pretextual stops earlier in the chapter, as long as a police officer can provide a valid reason for a stop, any racial motivation on his or her part is often legally irrelevant.

When data show that a law enforcement agency is improperly focusing its attention on members of minority groups, the remedies include

- A civil lawsuit against the law enforcement agency for violating provisions of the U.S. Constitution that require all citizens to be treated fairly and equally by the government.
- Law enforcement agency policies designed to stop the practice.

In addition, thirty states have passed laws that restrict racial profiling, and another seventeen states ban pretextual traffic stops when the pretext is race, ethnicity, gender, national origin, sexual orientation, or religion.[83] We will take a closer look at the issue of race-involved stop-and-frisk strategies in the *Policy Matters* feature at the end of the chapter.

Racial Profiling The practice of targeting people for police action based solely on their race, ethnicity, or national origin.

Immigration Law and Profiling   In 2010, the Arizona legislature passed a state law aimed at policing its large number of undocumented immigrants. The legislation, known as S.B. 1070, requires state and local police officers, "when practicable," to check the immigration status of someone they reasonably suspect to be in the country illegally.[84] Much to the disappointment of the law's many critics, in 2012 the United States Supreme Court upheld the so-called "papers, please" provision of S.B. 1070.[85] Thus, law enforcement agents in Arizona are empowered to check the immigration status of suspects who have been detained for other valid reasons, such as traffic stops or questioning about a crime.

In its decision, the Supreme Court seemed to hint that, if the implementation of S.B. 1070 resulted in blatant levels of racial profiling, the Court would revisit the constitutionality of the law.[86] Because of insufficient data, however, it has proved difficult to determine the exact impact of "papers, please" provisions in Arizona and the four other states that have passed similar legislation.[87]

▲ Using data gathered from red light cameras, a recent study found that the racial composition of those receiving traffic citations because of these cameras was similar to the racial composition of the neighborhood in which the violation occurred. **How might this technique be used to help determine whether racial profiling by law enforcement is occurring in any given geographical area?**

monticello/Shutterstock.com

Arrests

As happened in the *Terry* case, discussed earlier, a stop and frisk may lead to an **arrest.** An arrest is the act of apprehending a suspect for the purpose of detaining him or her on a criminal charge. It is important to understand the difference between a stop and an arrest. In the eyes of the law, a stop is a relatively brief intrusion on a citizen's rights, whereas an arrest involves a deprivation of liberty and calls for a full range of constitutional protections. (See this chapter's *Mastering Concepts—The Difference between a Stop and an Arrest.*) Consequently, while a stop can be made based on reasonable suspicion, a law enforcement officer needs probable cause, as defined earlier, to make an arrest.[88]

Elements of an Arrest

When is somebody under arrest? The easy—and incorrect—answer would be whenever the police officer says so. In fact, the state of being under arrest depends not only on the actions of the law enforcement officer but also on the perception of the suspect.

Suppose Mr. Smith is stopped by plainclothes detectives, driven to the police station, and detained for three hours for questioning. During this time, the police never tell Mr. Smith he is under arrest, and in fact, he is free to leave at any time. But if Mr. Smith or any other reasonable person *believes* he is not free to leave, then, according to the Supreme Court, that person is in fact under arrest and should receive the necessary constitutional protections.[89]

Criminal justice professor Rolando V. del Carmen of Sam Houston State University has identified four elements that must be present for an arrest to take place:

1. The *intent* to arrest. In a stop, though it may entail slight inconvenience and a short detention period, there is no intent on the part of the law enforcement officer to deprive the suspect of her or his freedom. Therefore, there is no arrest. As intent is a subjective term, it is sometimes difficult to determine whether the police officer

Arrest To deprive a person suspected of criminal activity of his or her liberty.

MASTERING CONCEPTS

The Difference between a Stop and an Arrest

Both stops and arrests are considered seizures because both police actions restrict an individual's freedom to "walk away." Both must be justified by a showing of reasonableness. You should be aware, however, of the differences between a stop and an arrest. **During a stop,** police can interrogate the person and make a limited search of his or her outer clothing. If certain events occur during the stop, such as the discovery of an illegal weapon, then officers may arrest the person. **If an arrest is made**, the suspect comes under police control and is protected by the U.S. Constitution in a number of ways that will be discussed later in the chapter.

PhotoDisc/Getty Images

	STOP	ARREST
Justification	Reasonable suspicion	Probable cause
Warrant	None	Required in some, but not all, situations
Intent of Officer	To investigate suspicious activity	To make a formal charge against the suspect
Search	May frisk, or "pat down," for weapons	May conduct a full search for weapons or evidence
Scope of Search	Outer clothing only	Area within the suspect's immediate control or "reach"

intended to arrest. In situations when the intent is unclear, courts often rely—as in our hypothetical case of Mr. Smith—on the perception of the arrestee.[90]

2. The *authority* to arrest. State laws give police officers the authority to place citizens under custodial arrest, or take them into *custody*, a concept defined later in the chapter.

3. *Seizure* or *detention.* A necessary part of an arrest is the detention of the subject. Detention is considered to have occurred as soon as the arrested individual submits to the control of the officer, whether peacefully or under the threat or use of force.

4. The *understanding* of the person that she or he has been arrested. Through either words—such as "you are now under arrest"—or actions, the person taken into custody must understand that an arrest has taken place. When a suspect has been forcibly subdued by the police, handcuffed, and placed in a patrol car, he or she is believed to understand that an arrest has been made. This understanding may be lacking if the person is intoxicated, insane, or unconscious.[91]

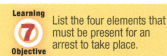

Learning **7** **Objective** List the four elements that must be present for an arrest to take place.

Arrests with a Warrant

When law enforcement officers have established probable cause to arrest an individual who is not in police custody, they obtain an arrest warrant for that person. An arrest warrant, similar to a search warrant, contains information such as the name of the person suspected and the crime he or she is suspected of having committed. (See Figure 7.3 for an example of an arrest warrant.) Judges or magistrates issue arrest warrants after first determining that the law enforcement officers have indeed established probable cause.

Arrest Warrant A written order, based on probable cause and issued by a judge or magistrate, commanding that the person named on the warrant be arrested by the police.

Entering a Dwelling
There is a perception that an arrest warrant gives law enforcement officers the authority to enter a dwelling without first announcing themselves. This is not accurate. In *Wilson v. Arkansas* (1995),[92] the Supreme Court reiterated

FIGURE 7.3 **Example of an Arrest Warrant**

United States District Court

DISTRICT OF _____

UNITED STATES OF AMERICA
V.

WARRANT FOR ARREST

CASE NUMBER:

To: The United States Marshal
and any Authorized United States Officer

YOU ARE HEREBY COMMANDED to arrest _____
_{name}

and bring him or her forthwith to the nearest magistrate to answer a(n)

☐ Indictment ☐ Information ☐ Complaint ☐ Order of Court ☐ Violation Notice ☐ Probation Violation Petition

charging him or her with (brief description of offense)

in violation of Title_____ United States Code, Section(s)_____

Name of Issuing Officer _____   Title of Issuing Officer _____

Signature of Issuing Officer _____   Date and Location _____

Bail fixed at $ _____   by _____
_{Name of Judicial Officer}

RETURN		
This warrant was received and executed with the arrest of the above-named defendant at _____		
DATE RECEIVED	NAME AND TITLE OF ARRESTING OFFICER	SIGNATURE OF ARRESTING OFFICER
DATE OF ARREST		

the common law requirement that police officers must knock and announce their identity and purpose before entering a dwelling.

Under certain conditions, known as **exigent circumstances,** law enforcement officers need not announce themselves. As determined by the courts, these circumstances arise when officers have a reasonable belief of any of the following:

- The suspect is armed and poses a strong threat of violence to the officers or others inside the dwelling.
- Persons inside the dwelling are in the process of destroying evidence or escaping because of the presence of the police.
- A felony is being committed at the time the officers enter.[93]

Exigent Circumstances Situations that require extralegal or exceptional actions by the police.

According to Peter Kraska, a professor at Eastern Kentucky University, the number of no-knock police raids based on exigent circumstances has increased from 2,000 to 3,000 per year in the mid-1980s to 50,000 per year today.[94]

The Waiting Period
The Supreme Court severely weakened the practical impact of the "knock-and-announce" rule with its decision in *Hudson v. Michigan* (2006).[95] In that case, Detroit police did not knock before entering the defendant's home with a warrant. Instead, they announced themselves and then waited only three to five seconds before making their entrance, not the fifteen to twenty seconds suggested by a prior Court ruling.[96] Hudson argued that the drugs found during the subsequent search were inadmissible because the law enforcement agents did not follow proper procedure.

By a 5–4 margin, the Court disagreed. In his majority opinion, Justice Antonin Scalia stated that an improper "knock and announce" is not unreasonable enough to provide defendants with a "get-out-of-jail-free card" by disqualifying evidence uncovered on the basis of a valid search warrant.[97] In other words, the exclusionary rule does not apply. Legal experts still advise, however, that police observe a reasonable waiting period after knocking and announcing to be certain that any evidence found during the subsequent search will stand up in court.[98]

Improper Stops and Arrests
What if a police officer makes a stop without reasonable suspicion, and that stop leads to a valid arrest? The Supreme Court addressed this issue in *Utah v. Strieff* (2016).[99] The case arose when a South Salt Lake, Utah, police officer stopped Edward Strieff as Strieff was leaving a house under surveillance for "narcotics activity." As often happens after a stop, the officer ran a warrant check and found that Strieff was wanted for a minor traffic violation. The officer arrested Strieff and, searching him, found a baggie containing illegal drugs.

Because no reasonable suspicion supported the initial stop, Strieff's lawyers argued that this evidence should be suppressed under the exclusionary rule. The Supreme Court reasoned, however, that the goal of the exclusionary rule is to deter *deliberate* police misconduct. In this situation, as Justice Clarence Thomas noted, the officer was "at most negligent."[100] Therefore, the Court ruled that the illegal drugs found on Strieff were admissible, creating what could be called a "negligence" exception to the exclusionary rule. Disagreeing with the majority opinion, Justice Sonia Sotomayor argued that "the Fourth Amendment does not tolerate an officer's unreasonable searches and seizures just because he did not know any better."[101]

Arrests without a Warrant
Arrest warrants are not always required, and in fact, most arrests are made on the scene without a warrant. A law enforcement officer may make a warrantless arrest in any of these circumstances:

1. The offense is committed in the presence of the officer.
2. The officer has probable cause to believe that the suspect has committed a particular crime.
3. The time lost in obtaining a warrant would allow the suspect to escape or destroy evidence, and the officer has probable cause to make an arrest.[102]

The type of crime also comes to bear. As a general rule, officers can make a warrantless arrest for a crime they did not see if they have probable cause to believe that a felony has been committed. For misdemeanors, the crime must have been committed in the presence

Warrantless Arrest An arrest made without a warrant for the action.

of the officer. According to a 2001 Supreme Court ruling, even an arrest for a misdemeanor that involves "gratuitous humiliations" imposed by a police officer "exercising extremely poor judgment" is valid as long as the officer can satisfy probable cause requirements.[103] That case involved a Texas mother who was handcuffed, taken away from her two young children, and placed in jail for failing to wear her seat belt.

The Interrogation Process and *Miranda*

After the Pledge of Allegiance, there is perhaps no recitation that comes more readily to the American mind than the *Miranda* warning:

> You have the right to remain silent. If you give up that right, anything you say can and will be used against you in a court of law. You have the right to speak with an attorney and to have the attorney present during questioning. If you so desire and cannot afford one, an attorney will be appointed for you without charge before questioning.

The *Miranda* warning is not a mere prop. It strongly affects one of the most important aspects of any criminal investigation—the **interrogation,** or questioning of a suspect from whom the police want to get information concerning a crime. The goal of an interrogation is to gain an *admission* or, preferably, a *confession*. An **admission** is a statement verifying information about some aspect of the underlying crime, while a **confession** is a statement in which the subject admits to being involved in an aspect of the crime.

The Legal Basis for *Miranda*

The Fifth Amendment guarantees protection against self-incrimination. In other words, as we shall see again in Chapter 10, a defendant cannot be required to provide information about his or her own criminal activity. A defendant's choice *not* to incriminate himself or herself cannot be interpreted as a sign of guilt by a jury in a criminal trial. A confession is by definition a statement of self-incrimination. How, then, to reconcile the Fifth Amendment with the critical need of law enforcement officers to gain confessions? The answer lies in the concept of **coercion,** or the use of physical or psychological duress to obtain a confession.

Setting the Stage for *Miranda*
The Supreme Court first ruled that a confession could not be physically coerced in a 1936 case concerning a defendant who was beaten and whipped until he confessed to a murder.[104] It was not until 1964, however, that the Court specifically recognized that the accused's due process rights should be protected during interrogation.

That year, the Court heard the case of *Escobedo v. Illinois,*[105] which involved a convicted murderer who had incriminated himself during a four-hour questioning session at a police station. Police officers ignored the defendant's requests to speak with his lawyer, who was actually present at the station while his client was being interrogated. The Court overturned the conviction, setting forth a five-pronged test in the process. This test established that if police were interrogating a suspect in custody, they could not deny the suspect's request to speak with an attorney and were required to warn the suspect of his or her constitutional right to remain silent under the Fifth Amendment. If any one of the five prongs was not satisfied, the suspect had effectively been denied his or her right to counsel under the Sixth Amendment.[106]

Interrogation The direct questioning of a suspect to gather evidence of criminal activity and to try to gain a confession.

Admission A statement acknowledging that certain facts concerning a crime are true but falling short of a confession.

Confession A statement acknowledging that the suspect participated in some aspect of a crime.

Coercion The use of physical force or mental intimidation to compel a person to do something—such as confess to committing a crime—against her or his will.

Miranda Rights The constitutional rights of accused persons taken into custody by law enforcement officials, including the right to remain silent and the right to counsel.

The *Miranda* Case   The limitations of the *Escobedo* decision quickly became apparent. All five of the prongs had to be satisfied for the defendant to enjoy the Sixth Amendment protections it offered. In fact, the accused rarely requested counsel, rendering the *Escobedo* test irrelevant no matter what questionable interrogation methods the police used to elicit confessions. Consequently, two years later, the Supreme Court handed down its *Miranda* decision,[107] establishing the *Miranda* rights and introducing the concept of what Columbia law professor H. Richard Uviller called *inherent coercion*. This term refers to the assumption that even if a police officer does not lay a hand on a suspect, the general atmosphere of an interrogation is coercive in and of itself.[108] (See the feature *Landmark Cases*—Miranda v. Arizona.)

LANDMARK CASES

Miranda v. Arizona

Learning Objective 8   Explain why the U.S. Supreme Court established the *Miranda* warning.

In 1963, a rape and kidnapping victim identified produce worker Ernesto Miranda as her assailant in a lineup. Phoenix detectives questioned Miranda for two hours concerning the crimes, at no time informing him that he had a right to have an attorney present. When the police emerged from the session, they had a signed statement by Miranda confessing to the crimes. He was subsequently convicted and sentenced to twenty to thirty years in prison. After the conviction was confirmed by the Arizona Supreme Court, Miranda appealed to the United States Supreme Court, claiming that he had not been warned that any statement he made could be used against him and had not been told that he had a right to counsel during the interrogation.

Miranda v. Arizona
United States Supreme Court
384 U.S. 436 (1966)

In the Words of the Court . . .

Chief Justice Warren, Majority Opinion

The cases before us raise questions which go to the roots of our concepts of American criminal jurisprudence: the restraints society must observe consistent with the Federal Constitution in prosecuting individuals for crime. More specifically, we deal with the admissibility of statements obtained from an individual who is subjected to custodial police interrogation and the necessity for procedures which assure that the individual is accorded his privilege under the Fifth Amendment to the Constitution not to be compelled to incriminate himself.

It is obvious that such an interrogation environment is created for no purpose other than to subjugate the individual to the will of his examiner. This atmosphere carries its own badge of intimidation. To be sure, this is not physical intimidation, but it is equally destructive of human dignity. The current practice of incommunicado interrogation is at odds with one of our Nation's most cherished principles—that the individual may not be compelled to incriminate himself. Unless adequate protective devices are employed to dispel the compulsion inherent in custodial surroundings, no statement obtained from the defendant can truly be the product of his free choice.

Decision

The Court overturned Miranda's conviction, stating that police interrogations are, by their very nature, coercive and therefore deny suspects their constitutional right against self-incrimination by "forcing" them to confess. Consequently, any person who has been arrested and placed in custody must be informed of his or her right to be free from self-incrimination and to be represented by counsel during any interrogation. In other words, suspects must be told that they *do not* have to answer police questions. To accomplish this, the Court established the *Miranda* warning, which must be read prior to questioning a suspect in custody.

FOR CRITICAL ANALYSIS
What is meant by the phrase "coercion can be mental as well as physical"? What role does the concept of "mental coercion" play in Chief Justice Warren's opinion?

Though the *Miranda* case is best remembered for the procedural requirement it established, at the time the Supreme Court was more concerned about the treatment of suspects during interrogation. The Court found that routine police interrogation strategies, such as leaving suspects alone in a room for several hours before questioning them, were inherently coercive.

Therefore, the Court reasoned, every suspect needed protection from coercion, not just those who had been physically abused. The *Miranda* warning is a result of this need. In theory, if the warning is not given to a suspect before an interrogation, the fruits of that interrogation, including a confession, are invalid.

When a *Miranda* Warning Is Required

As we shall see, a *Miranda* warning is not always necessary. Generally, *Miranda* requirements apply only when a suspect is in **custody.** In a series of rulings since *Miranda*, the Supreme Court has defined custody as an arrest or a situation in which a reasonable person would not feel free to leave.[109] Consequently, a **custodial interrogation** occurs when a suspect is under arrest or is deprived of her or his freedom in a significant manner. A *Miranda* warning is required before a custodial interrogation takes place. Thus, if four police officers enter a suspect's bedroom at 4:00 A.M., wake him, and form a circle around him, then they must give him a *Miranda* warning before questioning. Even though the suspect has not been arrested, he will "not feel free to go where he please[s]."[110]

The concept of custody is a fluid one, as the Court demonstrated with a 2012 ruling involving an imprisoned convict suspected of committing additional crimes. The inmate was taken from his cell to a conference room on a different floor of the prison, where he was questioned for five to seven hours without being read his *Miranda* rights. Even though the inmate was under armed guard and still in prison, the Court ruled that he was not in "custody" because the door to the room was open and he was told several times during the session that he was free to leave.[111]

When a *Miranda* Warning Is Not Required

A *Miranda* warning is not necessary in a number of situations:

1. When the police do not ask the suspect any questions that are *testimonial* in nature. Such questions are designed to elicit information that may be used against the suspect in court. Note that "routine booking questions," such as the suspect's name, address, height, and eye color, do not require a *Miranda* warning. Even though answering these questions may provide incriminating evidence, the Supreme Court has held that they are absolutely necessary if the police are to do their jobs.[112] (Imagine the officer not being able to ask a suspect her or his name.)
2. When the police have not focused on a suspect and are questioning witnesses at the scene of a crime.
3. When a person volunteers information before the police have asked a question.
4. When the suspect has given a private statement to a friend or some other acquaintance. *Miranda* does not apply to these statements so long as the government did not orchestrate the situation.
5. During a stop and frisk, when no arrest has been made.
6. During a traffic stop.[113]

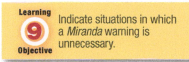

Learning Objective 9 Indicate situations in which a *Miranda* warning is unnecessary.

Custody The forceful detention of a person or the person's perception that he or she is not free to leave the immediate vicinity.

Custodial Interrogation The questioning of a suspect after that person has been taken into custody. In this situation, the suspect must be read his or her *Miranda* rights before interrogation can begin.

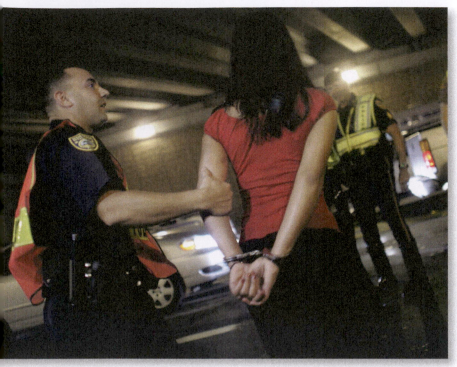

▲ Study the details of this photo of a Miami Beach, Florida, police officer and a suspect. **Why must the officer "Mirandize" the suspect before asking her any questions, even if the officer never formally places the suspect under arrest?** Joe Raedle/Getty Images News/Getty Images

In 1984, the Supreme Court also created a "public-safety exception" to the *Miranda* rule. The case involved a police officer who, after feeling an empty shoulder holster on a man he had just arrested, asked the suspect the location of the gun without informing him of his *Miranda* rights. The Court ruled that the gun was admissible as evidence because the police's duty to protect the public is more important than a suspect's *Miranda* rights.[114] In 2013, federal law enforcement agents relied on this exception to question Boston Marathon bomber Dzhokhar Tsarnaev from his hospital bedside without first "Mirandizing" him. Once the agents were satisfied that Tsarnaev knew of no other active plots or threats to public safety, they read the suspect his *Miranda* rights in the presence of a lawyer.[115]

Waiving *Miranda*   Suspects can *waive* their Fifth Amendment rights and speak to a police officer, but only if the waiver is made voluntarily. Silence on the part of a suspect does not mean that his or her *Miranda* protections have been relinquished. To waive their rights, suspects must state—either in writing or orally—that they understand those rights and that they will voluntarily answer questions without the presence of counsel.

To ensure that the suspect's rights are upheld, prosecutors are required to prove by a preponderance of the evidence that the suspect "knowingly and intelligently" waived his or her *Miranda* rights.[116] To make the waiver perfectly clear, police will ask suspects two questions in addition to giving the *Miranda* warning:

1. Do you understand your rights as I have read them to you?
2. Knowing your rights, are you willing to talk to another law enforcement officer or me?

If the suspect indicates that she or he does not want to speak to the officer, thereby invoking her or his right to silence, the officer must *immediately* stop any questioning.[117] Similarly, if the suspect requests a lawyer, the police can ask no further questions until an attorney is present.[118]

Clear Intent   The suspect must be absolutely clear about her or his intention to stop the questioning or have a lawyer present. In *Davis v. United States* (1994),[119] the Supreme Court upheld the interrogation of a suspect after he said, "Maybe I should talk to a lawyer." The Court found that this statement was too ambiguous, explaining that police officers should not be required to "read the minds" of suspects who make vague declarations.

Along these same lines, in *Berghuis v. Thompkins* (2010),[120] the Court upheld the conviction of a suspect who implicated himself in a murder after remaining mostly silent during nearly three hours of police questioning. The defendant claimed that he had invoked his *Miranda* rights by being uncommunicative with the interrogating officers. The Court disagreed, saying that silence is not enough—a suspect must actually state that he or she wishes to cut off questioning for the *Miranda* protections to apply.

The Weakening of *Miranda*

False Confession A confession of guilt when the confessor did not, in fact, commit the crime.

"*Miranda* has become embedded in routine police practice to the point where the warnings have become part of our national culture," wrote Chief Justice William Rehnquist over a decade ago.[121] This may be true, but, at the same time, many legal scholars believe that a series of Supreme Court rulings have eroded *Miranda*'s protections. "It's death by a thousand cuts," says Jeffrey L. Fisher of the National Association of Criminal Defense Lawyers, who believes the Court is "doing everything it can to ease the admissibility of confessions that police wriggle out of suspects."[122]

One such exception, created by the Supreme Court in 2004, is crucial to understanding the status of *Miranda* rights in current criminal law. The case involved a Colorado defendant who voluntarily told the police the location of his gun (which, being an ex-felon, he was not allowed to possess) without being read his rights.[123] The Court upheld the conviction, finding that the *Miranda* warning is only intended to prevent violations of the Fifth Amendment. Because only the gun, and not the defendant's testimony, was presented at trial, the police had not violated the defendant's constitutional rights.

In essence, the Court was ruling that the "fruit of the poisoned tree" doctrine, discussed earlier in this chapter, does not bar the admission of physical evidence that is discovered based on voluntary statements by a suspect who has not been "Mirandized." (See Figure 7.4 for a rundown of several other significant Court rulings that have weakened the *Miranda* requirements over the past decades.)

False Confessions

While observing more than two hundred interrogations over a nine-month period in northern California, University of San Francisco law professor Richard Leo noted that more than 80 percent of the suspects waived their *Miranda* rights.[124] Apparently, the suspects wanted to appear cooperative, a "willingness to please" that contributes to the troubling phenomenon of *false confessions* in the American criminal justice system.

Coercion and False Confessions A false confession occurs when a suspect admits to a crime that she or he did not actually commit. Given that juries tend to place a great deal of weight on confessions, sometimes to the exclusion of other evidence,

---

FIGURE 7.4 **Supreme Court Decisions Eroding *Miranda* Rights**

Moran v. Burbine (475 U.S. 412 [1986]). **This case established that police officers are not required to tell suspects undergoing custodial interrogation that their attorney is trying to reach them.** The Court ruled that events that the suspect could have no way of knowing about have no bearing on his ability to waive his *Miranda* rights.

Arizona v. Fulminante (499 U.S. 279 [1991]). **In this very important ruling, the Court held that a conviction is not automatically overturned if the suspect was coerced into making a confession.** If the other evidence introduced at the trial is strong enough to justify a conviction without the confession, then the fact that the confession was illegally gained can be, for all intents and purposes, ignored.

Texas v. Cobb (532 U.S. 162 [2001]). When a suspect refuses to waive his or her *Miranda* rights, a police officer cannot lawfully continue the interrogation until the suspect's attorney arrives on the scene. In this case, however, **the Court held that a suspect may be questioned without having a lawyer present if the interrogation does not focus on the crime for which he or she was arrested,** even though it does touch on another, closely related offense.

Florida v. Powell (559 U.S. 50 [2010]). Florida's version of the *Miranda* warning informs suspects that they have a right "to talk with an attorney," but does not clearly inform them of the right to a lawyer during police interrogation. The Court upheld Florida's warning, **ruling that different jurisdictions may use whatever version of the *Miranda* warning they please, as long as it reasonably conveys the essential information about a suspect's rights.**

Maryland v. Shatzer (559 U.S. 98 [2010]). **The Court announced a new rule that permits police to resume questioning of a suspect two weeks after that suspect has invoked her or his *Miranda* rights and been released from custody.** The Court reasoned that fourteen days "provides plenty of time for the suspect to get reacclimated to his normal life . . . and to shake off any residual coercive effect of his prior custody."

false confessions can have disastrous consequences for the defendant in court.[125] About one in four wrongful convictions overturned by DNA evidence resulted at least partially from a false confession.[126]

The Reid Technique According to Saul Kassin, a professor of psychology at Williams College in Williamstown, Massachusetts, there are three general types of false confessions:

1. *Voluntary.* The suspect is seeking attention, or is delusional and thinks he or she did commit the crime.
2. *Internalized.* The suspect is a vulnerable person, suffering from the stress of the interrogation, who comes to believe that he or she committed the crime.
3. *Compliant.* The suspect knows he or she is innocent, but decides—under police influence—that it is in his or her best interests to confess to the crime.

Kassin believes that the last two categories of false confessions are often "coerced."[127] Indeed, the Reid Technique, used widely by American law enforcement, is premised on the assumption that all interrogation subjects are guilty. Police officers trained in this method reject any denials during the interrogation. They are also taught to minimize the moral seriousness of the crime, and to present the suspect's actions as the lesser of two evils. ("Was this your idea, or did your buddies talk you into it?") When the suspect finally does admit to the crime, he or she is to be congratulated and immediately asked for corroborating details.[128]

Pressure Points Critics believe that the Reid Technique creates feelings of helplessness in the suspect and turns a confession into an "escape hatch" from the unpleasantness of the interrogation.[129] In 1985, for example, after forty hours of questioning with no attorney present, eighteen-year-old Christopher Abernathy, who was learning disabled, signed a written confession to having killed fifteen-year-old Kristina Hickey.

Almost immediately, Abernathy disavowed the confession, saying that he only made it because the interrogating officers said doing so was the only way he could go home and see his mother. Nonetheless, he was eventually sentenced to life in prison for the crime. Abernathy stayed behind bars until 2015, when a Cook County (Illinois) judge dismissed the charges against him based on the initial coercive questioning and more recent DNA evidence showing that someone else most likely killed Hickey.[130]

Another potential problem with the Reid Technique, noted earlier, is that it is predicated on the assumption that the suspect is guilty.[131] Because both guilty and innocent suspects show stress when being interrogated by police, the interrogator may be "fooled" by an innocent person's evasive and nervous behavior. An alternative method of police interrogation, which resembles a journalistic interview rather than psychological combat, is the subject of the feature *Comparative Criminal Justice—The PEACE Method.*

Recording Confessions

The mandatory videotaping of interrogations has been offered as a means to promote police accountability. Nineteen states, as well as federal agencies such as the Bureau of Alcohol, Tobacco, Firearms and Explosives, the Federal Bureau of Investigation, and the U.S. Marshals Service, mandate the recording of interrogations for certain felonies.[132]

In theory, such recordings will make clear any improper tactics used by law enforcement to gain a confession. In reality, this strategy might not live up to reformers' expectations. As Professor Jennifer Mnookin of the University of California, Los Angeles, points out, there is no guarantee that "judges or jurors can actually tell the difference between true and false confessions, even with the more complete record of interactions that recorded interrogations provide."[133]

The PEACE Method

Every police officer in England receives training in a nonconfrontational interrogation method that, in many ways, is the antithesis of the Reid Technique. Called Preparation and Planning, Engage and Explain, Account, Closure, and Evaluate (PEACE), this strategy allows a suspect first to tell his or her story without interruption. Then, the interrogating officer focuses her or his questioning on any inconsistencies between this story and the evidence. The PEACE method is based on the premise that lying—particularly about minute details—is difficult and that most untruthful suspects will be unable to keep their fabrications straight under rigorous questioning.

PEACE IN ACTION

Several years ago, British police used the PEACE method when questioning a man named David who was suspected of murdering his wife. In the first interview, a detective constable politely asked David for his version of events, and David spoke for an hour and a half, suggesting that his wife had run away to Spain.

In subsequent interviews, the detective constable pressed David on several key inconsistencies. For example, after David denied selling his wife's jewelry on a certain date, the officer asked him to explain getting a parking ticket near the jewelry shop on that day. When David claimed that his wife had sent him text messages while he was on a train to London by himself, the officer asked why cell phone records showed that both his and his wife's phones had been on the train at the same time. Although David never confessed to the crime, his obvious lies convinced a jury of his guilt, and he was convicted of murder.

FOR CRITICAL ANALYSIS

How might the PEACE method reduce false confessions? Should it replace the Reid Technique in the United States? Why or why not?

ETHICS CHALLENGE

Several years ago, police in Troy, New York, told a suspect that his son's life could be saved only if the suspect explained how the boy had injured his head. In fact, the child was already brain dead, which the suspect did not know when he admitted to slamming his son's head against a mattress. Law enforcement agents can use deception when interviewing suspects to gain a confession. Even so, did the Troy police behave ethically in this instance? Explain your answer.

The Identification Process

A confession is a form of self-identification; the suspect identifies herself or himself as the guilty party. If police officers are unable to gain a confession, they must use other methods to link the suspect with the crime. In fact, to protect against false confessions, police must use these other methods even if the suspect confesses.

Essential Procedures

Unless police officers witness the commission of the crime themselves, they must establish the identity of the suspect using three basic types of identification procedures:

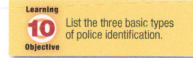

Learning Objective 10 List the three basic types of police identification.

1. *Showups,* which occur when a suspect who matches the description given by witnesses is apprehended near the scene of the crime within a reasonable amount of time after the crime has been committed. The suspect is usually returned to the crime scene for possible identification by witnesses.

▲ After spending thirty-four years in a Florida prison for rape, James Bain was freed after being exonerated by DNA evidence. At the time of the underlying crime, the victim told police that her attacker had sideburns. Investigators then put together a lineup of five or six men, of which only two—including Bain—had sideburns. The victim identified Bain as her attacker. **If you were Bain's defense attorney, how would you use this lineup procedure to create reasonable doubt about your client's guilt at trial?** AP Images/Steve Nesius

Booking The process of entering a suspect's name, offense, and arrival time into the police log following her or his arrest.

2. *Photo arrays*, which occur when no suspect is in custody but the police have a general description of the person. Witnesses and victims are shown "mug shots" of people with police records that match the description. Police will also present witnesses and victims with pictures of people they believe might have committed the crime.

3. *Lineups*, which entail lining up several physically similar people, one of whom is the suspect, in front of a witness or victim. The police may have each member of the lineup wear clothing similar to that worn by the criminal and repeat a phrase that was used during the crime. These visual and oral cues are designed to help the witness identify the suspect.

As with the other procedures discussed in this chapter, constitutional law governs the identification process, though some aspects are more tightly restricted than others. The Sixth Amendment right to counsel, for example, does not apply during showups or photo arrays. In showups, the police often need to establish a suspect quickly, and it would be unreasonable to expect them to wait for an attorney to arrive. According to the Supreme Court in *United States v. Ash* (1973),[134] however, the police must be able to prove this need for immediate identification, perhaps by showing that it was necessary to keep the suspect from fleeing the state.

As for photo arrays, courts have found that any procedure that does not require the suspect's presence does not require the presence of his or her attorney.[135] The lack of an attorney does not mean that police can "steer" a witness toward a positive identification with statements such as "Are you sure this isn't the person you saw robbing the grocery store?" Such actions would violate the suspect's due process rights.

Nontestimonial Evidence

Some observers feel that the standard **booking** procedure—the process of recording information about the suspect immediately after arrest—infringes on a suspect's Fifth Amendment rights. During booking, the suspect is photographed and fingerprinted, and blood samples may be taken. If these samples lead to the suspect's eventual identification, according to some, they amount to self-incrimination.

In *Schmerber v. California* (1966),[136] however, the Supreme Court held that such tests are not the equivalent of *testimonial* self-incrimination (where the suspect testifies verbally against himself or herself) and therefore do not violate the Fifth Amendment. Using similar legal reasoning, the Court has also determined that voice and handwriting samples gathered by police may be used to identify a suspect.[137]

Regulating Stops and Frisks

How Things Stand

At its peak in 2011, the New York City Police Department's (NYPD) stop-and-frisk strategy resulted in approximately 680,000 stops. That number, in itself, did not pose a constitutional problem. What did was the fact that 87 percent of those stopped were African American or Latino, of which 88 percent were neither arrested nor ticketed for an infraction.[138] In 2013, a federal judge found that members of minority groups living in the city were "likely targeted for stops based on a lesser degree of objectively founded suspicion than whites" and therefore ruled that the NYPD's stop-and-frisk tactics violated the Fourth Amendment.[139]

As a Result...

After the NYPD instituted new measures designed to discourage the practice, the number of overall stops in New York declined from 16,000 a week in January 2013 to fewer than 2,000 a week at the end of 2013 and have continued to fall.[140] Debate over the practice, however, has persisted. Is it, as one observer asks, "a valuable tool to catch criminals or an ugly wedge that makes minorities hate cops"?[141]

The fact that New York City's crime rate plummeted during the period when officers were most aggressively making stops led to the notion that the practice was a "valuable" crime-fighting tool. Given that the city's crime rates maintained their downward path after 2013, this argument has been widely discounted.[142] Instead, policing experts seem to agree that stop and frisk works when applied constitutionally rather than indiscriminately or, in the worst-case scenario, in a discriminatory manner. That is, the strategy is effective when officers make a stop only because they have reasonable suspicion that criminal activity is occurring or is about to occur.[143]

Up for Debate

"[In New York City], stop-and-frisk is used to help prevent crime in largely black and Latino neighborhoods, where largely black and Latino witnesses describe largely black and Latino suspects perpetrating crimes against largely black and Latino victims in a largely black and Latino city."[144]—*Editors, National Review*

"The problem is obvious: Most perpetrators of violent crime in New York might be young black and Latino men, but the vast majority of young blacks and Latinos aren't involved in crime. To treat them as presumptively criminal is to ignore factors outside of age and race that actually do contribute to violence."[145]
—*Jamelle Bouie, Slate chief political correspondent*

What's Your Take?

Review the discussion in this chapter on "The Elusive Description of Reasonable Suspicion" and "Race and Reasonable Suspicion" before answering the following questions.

1. Suppose a police department discovers a "hot spot" of crime (discussed in the preceeding chapter) in a neighborhood that is 95 percent Latino. How can police officers engage in stops and frisks in that neighborhood without exposing themselves to charges of discrimination?

2. A group of criminologists estimates that New York City's aggressive stop-and-frisk tactics may have led to a 2 percent decline in crime.[146] Do these findings justify police stops that may be based on a suspect's physical characteristics? Why or why not?

Digging Deeper...

Two of the nation's largest police departments have taken proactive steps to improve their stop-and-frisk strategies. In **New York City,** the strategy is called **"precision focused enforcement."** In **Chicago,** it relies on **"investigatory stop reports."** After researching these terms online, summarize the two strategies and consider the following policy implications: (1) Will the strategies increase the community's trust in police officers? (2) Are they constitutional according to the *Terry* ruling? Your written answer should be at least three paragraphs long.

For more information on these concepts, look back to the Learning Objective icons throughout the chapter.

Outline the four major sources that may provide probable cause. (a) Personal observation, usually based on an officer's personal training, experience, and expertise; (b) information gathered from informants, eyewitnesses, victims, police bulletins, and other sources; (c) evidence, which often has to be in plain view; and (d) association, which generally must involve a person with a known criminal background who is seen in a place where criminal activity is openly taking place.

Explain the exclusionary rule and the exceptions to it. This rule prohibits illegally seized evidence from being used against the accused in criminal court. Exceptions to the exclusionary rule are the "inevitable discovery" exception established in *Nix v. Williams* and the "good faith" exception established in *United States v. Leon* and *Arizona v. Evans*.

List the four categories of items that can be seized by use of a search warrant. (a) Items resulting from a crime, such as stolen goods; (b) inherently illegal items; (c) evidence of the crime; and (d) items used in committing the crime.

Explain when searches can be made without a warrant. Searches and seizures can be made without a warrant if they are incidental to an arrest (but they must be reasonable); when they are made with voluntary consent; when they involve the "movable vehicle" exception; when property has been abandoned; and when items are in plain view, under certain restricted circumstances (see *Coolidge v. New Hampshire*).

Describe the plain view doctrine and indicate one of its limitations. Under the plain view doctrine, police officers are justified in seizing an item if (a) the item is easily seen by an officer; (b) the officer is legally in a position to notice it; (c) the discovery of the item is unintended; and (d) the officer, without further investigation, immediately recognizes the illegal nature of the item. An item is not in plain view if the law enforcement agent needs to use technology such as a thermal imager to "see" it.

Distinguish between a stop and a frisk, and indicate the importance of the case *Terry v. Ohio*. Though the terms *stop* and *frisk* are often used in concert, they describe separate acts. A stop occurs when an officer briefly detains a person he or she reasonably believes to be suspicious. A frisk is the physical "pat-down" of a suspect. In *Terry v. Ohio*, the Supreme Court ruled that an officer must have "specific and articulable facts" before making a stop, but those facts may be "taken together with rational inferences."

List the four elements that must be present for an arrest to take place. (a) Intent, (b) authority, (c) seizure or detention, and (d) the understanding of the person that he or she has been arrested.

Explain why the U.S. Supreme Court established the *Miranda* warning. The Supreme Court recognized that police interrogations are, by their nature, coercive. Consequently, to protect a suspect's constitutional rights during interrogation, the Court ruled that the suspect must be informed of those rights before being questioned.

Indicate situations in which a *Miranda* warning is unnecessary. (a) When no questions that are testimonial in nature are asked of the suspect; (b) when there is no suspect and witnesses in general are being questioned at the scene of a crime; (c) when a person volunteers information before the police ask anything; (d) when a suspect has given a private statement to a friend without the government orchestrating it; (e) during a stop and frisk when no arrests have been made; (f) during a traffic stop; and (g) when a threat to public safety exists.

List the three basic types of police identification. (a) Showups, (b) photo arrays, and (c) lineups.

1. What are the two most significant legal concepts contained in the Fourth Amendment, and why are they important?

2. The Washington State Court of Appeals recently likened text messages to voice mail messages that can be overheard by anybody in a room. Using this logic, the court upheld a conviction based on text messages seized by police. Do you agree that people do not have a reasonable expectation of privacy when it comes to their text messaging? Why or why not?

3. A suspect discards his half-smoked cigarette on the sidewalk. The cigarette is picked up by a police officer, and the saliva on it allows law enforcement to obtain a sample of the suspect's DNA. Without a search warrant, should this evidence be allowed in court? Why or why not?

4. In Belgium, law enforcement agents are prohibited from entering private homes without consent from 9 P.M. to 5 A.M. What do you think is the reasoning behind this ban on nighttime raids? What might be some unintended consequences of the ban?

5. Responding to a call about a burglary at a vacant building, a police officer finds a homeless man named Ben sitting outside the alleged crime building. The officer asks Ben why a board covering a window of the building has been removed. Frist Ben says he doesn't know, but eventually admits that "I moved it so I could get inside and try and find some money." Should Ben's statement be allowed in court if he is charged with a crime? Why or why not?

KEY TERMS

admission 239
affidavit 222
arrest 235
arrest warrant 236
booking 246
coercion 239
confession 239
consent searches 225
custodial interrogation 241
custody 241
electronic surveillance 229

exclusionary rule 219
exigent circumstances 237
false confession 243
frisk 233
fruit of the poisoned tree 219
"good faith" exception 220
"inevitable discovery" exception 220
interrogation 239
Miranda rights 240
plain view doctrine 228
private search doctrine 221

probable cause 217
racial profiling 234
search 221
searches and seizures 217
searches incidental to arrests 224
search warrant 222
seizure 222
stop 233
warrantless arrest 238

1. *Rodriguez v. United States*, 575 U.S. _____ (2015).
2. *Illinois v. Caballes*, 543 U.S. 405 (2005).
3. *Michigan v. Summers*, 452 U.S. 692 (1981).
4. *Brinegar v. United States*, 338 U.S. 160 (1949).
5. Rolando V. del Carmen, *Criminal Procedure for Law Enforcement Personnel* (Monterey, Calif.: Brooks/Cole Publishing Co., 1987), 63–64.
6. *Maryland v. Pringle*, 540 U.S. 366 (2003).
7. 500 U.S. 44 (1991).
8. *United States v. Leon*, 468 U.S. 897 (1984).
9. Milton Hirsh and David Oscar Markus, "Fourth Amendment Forum," *Champion* (December 2002), 42.
10. 430 U.S. 387 (1977).
11. 467 U.S. 431 (1984).
12. 468 U.S. 897 (1984).
13. 514 U.S. 1 (1995).
14. *California v. Greenwood*, 486 U.S. 35 (1988).
15. *Ibid.*
16. 389 U.S. 347 (1967).
17. *Ibid.*, 361.
18. 486 U.S. 35 (1988).
19. *Ibid.*
20. *United States v. Jacobsen*, 466 U.S. 109, 117 (1984).
21. *United States v. Blanton*, 479 F.2d 327 (5th Cir. 1973).
22. 565 U.S. _____ (2012).
23. *Ibid.*
24. Quoted in James Vicini, "Supreme Court Limits Police Use of GPS to Track Suspects," *Reuters* (January 23, 2012).
25. *Coolidge v. New Hampshire*, 403 U.S. 443, 467 (1971).
26. *Millender v. Messerschmidt*, 620 F.3d 1016 (9th Cir. 2010).
27. del Carmen, *op. cit.*, 158.
28. *Katz v. United States*, 389 U.S. 347, 357 (1967).
29. 547 U.S. 398 (2006).
30. 414 U.S. 234–235 (1973).
31. 395 U.S. 752 (1969).
32. *Ibid.*, 763.
33. Carl A. Benoit, "Questioning 'Authority': Fourth Amendment Consent Searches," *FBI Law Enforcement Bulletin* (July 2008), 24.
34. *Bumper v. North Carolina*, 391 U.S. 543 (1968).
35. *State v. Stone*, 362 N.C. 50, 653 S.E.2d 414 (2007).
36. 412 U.S. 218 (1973).
37. *Ohio v. Robinette*, 519 U.S. 33 (1996).
38. Jayme W. Holcomb, "Knock and Talks," *FBI Law Enforcement Bulletin* (August 2006), 22–32.
39. *United States v. Cotterman*, 709 F.3d 952 (9th Cir. 2013).
40. *Birchfield v. North Dakota*, 579 U.S. _____. No. 14-1468. Supreme Court of the United States (June 23, 2016).
41. *Fernandez v. California*, 571 U.S. _____ (2014).
42. 267 U.S. 132 (1925).
43. *United States v. Ross*, 456 U.S. 798, 804–809 (1982); and *Chambers v. Maroney*, 399 U.S. 42, 44, 52 (1970).
44. 453 U.S. 454 (1981).
45. *Arizona v. Gant*, 556 U.S. 332 (2009).

46. Adam Liptak, "Justices Significantly Cut Back Officers' Searches of Cars of People They Arrest," *New York Times* (April 22, 2009), A12.
47. Dale Anderson and Dave Cole, "Search and Seizure after *Arizona v. Gant*," *Arizona Attorney* (October 2009), 15.
48. *Heien v. North Carolina*, 574 U.S. _____ (2014).
49. *Whren v. United States*, 517 U.S. 806 (1996).
50. *United States v. Ross*, 456 U.S. 798 (1982).
51. *Ibid.*, 824.
52. *California v. Acevedo*, 500 U.S. 565 (1991).
53. 403 U.S. 443 (1971).
54. *Kyollo v. United States*, 533 U.S. 27 (2001).
55. 388 U.S. 42 (1967).
56. 18 U.S.C. Sections 2510(7), 2518(1)(a), 2516 (1994).
57. Christopher K. Murphy, "Electronic Surveillance," in "Twenty-Sixth Annual Review of Criminal Procedure," *Georgetown Law Journal* (April 1997), 920.
58. *United States v. Nguyen*, 46 F.3d 781, 783 (8th Cir. 1995).
59. Joseph Siprut, "Privacy through Anonymity: An Economic Argument for Expanding the Right of Privacy in Public Places," *Pepperdine Law Review* 33 (2006), 311, 320.
60. "Taking Municipal Security to the Third Dimension," *Law Enforcement Technology* (September 2016), 34–37.
61. Bureau of Justice Statistics, *Local Police Departments, 2013: Equipment and Technology* (Washington, D.C.: U.S. Department of Justice, July 2015), Table 3, page 4.
62. Catherine Crump, quoted in Elizabeth Weise and Greg Toppo, "License-Plates Scanners: Love 'Em or Loathe 'Em," *USA Today* (July 19, 2013), 3A.
63. Brad Heath, "200 Imprisoned after Illegal Cellphone Tracking," *USA Today* (April 2016), 2A.
64. Todd Ruger, "Supreme Court Passes on Phone Tracking Case." *www.rollcall.com. Roll Call*: November 9, 2015, Web.
65. *California v. Riley*, 134 S.Ct. 2473 (2014).
66. *Ibid.*, 2485.
67. *Ibid.*, 2473.
68. 392 U.S. 1 (1968).
69. *Ibid.*, 20.
70. *Ibid.*, 21.
71. See *United States v. Cortez*, 449 U.S. 411 (1981); and *United States v. Sokolow*, 490 U.S. 1 (1989).
72. *United States v. Arvizu*, 534 U.S. 266 (2002).
73. *Ibid.*, 270.
74. *United States v. Place*, 462 U.S. 696 (1983).
75. *Hibel v. Sixth Judicial District Court*, 542 U.S. 177 (2004).
76. *Ibid.*, 182.
77. *Minnesota v. Dickerson*, 508 U.S. 366 (1993).
78. *People v. Boswell*, Ill.App.1st 122275 (2014).
79. *Arizona v. Johnson*, 555 U.S. 328 (2009).
80. *United States v. Avery*, 137 F.3d 343, 353 (6th Cir. 1997).
81. "Report of the Blue Ribbon Panel on Transparency, Accountability, and Fairness in Law Enforcement." *sfblueribbonpanel. com*. The City and County of San Francisco: July 2016, Web.

82. Lynn Langton and Matthew Durose, *Police Behavior during Traffic and Street Stops* (Washington, D.C.: U.S. Department of Justice, September 2013), Table 7, page 9.
83. *Born Suspect: Stop-and-Frisk Abuses and the Continued Fight to End Racial Profiling in America* (Baltimore, Md.: National Association for the Advancement of Colored People, September 2014), Appendix 1.
84. Arizona Revised Statutes Sections 11–1051(B), 13–1509, 13–2929(C).
85. *Arizona v. United States*, 567 U.S. ___(2012).
86. Julia Preston, "Immigration Ruling Leaves Issues Unresolved," *New York Times* (June 27, 2012), A14.
87. *Local Perspectives on State Immigration Policies* (Washington, D.C.: Police Executive Research Forum, July 2014), 9–12.
88. Rolando V. del Carmen and Jeffrey T. Walker, *Briefs of Leading Cases in Law Enforcement*, 2d ed. (Cincinnati, Ohio: Anderson, 1995), 38–40.
89. *Florida v. Royer*, 460 U.S. 491 (1983).
90. See also *United States v. Mendenhall*, 446 U.S. 544 (1980).
91. del Carmen, *op. cit.*, 97–98.
92. 514 U.S. 927 (1995).
93. Linda J. Collier and Deborah D. Rosenbloom, *American Jurisprudence*, 2d ed. (Rochester, N.Y.: Lawyers Cooperative Publishing, 1995), 122.
94. "Cops or Soldiers?" *The Economist* (March 22, 2014), 27.
95. 547 U.S. 586 (2006).
96. *United States v. Banks*, 540 U.S. 31, 41 (2003).
97. *Hudson v. Michigan*, 547 U.S. 586, 593 (2006).
98. Tom Van Dorn, "Violation of Knock-and-Announce Rule Does Not Require Suppression of All Evidence Found in Search," *The Police Chief* (October 2006), 10.
99. *Utah v. Strieff*, 579 U.S. _____ . No. 14–373. Supreme Court of the United States (June 20, 2016).
100. *Ibid.*, 2.
101. *Ibid.*, 20.
102. "Warrantless Searches and Seizures" in *Georgetown Law Journal Annual Review of Criminal Procedure, 2011* (Washington, D.C.: Georgetown Law Journal, 2011), 955.
103. *Atwater v. City of Lago Vista*, 532 U.S. 318, 346–347 (2001).
104. *Brown v. Mississippi*, 297 U.S. 278 (1936).
105. 378 U.S. 478 (1964).
106. *Ibid.*, 490–491.
107. *Miranda v. Arizona*, 384 U.S. 436 (1966).
108. H. Richard Uviller, *Tempered Zeal* (Chicago: Contemporary Books, 1988), 188–198.
109. *Orozco v. Texas*, 394 U.S. 324 (1969); *Oregon v. Mathiason*, 429 U.S. 492 (1977); and *California v. Beheler*, 463 U.S. 1121 (1983).
110. *Orozco, op. cit.*, 325.
111. *Howes v. Fields*, 132 S.Ct. 1181 (2012).
112. *Pennsylvania v. Muniz*, 496 U.S. 582 (1990).
113. del Carmen, *op. cit.*, 267–268.
114. *New York v. Quarles*, 467 U.S. 649 (1984).
115. Ethan Bronner and Michael S. Schmidt, "In Questions at First, No *Miranda* for Suspect," *New York Times* (April 23, 2013), A13.
116. *Moran v. Burbine*, 475 U.S. 412 (1986).

117. *Michigan v. Mosley,* 423 U.S. 96 (1975).
118. Fare v. Michael C., 442 U.S. 707, 723–724 (1979).
119. 512 U.S. 452 (1994).
120. 560 U.S. 370 (2010).
121. *Dickerson v. United States,* 530 U.S. 428 (2000).
122. Quoted in Jesse J. Holland, "High Court Trims *Miranda* Warning Rights Bit by Bit," *Associated Press* (August 2, 2010).
123. *United States v. Patane,* 542 U.S. 630 (2004).
124. Richard A. Leo, "Inside the Interrogation Room," *Journal of Criminal Law and Criminology* (1996), 266.
125. Saul M. Kassin and Lawrence S. Wrightsman, "Prior Confessions and Mock Juror Verdicts," *Journal of Social Psychology* (1980), 133–146.
126. "False Admissions or Confessions." *www.innocenceproject.org.* The Innocence Project: visited February 3, 2017, Web.
127. Saul M. Kassin, "Internalized False Confessions," in Michael P. Toglia, et al., eds., *Handbook of Eyewitness Psychology, Vol. 1* (New York: Psychology Press, 2007), 171.
128. Douglas Starr, "The Interview: Do Police Interrogation Techniques Produce False Confessions?" *The New Yorker* (December 9, 2013), 43–44.
129. *Ibid.,* 44.
130. "Christopher Abernathy." *www.law.umich.edu.* The National Registry of Exonerations: visited on February 3, 2017, Web.
131. Gregg McCrary, quoted in Starr, *op. cit.,* 46.
132. "Innocence Project, Wrongfully Convicted Floyd Bledsoe and Others Testify in Support of Kansas Bill that Would Require the Recording of Interrogations." *www.innocenceproject.org.* The Innocence Project: February 11, 2016.
133. Jennifer L. Mnookin, "Can a Jury Believe What It Sees?" *New York Times* (July 14, 2014), A19.
134. 413 U.S. 300 (1973).
135. *United States v. Barker,* 988 F.2d 77, 78 (9th Cir. 1993).
136. 384 U.S. 757 (1966).
137. *United States v. Dionisio,* 410 U.S. 1 (1973); and *United States v. Mara,* 410 U.S. 19 (1973).
138. Janell Ross, "Donald Trump Was Wrong about Stop and Frisk — and the Ruling that Called it Racial Profiling." *www.washingtonpost.com. Washington Post:* September 26, 2016, Web.
139. Joseph Goldstein, "Judge Rejects New York's Stop-and-Frisk Policy," *New York Times* (August 13, 2013), A1.
140. Mike Bostock and Ford Fessenden, "'Stop-and-Frisk' Is All But Gone from *New York.*" *www.nytimes.com. New York Times:* September 19, 2014, Web; and Al Baker, "New York Police Still Struggle to Follow Street-Stop Rules, Report Finds," *New York Times* (February 17, 2016), A20.
141. Josh Saul, "America Has a Stop-and-Frisk Problem. Just Look at Philadelphia." *www.newsweek.com. Newsweek:* May 18, 2016, Web.
142. Max Ehrenfreund, "Donald Trump Claims New York's Stop-and-Frisk Policy Reduced Crime. The Data Disagree." *www.washingtonpost.com. Washington Post:* September 22, 2016, Web.
143. Andrew Gelman, Jeffrey Fagan, and Alex Kiss, "An Analysis of the New York City Police Department's 'Stop-and-Frisk' Policy in the Context of Claims of Racial Bias," *Journal of the American Statistical Association* (2007), 813–823.
144. "Stop-and-Frisk Works." *www.nationalreview.com.* National Review: July 2, 2013, Web.
145. Jamelle Bouie, "What Donald Trump Means When He Talks About Stop-and-Frisk." *www.slate.com.* Slate: September 27, 2016, Web.
146. David Weisbud, et al., "Do Stop, Question, and Frisk Practices Deter Crime?" *Criminology & Public Policy* (February 2015), 31–56.

Courts and the Quest for Justice

To target your study and review, look for these numbered Learning Objective icons throughout the chapter.

Chapter Outline		Corresponding Learning Objectives
Functions of the Courts	**1**	Define and contrast the four functions of the courts.
The Basic Principles of the American Judicial System	**2**	Define *jurisdiction* and contrast geographic and subject-matter jurisdiction.
	3	Explain the difference between trial and appellate courts.
State Court Systems	**4**	Outline the levels of a typical state court system.
The Federal Court System	**5**	Outline the federal court system.
	6	Explain briefly how a case is brought to the United States Supreme Court.
Judges in the Court System	**7**	Explain the difference between the selection of judges at the state level and at the federal level.
	8	Describe one alternative, practiced in other countries, to the American method of choosing judges.
The Courtroom Work Group	**9**	List and describe the members of the courtroom work group.
	10	List the three basic features of an adversary system of justice.

Text Message

▲ Michelle Carter, shown here in a Taunton, Massachusetts, courtroom, was convicted of involuntary manslaughter for encouraging her boyfriend to kill himself. AP Images/Patrick Whittemore/*The Boston Herald*

"When are you doing it?" seventeen-year-old Michelle Carter asked her eighteen-year-old boyfriend, Carter Roy, in one of the thousands of texts the two shared. "You always say you're gonna do it, but you never do." On July 13, 2014, Roy finally did "it," committing suicide by carbon monoxide poisoning in his truck behind a Fairhaven, Massachusetts, K-Mart. Earlier that day, Carter had texted to Roy, "Tonight is the night," and "It's painless and quick." Furthermore, the two were speaking on the phone when Roy got out of his truck, afraid that the carbon monoxide was working. "I [expletive] told him to get back in," Carter apparently later admitted to a friend.

No criminal statute in Massachusetts applies specifically to Carter's behavior. Nonetheless, Bristol County prosecutors charged her with involuntary manslaughter for "strongly influencing" and "encouraging" Roy to commit suicide. New England School of Law professor David Siegel called the charge "a square peg in a round hole," noting that the state would need to prove that, with her goading, Carter consciously disregarded a "substantial and unjustifiable" risk of causing Roy's death. "What we have here is a young man who made a voluntary decision to end his own life," argued Joseph Cataldo, Carter's defense attorney. "His death was not caused by Michelle Carter."

According to Professor Siegel, prosecutors wanted to use the courts to "send a message" that, despite the lack of a specific law prohibiting it, Carter's behavior was unacceptable. In April 2016, a Massachusetts appeals court seemed to agree. Rejecting the defense's claim that no crime had taken place, the court ruled that there was sufficient evidence of a "direct, causal link" between Carter's actions and Roy's death for the case to go to trial. Thirteen months later, Juvenile Court Judge Lawrence Moniz determined that Carter created and then failed to set right the "toxic environment" that led to Roy's death, and found her guilty of involuntary manslaughter.

FOR CRITICAL ANALYSIS

1. "It's a sad story, a tragedy, but it's not manslaughter," said Michelle Carter's defense attorney of the situation described above. Do you agree? Why or why not?

2. Two years before his death, Carter Roy spent time in a mental institution. After his release, he tried to kill himself by overdosing on the pain reliever acetaminophen. Does this information help or hurt Carter's defense? Should it matter if she knew about Roy's suicide attempt? Explain your answers.

3. How would society benefit from a law that prohibits knowingly or recklessly encouraging a person to commit suicide? What might be some unintended consequences of such a law?

Functions of the Courts

After the Massachusetts appeals court ruled that Michelle Carter's manslaughter trial could move forward, Carter Roy's family expressed a sense of relieved anticipation. "I hope that justice will be served," said Roy's grandfather, Conrad Roy, Sr.[1]

Famed jurist Roscoe Pound once characterized "justice" as society's demand "that serious offenders be convicted and punished," while at the same time "the innocent and unfortunate are not oppressed."[2] This somewhat idealistic definition obscures the fact that there are two sides to each court proceeding. While Roy, Sr., understandably has strong feelings about Carter's fate, American legal traditions allow a person accused of any crime, no matter how heinous, the chance to prove his or her innocence before a neutral decision maker. On a practical level, then, a court is a place where arguments are settled. At best, the court provides a just environment in which the basis of the argument can be decided through the application of the law.

Courts have extensive powers in our criminal justice system: They can bring to bear the authority of the state to seize property and to restrict individual liberty. Given that the rights to own property and to enjoy personal freedom are enshrined in the U.S. Constitution, a court's *legitimacy* in taking such measures must be unquestioned by society. This legitimacy is based on two factors: impartiality and independence.[3] In theory, each party involved in a courtroom dispute must have an equal chance to present its case and must be secure in the belief that no outside factors are going to influence the decision rendered by the court. In reality, as we shall see over the next four chapters, it does not always work that way.

Due Process and Crime Control in the Courts

As mentioned in Chapter 1, the criminal justice system has two sets of underlying values: due process and crime control. Due process values focus on protecting the rights of the individual, whereas crime control values stress the punishment and repression of criminal conduct. The competing nature of these two value systems is often evident in the nation's courts.

Learning Objective 1 Define and contrast the four functions of the courts.

The Due Process Function   The primary concern of early American courts was to protect the rights of the individual against the power of the state. Memories of injustices suffered at the hands of the British monarchy were still strong, and most of the procedural rules that we have discussed in this textbook were created with the express purpose of giving the individual a "fair chance" against the government in any courtroom proceedings. Therefore, the due process function of the courts is to protect individuals from the unfair advantages that the government—with its immense resources—automatically enjoys in legal battles.

Seen in this light, constitutional guarantees such as the right to counsel, the right to a jury trial, and protection from self-incrimination are equalizers in the "contest" between the state and the individual. The idea that the two sides in a courtroom dispute are adversaries is fundamental in American courts, as you will see at the end of the chapter.

The Crime Control Function   Advocates of crime control distinguish between the court's obligation to be fair to the accused and its obligation to be fair to society. The crime control function of the courts emphasizes punishment and retribution—criminals must suffer for the harm done to society, and it is the courts' responsibility to see that they do so. Given this responsibility to protect the public, deter criminal behavior,

▲ Why is it important that American criminal courtrooms, such as this one in Cape May, New Jersey, are places of impartiality and independence?

AP Images/*The Press of Atlantic City,* Dale Gerhard

and "get criminals off the streets," the courts should not be concerned solely with giving the accused a fair chance.

Rather than using due process rules as "equalizers," then, the courts should use them as protection against blatantly unconstitutional acts. For example, a detective who beats a suspect with a tire iron to get a confession has obviously infringed on the suspect's constitutional rights. If, however, the detective uses trickery to gain a confession, the court should allow the confession to stand because it is not in society's interest that law enforcement agents be deterred from outwitting criminals.

The Rehabilitation Function

A third view of the court's responsibility is based on the "medical model" of the criminal justice system. In this model, criminals are analogous to patients, and the courts perform the role of physicians who dispense "treatment."[4] The criminal is seen as sick, not evil, and therefore treatment is morally justified. Of course, treatment varies from case to case, and some criminals require harsh penalties such as incarceration. In other cases, however, it may not be in society's best interest for the criminal to be punished according to the formal rules of the justice system. Perhaps the criminal can be rehabilitated to become a productive member of society and thus save taxpayers the costs of incarceration or other punishment.

The Bureaucratic Function

To a certain extent, the crime control, due process, and rehabilitation functions of a court are secondary to its bureaucratic function. In general, a court may have the goal of protecting society or protecting the rights of the individual, but on a day-to-day basis that court has the more pressing task of dealing with the cases brought before it. Like any bureaucracy, a court is concerned with speed and efficiency, and loftier concepts such as justice can be secondary to a judge's need to wrap up a particular case before six o'clock so that administrative deadlines can be met. Indeed, many observers feel that the primary adversarial relationship in the courts is not between the two parties involved but between the ideal of justice and the reality of bureaucratic limitations.[5]

The Basic Principles of the American Judicial System

One of the most often cited limitations of the American judicial system is its complex nature. In truth, the United States does not have a single judicial system, but fifty-two different systems—one for each state, the District of Columbia, and the federal government.

As each state has its own unique judiciary with its own set of rules, some of which may conflict with the federal judiciary, it is helpful at this point to discuss some basics—the concept of jurisdiction, trial and appellate courts, and the dual court system.

Jurisdiction

In Latin, *juris* means "law," and *diction* means "to speak." Thus, jurisdiction literally refers to the power "to speak the law." Before any court can hear a case, it must have jurisdiction over the persons involved in the case or its subject matter. The jurisdiction of every court, even the United States Supreme Court, is limited in some way.

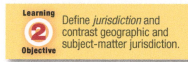

Learning 2 Objective — Define *jurisdiction* and contrast geographic and subject-matter jurisdiction.

Geographic Jurisdiction One limitation is geographic. Generally, a court can exercise its authority over residents of a certain area. A state trial court, for example, normally has jurisdictional authority over crimes committed in a particular area of the state, such as a county or a district. A state's highest court (often called the state supreme court) has jurisdictional authority over the entire state, and the United States Supreme Court has jurisdiction over the entire country. For the most part, criminal jurisdiction is determined by legislation. The U.S. Congress or a state legislature can determine what acts are illegal within the geographic boundaries it controls, thus giving federal or state courts jurisdiction over those crimes.

Federal versus State Jurisdiction Most criminal laws are state laws, so the majority of all criminal trials are heard in state courts. Many acts that are illegal under state law, however, are also illegal under federal law. What happens when more than one court system has jurisdiction over the same criminal act? As a general rule, when Congress "criminalizes" behavior that is already prohibited under a state criminal code, the federal and state courts both have jurisdiction over that crime unless Congress indicates otherwise in the initial legislation. Thus, concurrent jurisdiction, which occurs when two different court systems have simultaneous jurisdiction over the same case, is quite common.

For instance, both the federal courts and the South Carolina state court system have jurisdiction over Dylann Roof, who killed nine African American parishioners during bible study at a Charleston church in June 2015. South Carolina does not have a hate crimes law, and federal officials felt that the racial component of Roof's actions needed to be addressed. Thus, the federal government decided to pursue the case. In January 2017, a federal judge sentenced Roof to be executed after he was found guilty of, among other counts, federal hate crimes resulting in death. Three months later, South Carolina authorities allowed Roof to plead guilty to all related state charges, clearing the way for the defendant to begin his imprisonment on federal death row.[6]

State versus State Jurisdiction Multiple states can also claim jurisdiction over the same defendant or criminal act, depending on state legislation and the circumstances of the crime. For example, if Billy is standing in State A and shoots Frances, who is standing in State B, the two states could have concurrent jurisdiction to try Billy for murder. Similarly, if a property theft takes place in State A but police recover the stolen goods in State B, concurrent jurisdiction could exist. Some states have also passed laws stating that they have jurisdiction over their own citizens who commit crimes in other states, even if there is no other connection between the home state and the criminal act.[7]

The concept of jurisdiction encourages states to cooperate with each other regarding fugitives from the law. In 2016, for example, Cody Masiello was suspected by authorities

Jurisdiction The authority of a court to hear and decide cases within an area of the law or a geographic territory.

Concurrent Jurisdiction The situation that occurs when two or more courts have the authority to preside over the same criminal case.

of carjacking a driver at gunpoint in Seaside Heights, New Jersey. About three weeks after the alleged crime, Pennsylvania state troopers arrested Masiello across the state line in Saylorsburg. Pennsylvania officials subsequently *extradited* Masiello back to New Jersey to face the carjacking charges. **Extradition** is the formal process by which one legal authority, such as a state or a nation, transfers a fugitive or a suspect to another legal authority that has a valid claim on that person.

Multiple Trials   When different courts share jurisdiction over the same defendant, multiple trials can result. Between 2014 and 2016, for example, former professional football player Darren Sharper was sentenced in four different states—Arizona, California, Louisiana, and Nevada—after being convicted of drugging and raping a number of women in those states. Because officials in each state had probable cause to believe that he had committed crimes within state limits, each state had jurisdiction over him and the right to conduct a criminal trial.

Although some believe that such multiple trials are a waste of taxpayer money, state and county prosecutors often argue that local victims of crimes deserve the "sense of closure" that comes with criminal proceedings.[8] In addition, as you will see in Chapter 10, guilty verdicts can be appealed and reversed, and extra convictions serve as "insurance" against that possibility. In most situations, however, a conviction in one jurisdiction will end the prosecution of the same case in another jurisdiction. (Native American reservations in the United States operate under a unique, and sometimes controversial, geographic jurisdictional framework, which is examined in the *Policy Matters* feature at the end of the chapter.)

International Jurisdiction

Under international law, each country has the right to create and enact criminal law for its territory. Therefore, the notion that a nation has jurisdiction over any crimes committed within its borders is well established. The situation becomes more delicate when one nation feels the need to go outside its own territory to enforce its criminal law. International precedent does, however, provide several bases for expanding jurisdiction across international borders.

For example, anti-terrorism efforts have been guided by the principle that the United States has jurisdiction over persons who commit crimes against Americans even when the

▼ In 2017, Mexico extradited notorious drug trafficker Joaquin "El Chapo" Guzman, shown here with Mexican security forces, to the United States. **Should the possibility that Guzman was responsible for distributing large amounts of cocaine into this country give the American court system jurisdiction over him? Why or why not?** Susana Gonzalez/Bloomberg/Getty Images

former are citizens of foreign countries and live outside the United States. In 2016, for example, Spanish authorities agreed to extradite Ali Charaf Damache to the United States because of charges that he had recruited U.S. citizens to engage in international terrorist activities. Earlier, an Irish court had refused to extradite Damache—an Irish citizen—to the United States because Ireland's government disagrees with the American practice of placing prison inmates in solitary confinement.[9] Indeed, some countries, for legal and political reasons, will not extradite criminal suspects to the United States.

Nevertheless, the federal government feels it is legally justified in claiming jurisdiction over persons who commit crimes against U.S. citizens, even if these suspects have never set foot on American soil.[10] Furthermore, some behavior, such as piracy and genocide, is considered a crime against all nations collectively and, according to *universal jurisdiction*, can be prosecuted by any nation having custody of the wrongdoer.

Subject-Matter Jurisdiction   Jurisdiction over subject matter also acts as a limitation on the types of cases a court can hear. State court systems include courts of *general* (unlimited) *jurisdiction* and courts of *limited jurisdiction*. Courts of general jurisdiction have no restrictions on the subject matter they may address. These courts deal with the most serious felonies and civil cases. Courts of limited jurisdiction, also known as lower courts, handle misdemeanors and civil matters under a certain amount, usually $1,000.

Many states have created special subject-matter courts that only dispose of cases involving a specific crime. For example, a number of jurisdictions have established drug courts to handle an overload of illicit narcotics arrests. Furthermore, under the Uniform Code of Military Justice, the U.S. military has jurisdiction over active personnel who commit crimes, even if those crimes occur outside the course of duty.[11] In such cases, military officials can either attempt to *court-martial* the suspect in military court or allow civilian prosecutors to handle the case in state or federal court.

Trial and Appellate Courts

Another distinction is between courts of original jurisdiction and courts of appellate, or review, jurisdiction. Courts having *original jurisdiction* are courts of the first instance, or **trial courts.** Almost every case begins in a trial court. It is in this court that a trial (or a guilty plea) takes place, and the judge imposes a sentence if the defendant is found guilty. Trial courts are primarily concerned with *questions of fact*. They are designed to determine exactly what events occurred that are relevant to questions of the defendant's guilt or innocence.

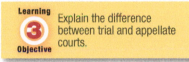

Learning Objective 3 Explain the difference between trial and appellate courts.

Courts having *appellate jurisdiction* act as reviewing courts, or **appellate courts.** In general, cases can be brought before appellate courts only on appeal by one of the parties in the trial court. (Note that because of constitutional protections against being tried twice for the same crime, prosecutors who lose in criminal trial court cannot appeal the verdict.) An appellate court does not use juries or witnesses to reach its decision. Instead, its judges make a decision on whether the lower court's ruling should be *affirmed* or *reversed*. If the ruling is reversed, it may also be *remanded* (sent back to the original court for a new trial). Appellate judges present written explanations for their decisions, and these **opinions** of the court are the basis for a great deal of the precedent in the criminal justice system.

It is important to understand that appellate courts do not determine the defendant's guilt or innocence—they make judgments only on questions of procedure. In other words, they are concerned with *questions of law* and normally accept the facts as established by the trial court. Only rarely will an appeals court question a jury's decision. Instead, the appellate judges will review how the facts and evidence were provided to the jury and rule on whether errors were made in the process.

The Dual Court System

As we saw in Chapter 1, America's system of federalism allows the federal government and the governments of the fifty states to hold separate authority in many areas. As a result, the federal government and each of the fifty states, as well as the District of Columbia, have their own separate court systems. Because of the split between the federal courts and the state courts, the United States is said to have a **dual court system.** (See Figure 8.1 to get a better idea of how federal and state courts operate as distinct yet parallel entities.)

Trial Courts Courts in which most cases begin and in which questions of fact are examined.

Appellate Courts Courts that review decisions made by lower courts, such as trial courts; also known as *courts of appeals*.

Opinions Written statements by appellate judges expressing the reasons for the court's decision in a case.

Dual Court System The separate but interrelated court system of the United States, made up of the courts on the national level and the courts on the state level.

FIGURE 8.1 The Dual Court System

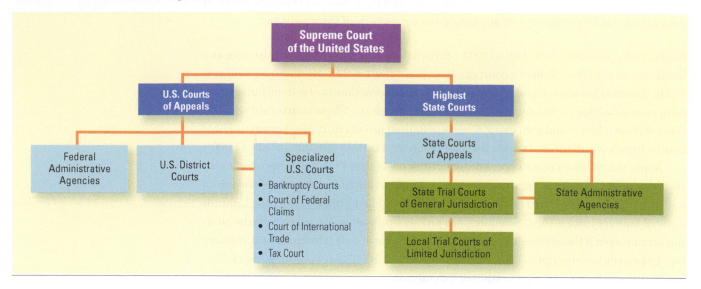

Federal and state courts both have limited jurisdiction. Generally, federal courts preside over cases involving violations of federal law, and state courts preside over cases involving violations of state law. The distinction is not always clear, however. Federal courts have jurisdiction over nearly five thousand crimes, many of which also can be found in state criminal codes. As we saw earlier in this section, when such *concurrent jurisdiction* exists, both sides can try the defendant under their own laws, or one side can step aside and let the other decide the fate of the defendant. Because the federal court system has greater resources than most state court systems, federal criminal charges often take precedence over state criminal charges for practical reasons.

ETHICS CHALLENGE

In 2003, U.S. troops directed tank fire at the Palestine Hotel in Baghdad, Iraq, believing that enemy combatants were taking shelter in the building. As it turned out, the hotel was the headquarters for a number of journalists, and the American military actions killed two members of the international media, including Spanish TV cameraman José Couso. Nearly a decade later, a Spanish judge indicted three U.S. soldiers in connection with Couso's death. Would it have been ethical for the American government to send the soldiers to Spain for a criminal trial? Why or why not?

State Court Systems

Typically, a state court system includes several levels, or tiers, of courts. State courts may include:

1. Lower courts, or courts of limited jurisdiction
2. Trial courts of general jurisdiction
3. Appellate courts
4. The state's highest court

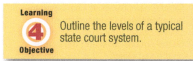

Learning
4 Objective
Outline the levels of a typical state court system.

As previously mentioned, each state has a different judicial structure, in which different courts have different jurisdictions, but there are enough similarities to allow for a general discussion. Figure 8.2 shows a typical state court system.

Courts of Limited Jurisdiction

Most states have local trial courts that are limited to trying cases involving minor criminal matters, such as traffic violations, prostitution, and drunk and disorderly conduct. Although these minor courts sometimes keep no written record of the trial proceedings and cases are decided by a judge rather than a jury, defendants have the same rights as in other trial courts. Most minor criminal cases are decided in these lower courts. Courts of limited jurisdiction can also be responsible for the preliminary stages of felony cases. Arraignments, bail hearings, and preliminary hearings often take place in these lower courts.

Magistrate Courts   One of the earliest courts of limited jurisdiction was the justice court, presided over by a *justice of the peace*, or JP. Today, more than half the states have abolished justice courts, though JPs still serve a useful function in some cities

---

FIGURE 8.2 **A Typical State Court System**

STATE SUPREME COURT
Court of final resort. Some states call it Court of Appeals, Supreme Judicial Court, or Supreme Court of Appeals.

INTERMEDIATE APPELLATE COURTS
About three-fourths of the states have intermediate appellate courts, which are intermediate appellate tribunals between the trial courts and the courts of final resort. A majority of cases are decided finally by these appellate courts.

SUPERIOR COURT
Highest trial court with general jurisdiction. Some states call it Circuit Court, District Court, Court of Common Pleas, or, in New York, Supreme Court.

PROBATE COURT
Some states call it Surrogate Court or Orphans' Court. It is a special court that handles wills, administration of estates, and guardianship of minors and incompetents.

COUNTY COURT *
These courts, sometimes called Common Pleas or District Courts, have limited jurisdiction in both civil and criminal cases.

MUNICIPAL COURT
In some cities, it is customary to have less important cases tried by municipal justices or municipal magistrates.

**JUSTICE OF THE PEACE†
AND POLICE MAGISTRATE**
Lowest courts in judicial hierarchy. Limited in jurisdiction in both civil and criminal cases.

DOMESTIC RELATIONS COURT
Also called Family Court or Children's Court.

*Courts of special jurisdiction, such as probate, family, or juvenile courts, and the so-called inferior courts, such as common pleas or municipal courts, may be separate courts or may be part of the trial court of general jurisdiction.

†Justices of the peace do not exist in all states. Their jurisdiction varies greatly from state to state when they do exist.

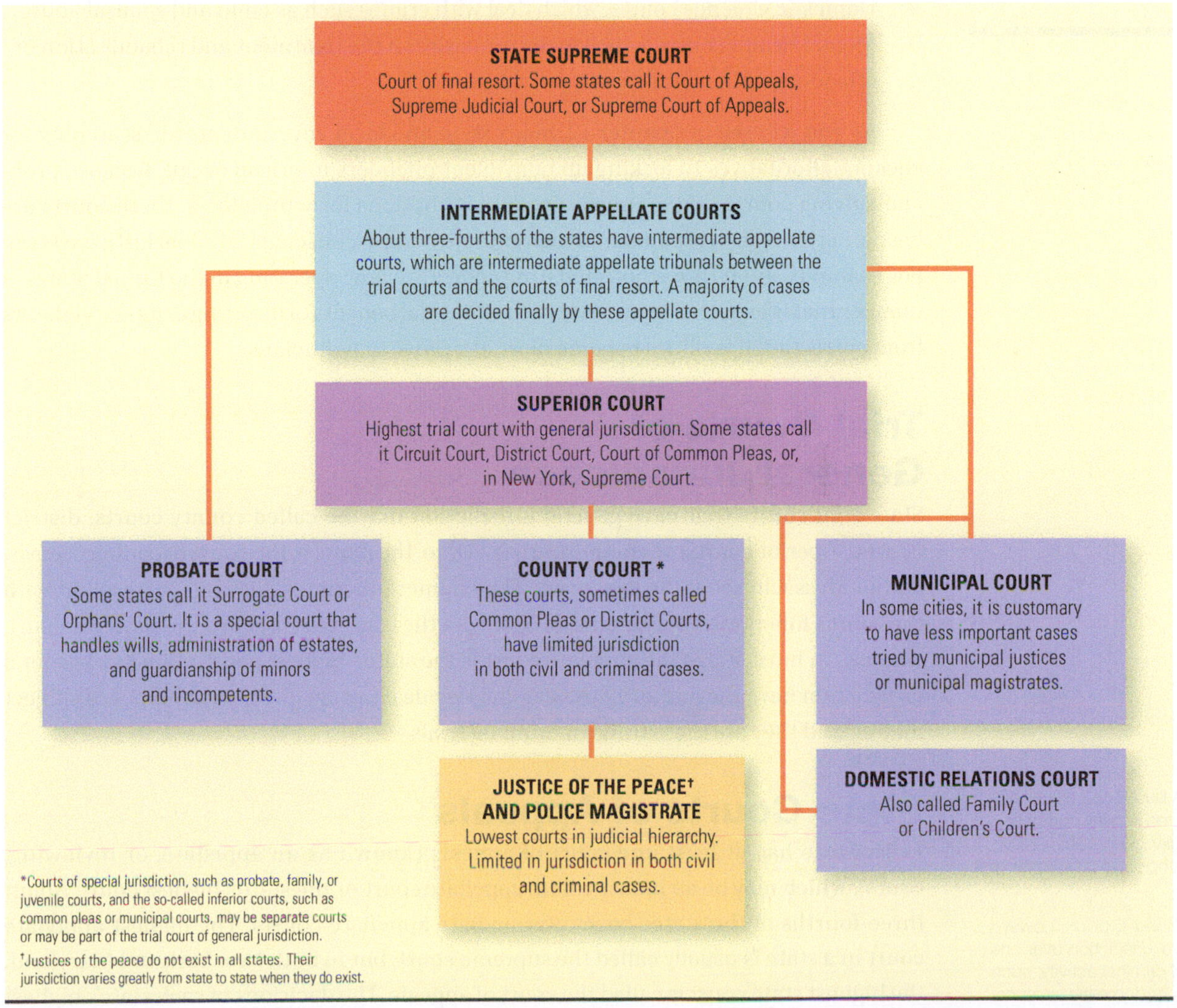

and rural areas, notably in Texas. The jurisdiction of justice courts is limited to minor disputes between private individuals and to crimes punishable by small fines or short jail terms.

The equivalent of a county JP in a city is known as a magistrate or, in some states, a municipal court judge. Magistrate courts have the same limited jurisdiction as do justice courts in rural settings. In most jurisdictions, magistrates are responsible for providing law enforcement agents with search and seizure warrants, discussed in Chapter 7.

Specialty Courts As mentioned earlier, many states have created courts that have jurisdiction over very narrowly defined areas of criminal justice. These so-called problem-solving courts not only remove many cases from the rest of the court system but also allow court personnel to become experts in a particular subject. Problem-solving courts include:

1. Drug courts, which deal only with illegal substance crimes.
2. Veterans courts, designed to handle factors that are often linked to criminal behavior by those who have served in the U.S. military, such as post-traumatic stress disorder and substance abuse.
3. Juvenile courts, which specialize in crimes committed by minors. (We will discuss juvenile courts in more detail in Chapter 15.)
4. Domestic violence courts, which deal with crimes such as child and spousal abuse.
5. Mental health courts, which focus primarily on the treatment and rehabilitation of offenders with mental health problems.

As you will see in Chapter 12, many state and local governments are searching for cheaper alternatives to locking up nonviolent offenders in prison or jail. Because problem-solving courts offer a range of treatment options for wrongdoers, these courts are becoming increasingly popular in today's more budget-conscious criminal justice system. For example, about three thousand drug courts are now operating in the United States, a number that is expected to increase as the financial benefits of diverting drug law violators from correctional facilities become more attractive to politicians.

Trial Courts of General Jurisdiction

State trial courts that have general jurisdiction may be called county courts, district courts, superior courts, or circuit courts. In Ohio, the name is the court of common pleas, and in Massachusetts, the trial court. (The name sometimes does not correspond with the court's functions. For example, in New York the trial court is called the supreme court, whereas in most states the supreme court is the state's highest court.) Courts of general jurisdiction have the authority to hear and decide cases involving many types of subject matter, and they are the setting for criminal trials.

State Courts of Appeals

Every state has at least one court of appeals (known as an appellate, or reviewing, court), which may be an intermediate appellate court or the state's highest court. About three-fourths of the states have intermediate appellate courts. The highest appellate court in a state is usually called the supreme court, but in both New York and Maryland, the highest state court is called the court of appeals. The decisions of each state's highest

Magistrate A public civil officer or official with limited judicial authority within a particular geographic area, such as the authority to issue an arrest warrant.

Problem-Solving Courts Lower courts that have jurisdiction over one specific area of criminal activity, such as illegal drugs or domestic violence.

court on all questions of state law are final. Only when issues of federal law or constitutional procedure are involved can the United States Supreme Court overrule a decision made by a state's highest court.

The Federal Court System

The federal court system is basically a three-tiered model consisting of (1) U.S. district courts (trial courts of general jurisdiction) and various courts of limited jurisdiction, (2) U.S. courts of appeals (intermediate courts of appeals), and (3) the United States Supreme Court.

Unlike state court judges, who are usually elected, federal court judges—including the justices of the Supreme Court—are appointed by the president of the United States, subject to the approval of the Senate. All federal judges receive lifetime appointments (because under Article III of the Constitution they "hold their offices during Good Behavior").

Learning
5
Objective
Outline the federal court system.

U.S. District Courts

On the lowest tier of the federal court system are the U.S. district courts, or federal trial courts. These are the courts in which cases involving federal laws begin and a judge or jury decides the case. Every state has at least one federal district court, and there is one in the District of Columbia. The number of judicial districts varies over time, primarily owing to population changes and corresponding caseloads. At the present time, there are ninety-four judicial districts. The federal system also includes other trial courts of limited jurisdiction, such as the Tax Court and the Court of International Trade.

U.S. Courts of Appeals

In the federal court system, there are thirteen U.S. courts of appeals—also referred to as U.S. circuit courts of appeals. The federal courts of appeals for twelve of the circuits hear appeals from the district courts located within their respective judicial circuits (see Figure 8.3). The Court of Appeals for the Thirteenth Circuit, called the Federal Circuit, has national appellate jurisdiction over certain types of cases, such as cases in which the U.S. government is a defendant. The decisions of the circuit courts of appeals are final unless a further appeal is pursued and granted. In that case, the matter is brought before the Supreme Court.

The United States Supreme Court

Alexander Hamilton, writing in *Federalist Paper No. 78* (1788), predicted that the United States Supreme Court would be the "least dangerous branch" of the federal government because it had neither the power of the purse nor the power of the sword. (That is, it could not raise any revenue, and it lacked an enforcement agency.)[12] Unless the other two branches of the government—the president and Congress—would accept its decisions, the Court would be superfluous.

Interpreting and Applying the Law   Despite Hamilton's pessimism, the Supreme Court has come to dominate the country's legal culture. Although the Court reviews a minuscule percentage of the cases decided in the United States each year, its decisions profoundly affect our lives.

The impact of Court decisions on the criminal justice system is equally far reaching: *Gideon v. Wainwright* (1963)[13] established every American's right to be represented by counsel in a criminal trial; *Miranda v. Arizona* (1966)[14] transformed pretrial

Source: Administrative Office of the United States Courts.

interrogations; *Furman v. Georgia* (1972)[15] ruled that the death penalty was unconstitutional; and *Gregg v. Georgia* (1976)[16] spelled out the conditions under which it could be allowed. As you have no doubt noticed from references in this textbook, the Court has addressed nearly every important facet of criminal law. The Supreme Court "makes" criminal justice policy in two important ways: through *judicial review* and through its authority to interpret the law.

Judicial Review Judicial review refers to the power of the Court to determine whether a law or action by the other branches of the government is constitutional. For example, until recently, in eleven states it was a crime for motorists suspected of drunk driving to refuse a blood alcohol test. As part of a case we touched on in the preceding chapter, in 2016 the Court found that these laws were unconstitutional because they forced suspects to choose between breaking the law and submitting to overly invasive warrantless searches of their bodies.[17] (See the feature *Discretion in Action—The Stolen Valor Act* to better understand how judicial review works.)

Statutory Interpretation As the final interpreter of the Constitution, the Supreme Court must also determine the meaning of certain statutory provisions when applied to specific situations. In 1994, for example, Congress passed a law that gives a victim of child pornography the ability to seek restitution from offenders to the extent that he or she has been harmed by the illegal behavior.[18] Twenty years later, the Court overturned

Judicial Review The power of a court—particularly the United States Supreme Court—to review the actions of the executive and legislative branches and, if necessary, declare those actions unconstitutional.

DISCRETION IN ACTION

The Stolen Valor Act

The Situation At a public meeting, Xavier Alvarez says, "I'm a retired Marine of twenty-five years. Back in 1987, I was awarded the Congressional Medal of Honor. I got wounded many times by the same guy." These statements are false, and Alvarez—an elected member of a local government board—is charged with violating the Stolen Valor Act. Under this federal law, it is a crime to lie about having received a military award, punishable by up to a year in prison.

Alvarez maintains that his remarks are protected by the First Amendment's guarantee of free speech. A trial judge rejects this argument, ruling that the Constitution does not protect statements that the speaker knows to be false. An appeals court reverses this decision, holding that if the Stolen Valor Act were upheld, "there would be no constitutional bar to criminalizing lying about one's height, weight, age, or financial status on Facebook." The federal government appeals, sending the issue to the United States Supreme Court.

The Law Under the doctrine of judicial review, the U.S. Supreme Court has the power to declare an act of Congress unconstitutional.

What Would You Do? Legally, the case rests on the concept of harm. That is, is the Stolen Valor Act necessary to protect against a specific type of harm? Alvarez argues that his statements, while reprehensible, hurt no one, and therefore are protected by the Constitution. The federal government argues that such lies do inflict a psychological harm on actual military medal recipients and their families.

On a policy level, the case raises questions about judicial review. The Stolen Valor Act was enacted by members of Congress, elected by citizens to carry out the wishes of the majority. Is it proper for unelected Supreme Court judges to thwart Congress in this manner? Taking both the legal and policy factors into account, if you were a Supreme Court justice, would you overturn the Stolen Valor Act or allow it to stand? Explain your answer.

To see how the United States Supreme Court ruled in this matter, go to Example 8.1 in Appendix B.

---

a $3.4 million award to a woman whose childhood rape had been videotaped and widely disseminated on the Internet. The offender in the case had pleaded guilty to having images of child pornography on his computer, including two images of the victim. The Court ruled that, under the 1994 law, the offender could not be held responsible for all of the damages the victim had suffered.[19]

Jurisdiction of the Supreme Court

The United States Supreme Court consists of nine justices—a chief justice and eight associate justices. The Supreme Court has original, or trial, jurisdiction only in rare instances (set forth in Article III, Section 2, of the Constitution). In other words, only rarely does a case originate at the Supreme Court level. Most of the Court's work is as an appellate court. It has appellate authority over cases decided by the U.S. courts of appeals, as well as over some cases decided in the state courts when federal questions are at issue.

Which Cases Reach the Supreme Court?

There is no absolute right to appeal to the United States Supreme Court. Although thousands of cases are filed with the Supreme Court each year, in 2015–2016, the Court heard only eighty-two. With a **writ of *certiorari*** (pronounced sur-shee-uh-*rah*-ree), the Supreme Court orders a lower court to send it the record of a case for review. A party can petition the Supreme Court to issue a writ of *certiorari*, but whether the Court will do so is entirely within its discretion. More than 90 percent of the petitions for writs of *certiorari* (or "certs," as they are popularly called) are denied. A denial is not a decision on the

Learning Objective 6 Explain briefly how a case is brought to the United States Supreme Court.

Writ of *Certiorari* A request from a higher court asking a lower court for the record of a case. In essence, the request signals the higher court's willingness to review the case.

merits of a case, nor does it indicate agreement with the lower court's opinion. Therefore, the denial of the writ has no value as a precedent.

The Court will not issue a writ unless at least four justices approve of it. This is called the **rule of four.** Although the justices are not required to give their reasons for refusing to hear a case, frequently the discretionary decision is based on whether the legal issue involves a "substantial federal question." Often, such questions arise when lower courts split on a particular issue.

For example, different federal and state courts have produced varying opinions on the question of whether the private search doctrine applies to digital storage devices, such as computers. Recall from the preceding chapter that under this doctrine, law enforcement officers do not need a warrant to go through personal items that have already been searched by a third-party civilian. Given how often private third-party searches of computer files turn up incriminating evidence, such as child pornography, many legal experts expect the Supreme Court to clarify this pressing legal question in the near future.[20]

Supreme Court Decisions   Like other appellate courts, the Supreme Court normally does not hear any evidence. The Court's decision in a particular case is based on the written record of the case and the written arguments (briefs) that the attorneys submit. The attorneys also submit **oral arguments**—arguments presented in person rather than on paper—to the Court, after which the justices discuss the case in *conference*. The conference is strictly private—only the justices are allowed in the room.

Majorities and Pluralities   When the Court has reached a decision, the chief justice, if in the majority, assigns the task of writing the Court's opinion to one of the justices. When the chief justice is not in the majority, the most senior justice voting with the majority assigns the writing of the Court's opinion. The opinion outlines the reasons for the Court's decision, the rules of law that apply, and the decision.

From time to time, the justices agree on the outcome of a case, but no single reason for that outcome gains five votes. When this occurs, the rationale that gains the most votes is called the *plurality* opinion. Plurality opinions are problematic, because they do not provide a strong precedent for lower courts to follow. Although still relatively rare, the incidence of plurality opinions has increased over the past fifty years as the Court has become more ideologically fractured.[21]

▼ John G. Roberts, Jr., pictured here, is the seventeenth chief justice of the United States Supreme Court. **What does it mean to say that Roberts and the eight associate members of the Court "make criminal justice policy"?** AP Images/Lawrence Jackson

Concurrence and Dissent   Often, one or more justices who agree with the Court's decision may do so for reasons different from those outlined in the majority opinion. These justices may write **concurring opinions** setting forth their own legal reasoning on the issue. Frequently, one or more justices disagree with the Court's conclusion. These justices may write **dissenting opinions** outlining the reasons why they feel the majority erred.

Although a dissenting opinion does not affect the outcome of the case before the Court, it may be important later. In a subsequent case concerning the same issue, a justice or attorney may use the legal reasoning in the dissenting opinion as the basis for an argument to reverse the previous decision and establish a new precedent.

Judges in the Court System

Supreme Court justices are the most visible and best-known American jurists, but in many ways they are unrepresentative of the profession as a whole. Few judges enjoy a three-room office suite fitted with a fireplace and a private bath, as does each Supreme Court justice. Few judges have four clerks to assist them. Few judges get a yearly vacation that stretches from July through September. Most judges, in fact, work at the lowest level of the system, in criminal trial courts, where they are burdened with overflowing caseloads and must deal daily with the pettiest of criminals.

One attribute a Supreme Court justice and a criminal trial judge in any small American city do have in common is the expectation that they will be just. Of all the participants in the criminal justice system, no single person is held to the same high standards as the judge. From her or his lofty perch in the courtroom, the judge is counted on to be "above the fray" of the bickering defense attorneys and prosecutors. When the other courtroom contestants rise at the entrance of the judge, they are placing the burden of justice squarely on the judge's shoulders.

The Roles and Responsibilities of Trial Judges

One of the reasons that judicial integrity is considered so important is the amount of discretionary power a judge has over the court proceedings. Nearly every stage of the trial process includes a decision or action to be taken by the presiding judge.

Before the Trial A great deal of the work done by a judge takes place before the trial even starts, free from public scrutiny. These duties, some of which you have seen from a different point of view in the section on law enforcement agents, include determining the following:

1. Whether there is sufficient probable cause to issue a search or arrest warrant.
2. Whether there is sufficient probable cause to authorize electronic surveillance of a suspect.
3. Whether enough evidence exists to justify the temporary incarceration of a suspect.
4. Whether a defendant should be released on bail, and if so, the amount of the bail.
5. Whether to accept pretrial motions by prosecutors and defense attorneys.
6. Whether to accept a plea bargain.

▼ Before the 2016 trial of alleged serial killer Lonnie Franklin, Jr., Los Angeles Superior Court Judge Kathleen Kennedy ruled that Franklin's defense attorneys could not present DNA evidence showing that another person committed the murders in question. Judge Kennedy, shown here, criticized the defense's expert in this matter as "woefully" incompetent. **Why must judges ensure that every person participating in a criminal trial is qualified to do so?** Al Seib/*Los Angeles Times*/Getty Images

During these pretrial activities, the judge takes on the role of the *negotiator*.[22] As most cases are decided through plea bargains rather than through trial proceedings, the judge often offers his or her services as a negotiator to help the prosecution and the defense "make a deal." The amount at which bail is set is often negotiated as well. Throughout the trial process, the judge usually spends a great deal of time in his or her *chambers*, or office, negotiating with the prosecutors and defense attorneys.

During the Trial When the trial starts, the judge takes on the role of *referee*. In this role, she or he is responsible for seeing that the trial unfolds according to the dictates of the law and that the participants in the trial do not overstep any legal or ethical bounds. Furthermore, the judge is expected to be neutral, determining the admissibility of testimony and evidence on a completely objective basis. The judge also acts as a *teacher* during the trial, explaining points of law to the jury. If the trial is not a jury trial, then the judge must also make decisions concerning the guilt or innocence of the defendant.

CJ & TECHNOLOGY

Lie Detection in Court

In 1935, Professor Leonarde Keeler relied on a polygraph test to show a jury that two defendants were lying when they denied attempting to kill a sheriff in Portage, Wisconsin. After the trial ended in convictions, Professor Keeler claimed that the "findings of the lie detector are as acceptable . . . as fingerprint testimony." Eight decades later, that prediction has yet to come true. Although polygraphs—devices that monitor changes in respiration, pulse, and blood pressure—are commonly used to determine truthfulness as part of police investigations and job screenings, the technology has not been permitted as evidence in criminal courtrooms. The problem is that polygraphs are often inaccurate and thus too unreliable for use in court.

Besides polygraph tests, other forms of lie-detector technology have also been developed. For example, some researchers presume that the brain "works harder" in telling a lie than in telling the truth. Therefore, functional magnetic resonance imaging, which (as we discussed in Chapter 2) measures blood flow in the brain, should be able to detect falsehoods. Most recently, software designed by researchers at the University of Michigan purports to use a speaker's words and gestures to determine whether he or she is telling the truth. Neither technology, however, has proven sufficiently dependable to convince "gatekeeper" judges to allow it as evidence in criminal trials.

Thinking about Lie Detection in Court

The University of Michigan software described above boasts a 75 percent accuracy rate in determining whether the subject is telling the truth. Are judges justified in keeping the potential results of this software out of court? Why or why not?

Sentencing At the close of the trial, if the defendant is found guilty, the judge must decide on the length of the sentence and the type of sentence. (Different types of sentences, such as incarceration, probation, and other forms of community-based corrections, will be discussed in Chapters 11 and 12.) The sentencing phase also gives the judge a chance to make personal comments about the proceedings, if he or she wishes.

In 2016, for instance, Kent County (Michigan) Circuit Court Judge Mark A. Trusock sentenced Charles Hanger, Jr., to between fourteen months and five years in prison for illegally hunting and killing eleven white-tailed deer out of season. Judge Trusock, himself a hunter, seemed particular outraged that Hanger's eighteen-year-old son was also involved in this wrongdoing. "So what are you teaching your son to do? To go out and violate all the laws?" Trusock said at Hanger's sentencing hearing. "It's people like you that give sportsmen in the state of Michigan a bad name."[23]

The Administrative Role   Judges are also *administrators* and are responsible for the day-to-day functioning of their courts. A primary administrative task of a judge is scheduling. Each courtroom has a **docket,** or calendar of cases, and it is the judge's responsibility to keep the docket current. This entails not only scheduling the trial, but also setting pretrial motion dates and deciding whether to grant attorneys' requests for *continuances*, or additional time to prepare for the trial.

Judges must also keep track of the immense paperwork generated by each case and manage the various employees of the court. Some judges are even responsible for the budgets of their courtrooms.[24] In 1939, Congress, recognizing the burden of such tasks, created the Administrative Office of the United States Courts to provide administrative assistance for federal court judges.[25] Most state court judges, however, do not have the luxury of similar aid, though they are supported by a court staff.

Appointment of Judges

In the federal court system, all judges are appointed by the president and confirmed by the Senate. Article II, Section 2, of the Constitution authorizes the president to appoint the justices of the Supreme Court with the advice and consent of the Senate. Subsequent laws enacted by Congress provide that the same procedure is used for appointing judges to the lower federal courts as well.

Federal Appointments   On paper, the federal appointment process is relatively simple. After selecting a nominee, the president submits the name to the Senate for approval. The Senate Judiciary Committee then holds hearings and makes its recommendation to the Senate, where a majority vote is needed to confirm the nomination.

Learning **7** **Objective** Explain the difference between the selection of judges at the state level and at the federal level.

In practice, the process does not always proceed smoothly. Given the importance of the Supreme Court in shaping the nation's laws and values, the appointment process for its justices is highly politicized. Presidents choose candidates who reflect the political beliefs of their party, and members of the opposing party in the Senate do their best to discredit these individuals. In recent years, heated debate over controversial issues such as abortion and gay rights has characterized the proceedings to the point that one commentator likens them to elections rather than the appointments envisioned by the nation's founders.[26]

State Appointments   As you will see, judges in most states are elected. A few states, however, employ selection methods similar to the federal appointment process. In New Jersey, for instance, all judges are appointed by the governor and confirmed by the upper chamber of the state legislature. Judges in these states, as would be expected, generally serve longer terms than their counterparts in nonappointment judicial systems.[27]

Patronage Issues   Appointed judges at both the federal and the state level are frequently regarded as products of *patronage*. In other words, appointed judges often obtain their positions because they belong to the same political party as the president (or governor, at the state level) and also have been active in supporting the candidates and ideology of the party in power. One of the most prevalent criticisms of appointing judges is that the system is based on "having friends in high places" rather than on merit.[28]

Election of Judges

As mentioned, in a few states, judges are appointed. Most states moved from an appointive to an elective system for judges in the mid-1800s, however. Today, a large majority of states choose at least some of their judges through elections.[29] Indeed, nearly 90 percent

Docket The list of cases entered on a court's calendar and thus scheduled to be heard by the court.

of all state judges face elections at some point in their judicial careers.[30] Nevertheless, the selection procedure varies widely from state to state.

Partisan versus Nonpartisan Elections

One difference among the states involves the role of party affiliation in the election of judges. In some states, such as Alabama, partisan elections are used to choose judges. In these elections, a judicial candidate declares allegiance to a political party, usually the Democrats or the Republicans, before the election. Other states, such as Kentucky, conduct nonpartisan elections that do not require a candidate to affiliate with a political party.

Merit Selection

In 1940, Missouri became the first state to combine appointment and election in a so-called merit selection process. When all jurisdiction levels are counted, nineteen states and the District of Columbia now utilize the Missouri Plan, as merit selection has been labeled. The Missouri Plan consists of three basic steps:

- When a vacancy on the bench arises, candidates are nominated by a nonpartisan committee of citizens.
- The names of the three most qualified candidates are sent to the governor or executive of the state judicial system, and that person chooses who will be the judge.
- A year after the new judge has been installed, a "retention election" is held so that voters can decide whether the judge deserves to keep the post.[31]

The goal of the Missouri Plan is to eliminate partisan politics from the selection procedure, while at the same time giving the citizens a voice in the process.

Regardless of how they are selected, the average term for state judges in this country is about seven years.[32] (For a review of the selection processes, see this chapter's *Mastering Concepts—The Selection of State and Federal Judges*.)

Judicial Decision Making

Two key concepts in the selection of judges are *independence* and *accountability*.[33] Some observers believe that judicial fairness depends on the judges' confidence that they will not be voted out of office as the result of an unpopular ruling. These observers support methods of selection that include appointment.[34] In contrast, other observers feel that judges are "politicians in robes" who make policy decisions every time they step to the bench. In their view, judges should be held accountable to those who are affected by their decisions and therefore should be chosen through elections, as legislators are.[35]

In fact, studies conducted in Pennsylvania and Washington State show that, as elections approach, judges begin handing down harsher-than-normal sentences for violent crimes.[36] The implication is that these judges are trying to impress upon voters that they are "tough on crime" rather than basing their sentencing decisions on the law and the facts. It would seem, then, that the most independent, and therefore least accountable, judges are those who hold lifetime appointments. These judges are influenced neither by the temptation to make popular decisions to impress voters nor by the need to follow the ideological or party line of the politicians who provided them with their posts.

The Removal of Judges

Besides losing an election, sitting judges can be removed from office for judicial misconduct, or behavior that diminishes public confidence in the judiciary.

Partisan Elections Elections in which candidates are affiliated with and receive support from political parties.

Nonpartisan Elections Elections in which candidates are presented on the ballot without any party affiliation.

Missouri Plan A method of selecting judges that combines appointment and election.

Judicial Misconduct A general term describing behavior—such as accepting bribes or consorting with known felons—that diminishes public confidence in the judiciary.

The Selection of State and Federal Judges

FEDERAL JUDGES	STATE JUDGES	
1. The president nominates a candidate and presents the nominee to the U.S. Senate. 2. The Senate Judiciary Committee holds hearings concerning the qualifications of the candidate and makes its recommendation to the full Senate. 3. The full Senate votes to confirm or reject the president's nominee.	**Partisan Elections** • Judicial candidates, supported by and affiliated with political parties, place their names before the voters for consideration for a particular judicial seat. • The electorate votes to decide who will retain or gain the seat. **Executive Appointment** • The governor nominates a candidate to the state legislature. • The legislature votes to confirm or reject the governor's nominee.	**Nonpartisan Elections** • Judicial candidates, not supported by or affiliated with political parties, place their names before the voters for consideration for a particular judicial seat. • The electorate votes to decide who will retain or gain the seat. **Missouri Plan** • A nominating commission provides a list of worthy candidates. • An elected official (usually the governor) chooses from the list submitted by the commission. • A year later, a "retention election" is held to allow voters to decide whether the judge will stay on the bench.

State Judicial Misconduct   Nearly every state has a *judicial conduct commission*, which consists of lawyers, judges, and other prominent citizens, and is often a branch of the state's highest court. This commission investigates charges of judicial misconduct and may recommend removal if warranted. The final decision to discipline a judge generally is made by the state supreme court.[37]

Several state judges are removed from office each year. A recent example is Tulare County (California) Superior Court Judge Valeriano Saucedo, who, according to state authorities, pressured a female clerk to have a "special friend" relationship with him. Saucedo also gave the clerk $26,000 in gifts, including a BMW, a trip to Disneyland, and cash. Finally, he lied to officials investigating the nature of his contacts with the clerk.[38]

The Impeachment Process   Such transgressions as those committed by Valeriano Saucedo, however deplorable, would be unlikely to result in a similar outcome if committed by a federal judge. Appointed under Article II of the U.S. Constitution, federal judges can be removed from office only if found guilty of "Treason, Bribery, or other high Crimes and Misdemeanors."

Before a federal judge can be **impeached**, the U.S. House of Representatives must be presented with specific charges of misconduct and vote on whether these charges merit further action. If the House votes to impeach by a simple majority (more than 50 percent), the U.S. Senate—presided over by the chief justice of the United States Supreme Court—holds a trial on the judge's conduct. At the conclusion of this trial, a two-thirds majority vote is required in the Senate to remove the judge.

This disciplinary action is extremely rare: Only eight federal judges have been impeached and convicted in the nation's history. U.S. District Court Judge Mark E. Fuller

Impeachment The formal process by which a public official is charged with misconduct that could lead to removal from office.

probably avoided becoming the ninth when he resigned in 2015. A special federal judicial committee had apparently found "grounds for impeachment" after Fuller was arrested a year earlier for physically abusing his wife in an Atlanta hotel room.[39] (See the feature *Comparative Criminal Justice—Back to School* to learn about France's preferred method for producing ethical judges.)

Diversity on the Bench

One of the supposed benefits of judicial elections is that they make judges more representative of the communities in which they serve. According to the Brennan Center for Justice in New York City, however, "Americans who enter the courtroom often face a predictable presence on the bench: a white male."[40]

State Court Diversity

Overall, about 58 percent of all state appellate judges are white males.[41] In many states, members of minority groups are underrepresented in comparison to the demographics of the general population. California, for example, is nearly 38 percent Latino and 15 percent Asian American. The state judiciary, however, is only 9.9 percent Latino and 6.5 percent Asian American.[42] In Texas, minority women make up 28 percent of the population but fill only 12 percent of judgeships, and, for minority men, the numbers are 29 percent and 14 percent, respectively.[43]

Federal Court Diversity

Members of minority groups are also underrepresented in the federal judiciary, though not to the same extent as in the states. Of the

Source: Central Intelligence Agency

COMPARATIVE CRIMINAL JUSTICE

Back to School

Learning Objective 8 Describe one alternative, practiced in other countries, to the American method of choosing judges.

Elections for judges are extremely rare outside the United States. Indeed, only two nations—Japan and Switzerland—engage in the practice, and then only in very limited situations. To the rest of the world, according to one expert, "American adherence to judicial elections is as incomprehensible as our rejection of the metric system." Much more common, for example, is the French system, crafted to provide extensive training for potential judges.

French judicial candidates must pass two exams. The first, open to law school graduates only, combines oral and written sections and lasts at least four days. In some years, only 5 percent of the applicants overcome this hurdle. Not surprisingly, the pressure is intense. "It gives you nightmares for years afterwards," says Jean-Marc Baissus, a judge in Toulouse. "You come out of [the exam] completely shattered." Those who do survive the first test enter a two-year program at the École Nationale de la Magistrature, a

judicial training academy. This school is similar to a police training academy in the United States, in that candidates spend half of their time in the classroom and the other half in the courtroom.

At the end of this program, judicial candidates are subject to a second examination. Only those who pass the exam may become judges. The result, in the words of Mitchel Lasser, a law professor at Cornell University, is that French judges "actually know what the hell they are doing. They've spent years in school taking practical and theoretical courses on how to be a judge." The French also pride themselves on creating judges who are free from the kind of political pressures faced by American judges who must go before the voters.

FOR CRITICAL ANALYSIS

Do you think that the French system of training judges is superior to the American system of electing them? Before explaining your answer, consider that French judges lack the practical courtroom experience of American judges, many of whom served as lawyers earlier in their careers.

approximately 1,700 federal judges in this country, about 13 percent are African American, 7 percent are Latino, and less than 3 percent are Asian American. Furthermore, about one-quarter are women.[44] Of the 111 justices who have served on the United States Supreme Court, two have been African American: Thurgood Marshall (1967–1991) and Clarence Thomas (1991–present). In 2009, Sonia Sotomayor became the first Latina appointed to the Court and the third woman, following Sandra Day O'Connor (1981–2006) and Ruth Bader Ginsburg (1993–present). A year later, Elena Kagan became the fourth woman appointed to the Court.

Promoting Judicial Diversity

Edward Chen, a federal judge for the Northern District of California, identifies a number of reasons for the low minority representation on the bench. Past discrimination in law schools has limited the pool of experienced minority attorneys who have the political ties, access to "old boy" networks, and career opportunities that lead to judgeships.[45] Only recently, as increased numbers of minorities have graduated from law schools, have rates of minority judges begun to creep slowly upward.

To further promote judicial diversity, the Brennan Center for Justice suggests that state judicial bodies:

1. Increase recruitment of minorities and women for open judicial seats.
2. Raise judicial salaries to attract diverse candidates from the legal community.
3. Appoint a diversity compliance officer to oversee efforts to include more minorities and women in the selection process.[46]

The Benefits of Judicial Diversity

There is a sense among criminal justice professionals that citizens are more likely to recognize the legitimacy of a diverse judiciary. That is, people tend to trust judges that resemble themselves.[47] The opposite may also be true. "There are reservations that a [minority] defendant facing a white, male judge [will have] . . . obviously that's going to reduce that person's confidence in the legal system," says Kevin Hart, executive director of the Utah Association of Criminal Defense Lawyers.[48]

Sherrilyn A. Ifill of the University of Maryland School of Law believes that "diversity on the bench" enriches our judiciary by introducing a variety of voices and perspectives into positions of power. By the same token, Ifill believes the lack of diversity in many trial and appeals courts has had a number of harmful consequences. These repercussions include more severe sentences for minority youths than for white youths who have committed similar crimes, disproportionate denial of bail to minority defendants, and disproportionate imposition of the death penalty on minority defendants accused of killing white victims.[49]

ETHICS CHALLENGE

In every state that has judicial elections, judges are allowed to receive campaign contributions from lawyers who appear before them in court. What ethical issues arise from this situation? Some states ban judges from making personal requests for funds, though such requests can still be made by the judges' campaign committees. Does this strategy remove—or at least lessen—the risk of corruption? Why or why not?

Shawn Davis Bailiff

Basically, there are two kinds of bailiffs: administrative bailiffs and criminal bailiffs. An administrative bailiff will handle paperwork, set up court dates, and answer questions about filings that the attorneys may have. A criminal bailiff is responsible for bringing the court to session, directing jurors, and overseeing court security, which involves keeping everybody—judges, attorneys, jurors, spectators, witnesses, and defendants—safe. In my case, I do double duty as an administrative and criminal bailiff.

Courtesy of Shawn Davis

Violence in the courtroom is rare. Most inmates are on their best behavior in front of the judge. It can flare up in an instant, however, and you have to be constantly on guard. One time, an inmate under my control made a run for it as we were transporting him back to the jail from his court appearance. His leg shackles broke, giving him a short-lived sense of freedom. We were able to tackle him in front of the courthouse just before he could jump into a waiting convertible. We later learned that the accomplice—the inmate's brother—was supposed to bring a handgun and shoot us as part of the escape plan. Another time, a defendant started taking off his shirt and tried to attack the victim, who had just given testimony. He was quickly tackled, cuffed, and carted off to jail.

SOCIAL MEDIA CAREER TIP Networking is crucial. Develop as many useful social media contacts as possible, and cultivate those contacts. Also, reciprocate. If you help others establish online contacts, they are likely to remember you and return the favor.

The Courtroom Work Group

Television dramas often depict the courtroom as a battlefield, with prosecutors and defense attorneys spitting fire at each other over the loud and insistent protestations of a frustrated judge. Consequently, many people are somewhat disappointed when they witness a real courtroom at work. Rarely does anyone raise his or her voice, and the courtroom professionals appear—to a great extent—to be cooperating with each other. In Chapter 6, we discussed the existence of a police subculture, based on the shared values of law enforcement agents. A courtroom subculture exists as well, centered on the **courtroom work group**.

The most important feature of any work group is that it is a *cooperative* unit, whose members establish shared values and methods that help the group efficiently reach its goals. Though cooperation is not a concept usually associated with criminal courts, it is in fact crucial to the adjudication process.

Members of the Courtroom Work Group

The courtroom work group is made up of those individuals who are involved with the defendant from the time she or he is arrested until sentencing. The most prominent members are the judge, the prosecutor, and the defense attorney (the latter two will

Courtroom Work Group The social organization consisting of the judge, prosecutor, defense attorney, and other court workers.

be discussed in detail in the next chapter). Three other court participants complete the work group:

1. The *bailiff of the court* is responsible for maintaining security and order in the judge's chambers and the courtroom. Bailiffs lead the defendant in and out of the courtroom and attend to the needs of the jurors during the trial. The bailiff, often a member of the local sheriff's department but sometimes an employee of the court, also delivers summonses in some jurisdictions.

2. The *clerk of the court* has an exhausting list of responsibilities. Any plea, motion, or other matter to be acted on by the judge must go through the clerk. The large amount of paperwork generated during a trial, including transcripts, photographs, evidence, and any other records, is maintained by the clerk. The clerk also issues subpoenas for jury duty and coordinates the jury selection process. In the federal court system, judges select clerks, while state clerks are either appointed or, in nearly a third of the states, elected.

3. *Court reporters* record every word that is said during the course of the trial. They also record any *depositions*, or pretrial question-and-answer sessions in which a party or a witness answers an attorney's questions under oath.

Formation of the Courtroom Work Group

The premise of the work group is based on constant interaction that fosters relationships among the members. As legal scholar David W. Neubauer describes:

> Every day, the same group of courthouse regulars assembles in the same courtroom, sits or stands in the same places, and performs the same tasks as the day before. The types of defendants and the nature of the crimes they are accused of committing also remain constant. Only the names of the victim, witnesses, and defendants are different.[50]

After a period of time, each member of a courtroom work group learns how the others operate. The work group establishes patterns of behavior and norms, and cooperation allows the adjudication process to function informally and smoothly.[51] In some cases, the members of the work group may even form personal relationships, which only strengthen the courtroom culture.

One way in which the courtroom work group differs from a traditional work group at a company such as Facebook, Inc., is that each member answers to a different sponsoring organization. Although the judge has ultimate authority over a courtroom, he or she is not the "boss" of the attorneys. The prosecutor is hired by the district attorney's office, the defense attorney by a private individual or the public defender's office, and the judge by the court system itself.

The Judge in the Courtroom Work Group

The judge is the dominant figure in the courtroom and therefore exerts the most influence over the values and norms of the work group. A judge who runs a "tight ship" follows procedure and restricts the freedom of attorneys to deviate from regulations, while a *"laissez-faire"* judge allows more leeway to members of the work group. A judge's personal philosophy also affects the court proceedings. If a judge has a reputation for being "tough on crime," both prosecutors and defense attorneys will alter their strategies accordingly.

▶ Two trial lawyers confer as their opponent reads over his notes during a criminal trial in Provo, Utah. **How is working in a courtroom similar to working in a corporate office? How is it different?**

Al Hartmann/Getty Images News/Getty Images

Although preeminent in the work group, a judge must still rely on other group members. To a certain extent, the judge is the least informed member of the trio. Like a juror, the judge learns the facts of the case as they are presented by the attorneys. If the attorneys do not properly present the facts, then the judge is hampered in making rulings.

Judges also have the power to discipline other members of the work group. Several years ago, for example, Superior Court judge Thomas Goethals removed several Orange County (California) prosecutors from a high-profile murder case the judge called "a comedy of errors." Along with other misdeeds, the prosecutors had apparently lied to the court about conspiring with the local sheriff's department to place the defendant in a jail cell next to an inmate acting as a government informant.[52]

The Adversary System

Two members of the courtroom work group—the prosecutor and the defense attorney—stand opposite each other in court and have opposing goals. That is, generally speaking, the goal of the prosecutor is to prove the defendant guilty, and the goal of the defense attorney is to prove the defendant innocent. For this reason, the American court system is often called an *adversary system*.

In strictly legal terms, three basic features characterize the adversary system:

1. A neutral and passive decision maker, either the judge or the jury.
2. The presentation of evidence from both parties.
3. A highly structured set of procedures (in the form of constitutional safeguards) that must be followed in the presentation of that evidence.[53]

"Ritualized Aggression"?   Some critics of the American court system believe that it has been tainted by overzealous prosecutors and defense attorneys. Gordon Van Kessel, a professor at Hastings College of Law in California, complains that American lawyers see themselves as "prize fighters, gladiators, or, more accurately, semantic warriors in a verbal battle," and bemoans the atmosphere of "ritualized aggression" that exists in the courts.[54]

Adversary System A legal system in which the prosecution and defense are opponents, or adversaries, and strive to "defeat" each other in court.

Our recent portrayal of the courtroom work group, however, seems to contradict this image of "ritualized aggression." As political scientists Herbert Jacob and James Eisenstein have written, "pervasive conflict is not only unpleasant; it also makes work more difficult."[55] The image of the courtroom work group as "negotiators" rather than "prize fighters" seems to be supported by the fact that more than nine out of every ten cases conclude with negotiated "deals" rather than trials. (We will cover these plea bargain procedures in the next chapter.)

Jerome Skolnick of the University of California at Berkeley found that work group members grade each other according to "reasonableness"[56]—a concept criminal justice scholar Abraham S. Blumberg embellished by labeling the defense attorney a "double agent." Blumberg believed that a defense attorney is likely to cooperate with the prosecutor in convincing a client to accept a negotiated plea of guilty because the defense attorney's main object is to finish the case quickly so as to collect the fee and move on.[57]

Truth versus Victory   Perhaps the most useful definition of the adversary process tempers Professor Van Kessel's criticism with the realities of the courtroom work group. University of California at Berkeley law professor Malcolm Feeley observes:

> In the adversary system the goal of the advocate is not to determine truth but to win, to maximize the interests of his or her side within the confines of the norms governing the proceedings. This is not to imply that the theory of the adversary process has no concern for the truth. Rather, the underlying assumption of the adversary process is that truth is most likely to emerge as a by-product of vigorous conflict between intensely partisan advocates, each of whose goal is to win.[58]

Blumberg took a more cynical view when he called the court process a "confidence game" in which "victory" is achieved when a defense attorney—with the implicit aid of the prosecutor and judge—is able to persuade the defendant to plead guilty.[59] As you read the next chapter, which deals with the various pretrial strategies employed by the prosecution and the defense, keep in mind Feeley's and Blumberg's positions concerning "truth" and "victory" in the American courts.

ETHICS CHALLENGE

In this section, we quoted a legal expert as saying, "In the adversary system the goal of the advocate is not to determine the truth but to win . . . ." Does this mean that prosecutors and defense attorneys should behave unethically in court? Why or why not?

Tribal Jurisdiction

How Things Stand

In 1978, the United States Supreme Court ruled that tribal courts did not have jurisdiction to prosecute non-Native Americans for crimes that took place on Indian land. Consequently, for any crime that involves a non-Indian defendant, jurisdiction rests with either the federal government or, in several states, the state government. In practice, according to Fred Urbina, the attorney general for the Pascua Yaqui tribe of Arizona, federal authorities are unlikely to seek conviction in these instances unless there has been "a major crime."[60]

As a Result...

Native Americans are victims of crime at a higher proportional rate than practically any other racial or ethnic minority group in the United States. In particular, female American Indians are at risk, with victimization rates for domestic violence, sexual assault, and murder that are much greater than national averages.[61] According to research sponsored by the National Institute of Justice, 97 percent of female American Indian violent crime victims and 90 percent of male American Indian violent crime victims were harmed by non-Native American offenders who are, by law, beyond the reach of tribal criminal justice courts.[62]

In many of these cases, victims do not report the crimes because there is little confidence that the federal government will conduct an investigation on reservation land. Indeed, one domestic violence victim, a member of the Southern Ute tribe in Colorado married to a non-Native American, describes how, "After one beating, my ex-husband called the tribal police and the sheriff's department himself, just to show me that no one could stop him."[63] Not surprisingly, many tribal leaders want Congress to remedy this situation by giving tribal criminal courts jurisdiction over non-Native American offenders who commit crimes on tribal land.

Up for Debate

"But under the laws of our land, you got to have a jury that is a reflection of society as a whole, and on an Indian reservation, it's going to be made up of Indians, right? So the non-Indian doesn't get a fair trial."[64] —*Charles Grassley, Republican senator from Iowa.*

"[Non-Native] perpetrators [on reservation land] think they can't be touched. They're invincible."[65] —*Sadie Young Bird, director of the Fort Berthold Indian Reservation Coalition against Violence*

What's Your Take?

Review the discussion in this chapter on "Jurisdiction" before answering the following questions.

1. The United States has unquestioned jurisdiction over non-U.S. citizens who are living in or visiting the country and have been charged with committing a crime. Does this fact help or hurt the argument that tribal courts should have jurisdiction over criminal activity involving non-Native Americans on tribal land? Explain your answer.

2. Although many tribes have passed legislation that mirrors the Bill of Rights, the U.S. Constitution does not apply on sovereign tribal lands. Consequently, defendants in criminal trials on these lands do not—technically—have the full range of protections offered in federal and state criminal courts.[66] Does this fact help or hurt the argument that tribal courts should have jurisdiction over criminal activity involving non-Native Americans on tribal land? Explain your answer.

Digging Deeper...

Section 904 of Congress's **2013 reauthorization of the Violence against Women Act** gives tribal courts the option to prosecute certain crimes committed by non-Native Americans on American Indian land. After researching this provision online, answer the following questions: 1) What crimes does Section 904 give tribal courts jurisdiction over? 2) To be prosecuted under Section 904, what special characteristics must a non-Native American offender have? 3) What specific civil rights protections does Section 904 guarantee for all non-Native American defendants in these cases? Given these limitations, how much practical impact do you think that Section 904 will have on tribal courts' jurisdiction over non-Native Americans in criminal matters? Your written answer should be at least three paragraphs long.

Jean-Erick PASQUIER/Gamma-Rapho/Getty Images

SUMMARY

For more information on these concepts, look back to the Learning Objective icons throughout the chapter.

Define and contrast the four functions of the courts. The four functions are (a) due process, (b) crime control, (c) rehabilitation, and (d) bureaucratic. The most obvious contrast is between the due process and crime control functions. The former is mainly concerned with the procedural rules that allow each accused individual to have a "fair chance" against the government in a criminal proceeding. For crime control, the courts are supposed to impose enough "pain" on convicted criminals to deter criminal behavior. For the rehabilitation function, the courts serve as "doctors" who dispense "treatment." In their bureaucratic function, courts are more concerned with speed and efficiency.

Define *jurisdiction* and contrast geographic and subject-matter jurisdiction. Jurisdiction relates to the power of a court to hear a particular case. Courts are typically limited in geographic jurisdiction— for example, to a particular state. Some courts are restricted in subject matter, such as a small claims court, which can hear only cases involving civil matters under a certain monetary limit.

Explain the difference between trial and appellate courts. Trial courts are courts of the first instance, where a case is first heard. Appellate courts review the proceedings of lower courts. Appellate courts do not have juries.

Outline the levels of a typical state court system. (a) At the lowest level are courts of limited jurisdiction; (b) next are trial courts of general jurisdiction, (c) then appellate courts, and (d) finally, the state's highest court.

Outline the federal court system. (a) At the lowest level are the U.S. district courts, in which trials are held, as well as various minor federal courts of limited jurisdiction; (b) next are the U.S. courts of appeals, otherwise known as circuit courts of appeals; and (c) finally, the United States Supreme Court.

Explain briefly how a case is brought to the United States Supreme Court. Cases decided in U.S. courts of appeals, as well as cases decided in the highest state courts (when federal questions arise), can be appealed to the Supreme Court. If at least four justices approve of a case filed with the Supreme Court, the Court will issue a writ of *certiorari*, ordering the lower court to send the Supreme Court the record of the case for review.

Explain the difference between the selection of judges at the state level and at the federal level. The president nominates all judges at the federal level, and the Senate must approve the nominations. A similar procedure is used in some states. In other states, all judges are elected on a partisan ballot or on a nonpartisan ballot. Some states use merit selection, or the Missouri Plan, in which a citizen committee nominates judicial candidates, the governor or executive of the state judicial system chooses among the top three nominees, and a year later a "retention election" is held.

Describe one alternative, practiced in other countries, to the American method of choosing judges. The practice of electing judges is quite rare, with the United States being one of the few countries that allows it. Other nations, including France, require candidates for judicial positions (generally law school graduates) to complete a rigorous training program that includes several difficult exams.

List and describe the members of the courtroom work group. (a) The judge; (b) the prosecutor, who brings charges in the name of the people (the state) against the accused; (c) the defense attorney; (d) the bailiff, who is responsible for maintaining security and order in the judge's chambers and the courtroom; (e) the clerk, who accepts all pleas, motions, and other matters to be acted on by the judge; and (f) the court reporter, who records what is said during a trial as well as at depositions.

List the three basic features of an adversary system of justice. (a) A neutral decision maker (judge or jury), (b) presentation of evidence from both parties, and (c) a highly structured set of procedures that must be used when evidence is presented.

1. Each state has legislation that makes cruelty to animals a crime. Nonetheless, in 2015, several members of Congress introduced the Preventing Animal Cruelty and Torture (PACT) Act. The PACT Act would give the federal government the ability to investigate and prosecute certain acts of animal abuse. What are some of the benefits and drawbacks of giving federal courts concurrent jurisdiction over a seemingly local crime such as animal abuse?

2. In 2010, authorities in Thailand extradited Russian citizen and alleged international arms dealer Viktor Bout to the United States. The evidence against Bout included an audio recording of a conversation he had with American agents posing as Colombian rebels. During this conversation, Bout agreed to furnish the "revolutionaries" with weapons for the purpose of killing American pilots. How does this evidence give the United States jurisdiction over Bout?

3. In 2012, the United States Supreme Court "denied cert" in the case of Joel Tenenbaum, who had been ordered to pay a recording company $675,000 in fines for illegally downloading thirty-one songs using a file-sharing website. Tenenbaum claimed that the fine was excessive and unfair. What does it mean for the Court to "deny cert"? In this instance, what might have been some reasons for the Court's refusal to consider Tenenbaum's case?

4. The United States Supreme Court does not allow its proceedings to be televised. Do you think that doing so would increase or diminish public confidence in the Court? Why?

5. Do you think that politicians should make a concerted effort to appoint greater numbers of minorities and women as judges? Why or why not?

adversary system 276
appellate courts 259
concurrent jurisdiction 257
concurring opinions 266
courtroom work group 274
dissenting opinions 266
docket 269
dual court system 259

extradition 258
impeachment 271
judicial misconduct 270
judicial review 264
jurisdiction 257
magistrate 262
Missouri Plan 270
nonpartisan elections 270

opinions 259
oral arguments 266
partisan elections 270
problem-solving courts 262
rule of four 266
trial courts 259
writ of *certiorari* 265

1. Quoted in "Teen Who Urged Suicide Via Text Will Stand Trial, Court Rules." *www.cbsnews.com. Crime Insider*: July 1, 2016, Web.

2. Roscoe Pound, "The Administration of Justice in American Cities," *Harvard Law Review 12* (1912).

3. Russell Wheeler and Howard Whitcomb, *Judicial Administration: Text and Readings* (Englewood Cliffs, N.J.: Prentice Hall, 1977), 3.

4. Larry J. Siegel, *Criminology: Instructor's Manual*, 6th ed. (Belmont, Calif.: West/Wadsworth Publishing Co., 1998), 440.

5. Gerald F. Velman, "Federal Sentencing Guidelines: A Cure Worse Than the Disease," *American Criminal Law Review 29* (Spring 1992), 904.

6. John Bacon, "Dylann Roof Pleads Guilty to State Murder Charges in Church Rampage." *www.usatoday.com. USA Today*: April 10, 2017, Web.

7. Wayne R. LaFave, "Section 4.6. Multiple Jurisdiction and Multiple Prosecution," *Substantive Criminal Law*, 2d ed. (C.J.S. Criminal Section 254), 2007.

8. William Wan, "Snipers to Be Tried in Maryland," *Baltimore Sun* (May 11, 2005), 1A.

9. "Spain Agrees to Extradite 'Jihad Jane' Recruiter to US to Face Terrorism Charges." *www.rt.com*. RT360: February 27, 2016, Web.

10. Anthony J. Colangelo, "Constitutional Limits on Extraterritorial Jurisdiction: Terrorism and the Intersection of National and International Law," *Harvard International Law Journal 48* (2007), 121–122.

11. 18 U.S.C. Section 3231; and *Solorio v. United States*, 483 U.S. 435 (1987).

12. Alexander Hamilton, Federalist Paper No. 78, in *The Federalist Papers*, ed. Clinton Rossiter (New York: New American Library, 1961), 467–470.

13. 372 U.S. 335 (1963).

14. 384 U.S. 436 (1966).

15. 408 U.S. 238 (1972).

16. 428 U.S. 153 (1976).

17. *Birchfield v. North Dakota*, 579 U.S. ___. No. 14-1468. Supreme Court of the United States (June 23, 2016).

18. Public Law Number 103-322, Section 16001, 108 Statute 2036 (1994); codified as amended at 18 U.S.C. Section 2259.

19. *Paroline v. United States*, 134 S.Ct. 1710 (2014).

20. Stephen Labrecque, "'Virtual Certainty' in a Digital World: The Sixth Circuit's Application of the Private Search Doctrine to Digital Storage Devices in *United States v. Lichtenberger*." *www.lawdigitalcommons. bc.edu. Boston College Law Review*: April 29, 2016), Web.

21. David R. Stras and James F. Spriggs II, "Explaining Plurality Opinions," *Georgetown Law Journal 99* (March 2010), 519.

22. Barry R. Schaller, *A Vision of American Law: Judging Law, Literature, and the Stories We Tell* (Westport, Conn.: Praeger, 1997).

23. Quoted in John Hogan, "Convicted Poacher Scolded by Judge for Giving Hunters 'A Bad Name.'" *www.freep.com. Detroit Free Press*: November 16, 2016, Web.

24. Harlington Wood, Jr., "Judiciary Reform: Recent Improvements in Federal Judicial Administration," *American University Law Review 44* (June 1995), 1557.

25. Pub. L. No. 76-299, 53 Stat. 1223, codified as amended at 28 U.S.C. Sections 601–610 (1988 & Supp. V 1993).

26. Richard Davis, *Electing Justice: Fixing the Supreme Court Nomination Process* (New York: Oxford University Press, 2005), 6–9.

27. Daniel R. Deja, "How Judges Are Selected: A Survey of the Judicial Selection Process in the United States," *Michigan Bar Journal 75* (September 1996), 904.

28. Edmund V. Ludwig, "Another Case against the Election of Trial Judges," *Pennsylvania Lawyer 19* (May/June 1997), 33.

29. American Judicature Society, "Methods of Judicial Selection." *www.judicialselection.us*. American Judicature Society: visited February 6, 2017, Web.

30. David K. Scott, "Zero-Sum Judicial Elections: Balancing Free Speech and Impartiality through Recusal Reform," *Brigham Young University Law Review* (2009), 481, 485.

31. James E. Lozier, "The Missouri Plan a.k.a. Merit Selection Is the Best Solution for Selecting Michigan's Judges," *Michigan Bar Journal 75* (September 1996), 918.

32. Ro Malega and Thomas H. Cohen, *State Court Organization*, 2011 (Washington, D.C.: U.S. Department of Justice, November 2013), 8.

33. Patrick Emery Longan, "Judicial Professionalism in a New Era of Judicial Selection," *Mercer Law Review* (Spring 2005), 913.

34. Andrew F. Hanssen, "Learning about Judicial Independence: Institutional Change in the State Courts," *Journal of Legal Studies* (2004), 431–474.

35. Brian P. Anderson, "Judicial Elections in West Virginia," *West Virginia Law Review* (Fall 2004), 243.

36. Gregory A. Huber and Stanford C. Gordon, "Accountability and Coercion: Is Justice Blind When It Runs for Office?" *American Journal of Political Science* (April 2004), 247–263; and Carlos Berdejo and Noam Yutchman, "Crime, Punishment, and Politics: An Analysis of Political Cycles in Criminal Sentencing." *http://faculty.haas. berkeley.edu/yuchtman/noam_yuchtman_ files/berdejo_yuchtman_sept_complete_ plus_app.pdf*. Haas School of Business, UC-Berkeley: September 2010, Web.

37. John Gardiner, "Preventing Judicial Misconduct: Defining the Role of Conduct Organizations," *Judicature 70* (1986), 113–121.

38. Reggie Ellis, "Court Denies Judge Saucedo Petition." *www.thesungazette.com. Foothills Sun-Gazette*: June 1, 2016, Web.

39. Andrew Kreig, "Wife-Beating Siegelman Judge Resigns, Ends Horrid Career with Civics Lesson." *www.justice-integrity.org*. Justice Integrity Project: June 4, 2015, Web.

40. Ciara Torres-Spelliscy, Monique Chase, and Emma Greenman, *Improving Judicial Diversity*, 2d ed. (New York: Brennan Center for Justice, 2010), 1.

41. Tracey E. George and Albert H. Yoon, *The Gavel Gap: Who Sits in Judgment on State Courts?* (Washington, D.C.: American Constitution Society for Law and Policy, 2016), 7.

42. "Demographic Data Provided by Justices and Judges Relative to Gender, Race/ Ethnicity, and Gender Identity/Sexual Orientation (Gov. Code, Section 12011.5(n))." *www.courts.ca.gov*. California Courts: December 31, 2015, Web.

43. "The Gavel Gap: Texas." *http://gavelgap.org/*. American Constitution Society for Law and Policy: visited February 7, 2016, Web.

44. "Diversity on the Bench." *www.fjc.gov*. Federal Judicial Center: visited February 7, 2016, Web.

45. Edward M. Chen, "The Judiciary, Diversity, and Justice for All," *California Law Review* (July 2003), 1109.

46. New York State Bar Executive Committee, *op. cit.*, 2.

47. Spelliscy, Chase, and Greenman, *op. cit.*, 36–42.

48. Quoted in Robert Gehrke, "Jury's Still Out on Effort to Diversify Utah Judicial Bench," *Salt Lake City Tribune* (July 10, 2016), A7.

49. Sherrilyn A. Ifill, "Racial Diversity on the Bench: Beyond Role Models and Public Confidence," *Washington and Lee Law Review* (Spring 2000), 405.

50. David W. Neubauer, *America's Courts and the Criminal Justice System*, 5th ed. (Belmont, Calif.: Wadsworth Publishing Co., 1996), 41.

51. Alissa P. Worden, "The Judge's Role in Plea Bargaining: An Analysis of Judges' Agreement with Prosecutors' Sentencing Recommendations," *Justice Quarterly 10* (1995), 257–278.

52. Christopher Goffard, "D.A. Is Removed from Scott Dekraai Murder Trial." *www.latimes. com. Los Angeles Times*: March 12, 2015, Web.

53. Johannes F. Nijboer, "The American Adversary System in Criminal Cases: Between Ideology and Reality," *Cardozo Journal of International and Comparative Law 5* (Spring 1997), 79.

54. Gordon Van Kessel, "Adversary Excesses in the American Criminal Trial," *Notre Dame Law Review 67* (1992), 403.

55. James Eisenstein and Herbert Jacob, *Felony Justice* (Boston: Little, Brown, 1977), 24.

56. Jerome Skolnick, "Social Control in the Adversary System," *Journal of Conflict Resolution 11* (1967), 52–70.

57. Abraham S. Blumberg, "The Practice of Law as Confidence Game: Organizational Cooption of a Profession," *Law and Society Review 4* (June 1967), 115–139.

58. Malcolm Feeley, "The Adversary System," in *Encyclopedia of the American Judicial System*, ed. Robert J. Janosik (New York: Scribners, 1987), 753.

59. Blumberg, *op. cit.*, 115.

60. Quoted in Lorelei Laird, "Indian Tribes Are Retaking Jurisdiction over Domestic Violence on Their Own Land." *www.abajournal. com. ABA Journal*: April 1, 2015, Web.

61. Senate Report Number 153, 112th Congress, 2d Session 7 (2012).

62. André B. Rosay, "Violence against American Indian and Alaskan Native Women and Men," *NIJ Journal* (September 2016), 42.

63. Quoted in Laird, *op. cit.*

64. Quoted in "Grassley on VAWA: 'The Non-Indian Doesn't Get a Fair Trial.'" *www. indiancountrymedianetwork.com. Indian Country Media Network*: February 21, 2013, Web.

65. Quoted in Sierra Crane-Murdoch, "On Indian Land, Criminals Can Get Away with Almost Anything." *www.theatlantic.com. The Atlantic*: February 22, 2013, Web.

66. *Duro v. Reina*, 495 U.S. 676, 693 (1990).

Pretrial Procedures:
The Adversary System in Action

To target your study and review, look for these numbered Learning Objective icons throughout the chapter.

Chapter Outline		Corresponding Learning Objectives
The Prosecution	**1**	Contrast the prosecutor's roles as an elected official and as a crime fighter.
The Defense Attorney	**2**	Delineate the responsibilities of defense attorneys.
	3	Explain why defense attorneys must often defend clients they know to be guilty.
Pretrial Detention	**4**	Identify the steps involved in the pretrial criminal process.
	5	Indicate the three main influences on a judge's decision to set bail.
Establishing Probable Cause	**6**	Identify the main difference between an indictment and an information.
The Prosecutorial Screening Process	**7**	Explain how a prosecutor screens potential cases.
Pleading Guilty	**8**	Indicate why prosecutors, defense attorneys, and defendants often agree to plea bargains.
	9	Describe some common criticisms of plea bargaining as an integral part of the American criminal justice system.

Puzzling Evidence

▲ In 2017, Miami, Florida, prosecutors dropped all charges against Deandre Charles relating to the murder of Rabbi Joseph Raskin.

Walter Michot/*Miami Herald*/Tribune News Service/Getty Images

Sixty-year-old Rabbi Joseph Raskin was visiting family in Miami during the summer of 2014 when he was shot and killed as he walked into a local synagogue. About sixteen months later, Miami police arrested fifteen-year-old Deandre Charles, and he was charged with first degree murder for Raskin's death. The prosecution seemingly had a wealth of evidence pointing to Charles as the killer. One witness said that, with his dying breath, Raskin identified "two black males" as his assailants. Another witness provided a hand-drawn sketch of the suspect. A confidential informant said that the offenders were driving a black Cadillac SUV, in which Charles was found three days later. DNA matching Charles's was found at the crime scene, and cell-phone records placed him there around the time of the shooting.

Taking advantage of a pretrial bail hearing, however, Charles's defense attorney, Adam Goodman, began poking holes in the prosecution's case. A forensics expert testified that "approximately half the world's population" would have been a match for the trace amounts of DNA at the crime scene. The witness's crude sketch only barely resembled the defendant. Charles's cell phone was actually in his brother's possession on the day of Raskin's death, and its proximity to the crime could not be proved. The murder weapon had been used in a different crime the day before, by a different person. Finally, the confidential informant who provided the information about the Cadillac SUV was unavailable to testify, having recently died.

A skeptical judge granted Charles bail, rare for a defendant charged with first degree murder. (We will discuss the bail process later in the chapter.) Then, about a year after his arrest, on January 17, 2017, prosecutors dropped all charges against Charles. In a statement, they admitted that they did not have "sufficient circumstantial evidence to prove the Defendant's guilt beyond a reasonable doubt." Charles "was not [at the crime scene] that day," said Goodman. "This was a travesty."

FOR CRITICAL ANALYSIS

1. Apparently, members of a local gang often kept guns at Deandre Charles's house. If you were Charles's defense attorney, how would you use this information to counteract evidence that your client's DNA was found on the murder weapon?

2. Before the confidential informant in this case died, prosecutors were reluctant to give his name to Charles's defense attorney. Is this a reasonable approach? Why would a defense attorney want to interview the confidential informant? Explain your answers.

3. Miami's tight-knit Orthodox Jewish community put a great deal of pressure on local authorities to find Rabbi Joseph Raskin's killer. How might this have influenced the prosecution's missteps in this case?

The Prosecution

As Deandre Charles's experience shows, the American adversary system is set in motion well before a criminal trial even starts. In fact, cases rarely make it as far as trial. Instead, the issue of guilt or innocence is usually negotiated beforehand, with the terms largely dictated by government lawyers called **public prosecutors.**

Prosecutorial Duties

The public prosecutor in federal criminal cases is called a U.S. attorney. In cases tried in state or local courts, the public prosecutor may be referred to as a *prosecuting attorney, state attorney, district attorney, county attorney,* or *city attorney.* Given their great autonomy, prosecutors are generally considered the most dominant figures in the American criminal justice system.

A Duty of Fairness

In some jurisdictions, the district attorney is the chief law enforcement officer, with broad powers over police operations. Prosecutors have the power to bring the resources of the state to bear against the individual and hold the legal keys to meting out or withholding punishment. Ideally, this power is balanced by a duty of fairness and a recognition that the prosecutor's ultimate goal is not to win cases, but to see that justice is done. In *Berger v. United States* (1935), Justice George Sutherland said of the prosecutor, "It is as much his duty to refrain from improper methods calculated to produce a wrongful conviction as it is to use every legitimate means to bring about a just one."[1]

The *Brady* Rule

To lessen the opportunity for "improper" behavior by prosecutors, the United States Supreme Court established the *Brady* rule more than half a century ago. This rule holds that prosecutors are not permitted to keep evidence from the defendant and her or his attorneys that may be useful in showing innocence.[2]

For example, in 1998 Michael Wearry was sentenced to death for killing a pizza-delivery driver named Eric Walber near Baton Rouge, Louisiana. Prosecutors had no physical evidence linking Wearry to the crime and relied heavily on the testimony of two jailhouse informants. As it turned out, one of the informants held a grudge against Wearry, while the other sought to trade his testimony for a lesser punishment in another crime. Furthermore, medical reports of Walber's death contradicted the prosecution's version of events. Because prosecutors failed to disclose any of this information to defense attorneys, in 2016 the United States Supreme Court reversed Wearry's conviction and granted him a new trial.[3]

The Office of the Prosecutor

When he or she is acting as an *officer of the law* during a criminal trial, there are limits on the prosecutor's conduct, as you will see in the next chapter. During the pretrial process, however, prosecutors hold a great deal of discretion in deciding the following:

1. Whether an individual who has been arrested by the police will be charged with a crime.
2. The level of the charges to be brought against the suspect.
3. If and when to stop the prosecution.

There are more than eight thousand prosecutors' offices around the country, serving state, county, and municipal jurisdictions. Even though the **attorney general** is the chief law enforcement officer in any state, she or he has limited control (and, in some states, no control) over prosecutors within the state's boundaries.

Public Prosecutors Individuals, acting as trial lawyers, who initiate and conduct cases in the government's name and on behalf of the people.

Attorney General The chief law officer of a state; also, the chief law officer of the nation.

Each jurisdiction has a chief prosecutor, who is sometimes appointed but more often elected. As an elected official, he or she typically serves a four-year term, though in some states, such as Alabama, the term is six years. In smaller jurisdictions, the chief prosecutor has several assistants, and they work closely together. In larger ones, the chief prosecutor may have numerous *assistant prosecutors*, many of whom he or she rarely meets.

Assistant prosecutors—for the most part, young attorneys recently graduated from law school—may be assigned to particular sections of the organization, such as criminal prosecutions in general or areas of *special prosecution*, such as narcotics or gang crimes. (See Figure 9.1 for the structure of a typical prosecutor's office.)

The Prosecutor as Elected Official

The chief prosecutor's autonomy is not absolute. As an elected official, she or he must answer to the voters. (There are exceptions: U.S. attorneys are nominated by the president and approved by the Senate, and chief prosecutors in Alaska, Connecticut, New Jersey, Rhode Island, and the District of Columbia are either appointed or hired as members of the attorney general's office.) In many jurisdictions, the prosecutor must declare a party affiliation and is expected to reward fellow party members with positions in the district attorney's office if elected.

The post of prosecutor is also considered a "stepping-stone" to higher political office, and many prosecutors have gone on to serve in legislatures or as judges. Sonia Sotomayor, the first Latina member of the United States Supreme Court, started her legal career in 1979 as an assistant district attorney in New York City. While at that job, she first came to public attention by helping to prosecute the "Tarzan Murderer," an athletic criminal responsible for at least twenty burglaries and four killings.

Elections and Impartiality
Just as judicial elections can raise concerns that judges' decisions may be influenced by politics, as we discussed in the previous chapter, the specter of an upcoming election can cast doubt on the impartiality of a prosecutor's decisions. For example, researchers have determined that during an election year, incumbent prosecutors in North Carolina are more likely to take cases to trial and less likely to allow defendants to plead guilty. In contrast, when that state's prosecutors do not face an election, fewer cases are taken to trial and more are plea bargained.[4]

Similar research in New York found that convictions won by prosecutors within six months of an election are 5 to 7 percent more likely to be later overturned by an appeals court. This is interpreted as evidence that prosecutors under electoral pressure are more apt to make mistakes while aggressively trying to win cases and attract positive publicity.[5]

FIGURE 9.1 The Baltimore City State's Attorney's Office

*F.I.V.E. is an acronym for "Firearms Investigation Violence Enforcement."

Source: Baltimore City State's Attorney's Office.

Community Pressures A prosecutor's electability is often enhanced by her or his involvement in high-profile cases. Such cases can be challenging for prosecutors to navigate, as Marilyn Mosby, Baltimore's chief prosecutor, recently discovered. Soon after Mosby was elected to her post in 2015, a twenty-five-year-old African American man named Freddie Gray died of spinal injuries he suffered while in the custody of the Baltimore Police Department. Daily protests by the city's black community followed, with many expressing outrage at what they saw as a trend of improper police use of force against members of minority groups. Only eighteen days after Gray's death, Mosby announced that six Baltimore police officers would face charges ranging from false imprisonment to second degree murder.

To justify the charges, Mosby argued that Gray had been wrongly arrested for carrying a legal folding knife and that he had not received proper medical attention for a spinal injury he suffered in a police van during transfer to the police station. After four trials failed to win convictions against the officers, however, Mosby's office dropped further efforts to prosecute the matter in July 2016. Legal experts questioned her judgment in moving forward without video or eyewitness testimony.[6] Others criticized Mosby for bowing to public pressure. "[I]t was a totally political prosecution," said one former city official. "I don't know why she was persuaded that she needed to bring the disorders to an end by charging the police."[7]

▲ About 80 percent of elected state and local prosecutors in the United States are white men, making Baltimore City State Attorney Marilyn Mosby, left, an exception to the rule. **Given the responsibilities of public prosecutors within the criminal justice system, how might society benefit from more diversity in the profession?** Mark Wilson/Getty Images News/ Getty Images

The Prosecutor as Crime Fighter

One of the reasons the prosecutor's post is a useful first step in a political career is that it is linked to crime fighting. Thanks to savvy public relations efforts and television police dramas such as *Law & Order*—with its opening line, "In the criminal justice system, the people are represented by two separate yet equally important groups: the police who investigate crime and the district attorneys who prosecute the offenders"—prosecutors are generally seen as law enforcement agents. Indeed, the prosecutors and the police do have a symbiotic relationship. Prosecutors rely on police to arrest suspects and gather sufficient evidence, and police rely on prosecutors to convict those who have been apprehended.

Learning Objective 1 Contrast the prosecutor's roles as an elected official and as a crime fighter.

Prosecutors and Police Despite, or perhaps because of, this mutual dependency, the relationship between the two branches of law enforcement is often strained. Part of this can be attributed to different backgrounds. Most prosecutors come from middle- or upper-class families, while police are often recruited from the working class. Furthermore, prosecutors are required to have a level of education that is not attained by most police officers. More important, however, is a basic divergence in the concept of guilt. For a police officer, a suspect is guilty if he or she has in fact committed a crime. For a prosecutor, a suspect is guilty if enough evidence can be legally gathered to prove such guilt in a court of law.

In other words, police officers often focus on *factual guilt*, whereas prosecutors are ultimately concerned with *legal guilt*.[8] Thus, police officers will feel a great deal of frustration when a suspect they "know" to be guilty is set free. Similarly, a prosecutor may become annoyed when police officers do not follow the letter of the law in gathering evidence, thereby greatly reducing the chances of conviction. To alleviate this tension, the Mecklenburg County (North Carolina) District Attorney's Office holds regular "round-table" meetings with local police to discuss the fate of recently arrested violent offenders.[9]

Prosecutors and Victims Because prosecutors have the responsibility of trying and convicting offenders, crime victims often see themselves as being on "the same side" as the prosecution. This perception is only strengthened when prosecutors publicly align themselves with victims. In fact, prosecutors do not represent crime victims. Understandably, most victims are focused primarily on the fate of the defendant who caused them harm. Prosecutors, in contrast, must balance the rights of the victims with those of the accused and the best interests of the public at large. Indeed, if a prosecutor becomes too involved in the personal tragedies of crime victims, he or she runs the risk of losing the neutrality that is the hallmark of the office.[10]

A prosecutor's duty of neutrality does not mean that he or she should ignore crime victims or their wishes. Practically, prosecutors rely on victims as sources of information and valuable witnesses. Believable victims are also quite helpful if a case goes to trial, as they may be able to elicit a sympathetic response from the jury.[11] Furthermore, as we saw in Chapter 3, federal and state victims' rights legislation requires the prosecutor to confer with victims at various stages of the criminal justice process.

CJ & TECHNOLOGY

Untested Rape Kits

In 2010, the Wayne County Prosecutor's Office found 11,000 untested rape kits in a Detroit police storage unit. These kits, prepared by forensic medical experts in the hours following a sexual assault, often contain DNA left by the offender. By September 2016, about 10,300 of the kits had been tested, leading to the identification of 770 serial rapists and over sixty convictions. According to Wayne County prosecutor Kym Worthy, DNA from the kits has been linked to crime scenes in thirty-nine other states, providing crucial evidence not just in sexual assaults but also "murders, armed robberies, [and] home invasions."

Nationwide, there is a backlog of about 400,000 untested rape kits, meaning that innumerable sexual assault offenders have escaped arrest and conviction. Given that most crime labs in the country are already overwhelmed with requests to test evidence, it seems that technology offers the best hope of reducing this backlog. Presently, lab technicians must laboriously separate the DNA of the victim from the DNA of the offender by slicing the cells of material in the rape kit, such as blood, semen, skin, or saliva, and testing each sample individually. A new process called *pressure cycling* immediately identifies the offender's semen, which significantly lessens the amount of time needed to get a usable DNA sample for database-matching purposes.

Thinking about Untested Rape Kits

How might the massive backlog of untested rape kits in this country discourage victims of sexual assault from reporting the crime to police?

The Defense Attorney

The media provide most people's perception of defense counsel: the idealistic public defender who nobly serves the poor, the "ambulance chaser," or the celebrity attorney in the $3,000 suit. These stereotypes, though not entirely fictional, tend to obscure the crucial role that the **defense attorney** plays in the criminal justice system.

Most persons charged with crimes have little or no knowledge of criminal procedure. Without assistance, they would be helpless in court. By acting as a staunch advocate for her

Defense Attorney The lawyer representing the defendant.

or his client, the defense attorney (ideally) ensures that the government proves every point against that client beyond a reasonable doubt, even for cases that do not go to trial. In sum, the defense attorney provides a counterweight against the state in our adversary system.

The Responsibilities of the Defense Attorney

The Sixth Amendment right to counsel is not limited to the actual criminal trial. In a number of instances, the United States Supreme Court has held that defendants are entitled to representation as soon as their rights may be denied, which, as we have seen, includes the custodial interrogation and lineup identification procedures.[12] Therefore, an important responsibility of the defense attorney is to represent the defendant at the various stages of the custodial process, such as arrest, interrogation, lineup, and arraignment. Other responsibilities include:

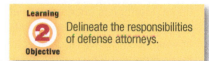

Learning Objective 2 Delineate the responsibilities of defense attorneys.

- Investigating the incident for which the defendant has been charged.
- Communicating with the prosecutor, which includes negotiating plea bargains.
- Preparing the case for trial.
- Submitting defense motions, including motions to suppress evidence.
- Representing the defendant at trial.
- Negotiating a sentence, if the client has been convicted.
- Determining whether to appeal a guilty verdict.[13]

Defending the Guilty

At one time or another in their careers, all defense attorneys will face a difficult question: Must I defend a client whom I know to be guilty? According to the American Bar Association's code of legal ethics, the answer is almost always, "yes."[14] The most important responsibility of the criminal defense attorney is to be an advocate for her or his client. As such, the attorney is obligated to use all ethical and legal means to achieve the client's desired goal, which is usually to avoid or lessen punishment for the charged crime.

As Supreme Court justice Byron White once noted, defense counsel has no "obligation to ascertain or present the truth." Rather, our adversary system insists that the defense attorney "defend the client whether he is innocent or guilty."[15] Indeed, if defense attorneys refused to represent clients whom they believed to be guilty, the Sixth Amendment guarantee of a criminal trial for all accused persons would be rendered meaningless. (To learn more about the difficult situations that can arise with a guilty defendant, see the feature *Discretion in Action—The Repugnant Client*.)

The Public Defender

Generally speaking, there are two different types of defense attorneys: (1) private attorneys, who are hired by individuals, and (2) **public defenders,** who work for the government. The distinction is not absolute, as many private attorneys accept employment as public defenders, too.

The modern role of the public defender was established by the Supreme Court's interpretation of the Sixth Amendment in *Gideon v. Wainwright* (1963).[16] In that case, the Court ruled that no defendant can be "assured a fair trial unless counsel is provided for him," and therefore the state must provide a public defender to those who cannot afford to hire one for themselves. Subsequently, the Court extended this protection to juveniles in *In re Gault* (1967)[17] and those faced with imprisonment for committing misdemeanors in *Argersinger v. Hamlin* (1972).[18] The impact of these decisions has been substantial: About 90 percent of all criminal defendants in the United States are represented by public defenders or other appointed counsel.[19]

Public Defenders Court-appointed attorneys who are paid by the state to represent defendants who cannot afford private counsel.

DISCRETION IN ACTION

The Repugnant Client

The Situation Gerard Marrone is the defense attorney for Levi Aron, charged with kidnapping, murdering, and dismembering eight-year-old Leiby Kletzky in Brooklyn, New

Learning Objective 3 Explain why defense attorneys must often defend clients they know to be guilty.

York. There is little question of Aron's guilt, as he provided the police with a signed confession

and has no alibi for his whereabouts at the time of the crime. Marrone is uncertain about whether he wants to continue representing this "horrific" client. "You can't look at your kids and then look at yourself in the mirror, knowing that a little boy, who's close in age to my eldest son, was murdered so brutally," Marrone said about his conflicted feelings.

The Law The Sixth Amendment requires that all criminal defendants are entitled to the right to assistance of counsel. Nonetheless, no state or federal law requires defense attorneys to represent clients they know to be

guilty of committing a crime. The American Bar Association (ABA) Model Rule of Professional Conduct, which provides informal guidance to the nation's lawyers, does not mandate representation of a client that an attorney finds "repugnant."

What Would You Do? Despite the ABA's advice about "repugnant" clients, the criminal justice system would not be able to function if lawyers refused to represent guilty defendants. Many believe that attorneys are ethically obligated to take on unpopular cases and clients to ensure the integrity of the American judicial system. At the same time, a lawyer must be guided by his or her own conscience. If a client is so repugnant to the lawyer as to impair the quality of representation, then perhaps the lawyer should drop the case. Given these opposing viewpoints, would you continue to represent Levi Aaron if you were in Gerard Marrone's position?

To see Gerard Marrone's eventual decision, go to Example 9.1 in Appendix B.

Eligibility Issues Although the Supreme Court's *Gideon* decision obligated the government to provide attorneys for indigent (poor) defendants, it offered no guidance on just how poor the defendant needs to be to qualify for a public defender. In theory, counsel should be provided for those who are unable to hire an attorney themselves without "substantial hardship."[20] In reality, each jurisdiction has its own guidelines, and a defendant refused counsel in one area might be entitled to it in another. New York State recently changed its standards so that any defendant with an annual income below about $30,000 is eligible for public counsel. Previously, these services were denied if the defendant owned a car or a house, often regardless of her or his income.[21]

Defense Counsel Programs In most areas, the county government is responsible for providing indigent defendants with attorneys. Three basic types of programs are used to allocate defense counsel:

1. *Assigned counsel programs*, in which local private attorneys are assigned clients on a case-by-case basis by the county.
2. *Contracting attorney programs*, in which a particular law firm or group of attorneys is hired to regularly assume the representative and administrative tasks of indigent defense.
3. *Public defender programs*, in which the county assembles a salaried staff of full-time or part-time attorneys and creates a public (taxpayer-funded) agency to provide services.[22]

Much to the surprise of many indigent defendants, these programs are not entirely without cost. Government agencies can charge fees for "free" legal counsel when the fees will not impose a "significant legal financial hardship" on the defendant. In at least forty-three states and the District of Columbia, therefore, local public defender offices have the option of charging some form of so-called cost recoupment.[23] In South Dakota, indigent defendants are billed $92 an hour for the services of a public defender, regardless of the outcome of the case. A defendant can be jailed for failing to cover these costs even if she or he is found innocent of the original charge.[24]

Effectiveness of Public Defenders
Under the U.S. Constitution, a defendant who is paying for her or his defense attorney has a right to choose that attorney without interference from the court.[25] This right of choice does not extend to indigent defendants. According to the United States Supreme Court, "[A] defendant may not insist on an attorney he cannot afford."[26] In other words, an indigent defendant must accept the public defender provided by the court system. (Note that, unless the presiding judge rules otherwise, a person can waive her or his Sixth Amendment rights and act as her or his own defense attorney.) This lack of control contributes to the widespread belief that public defenders do not provide an acceptable level of defense to indigents.

Statistics show, however, that conviction rates of defendants with private counsel and those represented by publicly funded attorneys are generally the same.[27] The main difference seems to be between private attorneys who are assigned indigent clients and full-time public defenders. A study of 3,412 Philadelphia indigent murder defendants found that, compared with private appointed counsel, public defenders reduced the conviction rate by 19 percent and the overall expected time served in prison by 24 percent.[28]

The main reason for this discrepancy, at least in Philadelphia, appears to be financial. Court-appointed defense attorneys in that city receive a flat fee for each client, which essentially works out to an average of $2 an hour. Furthermore, they are afforded limited public funds to investigate their clients' innocence. Philadelphia's public defenders, by contrast, are paid an annual salary and supported by a staff of investigators and various experts.[29]

Unreasonable Caseloads
The American Bar Association recommends that a public defender handle no more than 150 felony cases and 400 misdemeanor cases each year. Nationwide, about three-quarters of all county-based public defender programs exceed these limits.[30] Public defenders working in Fresno, California, for example, typically have as many as 700 clients at any given time, and an indigent defendant may wait as long as a month in jail before meeting her or his attorney for the first time.[31]

In early 2016, the public defender's office in Orleans Parish, Louisiana—which had forty-two lawyers for 22,000 cases—refused to take any new clients. "We simply don't have enough lawyers to handle the caseload," explained Derwyn Bunton, the parish's chief district defender.[32] By the end of the year, thirty-three of the forty-two public defender's offices in Louisiana had similar new case freezes, leading to a lawsuit in federal court claiming that the state was denying its poor citizens their constitutional right to counsel.[33]

The Strickland Standard
In one Louisiana murder trial, not only did the court-appointed defense attorney spend only eleven minutes preparing for trial on a charge that carried a mandatory life sentence, but she also represented the victim's father and

Annika Carlsten Public Defender

Courtesy of Annika Carlsten

My very first day on the job, I watched another attorney conduct *voir dire* (see Chapter 10) on a domestic violence assault. I wondered if I would ever be that comfortable and confident in court. Many years later, the cases have started to blur in my memory. That said, I will always remember my very first "not guilty" verdict. I was utterly convinced of my client's innocence, and very emotionally invested in winning the case for him. At the other end of the spectrum, I will never forget having to explain court proceedings to a man only hours after he accidentally shot and killed his child. Nothing in law school prepares you for that conversation. Nothing in life prepares you for that conversation.

Most of all, I believe passionately in the idea of what I do, in the principle of equal justice for everyone, regardless of money or circumstance. On a good day, I see that ideal fulfilled. On a great day, I feel like I personally have done something to make it so.

SOCIAL MEDIA CAREER TIP You need to differentiate yourself from everyone else online by providing unique, relevant, high-quality content on a regular basis. You should network with a purpose, not just to share fun things.

---

had been representing the victim at the time of his death. Not surprisingly, her defendant was found guilty. Such behavior raises a critical question: When a lawyer does such a poor job, has the client essentially been denied his or her Sixth Amendment right to assistance of counsel?

In *Strickland v. Washington* (1984),[34] the Supreme Court set up a two-pronged test to determine whether constitutional requirements have been met. To prove that prior counsel was not sufficient, a defendant must show that:

1. The attorney's performance was deficient, and
2. This deficiency *more likely than not* caused the defendant to lose the case.

In practice, it has been very difficult to prove the second prong of this test. A prosecutor can always argue that the defendant would have lost the case even if his or her lawyer had not been inept. Sometimes, however, such ineptness is so intolerable that it meets the *Strickland* standard and a remedy is necessary. In 2016, a Maryland judge ordered a new trial for Adnan Syed, who had been convicted and sentenced to life in prison sixteen years earlier for murdering his ex-girlfriend. At the original trial, Syed's attorney had failed to present evidence that Syed was not at the crime scene at the time of the murder. The attorney had also failed to cross-examine an expert witness who claimed that cell-phone records placed Syed at the scene of the crime.[35]

The Attorney-Client Relationship

The implied trust between an attorney and her or his client usually is not in question when the attorney has been hired directly by the defendant—as an "employee," the attorney well understands her or his duties. Relationships between public defenders and their clients, however, are often marred by suspicion on both sides. As Northwestern

University professor Jonathan D. Casper discovered while interviewing indigent defendants, many of them feel a certain amount of respect for the prosecutor. Like police officers, prosecutors are just "doing their job" by trying to convict the defendant. In contrast, the defendants' view of their own attorneys can be summed up in the following exchange between Casper and a defendant:

> Did you have a lawyer when you went to court the next morning?
> No, I had a public defender.[36]

This attitude is somewhat understandable. Given the caseloads that most public defenders carry, they may have as little as five or ten minutes to spend with a client before appearing in front of a judge. How much, realistically, can a public defender learn about the defendant in that time? Furthermore, the defendant is well aware that the public defender is being paid by the same source as the prosecutor and the judge. "Because you're part of the system, your indigent client doesn't trust you," admitted one court-appointed attorney.[37]

The situation handcuffs the public defenders as well. With so little time to spend on each case, they cannot validate the information provided by their clients. If the defendant says he or she has no prior offenses, the public defender often has no choice but to believe the client. Consequently, many public defenders later find that their clients have deceived them. Along with the high pressures of the job, a client's lack of cooperation and disrespect can limit whatever satisfaction a public defender may find in the profession.

Attorney-Client Privilege

To defend a client effectively, a defense attorney must have access to all the facts concerning the case, even those that may be harmful to the defendant. To promote the unrestrained flow of information between the two parties, legislatures and lawyers themselves have constructed rules of **attorney-client privilege.** These rules require that communications between a client and his or her attorney be kept confidential, unless the client consents to the disclosure.

The Privilege and Confessions

Attorney-client privilege does not stop short of confessions. Indeed, if, on hearing any statement that points toward guilt, the defense attorney could alert the prosecution or try to resign from the case, attorney-client privilege would be rendered meaningless. Even if the client says, "I have just killed seventeen women. I selected only pregnant women so I could torture them and kill two people at once. I did it. I liked it. I enjoyed it," the defense attorney must continue to do his or her utmost to serve that client.[38]

Attorney-Client Privilege
A rule of evidence requiring that communications between a client and his or her attorney be kept confidential, unless the client consents to disclosure.

▼ Defense attorney Jill Corey appears in Quincy, Massachusetts, District Court with her client, Andrew Fanguiaire, who was charged with possession of child pornography. **Why are the rules of attorney-client privilege necessary for a defense attorney to properly do his or her job?** Pat Greenhouse/*The Boston Globe*/Getty Images

Without attorney-client privilege, observes legal expert John Kaplan, lawyers would be forced to give their clients the equivalent of the *Miranda* warning before representing them.[39] In other words, lawyers would have to make clear what clients could or could not say in the course of preparing for trial, because any incriminating statement might be used against the client in court. Such a development would have serious ramifications for the criminal justice system.

The Exception to the Privilege   The scope of attorney-client privilege is not all-encompassing. In *United States v. Zolin* (1989),[40] the Supreme Court ruled that lawyers may disclose the contents of a conversation with a client if the client has provided information concerning a crime that has yet to be committed. This exception applies only to communications involving a crime that is ongoing or will occur in the future.

If the client reveals a past crime, the privilege is still in effect, and the attorney may not reveal any details of that particular criminal act. This aspect of the privilege can, admittedly, have tragic consequences. In 1956, for example, Darrel Parker was convicted of raping and killing his wife in Lincoln, Nebraska. These crimes had actually been committed by Wesley Peery, who admitted as much to his attorney. Parker spent fourteen years in prison, however, and was not exonerated until Peery died of a heart attack, allowing his attorney to make the confession public.

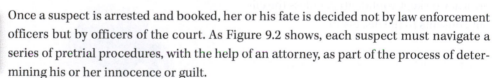

ETHICS CHALLENGE

Leon, the defendant, is on trial for having sex with an underage girl. Leon is represented by Daniel, the defense attorney, A jury finds Leon not guilty. A year later, as part of a dispute over legal fees, Daniel tells a judge that, in private conversations, Leon admitted to having sex with numerous underage girls, including members of his family. Should these conversations be covered by attorney-client privilege? Did Daniel behave unethically in sharing them with a court? Explain your answers.

Pretrial Detention

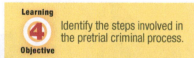

Once a suspect is arrested and booked, her or his fate is decided not by law enforcement officers but by officers of the court. As Figure 9.2 shows, each suspect must navigate a series of pretrial procedures, with the help of an attorney, as part of the process of determining his or her innocence or guilt.

The Initial Appearance

After a suspect has been booked, she or he is brought before a magistrate (see Chapter 8) for the **initial appearance.** As the U.S. Constitution does not specify how soon a defendant must be brought before a magistrate after arrest, it has been left to the judicial branch to determine the timing of the initial appearance. The Supreme Court has held that it must occur "promptly," which in most cases means within forty-eight hours of booking.[41]

During the initial appearance, the magistrate informs the defendant of the charges that have been brought against him or her and explains his or her constitutional rights—particularly, the right to remain silent (under the Fifth Amendment) and the right to be represented by counsel (under the Sixth Amendment). At this point, if the defendant cannot afford to hire a private attorney, a public defender may be appointed, or private counsel may be hired by the state to represent the defendant.

Initial Appearance An accused's first appearance before a judge or magistrate following arrest.

FIGURE 9.2 **The Steps Leading to a Trial**

Booking   After arrest, at the police station, the suspect is searched, photographed, finger-printed, and allowed at least one telephone call. After the booking, charges are reviewed, and if they are not dropped, a complaint is filed and a judge or magistrate examines the case for probable cause.

Initial Appearance   The suspect appears before the judge, who informs the suspect of the charges and of his or her rights. If the suspect requests a lawyer, one is appointed. The judge sets bail (conditions under which a suspect can obtain release pending disposition of the case).

Grand Jury   A grand jury determines if there is probable cause to believe that the defendant committed the crime. The federal government and about one-third of the states require grand jury indictments for at least some felonies.

Preliminary Hearing   In a preliminary hearing, the prosecutor presents evidence and the judge determines whether there is probable cause to hold the defendant over for trial.

Indictment   An indictment is the charging instrument issued by the grand jury.

Information   An information is the charging instrument issued by the prosecutor.

Arraignment   The suspect is brought before the trial court, informed of the charges, and asked to enter a plea.

Plea Bargain   A plea bargain is a prosecutor's promise of concessions (or promise to seek concessions) in return for the defendant's guilty plea. Concessions include a reduced charge and/or a lesser sentence.

Guilty Plea   In most jurisdictions, the majority of cases that reach the arraignment stage do not go to trial but are resolved by a guilty plea, often as the result of a plea bargain. The judge sets the case for sentencing.

Trial   If the defendant refuses to plead guilty, he or she proceeds to either a jury trial (in most instances) or a bench trial.

In misdemeanor cases, a defendant may decide to plead guilty and be sentenced during the initial appearance. Otherwise, the magistrate will usually release those charged with misdemeanors on their promise to return at a later date for further proceedings. For felony cases, however, the defendant is not permitted to make a plea at the initial appearance because a magistrate's court does not have jurisdiction to decide felonies.

Bail and Pretrial Release

At the initial appearance, in most cases the defendant will be released only if she or he posts **bail**—an amount paid by the defendant to the court and retained by the court until the defendant returns for further proceedings. Defendants who cannot afford bail are generally kept in a local jail or lockup until the date of their trial, though many jurisdictions are searching for alternatives to this practice because of overcrowded incarceration facilities.

The Purpose of Bail

Bail is provided for under the Eighth Amendment. The amendment does not, however, guarantee the right to bail. Instead, it states that "excessive bail shall not be required." This has come to mean that the bail amount must be reasonable compared with the seriousness of the wrongdoing. It does *not* mean that the amount of bail must be within the defendant's ability to pay.

At the same time, in theory, bail is not intended to be a punitive measure. That is, bail is not meant to be a sort of fine that a defendant must pay to avoid waiting for her or his trial in jail. Rather, bail is designed to provide an incentive for the accused to return to court and participate in her or his legal proceedings.

Setting Bail

There is no uniform system for setting bail. Each jurisdiction has its own *bail tariffs*, or general guidelines concerning the proper amount of bail. For misdemeanors, the police usually follow a preapproved bail schedule created by local judicial authorities. In felony cases, the primary responsibility to set bail lies with the judge. As Figure 9.3 shows, bail amounts generally rise according to the seriousness of the underlying offense, with murder suspects facing the highest cost of pretrial freedom.

Bail guidelines can be quite extensive. In Illinois, for example, a judge is required to take thirty-eight different factors into account when setting bail: Fourteen involve the crime itself, two refer to the evidence gathered, four to the defendant's record, nine to the defendant's flight risk and immigration status, and nine to the defendant's general character.[42] For the most part, however, judges are free to use such tariffs as loose guidelines, and they have a great deal of discretion in setting bail according to the circumstances in each case.

Judges and Bail Extralegal factors may also play a part in bail setting. University of New Orleans political scientist David W. Neubauer has identified three contexts that may influence a judge's decision-making process:[43]

1. *Uncertainty.* To a degree, predetermined bail tariffs are unrealistic, given that judges are required to set bail within forty-eight hours of arrest. It is often difficult to get information on the defendant in that period of time, and even if a judge can obtain a "rap sheet," or list of prior arrests ("priors"), she or he will probably not have an opportunity to verify its accuracy. Due to this uncertainty, most judges have no choice but to focus primarily on the seriousness of the crime in setting bail.

2. *Risk.* There is no way of knowing for certain whether a defendant released on bail will return for his or her court date or whether he or she will commit a crime while free. (In fact, recent statistics show that about 17 percent of released defendants fail to make a

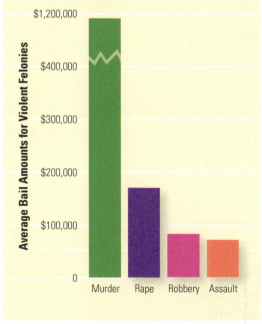

FIGURE 9.3 Average Bail Amounts for Violent Felonies

These figures represent the mean bail amounts for the seventy-five largest counties in the nation.

Source: Adapted from Bureau of Justice Statistics, *Felony Defendants in Large Urban Counties, 2009–Statistical Tables* (Washington, D.C.: U.S. Department of Justice, December 2013), Table 16, page 19.

scheduled court appearance. About 16 percent are rearrested while free on bail, and of those, 8 percent are rearrested for committing a felony.)[44] Judges are aware of the criticism they will come under from police groups, prosecutors, the press, and the public if a defendant commits a crime while out on bail. Consequently, a judge may prefer to "play it safe" in setting bail. In general, risk aversion also dictates why those who are charged with a violent crime such as murder are less likely to be released prior to trial than those who are charged with property crimes such as larceny or motor vehicle theft.

3. *Overcrowded jails.* As we will discuss in detail in Chapter 13, many of the nation's jails are overcrowded. This may force a judge to make a difficult distinction between those suspects she or he believes must be detained and those who might need to be detained. To save jail space, a judge might be more lenient in setting bail for members of the latter group.[45]

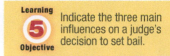

Preventive Detention   In addition to encouraging defendants to return to court, bail may sometimes serve another purpose: the protection of the community. That is, if a judge feels that the defendant would pose a threat if he or she were released before trial, the judge will set bail at a level the suspect cannot possibly afford. "The bail is really being set to keep the person in custody," admits Judge W. Kent Hamlin of Superior Court in Fresno County, California.[46] For example, in 2016, a judge set bail at $5.1 million for Damin Pashilk, a construction worker charged with seventeen counts of arson for allegedly setting a series of devastating fires in Northern California.

Alternatively, more than thirty states and the federal government have passed preventive detention legislation to achieve the same effect. These laws allow judges to act "in the best interests of the community" by denying bail to arrestees with prior records of violence, thus keeping them in custody prior to trial.[47]

Posting Bail   To gain pretrial release, a defendant must pay the full amount of the bail in cash to the court. The money, called a *cash bond*, will be returned when the suspect appears for trial.

Given the large amount of funds required, and the relative lack of wealth of many criminal defendants, a defendant can rarely post bail in cash. Another option is to use real property, such as a house, instead of cash as collateral. These property bonds are also rare because most courts require property valued at double the bail amount. Thus, if bail is set at $5,000, the defendant (or the defendant's family and friends) will have to produce property valued at $10,000.

Bail Bond Agents   If unable to post bail with cash or property, a defendant may arrange for a bail bond agent to post a bail bond on the defendant's behalf. The bond agent, in effect, promises the court that he or she will turn over to the court the full amount of bail if the defendant fails to return for further proceedings. The defendant usually must give the bond agent a certain percentage of the bail (frequently 10 percent) in cash. This amount, which is often not returned to the defendant later, is considered payment for the bond agent's assistance and assumption of risk. Depending on the amount of the bail bond, the defendant may also be required to sign over to the bond agent rights to certain property (such as a car, a valuable watch, or other asset) as security for the bond.

Although bail bond agents obviously provide a service for which there is demand, the process is widely viewed with distaste. Indeed, the Philippines is the only other nation

Preventive Detention The retention of an accused person in custody due to fears that she or he will commit a crime if released before trial.

Property Bonds An alternative to posting bail in cash, in which the defendant gains pretrial release by providing the court with property as assurance that he or she will return for trial.

Bail Bond Agent A businessperson who agrees, for a fee, to pay the bail amount if the accused fails to appear in court as ordered.

▲ If a defendant "skips" bail by failing to appear at trial, the bail bond agent sometimes hires a fugitive-recovery agent to find the defendant and return him or her to court. **Are there any circumstances under which a fugitive-recovery agent should be allowed to use deadly force in apprehending a runaway defendant? Explain your answer.** Chris Johnson/Hemera/Getty Images

where bail bonding is an accepted part of the pretrial release process. Four states—Illinois, Kentucky, Oregon, and Wisconsin—have abolished bail bonding for profit. The rationale for such reform focuses on three perceived problems with the practice:

1. Bail bond agents provide opportunities for corruption, as they may improperly influence officials who are involved in setting bail to inflate the bail.

2. Because they can refuse to post a bail bond, bail bond agents are, in essence, making a business decision concerning a suspect's pretrial release. This is considered the responsibility of a judge, not a private individual with a profit motive.[48]

3. About 40 percent of defendants released on bail are eventually found not guilty of any crime. These people, although innocent, have had to pay what amounts to a bribe if they wanted to stay out of jail before their trial.[49]

The states that have banned bail bond agents have established an alternative known as *10 percent cash bail*. This process requires the court, in effect, to take the place of the bond agent. An officer of the court will accept a deposit of 10 percent of the bail amount, refundable when the defendant appears at the assigned time. A number of jurisdictions allow for both bail bond agents and 10 percent cash bail, with the judge deciding whether a defendant is eligible for the latter.

Alternatives to Bail

One of the most consistent criticisms of bail is that the system is biased against low-income defendants who may not have the financial means to "buy" their temporary freedom. Numerous studies show that defendants detained in jail have worse trial outcomes than those who are able to gain pretrial release.[50] Furthermore, higher bail bond amounts make it more likely that members of minority groups will be kept in jail prior to their trials.[51]

Release on Recognizance   To remedy this situation, bail reformers want to increase the use of **release on recognizance (ROR),** in which the defendant is set free at no cost with the understanding that he or she will return at the time of the trial. Many jurisdictions are turning to pretrial risk assessment tools to determine which defendants should be eligible for ROR. For example, several local court systems in Colorado rely on the twelve factors listed in Figure 9.4 to measure the risk that a defendant will "jump" bail or be arrested on new charges while awaiting trial. A study of nearly two thousand defendants in Colorado found that ROR is just as effective as traditional bail bonds in protecting the public and ensuring appearance at trial, with significantly lower costs.[52]

Bail Reform   New Jersey has taken bail reform one step further by largely abolishing the practice. Starting on January 1, 2017, if a New Jersey judge finds that the defendant

Release on Recognizance (ROR) A judge's order that releases an accused person from jail with the understanding that he or she will return of his or her own will for further proceedings.

FIGURE 9.4 The Colorado Pretrial Assessment Tool (CPAT) Risk Factors

In Colorado, defendants in certain jurisdictions are given a score based on the twelve CPAT factors listed below. Based on this score, the defendant is assigned to one of four risk categories, and those deemed low risk have a much greater chance of being released on their own recognizance before trial.

1. Having a home phone or a cell phone
2. Owning or renting a residence
3. Contributing to residential payments
4. Past or current problems with alcohol
5. Past or current mental health treatment
6. Age at first arrest*

7. Past jail sentence
8. Past prison sentence
9. Having active warrants
10. Having other pending cases in court
11. Currently on probation or parole
12. History of bail "jumping"

*The lower the age of first arrest, the more likely the defendant is at risk to skip trial or reoffend.

Source: *The Colorado Bail Book: A Defense Practitioner's Guide to Adult Pretrial Release* (Denver: Colorado Criminal Defense Institute, September 2015), 7.

poses a minimal flight risk and little threat to public safety, then the defendant will most likely be released before trial.[53] In the first month under these new rules, of the 3,382 cases processed statewide, judges set bail only three times. An additional 283 defendants—almost all accused of serious crimes, or thought to be a flight risk, or both—were held without bail as a matter of preventive detention.[54] (The *Policy Matters* feature at the end of the chapter gives you a chance to decide whether you think this and similar bail reforms should serve as a model for the rest of the country.)

Establishing Probable Cause

Once the initial appearance has been completed and bail has been set, the prosecutor must establish *probable cause*. In other words, the prosecutor must show that a crime was committed and link the defendant to that crime. There are two formal procedures for establishing probable cause at this stage of the pretrial process: preliminary hearings and grand juries.

The Preliminary Hearing

During the **preliminary hearing,** the defendant appears before a judge or magistrate who decides whether the evidence presented is sufficient for the case to proceed to trial. Normally, every person arrested has a right to this hearing within a reasonable amount of time after his or her initial arrest—usually, no later than ten days if the defendant is in custody or within thirty days if he or she has gained pretrial release.

The Preliminary Hearing Process
The preliminary hearing is conducted in the manner of a mini-trial. Typically, a police report of the arrest is presented by a law enforcement officer, supplemented with evidence provided by the prosecutor. Because the burden of proving probable cause is relatively light (compared with proving guilt beyond a reasonable doubt), prosecutors rarely call witnesses during the preliminary hearing, saving them for the trial.

During this hearing, the defendant has a right to be represented by counsel, who may cross-examine witnesses and challenge any evidence offered by the prosecutor. In most

Preliminary Hearing An initial hearing in which a magistrate decides if there is probable cause to believe that the defendant committed the crime with which he or she is charged.

states, defense attorneys can take advantage of the preliminary hearing to begin the process of **discovery,** in which they are entitled to have access to any evidence in the possession of the prosecution relating to the case. Discovery is considered a keystone in the adversary process, as it allows the defense to see the evidence against the defendant prior to making a plea.

Waiving the Hearing

The preliminary hearing often seems rather perfunctory. It usually lasts no longer than five minutes, and the judge or magistrate rarely finds that probable cause does not exist. For this reason, defense attorneys commonly advise their clients to waive their right to a preliminary hearing. Once a judge has ruled affirmatively, in many jurisdictions the defendant is bound over to the **grand jury,** a group of citizens called to decide whether probable cause exists. In other jurisdictions, the prosecutor issues an **information,** which replaces the police complaint as the formal charge against the defendant for the purposes of a trial.

The Grand Jury

Learning Objective 6 Identify the main difference between an indictment and an information.

The grand jury does not determine the guilt or innocence of the defendant. Rather, it determines whether the evidence presented by the prosecution is sufficient to provide probable cause that a crime occurred. If a majority of the jurors find sufficient evidence, the grand jury will issue an **indictment** (pronounced in-*dyte*-ment). Like an information in a preliminary hearing, the indictment becomes the formal charge against the defendant.

The federal government and about one-third of the states require grand jury indictments to bring felony charges. In most of the other states, a grand jury is optional. When a grand jury is not used, the discretion of whether to charge is left to the prosecutor, who must then present his or her argument at the preliminary hearing.

Special Features of Grand Juries

Grand juries are *impaneled*, or created, for a period of time usually not exceeding three months. For the most part, grand jury proceedings are dominated by the prosecution, which can present a wide variety of evidence against the defendant, including photographs, documents, tangible objects, and the testimony of witnesses. Generally speaking, grand juries differ from trials, which we will discuss in the next chapter, in that:

1. Jurors can ask the district attorney and the judge questions about relevant law and can request that witnesses be recalled to the stand to testify a second time.

2. The defense cannot cross-examine prosecution witnesses, though it can present its own witnesses.

3. The proceedings are closed (secret). Witnesses can speak publicly, but only about their own testimony. Members of the grand jury are not allowed to speak to the media.

Recently, law enforcement worked closely with a grand jury to decide whether to bring terrorism-related charges against Noor Salman. Salman's husband, Omar Mateen, carried out the mass shooting that claimed forty-nine lives at an Orlando nightclub in June 2016. Federal investigators believed that Salman was aware of her husband's plans. After six months of reviewing the evidence, the grand jury charged Salman with obstruction of justice for lying to authorities concerning her knowledge of these plans.

A "Rubber Stamp" Once the federal jury launched its investigation into possible wrongdoing by Noor Salman, it was almost a foregone conclusion that charges would follow. Certainly, the procedural rules of the grand jury favor prosecutors. The exclusionary rule (see Chapter 7) does not apply in grand jury investigations, so prosecutors can present evidence that would be disallowed at any subsequent trial. Furthermore, the grand jury is given the prosecution's version of the facts, with the defense having only a limited ability to offer counterarguments.

In the words of one observer, a grand jury would indict a "ham sandwich" if the government asked it to do so.[55] Overall, defendants are indicted at a rate of more than 99 percent,[56] leading to the common characterization of the grand jury as little more than a "rubber stamp" for the prosecution.

▲ Several years ago, a St. Louis County, Missouri, grand jury failed to indict police officer Darren Wilson for fatally shooting an eighteen-year-old unarmed African American named Michael Brown. (This photo shows the hat Brown was wearing when he died.) **How might grand jury secrecy contribute to controversy surrounding a decision such as this one, which was widely criticized in the black community? Would you be in favor of legislation allowing grand jury members to speak publicly about a case? Why or why not?** St. Louis County Prosecutor's Office/Getty Images News/Getty Images

The Prosecutorial Screening Process

Some see the high government success rates in pretrial proceedings as proof that prosecutors successfully screen out weak cases before they get to a grand jury or preliminary hearing. If, however, grand juries have indeed abandoned their traditional duties in favor of "rubber stamping" most cases set in front of them, and preliminary hearings are little better, what is to keep prosecutors from using their charging powers indiscriminately?

Nothing, say many observers. Once the police have initially charged a defendant with committing a crime, the prosecutor can prosecute the case as it stands, reduce or increase the initial charge, file additional charges, or dismiss the case. In a system of government and law that relies on checks and balances, asked legal expert Kenneth Culp Davis, why should the prosecutor be "immune to review by other officials and immune to review by the courts?"[57] Though American prosecutors have far-ranging discretionary charging powers, however, it is not entirely correct to say that they are unrestricted. Controls are indirect and informal, but they do exist. (For information on another prosecutor-friendly system, see the feature *Comparative Criminal Justice—Japan's All-Powerful Prosecutors.*)

Case Attrition

Prosecutorial discretion includes the power *not* to prosecute cases. Figure 9.5 depicts the average outcomes of one hundred felony arrests in the United States. As you can see, of the sixty-five adult arrestees brought before the district attorney, only thirty-five are prosecuted, and only eighteen of these prosecutions lead to incarceration. This phenomenon is known as **case attrition,** and it is explained in part by prosecutorial discretion.

Scarce Resources

About half of the adult felony cases brought to prosecutors by police are dismissed through a *nolle prosequi* (Latin for "unwilling to pursue"). Another option is **deferred prosecution,** in which a prosecutor agrees to delay further legal action

Case Attrition The process through which prosecutors, by deciding whether to prosecute each person arrested, effect an overall reduction in the number of persons prosecuted.

Deferred Prosecution An alternative to prosecution in which the prosecutor agrees to delay criminal proceedings against a defendant as long as the defendant meets certain requirements for a predetermined amount of time.

Source: Central Intelligence Agency

Japan's All-Powerful Prosecutors

Prosecutors in the United States are generally believed to have a great deal of charging discretion. The discretionary power of American prosecutors, however, does not equal that of their Japanese counterparts. With the ability to "cherry pick" their cases, prosecutors in Japan routinely have annual conviction rates of about 99 percent.

THE "CONFESSION MILL"

One observer described the Japanese courts as a "confession mill." Unlike the American system, Japan has no arraignment procedure during which the accused can plead guilty or innocent. Instead, the focus of the Japanese criminal justice system is on extracting confessions of guilt: Police can hold and question suspects for up to twenty-three days without pressing charges. Furthermore, the suspect has no absolute right to counsel during the interrogation, and police are often able to get confessions that make for open-and-shut convictions. The prosecutor also has the "benevolent" discretion to drop the case altogether if the suspect expresses remorse.

In addition, the extraordinarily high conviction rate is a product of Japanese culture. To fail in an attempt to convict results in a loss of face, not only for the individual prosecutor but also for the court system as a whole. The Japanese Justice Ministry estimates that, to avoid the risk of losing, prosecutors decline to press charges against 35 percent of indictable suspects each year. Japanese judges—there are almost no juries—contribute to the high conviction rate by rarely questioning the manner in which prosecutors obtain confessions.

NO PLEA BARGAINING

Interestingly, given the amount of prosecutorial discretion, the Japanese criminal justice system does not allow for plea bargaining. The Japanese see the practice of "trading" a guilty plea for a lesser sentence as counterproductive, as a defendant may be tempted to confess to crimes she or he did not commit if the prosecution has a strong case. For the Japanese, a confession extracted after, say, twenty-three days of interrogation may be "voluntary," but a confession gained through a promise of leniency is "forced" and therefore in conflict with the system's goals of truth seeking and accuracy.

FOR CRITICAL ANALYSIS

Explain the fundamental differences between the American and Japanese criminal justice systems. Do you think the lack of a comparable adversary system weakens or strengthens the Japanese system in comparison with the American one?

---

as long as the defendant meets certain conditions. For example, if the charges involve possession of an illegal drug, the conditions may include getting substance abuse counseling and having no further contact with the criminal justice system for six months. If the defendant holds up his or her end of the agreement, then the case is usually dismissed, with the original charges expunged from the defendant's criminal record.

Why would the district attorney choose not to prosecute cases? In the section on law enforcement, you learned that the police do not have the resources to arrest every lawbreaker in the nation. Similarly, district attorneys do not have the resources to prosecute every arrest. They must choose how to distribute their scarce resources.

Screening Factors   Most prosecutors have a *screening* process for deciding when to prosecute and when not to prosecute. This process varies a bit from jurisdiction to jurisdiction, but most prosecutors consider several factors in making the decision:[58]

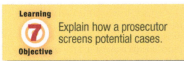
Learning
7 **Objective**
Explain how a prosecutor screens potential cases.

- The most important factor in deciding to prosecute is not whether the prosecutor believes the suspect is guilty but whether there is *sufficient evidence for conviction*. If prosecutors have strong physical evidence and a number of reliable and believable witnesses, they are quite likely to prosecute.
- Prosecutors also rely heavily on *offense seriousness* to guide their priorities, preferring to take on felony offenses rather than misdemeanors. In other words,

100 people arrested

35 juveniles go to juvenile court

65 adults considered for prosecution

30 cases dropped

30 put on probation or dismissed

35 cases accepted for prosecution

5 jump bail

30 cases go to trial

3 acquitted

23 plead guilty

4 found guilty

27 sentenced

9 placed on probation

Incarcerated: 18 adults 5 juveniles

Source: Adapted from Todd R. Clear, George F. Cole, and Michael D. Reisig, *American Corrections*, 11th ed. (Belmont, CA: Wadsworth, 2016), 131.

everything else being equal, a district attorney will prosecute a rapist instead of a jaywalker because the former presents a greater threat to society than does the latter. A prosecutor will also be more likely to prosecute someone with an extensive record of wrongdoing than a first-time offender.

- Sometimes a case is dropped even when it involves a serious crime and a wealth of evidence exists against the suspect. These situations usually involve *uncooperative victims*. As you saw in Chapter 3, domestic violence cases are particularly difficult to prosecute because the victims may want to keep the matter private, fear reprisals, or have a strong desire to protect their abuser. In one study of Chicago domestic violence cases, prosecutors won convictions 73 percent of time when the victim participated in court proceedings and only 23 percent of the time when the victim refused to cooperate.[59]

- *Unreliability of victims* can also affect a charging decision. If the victim of an alleged battery charge has an extensive criminal record and is unlikely to show up in court to testify, prosecutors may be reluctant to pursue the matter.

- A prosecutor may be willing to drop a case or reduce the charges against *a defendant who is willing to testify against other offenders*. Federal law encourages this kind of behavior by offering sentencing reductions to defendants who provide "substantial assistance in the investigation or prosecution of another person who has committed an offense."[60]

Often, prosecutors are motivated by a sense of doing "the right thing" for their communities. In the late 1980s, for example, Andrew Luger was a prosecutor in New York City when local police, looking for a cocaine stash house, found a dozen young women from Colombia trapped in a room containing little more than beds and condoms. Given that no state or federal human trafficking statute existed at the time, he had to charge those who forced the women into prostitution under labor laws.

Today, Luger is the U.S. attorney for the District of Minnesota, and he is intent on working "with law enforcement to protect the most vulnerable."[61] In 2016, his office indicted seventeen members of an international sex trafficking organization that transported hundreds of women from Thailand into the United States for commercial sex purposes. (To get a better idea of the difficulty of some charging decisions, see the feature *Discretion in Action—A Battered Woman*.)

Prosecutorial Charging and the Defense Attorney

For the most part, there is little the defense attorney can do when the prosecutor decides to charge a client. If a defense attorney feels strongly that the charge has been made in violation of the defendant's rights, he or she can, however, submit *pretrial motions* to the court requesting that a particular action be taken to protect his or her client. For example, a defense attorney has the option of filing a motion to dismiss the charges against her or his client completely because of lack of evidence.

Other common pretrial motions include the following:

1. Motions to suppress evidence obtained illegally.
2. Motions for a change of venue because the defendant cannot receive a fair trial in the original jurisdiction.

DISCRETION IN ACTION

A Battered Woman

The Situation For more than twenty years, John regularly beat his wife, Judy. He even put out cigarettes on her skin and slashed her face with glass. John was often unemployed and forced Judy into prostitution to earn a living. He regularly denied her food and threatened to maim or kill her. Judy left home several times, but John always managed to find her, bring her home, and punish her. Finally, Judy took steps to get John put in a psychiatric hospital. He told her that if anybody came for him, he would "see them coming" and cut her throat before they arrived. That night, Judy shot John three times in the back of the head while he was asleep, killing him. You are the prosecutor with authority over Judy.

The Law In your jurisdiction, a person can use deadly force in self-defense if it is necessary to kill an unlawful aggressor to save himself or herself from imminent death. (See Chapter 4 for a review of self-defense.) Voluntary manslaughter is the intentional killing of another human being without malice. It covers crimes of passion. First degree murder is premeditated killing, with malice. (Also, see Chapter 4 for a review of the different degrees of murder.)

What Would You Do? Will you charge Judy with voluntary manslaughter or first degree murder? Alternatively, do you believe she was acting in self-defense, in which case you will not charge her with any crime? Explain your choice.

To see how a Rutherford County, North Carolina, prosecutor decided a case with similar facts, go to Example 9.2 in Appendix B.

3. Motions to invalidate a search warrant.
4. Motions to dismiss the case because of a delay in bringing it to trial.
5. Motions to obtain evidence that the prosecution may be withholding.

As you will soon see, defense attorneys sometimes use these pretrial motions to pressure the prosecution into offering a favorable deal for their client.

ETHICS CHALLENGE

What are the potential ethical pitfalls of the practice, common among prosecutors, of reducing the charges against a defendant who is willing to testify against other offenders?

Pleading Guilty

Based on the information (delivered during the preliminary hearing) or indictment (handed down by the grand jury), the prosecutor submits a motion to the court to order the defendant to appear before the trial court for an **arraignment.** Due process of law, as guaranteed by the Fifth Amendment, requires that a criminal defendant be informed of the charges brought against her or him and be offered an opportunity to respond to those charges. The arraignment is one of the ways in which due process requirements are satisfied by criminal procedure law.

At the arraignment, the defendant is informed of the charges and must respond by pleading not guilty or guilty. In some but not all states, the defendant may also enter a plea of *nolo contendere,* which is Latin for "I will not contest it." The plea of *nolo contendere* is neither an admission nor a denial of guilt. (The consequences for someone who pleads guilty and for someone who pleads *nolo contendere* are the same in a criminal trial, but the latter plea cannot be used in a subsequent civil trial as an admission of guilt.) Most frequently, the defendant pleads guilty to the initial charge or to a lesser charge that has been agreed on through plea bargaining between the prosecutor and the defendant. If the defendant pleads guilty, no trial is necessary, and the defendant is sentenced based on the crime he or she has admitted committing.

Plea Bargaining in the Criminal Justice System

Plea bargaining most often takes place after the arraignment and before the beginning of the trial. In its simplest terms, it is a process by which the accused, represented by defense counsel, and the prosecutor work out a mutually satisfactory disposition of the case, subject to court approval.

Usually, plea bargaining involves the defendant's pleading guilty to the charges against her or him in return for a lighter sentence, but other variations are possible as well. The defendant can agree to plead guilty in exchange for having the charge against her or him reduced from, say, felony burglary to the lesser offense of breaking and entering. Or a person charged with multiple counts may agree to plead guilty if the prosecutor agrees to drop one or more of the counts. Whatever the particulars, the results of a plea bargain are generally the same: The prosecutor gets a conviction, and the defendant a lesser punishment.

In *Santobello v. New York* (1971),[62] the Supreme Court held that plea bargaining "is not only an essential part of the process but a highly desirable part for many reasons." Some

Arraignment A court proceeding in which the suspect is formally charged with the criminal offense stated in the indictment.

Nolo Contendere Latin for "I will not contest it." A plea in which a criminal defendant chooses not to challenge, or contest, the charges brought by the government.

Plea Bargaining The process by which the accused and the prosecutor work out a mutually satisfactory conclusion to the case, subject to court approval.

observers would agree, but with ambivalence. They understand that plea bargaining offers the practical benefit of saving court resources, but question whether it is the best way to achieve justice.[63]

Motivations for Plea Bargaining

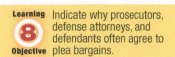

Learning Objective 8 Indicate why prosecutors, defense attorneys, and defendants often agree to plea bargains.

Given the high rate of plea bargaining—accounting for 97 percent of criminal convictions in state courts[64]—it follows that the prosecutor, defense attorney, and defendant each have strong reasons to engage in the practice.

Prosecutors and Plea Bargaining In most cases, a prosecutor has a single goal after charging a defendant with a crime: conviction. If a case goes to trial, no matter how certain a prosecutor may be that the defendant is guilty, there is always a chance that a jury or judge will disagree. Plea bargaining removes this risk. Furthermore, the prosecutorial screening process described earlier in the chapter is not infallible. Sometimes, a prosecutor will find that the evidence against the accused is weaker than first thought or will uncover new information that changes the complexion of the case. In these situations, the prosecutor may decide to drop the charges or, if he or she still feels that the defendant is guilty, turn to plea bargaining to "save" a questionable case.

The prosecutor's role as an administrator also comes into play. She or he may be interested in the quickest, most efficient manner to dispose of caseloads, and plea bargains reduce the time and money spent on each case. Personal philosophy can affect the proceedings as well. A prosecutor who feels that a mandatory minimum sentence for a particular crime, such as marijuana possession, is too strict may plea bargain in order to lessen the penalty. Similarly, some prosecutors will consider plea bargaining only in certain instances—for burglary and theft, for example, but not for more serious felonies such as rape and murder.

Defense Attorneys and Plea Bargaining Political scientist Milton Heumann has said that a defense attorney's most important lesson is that "most of his [or her] clients are guilty."[65] Given this stark reality, favorable plea bargains are often the best a defense attorney can do for clients, aside from helping them to gain acquittals. Some have suggested that defense attorneys have other, less savory motives for convincing a client to plead guilty, such as a desire to increase profit margins by quickly disposing of cases[66] or a wish to ingratiate themselves with the other members of the courtroom work group by showing their "reasonableness."[67]

Defendants and Plea Bargaining The plea bargain allows the defendant a measure of control over his or her fate. In September 2016, for example, Danny Heinrich pleaded guilty to federal child pornography charges that will keep him in prison for at least twenty years. As part of the plea bargain, prosecutors agreed not to charge Heinrich for murdering eleven-year-old Jacob Wetterling nearly twenty-seven years earlier—a crime for which, if convicted, he could have spent the rest of his life behind bars. As Figure 9.6 shows, defendants who plea bargain receive significantly lighter sentences on average than those who are found guilty at trial.

Victims and Plea Bargaining One of the major goals of the victims' rights movement has been to increase the role of victims in the plea bargaining process. In recent years, the movement has had some success in this area. About half of the states now allow for victim participation in plea bargaining. Many have laws similar to a North Carolina

FIGURE 9.6 **Sentencing Outcomes for Guilty Pleas**

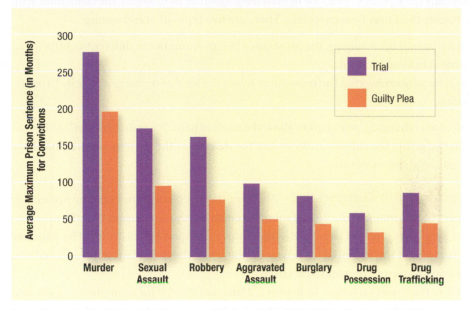

Source: Bureau of Justice Statistics, *Felony Sentences in State Courts, 2006—Statistical Tables* (Washington, D.C.: U.S. Department of Justice, December 2009), Table 4.3.

statute that requires the district attorney's office to offer victims "the opportunity to consult with the prosecuting attorney" and give their views on "plea possibilities."[68]

On the federal level, the Crime Victims' Rights Act grants victims the right to be "reasonably heard" during the process.[69] In the case just discussed, Jacob Wetterling's parents approved Danny Heinrich's relatively lenient plea bargain on the condition that he give a detailed confession of how he murdered Jacob and reveal the whereabouts of the boy's remains.[70]

In general, crime victims have mixed emotions regarding plea bargains. On the one hand, any form of "negotiated justice" that lessens the offender's penalty may add insult to the victim's emotional and physical injuries. On the other hand, trials can bring up events and emotions that some victims would rather not have to reexperience.

Plea Bargaining and the Adversary System

One criticism of plea bargaining is that it subverts the adversary system, the goal of which is to determine innocence or guilt. Although plea bargaining does value negotiation over conflict, it is important to remember that it does so in a context in which legal guilt has already been established. Even within this context, plea bargaining is not completely divorced from the adversary process.

Strategies to Induce a Plea Bargain   Earlier, we pointed out that the most likely reason why a prosecutor does not bring charges is the lack of a strong case. This is also the most common reason why a prosecutor agrees to a plea bargain once charges have been brought. Defense attorneys are well aware of this fact and often file numerous pretrial motions in an effort to weaken the state's case.

Even if the judge does not accept the motions, the defense may hope that the time required to process them will wear on the prosecutor's patience. As one district attorney has said, "[T]he usual defense strategy today is to bring in a stack of motions as thick as a Sunday newspaper; defense attorneys hope that we won't have the patience to ride them out."[71]

Prosecutors have their own methods of inducing a plea bargain. The most common is the ethically questionable practice of *overcharging*—that is, charging the defendant with more counts than may be appropriate. There are two types of overcharging:

1. In *horizontal overcharging*, the prosecutor brings a number of different counts for a single criminal incident.
2. In *vertical overcharging*, the prosecutor raises the level of a charge above its proper place.

After overcharging, prosecutors allow themselves to be "bargained down" to the correct charge, giving the defense attorney and the defendant the impression that they have achieved some sort of victory.

Protecting the Defendant

Watching the defense attorney and the prosecutor maneuver in this manner, the defendant often comes to the conclusion that the plea bargaining process is a sort of game with sometimes incomprehensible rules. The Supreme Court is aware of the potential for taking advantage of the defendant in plea bargaining and has taken steps to protect the accused.

Before the Court's decision in *Boykin v. Alabama* (1969),[72] for example, judges would often accept the defense counsel's word that the defendant wanted to plead guilty. In that case, the Court held that the defendant must make a clear statement that he or she accepts the plea bargain. As a result, many jurisdictions now ask the accused to sign a *Boykin* **form** waiving his or her right to a trial. (For a summary of other notable Supreme Court cases involving plea bargaining procedures, see Figure 9.7.)

Faulty Advice In 2012, the Supreme Court dramatically affected plea bargaining law by ruling that defendants have a constitutional right to effective representation during plea negotiations.[73] That year, the Court considered the plight of Anthony Cooper, who had shot a woman in Detroit. Based on faulty legal advice from his attorney, Cooper rejected

---

FIGURE 9.7 Notable United States Supreme Court Decisions on Plea Bargaining

The constitutional justification of the plea bargain as an accepted part of the criminal justice process has been fortified by these Supreme Court rulings.

Brady v. United States (397 U.S. 742 [1970]). In this case the defendant entered a guilty plea in order to avoid the death penalty. In allowing this action, the Court ruled that **plea bargains are a legitimate part of the adjudication process as long as they are entered into voluntarily and the defendant has full knowledge of the consequences of pleading guilty**.

North Carolina v. Alford (400 U.S. 25 [1970]). Although maintaining he was innocent of the first degree murder with which he was charged, Alford pleaded guilty to second degree murder in order to avoid the possibility of the death penalty that came with the original charges. After being sentenced to thirty years in prison, Alford argued that he was forced to plea bargain because of the threat of the death

penalty. The Court refused to invalidate Alford's guilty plea, **stating that plea bargains are valid even if the defendant claims innocence, as long as the plea was entered into voluntarily**.

Santobello v. New York (404 U.S. 257 [1971]). This case focused on the prosecutor's role in the plea bargain process. The Court ruled that **if a prosecutor promises a more lenient sentence in return for the defendant's guilty plea, the promise must be kept**.

Ricketts v. Adamson (483 U.S. 1 [1987]). In return for a reduction of charges, Ricketts agreed to plead guilty and to testify against a co-defendant in a murder case. When the co-defendant's conviction was reversed on appeal, Ricketts refused

to testify a second time. Therefore, the prosecutor rescinded the offer of leniency. The Court ruled that the prosecutor's action was justified, and that **defendants must uphold their side of the plea bargain in order to receive its benefits**.

United States v. Mezzanatto (513 U.S. 196 [1995]). The Court ruled that a prosecutor can refuse to plea bargain with a defendant unless the defendant agrees that any statements made by him or her during the bargaining process can be used against him or her in a possible trial. In other words, **if the defendant admits to committing the crime during plea bargain negotiations, and then decides to plead not guilty, the prosecution can use the admission as evidence during the trial**.

In 2016, nanny Yoselyn Ortega, center, rejected a plea deal offered by a New York City judge that would have given her thirty years to life in prison for killing two young children in her care. Instead, she faced the possibility of a life sentence without parole if found guilty at trial. **What might be some of the reasons for the fifty-three-year-old Ortega's decision to decline the judge's offer?**

Susan Watts/*New York Daily News*/Getty Images

a plea bargain that called for a sentence of four to seven years behind bars. Instead, he lost at trial and was sentenced to fifteen to thirty years. After hearing Cooper's appeal, the Court found that, in essence, defendants have a constitutional right to effective counsel during plea bargaining, just as they do during a trial.

A Second Chance to Plead Because of the Supreme Court's ruling, defendants like Anthony Cooper now have the opportunity to argue that had they received proper legal advice, they would have accepted the plea bargain rather than risk a trial. If a defendant successfully proves ineffective counsel during plea bargaining, he or she will be given another chance to make a favorable plea.[74]

The four members of the Court who dissented from this decision warned that it would give defendants who lose at trial an unfair opportunity to revisit a rejected plea bargain. "It's going to be tricky," agrees Stephanos Bibas, a law professor at the University of Pennsylvania. "There are going to be a lot of defendants who say after they're convicted that they really would have taken the plea."[75]

A "Necessary Evil"?

Viewed in its most negative light, plea bargaining seems to give the defendant either an unfair "discount" for pleading guilty or the risk of an unfair "penalty" for going to trial. The practice may also encourage innocent people to plead guilty if they feel there is even a slight chance that a jury or judge will decide against them. "I tell [clients], 'If you think ten years is too long to serve and the other option is to get twenty, I want you to think, how would you feel nine years from now?'" said one public defender. "Those aren't the options people should have."[76]

Furthermore, critics contend that plea bargaining gives prosecutors too much power to coerce defendants, either by overcharging or by claiming to have evidence that they know would actually be inadmissible at trial, such as contraband gained by an illegal search.[77] At the same time, practically speaking, the criminal justice system does not have the resources to try a high percentage of cases in court. "Because of plea bargaining, I guess we can say, 'Gee, the trains run on time,'" notes criminologist Franklin Zimring. "But do we like where they're going?"[78]

Learning Objective 9 Describe some common criticisms of plea bargaining as an integral part of the American criminal justice system.

Going to Trial

Despite the large number of defendants who eventually plead guilty, the plea of not guilty is fairly common at the arraignment. This is true even when the facts of the case seem stacked against the defendant. Generally, a not guilty plea in the face of strong evidence is part of a strategy to do one of the following:

1. Gain a more favorable plea bargain,
2. Challenge a crucial part of the evidence on constitutional grounds, or
3. Submit one of the affirmative defenses discussed in Chapter 4.

Of course, if either side is confident in the strength of its arguments and evidence, it will be more willing to go to trial. Both prosecutors and defense attorneys may favor a trial to gain publicity, and sometimes public pressure after an extremely violent or high-profile crime will force a chief prosecutor (who is, remember, normally an elected official) to take a weak case to trial. Also, some defendants may insist on their right to a trial, regardless of their attorneys' advice. In the next chapter, we will examine what happens to the roughly 3 percent of indictments that do lead to the courtroom.

ETHICS CHALLENGE

Paul is charged with forgery, a crime that carries a two- to ten-year prison term. The prosecutor threatens that, if Paul refuses a plea bargain, she will seek an indictment against him under state habitual crime legislation that carries a lifetime prison sentence. Is this ethical behavior on the prosecutor's part? Why or why not? (If you are curious to see how the United States Supreme Court ruled in a case with similar facts, search for *Bordenkircher v. Hayes* online.)

Policy Matters

For-Profit Bail

How Things Stand

Twenty-five years ago, release on recognizance was the most common form of pretrial release. Today, nearly two-thirds of all defendants must post bail to be released before trial, and 38 percent are held in jail until the disposition of their cases.[79] In addition, the average bail amount for those detained before trial was five times higher in 2009 than in 1990, reaching nearly $100,000.[80]

As a Result...

The United States detains more people before trial than any other country in the world—on a daily basis, about 500,000 jail inmates are behind bars because they cannot make bail.[81] In theory, the money bail system lessens the risk that defendants will fail to show up at trial by giving them a strong economic incentive to appear. Critics of the system maintain, however, that it operates on the basis of money rather than safety. As might be expected, the poorer a criminal defendant, the less likely she or he will be able to gain pretrial release. Consequently, defendants who can afford bail go free, regardless of the threat they pose to society, while defendants who cannot afford bail are locked up, regardless of the threat they pose.[82]

Because of this reality, the impact of for-profit bail falls disproportionately on members of low-income communities, for whom even a short stint behind bars has consequences such as loss of paychecks and jobs, possible evictions, and child care crises. Furthermore, a number of studies show that defendants who are free while awaiting trial are less likely to be convicted than are pretrial detainees.[83] Nevertheless, supporters of the money bail system, such as judges, prosecutors, and (naturally) bail bondspersons, contend that—whatever its faults—money bail is the best guarantor of both community safety and the appearance of the defendant at trial.

Up for Debate

"What has been demonstrated here is that usually only one factor determines whether a defendant stays in jail before he comes to trial. That factor is not guilt or innocence. It is not the nature of the crime. It is not the character of the defendant. That factor is, simply, money. How much money does the defendant have?"[84] —*Robert F. Kennedy, U.S. Attorney General (1961–1964)*

"Bail is probably the single most reliable assurance that someone will show up [for trial]."[85] —*Judge Steven White, president of the Alliance of California Judges*

What's Your Take?

Review the discussion in this chapter on "Pretrial Detention" before answering the following questions.

1. Bail conditions are not supposed to be punitive. At the same time, nearly half of all defendants who pay a nonrefundable bail bond to a bail bondsperson are eventually acquitted or have the charges against them dropped. Does this mean that bail often is, in reality, a punishment? Why or why not?

2. One Cleveland criminal court judge, defending her practice of setting money bail for poor defendants, says, "You're balancing risk. You can't throw the risk out the window just because somebody doesn't have any money."[86] Do you agree with the judge? Why or why not?

Digging Deeper...

Every afternoon in Washington, D.C., about 90 percent of the people who have been arrested are released without having to post bail. To learn more about this relative anomaly in the American criminal justice system, go online and search for the terms **Washington, D.C.** and **bail reform**. Afterward, explain how the pretrial system in our nation's capital works in the absence of bail. Does the concept of risk assessment factor into pretrial release decisions? Are there any evident drawbacks to the city's policy? Do you think it should be a national model for ending the practice of for-profit bail? Your answer should be at least three paragraphs long.

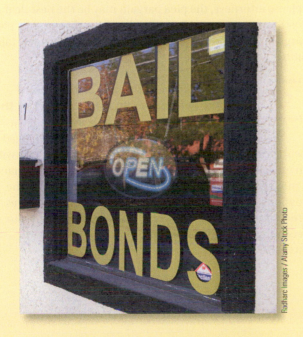

Radharc Images / Alamy Stock Photo

For more information on these concepts, look back to the Learning Objective icons throughout the chapter.

 Contrast the prosecutor's roles as an elected official and as a crime fighter. In most instances, the prosecutor is elected and therefore may feel obliged to reward members of her or his party with jobs. To win reelection or higher political office, the prosecutor may feel a need to bow to community pressures. As a crime fighter, the prosecutor is allied with the police, and indeed prosecutors are generally seen as law enforcement agents. Prosecutors, however, generally pursue cases only when they believe there is sufficient evidence to obtain a conviction.

 Delineate the responsibilities of defense attorneys. (a) Representation of the defendant during the custodial process, (b) investigation of the supposed criminal incident, (c) communication with the prosecutor (including plea bargaining), (d) preparation of the case for trial, (e) submission of defense motions, (f) representation of the defendant at trial, (g) negotiation of a sentence after conviction, and (h) appeal of a guilty verdict.

 Explain why defense attorneys must often defend clients they know to be guilty. In our adversary system, the most important responsibility of a defense attorney is to be an advocate for her or his client. This means ensuring that the client's constitutional rights are protected during criminal justice proceedings, regardless of whether the client is guilty or innocent.

 Identify the steps involved in the pretrial criminal process. (a) Suspect taken into custody or arrested; (b) initial appearance before a magistrate, at which time the defendant is informed of his or her constitutional rights and a public defender may be appointed or private counsel may be hired by the state to represent the defendant; (c) the posting of bail or release on recognizance; (d) preventive detention, if deemed necessary to ensure the safety of other persons or the community, or regular detention, if the defendant is unable to post bail; (e) preliminary hearing (mini-trial), at which the judge rules on whether there is probable cause and the prosecutor issues an information, or in the alternative (f) grand jury hearings, after which an indictment is issued against the defendant if the grand jury finds probable cause; (g) arraignment, in which the defendant is informed of the charges and must respond by pleading not guilty or guilty (or in some cases *nolo contendere*); and (h) plea bargaining.

 Indicate the three main influences on a judge's decision to set bail. (a) Uncertainty about the character and past criminal history of the defendant, (b) the risk that the defendant will commit another crime if out on bail, and (c) overcrowded jails, which may influence a judge to release a defendant on bail.

 Identify the main difference between an indictment and an information. An indictment is the grand jury's declaration that probable cause exists to charge a defendant with a specific crime. In jurisdictions that do not use grand juries, the prosecution issues an information as the formal charge of a crime.

 Explain how a prosecutor screens potential cases. (a) Is there sufficient evidence for conviction? (b) What is the priority of the case? The more serious the alleged crime, the higher the priority. The more extensive the defendant's criminal record, the higher the priority. (c) Are the victims cooperative? Violence against family members often yields uncooperative victims, so these cases are rarely prosecuted. (d) Are the victims reliable? (e) Might the defendant be willing to testify against other offenders?

 Indicate why prosecutors, defense attorneys, and defendants often agree to plea bargains. For prosecutors, a plea bargain removes the risk of losing the case at trial, particularly if the evidence against the defendant is weak. For defense attorneys, the plea bargain may be the best deal possible for a potentially guilty client. For defendants, plea bargains give a measure of control over a highly uncertain future.

 Describe some common criticisms of plea bargaining as an integral part of the American criminal justice system. Plea bargaining is seen by some as a double-edged sword: On the one hand, it provides guilty defendants with an unfair "discount" for pleading guilty. On the other hand, it punishes those defendants who do go to trial with the possibility of a harsher sentence. The practice also gives prosecutors too much power to coerce a defendant into accepting a deal that may not be in his or her best interests.

QUESTIONS FOR CRITICAL ANALYSIS

1. According to the United States Supreme Court, prosecutors cannot face civil lawsuits for misconduct, even if they have deliberately sent an innocent person to prison. In practical terms, why do you think prosecutors are protected in this manner? Do you think the Supreme Court should lift this immunity for prosecutors? Why or why not?

2. Why might the practice of charging low-income defendants fees for the services of public defenders go against the Supreme Court's ruling in *Gideon v. Wainwright?*

3. Between 2012 and 2016, in an attempt to reduce the city's skyrocketing violent crime rates, Chicago judges doubled the bail amount (from $25,000 to $50,000) for defendants charged with gun-related crimes. What is the theory behind this strategy for reducing firearm-related crimes? In fact, the strategy failed; these defendants gained pretrial release twice as often in 2016 as in 2012. Explain how this seeming statistical inconsistency could happen in a system with monetary bail and bail bondspersons.

4. In practice, the constitutional right to a lawyer does not cover initial bail hearings. What are the disadvantages for an indigent defendant who is not represented by a lawyer at this point in the pretrial process?

5. Review the Supreme Court's ruling, discussed in the last section of this chapter, that defendants have a constitutional right to effective representation during plea negotiations. Do you think the Court made the proper ruling? Why or why not?

KEY TERMS

arraignment 305
attorney-client privilege 293
attorney general 285
bail 296
bail bond agent 297
Boykin form 308
case attrition 301
defense attorney 288

deferred prosecution 301
discovery 300
grand jury 300
indictment 300
information 300
initial appearance 294
nolo contendere 305
plea bargaining 305

preliminary hearing 299
preventive detention 297
property bonds 297
public defenders 289
public prosecutors 285
release on recognizance (ROR) 298

NOTES

1. 295 U.S. 78 (1935).
2. *Brady v. Maryland*, 373 U.S. 83 (1963).
3. *Wearry v. Cain*, 577 U.S. _____, No. 14-10008. Supreme Court of the United States (March 7, 2016).
4. Siddhartha Bandyopadhyay and Bryan C. McCannon, "The Effect of the Election of Public Prosecutors on Criminal Trials," *Public Choice* (October 2010), 1–2.
5. Bryan C. McCannon, "Prosecutor Elections, Mistakes, and Appeals," *Journal of Empirical Legal Studies* (December 2013), 696–714.
6. Jess Bidgood, "Stakes Rise for Prosecutors Trying Officer in Freddie Gray Case for Murder," *New York Times* (June 9, 2016), A11.
7. Quoted in Sheryl Gay Stolberg, "2 Trials, 0 Convictions: Baltimore Prosecutor Is in a Bind," *New York Times* (May 25, 2016), A10.

8. Herbert Packer, *Limits of the Criminal Sanction* (Stanford, Calif.: Stanford University Press, 1968), 166–167.
9. William T. Stetzer, "A Collaborative Approach to Plea Offers," *The Police Chief* (April 2014), 26–29.
10. Bennett L. Gershman, "Prosecutorial Ethics and Victims' Rights: The Prosecutor's Duty of Neutrality," *Lewis & Clark Law Review* 9 (2005), 561.
11. *Ibid.*, 560–561.
12. *Gideon v. Wainwright*, 372 U.S. 335 (1963); *Massiah v. United States*, 377 U.S. 201 (1964); *United States v. Wade*, 388 U.S. 218 (1967); *Argersinger v. Hamlin*, 407 U.S. 25 (1972); and *Brewer v. Williams*, 430 U.S. 387 (1977).
13. Larry Siegel, *Criminology*, 6th ed. (Belmont, Calif.: West/Wadsworth Publishing Co., 1998), 487–488.

14. Center for Professional Responsibility, *Model Rules of Professional Conduct* (Washington, D.C.: American Bar Association, 2003), Rules 1.6 and 3.1.
15. *United States v. Wade*, 388 U.S. 218, 256–258 (1967).
16. 372 U.S. 335 (1963).
17. 387 U.S. 1 (1967).
18. 407 U.S. 25 (1972).
19. Laurence A. Benner, "Eliminating Excessive Public Defender Workloads," *Criminal Justice* (Summer 2011), 25.
20. "Providing Defense Services: Standard 5-7.1. *www.americanbar.org*. American Bar Association: visited February 11, 2017, Web.
21. "The Court Decides, and Doesn't: A Big Victory for Public Defense in New York," *New York Times* (June 24, 2016), A26.

22. Bureau of Justice Statistics, *County-Based and Local Public Defender Offices, 2007* (Washington, D.C.: U.S. Department of Justice, September 2010), 3.

23. "State-by-State Court Fees." *www.npr.org*. *National Public Radio*: May 19, 2014, Web.

24. Mark Walker, "In S.D. Right to an Attorney Comes with a Price." *www.argusleader. com*. Argus Leader: March 4, 2016, Web.

25. *United States v. Gonzalez-Lopez*, 548 U.S. 140 (2006).

26. *Wheat v. United States*, 486 U.S. 153, 159 (1988).

27. Richard Hartley, Holly V. Miller, and Cassie Spohn, "Do You Get What You Pay For? Type of Counsel and Its Effect on Criminal Court Outcomes," *Journal of Criminal Justice* (September–October 2010), 1063–1070.

28. James M. Anderson and Paul Heaton, *Measuring the Effect of Defense Counsel on Homicide Case Outcomes: Executive Summary* (Santa Monica, Calif.: RAND Corporation, December 2012), 1.

29. Peter A. Joy and Kevin C. McMunigal, "Does a Lawyer Make a Difference? Public Defender v. Appointed Counsel," *Criminal Justice* (Spring 2012), 46–47.

30. *County-Based and Local Public Defender Offices, 2007, op. cit.*, 1.

31. "ACLU Sues over Failing Public Defense System in Fresno County, California." *www.aclu.org*. American Civil Liberties Union: July 15, 2015, Web.

32. Derwyn Burton, "No Lawyers to Spare for Poor in New Orleans," *New York Times* (February 19, 2016), A31.

33. Lorelei Laird, "Class Action Lawsuit Alleges Louisiana Public Defender Funding System Denies Right to Counsel." *www.abajournal.com*. *ABA Journal:* February 7, 2017, Web.

34. 466 U.S. 668 (1984).

35. Euan McKirdy, Emanuella Grinberg, and Lauren DelValle, "'Serial' Podcast's Adnan Syed's New Trial Appealed." *www.cnn.com*. CNN: August 2, 2016, Web.

36. Jonathan D. Casper, *American Criminal Justice: The Defendant's Perspective* (Englewood Cliffs, N.J.: Prentice Hall, 1972), 101.

37. Quoted in Mark Pogrebin, *Qualitative Approaches to Criminal Justice* (Thousand Oaks, Calif.: Sage Publications, 2002), 173.

38. Randolph Braccialarghe, "Why Were Perry Mason's Clients Always Innocent?" *Valparaiso University Law Review* (Fall 2004), 65.

39. John Kaplan, "Defending Guilty People," University of Bridgeport Law Review (1986), 223.

40. 491 U.S. 554 (1989).

41. *Riverside County, California v. McLaughlin*, 500 U.S. 44 (1991).

42. Illinois Annotated Statutes Chapter 725, Paragraph 5/110-5.

43. David W. Neubauer, *America's Courts and the Criminal Justice System*, 5th ed. (Belmont, Calif.: Wadsworth Publishing Co., 1996), 179–181.

44. Quoted in Shaila Dewan, "Poor, Accused and Punished by Bail System," *New York Times* (June 11, 2015), A1.

45. Roy Flemming, C. Kohfeld, and Thomas Uhlman, "The Limits of Bail Reform: A Quasi Experimental Analysis," *Law and Society Review 14* (1980), 947–976.

46. *Bail Fail: Why the U.S. Should End the Practice of Using Money for Bail* (Washington, D.C.: Justice Policy Institute, September 2012), 7.

47. Bureau of Justice Statistics, *Felony Defendants in Large Urban Counties, 2009—Statistical Tables* (Washington, D.C.: U.S. Department of Justice, December 2013), Table 18, page 21; and Table 19, page 21.

48. John S. Goldkamp and Michael R. Gottfredson, *Policy Guidelines for Bail: An Experiment in Court Reform* (Philadelphia: Temple University Press, 1985), 18.

49. Adam Liptak, "Illegal Globally, Bail Profit Remains Pillar of U.S. Justice," *New York Times* (January 28, 2008), A1.

50. *Bail Fail, op. cit.*, 13.

51. Jeremy Ball and Lisa Bostaph, "He Versus She: A Gender-Specific Analysis of Legal and Extralegal Effects on Pretrial Release for Felony Defendants," *Women & Criminal Justice* 19 (2009), 95–119.

52. Michael R. Jones, *Unsecured Bonds: The As Effective and Most Efficient Pretrial*

Release Option (Washington, D.C.: Pretrial Justice Institute, October 2013).

53. Ben Horowitz, "Bail Reform to Require 'Extraordinary Amount of Resources,' Judge Says." *www.nj.com. NJ.com:* September 10, 2015, Web.

54. Lisa W. Foderaro, "Mercy vs. Risk as New Jersey Cuts Cash Bail," *New York Times* (February 7, 2017), A1.

55. New York Court of Appeals Judge Sol Wachtler, quoted in David Margolik, "Law Professor to Administer Courts in State," *New York Times* (February 1, 1985), B2.

56. Sam Skolnick, "Grand Juries: Power Shift?" *The Legal Times* (April 12, 1999), 1.

57. Kenneth C. Davis, *Discretionary Justice: A Preliminary Inquiry* (Baton Rouge, La.: Louisiana State University Press, 1969), 189.

58. Bruce Frederick and Don Stemen, *The Anatomy of Discretion: An Analysis of Prosecutorial Decision Making—Summary Report* (New York: Vera Institute of Justice, December 2012), 4–16.

59. Carolyn C. Hartley and Lisa Frohmann, *Cook County Target Abuser Call (TAC): An Evaluation of a Specialized Domestic Violence Court* (Washington, D.C.: National Institute of Justice, August 2003).

60. 18 U.S.C. Section 3553(e) (2006).

61. Quoted in Rubén Rosario, "This Is Why Minnesota's Federal Prosecutor Focuses on Sex Trafficking." *www.twincities.com. Twin Cities Pioneer Press:* May 20, 2016, Web.

62. 404 U.S. 257 (1971).

63. Fred C. Zacharias, "Justice in Plea Bargaining," *William and Mary Law Review* 39 (March 1998), 1121.

64. Bureau of Justice Statistics, *Prosecutors in State Courts, 2007—Statistical Tables* (Washington, D.C.: U.S. Department of Justice, December 2011), 2.

65. Milton Heumann, *Plea Bargaining: The Experiences of Prosecutors, Judges, and Defense Attorneys* (Chicago: University of Chicago Press, 1978), 58.

66. Albert W. Alschuler, "The Defense Attorney's Role in Plea Bargaining," *Yale Law Journal* 84 (1975), 1200.

67. Stephen J. Schulhofer, "Plea Bargaining as Disaster," *Yale Law Journal 101* (1992), 1987.

68. North Carolina General Statutes Section 15A-832(f) (2003).

69. 18 U.S.C. Section 3771 (2004).

70. "Man Admits Abducting, Killing Jacob Wetterling," *Associated Press* (September 7, 2016).

71. Albert W. Alschuler, "The Prosecutor's Role in Plea Bargaining," *University of Chicago Law Review* 36 (1968), 53.

72. 395 U.S. 238 (1969).

73. *Lafler v. Cooper,* 132 S.Ct. 1376 (2012); and *Missouri v. Frye,* 132 S.Ct. 1399 (2012).

74. Laurence Benner, "Expanding the Right to Effective Counsel at Plea Bargaining," *Criminal Justice* (Fall 2012), 4–11.

75. Quoted in Adam Liptak, "Justices' Ruling Expands Rights of Accused in Plea Bargains," *New York Times* (March 22, 2012), A1.

76. Quoted in Erik Eckholm, "Prosecutors Draw Fire for Sentences Called Harsh," *New York Times* (December 6, 2013), A19.

77. H. Mitchell Caldwell, "Coercive Plea Bargaining: The Unrecognized Scourge of the Justice System." *www.scholarship. law.edu.* Catholic University Law Review: 2011, Web.

78. Quoted in "Is Plea Bargaining a Cop-Out?" *www.aldeilis.net. Time:* August 28, 1978, Web.

79. *Felony Defendants in Large Urban Counties, 2009—Statistical Tables, op. cit,* 1.

80. Bureau of Justice Statistics, *Felony Defendants in Large Urban Counties, 1990* (Washington, D.C.: U.S. Department of Justice, May 1993), Table 11, page 9; and Table 16, page 19.

81. Timothy R. Schnacke, *Fundamental of Bail: A Resource Guide for Pretrial Practitioners and a Framework for American Pretrial Reform* (Washington, D.C.: National Institute of Corrections, September 2014), 1.

82. *Bail Fail, op. cit.,* 1.

83. Mary T. Phillips, *Pretrial Detention and Case Outcomes, Part 2: Felony Cases* (New York: New York City Criminal Justice Agency, 2008).

84. Quoted in *Bail Fail, op. cit.,* 1.

85. Quoted in Dewan, *op. cit.*

86. Nancy Margaret Russo, quoted in *ibid.*

MEGAN E. SHANAHAN, JUDGE

The Criminal Trial

To target your study and review, look for these numbered Learning Objective icons throughout the chapter.

Chapter Outline		Corresponding Learning Objectives
Special Features of Criminal Trials	**1**	Identify the basic protections enjoyed by criminal defendants in the United States.
	2	Explain what "taking the Fifth" really means.
Jury Selection	**3**	List the requirements normally imposed on potential jurors.
	4	Contrast challenges for cause and peremptory challenges during *voir dire*.
The Trial	**5**	List the standard steps in a criminal jury trial.
	6	Describe the difference between direct and circumstantial evidence, and explain why evidence of a defendant's "evil character" is often excluded from trial.
	7	Identify the primary method that defense attorneys use in most trials to weaken the prosecution's case against their client.
The Final Steps of the Trial and Postconviction Procedures	**8**	Delineate circumstances in which a criminal defendant may be tried a second time for the same act.
	9	List the five basic steps of an appeal.

The Holdout

▲ A photograph of six-year-old Etan Patz hangs on an angel figurine as part of a memorial held for the boy several years ago in the SoHo neighborhood of New York City. AP Images/Mark Lennihan

and more." Hernandez's attorneys claimed that this confession was a fantasy made up by their client, who was suffering from mental problems. For Sirois, the holdout juror, the main issue was that police interviewed Hernandez for more than six hours before turning on the videotape and getting the confession. "We needed to see the full interrogation to determine if the story [the defendant] eventually told police originated with him or if it was coached to him by the detectives," said Sirois.

Following the mistrial, the other jurors expressed hope that prosecutors would retry Hernandez and find a resolution "for the Patz family, for the Hernandez family, [and] for the City of New York." They got their wish. On February 14, 2017, after a second, three-month trial and nine days of jury deliberation, a different set of jurors found Hernandez guilty of murdering Etan. Eventually, he was sentenced to life in prison without parole.

Three times, the judge asked the jurors to come up with a verdict. Three times, the jurors failed to do so. Consequently, on May 8, 2015, after a four-month trial and eighteen days of jury deliberation, Justice Maxwell Riley had no choice but to declare a mistrial in the murder case of Pedro Hernandez. Thirty-three years earlier, in his own words, Hernandez had lured six-year-old Etan Patz into the basement of the New York City bodega where he worked and strangled the boy. Eleven of the jurors accepted this confession as proof of Hernandez's guilt. One did not. "Ultimately I couldn't find enough evidence that was not circumstantial to convict," Adam Sirois, the holdout, said afterwards. "I couldn't get there."

In fact, Etan's body was never found. Neither were the boy's clothes or the small tote bag that he was carrying when he disappeared. Prosecutors had no forensic evidence from a crime scene. The only proof they could offer was a videotaped confession in which the defendant said, "Something took over me and I squeezed [Patz] more

FOR CRITICAL ANALYSIS

1. Do you agree with the policy that jurors must vote unanimously to find a defendant such as Pedro Hernandez guilty? Or should an 11–1 vote, as occurred in Hernandez's first trial, be sufficient? Explain your answer.

2. Hernandez's attorney provided evidence at trial suggesting that Jose Ramos, a convicted child molester with connections to the Patz family, killed Etan. Should the defense be allowed to raise the possibility at trial that a different culprit committed the crime? Why or why not?

3. Adam Sirois, the holdout juror, said he felt "duped" after a district attorney explained that police did not videotape the first six hours of Hernandez's interrogation because it would be "disruptive to the process." Do you think this is a valid reason for Sirois to find Hernandez not guilty? Explain your answer.

Special Features of Criminal Trials

In 1979, Etan Patz's highly publicized disappearance changed many parents' attitudes about letting their children walk city streets alone. Etan's photo was one of the first to appear on a milk carton, and the date he vanished became National Missing Children's Day. It is not surprising, then, that both of Pedro Hernandez's trials attracted national attention. Those who followed the proceedings might have gotten a skewed version of how the criminal justice system works, however.

According to the *"wedding cake" model* of our court system, only the top, and smallest, "layer" of trials comes close to meeting constitutional standards of procedural justice.[1] In these celebrity trials, such as Hernandez's, committed (and expensive) attorneys argue minute technicalities for days, with numerous (and expensive) expert witnesses taking the stand for both sides. On the bottom, largest layer of the wedding cake, the vast majority of defendants are dealt with informally, and the end goal seems to be speed rather than justice. Indeed, misdemeanor cases comprise about 80 percent of criminal court dockets, and for these defendants "convictions are largely a function of being selected for arrest."[2]

Ideally, of course, criminal trial procedures are designed to protect *all* criminal defendants against the power of the state by providing them with a number of rights. Many of the significant rights of the accused are spelled out in the Sixth Amendment, which reads, in part, as follows:

> In all criminal prosecutions, the accused shall enjoy the right to a speedy and public trial, by an impartial jury of the State and the district wherein the crime shall have been committed, . . . and to be informed of the nature and cause of the accusation; to be confronted with the witnesses against him; to have compulsory process for obtaining witnesses in his favor; and to have the Assistance of Counsel for his defense.

Learning Objective 1 Identify the basic protections enjoyed by criminal defendants in the United States.

In the last chapter, we discussed the Sixth Amendment's guarantee of the right to counsel. In this section, we will examine the other important aspects of the criminal trial, beginning with two protections explicitly stated in the Sixth Amendment: the right to a speedy trial by an impartial jury.

A "Speedy" Trial

As you have just read, the Sixth Amendment requires a speedy trial for those accused of a criminal act. The reason for this requirement is obvious: Depending on various factors, the defendant may lose his or her right to move freely and may be incarcerated prior to trial. Also, the accusation that a person has committed a crime jeopardizes that person's reputation in the community. If the defendant is innocent, the sooner the trial is held, the sooner his or her innocence can be established in the eyes of the court and the public.

The Definition of a Speedy Trial
The Sixth Amendment does not specify what is meant by the term *speedy*. The United States Supreme Court has refused to quantify "speedy" as well, ruling instead in *Barker v. Wingo* (1972)[3] that only in situations in which the delay is unwarranted and proved to be prejudicial can the accused claim a violation of Sixth Amendment rights.

Speedy-Trial Laws
To meet constitutional requirements, all fifty states have their own speedy-trial statutes. For example, under New York law, a felony defendant must be tried within six months of arrest and a misdemeanor defendant must be tried within

either sixty days or ninety days of arrest, depending on the offense.[4] Keep in mind, however, that a defendant does not automatically go free if her or his trial is not "speedy" enough. For example, in 2016, despite the state law just cited, the average wait for a jury trial on a misdemeanor charge in the New York City borough of the Bronx was 827 days. None of the defendants affected were set free because of the delays, as unconstitutional as they may seem. That step would require judicial action, which was not forthcoming for the Bronx defendants.[5]

Nearly half of all criminal trials in state courts are settled within three months of the defendant's arrest. About 15 percent take more than a year to adjudicate.[6] At the national level, the Speedy Trial Act of 1974[7] (amended in 1979) specifies the following time limits for those in the federal court system:

1. No more than thirty days between arrest and indictment.
2. No more than ten days between indictment and arraignment.
3. No more than sixty days between arraignment and trial.

Both federal and state law allow extra time for hearings on pretrial motions, mental competency examinations, and other procedural actions. The resulting intervals can be considerable, particularly when it comes to high-profile trials. For example, in the case that opened this chapter, Pedro Hernandez's first trial started almost three years after he was arrested for murdering Etan Patz.

Statutes of Limitations   The Sixth Amendment's guarantee of a speedy trial does not apply until a person has been accused of a crime. Citizens are protected against unreasonable delays before accusation by **statutes of limitations.** These legislative time limits require prosecutors to charge a defendant with a crime within a certain amount of time after the illegal act took place. If the statute of limitations on a particular crime is ten years, and the police do not identify a suspect until ten years and one day after the criminal act occurred, then that suspect cannot be charged with that particular offense.

In general, murder and other offenses that carry the death penalty are not governed by statutes of limitations. This exception provides police with the ability to conduct cold case investigations that last for decades. The problem with prosecuting such cases, of course, is that so much time has passed since the criminal act that witnesses may be missing or dead, memories may be unreliable, and other evidence may have been lost. Despite such concerns, there is public support for extending or prohibiting statutes of limitations for sex-related crimes, the subject of the *Policy Matters* feature at the end of this chapter.

The Role of the Jury

The Sixth Amendment also states that anyone accused of a crime shall be judged by "an impartial jury." In *Duncan v. Louisiana* (1968),[8] the Supreme Court solidified this right by ruling that in all felony cases, the defendant is entitled to a **jury trial.** The Court has, however, left it to the individual states to decide whether juries are required for misdemeanor cases.[9] If the defendant waives her or his right to trial by jury, a **bench trial** takes place in which a judge decides questions of legality and fact, and no jury is involved.

Jury Size   The predominant American twelve-person jury is not the result of any one law—the Constitution does not require that the jury be a particular size. Historically, the number was inherited from the size of English juries, which was fixed at twelve during the fourteenth century.

Statutes of Limitations Laws limiting the amount of time prosecutors have to bring criminal charges against a suspect after the crime has occurred.

Jury Trial A trial before a judge and a jury.

Bench Trial A trial conducted without a jury, in which a judge makes the determination of the defendant's guilt or innocence.

In 1970, responding to a case that challenged Florida's practice of using a six-person jury in all but capital cases, the Supreme Court ruled that the accused did not have the right to be tried by a twelve-person jury. Indeed, the Court labeled the number twelve "a historical accident, wholly without significance except to mystics."[10]

In *Ballew v. Georgia* (1978),[11] however, the Court did strike down attempts to use juries with fewer than six members, stating that a jury's effectiveness was severely hampered below that limit. About half the states allow fewer than twelve persons on criminal juries, though rarely for serious felony cases. In federal courts, defendants are entitled to have the case heard by a twelve-member jury unless both parties agree in writing to a smaller jury.

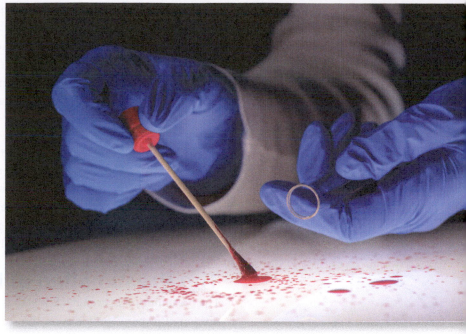

▲ The collection of DNA in hair, saliva, and, as shown here, blood, allows crime labs to more accurately and easily match a suspect to evidence at a crime scene. **What are the arguments for and against abolishing statutes of limitations for** *any* **crime in which DNA evidence is available?** igorstevanovic/Shutterstock.com

Unanimity In most jurisdictions, jury verdicts in criminal cases must be *unanimous* for acquittal or conviction. If the jury cannot reach unanimous agreement on whether to acquit or convict the defendant, the result is a *hung jury*. When this occurs, the prosecution has the option to retry the case, which is what happened with defendant Pedro Hernandez in the case discussed in the opening of this chapter.

The Supreme Court has held that unanimity is not a rigid requirement. It declared that jury verdicts must be unanimous in federal criminal trials, but has given states leeway to set their own rules.[12] As a result, Louisiana and Oregon continue to require only ten votes for conviction in criminal cases.

The Privilege against Self-Incrimination

In addition to the Sixth Amendment, which specifies the protections we have just discussed, the Fifth Amendment to the Constitution also provides important safeguards for the defendant. The Fifth Amendment states that no person "shall be compelled in any criminal case to be a witness against himself." Therefore, a defendant has the right not to testify at his or her own trial—in popular parlance, to "take the Fifth." Because defense attorneys often are wary of exposing their clients to prosecutor's questions in court, defendants rarely take the witness stand.

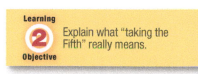

Learning Objective 2 Explain what "taking the Fifth" really means.

Prejudicing the Jury It is important to note not only that the defendant has the right to "take the Fifth," but also that the decision to do so should not prejudice the jury in the prosecution's favor. The Supreme Court came to this controversial conclusion while reviewing *Adamson v. California* (1947),[13] a case involving the convictions of two defendants who had declined to testify in their own defense against charges of robbery, kidnapping, and murder. The prosecutor in the *Adamson* proceedings frequently and insistently brought this silence to the notice of the jury in his closing argument, insinuating that if the pair had been innocent, they would not have been afraid to testify.

Acquittal A declaration following a trial that the individual accused of the crime is innocent in the eyes of the law and thus is absolved from the charges.

The Court ruled that such tactics effectively invalidated the Fifth Amendment by using the defendants' refusal to testify as a ploy to insinuate guilt. As a result, judges are required to inform the jury that an accused's decision to remain silent cannot be held against him or her. This protection only covers post-arrest and trial silence, however. In 2013, the Supreme Court ruled that prosecutors can inform a jury that a defendant refused to answer police questions *before* being arrested, a process detailed in Chapter 6.[14]

Witnesses in Court Witnesses are also protected by the Fifth Amendment and may refuse to testify on the ground that such testimony would reveal their own criminal wrongdoing. In practice, however, witnesses are sometimes granted *immunity* before testifying, meaning that no information they disclose can be used to bring criminal charges against them. Witnesses who have been granted immunity cannot refuse to answer questions in court on the basis of self-incrimination.

The Presumption of Innocence

The presumption in criminal law is that a defendant is innocent until proved guilty. The burden of proving guilt falls on the state (the public prosecutor). Even if a defendant did in fact commit the crime, she or he will be "innocent" in the eyes of the law unless the prosecutor can substantiate the charge with sufficient evidence to convince a jury (or judge, in a bench trial) of the defendant's guilt.

Sometimes, especially when a case involves a high-profile crime, pretrial publicity may have convinced many members of the community—including potential jurors—that a defendant is guilty. In these instances, a judge has the authority to change the venue of the trial to increase the likelihood of an unbiased jury. For example, the case of Justin Ross Harris, charged with intentionally killing his infant son by leaving the boy in the back seat of an overheated SUV, received intense local media scrutiny. As a result, a Cobb County, Georgia, judge moved Harris's 2016 trial to coastal Glynn County, about 275 miles south of Atlanta, where the alleged crime occurred.

"People in Atlanta think all of Georgia is paying attention to what happens in Atlanta," said one former state district attorney of the move. "But the rest of Georgia couldn't care less most of the time, especially about crime."[15] (The feature *Comparative Criminal Justice—Presumed Guilty* describes a system in which defendants do not receive the same procedural protections as defendants in the United States.)

A Strict Standard of Proof

In a criminal trial, the defendant is not required to prove his or her innocence. As mentioned earlier, the burden of proving the defendant's guilt lies entirely with the state. Furthermore, the state must prove the defendant's guilt *beyond a reasonable doubt*. In other words, the prosecution must show that, based on all the evidence, the defendant's guilt is clear and unquestionable. Explaining his reservations about Pedro Hernandez's guilt in the case that opened this chapter, holdout juror Adam Sirois said that, despite the defendant's confessions, "I could not get beyond reasonable doubt."[16]

In *In re Winship* (1970),[17] a case involving the due process rights of juveniles, the Supreme Court ruled that the Constitution requires the reasonable doubt standard because it reduces the risk of convicting innocent people and therefore reassures Americans of the law's moral force and legitimacy. This high standard of proof in criminal cases reflects a fundamental social value—the belief that it is worse to convict an innocent individual than to let a guilty one go free. The consequences to the life, liberty, and reputation

Presumed Guilty

The presumption of innocence is a cornerstone of criminal justice in the United States, but that has not traditionally been the case with its neighbor to the south. Under Mexico's long-established "inquisitorial model," trials are closed to the public. A single judge, rather than a jury, decides the defendant's fate, relying on written arguments and evidence presented by the prosecution and the defense. Indeed, Mexican judges often make decisions of innocence or guilt without ever seeing the defendant in court.

LACK OF CONFIDENCE

An estimated nine of every ten arrests in Mexico are made without the benefit of scientific evidence such as fingerprint or DNA matches. In six out of every ten cases, suspects are arrested within three hours of the crime, raising at least the possibility of hasty police work open to challenge by a defense attorney. Research conducted in 2012 by Mexico City's *Centro de Investigación y Docencia Económica*, however, found that 43 percent of those incarcerated for drug crimes in the country were not represented by a lawyer leading up to trial.

That same year, in a poll conducted by the Mexican Ministry of the Interior, only 6 percent of the respondents expressed confidence in the criminal justice system. This is one reason that Mexicans routinely fail to report criminal activity to the police. As a result, only 7 percent of crimes in Mexico are investigated, and fewer than 2 percent are solved.

FOR CRITICAL ANALYSIS

The Mexican criminal courts are presently undergoing major reforms. In the near future, all of the country's criminal trials will be open to the public, will be heard by a three-judge panel, and will feature oral arguments by attorneys on both sides. A stated goal of the changes is to ensure that those charged with crimes in Mexico are presumed innocent until proved guilty. In what ways might these reforms increase public confidence in the Mexican criminal justice system?

---

of an accused person from an erroneous conviction for a crime are substantial, and this has been factored into the process. Placing a high standard of proof on the prosecutor reduces the margin of error in criminal cases (at least in one direction).

Jury Selection

The initial step in a criminal trial involves choosing the jury. The framers of the Constitution ensured that the importance of the jury would not be easily overlooked. The right to a trial by jury is explicitly mentioned no fewer than three times in the Constitution: in Section 2 of Article III, in the Sixth Amendment, and again in the Seventh Amendment. The use of a peer jury not only provided safeguards against the abuses of state power that the framers feared, but also gave Americans a chance—and a duty—to participate in the criminal justice system.

In the early years of the country, a jury "of one's peers" meant a jury limited to white, landowning males. Now, as the process has become fully democratized, there are still questions about what "a jury of one's peers" actually means and how effective the system has been in providing the necessary diversity in juries.

Initial Steps:
The Master Jury List and *Venire*

The main goal of jury selection is to produce a cross section of the population in the jurisdiction where the crime was committed. As we saw earlier, sometimes a defense attorney may argue that his or her client's trial should be moved to another community to protect against undue prejudice. In practice, judges, mindful of the intent of the Constitution, are hesitant to grant such pretrial motions.

A Jury of Peers

The belief that trials should take place in the community where the crime was committed is central to the purpose of selecting a jury of the defendant's "peers." The United States is a large, diverse nation, and the outlook of its citizens varies accordingly. Two very different cases, one tried in rural Maine and the other in San Francisco, illustrate this point.[18]

In Maine, the defendant had accidentally shot and killed a woman standing in her backyard because he had mistaken her white mittens for a deer's tail. His attorney argued that it was the responsibility of the victim to wear bright-colored clothing in the vicinity of hunters during hunting season. The jury agreed, and the defendant was acquitted of manslaughter. In the San Francisco case, two people were charged with distributing sterile needles to intravenous drug users. Rather than denying that the defendants had distributed the needles, the defense admitted the act but insisted that it was necessary to stem the transmission of AIDS and, thus, to save lives. The jury voted 11–1 to acquit, causing a mistrial.

These two outcomes may surprise or even anger people in other parts of the country, but they reflect the values of the regions where the alleged crimes were committed. Thus, a primary goal of the jury selection process is to ensure that the defendant is judged by members of her or his community—peers in the true sense of the word.

The Master Jury List

Besides having to live in the jurisdiction where the case is being tried, there are very few restrictions on eligibility to serve on a jury. State legislatures generally set the requirements, and they are similar in most states. For the most part, jurors must be

1. Citizens of the United States.
2. Eighteen years of age or over.
3. Free of felony convictions.
4. Healthy enough to function in a jury setting.
5. Sufficiently intelligent to understand the issues of a trial.
6. Able to read, write, and comprehend the English language (with one exception— New Mexico does not allow non-English-speaking citizens to be eliminated from jury lists simply because of their lack of English-language skills).

▼ A Boston jury waits to be dismissed after finding Christian K. Gerhartsreiter guilty of kidnapping his seven-year-old daughter during a supervised visit. **Why is it important for a defendant to be tried by a jury of her or his "peers"?** AP Images/CJ Gunther

The **master jury list,** sometimes called the *jury pool*, is made up of all the eligible jurors in a community. This list is usually drawn from voter-registration lists or driver's license rolls, which have the benefit of being easily available and up-to-date.

Venire   The next step in gathering a jury is to draw together the **venire** (Latin for "to come"). The *venire* is composed of all those people who are notified by the clerk of the court that they have been selected for jury duty. Those selected to be part of the *venire* are ordered to report to the courthouse on the date specified by the notice.

Some people are excused from answering this summons. Persons who do not meet the qualifications just listed either need not appear in court or, in some states, must appear only in order to be officially dismissed by court officials. Also, people in some professions, including teachers, physicians, and judges, can receive exemptions due to the nature of their work. Each court sets its own guidelines for the circumstances under which it will excuse jurors from service, and these guidelines can be as strict or as lenient as the court desires.

Voir Dire

At the courthouse, prospective jurors are gathered, and the process of selecting those who will actually hear the case begins. This selection process is not haphazard. The court ultimately seeks jurors who are free of any biases that may affect their willingness to listen to the facts of the case impartially. To this end, both the prosecutor and the defense attorney have some input into the ultimate makeup of the jury. Each attorney questions prospective jurors in a proceeding known as **voir dire** (French for "to speak the truth"). During *voir dire*, jurors are required to provide the court with a significant amount of personal information, including home address, marital status, employment status, arrest record, and life experiences.

Questioning Potential Jurors   The *voir dire* process involves both written and oral questioning of potential jurors. Attorneys fashion their inquiries in such a manner as to uncover any biases on the parts of prospective jurors and to find persons who might identify with the plights of their respective sides. As one attorney noted, though a lawyer will have many chances to talk to a jury as a whole, *voir dire* is his or her only chance to talk with the individual jurors. (To better understand the specific kinds of questions asked during this process, see Figure 10.1.)

FIGURE 10.1 **Sample Juror Questionnaire**

In the murder trial of Pedro Hernandez, featured at the beginning of the chapter, defense attorneys planned to show that their client's mental problems made him particularly susceptible to giving police a false confession. Therefore, as the following excerpts from the juror questionnaire shows, the lawyers were interested in learning potential jurors' views on the subject of mental illness.

87. Have you, a family member, or a close friend ever seen a mental health professional, therapist, or counselor for emotional, psychological, or psychiatric difficulties?

89. Have you, a family member, or a close friend ever taken medication for psychiatric, psychological, or emotional difficulties?

93. Do you recall reading any books, magazines, or newspaper articles or seeing any television programs or movies about psychiatrists, psychologists, or other mental health professionals?

94. Is there anything about your answers to [these] questions that makes you believe you cannot be a fair and impartial juror in this matter?

Source: Supreme Court of the State of New York, County of New York

Master Jury List The list of citizens in a court's district from which a jury can be selected; compiled from voter-registration lists, driver's license lists, and other sources.

Venire The group of citizens from which the jury is selected.

Voir Dire The preliminary questions that the trial attorneys ask prospective jurors to determine whether they are biased or have any connection with the defendant or a witness.

A potential juror's failure to be forthcoming during *voir dire* can have serious consequences. Several years ago, after Cory Batey and Brandon Vandenburg were convicted of sexually assaulting a woman on the campus of Vanderbilt University in Nashville, Tennessee, a judge nullified the results of the trial. One of the jurors, it turned out, had failed to disclose that he had been a victim of sex crimes as a teenager. Judge Monte D. Watkins decided that this omission raised a presumption of bias on the juror's part, and ordered that both defendants be retried.[19]

Challenging Potential Jurors

During *voir dire*, the attorney for each side may exercise a certain number of challenges to prevent particular persons from serving on the jury. Both sides can exercise two types of challenges: challenges "for cause" and peremptory challenges.

Challenges for Cause   If a defense attorney or prosecutor concludes that a prospective juror is unfit to serve, the attorney may exercise a **challenge for cause** and request that that person not be included on the jury. Attorneys must provide the court with a sound, legally justifiable reason for why potential jurors are "unfit" to serve. For example, jurors can be challenged for cause if they are mentally incompetent or are proved to have a prior link—be it personal or financial—with the defendant or victim.

Jurors can also be challenged if they express opinions that would prejudice them for or against the defendant. In addition, the Supreme Court has ruled that individuals may be legally excluded from a jury in a capital case if they would under no circumstances vote for a guilty verdict if it carried the death penalty.[20] At the same time, potential jurors cannot be challenged for cause if they have "general objections" or have "expressed conscientious or religious scruples" against capital punishment.[21] The final responsibility for deciding whether a potential juror should be excluded rests with the judge, who may choose not to act on an attorney's request.

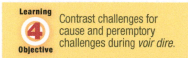

Learning Objective 4 — Contrast challenges for cause and peremptory challenges during *voir dire*.

Peremptory Challenges   Each attorney may also exercise a limited number of **peremptory challenges.** These challenges are based solely on an attorney's subjective reasoning, and the attorney usually is not required to give any legally justifiable reason for wanting to exclude a particular person from the jury. Because of the rather random nature of peremptory challenges, each state limits the number that an attorney may utilize: between five and ten for felony trials (depending on the state) and between ten and twenty for trials that could possibly result in the death penalty (also depending on the state). Once an attorney's peremptory challenges are used up, he or she must accept forthcoming jurors, unless a challenge for cause can be used.

An attorney's decision to exclude a juror may sometimes seem whimsical. One state prosecutor who litigated drug cases was known to use a peremptory challenge whenever he saw a potential juror with a coffee mug or backpack bearing the insignia of the local public broadcasting station. The attorney presumed that this was evidence that the potential juror had donated funds to the public station, and that anybody who would do so would be too "liberal" to give the government's case against a drug offender a favorable hearing.[22] Lawyers have been known to similarly reject potential jurors for reasons of demeanor, dress, and posture.

Jury Consultants

To ensure that the jury is as sympathetic to their clients as possible, trial lawyers sometimes will hire a *jury selection consultant* to help with the *voir dire* process. These experts provide a number of services, from investigating the background of potential jurors to running mock trials that assist in determining what types of jurors will be most likely to provide the desired outcome.[23] As you might imagine, these services can be quite expensive, with fees reaching tens of thousands of dollars. A less costly alternative for attorneys is to conduct their own research by scouring Facebook, Snapchat, and Twitter for valuable information on potential jurors' media habits, interests, hobbies, and religious affiliations.

Race and Gender Issues in Jury Selection

For many years, prosecutors used their peremptory challenges as an instrument of segregation in jury selection. Prosecutors were able to keep African Americans off juries in cases in which an African American was the defendant. The argument that African Americans—or members of any other minority group—would be partial toward one of their own was tacitly supported by the Supreme Court. Despite its own assertion, made in *Swain v. Alabama* (1965),[24] that blacks have the same right to appear on a jury as whites, the Court mirrored the apparent racism of society as a whole by protecting the questionable actions of many prosecutors.

The *Batson* Reversal The Supreme Court reversed this policy in 1986 with *Batson v. Kentucky*.[25] In that case, the Court declared that the Constitution prohibits prosecutors from using peremptory challenges to strike possible jurors on the basis of race. Under the *Batson* ruling, the defendant must prove that the prosecution's use of a peremptory challenge was racially motivated. Doing so requires a number of legal steps:[26]

1. First, the defendant must make a *prima facie* case that there has been discrimination during *venire*. (*Prima facie* is Latin for "at first sight." Legally, it refers to a fact that is presumed to be true unless contradicted by evidence.)
2. To do so, the defendant must show that he or she is a member of a recognizable racial group and that the prosecutor has used peremptory challenges to remove members of this group from the jury pool.
3. Then, the defendant must show that these facts and other relevant circumstances raise the possibility that the prosecutor removed the prospective jurors solely because of their race.
4. If the court accepts the defendant's charges, the burden shifts to the prosecution to prove that its peremptory challenges were race neutral. If the court finds against the prosecution, it rules that a *Batson* violation has occurred.

The Court has revisited the issue of race a number of times in the years since its *Batson* decision. In *Powers v. Ohio* (1991),[27] it ruled that a defendant may contest race-based peremptory challenges even if the defendant is not of the same race as the excluded jurors. In *Georgia v. McCollum* (1992),[28] the Court placed defense attorneys under the same restrictions as prosecutors when making race-based peremptory challenges.

Continuing Concerns In 2016, the Court reaffirmed its *Batson* decision of thirty years earlier, overturning the conviction of an African American death row inmate because Georgia prosecutors had improperly picked an all-white jury for his murder trial.[29] As reflected by the Court's nearly unanimous decision, the evidence of bias in this case was fairly obvious.

Collins E. Ijoma Trial Court Administrator

As the trial court administrator, I serve principally as the chief administrative officer for the largest trial and municipal court system in New Jersey. We provide technical and managerial support to the court (more than sixty superior court judges and thirty-six municipal court judges) on such matters as personnel, program development, case flow, resources, and facilities management. This description may sound "highfalutin" considering that most people can only describe a

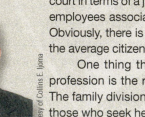

court in terms of a judge, one or two courtroom staff, and a few other employees associated with the visible activities in the courthouse. Obviously, there is a lot more going on behind the scenes of which the average citizen is not aware.

One thing that keeps me going and enthused about this profession is the resolve and dedication of our judges and staff. The family division embraces a host of issues, and in some cases those who seek help are hurting and desperate. The court may be their only hope.

Courtesy of Collins E. Ijoma

SOCIAL MEDIA CAREER TIP Many businesses and organizations have their own career websites for potential employees. Some have even set up *talent communities* to interact with applicants. Explore these options if you have a specific job in mind.

For example, during *voir dire*, the prosecutors marked the names of black prospective jurors with a "B" and highlighted those names in green. One prospective thirty-four-year-old African American juror was removed for the supposedly race-neutral reason that she was too close in age to the eighteen-year-old defendant. However, prosecutors failed to strike eight white prospective jurors who were younger than thirty-six. One of them, a twenty-one-year-old woman, made it onto the jury.[30]

Rulings of this kind do not mean that a black defendant can never be judged by a jury made up entirely of whites. Rather, they indicate that attorneys cannot use peremptory challenges to reject a prospective juror because of her or his race. And in spite of such rulings, there is evidence that African Americans are still being kept off juries, particularly in parts of the South.[31] "Anyone with any sense at all can think up a race-neutral reason [to exclude a potential minority juror] and get away with it," says Atlanta defense attorney Stephen B. Bright.[32]

Women on the Jury

In *J.E.B. v. Alabama ex rel. T.B.* (1994),[33] the Supreme Court extended the principles of the *Batson* ruling to cover gender bias in jury selection. The case was a civil suit for paternity and child support brought by the state of Alabama. Prosecutors used nine of their ten challenges to remove men from the jury, while the defense made similar efforts to remove women. When challenged, the state defended its actions by referring to what it called the rational belief that men and women might have different views on the issues of paternity and child support. The Court disagreed and held this approach to be unconstitutional.

Alternate Jurors

Because unforeseeable circumstances or illness may necessitate that one or more of the sitting jurors be dismissed, the court may also seat several *alternate jurors* who will hear the entire trial. Depending on the rules of the particular jurisdiction, two or three alternate jurors may be present throughout the trial. If a juror has to be excused in the middle of the trial, an alternate may take his or her place without disrupting the proceedings.

The Trial

Once the jury members have been selected, the judge swears them in and the trial itself can begin. (See Figure 10.2 for a preview of the stages of a jury trial that will be detailed in this section.) A rather pessimistic truism among attorneys is that every case "has been won or lost when the jury is sworn." This reflects the belief that jurors' values are the major, if not dominant, factor in the decision of guilt or innocence.[34]

In actuality, it is difficult to predict how a jury will go about reaching a decision. Despite a number of studies on the question, researchers have not been able to identify any definitive consistent patterns of jury behavior. Sometimes, jurors in a criminal trial will follow instructions to find a defendant guilty unless there is a reasonable doubt, and sometimes they seem to follow instinct or prejudice and apply the law any way they choose.

Learning **5** **Objective** List the standard steps in a criminal jury trial.

FIGURE 10.2 **The Steps of a Jury Trial**

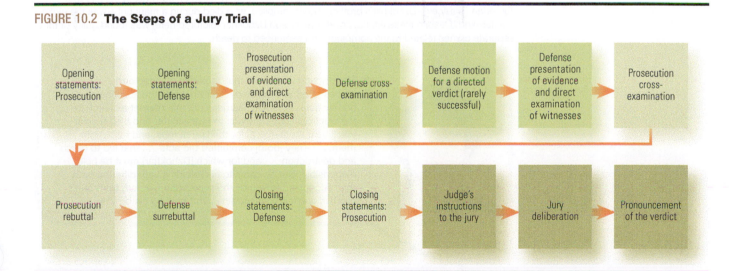

Opening Statements

Attorneys may choose to open the trial with a statement to the jury, though they are not required to do so. In these opening statements, the attorneys give a brief version of the facts and the supporting evidence that they will present during the trial. Because some trials can last for weeks or even months, it is extremely helpful for jurors to hear a summary of what will unfold. In short, the opening statement is a kind of "road map" that describes the destination that each attorney hopes to reach and outlines how she or he plans to reach it.

The danger for attorneys is that they will offer evidence during the trial that might contradict an assertion made during the opening statement. This may cause jurors to disregard the evidence or shift their own thinking further away from the narrative being offered by the attorney.[35] (For an example of an opening statement, see Figure 10.3.)

The Role of Evidence

Once the opening statements have been made, the prosecutor begins the trial proceedings by presenting the state's *evidence* against the defendant. Evidence is anything that is used to prove the existence or nonexistence of a fact. Courts have complex rules about what types of evidence may be presented and how the evidence may be brought out during the trial. For the most part, evidence can be broken down into two categories: testimony and real evidence. Testimony consists of statements by competent witnesses. Real evidence, presented to the court in the form of exhibits, includes any physical items—such as the murder weapon or a bloodstained piece of clothing—that affect the case.

Rules of evidence are designed to ensure that testimony and exhibits presented to the jury are relevant, reliable, and not unfairly prejudicial against the defendant. One of the tasks of the defense attorney is to challenge evidence presented by the prosecution by establishing that the evidence is not reliable. Of course, the prosecutor also tries to demonstrate the irrelevance or unreliability of evidence presented by the defense. The final decision on whether evidence is allowed before the jury rests with the judge, in keeping with his or her role as the "referee" of the adversary system.

FIGURE 10.3 **The Opening Statement**

At Dzhokhar Tsarnaev's trial for his role in the 2013 Boston Marathon bombings, his defense team admitted their client's guilt while at the same time trying to lessen his punishment. As this opening statement by defense attorney Judy Clarke shows, the strategy relied on convincing the jury that Tamerlan Tsarnaev—Dzhokhar's brother and accomplice, who died during a manhunt—was the plot's mastermind. Despite these efforts, several years ago Dzhokhar (pictured here) was found guilty of thirty separate crimes related to the bombings and sentenced to death.

The evidence will show that Tamerlan planned and orchestrated and enlisted his brother into these series of horrific acts. Tamerlan Tsarnaev did the Internet research on the electronic components, the transmitter and the receiver you'll hear more about, for the two bombs, and he bought them. . . . They [both] committed the acts . . . that led to death and destruction . . . and for which [Dzhokhar] must be held responsible. But he came to his role by a very different path than suggested to you by the prosecution: a path born of his brother, created by his brother, and paid by his brother.

FBI/Getty Images News/Getty Images

Source: United States District Court for the District of Massachusetts

Testimonial Evidence　A person who is called to testify on factual matters that would be understood by the average citizen is referred to as a **lay witness.** If asked about the condition of a victim of an assault, for example, a lay witness could relate certain facts, such as "she was bleeding from her forehead" or "she was unconscious on the ground for several minutes." A lay witness could not, however, give information about the medical extent of the victim's injuries, such as whether she suffered from a fractured skull or internal bleeding. Coming from a lay witness, such testimony would be inadmissible.

Expert Witnesses　When the matter in question requires scientific, medical, or technical skill beyond the scope of the average person, prosecutors and defense attorneys may call an **expert witness** to the stand. The expert witness is an individual who has professional training, advanced knowledge, or substantial experience in a specialized area, such as medicine, computer technology, or ballistics. The rules of evidence state that expert witnesses may base their opinions on three types of information:

1. Facts or data of which they have personal knowledge.
2. Material presented at trial.
3. Secondhand information given to the expert outside the courtroom.[36]

Expert witnesses are considered somewhat problematic for two reasons. First, they may be chosen for their "court presence"—whether they speak well or will appear sympathetic to the jury—rather than their expertise. Second, attorneys pay expert witnesses for their services. Given human nature, the attorneys expect a certain measure of cooperation from an expert they have hired, and an expert witness has an interest in satisfying the attorneys so that he or she will be hired again.[37] Under these circumstances, some have questioned whether the courts can rely on the professional nonpartisanship of expert witnesses.[38]

Challenging Expert Testimony　If a trial lawyer wants to challenge an expert witness's validity or reliability, he or she must follow guidelines established by a Supreme Court decision from 1993. These guidelines call on the judge to determine whether the technique on which the expert witness is relying has been accepted by the scientific community at large.[39] Such challenges are fairly commonplace and have been used to question expert analysis of DNA evidence and polygraph tests.

This procedure has also been employed in efforts to undermine the legitimacy of fingerprint matches. The predominant method of fingerprint identification, known as ACE-V (Analysis Comparison Evaluation Verification), relies on infrared or X-ray imaging of secretions from the body to produce fingerprint matches. If these samples are incomplete or in some way damaged, a faulty match between the print lifted from a crime scene and that of a suspect may result. Several scientific studies have shown that fingerprint matching is not infallible, though error rates are quite low at less than 1 percent.[40]

Because of such small error rates, challenges to the reliability of fingerprint matches almost always fail.[41] Defense attorneys have, however, had success questioning the link between their clients and fingerprints found on movable objects. In these cases, since prosecutors cannot prove *when* a fingerprint was left on an object, courts have found that a match does not prove the defendant's presence at a crime scene beyond a reasonable doubt.[42]

Direct versus Circumstantial Evidence　Two types of testimonial evidence may be brought into court: direct evidence and circumstantial evidence. **Direct evidence** is evidence that has been witnessed by the person giving testimony. "I saw Bill

Lay Witness A witness who can truthfully and accurately testify on a fact in question without having specialized training or knowledge.

Expert Witness A witness with professional training or substantial experience qualifying her or him to testify on a certain subject.

Direct Evidence Evidence that establishes the existence of a fact that is in question without relying on inference.

Learning 6 Objective Describe the difference between direct and circumstantial evidence, and explain why evidence of a defendant's "evil character" is often excluded from trial.

shoot Chris" is an example of direct evidence. **Circumstantial evidence** is indirect evidence that, even if believed, does not establish the fact in question but only the degree of likelihood of the fact. In other words, circumstantial evidence can create an inference that a fact exists.

Suppose, for example, that the defendant owns a gun that shoots bullets of the type found in the victim's body. This circumstantial evidence, by itself, does not establish that the defendant committed the crime. Combined with other circumstantial evidence, however, it may do just that. For instance, if other circumstantial evidence indicates that the defendant had a motive for harming the victim and was at the scene of the crime when the shooting occurred, the jury might conclude that the defendant committed the crime.

The "CSI Effect"

When possible, defense attorneys will almost always make the argument that the state has failed to present any evidence other than circumstantial evidence against their client. This tactic has been aided by a phenomenon known as the "CSI effect," taking its name from the popular television series *CSI: Crime Scene Investigation* and its spin-offs. Apparently, these shows have fostered unrealistic notions among jurors as to what high-tech forensic science can accomplish as part of a criminal investigation. In reality, the kind of physical evidence used to solve crimes on television programs like *CSI* is often not available to the prosecution, which must rely instead on witnesses and circumstantial evidence.

To test the CSI effect, researchers from several Virginia universities interviewed sixty jurors who had just heard cases involving the crime of malicious wounding. Ninety-five percent of these jurors reported that they watched *CSI*, and 60 percent of the jurors said that they believed the scientific methods depicted on the show accurately represented the forensic techniques used by real-life police investigators. The survey also found that a juror's belief in the authenticity of the *CSI* shows was a "significant predictor" that they would vote to acquit the defendant.[43]

Relevance

Evidence will not be admitted in court unless it is relevant to the case being considered. **Relevant evidence** is evidence that tends to prove or disprove a fact in question. Forensic proof that the bullets found in a victim's body were fired from a gun discovered in the suspect's pocket at the time of arrest, for example, is certainly relevant. The suspect's prior record, showing a conviction for armed robbery ten years earlier, is, as we shall soon see, irrelevant to the case at hand and in most instances will be ruled inadmissible by the judge.

Prejudicial Evidence

Evidence may be excluded if it would tend to distract the jury from the main issues of the case, mislead the jury, or cause jurors to decide the issue on an emotional basis. For example, several years ago, during the murder trial of former professional football player Aaron Hernandez, Judge Susan Garsh ruled that texts sent by Odin Lloyd, the victim, to his sister on the night of Odin's death were inadmissible. The texts read, "U saw who I'm with," and "NFL [National Football League]," referring to Hernandez. Judge Garsh kept this evidence from the jury because the texts suggested, without proof, that Lloyd was warning his sister that Hernandez was responsible for any harm that might befall him that night.[44]

Evil Character Defense attorneys are likely to have some success precluding prosecutors from using prior purported criminal activities or actual convictions to show that the defendant has criminal propensities or an "evil character."[45] During the trial of Aaron

Circumstantial Evidence Indirect evidence that is offered to establish, by inference, the likelihood of a fact that is in question.

Relevant Evidence Evidence tending to make a fact in question more or less probable than it would be without the evidence. Only relevant evidence is admissible in court.

Hernandez, mentioned earlier, the prosecution was denied the opportunity to tell the jury that the defendant faced a civil lawsuit for shooting another friend following an argument in a South Florida nightclub two years earlier. "This case is about Odin Lloyd and no one else," said Hernandez's defense attorney while arguing against the introduction of this evidence.[46]

Concerns of this kind are codified in the Federal Rules of Evidence, which state that evidence of "other crimes, wrongs, or acts is not admissible to prove the character of a person in order to show action in conformity therewith." Such evidence is allowed only when it does not apply to character construction and focuses instead on "motive, opportunity, intent, preparation, plan, knowledge, identity, or absence of mistake or accident."[47]

Although this legal concept has come under a great deal of criticism, it is consistent with the presumption-of-innocence standards discussed earlier. Arguably, if a prosecutor is allowed to establish that the defendant has shown antisocial or even violent traits in the past, this will prejudice the jury against the defendant in the present trial. Even if the judge instructs jurors that this prior evidence is irrelevant, human nature dictates that it will probably have a "warping influence" on the jurors' perception of the defendant.[48] Therefore, whenever possible, defense attorneys will keep such evidence from the jury.

▲ Several years ago, Aaron Hernandez—shown here in a Bristol County, Massachusetts, courtroom—was found guilty of fatally shooting Odin Lloyd and sentenced to life in prison without parole. During his trial, Judge Susan Garsh ruled that a photograph from the celebrity gossip website TMZ that depicted Hernandez holding a gun was inadmissible as evidence. **Why do you think the judge made this decision?** John Tlumacki/*The Boston Globe*/Getty Images

Evidence of the Victim's Behavior Along these same lines, courts frown on the defense practice of portraying the victim in a negative light. In one case, for example, a judge banned school records showing that the alleged murder victim had been suspended from high school for marijuana possession.[49] Such evidence, it can be argued, not only is irrelevant, but also implies that the victim somehow deserved her or his fate.

Nonetheless, in sexual assault cases, defense attorneys have found that if they can get evidence of the defendant's prior behavior into court, they have a greater chance of acquittal. Historically, because of a pervasive attitude labeled the "chastity requirement" by one observer, rape victims who were perceived to be sexually virtuous were much more likely to be believed by jurors than those who had been sexually active.[50] If a woman had consented to sex before, so the line of thought went, she was more likely to do so again.

Consequently, defense attorneys focused on the accuser's sexual past, convincing juries that consent had been given in the present instance by establishing a pattern of consent in past ones. As the feature *Myth vs. Reality—Rape Shield Laws* suggests, extensive legislative efforts to reverse this trend and make the courtroom "safe" for rape victims have been largely, if not entirely, successful.

The Prosecution's Case

Because the burden of proof is on the state, the prosecution is generally considered to have a more difficult task than the defense. The prosecutor attempts to establish guilt beyond a reasonable doubt by presenting the *corpus delicti* (Latin for "body of the offense") of the crime to the jury. *Corpus delicti* is a legal term that refers to the substantial facts that show a crime has been committed. By establishing such facts through the presentation of relevant and nonprejudicial evidence, the prosecutor hopes to convince the jury of the defendant's guilt.

Rape Shield Laws

The Myth Criminal statutes of every state and the federal government include rape shield laws meant to keep evidence about a victim's reputation and previous sexual conduct out of the courtroom. Consequently, victims of sex crimes can report these crimes to the police secure in the knowledge that their private lives will not be exposed in court for public consumption.

The Reality In most instances, rape shield laws have blocked defense attorneys from using an accuser's sexual past to create doubt concerning consent in the case at hand. Rape shield laws do, however, contain certain exceptions that allow the defense to use evidence of the accuser's prior sexual conduct to undermine the credibility of his or her testimony.

For example, Federal Rule 412 states that evidence of "other sexual behavior" or the "sexual disposition" of a rape complainant is inadmissible *except* in specified situations. The evidence may be admitted if it is offered to prove that a person other than the accused was the source of semen, injury, or other physical evidence. In addition, evidence of specific instances of the victim's sexual behavior with respect to the defendant may be admitted. Finally, the defense must show that the exclusion of the evidence would violate the constitutional rights of the defendant to confront his or her accuser.

FOR CRITICAL ANALYSIS

A woman accuses two men of raping her in the back seat of a car. Both defendants claim that the sexual activity was consensual. At their trial, the defendants want to present the following evidence from that night: (1) a fourth person had witnessed the accuser flirting aggressively with numerous men at a local bar; (2) the accuser had openly tried to seduce the older brother of one of the defendants; and (3) another witness had seen the accuser sitting on a soda crate in front of the defendants, one of whom was zipping up his pants. Given the goals of rape shield laws and the exceptions discussed in this feature, which evidence, if any, concerning the above incident should be admitted before the jury? Why?

Direct Examination of Witnesses Witnesses are crucial to establishing the prosecutor's case against the defendant. The prosecutor will call witnesses to the stand and ask them questions pertaining to the sequence of events that the trial is addressing. This form of questioning is known as **direct examination.** During direct examination, the prosecutor will usually not be allowed to ask *leading questions*— questions that might suggest to the witness a particular desired response.

A leading question might be something like "So, Mrs. Williams, you noticed the defendant threatening the victim with a broken beer bottle?" If Mrs. Williams answers "yes" to this question, she has, in effect, been "led" to the conclusion that the defendant was, in fact, threatening with a broken beer bottle. The fundamental purpose behind testimony is to establish what actually happened, not what the trial attorneys would like the jury to believe happened. (A properly worded query would be, "Mrs. Williams, please describe the defendant's manner toward the victim during the incident.")

Competence and Reliability of Witnesses The rules of evidence include certain restrictions and qualifications pertaining to witnesses. Witnesses must have sufficient mental competence to understand the significance of testifying under oath. They must also be reliable in the sense that they are able to give a clear and sound description of the events in question. If not, the prosecutor or defense attorney will make sure that the jury is aware of these shortcomings through *cross-examination.*

Direct Examination The examination of a witness by the attorney who calls the witness to the stand to testify.

Confrontation Clause The part of the Sixth Amendment that guarantees all defendants the right to confront witnesses testifying against them during the criminal trial.

Cross-Examination The questioning of an opposing witness during trial.

Cross-Examination

After the prosecutor has directly examined her or his witnesses, the defense attorney is given the chance to question these witnesses. The Sixth Amendment states, "In all criminal prosecutions, the accused shall enjoy the right . . . to be confronted with witnesses against him." This **confrontation clause** gives the accused, through his or her attorneys, the right to cross-examine witnesses. **Cross-examination** refers to the questioning of an opposing witness during trial, and both sides of a case are allowed to conduct cross-examination.

Questioning Witnesses Cross-examination allows the attorneys to test the truthfulness of opposing witnesses and usually entails efforts to create doubt in the jurors' minds that a witness is reliable (see Figure 10.4). After the defense has cross-examined a prosecution witness, the prosecutor may want to reestablish any reliability that might have been lost. The prosecutor can do so by again questioning the witness, a process known as *redirect examination*. Following the redirect examination, the defense attorney will be given the opportunity to ask further questions of prosecution witnesses, or *recross examination*. Thus, each side has two opportunities to question a witness. The attorneys need not do so, but only after each side has been offered the opportunity will the trial move on to the next witness or the next stage.

Hearsay Cross-examination is also linked to problems presented by *hearsay* evidence. **Hearsay** can be defined as any testimony given about a statement made by someone else. An example of hearsay would be: "Jenny told me that Bill told her that he was the killer." Literally, it is what someone heard someone else say. For the most part, hearsay is not admissible as evidence. When a witness offers hearsay, the person making the original remarks is not in court and therefore cannot be cross-examined. If such testimony were allowed, the defendant's Sixth Amendment right to confront witnesses against him or her would be violated.

There are a number of exceptions to the hearsay rule, and as a result a good deal of hearsay evidence finds its way into criminal trials. For example, a hearsay statement is usually admissible if there seems to be little risk of a lie. Therefore, a statement made by someone who believes that his or her death is imminent—a "dying declaration" or a suicide note—is often allowed in court even though it is hearsay.[51] Similarly, the rules of most states allow hearsay when the statement contains an admission of wrongdoing *and* the speaker is not available to testify in court. The logic behind this exception is that a person generally does not make a statement against her or his own best interests unless it is true.[52]

> **Hearsay** An oral or written statement made by an out-of-court speaker that is later offered in court by a witness (not the speaker) concerning a matter before the court.

FIGURE 10.4 The Cross-Examination

During Michael Dunn's trial for the murder of Jordan Davis outside a convenience store in Jacksonville, Florida, the defendant claimed he had fatally shot Davis in self-defense. Crucially, Dunn insisted that Davis had pointed a shotgun at him, though no such weapon was found at the crime scene. When Dunn took the stand, the prosecution cross-examined him about what he said to his fiancée, Rhonda Rouer, following the shooting.

Prosecutor: How did you describe the weapon [to her]? Did you say [Davis and his friends] had a sword? Did you say they had a machete?

Dunn: Gun.

Prosecutor: A gun. You used the word "gun"?

Dunn: Multiple times.

Later in the trial, the prosecution called Rouer (pictured here) as a witness. In her testimony, she stated that Dunn never mentioned that he had been threatened with a shotgun, or any other kind of weapon, during the confrontation. Dunn was convicted of first degree murder and sentenced to life in prison without parole.

AP Images/*Florida Times-Union*, Bob Mack

Motion for a Directed Verdict

After the prosecutor has finished presenting evidence against the defendant, the government will inform the court that it has rested the people's case. At this point, the defense may make a motion for a directed verdict (also known as a *motion for judgment as a matter of law* in federal courts). Through this motion, the defense is basically saying that the prosecution has not offered enough evidence to prove that the accused is guilty beyond a reasonable doubt. If the judge grants this motion, which rarely occurs, then a judgment will be entered in favor of the defendant, and the trial is over.

The Defendant's Case

Assuming that the motion for a directed verdict is denied, the defense attorney may offer the defendant's case. Because the burden is on the state to prove the accused's guilt, the defense is not required to offer any case at all. It can simply "rest" without calling any witnesses or producing any real evidence, and ask the jury to decide the merits of the case on what it has seen and heard from the prosecution.

Placing the Defendant on the Stand

If the defense does present a case, its first—and often most important—decision is whether the defendant will take the stand in her or his own defense. Because of the Fifth Amendment protection against self-incrimination, the defendant is not required to testify.

Therefore, the defense attorney must make a judgment call. He or she may want to put the defendant on the stand if the defendant is likely to appear sympathetic to the jury, or is well spoken and able to aid the defense's case. With a less sympathetic or less effective defendant, the defense attorney may decide that exposing the defendant before the jury presents too large a risk. Also, if the defendant testifies, she or he is open to cross-examination under oath from the prosecutor.

Creating a Reasonable Doubt

Defense lawyers most commonly defend their clients by attempting to expose weaknesses in the prosecutor's case. Remember that if the defense attorney can create reasonable doubt concerning the client's guilt in the mind of just a single juror, the defendant has a good chance of gaining an acquittal or at least a *hung jury*, a circumstance explained later in the chapter.

Even if the prosecution can present seemingly strong evidence, a defense attorney may succeed by creating reasonable doubt. In an illustrative case, Jason Korey bragged to his friends that he had shot and killed Joseph Brucker in Pittsburgh, Pennsylvania, and a great deal of circumstantial evidence linked Korey to the killing. The police, however, could find no direct evidence. They could not link Korey to the murder weapon, nor could they match his footprints to those found at the crime scene. Michael Foglia, Korey's defense attorney, explained his client's bragging as an attempt to gain attention, not a true statement. Though this explanation may strike some as unlikely, in the absence of physical evidence it did create doubt in the jurors' minds, and Korey was acquitted. (For a better idea of how this strategy works in court, see the feature *Discretion in Action— Shadow of a Doubt?*)

Other Defense Strategies

The defense can choose among a number of strategies to generate reasonable doubt in the jurors' minds. It can present an *alibi defense*, by submitting evidence that the accused was not at or near the scene of the crime at the time the crime was committed. Another option is to attempt an *affirmative defense*,

DISCRETION IN ACTION

Shadow of a Doubt?

The Situation Twelve-year-old Garrett was killed in his mother's apartment moments after he returned from a nearby afternoon basketball game. The boy screamed for help, according to neighbors, before being strangled to death. Oral, the local soccer coach, is eventually charged with Garrett's murder. Oral insists he is innocent. No direct evidence—such as fingerprints, trace DNA samples, or witnesses—places Oral at the crime scene.

In court, prosecutors rely heavily on security camera footage that shows Garrett walking by Oral's car in a parking lot. Oral's car then briefly follows Garrett and turns left, toward the boy's apartment, instead of right, toward Oral's home. As for motive, prosecutors contend that Oral was punishing Garrett's mother, who had recently broken up with him. At trial, Garrett's mother testifies that she ended the relationship in part because Garrett did not like Oral.

The Law To find a defendant guilty, a judge or jury must find *beyond a reasonable doubt* that she or he committed a crime.

What Would You Do? You are Oral's defense attorney. Your job is to create reasonable doubt in the jurors' minds that your client killed Garrett. Oral tells you that he was in the parking lot scouting a local soccer team on a field that the boy passed on the way home. You also discover that a police dog brought to the crime scene followed a scent to a nearby river nowhere near your client's house and that video footage shows a white man in a hoodie near Garrett's home at the time of the murder. (Oral is African American.) Finally, your client was not arrested until two-and-a-half years after Garrett's death.

Taking all these factors into consideration, what argument will you make before the jury to create reasonable doubt?

Learning Objective 7 Identify the primary method that defense attorneys use in most trials to weaken the prosecution's case against their client.

To see how a defense attorney argued in a case with similar facts that took place in Potsdam, New York, go to Example 10.1 in Appendix B.

by presenting facts that add to the ones offered by the prosecution. Possible affirmative defenses, which we discussed in detail in Chapter 4, include self-defense, insanity, duress, and entrapment.

With an affirmative defense strategy, the defense attempts to prove that the defendant should be found not guilty because of certain circumstances surrounding the crime. An affirmative strategy can be difficult to carry out because it forces the defense to prove the reliability of its own evidence, not simply disprove the evidence offered by the prosecution.

The defense is often willing to admit that a certain criminal act took place, especially if the defendant has already confessed. In this case, the primary question of the trial becomes not whether the defendant is guilty, but what the defendant is guilty of. In these situations, the defense strategy focuses on obtaining the lightest possible penalty for the defendant, as we saw with Dzhokhar Tsarnaev in Figure 10.3. This strategy is partially responsible for the high percentage of proceedings that end in plea bargains, discussed in the previous chapter.

Rebuttal and Surrebuttal

After the defense closes its case, the prosecution is permitted to bring new evidence forward that was not used during its initial presentation to the jury. This is called the **rebuttal** stage of the trial. When the rebuttal stage is finished, the defense is given the opportunity to cross-examine the prosecution's new witnesses and introduce new witnesses of its own. This final act is part of the *surrebuttal*. After these stages have been completed, the defense may offer another motion for a directed verdict, asking the judge to find in the defendant's favor. If this motion is rejected, and it almost always is, the case is closed, and the opposing sides offer their closing arguments.

Rebuttal Evidence given to counteract or disprove evidence presented by the opposing party.

Closing Arguments Arguments
made by each side's attorney after the
cases for the plaintiff and defendant
have been presented.

Closing Arguments

In their **closing arguments,** the attorneys summarize their presentations and argue one final time for their respective cases. In most states, the defense attorney goes first, and then the prosecutor. (In Colorado, Kentucky, and Missouri, the order is reversed.) An effective closing argument includes all of the major points that support the government's or the defense's case. It also emphasizes the shortcomings of the opposing party's case.

Jurors will view a closing argument with some skepticism if it merely recites the central points of a party's claim or defense without also responding to the unfavorable facts or issues raised by the other side. Of course, neither attorney wants to focus too much on the other side's position, but the elements of the opposing position do need to be acknowledged and their flaws highlighted. (For an example of a closing argument, see Figure 10.5.)

One danger in the closing arguments is that an attorney will become too emotional and make remarks that are later deemed by appellate courts to be prejudicial. Furthermore, lawyers are not permitted to introduce any additional facts during a closing statement. If allowed to do so, lawyers would be able to "sneak in" new evidence without giving the opposing party a chance to challenge that evidence.[53] Once both attorneys have completed their remarks, the case is submitted to the jury, and the attorneys' role in the trial is, for the moment, complete.

ETHICS CHALLENGE

As you learned in this section, expert witnesses are paid for their testimony by either the prosecution or the defense. In your opinion, what ethical problems, if any, does this common practice raise? What role does cross-examination play in limiting any potential problems with partisan expert witnesses?

FIGURE 10.5 **The Closing Argument**

Defense attorneys for Keith Kidwell, charged with murdering convenience store worker Crayton Nelms in Bull City, North Carolina, argued that the case against their client was "flawed to the core." In her closing argument, District Attorney Tracey Cline focused on one particular piece of evidence to contradict this assertion:

Inside that [store] that morning, there were footprints, shoe impressions. All the ones that were in blood—and I'm not talking about what the kids put on their face at Halloween. Real blood. Blood that had once run warm inside a body. But all of the shoe prints in blood can be traced to Mr. Kidwell's shoes. Outside sole design, same physical size, general wear, similar features. Scientific words. You, each of you, had in your hands the picture of that bloody shoe print on Mr. Nelms' back and matched it up—I said matched—with [Kidwell's] shoe. Coincidence?

The jury found Kidwell guilty of first degree murder, and he was sentenced to life in prison without the possibility of parole.

Source: For a complete transcript of Cline's closing argument, go to **media2.newsobserver.com/smedia/2011/09/05/09/47/qSaKF .So.156.pdf.**

The Final Steps of the Trial and Postconviction Procedures

After closing arguments, the outcome of the trial is in the hands of the jury. In this section, we examine the efforts to give jurors the means necessary to make informed decisions about the guilt or innocence of the accused. We also look at the posttrial motions that can occur when the defense feels that the jurors, prosecution, or trial judge made errors that necessitate remedial legal action.

Jury Instructions

Before the jurors begin their deliberations, the judge gives the jury a **charge**, summing up the case and instructing the jurors on the rules of law that apply to the issues in the case. These charges, also called jury instructions, are usually prepared during a special *charging conference* involving the judge and the trial attorneys. In this conference, the attorneys suggest the instructions they would like the jurors to receive, but the judge makes the final decision as to the charges submitted. If the defense attorney disagrees with the charges sent to the jury, he or she can enter an objection, thereby setting the stage for a possible appeal.

The judge usually begins by explaining basic legal principles, such as the need to find the defendant guilty beyond a reasonable doubt. Then the jury instructions narrow to the specifics of the case at hand, and the judge explains to the jurors what facts the prosecution must have proved to obtain a conviction. If the defense strategy centers on an affirmative defense such as insanity or entrapment, the judge will discuss the relevant legal principles that the defense must have proved to obtain an acquittal.

The final segment of the charges discusses possible verdicts. These always include "guilty" and "not guilty," but some cases also allow for the jury to find "guilt by reason of insanity" or "guilty but mentally ill." Juries are often charged with determining the seriousness of the crime as well, such as deciding whether a homicide is murder in the first degree, murder in the second degree, or manslaughter.

Jury Deliberation

After receiving the charge, the jury begins its deliberations. Jury deliberation is a somewhat mysterious process, as it takes place in complete seclusion. Most of what is known about how a jury deliberates comes from mock trials or interviews with jurors after the verdict has been reached. A general picture of the deliberation process constructed from this research shows that jurors are not necessarily predisposed to argue with one another over the fate of the defendant. In approximately three out of every ten cases, the initial vote by the jury led to a unanimous decision. In 90 percent of the remaining cases, the majority eventually dictated the decision.[54]

One of the most important instructions that a judge normally gives the jurors is that they should seek no outside information during deliberation. The idea is that jurors should base their verdict *only* on the evidence that the judge has deemed admissible. In extreme cases, the judge will order that the jury be *sequestered*, or isolated from the public, during the trial and deliberation stages of the proceedings. **Sequestration** is used when deliberations are expected to be lengthy, or when the trial is attracting a high amount of interest and the judge wants to keep the jury from being unduly influenced. Juries are usually sequestered in hotels and kept under the watch and guard of officers of the court.

Charge The judge's instructions to the jury following the attorneys' closing arguments.

Sequestration The isolation of jury members during a trial to ensure that their judgment is not tainted by information other than what is provided in the courtroom.

The importance of *total* sequestration is reflected in a Colorado Supreme Court decision to overturn the death penalty of a man who was sentenced after the jurors consulted a Bible during deliberations. The court held that a Bible constituted an improper outside influence and a reliance on a "higher authority."[55]

CJ & TECHNOLOGY

Wireless Devices in the Courtroom

One former juror, fresh from trial, complained that the members of the courtroom work group had not provided the jury with enough information to render a fair verdict. "We felt deeply frustrated at our inability to fill those gaps in our knowledge," he added. Until recently, frustrated jury members have lacked the means to carry out their own investigations in court. Today, however, jurors with smartphones and tablet computers can easily access news stories and online research tools. With these wireless devices, they can look up legal terms, blog and tweet about their experiences, and sometimes even try to contact other participants in the trial through "friend" requests on social media websites.

This access can cause serious problems for judges, whose responsibility it is to ensure that no outside information taints the jury's decision. Over the past several years, jurors have used smartphones to pull up images of a crime scene on Google Earth, measure the distance between a defendant's home and the crime scene on MapQuest, and look up the definitions of technical terms such as *reasonable doubt* and *retinal detachment*. In many such cases, the presiding judge feels obligated to declare a mistrial, as these instances of juror misconduct could have improperly influenced the final verdict.

Thinking about Wireless Devices in the Courtroom

The Sixth Amendment guarantees the accused the right to trial by an "impartial jury." How does the use of wireless devices in the courtroom threaten this right?

The Verdict

Once it has reached a decision, the jury issues a **verdict.** The most common verdicts are guilty and not guilty, though, as we have seen, juries may signify different degrees of guilt if instructed to do so. Following the announcement of a guilty or not guilty verdict, the jurors are discharged, and the jury trial proceedings are finished.

Hung Juries When a jury in a criminal trial is unable to agree on a unanimous verdict—or a majority verdict, in certain states—it returns with no decision. This is known as a **hung jury.** Following a hung jury, the judge will declare a mistrial, and the case will be tried again in front of a different jury if the prosecution decides to pursue the matter a second time. As you may recall, this is what happened with defendant Pedro Hernandez, whose multiple trials for the murder of six-year-old Etan Patz we discussed at the opening of the chapter.

A judge can do little to reverse a hung jury, considering that "no decision" is just as legitimate a verdict as guilty or not guilty. In some states, however, if there are only a few dissenters to the majority view, a judge can send the jury back to the jury room under a set of rules set forth more than a century ago by the Supreme Court in *Allen v. United States* (1896).[56] The **Allen charge,** as this instruction is called, asks the jurors in the minority to reconsider the majority opinion. Many jurisdictions do not allow *Allen* charges on the ground that they improperly coerce jurors with the minority opinion to change their minds.[57]

Jury Nullification For all of the attention they receive, hung juries are relatively rare. Juries are unable to come to a decision in only about 6 percent of all cases.[58] Furthermore, juries may be more lenient (or easy to "trick") than is generally perceived. One

Verdict A formal decision made by the jury.

Hung Jury A jury whose members are so irreconcilably divided in their opinions that they cannot reach a verdict.

***Allen* Charge** An instruction by a judge to a deadlocked jury with only a few dissenters that asks the jurors in the minority to reconsider the majority opinion.

study found that juries were six times more likely than judges (in bench trials) to acquit a person who turns out to be guilty.[59] This statistic raises the question of *jury nullification*, which occurs when jurors "nullify" by using their own judgment to reach a verdict rather than following judicial instructions or the law.

Although there is no way to measure the amount of jury nullification in American courts, it is believed to occur most often in cases involving controversial issues such as race, drug offenses, and overreach of federal criminal law. In 2016, for example, a Portland, Oregon, jury found brothers Ammon and Ryan Bundy not guilty of conspiracy to impede federal officers by force, threat, or intimidation. The defendants and several of their followers had occupied the headquarters of the Malheur National Wildlife Refuge in southeast Oregon for forty-one days to protest the federal government's management of public lands.

Despite the fact that the defendants were armed and did significant damage to the building—actions caught on videotape and presented at trial—prosecutors were unable to convince jurors that the occupation was a criminal act. "I think the jury . . . saw that these were well-meaning, well-intentioned individuals," said one of the occupiers' defense attorneys.[60]

▲ In 2016, New Hampshire's legislature considered a bill that would have required judges to inform juries of their right to vote "not guilty" when "a guilty verdict will yield an unjust result." **What is your opinion of this proposed legislation to—essentially—legitimize the practice of jury nullification?** Enigma/Alamy Stock Photo

Appeals

Even if a defendant is found guilty, the trial process is not necessarily over. In our criminal justice system, a person convicted of a crime has a right to appeal. An **appeal** is the process of seeking a higher court's review of a lower court's decision for the purpose of correcting or changing the lower court's judgment. A defendant who loses a case in a trial court cannot automatically appeal the conviction. The defendant normally must first be able to show that the trial court acted improperly on a question of law.

At the state level, an appellate court upholds the decision of the trial court in 52 percent of all appeals.[61] Common reasons for appeals include the introduction of tainted evidence by the prosecution or faulty jury instructions delivered by the trial judge. In 2017, for example, Justin Ross Harris appealed his conviction for killing his young son by leaving the boy in a hot car, mentioned earlier in the chapter. Among other issues, Harris's lawyers claimed that the trial judge created an "unduly prejudicial atmosphere" by showing the jury "ghoulish images of a dead child with his eyes open" and "macabre autopsy photos."[62]

Double Jeopardy

The appeals process is available only to the defense. If a jury finds the accused not guilty, the prosecution cannot appeal to have the decision reversed. To do so would infringe on the defendant's Fifth Amendment rights against multiple trials for the same offense. This guarantee against being tried a second time for the same crime is known as protection from **double jeopardy**. The prohibition against double jeopardy means that once a criminal defendant is found not guilty of a particular crime, the government may not reindict the person and retry him or her for the same crime.

Appeal The process of seeking a higher court's review of a lower court's decision for the purpose of correcting or changing this decision.

Double Jeopardy To twice place at risk (jeopardize) a person's life or liberty. Constitutional law prohibits a second prosecution in the same court for the same criminal offense.

The basic idea behind the double jeopardy clause, in the words of Supreme Court Justice Hugo Black, is that the state should not be allowed to

> make repeated attempts to convict an individual for an alleged offense, thereby subjecting him to embarrassment, expense, and ordeal and compelling him to live in a continuing state of anxiety and insecurity, as well as enhancing the possibility that though innocent he may be found guilty.[63]

The American prohibition against double jeopardy is not, however, absolute. There are several circumstances in which, for practical purposes, a defendant can find herself or himself back in court after a jury has failed to find her or him guilty of committing a particular crime:

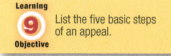

Learning Objective 8 Delineate circumstances in which a criminal defendant may be tried a second time for the same act.

1. One state's prosecution will not prevent a different state or the federal government from prosecuting the same crime.
2. Acquitted defendants can be sued in *civil court* for circumstances arising from the alleged wrongdoing on the theory that they are not being tried for the same *crime* twice.
3. A hung jury is not an acquittal for purposes of double jeopardy. So, if a jury is deadlocked, the government is free to set a new trial.

The Appeals Process   There are two basic reasons for the appeals process. The first is to correct an error made during the initial trial. The second is to review policy. Because of this second function, the appellate courts are an important part of the flexible nature of the criminal justice system. When existing law has ceased to be effective or no longer reflects the values of society, an appellate court can effectively change the law through its decisions and the precedents that it sets.[64] A classic example was the *Miranda v. Arizona* decision (see Chapter 7), which, although it failed to change the fate of the defendant (he was found guilty on retrial), had a far-reaching impact on custodial interrogation of suspects.

It is also important to understand that once the appeals process begins, the defendant is no longer presumed innocent. The burden of proof has shifted, and the defendant is obligated to prove that her or his conviction should be overturned. The method of filing an appeal differs slightly among the fifty states and the federal government, but the five basic steps are similar enough for summarization in Figure 10.6. For the most part, defendants are not required to exercise their right to appeal. The one exception involves the death sentence. Given the seriousness of capital punishment, the defendant is required to appeal the case, regardless of his or her wishes.

Learning Objective 9 List the five basic steps of an appeal.

Wrongful Convictions

The appeals process is primarily concerned with "legal innocence." That is, appeals courts focus on how the law was applied in a case, rather than on the facts of the case. But what if a defendant who is factually innocent has been found guilty at trial? For the most part, such **wrongful convictions** can be righted only with the aid of new evidence suggesting that the defendant was not, in fact, guilty. When such new evidence is uncovered, a prosecutor's office can choose to reopen the case and redress the initial injustice.

DNA Exoneration   In Chapter 6, we saw how DNA fingerprinting has been a boon for law enforcement. According to the Innocence Project, a New York–based legal group, as of February 2017, the procedure has also led to the exoneration of 394 convicts in the United States.[65]

Wrongful Convictions The conviction, either by verdict or by guilty plea, of a person who is factually innocent of the charges.

FIGURE 10.6 The Steps of an Appeal

1. The defendant, or *appellant*, files a **notice of appeal**—a short written statement outlining the basis of the appeal.

2. The appellant transfers the trial court record to the appellate court. This record contains items such as evidence and a transcript of the testimony.

3. Both parties file **briefs**. A brief is a written document that presents the party's legal arguments.

4. Attorneys from both sides present **oral arguments** before the appellate court.

5. Having heard from both sides, the judges of the appellate court retire to deliberate the case and make their decision. As described in Chapter 8, this decision is issued as a **written opinion**. Appellate courts generally do one of the following:
   - **Uphold** the decision of the lower court.
   - **Modify** the lower court's decision by changing only a part of it.
   - **Reverse** the decision of the lower court.
   - **Reverse and remand** the case, meaning that the matter is sent back to the lower court for further proceedings.

For example, in 1982 Keith Harward was wrongly convicted of beating a man to death in Newport News, Virginia, and raping his wife while their children slept in a nearby bedroom. Harward subsequently spent thirty-three years in prison before a court ordered DNA testing of items from the crime scene, including a rape kit and a towel draped over the female victim. This testing implicated another suspect, who had died in prison a decade earlier, and in April 2016 the Virginia Supreme Court ordered Harward's release.

The Causes of Wrongful Convictions

Keith Harward was not a suspect in the rape and murder just described until a girlfriend accused him of biting her during a fight. Then, after undergoing hypnosis, a witness told Newport News police that he had seen Harward on the night of the crimes wearing clothes splattered with paint or blood. At trial, the only evidence directly linking Harward to the crimes was provided by two experts in forensic dentistry, who matched the defendant's tooth patterns to wounds on photographs of the victim.

Harward's case highlights two of the five most common reasons[66] for wrongful convictions later overturned by DNA evidence:

1. *Eyewitness misidentification*, which research shows to be a factor in nearly three-fourths of all cases in which a falsely convicted person has been exonerated by DNA evidence.[67]

2. *False confessions*, which are often the result of overly coercive police interrogation techniques (see Chapter 7) or a suspect's mental illness.

3. *Faulty forensic evidence* produced by crime labs, which analyze evidence of everything from bite marks to handwriting samples to ballistics. Since the arrest of Keith Harward in 1982, at least twenty-four other defendants whose convictions were based wholly or partly on bite-mark evidence have been exonerated.[68]

4. *False informant testimony*, provided by "jailhouse snitches" and other offenders who are motivated to lessen their own punishment by incriminating other suspects.

5. *Law enforcement misconduct* by overzealous or corrupt police officers and prosecutors.

Numerous jurisdictions are taking steps to lessen the probability that these factors will result in wrongful convictions. Texas law enforcement agencies, for example, are increasingly replacing traditional simultaneous police lineups with sequential lineups. In simultaneous lineups, eyewitnesses view all the suspects at once, while in sequential lineups, they

see only one lineup member at a time.[69] Studies show that the traditional method is flawed because it encourages eyewitnesses to simply choose the lineup member who most closely resembles the offender, rather than focusing on accurately identifying the actual offender.[70]

Nearly thirty prosecutor's offices around the nation have set up conviction-review units to aid defense attorneys in investigating possible wrongful convictions and, if necessary, to take steps to overturn them.[71] Perhaps most interestingly, a recent New York appellate court ruling allows convicts in parts of that state to use appeals courts to prove "actual innocence."[72] This is a departure from the typical practice because, as noted earlier, the American appeals process is primarily designed to review matters of law, not matters of fact such as guilt or innocence.

▲ In 2016, after spending more than thirty-three years behind bars, Keith Harward was released from a Virginia prison when DNA evidence proved him innocent of the murder and rape for which he was initially convicted. **Should prosecutors be punished for bringing charges against defendants such as Harward who turn out to be innocent? If so, what would be an appropriate punishment? Explain your answers.** AP Images/Daniel Sangjib Min/ *Richmond Times-Dispatch*

Habeas Corpus In 2009, the United States Supreme Court ruled that convicts have no constitutional right to DNA testing that may prove their innocence.[73] Nonetheless, most states allow prisoners access to such testing if there is a reasonable possibility of a wrongful conviction.

In addition, even after the appeals process is exhausted, a convict may have access to a procedure known as *habeas corpus* (Latin for "you have the body"). *Habeas corpus* is a judicial order that commands a corrections official to bring a prisoner before a federal court so that the court can hear the convict's claim that he or she is being held illegally. A writ of *habeas corpus* differs from an appeal in that it can be filed only by someone who is imprisoned. In recent years, defense attorneys have successfully used the *habeas corpus* procedure for a number of their death row clients who have new DNA evidence proving their innocence.[74]

According to federal law, *habeas corpus* petitions must be filed no later than a year after the date of conviction. This restriction has proved problematic for inmates and their lawyers who may come across evidence of innocence after the deadline has passed. In 2013, the Supreme Court provided an exception to the one-year deadline rule in situations where the convict can prove that "it is more likely than not that no reasonable juror would have convicted him in light of the new evidence."[75]

Habeas Corpus An order that requires corrections officials to bring an inmate before a court or a judge and explain why he or she is being held in prison.

ETHICS CHALLENGE

Ralph Armstrong is convicted for the rape and murder of a student at the University of Wisconsin–Madison. During Ralph's appeal, a woman calls the local district attorney and reports that Stephen, Ralph's younger brother, told her that he committed the crime. The prosecutor does not investigate this lead, nor does he inform Ralph's defense team of the woman's phone call. Ralph spends twenty-eight years behind bars before he is exonerated by DNA testing. What are some of the reasons that a prosecutor would behave in such a clearly unethical manner?

Statutes of Limitations for Sex Crimes

How Things Stand

Twenty states have no statute of limitations for the crime of rape. In twelve states, the statute of limitations for this crime is between ten and twenty years. In the remainder of the states the rape charges must be filed within a decade or less.

As a Result...

In theory, statutes of limitations for sex crimes reflect the American criminal justice system's commitment to proving a defendant's guilt beyond a reasonable doubt. The longer the delay between criminal act and prosecution, the more difficult it will be to establish that guilt. As Ryan W. Scott, a law professor at Indiana University, points out, "After a certain time, it becomes harder to get reliable evidence, physical evidence deteriorates, and the memories of witnesses fade."[76]

Even so, the laws do seem to lead to unfair results. In 2014, for example, a man named Bart Bareither walked into the Marion County (Indiana) Sheriff's Department and admitted to raping a woman nine years earlier. Because the statute of limitations for rape in Indiana is five years, however, prosecutors could not press charges. "I was completely devastated," said Bareither's victim on learning what had happened.[77] Critics of statutes of limitation for sex crimes say that, besides inflicting this sort of damage, the laws also discourage victims from reporting such crimes in the first place. Between 2014 and 2016, legislatures in six states extended or eliminated their statutes of limitations for sex-related crimes.[78]

Up for Debate

"The need for justice and the need for healing do not suddenly go away after some arbitrary number of years has passed."[79] —*Katie Hanna, executive director of the Ohio Alliance to End Sexual Violence.*

"We believe in fresh starts. We believe in people rehabilitating. Going back twenty years [to prosecute a crime] . . . feels unfair to many people. People should be judged on the basis on who they are now."[80] —*Richard E. Myers, professor at University of North Carolina School of Law*

What's Your Take?

Review the discussion in this chapter on "Special Features of Criminal Trials" before answering the following questions.

1. One critic of extending or eliminating statutes of limitations for sex-related crimes writes, "It's not that America likes criminals, it's that with each passing year, the odds increase that a criminal prosecution puts an innocent person in jail."[81] Do you agree with this reasoning? Why or why not?

2. What is your opinion of the legal argument that in cases where DNA evidence of a sex crime exists, statutes of limitations should *always* be ignored, regardless of the amount of time that has elapsed since the criminal act?

Digging Deeper...

According to federal statistics, rape and sexual assaults are the least reported of all violent crimes.[82] Recently, however, in the wake of **high-profile sexual assault claims against actor and comedian Bill Cosby,** law enforcement officials are noticing a reversal of this trend, called the **"Cosby effect."** Go online and research the various charges against Cosby. How many were allowed to go forward under various state statutes of limitations? Why might victims be reluctant to report sex-related crimes, and how has the "Cosby effect" apparently helped to overcome this reluctance? Your answer should be at least three paragraphs long.

For more information on these concepts, look back to the Learning Objective icons throughout the chapter.

 Identify the basic protections enjoyed by criminal defendants in the United States. According to the Sixth Amendment, a criminal defendant has the right to a speedy and public trial by an impartial jury in the community where the crime was committed. Additionally, a person accused of a crime must be informed of the nature of the crime and be confronted with the witnesses against him or her. Further, the accused must be able to summon witnesses in her or his favor and have the assistance of counsel.

 Explain what "taking the Fifth" really means. The Fifth Amendment states that no person "shall be compelled in any criminal case to be a witness against himself." Thus, defendants do not have to testify if their testimony would implicate them in the crime. Witnesses may refuse to testify on this same ground. (Witnesses, though, are often granted immunity and thereafter can no longer take the Fifth.) In the United States, silence on the part of a defendant cannot be used by the jury in forming its opinion about guilt or innocence.

 List the requirements normally imposed on potential jurors. They must be (a) citizens of the United States; (b) over eighteen years of age; (c) free of felony convictions; (d) healthy enough to function on a jury; (e) sufficiently intelligent to understand the issues at trial; and (f) able to read, write, and comprehend the English language.

 Contrast challenges for cause and peremptory challenges during *voir dire*. A challenge for cause occurs when an attorney provides the court with a legally justifiable reason why a potential juror should be excluded—for example, the juror does not understand English. In contrast, peremptory challenges do not require any justification by the attorney and are usually limited to a small number. They cannot, however, be based, even implicitly, on race or gender.

 List the standard steps in a criminal jury trial. (a) Opening statements by the prosecutor and the defense attorney; (b) presentation of evidence, usually in the form of questioning by the prosecutor, known as direct examination; (c) cross-examination by the defense attorney of the same witnesses; (d) at the end of the prosecutor's presentation of evidence, motion for a directed verdict by the defense (also called a motion for judgment as a matter of law in the federal courts), which is normally denied by the judge; (e)

presentation of the defendant's case, which may include putting the defendant on the stand and direct examination of the defense's witnesses; (f) cross-examination by the prosecutor; (g) after the defense closes its case, rebuttal by the prosecution, which may involve new evidence; (h) cross-examination of any new prosecution witnesses by the defense and possible introduction of new defense witnesses, called the surrebuttal; (i) closing arguments by both the defense and the prosecution; (j) the charging of the jury by the judge, during which the judge sums up the case and instructs the jurors on the rules of law that apply; (k) jury deliberations; and (l) presentation of the verdict.

 Describe the difference between direct and circumstantial evidence, and explain why evidence of a defendant's "evil character" is often excluded from trial. Direct evidence is evidence witnessed by the person giving testimony. Circumstantial evidence is indirect evidence that can create an inference that a fact exists but does not directly establish the fact. "Evil character" evidence, which often refers to prior criminal acts by the defendant, is excluded because it tends to prejudice the jury against the defendant in the case at hand.

 Identify the primary method that defense attorneys use in most trials to weaken the prosecution's case against their client. To find a defendant guilty, a jury must believe beyond a reasonable doubt that he or she committed the crime. Therefore, defense attorneys will often present arguments and evidence designed to raise a reasonable doubt of guilt in the jurors' minds.

 Delineate circumstances in which a criminal defendant may be tried a second time for the same act. A defendant who is acquitted in a criminal trial may be sued in a civil case for essentially the same act. When an act is a crime under both state and federal law, a defendant who is acquitted in state court may be tried in federal court for the same act, and vice versa.

 List the five basic steps of an appeal. (a) The filing of a notice of appeal; (b) the transfer of the trial court record to the appellate court; (c) the filing of briefs; (d) the presentation of oral arguments; and (e) the issuance of a written opinion by the appellate judges, upholding the decision of the lower court, modifying part of the decision, reversing the decision, or reversing and remanding the case to the trial court.

QUESTIONS FOR CRITICAL ANALYSIS

1. Why is it important for the judge to tell jurors that a defendant's decision to remain silent during the trial cannot be taken as a sign of guilt?

2. During *voir dire* for the trial of a police officer charged with manslaughter, a potential juror fails to indicate that his father once served seven years in prison. This person winds up on the jury, which finds the police officer guilty. Once this information becomes known, should the judge declare a mistrial? Why or why not?

3. Police find a critically wounded man lying in the parking lot of a gas station. When they ask him what happened, he indicates that Mr. X shot him. Then, the man dies. Should the dead man's identification of Mr. X be allowed in court? Or is it inadmissible hearsay? Explain your answer. (To see how the United States Supreme Court ruled in a similar case, go to **www. scotusblog.com/case-files/ cases/michigan-v-bryant.**)

4. Texas has a law called the Timothy Cole Compensation Act, under which people who are wrongfully convicted of crimes may collect $80,000 from the state for each year of unwarranted imprisonment. Do you think this is fair? Why or why not? What are the goals of this kind of legislation?

5. Several years ago, following the conviction of Miguel Angel Peña-Rodriguez for attempted sexual assault, a juror showed bias during deliberations. Among other things, the juror said, "I think he did it because he's Mexican and Mexican men take whatever they want." Even though jury deliberations are meant to be kept secret, Rodriguez's lawyers wanted the statements made public and demanded that their client be retried by an unbiased jury. Which is more important: the right to trial by an impartial jury or the need for secrecy in jury deliberations? Explain your answer.

KEY TERMS

acquittal 321
Allen charge 340
appeal 341
bench trial 320
challenge for cause 326
charge 339
circumstantial evidence 332
closing arguments 338
confrontation clause 334
cross-examination 334
direct evidence 331
direct examination 334

double jeopardy 341
evidence 330
expert witness 331
habeas corpus 344
hearsay 335
hung jury 340
jury trial 320
lay witness 331
master jury list 325
motion for a directed verdict 336
opening statements 330
peremptory challenges 326

real evidence 330
rebuttal 337
relevant evidence 332
sequestration 339
statute of limitations 320
testimony 330
venire 325
verdict 340
voir dire 325
wrongful conviction 342

1. Lawrence M. Friedman and Robert V. Percival, *The Roots of Justice* (Chapel Hill, N.C.: University of North Carolina Press, 1981).

2. Alexandra Natapoff, "Misdemeanors," *Southern California Law Review* 85 (2012), 105.

3. 407 U.S. 514 (1972).

4. New York Criminal Procedure Law Section 30.30, "Speedy trial; time limitations." *http://codes.findlaw.com/ny/criminal-procedure-law/cpl-sect-30-30.html*. FindLaw: visited on February 12, 2017, Web

5. "A Nightmare Court, Worthy of Dickens," *New York Times* (May 12, 2016), A26.

6. Bureau of Justice Statistics, *Felony Defendants in Large Urban Counties, 2009—Statistical Tables* (Washington, D.C.: U.S. Department of Justice, December 2013), Table 20, page 23.

7. 18 U.S.C. Section 3161.

8. 391 U.S. 145 (1968).

9. *Blanton v. Las Vegas*, 489 U.S. 538 (1989).

10. *Williams v. Florida*, 399 U.S. 102 (1970).

11. 435 U.S. 223 (1978).

12. *Apodaca v. Oregon*, 406 U.S. 404 (1972); and *Lee v. Louisiana*, No. 07-1523 (2008).

13. 332 U.S. 46 (1947).

14. *Salinas v. Texas*, 570 U.S. _____ (2013).

15. Quoted in Ross Bynum, "Trial of Dad in Boy's Hot Car Death Restarts 275 Miles Away." *www.bigstory.ap.org. Associated Press:* September 10, 2016, Web.

16. Quoted in James C. McKinley, Jr., "Jurors in Patz Case Fall a Vote Shy of a Conviction," *New York Times* (May 9, 2015), A1.

17. 397 U.S. 358 (1970).

18. James P. Levine, "The Impact of Local Political Cultures on Jury Verdicts," *Criminal Justice Journal* 14 (1992), 163–164.

19. Stacey Barchenger, "Judge Grants Mistrial in Vanderbilt Rape Case." *www.tennessean.com. The Tennessean:* June 23, 2015, Web.

20. *Lockhart v. McCree*, 476 U.S. 162 (1986).

21. *Witherspoon v. Illinois*, 391 U.S. 510 (1968).

22. John Kaplan and Jon R. Waltz, *The Trial of Jack Ruby* (New York: Macmillan, 1965), 91–94.

23. John W. Clark III, "The Utility of Jury Consultants in the Twenty-First Century," *Criminal Law Bulletin* (Spring 2006), 3.

24. 380 U.S. 224 (1965).

25. 476 U.S. 79 (1986).

26. Eric L. Muller, "Solving the Batson Paradox: Harmless Error, Jury Representation, and the Sixth Amendment," *Yale Law Journal* 106 (October 1996), 93.

27. 499 U.S. 400 (1991).

28. 502 U.S. 1056 (1992).

29. *Foster v. Chatman,* 578 U.S. _____. No. 14-8349. Supreme Court of the United States (May 23, 2016).

30. *Ibid.*, 21.

31. Adam Liptak, "New Questions on Racial Gap in Filling Juries," *New York Times* (August 17, 2015), A1.

32. Quoted in Shaila Dewan, "Study Finds Blacks Blocked from Southern Juries," *New York Times* (June 2, 2010), 14.

33. 511 U.S. 127 (1994).

34. Harry Kalven and Hans Zeisel, *The American Jury* (Boston: Little, Brown, 1966), 163–167.

35. Nancy Pennington and Reid Hastie, "The Story Model for Juror Decision Making," in *Inside the Juror: The Psychology of Juror Decision Making* (Cambridge, Mass.: Harvard University Press, 1983), 192, 194–195.

36. Federal Rule of Evidence 703.

37. Richard A. Epstein, "Judicial Control over Expert Testimony: Of Deference and Education," *Northwestern University Law Review* 87 (1993), 1156.

38. L. Timothy Perrin, "Expert Witnesses under Rules 703 and 803(4) of the Federal Rules of Evidence: Separating the Wheat from the Chaff," *Indiana Law Journal* 72 (Fall 1997), 939.

39. *Daubert v. Merrell Dow Pharmaceuticals*, 509 U.S. 579 (1993).

40. Committee on Identifying the Needs of the Forensic Science Community, *Strengthening Forensic Science in the United States: A Path Forward* (Washington, D.C.: National Academies Press, 2009), 269–278; Bradford T. Ulery, et al., "Accuracy and Reliability of Forensic Latent Fingerprint Decisions," *Proceedings of the National Academy of Sciences Early Edition* (April 5, 2011), 1–6; and Jason M. Tanger, Matthew B. Thompson, and Duncan J. McCarthy, "Identifying Fingerprint Expertise," *Psychological Science* (August 16, 2011), 995–997.

41. Lyn Haber and Ralph Norman Haber, "Scientific Validation of Fingerprint Evidence under Daubert," *Law, Probability, and Risk* 7 (2008), 87–109.

42. "Highlighting the Limits to Fingerprint Evidence." *www.federalevidence.com.* Federal Evidence Review: February 26, 2014, Web.

43. Corey Call, et al., "Seeing Is Believing: The CSI Effect among Jurors in Malicious Wounding Cases," *Journal of Social, Behavioral, and Health Sciences* 7 (2013), 60, 62.

44. Maria Cramer, "Victim's Text Messages Tossed in Aaron Hernandez Case." *www.bostonglobe.com. Boston Globe*: December 12, 2014, Web.

45. Thomas J. Reed, "Trial by Propensity: Admission of Other Criminal Acts Evidenced in Federal Criminal Trials," *University of Cincinnati Law Review* 50 (1981), 713.

46. Quoted in Dan Wetzel, "Aaron Hernandez Avoids Major Defeat." *www.sports.yahoo.com. Yahoo Sports:* March 4, 2015, Web.

47. Reed, *op. cit.*, 713.

48. *People v. Zackowitz*, 254 N.Y. 192 (1930).

49. Tracy Connor, James Novogrod, and Tom Winter, "Judge Denies Delay, Bars Evidence in George Zimmerman Trial—For Now." *www.usnews.newsvine.com. NBC News*: May 28, 2013, Web.

50. Michelle J. Anderson, "From Chastity Requirement to Sexuality License: Sexual Consent and a New Rape Shield Law," *George Washington Law Review* (February 2002), 51.

51. Federal Rules of Procedure, Rule 804(b)(2).

52. Arthur Best, *Evidence: Examples and Explanations*, 4th ed. (New York: Aspen Law & Business, 2001), 89–90.

53. *United States v. Wright*, 625 F.3d 583, 611 (9th Cir. 2010).

54. David W. Broeder, "The University of Chicago Jury Project," *Nebraska Law Review* 38 (1959), 744–760.

55. *People v. Haran*, 109 P.3d 616 (Colo. 2005).

56. 164 U.S. 492 (1896).

57. *United States v. Fioravanti*, 412 F.2d 407 (3d Cir. 1969).

58. William S. Neilson and Harold Winter, "The Elimination of Hung Juries: Retrials and Nonunanimous Verdicts," *International Review of Law and Economics* (March 2005), 2.

59. Joseph L. Gastwirth and Michael D. Sinclair, "Diagnostic Test Methodology in the Design and Analysis of Judge-Jury Agreement Studies," *Jurimetrics Journal* 39 (Fall 1998), 59.

60. Quoted in Matt Pearce, "Leaders of Oregon Wildlife Refuge Standoff Are Acquitted of Federal Charges." *www.latimes.com. Los Angeles Times:* October 27, 2016, Web.

61. Bureau of Justice Statistics, *Criminal Appeals in State Courts* (Washington, D.C.: U.S. Department of Justice, September 2015), 1.

62. Bill Rankin, "Ross Harris Launches Appeal of Murder Conviction." *www.myajc.com. Atlanta Journal-Constitution:* January 4, 2017, Web.

63. *Green v. United States*, 355 U.S. 184 (1957).

64. David W. Neubauer, *America's Courts and the Criminal Justice System*, 5th ed. (Belmont, Calif.: Wadsworth Publishing Co, 1996), 254.

65. "Exonerated by DNA." *www.innocenceproject.org.* The Innocence Project: visited February 14, 2017, Web.

66. "The National Registry of Exonerations." *www.law.umich.edu.* Michigan Law School & Northwestern Law School: visited February 14, 2017, Web.

67. "Eyewitness Misidentification." *www.innocenceproject.org.* The Innocence Project: visited February 14, 2017, Web.

68. Erik Eckholm, "Inmate Freed as Bite Marks Are Refuted," *New York Times* (April 9, 2016), A10.

69. Paul Kix, "Recognition," *New Yorker* (January 18, 2016), 41.

70. Nancy K. Steblay, "Reduction of False Convictions through Improved Identification Procedures: Further Refinements for Street Practice and Public Policy." *www.njcrs.gov.* National Criminal Justice Reference Service: January 2, 2012, Web.

71. Stephanie Clifford, "A Shot to the Heart," *New Yorker* (October 24, 2016), 30.

72. *People v. Hamilton*, 79 N.Y.S.2d 97 (App. Div. 2014).

73. *District Attorney's Office v. Osborne*, 557 U.S. 52 (2009).

74. Theresa Hsu Schriever, "In Our Own Backyard: Why California Should Care about Habeas Corpus," *McGeorge Law Review* 45 (2014), 764–798.

75. *McQuiggin v. Perkins*, 133 S.Ct. 1924, 1932 (2013).

76. Quoted in Tim Evans, "Indiana Law Lets Rapists Go Free," *www.usatoday.com. Indianapolis Star:* February 16, 2016, Web.

77. Quoted in *ibid*.

78. Sydney Ember and Graham Bowley, "After Bill Cosby, States Shift on Statutes of Limitations in Sexual Assault Cases," *New York Times* (November 7, 2016), A1.

79. Quoted in Evans, *op. cit.*

80. Quoted in Katie Rose Guest Pryal, "Here's How America's Confusing and Outdated Rape Statutes of Limitations Are Hurting Victims." *www.qz.com. Quartz:* February 22, 2016, Web.

81. Joe Patrice, "Bill Cosby and Eliminating Statutes of Limitations: A Truly Terrible Idea." *www.abovethelaw.com. Above the Law:* January 4, 2016, Web.

82. Bureau of Justice Statistics, *Criminal Victimization, 2015* (Washington, D.C.: U.S. Department of Justice, October 2016), Table 5, page 7.

Punishment and Sentencing

To target your study and review, look for these numbered Learning Objective icons throughout the chapter.

Chapter Outline		Corresponding Learning Objectives
The Purpose of Sentencing	**1**	List and contrast the four basic philosophical reasons for sentencing criminals.
The Structure of Sentencing	**2**	Contrast indeterminate with determinate sentencing.
	3	Explain why there is a difference between the sentence imposed by a judge and the actual sentence served by the prisoner.
	4	State who has input into the sentencing decision and list the factors that determine a sentence.
Inconsistencies in Sentencing	**5**	Explain some of the reasons why sentencing reform has occurred.
Sentencing Reform	**6**	Describe the goal of mandatory minimum sentencing guidelines and explain why these laws have become unpopular in recent years.
Capital Punishment	**7**	Identify the two stages that make up the bifurcated process of death penalty sentencing.
	8	Explain why the U.S. Supreme Court abolished the death penalty for juvenile offenders.
	9	Describe the main issues of the death penalty debate.

Questionable Judgment

▲ Brock Turner leaves the Santa Clara County (California) Jail on September 2, 2016, after serving only half of a six-month sentence for sexual assault. REUTERS/Stephen Lam

"In 2006, I sentenced a man to eighteen years in prison," federal district Judge Stefan Underhill wrote a decade later. "I have been wrestling with that decision ever since." Judge Underhill worried that neither society nor the defendant—a gang enforcer who killed a potential witness before turning his life around—benefited from such a long stint behind bars. This admission gained little attention, as judges rarely face public disapproval for being too harsh when sentencing, particularly for a confessed murderer.

Excessive judicial leniency, however, is another story. In 2016, for example, Santa Clara County (California) Judge Aaron Persky came under withering criticism for sentencing Stanford University freshman and first-time offender Brock Turner to six months in jail. Turner had been found guilty of raping a twenty-three-year-old woman behind a dumpster on the Stanford campus. Judge Persky defended his decision by saying that Turner had "less moral culpability" because he was drunk at the time of the

assault. Court documents seemed to show that the judge took into consideration Turner's considerable skill as a collegiate swimmer in handing down the light sentence. The victim responded, "How fast Brock swims does not lessen the severity of what happened to me, and should not lessen the severity of his punishment."

Five months later, Judge John McKeon of Valley County (Montana) District Court faced comparable public outrage after he sentenced a father to sixty days in jail for repeatedly raping his twelve-year-old daughter. The judge relied on a state law that recommends probation for sex offenders if such a disposition "affords a better opportunity for rehabilitation of the offender and for the ultimate protection of the victim and society." Reacting to an online petition to remove him from office that had collected about 265,000 supporters, Judge McKeon said that though his ruling was not "popular," it was "just and proper." More than 1.3 million people signed a similar online petition to remove Judge Persky as part of the Brock Turner sentencing controversy.

FOR CRITICAL ANALYSIS

1. Judge Stefan Underhill had two reasons for thinking the confessed murderer he sentenced to eighteen years deserved leniency. First, the offender showed remorse. Second, he gave prosecutors valuable information about the criminal activity of his fellow gang members. How much influence should either of these factors have on a murder sentence?

2. Judge Aaron Persky justified his sentencing decision by saying that a long prison term would not make Brock Turner any *less* likely to commit another violent crime in the future. Do you agree with this reasoning?

3. The mother of the victim in the Montana incest case requested that the defendant not be punished too harshly. "He is not a monster, just a man that really screwed up," she told the court. How much weight should judges gives the wishes of victims or victims' family members in making sentencing decisions?

The Purpose of Sentencing

Professor Herbert Packer has said that punishing criminals serves two ultimate purposes: the "deserved infliction of suffering on evil doers" and "the prevention of crime."[1] Even this straightforward assessment raises several questions. How does one determine the sort of punishment that is "deserved"? How can we be sure that certain penalties "prevent" crime? Should criminals be punished solely for the benefit of society, or should their well-being also be taken into consideration? Why did Brock Turner and the Montana father receive such light sentences for acts that have resulted in many other defendants spending decades behind bars?

Sentencing laws indicate how any given society has answered these questions, but do not tell us why they were answered in that manner. To understand why, we must first consider the four basic philosophical reasons for sentencing—retribution, deterrence, incapacitation, and rehabilitation.

Retribution

The oldest and most common justification for punishing someone is that he or she "deserved it"—as the Old Testament states, "an eye for an eye and a tooth for a tooth." Under a system of justice that favors **retribution,** a wrongdoer who has freely chosen to violate society's rules must be punished for the infraction. Retribution relies on the principle of **just deserts,** which holds that the severity of the punishment must be in proportion to the severity of the crime. Retributive justice is not the same as *revenge*. Whereas revenge implies that the wrongdoer is punished only with the aim of satisfying a victim or victims, retribution is more concerned with the needs of society as a whole.

The *principle of willful wrongdoing* is central to the idea of retribution. According to this principle, society is morally justified in punishing someone only if that person was aware that he or she committed a crime. Therefore, animals, children, and people who are mentally incapacitated are not responsible for their criminal actions, even though they may be a threat to the community.[2] Furthermore, the principles of retribution reject any wide-reaching social benefit as a goal of punishment. The philosopher Immanuel Kant (1724–1804), an early proponent of retribution in criminal justice, believed that punishment by a court

> can never be inflicted merely as a means to promote some other good for the criminal himself or for civil society. It must always be inflicted upon him only because he has committed a crime. For a man can never be treated merely as a means to the purposes of another.[3]

In other words, punishment is an end in itself and cannot be justified by any future good that may result from a criminal's suffering.

One problem with retributive ideas of justice lies in proportionality. Whether or not one agrees with the death penalty, the principle behind it is easy to fathom: The punishment (death) often fits the crime (murder). But what about the theft of an automobile? How does one fairly determine the amount of time the thief must spend in prison for that crime? Should the type of car or the wealth of the car owner matter? Theories of retribution often have a difficult time providing answers to such questions.

Deterrence

Whereas the goal of retribution is only to punish the wrong-doer, the goal of **deterrence** is to prevent future crimes. By "setting an example," society is sending a message to potential criminals that certain actions will not be tolerated. Jeremy Bentham, a

Learning Objective 1 List and contrast the four basic philosophical reasons for sentencing criminals.

Retribution The philosophy that those who commit criminal acts should be punished for breaking society's rules to the extent required by just deserts.

Just Deserts A sanctioning philosophy based on the assertion that criminal punishment should be proportionate to the severity of the crime.

Deterrence The strategy of preventing crime through the threat of punishment.

▲ A Los Angeles judge recently sentenced Dr. Hsui-Ying Tseng to thirty years to life in prison for improperly prescribing drugs to three of her patients who fatally overdosed. Tseng is the first doctor to be convicted of murder in the United States for overprescribing medication. **How does the theory of deterrence justify Tseng's punishment?**

Irfan Khan/*Los Angeles Times*/Getty Images

nineteenth-century British reformer who first articulated the principles of deterrence, felt that retribution was counterproductive because it does not serve the community. He believed that a person should be punished only when punishment is in society's best interests and that the severity of the punishment should be based on its deterrent value, not on the severity of the crime.[4]

General and Specific Deterrence

Deterrence can take two forms: general and specific. The basic idea of *general deterrence* is that by punishing one person, society discourages others from committing a similar crime. *Specific deterrence* assumes that an individual, after being punished once for a certain act, will be less likely to repeat that act because she or he does not want to be punished again.[5] Proponents of harsh sentences for nonviolent drug crimes often rely on general deterrence principles to argue that such punishments discourage illegal drug possession and distribution by others.[6]

Both forms of deterrence have proved problematic in practice. General deterrence assumes that a person commits a crime only after a rational decision-making process in which he or she implicitly weighs the benefits of the crime against the possible costs of the punishment. This is not necessarily the case, especially for young offenders who tend to value the immediate rewards of crime over the possible future consequences. The argument for specific deterrence is somewhat weakened by the fact that a relatively small number of habitual offenders are responsible for the majority of certain criminal acts.

Low Probability of Punishment

Another criticism of deterrence is that for most offenses, wrongdoers are unlikely to be caught, sentenced, and imprisoned. According to the National Crime Victimization Survey, only 47 percent of all violent crimes and 35 percent of all property crimes are even reported to the police.[7] Of those reported, only 46 percent of violent crimes and 19 percent of property crimes result in an arrest.[8] Then, as we saw in Chapter 9, case attrition further whittles down the number of arrestees who face trial and the possibility of imprisonment.

Furthermore, studies show that potential offenders are generally unaware of the likely punishment for any given crime, and they underestimate the already low probability of being caught by law enforcement.[9] Professors Paul H. Robinson of the University of Pennsylvania Law School and John M. Darley of Princeton University note that this low probability of punishment could be offset by making the punishment so severe that even the slightest chance of apprehension could act as a deterrent—for example, an eighty-five-year prison term for shoplifting or the loss of a hand for burglary.[10] Or punishments could be "advertised" to have a greater deterrent impact. In Iran, criminals are sometimes hanged in public, and Chinese authorities broadcast death sentence proceedings on national television. Our society is, however, unwilling to accept such practices.

Incapacitation

"Wicked people exist," said James Q. Wilson. "Nothing avails except to set them apart from innocent people."[11] Wilson's blunt statement summarizes the justification for **incapacitation** as a form of punishment. As a purely practical matter, incarcerating criminals guarantees that they will not be a danger to society, at least for the length of their prison terms. Such reasoning is partially responsible for the dramatic increase of life sentences without the possibility of parole in the criminal justice system. Since 1984, the inmate population serving life without parole has quadrupled, to nearly 160,000, encompassing one of every nine individuals behind bars in the United States.[12] (See the feature *Comparative Criminal Justice—"Forgotten Human Waste"* to learn about Europe's philosophy regarding the incapacitation of violent offenders for life.)

The Impact of Incapacitation Several studies do support incapacitation's efficacy as a crime-fighting tool. Criminologist Isaac Ehrlich of the University at Buffalo estimated that a 1 percent increase in sentence length will produce a 1 percent decrease in the crime rate.[13] More recently, Avinash Singh Bhati of the Urban Institute in Washington, D.C., found that higher levels of incarceration lead to fewer violent crimes but have little impact on property crime rates.[14]

Incapacitation as a theory of punishment does suffer from several weaknesses. Unlike retribution, it offers no proportionality with regard to a particular crime. Giving a burglar a life sentence would certainly ensure that she or he would not commit another burglary. Does that justify such a severe penalty? Furthermore, incarceration protects society only

---

 COMPARATIVE CRIMINAL JUSTICE

Source: Central Intelligence Agency

"Forgotten Human Waste"

In 1979, James Murray was sentenced to life in prison for murdering a six-year-old on the Caribbean island of Curaçao, which is part of the Netherlands. Although Murray asked several times to be pardoned by the Dutch king (his only hope for early release), these requests were denied. Murray was finally released after being diagnosed with terminal cancer. Following Murray's death in 2014, the European Court of Human Rights (ECHR) criticized the Netherlands' practice of sentencing violent offenders to life in prison as inhumane. According to the ECHR, no person deserves to be treated as "forgotten human waste" in this manner.

TIME FOR A CHANGE
The ECHR oversees the provisions of a human rights treaty signed by most countries in Europe, including the Netherlands. Earlier in this decade, the ECHR ruled that the practice of life imprisonment was contrary to the treaty, which prohibits torture and inhuman or degrading punishment. This ruling aligned with federal law in most European countries—except for the Netherlands. With thirty-three inmates serving life sentences without any prospects for release, the Dutch remained an exception to the rule.

That changed in 2016, when the *Hoge Raad*, the Supreme Court of the Netherlands, decided to move the country toward European norms. Starting the next year, all Dutch inmates sentenced to life would be afforded a "right to review" after twenty-five years to determine whether their continued imprisonment could still be justified. In addition, Dutch corrections officials were ordered to prepare such prisoners for eventual release, regardless of the seriousness of their crimes.

FOR CRITICAL ANALYSIS
What is your opinion of the European philosophy that all life imprisonment sentences—even for the worst of violent offenders—are "inhuman and degrading" and should be prohibited?

until the criminal is freed. Many studies have shown that, on release, offenders may actually be more likely to commit crimes than before they were imprisoned.[15] In that case, incapacitation may increase likelihood of crime, rather than diminish it.

Selective and Collective Incapacitation   Some observers believe that strategies of *selective incapacitation* should be favored over strategies of *collective incapacitation* for the best results. With collective incapacitation, all offenders who have committed a similar crime are imprisoned for the same time period. Selective incapacitation, in contrast, provides longer sentences for individuals, such as career criminals, who are considered more likely to commit further crimes if and when they are released.

The problem with selective incapacitation lies in the difficulty of predicting just who is at the greatest risk to commit future crimes. Studies have shown that even the most effective methods of trying to predict future criminality are correct less than half of the time.[16]

Rehabilitation

For many, rehabilitation is the most "humane" goal of punishment. This line of thinking reflects the view that crime is a "social phenomenon" caused not by the inherent criminality of a person, but by factors in that person's surroundings. By removing wrongdoers from their environment and intervening to change their values and personalities, the rehabilitative model suggests that criminals can be "treated" and possibly even "cured" of their proclivities toward crime. Although studies of the effectiveness of rehabilitation are too varied to be easily summarized, it does appear that, in most instances, criminals who receive treatment are less likely to reoffend than those who do not.[17]

For the better part of the past four decades, the American criminal justice system has been characterized by a notable rejection of many of the precepts of rehabilitation in favor of retributive, deterrent, and incapacitating sentencing strategies that "get tough on crime." Recently, however, more jurisdictions are turning to rehabilitation as a cost-effective (and, possibly, crime-reducing) alternative to punishment, a topic that we will explore more fully in the next few chapters.

Furthermore, the American public may be more accepting of rehabilitative principles than many elected officials think. A recent national survey by the Pew Research Center found that more than 80 percent of respondents supported job training and drug treatment programs for nonviolent prison inmates.[18] In addition, according to Gallup, in 2016, only 45 percent of Americans thought that the criminal justice system was not "tough enough" on criminals, compared with 65 percent in 2003.[19] (See the accompanying *Mastering Concepts* feature for an overview of the four main sentencing philosophies.)

Restorative Justice

On many reservations across the United States, Native Americans practice a "peacemaking" approach to criminal justice. Unlike the adversary system of the mainstream court system, peacemaking focuses on dispute resolution and the needs of the community rather than the rights of individual offenders. In a Navajo peacemaking session, for example, members of the community, including the victim, describe the harm suffered because of the act in question. Then, the participants, as a group, decide on the proper *nalyeeh*, loosely translated as payment, that the offender (or the offender's family) owes the community.[20]

The goal of *nalyeeh*, which may or may not include money, is to make the injured party and the community "feel better," in the words of one Navajo judge.[21] In Native American jurisdictions, these principles have been applied to resolve criminal issues from domestic

Rehabilitation The philosophy that society is best served when wrongdoers are provided the resources needed to eliminate their criminal behavior.

Sentencing Philosophies

Several years ago, Judge John Baricevic sentenced Thomas Kelley to seven years behind bars for cooking methamphetamine in a house where a one-year-old child was present. Even though Kelley was a nonviolent drug offender—a class of criminal that is increasingly being diverted from prison—the judge's decision was in keeping with the four main philosophies of sentencing.

PHILOSOPHY	BASIC PRINCIPLE	EXPLANATION
Retribution	Punishment is society's means of expressing condemnation of illegal acts such as drug crimes.	According to a prosecutor, Thomas Kelley was not punished "for being an addict" but rather "for making a decision that put people at risk."
Deterrence	Harsh sentences for drug crimes may convince others not to engage in that illegal behavior.	Prosecutors said that Kelley's example would prevent others from making drugs in the presence of children, which constitutes a threat to "public safety."
Incapacitation	Incarcerated criminals are not a threat to the general society for the duration of their time behind bars.	Kelley will be unable to commit any drug-related crimes while incarcerated.
Rehabilitation	Prison programs can help inmates change their behavior so that they no longer pose a threat to themselves or others.	In prison, Kelley will be able to receive vocational training and substance abuse treatment. "You can come out better or you can come out worse," Judge Baricevic told the defendant. "That's your choice."

Source: Beth Hundsdorfer, "Belleville Man Admits Addiction, Receives Seven-Year Prison Sentence," www.bnd.com. Belleville News-Democrat: December 15, 2015, Web.

violence to gang activity to driving while intoxicated. They are also spreading to the non-tribal criminal justice system as part of the **restorative justice** movement in this country.

A Different Approach   Restorative justice strategies attempt to repair the damage that a crime does to the victim, the victim's family, and society as a whole. This outlook relies on the efforts of the offender to "undo" the harm caused by the criminal act through an apology and **restitution,** or monetary compensation for losses suffered by the victim. Five features differentiate restorative justice from the mainstream criminal justice system:

1. *Offender involvement.* Offenders are given the opportunity to take responsibility for and address the reasons behind their behavior in ways that do not involve the corrections system.
2. *Victim involvement.* Victims have a voice in determining how the offender should atone for her or his crime.
3. *Victim-offender interaction.* On a voluntary basis, victims and offenders meet to discuss and better understand the circumstances of the crime. This meeting allows the victim to express her or his feelings related to the offense.
4. *Community involvement.* Community members also affected by the crime can participate in the process and request an apology and restitution from the offender.
5. *Problem-solving practices.* Participants in the process—including victims, offenders, and community members—can develop strategies for solving the problems that led to the crime in question.[22]

Although restorative justice is theoretically available for all types of criminal behavior, it almost always involves property crime, public order crime, and, particularly, offenses committed by juveniles. Rarely, if ever, will restorative justice principles be applied to violent crime.

Restorative Justice An approach to punishment designed to repair the harm done to the victim and the community by the offender's criminal act.

Restitution Monetary compensation for damages done to the victim by the offender's criminal act.

Indeterminate Sentencing
Imposition of a sentence that
prescribes a range of years rather
than a specified number of years to be
served.

Restorative Justice Legislation

About thirty-five states have passed legislation that relies on restorative justice principles and uses the language of the movement. For the most part, these laws involve alternatives to the state juvenile justice system, victim participation in the justice process, and the requirement that offenders pay restitution directly to victims or into a victims' fund.[23] On the federal level, the Victims of Crime Act of 1984 established the Crime Victims Fund to provide financial aid for crime victims.[24] This program—financed by fines and penalties assessed on convicted federal offenders—distributes grants to state governments, which in turn pass the funds on to victims.

Victim-Offender Dialogue

Principles of restorative justice are also infiltrating the American corrections system. For example, the practice of *victim-offender dialogue (VOD)* encourages face-to-face meetings between victims and offenders in a secure setting at the offender's prison. VOD allows victims to speak directly to offenders about the criminal incident and how it has affected their lives. It also gives the offender a chance to apologize directly to the victim. Today, more than half of state corrections departments support VOD programs within their prisons.[25]

Although restorative justice still suffers from the suspicion among criminal justice professionals that it is too vague and "touchy-feely" to be useful,[26] that perception is changing. According to Stanley Garnett, a district attorney in Boulder, Colorado, "[S]tats don't lie—recidivism drops significantly when restorative justice processes are employed."[27]

ETHICS CHALLENGE

In Iran, convicted criminals can buy their freedom from their victims. Several years ago, for example, a man found guilty of murdering a rival during a knife fight had the charges against him dropped after he paid the victim's family $50,000. Does this practice have any ethical benefits for society? How does it differ from the American practice of restitution, described in this section? Explain your answers.

The Structure of Sentencing

Philosophy not only is integral to explaining *why* we punish criminals, but also influences *how* we do so. The history of criminal sentencing in the United States has been characterized by shifts in institutional power among the three branches of the government. When public opinion moves toward more severe strategies of retribution, deterrence, and incapacitation, *legislatures* have responded by asserting their power over determining sentencing guidelines. In contrast, periods of rehabilitation are marked by a transfer of this power to the *administrative* and *judicial* branches.

Legislative Sentencing Authority

Because legislatures are responsible for making laws, these bodies are also initially responsible for passing the criminal codes that determine the length of sentences.

Learning
2
Objective
Contrast indeterminate with
determinate sentencing.

Indeterminate Sentencing

Penal codes with indeterminate sentencing policies set a minimum and maximum amount of time that a person must spend in prison. For example, the indeterminate sentence for aggravated assault could be three to nine years, or six to twelve years, or twenty years to life. Within these parameters, a judge can prescribe a particular term, after which an administrative body known as the *parole board* decides at what point the offender is to be released. A prisoner is aware that he or she is eligible for *parole* as soon as the minimum time has been served and that good behavior can further shorten the sentence.

Determinate Sentencing

Disillusionment with the somewhat vague nature of indeterminate sentencing often leads politicians to support **determinate sentencing,** or fixed sentencing. As the name implies, in determinate sentencing an offender serves exactly the amount of time to which she or he is sentenced (minus "good time," described below). For example, if the legislature deems that the punishment for a first-time armed robber is ten years, then the judge has no choice but to impose a sentence of ten years, and the criminal will serve ten years minus good time before being freed.

"Good Time" and Truth in Sentencing

Often, the amount of time prescribed by a judge bears little relation to the amount of time the offender actually spends behind bars. In states with indeterminate sentencing, parole boards have broad powers to release prisoners once they have served the minimum portion of their sentence. Furthermore, most states offer prisoners the opportunity to reduce their sentences by doing **"good time"**—or behaving well—as determined by prison administrators. (See Figure 11.1 for an idea of the effects of good-time regulations and other early-release programs on state prison sentences.)

Sentence-reduction programs promote discipline within a correctional institution and reduce overcrowding, so many prison officials welcome them. The public, however, may react negatively to news that a violent criminal has served a shorter term than ordered by a judge and pressure elected officials to "do something." In Illinois, for example, some inmates were serving less than half their sentences by receiving a one-day reduction in their term for each day of "good time." Under pressure from victims' groups, the state legislature passed a **truth-in-sentencing law** that requires murderers and others convicted of serious crimes to complete at least 85 percent of their sentences with no time off for good behavior.[28]

As their name suggests, the primary goal of these laws is to provide the public with more accurate information about the actual amount of time an offender will spend behind

Determinate Sentencing Imposition of a sentence that is fixed by a sentencing authority and cannot be reduced by judges or other corrections officials.

"Good Time" A reduction in time served by prisoners based on good behavior, conformity to rules, and other positive behavior.

Truth-in-Sentencing Law Legislative attempts to ensure that convicts will serve approximately the terms to which they were initially sentenced.

Learning Objective 3 Explain why there is a difference between the sentence imposed by a judge and the actual sentence served by the prisoner.

FIGURE 11.1 Average Sentence Length and Estimated Time to Be Served in State Prison

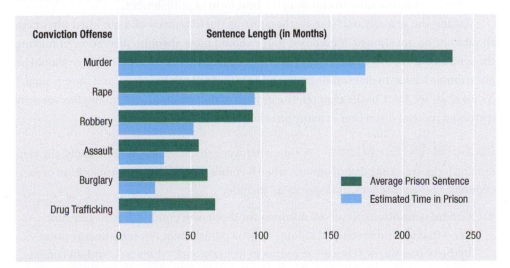

Source: *National Corrections Reporting Program: Sentence Length of State Prisoners, by Offense, Admission Type, Sex, and Race,* "Table 9: First Releases from State Prison, 2009." *www.bjs.gov.* Bureau of Justice Statistics: May 5, 2011, Web.

bars. The laws also keep convicts incapacitated for longer periods of time. Fifteen years after Illinois passed its truth-in-sentencing law, those murderers subject to the legislation were spending an average of seventeen months more in prison than those not subject to the legislation. For sex offenders, the difference was 3.5 years.[29] Today, forty states have instituted some form of truth-in-sentencing laws, though the continued popularity of such statutes is being undermined by the pressures of overflowing prisons.

Administrative Sentencing Authority

Parole is a condition of early release in which a prisoner is released from a correctional facility but is not freed from the legal custody and supervision of the state. Generally, after an inmate has been released on parole, he or she is supervised by a parole officer for a specified amount of time. The decision of whether to parole an inmate lies with the parole board. Parole is a crucial aspect of the criminal justice system and will be discussed in detail in Chapter 12.

For now, it is important to understand the role rehabilitation theories play in *administrative sentencing authority*. The formation in 1910 of the U.S. Parole Commission and similar commissions in the fifty states implied that the judge, though a legal expert, was not trained to determine when an inmate had been rehabilitated. Therefore, the commission argued, sentencing power should be given to experts in human behavior, who were qualified to determine whether a convict was fit to return to society.[30]

Judicial Sentencing Authority

During the pretrial procedures and the trial itself, the judge's role is somewhat passive and reactive. She or he is primarily a "procedural watchdog," ensuring that the rights of the defendant are not infringed while the prosecutor and defense attorney dictate the course of action. At a traditional sentencing hearing, however, the judge is no longer an arbiter between the parties. She or he is now called on to exercise the ultimate authority of the state in determining the defendant's fate.

When theories of rehabilitation hold sway over the criminal justice system, indeterminate sentencing practices are guided by the theory of "individualized justice." Just as a physician gives specific treatment to individual patients depending on their particular health needs, the hypothesis goes, a judge needs to consider the specific circumstances of each individual offender in choosing the best form of punishment.

Taking the analogy one step further, just as the diagnosis of a qualified physician should not be questioned, a qualified judge should have absolute discretion in making the sentencing decision. *Judicial discretion* rests on the assumption that a judge should be given ample leeway in determining punishments that fit both the crime and the criminal.[31] As we shall see later in the chapter, the growth of determinate sentencing has severely restricted judicial discretion in many jurisdictions.

Judicial Dispositions Within whatever legislative restrictions apply, the sentencing judge has a number of options when it comes to choosing the proper form of punishment. These sentences, or *dispositions*, include:

1. *Capital punishment.* Reserved normally for those who commit first degree murder—that is, a premeditated killing—capital punishment is a sentencing option in thirty-one states. It is also an option in federal court, where a defendant can be put to death for murder, as well as for trafficking in a large amount of illegal drugs, *espionage* (spying), and treason (betraying the United States).

Ellen Kalama Clark Superior Court Judge

My favorite thing about my work is making a difference in people's lives. This is especially true in juvenile court, which is my favorite assignment. For example, early one morning I was walking to the juvenile court building when I saw a group of teenage boys heading toward me. Some of them I recognized from being in court, and they recognized me. A couple avoided eye contact, one looked me straight in the eye rather defiantly, and the last one kind of smirked. As we got closer to each other, the last boy—a tall, stocky kid—stopped, and the group just about blocked the sidewalk. It made me nervous.

The boy then leaned forward toward me and said, not in an intimidating manner but certainly meaning to get my attention, "Hey, Judge." I said good morning. He then broke into a big smile and said, "I got my GED [general equivalency diploma]! And I'm staying out of trouble." I didn't remember his name or his offense, but I was absolutely thrilled that he had accomplished those things, that he would want me to know that, and that he was bragging about it in front of his friends. I consider this a great success story.

Courtesy of Ellen Kalama Clark

FASTFACTS

Judge

Job description:
- Preside over trials and hearings in federal, state, and local courts.

What kind of training is required?
- A law degree and several years of legal experience.
- Judges are either appointed or elected.

Annual salary range?
- $118,000–$205,000

SOCIAL MEDIA CAREER TIP Think about your online presence as your online personal brand. You create this online personal brand through the sum of all the posts you make on different websites and social media tools.

2. *Imprisonment.* Whether for the purpose of retribution, deterrence, incapacitation, or rehabilitation, a common form of punishment in American history has been imprisonment. In fact, it is used so commonly today that judges—and legislators—are having to take factors such as prison overcrowding into consideration when making sentencing decisions. The issues surrounding imprisonment will be discussed in Chapters 13 and 14.

3. *Probation.* One of the effects of prison overcrowding has been a sharp rise in the use of probation, in which an offender is permitted to live in the community under supervision and is not incarcerated. (Probation is covered in Chapter 12.) *Alternative sanctions* (also discussed in Chapter 12) combine probation with other dispositions, such as electronic monitoring, house arrest, boot camps, and shock incarceration.

4. *Fines.* Fines can be levied by judges in addition to incarceration and probation or independently of other forms of punishment. Fines are generally considered a form of judicial leniency for nonviolent offenders. This disposition has, however, come under criticism recently for its often stark alternatives: pay or go to jail.[32] Although technically unconstitutional,[33] the widespread practice of incarcerating those who cannot pay their fines unavoidably discriminates against indigent defendants.

Whereas fines are payable to the government, restitution and community service are seen as reparations to the injured party or to the community. As noted earlier, restitution is a direct payment to the victim or victims of a crime. Community service consists of "good works"—such as cleaning up highway litter or tutoring disadvantaged youths—that benefit the entire community.

Along with restitution, *apologies* play an important role in restorative justice, discussed previously. An apology is seen as an effort by the offender to recognize the wrongness of her or his conduct and acknowledge the impact that it has had on the victim and the community. (See the feature *Discretion in Action—Pledge Night* to learn more about one judge's sentencing decision.)

Creative Punishments   In some jurisdictions, judges have a great deal of discretionary power and can impose sentences that do not fall into any of the categories listed above. This "creative sentencing," as it is sometimes called, has produced some interesting results. Over the past few years, Painesville (Ohio) Municipal Court Judge Michael Cicconetti has sentenced a man who solicited a prostitute to wear a chicken suit and ordered a woman who mistreated her dog to pick up garbage in a dump. Judge Cicconetti also recently gave an eighteen-year-old who failed to pay a taxi driver for a thirty-mile ride a choice—spend thirty days in jail or walk thirty miles. (She chose the walk.)[34] Though these types of punishments are often ridiculed, many judges see them as a viable alternative to incarceration for less dangerous offenders.

DISCRETION IN ACTION

Pledge Night

The Situation Michael was a nineteen-year-old pledge of the Pi Delta Psi fraternity. At an early December weekend retreat in Pennsylvania's Pocono Mountains, Michael and the other pledges were blindfolded, outfitted with backpacks weighted with sand, and forced to cross a frozen yard while taking blows from fraternity members. During the ritual, Michael kicked one of the men tackling him. In retaliation, fraternity members struck him more forcefully and pushed him to the ground, each knock amplified by the weight of the backpack.

Michael lost consciousness. While some of the fraternity members searched the Internet for terms like "Concussion can't wake up," others tried to hide evidence linking them to his injuries. After an hour, three members took Michael to a nearby hospital, where he eventually died from brain damage. A doctor at the hospital determined that his head injuries were so severe that they would have required "hundreds of pounds" of force. At trial, one of the fraternity members known to have struck Michael was found guilty of third degree murder, or "acting with extreme indifference to human life."

The Law Under state sentencing guidelines, the penalties for third degree murder without a deadly weapon can range from six to forty years in prison. These guidelines are, however, not mandatory.

What Would You Do? You are the sentencing judge in this trial. You have several factors to consider. The defendant had no previous criminal record. As his lawyer argued, "This was a scared kid who clearly had no intention to commit any crimes that weekend. When the accident occurred, he used bad judgment." At the same time, the defendant did help try to cover up the crime and lied to police about his involvement in Michael's death. Furthermore, a harsh punishment would send the message that the criminal justice system does not condone violent fraternity hazing. Choosing from the dispositions in the text, how would you sentence the defendant?

To see how a judge in Monroe County, Pennsylvania, decided the outcome of a similar case, go to Example 11.1 in Appendix B.

The Sentencing Process

The decision of how to punish a wrongdoer is the end result of what Yale Law School professor Kate Stith and federal appeals court judge José A. Cabranes call the "sentencing ritual."[35] The two main participants in this ritual are the judge and the defendant, but prosecutors, defense attorneys, and probation officers also play roles in the proceedings. Individualized justice requires that the judge consider all the relevant circumstances in making sentencing decisions. Therefore, judicial discretion is often tantamount to *informed* discretion—without the aid of the other members of the courtroom work group, the judge would not have sufficient information to make the proper sentencing choice.

Learning Objective 4 State who has input into the sentencing decision and list the factors that determine a sentence.

The Presentence Investigative Report

For judges operating under indeterminate sentencing guidelines, information in the presentence investigative report is a valuable component of the sentencing ritual. Compiled by a probation officer, the report describes the crime in question, notes the suffering of any victims, and lists the defendant's prior offenses (as well as any alleged but uncharged criminal activity). The report also contains a range of personal data such as family background, work history, education, and community activities—information that is not admissible as evidence during trial. In putting together the presentence investigative report, the probation officer is supposed to gain a "feel" for the defendant and communicate these impressions of the offender to the judge.

The report also includes a sentencing recommendation. For example, as part of the case discussed in the opening of this chapter, a county probation officer recommended a "moderate jail sentence" for Brock Turner. Her presentence report cited Turner's "lack of a criminal history, his youthful age, and his expressed remorse and empathy toward the victim."[36] This practice has been criticized as giving probation officers too much power in the sentencing process, because less diligent judges might simply rely on the recommendation in determining punishment.[37] For the most part, however, judges do not act as if they were bound by the presentence investigative report.

The Prosecutor and Defense Attorney

To a certain extent, the adversary process does not end when the guilt of the defendant has been established. Both the prosecutor and the defense attorney are interviewed in the process of preparing the presentence investigative report, and both will try to present a version of the facts consistent with their own sentencing goals. The defense attorney in particular has a duty to make sure that the information contained in the report is accurate and not prejudicial toward his or her client. Depending on the norms of any particular courtroom work group, prosecutors and defense attorneys may petition the judge directly for certain sentences.

Sentencing and the Jury

Juries also play an important role in the sentencing process. As we will see later in the chapter, it is the jury, and not the judge, that generally decides whether a convict eligible for the death penalty will in fact be executed. Additionally, six states—Arkansas, Kentucky, Missouri, Oklahoma, Texas, and Virginia—allow juries, rather than judges, to make the sentencing decision even when the death penalty is not an option. In these states, the judge gives the jury instructions on the range of penalties available, and then the jury makes the final decision.[38]

Presentence Investigative Report An investigative report on an offender's background that assists a judge in determining the proper sentence.

Factors of Sentencing

The sentencing ritual strongly lends itself to the concept of individualized justice. With inputs—sometimes conflicting—from the prosecutor, attorney, and probation officer, the judge can be reasonably sure of getting the "full picture" of the crime and the criminal. In making the final decision, however, most judges consider two factors above all others: the seriousness of the crime and any mitigating or aggravating circumstances.

The Seriousness of the Crime
As would be expected, the seriousness of the crime is the primary factor in a judge's sentencing decision. The more serious the crime, the harsher the punishment, for society demands no less. Each judge has his or her own methods of determining the seriousness of the offense. Many judges simply consider the "conviction offense," basing their sentence on the crime for which the defendant was convicted.

Other judges—some mandated by statute—focus instead on the **"real offense"** in determining the punishment. The "real offense" is based on the actual behavior of the defendant, regardless of the official conviction. For example, through a plea bargain, a defendant may plead guilty to simple assault when in fact he hit his victim in the face with a baseball bat. A judge, after reading the presentence investigative report, could decide to sentence the defendant as if he had committed aggravated assault, which is the "real offense." Though many prosecutors and defense attorneys are opposed to "real offense" procedures, which can render a plea bargain meaningless, there is considerable belief in criminal justice circles that they bring a measure of fairness to the sentencing decision.[39]

Mitigating and Aggravating Circumstances
When deciding the severity of punishment, judges and juries are often required to evaluate the *mitigating* and *aggravating circumstances* surrounding the case. **Mitigating circumstances** are those circumstances, such as the fact that the defendant was coerced into committing the crime, that allow a lighter sentence to be handed down. In contrast, **aggravating circumstances,** such as a prior record, blatant disregard for the safety of others, or the use of a weapon, can lead a judge or jury to inflict a harsher penalty than might otherwise be warranted (see Figure 11.2).

Aggravating circumstances play an important role in a prosecutor's decision to charge a suspect with capital murder. The criminal code of every state that employs the death penalty contains a list of aggravating circumstances that make an offender eligible for execution. Most of these codes require that the murder take place during the commission of a felony, or create a grave risk of death for multiple victims, or interfere with the duties of law enforcement.[40] As you will see later in the chapter, mitigating factors such as mental illness and youth can spare an otherwise death-eligible offender from capital punishment.

Judicial Philosophy
Most states and the federal government spell out mitigating and aggravating circumstances in statutes, but there is room for judicial discretion in applying the law to particular cases. Judges are not uniform, or even consistent, in their opinions of which circumstances are mitigating or aggravating. One judge may believe that a fourteen-year-old is not fully responsible for his or her actions, while another may believe that teenagers should be treated as adults by criminal courts. A recent study of sentencing practices in Florida suggests that defendants who look less "trustworthy" are subjected to harsher sentences from state judges.[41]

FIGURE 11.2 Aggravating and Mitigating Circumstances

AGGRAVATING CIRCUMSTANCES	MITIGATING CIRCUMSTANCES
• An offense involved multiple participants, and the offender was the leader of the group.	• An offender acted under strong provocation, or other circumstances in the relationship between the offender and the victim make the offender's behavior less serious and therefore less deserving of punishment.
• A victim was particularly vulnerable.	
• A victim was treated with particular cruelty for which an offender should be held responsible.	• An offender played a minor or passive role in the offense or participated under circumstances of coercion or duress.
• The offense involved injury or threatened violence to others and was committed to gratify an offender's desire for pleasure or excitement.	• An offender, because of youth or physical impairment, lacked substantial capacity for judgment when the offense was committed.
• The degree of bodily harm caused, attempted, threatened, or foreseen by an offender was substantially greater than average for the given offense.	
• The degree of economic harm caused, attempted, threatened, or foreseen by an offender was substantially greater than average for the given offense.	
• The amount of contraband materials possessed by the offender or under the offender's control was substantially greater than average for the given offense.	

Source: American Bar Association.

ETHICS CHALLENGE

Several years ago, the Southern Poverty Law Center filed an ethics complaint against a judge in rural Alabama for giving defendants who could not pay fines the option of donating blood instead. If the defendant could not afford the fine and did not want to give blood, she or he faced jail time. Do you agree with one ethics expert who said that this practice "is wrong in about 3,000 ways?" Why or why not?

Inconsistencies in Sentencing

For some, the natural differences in judicial philosophies, when combined with a lack of institutional control, raise important questions. Why should a bank robber in South Carolina and a bank robber in Michigan receive different sentences? Even federal indeterminate sentencing guidelines seem overly vague: a bank robber can receive a prison term from one day to twenty years, depending almost entirely on the judge.[42] Furthermore, if judges have freedom to use their discretion, do they not also have the freedom to misuse it?

Purported improper judicial discretion is often the first reason given for two phenomena that plague the criminal justice system: *sentencing disparity* and *sentencing discrimination*. Though the two terms are often used interchangeably, they describe different statistical occurrences—the causes of which are open to debate.

Learning **Objective** Explain some of the reasons why sentencing reform has occurred.

Sentencing Disparity

Justice would seem to demand that those who commit similar crimes should receive similar punishments. Sentencing disparity occurs when this expectation is not met in one of three ways:

1. Criminals receive similar sentences for different crimes of unequal seriousness.
2. Criminals receive different sentences for similar crimes.
3. Mitigating or aggravating circumstances have a disproportionate effect on sentences.

Most of the blame for sentencing disparities is placed at the feet of the judicial profession. Even with the restrictive presence of the sentencing reforms we will discuss shortly, judges have a great deal of influence over the sentencing decision, whether they are making that decision themselves or instructing the jury on how to do so. Like other members of the criminal justice system, judges are individuals, and their discretionary sentencing decisions reflect that individuality. Besides judicial discretion, several other causes have been offered as explanations for sentencing disparity, including differences between geographic jurisdictions and between federal and state courts.

Geographic Disparities

For offenders, the amount of time spent in prison often depends as much on where the crime was committed as on the crime itself. A comparison of the sentences for drug trafficking reveals that someone convicted of the crime in Washington State faces an average of 64 months in prison, whereas a similar offender in Mississippi can expect an average of 121 months.[43] The average sentences imposed in the Fourth Circuit, which includes North Carolina, South Carolina, Virginia, and West Virginia, are consistently harsher than those in the Ninth Circuit, comprising most of the western states: 31 months longer for convictions related to firearms and 34 months longer for all offenses.[44] Such disparities can be attributed to a number of different factors, including local attitudes toward crime and financial resources available to cover the expenses of incarceration.

Federal versus State Court Disparities

Because of different sentencing guidelines, the punishment for the same crime in federal and state courts can also be dramatically different. In North Carolina, for example, a defendant convicted of distributing child pornography in state court will rarely face a prison sentence of more than two years. If it is a first offense, he or she will most likely be placed on probation. Federal courts, however, have a mandatory five-year minimum prison term for any child pornography distribution conviction, with punishments often reaching twenty years because of aggravating circumstances.[45] Figure 11.3 shows the sentencing disparities for certain crimes in the two systems.

Sentencing Discrimination

Sentencing discrimination occurs when disparities can be attributed to extralegal variables such as the defendant's gender, race, or economic standing.

Race and Sentencing

At first glance, racial discrimination would seem to be rampant in sentencing practices. Research by Cassia Spohn of Arizona State University and David Holleran of the College of New Jersey suggests that minorities pay a "punishment penalty" when it comes to sentencing.[46] In Chicago, Spohn and Holleran found that

Sentencing Disparity A situation in which those convicted of similar crimes do not receive similar sentences.

Sentencing Discrimination A situation in which the length of a sentence appears to be influenced by a defendant's race, gender, economic status, or other factor not directly related to the crime he or she committed.

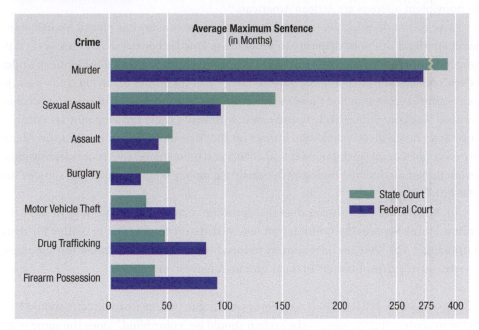

FIGURE 11.3 **Average Maximum Sentences for Selected Crimes in State and Federal Courts**

Source: Bureau of Justice Statistics, *Felony Defendants in Large Urban Counties, 2009–Statistical Tables* (Washington, D.C.: U.S. Department of Justice, December 2013), Table 25, page 30; and "Statistical Information Packet, Fiscal Year 2009, First Circuit," Table 7. *www.ussc.gov*. United States Sentencing Commission: 2010, Web.

convicted African Americans were 12.1 percent more likely and convicted Latinos were 15.3 percent more likely to go to prison than convicted whites. Another report released by the Illinois Disproportionate Justice Impact Study Commission found that African Americans were nearly five times more likely to be sentenced to prison than whites for low-level drug crimes in that state.[47]

Nationwide, sentences imposed on African American males are about 20 percent more severe than those imposed on white males for similar crimes.[48] Black and Latino defendants are also significantly more likely to be incarcerated than white defendants for comparable wrongdoing.[49] Furthermore, race seems to play a meaningful role in determining which capital crimes are punished by death sentences.[50]

Sentencing Bias?   Such numbers, while significant, may not be the result of blatant sentencing bias. For example, the large numbers of Latinos in federal prison are a direct result of immigration laws, which disproportionately target that demographic. Furthermore, Spohn and Holleran found that the rate of imprisonment rose significantly for minorities who were young and unemployed. This led them to conclude that the disparities between races were not the result of "conscious" discrimination on the part of the sentencing judges. Rather, faced with limited time to make decisions and limited information about the offenders, the judges would resort to stereotypes, considering not just race, but age and unemployment as well.[51]

Another study, published in 2006, found that older judges and judges who were members of minority groups in Pennsylvania were less likely to send offenders to prison, regardless of their race.[52] Such research findings support the argument in favor of diversity among judges, discussed in Chapter 8. One white male judge, speaking anonymously, attributed racial disparities in sentencing to bias that "affects everyone's perceptions" rather than "overt, purposeful discrimination" among his peers.[53]

Length of Sentence Further evidence suggests that race has an impact on length of sentences. Nationwide, about 65 percent of inmates serving life sentences without parole for nonviolent offenses are African American.[54]

Over recent decades, the issue of crack cocaine sentencing has placed a particularly harsh spotlight on racial disparity in sentencing. Powder cocaine and crack, a crystallized form of the drug that is smoked rather than inhaled, are chemically identical. Under federal legislation passed in 1986, however, sentences for crimes involving crack were, in some instances, one hundred times more severe than for crimes involving powder cocaine. Because blacks are more likely to use crack, with white users favoring powder cocaine, these laws had a disproportionate impact on the African American community. About 80 percent of federal crack defendants are black and therefore received considerably more severe punishments than their powder-favoring, mostly white, counterparts under the 1986 law.[55]

In 2010, Congress reduced the crack/powder cocaine disparity,[56] and in 2014 the United States Sentencing Commission lessened its recommended penalties for drug trafficking.[57] The changes retroactively reduced the sentences of almost ten thousand inmates, nearly three-quarters of them African American or Latino.[58]

Women and Sentencing

Few would argue that race or ethnicity should be a factor in sentencing decisions—the system should be "color-blind." Does the same principle apply to women? In other words, should the system be "gender-blind" as well—at least on a policy level? Congress answered that question in the Sentencing Reform Act of 1984, which emphasized the ideal of gender-neutral sentencing.[59] In practice, however, this ideal has not been realized.

Gender Differences Women who are convicted of crimes are less likely to go to prison than men, and those who are incarcerated tend to serve shorter sentences. According to government data, on average, a woman receives a sentence that is twenty-nine months shorter than that of a man for a violent crime and nine months shorter for a property crime.[60] When adjusting for comparable arrest offenses, criminal histories, and other presentencing factors, Sonja B. Starr of the University of Michigan Law School found that male convicts receive sentences that are 60 percent more severe than those for women.[61]

The Chivalry Effect One study attributes gender differences in sentencing to certain characteristics of female criminality. Women who commit property crimes are usually accessories, and women who commit violent crimes are usually reacting to physical abuse. In both situations, the mitigating circumstances lead to lesser punishment.[62]

Other evidence suggests that a *chivalry effect*, or the idea that women should be treated more leniently than men, plays a large role in sentencing decisions. Several self-reported studies have shown that judges may treat female defendants more "gently" than males and that with women, judges are influenced by mitigating factors, such as marital status and family background, that they would ignore with men.[63]

In certain situations, however, a woman's gender may seem to work against her. In 2016, for example, married couple Christopher and Lonna Barton pleaded guilty to selling "Molly," a synthetic hallucinogen and amphetamine. A Baker County (Florida) judge sentenced Christopher to three years in prison and Lonna to seven years in prison. Explaining the discrepancy, Lonna's defense attorney said he believed that his client had received extra punishment because, in separate proceedings, she had been found guilty of neglect that contributed to the death of her infant son.[64] According to Keith Crew, a professor of sociology and criminology at the University of Northern Iowa, defendants who are seen as bad mothers often "get the hammer" from judges and juries.[65]

Sentencing Reform

Judicial discretion, then, has both positive and negative aspects. Although it allows judges to impose a wide variety of sentences to fit specific criminal situations, it appears to fail to rein in some judges' subjective biases, which can lead to disparity and perhaps discrimination. Critics of judicial discretion believe that its costs (the lack of equality) outweigh its benefits (providing individualized justice). As Columbia law professor John C. Coffee noted:

> If we wish the sentencing judge to treat "like cases alike," a more inappropriate technique for the presentation could hardly be found than one that stresses a novelistic portrayal of each offender and thereby overloads the decisionmaker in a welter of detail.[66]

In other words, Professor Coffee feels that judges are given too much information in the sentencing process, making it impossible for them to be consistent in their decisions. It follows that limiting judicial discretion would not only simplify the process but lessen the opportunity for disparity or discrimination. This attitude has spread through state and federal legislatures, causing extensive changes in sentencing procedures within the American criminal justice system.

Sentencing Guidelines

In an effort to eliminate the inequities of disparity by removing judicial bias from the sentencing process, many states and the federal government have turned to **sentencing guidelines,** which require judges to dispense legislatively determined sentences based on factors such as the seriousness of the crime and the offender's prior record.

State Sentencing Guidelines

About twenty states employ some form of sentencing guidelines. In general, these guidelines remove discretionary power from state judges by turning sentencing into a mathematical exercise. Members of the courtroom work group use a *grid* to determine the proper sentence. Figure 11.4 shows the grid established by the Massachusetts sentencing commission. One axis ranks the type of crime, while the other identifies the offender's criminal history. The pink boxes indicate the "incarceration zone." A prison sentence is required for crimes in this zone. The yellow boxes identify the "discretionary zone," in which the judge can decide between incarceration and intermediate sanctions, which you will learn about in the next chapter. The green boxes indicate the "intermediate sanction zone," in which only intermediate sanctions are to be levied.

▲ A judge in Pontiac, Michigan, gave seventy-five-year-old Sandra Layne a harsher sentence than required by state guidelines for the second-degree murder of her seventeen-year-old grandson. **How might a woman's gender work against her in sentencing situations involving family-related violent crimes?**

AP Images/*The Oakland Press*, Vaughn Gurganian

Sentencing Guidelines Legislatively determined guidelines that judges are required to follow when sentencing those convicted of specific crimes.

FIGURE 11.4 **Massachusetts's Sentencing Guidelines**

Sentencing Guidelines Grid

Level	Illustrative Offenses	Sentence Range				
		A No/Minor Record	B Moderate Record	C Serious Record	D Violent/Repetitive	E Serious Violent
9	Murder	Life	Life	Life	Life	Life
8	Manslaughter (Voluntary) / Rape of a Child with Force / Aggravated Rape / Armed Burglary	96–144 Months	108–162 Months	120–180 Months	144–216 Months	204–306 Months
7	Armed Robbery / Rape / Mayhem	60–90 Months	68–102 Months	84–126 Months	108–162 Months	160–240 Months
6	Manslaughter (Involuntary) / Armed Robbery (No Gun) / A&B DW* (Significant Injury)	40–60 Months	45–67 Months	50–75 Months	60–90 Months	80–120 Months
5	Unarmed Robbery / Unarmed Burglary / Stalking in Violation of Order / Larceny ($50,000 and over)	12–36 Months IS-IV IS-III IS-II	24–36 Months IS-IV IS-III IS-II	36–54 Months	48–72 Months	60–90 Months
4	Larceny (from a Person) / A&B DW (Moderate Injury)* / B&E** (Dwelling) / Larceny ($10,000 to $50,000)	0–24 Months IS-IV IS-III IS-II	3–30 Months IS-IV IS-III IS-II	6–30 Months IS-IV IS-III IS-II	20–30 Months	24–36 Months
3	A&B DW (Minor or No Injury) / B&E (Not Dwelling) / Larceny ($250 to $10,000)	0–12 Months IS-IV IS-III IS-II IS-I	0–15 Months IS-IV IS-III IS-II IS-I	0–18 Months IS-IV IS-III IS-II IS-I	0–24 Months IS-IV IS-III IS-II	6–24 Months IS-IV IS-III IS-II
2	Assault / Larceny (under $250)	IS-III IS-II IS-I	0–6 Months IS-III IS-II IS-I	0–6 Months IS-III IS-II IS-I	0–9 Months IS-IV IS-III IS-II IS-I	0–12 Months IS-IV IS-III IS-II IS-I
1	Driving after Suspended License / Disorderly Conduct / Vandalism	IS-II IS-I	IS-III IS-II IS-I	IS-III IS-II IS-I	0–3 Months IS-IV IS-III IS-II IS-I	0–6 Months IS-IV IS-III IS-II IS-I
	Criminal History Scale	A No/Minor Record	B Moderate Record	C Serious Record	D Violent/Repetitive	E Serious Violent

*A&B DW = Assault and Battery, Dangerous Weapon
**B&E = Breaking and Entering

The numbers in each cell represent the range from which the judge selects the maximum sentence ("not more than"). The minimum sentence ("not less than") is two-thirds of the maximum sentence and constitutes the initial parole eligibility date.

Sentencing Zones

- Incarceration Zone
- Discretionary Zone (incarceration/intermediate sanction)
- Intermediate Sanction Zone

Intermediate Sanction Levels

IS-IV	24-Hour Restriction
IS-III	Daily Accountability
IS-II	Standard Supervision
IS-I	Financial Accountability

Source: "Massachusetts Sentencing Grid." *www.mass.gov.* Massachusetts Court System: visited February 18, 2017, Web.

Certain crimes are "staircased" in the Massachusetts grid, meaning that the same crime can result in different punishments based on factors other than criminal history.[67] For example, assault and battery with a dangerous weapon (A&B DW) resulting in no injury or a minor injury is at level 3. When the crime results in a moderate but not life-threatening injury, it is at level 4. But when the injury is life threatening, the crime is at level 6—squarely in the "incarceration zone"—regardless of the defendant's criminal history.

Federal Sentencing Guidelines

In 1984, Congress passed the Sentencing Reform Act (SRA),[68] paving the way for federal sentencing guidelines that went into effect three years later. Similar in many respects to the state guidelines, the SRA also eliminated parole for federal prisoners and severely limited early release from prison due to good behavior.[69] The impact of the SRA and the state guidelines was dramatic. Sentences became harsher—by 2004, the average federal prison sentence was fifty months, more than twice as long as in 1984.[70]

Much to the disappointment of supporters of sentencing reform, a series of United States Supreme Court decisions handed down midway though the first decade of the 2000s held that federal sentencing guidelines were advisory only.[71] Five years after these Court decisions, according to the U.S. Sentencing Commission, African American defendants were receiving sentences about 20 percent longer than white males who were convicted of similar crimes.[72] Similarly, a study released in 2015 shows that judicial leniency for white males and all women has increased significantly in federal courts, with sentence lengths moving in the opposite direction for black males.[73]

Judicial Departures

In essence, the Supreme Court decisions just mentioned gave federal judges the ability to "depart" from federal sentencing guidelines. Federal judges are taking advantage of this discretion, deviating from sentencing guidelines in almost half of all cases before them.[74] This "escape hatch" of judicial discretion, called a **departure,** is available to state judges as well as their federal counterparts. Judges in Massachusetts, for example, can depart from the grid in Figure 11.4 if a case involves mitigating or aggravating circumstances.[75]

Mandatory Sentencing Guidelines

In an attempt to close even the limited loophole of judicial discretion offered by departures, politicians (often urged on by their constituents) have passed sentencing laws even more contrary to the idea of individualized justice. These **mandatory** (minimum) **sentencing guidelines** further limit a judge's power to deviate from determinate sentencing laws by setting firm standards for certain crimes.

> **Learning 6 Objective** Describe the goal of mandatory minimum sentencing guidelines and explain why these laws have become unpopular in recent years.

State and Federal Mandatory Minimums

The mandatory minimum "movement" started in the early 1970s in New York state, which was experiencing a wave of heroin-related crime. Governor Nelson Rockefeller pushed through a series of mandatory drug sentences, the most draconian being a fifteen-years-to-life punishment for anyone convicted of possessing four ounces of any illegal narcotic other than marijuana.[76] Today, nearly every state has mandatory sentencing laws, most related to crimes involving the sale or possession of illegal drugs.

The federal government passed its Anti-Drug Abuse Act[77] in the mid-1980s, in response to the cocaine overdose death of a well-known basketball player named Len Bias. Federal mandatory minimums are guided by a set of "triggers" based on the amount of drugs involved, the offender's criminal history, and many other attendant circumstances. These triggers include selling drugs to someone under twenty-one years of age, using a minor as part of "drug operations," and carrying a firearm during the drug-related crime.[78] This legislation has given a great deal of power to federal prosecutors, who,

Departure A stipulation in many federal and state sentencing guidelines that allows a judge to adjust his or her sentencing decision based on the special circumstances of a particular case.

Mandatory Sentencing Guidelines Statutorily determined punishments that must be applied to those who are convicted of specific crimes.

by using their discretion to add penalty enhancements, are able to coerce defendants into plea bargaining rather than risking a lengthy prison sentence.[79]

"Three-Strikes" Legislation

Habitual offender laws are a form of mandatory sentencing found in twenty-six states and used by the federal government. Also known as "three-strikes-and-you're-out" laws, these statutes require that any person convicted of a third felony must serve a lengthy prison sentence. In many cases, the underlying crime does not have to be of a violent or dangerous nature.

Under Washington's habitual offender law, for example, a "persistent offender" is automatically sentenced to life even if the third felony offense happens to be "vehicular assault" (an automobile accident that causes injury), unarmed robbery, or attempted arson, among other lesser felonies.[80] Consequently, about 44 percent of the nearly 670 inmates serving life without parole in that state were sentenced for a third strike.[81] In California, convicts have been sent to prison for life for third offenses that include shoplifting a pair of tube socks, stealing a slice of pizza, and possessing .14 grams of methamphetamine.[82]

The Supreme Court validated the most punitive aspects of habitual offender laws with its decision in *Lockyer v. Andrade* (2003).[83] That case involved the sentencing under California's "three-strikes" law of Leandro Andrade to fifty years in prison for stealing $153 worth of videotapes. Writing for the majority in a bitterly divided 5–4 decision, Justice Sandra Day O'Connor concluded that Andrade's punishment was not so "objectively" unreasonable that it violated the Constitution.[84] Basically, the justices who upheld the law said that if the California legislature—and by extension the California voters—felt that the law was reasonable, then the judicial branch was in no position to disagree.

Reforming Mandatory Minimums

Somewhat ironically, in 2012 California voters decided that the state's three-strikes law was indeed unreasonable. That year, by a two-thirds vote, Californians passed a ballot initiative revising the law. Now, a life sentence will be imposed only when the third felony conviction is for a serious or violent crime. Furthermore, the measure authorizes judges to resentence those approximately 3,000 inmates who are serving life prison terms in California prisons because of a nonviolent "third strike." As of February 2016, about 2,100 of these inmates had been released from prison.[85]

The California ballot initiative reflects nationwide discontent with mandatory minimum sentencing statutes. These laws are often unpopular with judges because of the limitations they place on judicial discretion. They are also seen as contributing heavily to the explosive, and costly, growth of the U.S. prison population since the 1980s, which we will discuss in Chapter 13. In addition, the country's minority population seems to have borne the brunt of harsh sentencing legislation—nearly 70 percent of all convicts subject to mandatory minimum sentences are African American or Latino.[86]

In response to these issues, nearly thirty states have reformed their mandatory sentencing laws since 2000. In general, these reforms take one of three approaches:[87]

1. *Expanding judicial discretion.* In Iowa, judges can depart from mandatory minimum sentences for certain drug crimes when no violence or threat of violence was present.[88]

▼ Through a ballot initiative, California voters decided to revise the state's "three strikes" law so that only a violent or serious third felony will trigger the automatic life sentence. **Do you think that the new version of California's habitual offender law is fairer than the old one? Why or why not?**

Jim West/Alamy Stock Photo

2. *Limiting habitual offender "triggers."* In Nevada, misdemeanor convictions no longer count toward a five-year mandatory minimum sentence for a third conviction.[89]

3. *Repealing or revising mandatory minimum sentences.* In 2009, New York repealed the "Rockefeller drug laws," eliminating mandatory minimum sentences for low-level drug offenders.[90]

On the federal level, the U.S. Congress is considering several bills that would allow federal judges to depart from mandatory minimum sentences for nonviolent drug offenses.[91]

Victim Impact Evidence

The final piece of the sentencing puzzle involves victims and victims' families. As mentioned in Chapter 3, crime victims traditionally were banished to the peripheries of the criminal justice system. This situation has changed dramatically with the emergence of the victims' rights movement over the past several decades. Victims are now given the opportunity to testify—in person or through written testimony—during sentencing hearings about the suffering they experienced as the result of the crime. These victim impact statements (VISs) have proved extremely controversial, however, and legal experts have had a difficult time determining whether they cause more harm than good.

Balancing the Process

The Crime Victims' Rights Act gives victims the right to be reasonably heard during the sentencing process,[92] and many state victims' rights laws contain similar provisions.[93] In general, these laws allow a victim to tell his or her side of the story to the sentencing body, be it a judge, jury, or parole officer. In nonmurder cases, the victim can personally describe the physical, financial, and emotional impact of the crime. When the charge is murder or manslaughter, relatives or friends can give personal details about the victim and describe the effects of her or his death. In almost all instances, the goal of the VIS is to increase the harshness of the sentence.

Most of the debate surrounding VISs centers on their use in the sentencing phases of death penalty cases. Supporters point out that the defendant has always been allowed to present character evidence in the hope of dissuading a judge or jury from capital punishment. According to some, a VIS balances the equation by giving survivors a voice in the process.

Presenting a VIS is also said to have psychological benefits for victims, who are no longer forced to sit in silence as decisions that affect their lives are made by others.[94] Finally, on a purely practical level, a VIS may help judges and juries make informed sentencing decisions by providing them with an understanding of all of the consequences of the crime. (For an example of a victim impact statement from a recent death penalty case, see Figure 11.5.)

The Risks of Victim Evidence

Opponents of the use of VISs claim that they interject dangerously prejudicial evidence into the sentencing process, which should be governed by reason, not emotion. The inflammatory nature of a VIS, they say, may distract judges and juries from the facts of the case, which should be the only basis for a sentence.[95]

In fact, research has shown that hearing victim impact evidence makes jurors more likely to impose the death penalty.[96] The Supreme Court, however, has given its approval to the use of VISs, allowing judges to decide whether the statements are admissible on a case-by-case basis, just as they do with any other type of evidence.[97]

FIGURE 11.5 Victim Impact Statement (VIS)

In July 2015, a Colorado jury found James Holmes (see photo) guilty on twenty-four counts of first degree murder, two for each of the twelve victims he fatally shot inside an Aurora movie theater three years earlier. At least one hundred victims and witnesses testified at his sentencing hearing, including Kristian Cowden, whose father, Gordon Cowden, was killed by Holmes. A portion of her VIS is reprinted here.

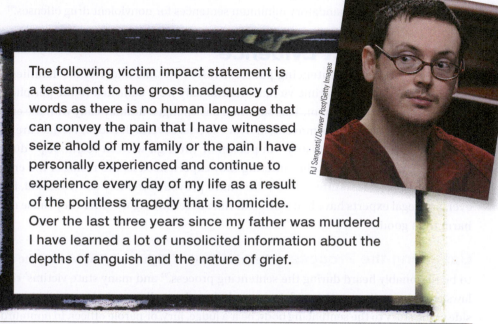

The following victim impact statement is a testament to the gross inadequacy of words as there is no human language that can convey the pain that I have witnessed seize ahold of my family or the pain I have personally experienced and continue to experience every day of my life as a result of the pointless tragedy that is homicide.
Over the last three years since my father was murdered I have learned a lot of unsolicited information about the depths of anguish and the nature of grief.

RJ Sangosti/Denver Post/Getty Images

ETHICS CHALLENGE

Critics contend that victim impact statements unethically introduce the idea of a victim's "social value" into the courtroom. That is, judges and juries may feel compelled to base the punishment on the worthiness of the victim (his or her standing in the community, role as a family member, and the like) rather than the circumstances of the crime. What is your opinion of this argument?

Capital Punishment

Few topics in the criminal justice system inspire such heated debate as **capital punishment,** or the use of the death penalty. Opponents such as legal expert Stephen Bright wonder whether "there comes a time when a society gets beyond some of the more primitive forms of punishment."[98] They point out that the United States is the sole Western democracy that continues the practice, putting it among China, Iran, Iraq, and Saudi Arabia on the list of nations that carry out the most executions.[99]

Critics also claim that a process whose subjects are chosen by "luck and money and race" cannot serve the interests of justice.[100] Proponents believe that the death penalty serves as the ultimate deterrent for violent criminal behavior and that the criminals who are put to death are the "worst of the worst" and deserve their fate.

Today, about 2,900 convicts are living on "death row" in American prisons, meaning they have been sentenced to death and are awaiting execution. In the 1940s, as many as two hundred people were put to death in the United States in one year. As Figure 11.6

Capital Punishment The use of the death penalty to punish wrongdoers for certain crimes.

FIGURE 11.6 **Executions in the United States, 1976 to 2016**

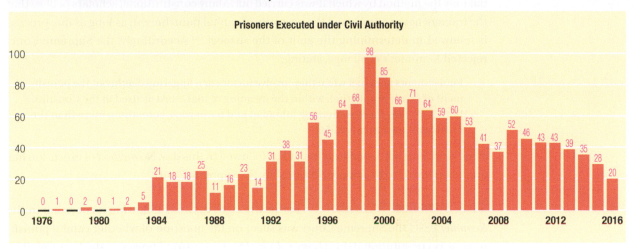

Source: Death Penalty Information Center.

shows, the most recent high-water mark was ninety-eight in 1999. Despite declines since then, certain states and the federal government still regularly seek the death penalty for offenders convicted of capital crimes. Consequently, the questions that surround the death penalty—Is it fair? Is it humane? Does it deter crime?—will continue to mobilize both its supporters and its detractors.

Methods of Execution

In its early years, when the United States adopted the practice of capital punishment from England, it also adopted English methods, which included drawing and quartering and boiling the convict alive. By the nineteenth century, these techniques had been deemed "barbaric" and were replaced by hanging. Indeed, the history of capital punishment in America is marked by attempts to make the act more humane. The 1890s saw the introduction of electrocution as a less painful method of execution than hanging, and in 1890 in Auburn Prison, New York, William Kemmler was the first American to die in an electric chair.

The "chair" remained the primary form of execution until 1977, when Oklahoma became the first state to adopt lethal injection. Today, this method dominates executions in all thirty-one states that employ the death penalty. Fourteen states authorize at least two different methods of execution, meaning that electrocution (eight states), lethal gas (five states), hanging (three states), and the firing squad (two states) are still used on very rare occasions.[101]

For about three decades, states used a similar three-drug process to carry out lethal injections. The process—which involves a sedative, a paralyzing agent, and a drug that induces heart failure—was designed to be as painless as possible for the condemned convict. More recently, however, the companies that manufacture these three drugs have refused to sell them for execution purposes. This has forced state officials to experiment with untested replacement drugs, a development that—as we shall soon see—has added an element of uncertainty to capital punishment in the United States.

The Death Penalty and the Supreme Court

In 1890, William Kemmler challenged his sentence to die in New York's new electric chair (for murdering his mistress) by arguing that electrocution infringed on his Eighth Amendment rights against cruel and unusual punishment.[102] Kemmler's challenge is historically significant in that it did not implicate the death penalty itself as being cruel and unusual, but only the method by which it was carried out. Many constitutional scholars believe that the framers never questioned the necessity of capital punishment, as long as due process is followed in determining the guilt of the suspect.[103] Accordingly, the Supreme Court rejected Kemmler's challenge, stating:

> Punishments are cruel when they involve torture or a lingering death; but the punishment of death is not cruel, within the meaning of that word as used in the Constitution. It implies there something inhuman and barbarous, something more than the mere extinguishment of life.[104]

Thus, the Court set a standard that it has followed to this day. No *method* of execution has ever been found to be unconstitutional by the Supreme Court.

The *Weems* Standard

For nearly eight decades following its decision in the *Kemmler* case, the Supreme Court was silent on the question of whether capital punishment was constitutional. In *Weems v. United States* (1910),[105] however, the Court made a ruling that would significantly affect the debate on the death penalty. In this case, the defendant had been sentenced to fifteen years of hard labor, a heavy fine, and a number of other penalties for the relatively minor crime of falsifying official records. The Court overturned the sentence, ruling that the penalty was too harsh considering the nature of the offense. Ultimately, in the *Weems* decision, the Court set three important precedents concerning sentencing:

1. Cruel and unusual punishment is defined by the changing norms and standards of society and therefore is not based on historical interpretations.
2. Courts may decide whether a punishment is unnecessarily cruel with regard to physical pain.
3. Courts may decide whether a punishment is unnecessarily cruel with regard to psychological pain.[106]

"Cruel and Unusual" Concerns

In *Baze v. Rees* (2008),[107] the Supreme Court ruled that the mere possibility of pain "does not establish the sort of 'objectively intolerable risk of harm' that qualifies as cruel and unusual" punishment. That ruling, however, applied to the three-drug process described earlier. For a variety of reasons, manufacturers in America and Europe now refuse to sell those drugs to the states. Consequently, state corrections systems have been forced to try new lethal injection protocols, with controversial results. In December 2016, using a replacement anesthetic called midazolam, Alabama authorities took thirty minutes to execute convicted murderer Robert Smith, Jr. For thirteen minutes, Smith, who was supposed to be heavily sedated, coughed and moved, raising questions of whether he was conscious during the procedure.

Similarly lengthy ordeals by condemned convicts in Arizona, Oklahoma, and Ohio bolstered claims by medical experts that midazolam cannot be relied upon to mask the pain suffered during lethal injection.[108] Nevertheless, in 2015 the Supreme Court approved use of the drug, once

▼ In 2016, Pfizer, the world's second largest pharmaceutical company, announced that it would stop providing state corrections departments with drugs that are used to carry out lethal injections. **If a state can no longer obtain such drugs, is it acceptable to use a different execution method, such as a firing squad or hanging? Why or why not?**

Mario Tama/Getty Images News/Getty Images

again holding that a method of capital punishment was not cruel and unusual.[109] Writing for the Court's 5–4 majority, Justice Samuel Alito pointed out that rejecting all available means for executions would be the same as ending the practice, which remains constitutional. In her dissent, Justice Sonia Sotomayor accused her colleagues of sanctioning "the chemical equivalent of being burned alive."[110]

Death Penalty Sentencing

In the 1960s, the Supreme Court became increasingly concerned about what it saw as serious flaws in the way the states administered capital punishment. Finally, in 1967, the Court put a moratorium on executions until it could "clean up" the process. The chance to do so came with the *Furman v. Georgia* case, decided in 1972.[111]

The Bifurcated Process

In its *Furman* decision, by a 5–4 margin, the Supreme Court essentially held that the death penalty, as administered by the states, violated the Eighth Amendment. Justice Potter Stewart was particularly eloquent in his concurring opinion, stating that the sentence of death was so arbitrary as to be comparable to "being struck by lightning."[112] Although the *Furman* ruling invalidated the death penalty for more than six hundred offenders on death row at the time, it also provided the states with a window to make the process less arbitrary, thereby bringing their death penalty statutes up to constitutional standards.

The result was a two-stage, or *bifurcated*, procedure for capital cases. In the first stage, a jury determines the guilt or innocence of the defendant for a crime that has, by state statute, been determined to be punishable by death. If the defendant is found guilty, the jury reconvenes in the second stage and considers all aggravating and mitigating factors to decide whether the death sentence is in fact warranted. (See this chapter's second *Mastering Concepts* feature to get a better idea of how these two stages work.) Therefore, even if a jury finds the defendant guilty of a crime, such as first degree murder, that *may be* punishable by death, in the second stage it can decide that the circumstances surrounding the crime justify only a punishment of life in prison.

Today, thirty-one states and the federal government have capital punishment laws based on the bifurcated process. State governments are responsible for almost all executions in this country. The federal government has carried out only three death sentences since 1963, and usually seeks capital punishment only for high-profile defendants such as

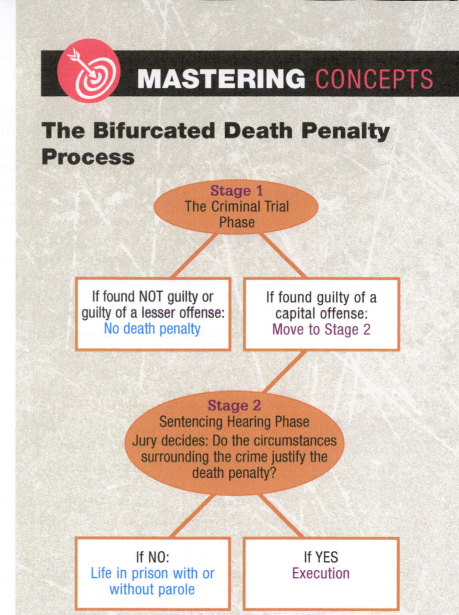

MASTERING CONCEPTS

The Bifurcated Death Penalty Process

Stage 1
The Criminal Trial Phase

If found NOT guilty or guilty of a lesser offense:
No death penalty

If found guilty of a capital offense:
Move to Stage 2

Stage 2
Sentencing Hearing Phase
Jury decides: Do the circumstances surrounding the crime justify the death penalty?

If NO:
Life in prison with or without parole

If YES
Execution

Learning Objective 7 Identify the two stages that make up the bifurcated process of death penalty sentencing.

Dylann Roof, sentenced to die in 2017 for killing nine African American parishioners at a church in Charleston, South Carolina, two years earlier.

The Jury's Role

The Supreme Court reaffirmed the important role of the jury in death penalties in *Ring v. Arizona* (2002).[113] The case involved Arizona's bifurcated process: After the jury determined a defendant's guilt or innocence, it would be dismissed, and the judge alone would decide whether execution was warranted. The Court found that this procedure violated the defendant's Sixth Amendment right to a jury trial, ruling that juries must be involved in *both* stages of the bifurcated process. The decision invalidated death penalty laws in Arizona, Colorado, Idaho, Montana, and Nebraska, forcing legislatures in those states to hastily revamp their procedures.

In most circumstances, a jury's decision to execute a defendant must be unanimous. For example, James Holmes, discussed in Figure 11.5, avoided the death penalty because a single juror felt that, due to his mental illness, Holmes should serve life in prison instead. The only state that routinely allows a measure of judicial discretion when it comes to capital punishment is Alabama, where jurors only recommend the final sentencing outcome in capital cases, pending a judge's approval. This practice may, however, be resting on uncertain legal ground. The Supreme Court recently struck down the part of Florida's execution procedure that gave judges rather than juries the final say in death penalty decisions.[114]

Mitigating Circumstances

Several mitigating circumstances will prevent a defendant found guilty of first degree murder from receiving the death penalty.

Insanity

In 1986, the United States Supreme Court held that the Constitution prohibits the execution of a person who is insane. The Court failed to provide a test for insanity other than Justice Lewis F. Powell's statement that the Eighth Amendment "forbids the execution only of those who are unaware of the punishment they are about to suffer and why they are to suffer it."[115] Consequently, each state must come up with its own definition of "insanity" for death penalty purposes. A state may also force convicts on death row to take medication that will make them sane enough to be aware of the punishment they are about to suffer and why they are about to suffer it.[116]

Intellectual Disability

The Supreme Court's change of mind on the question of whether a convict with intellectual disabilities may be put to death underscores the continuing importance of the *Weems* test. In 1989, the Court rejected the argument that execution of a mentally handicapped person was "cruel and unusual" under the Eighth Amendment.[117] At the time, only two states barred execution of those with intellectual disablities. Thirteen years later, eighteen states had such laws, and the Court decided that this increased number reflected "changing norms and standards of society." In *Atkins v. Virginia* (2002),[118] the Court used the *Weems* test as the main rationale for barring the execution of the mentally handicapped.

The *Atkins* ruling did not end controversy in this area, however, as it allowed state courts to make their own determinations concerning which inmates qualified as "mentally impaired" for death penalty purposes. In 2014, the Supreme Court disallowed one method of doing so by ruling that states cannot designate a fixed IQ score to determine whether a capital offender has intellectual disablities. While overturning Florida's "inflexible bright-line cutoff" of an IQ below 71, Justice Anthony Kennedy wrote that, "Intellectual disability is a condition, not a number."[119]

Age   Following the *Atkins* case, many observers, including four Supreme Court justices, hoped that the same reasoning would be applied to the question of whether convicts who committed the relevant crime when they were juveniles may be executed. These hopes were realized in 2005 when the Court issued its *Roper v. Simmons* decision, which effectively ended the execution of those who committed crimes as juveniles.[120]

As in the *Atkins* case, the Court relied on the "evolving standards of decency" test, noting that a majority of the states, as well as every other civilized nation, prohibited the execution of offenders who committed their crimes before the age of eighteen. (See the feature *Landmark Cases*—Roper v. Simmons.) The *Roper* ruling required that seventy-two

LANDMARK CASES

Roper v. Simmons

Learning Objective 8 Explain why the U.S. Supreme Court abolished the death penalty for juvenile offenders.

When he was seventeen years old, Christopher Simmons abducted Shirley Cook, used duct tape to cover her eyes and mouth and bind her hands, and threw her to her death in a river. Although he bragged to his friends that he would "get away with it" because he was a minor, he was found guilty of murder and sentenced to death by a Missouri court. After the United States Supreme Court held, in 2002, that "evolving standards of decency" rendered the execution of mentally disabled persons unconstitutional, Simmons appealed his own sentence. His case gave the Court a chance to apply the "evolving standards of decency" test to death sentences involving offenders who were juveniles at the time they committed the underlying capital crime.

Roper v. Simmons
United States Supreme Court
543 U.S. 551 (2005)

In the Words of the Court . . .

Justice Kennedy, Majority Opinion

The evidence of national consensus against the death penalty for juveniles is similar, and in some respects parallel, to the evidence *Atkins* held sufficient to demonstrate a national consensus against the death penalty for the mentally retarded.

Three general differences between juveniles under 18 and adults demonstrate that juvenile offenders cannot with reliability be classified among the worst offenders. First, as any parent knows and as the scientific and sociological studies * * * tend to confirm, "[a] lack of maturity and an underdeveloped sense of responsibility are found in youth more often than in adults and are more understandable among the young. These qualities often result in impetuous and ill-considered actions and decisions." * * * In recognition of the comparative immaturity and irresponsibility of juveniles, almost every State prohibits those under 18 years of age from voting, serving on juries, or marrying without parental consent.

The second area of difference is that juveniles are more vulnerable or susceptible to negative influences and outside pressures, including peer pressure. * * * The third broad difference is that the character of a juvenile is not as well formed as that of an adult. The personality traits of juveniles are more transitory, less fixed.

These differences render suspect any conclusion that a juvenile falls among the worst offenders. * * * Retribution is not proportional if the law's most severe penalty is imposed on one whose culpability or blameworthiness is diminished, to a substantial degree, by reason of youth and immaturity.

Decision

The Court found that, applying the Eighth Amendment in light of "evolving standards of decency," the execution of offenders who were under the age of eighteen when their crimes were committed was cruel and unusual punishment and therefore unconstitutional.

FOR CRITICAL ANALYSIS

In his majority opinion, Justice Kennedy noted that a number of countries, including China, Iran, and Pakistan, had recently ended the practice of executing juveniles, leaving the United States "alone in a world that has turned its face against the practice." What impact, if any, should international customs have on American criminal law?

convicted murderers in twelve states be resentenced and took the death penalty "off the table" for dozens of pending cases in which prosecutors were seeking capital punishment for juvenile criminal acts.

Debating the Sentence of Death

Of the topics covered in this textbook, few inspire such passionate argument as the death penalty. Many advocates believe that execution is "just deserts" for those who commit heinous crimes. In the words of sociologist Ernest van den Haag, death is the "only fitting retribution for murder that I can think of."[121] Opponents worry that retribution is simply another word for vengeance and question whether a governmental body has the moral authority to "kill those whom it has imprisoned."[122] The continuing debate over capital punishment tends to focus on several key issues: deterrence, fallibility, arbitrariness, and discrimination.

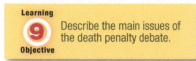

Learning Objective 9 Describe the main issues of the death penalty debate.

Deterrence   Those advocates of the death penalty who wish to show that the practice benefits society often turn to the idea of deterrence. In other words, they believe that by executing convicted criminals, the criminal justice system discourages potential criminals from committing similar violent acts. Numerous studies support these claims. For example, researchers from Sam Houston State University and Duke University estimated that as many as sixty murders were deterred by executions carried out from January 1994 to December 2005 in Texas, the nation's most active capital punishment state.[123]

The main problem with studies that support the death penalty, say its critics, is that there are too few executions carried out in the United States each year to adequately determine their impact.[124] (In 2015, there was one execution in the United States for every 396 murder arrests.) Furthermore, each study that "proves" the deterrent effect of the death penalty seems be matched by one that "disproves" the same premise.[125]

In the end, the deterrence debate follows a familiar pattern. Opponents of the death penalty claim that murderers rarely consider the consequences of their act, and therefore it makes no difference whether capital punishment exists or not. Proponents counter that this proves the death penalty's deterrent value, because if the murderers *had* considered the possibility of execution, they would not have committed their crimes.

Fallibility   In a sense, capital punishment acts as the ultimate specific deterrent by rendering those executed incapable of committing further crimes. Incapacitation as a justification for the death penalty, though, rests on two questionable assumptions: (1) every convicted murderer is likely to recidivate, and (2) the criminal justice system is *infallible*. In other words, the system never convicts someone who is actually not guilty.

Wrongful Deaths?   Although several executions from the 1980s and 1990s are coming under increased scrutiny,[126] no court has ever found that an innocent person has been executed in the United States. According to the Death Penalty Information Center, however, between 1973, when the Supreme Court had temporarily suspended capital punishment, and January 2017, 157 American men and women who had been convicted of capital crimes and sentenced to death—though not executed—were exonerated and released. Over that same time period, 1,446 executions took place, meaning that for about every nine convicts put to death during that period, approximately one death row inmate was found innocent.[127]

Defense Issues   The single factor that contributes the most to the criminal justice system's fallibility in this area is widely believed to be unsatisfactory legal representation. Many states and counties cannot or will not allocate adequate funds for death penalty cases, meaning that indigent capital defendants are often provided with a less-than-vigorous defense.

The case of convicted murderer Ronald Rompilla highlights the consequences of poor counsel in a capital case. During the sentencing phase of his trial, Rompilla's lawyers made two serious errors. First, they failed to challenge the prosecution's characterization of Rompilla's previous conviction for rape and assault. In fact, they never even looked at the file of that case. Second, they failed to provide the Pennsylvania jury with mitigating factors that would argue against a death sentence, such as their client's troubled childhood, severe alcoholism, and other mental illnesses. Not surprisingly, the jury ordered Rompilla's execution, a sentence that was eventually overturned by the United States Supreme Court due to his ineffective counsel.[128]

Arbitrariness   Despite the bifurcated process required by the Supreme Court's *Furman* ruling (discussed earlier), a significant amount of arbitrariness appears to remain in the system. The chances of a defendant in a capital trial being sentenced to death seem to depend heavily on the quality of the defense counsel, as we have just seen, and the jurisdiction where the crime was committed.

As Figure 11.7 shows, a convict's likelihood of being executed is strongly influenced by geography. Five states (Florida, Missouri, Oklahoma, Texas, and Virginia) account for more than two-thirds of all executions, while nineteen states and the District of Columbia do not provide for capital punishment within their borders. In addition, because the decision to seek the death penalty is made on a local level by local prosecutors, the practice is not consistent within states that allow it. For example, Louisiana's Caddo Parish accounts

FIGURE 11.7 **Executions by State, 1976–2016**

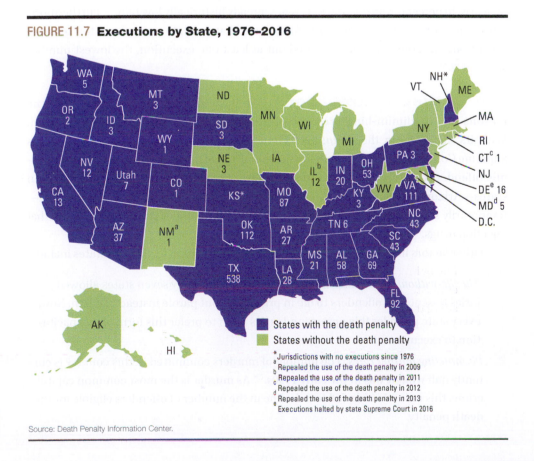

| | States with the death penalty |
| | States without the death penalty |

* Jurisdictions with no executions since 1976
a Repealed the use of the death penalty in 2009
b Repealed the use of the death penalty in 2011
c Repealed the use of the death penalty in 2012
d Repealed the use of the death penalty in 2013
e Executions halted by state Supreme Court in 2016

Source: Death Penalty Information Center.

for 5 percent of the state's population and 5 percent of its homicides but imposes almost half of its death penalties.[129]

Discriminatory Effect

Whether or not capital punishment is imposed arbitrarily, some observers claim that it is not done without bias. A disproportionate number of those executed since 1976—just over one-third—have been African American, and today 42 percent of all inmates on death row are black.[130] Another set of statistics also continues to be problematic. That is, in 284 cases involving interracial murders in which the defendant was executed between 1976 and February 2017, the defendant was African American and the victim was white. Over that same time period, only 20 cases involved a white defendant and a black victim.[131] In fact, although slightly less than half of murder victims are white, three out of every four executions involve white victims.[132]

In *McCleskey v. Kemp* (1987),[133] the defense attorney for an African American sentenced to death for killing a white police officer used similar statistics to challenge Georgia's death penalty law. A study of two thousand Georgia murder cases showed that although African Americans were the victims of six out of every ten murders in the state, more than 80 percent of the cases in which death was imposed involved murders of whites.[134] In a 5–4 decision, the United States Supreme Court rejected the defense's claims, ruling that statistical evidence did not prove discriminatory intent on the part of Georgia's lawmakers.

The Future of the Death Penalty

As noted earlier in the chapter, the number of executions carried out each year in the United States has decreased dramatically since 1999. Other statistics also indicate a decline in death penalty activity. In 2016, only 30 people were sentenced to death, a drop of nearly 40 percent from the previous year's already historically low tally.[135] Furthermore, 2016 marked the first year in nearly forty years that no state carried out ten or more executions, and only five states carried out at least one execution, the lowest number since 1992.[136]

The Decline in Executions

We have already addressed some of the reasons for the diminishing presence of executions in the criminal justice system. With its decisions in the *Atkins* (2002) and *Roper* (2005) cases, the United States Supreme Court removed the possibility that hundreds of mentally handicapped and juvenile offenders could be sentenced to death. Over the past several years, at least seven states—Arizona, Arkansas, Louisiana, Mississippi, Montana, Ohio, and Oklahoma—temporarily shut down their death chambers to deal with issues surrounding their lethal injection drugs.

Other factors in the declining use of capital punishment in the United States include:

1. *The life-without-parole alternative.* In the early 1970s, only seven states allowed juries to sentence offenders to life in prison without parole instead of death. Now, every state provides this option, and juries seem to prefer this form of incapacitation to execution.[137]

2. *Plummeting murder rates.* The number of murders committed in this country is currently half what it was in the early 1990s.[138] As murder is the most common capital crime, this reduction has led to a decline in the number of offenders eligible for the death penalty.

3. *High costs.* Because of the costs of intensive law enforcement investigations, extensive *voir dire* (see Chapter 10), and lengthy appellate reviews, pursuing capital punishment can be very expensive for states. Nevada recently determined that its death penalty cases cost twice as much as similar cases without the death penalty, resulting in a $76 million price tag for state taxpayers between 1976 and 2014.[139]

Changing Norms and Standards

In August 2016, Delaware's Supreme Court ruled that the state's death penalty procedures were unconstitutional because they gave judges too great a role in the capital punishment sentencing process.[140] As a result of this ruling, Delaware became the seventh state to end capital punishment since 2004, along with Connecticut, Illinois, Maryland, New Jersey, New Mexico, and New York. In addition, the majority of states that do carry out executions have not done so in recent years. According to the Pew Research Center, in 2016 public support for the death penalty dipped below 50 percent for the first time in forty years.[141] Under the circumstances, is it possible that the "norms and standards" of our society are turning against capital punishment, raising the possibility of a new evaluation under the *Weems* test?

Probably not. Only two Supreme Court justices—Stephen Breyer and Ruth Bader Ginsberg—have openly questioned the constitutionality of capital punishment.[142] In 2016, the Court refused to hear a case on whether the practice violates the Eighth Amendment's prohibition on cruel and unusual punishment.[143] Also in 2016, the residents of Nebraska voted to reinstate the death penalty after a year-long hiatus. Finally, public support for executions tends to rise when the penalty is linked with certain crimes, such as the killing of children or law enforcement officers.[144] As highlighted in the *Policy Matters* feature that follows, future strategies for capital punishment in the United States may focus not on rejection but rather on reform.

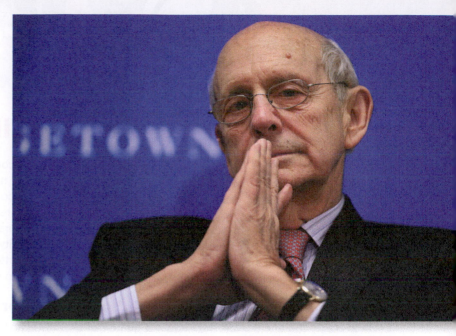

▲ Supreme Court associate justice Stephen Breyer has argued that the length of time between the sentence of death and execution—an average of eighteen years—constitutes cruel and unusual punishment. **Generally speaking, why do defendants routinely spend decades on death row before their cases are resolved? Do you agree that these delays render capital punishment unconstitutional? Explain your answers.**

Chip Somodevilla/Getty Images News/Getty Images

Pat Greenhouse/The Boston Globe/Getty Images

Death Penalty Reform in California

How Things Stand

Delay and cost are built into California's death penalty procedures. Under the state constitution, offenders sentenced to death are guaranteed a publicly funded defense attorney to guide them through a lengthy appeals process. Each such case must be reviewed by the California Supreme Court. If the Court upholds the execution, the defendant can challenge the ruling with the help of a different defense attorney. Even if this step is unsuccessful, the defendant has a final right of appeal to the federal courts.

On average, the entire affair lasts about a quarter of a century—and still often does not result in death. Since 2006, thanks to problems with its three-drug lethal injection protocol, the state has lacked a court-approved method for carrying out executions. A new lethal injection protocol, proposed in 2015, could be years away from implementation.[145]

As a Result...

California taxpayers are spending $150 million a year on an ineffective system.[146] More than nine hundred offenders have been sentenced to die in the state since 1978, but only thirteen executions have taken place. Approximately 750 prisoners are housed on California's death row—the largest such number in the nation—with a dozen having been there for more than three decades.[147] Indeed, approximately fifty death row inmates have died of drug overdose, cancer, suicide, or other causes since the state's last execution in 2006.

According to one federal judge, California's death penalty system has become so arbitrary and unpredictable that it is unconstitutional. Those on state death row, wrote the judge, are experiencing a punishment that "no rational jury or legislature could ever impose: life in prison, with the remote possibility of death."[148] Indeed, in the words of a commission of experts, California's administration of the death penalty is "close to collapse," with no easy solution in sight.[149]

Up for Debate

"You no longer have to be against the death penalty in theory to be against the way the death penalty is practiced in the United States. We used to look at it dogmatically, and now we are looking at it pragmatically."[150]—*Robert Dunham, executive director of the Death Penalty Information Center*

"[A majority of Americans support the death penalty because] the very worst murderers just plain deserve it. That remains true even after long delays."[151]—*Kent S. Scheidegger, legal director of the Criminal Justice Legal Foundation*

What's Your Take?

Review the discussion in this chapter on "Capital Punishment" before answering the following questions.

1. In 2012, a ballot initiative to end capital punishment in California failed by four percentage points. Would you have voted in favor of or against the death penalty? Why?

2. Every offender sentenced to death in the United States is guaranteed the chance to appeal his or her punishment. Why do you think this is the case? Does it make the process fairer? Explain your answers.

Digging Deeper...

In 2016, **Californians were given the chance to "end or mend"** their death penalty system by voting on two competing ballot measures: **Proposition 62** and **Proposition 66**. Research these two measures online and provide a short summary of their key points. Then, explain which measure prevailed and why. Finally, consider the assertion made by one observer that the voters in "California just made a mistake the size of Texas" with their choice.[152] Do you agree with this statement? Your answer should be at least three paragraphs long.

AP Images/Sue Ogrocki

For more information on these concepts, look back to the Learning Objective icons throughout the chapter.

List and contrast the four basic philosophical reasons for sentencing criminals. (a) Retribution, (b) deterrence, (c) incapacitation, and (d) rehabilitation. Under the principle of retributive justice, the severity of the punishment is proportional to the severity of the crime. Punishment is an end in itself. In contrast, the deterrence approach seeks to prevent future crimes by setting an example. Punishment is based on its deterrent value and not necessarily on the severity of the crime. The incapacitation theory of punishment simply argues that a criminal in prison cannot inflict further harm on society. In contrast, the rehabilitation theory asserts that criminals can be rehabilitated in the appropriate prison environment.

Contrast indeterminate with determinate sentencing. Indeterminate sentencing policies set a minimum and maximum amount of time that an offender must spend in prison. Within these limits, a judge may prescribe a specific term. Determinate sentencing requires the offender to serve a fixed amount of time, although this may be reduced for "good time."

Explain why there is a difference between the sentence imposed by a judge and the actual sentence served by the prisoner. Although, under indeterminate sentencing, judges may decide on specific sentences for offenders, thereafter it is parole boards that decide when prisoners will be released after the minimum sentence is served.

State who has input into the sentencing decision and list the factors that determine a sentence. The prosecutor, defense attorney, probation officer, and judge provide inputs. The factors considered in sentencing are (a) the seriousness of the crime, (b) mitigating circumstances, (c) aggravating circumstances, and (d) judicial philosophy.

Explain some of the reasons why sentencing reform has occurred. One reason for reform is sentencing disparity, a situation in which those convicted of similar crimes receive dissimilar sentences (often due to a particular judge's sentencing philosophy). Sentencing discrimination has also occurred on the basis of defendants' gender, race, or economic standing.

Describe the goal of mandatory minimum sentencing guidelines and explain why these laws have become unpopular in recent years. Mandatory minimum sentencing guidelines set fixed punishments for certain crimes. For the most part, these sentences are immune from judicial discretion. For that reason, they are unpopular with judges, who feel the laws do not recognize the individual aspects of each case. The guidelines also are believed to contribute to America's immense prison population and the racial imbalance of those behind bars.

Identify the two stages that make up the bifurcated process of death penalty sentencing. The first stage of the bifurcated process requires a jury to find the defendant guilty or not guilty of a crime that is punishable by execution. If the defendant is found guilty, then, in the second stage, the jury reconvenes to decide whether the death sentence is warranted.

Explain why the U.S. Supreme Court abolished the death penalty for juvenile offenders. In its *Roper v. Simmons* decision, the Supreme Court ruled that "evolving standards of decency" no longer justified the execution of juvenile offenders. Such offenders are understood to be less blameworthy than adults because of various issues relating to immaturity and irresponsibility.

Describe the main issues of the death penalty debate. Many of those who favor capital punishment believe that it is "just deserts" for the most violent of criminals. Those who oppose it see the act as little more than revenge. There is also disagreement over whether the death penalty acts as a deterrent. The relatively high number of death row inmates who have been found innocent has raised questions about the fallibility of the process, while certain statistics seem to show that execution is rather arbitrary. Finally, many observers contend that capital punishment is administered unfairly with regard to members of minority groups.

1. Suppose that the U.S. Congress passed a new law that punished shoplifting with a mandatory eighty-five-year prison term. What would be the impact of the new law on shoplifting nationwide? Would such a harsh law be justified by its deterrent effect? What about imposing a similarly extreme punishment on a more serious crime—a mandatory sentence of life in prison for, say, drunk driving? Would such a law be in society's best interest? Why or why not?

2. Why are truth-in-sentencing laws generally popular among victims' rights advocates? Why might these laws not be so popular with prison administrators or government officials charged with balancing a state budget?

3. Harold is convicted of unarmed burglary after a trial in Boston, Massachusetts. He has no prior convictions. According to the grid in Figure 11.4, what punishment do the state guidelines require? What would his punishment be if he had a previous conviction for armed robbery, which would mean that he had a "serious" criminal record?

4. Defense attorneys are increasingly likely to submit expensive biographical videos of their clients during sentencing in hopes of gaining a more lenient sentence. Lawyers say that such videos give judges and juries a sense of the "totality of the defendant." What might be some of the criticisms of this practice, particularly among public defenders?

5. What might be some of the unintended consequences of the United States Supreme Court ruling, discussed in this chapter, that states may not use a fixed IQ score to determine whether a convict is mentally handicapped for purposes of execution?

aggravating circumstances 364
capital punishment 374
departure 371
determinate sentencing 359
deterrence 353
"good time" 359
habitual offender laws 372
incapacitation 355

indeterminate sentencing 358
just deserts 353
mandatory sentencing guidelines 371
mitigating circumstances 364
presentence investigative report 363
"real offense" 364
rehabilitation 356
restitution 357

restorative justice 357
retribution 353
sentencing discrimination 366
sentencing disparity 366
sentencing guidelines 369
truth-in-sentencing laws 359
victim impact statement (VIS) 373

1. Herbert L. Packer, "Justification for Criminal Punishment," in *The Limits of Criminal Sanction* (Palo Alto, Calif.: Stanford University Press, 1968), 36–37.

2. Jami L. Anderson, "Reciprocity as a Justification for Retributivism," *Criminal Justice Ethics* (Winter/Spring 1997), 13–14.

3. Immanuel Kant, *Metaphysical First Principles of the Doctrine of Right*, trans. Mary Gregor (Cambridge, UK: Cambridge University Press, 1991), 331.

4. Jeremy Bentham, *An Introduction to the Principles of Morals and Legislation 1789* (New York: Hafner Publishing Corp., 1961).

5. Brian Forst, "Prosecution and Sentencing," in *Crime*, ed. James Q. Wilson and Joan Petersilia (San Francisco: ICS Press, 1995), 376.

6. Frank O. Bowman III, "Playing '21' with Narcotics Enforcement: A Response to Professor Carrington," *Washington and Lee Law Review* 52 (1995), 972.

7. Bureau of Justice Statistics, *Criminal Victimization, 2015* (Washington, D.C.: U.S. Department of Justice, October 2016), Table 4, page 6.

8. Federal Bureau of Investigation, *Crime in the United States, 2015*, Table 25. *ucr.fbi.gov*. U.S. Department of Justice: 2016, Web.

9. Justin T. Pickett and Sean Patrick Roche, "Arrested Development: Misguided Direction in Deterrence Theory and Policy," *Criminology & Public Policy* (August 2016), 727–751.

10. Paul H. Robinson and John M. Darley, "The Utility of Desert," *Northwestern University Law Review* 91 (Winter 1997), 453.

11. James Q. Wilson, *Thinking about Crime* (New York: Basic Books, 1975), 235.

12. Ashley Nellis, *Life Goes On: The Historic Rise of Life Sentences in America* (Washington, D.C.: The Sentencing Project, September 2013), 1.

13. Isaac Ehrlich, "Participation in Illegitimate Activities: A Theoretical and Empirical Investigation," *Journal of Political Economy* 81 (May/June 1973), 521–564.

14. Avinash Singh Bhati, *An Information Theoretic Method for Estimating the Number of Crimes Averted by Incapacitation* (Washington, D.C.: Urban Institute, July 2007), 18–33.

15. Todd Clear, *Harm in Punishment* (Boston: Northeastern University Press, 1980).

16. Jan Chaiken, Marcia Chaiken, and William Rhodes, "Predicting Violent Behavior and Classifying Violent Offenders," in *Understanding and Preventing Violence*, ed. Albert J. Reiss Jr., and Jeffrey A. Roth (Washington, D.C.: National Academy Press, 1994).

17. Patricia M. Clark, "An Evidence-Based Intervention for Offenders," *Corrections Today* (February/March 2011), 62–64.

18. "Voters Want Big Changes in Federal Sentencing, Prison System." *www.pewtrusts.org*. The Pew Charitable Trusts: March 8, 2016, Web.

19. Justin McCarthy, "Americans' Views Shift on Toughness of Justice System." *www.gallup.com*. Gallup: October 20, 2016, Web.

20. Robert V. Wolf, *Widening the Circle: Can Peacemaking Work Outside of Tribal Communities?* (New York: Center for Court Innovation, 2012), 2–8.

21. Quoted in *ibid.*, 8.

22. Kimberly S. Burke, *An Inventory and Examination of Restorative Justice Practices for Youth in Illinois* (Chicago: Illinois Criminal Justice Information Authority, April 2013), 6–7.

23. Rebecca Beitsch, "States Consider Restorative Justice as Alternative to Mass Incarceration." *www.pbs.org*. PBS NewsHour: July 20, 2016.

24. 42 U.S.C. Section 10601 (2006).

25. Josh Allen, "Jon Wilson Helps Crime Victims Talk with Their Offenders," *The Christian Science Monitor Weekly* (April 9, 2012), 45.

26. Diana McKibben and Phil Penko, "Does Restorative Justice Have a Realistic Place in Today's Criminal Justice System?" *The Police Chief* (December 2015), 72–77.

27. Quoted in Molly Rowan Leach, "The Political Rise of Restorative Justice." *www.huffingtonpost.com*. Huffington Post: March 26, 2014, Web.

28. Gregory W. O'Reilly, "Truth-in-Sentencing: Illinois Adds Yet Another Layer of 'Reform' to Its Complicated Code of Corrections," *Loyola University of Chicago Law Journal* (Summer 1996), 986, 999–1000.

29. David E. Olson, et al., *Final Report: The Impact of Illinois' Truth-in-Sentencing Law on Sentence Lengths, Time to Serve and Disciplinary Incidents of Convicted Murderers and Sex Offenders* (Chicago: Illinois Criminal Justice Information Authority, June 2009), 4–5.

30. Marvin Zalman, "The Rise and Fall of the Indeterminate Sentence," *Wayne Law Review* 24 (1977), 45, 52.

31. Paul W. Keve, *Crime Control and Justice in America: Searching for Facts and Answers* (Chicago: American Library Association, 1995), 77.

32. *Debtor's Prisons in New Hampshire* (Concord, N.H.: American Civil Liberties Union of New Hampshire, September 23, 2015).

33. *Bearden v. Georgia*, 462 U.S. 660 (1983).

34. Aris Pinedo, Jasmine Brown, and Alexa Valiente, "Why an Ohio Judge Is Using Unusual Punishments to Keep People Out of Jail." *www.abcnews.com*. ABC News: September 1, 2015, Web.

35. Kate Stith and José A. Cabranes, "Judging under the Federal Sentencing Guidelines," *Northwestern University Law Review* 91 (Summer 1997), 1247.

36. Quoted in Jacqueline Lee, "Brock Turner Case: Probation Department's Report Spared Scrutiny." *www.mercurynews.com*. Mercury News: December 19, 2016, Web.

37. Mark M. Lanier and Claud H. Miller III, "Attitudes and Practices of Federal Probation Officers towards Pre-Plea/Trial Investigative Report Policy," *Crime & Delinquency* 41 (July 1995), 365–366.

38. Nancy J. King and Rosevelt L. Noble, "Felony Jury Sentencing in Practice: A Three-State Study," *Vanderbilt Law Review* (2004), 1986.

39. Julie R. O'Sullivan, "In Defense of the U.S. Sentencing Guidelines Modified Real-Offense System," *Northwestern University Law Review* 91 (1997), 1342.

40. "Aggravating Factors for Capital Punishment by State." *www.deathpenaltyinfo.org*. Death Penalty Information Center: visited February 16, 2017, Web.

41. John Paul Wilson and Nicholas O. Rule, "Facial Trustworthiness Predicts Extreme Criminal-Sentencing Outcomes," *Psychological Science* (August 2015), 1325–1331

42. 18 U.S.C. Section 2113(a) (1994).

43. "Statistical Information Packet, Fiscal Year 2015, Washington," Table 7. *www.ussc.gov*. United States Sentencing Commission: 2016, Web; and "Statistical Information Packet, Fiscal Year 2015, Mississippi," Table 7. *www.ussc.gov*. United States Sentencing Commission: 2016, Web.

44. "Statistical Information Packet, Fiscal Year 2015, Fourth Circuit," Table 7. *www.ussc.gov*. United States Sentencing Commission: 2016, Web; and "Statistical Information Packet, Fiscal Year 2015, Ninth Circuit," Table 7. *www.ussc.gov*. United States Sentencing Commission: 2016, Web.

45. Keith Williams, "Practical Child Porn Defense: Fighting the Pitchfork Mentality," *Aspatore* (July 2012), 3911.

46. Cassia Spohn and David Holleran, "The Imprisonment Penalty Paid by Young, Unemployed Black and Hispanic Male Offenders," *Criminology* 35 (2000), 281.

47. "Key Findings and Recommendations." *www.illinoissenatedemocrats.com*. Illinois Disproportionate Justice Impact Study Commission: 2011, Web.

48. "Report on the Continued Impact of United States v. Booker on Federal Sentencing." *www.ussc.gov*. United States Sentencing Commission: December 2012, Web.

49. Xia Wang, et al., "Assessing the Differential Effects of Race and Ethnicity on Sentence Outcomes under Different Sentencing Systems," *Crime and Delinquency* (February 2013), 87–114.

50. David C. Baldus and George Woodworth, "Race Discrimination and the Legitimacy of Capital Punishment: Reflections on the Interaction of Fact and Perception," *DePaul Law Review* (2004), 1411.

51. Spohn and Holleran, *op. cit.*, 301.

52. Brian Johnson, "The Multilevel Context of Criminal Sentencing: Integrating Judge- and County-Level Influences," *Criminology* (May 2006), 259–298.

53. Quoted Matthew Clair and Alix S. Winter, "How Judges Think about Racial Disparities: Situational Decision Making in the Criminal Justice System," *Criminology* (May 2016), 340.

54. *A Living Death: Life without Parole for Nonviolent Offenses* (New York: American Civil

Liberties Union, November 2013), Table 10, page 28.

55. Solomon Moore, "Justice Department Seeks Equity in Sentences for Cocaine," *New York Times* (April 30, 2009), A17.

56. Pub. L. No. 111-220, Section 2, 124 Stat. 2372.

57. "Materials on 2014 Drug Guidelines Amendment." *www.ussc.gov*. United States Sentencing Commission: visited February 17, 2017, Web.

58. Julie H. Davis and Gardiner Harris, "Obama Issues Reductions of Sentences in Drug Cases," *New York Times* (July 14, 2015), A11.

59. 28 U.S.C. Section 991 (1994).

60. Bureau of Justice Statistics, *Felony Sentences in State Courts, 2006—Statistical Tables* (Washington, D.C.: U.S. Department of Justice, December 2009), Table 3.5, page 20.

61. Sonja B. Starr, "Estimating Gender Disparities in Federal Criminal Cases." *repository. law.umich.edu*. University of Michigan Law School: August 1, 2012, Web.

62. Clarice Feinman, *Women in the Criminal Justice System*, 3d ed. (Westport, Conn.: Praeger, 1994), 35.

63. Darrell Steffensmeier, John Kramer, and Cathy Streifel, "Gender and Imprisonment Decisions," *Criminology 31* (1993), 411.

64. Larry Hannah, "Lonzie Barton's Mother Sentenced to 7 Years in Baker Drug Case; Will Serve 12 Years Total." *www.jacksonville. com. Florida Times-Union*: March 22, 2016, Web.

65. Quoted in Kareem Fahim and Karen Zraick, "Seeing Failure of Mother as Factor in Sentencing," *New York Times* (November 17, 2008), A24.

66. John C. Coffee, "Repressed Issues of Sentencing," *Georgetown Law Journal 66* (1978), 987.

67. *Sentencing Guidelines: Massachusetts Sentencing Guidelines* (Boston: Massachusetts Sentencing Commission, February 1998), 5.

68. Pub. L. No. 98-473, 98 Stat. 1987, codified as amended at 18 U.S.C. Sections 3551–3742 and 28 U.S.C. Sections 991–998 (1988).

69. Julia L. Black, "The Constitutionality of Federal Sentences Imposed under the Sentencing Reform Act of 1984 after Mistretta v.

United States," *Iowa Law Review 75* (March 1990), 767.

70. *Fifteen Years of Guidelines Sentencing: An Assessment of How Well the Federal Criminal Justice System Is Achieving the Goals of Sentencing Reform* (Washington, D.C.: U.S. Sentencing Commission, November 2004), 46.

71. *Blakely v. Washington*, 542 U.S. 296 (2004); *United States v. Booker*, 543 U.S. 220 (2005); and *Gall v. United States*, 552 U.S. 38 (2007).

72. *Demographic Differences in Federal Sentencing Practices: An Update of the Booker Report's Multivariate Regression Analysis* (Washington, D.C.: U.S. Sentencing Commission, March 2010), C-3.

73. William Rhodes, et al., *Federal Sentencing Disparity: 2005–2012* (Washington, D.C.: Bureau of Justice Statistics, October 22, 2015), 38–43.

74. "Table N: National Comparison of Sentence Imposed and Position Relative to the Guideline Range, Fiscal Year 2013." *www .ussc.gov*. United States Sentencing Commission: 2013, Web.

75. Neal B. Kauder and Brian J. Ostrom, *State Sentencing Guidelines: Profiles and Continuum* (Williamsburg, Va.: National Center for State Courts, 2008), 15.

76. N.Y. Penal Law Sections 220.21, 60.5, 70.0(3) (1973).

77. Public Law Number 99–570 (1986).

78. 21 U.S.C. Section 859(b) (1986); 21 U.S.C. Section 861(a) (1986); and 18 U.S.C. Section 924(c)(1)(A)(i) (1998).

79. Todd R. Clear, George F. Cole, and Michael D. Reisig, *American Corrections*, 7th ed. (Belmont, Calif.: Thomson Wadsworth, 2006), 68–69.

80. Washington Revised Code Annotated Section 9.94A.030.

81. Nina Shapiro, "Should Washington Bring Back Parole?" *www.seattletimes.com. Seattle Times*: November 10, 2015, Web.

82. Matt Taibbi, "Cruel and Unusual Punishment: The Shame of Three Strikes Laws." *www.rollingstone.com. Rolling Stone*: March 27, 2013, Web.

83. *Lockyer v. Andrade*, 270 F.3d 743 (9th Cir. 2001).

84. *Ibid.*, 76.

85. Rob Kuznia, "An Unprecedented Experiment in Mass Forgiveness." *www.washingtonpost .com. Washington Post*: February 8, 2016, Web.

86. *United States Sentencing Commission, Report to Congress: Mandatory Minimum Penalties in the Federal Criminal Justice System* (Washington, D.C.: United States Sentencing Commission, October 2011), xxviii.

87. "Recent State-Level Reforms to Mandatory Minimums Laws." *www.famm.org*. Families against Mandatory Minimums: June 1, 2016, Web.

88. Kathy A. Bolton, "Branstad Signs Bill Allowing Early Release of Hundreds of Drug Felons," *www.desmoinesregister.com. Des Moines Register*: May 12, 2016, Web.

89. Nevada House Bill Number 239 (2009).

90. Jim Parsons, et al., *End of an Era? The Impact of Drug Reform in New York City* (New York: Vera Institute of Justice, 2015).

91. Scott Shackford, "Here's What to Expect from the Latest Attempt at Federal Sentencing Reform." *www.reason.com. Reason*: May 11, 2016, Web.

92. Justice for All Act of 2004, Pub. L. No. 108–405, 118 Stat. 2260.

93. Paul G. Cassell, "In Defense of Victim Impact Statements," *Ohio State Journal of Criminal Law* (Spring 2009), 614.

94. Edna Erez, "Victim Voice, Impact Statements, and Sentencing: Integrating Restorative Justice and Therapeutic Jurisprudence Principles in Adversarial Proceedings," *Criminal Law Bulletin* (September/October 2004), 495.

95. Bryan Myers and Edith Greene, "Prejudicial Nature of Impact Statements," *Psychology, Public Policy, and Law* (December 2004), 493.

96. Bryan Myers and Jack Arbuthnot, "The Effects of Victim Impact Evidence on the Verdicts and Sentencing Judgments of Mock Jurors," *Journal of Offender Rehabilitation* (1999), 95–112.

97. *Payne v. Tennessee*, 501 U.S. 808 (1991).

98. Comments made at the Georgetown Law Center, "The Modern View of Capital Punishment," *American Criminal Law Review 34* (Summer 1997), 1353.

99. "America and Its Fellow Executioners," *New York Times* (January 10, 2016), SR10.

100. David Bruck, quoted in Bill Rankin, "Fairness of the Death Penalty Is Still on Trial," *Atlanta Journal-Constitution* (July 29, 1997), A13.

101. "Methods by State." *www.deathpenaltyinfo.org*. Death Penalty Information Center: visited February 17, 2017, Web.

102. Larry C. Berkson, *The Concept of Cruel and Unusual Punishment* (Lexington, Mass.: Lexington Books, 1975), 43.

103. John P. Cunningham, "Death in the Federal Courts: Expectations and Realities of the Federal Death Penalty Act of 1994," *University of Richmond Law Review* 32 (May 1998), 939.

104. *In re Kemmler*, 136 U.S. 447 (1890).

105. 217 U.S. 349 (1910).

106. Pamela S. Nagy, "Hang by the Neck until Dead: The Resurgence of Cruel and Unusual Punishment in the 1990s," *Pacific Law Journal 26* (October 1994), 85.

107. 553 U.S. 35 (2008).

108. Rose Carmen Goldberg, "Safe and Effective for Human Executions?" *www.stanfordlawreview.com. Stanford Law Review*: May 2015, Web.

109. *Glossip v. Gross*, 576 U.S. ____ (2015).

110. *Ibid.*, No. 14–7955. Supreme Court of the United States (June 29, 2015), 28.

111. 408 U.S. 238 (1972).

112. 408 U.S. 309 (1972) (Stewart, concurring).

113. 536 U.S. 584 (2002).

114. *Hurst v. Florida*, 577 U.S. ____ (2016).

115. *Ford v. Wainwright*, 477 U.S. 399, 422 (1986).

116. Vidisha Barua, "'Synthetic Sanity': A Way around the Eighth Amendment?" *Criminal Law Bulletin* (July/August 2008), 561–572.

117. *Penry v. Lynaugh*, 492 U.S. 302 (1989).

118. 536 U.S. 304 (2002).

119. *Hall v. Florida*, 134 S.Ct. 1986, 2001 (2014).

120. 543 U.S. 551 (2005).

121. Ernest van den Haag, "The Ultimate Punishment: A Defense," *Harvard Law Review* 99 (1986), 1669.

122. Bryan Stevenson, "Close to Death: Reflections on Race and Capital Punishment in America," in *Debating the Death Penalty: Should America Have Capital Punishment?* ed. Hugo Bedau and Paul Cassell (New York: Oxford University Press, 2004), 97.

123. Kenneth C. Land, Raymond H. C. Teske, Jr., and Hui Zheng, "The Short-Term Effects of Executions on Homicides: Deterrence, Displacement, or Both?" *Criminology* (November 2009), 1009–1043.

124. Oliver Roeder, Lauren-Brooke Eisen, and Julia Bowling, *What Caused the Crime Decline?* (New York: Brennan Center for Justice, 2015), 43.

125. Tomislav V. Kovandzic, Lynne M. Vieraitis, and Denise Paquette Boots, "Does the Death Penalty Save Lives? New Evidence from State Panel Data, 1977 to 2006," *Criminology & Public Policy* (November 2009), 803–843.

126. Roger C. Barnes, "Death Penalty Undermines Justice," *San Antonio Express-News* (July 12, 202), 6B.

127. "Innocence and the Death Penalty." *www.deathpenaltyinfo.org*. Death Penalty Information Center: visited February 18, 2017, Web.

128. *Rompilla v. Beard*, 545 U.S. 375 (2005).

129. *Tucker v. Louisiana*, 578 U.S. ____ (2016), No. 15-946. Supreme Court of the United States (May 31, 2016), 1.

130. Deborah Fins, *Death Row U.S.A.* (New York: NAACP Legal Defense and Educational Fund, Summer 2016), 1.

131. "National Statistics on the Death Penalty and Race." *www.deathpenaltyinfo.org*. Death Penalty Information Center: visited February 18, 2017, Web.

132. *Ibid.*

133. 481 U.S. 279 (1987).

134. David C. Baldus, George Woodworth, and Charles A. Pulaski, *Equal Justice and the Death Penalty: A Legal and Empirical Analysis* (Boston: Northeastern University Press, 1990), 140–197, 306.

135. *The Death Penalty in 2016 Year End Report* (Washington, D.C.: Death Penalty Information Center, December 2016), 1.

136. *Ibid.*, 3

137. Craig Haney, "Floridians Pefer Life without Parole over Capital Punishment for Murderers." *www.tampabay.com*. Tampa Bay Times: August 16, 2016, Web.

138. *Crime in the United States, 2015, op. cit.*, Table 1.

139. Legislative Auditor, *Performance Audit: Fiscal Costs of the Death Penalty* (Carson City, Nev.: State of Nevada, 2014), 1.

140. Jessica M. Reyes, "Top Court: Delaware's Death Penalty Law Unconstitutional." *www.delawareonline.com. The News Journal*: August 3, 2016, Web.

141. *Tucker v. Louisiana, op. cit.*

142. Mark Berman, "Justices Breyer and Ginsburg: 'It Is Highly Likely' the Death Penalty Is Unconstitutional." *www.washingtonpost.com. Washington Post*: June 29, 2015, Web.

143. *Tucker v. Louisiana, op. cit.*

144. Dan Boyd, "65% Support Bringing Back Death Penalty," *Albuquerque Journal* (October 3, 2016), A1.

145. Tracy Connor, "California Unveils Lethal Injection Plan after Long Execution Delay." *www.nbcnews.com. NBCNews*: November 6, 2015, Web.

146. Jennifer Medina, "California Voters Face Choice: End Death Penalty, or Speed It Up," *New York Times* (September 21, 2016), A14.

147. "California Passes Death Penalty Reform to Speed Executions," *Associated Press* (November 23, 2016).

148. "Judge Orders California's Death Penalty Unconstitutional." *www.latimes.com. Los Angeles Times*: July 16, 2014, Web.

149. Maura Dolan, "Death Row Report Sees Failed System." *www.latimes.com. Los Angeles Times*: July 1, 2008, Web.

150. Quoted in Medina, *op. cit.*

151. Quoted in Erik Eckholm and John Schwartz, "California Death Penalty Is Unconstitutional, Federal Judge Rules," *New York Times* (July 17, 2014), A11.

152. Ana Zamora, quoted in "California Passes Death Penalty Reform to Speed Executions," *op. cit.*

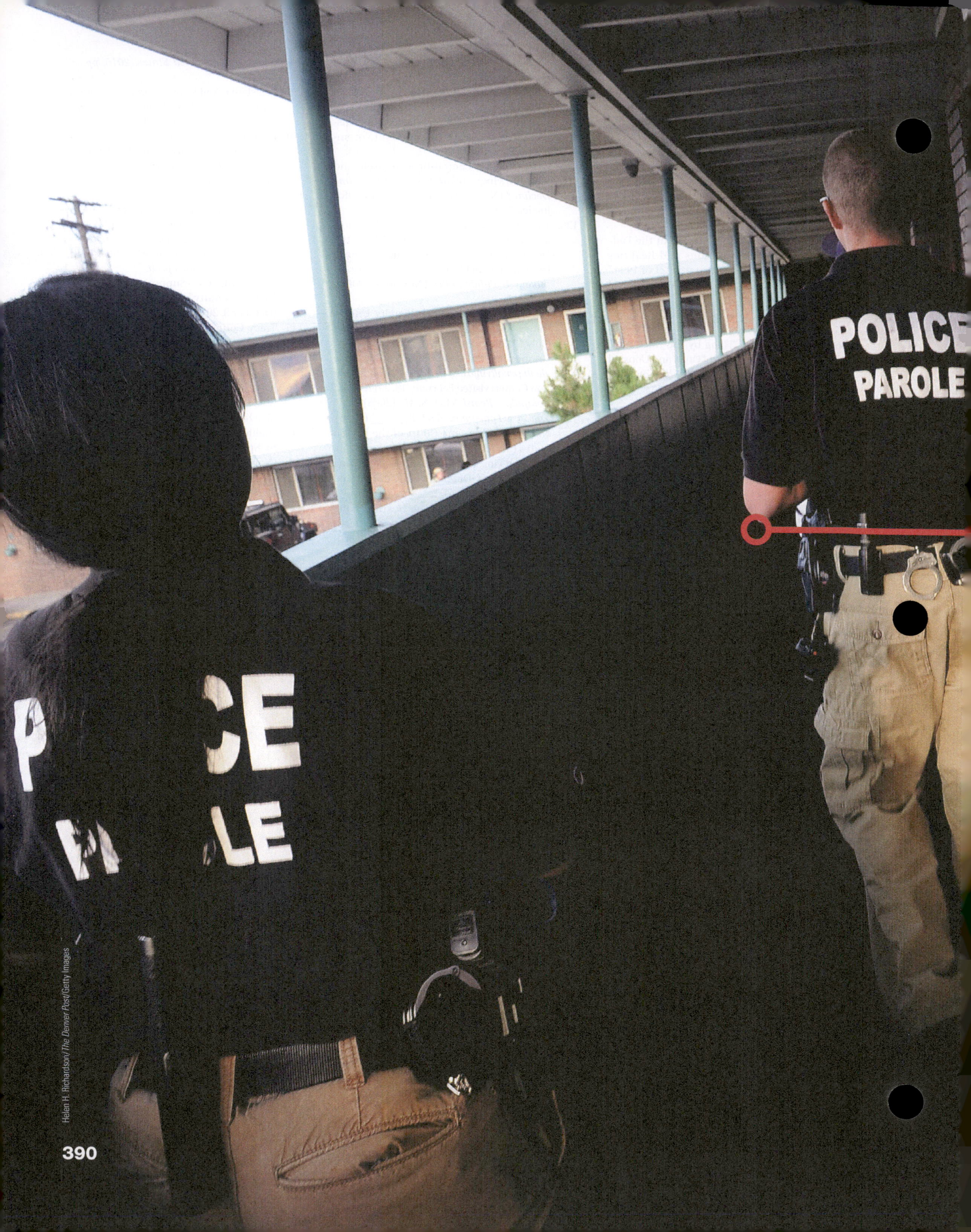

Helen H. Richardson/*The Denver Post*/Getty Images

12

Probation, Parole, and Intermediate Sanctions

To target your study and review, look for these numbered Learning Objective icons throughout the chapter.

Chapter Outline		Corresponding Learning Objectives
The Justifications for Community Corrections	**1**	Explain the justifications for community-based corrections programs.
Probation: Doing Time in the Community	**2**	Explain several alternative sentencing arrangements that combine probation with incarceration.
	3	Specify the conditions under which an offender is most likely to be denied probation.
	4	Describe the three general categories of conditions placed on a probationer.
The Parole Picture	**5**	Identify the main differences between probation and parole.
	6	Explain which factors influence the decision to grant parole.
Intermediate Sanctions	**7**	Contrast day reporting centers with intensive supervision probation.
	8	List the three levels of home monitoring.
The Paradox of Community Corrections	**9**	Summarize the paradox of community corrections.

A Significant Departure

▲ In May 2016, Judge Frederick Block decided that a defendant found guilty of importing and possessing 1.3 pounds of cocaine deserved a punishment of probation rather than incarceration. wawritto/Shutterstock.com

According to nineteen-year-old Chevelle Nesbeth, the only reason she visited Jamaica was to please her boyfriend. Also according to Nesbeth, friends in Jamaica purchased her round-trip ticket and asked her to bring two suitcases back to the United States as a favor. As Nesbeth tells the story, she was as surprised as anyone when a search of this luggage at New York City's Kennedy International Airport uncovered about 1.3 pounds of cocaine. A federal jury, unimpressed with her apparent naïveté, found Nesbeth guilty of importation and possession of a controlled substance with intent to distribute.

Under federal sentencing guidelines, Nesbeth should have spent from thirty-three to forty-one months in prison for her crimes. Senior District Judge Frederick Block decided to depart from those guidelines, however, and spared Nesbeth any incarceration. Instead, on May 25, 2016, he sentenced her to a year of probation, six months

of home confinement, and one hundred hours of community service. Judge Block did call Nesbeth's criminal conduct "inexcusable." At the same time, he emphasized that her wrongdoing was "a marked deviation from an exemplary law-abiding life." Prior to her arrest, Nesbeth was attending school and planned to become a teacher. "She has a record of prior good works counseling and tending to young children," the judge noted. "She apparently was under the influence of her boyfriend, and there is no evidence that she was even to be paid for her crime or was motivated by financial gain."

Even without going to prison, Judge Block explained, Nesbeth was going to be severely punished for her wrongdoing. Because of her conviction, Nesbeth would temporarily lose her driver's license and become ineligible for student loans and work assistance. She and her family would be denied federally assisted housing and other benefits such as food stamps, potentially for the remainder of her life. Justifying his seemingly lenient ruling, the judge criticized these "collateral consequences" as serving "no useful function other than to further punish criminal defendants after they have completed their court-imposed sentences."

FOR CRITICAL ANALYSIS

1. Which is in society's best interests—that Chevelle Nesbeth be sent to prison, or that she remain in the community while serving her term of probation? Explain your answer.

2. Do you agree with Judge Frederick Block that the "collateral consequences" of Nesbeth's conviction are punishment enough? Why or why not? How would your answer change if she had been guilty of a violent crime such as aggravated assault?

3. Is it proper that judges deviate from legislative sentencing guidelines? Are judges or lawmakers in a better position to determine proper sentences? Explain your answers.

The Justifications for Community Corrections

After Judge Frederick Block refused to send Chevelle Nesbeth to prison for smuggling cocaine, the *New York Post* ran an editorial with the headline, "Brooklyn Judge Attempts to Rewrite Laws with an Outrageous Wrist-Slap for Felon."[1] In fact, as this chapter will make clear, the law allows a range of sentencing possibilities for American judges, including numerous options that keep offenders out of prison and jail. For instance, about 3.8 million offenders are presently serving their sentences in the community on *probation* rather than behind bars. In addition, approximately 870,000 convicts in the United States have been *paroled*, meaning that they are finishing their prison sentences "on the outside" under the supervision of correctional officers.[2]

America, says University of Minnesota law professor Michael Tonry, is preoccupied with the "absolute severity of punishment" and the "widespread view that only imprisonment counts."[3] Consequently, **community corrections** such as probation and parole are often considered a less severe, and therefore a less worthy, alternative to imprisonment. In reality, community corrections are crucial to our criminal justice system. One in fifty-three adults in this country is living under community supervision,[4] and few criminal justice matters are more pressing than the need to successfully reintegrate these offenders into society.

Reintegration

A very small percentage of all convicted offenders have committed crimes that warrant life imprisonment or capital punishment. Most, at some point, will return to the community. Consequently, according to one group of experts, the task of the corrections system

> includes building or rebuilding solid ties between the offender and the community, integrating or reintegrating the offender into community life—restoring family ties, obtaining employment and an education, securing in the larger sense a place for the offender in the routine functioning of society.[5]

Considering that some studies have shown higher recidivism rates for offenders who are subjected to prison culture, a frequent justification of community-based corrections is that they help to reintegrate the offender into society.

Reintegration has a strong theoretical basis in rehabilitative theories of punishment. An offender is generally considered to be "rehabilitated" when he or she no longer represents a threat to other members of the community and therefore is believed to be fit to live in that community. In the context of this chapter and the two that follow, it will also be helpful to see reintegration as a process through which criminal justice officials such as probation and parole officers provide the offender with incentives to follow the rules of society.

These incentives can be positive, such as enrolling the offender in a drug treatment program. They can also be negative—in particular, the threat of return to prison or jail for failure to comply. In all instances, criminal justice professionals must carefully balance the needs of the individual offender against the rights of law-abiding members of the community.

Diversion

Another justification for community-based corrections, based on practical considerations, is *diversion*, a strategy introduced in Chapter 1. As you are already aware, many criminal offenses fall into the category of "petty," and it is well-nigh impossible, as well as unnecessary, to imprison every offender for every offense. Diversion programs not only relieve the pressure on overloaded courts and overcrowded jails and prisons, but also spare

Community Corrections The correctional supervision of offenders in the community as an alternative to sending them to prison or jail.

Reintegration A goal of corrections that focuses on preparing the offender for a return to the community unmarred by further criminal behavior.

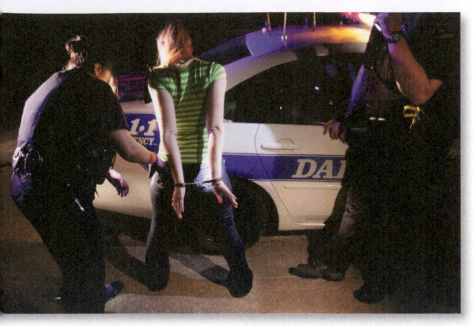

▲ In Dallas, street prostitutes such as the one shown here are often treated as crime victims and offered access to treatment and rehabilitation programs. **How might society benefit if such offenders are kept out of jail or prison through these kinds of diversion programs?** AP Images/LM Otero

low-risk, nonviolent offenders the "collateral consequences" of a conviction, as described in the opening of this chapter. In addition, the programs provide offenders with job training, counseling, and substance abuse treatment, thereby addressing the root causes of criminal behavior. Prosecutors in Cook County, Illinois, divert approximately five thousand participants from the criminal justice system on an annual basis, with 86 percent of felony defendants staying crime free for at least a year after completing the program.[6]

In his "strainer" analogy, corrections expert Paul H. Hahn likens this process to the workings of a kitchen strainer. With each "shake" of the corrections "strainer," the less serious offenders are diverted from incarceration. At the end, only the most serious convicts remain in prison.[7] The diversionary role of community-based punishments has become more pronounced as prisons and jails have filled up over the past several decades. In fact, probationers and parolees now account for about 70 percent of all adults in the American corrections systems.[8]

The "Low-Cost Alternative"

Not all of the recent expansion of community corrections can be attributed to acceptance of its theoretical underpinnings. Many politicians and criminal justice officials who do not look favorably on ideas such as reintegration and diversion have embraced programs to keep nonviolent offenders out of prison. The reason is simple: economics. The cost of constructing and maintaining prisons and jails, as well as housing and caring for inmates, has placed a great deal of pressure on corrections budgets across the country. States spend between $48 billion and $53 billion a year on their corrections systems, most of which goes to prison operating costs.[9]

Community corrections offer an enticing financial alternative to imprisonment. The Bureau of Prisons estimates that the federal government saves about $25,600 annually by shifting a nonviolent offender from incarceration to supervised release.[10] The average yearly cost of housing an inmate in North Carolina is $29,003, compared with $1,170 for community corrections.[11] The substance abuse programs affiliated with Cook County's diversion efforts, discussed above, save the county an estimated $1.5 million annually by keeping drug offenders out of jail.[12]

ETHICS CHALLENGE

Some jurisdictions charge mandatory fees to participate in a diversion program. For example, a woman in Topeka, Kansas, who struck a girl while driving—causing the victim brain damage and the loss of a leg—paid about $1,100 in fees to take part in one such program, leading to a dismissal of reckless battery charges. What are some ethical problems that arise when such fees are required of offenders, regardless of their ability to pay?

Probation: Doing Time in the Community

As Figure 12.1 shows, **probation** is the most common form of punishment in the United States. Although it is administered differently in various jurisdictions, probation can be generally defined as

> the legal status of an offender who, after being convicted of a crime, has been directed by the sentencing court to remain in the community under the supervision of a probation service for a designated period of time and subject to certain conditions imposed by the court or by law.[13]

The theory behind probation is that the legal system can treat certain offenders more economically and humanely by putting them under controls while still allowing them to live in the community. One of the advantages of probation has been that it provides for the rehabilitation of the offender while saving society the costs of incarceration. Despite probation's widespread use, certain participants in the criminal justice system question its ability to reach its rehabilitative goals. Critics point to the immense number of probationers, some of whom are violent felons, as evidence that the system has outgrown its idealistic principles.[14]

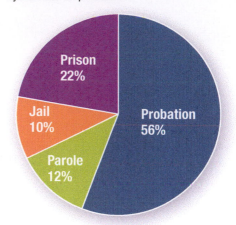

FIGURE 12.1 Probation in American Corrections

As you can see, the majority of convicts under the control of the American corrections system are on probation.

Source: Bureau of Justice Statistics, *Correctional Populations in the United States, 2015* (Washington, D.C.: U.S. Department of Justice, December 2016), Table 1, page 2.

Sentencing and Probation

Probation is basically an arrangement between sentencing authorities and the offender. In traditional probation, the offender agrees to comply with certain terms for a specified amount of time in return for serving the sentence in the community. One of the primary benefits for the offender, besides not being sent to a correctional facility, is that the length of the probationary period is usually considerably shorter than the length of a prison term (see Figure 12.2).

The traditional form of probation is not the only arrangement that can be made. A judge can hand down a **suspended sentence,** under which a defendant who has been convicted and sentenced to be incarcerated is not required to serve the sentence immediately. Instead, the judge puts the offender on notice, keeping open the option of reinstating the original sentence and sending the offender to prison or jail if he or she reoffends. In practice, suspended sentences are quite similar to probation.

> **Learning 2 Objective** Explain several alternative sentencing arrangements that combine probation with incarceration.

Alternative Sentencing Arrangements
Judges can also combine probation with incarceration. Such sentencing arrangements include:

- *Split sentences.* In **split sentence probation,** also known as *shock probation*, the offender is sentenced to a specific amount of time in prison or jail, to be followed by a period of probation.
- *Shock incarceration.* In this arrangement, an offender is sentenced to prison or jail with the understanding that after a period of time, she or he may petition the court to be released on probation. Shock incarceration is discussed more fully later in the chapter.
- *Intermittent incarceration.* With intermittent incarceration, the offender spends a certain amount of time each week, usually during the weekend, in a jail, workhouse, or other government institution.

Split sentences are sometimes used by judges, as they combine the "treatment" aspects of probation with the "punishment" aspects of incarceration. According to the

Probation A criminal sanction in which a convict is allowed to remain in the community rather than be imprisoned.

Suspended Sentence A judicially imposed condition in which an offender is sentenced after being convicted of a crime, but is not required to begin serving the sentence immediately.

Split Sentence Probation A sentence that consists of incarceration in a prison or jail, followed by a probationary period in the community.

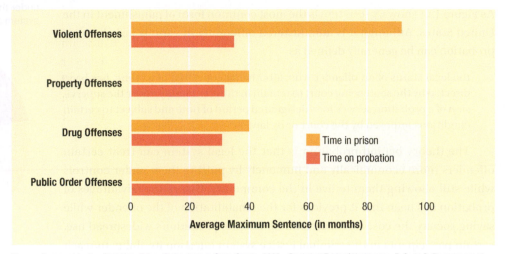

FIGURE 12.2 **Average Length of Sentence: Prison versus Probation**

As you can see, the average probation sentence is much shorter than the average prison sentence for most crimes.

Source: Bureau of Justice Statistics, *Felony Defendants in State Courts, 2009—Statistical Tables* (Washington, D.C.: U.S. Department of Justice, December 2013), Table 25, page 30; and Table 27, page 31.

United States Sentencing Commission, about 3 percent of all sentences handed down by federal judges are split sentences.[15]

Choosing Probation

Generally, research has shown that offenders are most likely to be denied probation if they:

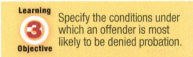

Learning Objective 3 Specify the conditions under which an offender is most likely to be denied probation.

- Are convicted on multiple charges.
- Were on probation or parole at the time of the arrest.
- Have two or more prior convictions.
- Are addicted to narcotics.
- Seriously injured the victim of the crime.
- Used a weapon during the commission of the crime.[16]

As might be expected, the chances of a felon being sentenced to probation are highly dependent on the seriousness of his or her crime. Only 19 percent of probationers in the United States have committed a violent crime, including domestic violence and sex offenses. The majority of probationers have been convicted of property crimes, drug offenses, or public order crimes such as drunk driving.[17]

Probation permits the judicial system to recognize that some offenders are less blameworthy than others. In 2016, for example, Lyvette Crespo pleaded guilty to voluntary manslaughter for killing her husband, Daniel, who had apparently been abusing her for many years. A Los Angeles judge sentenced Crespo to only ninety days in jail, along with five years' probation, five hundred hours of community service, and completion of an anger management course. "Not every case is deserving of the max sentence," said an approving local prosecutor of Crespo's punishment, which could have been up to eleven years behind bars.[18]

Probation Demographics

As in other areas of the criminal justice system, African Americans make up a higher percentage of the national probation population (30 percent) than the general population (13 percent). Fifty-three percent of probationers are white, and 13 percent are Latino.[19] The percentage of female probationers is significantly higher than female prison inmates (25 percent to 7 percent),[20] which is in keeping with the gender sentencing trends we discussed in the preceding chapter. More detailed surveys of probationers reveal that they tend to be between the ages of twenty-one and thirty-nine, single, high school graduates, and have annual incomes of less than $20,000.[21]

Revocation The formal process that follows the failure of a probationer or parolee to comply with the terms of his or her probation or parole, often resulting in the offender's incarceration.

Conditions of Probation

A judge may decide to impose certain conditions as part of a probation sentence. These conditions represent a "contract" between the judge and the offender, in which the latter agrees that if she or he does not follow certain rules, probation may be *revoked* (see Figure 12.3). **Revocation** is the formal process by which probation is ended and a probationer is punished for his or her wrongdoing, often by being sent to jail or prison for the original term decided by the court.

Judges have a great deal of discretion to impose any terms of probation that they feel are necessary. In 2017, for example, an Idaho judge required a nineteen-year-old convicted of statutory rape to abstain from extramarital sex during the term of his probation. That same year, a federal judge ordered a white-collar criminal with a history of alcoholism not only to refrain from any drug or alcohol use as a condition of probation, but also to stay out of bars and disassociate himself from anybody he knew to be a consumer of alcohol.[22]

Principles of Probation

A judge's personal philosophy is often reflected in the probation conditions that she or he creates for probationers. In *In re Quirk* (1997),[23] for example, the Louisiana Supreme Court upheld the ability of a trial judge to impose church attendance as a condition of probation. Though judges have a great deal of discretion in setting the conditions of probation, they do operate under several guiding principles. First, the conditions must be related to the dual purposes of probation, which most federal and state courts define as (1) the rehabilitation of the probationer and (2) the protection of the community. Second, the

FIGURE 12.3 Conditions of Probation

**UNITED STATES DISTRICT COURT
FOR THE
DISTRICT OF COLUMBIA**

To: _____ No. 84-417

Address: 1440 N St., N.W., #10, Wash., D.C.

In accordance with authority conferred by the United States Probation Law, you have been placed on probation this date, January 25, 2018 for a period of one year by the Hon. Thomas F. Hogan United States District Judge, sitting in and for this District Court at Washington, D.C.

CONDITIONS OF PROBATION

It is the order of the Court that you shall comply with the following conditions of probation:

(1)-You shall refrain from violation of any law (federal, state, and local). You shall get in touch immediately with your probation officer if arrested or questioned by a law enforcement officer.

(2)-You shall associate only with law-abiding persons and maintain reasonable hours.

(3)-You shall work regularly at a lawful occupation and support your legal dependents, if any, to the best of your ability. When out of work you shall notify your probation officer at once. You shall consult him prior to job changes.

(4)-You shall not leave the judicial district without permission of the probation officer.

(5)-You shall notify your probation officer immediately of any change in your place of residence.

(6)-You shall follow the probation officer's instructions.

(7)-You shall report to the probation officer as directed.

(8)-You shall not possess a firearm (handgun or rifle) for any reason.

The special conditions ordered by the Court are as follows:

Imposition of sentence suspended, one year probation, Fine of $75 on each count.

I understand that the Court may change the conditions of probation, reduce or extend the period of probation, and at any time during the probation period or within the maximum probation period of 5 years permitted by law, may issue a warrant and revoke probation for a violation occurring during the probation period.

I have read or had read to me the above conditions of probation. I fully understand them and I will abide by them.

_____ Date _____
Probationer

You will report as follows: _____ as directed by your Probation Officer
_____ Date _____
U.S. Probation Officer

conditions must not violate the U.S. Constitution, as probationers are generally entitled to the same constitutional rights as other prisoners.[24]

Of course, probationers do give up certain constitutional rights when they consent to the terms of probation. Most probationers, for example, agree to spot checks of their homes for contraband such as drugs or weapons, and they therefore have a diminished expectation of privacy.

In *United States v. Knights* (2001),[25] the United States Supreme Court upheld the actions of deputy sheriffs in Napa County, California, who searched a probationer's home without a warrant or probable cause. The unanimous decision was based on the premise that because those on probation are more likely to commit crimes, law enforcement agents "may therefore justifiably focus on probationers in a way that [they do] not on the ordinary citizen."[26]

Types of Conditions   Obviously, probationers who break the law are very likely to have their probation revoked. Other, less serious infractions may also result in revocation. The conditions placed on a probationer fall into three general categories:

Learning Objective 4 Describe the three general categories of conditions placed on a probationer.

- *Standard conditions*, which are imposed on all probationers. These include reporting regularly to the probation officer, notifying the agency of any change of address, not leaving the jurisdiction without permission, and remaining employed.
- *Punitive conditions*, which usually reflect the seriousness of the offense and are intended to increase the punishment of the offender. Such conditions include fines, community service, restitution, drug testing, and home confinement (discussed later).
- *Treatment conditions*, which are imposed to reverse patterns of self-destructive behavior. Such treatment generally includes counseling for drug and alcohol abuse, anger management, and therapy for mental health issues, and is a component of approximately 27 percent of probation sentences in this country.[27]

Some observers feel that judges have too much discretion in imposing overly restrictive conditions that no person, much less one who has exhibited antisocial tendencies, could meet. Citing prohibitions on drinking liquor, gambling, and associating with "undesirables," as well as requirements such as meeting early curfews, the late University of Delaware professor Carl B. Klockars claimed that if probation rules were taken seriously, "very few probationers would complete their terms without violation."[28]

As the majority of probationers do complete their terms successfully,[29] Klockars's statement suggests that either probation officers are unable to determine that violations are taking place, or many of them are exercising a great deal of discretion in reporting minor probation violations. Perhaps the officers realize that violating probationers for every single "slip-up" is unrealistic and would add to the already significant problem of jail and prison overcrowding.

The Supervisory Role of the Probation Officer

The probation officer has two basic roles. The first is investigative and consists of conducting the presentence investigation (PSI), which was discussed in Chapter 11. The second is supervisory and begins as soon as the offender has been sentenced to probation. In smaller probation agencies, individual officers perform both tasks. In larger jurisdictions, the trend has been toward separating the responsibilities, with *investigating officers* handling the PSI and *line officers* concentrating on supervision.

Peggy McCarthy Lead Probation Officer

The best thing about my job is that every day is different. I may be in court first thing in the morning, and then in my office meeting with defendants or developing case plans. In the afternoon, I may be at the jail taking statements for court reports or out in the field seeing my defendants. If I work a late shift, I may be visiting counseling agencies or talking to collateral sources or doing surveillance. I may be organizing a search on a defendant's home or making an arrest. I may be working with the police to solve crimes or locate absconders. Or I may simply be completing administrative duties like filing or returning phone calls to defendants and/or their family members. Anything can happen at any time, and I have to be ready to respond. If a probation officer gets bored, something is wrong.

I take a great deal of pride in assisting defendants with the difficult task of making positive change in their lives. The rewards may be few and far between, but when a defendant with a history of substance abuse stays clean and sober for a year, when a gang-affiliated defendant secures a job and no longer associates with negative peers, or when a defendant who admittedly never liked school obtains a GED or diploma, that is when I realize that what I'm doing day in and day out is 100 percent worthwhile.

Courtesy of Peggy McCarthy

SOCIAL MEDIA CAREER TIP Manage your online reputation—or someone else will do it for you. Monitor your profile using tools such as Pipl and ZabaSearch. Check BoardReader and Omgili for information on what people are saying about you on message boards.

FAST FACTS

Lead probation officer

Job description:
- Work with offenders or clients who have been sentenced to probation.
- Work with the courts. Investigate backgrounds, write presentence reports, and recommend sentences.

What kind of training is required?
- Bachelor's degree in criminal justice, social work/psychology, or related field.
- Must be at least 21 years of age, have no felony convictions, and have strong writing and interview skills. Experience in multicultural outreach a plus.

Annual salary range?
- $30,000–$80,000

One of the most difficult aspects of a probation officer's supervisory duties is an unavoidable *role conflict*. On the one hand, the probation officer has the task of guiding the probationer to a successful completion of the probationary term. On the other hand, the probation officer must protect the community from the probationer, who has already shown that he or she is capable of breaking the law. Operating under vague institutional guidelines, probation officers must rely mostly on their own discretion to navigate the complexities of their profession.[30]

The Use of Authority Not surprisingly, research shows that the ideal officer-offender relationship is based on mutual respect, honesty, and trust. In reality, these conditions are often hard to maintain between probation officers and their clients. Any incentive an offender might have to be completely truthful with a line officer is marred by one simple fact: Self-reported wrongdoing can be used to revoke probation. Even probation officers whose primary mission is to rehabilitate are under institutional pressure to punish their clients for violating conditions of probation. One officer deals with this situation by telling his clients

that I'm here to help them, to get them a job, and whatever else I can do. But I tell them too that I have a family to support and that if they get too far off track, I can't afford to put my job on the line for them. I'm going to have to violate them.[31]

In the absence of trust, most probation officers rely on their **authority** to guide an offender successfully through the sentence. An officer's authority, or ability to influence a person's actions without resorting to force, is based partially on her or his power to revoke probation. It also reflects her or his ability to impose a number of lesser sanctions. For example, if a probationer fails to attend a required alcohol treatment program, the officer can send him or her to a "lockup," or detention center, overnight. To be successful, a probation officer must establish this authority early in the relationship, as it is the primary tool for persuading the probationer to behave in an acceptable manner.

The Caseload Dilemma   Even the most balanced, "firm but fair" approach to probation can be defeated by the problem of excessive *caseloads*. A **caseload** is the number of clients a probation officer is responsible for at any one time. Heavy probation caseloads seem inevitable. Unlike a prison cell, a probation officer can always take "just one more" client. Furthermore, the ideal caseload size is very difficult to determine because different offenders require different levels of supervision.

The consequences of disproportionate probation officer–probationer ratios are, in many instances, predictable. When burdened with large caseloads, probation officers find it practically impossible to rigorously enforce the conditions imposed on their clients. Lack of surveillance leads to lack of control, which can undermine the very basis of a probationary system.

Federal probation officers in western Oklahoma, for example, oversee about nine hundred probationers each, an increase of 17 percent since 2010. With fewer officers per probationer, fewer probation violations are being uncovered. "There is a tie between revocation rates going down and a shortage of officers in the community checking on people," said Steve Skinner, chief of the federal probation office in Oklahoma City.[32] In some cases, jurisdictions have tried to alleviate caseload pressure by engaging private probation services, contributing to a problem discussed in the feature *Myth vs. Reality—Modern-Day Debtor's Prisons?*

Revocation of Probation

The probation period can end in one of two ways. Either the probationer successfully fulfills the conditions of the sentence, or the probationer misbehaves and probation is revoked, resulting in a prison or jail term. As mentioned, probationers who break the law will generally have their probation revoked. The decision of whether to revoke after a **technical violation**—such as failing to report a change of address or testing positive for drug use—is often made at the discretion of the probation officer.

Probation and the Constitution   As we have seen, probationers do not always enjoy the same protections under the U.S. Constitution as other members of society. The United States Supreme Court has not stripped these offenders of all rights, however. In *Mempa v. Rhay* (1967),[33] the Court ruled that probationers were entitled to an attorney during the revocation process. Then, in *Morrissey v. Brewer* (1972) and *Gagnon v. Scarpelli* (1973),[34] the Court established a three-stage procedure by which the "limited" due process rights of probationers must be protected in potential revocation situations:

- *Preliminary hearing.* In this appearance before a "disinterested person" (often a judge), the facts of the violation or arrest are presented, and it is determined whether probable cause for revoking probation exists. This hearing can be waived by the probationer.

Authority The power conferred on an agent of the law to enforce obedience.

Caseload The number of individual probationers or parolees under the supervision of a probation or parole officer.

Technical Violation An action taken by a probationer or parolee that, although not criminal, breaks the terms of probation or parole as designated by the court.

- *Revocation hearing.* During this hearing, the probation agency presents evidence to support its claim of violation, and the probationer can attempt to refute this evidence. The probationer has the right to know the charges being brought against him or her. Furthermore, probationers can testify on their own behalf and present witnesses in their favor, as well as confront and cross-examine adverse witnesses. A "neutral and detached" body must hear the evidence and rule on the validity of the proposed revocation.

- *Revocation sentencing.* If the presiding body rules against the probationer, then the judge must decide whether to impose incarceration and for what length of time. In a revocation hearing dealing with technical violations, the judge will often reimpose probation with stricter terms or intermediate sanctions.

In effect, this is a "bare-bones" approach to due process. Most of the rules of evidence that govern regular trials do not apply to revocation hearings. Probation officers are not, for example, required to read offenders their *Miranda* rights before questioning them about crimes they may have committed during probation. In *Minnesota v. Murphy* (1984),[35] the Supreme Court ruled that a meeting between probation officer and client does not equal custody and, therefore, the Fifth Amendment protection against self-incrimination does not apply, either.

Limiting Revocation Probation (and parole) revocation accounts for a significant portion of prison admissions in many states. Research shows, however, that revoking probation for technical violations does not increase community safety. Indeed, a low-level offender sent to prison for a technical violation is more likely to reoffend than if he or she is able to avoid incarceration.[36]

Consequently, policy makers recently have been focusing on **graduated sanctions** to keep those who violate the terms of their probation out of jail or prison. These sanctions move upward on a scale of severity, punishing offenders more harshly with each misstep. So, for example, in Kansas, at the discretion of a judge, probationers may be punished according to the following scale:

1. First technical violation = a modification of the terms of probation.
2. Second technical violation = a short stint in jail, not more than six days per month for three consecutive months.

MYTH VS REALITY

Modern-Day Debtor's Prisons?

The Myth During this country's early years, someone who was unable to pay his or her debts—public or private—was routinely placed behind bars until that debt was satisfied. In 1833, the federal government banned these so-called "debtor's prisons," and today most states specifically prohibit the criminalization of poverty. (For example, Georgia's constitution holds that "There shall be no imprisonment for debt.") Therefore, debtor's prisons no longer exist in the United States.

The Reality At the time he was sentenced to probation and ordered to pay a $200 fine for stealing a can of beer, Thomas Barrett of Augusta, Georgia, was unemployed and living on food stamps. A private probation service (PPS) administered Barrett's community supervision, charging him $360 per month. Despite selling his blood plasma, Barrett eventually owed the PPS more than $1,000 in fees and, unable to pay, was jailed.

Apart from hiring PPSs, hundreds of states and localities across the country have tried to defray the costs of incarceration with a variety of court-imposed fees and surcharges. If these fees go unpaid, a judge can send the defendant to jail as punishment. Particularly for poorer defendants, this can lead to a vicious cycle: Behind bars, they cannot earn the paycheck needed to cover the unpaid fees.

In 2016, the city of Jennings, Missouri, settled a lawsuit by agreeing to disburse $4.7 million as compensation to nearly two thousand people jailed for not paying fines and fees related to traffic violations and other petty infractions. "It's 100 percent true that we have debtor's prisons in 2016," says one public defender, decrying the common practice of keeping people in jail "not because of what they've done, but because they're poor."

FOR CRITICAL ANALYSIS

As noted in Chapter 11, the United States Supreme Court ruled three decades ago that courts could not imprison defendants who were unable to pay court-imposed fines. As part of that ruling, the Court indicated that courts could imprison defendants who "willfully" refused to pay such fines. How can a court distinguish between "unable" and "unwilling" defendants in these cases? Can you think of any alternatives to jail for poor defendants who are unable to pay their fines? Explain your answers.

Graduated Sanctions A series of punishments that become more severe with each subsequent act of wrongdoing.

3. Third technical violation = imprisonment for three months.
4. Fourth technical violation = imprisonment for four months.
5. Fifth technical violation = parole revocation and restoration of original sentence.[37]

Kansas also offers certain low-level offenders the chance to end their probationary term after one year, regardless of the length of the sentence, if they have complied with their conditions during that time.[38] A number of states offer similar incentives, which serve the dual purpose of providing motivation for good behavior and reducing probation officer caseloads.

▲ An airplane drops retardant onto the Cold Springs Fire, which burned five hundred acres and destroyed eight homes in northern Colorado in July 2016. Two men who pleaded guilty to arson for starting the fire were sentenced to a split sentence that included two years' jail time and four years' probation. **Was this an appropriate punishment? Which sentence do you think more effectively reduces the likelihood of recidivism: a split sentence or probation only? Explain your answers.** Andy Cross/*The Denver Post*/Getty Images

Does Probation Work?

On August 27, 2016, Rodney Earl Sanders admitted to killing two nuns in Holmes County, Mississippi. A year earlier, Sanders had been arrested for felony driving-under-the-influence and was free on probation. Indeed, probationers are responsible for a significant amount of crime. According to the most recent data, 11 percent of all suspects arrested for violent crimes (and 13 percent of those arrested for murder) were on probation at the time of their apprehension.[39] Such statistics raise a critical question—is probation worthwhile?

To evaluate the effectiveness of probation, we must look again at its purpose. Generally, as we saw earlier, the goal of probation is to reintegrate and divert as many offenders as possible while at the same time protecting the public. Specifically, probation and other community corrections programs are evaluated by their success in preventing *recidivism*—the eventual rearrest of the probationer.[40] Given that most probationers are first-time, nonviolent offenders, the system is not designed to prevent relatively rare outbursts of violence, such as the murder committed by Rodney Earl Sanders.

Risk Factors for Recidivism

About 8 percent of all probationers exit probation by being sent to prison or jail.[41] There are several risk factors that make a probationer more likely to recidivate, including:

1. *Antisocial personality patterns*, meaning that the probationer is impulsive, pleasure seeking, restlessly aggressive, or irritable.
2. *Procriminal attitudes* such as negative opinions of authority and the law, as well as a tendency to rationalize prior criminal behavior.
3. *Social supports for crime*, including friends who are offenders and a living environment lacking in positive role models.[42]

Other important risk factors for recidivism include substance abuse and unemployment. By concentrating resources on those probationers who exhibit these risk factors, probation departments can succeed in lowering caseloads and overall recidivism rates.

Jurisdictions are increasingly using crime-prediction software to determine which probationers are at the greatest risk of recidivating and therefore need greater levels of supervision. A risk-prediction tool used by Philadelphia's Adult Probation and Parole Department (APPD), for example, employs a sophisticated statistical technique called "random forest modeling" to evaluate each offender according to factors such as criminal history, number of years since the last serious offense, and ZIP code. Based on this evaluation, APPD assigns the offender to one of three risk categories. Its high-risk probationers are thirteen times more likely to recidivate than low-risk probationers, and are supervised accordingly.[43]

"Swift and Certain"   One of the problems with traditional methods of sanctioning probation violations is the length of the proceedings. If, for example, a probationer fails a drug test, it may take months before a penalty is enforced, weakening the link between wrongdoing and punishment. As criminologist James Q. Wilson pointed out, a parent does not discipline a child by saying, "Because [you've misbehaved], you have a 50-50 chance nine months from now of being grounded."[44]

A number of probation departments have implemented strategies that operate on the principle of providing "swift and certain" sanctions for probation violations. Perhaps the most successful of these strategies is Hawaii's Opportunity Probation with Enforcement (HOPE) program. The rules of HOPE are simple. Each substance abuse probationer must call the courthouse every day to learn if she or he is required to come in for a urine test for drugs, or *urinalysis*. If drugs are found in the probationer's system during one of these frequent tests, a short jail term—one to two weeks—is automatically imposed.[45] HOPE has resulted in large reductions in positive drug tests by probationers, and its 2,200 participants are significantly less likely to be rearrested than those not in the program.[46]

Following the HOPE model, South Dakota's 24/7 Sobriety Project requires probationers convicted of alcohol-related offenses to wear alcohol-monitoring bracelets or submit to daily breathalyzer tests. Offenders who skip or fail these tests are immediately sent to jail for a short stay. Data show that, from 2005 to 2010, when more than 17,000 South Dakota residents participated in the program, repeat DUI arrests in the state declined 12 percent and domestic violence arrests declined 9 percent.[47]

ETHICS CHALLENGE

You may have noticed that one of the factors used in Philadelphia to determine a probationer's risk category is his or her residential ZIP code. Why have some observers criticized this tactic as a form of racial and ethnic discrimination? Should the use of ZIP codes in offender risk-assessment strategies be prohibited because it is unethical? Why or why not?

The Parole Picture

At any given time, about 870,000 Americans are living in the community on **parole**—the *conditional* release of a prisoner after a portion of his or her sentence has been served behind bars. Parole allows the corrections system to continue to supervise an offender who is no longer incarcerated. As long as parolees follow the conditions of their parole, they are allowed to finish their terms outside the prison. If parolees break the terms of their early release, however, they face the risk of being returned to a penal institution.

Parole The conditional release of an inmate before his or her sentence has expired.

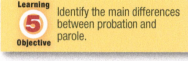

Parole Contract An agreement between the state and the offender that establishes the conditions of parole.

Parole is based on three concepts:[48]

1. *Grace.* The prisoner has no right to be given an early release, but the government has granted her or him that privilege.
2. *Contract of consent.* The government and the parolee enter into an arrangement whereby the latter agrees to abide by certain conditions in return for continued freedom.
3. *Custody.* Technically, though no longer incarcerated, the parolee is still the responsibility of the state. Parole is an extension of corrections.

Because of good-time credits and parole, most prisoners do not serve their entire sentence in prison. In fact, the average felon serves only about half of the term handed down by the court.

Comparing Probation and Parole

Both probation and parole operate under the basic assumption that the offender serves her or his time in the community rather than in a prison or jail. The main differences between the two concepts—which sound confusingly similar—involve their circumstances. Probation is a sentence handed down by a judge following conviction and usually does not include incarceration. Parole is a conditional release from prison and occurs after an offender has already served some time in a correctional facility. (See *Mastering Concepts—Probation versus Parole* for clarification.)

Conditions of Parole

In many ways, parole supervision is similar to probation supervision. Like probationers, offenders who are granted parole are placed under the supervision of community corrections officers and required to follow certain conditions. Parole conditions often mirror probation conditions. All parolees, for example, must comply with the law, and they are generally responsible for reporting to their parole officer at certain intervals.

The frequency of these visits, along with the other terms of parole, is spelled out in the **parole contract,** which sets out the agreement between the state and the paroled offender. Under the terms of the contract, the state agrees to conditionally release the inmate, and the future parolee agrees that her or his conditional release will last only as long as she or he abides by the contract. (See Figure 12.4 for a list of standard parole conditions.)

FIGURE 12.4 **Standard Conditions of Parole**

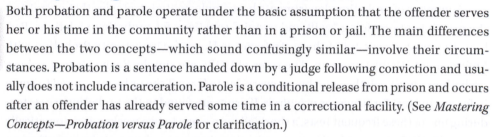

The parolee must do the following:

- Stay within a certain area.
- Obtain permission before changing residence or employment.
- Obtain and maintain employment.
- Maintain acceptable, nonthreatening behavior.
- Not possess firearms or weapons.
- Report any arrest within twenty-four hours.
- Not use illegal drugs or alcohol or enter drinking establishments.
- Not break any state or local laws.
- Allow contacts by parole officers at home or employment without obstruction.
- Submit to search of person, residence, or motor vehicle at any time by parole officers.

Parole Revocation

About a quarter of parolees return to prison before the end of their parole period, most because they were convicted of a new offense or had their parole revoked.[49] Property crimes are the most common reason that both male and female parolees return to incarceration, and men on parole are twice as likely as their female counterparts to have their parole revoked for a violent crime.[50] Parole revocation is similar in many aspects to probation revocation. If the parolee commits a new crime, then a return to prison is very likely. If, however, the individual commits a technical violation by breaking a condition of parole, then parole authorities have discretion as to whether revocation proceedings should be initiated. A number of states, including Arkansas, Connecticut,

Probation versus Parole

Probation and parole have many aspects in common. In fact, probation and parole are so similar that many jurisdictions combine them into a single agency. There are, however, some important distinctions between the two systems, as noted below.

	PROBATION	PAROLE
Basic Definition	An **alternative to imprisonment** in which a person who has been convicted of a crime is allowed to serve his or her sentence in the community subject to certain conditions and supervision by a probation officer.	An **early release** from a correctional facility, in which the convicted offender is given the chance to spend the remainder of her or his sentence under supervision in the community.
Timing	The offender is sentenced to a probationary term in place of a prison or jail term. If the offender breaks the conditions of probation, he or she is sent to prison or jail. Therefore, **probation generally occurs** *before* **imprisonment**.	Parole is a form of early release. Therefore, **parole occurs** *after* **an offender has spent time behind bars.**
Authority	**Probation is under the domain of the judiciary.** A judge decides whether to sentence a convict to probation, and a judge determines whether a probation violation warrants revocation and incarceration.	**Parole often falls under the domain of the parole board.** This administrative body determines whether the prisoner qualifies for early release and the conditions under which the parole must be served.
Characteristics of Offenders	As a number of studies have shown, probationers are normally less involved in the criminal lifestyle. Most of them are **first-time offenders who have committed nonviolent crimes.**	Many parolees have **spent months or even years in prison** and, besides abiding by conditions of parole, must make the difficult transition to "life on the outside."

Georgia, and Texas, have recently have taken steps to avoid reincarcerating parolees for technical violations as part of their continuing efforts to reduce prison populations.[51]

When authorities do attempt to revoke parole for a technical violation, they must provide the parolee with a revocation hearing.[52] Although this hearing does not provide the same due process protections as a criminal trial, the parolee does have the right to be notified of the charges, to present witnesses, to speak in his or her defense, and to question any hostile witnesses (so long as such questioning would not place these witnesses in danger). In the first stage of the hearing, the parole authorities determine whether there is probable cause that a violation occurred. Then, they decide whether to return the parolee to prison.

Probation and Parole Officers   Unlike police officers or sheriffs' deputies, probation and parole officers generally do not wear uniforms. Instead, they have badges that identify their position and agency. The duties of probation officers and parole officers are so similar that many small jurisdictions combine the two posts into a single position.

Given the supervisory nature of their professions, probation and parole officers are ultimately responsible for protecting the community by keeping their clients from committing crimes. There is also an element of social work in their duties, and these officers must constantly balance the needs of the community with the needs of the offender.[53] Parole officers in particular are expected to help the parolee readjust to life outside the correctional institution by helping her or him find a place to live and a job, and seeing that she or he receives any treatment that may be necessary.

Discretionary Release

As you may recall from Chapter 11, corrections systems are classified by sentencing procedure—indeterminate or determinate. Indeterminate sentencing occurs when the legislature sets a range of punishments for particular crimes, and the judge and the parole board exercise discretion in determining the actual length of the prison term. For that reason, states with indeterminate sentencing are said to have systems of **discretionary release.**

Eligibility for Parole

Under indeterminate sentencing, parole is not a right but a privilege. This is a crucial point, as it establishes the terms of the relationship between the inmate and the corrections authorities during the parole process. In *Greenholtz v. Inmates of the Nebraska Penal and Correctional Complex* (1979),[54] the Supreme Court ruled that inmates do not have a constitutionally protected right to expect parole, thereby giving states the freedom to set their own standards for determining parole eligibility. In most states that have retained indeterminate sentencing, a prisoner is eligible to be considered for parole release after serving a legislatively determined percentage of the minimum sentence—usually one-half or two-thirds—less any good time or other credits.

Not all convicts are eligible for parole. As we saw in Chapter 11, offenders who have committed the most serious crimes often receive life sentences without the possibility of early release. In general, life without parole is reserved for those who have been found guilty of first degree murder or are defined by statute as habitual offenders. In addition, about 3,300 inmates convicted of nonviolent drug and property crimes have also received this sentence.[55] Today, about one-third of convicts serving life sentences have no possibility of parole.[56]

Parole Procedures

A convict does not apply for parole. Rather, different jurisdictions have different procedures for determining discretionary release dates. In many states, the offender is eligible for discretionary release at the end of his or her minimum sentence minus good-time credits (see Chapter 11). In 2016, for example, Patrick Durocher was sentenced to three to five years in prison for sexually assaulting a woman on the campus of the University of Massachusetts Amherst. This means that Durocher will become eligible for parole after serving three years, less good time. In other states, parole eligibility is measured at either one-third or one-half of the maximum sentence, or it is a matter of discretion for the parole authorities.

In most, but not all, states, the responsibility for making the parole decision falls to the **parole board,** whose members are generally appointed by the governor. According to the American Correctional Association, the parole board has four basic roles:

1. To decide which offenders should be placed on parole.
2. To determine the conditions of parole and aid in the continuing supervision of the parolee.
3. To discharge the offender when the conditions of parole have been met.
4. If a violation occurs, to determine whether parole privileges should be revoked.[57]

Most parole boards are small, made up of three to seven members. In many jurisdictions, board members' terms are limited to between four and six years. The requirements for board members vary. Nearly half the states have no prerequisites, while others require a bachelor's degree or some expertise in the field of criminal justice.

Discretionary Release The release of an inmate into a community supervision program at the discretion of the parole board within limits set by state or federal law.

Parole Board A body of appointed civilians that decides whether a convict should be granted conditional release before the end of his or her sentence.

The Parole Decision Parole boards use a number of criteria to determine whether a convict should be given discretionary release. These criteria include:

1. The nature and circumstances of the underlying offense and the offender's current attitude toward it.
2. The offender's prior criminal record.
3. The offender's attitude toward the victim and the victim's family members.
4. The offender's physical, mental, and emotional health.
5. The offender's behavior behind bars, including his or her participation in programs for self-improvement.[58]

In a system that uses discretionary parole, the actual release decision is made at a **parole grant hearing.** During this hearing, the entire board or a subcommittee reviews relevant information on the convict. Sometimes, but not always, the offender is interviewed. "I really am sorry for all the crimes I committed," Darryl Dent told a New York parole board in March 2016. Dent was serving five to eleven years behind bars for stealing a wallet, his eighth petty theft conviction. "I'm tired of coming to jail. I'm 56 years old, and I don't want to spend the rest of my life in jail."[59]

Because the board members have only limited knowledge of each offender, key players in the case are often notified in advance of the parole hearing and asked to provide comments and recommendations. These participants include the sentencing judge, the attorneys at the trial, the victims, and any law enforcement officers who may be involved. After these preparations, the typical parole hearing itself is very short—usually lasting just a few minutes. In most jurisdictions, there is little time for more lengthy proceedings. The New York parole board that ultimately rejected Darryl Dent's parole, for example, holds about twelve thousand hearings a year, conducting as many as forty in a single day.[60]

Parole Denial When parole is denied, the reasons usually involve poor prison behavior by the offender and/or the severity of the underlying crime.[61] After a parole denial, the entire process will generally be replayed at the next "action date," which depends on the nature of the offender's crimes and all relevant laws. In 2016, for example, seventy-two-year-old Sirhan Sirhan was denied parole for the fifteenth time. Nearly five decades earlier, Sirhan had been convicted of murdering Senator Robert F. Kennedy at the Ambassador Hotel in Los Angeles and sentenced to life in prison. At his most recent parole hearing, Sirhan claimed that he did not remember shooting Kennedy, leading the California parole board to conclude that he did not show adequate remorse or understand the enormity of his crime.[62]

On rare occasions, a state governor will veto the decision of a parole board to grant supervised release. In 2016, for example, a California parole board recommended the release of sixty-six-year-old Leslie Van Houten, whose parole had been denied nineteen times for a double murder that took place in 1969. Over the course of nearly five decades behind bars, Van Houten had been a model inmate, earning her bachelor's and master's degrees in prison and running a self-help group for incarcerated women. California governor Jerry Brown blocked Van Houten's parole, however, saying that "her role in these extraordinarily brutal crimes . . . cannot be overlooked and lead me to believe she remains an unacceptable risk to society if released."[63] (See the feature *Discretion in Action—Cause for Compassion?* to learn more about the process of discretionary release.)

Parole Grant Hearing A hearing in which the entire parole board or a subcommittee reviews information, meets the offender, and hears testimony from relevant witnesses to determine whether to grant parole.

DISCRETION IN ACTION

Cause for Compassion?

The Situation Thirty-seven years ago, Susan was convicted of first degree murder and sentenced to life in prison for taking part in a grisly killing spree in Los Angeles. Over the course of two days, Susan and her accomplices killed seven people. Susan stabbed one of the victims—a pregnant woman—sixteen times and wrote the word "PIG" on a door using another victim's blood. During her trial, Susan testified that she "was stoned, man, stoned on acid" at the time of her crimes. Now sixty-one years old, Susan is before your parole board, requesting release from prison. For most of her time behind bars, she has been a model prisoner, and she has apologized numerous times for her wrongdoing. Furthermore, her left leg has been amputated, the left side of her body is paralyzed, and she has been diagnosed with terminal brain cancer.

The Law You have a great deal of discretion in determining whether a prisoner should be paroled. Some of the factors

you should consider are the threat the prisoner would pose to the community if released, the nature of the offense, and the level of remorse. In addition, California allows for "compassionate release" when an inmate is "terminally ill."

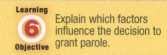

Learning Objective **6** Explain which factors influence the decision to grant parole.

What Would You Do? Susan obviously poses no threat to the community and is a viable candidate for compassionate release. Should she be set free on parole? Or are some crimes so horrific that the convict should never be given parole, no matter what the circumstances? Explain your vote.

To see how a California parole board voted in a similar situation, go to Example 12.1 in Appendix B.

Parole Guidelines

Nearly twenty states have moved away from discretionary release systems to procedures that provide for **mandatory release.** Under mandatory release, offenders leave prison only when their prison terms have expired, minus adjustments for good time. No parole board is involved in this type of release, which is designed to eliminate discretion from the process.

Instead, in mandatory release, corrections officials rely on **parole guidelines** to determine the early release date. Similar to sentencing guidelines (see Chapter 11), parole guidelines determine a potential parolee's risk of recidivism using a mathematical equation. Under this system, inmates and corrections authorities know the *presumptive parole date* soon after the inmate enters prison. So long as the offender does not experience any disciplinary or other problems while incarcerated, he or she can be fairly sure of the time of release.

Note that a number of states and the federal government claim to have officially "abolished" parole through truth-in-sentencing laws. (As described in Chapter 11, this form of legislation requires certain statutorily determined offenders to serve at least 85 percent of their prison terms.) For the most part, however, these laws simply emphasize prison terms that are "truthful," not necessarily "longer." Mechanisms for parole, by whatever name, are crucial to the criminal justice system for several reasons. First, they provide inmates with an incentive to behave properly in the hope of an early release. Second, they reduce the costs related to incarceration by keeping down the inmate population, a critical concern for prison administrators.[64]

Victims' Rights and Parole

Over the past several decades, the community corrections system has expanded to better encompass the wants and needs of victims. Many probation and parole departments now have employees responsible for assisting victims in areas such as collecting restitution or compensation and providing information about the status and location of offenders.[65]

Mandatory Release Release from prison that occurs when an offender has served the full length of his or her sentence, minus any adjustments for good time.

Parole Guidelines Standards that are used in the parole process to measure the risk that a potential parolee will recidivate.

The federal Crime Victims' Rights Act provides victims with the right to be reasonably notified of any parole proceedings and the right to attend and be reasonably heard at such proceedings.[66] A number of states offer similar assurances of victim participation in the parole process. Generally, victim testimony before a parole board focuses on the emotional, physical, and financial hardship experienced by the victim or the victim's family because of the offender's criminal act. Given the moral power of such testimony, it is somewhat surprising to learn that victim input appears to have little effect on the parole decision. Instead, parole boards prefer to rely on the traditional criteria for determining parole, described earlier in this section.[67]

▲ Paul Schrade reacts with frustration during the 2016 parole hearings for Sirhan Sirhan in San Diego. Even though Schrade was wounded when Sirhan assassinated Senator Robert F. Kennedy nearly fifty years earlier, as described in the text, Schrade has forgiven Sirhan and argued that he should be granted parole. **How much weight should parole boards place on the wishes of victims when making the decision to grant or deny parole?** AP Photo/ Gregory Bull

Intermediate Sanctions

Many observers feel that the most widely used sentencing options—imprisonment and probation—fail to reflect the immense diversity of crimes and criminals. **Intermediate sanctions** provide a number of additional sentencing options for wrongdoers who require stricter supervision than that supplied by probation, but for whom imprisonment would be unduly harsh and counterproductive. The intermediate sanctions discussed in this section are designed to match the specific punishment and treatment of an individual offender with a corrections program that reflects that offender's situation.

Dozens of different variations of intermediate sanctions are handed down each year. To cover the spectrum succinctly, two general categories of such sanctions will be discussed in this section: those administered primarily by the courts and those administered primarily by corrections departments, including day reporting centers, intensive supervision probation, shock incarceration, and home confinement. Remember that none of these sanctions is exclusive. They are often combined with imprisonment and probation and parole, and with each other.

Judicially Administered Sanctions

The lack of sentencing options is most frustrating for the person who, in the majority of cases, does the sentencing—the judge. Consequently, when judges are given the discretion to "color" a punishment with intermediate sanctions, they will often do so. In addition to imprisonment and probation, a judge has five sentencing options:

1. Fines.
2. Community service.
3. Restitution.
4. Pretrial diversion programs.
5. Forfeiture.

Fines, community service, and restitution were discussed in Chapter 11. In the context of intermediate sanctions, it is important to remember that these punishments are generally combined with incarceration or probation. For that reason, some critics feel the

Intermediate Sanctions Sanctions that are more restrictive than probation and less restrictive than imprisonment.

retributive or deterrent impact of such punishments is severely limited. Many European countries, in contrast, rely heavily on fines as the sole sanction for a variety of crimes. (See the feature *Comparative Criminal Justice—Swedish Day-Fines*.)

Pretrial Diversion Programs

Not every criminal violation requires the courtroom process. Consequently, some judges have the discretion to order an offender into a **pretrial diversion program** during the preliminary hearing. (As illustrated in the earlier example from Cook County, Illinois, prosecutors can also offer an offender the opportunity to join such a program in return for reducing or dropping the initial charges.) These programs represent an "interruption" of the criminal proceedings and are generally reserved for young or first-time offenders who have been arrested on charges of illegal drug use, child or spousal abuse, or sexual misconduct. Pretrial diversion programs usually include extensive counseling, often in a treatment center. If the offender successfully follows the conditions of the program, the criminal charges are dropped.

Pretrial Diversion Program An alternative to trial offered by a judge or prosecutor, in which the offender agrees to participate in a specified counseling or treatment program in return for withdrawal of the charges.

Problem-Solving Courts

Many judges have found opportunities to divert low-level offenders by presiding over problem-solving courts. In these comparatively informal courtrooms, judges attempt to address problems such as drug addiction, mental illness,

COMPARATIVE CRIMINAL JUSTICE

Source: Central Intelligence Agency

Swedish Day-Fines

Few ideals are cherished as highly in our criminal justice system as equality. Most Americans take it for granted that individuals guilty of identical crimes should face identical punishments. From an economic perspective, however, this emphasis on equality renders our system decidedly unequal. Take two citizens, one a millionaire investment banker and the other a checkout clerk earning the minimum wage. Driving home from work one afternoon, each is caught by a traffic officer doing 80 miles per hour in a 55-mile-per-hour zone. The fine for this offense is $150. This amount, though equal for both, has different consequences. It represents mere pocket change for the investment banker, but a significant chunk out of the checkout clerk's weekly paycheck.

Restricted by a "tariff system" that sets specific amounts for specific crimes, regardless of the financial situation of the convict, American judges often refrain from using fines as a primary sanction. They may assume that poor offenders cannot pay the fine and may worry that a fine will allow wealthier offenders to "buy" their way out of a punishment.

PAYING FOR CRIME

In searching for a way to make fines more effective sanctions, many reformers have seized on the concept of the "day-fine," as practiced in Sweden and several other European countries. In this system, which was established in the 1920s and 1930s, the fine amount is linked to the monetary value of the offender's daily income. Depending on the seriousness of the crime, a Swedish offender will be sentenced to 1 to 120 day-fines or, as combined punishment for multiple crimes, up to 200 day-fines.

For each day-fine unit assessed, the offender is required to pay one-thousandth of her or his annual gross income (minus a deduction for basic living expenses, as determined by the Prosecutor General's Office) to the court. Consequently, the day-fine system not only reflects the degree of the crime, but also ensures that the economic burden will be equal for those with different incomes. (For example, in neighboring Finland, which has a similar system, a millionaire was recently fined the equivalent of about $58,000 for driving 64 miles per hour in a 50-mile-per-hour zone.)

Swedish police and prosecutors can levy day-fines without court involvement. As a result, plea bargaining is nonexistent, and more than 80 percent of all offenders are sentenced to intermediate sanctions without a trial. The remaining cases receive full trials, with a non-conviction rate of only 6 percent, compared with 26 percent in the United States.

FOR CRITICAL ANALYSIS

Do you think a "day-fine" system would be feasible in the United States? Why might it be difficult to implement in this country?

and homelessness that often lead to the eventual rearrest of the offender. About three thousand problem-solving courts are operating in the United States.

Drug Courts Although problem-solving courts cover a wide variety of subjects, from domestic violence to juvenile crime to mental illness, the most common problem-solving courts are drug courts. The specific procedures of drug courts vary widely, but most follow a general pattern. Either after arrest or on conviction, the offender is given the option of entering a drug court program or continuing through the standard courtroom process. Those who choose the former come under the supervision of a judge who will oversee a mixture of treatment and sanctions designed to cure their addiction. When offenders successfully complete the program, the drug court rewards them by dropping all charges. Drug courts operate on the assumption that when a criminal addict's drug use is reduced, his or her drug-fueled criminal activity will also decline.

▲ In Pinellas County, Florida, Judge Dee Anna Farnell congratulates graduates of her drug court program. **How does society benefit when an offender successfully completes a drug court program rather than being sent to prison or jail?** Scott Keeler/ZUMA Press/Largo/FL/USA/Newscom

In response to the opiate addiction crisis that we discussed in Chapter 2, drug courts in New Jersey, New York, and West Virginia have incorporated medication-assisted treatment (MAT) into their operations. MAT is based on providing addicts with alternative drugs such as methadone and buprenorphine to help lessen the symptoms of withdrawal from opiates. In Indiana, mandatory MAT can be included as a condition of probation or parole.[68]

Diversion and Restorative Justice Judges are also taking advantage of the positive policy implications of specialty courts to insert principles of restorative justice, which we discussed in Chapter 11, into their diversion efforts. For example, more judges are using *community dispute resolution centers* to move certain misdemeanors and minor criminal matters out of the court system completely. At these centers, specialists help the parties involved in a dispute—such as one involving vandalism or noise complaints—by *mediating,* or negotiating, a satisfactory outcome for both sides. In 2014 and 2015, New York judges, prosecutors, and police officers referred almost 3,500 criminal cases to community dispute resolution centers, thus diverting the participants from the formal court system.[69]

Forfeiture

In 1970, Congress passed the Racketeer Influenced and Corrupt Organizations Act (RICO) in an attempt to prevent the use of legitimate business enterprises as shields for organized crime.[70] As amended, RICO and other statutes allow judges to implement *forfeiture* proceedings in certain criminal cases. **Forfeiture** is a process by which the government seizes property gained from or used in criminal activity. For example, if a person is convicted for smuggling cocaine into the United States from South America, a judge can order the seizure of not only the narcotics, but also the speedboat used to deliver the drugs to a pickup point off the coast of South Florida. In *Bennis v. Michigan* (1996),[71] the Supreme Court ruled that a person's home or car could be forfeited even though the owner was unaware that the property was connected to illegal activity.

Forfeiture The process by which the government seizes private property attached to criminal activity.

Once property is forfeited, the government has several options. It can sell the property, with the proceeds going to the state and/or federal law enforcement agencies involved in the seizure. Alternatively, the government agency can use the property directly in further crime-fighting efforts or award it to a third party, such as an informant. Forfeiture is financially rewarding for both federal and local law enforcement agencies. The U.S. Marshals Service manages about $3.1 billion worth of contraband and property impounded from criminals and criminal suspects. In 2015, the agency shared about $365 million of these funds with state and local law enforcement agencies, with an additional $605 million going to crime victims.[72] (In the *Policy Matters* feature at the end of the chapter, we examine the question of whether the government should be able to confiscate property in the absence of criminal guilt.)

Day Reporting Centers

Day reporting centers (DRCs) are mainly tools to reduce jail and prison overcrowding. Although the offenders are allowed to live in the community rather than jail or prison, they must spend all or part of each day at a reporting center. In general, being sentenced to a DRC is an extreme form of supervision. With offenders under a single roof, they are much more easily monitored and controlled. DRCs are instruments of rehabilitation as well. They often feature treatment programs for drug and alcohol abusers and provide counseling for a number of psychological problems, such as depression and anger management.

Critics of DRCs contend that the centers allow offenders to "network" with other individuals who have criminal histories and drug or alcohol abuse issues.[73] A survey of DRCs in New Jersey seems to support these suspicions. Over a ninety-day period, male DRC participants were twice as likely to be arrested for a new offense and 41 percent less likely to find jobs compared with similar male offenders on parole. Furthermore, six months following the study period, DRC participants were slightly more likely to be convicted of a new offense and significantly more likely to fail a drug test than were parolees.[74]

Intensive Supervision Probation

Over the past several decades, a number of jurisdictions have turned to **intensive supervision probation (ISP)** to solve the problems associated with burdensome caseloads discussed earlier in the chapter. ISP offers a more restrictive alternative to regular probation, with higher levels of face-to-face contact between offenders and officers and frequent modes of control such as urine tests for drugs. In New Jersey, for example, ISP officers have caseloads of only 20 offenders (compared with 115 for other probation officers in the state) and are provided with additional resources to help them keep tabs on their charges.[75] Different jurisdictions have different methods of determining who is eligible for ISP, but a majority of states limit ISP to offenders who do not have prior probation violations.

The main goal of ISP is to provide prisonlike control of offenders while keeping them out of prison. Critics of ISP believe that it "causes" high failure rates, as more supervision increases the chances that an offender will be caught breaking conditions of probation.[76] One comparison of ISP with DRCs, however, found the intensive supervision of ISP to be more effective. In the six months following termination of the program, DRC participants were more likely to be convicted for a new offense and to test positive for drugs than their ISP counterparts. The study suggests that when combined with services such as outpatient drug treatment and educational training, ISP can be effective in producing low rates of recidivism.[77]

Learning Objective 7 Contrast day reporting centers with intensive supervision probation.

Shock Incarceration

As the name suggests, **shock incarceration** is designed to "shock" criminals into compliance with the law. Following conviction, the offender is first sentenced to a prison or jail term. Then, usually within ninety days, he or she is released and resentenced to probation.

The theory behind shock incarceration is that by getting a taste of the brutalities of the daily prison grind, the offender will be shocked into a crime-free existence.

In the past, shock incarceration was targeted primarily toward youthful, first-time offenders, who were thought to be more likely to be "scared straight" by a short stint behind bars. More recent data show, however, that 20 percent of all adults sentenced to probation spend some time in jail or prison before being released into the community.[78] Critics of shock incarceration are dismayed by this trend. They argue that the practice needlessly disrupts the lives of low-level offenders who would not otherwise be eligible for incarceration and exposes them to the mental and physical hardships of prison life.[79] Furthermore, there is little evidence that shock probationers fare any better than regular probationers when it comes to recidivism rates.[80]

Impact incarceration programs, or *boot camps*, are a variation on traditional shock incarceration. Instead of spending the "shock" period of incarceration in prison or jail, offenders are sent to a boot camp. Modeled on military basic training, these camps are generally located within prisons and jails, though some can be found in the community. The programs emphasize strict discipline, manual labor, and physical training. They are designed to instill self-responsibility and self-respect in participants, thereby lessening the chances that they will return to a life of crime. More recently, boot camps have also emphasized rehabilitation, incorporating such components as drug and alcohol treatment programs, anger management courses, and vocational training.

▲ A correctional officer checks the beard growth of an inmate at the Moriah Shock Incarceration Facility in Mineville, New York. **In theory, why would boot camps such as this one benefit first-time nonviolent offenders more than a jail or prison sentence?** AP Images/ Mike Groll

Home Confinement and Electronic Monitoring

Various forms of home confinement—in which offenders serve their sentences not in a government institution but at home—have existed for centuries. It has often served as a method of political control, used by totalitarian regimes to isolate and silence dissidents, and it continues to be used in this way. For purposes of general law enforcement, home confinement was impractical until relatively recently. After all, one could not expect offenders to keep their promises to stay at home, and the personnel costs of guarding them were prohibitive.

In the 1980s, however, the advent of electronic monitoring, which uses technology to guard the prisoner, made home confinement more viable. Today, all fifty states and the federal government have home monitoring programs, with about 125,000 offenders, including probationers and parolees, participating at any one time.[81]

The Levels of Home Monitoring

Home monitoring has three general levels of restriction:

1. *Curfew*, which requires offenders to be in their homes at specific hours, usually at night.
2. *Home detention*, which requires that offenders remain home at all times, with exceptions being made for education, employment, counseling, and other specified activities such as the purchase of food or, in some instances, attendance at religious services.

Home Confinement A community-based sanction in which offenders serve their terms of incarceration in their homes.

Electronic Monitoring A supervision technique in which the offender's whereabouts are kept under surveillance by an electronic device.

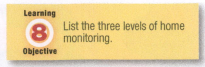
Learning
8 Objective
List the three levels of home monitoring.

3. *Home incarceration*, which requires the offender to remain home at all times, save for medical emergencies.

Under ideal circumstances, home confinement serves many of the goals of intermediate sanctions. It protects the community. It saves public funds and space in correctional facilities by keeping convicts out of institutional incarceration. It meets public expectations of punishment for criminals. Uniquely, home confinement also recognizes that convicts, despite their crimes, play important roles in the community, and allows them to continue in those roles. An offender, for example, may be given permission to leave confinement to care for elderly parents.

Home confinement is also lauded for giving sentencing officials the freedom to match the punishment with the needs of the offender. In 2016, for example, Rajat Gupta was allowed to serve the final six months of a two-year prison sentence for stock market fraud at his New York City apartment. Wearing an electronic ankle bracelet, Gupta could leave home to work, visit the doctor, or attend religious services. Indeed, home confinement is a popular punishment for white-collar criminals, who often need to earn funds to pay off significant court-ordered fines—nearly $20 million in Gupta's case.[82]

Types of Electronic Monitoring According to some reports, the inspiration for electronic monitoring was a *Spider-Man* comic book in which the hero was trailed by the use of an electronic device on his arm. In 1979, a New Mexico judge named Jack Love, having read the comic, convinced an executive at Honeywell, Inc., to begin developing similar technology to supervise convicts.[83]

Two major types of electronic monitoring grew out of Love's initial concept. The first is a "programmed contact" system, in which the offender is contacted periodically by voice or text to verify his or her whereabouts. Verification may be obtained via a computer that uses voice or visual identification techniques, or the offender may be required to enter a code in an electronic box when called. The second is a "continuously signaling" device, worn around the convict's wrist, ankle, or neck. A transmitter in the device sends out a continuous signal to a "receiver-dialer" device located in the offender's dwelling. If the receiver device does not detect a signal from the transmitter, it informs a central computer, and the police are notified.

▼ How might being required to wear an electronic ankle bracelet (such as the one shown here) negatively affect an offender's ability to find and keep a job? Should such difficulties influence a judge's decision to impose this particular intermediate sanction? Why or why not? AP Images/Wilfredo Lee

Technological Advances in Electronic Monitoring As electronic monitoring technology has evolved, the ability of community corrections officials to target specific forms of risky behavior has greatly increased. Michigan courts, for example, routinely place black boxes in the automobiles of repeat traffic violators. Not only do these boxes record information about the offenders' driving habits for review by probation officers, but they also emit a loud beep when the car goes too fast or stops too quickly. Another device—an ankle bracelet—is able to test a person's sweat for alcohol levels and transmit the results over the Internet.

Effectiveness of Electronic Monitoring Because most participants in home confinement programs are low-risk offenders, their recidivism rates are quite low. Even so, numerous studies indicate that electronically monitored offenders have significantly lower rates of revocation for technical violations or arrests for new crimes than do comparable offenders not on electronic supervision.[84] The devices can also be an aid to law enforcement. For example, Orange County, California, police were able to use data from the ankle monitor worn by sex offender Steven Gordon to establish that he was in the vicinity of three prostitutes at the times of their violent deaths. In 2016, that evidence helped prosecutors gain multiple murder convictions against Gordon.

One concern about electronic monitoring is that offenders are often required to defray program costs. In Richland County, South Carolina, such costs include $300 a month plus a $180 setup fee. If offenders are unable to meet their payments, they can be sent to jail. "People are pleading guilty because it's cheaper to be on probation than it is to be on electronic monitoring," says Jack Duncan, a local public defender.[85]

This form of intermediate sanction may also cause problems in the personal and financial lives of offenders. In one Florida survey, 43 percent of respondents, all of whom were electronically monitored offenders, complained that the devices had a negative effect on their relationships with intimate partners. A number of these respondents also noted the sense of shame that wearing such devices caused them, since many people assume that those who wear monitoring devices are sex offenders.[86]

CJ & TECHNOLOGY

Global Positioning System (GPS)

Global positioning system (GPS) technology is a form of tracking technology that relies on twenty-four military satellites orbiting thousands of miles above the earth. The satellites transmit signals to each other and to a receiver on the ground, allowing a monitoring station to determine the location of a receiving device to within a few feet. GPS provides a much more precise level of supervision than regular electronic monitoring. The offender wears a transmitter, similar to a traditional electronic monitor, around his or her ankle or wrist. This transmitter communicates with a portable tracking device, a small box that uses the military satellites to determine the probationer's movements.

GPS technology can be used either "actively" to constantly monitor the subject's whereabouts or "passively" to ensure that the offender remains within the confines of a limited area determined by a judge or probation officer. Inclusion and exclusion zones are also important to GPS supervision. Inclusion zones are areas such as a home or workplace where the offender is expected to be at certain times. Exclusion zones are areas such as parks, playgrounds, and schools where the offender is not permitted to go. GPS-linked computers can alert officials immediately when an exclusion zone has been breached and create a computerized record of the probationer's movements for review at a later time.

Despite the benefits of this technology, it is rarely used in the context of community corrections. According to the Bureau of Justice Statistics, only about eight thousand probationers are currently being tracked by GPS.

Thinking about GPS

How might GPS monitoring be used to improve and overhaul the American bail system, covered in Chapter 9?

Widening the Net

As we have seen, most of the convicts chosen for intermediate sanctions are low-risk offenders. From the point of view of the corrections official doing the choosing, this makes sense. Such offenders are less likely to commit crimes and attract negative publicity. This selection strategy, however, appears to invalidate one of the primary reasons intermediate sanctions exist: to reduce prison and jail populations. If most of the offenders in intermediate sanctions programs would otherwise have received probation, then the effect on these populations is nullified. Indeed, studies have shown this to be the case.[87]

At the same time, intermediate sanctions broaden the reach of the corrections system. In other words, they increase rather than decrease the amount of control the state exerts over the individual. Suppose a person is arrested for a misdemeanor such as shoplifting and, under normal circumstances, would receive probation. With access to intermediate sanctions, the judge may add a period of home confinement to the sentence. Critics contend that such practices **widen the net** of the corrections system by increasing the number of citizens who are under the control and surveillance of the state and also *strengthen the net* by increasing the government's power to intervene in the lives of its citizens[88] Technological advances—such as the black boxes in automobiles, sweat-testing ankle bracelets, and GPS devices mentioned in this chapter—will only accelerate the trend.

The Paradox of Community Corrections

Despite their many benefits, including cost savings, treatment options, and the ability to divert hundreds of thousands of nonviolent wrongdoers from prisons and jails, community-based corrections programs suffer from a basic pardox. That is, the more effectively offenders are controlled, the more likely they are to be caught violating the terms of their conditional release. As you may have noticed, the community supervision programs discussed in this chapter are evaluated according to rates of recidivism and revocation, with low levels of each reflecting a successful program. Increased control and surveillance, however, will necessarily raise the level of violations, thus increasing the probability that any single violation will be discovered. Therefore, as factors such as the number of conditions placed on probationers and the technological proficiency of electronic monitoring devices increase, so, too, will the number of offenders who fail to meet the conditions of their community-based punishment.

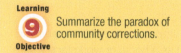

Learning Objective 9 Summarize the paradox of community corrections.

One observer calls this the "quicksand" effect of increased surveillance. Instead of helping offenders leave the corrections system, increased surveillance pulls them more deeply into it.[89] Given that, as we have noted throughout this chapter, policymakers are relying on community corrections to *decrease* the costs associated with corrections, many states are taking active steps to counteract the quicksand effect.

For example, a legislative task force recently determined that Arkansas's prison population, already one of the fastest growing in the country, is destined to continue its upward path unless the state makes significant changes to its corrections culture. In 2016, nearly half of Arkansas's prison inmates were either probation or parole violators. A third of these inmates were incarcerated because of a technical violation rather than an arrest. Consequently, the task force recommended that the state limit the amount of time served behind bars for technical violations and fund a system of community-based treatment intervention services designed to reduce the presence of these nonviolent offenders in Arkansas prisons.[90]

ETHICS CHALLENGE

Participants in intensive supervision probation in Lake County, Illinois, must agree to the following conditions: (1) no use of any over-the-counter medications, hygiene products, or other products that contains alcohol and (2) no residence in any location where alcoholic beverages are present or regularly consumed. How do such conditions contribute to the paradox of community corrections, discussed above? Is it ethical to require probationers to comply with such conditions? Why or why not?

Policy Matters

Civil Forfeiture

How Things Stand

With criminal forfeiture, as described in the text, the government seizes property gained from or used in criminal activity. Such forfeiture can occur only after a defendant is convicted of the crime in question. But with *civil forfeiture*, as implemented by the federal government and almost every state government, law enforcement agencies can confiscate property from a person suspected of a crime without necessarily charging the owner with wrongdoing. Furthermore, the governmental agency can keep that property even if the owner is charged and ultimately found not guilty of the crime. In general, the government need only prove a "substantial connection" between the property and the underlying crime for civil forfeiture to apply.

As a Result...

Between 1985 and 2013, the U.S. Department of Justice's Asset Forfeiture Funds grew from $27 million to over $2 billion.[91] In 2014, civil forfeitures reached approximately $4.5 billion, more than the value of all property theft reported by Americans that year.[92] Proponents of civil forfeiture insist that the practice gives law enforcement a powerful tool to fight drug dealers and white-collar criminals by allowing the police to more easily confiscate the illegal gains of these criminal activities. Furthermore, as the New Mexico Department of Safety has noted, its prohibition would result in "less training, less resources, less equipment, and a reduction of criminal investigations" due to lack of funds.[93]

Most of the criticism surrounding civil forfeiture involves due process concerns. That is, our legal system generally requires that a person be found guilty of committing a crime before she or he can be punished for that crime. In addition, the policy has been tainted by instances of police misconduct. In 2012, for example, officials in Shelby County, Texas, admitted that they had improperly seized approximately $3 million from at least 140 motorists who were never arrested or charged with any criminal wrongdoing after being stopped by local police. In one instance, officers took into custody the sixteen-month-old son of a driver who refused to give them $50,000 in cash he was carrying to buy restaurant equipment.[94]

Up for Debate

"Everybody knows there are bad eggs out there. But we don't stop prosecuting people for murder just because some district attorneys have made mistakes."[95] —*Karen Morris, supervisor of the Harris County (Texas) district attorney's forfeiture unit*

"[C]ivil forfeiture [is] a form of legalized theft in which the government takes property allegedly linked to crime without even charging the owner, let alone convicting him."[96] —*Jacob Sullum, Forbes Magazine*

What's Your Take?

Review the discussion in this chapter on "Intermediate Sanctions" before answering the following questions.

1. For many local district attorney's offices and law enforcement agencies, funds collected through civil forfeiture cover a significant percentage of the annual operating budget. Does this fact make you more likely or less likely to support the practice? Why?

2. A son borrows his mother's car and is arrested for driving under the influence. In accord with state civil forfeiture law, the local prosecutor confiscates the car and sells it. Is this a fair outcome? Does it matter if the mother knows that her son has driven drunk before? Explain your answers.

Digging Deeper...

In 2016, the governments of **Montana** and **New Mexico** took drastic steps to **curtail civil forfeiture** within state borders. After researching these legislative efforts online, provide a short description of each state law. How are they similar? How are they different? How do they address the issues of due process and police misconduct mentioned above? Would you support making either a model for nationwide civil forfeiture reform? Your answer should be at least three paragraphs long.

For more information on these concepts, look back to the Learning Objective icons throughout the chapter.

 Explain the justifications for community-based corrections programs. One justification involves reintegration of the offender into society. Reintegration restores family ties, encourages employment and education, and secures a place for the offender in the routine functioning of society. Other justifications involve diversion and cost savings. By diverting criminals to alternative modes of punishment, further overcrowding of jail and prison facilities can be avoided, as can the costs of incarcerating the offenders.

 Explain several alternative sentencing arrangements that combine probation with incarceration. With a suspended sentence, a convicted offender is not required to serve the sentence, but the judge has the option of reinstating the sentence if the person reoffends. Three other general types of sentencing arrangements are: (a) split sentence probation, in which the judge specifies a certain time in jail or prison followed by a certain time on probation; (b) shock incarceration, in which a judge sentences an offender to be incarcerated, but allows that person to petition the court to be released on probation; and (c) intermittent incarceration, in which an offender spends a certain amount of time each week in jail or in a halfway house or another government institution.

 Specify the conditions under which an offender is most likely to be denied probation. The offender (a) has been convicted of multiple charges, (b) was on probation or parole when arrested, (c) has two or more prior convictions, (d) is addicted to narcotics, (e) seriously injured the victim of the crime, or (f) used a weapon while committing the crime.

 Describe the three general categories of conditions placed on a probationer. (a) Standard conditions, such as requiring that the probationer notify the agency of a change of address, not leave the jurisdiction without permission, and remain employed; (b) punitive conditions, such as restitution, community service, and home confinement; and (c) treatment conditions, such as required drug or alcohol treatment.

 Identify the main differences between probation and parole. Probation is a sentence handed down by a judge that generally acts as an alternative to incarceration. Parole is a form of early release from prison determined by a parole authority, often a parole board. Probationers are usually first-time offenders who have committed nonviolent crimes, while parolees have often spent significant time in prison.

 Explain which factors influence the decision to grant parole. In deciding whether to grant parole, parole board members primarily consider the severity of the underlying crime and the threat the offender will pose to the community if released. Other factors include the offender's level of remorse and his or her behavior while incarcerated.

 Contrast day reporting centers with intensive supervision probation. In a day reporting center, the offender is allowed to remain in the community, but must spend all or part of each day at the reporting center. While at the center, offenders meet with probation officers, submit to drug tests, and attend counseling and education programs. With intensive supervision probation (ISP), more restrictions are imposed, and there is more face-to-face contact between offenders and probation officers. ISP may also include electronic surveillance.

 List the three levels of home monitoring. (a) Curfew, which requires that the offender be at home during specified hours; (b) home detention, which requires that the offender be at home except for education, employment, and counseling; and (c) home incarceration, which requires that the offender be at home at all times except for medical emergencies.

 Summarize the paradox of community corrections. The more effective a probation or parole department is in controlling and supervising its clients, the more likely it is that those clients will be caught violating the conditions of their supervision. This makes it more likely that the probationer or parolee will be incarcerated, thus defeating the diversion and treatment purposes of community corrections.

QUESTIONS FOR CRITICAL ANALYSIS

1. Several years ago, an eighty-six-year-old man was found guilty of fatally shooting his eighty-one-year-old wife. The victim was suffering from a painful health condition and had begged her husband to end her life. An Arizona judge sentenced the defendant to two years' probation. Do you agree with this punishment? Why or why not?

2. Why might probationers and parolees want to limit their social media activity? Give an example of a circumstance in which a Facebook posting could cause probation or parole to be revoked.

3. Review our earlier discussion of Hawaii's Opportunity Probation with Enforcement (HOPE). What might be some of the reasons participants in the program are less likely to fail a second urinalysis?

4. A number of courts have held that GPS monitoring, described in this chapter's *CJ & Technology* feature, is a form of regulation rather than punishment, and therefore is not subject to constitutional safeguards. Do you agree that GPS monitoring is not a punitive measure? Why or why not?

5. In your own words, explain what the phrase "widening the net" means. What might be some of the unintended consequences of increasing the number of offenders who are supervised by corrections officers in the community?

KEY TERMS

authority 400
caseload 400
community corrections 393
day reporting center (DRC) 412
discretionary release 406
electronic monitoring 413
forfeiture 411
graduated sanctions 401
home confinement 413

intensive supervision probation (ISP) 412
intermediate sanctions 409
mandatory release 408
parole 403
parole board 406
parole contract 404
parole grant hearing 407
parole guidelines 408

pretrial diversion program 410
probation 395
reintegration 393
revocation 397
shock incarceration 412
split sentence probation 395
suspended sentence 395
technical violation 400
widen the net 416

NOTES

1. "Brooklyn Judge Attempts to Rewrite Laws with an Outrageous Wrist-Slap for Felon." *www.nypost.com. New York Post:* May 25, 2016, Web.

2. Bureau of Justice Statistics, *Probation and Parole in the United States, 2015* (Washington, D.C.: U.S. Department of Justice, December 2016), 1.

3. Michael Tonry, *Sentencing Matters* (New York: Oxford Press, 1996), 28.

4. *Probation and Parole in the United States, 2015, op. cit.,* 1.

5. Corrections Task Force of the President's Commission on Law Enforcement and Administration of Justice (1967).

6. Shaila Dewan and Andrew W. Lehren, "Spared from a Criminal Record, as Long as You Can Pay," *New York Times* (December 12, 2016), A1.

7. Paul H. Hahn, *Emerging Criminal Justice: Three Pillars for a Proactive Justice System* (Thousand Oaks, Calif.: Sage Publications, 1998), 106–108.

8. Bureau of Justice Statistics, *Correctional Populations in the United States, 2015* (Washington, D.C.: U.S. Department of Justice, December 2016), Table 1, page 2.

9. Bureau of Justice Statistics, *State Corrections Expenditures, FY 1982–2010* (Washington, D.C.: U.S. Department of Justice, April 2014), 1.

10. "Supervision Costs Significantly Less Than Incarceration in Federal System." *http://www.uscourts.gov/news/2013/07/18/supervision-costs-significantly-less-incarceration-federal-system. United States Courts:* July 18, 2013, Web.

11. "Cost of Corrections." *www.ncdps.gov.* North Carolina Public Department of Public Safety: June 30, 2016, Web.

12. Dewan and Lehren, *op. cit.*

13. Paul W. Keve, *Crime Control and Justice in America* (Chicago: American Library Association, 1995), 183.

14. Gerald Bayens and John Ortiz Smykla, *Probation, Parole, & Community-Based Corrections* (New York: McGraw-Hill, 2013), 186–217.

15. *Alternative Sentencing in the Federal Criminal Justice System* (Washington, D.C.: United States Sentencing Commission, May 2015), 4.

16. Joan Petersilia and Susan Turner, *Prison versus Probation in California: Implications for Crime and Offender Recidivism* (Santa Monica, Calif.: RAND Corporation, 1986).

17. *Probation and Parole in the United States, 2015, op. cit.,* Table 4, page 5.

18. Quoted in Marisa Gerber, "Under a Plea Deal, the Wife of Slain Bell Gardens Mayor Gets 90 Days in Jail for His Killing." *www.latimes.com. Los Angeles Times:* November 30, 2016, Web.

19. *Probation and Parole in the United States, 2015, op. cit.,* Table 4, page 5.

20. *Ibid.;* and Bureau of Justice Statistics, *Prisoners in 2015* (Washington, D.C.: U.S. Department of Justice, December 2016), Table 1, page 2.

21. Sharyn Adams, Lindsay Bostwick, and Rebecca Campbell, *Examining Illinois Probationer Characteristics and Outcomes* (Chicago: Illinois Criminal Justice Information Authority, September 2011), Table 1, pages 16–17.

22. Debra C. Weiss, "Judge Makes Celibacy Outside of Marriage a Condition of Probation." *www.abajournal.com. ABA Journal:* February 7, 2017, Web; and Milton J. Valencia, "Judge Calls Ex-Lobbyist a Liar, Prepares Strict Probation Terms." *www.bostonglobe. com.* Boston Globe: January 6, 2017, Web.

23. 705 So.2d 172 (La. 1997).

24. Neil P. Cohen and James J. Gobert, *The Law of Probation and Parole* (Colorado Springs, Colo.: Shepard's/McGraw-Hill, 1983), Section 5.01, 183–184; Section 5.03, 191–192.

25. 534 U.S. 112 (2001).

26. *Ibid.,* 113.

27. Bureau of Justice Statistics, *Felony Defendants in Large Urban Counties, 2009— Statistical Tables* (Washington, D.C.: U.S. Department of Justice, December 2013), Table 28, page 32.

28. Carl B. Klockars, Jr., "A Theory of Probation Supervision," *Journal of Criminal Law, Criminology, and Police Science 63* (1972), 550–557.

29. *Probation and Parole in the United States, 2015, op. cit.,* Table 3, page 4.

30. Todd R. Clear, George F. Cole, and Michael D. Reisig, *American Corrections,* 11th ed. (Belmont, Calif.: Wadsworth Cengage Learning, 2016), 206.

31. Klockars, *op. cit.,* 551.

32. Quoted in Gary Fields, "Changes in Sentencing Policy Raise Pressure on Probation Officers." *www.wsj.com. Wall Street Journal:* July 5, 2016, Web.

33. 389 U.S. 128 (1967).

34. *Morrissey v. Brewer,* 408 U.S. 471 (1972); and *Gagnon v. Scarpelli,* 411 U.S. 778 (1973).

35. 465 U.S. 420 (1984).

36. L.M. Vieraitis, et al., "The Criminogenic Effects of Imprisonment: Evidence from State Panel Data, 1974–2002," *Criminology and Public Policy 6* (2007), 589–622.

37. Kansas House Bill 2170 (2013).

38. *Ibid.*

39. *Felony Defendants in Large Urban Counties, 2009—Statistical Tables, op. cit.,* Table 6, page 10.

40. Jennifer L. Skeem and Sarah Manchak, "Back to the Future: From Klockars' Model of Effective Supervision to Evidence-Based Practice in Probation," *Journal of Offender Rehabilitation 47* (2008), 231.

41. *Probation and Parole, 2015, op. cit.,* Table 3, page 4.

42. Pamela M. Casey, Roger K. Warren, and Jennifer K. Elek, *Using Offender Risk and Needs Assessment Information at Sentencing* (Williamsburg, Va.: National Center for State Courts, 2011), Table 1, page 5.

43. Nancy Ritter, "Predicting Recidivism Risk: New Tool in Philadelphia Shows Great Promise," *NIJ Journal* (February 2013), 4–13.

44. James Q. Wilson, "Making Justice Swifter," *City Journal 7* (1997), 4.

45. Graeme Wood, "Prison without Walls," *The Atlantic* (September 2010), 92–93.

46. Angela Hawken, et al., *HOPE II: A Follow-Up to Hawaii's HOPE Evaluation* (Washington, D.C.: National Institute of Justice, May 2016).

47. Greg Midgette, *A New Approach to Reducing Heavy Drinking and Alcohol-Involved Crime?* (Santa Monica, Calif.: RAND Corporation, 2016), 2.

48. *Clear, Cole, and Reisig, op. cit.,* 413.

49. *Probation and Parole in the United States, 2015, op cit.* Table 5, page 6.

50. Bureau of Justice Statistics, *Probation and Parole in the United States, 2012* (Washington, D.C.: U.S. Department of Justice, December 2013), Table 7, page 9.

51. Nicole D. Porter, *The State of Sentencing 2015: Developments in Policy and Practice* (Washington, D.C.: The Sentencing Project, 2015), 5.

52. *Morrissey v. Brewer,* 408 U.S. 471 (1972).

53. Todd R. Clear and Edward Latessa, "Probation Officer Roles in Intensive Supervision: Surveillance versus Treatment," *Justice Quarterly 10* (1993), 441–462.

54. 442 U.S. 1 (1979).

55. American Civil Liberties Union, *A Living Death: Life without Parole for Nonviolent Offenses* (November 2013), 2.

56. Marie Gottschalk, "Days without End: Life Sentences and Penal Reform." *www.prison-legalnews.org.* Prison Legal News: April 11, 2013, Web.

57. William Parker, *Parole: Origins, Development, Current Practices, and Statutes* (College Park, Md.: American Correctional Association, 1972), 26.

58. Clear, Cole, and Reisig, *op. cit.,* 387.

59. Quoted in Michael Winerip, Michael Schwartz, and Robert Gebeloff, "For Blacks Facing Parole, Signs of Broken System in New York," *New York Times* (December 5, 2016), A1.

60. *Ibid.*

61. Clear, Cole, and Reisig, *op. cit.,* 393.

62. Peter Holley, "Sirhan Sirhan Denied Parole Despite a Kennedy Confidant's Call for the Assassin's Release." *www.washingtonpost. com. Washington Post:* February 11, 2016.

63. Quoted in Jonathan J. Cooper, "California Governor Denies Parole for Manson Follower." *www.bigstory.ap.org. Associated Press:* July 22, 2016, Web.

64. Mark P. Rankin, Mark H. Allenbaugh, and Carlton Fields, "Parole's Essential Role in

Bailing Out Our Nation's Criminal Justice Systems," *Champion* (January 2009), 47–48.

65. "Council of State Government/American Probation and Parole Association." *www.appa-net.org*. American Probation and Parole Association: 2012, Web.

66. 18 U.S.C. Section 3771(a)(4) (2006).

67. Joel M. Caplan, "Parole Release Decisions: Impact of Victim Input on a Representative Sample of Inmates," *Journal of Criminal Justice* (May–June 2010), 291–300.

68. Rebecca Silber, Ram Subramanian, and Maia Spotts, *Justice in Review: New Trends in State Sentencing and Corrections 2014–2015* (New York: Vera Institute of Justice, May 2016), 13.

69. Community Dispute Resolution Centers Program, "2014–2015 Annual Report." *www.nycourts.gov*. New York Unified Court System: 2016, Web.

70. 18 U.S.C. Sections 1961–1968.

71. 516 U.S. 442 (1996).

72. "Fact Sheet: Asset Forfeiture 2016." *https://www.usmarshals.gov/*. U.S. Marshals Service: March 11, 2016, Web.

73. Douglas J. Boyle, et al., "Overview of: 'An Evaluation of Day Reporting Centers for Parolees: Outcomes of a Randomized Trial,'" *Criminology & Public Policy* (February 2013), 136.

74. Philip Bulman, *Day Reporting Centers in New Jersey: No Evidence of Reduced Recidivism* (Washington, D.C.: National Institute of Justice, 2013), 1–2.

75. *ISP Fact Sheet: Intensive Supervision Program* (Trenton, N.J.: Administrative Office of the Courts, February 2015), 1–2.

76. Joan Petersilia and Susan Turner, "Intensive Probation and Parole," *Crime and Justice 17* (1993), 281–335.

77. Douglas J. Boyle, et al., *Outcomes of a Randomized Trial of an Intensive Community Corrections Program—Day Reporting Center—for Parolees, Final Report for the National Institute of Justice* (Washington, D.C.: U.S. Department of Justice, October 2011), 3–4.

78. *Probation and Parole in the United States, 2010*, Appendix table 3, page 31.

79. Clear, Cole, and Reisig, *op. cit.*, 238

80. Paul Stageberg and Bonnie Wilson, *Recidivism among Iowa Probationers* (Des Moines, Iowa: The Iowa Division of Criminal and Juvenile Justice Planning, July 2005); and Paul Koniceck, *Five Year Recidivism Follow-Up Offender Releases* (Columbus, Ohio: Ohio Department of Rehabilitation and Correction, August 1996).

81. Stephanie Fahy, et al., "Use of Electronic Offender-Tracking Devices Expands Sharply." *www.pewtrusts.org*. The Pew Charitable Trusts: September 7, 2016, Web.

82. Anita Raghavanjan, "Rajat Gupta to Finish Insider Trading Sentence at His Home," *New York Times* (January 21, 2016), B3.

83. Josh Kurtz, "New Growth in a Captive Market," *New York Times* (December 31, 1989), 12.

84. Matthew DeMichele, "Electronic Monitoring: It Is a Tool, Not a Silver Bullet," *Criminology & Public Policy* (August 2014), 95–96.

85. Quoted in Eric Markowitz, "Chain Gang 2.0: If You Can't Afford This GPS Ankle Bracelet, You Get Thrown in Jail." *www.ibtimes.com*. International Business Times: September 21, 2015, Web.

86. National Institute of Justice, *Electronic Monitoring Reduces Recidivism* (Washington, D.C.: U.S. Department of Justice, 2011), 2.

87. Michael Tonry and Mary Lynch, "Intermediate Sanctions," in *Crime and Justice*, vol. 20, ed. Michael Tonry (Chicago: University of Chicago Press, 1996), 99.

88. Dennis Palumbo, Mary Clifford, and Zoann K. Snyder-Joy, "From Net Widening to Intermediate Sanctions: The Transformation of Alternatives to Incarceration from Benevolence to Malevolence," in *Smart Sentencing: The Emergence of Intermediate Sanctions*, ed. James M. Byrne, Arthur Lurigio, and Joan Petersilia (Newbury Park, Calif.: Sage, 1992), 231.

89. Keve, *op. cit.*, 207.

90. Andy Barbee, Jessica Gonzales, and Ben Shelor, *Justice Reinvestment in Arkansas* (Lexington, Ky.: The Council of State Governments: August 25, 2016).

91. Nick Sibilla, "Civil Forfeiture Now Requires a Criminal Conviction In Montana and New Mexico." *www.forbes.com*. Forbes: July 2, 2015, Web.

92. Martin Armstrong, "Police Civil Asset Forfeitures Exceed All Burglaries in 2014." *www.armstrongeconomics.com*. Armstrong Economics: November 17, 2015, Web.

93. Sheila Dewan, "Bill to End Civil Forfeiture in New Mexico Awaits Move by Governor Martinez," *New York Times* (April 10, 2015), A16.

94. Elora Mukherjee, "Settlement Means No More Highway Robbery in Tenaha, Texas," *ACLU* (August 9, 2012), at *www.aclu.org/blog/settlement-means-no-more-highway-robbery-tenaha-texas*.

95. Quoted in Jacob Gershman, "Efforts to Curb Asset Seizures by Law Enforcement Hit Headwinds." *www.wsj.com*. Wall Street Journal: June 3, 2015, Web.

96. Jacob Sullum, "Despite Holder's Forfeiture Reform, Cops Still Have a License to Steal." *www.forbes.com*. Forbes: January 22, 2015, Web.

13

Prisons and Jails

To target your study and review, look for these numbered Learning Objective icons throughout the chapter.

Chapter Outline		Corresponding Learning Objectives
A Short History of American Prisons	**1**	Contrast the Pennsylvania and the New York penitentiary theories of the 1800s.
	2	Explain the three general models of prisons.
Prison Organization and Management	**3**	Describe the formal prison management system, and indicate the three most important aspects of prison governance.
	4	List and briefly explain the four types of prisons.
Inmate Population Trends	**5**	Identify some factors that have caused the prison population to grow dramatically in the last several decades.
	6	Indicate some of the consequences of our high rates of incarceration.
Private Prisons	**7**	Describe the arguments for and against private prisons.
Jails	**8**	Summarize the distinction between jails and prisons, and indicate the importance of jails in the American corrections system.
	9	Identify three conditions common among jail inmates that make the management of jails difficult for sheriffs' departments.

Downsizing?

▲ About 2.2 million inmates are incarcerated in prisons and jails in the United States, including these prisoners waiting in line at San Quentin State Prison in San Quentin, California. Justin Sullivan/Getty Images News/Getty Images

measures had led to an 18 percent drop in South Carolina's prison population and $18 million in corrections savings. Overall, between 2006 and 2016, twenty-eight states saw their prison populations decline, contributing to a small but significant trend in American corrections: fewer inmates. In 2015, the U.S. prison population fell by just over 2 percent, hitting its lowest level since 2005 and continuing a six-year downward course.

To be sure, these decreases do little to threaten our nation's title as "the globe's leading incarcerator." About 2.2 million Americans are in prison and jail. The United States locks up six times as many of its citizens as Canada does, and eight times as many as a number of European democracies. Still, the fact that politicians are willing to accept policies that reduce the number of inmates represents a sea change in the country's corrections strategies. "We're talking about using a scarce resource—beds in jails and prisons—in the most effective way. I would say to people, 'Who would you rather have [incarcerated]—a bank robber or an addict who is aggressively panhandling downtown?'" says Benjamin David, a district attorney from North Carolina. "This is not a political issue, it is a moral issue."

To reform its criminal justice system, Maryland's legislature took two massive steps in 2016. First, nonviolent offenders who had been given severe prison sentences in the past would be eligible for early release. Second, mandatory minimum sentences for newly convicted nonviolent offenders were rescinded, meaning that those found guilty of intent to distribute illegal drugs would no longer automatically face ten years in prison. As a result, Maryland expects to reduce its prison population by nearly two thousand and save at least $80.5 million dollars in incarceration costs over the next decade.

Maryland is hardly the only state to have taken dramatic measures with regard to corrections and criminal justice. In 2010, South Carolina eliminated some mandatory minimums, changed low-level property crimes from felonies to misdemeanors, and made it less likely for probation and parole violators to be incarcerated. By 2016, these

FOR CRITICAL ANALYSIS

1. Do you agree with the assertion that reducing the number of inmates in the United States is a moral issue instead of a political issue? Why or why not?

2. What might be some unintended consequences of providing an early release for large numbers of nonviolent property crime and drug offenders?

3. How do you think declining national crime rates over the past two decades, as discussed in Chapter 3, have contributed to an atmosphere in which politicians are less worried about being depicted as "soft on crime"?

A Short History of American Prisons

Today's high rates of imprisonment—often referred to as evidence of "mass incarceration" in the United States—are the result of many criminal justice strategies that we have discussed in this textbook. These include truth-in-sentencing guidelines, relatively long sentences for gun and drug crimes, "three-strikes" habitual offender laws, and judicial freedom to incarcerate convicts for relatively minor criminal behavior. At the base of all these policies is a philosophy that sees prisons primarily as instruments of punishment. The loss of freedom imposed on inmates is the penalty for the crimes they have committed. Punishment has not, however, always been the main reason for incarceration in this country.

English Roots

The prisons of eighteenth-century England, known as "bridewells" after London's Bridewell Palace, had little to do with punishment. These facilities were mainly used to hold debtors or those awaiting trial, execution, or banishment from the community. (In many ways, as will be made clear, these facilities resembled the modern jail.) English courts generally imposed one of two sanctions on convicted felons: they turned them loose, or they executed them.[1] To be sure, most felons were released, pardoned either by the court or the clergy after receiving a whipping or a branding.

The correctional system in the American colonies differed very little from that of their motherland. If anything, colonial administrators were more likely to use corporal punishment than their English counterparts, and the death penalty was not uncommon in early America. The one dissenter was William Penn, who adopted the "Great Law" in Pennsylvania in 1682. Based on Quaker ideals of humanity and rehabilitation, this criminal code forbade the use of torture and mutilation as forms of punishment.

Instead, felons were ordered to pay restitution of property or goods to their victims. If the offenders did not have sufficient property to make restitution, they were placed in a prison, which was primarily a "workhouse."[2] The death penalty was still allowed under the "Great Law," but only in cases of premeditated murder. Penn proved to be an exception, however, and the path to reform was much slower in the colonies than in England.

Walnut Street Prison: The First Penitentiary

On William Penn's death in 1718, the "Great Law" was rescinded in favor of a harsher criminal code, similar to those of the other colonies. At the time of the American Revolution, however, the Quakers were instrumental in the first broad swing of the incarceration pendulum from punishment to rehabilitation. In 1776, Pennsylvania passed legislation ordering that offenders be reformed through treatment and discipline rather than simply beaten or executed.[3] Several states, including Massachusetts and New York, quickly followed Pennsylvania's example.

Pennsylvania continued its reformist ways by opening the country's first **penitentiary** in a wing of Philadelphia's Walnut Street Jail in 1790. The penitentiary operated on the assumption that silence and labor provided the best hope of rehabilitating the criminal spirit. Remaining silent would force the prisoners to think about their crimes, and eventually the weight of conscience would lead to repentance. At the same time, enforced labor would attack the problem of idleness—regarded as the main cause of crime by penologists of the time.[4] Consequently, inmates at Walnut Street were isolated from one another in solitary rooms and kept busy with constant menial chores.

Penitentiary An early form of correctional facility that emphasized separating inmates from society and from each other.

Learning Objective 1 Contrast the Pennsylvania and the New York penitentiary theories of the 1800s.

Eventually, the penitentiary at Walnut Street succumbed to the same problems that continue to plague institutions of confinement: overcrowding and excessive costs. As an influx of inmates forced more than one person to be housed in a room, maintaining silence became nearly impossible. By the early 1800s, officials could not find work for all of the convicts, so many were left idle.

The Great Penitentiary Rivalry: Pennsylvania versus New York

The apparent lack of success at Walnut Street did little to dampen enthusiasm for the penitentiary concept. Throughout the first half of the nineteenth century, a number of states reacted to prison overcrowding by constructing new penitentiaries. Each state tended to have its own peculiar twist on the roles of silence and labor, and two such systems—those of Pennsylvania and New York—emerged to shape the debate over the most effective way to run a prison.

The Pennsylvania System

After the failure of Walnut Street, Pennsylvania constructed two new prisons: the Western Penitentiary near Pittsburgh (opened in 1826) and the Eastern Penitentiary in Cherry Hill, near Philadelphia (1829). The Pennsylvania system took the concept of silence as a virtue to new extremes. Based on the idea of **separate confinement,** these penitentiaries were constructed with back-to-back cells facing outward from the center. (See Figure 13.1 for the layout of the original Eastern Penitentiary.) To protect each inmate from the corrupting influence of the others, prisoners worked, slept, and ate alone in their cells. Their only contact with other human beings came in the form of religious instruction from a visiting clergyman or prison official.[5]

The New York System

If Pennsylvania's prisons were designed to transform wrongdoers into honest citizens, those in New York focused on obedience. When New York's Newgate Prison (built in 1791) became overcrowded, the state authorized the construction of Auburn Prison, which opened in 1816. Auburn initially operated under many of the same assumptions that guided the penitentiary at Walnut Street. Solitary confinement, however, seemed to lead to an inordinate amount of sickness, insanity, and even suicide among inmates, and it was abandoned in 1822. Nine years later, Elam Lynds became warden at Auburn and instilled the **congregate system,** also known as the Auburn system. Like Pennsylvania's separate confinement system, the congregate system was based on silence and labor. At Auburn, however, inmates worked and ate together, with silence enforced by prison guards.[6]

If either state can be said to have "won" the debate, it was New York. The Auburn system proved more popular, and a majority of the new prisons built during the first half of the nineteenth century followed New York's lead, though mainly for economic reasons rather than philosophical ones. New York's penitentiaries were cheaper to build because they did not require so much space. Furthermore, inmates in New York were employed in workshops, whereas those in Pennsylvania toiled alone in their cells. Consequently, the Auburn system was better positioned to exploit prison labor in the early years of widespread factory production.

FIGURE 13.1 The Eastern Penitentiary

As you can see, the Eastern Penitentiary was designed in the form of a "wagon wheel," known today as the radial style. The back-to-back cells in each "spoke" of the wheel faced outward from the center to limit contact between inmates.

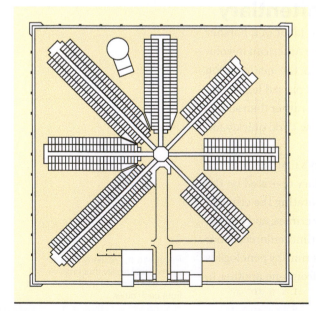

The Reformers and the Progressives

The Auburn system did not go unchallenged. In the 1870s, a group of reformers argued that fixed sentences, imposed silence, and isolation did nothing to improve prisoners. These critics proposed that penal institutions should offer the promise of early release as a prime tool for rehabilitation. Echoing the views of the Quakers a century earlier, the reformers presented an ideology that would heavily influence American corrections for the next century.

This "new penology" was put into practice at New York's Elmira Reformatory in 1876. At Elmira, good behavior was rewarded by early release, and misbehavior was punished with extended time under a three-grade system of classification. On entering the institution, the offender was assigned a grade of 2. If the inmate followed the rules and completed work and school assignments, after six months he was moved up to grade 1, the necessary grade for release. If, however, the inmate broke institutional rules, he was lowered to grade 3. A grade 3 inmate needed to behave properly for three months before he could return to grade 2 and begin to work back toward grade 1 and eventual release.[7]

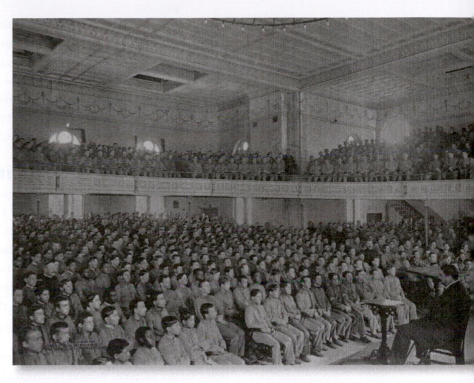

▲ Inmates of the Elmira Reformatory in New York attend a presentation at the prison auditorium. **To what extent do you believe that treatment should be a part of the incarceration of criminals?** Library of Congress/Corbis Historical/VCG/Getty Images

Although other penal institutions did not adopt the Elmira model, its theories came into prominence in the first two decades of the twentieth century thanks to the Progressive movement in criminal justice. The Progressives—linked to the positivist school of criminology discussed in Chapter 2—believed that criminal behavior was caused by social, economic, and biological factors and, therefore, a corrections system should have a goal of treatment, not punishment. Consequently, they trumpeted a **medical model** for prisons, which held that institutions should offer a variety of programs and therapies to cure inmates of their "ills," whatever the root causes. The Progressives were largely responsible for the spread of indeterminate sentences (Chapter 11), probation (Chapter 12), intermediate sanctions (Chapter 12), and parole (Chapter 12) in the first half of the twentieth century.

The Reassertion of Punishment

Even though the Progressives had a great influence on the corrections system as a whole, their theories had little impact on the prisons themselves. Many of these facilities had been constructed in the nineteenth century and were impervious to change. More important, prison administrators usually did not agree with the Progressives and their followers, so the day-to-day lives of most inmates varied little from the congregate system of Auburn Prison.

Academic attitudes began to shift away from the Progressives in the mid-1960s. Then, in 1974, the publication of Robert Martinson's famous "What Works?" essay provided opponents of the medical model with statistical evidence that rehabilitation efforts did nothing to lower recidivism rates.[8] This is not to say that Martinson's findings went unchallenged. A number of critics argued that rehabilitative programs could be successful.[9] In fact, Martinson himself retracted most of his claims in a little-noticed

Medical Model A model of corrections in which the psychological and biological roots of an inmate's criminal behavior are identified and treated.

article published five years after his initial report.[10] Attempts by Martinson and others to "set the record straight" went largely unnoticed, however, as crime rose sharply in the early 1970s. This trend led many criminologists and politicians to champion "get tough" measures to deal with criminals they now considered "incurable." By the end of the 1980s, the legislative, judicial, and administrative strategies that we have discussed throughout this text had positioned the United States for an explosion in inmate populations and prison construction unparalleled in the nation's history.

The Role of Prisons in Modern Society

For reasons that we will explain later in the chapter, the number of federal and state prisoners quadrupled between 1980 and 2010.[11] This increase reflects the varied demands placed on the modern American penal institution. As University of Connecticut sociologist Charles Logan once noted, Americans expect prisons to "correct the incorrigible, rehabilitate the wretched, . . . restrain the dangerous, and punish the wicked."[12] Basically, prisons exist to make society a safer place. Whether this is to be achieved through retribution, deterrence, incapacitation, or rehabilitation—the four justifications of corrections introduced in Chapter 11—depends on the operating philosophy of the individual penal institution.

Models of Organization

Three general models of prisons have emerged to describe the different schools of thought behind prison organization:

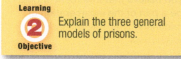

- The *custodial model* is based on the assumption that prisoners are incarcerated for reasons of incapacitation, deterrence, and retribution. All decisions within the prison—such as what form of recreation to provide the inmates—are made with an eye toward security and discipline, and the daily routine of the inmates is highly controlled. The custodial model has dominated the most restrictive prisons in the United States since the 1930s.
- The *rehabilitation model* stresses the ideals of individualized treatment that we discussed in Chapter 11. Security concerns are often secondary to the well-being of the individual inmate, and a number of treatment programs are offered to aid prisoners in changing their criminal and antisocial behavior. The rehabilitation model came into prominence during the 1950s and enjoyed widespread popularity until it began to lose general acceptance in the 1970s and 1980s.
- In the *reintegration model*, the correctional institution serves as a training ground for the inmate to prepare for existence in the community. Prisons that have adopted this model give the prisoners more responsibility during incarceration and offer halfway houses and work programs to help them reintegrate into society. This model is becoming more influential, as corrections officials react to problems such as prison overcrowding.[13]

Differing Perspectives

Critical views of the prison's role in society are at odds with these three "ideal" perspectives. Professor Alfred Blumstein argues that prisons create new criminals, especially with regard to nonviolent drug offenders. Not only do these nonviolent felons become socialized to the criminal lifestyle while in prison, but the stigma of incarceration makes it more difficult for them to obtain employment on release. Their only means of sustenance "on the outside" is to apply the criminal methods they learned in prison.[14] A study by criminal justice professors Cassia Spohn of Arizona State University and David Holleran of the College of New Jersey found that convicted drug offenders who were sentenced to prison were 2.2 times more likely to be incarcerated for a new offense than those sentenced to probation.[15]

Prison Organization and Management

The United States has a dual prison system that parallels its dual court system, which we discussed in Chapter 8. The Federal Bureau of Prisons (BOP) currently operates about one hundred confinement facilities, ranging from prisons to immigration detention centers to community corrections institutions.[16] In the federal corrections system, a national director, appointed by the president, oversees six regional directors and a staff of nearly 40,000 employees. All fifty states also operate state prisons, which number about 1,700 and make up more than 90 percent of the country's correctional facilities.[17] Governors are responsible for the organization and operation of state corrections systems, which vary widely based on each state's geography, demographics, and political culture.

Generally, offenders sentenced in federal court for breaking federal law serve their time in federal prisons, and offenders sentenced in state court for breaking state law serve their time in state prisons. As you can see in Figure 13.2, federal prisons hold relatively few violent felons, because relatively few federal laws involve violent crime. At the same time, federal prisons are much more likely to hold public order offenders, a group that includes violators of federal immigration law.

FIGURE 13.2 **Types of Offenses of Federal and State Prison Inmates**

As the comparison below shows, state prisoners are most likely to have been convicted of violent crimes, while federal prisoners are most likely to have been convicted of drug and public order offenses.

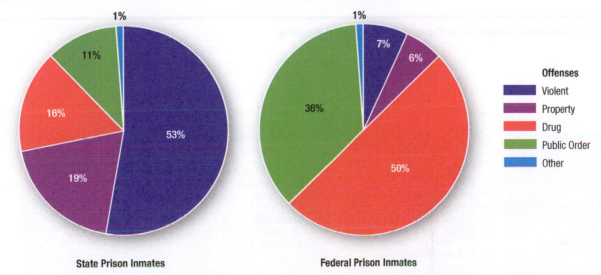

State Prison Inmates

Federal Prison Inmates

Offenses
- Violent
- Property
- Drug
- Public Order
- Other

Source: Bureau of Justice Statistics, *Prisoners in 2015* (Washington, D.C.: U.S. Department of Justice, December 2016), Table 9, page 14; and Table 10, page 15.

Warden The prison official who is ultimately responsible for the organization and performance of a correctional facility.

Prison Administration

Whether the federal government or a state government operates a prison, its administrators have the same general goals, summarized by Charles Logan as follows:

> The mission of a prison is to keep prisoners—to keep them in, keep them safe, keep them in line, keep them healthy, and keep them busy—and to do it with fairness, without undue suffering and as efficiently as possible.[18]

Considering the environment of a prison—an enclosed world inhabited by people who are generally violent and angry and would rather be anywhere else—Logan's mission statement is somewhat unrealistic. A prison staff must supervise the daily routines of hundreds or thousands of inmates, a duty that includes providing them with meals, education, vocational programs, and different forms of leisure. The smooth operation of this supervision is made more difficult—if not, at times, impossible—by budgetary restrictions, overcrowding, and continual inmate turnover.

Learning 3 Objective Describe the formal prison management system, and indicate the three most important aspects of prison governance.

Formal Prison Management   In some respects, the management structure of a prison is similar to that of a police department, as discussed in Chapter 6. Both systems rely on a hierarchical (top-down) *chain of command* to increase personal responsibility. Both assign different employees to specific tasks, though prison managers have much more direct control over their subordinates than do police managers. The main difference is that police departments have a *continuity of purpose* that is sometimes lacking in prison organizations. All members of a police force are, at least theoretically, working to reduce crime and apprehend criminals. In a prison, this continuity is less evident. An employee in the prison laundry service and one who works in the visiting center have little in common. In some instances, employees may even have cross-purposes: A prison guard may want to punish an inmate, while a counselor in the treatment center may want to rehabilitate her or him.

Consequently, a strong hierarchy is crucial for any prison management team that hopes to meet Charles Logan's expectations. As Figure 13.3 shows, the **warden** (also known as a superintendent) is ultimately responsible for the operation of a prison. He or she oversees deputy wardens, who in turn manage the various organizational lines of the institution. The custodial employees, who deal directly with the inmates and make up more than half of a prison's staff, operate under a militaristic hierarchy, with a line of command passing from the deputy warden to the captain to the correctional officer.

FIGURE 13.3 **Organizational Chart for a Typical Correctional Facility**

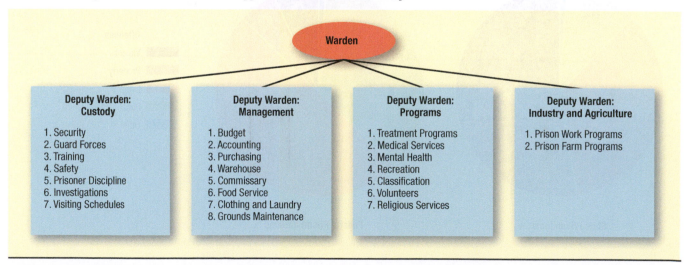

Berry Larson Prison Warden

Before I began my career as a correctional officer for the Arizona Department of Corrections, I had several people question my desire to work inside a prison. Why would I want to stick myself somewhere so unpleasant and stressful? While at the training academy, however, we were taught that "approach determines response." I found that to be very true during my time as a correctional officer. It is all about the way you carry yourself and the way you relate to the inmates. An inmate can tell if you are trying to be someone you are not. They can also tell if you are afraid. I never had to use physical force once in all the time I was a correctional officer—officer presence and nonverbal/verbal communication is usually sufficient to handle any situation, as long as you keep control of your emotions.

As warden of the Arizona State Prison Complex–Lewis, my duties include touring the units; attending special events such as inmate graduations for GED and vocational programs; managing emergency situations such as power outages, fights and assaults, and staff injuries; and eradicating all criminal activity from the facility. Many, if not most, of our inmates came to us in pretty bad shape—little or no education, a substance abuse history, or mental health or behavioral issues. These young men have spent their lives watching television and playing video games and simply do not have the skills to be successful in life. We try to remedy the situation by providing them with educational and vocational programs and "life-skills" classes that promote civil and productive behavior.

Courtesy of Berry Larson

FASTFACTS

Prison warden

Job description:

- A prison warden is the chief managing officer of an adult correctional institution.

What kind of training is required?

- Bachelor's degree in criminal justice, corrections, law enforcement, or a related field.
- One or more years of work experience in the management of a major division of a correctional institution.

Annual salary range?

- $38,000–$100,000 (depending on size of institution and geographic region)

SOCIAL MEDIA CAREER TIP Regularly reevaluate your social media tools and the methods you use to keep up to date in your fields of interest. If you are still using the same tools as a year ago, you probably aren't keeping up with the latest developments in Internet technology.

Governing Prisons The implications of prison mismanagement can be severe. While studying a series of prison riots, sociologists Bert Useem and Peter Kimball found that breakdown in managerial control commonly preceded such acts of mass violence.[19] During the 1970s, for example, conditions at the State Penitentiary in New Mexico deteriorated significantly. Inmates were increasingly the targets of random and harsh treatment at the hands of the prison staff, while at the same time a reduction in structured activities left prison life "painfully boring."[20] The result, in 1980, was one of the most violent prison riots in the nation's history.

What sort of prison management is most suited to avoid such situations? Most prisons in the United States operate under an authoritarian management structure, characterized by a strong leader, extensive control of the prison environment, and harsh discipline for misbehaving inmates.[21] Political scientist John DiIulio believes that, in general, the sound governance of correctional facilities is a matter of order, amenities, and services:

- *Order* can be defined as the absence of misconduct such as murder, assault, and rape. Many observers, including DiIulio, believe that, having incarcerated a person, the state has a responsibility to protect that person from disorder in the correctional institution.

- *Amenities* are those comforts that make life "livable," such as clean living conditions, acceptable food, and entertainment. One theory of incarceration holds that inmates

Classification The process through which prison officials screen each incoming inmate to best determine that inmate's security and treatment needs.

Custody Level As a result of the classification process, the security designation given to new inmates, crucial in helping corrections officials determine which correctional facility is best suited to the individual offender.

should not enjoy a quality of life comparable to life outside prison. Without the basic amenities, however, prison life becomes unbearable, and inmates are more likely to lapse into disorder.

- *Services* include programs designed to improve an inmate's prospects on release, such as vocational training, remedial education, and drug treatment. Again, many feel that a person convicted of a crime does not deserve to participate in these kinds of programs, but they have two clear benefits. First, they keep the inmate occupied and focused during her or his sentence. Second, they reduce the chances that the inmate will go back to a life of crime after she or he returns to the community.[22]

According to DiIulio, in the absence of order, amenities, and services, inmates will come to see their imprisonment as not only unpleasant but unfair, and they will become much more difficult to control.[23] Furthermore, weak governance encourages inmates to come up with their own methods of regulating their lives. As we shall see in the next chapter, the result is usually high levels of violence and the expansion of prison gangs and other unsanctioned forms of authority.

Classification   One of the most important aspects of prison administration occurs soon after a defendant has been convicted of a crime and sentenced to be incarcerated. In this **classification** process, an inmate's mental, physical, and security needs are evaluated to help determine the best correctional facility "fit." The classification process usually takes four to eight weeks, and is overseen by a corrections counselor, also known as a case manager. During this period, the inmate undergoes numerous tests and interviews to identify education levels, medical issues, drug/alcohol addictions, and any behavioral "red flags."

Taking the results of the process into consideration, prison administrators generally rely on three broad criteria for classification purposes:

1. The seriousness of the crime committed.
2. The risk of future criminal or violent conduct.
3. The need for treatment and rehabilitation programs.[24]

Classification is not a one-time operation. Inmates can, and often do, change their behavior patterns during the course of their incarceration. If an inmate acts more violently, or, conversely, shows an increasingly positive attitude, that inmate will need to be *reclassified*. Furthermore, the successful completion of prison rehabilitation programs may require an adjustment in the inmate's release plan, discussed in the next chapter.[25]

Types of Prisons

Following the classification process, an inmate is assigned a **custody level.** Corrections officials rely on this custody level to place the inmate in the appropriate correctional facility. In the federal prison system, an offender's custody level determines whether she or he is sent to one of six different types of prisons. Inmates in level 1 facilities are usually non-violent and require the least amount of security, while inmates in level 6 facilities are the most dangerous and require the harshest security measures. (Many states also use the six-level system, an example of which can be seen in Figure 13.4.)

To simplify matters, most correctional facilities are designated as being one of three security levels—minimum, medium, or maximum. A fourth level—the supermaximum-security prison, known as the "supermax"—is relatively rare and extremely controversial due to its hyper-harsh methods of punishing and controlling the most dangerous prisoners.

Learning Objective 4 List and briefly explain the four types of prisons.

FIGURE 13.4 Security Levels of Correctional Facilities in Virginia

The security levels of correctional facilities in Virginia are graded from level 1 to level 6. As you can see, level 1 facilities are for those inmates who pose the least amount of risk to fellow inmates, staff members, and themselves. Level 6 facilities are for those who are considered the most dangerous by the Virginia Department of Corrections.

LEVEL 1 - LOW
No first or second degree murder, robbery, sex-related crime, kidnapping/abduction, felonious assault (current or prior), flight/escape history, carjacking, or malicious wounding. No disruptive behavior.

LEVEL 1 - HIGH
No first or second degree murder, robbery, sex-related crime, kidnapping/abduction, felonious assault (current or prior), flight/escape history. No disruptive behavior for at least past 24 months.

LEVEL 2
For initial assignment only. No escape history for past 5 years. No disruptive behavior for at least past 24 months prior to transfer to any less secure facility.

LEVEL 3
Single, multiple, and life+ sentences.* Must have served 20 consecutive years on sentence. No disruptive behavior for at least past 24 months prior to transfer to any less secure facility.

LEVEL 4
Single, multiple, and life+ sentences. No disruptive behavior for at least past 24 months prior to transfer to any less secure facility.

LEVEL 5
Same as level 4 except with fewer opportunities to participate in programs and jobs, fewer visitation and phone access privileges, and less freedom of movement within the facility. No disruptive behavior for at least past 24 months prior to transfer to any less secure facility.

LEVEL 6
Single, multiple, and life+ sentences. Profile of inmates: disruptive, assaultive, severe behavior problems, predatory-type behavior, escape risk. No disruptive behavior for at least past 24 months prior to transfer to any less secure facility.

* "Life +" means a life sentence plus extra years in case of an early release.

Source: Virginia Department of Corrections.

Maximum-Security Prisons

In a certain sense, the classification of prisoners today owes a debt to the three-grade system developed at the Elmira Reformatory, discussed earlier in the chapter. Once wrongdoers enter a corrections facility, they are constantly graded on behavior. Those who serve "good time," as we have seen, are often rewarded with early release. Those who compile extensive misconduct records are usually housed, along with violent and repeat offenders, in **maximum-security prisons.**

The names of these institutions—Folsom, San Quentin, Sing Sing, Attica—conjure up foreboding images of concrete and steel jungles, with good reason. Maximum-security prisons are designed with full attention to security and surveillance. In these institutions, inmates' lives are programmed in a militaristic fashion to keep them from escaping or from harming themselves or the prison staff. About a quarter of the prisons in the United States are classified as maximum security, and these institutions house about a third of the country's prisoners.

The Design Maximum-security prisons tend to be large—holding more than a thousand inmates—and they have similar features. The entire operation is usually surrounded by concrete walls that stand twenty to thirty feet high and have also been sunk deep into the ground to deter tunnel escapes. Fences reinforced with razor-ribbon barbed wire that can be electrically charged may supplement these barriers. The prison walls are studded with watchtowers, from which guards armed with shotguns and rifles survey the movement of prisoners below.

The designs of these facilities, though similar, are not uniform. Though correctional facilities built using the radial design pioneered by the Eastern Penitentiary still exist, several other designs have become prominent in more recently constructed institutions. For an overview of these designs, including the radial design, see Figure 13.5.

Maximum-Security Prisons
A correctional institution designed and organized to control and discipline dangerous felons, as well as prevent escape.

FIGURE 13.5 Prison Designs

The Radial Design

The wagon wheel form of the radial design was created with the dual goals of separation and control. Inmates are separated from one another in their cells on the "spokes" of the wheel, and prison officials can control the activities of the inmates from the control center in the "hub" of the wheel.

The Telephone-Pole Design

The main feature of this design is a long central corridor that serves as a means for transporting inmates from one part of the facility to another. Branching off from this main corridor are the functional areas of the facility: housing, food services, workshops, a treatment programs room, and other services.

The Courtyard Style

In the courtyard-style prison, a courtyard replaces the transportation function of the "pole" in the telephone-pole prison. The prison buildings form a square around the courtyard, and to get from one part of the facility to another, the inmates go across the courtyard.

The Campus Style

Some of the newer minimum-security prisons have adopted the campus style, which had previously been used in correctional facilities for women and juveniles. As on a college campus, housing units are scattered among functional units such as the dining room, recreation area, and treatment centers.

Source: Text adapted from Todd R. Clear, George F. Cole, and Michael D. Reisig, *American Corrections*, 11th ed. (Boston: Cengage Learning, 2016), 261–262.

Inmates live in cells, most of them with dimensions similar to those found in the Topeka Correctional Facility, a maximum-security prison in Topeka, Kansas: eight feet by fourteen feet with cinder block walls. The space contains bunks, a toilet, a sink, and possibly a cabinet or closet. Cells are located in rows of *cell blocks*, each of which forms its own security unit, set off by a series of gates and bars. A maximum-security institution is essentially a collection of numerous cell blocks, each constituting its own prison within a prison.

Most prisons, regardless of their design, have cell blocks that open into sprawling prison yards, where the inmates commingle daily. The "prison of the future," however, rejects this layout. Instead, it relies on a podular design, as evident at the Two Rivers Correctional Institution in Umatilla, Oregon. (Podular design is discussed in more detail later in the chapter.) At Two Rivers, which opened about a decade ago, fourteen housing units, called pods, contain ninety-six inmates each. Each unit has its own yard, so inmates rarely, if ever, interact with members of other pods. This design gives administrators the flexibility to, for example, place violent criminals in pod A and white-collar criminals in pod B without worrying about mixing the two different security levels.[26]

Security Measures Within maximum-security prisons, inmates' lives are dominated by security measures. Whenever they move from one area of the prison to another, they do so in groups and under the watchful eye of armed correctional officers. Television surveillance cameras may be used to monitor their every move, even when sleeping, showering, or using the toilet. They are subject to frequent pat-downs or strip searches at the guards' discretion. Constant "head counts" ensure that every inmate is where he or she should be. Tower guards—many of whom have orders to shoot to kill in the case of a disturbance or escape attempt—constantly look down on the inmates as they move around outdoor areas of the facility.

Supermax Prisons
About thirty states and the Federal Bureau of Prisons (BOP) operate **supermax** (short for supermaximum-security) **prisons,** which are supposedly reserved for the "worst of the worst" of America's corrections population. Many of the inmates in these facilities are deemed high risks to commit murder behind bars—about a quarter of the occupants of the BOP's U.S. Penitentiary Administrative Maximum (ADX) in Florence, Colorado, have killed other prisoners or assaulted correctional officers elsewhere.

Supermax prisons are also used as punishment for offenders who commit serious disciplinary infractions in maximum-security prisons or who become involved with prison gangs. In addition, a growing number of supermax occupants are either high-profile individuals who would be at constant risk of attack in a general prison population or convicted terrorists such as Zacarias Moussaoui, who helped plan the attacks of September 11, 2001; Ted "the Unabomber" Kaczynski; and Terry Nichols, who was involved in the bombing of a federal office building in Oklahoma City in 1995. Although different jurisdictions have different definitions of what constitutes a supermax, the most reliable surveys estimate that about sixty such facilities exist in the United States, holding approximately 25,000 inmates.[27]

A Controlled Environment The main purpose of a supermax prison is to strictly control the inmates' movement, thereby limiting (or eliminating) situations that could lead to breakdowns in discipline. The conditions at California's Security Housing Unit (SHU) at Pelican Bay State Prison are representative of most supermax institutions. Prisoners are confined to their one-person cells for twenty-three hours each day under video camera surveillance. They receive meals through a slot in the door. The cells measure eight by ten feet in size and are windowless. Fluorescent lights are continuously on, day and night, making it difficult for inmates to enjoy any type of privacy or sleep.[28]

For the most part, supermax prisons operate in a state of perpetual **lockdown,** in which all inmates are confined to their cells and social activities such as meals, recreational sports, and treatment programs are nonexistent. For the sixty minutes of each day that SHU inmates are allowed out of their cells (compared with twelve to sixteen hours in regular maximum-security prisons), they may either shower or exercise in an enclosed, concrete "yard" covered by plastic mesh. Prisoners are strip-searched before and after leaving their cells, and are placed in waist restraints and handcuffs on their way to and from the "yard" and showers.[29]

Supermax Syndrome Many prison officials support the proliferation of supermax prisons because they provide increased security for the most dangerous inmates. These proponents believe that the harsh reputation of the facilities will deter convicts from

Supermax Prison A highly secure, freestanding correctional facility—or such a unit within a correctional facility—that manages offenders who would pose a threat to the security and safety of other inmates and staff members if housed in the general inmate population.

Lockdown A disciplinary action taken by prison officials in which all inmates are ordered to their quarters and nonessential prison activities are suspended.

▲ **What security measures can you identify from this photo of a cell block at Arizona State Prison in Florence, Arizona?** AP Images/Matt York

misbehaving for fear of transfer to a supermax. Nevertheless, the supermax has aroused a number of criticisms. Amnesty International and other human rights groups assert that the facilities violate standards for proper treatment of prisoners. At Wisconsin's Supermax Correctional Facility, for example, the cells have no air-conditioning or windows, and average temperatures during the summer top 100 degrees.[30]

Furthermore, while studying prisoners at California's Pelican Bay facility, a Harvard University psychiatrist found that 80 percent suffered from what he called "SHU [security housing unit] syndrome," a condition brought on by long periods of isolation.[31] Further research on SHU syndrome shows that supermax inmates exhibit a number of psychological problems, including intense anxiety, hallucinations, and acute confusion.[32] We will take a closer look at the merits and drawbacks of solitary confinement, a method of inmate punishment that extends well beyond supermax prisons, in the next chapter.

Medium- and Minimum-Security Prisons

Medium-security prisons hold about 45 percent of the prison population and minimum-security prisons 20 percent. Inmates at medium-security prisons have for the most part committed less serious crimes than those housed in maximum-security prisons and are not considered high risks for escaping or causing harm. Consequently, medium-security institutions are not designed for control to the same extent as maximum-security prisons and have a more relaxed atmosphere. These facilities also offer more educational and treatment programs and allow for more contact between inmates. Medium-security prisons are rarely walled, relying instead on high fences. Prisoners have more freedom of movement within the structures, and the levels of surveillance are much lower. Living quarters are less restrictive as well—many of the newer medium-security prisons provide dormitory housing.

A minimum-security prison seems at first glance to be more like a college campus than an incarceration facility. Most of the inmates at these institutions are first-time offenders who are nonviolent and well behaved. A high percentage are white-collar criminals. In addition, inmates are often transferred to minimum-security prisons as a reward for good behavior in other facilities. Therefore, security measures are lax compared with even medium-security prisons. Unlike medium-security institutions, minimum-security prisons sometimes do not have armed guards. Prisoners are provided with amenities such as televisions and computers in their rooms. They also enjoy freedom of movement, and are allowed off prison grounds for educational or employment purposes to a much greater extent than those held in more restrictive facilities.

Some critics have likened minimum-security prisons to "country clubs," but in the corrections system, everything is relative. A minimum-security prison may seem like a vacation spot when compared with the horrors of Sing Sing, but it still represents a restriction of personal freedom and separates the inmate from the outside world. (The feature *Comparative Criminal Justice—Prison Lite* provides a look at Norway's approach to incarceration, in which even the worst offenders are afforded the minimum-security experience.)

Medium-Security Prisons
A correctional institution that houses less dangerous inmates and therefore uses less restrictive measures to prevent violence and escapes.

Minimum-Security Prison
A correctional institution designed to allow inmates, most of whom pose low security risks, a great deal of freedom of movement and contact with the outside world.

Source: Central Intelligence Agency

Prison Lite

In Norway, incarceration is based on the premise that loss of liberty is punishment enough for offenders. Consequently, the prisons themselves are made as pleasant as possible. For example, Halden prison, which houses murderers and rapists, provides amenities such as a recording studio, a "kitchen laboratory" for cooking classes, and a two-bedroom house where inmates can house their families for overnight visits. An inmate at the Skien maximum-security island prison compares his incarceration to "living in a village." He adds, "Everybody has to work. But we have free time so we can do some fishing, or in summer we can swim off the beach. We know we are prisoners but here we feel like people."

Norway's methods have, it appears, created certain expectations among its inmates. After spending several months behind bars following a conviction on multiple counts of murder, one Norwegian prisoner wrote a letter to authorities protesting the conditions of his imprisonment. Among the complaints: not enough butter for his bread, cold coffee, and no skin moisturizer. By at least one measurement, however, Norway's "prison lite" strategy is effective, as the country has a five-year recidivism rate of only 20 percent—one of the lowest such rates in the world.

FOR CRITICAL ANALYSIS

In the United States, life behind bars has long been predicated on the *principle of least eligibility*, which holds that the least advantaged members of society outside prison should lead a better existence than any prison or jail inmate. Do you favor the American or the Norwegian approach to prison conditions? Why?

Inmate Population Trends

As Figure 13.6 shows, the number of Americans in prison or jail has increased dramatically in the past several decades. A number of different factors, described below, have been offered as reasons for this long-term trend, which has only recently begun to level off.

Factors in Prison Population Growth

John Pfaff, an expert on sentencing from Fordham University's School of Law, attributes much of the growth in the U.S. prison population to a greater willingness on the part of prosecutors to bring felony—rather than misdemeanor—charges against arrestees.[33] Other experts point to the enhancement and stricter enforcement of the nation's drug laws. In 1980, about 19,000 drug offenders were incarcerated in state prisons and 4,800 drug offenders were in federal prisons. Thirty-five years later, state prisons held about 209,000 inmates who had been arrested for drug offenses, and the number of drug offenders in federal prisons had risen to approximately 97,000 (representing about half of all inmates in federal facilities).[34]

Learning 5 Objective Identify some factors that have caused the prison population to grow dramatically in the last several decades.

Increased Probability of Incarceration For most of the 1980s, crime rates in the United States were much higher than they are today. In addition, during that decade, the likelihood of incarceration in a state prison after arrest increased fivefold for drug offenses, threefold for weapons offenses, and twofold for crimes such as sexual assault, burglary, auto theft, and larceny.[35] With more convicted offenders facing greater probability of imprisonment, the state inmate population was bound to grow.[36] In the federal criminal justice system, this trend has persisted. The proportion of convicted defendants being sent to federal prison rose from 54 percent in 1988 to 87 percent in 2015.[37]

Inmates Serving More Time In Chapter 11, we discussed a number of "get tough" sentencing laws passed in reaction to the crime wave of the 1970s and 1980s. These measures, including sentencing guidelines, mandatory minimum sentences, and truth-in-sentencing laws, have significantly increased the length of prison terms in the United

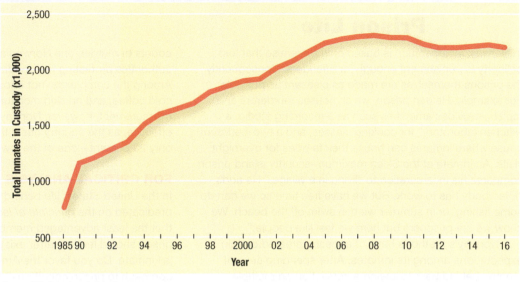

FIGURE 13.6 **The Inmate Population of the United States**

The total number of inmates in the United States has risen from 744,208 in 1985 to about 2.2 million in 2016.

Source: U.S. Department of Justice.

States.[38] Overall, inmates released from state prison in 2009 spent an average of nine months—about 36 percent—longer behind bars than inmates released in 1990.[39] On the federal level, in the fifteen years after the passage of the Sentencing Reform Act of 1984, the average time served in federal prison increased more than 50 percent.[40]

Federal Prison Growth The number of inmates in the federal prison population declined by about 7 percent (or 14,112 prisoners) in 2015.[41] This decrease is too small, however, to offset the longer-term expansion of the federal corrections system. Between 2000 and 2015, the federal prison population grew 56 percent, from about 125,000 to over 196,000.[42]

As already mentioned, an increase in federal drug offenders is largely responsible for the growth of the federal prison population. Because of mandatory minimum sentencing laws, federal drug traffickers spend an average of seventy-four months behind bars, considerably longer than those sentenced to state prisons.[43] Other factors driving federal prison population growth include the following:

1. Starting in 1987, Congress *abolished parole* in the federal corrections system, meaning that federal inmates must serve their entire sentences, minus good time credits.[44]

2. The number of federal inmates sentenced for *immigration violations* (covered by federal law rather than state law) increased by more than 850 percent from 1990 to 2015.[45]

3. In 2017, nearly 12,700 *female offenders* were behind bars in federal prison, about 75 percent more than in 1995.[46] Indeed, there were about the same number of women in federal prison for drug offenses in 2012 as there were for all offenses in 1995.[47]

Decarceration

To significantly reverse the trend of prison population growth, says Michael Tonry, a criminal justice professor at the University of Minnesota, there must be a national consensus that "too many people have been sent to prison for too long."[48] As we saw at the beginning of this chapter, policymakers in numerous jurisdictions have embraced strategies of *decarceration*, or the lowering of incarceration rates. In general, decarceration policies rely on three methods to reduce the number of offenders in prison:

1. Decreasing the probability that non-violent offenders will be sentenced to prison.

2. Increasing the rate of release of nonviolent offenders from prison.

3. Decreasing the rate of imprisonment for probation and parole violators.[49]

A Limited Focus For the most part, decarceration strategies have focused on reducing the number of nonviolent offenders behind bars. More than half the states have enacted "front-end" reforms to divert these offenders from prison or to shorten their length of incarceration.[50] Along those same lines, as many as 46,000 nonviolent federal offenders are expected to gain early release under federal sentencing guidelines established in 2015.[51]

In response to a U.S. Supreme Court case discussed in the next chapter, California implemented a "realignment" strategy to reduce its rates of imprisonment. As a result of this realignment, in which nearly 60,000 low-level offenders were released into some form of community corrections, the state's prison inmate population declined by 51 percent from 2006 to 2015.[52] Besides California, three other states (New Jersey, New York, and Rhode Island) have decreased their prison populations by over 20 percent in the twenty-first century.[53] In general, states are relying on *evidence-based practices*, or those strategies supported by statistical research, to decarcerate.

Experts caution that decarceration policies that focus only on nonviolent offenders have their limits. "If you released every person in prison on a drug charge today," says criminologist John Pfaff, "[the United States would] still be the world's largest incarcerating country."[54] To truly reverse America's incarceration trends, decarceration policies in the future will need to concentrate on freeing violent criminals from prison. California has taken several steps in this direction. Its legislature recently mandated new parole hearings for certain inmates convicted of violent crimes before the age of twenty-three, and Governor Jerry Brown has approved parole for 2,300 offenders serving life sentences for murder.

Public Safety Issues Many observers believe that America's high rate of incarceration has contributed significantly to the drop in the nation's crime rates,[55] an assertion discussed in the feature *Myth vs Reality—Does Putting Criminals in Prison Reduce Crime?* In these circles, there is concern that the decarceration movement discussed above will reverse the nation's positive crime trends. "People come out of prison hardened and angry and more likely to offend," says Ronald Teachman, formerly the police chief in South Bend, Indiana.[56]

To determine whether releasing low-level offenders necessarily leads to increased criminal activity, researchers are closely watching crime rates in California. In November 2014, California voters passed Proposition 47, which downgraded a number of

▲ Immigration detainees wait for their cases to be disposed of at the Central Arizona Detention Center in Florence. **Why has heightened enforcement of immigration law increased the inmate population at federal correctional facilities while having little or no impact on the inmate populations in state prisons?** John Moore/Getty Images News/ Getty Images

MYTH vs REALITY

Does Putting Criminals in Prison Reduce Crime?

The Myth Since the early 1990s, crime rates in the United States have been stable or declining. During most of that same period, as seen in Figure 13.6 earlier in the chapter, the number of imprisoned Americans climbed precipitously. Thus, it seems clear that crime falls when the prison population rises.

This perception is supported by the theories of deterrence and incapacitation, which we covered in Chapter 11. First, the threat of prison deters would-be criminals from committing crimes. Second, a prison inmate is incapable of committing crimes against the public because he or she has been separated from the community.

The Reality Numerous statistical examples discredit a direct, sustained link between decreased crime rates and increased prison populations. According to the Pew Charitable Trusts, for example, the ten states with the largest declines in imprisonment from 2010 to 2015 saw their crime rates *decrease* by an average of 14.4 percent over that time period. By the same token, North Dakota and New Hampshire, the two states with the greatest increase in violent crime from 2006 to 2014, increased their prison populations slightly during those years.

According to one theory, massive incarceration accounted for about a quarter of the crime drop of the 1990s, as many of the most violent offenders were removed from society and remain behind bars. Since then, however, a large percentage of new prison admissions have been drug law offenders and probation/parole violators. The data tell us that removing these sorts of criminals from the community has a relatively limited effect on violent and property crime rates. In fact, their absence from their homes may even contribute to criminal activity. As we discussed in Chapter 2, many criminologists believe that widespread family disruption greatly increases the incidence of crime in a community.

Additionally, some experts believe that prisons are "schools of crime" that "teach" low-level offenders to be habitual criminals. If this is true, many inmates are more likely to commit crimes after their release from prison than they would have been if they had never been incarcerated in the first place.

FOR CRITICAL ANALYSIS

Critics of decarceration insist that that freeing large numbers of low-level offenders from prison will inevitably start a "vicious cycle" leading to increases in both property and violent crime. What is your opinion of these warnings?

nonviolent felonies involving less than $950—including grand theft, shoplifting, writing bad checks, receiving stolen property, and drug possession—to misdemeanors. Because this change in state law was applied retroactively, inmates serving time for these crimes were eligible for immediate release from prison. By December 2016, about 13,500 prisoners who had committed crimes covered by Proposition 47 were freed from incarceration.[57]

As would be expected, the number of felony arrests in California dropped nearly 30 percent between 2014 and 2015 as a result of Proposition 47's changes in classification. In addition, the number of plea bargains in the state has decreased as offenders—not facing the threat of prison time—have less incentive to avoid trial.[58] It is still too early to determine the impact of Proposition 47 on violent crime. In another area, however, early release does not seem to have greatly impacted criminal activity. Only 2 percent of the "lifers" paroled by Governor Brown in California have gone on to commit new crimes.[59]

The Consequences of America's High Rates of Incarceration

Proponents of decarceration point out that mass incarceration can have severe social repercussions for communities and the families that make up those communities. About 2.7 million minors in this country—one in twenty-eight—have a parent in prison.[60] These children are at an increased risk of suffering from poverty, depression, and academic problems, as well as higher levels of juvenile delinquency and eventual incarceration themselves.[61] Studies also link high imprisonment rates to increased incidence of sexually transmitted diseases and teenage pregnancy, as the separation caused by incarceration wreaks havoc on interpersonal relationships.[62] In addition, of course, incarceration has a harmful impact on offenders themselves. After being released from prison or jail, these men and women suffer from higher rates of physical and mental health problems than the rest of the population, and are more likely to struggle with addiction, unemployment, and homelessness.[63]

Because of the demographics of the U.S. prison population, these problems have a disproportionate impact on members of minority groups. African American males are

Learning Objective 6 Indicate some of the consequences of our high rates of incarceration.

incarcerated at a rate more than six times that of white males and about two and a half times that of Latino males.[64] This disparity appears to contribute to racial wealth inequality in the United States. A recent study determined that the incarceration of a family member leads to a 64 percent decline in household income, leaving African Americans relatively more susceptible to this form of economic hardship.[65] (The *Policy Matters* feature at the end of the chapter addresses another consequence of incarceration that disproportionately impacts the nation's black communities: disenfranchisement, or loss of the right to vote.)

Private Prisons Correctional facilities operated by private corporations instead of the government and, therefore, reliant on profits for survival.

ETHICS CHALLENGE

Another consequence of mass incarceration is that it leaves many ex-felons unable to find a place to live. The Fair Housing Act does not include criminals as a protected class, meaning that, in many circumstances, landlords can refuse to rent an apartment or house to someone with a criminal record. What are the ethical implications of this situation? Explain.

Private Prisons

As the prison population soared at the end of the twentieth century, state corrections officials faced a serious problem: too many inmates, not enough prisons. "States couldn't build space fast enough," explains corrections expert Martin Horn. "And so they had to turn to the private sector."[66] With corrections exhibiting every appearance of "a recession-proof industry," American businesses eagerly entered the market.

Today, private prisons, or prisons run by private firms to make a profit, are an important part of the criminal justice system. About two dozen private companies operate more than two hundred facilities across the United States. The two largest corrections firms, Corrections Corporation of America (CCA) and the GEO Group, Inc., manage approximately 190 correctional facilities and generate about $3.3 billion in annual revenue combined. By 2015, private penal institutions housed about 126,000 inmates, representing 8.3 percent of all prisoners in the state and federal corrections systems.[67]

Why Privatize?

It would be a mistake to automatically assume that private prisons are less expensive to run than public ones. Nevertheless, the incentive to privatize is primarily financial.

Cost Efficiency   Private prisons can often be run more cheaply and efficiently than public ones for the following reasons:

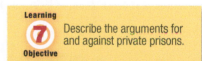

Learning 7 Objective Describe the arguments for and against private prisons.

- *Labor costs.* The wages of public employees account for nearly two-thirds of a prison's operating expenses. Although private corrections firms pay base salaries comparable to those of public prison employees, their nonunionized staffs receive lower levels of overtime pay, workers' compensation claims, sick leave, and health-care insurance.
- *Competitive bidding.* Because of the profit motive, private corrections firms have an incentive to buy goods and services at the lowest possible price.
- *Less red tape.* Private corrections firms are not part of the government bureaucracy and therefore do not have to contend with the massive amount of paperwork that can clog government organizations.[68]

In 2015, the Bureau of Prisons estimated that, on average, it costs the federal government about $80 a day to house an inmate, compared with about $63 a day in a privately operated prison.[69] Similarly, research conducted at Temple University found that, by replacing public correctional facilities with private ones, states could save up to 45 percent in operating costs per prison.[70]

Overcrowding and Outsourcing

Private prisons are becoming increasingly attractive to state governments faced with the competing pressures of tight budgets and overcrowded corrections facilities. Lacking the funds to alleviate overcrowding by building more prisons, state officials are turning to the private institutions for help. Several years ago, for example, the Oklahoma Corrections Department spent $2 million to purchase beds at private institutions to handle a prison population that was at 112 percent of capacity.[71] Often, the private prison is out of state, which leads to the "outsourcing" of inmates. Washington State recently alleviated its prison overcrowding problems by sending about a thousand inmates to private institutions in Michigan.[72]

The Argument against Private Prisons

The assertion that private prisons offer economic benefits is not universally accepted. A number of studies have found that private prisons are no more cost-effective than public ones.[73] Furthermore, opponents of private prisons worry that, despite the assurances of corporate executives, private corrections companies will "cut corners" to save costs, denying inmates important security guarantees in the process.

Safety Concerns

Criticism of private prisons is somewhat supported by the anecdotal evidence. Certainly, these institutions have been the setting for a number of violent incidents over the past several years. In 2015, the Arizona State Prison in Kingman—operated by Management and Training Corporation (MTC)—experienced a riot that required the evacuation of 1,200 inmates. According to prisoners, the disturbance was the result of pent-up frustration caused by constant use of pepper spray by correctional officers.[74] In 2016, the Mississippi Department of Corrections shut down an MTC-operated facility in Walnut Grove. That prison had been plagued by inmate sexual misconduct and gladiator-style fights between prisoners with correctional officers wagering on the outcome.[75]

Apart from anecdotal evidence, various studies have also uncovered disturbing patterns of misbehavior at private prisons. For example, in the year after CCA took over operations of Ohio's Lake Erie Correctional Institution from the state corrections department, the number of assaults against correctional officers and inmates increased by over 40 percent.[76] In addition, research conducted by Curtis R. Blakely of the University of South Alabama and Vic W. Bumphus of the University of Tennessee at Chattanooga found that a prisoner in a private correctional facility was twice as likely to be assaulted by a fellow inmate as a prisoner in a public one.[77]

▼ Tennessee's newest prison, the Trousdale Turner Correctional Center, opened in 2015 and is operated by the Corrections Corporation of America (CCA). The state has a five-year, $276 million contract to cover the prison's operating costs, regardless of how many inmates are housed there. **How might this arrangement hamper efforts in Tennessee to reduce the state's prison population?** AP Images/Mark Humphrey

Philosophical Concerns   Other critics see private prisons as inherently unjust, even if they do save tax dollars or provide enhanced services. These observers believe that corrections is not simply another industry, like garbage collection or road maintenance, and that only the government has the authority to punish wrongdoers. In the words of John DiIulio:

> It is precisely because corrections involves the deprivation of liberty, precisely because it involves the legally sanctioned exercise of coercion by some citizens over others, that it must remain wholly within public hands.[78]

Furthermore, some observers note, if a private corrections firm receives a fee from the state for each inmate housed in its facility, does that not give management an incentive to increase the amount of time each prisoner serves? Though government parole boards make the final decision on an inmate's release from private prisons, the company could manipulate misconduct and good behavior reports to maximize time served and, by extension, maximize profits.[79] "You can put a dollar figure on each inmate that is held at a private prison," says Alex Friedmann of *Prison Legal News*. "They are treated as commodities. And that's very dangerous and troubling when a company sees the people it incarcerates as nothing more than a money stream."[80]

The Future of Private Prisons

The private prison industry will continue to play an important role in American corrections for two reasons. First, states experiencing shrinking corrections budgets and congested prisons rely on private correctional institutions to handle their inmate population overflow.

Second, the federal government contracts with private facilities to house about two-thirds of the undocumented immigrants taken into custody by U.S. Immigration and Customs Enforcement. In 2016, private prisons held an average of about 20,000 such detainees on a typical day.[81] This figure seems poised to increase because of an immigration law "crackdown" announced by the Department of Homeland Security in early 2017. As part of this strategy, the federal government will rely on private prisons to detain increasing numbers of noncitizens.[82]

CJ & TECHNOLOGY

Video Visits

Thousands of prisons and jails in the United States offer "video visitation" to inmates. These communications take place via closed-circuit video systems located within the corrections facility. Administrators favor video visits because they promote safety and require less work for correctional staffers, who do not need to transport an inmate to a visiting area. There is also a profit motive. For example, Securus Technologies, which provides video communications to thousands of jails, typically charges a dollar a minute for such teleconferences. Twenty percent of this fee goes back to the correctional facility.

Opponents of visual visitation condemn the burden that these costs place on inmates' families, many of which are low income. They also point out that the practice tends to displace face-to-face visits, which have a number of benefits. Research shows that seeing friends and family members in person creates social bonds, lessens stress, and even reduces recidivism among inmates.

Thinking about Video Visits

In some instances, Securus has required that, before using its services, a jail must ban all in-person visitation, forcing inmates to rely on the video feeds to contact loved ones. What is your opinion of this situation, in which a private company is essentially dictating correctional policy?

Jails

Learning 8 Objective

Summarize the distinction between jails and prisons, and indicate the importance of jails in the American corrections system.

Although prisons and prison issues dominate the public discourse on corrections, there is an argument to be made that jails are the dominant penal institutions in the United States. In general, a prison is a facility designed to house people convicted of felonies for lengthy periods of time, while a jail is authorized to hold pretrial detainees and offenders who have committed misdemeanors. On any given day, about 730,000 inmates are in jail in this country, and jails admit approximately 11.7 million persons over the course of a year.[83] Nevertheless, jail funding is often the lowest priority for the tight budgets of local governments, leading to severe overcrowding and other dismal conditions.

Many observers see this negligence as having far-reaching consequences for criminal justice. Jail is often the first contact that citizens have with the corrections system. It is at this point that treatment and counseling have the best chance to deter future criminal behavior.[84] By failing to take advantage of this opportunity, says Professor Franklin Zimring of the University of California, Berkeley School of Law, corrections officials have created a situation in which "today's jail folk are tomorrow's prisoners."[85] (To better understand the role that these two correctional institutions play in the criminal justice system, see *Mastering Concepts—The Main Differences between Prisons and Jails*.)

The Jail Population

Like their counterparts in state prisons, jail inmates are overwhelmingly young male adults. About 48 percent of jail inmates are white, 35 percent are African American, and 14 percent are Latino.[86] The main difference between state prison and jail inmates involves their criminal activity. As Figure 13.7 shows, jail inmates are more likely to have been convicted of nonviolent crimes than their counterparts in state prison.

Pretrial Detainees A significant number of those detained in jails—about 435,000 inmates on any given day[87]—technically are not prisoners. They are **pretrial detainees** who have been arrested by the police and, for a variety of reasons that we

Jail A facility, usually operated by the county government, used to hold persons awaiting trial or those who have been found guilty of minor crimes (mostly misdemeanors).

Pretrial Detainees Individuals who cannot post bail after arrest and are therefore forced to spend the time prior to their trial incarcerated in jail.

MASTERING CONCEPTS

The Main Differences between Prisons and Jails

PRISONS	JAILS
1. . . . are operated by the federal and state governments.	. . . are operated by county and city governments.
2. . . . hold inmates who may have lived quite far away before being arrested.	. . . hold mostly inmates from the local community.
3. . . . house only those who have been convicted of a crime.	. . . house those who are awaiting trial or have recently been arrested, in addition to convicts.
4. . . . generally hold inmates who have been found guilty of serious crimes and received sentences of longer than one year.	. . . generally hold inmates who have been found guilty of minor crimes and are serving sentences of less than a year.
5. . . . often offer a wide variety of rehabilitation and educational programs for long-term prisoners.	. . . due to smaller budgets, tend to focus only on the necessities of safety, food, and clothing.

FIGURE 13.7 Types of Offenses of Prison and Jail Inmates

As the comparison below shows, jail inmates are more likely than state prisoners to have been convicted of nonviolent crimes. This underscores the main function of jails: to house less serious offenders for a relatively short period of time.

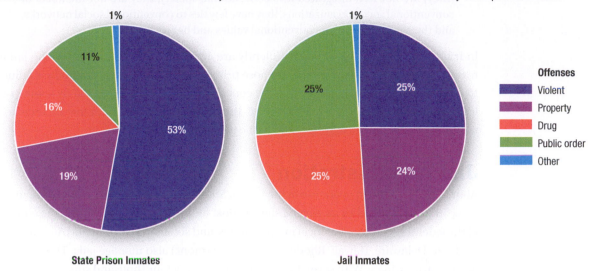

State Prison Inmates

Jail Inmates

Offenses
- Violent
- Property
- Drug
- Public order
- Other

Source: Bureau of Justice Statistics, *Prisoners in 2015* (Washington, D.C.: U.S. Department of Justice, September 2014), Table 9, page 14; and Bureau of Justice Statistics, *Profile of Jail Inmates, 2002* (Washington, D.C.: U.S. Department of Justice, July 2004), 1.

discussed in Chapter 9, are unable to post bail. Pretrial detainees are, in many ways, walking legal contradictions. According to the U.S. Constitution, they are innocent until proved guilty. At the same time, by being incarcerated while awaiting trial, they are denied a number of personal freedoms and are subjected to the poor conditions of many jails.

In *Bell v. Wolfish* (1979), the Supreme Court rejected the notion that this situation is inherently unfair by refusing to give pretrial detainees greater legal protections than sentenced jail inmates have.[88] In essence, the Court recognized that treating pretrial detainees differently from convicted jail inmates would place too much of a burden on corrections officials and was therefore impractical.[89]

Sentenced Jail Inmates According to the U.S. Department of Justice, about 38 percent of those in jail have been convicted of their current charges.[90] In other words, they have been found guilty of a crime, usually a misdemeanor, and sentenced to time in jail. The typical jail term lasts between thirty and ninety days, and rarely does a prisoner spend more than one year in jail for any single crime. Often, a judge will credit the length of time the convict has spent in detention waiting for trial—known as **time served**—toward his or her sentence. This practice acknowledges two realities of jails:

1. Terms are generally too short to allow the prisoner to gain any benefit (that is, rehabilitation) from the jail's often limited or nonexistent treatment facilities. Therefore, the jail term can serve no purpose except to punish the wrongdoer. (Judges who believe jail time can serve purposes of deterrence and incapacitation may not agree with this line of reasoning.)
2. Jails are chronically overcrowded, and judges need to clear space for new offenders.

Other Jail Inmates Pretrial detainees and those convicted of misdemeanors make up the majority of the jail population. Jail inmates also include probation and parole violators, mentally ill inmates, juveniles awaiting transfer to juvenile authorities, and immigration law violators being held for the federal government. Increasingly, jails are also called on to handle the overflow from state prisons that have reached or surpassed their population capacities.

Time Served The period of time a person denied bail (or unable to pay it) has spent in jail prior to his or her trial.

The Sociology of Jail   According to sociologist John Irwin, the unofficial purpose of a jail is to manage society's "rabble," so called because

> [they] are not well integrated into conventional society, they are not members of conventional social organizations, they have few ties to conventional social networks, and they are carriers of unconventional values and beliefs.[91]

In Irwin's opinion, rabble who act violently are arrested and sent to prison. The jail is reserved for merely offensive rabble, whose primary threat to society lies in their failure to conform to its behavioral norms. This concept of rabble has been used by some critics of American corrections to explain the disproportionate number of low-income and minority offenders who may be found in the nation's jails at any time.

Jail Administration

About 3,300 jails are in operation in the United States. The vast majority of these are managed on a county level by an elected sheriff. Most of the remainder are under the control of the federal government or local municipalities, and six state governments (Alaska, Connecticut, Delaware, Hawaii, Rhode Island, and Vermont) also manage jails. The capacity of jails varies widely. With seven facilities encompassing four thousand square miles, the Los Angeles County Jail houses a daily average of about 19,000 inmates. Jails that large are, however, the exception rather than the rule. About half of all jails in this country house fewer than five hundred inmates.[92]

Many jails operate on the principle of a **fee system,** in which a government agency reimburses the sheriff's department for the daily cost of housing and feeding each inmate. This practice is often problematic, because once the daily fee per inmate has been established (at, say, $8), the sheriff is free to divert some of those funds to other areas of need in her or his department. Also, it is not uncommon for sheriffs' departments to charge inmates "pay-to-stay" fees for aspects of their incarceration such as food, clothing, and medical and dental care.

The "Burden" of Jail Administration   Given that the public's opinion of jails ranges from negative to indifferent, some sheriffs neglect their jail management duties. Instead, they focus on high-visibility issues such as putting more law enforcement officers on the streets and improving security in schools. In fact, a jail usually receives publicity only after an escape or an incident in which inmates are abused by jailers.

Nonetheless, with their complex and diverse populations, jails are often more difficult to manage than prisons. Jails hold people who have never been incarcerated before and who exhibit a range of behavior—from nonviolent to extremely violent—that only adds to the unpredictable atmosphere. Jail inmates have a number of other problems, including:

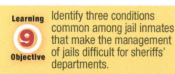

Learning Objective 9 Identify three conditions common among jail inmates that make the management of jails difficult for sheriffs' departments.

1. *Mental illness.* About 60 percent of jail inmates have a history of mental illness, including symptoms of schizophrenia, depression, hallucinations, and suicidal tendencies.[93]
2. *Physical health problems and disabilities.* More than one-third of jail inmates report having a current medical problem such as an injury or ailments such as arthritis, asthma, or sexually transmitted diseases.[94] Furthermore, about 40 percent have disabilities in areas such as hearing, vision, and cognition.[95]
3. *Substance abuse and dependency.* About two-thirds of jail inmates are dependent on alcohol or other drugs, and half of all convicted jail inmates were under the influence of drugs or alcohol at the time of their arrest.[96]

Given that most jails lack the resources and facilities to properly deal with these problems, the task of managing jail inmate populations falls disproportionately on untrained prison staff. Speaking of mentally ill inmates at Rikers Island, New York City's main jail complex, one corrections official said, "They need medication, treatment, [and] psychological help. They don't need a corrections officer."[97] In response to these challenges, jails in cities such as Chicago, Miami, New York, and Los Angeles have recently taken drastic steps to improve living conditions for at-need inmate populations (see Figure 13.8).

One problem that consistently plagues jails is the inability to live up to the American Correctional Association's requirement that they "operate effectively as self-contained communities in which all necessary goods are provided in a safe, secure, and controlled manner."[98] Given the challenges just mentioned, many jails need expensive upgrades to (1) add bed space for increased inmate populations and (2) provide better health and psychiatric care. So, for example, the new Muskegon (Michigan) County Jail, which opened in 2015, has 600 inmate beds (up from 370 in the old jail) and a "medical triage" center to better determine the health needs of inmates during the intake process.[99]

The Challenges of Overcrowding   Overcrowding exacerbates the difficulties involved in jail management. Cells intended to hold one or two people are packed with up to six. Inmates are forced to sleep in hallways. Treatment facilities, when they exist, are overwhelmed. In such stressful situations, tempers flare, leading to violent, aggressive behavior. The jails most likely to suffer from such issues are those in heavily populated metropolitan areas with large numbers of "pass through" pretrial detainees.[100]

Given the emphasis on reducing prison populations discussed throughout this chapter, there are concerns that jails will be forced to house more low-level offenders in the future than they have in the past. As most jurisdictions do not have the resources to build new jails, administrators will have to come up with creative ways to alleviate possible overcrowding. Two possible solutions involve pretrial procedures we discussed in Chapter 9:

1. Increasing options for pretrial release.

2. Speeding up trials so that detainees do not need to spend as much time waiting in jail for court proceedings to begin.[101]

FIGURE 13.8 Miami-Dade County's Criminal Mental Health Project

On any given day, the Miami-Dade County Jail houses about 1,200 inmates who suffer from a *serious mental illness* (or SMI, which includes schizophrenia, bipolar disorder, and major depression), making it the largest psychiatric facility in the state of Florida. To combat this problem, local criminal justice officials have established the following two strategies to divert nonviolent offenders with an SMI from the jail.

STRATEGY #1: PRE-BOOKING DIVERSION	STRATEGY #2: POST-BOOKING DIVERSION
● Provide local police officers with forty hours of Crisis Intervention Team (CIT) training, which helps them recognize SMI symptoms and de-escalate crises involving offenders with mental illnesses.	● All defendants booked into the jail are screened for possible SMI symptoms and, if necessary, referred to the corrections health services psychiatric staff for a more thorough evaluation.
● When appropriate, offenders suffering from an SMI will be taken to a local psychiatric treatment center rather than being arrested and put in jail.	● Those defendants who meet the criteria (nonviolent offender convicted of a misdemeanor, SMI diagnosis) are transferred from the jail to a community-based crisis stabilization facility.
	● With the consent of the defendant, she or he will receive community-based treatment and help in finding housing.

Source: Eleventh Judicial Circuit of Florida.

▲ How does the layout of this direct supervision jail differ from that of the maximum-security prison pictured earlier in the chapter? What do these differences tell you about the security precautions needed for jail inmates as opposed to prison inmates? Photo courtesy Bergen County Sheriff's Office, Bergen, NJ

Also, community corrections—the subject of the previous chapter—can be useful in reducing jail inmate populations. In 2015, about 57,000 offenders sentenced to jail terms were supervised in the community, with nearly a quarter subjected to electronic monitoring.[102]

New-Generation Jails

For most of the nation's history, the architecture of a jail was secondary to its purpose of keeping inmates safely locked away. Consequently, most jails in the United States continue to resemble those from the days of the Walnut Street Jail in Philadelphia. In this *traditional*, or *linear*, *design*, jail cells are located along a corridor. To supervise the inmates while they are in their cells, custodial officers must walk up and down the corridor, so the number of offenders they can see at any one time is severely limited. With this limited supervision, inmates can more easily break institutional rules.

Podular Design   In the 1970s, planners at the Bureau of Federal Prisons decided to upgrade the traditional jail design with the goal of improving conditions for both the staff and the inmates. The result was the **new-generation jail,** which differs significantly from its predecessors.[103] The layout of the new facilities makes it easier for the staff to monitor cell-confined inmates. The basic structure of the new-generation jail is based on a podular design. Each "pod" contains "living units" for individual prisoners. These units, instead of lining up along a straight corridor, are often situated in a triangle so that a staff member in the center of the triangle has visual access to nearly all the cells.

Daily activities such as eating and showering take place in the pod, which also has an outdoor exercise area. Treatment facilities are also located in the pod, allowing greater access for the inmates. During the day, inmates stay out in the open and are allowed back in their cells only when given permission. The officer locks the door to the cells from his or her control terminal.

Direct Supervision Approach   The podular design also enables a new-generation jail to be managed using a **direct supervision approach.**[104] One or more jail officers are stationed in the living area of the pod and are therefore in constant interaction with all prisoners in that particular pod. Some new-generation jails even provide a desk in the center of the living area, which sends a very different message to the prisoners than the traditional control booth. Theoretically, jail officials who have constant contact with inmates will be able to stem misconduct quickly and efficiently, and will also be able to recognize "danger signs" from individual inmates and stop outbursts before they occur. (As noted earlier in the chapter, corrections officials are using aspects of podular design when building new prisons, for many of the same reasons that the trend has been popular in jails.)

New-Generation Jail A type of jail that is distinguished architecturally from its predecessors by a design that encourages interaction between inmates and jailers and that offers greater opportunities for treatment.

Direct Supervision Approach A process of prison and jail administration in which correctional officers are in continuous visual contact with inmates during the day.

ETHICS CHALLENGE

Jail officials routinely strip-search new inmates to (1) detect lice and other contagious diseases, (2) look for evidence of gang membership such as tattoos, and (3) prevent smuggling of drugs and weapons. These strip searches are highly invasive, often including close examination of the subject's genitals and rectum. Are there any ethical issues with conducting such searches on jail entrants who have not been convicted of a crime? Explain your answer.

Policy Matters

The Right to Vote

How Things Stand

Maine and Vermont are the only two states that have no restrictions on allowing those convicted of felonies to vote. At the other end of the spectrum, in Florida, Iowa, and Kentucky, felons permanently lose their right to vote. The remaining states have a variety of rules regarding felon disenfranchisement, with some allowing probationers and parolees the right to vote and others requiring government action to reinstate this right to a limited class of offenders.[105]

As a Result...

An estimated 6.1 million Americans, or 2.5 percent of the nation's voting population, are not able to participate in our democracy because of past criminal activities. In six states (Alabama, Florida, Kentucky, Mississippi, Tennessee, and Virginia), more than 7 percent of the adult population is prohibited from voting.[106] Because members of minority groups make up a disproportionate percentage of ex-convicts in this country, these groups are also disproportionately impacted by state disenfranchisement laws. According to The Sentencing Project, one of every thirteen African American adults is disenfranchised in the United States because of her or his criminal record.[107]

Indeed, some historians believe that the nation's first laws barring felons from voting, passed following the Civil War (1861–1865), were expressly designed to remove African Americans from the political process.[108] In Alabama, a recent lawsuit alleges that the state law prohibiting a person from voting if she or he has been "convicted of a felony involving moral turpitude" is biased against minority residents. The suit claims that Alabama's vague law disenfranchises about 15 percent of the state's African American adult population, while similarly impacting only 5 percent of its white adult population.[109]

Up for Debate

"If you won't follow the law yourself, then you can't make the law for everyone else, which is what you do—directly or indirectly—when you vote."[110]—*Roger Clegg, president of the Center for Equal Opportunity.*

"Like the antiquated laws that excluded women, people of color, and the poor from the ballot box, felon disenfranchisement laws are an anti-democratic tool with a sordid history of discrimination."[111]—*Janai S. Nelson, associate director counsel at the NAACP Legal Defense Fund.*

What's Your Take?

Review the discussions in this chapter on "The Role of Prisons in Modern Society" and "The Consequences of America's High Rates of Incarceration" before answering the following questions.

1. Do you prefer the custodial model or the reintegration model when it comes to American prisons? How does your answer influence your opinion of state laws that disenfranchise felons?

2. In some states, disenfranchisement is based on the seriousness of the underlying conviction. For example, a felon convicted of attempted murder might be kept from voting, but a felon convicted of drug possession would be allowed to vote. Do you agree with this policy? If so, where would you "draw the line" between crimes that triggered disenfranchisement? Explain your answers.

Digging Deeper...

In 2016, **Virginia governor Terry McAuliffe** attempted to restore the vote to thousands of ex-felons living in the state. Go online to learn more about these **voting reform** efforts. How successful was McAuliffe in expanding voting rights before the 2016 presidential election? What were the arguments made by those on each side of the issue? What role did race and party politics play in the controversy? Your answer should be at least three paragraphs long.

SUMMARY

For more information on these concepts, look back to the Learning Objective icons throughout the chapter.

 Contrast the Pennsylvania and the New York penitentiary theories of the 1800s. Basically, the Pennsylvania system imposed total silence on its prisoners. Based on the concept of separate confinement, penitentiaries were constructed with back-to-back cells facing both outward and inward. Prisoners worked, slept, and ate alone in their cells. In contrast, New York used the congregate system: Silence was imposed, but inmates worked and ate together.

 Explain the three general models of prisons. (a) The custodial model assumes that the prisoner is incarcerated for reasons of incapacitation, deterrence, and retribution. (b) The rehabilitation model puts security concerns second and the well-being of the individual inmate first. As a consequence, treatment programs are offered to prisoners. (c) The reintegration model sees the correctional institution as a training ground for preparing convicts to reenter society.

 Describe the formal prison management system, and indicate the three most important aspects of prison governance. The formal prison management system is militaristic with a hierarchical (top-down) chain of command; the warden (or superintendent) is on top, then deputy wardens, and last, custodial employees. Sound governance of a correctional facility requires officials to provide inmates with a sense of order, amenities such as clean living conditions and acceptable food, and services such as vocational training and remedial education programs.

 List and briefly explain the four types of prisons. (a) Maximum-security prisons, which are designed mainly with security and surveillance in mind. Such prisons are usually large and consist of cell blocks, each of which is set off by a series of gates and bars. (b) Medium-security prisons, which offer considerably more educational and treatment programs and allow more contact between inmates. Such prisons are usually surrounded by high fences rather than by walls. (c) Minimum-security prisons, which permit prisoners to have televisions and computers and often allow them to leave the grounds for educational and employment purposes. (d) Supermaximum-security (supermax) prisons, in which prisoners are confined to one-person cells for up to twenty-three hours per day under constant video camera surveillance.

 Identify some factors that have caused the prison population to grow dramatically in the last several decades. Factors include the willingness of prosecutors to bring felony rather than misdemeanor charges, the enhancement and stricter enforcement of drug laws, the increased probability of incarceration, the increase in time served for each crime, and the expansion of the federal prison system.

 Indicate some of the consequences of our high rates of incarceration. Some people believe that the reduction in the country's crime rate is a direct result of increased incarceration rates. Others believe that high incarceration rates are having increasingly negative social consequences, such as financial hardships, reduced supervision and discipline of children, and a general deterioration of the family structure when one parent is in prison.

 Describe the arguments for and against private prisons. Proponents of private prisons contend that they can be run more cheaply and efficiently than public ones. Opponents of prison privatization dispute such claims. They also argue that private prisons are financially motivated to deny inmates the same protections and rights they receive in public correctional facilities.

 Summarize the distinction between jails and prisons, and indicate the importance of jails in the American corrections system. Generally, a prison is for those convicted of felonies who will serve lengthy periods of incarceration, whereas a jail is for those who have been convicted of misdemeanors and will serve less than a year of incarceration. Jails also hold individuals awaiting trial, juveniles awaiting transfer to juvenile authorities, probation and parole violators, and mentally ill inmates. In any given year, almost 12 million people are admitted to jails. It is at this point that treatment and counseling have the best chance to deter future criminal behavior on the part of these low-level offenders.

 Identify three conditions common among jail inmates that make the management of jails difficult for sheriffs' departments. More than half of jail inmates suffer from mental illness. Many also exhibit medical problems or have physical disabilities. In addition, the majority of jail inmates are dependent on alcohol or other drugs.

QUESTIONS FOR CRITICAL ANALYSIS

1. By most measures, the United States imprisons more of its citizens than any other country in the world. Economic considerations aside, what is your opinion of our dramatically high incarceration rates?

2. Would you be in favor of a policy that prohibited corrections administrators from housing inmates with a preexisting mental illness in supermax prisons? Why or why not?

3. Do you agree with the argument that private prisons are inherently unjust, no matter what costs they may save taxpayers? Why or why not?

4. Why have pretrial detainees been called "walking legal contradictions"? What are the practical reasons why pretrial detainees will continue to be housed in jails prior to trial, regardless of whether their incarceration presents any constitutional irregularities?

5. Experience shows that building new jails does little or nothing to alleviate jail overcrowding. Why might this be the case?

KEY TERMS

classification 432

congregate system 426

custody level 432

direct supervision approach 448

fee system 446

jail 444

lockdown 435

maximum-security prison 433

medical model 427

medium-security prison 436

minimum-security prison 436

new-generation jail 448

penitentiary 425

pretrial detainees 444

private prisons 441

separate confinement 426

supermax prison 435

time served 445

warden 430

NOTES

1. James M. Beattie, *Crime and the Courts in England, 1660–1800* (Princeton, N.J.: Princeton University Press, 1986), 506–507.

2. Samuel Walker, *Popular Justice* (New York: Oxford University Press, 1980), 11.

3. Michael Meranze, *Laboratories of Virtue: Punishment, Revolution, and Authority in Philadelphia, 1760–1835* (Chapel Hill: University of North Carolina Press, 1996), 55.

4. Negley K. Teeters, *The Cradle of the Penitentiary: The Walnut Street Jail at Philadelphia, 1773–1835* (Philadelphia: Pennsylvania Prison Society, 1955), 30.

5. Negley K. Teeters and John D. Shearer, *The Prison at Philadelphia's Cherry Hill* (New York: Columbia University Press, 1957), 142–143.

6. Henry Calvin Mohler, "Convict Labor Policies," *Journal of the American Institute of Criminal Law and Criminology* 15 (1925), 556–557.

7. Zebulon Brockway, *Fifty Years of Prison Service* (Montclair, N.J.: Patterson Smith, 1969), 400–401.

8. Robert Martinson, "What Works? Questions and Answers about Prison Reform," *Public Interest* 35 (Spring 1974), 22.

9. See Ted Palmer, "Martinson Revisited," *Journal of Research on Crime and Delinquency* (1975), 133; and Paul Gendreau and Bob Ross, "Effective Correctional Treatment: Bibliotherapy for Cynics," *Crime & Delinquency* 25 (1979), 499.

10. Robert Martinson, "New Findings, New Views: A Note of Caution Regarding Sentencing Reform," *Hofstra Law Review* 7 (1979), 243.

11. Byron Eugene Price and John Charles Morris, eds., *Prison Privatization: The Many Facets of a Controversial Industry*, Volume 1 (Santa Barbara, Calif.: Praeger, 2012), 58.

12. Charles H. Logan, *Criminal Justice Performance Measures in Prisons* (Washington, D.C.: U.S. Department of Justice, 1993), 5.

13. Todd R. Clear and George F. Cole, *American Corrections*, 4th ed. (Belmont, Calif.: Wadsworth Publishing Co., 1997), 245–246.

14. Alfred Blumstein, "Prisons," in *Crime*, eds. James Q. Wilson and Joan Petersilia (San Francisco: ICS Press, 1995), 392.

15. Cassia Spohn and David Holleran, "The Effect of Imprisonment on Recidivism Rates of Felony Offenders: A Focus on Drug Offenders," *Criminology* (May 1, 2002), 329–357.

16. Bureau of Justice Statistics, *Census of State and Federal Correctional Facilities, 2005* (Washington, D.C.: U.S. Department of Justice, October 2008), 2.

17. *Ibid.*

18. Charles H. Logan, "Well Kept: Comparing Quality of Confinement in a Public and Private Prison," *Journal of Criminal Law and Criminology* 83 (1992), 580.

19. Bert Useem and Peter Kimball, *Stages of Siege: U.S. Prison Riots, 1971–1986* (New York: Oxford University Press, 1989).

20. Bert Useem, "Disorganization and the New Mexico Prison Riot of 1980," *American Sociology Review* 50 (1985), 685.

21. Peter M. Carlson and John J. DiIulio, Jr., "Organization and the Management of the Prison," in *Prison and Jail Administration: Practice and Theory*, 3rd ed., ed. Peter M. Carlson (Burlington, Mass.: Jones & Bartlett Learning, 2015), 272.

22. John J. DiIulio, *Governing Prisons* (New York: Free Press, 1987), 12.

23. *Ibid.*

24. Todd R. Clear, George F. Cole, and Michael D. Reisig, *American Corrections*, 11th ed. (Boston: Wadsworth Cengage Learning, 2016), 155–156.

25. Peter M. Carlson, "Inmate Classification," in *Prison and Jail Administration: Practice and Theory*, 3rd ed., *op. cit.*, 53–57.

26. Douglas Page, "The Prison of the Future," *Law Enforcement Technology* (January 2012), 11–13.

27. Daniel P. Mears, "Supermax Prisons: The Policy and the Evidence," *Criminology and Public Policy* (November 2013), 684.

28. Keramet Reiter, *Parole, Snitch, or Die: California's Supermax Prisons and Prisoners, 1987–2007* (Berkeley: University of California Institute for the Study of Social Change, 2010), 1.

29. "Facts about Pelican Bay's SHU," *California Prisoner* (December 1991).

30. *Jones-El et al. v. Berge and Lichter*, 164 F.Supp.2d 1096 (2001).

31. Robert Perkinson, "Shackled Justice: Florence Federal Penitentiary and the New Politics of Punishment," *Social Justice* (Fall 1994), 117–123.

32. Terry Kuppers, *Prison Madness: The Mental Health Crisis behind Bars and What We Must Do about It* (San Francisco: Jossey-Bass, 1999), 56–64.

33. David Brooks, "The Prison Problem," *New York Times* (September 29, 2015), A27.

34. Bureau of Justice Statistics, *Prisoners in 2015* (Washington, D.C.: U.S. Department of Justice, December 2016), Table 9, page 14; and Table 10, page 15.

35. Allen J. Beck, "Growth, Change, and Stability in the U.S. Prison Population, 1980–1995," *Corrections Management Quarterly* (Spring 1997), 9–10.

36. John Pfaff, "The Micro and Macro Causes of Prison Growth," *Georgia State Law Review* (Summer 2012), 1237–1271.

37. "Table D-5: U.S. District Courts—Criminal Defendants Sentenced after Conviction, by Offense, during the 12-Month Period Ending September 30, 2015." *www.uscourts.gov*. U.S. District Courts: 2016, Web.

38. Joan Petersilia, "Beyond the Prison Bubble," *Wilson Quarterly* (Winter 2011), 27.

39. *Time Served: The High Cost, Low Return of Longer Prison Terms* (Washington, D.C.: The Pew Center on the States, June 2012), 2.

40. *Fifteen Years of Guidelines Sentencing: An Assessment of How Well the Federal Criminal Justice System Is Achieving the Goals of Sentencing Reform* (Washington, D.C.: U.S. Sentencing Commission, November 2004), 46.

41. *Prisoners in 2015, op. cit.*, Table 1, page 3.

42. *Ibid.*

43. Julie Samuels, Nancy La Vigne, and Samuel Taxy, *Stemming the Tide: Strategies to Reduce the Growth and Cut the Cost of the Federal Prison System* (Washington, D.C.: Urban Institute, November 2013), 1.

44. Comprehensive Crime Control Act of 1984, Public Law Number 98–473.

45. *Prisoners in 2015, op. cit.*, Appendix table 6, page 31.

46. "Inmate Gender." *www.bop.gov*. Federal Bureau of Prisons: January 28, 2017, Web.

47. Bureau of Justice Statistics, *Prisoners in 2012: Trends in Admissions and Releases, 1991–2012* (Washington, D.C.: U.S. Department of Justice, December 2013), Appendix table 10, page 43; and Bureau of Justice Statistics, *Prison and Jail Inmates 1995* (Washington, D.C.: U.S. Department of Justice, August 1996), Table 6, page 6.

48. Quoted in Jeremy Travis, "Assessing the State of Mass Incarceration: Tipping Point or the New Normal?" *Criminology & Public Policy* (November 2014), 571.

49. Rosemary Gartner, Anthony N. Doob, and Franklin E. Zimring, "The Past as Prologue? Decarceration in California Then and Now," *Criminology & Public Policy* (May 2011), 294–296.

50. Samantha Harvell, Jeremy Welsh-Loveman, and Hanna Love, *Reforming Sentencing and Corrections Policy* (Washington, D.C.: Urban Institute, December 2016), 6.

51. "What You Need to Know about the New Federal Prison Release." *www.themarshallproject.org*. The Marshall Project: October 29, 2015, Web.

52. "The Right Choices," *The Economist* (June 20, 2015), 26.

53. "Prison Population Trends 1999–2014: Broad Variation among States in Recent Years," *www.sentencingproject.org*. The Sentencing Project: February 16, 2016, Web.

54. Quoted in Leon Neyfakh, "Why Are So Many Americans in Prison?" *www.slate.com*. *Slate:* February 6, 2015, Web.

55. Dan Seligman, "Lock 'Em Up," *Forbes* (May 23, 2005), 216–217.

56. Quoted in Michael S. Schmidt, "U.S. to Begin Freeing 6,000 from Prisons," *New York Times* (October 7, 2015), A1.

57. "Freed but Forgotten." *www.usatoday.com* *USA Today:* December 14, 2016, Web.

58. "California Crime Initiative Leads to Lowest Arrest Rate in State's History," *Associated Press* (August 22, 2016).

59. Rob Kuznia, "An Unprecedented Experiment in Mass Forgiveness." *www.washingtonpost.com*. *Washington Post:* February 8, 2016, Web.

60. Bureau of Justice Statistics, *Parents in Prison and Their Minor Children* (Washington, D.C.: U.S. Department of Justice, March 2010), 1.

61. John Tierney, "Prison and the Poverty Trap," *New York Times* (February 19, 2013), D1.

62. *Ibid.*

63. *Rethinking the Blues: How We Police in the U.S. and at What Cost* (Washington, D.C.: Justice Policy Institute, May 2012), 34.

64. *Prisoners in 2015, op. cit.*, Table 5, page 8.

65. Bryan L. Sikes and Michelle Morato, "A Wealth of Inequalities: Mass Incarceration, Employment, and Racial Disparities in U.S. Household Wealth, 1996 to 2011," *The Russell Sage Foundation Journal of the Social Sciences* (October 2016), 129–152.

66. Quoted in Scott Cohn, "Private Prison Industry Grows Despite Critics." *www.nbcnews.com*. *CNBC.com:* October 18, 2011, Web.

67. *Prisoners in 2015, op. cit.* Appendix table 2, page 28.

68. "A Tale of Two Systems: Cost, Quality, and Accountability in Private Prisons," *Harvard Law Review* (May 2002), 1872.

69. "Federal Prison System per Capita Costs." *www.bop.gov*. Bureau of Prisons: 2015, Web.

70. Simon Hakin and Erwin A. Blackstone, *Prison Break: A New Approach to Public Cost and Safety* (Oakland, Calif.: The Independent Institute, June 2014), 4.

71. Jennifer Palmer, "Adding Beds Isn't Enough to Address Oklahoma Prison Overcrowding, Experts Say." *www.newsok.com. The Oklahoman:* October 25, 2015, Web.

72. Jennifer Sullivan, "Overcrowding to Force State to Export Prisoners to Michigan." *www.seattletimes.com. Seattle Times:* June 2, 2015, Web.

73. Gerald G. Gaes, "The Current Status of Prison Privatization Research on American Prisons." *www.works.bepress.com. Selected Works:* 2012, Web.

74. "Prisoners, Sheriffs Say Abuse Led to Prison Riot in Kingman," *Associated Press* (August 13, 2015).

75. Timothy Williams, "Privately Run Mississippi Prison, Ruled a Scene of Horror and Corruption, Closes," *New York Times* (September 16, 2016), A12.

76. Gregory Geisler, *CIIC: Lake Erie Correctional Institution* (Columbus, Ohio: Correctional Institution Inspection Committee, January 2013), 16.

77. Curtis R. Blakely and Vic W. Bumphus, "Private and Public Sector Prisons," *Federal Probation* (June 2004), 27.

78. John DiIulio, "Prisons, Profits, and the Public Good: The Privatization of Corrections," in *Criminal Justice Center Bulletin* (Huntsville, Tex.: Sam Houston State University, 1986).

79. David M. Siegel, "Internalizing Private Prison Externalities: Let's Start with the GED," *New England Law* (February 4, 2016), 4–5.

80. Quoted in Cohn, *op. cit.*

81. Brian Bennett, "U.S. Rethinks Immigrant Holding Sites," *Los Angeles Times* (September 6, 2016), A1.

82. Fredreka Schouten, "Private Prisons Bank on Trump," *USA Today* (February 24, 2017), 1A.

83. Bureau of Justice Statistics, *Jail Inmates in 2015* (Washington, D.C.: U.S. Department of Justice, December 2016), 1.

84. Arthur Wallenstein, "Jail Crowding: Bringing the Issue to the Corrections Center Stage," *Corrections Today* (December 1996), 76–81.

85. Quoted in Fox Butterfield, "'Defying Gravity,' Inmate Population Climbs," *New York Times* (January 19, 1998), A10.

86. *Jail Inmates in 2015, op. cit.*, Table 3, page 4.

87. *Ibid.*

88. 441 U.S. 520 (1979).

89. *Ibid.*, at 546.

90. *Jail Inmates in 2015, op. cit.*, Table 3, page 4.

91. John Irwin, *The Jail: Managing the Underclass in American Society* (Berkeley: University of California Press, 1985), 2.

92. Bureau of Justice Statistics, *Census of Jails: Population Changes, 1993–2013* (Washington, D.C.: U.S. Department of Justice, December 2015), 3.

93. Doris J. James and Lauren E. Glaze, *Bureau of Justice Statistics Special Report: Mental Health Problems of Prison and Jail Inmates* (Washington, D.C.: U.S. Department of Justice, September 2006), 1.

94. Bureau of Justice Statistics, *Medical Problems of State and Federal Prison and Jail Inmates, 2011–2012* (Washington, D.C.: U.S. Department of Justice, October 2016), 11.

95. Bureau of Justice Statistics, *Disabilities among Prison and Jail Inmates, 2011–12* (Washington, D.C.: U.S. Department of Justice, December 2015), 1.

96. Jennifer C. Karberg and Doris J. James, *Bureau of Justice Statistics Special Report: Substance Dependence, Abuse, and Treatment of Jail Inmates, 2002* (Washington, D.C.: U.S. Department of Justice, July 2005), 1.

97. Quoted in Michael Schwirtz, "Rikers Island Struggles with a Surge in Violence and Mental Illness," *New York Times* (March 19, 2014), A1.

98. Quoted in Sara Scullin, "Building to a Better Blueprint," *Law Enforcement Technology* (June 1015), 21.

99. Heather L. Peters, "Tour of New Muskegon County Jail Brings Out Hundreds of Curious Citizens," *www.mlive.com.* Mlive.com: August 22, 2015, Web.

100. Clear, Cole, and Reisig, *op. cit.*, 183.

101. Mark Cuniff, *Jail Crowding: Understanding Jail Population Dynamics* (Washington, D.C.: National Institute of Corrections, January 2002), 36.

102. *Jail Inmates in 2015, op. cit.*, 8.

103. R. L. Miller, "New Generation Justice Facilities: The Case for Direct Supervision," *Architectural Technology* 12 (1985), 6–7.

104. David Bogard, Virginia A. Hutchinson, and Vicci Persons, *Direct Supervision Jails: The Role of the Administrator* (Washington, D.C.: National Institute of Corrections, February 2010), 1–2.

105. "6 Million Lost Voters: State-Level Estimates of Felony Disenfranchisement, 2016. Table 1." *www.sentencingproject.org.* The Sentencing Project: October 6, 2016, Web.

106. *Ibid.*

107. *Ibid.*

108. Angela Behrens, Christopher Uggen, and Jeff Manza, "Ballot Manipulation and the 'Menace of Negro Domination': Racial Threat and Felon Disenfranchisement in the United States, 1850–2002," *American Journal of Sociology* (November 2003), 559.

109. Campbell Robertson, "Suit Accuses Alabama of Bias in Law that Bars Some Felons from Voting," *New York Times* (September 27, 2016), A10.

110. Roger Clegg, "If You Can't Follow the Laws, You Shouldn't Help Make Them." *www.nytimes.com. New York Times:* April 22, 2016, Web.

111. Janai S. Nelson, "Felon Disenfranchisement Is Anti-Democratic." *www.nytimes.com. New York Times:* April 22, 2016, Web.

RECEIVING & RELEASE

ATTENTION
PROPERTY TO R&R
LAYOVER PROPERTY.

ATTENTION
DO NOT UNLOAD YOUR VEHICLE WITHOUT
AUTHORIZATION FROM R&R STAFF.

A
DELI
MED

RCCC

454

14

The Prison Experience and Prisoner Reentry

To target your study and review, look for these numbered Learning Objective icons throughout the chapter.

Chapter Outline		Corresponding Learning Objectives
Prison Culture	**1**	Explain the concept of prison as a total institution.
	2	Describe a risk run by corrections officials who fail to provide adequate medical care to the inmates under their control.
Prison Violence	**3**	Indicate some of the reasons for violent behavior in prisons.
Correctional Officers and Discipline	**4**	List the circumstances in which courts have found that the "legitimate security interests" of a jail or prison justify the use of force by correctional officers.
	5	Describe the hands-off doctrine of prisoner law and indicate two standards used to determine if prisoners' rights have been violated.
Inside a Women's Prison	**6**	Explain the aspects of imprisonment that prove challenging for incarcerated mothers and their children.
Return to Society	**7**	Contrast parole, expiration release, pardon, and furlough.
	8	Explain the goal of prisoner reentry programs.
	9	Indicate typical conditions for release for a paroled sex offender.

Two Strikes

▲ A prisoner pushes a bin of greens inside a food processing plant at the Louisiana State Penitentiary in Angola, where inmate workers are paid as little as two cents an hour. AP Images/Gerald Herbert

In 2016, a coalition of community leaders and prison inmates calling themselves the Free Alabama Movement released a document entitled "Our Freedom Bill." Among other stipulations, this manifesto demanded the elimination of "all laws that permit slavery" in Alabama. This request was not quite as extreme as it might have seemed. While the Thirteenth Amendment to the U.S. Constitution, ratified in 1865, did abolish slavery, it provided an exception for jobs performed "as a punishment for a crime." As a result of this loophole, almost every prison inmate in the United States, if physically and mentally able, works for little or no compensation.

The variety of prison employment is enormous, from on-site maintenance and kitchen duty, to firefighting, to building products for companies such as McDonald's, Wal-Mart, and Victoria's Secret. At the most, inmates in federal prisons receive salaries of up to $1.14 an hour. At the least, a number of states, including Alabama, do not pay inmates at all. To draw attention to this version of "slavery," on September 9, 2016, members of the Free Alabama Movement at the William C. Holman Correctional Facility in Atmore organized a strike. That day, about 75 inmates at Holman refused to work. Over the next several weeks, as news of this action spread through social media, approximately 24,000 prisoners in twelve other states joined the cause.

The inmate work strike was not the only sign of labor unrest at Holman prison that month. On September 24, nine correctional officers stayed home to protest the institution's chronic understaffing. Holman had already experienced a number of violent riots that year, and on September 1, an inmate had fatally stabbed a correctional officer following a dispute over food portions. "Officers are refusing to go in the cells because of the violence and won't respond to emergency situations because they think it's too dangerous," said one inmate, who claimed that four stabbings a day were taking place at Holman. "Basically, prisoners are just policing themselves."

FOR CRITICAL ANALYSIS

1. Do you think it is fair that inmates receive low wages, or no wages, for doing work while incarcerated? Why or why not? What benefits besides being paid could be associated with prison work?

2. At a prison in South Carolina, inmates who took part in the work strike were punished by losing telephone and visitation privileges, and some were locked in solitary confinement. Do you think such disciplinary steps are justified? Why or why not?

3. Most Alabama prisons house their inmates in large dormitories, with 90 to 150 offenders in each room. Single beds and bunks are often only two feet apart. Why might this environment be more conducive to violence than if inmates lived in separate cells?

Prison Culture

In this chapter, we will look at the life of the imprisoned convict, starting with the realities of an existence behind bars and finishing with the challenges of returning to free society. Along the way, we will discuss violence in prison, correctional officers, women's prisons, different types of release, and several other issues that are at the forefront of American corrections today. To start, we must understand the forces that shape prison culture and how those forces affect the overall operation of the correctional facility.

Any institution, whether a school, a bank, or a police department, has an organizational culture—a set of values that help the people in the organization understand what actions are acceptable and what actions are unacceptable. According to a theory put forth by the influential sociologist Erving Goffman, prison cultures are unique because prisons are **total institutions** that encompass every aspect of an inmate's life. Unlike a student or a bank teller, a prisoner cannot leave the institution or have any meaningful interaction with outside communities. Others arrange every aspect of daily life, and all prisoners are required to follow this schedule in the same manner.[1]

Inmates develop their own argot, or way of speaking. They also have their own way of expressing themselves through body art (see Figure 14.1). They create their own economy, which, in the absence of currency, is based on the barter of valued commodities such as food, contraband, and sexual favors. They establish methods of determining power, many of which, as we shall see, involve violence. Isolated and heavily regulated, prisoners create a social existence that is, out of both necessity and design, separate from the outside world.

Total Institution An institution, such as a prison, that provides all of the necessities for existence to those who live within its boundaries.

FIGURE 14.1 Prison Tattoos

Using makeshift needles and ink from contraband pens or melted plastic, many inmates have become proficient at the art of tattooing. These tattoos help establish the inmate's place in prison culture by symbolizing concepts such as toughness, racism, and the length of time spent behind bars.

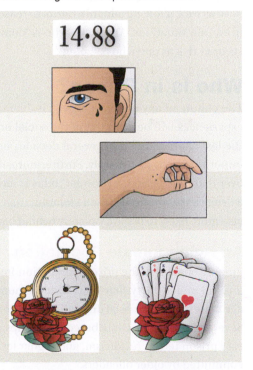

1488 These numbers are worn by inmates who consider themselves white supremacists or Nazi sympathizers. The number 14 refers to the number of words in a speech made by white supremacist David Lane; 88 refers to the doubling of the eighth letter of the alphabet, as in "Heil Hitler."

A teardrop Depending on the location of the prison, a teardrop can indicate that the wearer is serving a lengthy prison sentence or that the wearer has committed murder.

Three dots Typically found on the hands or around the eyes, this logo refers to *"mi vida loca,"* or "my crazy life." It acknowledges an allegiance to the gang lifestyle.

A clock with no hands This image indicates that the wearer is spending a lengthy amount of time behind bars.

Playing cards Playing cards, as well as card suits (spades, clubs, hearts, and diamonds), have two meanings: (1) literally, that the inmate likes to participate in games of chance, such as poker, and (2) figuratively, that the inmate takes risks in real life.

Source: Correctionsone.com.

Adapting to Prison Society

On arriving at prison, each convict attends an orientation session and receives a "Resident's Handbook." The handbook provides information such as meal and official count times, disciplinary regulations, and visitation guidelines. The norms and values of the prison society, however, cannot be communicated by the staff or learned from a handbook. As first described by Donald Clemmer in his classic 1940 work, *The Prison Community*, the process of prisonization—or adaptation to the prison culture—advances as the inmate gradually understands what constitutes acceptable behavior in the institution, as defined not by the prison officials but by other inmates.[2]

In studying prisonization, criminologists have focused on two areas: how prisoners change their behavior to adapt to life behind bars, and how life behind bars has changed because of inmate behavior. Sociologist John Irwin has identified several patterns of inmate behavior, each one driven by the inmate's personality and values:

1. Professional criminals adapt to prison by "doing time." In other words, they follow the rules and generally do whatever is necessary to speed up their release and return to freedom.

2. Some convicts, mostly state-raised youths or those frequently incarcerated in juvenile detention centers, are more comfortable inside prison than outside. These inmates serve time by "jailing," or establishing themselves in the power structure of prison culture.

3. Other inmates take advantage of prison resources such as libraries or drug treatment programs by "gleaning," or working to improve themselves to prepare for a return to society.

4. Finally, "disorganized" criminals exist on the fringes of prison society. These inmates may have mental impairments or low levels of intelligence, and find it impossible to adapt to prison culture on any level.[3]

The process of categorizing prisoners has a theoretical basis, but it serves a practical purpose as well, allowing administrators to reasonably predict how different inmates will act in certain situations. An inmate who is "doing time" generally does not present the same security risk as one who is "jailing."

Who Is in Prison?

The culture of any prison is heavily influenced by its inmates. Their values, beliefs, and experiences will be reflected in the social order that exists behind bars. As we noted in the last chapter, the past several decades have seen incarceration rates of women and minority groups rise sharply. Furthermore, the arrest patterns of inmates have changed over that time period. A prisoner today is much more likely to have been incarcerated on a drug charge or immigration violation than was the case in the 1980s. Today's inmate is also more likely to behave violently behind bars—a situation that will be addressed shortly.

An Aging Inmate Population   In recent years, the most significant demographic change in the prison population involves age. Though the majority of inmates are still under thirty-four years old, the number of state and federal prisoners over the age of forty has increased dramatically since the mid-1990s, as you can see in Figure 14.2. Several factors have contributed to this upsurge, including longer prison terms, mandatory prison terms, recidivism, and higher levels of crimes—particularly violent crimes—committed by older offenders.[4]

Prisonization The socialization process through which a new inmate learns the accepted norms and values of the prison culture.

An Ailing Inmate Population Overall, about half of those incarcerated in the United States (including federal and state prisoners and jail inmates) report having a chronic medical condition such as cancer, high blood pressure, diabetes, or asthma.[5] Furthermore, given the frailties of older inmates, prisons and jails are now holding more people with medical issues than in the past. Poor health is the cause of nine of ten inmate deaths in state prisons, with heart disease and cancer accounting for over half of these fatalities.[6] Not surprisingly, the mortality rates of inmates fifty-five and older from heart disease and cancer are significantly higher than those of any other age group.[7]

Corrections budgets are straining under the financial pressures caused by the health-care needs of aging inmates. In the federal prison system, the annual cost of housing an inmate who has health problems—many of whom are over fifty-five years of age—is more than twice the cost of housing a prisoner in the general population.[8] About half of the nearly $60 million that Virginia spends annually on off-site prison medical treatment goes for the care of older inmates.[9] Given the burden of inmate medical costs, state corrections officials may be tempted to cut such services whenever possible. As the feature *Landmark Cases*—Brown v. Plata shows, however, prisoners have a constitutional right to adequate health care.

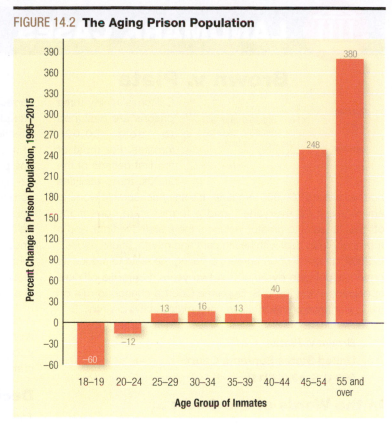

FIGURE 14.2 **The Aging Prison Population**

Sources: Bureau of Justice Statistics, *Prisoners in 2003* (Washington, D.C.: U.S. Department of Justice, November 2004), Table 10, page 8; Bureau of Justice Statistics, *Prisoners in 2015* (Washington, D.C.: U.S. Department of Justice, December 2016), Table 8, page 13.

Mental Illness behind Bars Another factor in rising correctional health-care costs is the high incidence of mental illness in American prisons and jails. During the 1950s and 1960s, nearly 600,000 mental patients lived in public hospitals, often against their will. A series of scandals spotlighting the poor medical services and horrendous living conditions in these institutions led to their closure and the elimination of much of the nation's state-run mental health infrastructure.[10] Many mentally ill people now receive no supervision whatsoever, and some inevitably commit deviant or criminal acts.

As a result, in the words of criminal justice experts Katherine Stuart van Wormer and Clemens Bartollas, jails and prison have become "the dumping grounds for people whose bizarre behavior lands them behind bars."[11] According to the federal government, half of state prison inmates and 60 percent of jail inmates have experienced mental health problems such as depression or psychosis at a recent point in their lives.[12] As with aging and ailing prisoners, correctional facilities are required by law to provide treatment to mentally ill inmates, thus driving the costs associated with their confinement well above the average. For reasons that should become clear over the course of this chapter, correctional facilities are not designed to foster mental well-being, and indeed inmates with mental illnesses often find that their problems are exacerbated by the prison environment.[13]

LANDMARK CASES

Brown v. Plata

Learning Objective 2 Describe a risk run by corrections officials who fail to provide adequate medical care to the inmates under their control.

California's thirty-three prisons are designed to hold 80,000 inmates. For most of the first decade of the 2000s, these facilities housed around 160,000 inmates. "It's an unacceptable working environment for everyone," said a former state corrections official. "It leads to greater violence, more staff overtime, and a total inability to deal with health care and mental illness issues." In 2009, a federal court agreed, ordering the state to reduce its prison population by 30,000 in two years. California officials appealed, giving the U.S. Supreme Court a chance to rule on the importance of medical care for inmates in this country.

Brown v. Plata
United States Supreme Court
563 U.S. 493 (2011)

In the Words of the Court ...

Justice Kennedy, Majority Opinion

For years the medical and mental health care provided by California's prisons has fallen short of minimum constitutional requirements and has failed to meet prisoners' basic health needs. Needless suffering and death have been the well documented result.

Prisoners are crammed into spaces neither designed nor intended to house inmates. As many as 200 prisoners may live in a gymnasium, monitored by as few as two or three correctional officers. * * * The consequences of overcrowding include "increased, substantial risk for transmission of infectious illness" and a suicide rate "approaching an average of one per week." * * * A correctional officer testified that, in one prison, up to 50 sick inmates may be held together in a 12- by 20-foot cage for up to five hours awaiting treatment. The number of staff is inadequate, and prisoners face significant delays in access to care. A prisoner with severe abdominal pain died after a 5-week delay in referral to a specialist; a prisoner with "constant and extreme" chest pain died after an 8-hour delay in evaluation by a doctor; and a prisoner died of testicular cancer after a "failure of MDs to work up for cancer in a young man with 17 months of testicular pain."

A prison that deprives prisoners of basic sustenance, including adequate medical care, is incompatible with the concept of human dignity and has no place in civilized society.

Decision

The Court found that severe overcrowding in California state prisons denied inmates satisfactory levels of mental and physical health care and therefore amounted to unconstitutional cruel and unusual punishment. It ordered the state to reduce the prison population to 137.5 percent of capacity—about 110,000 inmates—by June 2013. (As of May 2017, California's prison population stood at about 130,000.)

FOR CRITICAL ANALYSIS
In his dissent, Justice Alito wrote, "I fear that today's decision will lead to a grim roster of victims." What might be some of the reasons behind this fear? What steps could California corrections officials take to alleviate Alito's worries?

Rehabilitation and Prison Programs

In Chapter 11, we saw that rehabilitation is one of the basic theoretical justifications for punishment. **Prison programs,** which include any organized activities designed to foster rehabilitation, benefit inmates in several ways. On a basic level, these programs get prisoners out of their cells and alleviate the boredom that marks prison and jail life. The programs also help inmates improve their health and skills, giving them a better chance of reintegration into society after release. Consequently, nearly every federal and state prison in the United States offers some form of rehabilitation.[14]

Prison programs are limited, however. Many state inmates suffering from mental illness would benefit from medication and twenty-four-hour psychiatric care. Yet these services are quite rare behind bars, mostly due to their high costs.[15] In addition, as many state prison systems face budget restraints, rehabilitation programs are increasingly subject to a

Prison Programs Organized activities for inmates that are designed to improve their physical and mental health, provide them with vocational skills, or simply keep them busy while incarcerated.

cost-benefit analysis. In other words, for each dollar spent on a program, how many dollars are saved? These savings can be difficult to calculate, but researchers have become skilled at measuring reductions in future criminal behavior—and the costs such behavior would have imposed on society—to determine the usefulness of prison programs.

Substance Abuse Treatment

As we have seen throughout this textbook, there is a strong link between crime and abuse of drugs and alcohol. According to the National Center on Addiction and Substance Abuse (CASA) at New York's Columbia University, 1.5 million prison and jail inmates in the United States meet the medical criteria for substance abuse or addiction. Also according to CASA, only 11 percent of these inmates have received any type of professional treatment behind bars.[16] The most effective substance abuse programs for prisoners require trained staff, lengthy periods of therapy, expensive medication, and community aftercare, and carry a price tag of nearly $10,000 per inmate. If every eligible prisoner in the United States received such treatment, the cost would be $12.6 billion.

Researchers at CASA contend, however, that "the nation would break even in a year" if just one in ten of these inmates remained substance and crime free and employed for one year after release from prison.[17] One method that seems to have had success in this area is therapeutic community (TC) treatment, in which former substance abusers help current addicts change the harmful behavior patterns that lead to drug and alcohol abuse. The Cornerstone program in Oregon, for example, provides prerelease TC to inmates, followed by a six-month program in the community. Full-term participants have showed considerably lower recidivism rates than those who dropped out of Cornerstone before finishing the program.[18]

Vocational and Educational Programs

Even if an ex-convict does stay substance free, he or she will have a difficult time finding a steady paycheck. Employers are only about half as likely to hire job applicants with criminal records as they are those with "clean sheets."[19] To overcome this handicap, more than half of all American prisons offer *vocational* training, or prison programs that provide inmates with skills necessary to find a job. Such programs commonly provide instruction in blue-collar fields such as landscaping, automobile repair, and electrical work. Nine out of ten prisons also attempt to educate their inmates, offering literacy training, GED (general equivalency degree) programs, and other types of instruction.[20]

Impact on Recidivism Some evidence suggests that such efforts can have a positive effect on rates of reoffending. A recent study by the nonprofit Rand Corporation, summarizing thirty years of research, found that ex-inmates who participated in education programs from behind bars had a 43 percent lower chance of reoffending within three years after release than those who did not.[21] The same study found that participation in vocational training improved an inmate's chances of finding post-release employment by 28 percent.[22]

Evidence of the benefits of prison work offer a counterpoint to the position taken by members of the Free Alabama Movement, described in the opening of this chapter, who say that making prisoners work for low or no wages is inherently exploitative. Research shows that inmates who work in prison are more likely to find a job on release and to keep that job for a longer period of time.[23] In addition, prison work can have psychological benefits. "Employed inmates seem less like caged animals," said one ex-convict, who served time at the York Correctional Institution in Niantic, Connecticut. "While they paid me less than two dollars a day, my supervisors valued me as a person and an employee, at a time when no one else did, including myself."[24]

Therapeutic Community (TC)
A group-based form of substance abuse treatment that focuses on identifying the underlying social and psychological problems of abusers to help change negative behaviors linked to drug and alcohol addiction.

Pell Grants   At one time, the federal government provided grants that helped eligible inmates earn college degrees while in prison. This Pell Grant program was discontinued in 1994 after critics successfully argued that any available educational funds should go to non-prisoners.[25] In 2016, however, the U.S. Department of Education announced the Second Chance Pell Pilot program. This "experiment" will give 12,000 inmates eligible for release within five years the opportunity to earn associate's or bachelor's degrees while still incarcerated. In justifying the program, the then secretary of education Arne Duncan referred to the RAND study mentioned earlier, which estimated that for every dollar spent on correctional education, four to five dollars were saved on reincarceration costs.[26]

Prison Violence

Prisons and jails are dangerous places to live. Prison culture is predicated on violence—one observer calls the modern penal institution an "unstable and violent jungle."[27] Correctional officers use the threat of violence (and, at times, actual violence) to control the inmate population. Sometimes, the inmates strike back. According to the Bureau of Labor Statistics, because of inmate assaults, correctional officers have one of the most dangerous jobs in the United States.[28]

Among the prisoners, violence is used to establish power and dominance. On occasion, this violence leads to death. Although misconduct varies from institution to institution, overall rates of inmate-on-inmate assault are two to three times higher than arrest rates for assault in the general U.S. adult population.[29] With nothing but time on their hands, prisoners have been known to fashion deadly weapons out of everyday items such as toothbrushes and mop handles. Many inmates also bring the "code of the street," with its fixation on "respect, toughness, and retribution," into prison, making them likely both to engage in violent acts behind bars and to be victims of such violence.[30]

Violence in Prison Culture

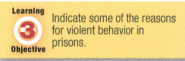

Learning Objective 3
Indicate some of the reasons for violent behavior in prisons.

Until the 1970s, prison culture emphasized "noninterference" and did not support inmate-on-inmate violence. Prison "elders" would themselves punish any of their peers who showed a proclivity toward assaulting fellow inmates. Today, in contrast, violence is used to establish the prisoner hierarchy by separating the powerful from the weak. Humboldt State University's Lee H. Bowker has identified several other reasons for violent behavior:

- It provides a deterrent against being victimized, as a reputation for violence may eliminate an inmate as a target of assault.
- It enhances self-image in an environment that does not respect other attributes, such as intelligence.

- In the case of rape, it gives sexual relief.
- It serves as a means of acquiring material goods through extortion or outright robbery.[31]

The **deprivation model** can be used to explain the high level of prison violence. According to this model, the stressful and oppressive conditions of prison life lead to aggressive behavior on the part of inmates. Prison researcher Stephen C. Light found that when conditions such as overcrowding worsen, inmate misconduct often increases.[32] In these circumstances, the violent behavior may not have any express purpose—it may just be a means of relieving tension.

Riots

The deprivation model is helpful in explaining collective violence but leaves some questions unanswered. As far back as the 1930s, sociologist Frank Tannenbaum noted that harsh prison conditions can cause tension to build among inmates until it eventually explodes in the form of mass violence.[33] Living conditions among prisons are fairly constant, however, so how can the seemingly spontaneous outbreak of prison riots be explained?

Researchers have addressed the seeming randomness of prison violence by turning to the concept of **relative deprivation.** These theories focus on the gap between what is expected in a certain situation and what is achieved. Criminologist Peter C. Kratcoski has argued that because prisoners enjoy such meager privileges to begin with, any further deprivation can spark disorder.[34] A number of prison experts have noted that collective violence occurs in response to heightened measures of security at corrections facilities.[35] Thus, the violence is primarily a reaction to additional reductions in freedom for inmates, who enjoy very little freedom to begin with.

Riots, which have been defined as situations in which a number of prisoners are beyond institutional control for a significant amount of time, are relatively rare. These incidents are marked by extreme levels of inmate-on-inmate violence and can often be attributed, at least in part, to poor living conditions and inadequate prison administration.

Alabama's Holman Correctional Facility, featured in the opening of this chapter, experienced no fewer than three riots in 2016, including one in which an inmate stabbed the warden. Designed to hold about six hundred inmates, Holman houses around one thousand in its general population, and prisoners have easy access to contraband weapons. "All I have is chemical spray and a baton, and the inmates have knives," said a Holman correctional officer, explaining why he and his colleagues are reluctant to administer discipline in the facility.[36]

Prison Rape

Prison rape, like rape in general, is considered primarily an act of violence rather than sex. Inmates subject to rape ("punks") are near the bottom of the **prison power structure** and, in some instances, may accept rape by one particularly powerful inmate in return

▲ A correctional official displays a set of homemade knives, also known as *shivs*, made by inmates at Attica Correctional Facility in Attica, New York. **How does the deprivation model explain high levels of prison violence?** AP Images/David Duprey

Deprivation Model A theory that inmate aggression is the result of the frustration inmates feel at being deprived of freedom, consumer goods, sex, and other staples of life outside the institution.

Relative Deprivation The theory that inmate aggression is caused when freedoms and services that the inmate has come to accept as normal are decreased or eliminated.

for protection from others.[37] Abused inmates often suffer from rape trauma syndrome and a host of other psychological ailments, including suicidal tendencies. Many prisons do not offer sufficient medical treatment for rape victims, nor does the prison staff take the necessary measures to protect obvious targets of rape—young, slightly built, nonviolent offenders.

According to the most recent inmate survey, 3.1 percent of heterosexual inmates, 14 percent of homosexual inmates, and 40 percent of transgender inmates reported having been sexually assaulted by other inmates or prison staff.[38] The total number of rapes measured in this survey—about 80,000—is almost certainly an underrepresentation, as many such assaults go unreported due to shame or fear of retaliation. With the Prison Rape Elimination Act, passed in 2003, Congress set fifty-two standards in areas such as evidence collection and crisis counseling aimed at combating this problem.[39] By September 2016, twelve states had adopted these "best practices" for their correctional institutions.[40]

Issues of Race and Ethnicity

"As a white person, I can't use or touch anything that a black person has used or touched," says ex-convict Steven Czifra of his life in a California prison. "If I drop my soap on the floor next to my bunk," Czifra explains, "I have to throw it away" because a black inmate probably has walked on the floor.[41]

Czifra is describing the "etiquette" observed in the prison between whites and blacks. Race plays a major role in prison life, and prison violence is often an outlet for racial tension. As prison populations have changed over the past decades, with African Americans and Latinos becoming the majority in many penal institutions, issues of race and ethnicity have become increasingly important to prison administrators and researchers.

Separate Worlds

As early as the 1950s, researchers were noticing different group structures in inmate life. At that time, for example, prisoners at California's Soledad Prison informally segregated themselves according to geography as well as race: Tejanos (Mexicans raised in Texas), Chicanos, blacks from California, blacks from the South and Southwest, and the majority whites all formed separate social worlds.[42] Leo Carroll, professor of sociology at the University of Rhode Island, has written extensively about how today's prisoners are divided into hostile groups, with race determining nearly every aspect of an inmate's life, including friends, job assignments, and cell location.[43]

Prison Segregation

More than four decades ago, the United States Supreme Court put an end to the widespread practice of prison segregation, under which correctional officials would place inmates in cells or blocks with those of a similar race or ethnicity.[44] According to the Supreme Court's ruling, prison segregation was unconstitutional because government officials were discriminating against individuals based on their skin color.

Years after this ruling, however, the California Department of Corrections began implementing an unwritten policy of putting all new and transferred male inmates in cells with inmates of the same race or ethnicity for the first sixty days of incarceration. The goal of this policy was to determine if an inmate was a member of a race-based gang before allowing him to live in integrated quarters. In 2005, the Supreme Court struck down California's version of prison segregation.[45] The Court did, however, leave prison officials with an "out": They can still segregate prisoners in an "emergency situation."[46]

Prison Segregation The practice of separating inmates based on a certain characteristic, such as race or ethnicity.

Prison Gangs and Security Threat Groups (STGs)

In 2014, in response to legal action, the California Department of Corrections agreed to refrain from segregating inmates by race, even during an "emergency situation."[47] The lawsuit was brought by inmates claiming that state corrections officials unfairly used race to determine which of them was involved in prison gang activity.

In reality, corrections officials routinely rely on racial and ethnic identification as a shortcut to identify members of prison gangs, or cliques of inmates who join together in an organizational structure to engage in illegal activity. Gang affiliation is often the cause of inmate-on-inmate violence. For decades, the California prison system has been plagued by feuds involving various gangs, such as the Mexican Mafia, composed of U.S.-born inmates of Mexican descent, and their enemies, a spin-off organization called La Nuestra Familia.

In part, the prison gang is a natural result of life in the modern prison. As one expert says of these gangs:

> Their members have done in prison what many people do elsewhere when they feel personally powerless, threatened, and vulnerable. They align themselves with others, organize to fight back, and enhance their own status and control through their connection to a more powerful group.[48]

In addition to their important role in the social structure of correctional facilities, prison gangs participate in a wide range of illegal economic activities within these institutions, including prostitution, drug selling, gambling, and loan sharking. A study released in 2011 by Alan J. Drury and Matt DeLisi of Iowa State University found that gang members were more likely to be involved in prison misconduct than inmates who had been convicted of murder.[49]

The Prevalence of Prison Gangs

There is little question that the nation's correctional institutions are hotbeds of gang activity. The most recent research conducted by the National Gang Crime Research Center places the proportion of gang members in state prisons and local jails at 30 percent of male inmates and 9 percent of female inmates. In the same survey, 87 percent of corrections officials answered "yes" to the question, "Do you believe that some inmates may have voluntarily joined or may have been recruited into a gang while incarcerated?"[50]

In many instances, prison gangs are extensions of street gangs. In fact, with the help of corrupt correctional officers and contraband cell phones, gang members "at sea" (behind bars) often are able to coordinate criminal activities with gang members "on land" (on the streets). This relationship serves a mixture of practical and economic purposes. Gang members incarcerated with lengthy sentences will offer protection to other gang members serving shorter terms. On release, the latter will provide financial support to the families of their still-incarcerated counterparts.[51] (See Figure 14.3 for a rundown of several major prison gangs presently active in the American corrections system.)

Combating Prison Gangs

In their efforts to combat the influence of prison gangs, over the past decade correctional officials have increasingly turned to the security threat group (STG) model. Generally speaking,

Prison Gang A group of inmates who band together within the corrections system to engage in social and criminal activities.

Security Threat Group (STG) A group of three or more inmates who engage in activity that poses a threat to the safety of other inmates or the prison staff.

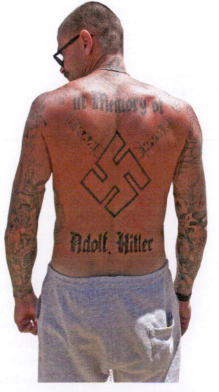

▼ A member of the Aryan Brotherhood in California's Calipatria State Prison. This particular prison gang espouses white supremacy, but for the most part its leadership focuses on illegal activities such as extortion and drug trafficking. **Why might an inmate join a prison gang?**

Mark Allen Johnson/ZUMA Press/Calipatria/CA/USA/Newscom

FIGURE 14.3 **The Top Prison Gangs in the United States**

Certain prison gangs, such as the Crips and the Bloods, are offshoots of street gangs and gained influence behind bars because so many of their members have been incarcerated. Others, such as the Aryan Brotherhood and the Mexican Mafia, formed in prison and expanded to the streets. Listed here are seven of the most dangerous gangs operating in the American prison system today.

Aryan Brotherhood
White
Origins: Prison gang, formed in San Quentin State Prison in 1967, as white protection against blacks.
Allies: Mexican Mafia
Rivals: Black Guerrilla Family

REUTERS/Alamy Stock Photo

Signs/Symbols: Swastika, SS lightning bolts, numbers 666 (Satan, evil) and 88 (H is the eighth letter of the alphabet, so 88 stands for HH, as in "Heil Hitler"), letters AB, shamrock (a symbol of their original Irish membership), Nordic dagger on shield with lightning bolts.

Black Guerrilla Family
African American
Origins: Prison gang, founded by incarcerated Black Panthers in San Quentin State Prison in the mid-1960s.
Allies: La Nuestra Familia
Rivals: Aryan Brotherhood
Signs/Symbols: Crossed sabers, machetes, rifles, shotguns with the letters BGF, a black dragon squeezing the life out of a prison guard by a prison tower.

Bloods
African American
Origins: Street gang, formed in Los Angeles in the 1960s, as a defense against the Crips.
Allies: People Nation (Chicago gang), La Nuestra Familia
Rivals: Crips, Aryan Brotherhood
Signs/Symbols: The color red, red bandannas or rags, the word "Piru" (the original Blood gang), crossed-out "c" in words as disrespect for Crips, other anti-Crip graffiti, hand signal spells "blood."

Crips
African American
Origins: Street gang, formed in the Central Avenue area of Los Angeles in the late 1960s.
Allies: Black Guerrilla Family, La Nuestra Familia
Rivals: Bloods, Aryan Brotherhood, Vice Lords
Signs/Symbols: The color blue, blue bandannas and rags, use the letter "c" in place of "b" in writing as disrespect for Bloods, calling each other Cuzz, calling themselves Blood Killas (BK), wearing British Knight (BK) tennis shoes.

Mexican Mafia (EMC)
Mexican American/Latino
Origins: Prison gang, formed in Los Angeles in the Deuel Vocational Institution in the late 1950s. Foot soldiers and related Southern California street gangs are called Sureños.
Allies: Aryan Brotherhood
Rivals: Black Guerrilla Family, La Nuestra Familia
Signs/Symbols: The national symbol of Mexico, an eagle and a snake, on a flaming circle, lying on crossed knives. The color blue, the number 13.

Mara Salvatrucha 13 (MS-13)
Latino
Origins: Largest street gang in North America, originated in El Salvador and formed in Los Angeles in the 1980s.
Allies: Mexican Mafia
Rivals: MS-18 (LA gang)

Yuri Cortez/AFP/Getty Images

Signs/Symbols: Most Mara Salvatrucha members are covered in tattoos, even on their faces. Common markings include MS, 13, Salvadorian Pride, Devil Horns.

La Nuestra Familia
Mexican American/Latino
Origins: Prison gang, formed in Soledad Prison in the late 1960s, as a reaction to the Mexican Mafia. Based in Northern California, foot soldiers outside of prison are called Norteños.
Allies: Black Guerrilla Family, Bloods, Crips
Rivals: Mexican Mafia, Mara Salvatrucha
Signs/Symbols: Large tattoos, often on the entire back. The initials NF, LNF, ENE, and F. The number 14 for N, the fourteenth letter in the alphabet, stands for Norte or Norteño. The color red, Nebraska cornhuskers' caps with the letter N. A sombrero with a dagger is a common NF symbol.

Sources: "Gangs or Us," at www.gangsorus.com/index.html; and "Prison Gang Profiles," at www.insideprison.com/prison_gang_profiles.asp.

an STG is an identifiable group with three or more individuals and a leadership structure that poses a threat to the safety of other inmates or members of the corrections community. About two-thirds of all prisons have a correctional officer who acts as an STG coordinator.[52] This official is responsible for the classification of individuals who are likely to be involved in STG (though not necessarily prison gang) activity and for taking measures to protect the prison community from these individuals.

In many instances, these measures are punitive. Prison officials, for example, have reduced overall levels of violence significantly by putting gang members in solitary confinement, away from the general prison population. Other punitive measures include restrictions on privileges such as family visits and prison program participation, as well as delays of parole eligibility.[53]

Contraband Cell Phones

One piece of technology has made the task of controlling prison gangs extremely difficult: the cell phone. Although inmates are prohibited from possessing these devices, cell phones are routinely used to arrange attacks, plan escapes, and operate illegal money-making schemes from behind bars. The phones are usually smuggled in by visitors, who hide them in locations as varied as babies' diapers, food packages, soda cans, and body cavities. In Georgia, corrections officials found cell-phone parts stuffed into the body of a dead cat that had been thrown over a prison fence, and there have been numerous reports nationwide of drones being used to deliver the phones into prison yards.

Earlier this decade, forty-four inmates and correctional officers at the Baltimore City Detention Center were arrested for helping to operate the Black Guerrilla Family gang from within the prison using cell phones. In response, the state of Maryland started a managed access program to deal with the problem. This "cellular umbrella" antenna technology is designed to analyze all calls made from the prison and instantly block any that originate from a contraband phone. Authorities at the Mississippi State Penitentiary in Parchman estimate that between 2010 and 2015, its managed-access system, while not 100 percent effective, captured more than six million illicit transmissions.

Thinking about Contraband Cell Phones

It would be much easier—and cheaper—for corrections officials to combat contraband cell phones by disrupting *all* cell-phone activity in a prison or jail. However, this practice—called "jamming"—is illegal under federal law. What do you think is the reasoning behind this blanket prohibition of jamming?

Correctional Officers and Discipline

Ideally, the presence of correctional officers—the standard term used to describe prison guards—has the effect of lessening violence in American correctional institutions. Practically speaking, this is indeed the case. Without correctional officers, the prison would be a place of anarchy. But in the highly regulated, oppressive environment of the prison, correctional officers must use the threat of violence, if not actual violence, to instill discipline and keep order. Thus, the relationship between prison staff and inmates is marked by mutual distrust. Consider the two following statements, the first made by a correctional officer and the second by a prisoner:

> [My job is to] protect, feed, and try to educate scum who raped and brutalized women and children . . . who, if I turn my back, will go into their cell, wrap a blanket around their cellmate's legs, and threaten to beat or rape him if he doesn't give sex, carry contraband, or fork over radios, money, or other goods willingly. And they'll stick a shank in me tomorrow if they think they can get away with it.[54]

> The pigs in the state and federal prisons . . . treat me so violently, I cannot possibly imagine a time I could ever have anything but the deepest, aching, searing hatred for them. I can't begin to tell you what they do to me. If I were weaker by a hair, they would destroy me.[55]

It may be difficult for an outsider to understand the emotions that fuel such sentiments. French philosopher Michel Foucault points out that discipline, both in prison and in the general community, is a means of social organization as well as punishment.[56] Discipline is imposed when a person behaves in a manner that is contrary to the values of the dominant social group. Correctional officers and inmates have different concepts of the ideal structure of prison society, and, as the two quotations just cited demonstrate, this conflict generates intense feelings of fear and hatred, which often lead to violence.

Prison Employment

There are numerous benefits to a career as a correctional officer. Because the position is a civil service (government) job, it offers steady benefits and employment security. In some states, such as California and New York, salaries can reach $70,000. Furthermore, because of a professionalism movement in hiring, the standards of correctional officers have risen dramatically in the past few decades.[57]

Becoming a Correctional Officer

Most prospective correctional officers are required to pass the civil service exam in their state of employment. Furthermore, as with police cadets, correctional officers usually go through a military-style training program prior to deployment in a prison. This program incorporates classwork and physical training, including instruction in areas such as self-defense, inmate control, and protection against communicable disease. Like police cadets, correctional officer trainees also go through a period of supervision with an experienced co-worker, in which they learn not only the job's specific techniques and procedures, but also about the prison environment and subculture.[58]

Correctional Officer Diversity

In the not-too-distant past, prisons and jails drew their employees mainly from the communities in which they were located. Given that these rural areas were (and still are) mostly white, so were the vast majority of correctional officers.[59] (Women, as we will soon discuss, were also eliminated from most recruiting efforts.) Today, for many of the same reasons detailed in Chapter 5 regarding law enforcement officers, the field is considerably more diverse. According to the U.S. Bureau of Labor Statistics, about 28 percent of correctional officers are women, 25 percent are African American, and 13 percent are Latino.[60]

▼ A number of California correctional facilities, including Chino State Prison (pictured here), suffer from chronic overcrowding. **How does overcrowding make it more difficult for correctional officers to "keep the peace" in a prison or jail?** Kevork Djansezian/Getty Images News/Getty Images

Rank and Duties

The custodial staff at most prisons is organized according to four general ranks—captain, lieutenant, sergeant, and officer. In keeping with the militaristic model, captains are primarily administrators who deal directly with the warden on custodial issues. Lieutenants are the disciplinarians of the prison, responsible for policing and transporting the inmates. Sergeants oversee platoons of officers in specific parts of the prison, such as various cell blocks or work spaces.

Lucien X. Lombardo, professor of sociology and criminal justice at Old Dominion University, has identified six general job categories among correctional officers:[61]

1. *Block officers.* These employees supervise cell blocks containing as many as four hundred inmates, as well as the

correctional officers on block guard duty. In general, the block officer is responsible for the well-being of the inmates. He or she tries to ensure that the inmates do not harm themselves or other prisoners and also acts as something of a camp counselor, dispensing advice and seeing that inmates understand and follow the rules of the facility.

2. *Work detail supervisors.* In most penal institutions, the inmates work in the cafeteria, the prison store, the laundry, and other areas. Work detail supervisors oversee small groups of inmates as they perform their tasks.

3. *Industrial shop and school officers.* These officers perform maintenance and security functions in workshop and educational programs. Their primary responsibility is to make sure that inmates are on time for these programs and do not cause any disturbances during the sessions.

4. *Yard officers.* Officers who work the prison yard usually have the least seniority, befitting the assignment's reputation as dangerous and stressful. These officers must be constantly on alert for breaches in prison discipline or regulations in the relatively unstructured environment of the prison yard.

5. *Tower guards.* These officers spend their entire shifts, which usually last eight hours, in isolated, silent posts high above the grounds of the facility. Although their only means of communication are walkie-talkies or cellular devices, the safety benefits of the position can outweigh the loneliness that comes with the job.

6. *Administrative building assignments.* Officers who hold these positions provide security at prison gates, oversee visitation procedures, act as liaisons for civilians, and handle administrative tasks such as processing the paperwork when an inmate is transferred from another institution.

Discipline

Inmate discipline policies have three general goals:

1. To ensure a safe and orderly living environment.
2. To instill respect for authority of correctional officers and administrators.
3. To teach values and respectful behavior that influence the inmate's attitude when she or he is released from prison.[62]

As Erving Goffman noted in his essay on the "total institution," in the general society adults are rarely placed in a position where they are "punished" as a child would be.[63] Therefore, the strict disciplinary measures imposed on prisoners come as something of a shock and can provoke strong defensive reactions. Correctional officers who must deal with these responses often find that disciplining inmates is the most difficult and stressful aspect of their job. (To learn more about the potential hazards for correctional officers in dealing with inmates, see the feature *Discretion in Action—"Downing a Duck."*)

Sanctioning Prisoners

As mentioned earlier, one of the first items that an inmate receives on entering a correctional facility is a manual that details the rules of the prison or jail, along with the punishment that will result from rule violations. These handbooks can be quite lengthy—running one hundred pages in some instances—and specific. Not only will a prison manual prohibit obvious misconduct such as violent or sexual activity, gambling, and possession of drugs or currency, but it also addresses matters of daily life such as personal hygiene, dress codes, and conduct during meals.

Correctional officers enforce the prison rules in much the same way that a highway patrol officer enforces traffic regulations. For a minor violation, the inmate may be "let

GETTING
Linked in™

Hundreds of correctional facilities across the United States are posting job advertisements for **correctional officers** at any given time. To better understand the wide variety of possibilities in this profession, enter the term **"correctional officer"** into LinkedIn's search engine.

DISCRETION IN ACTION

"Downing a Duck"

The Situation You have just been hired as a correctional officer at a maximum-security prison. Most of the inmates at the facility are violent criminals serving lengthy sentences. During your first week, the inmates in your cell block do a poor job of keeping their living quarters clean, causing you to get a negative performance review and a tongue-lashing from your supervisor. An inmate named Rick consoles you and promises that he will use his influence to ensure that the other inmates "make you look good." He does so. Later, you are threatened by two prisoners who threaten to "get" you. Rick steps in and defuses the situation. You are grateful and begin to look at Rick as something of a friend.

When another inmates dies of a heart attack, Rick comes to you and asks for a favor. He and some other inmates have taken up a collection for the inmate's widow, and he wants you to deliver the money, with a sympathy card, to her on the outside.

The Law Prison regulations strictly prohibit inmates from possessing any form of money or currency. State law prohibits correctional officers from transporting any contraband outside the prison.

What Would You Do? Clearly, you are legally required not only to refuse Rick's request, but also to report him and the other inmates for possession of cash. You also remember advice from a colleague, who warned that inmates are skilled at manipulating inexperienced correctional officers, a strategy called "downing a duck." At the same time, Rick has made your job much easier, and it is possible that he saved your life. While Rick's request may technically be against the rules, he is hardly asking you to do something immoral or unethical. How do you respond?

To see how prison employees in upstate New York reacted to friendly overtures from a pair of inmates, go to Example 14.1 in Appendix B.

---

off easy" with a verbal warning. More serious infractions will result in a "ticket," or a report forwarded to the institution's disciplinary committee.[64] The disciplinary committee generally includes several correctional officers and, in some instances, outside citizens or even inmates.

Although, as we shall see, the United States Supreme Court has ruled that inmates must be given a "fair hearing" before being disciplined, the Court denied inmates the right to confront adverse witnesses or consult a lawyer during these hearings.[65] In practice, then, an inmate has very little ability to challenge the committee's decision. Depending on the seriousness of the violation, sanctions can range from a loss of privileges such as visits from family members to the unpleasantness of solitary confinement, a controversial practice featured in the chapter-ending *Policy Matters* feature.

Most correctional officers prefer to rely on the "you scratch my back and I'll scratch yours" model for controlling inmates. In other words, as long as the prisoner makes a reasonable effort to conform to institutional rules, the correctional officer will refrain from taking disciplinary steps. Of course, the staff-inmate relationship is not always marked by cooperation, and correctional officers often find themselves in situations where they must use force.

Use of Force

Generally, courts have been unwilling to put too many restrictions on the use of force by correctional officers. As we saw earlier with police officers, correctional officers are given great leeway to use their experience to determine when force is warranted. In *Whitley v. Albers* (1986),[66] the Supreme Court held that the use of force by prison officials violates an inmate's Eighth Amendment protections only if the force amounts to "the unnecessary and wanton infliction of pain."

Excessive force can be considered "necessary" if the legitimate security interests of the penal institution are at stake. Consequently, an appeals court ruled that when officers at a Maryland prison formed an "extraction team" to remove the leader of a riot from his cell, beating him in the process, the use of force was justified given the situation.[67]

Legitimate Security Interests Courts have found that the "legitimate security interests" of a prison or jail justify the use of force when the correctional officer is

1. Acting in self-defense.
2. Acting to defend the safety of a third person, such as a member of the prison staff or another inmate.
3. Upholding the rules of the institution.
4. Preventing a crime such as assault, destruction of property, or theft.
5. Preventing an escape effort.[68]

Learning 4 Objective List the circumstances in which courts have found that the "legitimate security interests" of a jail or prison justify the use of force by correctional officers.

In addition, most prisons and jails have written policies that spell out the situations in which their employees may use force against inmates. Following the lead of their counterparts in law enforcement, administrators in numerous correctional facilities are equipping their correctional officers with body cameras to provide more transparency in actual and alleged use-of-force incidents.

The "Malicious and Sadistic" Standard The judicial system has not given correctional officers total freedom of discretion to apply force. In *Hudson v. McMillan* (1992),[69] the Supreme Court ruled that minor injuries suffered by a convict at the hands of a correctional officer following an argument did violate the inmate's rights, because there was no security concern at the time of the incident. In other words, the issue is not *how much* force was used, but whether the officer used the force as part of a good faith effort to restore discipline or acted "maliciously and sadistically" to cause harm.

Civil Actions Inmates have the right to sue correctional officers in federal court to address grievances.[70] In 2015, the Supreme Court made it more likely that inmates who sued correctional officers for excessive use of force would succeed. The case involved the use, by Wisconsin jail officials, of a stun gun on an inmate who was handcuffed and taken from his cell for refusing to remove a piece of paper covering a light fixture. The Court held that, to succeed in his suit, the inmate did not need to prove that the correctional officers were aware that their use of force was unjustified under the circumstances. Instead, the inmate need only prove that the use of force was "objectively unreasonable," a much easier standard to meet.[71]

Female Correctional Officers

Security concerns were the main reason that, for many years, prison administrators refused to hire women as correctional officers in men's prisons. The consensus was that women were not physically strong enough to subdue violent male inmates and that their mere presence in the predominantly masculine prison world would cause disciplinary breakdowns.[72] As a result, in the 1970s a number of women brought lawsuits against state corrections systems, claiming that they were being discriminated against on the basis of their gender. For the most part, these legal actions were successful in opening the doors to men's prisons for female correctional officers (and vice versa).[73] Today, more than 100,000 women work as correctional officers in prison and jails, many of them in constant close contact with male inmates.[74]

As it turns out, female correctional officers have proved just as effective as their male counterparts in maintaining discipline in men's prisons. As reported in one study of Texas maximum-security prisons, inmates felt that female correctional officers were

▲ Women make up a small—if not tiny—percentage of the security staff at most jails in the United States, including the Baltimore County (Maryland) Detention Center shown here. **What are some of the challenges that face female correctional officers in men's prisons and jails?** Kim Hairston/ *Baltimore Sun*/MCT/Tribune News Service/Getty Images

Learning Objective 5 Describe the hands-off doctrine of prisoner law and indicate two standards used to determine if prisoners' rights have been violated.

"Hands-Off" Doctrine The unwritten judicial policy that favors noninterference by the courts in the administration of prisons and jails.

"Deliberate Indifference" The standard for establishing a violation of an inmate's Eighth Amendment rights, requiring that prison officials were aware of harmful conditions in a correctional institution and failed to take steps to remedy those conditions.

as competent as their male counterparts and exhibited "calm and cool" in pressurized situations.[75] Further evidence suggests that this calming influence on male inmates can lower levels of prison violence.[76]

Protecting Prisoners' Rights

The general attitude of the law toward inmates is summed up by the Thirteenth Amendment to the U.S. Constitution, which we mentioned in this chapter's opening feature:

Neither slavery nor involuntary servitude, except as a punishment for crime whereof the party shall have been duly convicted, shall exist within the United States.

In other words, inmates do not have the same guaranteed rights as other Americans. For most of the nation's history, courts have followed the spirit of this amendment by applying the **"hands-off" doctrine** of prisoner law. This (unwritten) doctrine assumes that the care of inmates should be left to prison officials and that it is not the place of judges to intervene in penal administrative matters.

At the same time, the United States Supreme Court has stated that "[t]here is no iron curtain between the Constitution and the prisons of this country."[77] Consequently, as with so many other areas of the criminal justice system, the treatment of prisoners is based on a balancing act—here, between the rights of prisoners and the security needs of the correctional institutions. Because inmates do not enjoy the same civil rights as other members of society, American courts tend to place more weight on security concerns. In 1984, for example, the Supreme Court ruled that arbitrary searches of prison cells are allowed under the Fourth Amendment because inmates have no reasonable expectation of privacy[78] (see Chapter 7 for a review of this expectation).

The "Deliberate Indifference" Standard As for those constitutional rights that inmates do retain, in 1976 the Supreme Court established the **"deliberate indifference"** standard. In the case in question, *Estelle v. Gamble,*[79] an inmate had claimed to be the victim of medical malpractice. In his majority opinion, Justice Thurgood Marshall wrote that prison officials violated a convict's Eighth Amendment rights if they "deliberately" failed to provide him or her with necessary medical care. At the time, the decision was hailed as a victory for prisoners' rights, and it continues to ensure that a certain level of health care is provided.

In 2016, for example, a U.S. District Court ruled that that prison officials at the Wallace Pack Unit in Navasota, Texas, were "deliberately indifferent" when they failed to provide inmates with drinking water that met "contemporary standards of decency." The facility's water supply contained between 2 and 4.5 times the amount of arsenic permitted by the federal Environmental Protection Agency.[80] In general, however, courts have found it difficult to define "deliberate" in this context. Does it mean that prison officials "should have known" that an inmate was placed in harm's way, or does it mean that officials purposefully placed the inmate in that position?

The Supreme Court seems to have taken the latter position. In *Wilson v. Seiter* (1991),[81] for example, inmate Pearly L. Wilson filed a lawsuit alleging that certain conditions of his confinement—including overcrowding; excessive noise; inadequate heating, cooling, and ventilation; and unsanitary bathroom and dining facilities—were cruel and unusual. The Court ruled against Wilson, stating that he had failed to prove that these conditions, even if they existed, were the result of "deliberate indifference" on the part of prison officials.

"Identifiable Human Needs"   In its *Wilson* decision, the Supreme Court created the "identifiable human needs" standard for determining Eighth Amendment violations. The Court asserted that a prisoner must show that the institution has denied her or him a basic need such as food, warmth, or exercise.[82] The Court mentioned only these three needs, however, forcing the lower courts to determine for themselves what other needs, if any, fall into this category.

Because of the Supreme Court's *Estelle* decision, described above, prisoners do have a well-established right to "adequate" medical care. "Adequate" has been interpreted to mean a level of care comparable to what the inmate would receive if he or she were not behind bars.[83]

So, for example, several years ago, California agreed to provide sex reassignment surgery for transgender inmate Shiloh Quine, who is serving a life sentence without parole for murder. The state's medical expert had ruled that the medial procedure was necessary to "alleviate severe pain caused by her gender dysphoria."[84] Furthermore, as noted earlier in the chapter, the Supreme Court asserted that the overcrowding of California's state prisons was so severe that it denied inmates satisfactory levels of health care.[85]

The First Amendment in Prison   The First Amendment reads, in part, that the federal government "shall make no law respecting an establishment of religion, or prohibiting the free exercise thereof; or abridging the freedom of speech." In the 1970s, the prisoners' rights movement forced open the "iron curtain" to allow the First Amendment behind bars. In 1974, for example, the Supreme Court held that prison officials can censor inmate mail only if doing so is necessary to maintain prison security.[86] The decade also saw court decisions protecting inmates' access to group worship, instruction by clergy, special dietary requirements, religious publications, and other aspects of both mainstream and non-mainstream religions.[87]

Judges will limit some of these protections when an obvious security interest is at stake. In 2010, for example, a Pennsylvania prison was allowed to continue banning religious headscarves because of legitimate concerns that the scarves could be used to conceal drugs or strangle someone.[88] In contrast, a federal judge ruled in 2015 that jail inmates in Chicago have a First Amendment right to read newspapers. The Cook County sheriff's department had banned these items in city jails over concerns that they could be used to fashion paper-maché weapons, fuel fires, and clog toilets.[89]

Inside a Women's Prison

When the first women's prison in the United States opened in 1839 on the grounds of New York's Sing Sing institution, the focus was on rehabilitation. Prisoners were prepared for a return to society with classes on reading, knitting, and sewing. Early women's reformatories had few locks or bars, and several included nurseries for the inmates' young children.

Today, the situation is dramatically different. "Women's institutions are literally men's institutions, only we pull out the urinals," remarks Meda Chesney-Lind, a criminologist at the University of Hawaii.[90] Following a recently concluded, decade-long study of conditions in women's prisons, researchers at the University of Cincinnati identified six specific concerns relating to female inmates:

1. They often suffer from lack of *self-efficacy*, meaning that they do not feel able to meet personal goals, and believe that they are not in control of their own lives.

2. Their criminal behavior is linked to *parental stress*—specifically, the financial strain of raising children and the possibility of losing custody of children due to antisocial behavior such as crime and substance abuse.

3. They are more likely than male offenders to suffer from *mental health problems* such as depression, anxiety, and self-injurious behaviors.

4. They are more likely than male offenders to have been *victims of physical and sexual abuse* as children and adults.

5. Before arrest, they were involved in *unhealthy relationships* with family members, spouses, or romantic partners that contributed to their criminal behavior.

6. Their lives are marked by *poverty and homelessness*, often brought on by substance abuse, child care responsibilities, and lack of educational and work skills.[91]

These concerns—when combined with the fact that most female inmates are nonviolent offenders—suggest that women's prisons require a different management style than men's prisons.

Characteristics of Female Inmates

Male inmates outnumber female inmates by approximately twelve to one, and there are only about a hundred women's correctional facilities in the United States. Consequently, most research concerning the American corrections system focuses on male inmates and men's prisons. Enough data exist, however, to provide a useful portrait of women behind bars. Female inmates are typically low income and undereducated, and have a history of unemployment. Female offenders are much less likely than male offenders to have committed a violent offense. Most are incarcerated for a nonviolent drug or property crime.[92] As Figure 14.4 shows, the demographics of female prisoners are similar to those of their male counterparts. That is, the majority of female inmates are under the age of forty, and the population is disproportionately African American.

A History of Abuse The single factor that most distinguishes female prisoners from their male counterparts is a history of physical or sexual abuse. A self-reported study conducted by the federal government indicates that 55 percent of female jail inmates have been abused at some point in their lives, compared with only 13 percent of male jail inmates.[93] Fifty-seven percent of women in state prisons and 40 percent of women in federal prisons report some form of past abuse—both figures are significantly higher than those for male prisoners.[94] Health experts believe that these levels of abuse are related to the significant amount of drug and alcohol addiction that plagues the female prison population, as well as to the mental illness problems that such addictions can cause or exacerbate.[95]

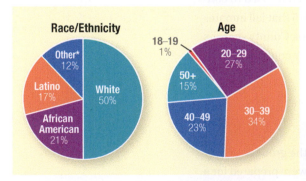

FIGURE 14.4 Female Prisoners in the United States by Race, Ethnicity, and Age

*Includes American Indians, Alaska Natives, Native Hawaiians, other Pacific Islanders, and persons identifying two or more races.

Source: Bureau of Justice Statistics, *Prisoners in 2015* (Washington, D.C.: U.S. Department of Justice, December 2016), Table 8, page 13.

Other Health Problems   In fact, about 25 percent of women in state prisons have been diagnosed with mental disorders, such as post-traumatic stress disorder (PTSD), depression, and substance abuse. PTSD, in particular, is found in women who have experienced sexual or physical abuse.[96] Furthermore, more women than men enter prisons and jails with health problems due to higher instances of poverty, inadequate health care, and substance abuse.[97] Not only do women prisoners have high rates of breast and cervical cancer, but they are also 50 percent more likely than men to be HIV positive and are at significantly greater risk for lung cancer.[98]

All these data suggest that administrators at women's prisons should focus less on security than their counterparts at male correctional institutions, and more on treatment and rehabilitation.[99] Moving On, a therapeutic prison program specifically designed for women, has had success in helping female inmates repair the damage done by past relationships. Composed of group and one-on-one discussions, role-playing, writing exercises, and self-assessments, Moving On focuses on improving communication skills and expressing emotions in a healthful and constructive manner.[100]

The Motherhood Problem

Drug and alcohol use within a women's prison can be a function of the anger and depression many inmates experience due to being separated from their children. An estimated 147,000 American children have a mother in state prison, and the problem is much more pronounced for African American and Latino children than for white children.[101] Given the scarcity of women's correctional facilities, inmates are often housed at great distances from their children. One study found that almost two-thirds of women in federal prison are more than five hundred miles from their homes.[102]

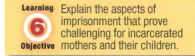

Learning Objective 6   Explain the aspects of imprisonment that prove challenging for incarcerated mothers and their children.

Further research indicates that an inmate who serves her sentence more than fifty miles from her residence is much less likely to receive phone calls or personal visits from family members. For most inmates and their families, the costs of "staying in touch" are too high.[103] This kind of separation can have serious consequences for the children of inmates. When a father goes to prison, his children are likely to live with their mother. When a mother is incarcerated, however, her children are likely to live with other relatives or, in about 11 percent of the cases, be sent to foster care.[104]

Only nine states provide facilities where inmates and their infant children can live together, and in these facilities nursery privileges generally end once the child is eighteen months old. Even this limited contact seems to be of great benefit to the mother. A ten-year study released in 2009 showed that the recidivism rate for mothers separated from newborns was 50 percent, compared with only 17 percent for mothers who had nursery privileges.[105] "Nothing has made me want to change before," said one incarcerated mother. "Kids make you want to change."[106]

The Culture of Women's Prisons

After spending five years visiting female inmates in the Massachusetts Correctional Institution (MCI) at Framingham, journalist Cristina Rathbone observed that the medium-security facility seemed "more like a high school than a prison."[107] The prisoners were older and tougher than high school girls, but they still divided into cliques, with the "lifers" at the top of the hierarchy and "untouchables" such as child abusers at the bottom. Unlike in men's prisons, where the underground economy revolves around drugs and weapons, at MCI-Framingham the most treasured contraband items are clothing, food, and makeup.[108]

▲ An inmate at the Decatur Correctional Center in Decatur, Illinois, plays with her three-month-old daughter. As part of the Moms with Babies program at this minimum security facility, incarcerated mothers can live with their infant children for up to two years while serving their sentences. **Why might this type of program reduce recidivism rates among participating inmates?**

Scott Olson/Getty Images News/Getty Images

The Pseudo-Family   Although both men's and women's prisons are organized with the same goals of control and discipline, the cultures within the two institutions are generally very different. As we have seen, male prison society operates primarily on the basis of power. Deprived of the benefits of freedom, male prisoners tend to create a violent environment that bears little relation to life on the outside.[109] In contrast, researchers have found that women prisoners prefer to re-create their outside identities by forming social networks that resemble, as noted earlier, high school cliques or, more commonly, the traditional family structure.[110] In these pseudo-families, inmates often play specific roles, with the more experienced convicts acting as "mothers" to younger, inexperienced "daughters." As one observer noted, the younger women rely on their "moms" for emotional support, companionship, loans, and even discipline.[111]

Sexual Violence and Prison Staff   Compared with men's prisons, women's prisons have extremely low levels of race-based, gang-related physical aggression.[112] Furthermore, though rates of sexual victimization can be high, most such episodes involve abusive sexual contacts such as unwanted touching rather than sexual assault or rape.[113]

One form of serious prison violence that does plague women prisoners, however, is sexual misconduct by prison staff. Although no large-scale study on sexual abuse of female inmates by male correctional officers exists, a number of state-level studies suggest that it is widespread.[114] Dr. Kerry Kupers, who has studied the effects of prison sexual assault, believes that it contributes to the PTSD, depression, anxiety, and other mental illnesses suffered by so many women prisoners.[115]

ETHICS CHALLENGE

A number of states place pregnant inmates in handcuffs or other forms of restraint as part of the procedure for childbirths that take place while the inmates are incarcerated. What might be some of the reasons for this practice? Do you feel it is an ethical way to treat these women during and after labor? Why or why not?

Return to Society

On August 28, 2016, according to Chicago police, Derren Sorrells took aim at a man driving a car, fired, and missed. The bullet struck and killed a young mother who was pushing a stroller down a nearby sidewalk. Sorrells, who had earlier been sentenced to six years behind bars for possession of a stolen vehicle, had been paroled from prison only two weeks earlier.

In contrast, two years after serving a decade in federal prison for drug distribution, Dquan Rosario earned a job as an emergency medical technician in Essex County, New Jersey. "Instead of peddling drugs that are destroying lives, he's saving lives," said one of Rosario's supporters. "He's making the community better."[116]

Each year, about 640,000 inmates are released from American prisons. The challenge for ex-inmates is to ensure that their post-release experience mirrors that of Dquan Rosario rather than that of Derren Sorrells. More than in the past, however, ex-convicts are not facing this challenge alone. Given the benefits to society of reducing recidivism, corrections officials and community leaders are making unprecedented efforts to help newly released prisoners establish crime-free lives.

Types of Prison Release

The majority of all inmates leaving prison—about two-thirds—do so through one of the parole mechanisms discussed in Chapter 12. Of the remaining third, most are given an **expiration release.**[117] Also known as "maxing out," expiration release occurs when an inmate has served the maximum amount of time on the initial sentence, minus reductions for good-time credits, and is not subjected to community supervision.

Another, quite rare unconditional release is a **pardon,** a form of executive clemency. The president (on the federal level) and the governor (on the state level) can grant a pardon, or forgive a convict's criminal punishment. Most states have a board of pardons— affiliated with the parole board—that makes recommendations to the governor in cases in which it believes a pardon is warranted. The majority of pardons involve obvious miscarriages of justice, though sometimes a governor will pardon an individual to remove the stain of conviction from her or his criminal record.

Learning Objective 7 Contrast parole, expiration release, pardon, and furlough.

Certain temporary releases also exist. Some inmates, who qualify by exhibiting good behavior and generally proving that they do not represent a risk to society, are allowed to leave the prison on **furlough** for a certain amount of time, usually between a day and a week. At times, a furlough is granted because of a family emergency, such as a funeral. Furloughs can be particularly helpful for an inmate who is nearing release and can use them to ease the readjustment period. Finally, certain alternative sentencing arrangements, discussed in Chapter 12, involve combinations of imprisonment and probation release. Generally, however, as you have seen, probationers experience community supervision in place of a prison term.

The Challenges of Reentry

What steps can corrections officials take to lessen the possibility that ex-convicts will reoffend following their release? Efforts to answer that question have focused on programs that help inmates make the transition from prison to the outside. In past years, these programs would have come under the general heading of "rehabilitation," but today corrections officials and criminologists refer to them as part of the strategy of **prisoner reentry.**

The concept of reentry has come to mean many things to many people. For our purposes, keep in mind the words of Joan Petersilia of the University of California at Irvine, who defines *reentry* as encompassing "all activities and programming conducted to prepare ex-convicts to return safely to the community and to live as law abiding citizens."[118] In other words, whereas rehab is focused on the individual offender, *reentry* encompasses the released convict's relationship with society.

Expiration Release The release of an inmate from prison at the end of his or her sentence without any further correctional supervision.

Pardon An act of executive clemency that overturns a conviction and erases mention of the crime from the person's criminal record.

Furlough Temporary release from a prison for purposes of vocational or educational training, to ease the shock of release, or for personal reasons.

Prisoner Reentry A corrections strategy designed to prepare inmates for a successful return to the community and to reduce their criminal activity after release.

▲ An Indiana Department of Corrections inmate works at the deli of a state reentry facility, learning skills that give him a better chance to reintegrate back into society after his release from prison. **Should all inmates be eligible for such reentry programs, regardless of the seriousness of the crimes they committed? Why or why not?** AP Photo/John Harrell

Barriers to Reentry   Perhaps the largest obstacle to successful prisoner reentry is the simple truth that life behind bars is very different from life on the outside. As one inmate explains, the "rules" of prison survival are hardly compatible with good citizenship:

> An unexpected smile could mean trouble. A man in uniform was not a friend. Being kind was a weakness. Viciousness and recklessness were to be respected and admired.[119]

The prison environment also insulates inmates. They are not required to make the day-to-day decisions that characterize a normal existence beyond prison walls. Bruce Western, a Harvard sociologist, describes one freed female offender who "frequently forgot to eat breakfast or lunch for several months because she was used to being called to meals in prison."[120]

Depending on the length of incarceration, a released inmate must adjust to an array of economic, technological, and social changes that took place while she or he was behind bars. Common acts such as using an ATM or a smartphone may be completely alien to someone who has just completed a long prison term. According to Ann Jacobs, director of the Prisoner Reentry Institute at New York's John Jay College of Criminal Justice, ex-convicts often perceive themselves as "imposters" who are "incapable of living a normal life."[121]

Housing and Employment   Other obstacles hamper reentry efforts. Housing can be difficult to secure, as many private property owners refuse to rent to someone with a criminal record, and federal and state laws restrict public housing options for ex-convicts. Finding affordable housing is, in turn, closely linked with another crucial and difficult step in the reentry process—finding a job.[122]

The Council of State Governments has tabulated more than 46,000 federal and state restrictions imposed on convicted felons, about three-quarters of which are employment-related.[123] Furthermore, background checks of potential employees are commonplace in corporate America. As a result, according to research conducted by the Ella Baker Institute, about a quarter of former inmates remain unemployed five years after their release, with the vast majority of the rest able to find only part-time or temporary work.[124]

These economic barriers can be complicated by the physical and mental condition of the freed convict. We have already discussed the high incidence of substance abuse among prisoners and the health-care needs of aging inmates. We have also described the high incidence of mental illness among prisoners. One study concluded that as many as one in five Americans leaving jail or prison is seriously mentally ill.[125] (See Figure 14.5 for a list of the hardships commonly faced by former inmates in their first year out of prison.)

The Threat of Relapse   Regardless of their ability to find a job or housing, many ex-convicts are fated to run afoul of the criminal justice system. Psychologists Edward Zamble and Vernon Quinsey explain the phenomenon as a *relapse process*.[126] Take the hypothetical example of an ex-convict who gets in a minor automobile accident while driving from his home to his job one morning. The person in the other car gets out and starts yelling at the ex-convict, who "relapses" and reacts just as he would have in prison—by punching the other person in the face. The ex-convict is then convicted of assault and battery and given a harsh prison sentence because of his criminal record.

Desistance The process through which criminal activity decreases and reintegration into society increases over a period of time.

Promoting Desistance   One ex-inmate compared the experience of being released to entering a "dark room, knowing that there are steps in front of you and waiting to fall."[127] The goal of reentry is to act as a flashlight for convicts by promoting **desistance,** a general term used to describe continued abstinence from offending and reintroduction of offenders into society. Certainly, the most important factor in the process is the individual convict. She or he has to *want* to desist and take steps to do so. In most cases, however, ex-inmates are going to need help—help getting an education, help finding and keeping a job, and help freeing themselves from harmful addictions to drugs and alcohol. Corrections officials are in a good position to offer this assistance, and their efforts in doing so form the backbone of the reentry movement.

Reentry planning starts behind bars. In addition to the rehabilitation-oriented prison programs discussed earlier in the chapter, most correctional facilities offer "life skills" classes to inmates. This counseling covers topics such as finding and keeping a job, locating a residence, understanding family responsibilities, and budgeting. After release, however, former inmates often find it difficult to continue with educational programs and

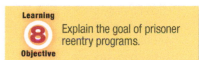

Learning Objective 8 Explain the goal of prisoner reentry programs.

FIGURE 14.5 **Prisoner Reentry Issues**

Researchers from the Urban Institute in Washington, D.C., asked nearly three hundred former prisoners (all male) in the Cleveland, Ohio, area about the most pressing issues they faced in their first year after release. The answers provide a useful snapshot of the many challenges of reentry.

1. **Housing.** Nearly two-thirds of the men were living with family members, and about half considered their housing situation "temporary." Many were concerned about their living environment: Half said that drug dealing was a major problem in their neighborhoods, and almost 25 percent were living with drug and alcohol abusers.

2. **Employment.** After one year, only about one-third of the former inmates had a full-time job, and another 11 percent were working part time.

3. **Family and friends.** One in four of the men identified family support as the most important thing keeping them from returning to criminality. Another 16 percent said that avoiding certain people and situations was the most crucial factor in their continued good behavior.

4. **Programs and services.** About two-thirds of the former inmates had taken part in programs and services such as drug treatment and continuing education.

5. **Health.** More than half of the men reported suffering from a chronic health condition, and 29 percent showed symptoms of depression.

6. **Substance use.** About half of the men admitted to weekly drug use or alcohol intoxication. Men who had strong family ties and those who were required to maintain telephone contact with their parole officers were less likely to engage in frequent substance use.

7. **Parole violation and recidivism.** More than half of the former inmates reported that they had violated the conditions of their parole, usually by drug use or having contact with other parolees. Fifteen percent of the men returned to prison in the year after release. Four out of five of the returns were the result of a new crime.

Source: Christy A. Visher and Shannon M. E. Courtney, *One Year Out: Experience of Prisoners Returning to Cleveland* (Washington, D.C.: Urban Institute, April 2007), 2.

Julie Howe Halfway House Program Manager

Early on in my career, I felt a bit intimidated by the clients simply because of my discomfort, not by their behavior. I started out very stern and learned later that it was better to start strong and to lighten up later rather than the reverse. The clients respect you more and know to take you seriously. My first client as a case manager was a real eye-opener. He was in his fifties, and I was in my early twenties. Earning his trust was quite a challenge. In the end, he learned to respect me, and I learned different techniques when working with offenders.

My favorite part of my job is that I know that I have an impact on people's lives. If I can assist someone to become sober, responsible, employed, and self-sufficient, I am also having an impact on the community and those whom my clients' lives touch. I never get tired of hearing clients say thanks and knowing their lives are forever changed when they realize their potential and value. I also love that I have the opportunity to influence the behavior of others and shape their future. What an awesome responsibility!

Courtesy of Julie Howe

SOCIAL MEDIA CAREER TIP Don't misrepresent facts or tell lies of omission online. Doing so in front of millions of online viewers virtually ensures that you will be caught, and such untruths can fatally damage career possibilities.

---

counseling as they struggle to readjust to life outside prison. Consequently, parole supervising agencies operate a number of programs to facilitate offenders' desistance efforts while, at the same time, protecting the community to the greatest extent possible.

Community-Based Reentry Programs As is made clear in Figure 14.5, work and lodging are crucial components of desistance. Corrections officials have several options in helping certain parolees—usually low-risk offenders—find employment and a place to live during the supervision period. Nearly a third of correctional facilities offer **work release programs,** in which prisoners nearing the end of their sentences are given permission to work at paid employment in the community.[128]

Inmates on work release either return to the correctional facility in the evening or, under certain circumstances, live in community residential facilities known as **halfway houses.** These facilities, also available to other parolees and those who have finished their sentences, are often remodeled hotels or private homes. They provide a less institutionalized living environment than a prison or jail for a small number of offenders (usually between ten and twenty-five). Halfway houses can be tailored to the needs of the former inmates. Many communities, for example, offer substance-free transitional housing for those whose past criminal behavior was linked to drug or alcohol abuse.

What Works in Reentry Research conducted by the Pew Center on the States found that 43 percent of ex-prisoners are back in prison or jail within three years of their release dates.[129] According to a study by professors Alfred Blumstein of Carnegie Mellon University

Work Release Program Temporary release of convicts from prison for purposes of employment. The offenders may spend their days on the job, but must return to the correctional facility at night and during the weekend.

Halfway House A community-based form of early release that places inmates in residential centers and allows them to reintegrate with society.

and Kiminori Nakamura of the University of Maryland, however, after ten to thirteen years in the community, ex-inmates pose the same risk of offending as do those without a criminal record.[130]

How can society help released prisoners go at least a decade without reoffending? In general, reentry planning produces positive results when it focuses on reducing substance abuse and promoting employment. To that end, a number of jurisdictions have established *reentry courts*, in which a judge ensures that inmates have been following their reentry requirements.

As noted earlier in the chapter, the reluctance of employers to consider hiring an ex-convict is a severe hurdle for many released inmates. Two policies have emerged to remedy this situation:

1. Expungement laws, which allow low-level criminals to remove offenses from their criminal records so that these crimes will not be uncovered by employer background checks.
2. "Ban the box" laws, which prohibit public employers from inquiring into the criminal backgrounds of potential employees by having a "criminal history box" on their application forms.[131]

Several dozen municipalities, fourteen states, and the federal government have passed "ban the box" legislation, and numerous corporations no longer make inquiries about criminal records early in the hiring process. Still, those with criminal convictions and arrest records will continue to find barriers to employment, given how easily such information is found online. "Criminal background screening is an important tool—nearly the only tool—that employers have to protect their customers, their employees, and themselves from criminal behavior," says Todd McCracken, president of the National Small Business Association.[132]

The Special Case of Sex Offenders

Despite the beneficial impact of reentry efforts, one group of wrongdoers has consistently been denied access to such programs: those convicted of sex crimes. The eventual return of these offenders to society causes such high levels of community anxiety that the criminal justice system has not yet figured out what to do with them.

Fear of Sex Offenders   Outraged that a halfway house for sex offenders was operating in their midst, residents of a Mesa, Arizona, neighborhood posted signs reading, "Sex Offenders, Felons, and Pedophiles," with arrows pointing toward the home. "It's a safety issue," explained one neighbor. "There is still that lingering effect that they could possibly strike again."[133] Such attitudes reflect the widespread belief that convicted sex offenders cannot be "cured" of their criminality and therefore are destined to continue committing sex offenses after their release from prison.

It is true that the medical health profession has had little success in treating the "urges" that lead to sexually deviant or criminal behavior.[134] This has not, however, translated into rampant recidivism among sex offenders compared with other types of criminals. According to the U.S. Department of Justice, the rearrest rates of rapists (46 percent) and those convicted of other forms of sexual assault (41 percent) are among the lowest for all offenders.[135]

Furthermore, after analyzing eighty-two recidivism studies, Canadian researchers R. Karl Hanson and Kelly Morton-Bourgon found that only 14 percent of sex offenders were apprehended for another sex crime after release from prison or jail. On average, such

Residency Restrictions

The Myth More than half of the states and hundreds of municipalities have passed residency restrictions for convicted sex offenders. These laws ban sex offenders from living within a certain distance of places where children naturally congregate. In New Jersey, for example, "high-risk" offenders cannot take up residence within 3,000 feet of any school, park or campground, church, theater, bowling alley, library, or convenience store. (For medium- and low-risk offenders, the distances are 2,500 feet and 1,000 feet, respectively.) These laws are premised on the belief that forbidding sex offenders from residing near schools and other areas that attract large groups of children decreases their access to these children, thus reducing the risk that they will reoffend.

The Reality Residency requirements are reassuring to parents and are generally very popular with the public. Many criminologists, however, see them as problematic. The overlapping "off-limits zones" created by residency requirements can dramatically limit where a sex offender can find affordable housing. In Milwaukee, for example, the number of homeless sex offenders spiked from about 15 to about 230 after the city passed a residency restriction ordinance several years ago. Research shows that without a permanent home, the lives of these offenders become less stable, making them more likely to reoffend.

Residency restrictions also push sex offenders into less populated areas, which makes it much more difficult for law enforcement and corrections agents to keep tabs on them. "Somebody might feel safer today because this one person doesn't live on their block. But as a community, we are not safer," said Holly Patzer, executive director of Wisconsin Community Services.

FOR CRITICAL ANALYSIS

Studies have shown that strangers commit only about 10 percent of all sexual offenses against children. The perpetrators of such crimes are much more likely to be family members, friends, or other acquaintances. Do these data strengthen or weaken the argument that residency requirements protect the community? Why?

offenders were significantly more likely to be rearrested for nonsexual criminal activity, if they were rearrested at all.[136]

Conditions of Release Whatever their recidivism rates, sex offenders are subject to extensive community supervision after being released from prison. Generally, they are supervised by parole officers and live under the same threat of revocation as other parolees. Specifically, many sex offenders—particularly child molesters—have the following special conditions of release:

- No contact with children under the age of eighteen.
- Psychiatric treatment.
- Must stay a certain distance from schools or parks where children are present.
- Cannot own toys that may be used to lure children.
- Cannot have a job or participate in any activity that involves children.

In New York State, paroled sex offenders must agree not to "engage in any Internet-enabled gaming activities to include Pokémon Go." This stipulation, designed to protect children who play such games, has been criticized as having "no meaningful public safety benefit" by the New York Civil Liberties Union.[137] (See the feature *Myth vs Reality—Residency Restrictions* to explore another condition of release for sex offenders that is often more popular with parents than with civil liberties advocates.)

Sex Offender Notification Law Legislation that requires law enforcement authorities to notify people when convicted sex offenders are released into their neighborhood or community.

Sex Offender Notification Laws

Perhaps the most dramatic step taken by criminal justice authorities to protect the public from sex crimes involves *sex offender registries*, or databases that contain sex offenders' names, addresses, photographs, and other information. The movement to register sex offenders started in the mid-1990s, after seven-year-old Megan Kanka of Hamilton Township, New Jersey, was raped and murdered by a twice-convicted pedophile (an adult sexually attracted to children) who had moved into her neighborhood after being released from prison on parole.

The next year, in response to public outrage, the state passed a series of laws known collectively as the New Jersey Sexual Offender Registration Act, or "Megan's Law."[138] Today, all fifty states and the federal government have a **sex offender notification law,** which requires local law authorities to alert the public when a sex offender has been released into the community.

Active and Passive Notification   No two sex offender notification laws have exactly the same provisions, but all are designed with the goal of allowing the public to learn the identities of convicted sex offenders living in their midst. In general, the laws demand that a paroled sex offender notify local law enforcement authorities on taking up residence in a state. In Georgia, for example, paroled sex offenders are required to present themselves to both the local sheriff and the superintendent of the public school district where they plan to live.[139] This registration process must be renewed every time the parolee changes address.

The authorities, in turn, notify the community of the sex offender's presence through the use of one of two models. Under the "active" model, the authorities directly notify the community or community representatives. Traditionally, this notification has taken the form of bulletins or posters, distributed and posted within a certain distance from the offender's home. Now, however, a number of states use e-mail alerts to fulfill notification obligations. In the "passive" model, information on sex offenders is made open and available for public scrutiny.

Prevalence of Sex Offender Registries   In 2006, Congress passed the Adam Walsh Child Protection and Safety Act, which established a national registry of sex offenders.[140] In addition, all fifty states operate sex offender registries with data on registered sex offenders in their jurisdictions. (For an idea of how this process works, you can visit the Federal Bureau of Investigation's Sex Offender Registry website.) The total number of registered sex offenders in the United States is about 800,000.

Civil Confinement   To many, any type of freedom, even if encumbered by notification requirements, is too much freedom for a sex offender. "The issue is, what can you do short of putting them all in prison for the rest of their lives?" complained one policymaker.[141]

In fact, a number of states have devised a legal method to keep sex offenders off the streets for, if not their entire lives, then close to it. These civil confinement laws allow corrections officials to lock up sex offenders in noncorrectional facilities such as psychiatric hospitals after the conclusion of their prison terms. Under these laws, corrections officials can keep sexual criminals confined for an unspecified amount of time as long as they are deemed a danger to society. In practice, civil confinement laws essentially give the state the power to detain this class of criminal indefinitely—a power upheld by the United States Supreme Court in 2010.[142]

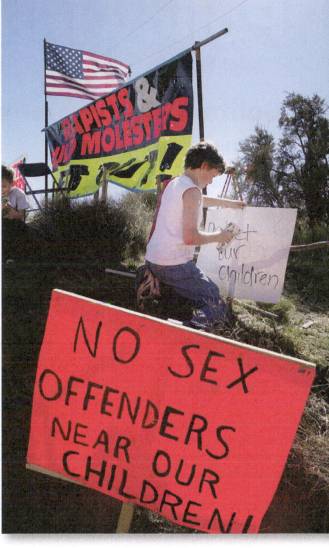

▲ Residents of Phelan, California, protest the opening of a proposed group home for sex offenders in their neighborhood. **What are some of the reasons that community members fear the nearby presence of freed sex offenders? Are these fears justified? Why or why not?** AP Images/Francis Specker

Civil Confinement The practice of confining individuals against their will if they present a danger to the community.

ETHICS CHALLENGE

Most universities include questions about an applicant's criminal record as part of the admissions process. Is this practice ethical? Why would such information be relevant? Explain your answers.

Solitary Confinement

How Things Stand

Solitary confinement, also known as restrictive housing, refers to the disciplinary practice of confining inmates by themselves in small cells for more than twenty-two hours each day over the course of weeks, months, or even years. Inmates are not sentenced to solitary confinement by a judge, and for most of them, the assignment has no connection with their original offense. Rather, prison officials use solitary confinement to separate prisoners deemed too dangerous to house with the general population. For the most part, these inmates either have engaged in serious misconduct (subject to *punitive segregation*), are likely to be targeted by other inmates (*protective segregation*), or are members of gangs and pose a threat to other inmates (*administrative segregation*).[143]

As a Result...

On any given day, between 80,000 and 100,000 federal and state inmates are "in solitary" in the United States.[144] Many prison administrators believe that the practice is a vital tool for maintaining order and discipline, particularly in institutions that are overcrowded and charged with controlling large numbers of violent offenders. They insist that it protects prison staff and inmates alike by removing dangerous convicts from the general inmate population.[145]

Criticism of solitary confinement focuses on its psychological impact on prisoners, particularly those with preexisting mental illnesses or those who are isolated for lengthy periods of time. After interviewing random solitary confinement inmates at California's Pelican Bay State Prison, psychologist Craig Haney found that 63 percent who had been isolated for more than ten years felt close to an "impending breakdown." These inmates also suffered from anxiety, paranoia, deep depression, and hallucinations.[146] Finally, many inmates are released directly from restrictive housing to the community without any transition period, leading to fears that they pose a particular danger to the public.[147]

Up for Debate

"It's a standard psychological concept, if you put people in isolation, they will go insane."[148] — *Sandra Schank, psychiatrist*

"Today's disciplinary confinement policies have evolved over decades of experience, and it is simply wrong to unilaterally take the tools away from law enforcement officers who face dangerous situations on a daily basis."[149] — *New York State Correctional Officers & Police Benevolent Association*

What's Your Take?

Review the discussion in this chapter on "Discipline" and "Protecting Prisoners' Rights" before answering the following questions.

1. As noted in the text, to show that prison officials have violated an inmate's Eighth Amendment rights, the inmate must prove that there was "deliberate indifference." Do you think that solitary confinement, in general, meets this standard? What if the confinement is essentially permanent? What if the inmate has a preexisting mental illness? Explain your answers.

2. As you saw earlier in the chapter, prison gangs pose numerous problems for prison administrators and correctional officers. Can you make the argument that lengthy solitary confinement is a reasonable disciplinary policy when it comes to prison gang members? Why or why not?

Digging Deeper...

Most states have no legislation that controls the use of solitary confinement. If you search online for **solitary confinement reform**, however, you will find that there have been some efforts in this direction in **California, Colorado, New York, and Washington State**. If you were to draft a model law for solitary confinement, what elements from these states' policies would it contain? Would you give prison officials a "free hand" in this area of prison discipline? Or would you restrict their discretion in determining who is placed in solitary, the length of the punishment, and the infractions to which it applies? Your answer should be at least three paragraphs long.

For more information on these concepts, look back to the Learning Objective icons throughout the chapter.

 Explain the concept of prison as a total institution. Though many people spend time in partial institutions—schools, companies where they work, and religious organizations—only in prison is every aspect of an inmate's life controlled, and that is why prisons are called total institutions. Every detail for every prisoner is fully prescribed and managed.

 Describe a risk run by corrections officials who fail to provide adequate medical care to the inmates under their control. In the first decade of the 2000s, medical care for inmates in California's prison system was severely compromised by extreme overcrowding. As a result, the U.S. Supreme Court ordered state corrections officials to release 30,000 inmates so that standards of health care in the prison could be more compatible "with the concept of human dignity."

 Indicate some of the reasons for violent behavior in prisons. (a) To separate the powerful from the weak and establish a prisoner hierarchy; (b) to minimize one's own probability of being a target of assault; (c) to enhance one's self-image; (d) to obtain sexual relief; and (e) to obtain material goods through extortion or robbery.

 List the circumstances in which courts have found that the "legitimate security interests" of a jail or prison justify the use of force by correctional officers. A correctional officer is justified in using force if she or he is (a) acting in self-defense; (b) protecting another prison employee or inmate; (c) upholding the rules of the correctional facility; (d) preventing an inmate from committing a crime; or (e) preventing an inmate from attempting to escape.

 Describe the hands-off doctrine of prisoner law and indicate two standards used to determine if prisoners' rights have been violated. The hands-off doctrine assumes that the care of prisoners should be left to prison officials and that it is not the place of judges to intervene. Nonetheless, the Supreme Court has created two standards to be used by the courts in determining whether a prisoner's Eighth Amendment protections against cruel and unusual punishment have been violated. Under the "deliberate indifference" standard, prisoners must show that prison officials were aware of harmful conditions at the facility and failed to remedy them. Under the "identifiable human needs" standard, prisoners must show that they were denied a basic need such as food, warmth, or exercise.

 Explain the aspects of imprisonment that prove challenging for incarcerated mothers and their children. Besides the anxiety that results from any separation of parent and child, incarcerated mothers often find it difficult to stay in contact with their children due to long distances between the prison and home. Furthermore, when a mother is imprisoned, her children are more likely not only to be separated from their father, but also to wind up in foster care.

 Contrast parole, expiration release, pardon, and furlough. Parole is an early release program for those incarcerated. Expiration release occurs when the inmate has served the maximum time for her or his initial sentence minus good-time credits. A pardon can be given only by the president or one of the fifty governors. Furlough is a temporary release while in jail or prison.

 Explain the goal of prisoner reentry programs. Based on the ideals of promoting desistance, these programs have two main objectives: (a) to prepare a prisoner for a successful return to the community, and (b) to protect the community by reducing the chances that the ex-convict will continue her or his criminal activity after release from prison.

 Indicate typical conditions for release for a paroled sex offender. (a) Have no contact with children under the age of eighteen; (b) continue psychiatric treatment; (c) keep away from schools or parks where children are present; (d) cannot own toys that may be used to lure children; and (e) cannot have a job or participate in any activity that involves children.

QUESTIONS FOR CRITICAL ANALYSIS

1. Can prison treatment and rehabilitation programs be justified for reasons that have nothing to do with their potential cost and safety benefits for society? In other words, does the American criminal justice system have a responsibility to individual inmates to "improve" them during incarceration?

2. Several years ago, an inmate sued the Florida Department of Corrections, claiming that his soy-based diet was cruel and unusual punishment. Under what circumstances, if any, do you think that unpleasant prison food can violate an inmate's constitutional rights?

3. Do you agree with prison policies that prohibit male correctional officers from patting down and strip-searching female inmates? Why or why not? Under what circumstances might such policies be unrealistic?

4. How does the process of prisonization differ between male and female inmates?

5. What is the main justification for legislation that prohibits convicted sex offenders from accessing Facebook and online video games? What is your opinion of such legislation?

KEY TERMS

civil confinement 483
"deliberate indifference" 472
deprivation model 463
desistance 479
expiration release 477
furlough 477
halfway house 480

"hands-off" doctrine 472
"identifiable human needs" 473
pardon 477
prisoner reentry 477
prison gang 465
prisonization 458
prison programs 460

prison segregation 464
relative deprivation 463
security threat group (STG) 465
sex offender notification law 482
therapeutic community (TC) 461
total institution 457
work release program 480

1. Erving Goffman, "On the Characteristics of Total Institutions," in *Asylums: Essays on the Social Situation of Mental Patients and Other Inmates* (New York: Doubleday, 1961), 6.

2. Donald Clemmer, *The Prison Community* (Boston: Christopher, 1940).

3. John Irwin, *Prisons in Turmoil* (Boston: Little, Brown, 1980), 67.

4. Jeremy Luallen and Ryan Kling, "A Method for Analyzing Changing Prison Populations: Explaining the Growth of the Elderly in Prison," *Evaluation Review* (December 2014), 459–486.

5. Bureau of Justice Statistics, *Medical Problems of State and Federal Prisoners and Jail Inmates, 2011–12* (Washington, D.C.: U.S. Department of Justice, February 2015), 1.

6. Bureau of Justice Statistics, *Mortality in Local Jails and State Prisons, 2000–2013—Statistical Tables* (Washington, D.C.: U.S. Department of Justice, August 2015), Table 16, page 20.

7. *Ibid.*, Table 23, page 23.

8. Michael E. Horowitz, "Top Management and Performance Challenges Facing the Department of Justice–2014." *www.oig.justice.gov.* Office of the Inspector General, 2014, Web.

9. Michael Ollove, "Elderly Inmates Burden State Prisons," *www.pewtrusts.org.* The Pew Charitable Trusts: March 17, 2016, Web.

10. Michael Vitiello, "Addressing the Special Problems of Mentally Ill Prisoners: A Small Piece of the Solution to Our Nation's Prison Crisis," *Denver University Law Review* (Fall 2010), 57–62.

11. Katherine Stuart van Wormer and Clemens Bartollas, *Women and the Criminal Justice System*, 3d ed. (Upper Saddle River, N.J.: Pearson Education, 2011), 143.

12. Bureau of Justice Statistics, *Mental Health Problems of Prison and Jail Inmates* (Washington, D.C.: U.S. Department of Justice, December 2006), Table 1, page 3.

13. William Kanapaux, "Guilty of Mental Illness." *www.psychiatrictimes.com. Psychiatric Times:* January 1, 2004, Web.

14. Bureau of Justice Statistics, *Census of State and Federal Correctional Facilities, 2005* (Washington, D.C.: U.S. Department of Justice, October 2008), 15.

15. Todd R. Clear, George F. Cole, and Michael D. Reisig, *American Corrections*, 11th ed (Boston: Wadsworth Cengage Learning, 2016), 362.

16. *Behind Bars II: Substance Abuse and America's Prison Population* (New York: The National Center on Addiction and Substance Abuse at Columbia University, February 2010), 4.

17. *Ibid.*, 83–84.

18. James A. Inciardi, James E. Rivers, and Duane C. McBride, "Drug Treatment," in *Prison and Jail Administration: Practice and Theory*, 3d ed., ed. Peter M. Carlson (Burlington, Mass.: Jones & Bartlett Learning, 2015), 202–204.

19. Devah Pager and Bruce Western, *Investigating Prisoner Reentry: The Impact of Conviction Status on the Employment Prospects of Young Men* (Washington, D.C.: National Institute of Justice, October 2009), 6.

20. *Census of State and Federal Correctional Facilities, 2005, op. cit.*, 6.

21. Lois M. Davis, et al., *Evaluating the Effectiveness of Correctional Education* (Santa Monica, Calif.: The Rand Corporation, 2013), xvi.

22. *Ibid.*, xvii.

23. Marilyn C. Moses and Cindy J. Smith, "Factories behind Fences: Do Prison 'Real Work' Programs Work?" *www.nij.gov.* National Institute of Justice: June 2007, Web.

24. Chandra Bozelko, "My Prison Job Wasn't About the Money." *www.wsj.com. Wall Street Journal:* October 11, 2015, Web.

25. Wendy Erisman and Jeanne B. Contardo, *Learning to Reduce Recidivism: A 50-State Analysis of Postsecondary Correctional Education Policy* (Washington, D.C.: Institute for Higher Education Policy, 2005), 1.

26. Danielle Douglas-Gabriel, "12,000 Inmates to Receive Pell Grants to Take College Classes." *www.washingtonpost.com. Washington Post:* June 24, 2016, Web.

27. Robert Johnson, *Hard Time: Understanding and Reforming the Prison*, 2d ed. (Belmont, Calif.: Wadsworth, 1996), 133.

28. Srinivas Konda, et al., "U.S. Correctional Officers Killed or Injured on the Job," *Corrections Today* (November/December 2013), 122–123.

29. Benjamin Steiner and Calli M. Cain, "The Relationship Between Inmate Misconduct, Institutional Violence, and Administrative Segregation: A Systematic Review of the Evidence," in *Restrictive Housing in the U.S.: Issues, Challenges, and Future Directions* (Washington, D.C.: National Institute of Justice, 2016), 166–167.

30. Daniel P. Mears, et al., "The Code of the Street and Inmate Violence: Investigating the Salience of Imported Belief Systems," *Criminology* (August 2013), 695–728.

31. Lee H. Bowker, *Prison Victimization* (New York: Elsevier, 1981), 31–33.

32. Stephen C. Light, "The Severity of Assaults on Prison Officers: A Contextual Analysis," *Social Science Quarterly* 71 (1990), 267–284.

33. Frank Tannenbaum, *Crime and Community* (Boston: Ginn & Co., 1938).

34. Randy Martin and Sherwood Zimmerman, "A Typology of the Causes of Prison Riots and an Analytical Extension to the 1986 Virginia Riot," *Justice Quarterly* 7 (1990), 711–737.

35. Bert Useem, "Disorganization and the New Mexico Prison Riot of 1980," *American Sociological Review* 50 (1985), 677–688.

36. Quoted in Christopher Harress, "Brutal Murder Underlines Increasingly Dangerous Conditions in Alabama Prison System." *www.al.com. AL.com:* October 7, 2016, Web.

37. James E. Robertson, "The Prison Rape Elimination Act of 2003: A Primer," *Criminal Law Bulletin* (May/June 2004), 270–273.

38. Deborah Sontag, "Push to End Prison Rape Loses Earlier Momentum," *New York Times* (May 13, 2015), A1.

39. 42 U.S.C. Sections 15601–15609 (2006).

40. "Only a Dozen States in Full Compliance with Federal Prison Rape Law." *www.thecrimereport.org. The Crime Report:* September 12, 2016, Web.

41. Quoted in Larissa MacFarquhar, "Out and Up," *New Yorker* (December 12, 2016), 60.

42. Irwin, *op. cit.*, 47.

43. Leo Carroll, "Race, Ethnicity, and the Social Order of the Prison," in *The Pains of Imprisonment*, ed. R. Johnson and H. Toch (Beverly Hills, Calif.: Sage, 1982).

44. *Lee v. Washington*, 390 U.S. 333 (1968).

45. *Johnson v. California*, 543 U.S. 499 (2005).

46. *Ibid.*, at 508.

47. Paige St. John, "California Prisons to End Race-Based Policy for Inmate Violence." *www.latimes.com. Los Angeles Times:* October 23, 2014, Web.

48. Craig Haney, "Psychology and the Limits of Prison Pain," *Psychology, Public Policy, and Law* (December 1977), 499.

49. Alan J. Drury and Matt DeLisi, "Gangkill: An Exploratory Empirical Assessment of Gang Membership, Homicide Offending, and Prison Misconduct," *Crime & Delinquency* (January 2011), 130–146.

50. George W. Knox, "The Problem of Gangs and Security Threat Groups (STGs) in American Prisons and Jails Today: Recent Findings from the 2012 NGCRC National Gang/STG Survey." *www.ngcrc.com.* National Gang Crime Research Center: 2012, Web.

51. *2013 National Gang Report* (Washington, D.C.: National Gang Intelligence Center, 2013), 15.

52. George W. Knox, "The Problem of Gangs and Security Threat Groups (STGs) in American Prisons Today: Recent Research Findings from the 2004 Prison Gang Survey." *www.ngcrc.com.* National Gang Crime Research Center: 2006, Web.

53. John Winterdyk and Rick Ruddell, "Managing Prison Gangs: Results from a Survey of U.S. Prison Systems," *Journal of Criminal Justice* 38 (2010), 733–734.

54. Quoted in John J. DiIulio, Jr., *No Escape: The Future of American Corrections* (New York: Basic Books, 1991), 268.

55. Jack Henry Abbott, *In the Belly of the Beast* (New York: Vintage Books, 1991), 54.

56. Michel Foucault, *Discipline and Punish: The Birth of the Prison* (New York: Pantheon Books, 1977), 128.

57. Clear, Cole, and Reisig, *op. cit.*, 340.

58. *Ibid.*, 342.

59. Peter M. Carlson and Lindsey Battles, "Changing Diversity of Correctional Officers," in *Prison and Jail Administration: Practice and Theory*, 3d ed., *op. cit.*, 260.

60. "Labor Force Statistics from the Current Population Survey: Employed Persons by Detailed Occupation, Sex, Race, and Hispanic or Latino Ethnicity." *www.bls.gov.* Bureau of Labor Statistics: 2016, Web.

61. Lucien X. Lombardo, *Guards Imprisoned: Correctional Officers at Work* (Cincinnati, Ohio: Anderson Publishing Co., 1989), 51–71.

62. Clair A. Crip, "Inmate Disciplinary Procedures," in *Prison and Jail Administration: Practice and Theory*, 3d ed., *op. cit.*, 344.

63. Goffman, *op. cit.*, 7.

64. Clear, Cole, and Reisig, *op. cit.*, 340.

65. *Wolff v. McDonnell*, 418 U.S. 539 (1974).

66. 475 U.S. 312 (1986).

67. *Stanley v. Hejirika*, 134 F.3d 629 (4th Cir. 1998).

68. Christopher R. Smith, *Law and Contemporary Corrections* (Belmont, Calif.: Wadsworth, 1999), Chapter 6.

69. 503 U.S. 1 (1992).

70. *Cooper v. Pate*, 378 U.S. 546 (1964).

71. *Kingsley v. Hendrickson*, 576 U.S. ___ (2015).

72. Van Wormer and Bartollas, *op. cit.*, 387.

73. Cristina Rathbone, *A World Apart: Women, Prison, and a Life behind Bars* (New York: Random House, 2006), 46.

74. Labor Force Statistics from the Current Population Survey: Employed Persons by Detailed Occupation, Sex, Race, and Hispanic or Latino Ethnicity," *op. cit.*

75. Kelly A. Cheeseman, Janet L. Mullings, and James W. Marquart, "Inmate Perceptions of Security Staff across Various Custody Levels," *Corrections Management Quarterly* (Spring 2001), 44.

76. Michael H. Jaime and Armand R. Burruel, "Labor Relations in Corrections," in *Prison and Jail Administration: Practice and Theory*, 3d ed., *op. cit.*, 264.

77. *Wolff v. McDonnell*, 539.

78. *Hudson v. Palmer*, 468 U.S. 517 (1984).

79. 429 U.S. 97 (1976).

80. Juan A. Lozano, "Judge: Texas Prison's Water Violates Standards of Decency." *www.bigstory.ap.org. Associated Press*: June 22, 2016, Web.

81. 501 U.S. 294 (1991).

82. *Wilson v. Seiter*, 501 U.S. 294, 304 (1991).

83. *Woodall v. Foti*, 648 F.2d, 268, 272 (5th Cir. 1981).

84. Paige St. John, "In a First, California Agrees to Pay for Transgender Inmate's Sex Reassignment." *www.latimes.com. Los Angeles Times*: August 10, 2015, Web.

85. *Brown v. Plata*, 563 U.S. ___ (2011).

86. *Procunier v. Martinez*, 416 U.S. 396 (1974).

87. *Cruz v. Beto*, 405 U.S. 319 (1972); *Gittlemacker v. Prasse*, 428 F.2d 1 (3d Cir. 1970); and *Kahane v. Carlson*, 527 F.2d 492 (2d Cir. 1975).

88. Maryclaire Dale, "Court Says Pa. Prison Can Ban Muslim Scarf," *Associated Press* (August 2, 2010).

89. Elizabeth Nolan Brown, "Jail Newspaper Ban Not Justified by Threat of Clogged Toilets and Paper Mâché Weapons." *www.reason.com. Reason*: July 8, 2015, Web.

90. Quoted in Alexandra Marks, "Martha Checks in Today," *Seattle Times* (October 8, 2004), A8.

91. Emily M. Wright, et al., "Gender-Responsive Lessons Learned and Policy Implications for Women in Prison: A Review," *Criminal Justice and Behavior* (September 2012), 1612–1632.

92. Bureau of Justice Statistics, *Sourcebook of Criminal Justice*, 3d ed. (Washington, D.C.: U.S. Department of Justice, 2003), Table 6.56, page 519; and Bureau of Justice Statistics, *Prisoners in 2015* (Washington, D.C.: U.S. Department of Justice, December 2016) Table 9, page 14.

93. Bureau of Justice Statistics, *Profile of Jail Inmates, 2002* (Washington, D.C.: U.S. Department of Justice, July 2004), 10.

94. Bureau of Justice Statistics, *Prior Abuse Reported by Inmates and Probationers* (Washington, D.C.: U.S. Department of Justice, April 1999), 2.

95. *Caught in the Net: The Impact of Drug Policies on Women and Families* (Washington, D.C.: American Civil Liberties Union, 2004), 18–19.

96. Allen J. Beck and Laura M. Maruschak, *Mental Health Treatment in State Prisons, 2000* (Washington, D.C.: U.S. Department of Justice, July 2001), 1.

97. Barbara Bloom, Barbara Owen, and Stephanie Covington, *Gender Responsive Strategies: Research, Practice, and Guiding Principles for Women Offenders* (Washington, D.C.: National Institute of Corrections, 2003), 6.

98. *Ibid.*, 7.

99. Wright, et al., *op. cit.*, 1618–1624.

100. Grant Duwe and Valerie Clark, "Importance of Program Integrity: Outcome Evaluation of a Gender-Responsive, Cognitive-Behavioral Program for Female Offenders," *Criminology & Public Policy* (May 2015), 304–308.

101. Bureau of Justice Statistics, *Parents in Prison and Their Minor Children* (Washington, D.C.: U.S. Department of Justice, March 2010), 2.

102. Kelly Bedard and Eric Helland, "Location of Women's Prisons and the Deterrent Effect of 'Harder' Time," *International Review of Law and Economics* (June 2004), 152.

103. *Ibid.*

104. Sarah Schirmer, Ashley Nellis, and Marc Mauer, *Incarcerated Parents and Their Children: Trends 1991–2007* (Washington, D.C.: The Sentencing Project, February 2009), 5.

105. Joseph R. Carlson, "Prison Nurseries: A Pathway to Crime-Free Futures," *Corrections Compendium* (Spring 2009), 17–24.

106. Quoted in Sarah Yager, "Prison Born." *www.theatlantic.com. The Atlantic*: July/August 2015, Web.

107. Rathbone, *op. cit.*, 4.

108. *Ibid.*, 158.

109. Van Wormer and Bartollas, *op. cit.*, 137–138.

110. Barbara Bloom and Meda Chesney-Lind, "Women in Prison," in *It's a Crime: Women and Justice*, 4th ed., ed. Roslyn Muraskin (Upper Saddle River, N.J.: Prentice Hall, 2007), 542–563.

111. Piper Kerman, *Orange Is the New Black: My Year in a Women's Prison* (New York: Spiegal and Grau, 2011), 131.

112. Barbara Owen, et al., "Gendered Violence and Safety: A Contextual Approach to Improving Security in Women's Facilities." *www.ncjrs.gov*. National Criminal Justice Reference Service: December 2008, Web.

113. Nancy Wolff, Cynthia Blitz, Jing Shi, Jane Siegel, and Ronet Bachman, "Physical Violence inside Prisons: Rates of Victimization," *Criminal Justice and Behavior* 34 (2007), 588–604.

114. Van Wormer and Bartollas, *op. cit.*, 146–148.

115. Cited in Bloom, Owen, and Covington, *op. cit.*, 26.

116. Quoted in S. P. Sullivan, "Obama Tells N.J. Inmate's Recovery Story during Newark Stop." *www.nj.com. NJ.com*: November 3, 2015, Web.

117. *Prisoners in 2015, op. cit.*, Table 7, page 11.

118. Joan Petersilia, *When Prisoners Come Home: Parole and Prisoner Reentry* (New York: Oxford University Press, 2003), 39.

119. Victor Hassine, *Life without Parole: Living in Prison Today*, ed. Thomas J. Bernard and Richard McCleary (Los Angeles: Roxbury Publishing Co., 1996), 12.

120. Bruce Western, et al., "Stress and Hardship after Prison," *American Journal of Sociology* (March 2015), 1526.

121. Quoted in Jon Mooallem, "You Just Got Out of Prison. Now What?" *New York Times Sunday Magazine* (July 29, 2015), 38.

122. "Public Housing for People with Criminal Histories." *https://www.vera.org/publications/public-housing-for-people-with-criminal-histories-fact-sheet*. Vera Institute of Justice, 2015, Web.

123. "National Inventory of the Collateral Consequences of Conviction." *https://niccc.csgjusticecenter.org*. The Council of State Governments: visited March 4, 2017, Web.

124. Saneta deVuono-Powell, et al., *Who Pays? The True Cost of Incarceration on Families* (Oakland, Calif.: Ella Baker Center, 2015), 20.

125. *Ill Equipped: U.S. Prisons and Offenders with Mental Illness* (New York: Human Rights Watch, 2003).

126. Edward Zamble and Vernon Quinsey, *The Criminal Recidivism Process* (Cambridge, England: Cambridge University Press, 1997).

127. Quoted in Kevin Johnson, "After Years of Solitary, Freedom Is Hard to Grasp," *USA Today* (June 9, 2005), 2A.

128. *Census of State and Federal Correctional Facilities, 2005, op. cit.*, Table 6, page 5.

129. Pew Center on the States, *State of Recidivism: The Revolving Door of America's Prisons* (Washington, D.C.: The Pew Charitable Trusts, April 2011), 2.

130. Alfred Blumstein and Kiminori Nakaruma, "Redemption in the Presence of Widespread Criminal Background Checks," *Criminology* (May 2009), 327–359.

131. *The State of Sentencing 2014: Developments in Policy and Practice* (Washington, D.C.: The Sentencing Project, February 2015), 8–9.

132. Quoted in Binyamin Appelbaum, "Out of Trouble, Out of Work," *New York Times* (March 1, 2015), BU1.

133. Quoted in MaryEllen Resendez, "Neighbors Continue Battle against Sex Offender Halfway House in Mesa." *www.abc15.com. ABC15 Arizona*: February 8, 2016, Web.

134. Belinda Brooks Gordon and Charlotte Bilby, "Psychological Interventions for Treatment of Adult Sex Offenders," *British Medical Journal* (July 2006), 5–6.

135. Bureau of Justice Statistics, *Recidivism of Prisoners Released in 1994* (Washington, D.C.: U.S. Department of Justice, June 2002), Table 9, page 8.

136. R. Karl Hanson and Kelly Morton-Bourgon, "The Characteristics of Persistent Sexual Offenders: A Meta-Analysis of Recidivism Studies, *Journal of Consulting and Clinical Psychology* 73 (2005), 1154–1163.

137. Quoted in Eli Rosenberg, "In a Safeguard for Children, Some Civil Liberties Groups See Concerns," *New York Times* (August 22, 2016), A14.

138. New Jersey Revised Statute Section 2C:7-8(c) (1995).

139. Georgia Code Annotated Section 42-9-44.1(b)(1).

140. Public Law Number 109–248, Section 116, 120 Statute 595 (2006).

141. Abby Goodnough, "After Two Cases in Florida, Crackdown on Molesters," *Law Enforcement News* (May 2004), 12.

142. *United States v. Comstock*, 560 U.S. 126 (2010).

143. Ryan M. Labrecque, *The Effect of Solitary Confinement on Institutional Misconduct* (Cincinnati, Ohio: University of Cincinnati, Division of Research and Advanced Studies, 2015), 1.

144. Liman Program & Association of State Correctional Administrators, *Time-In-Cell: ASCA-Liman 2014 National Survey of Administrative Segregation in Prison* (New Haven, Conn.: Yale Law School, 2015).

145. Maureen L. O'Keefe, "Administrative Segregation from Within: A Corrections Perspective," *The Prison Journal* 88 (2008), 123–143.

146. Erica Goode, "Solitary Confinement: Punished for Life," *New York Times* (August 4, 2015), D1.

147. "Resolution on the Release of Inmates Directly from Solitary Confinement." *www.alec.org*. American Legislature Exchange Council: July 1, 2014, Web.

148. Quoted in Susie Neilson, "How to Survive Solitary Confinement." *www.nautil.us. Nautilus*: January 28, 2016, Web.

149. Quoted in Timothy Williams, "Prison Officials Join Movement to Curb Solitary Confinement," *New York Times* (September 3, 2015), A1.

The Juvenile Justice System

To target your study and review, look for these numbered Learning Objective icons throughout the chapter.

Chapter Outline		Corresponding Learning Objectives
The Evolution of American Juvenile Justice	**1**	Describe the child-saving movement and its relationship to the doctrine of *parens patriae*.
	2	List the four major differences between juvenile courts and adult courts.
	3	Identify and briefly describe the single most important U.S. Supreme Court case with respect to juvenile justice.
Determining Delinquency Today	**4**	Describe the reasoning behind recent U.S. Supreme Court decisions that have lessened the harshness of sentencing outcomes for violent juvenile offenders.
Trends in Juvenile Delinquency	**5**	Define *bullying*, and list the four components that are often present in this sort of behavior.
Factors in Juvenile Delinquency	**6**	Describe the one variable that always correlates highly with juvenile crime rates.
First Contact: The Police and Pretrial Procedures	**7**	List the factors that normally determine what police do with juvenile offenders.
	8	Describe the four primary components of pretrial juvenile justice procedure.
Trying and Punishing Juveniles	**9**	Explain the distinction between an adjudicatory hearing and a disposition hearing.

Bad Thing. Good Kid?

▲ In Indiana, juvenile court judges have the ability to remove an eighteen-year-old violent juvenile offender from adult prison if there is evidence that the young inmate can be rehabilitated. AP Images/Daniel Mears/*Detroit News*

"I know I committed a truly horrible crime and I am sorry for that," said Paul Gingerich, his voice breaking while he addressed a courtroom in Kosciusko County, Indiana. "I will never stop being sorry and I know sorry will never be enough." Six years earlier, in the same courtroom, a twelve-year-old Gingerich had pleaded guilty to shooting and killing Phil Danner, the stepfather of his fifteen-year-old friend Colt Lundy. (Gingerich and Lundy, who also took part in the murder, wanted to run away together and saw Danner as an impediment to these plans.) For his crimes, a judge sentenced Gingerich to twenty-five years behind bars.

The decision to punish such a young boy so harshly spurred calls for the reform of Indiana's juvenile justice system. As a result, the state legislature passed "Paul's Law," named in honor of Gingerich. This statute gives Indiana judges the discretion to remove violent juvenile offenders from adult prison at the age of eighteen if

there is evidence that the offender is susceptible to changing her or his ways. "Adolescent development research proves that children are fundamentally different than adults," said a supporter of Paul's Law. "They are more prone to risk-taking behavior, more susceptible to peer pressure, and they are uniquely capable of rehabilitation."

In 2016, an eighteen-year-old Gingerich petitioned to have his sentence readjusted under Paul's Law. He had spent the five years since Danner's murder in the Pendleton Juvenile Correctional Facility, amassing an impressive record of good behavior and successful therapy. After hearing evidence of Gingerich's rehabilitation, Judge James Heuer decided that the young man would spend only three hundred days in adult prison before serving the remainder of his sentence—nearly two decades—under home detention. "I am willing to bet the mortgage on Paul Gingerich," said Monica Foster, his lawyer, noting that any misstep would land her client back behind bars. "He is a good kid who did a very bad thing."

FOR CRITICAL ANALYSIS

1. What is your opinion of Judge James Hueur's decision to spare Paul Gingerich from having to spend the remainder of his sentence in adult prison?

2. Much juvenile justice reform is based on the assumption that young people who commit murder should be given a chance to rehabilitate themselves because they were not old enough to fully appreciate the magnitude of their crimes. Do you agree with this reasoning? Why or why not?

3. Even though he was initially charged as an adult, Indiana corrections officials decided against sending twelve-year-old Gingerich to an adult prison. Instead, they placed him in a juvenile facility. What might have been some of the reasons for this decision?

The Evolution of American Juvenile Justice

A difficult question—asked every time a youthful offender such as Paul Gingerich commits a heinous act of violence—lies at the heart of the juvenile justice debate: Should such acts by youths be given the same weight as those committed by adults, or should they be seen as "mistakes" that can be corrected by care and counseling?

From its earliest days, the American juvenile justice system has operated as an uneasy compromise between "rehabilitation and punishment, treatment and custody."[1] At the beginning of the 1800s, juvenile offenders were treated the same as adult offenders—they were judged by the same courts and sentenced to the same severe penalties. This situation began to change soon after, as urbanization and industrialization created an immigrant underclass that was, at least in the eyes of many reformers, predisposed to deviant activity. Certain members of the Progressive movement, known as the child savers, began to take steps to "save" children from these circumstances, introducing the idea of rehabilitating delinquents in the process.

The Child-Saving Movement

In general, the child savers favored the doctrine of *parens patriae,* which holds that the state has not only a right but also a duty to care for children who are neglected, delinquent, or in some other way disadvantaged. Juvenile offenders, the child savers believed, required treatment, not punishment, and they were horrified at the thought of placing children in prisons with hardened adult criminals. In 1967, then Supreme Court justice Abe Fortas said of the child savers:

Learning Objective 1 Describe the child-saving movement and its relationship to the doctrine of *parens patriae.*

> They believed that society's role was not to ascertain whether the child was "guilty" or "innocent," but "What is he, how has he become what he is, and what had best be done in his interest and in the interest of the state to save him from a downward career." The child—essentially good, as they saw it—was made "to feel that he is the object of [the government's] care and solicitude," not that he was under arrest or on trial.[2]

Child-saving organizations convinced local legislatures to pass laws that allowed them to take control of children who exhibited criminal tendencies or had been neglected by their parents. To separate these children from the environment in which they were raised, the organizations created a number of institutions, the best known of which was New York's House of Refuge. Opening in 1825, the House of Refuge implemented many of the same reformist measures popular in the penitentiaries of the time, meaning that its charges were subjected to the healthful influences of hard study and labor. Although the House of Refuge was criticized for its harsh discipline (which caused many boys to run away), similar institutions sprang up throughout the Northeast during the middle of the 1800s.

The Illinois Juvenile Court

The efforts of the child savers culminated with the passage of the Illinois Juvenile Court Act in 1899. The Illinois legislature created the first court specifically for juveniles, guided by the principles of *parens patriae* and based on the belief that children are not fully responsible for criminal conduct and are capable of being rehabilitated.[3]

Parens Patriae A doctrine that holds that the state has a responsibility to look after the well-being of children and to assume the role of parent if necessary.

The Illinois Juvenile Court and those in other states that followed in its path were (and, in many cases, remain) drastically different from adult courts:

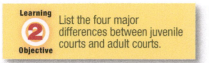
Learning Objective **2** List the four major differences between juvenile courts and adult courts.

- *No juries.* The matter was decided by judges who wore regular clothes instead of black robes and sat at a table with the other participants rather than behind a bench. Because the primary focus of the court was on the child and not the crime, the judge had wide discretion in disposing of each case.
- *Different terminology.* To reduce the stigma of criminal proceedings, "petitions" were issued instead of "warrants." The children were not "defendants" but "respondents," and they were not "found guilty" but "adjudicated delinquent."
- *No adversarial relationship.* Instead of trying to determine guilt or innocence, the parties involved in the juvenile court worked together in the best interests of the child, with the emphasis on rehabilitation rather than punishment.
- *Confidentiality.* To avoid "saddling" the child with a criminal past, juvenile court hearings and records were kept sealed, and the proceedings were closed to the public.

By 1945, every state had a juvenile court system modeled after the first Illinois court. For the most part, these courts were able to operate without interference until the 1960s and the onset of the juvenile rights movement.

Status Offending

Status Offender A juvenile who has engaged in behavior deemed unacceptable for those under a certain statutorily determined age.

Juvenile Delinquency Illegal behavior committed by a person who is under an age limit specified by statute.

After the first juvenile court was established in Illinois, the Chicago Bar Association described its purpose as, in part, to "exercise the same tender solicitude and care over its neglected wards that a wise and loving parent would exercise with reference to his [or her] own children under similar circumstances."[4] In other words, the state was given the responsibility of caring for those minors whose behavior seemed to show that they could not be controlled by their parents.

As a result, many **status offenders** found themselves in the early houses of refuge, and these offenders continue to be placed in state-run facilities today. A status offense is an act that, when committed by a juvenile, is considered illegal and grounds for possible state custody. The same act, when committed by an adult, does not warrant law enforcement action. (See Figure 15.1 for an idea of which status offenses are most commonly brought to the attention of authorities.)

FIGURE 15.1 Status Offenses

About 109,000 status offenses are processed by juvenile courts in the United States each year. The most common, as this graph shows, are truancy (skipping school) and liquor-related offenses.

Miscellaneous 8%
Running away from home 8%
Curfew violations 9%
Ungovernability* 9%
Liquor law violations 15%
Truancy 51%

* Being beyond the control of parents, teachers, or other adult authority figures.

Source: Sarah Hockenberry and Charles Puzzanchera, *Juvenile Court Statistics, 2013* (Pittsburgh, Pa.: National Center for Juvenile Justice, July 2015), 66.

Juvenile Delinquency

In contrast to status offending, **juvenile delinquency** refers to conduct that would also be criminal if committed by an adult. According to federal law and the laws of most states, a juvenile delinquent is someone who has not yet reached his or her eighteenth birthday—the age of adult criminal responsibility—at the time of the offense in question. In two states (New York and North Carolina), persons aged sixteen are considered adults, and five other states confer adulthood on seventeen-year-olds for purposes of criminal law.

Under certain circumstances, discussed later in this chapter, children under these ages can be tried in adult courts and incarcerated in adult prisons and jails. Remember, from the opening of this chapter, that Paul Gingerich was twelve years old when he was charged as an adult and sentenced to a long term in prison for his role in the murder of Phil Danner. By contrast, in most cases, an offender who is adjudicated as a juvenile and held in a juvenile corrections facility cannot be held past her or his eighteenth or twenty-first birthday, depending on the jurisdiction, regardless of the seriousness of the underlying wrongdoing.

Constitutional Protections and the Juvenile Court

Though the ideal of the juvenile court seemed to offer the "best of both worlds" for juvenile offenders, in reality the lack of procedural protections led to many children being arbitrarily punished not only for crimes, but for status offenses as well. Juvenile judges were treating all violators similarly, which led to many status offenders being incarcerated in the same institutions as violent delinquents. In response to a wave of lawsuits demanding due process rights for juveniles, the United States Supreme Court issued several rulings in the 1960s and 1970s that significantly changed the juvenile justice system.

▲ Students at Simon Elementary School in Washington, D.C., show off numbered index cards that can be turned in for various prizes such as pencils, snacks, or backpacks. This daily raffle is part of an effort to combat truancy in the city's school system. **What is the primary difference between a status offense such as truancy and an act of juvenile delinquency?** Evelyn Hockstein/*Washington Post*/Getty Images

Kent v. United States   The first decision to extend due process rights to children in juvenile courts was *Kent v. United States* (1966).[5] The case concerned sixteen-year-old Morris Kent, who had been arrested for breaking into a woman's house, stealing her purse, and raping her. Because Kent was on juvenile probation, the state sought to transfer his trial for the crime to an adult court.

Without giving any reasons for his decision, the juvenile judge consented to this strategy, and Kent was sentenced in the adult court to a thirty- to ninety-year prison term. The Supreme Court overturned the sentence, ruling that juveniles have a right to counsel and a hearing in any instance in which the juvenile judge is considering sending the case to an adult court. The Court stated that, in such cases, a child receives "the worst of both worlds," getting neither the "protections accorded to adults" nor the "solicitous care and regenerative treatment" offered in the juvenile system.[6]

In re Gault   The *Kent* decision provided the groundwork for *In re Gault* one year later. Considered by many to be the single most important case concerning juvenile justice, *In re Gault* involved a fifteen-year-old boy who was arrested for allegedly making a lewd phone call while on probation.[7] In its decision, the Supreme Court held that juveniles facing a loss of liberty were entitled to many of the same basic procedural safeguards granted to adult offenders in this country. (See the feature *Landmark Cases*—In re Gault for more information on this case.)

Other Important Court Decisions   Over the next ten years, the Supreme Court handed down three more important rulings on juvenile court procedure. The ruling in *In re Winship* (1970)[8] required the government to prove "beyond a reasonable doubt" that a juvenile had committed an act of delinquency, raising the burden of proof from a "preponderance of the evidence." In *Breed v. Jones* (1975),[9] the Court held that the Fifth Amendment's double jeopardy clause prevented a juvenile from being tried in an adult court for a crime that had already been adjudicated in juvenile court. In contrast, the

In re Gault

 Learning Objective 3 Identify and briefly describe the single most important U.S. Supreme Court case with respect to juvenile justice.

In 1964, fifteen-year-old Gerald Gault and a friend were arrested for making lewd telephone calls to a neighbor in Gila County, Arizona. Gault, who was on probation, was placed under custody with no notice given to his parents. The juvenile court in his district held a series of informal hearings to determine Gault's punishment. During these hearings, no records were kept, Gault was not afforded the right to counsel, and the complaining witness was never made available for questioning. At the close of the hearing, the judge sentenced Gault to remain in Arizona's State Industrial School until the age of twenty-one. Gault's lawyers challenged this punishment, arguing that the proceedings had denied their client his due process rights. Eventually, the matter reached the United States Supreme Court.

In re Gault
United States Supreme Court
387 U.S. 1 (1967)

In the Words of the Court . . .

Justice Fortas, Majority Opinion

From the inception of the juvenile court system, wide differences have been tolerated—indeed insisted upon—between the procedural rights accorded to adults and those of juveniles. In practically all jurisdictions, there are rights granted to adults which are withheld from juveniles.

The absence of substantive standards has not necessarily meant that children receive careful, compassionate, individualized treatment. The absence of procedural rules based upon constitutional principle has not always produced fair, efficient, and effective procedures. Departures from established principles of due process have frequently resulted not in enlightened procedure, but in arbitrariness.

Ultimately, however, we confront the reality of that portion of the Juvenile Court process with which we deal in this case. A boy is charged with misconduct. The boy is committed to an institution where he may be restrained of liberty for years.* * * His world becomes "a building with whitewashed walls, regimented routine and institutional hours. . . ." Instead of mother and father and sisters and brothers and friends and classmates, his world is peopled by guards, custodians, state employees, and "delinquents" confined with him for anything from waywardness to rape and homicide. In view of this, it would be extraordinary if our Constitution did not require the procedural regularity and the exercise of care implied in the phrase "due process." Under our Constitution, the condition of being a boy does not justify a kangaroo court.

★ ★ ★ ★

Decision

The Court held that juveniles were entitled to the basic procedural safeguards afforded by the U.S. Constitution, including the right to advance notice of charges, the right to counsel, the right to confront and cross-examine witnesses, and the privilege against self-incrimination. The decision marked a turning point in juvenile justice in this country: No longer would informality and paternalism be the guiding principles of juvenile courts. Instead, due process would dictate the adjudication process, much as in an adult court.

FOR CRITICAL ANALYSIS

What might be some of the negative consequences of the *In re Gault* decision for juveniles charged with committing delinquent acts? Can you think of any reasons why juveniles should not receive the same due process protections as adult offenders?

---

decision in *McKeiver v. Pennsylvania* (1971)[10] represented an instance in which the Court did not move the juvenile court further toward the adult model. In that case, the Court ruled that the Constitution did not give juveniles the right to a jury trial.

Determining Delinquency Today

In the eyes of many observers, the net effect of the Supreme Court decisions during the 1966–1975 period was to move juvenile justice away from the ideals of the child savers. As a result of these decisions, many young offenders would find themselves in a formalized system that is often indistinguishable from its adult counterpart. At the same time, though the Court has recognized that minors charged with crimes possess certain constitutional rights, it has failed to dictate at what age these rights should be granted. Consequently, the legal status of children in the United States varies depending on where they live, with each state making its own policy decisions on the crucial questions of age and competency.

The Age Question

In Chapter 4, we saw that early American criminal law recognized infancy as a defense against criminal charges. At that time, on attaining fourteen years of age, a youth was considered an adult and treated accordingly by the criminal justice system. During the "get tough on crime" movement of the 1990s, many states took steps that promoted sending young offenders to adult courts. Recently, however, states are moving in the opposite direction. From 2009 to 2016, six states raised the age at which offenders are treated as adults from seventeen to eighteen. Today, forty-three states treat offenders under the age of eighteen as juveniles (see Figure 15.2).

The consequences of this shift are significant. Suppose, for example, that a seventeen-year-old gets into a fight at school. In Alabama, where the juvenile age limit is eighteen, her parents will be notified, and if necessary, her case will be handled by a juvenile court. In neighboring Georgia, where the age limit is seventeen, she might be arrested, charged with battery, and housed in a local jail until she can post bail. There is a good chance she will be expelled from school for missing multiple days of class, and she will almost certainly be burdened with an arrest record for the rest of her life.

Regardless of a state's age limits, young offenders of *any* age who commit violent crimes can be *transferred* to adult court by means of a process we will discuss later in the chapter. Those defendants can, and often do, receive lengthy sentences to be served in adult prisons.

When young offenders who remain in juvenile court are found guilty, they receive "limited" sentences that usually expire when they turn eighteen or twenty-one. In addition, young offenders who are processed in the juvenile justice system have significantly lower recidivism rates than those sent to the adult system.[11]

The Culpability Question

Many researchers believe that by the age of fourteen, an adolescent has the same ability as an adult to make a competent decision. Nevertheless, according to some observers, a juvenile's capacity to understand the difference between "right" and "wrong" does not mean that she or he should be held to the same standards of competency as an adult.

FIGURE 15.2 **Age Limit for Juvenile Court Jurisdiction**

For the majority of states, eighteen years is the age under which youthful offenders will be considered juveniles and have their cases adjudicated in juvenile court.

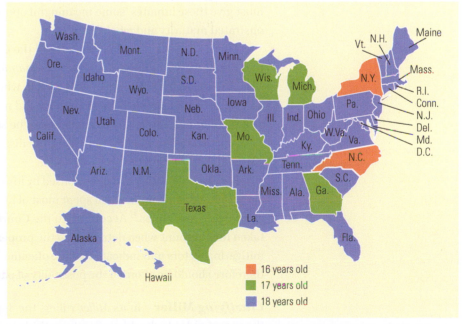

- 16 years old
- 17 years old
- 18 years old

Source: "Juvenile Age of Jurisdiction and Transfer to Adult Court Laws." *www.ncsl.org*. National Conference of State Legislatures: February 1, 2017, Web.

Juvenile Behavior   A study released in 2003 by the Research Network on Adolescent Development and Juvenile Justice found that 33 percent of juvenile defendants in criminal courts had the same low level of understanding of legal matters as mentally ill adults who had been found incompetent to stand trial.[12] Legal psychologist Richard E. Redding believes that

> adolescents' lack of life experience may limit their real-world decision-making ability. Whether we call it wisdom, judgment, or common sense, adolescents may not have nearly enough.[13]

Juveniles are generally more impulsive, more likely to engage in risky behavior, and less likely to calculate the long-term consequences of any particular action. Furthermore, adolescents are far more likely to respond to peer pressure than are adults, meaning that they often engage in the same criminal or delinquent behavior as their friends.[14] Accordingly, they are arrested as part of a group at much higher rates than adults.[15] Furthermore, juveniles are less likely than adults to display remorse immediately following a violent act. As a result, they are often penalized by the courts for showing "less grief than the system demands."[16]

Diminished Guilt   The "diminished culpability" of juveniles was one of the reasons given by the United States Supreme Court in its landmark decision in *Roper v. Simmons* (2005).[17] As we saw in Chapter 11, that case forbade the execution of offenders who were under the age of eighteen when they committed their crimes. In his majority opinion, Justice Anthony Kennedy wrote that because minors cannot fully comprehend the consequences of their actions, the two main justifications for the death penalty—retribution and deterrence—do not "work" with juvenile wrongdoers.[18]

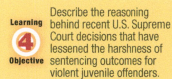

Learning Objective 4 Describe the reasoning behind recent U.S. Supreme Court decisions that have lessened the harshness of sentencing outcomes for violent juvenile offenders.

Life Imprisonment Issues   The Supreme Court applied the same reasoning in two later cases that have dramatically affected the sentencing of violent juvenile offenders. First, in *Graham v. Florida* (2010),[19] the Court held that juveniles who commit crimes that do not involve murder may not be sentenced to life in prison without the possibility of parole. According to Justice Kennedy, who wrote the majority opinion, state officials must give these inmates "some meaningful opportunity to obtain release based on demonstrated maturity and rehabilitation."[20]

Then, with *Miller v. Alabama* (2012),[21] the Court banned laws in twenty-eight states that made life-without-parole sentences *mandatory* for juveniles convicted of murder. The case focused on the fate of Evan Miller, who was fourteen years old when he killed a neighbor with a baseball bat. The ruling did not signify that juvenile offenders such as Miller could not, under any circumstances, be sentenced to life without parole. Rather, the Court stated that judges must have the discretion to weigh the mitigating factors in each individual case.

For example, Miller had been abused by his stepfather and neglected by his alcoholic and drug-addicted mother, had spent most of his life in foster care, and had tried to commit suicide four times.[22] According to the Court, this type of personal history must be taken into account when determining the proper sentence for a juvenile murderer. Such mitigating factors may indicate that the offender has the potential to be rehabilitated and therefore should be afforded the possibility of parole.

Clarifying **Miller**   In its *Miller* ruling, the Supreme Court failed to indicate whether the new standards should apply retroactively to inmates already serving mandatory life-without-parole terms for crimes committed as juveniles. The Court clarified this matter in

2016, holding that each of the approximately two thousand such offenders imprisoned in this nation should be given a new chance at release.[23]

Discussing this ruling, Justice Kennedy clearly indicated his distaste for sending juveniles to prison for the remainder of their lives. "A sentencer might encounter the rare juvenile offender who exhibits such irretrievable depravity that rehabilitation is impossible and life without parole is justified," he stated. But, given young people's "diminished culpability and heightened capacity for change," the "appropriate occasions for sentencing juveniles to this harshest possible penalty will be uncommon."[24]

▲ Isaiah Sweet, center, was sentenced to life in prison without parole for murdering his grandparents with an assault rifle when he was seventeen years old. In 2016, the Iowa Supreme Court overturned Sweet's sentence, ruling that sending juveniles to prison for life without parole amounts to cruel and unusual punishment and is therefore unconstitutional. **Do you agree with the court's decision? Why or why not?** AP images/*Dubuque Telegraph Herald*, Dave Kettering

Trends in Juvenile Delinquency

When asked, juveniles will admit to a wide range of illegal or dangerous behavior, including carrying weapons, getting involved in physical fights, driving after drinking alcohol, and stealing or deliberately damaging school property.[25] Has the juvenile justice system been effective in controlling and preventing this kind of misbehavior, as well as more serious acts? Answering this question requires us to examine recent trends in the extent of juvenile delinquency.

Delinquency by the Numbers

According to the Uniform Crime Reporting program, in 2015, juveniles accounted for 10.2 percent of violent crime arrests and 8.5 percent of criminal activity arrests in general.[26] As Figure 15.3 shows, juvenile arrest rates for violent crimes have fluctuated dramatically over the past three decades. In the 2000s, with a few exceptions, juvenile crime in the United States has decreased at a rate similar to that of adult crime, as discussed earlier in this textbook. From 2004 to 2013, juvenile court delinquency caseloads declined by 37 percent.[27] Not surprisingly, the drop in juvenile arrests and court appearances has led to fewer juveniles behind bars. The national population of juvenile inmates decreased 52 percent between 1997 and 2014, allowing officials in some states, including California, Ohio, and Texas, to close juvenile detention facilities.[28]

The Decline of Juvenile Crime   A number of theories have been put forth to explain the downturn in juvenile offending. Some observers point to the increase in police action against "quality-of-life" crimes such as loitering, which they believe stops juveniles before they have a chance to commit more serious crimes. Similarly, about 80 percent of American municipalities enforce juvenile curfews, which restrict the movement of minors during certain hours, usually after dark.[29] In 2015, law enforcement made about 45,000 arrests for curfew and loitering law violations.[30]

Furthermore, hundreds of local programs designed to educate children about the dangers of drugs and crime operate across the country. The results of such

FIGURE 15.3 **Arrest Rates of Juveniles**

After rising dramatically in the mid-1990s, juvenile arrest rates for violent crimes have—with a few exceptions—continued to drop steadily in the 2000s.

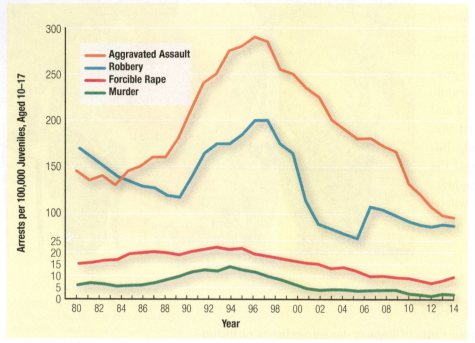

Source: "Statistical Briefing Book: Juvenile Arrest Rates." *www.ojjdp.gov.* Office of Juvenile Justice and Delinquency Prevention: visited March 22, 2017, Web.

community-based efforts are difficult, if not impossible, to measure—it cannot be assumed that children would have become delinquent if they had not participated. Nevertheless, these programs are generally considered a crucial element of keeping youth crime under control.[31]

Race and Juvenile Offending

As is the case in the criminal justice system, African Americans are overrepresented in the juvenile justice system. The total delinquency case rate for black juveniles is more than double that for white juveniles.[32] African American youths are more likely to be arrested for every major category of crime than are white youths, and more than six in every ten juvenile offenders in state custody is a member of a minority group.[33] Furthermore, black students are three times more likely to face school disciplinary action—discussed later in the chapter—than are white students.[34]

Gender and Juvenile Offending

Although overall rates of juvenile offending have been dropping, arrest rates for girls are declining more slowly than those for boys. Between 1997 and 2013, the number of cases involving males in delinquency courts declined 47 percent, while the female caseload declined by 34 percent.[35] Self-reported studies show, however, that there has been little change in girls' violent behavior over the past few decades.[36] How, then, do we explain why delinquency rates for girls have changed and why the change is different from that for boys?

Detention Trends Evidence shows that law enforcement officers are more likely to apprehend girls than boys for status offenses and nonviolent behavior. According to the most recent statistics, 37 percent of girls detained by juvenile justice authorities were being held for status offenses and technical violations of probation, compared with 25 percent of boys.[37] Furthermore, 21 percent of girls detained by authorities were taken into custody for simple assault and public order offenses, compared to just 12 percent of boys.[38] Criminologists who focus on issues of gender hypothesize that such behavior is considered normal for boys, but is seen as deviant for girls and therefore more deserving of punishment.[39]

Family- and Gender-Based Delinquency A significant amount of data also suggest that police are much more likely to make arrests in situations involving domestic violence than was the case several decades ago. Experts have found that girls are four times more apt to fight with parents or siblings than are boys, who usually engage in violent encounters with strangers. Consequently, a large percentage of female juvenile arrests for assault arise out of family disputes—arrests that until relatively recently would not have been made.[40] Finally, because girls are more likely to be exploited in sex trafficking operations, they represent a significant majority of juveniles arrested for prostitution and commercialized vice.[41]

School Violence

One late Monday morning in February 2016, fourteen-year-old James Austin Hancock brought a .380-caliber handgun into the cafeteria of the Madison Junior-Senior High School in Madison Township, Ohio. Hancock opened fire, wounding four classmates before fleeing. The incident was every student's (and teacher's and parent's) worst nightmare. Like other episodes of school violence, it received heavy media coverage, fanning fears that our schools are unsafe.

Safe Schools?   Research does show that juvenile victimization and delinquency rates increase during the school day, and the most common juvenile crimes, such as simple assaults, are most likely to take place on school grounds.[42] In spite of well-publicized shootings such as the one carried out by James Austin Hancock, however, violent crime is not commonplace in American schools. In fact, less than one-half of one percent of students are the victims of serious violent crimes such as aggravated assault, robbery, and rape at school.[43]

Although serious violence on campus is rare, 65 percent of American schools do experience at least one such incident each school year, and about 450,000 fights not involving a weapon take place at schools annually.[44] Furthermore, physical bullying, threats, and weapon-carrying are relatively commonplace in the learning environment, particularly when groups of students gather without adult supervision.[45] Indeed, research shows that juveniles are most likely to be victims of violent crime on school days between 3 P.M. and 4 P.M.—in other words, just after the end of classes.[46]

Security Measures   Victimization rates of students for nonfatal crimes have declined significantly over the past twenty-five years.[47] In part, this downturn reflects general crime trends. Additionally, since the fatal shootings of fourteen students and a teacher at Columbine High School near Littleton, Colorado, in 1999, many schools have improved security measures. From 1999 to 2013, the percentage of American schools using security cameras to monitor their campuses increased from 19 to 64 percent. In addition, three-quarters of public schools control access to school buildings by locking or monitoring their doors.[48]

Educators are increasingly using the "smart policing" measures we discussed in Chapter 6 to identify potential threats to school safety. For example, every school in Virginia is required by state law to have a "threat assessment" team that attempts to forecast potential student victimization situations.[49] Furthermore, many districts rely on law enforcement officers to patrol school grounds, a controversial practice that we will cover in the *Policy Matters* feature at the end of the chapter.

Disciplinary Measures   The Columbine shootings also led many schools to adopt "zero tolerance" policies when it comes to student behavior. These policies require strict punitive measures, such as suspension, expulsion, or referral to the police, for *any* breach of the school's disciplinary code. As a result, according to research conducted by the Vera Institute of Justice, one in nine secondary school students are suspended or expelled each year.[50]

The many critics of zero-tolerance policies point out that only 5 percent of serious school disciplinary actions involve possession of a weapon.[51] Examples of less-serious student behavior resulting in expulsion include incidents in which a seven-year-old ate a Pop-Tart into the shape of a gun, a young boy fired an imaginary bow and arrow, and a six-year-old boy kissed a six-year-old girl on the hand.[52] This trend of reacting harshly to minor infractions may have serious repercussions for society. Students who have been expelled for any amount of time are at a much greater risk for future involvement in the juvenile justice system than those who have not faced such disciplinary measures.[53]

CJ & TECHNOLOGY

Gunshot Detectors in Schools

The sad—and frightening—reality concerning school shootings is that they are almost impossible to predict, making them very difficult to stop. An estimated two-thirds of such incidents in American schools are over before police are able to engage the shooter. The challenge, then, is to link schools with local law enforcement agencies to speed up the response time to active shooters.

With this goal in mind, several years ago California's Newark Memorial High School became the first school in the United States to install gunshot-detection sensors on campus grounds. This technology uses microphones, computer software, a clock, and satellite positioning technology to pinpoint the precise location and time of gunfire. When the system is "triggered" by a gunshot, the school's security camera immediately provides a live feed of the event to a local law enforcement agency. Ideally, this will give police a good idea of the suspect's description and location, as well as the danger posed to students and staff. "[The technology] won't stop a school shooting but it'll get us to the shooter quicker," says Newark Police Commander Mike Carroll.

Thinking about Gunshot Detectors in Schools

Suppose a school attack involves a knife, a hidden bomb, or some other "silent" weapon. What kind of technological "trigger" could be used to alert local law enforcement in these situations?

Bullying

A disproportionate number of young people who do bring guns or other weapons to school report that they have been *bullied* by other students.[54] **Bullying** can be broadly defined as repeated, aggressive behavior that contains at least one of the following elements:

1. *Physical abuse,* such as hitting, punching, or damaging the subject's property.
2. *Verbal abuse,* such as teasing, name calling, intimidation, or homophobic or racist remarks.
3. *Social and emotional abuse,* such as spreading false rumors, social exclusion, or playing jokes designed to humiliate.
4. *Cyber abuse,* which includes any form of bullying that takes place online or through the use of devices such as smartphones. (We will explore the issue of *cyberbullying* more fully in the next chapter's discussion of cyber crime.)

Changing Perspectives Bullying has traditionally been seen more as an inevitable rite of passage among adolescents than as potentially criminal behavior. In recent years, however, society has become more aware of the negative consequences of bullying, underscored by a number of high-profile "bullycides." In October 2016,

Bullying Overt acts taken by students with the goal of intimidating, harassing, or humiliating other students.

for example, eleven-year-old Bethany Thompson fatally shot herself in Cable, Ohio, apparently after enduring sustained teasing for having a "crooked smile" because of a brain tumor operation. According to research conducted at Yale University, juveniles who have been bullied are between two and nine times more likely to commit suicide than those who have not been bullied.[55]

Legal Responses   According to data gathered by the federal government, 28 percent of students aged twelve to eighteen have been victims of bullying.[56] In particular, LGBT (lesbian, gay, bisexual, and transgender) students are targeted—two-thirds report having been bullied within the previous year.[57] As a response to this problem, nearly every state has passed anti-bullying legislation. These laws focus mostly on "soft" measures, such as training school personnel how to recognize and respond to bullying.[58]

With a few exceptions, state legislatures have been reluctant to take "harder" measures, such as specifically labeling bullying a crime. Consequently, parents of bullied children have had to turn to civil courts for "justice" in this matter. Several years ago, for example, the parents of a fourteen-year-old Missouri boy who committed suicide after being taunted about his sexual orientation were awarded $300,000 because of the "deliberate indifference" of school officials. According to one estimate, about a hundred successful anti-bullying lawsuits have been filed over the past two decades, with a number of plaintiffs awarded more than $1 million in damages.[59]

ETHICS CHALLENGE

A municipal ordinance in Shawano, Wisconsin, allows city officials to fine parents who are told that their children are behaving like bullies and who do nothing to stop the behavior. The penalty for a first offense is $366. What is your opinion of this law? Is it ethical? Is it enforceable? Explain your answers.

Factors in Juvenile Delinquency

As we discussed in Chapter 2, an influential study conducted by Professor Marvin Wolfgang and several colleagues in the early 1970s introduced the "chronic 6 percent" to criminology. The researchers found that out of one hundred boys, six will become chronic offenders, meaning that they will be arrested five or more times before their eighteenth birthdays. Furthermore, the researchers determined that these chronic offenders are responsible for half of all crimes and two-thirds of all violent crimes within any given cohort (a group of persons who have similar characteristics).[60]

Does this "6 percent rule" mean that no matter what steps society takes, six out of every hundred juveniles are "bad seeds" and will act delinquently? Or does it point to a situation in which a small percentage of children may be more likely to commit crimes under certain circumstances?

Most criminologists favor the second interpretation. In this section, we will examine the four factors that have traditionally been used to explain juvenile criminal behavior and violent crime rates: age, substance abuse, family problems, and gangs. Keep in mind, however, that the factors influencing delinquency are not limited to these areas (see Figure 15.4). Researchers are constantly interpreting and reinterpreting statistical evidence to provide fresh perspectives on this very important issue.

FIGURE 15.4 Risk Factors for Juvenile Delinquency

The characteristics listed here are generally accepted as "risk factors" for juvenile delinquency. In other words, if one or more of these factors are present in a juvenile's life, he or she has a greater chance of exhibiting delinquent behavior—though such behavior is by no means a certainty.

Family	• Single parent/lack of parental role model • Parental or sibling drug/alcohol abuse • Extreme economic deprivation • Family members in a gang or in prison
School	• Academic frustration/failure • Learning disability • Negative labeling by teachers • Disciplinary problems
Community	• Social disorganization (refer to Chapter 2) • Presence of gangs and obvious drug use in the community • Availability of firearms • High crime/constant feeling of danger • Lack of social and economic opportunities
Peers	• Delinquent friends • Friends who use drugs or who are members of gangs • Lack of "positive" peer pressure
Individual	• Mental illness • Tendency toward aggressive behavior • Inability to concentrate or focus/easily bored/hyperactive • Alcohol or drug use • Fatalistic/pessimistic viewpoint

Learning Objective 6 Describe the one variable that always correlates highly with juvenile crime rates.

Aging Out A term used to explain the fact that criminal activity declines with age.

Age of Onset The age at which a juvenile first exhibits delinquent behavior.

The Age-Crime Relationship

Crime statistics are fairly conclusive on one point: The older a person is, the less likely he or she will exhibit criminal behavior. Self-reported studies confirm that most people are involved in some form of criminal behavior—however "harmless"—during their early years. In fact, Terrie Moffitt of Duke University has said that "it is statistically aberrant to refrain from crime during adolescence."[61] So why do the vast majority of us not become chronic offenders?

According to many criminologists, particularly Travis Hirschi and Michael Gottfredson, any group of at-risk persons—regardless of gender, race, intelligence, or class—will commit fewer crimes as they grow older.[62] This process is known as **aging out** (or, sometimes, *desistance*, a term we introduced in the preceding chapter). Professor Robert J. Sampson and his colleague John H. Laub believe that this phenomenon is explained by certain events, such as marriage, employment, and military service, that force delinquents to "grow up" and forgo criminal acts.[63]

Another view sees the **age of onset,** or the age at which a youth begins delinquent behavior, as a consistent predictor of future criminal behavior. One study compared recidivism rates between juveniles first judged to be delinquent before the age of fifteen and those first adjudicated delinquent after the age of fifteen. Of the seventy-one subjects who made up the first group, 32 percent became chronic offenders. Of the sixty-five who made up the second group, none became chronic offenders.[64]

Furthermore, according to the Office of Juvenile Justice and Delinquency Prevention, the earlier a youth enters the juvenile justice system, the more likely he or she will become a violent offender.[65] This research suggests that juvenile justice resources should be concentrated on the youngest offenders, with the goal of preventing crime and reducing the long-term risks for society.

Substance Abuse

As we have seen throughout this textbook, substance abuse plays a strong role in criminal behavior for adults. The same can certainly be said for juveniles.

A Strong Correlation
Drug use is associated with a wide range of antisocial and illegal behaviors by juveniles, from school suspensions to large-scale theft.[66] Nearly all young offenders (94 percent) entering juvenile detention self-report drug use at some point in their lives, and 85 percent have used drugs in the previous six months.[67] According to the Arrestee Drug Abuse Monitoring Program, nearly 60 percent of male juvenile detainees and 46 percent of female juvenile detainees test positive for drug use at the time of their offense.[68]

Drug use is a particularly strong risk factor for girls. Some 75 percent of young women incarcerated in juvenile facilities report regular drug and alcohol use—starting at the age of fourteen—and one study found that 87 percent of female teenage offenders need substance abuse treatment.[69]

Strong Causation?   The correlation between substance abuse and offending for juveniles seems obvious. Does this mean that substance abuse *causes* juvenile offending? Researchers make the point that most youths who become involved in antisocial behavior do so before their first experience with alcohol or drugs. Therefore, it would appear that substance abuse is a form of delinquent behavior rather than its cause.[70] Still, one study of adolescent offenders did find that substance abuse treatment reduces criminal behavior in the short term, suggesting that, at the least, the use of illegal drugs is an integral component of the juvenile delinquent lifestyle.[71]

Child Abuse and Neglect

Abuse by parents also plays a substantial role in juvenile delinquency. Child abuse can be broadly defined as the infliction of physical, emotional, or sexual damage on a child. Child neglect is a form of abuse that occurs when caregivers deprive a child of necessities such as love, shelter, food, and proper care. According to the National Survey of Children's Exposure to Violence, one in ten children in the United States experiences mistreatment at the hands of a close family member before reaching eighteen years of age.[72]

Children in homes characterized by violence or neglect suffer from a variety of physical, emotional, and mental health problems at a much greater rate than their peers.[73] This, in turn, increases their chances of engaging in delinquent behavior. One survey of violent juveniles showed that 75 percent had been subjected to severe abuse by a family member and 80 percent had witnessed violence in their homes.[74] Nearly half of all juveniles—and 80 percent of girls—sentenced to life in prison suffered high rates of abuse.[75]

Cathy Spatz Widom, a professor of psychology at John Jay College of Criminal Justice, compared the arrest records of two groups of subjects—one made up of 908 cases of substantiated parental abuse and neglect, and the other made up of 667 children who had not been abused or neglected. Widom found that those who had been abused or neglected were 53 percent more likely to be arrested as juveniles than those who had not.[76] Simply put, according to researchers Janet Currie of Columbia University and Erdal Tekin of Georgia State University, "child maltreatment roughly doubles the probability that an individual engages in many types of crime."[77]

Gangs

When youths cannot find the stability and support they require in the family structure, they often turn to their peers. This is just one explanation for why juveniles join youth gangs. Although jurisdictions may have varying definitions, for general purposes a youth gang is viewed as a group of three or more persons who (1) self-identify as an entity separate from the community by adopting special clothing, vocabulary, hand signals, and names and (2) engage in criminal activity. According to research conducted by criminologists David C. Pyrooz and Gary Sweeten, there are just over a million gang members between the ages of five and seventeen in the United States.[78]

A study of criminal behavior among juveniles in Seattle found that gang members were considerably more likely to commit crimes than at-risk youths who shared

Child Abuse Mistreatment of children involving physical, emotional, or sexual damage.

Child Neglect A form of child abuse in which the child is denied certain necessities such as shelter, food, care, and love.

Youth Gang A self-formed group of youths with several identifiable characteristics, including a gang name and other recognizable symbols, a geographic territory, and participation in illegal activities.

many characteristics with gang members but were not affiliated with any gang (see Figure 15.5). The survey also found that gang members were much more likely to own firearms or have friends who did than non–gang members.[79] In addition, on reaching adulthood, youth gang members have worse outcomes than their peers in a number of areas, including drug abuse, likelihood of arrest and incarceration, and general health.[80]

Who Joins Gangs?

The average gang member is eighteen years old, though members are often older in cities with long traditions of gang activity, such as Chicago and Los Angeles. Although it is difficult to determine with any certainty the makeup of gangs as a whole, one recent survey found that 53 percent of all gang members in the United States are Latino, 32 percent are African American, and 10 percent are white, with the remaining 5 percent belonging to other racial or ethnic backgrounds.[81]

Though gangs tend to have racial or ethnic characteristics—that is, one group predominates in each gang—many researchers do not believe that race or ethnicity is the dominant factor in gang membership. Instead, gang members seem to come from lower-class or working-class communities, mostly in urban areas but with an increasing number from the suburbs and rural counties.

A small percentage of youth gang members are female. In many instances, girls associate themselves with gangs, even though they are not considered members. Generally, girls assume subordinate gender roles in youth gangs, providing emotional, physical, and sexual services for the dominant males.[82] Still, almost half of all youth gangs report having female members, and involvement of girls in gangs appears to be increasing.[83]

Why Join Gangs?

The decision to join a gang, like the decision to engage in any sort of antisocial or criminal behavior, is a complex one, and the factors that go into it vary

---

FIGURE 15.5 Comparison of Gang and Nongang Delinquent Behavior

Taking self-reported surveys of subjects aged thirteen to eighteen in the Seattle area, researchers for the Office of Juvenile Justice and Delinquency Prevention found that gang members were much more likely to exhibit delinquent behavior than non–gang members.

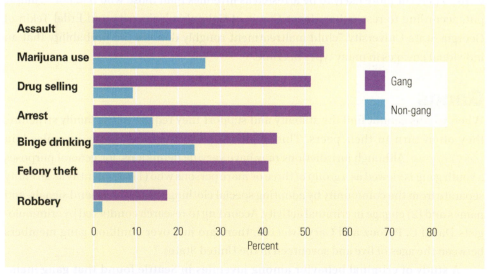

Source: Karl G. Hill, Christina Lui, and J. David Hawkins, *Early Precursors of Gang Membership: A Study of Seattle Youth* (Washington, D.C.: Office of Juvenile Justice and Delinquency Prevention, December 2001), Figure 1, page 2.

depending on the individual. Generally, however, the reasons for gang membership involve one or more of the following:

1. *Identity.* Being part of a gang often confers a status that the individual feels he or she could not attain outside the gang.

2. *Protection.* Many gang members live in neighborhoods marked by high levels of crime and violence, and a gang guarantees support and retaliation in case of an attack.

3. *Fellowship.* The gang often functions as an extension of the family and provides companionship that may not be available at home.

4. *Criminal activity.* Many gang members enjoy financial rewards because of the gang's profits and protection.

5. *Intimidation.* Some gang members are pressured or forced to join the gang, often to act as "foot soldiers" in the gang's criminal enterprises.[84]

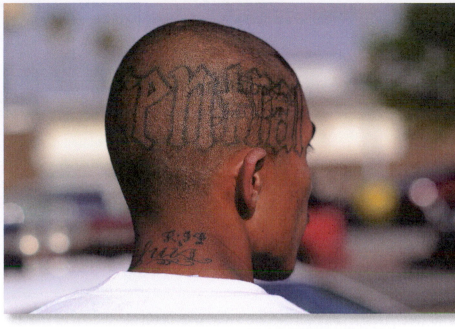

▲ In Los Angeles, a gang member signifies his allegiance to the "Street Villains" through a series of elaborate tattoos. **What role does identity play in a juvenile's decision to join a gang?** Kevork Djansezian/Getty Images News/Getty Images

To help gang members leave their gang, "desistance experts" often focus on counteracting the same pressures that initially led to gang membership. For example, gang members with intimate partners and children are encouraged to commit to their "real family" rather than their "gang family." Help in gaining legal employment can also reduce some of the financial incentives for gang members to continue their illegal activities.[85]

First Contact: The Police and Pretrial Procedures

In an attempt to stem the tide of violent crime in their city, Chicago police officers spend hours monitoring the social media accounts of local gang members, who often use that format to boast about past and future criminal activity. Most commonly, however, contact between juvenile offenders and law enforcement takes place on the streets, initiated by a police officer on patrol who either apprehends the juvenile while he or she is committing a crime or answers a call for service. The youth is then passed on to an officer of the juvenile court, who must decide how to handle the case. (See Figure 15.6 for an overview of the juvenile justice process.)

Police Discretion and Juvenile Crime

Police arrest about 580,000 youths under the age of eighteen each year.[86] In most states, police officers must have probable cause to believe that the minor has committed an offense, just as they would if the suspect was an adult. Police power with regard to juveniles is greater than with adults, however, because police can take youths into custody for status offenses, such as possession of alcohol or truancy. In these cases, the officer is acting *in loco parentis*, or in the place of the parent. The officer's role is not necessarily to punish the youths, but to protect them from harmful behavior.

FIGURE 15.6 The Juvenile Justice Process

This diagram shows the possible tracks that a young person may take after her or his first contact with the juvenile justice system (usually a police officer).

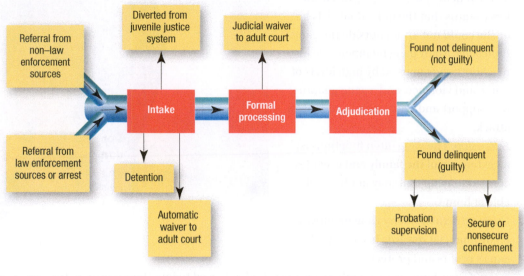

Source: Office of Juvenile Justice and Delinquency Prevention.

Low-Visibility Decision Making

Police officers also have a great deal of discretion in deciding what to do with juveniles who have committed crimes or status offenses. Juvenile justice expert Joseph Goldstein labels this discretionary power **low-visibility decision making** because it relies on factors that the public is not generally in a position to understand or criticize. When a grave offense has taken place, a police officer may decide to formally arrest the juvenile, send him or her to juvenile court, or place the youth under the care of a social-service organization. In less serious situations, the officer may simply issue a warning or take the offender to the police station and release the child into the custody of her or his parents.

In making these discretionary decisions, police generally consider the following factors:

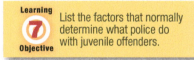

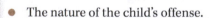

- The nature of the child's offense.
- The offender's past history of involvement with the juvenile justice system.
- The setting in which the offense took place.
- The ability and willingness of the child's parents to take disciplinary action.
- The attitude of the offender.
- The offender's gender.

Law enforcement officers notify the juvenile court system that a particular young person requires its attention through a process known as a **referral.** Anyone with a valid reason, including parents, relatives, welfare agencies, and school officials, can refer a juvenile to the juvenile court. The vast majority of cases in juvenile courts, however, are referred by the police.[87]

Arrests and Minority Youths

As noted earlier in the chapter, members of minority groups are disproportionately represented in juvenile arrests. Furthermore, the referral rate for black juveniles is more than double the referral rate for white juveniles.[88] A great deal of research, much of it contradictory, has been done to determine whether

Low-Visibility Decision Making A term used to describe the discretionary power police have in determining what to do with misbehaving juveniles.

Referral The notification process through which a law enforcement officer or other concerned citizen makes the juvenile court aware of a juvenile's unlawful or unruly conduct.

these statistics reflect inherent racism in the juvenile justice system or whether social factors are to blame.[89] One large-scale study, performed by federal government crime researchers Carl E. Pope and Howard Snyder using the National Incident-Based Reporting System, found that nonwhite offenders were no more likely than white offenders to be arrested for the same delinquent behavior.[90]

Failing the "Attitude Test" In general, though, as Figure 15.7 shows, police officers do seem more likely to arrest members of minority groups. Although this may be partially attributed to the social factors discussed in Chapter 2, it also appears that minority youths often fail the "attitude test" during interactions with police officers. After the seriousness of the offense and past history, the most important factor in the decision of whether to arrest or release appears to be the offender's attitude. An offender who is polite and apologetic generally has a better chance of being released. If the juvenile is hostile or unresponsive, the police are more likely to place him or her in custody for even a minor offense.[91]

Furthermore, police officers who do not live in the same community with minority youths may misinterpret normal behavior as disrespectful or delinquent and act accordingly.[92] This "culture gap" is of crucial importance to police-juvenile relations and underscores the community-oriented policing goal of having law enforcement agents be more involved in the communities they patrol.

Intake

As noted earlier, if, following arrest, a police officer feels the offender warrants the attention of the juvenile justice process, the officer will refer the youth to juvenile court. Once this step has been taken, a complaint is filed with a special division of the juvenile court, and the **intake** process begins. Intake may be followed by diversion to a community-based program, transfer to an adult court, or detention to await trial in juvenile court. Thus, intake, diversion, transfer, and detention are the four primary components of pretrial juvenile justice procedure.

Intake The process by which an official of the court must decide whether to file a petition, release the juvenile, or place the juvenile under some other form of supervision.

FIGURE 15.7 Juvenile Arrest Rates by Race

Using the FBI's Uniform Crime Report, statisticians can determine the rates of arrest for persons aged ten to seventeen in the United States. As you can see, the rate of arrests per 100,000 juveniles remains considerably higher for African Americans than for other racial groups.

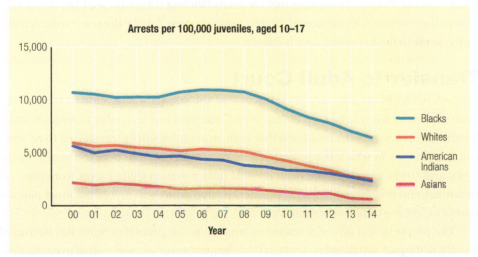

Source: "Statistical Briefing Book: Juvenile Arrest Rates." www.ojjdp.gov. Office of Juvenile Justice and Delinquency Prevention: visited March 22, 2017, Web.

During intake, an official of the juvenile court—usually a probation officer, but sometimes a judge—must decide, in effect, what to do with the offender. The intake officer has several options during intake.

1. Simply dismiss the case, releasing the offender without taking any further action. This occurs in about one in three cases, usually because the judge cannot determine a sufficient reason to continue.[93]
2. Divert the offender to a social-services program, such as drug rehabilitation or anger management.
3. File a **petition** for a formal court hearing. The petition is the formal document outlining the charges against the juvenile.
4. Transfer the case to an adult court, where the offender will be tried as an adult.

With regard to status offenses, judges have sole discretion to decide whether to process the case or *divert* the youth to another juvenile service agency.

Pretrial Diversion

In the early 1970s, Congress passed the first Juvenile Justice and Delinquency Prevention (JJDP) Act, which ordered the development of methods "to divert juveniles from the traditional juvenile justice system."[94] Within a few years, hundreds of diversion programs had been put into effect. Today, diversion refers to the process of removing low-risk offenders from the formal juvenile justice system by placing them in community-based rehabilitation programs.

Diversion programs vary widely, but fall into three general categories:

1. *Probation.* In this program, the juvenile is returned to the community, but placed under the supervision of a juvenile probation officer. If the youth breaks the conditions of probation, he or she can be returned to the formal juvenile system.
2. *Treatment and aid.* Many juveniles have behavioral or medical conditions that contribute to their delinquent behavior, and many diversion programs offer remedial education, drug and alcohol treatment, and other forms of counseling to alleviate these problems.
3. *Restitution.* In these programs, the offender "repays" her or his victim, either directly or symbolically through community service.[95]

Proponents of diversion programs include many labeling theorists (see Chapter 2), who believe that contact with the formal juvenile justice system "labels" the youth a delinquent, which leads to further delinquent behavior.

Transfer to Adult Court

One side effect of diversionary programs is that the youths who remain in the juvenile courts are more likely to be seen as "hardened" and thus less amenable to rehabilitation. This, in turn, increases the likelihood that such an offender will be transferred to an adult court, a process in which the juvenile court waives jurisdiction over the youth. In the 1980s and 1990s, when the American juvenile justice system shifted away from ideals of treatment and toward punishment, transfer to adult court was one of the most popular means of "getting tough" on delinquents.

The proportion of juveniles waived to adult court for property crimes has decreased steadily in the past two decades. About 4,000 delinquent cases are now waived to adult criminal court each year—less than 1 percent of all cases that reach juvenile court. This figure is down significantly from 1994, when the number of such cases peaked at 13,600.[96] As might be

Petition The document filed with a juvenile court alleging that the juvenile is a delinquent or a status offender and requesting that the court either hear the case or transfer it to an adult court.

expected, the majority of transfer cases involve juveniles, such as Paul Gingerich, who have committed a violent offense.[97] In the opening of this chapter, we discussed how Gingerich was charged as an adult for, at the age of twelve, participating in the murder of a friend's stepfather.

Methods of Transfer

There are three types of transfer laws, and most states use more than one of them, depending on the jurisdiction and the seriousness of the offense. Juveniles are most commonly transferred to adult courts through judicial waiver, in which the juvenile judge is given the power to determine whether a young offender's case will be waived to adult court. The judge makes this decision based on the offender's age, the nature of the offense, and any criminal history. All but five states employ judicial waiver.

Twenty-nine states have taken the waiver responsibility out of judicial hands through automatic transfer, also known as *legislative waiver*. In these states, the legislatures have designated certain conditions—usually involving serious crimes such as murder and rape—under which a juvenile case is automatically "kicked up" to adult court. In Rhode Island, for example, a juvenile aged sixteen or older with two prior felony adjudications will automatically be transferred on being accused of a third felony.[98]

Fifteen states also allow for prosecutorial waiver, in which prosecutors are allowed to choose whether to initiate proceedings in juvenile or criminal court when certain age and offense conditions are met. (See *Discretion in Action—Juvenile Drunk Driving* for further insight into prosecutorial waiver procedures.)

Reverse Transfer

In twenty-five states, criminal court judges also have the freedom to send juveniles who were transferred to adult court back to juvenile court. Known as *reverse transfer* statutes, these laws are designed to provide judges with a measure of discretion even when automatic transfer takes place. This process is popular with those who want to reduce the number of juveniles waived to adult court. For example, Arizona has expanded the number of offenses eligible for reverse transfer and has given certain nonviolent juvenile offenders the ability to request a reverse transfer hearing.[99]

Judicial Waiver The process in which the juvenile judge, based on the facts of the case at hand, decides that the alleged offender should be transferred to adult court.

Automatic Transfer The process by which a juvenile is transferred to adult court as a matter of state law.

Prosecutorial Waiver A procedure used in situations where the prosecutor has discretion to decide whether a case will be heard by a juvenile court or an adult court.

DISCRETION IN ACTION

Juvenile Drunk Driving

The Situation James, a seventeen-year-old high school senior, gets behind the wheel of his father's car with a blood alcohol concentration of .12, well over the state limit for driving under the influence (DUI). He slams headfirst into another car, killing the driver. Initially, he is charged with vehicular homicide as a juvenile.

The Law In this state, prosecutors have the discretion to waive juvenile offenders to adult court if the alleged offender is sixteen years old or older at the time of the alleged offense and is charged with a felony, such as vehicular manslaughter.

What Would You Do? You are a prosecutor with the discretionary power to transfer James from juvenile court to adult court. On the one hand, James has no previous criminal record, did not intend to kill his victim, and has shown extreme remorse for his actions. Furthermore, he is a juvenile and, as such, is seen by the law as less culpable than an adult. On the other hand, his careless actions resulted in a homicide, and trying him as an adult might deter other juveniles from committing DUI crimes. Do you keep James in juvenile court or waive him to adult court? Why?

To learn what a prosecutor in Denver, Colorado, did in a similar situation, see Example 15.1 in Appendix B.

Detention The temporary custody of a juvenile in a secure facility after a petition has been filed and before the adjudicatory process begins.

Detention Hearing A hearing to determine whether a juvenile should be detained, or remain detained, while waiting for the adjudicatory process to begin.

Transfer and Adult Corrections   Proponents of transferring juveniles to the adult justice system contend that violent juvenile offenders pose a risk to nonviolent offenders in juvenile detention centers. Thus, their removal makes the juvenile justice system safer. Critics of the practice point out that, by the same token, adult prisons and jails can be very dangerous places for young offenders. Acknowledging that young offenders are at a high risk for sexual assault victimization, the Prison Rape Elimination Act requires that juvenile prison and jail inmates be housed separately from the general inmate population.[100]

Data indicate that juveniles transferred to adult correctional facilities have higher recidivism rates than those who remain in the juvenile justice system.[101] Experts have several theories to explain this pattern, including decreased opportunities for family support in adult correctional facilities and the negative effects of being in close contact with older, more experienced prisoners.[102] "You can learn a whole lot more bad things in here than good," said one juvenile inmate from his cell in an Arizona adult prison.[103] In part as a result of these concerns, the number of juvenile inmates in adult facilities has declined from approximately five thousand in 1997 to fewer than one thousand today.[104]

Detention

If a decision is made that the offender will face adjudication in a juvenile court, the intake official must decide what to do with him or her until the start of the trial. Generally, the juvenile is released into the custody of parents or a guardian—most jurisdictions favor this practice in lieu of setting money bail for youths. The intake officer may also place the offender in **detention,** or temporary custody in a secure facility, until the disposition process begins. Once a juvenile has been detained, most jurisdictions require that a **detention hearing** be held within twenty-four hours. During this hearing, the offender has several due process safeguards, including the right to counsel, the right against self-incrimination, and the right to cross-examine and confront witnesses.

In justifying its decision to detain, the court will usually address one of three issues:

1. Whether the child poses a danger to the community.
2. Whether the child will return for the adjudication process.
3. Whether detention will provide protection for the child.

The Supreme Court upheld the practice of preventive detention (see Chapter 9) for juveniles in *Schall v. Martin* (1984)[105] by ruling that youths can be detained if they are deemed a "risk" to the safety of the community or to their own welfare. About one-third of juveniles involved in violent offenses are detained before trial.[106]

ETHICS CHALLENGE

Police suspect that a seven-year-old named Patrick has knowledge concerning the murder of an eleven-year-old girl. After Patrick waives his *Miranda* rights without his parents present, he tells a detective that he threw a rock at the victim's head. Is it ethical for police to treat juveniles the same as adults when it comes to *Miranda* proceedings, which we covered in Chapter 7? At what age can a juvenile be expected to understand the concepts of the right to remain silent and the right to an attorney? Explain your answers. (To learn more about the Supreme Court's approach to this topic, search for *Fare v. Michael C.* [1979] and *J.D.B. v. North Carolina* [2011] online.)

Trying and Punishing Juveniles

In just over half of all referred cases, the juvenile is eventually subject to formal proceedings in juvenile court.[107] As noted earlier, changes in the juvenile justice system since *In re Gault* (1967) have led many to contend that juvenile courts have become indistinguishable, both theoretically and practically, from adult courts.[108] About half the states, for example, permit juveniles to request a jury trial under certain circumstances. As this chapter's *Mastering Concepts* feature explains, however, juvenile justice proceedings can still be distinguished from the adult system of criminal justice, and these differences are evident in the adjudication and disposition of the juvenile trial.

MASTERING CONCEPTS

The Juvenile Justice System versus the Criminal Justice System

AP Images/Newspaper Member/
Columbus Dispatch/James D. DeCamp

When the juvenile justice system was first established in the United States, its participants saw it as being separate from the adult criminal justice system. Indeed, the two systems remain separate in many ways. There are, however, a number of similarities between juvenile and adult justice. Here, we summarize both the similarities and the differences.

SIMILARITIES	DIFFERENCES		
		Juvenile System	**Adult System**
• The right to receive the *Miranda* warnings.	**Purpose**	Rehabilitation of the offender.	Punishment.
• Procedural protections when making an admission of guilt.	**Arrest**	Juveniles can be arrested for acts (status offenses) that are not criminal for adults.	Adults can be arrested only for acts made illegal by the relevant criminal code.
• Prosecutors and defense attorneys play equally important roles.	**Wrongdoing**	Considered a "delinquent act."	A crime.
• The right to be represented by counsel at the crucial stages of the trial process.	**Proceedings**	Informal; closed to public.	Formal and regimented; open to public.
• Access to plea bargains.	**Information**	Courts may NOT release information to the press.	Courts MUST release information to the press.
• The right to a hearing and an appeal.	**Parents**	Play significant role.	Play no role.
• The standard of evidence is proof beyond a reasonable doubt.	**Release**	Into parent/guardian custody.	May post bail when appropriate.
	Jury trial	In some states, juveniles do NOT have this right.	All adults have this right.
• Offenders can be placed on probation by the judge.	**Searches**	Juveniles can be searched in school without probable cause.	No adult can be searched without probable cause.
• Offenders can be held before adjudication if the judge believes them to be a threat to the community.	**Records**	Juvenile records are sealed at age of adult criminal responsibility.	Adult criminal records are, for the most part, permanent.
• Following trial, offenders can be sentenced to community supervision.	**Sentencing**	Juveniles are placed in separate facilities from adults.	Adults are placed in county jails or state or federal prisons.
	Death penalty	No death penalty.	Death penalty for certain serious crimes under certain circumstances.

Learning 9 Objective Explain the distinction between an adjudicatory hearing and a disposition hearing.

Adjudication

During the adjudication stage of the juvenile justice process, a hearing is held to determine whether the offender is delinquent or in need of some form of court supervision. Most state juvenile codes dictate a specific set of procedures that must be followed during the **adjudicatory hearing,** with the goal of providing the respondent with "the essentials of due process and fair treatment." Consequently, the respondent in an adjudicatory hearing has the right to notice of charges, counsel, and confrontation and cross-examination, along with the privilege against self-incrimination. Furthermore, "proof beyond a reasonable doubt" must be established to find the child delinquent. When the child admits guilt—that is, admits to the charges of the initial petition—the judge must ensure that the admission was voluntary.

At the close of the adjudicatory hearing, the judge is generally required to rule on the legal issues and evidence that have been presented. Based on this ruling, the judge determines whether the respondent is delinquent or in need of court supervision. Alternatively, the judge can dismiss the case based on a lack of evidence. It is important to remember that finding a child delinquent is *not* the same as convicting an adult of a crime. A delinquent does not face the same restrictions imposed on adult convicts in some states, such as limits on the right to vote and to run for political office.

Disposition

Once a juvenile has been adjudicated delinquent, the judge must decide what steps will be taken toward treatment and/or punishment. Most states provide for a *bifurcated* process in which a separate **disposition hearing** follows the adjudicatory hearing. Depending on state law, the juvenile may be entitled to counsel at the disposition hearing.

Sentencing Juveniles

In an adult trial, the sentencing phase is primarily concerned with protecting the community from the convict. In contrast, a juvenile judge uses the disposition hearing to determine a sentence that will serve the needs of the child. For assistance in this crucial process, the judge will order the probation department to gather information on the juvenile and present it in the form of a **predisposition report.** The report usually contains information concerning the respondent's family background, the facts surrounding the delinquent act, and interviews with social workers, teachers, and other important figures in the child's life.

Judicial Discretion

In keeping with the rehabilitative tradition of the juvenile justice system, juvenile judges generally have a great deal of discretion in choosing one of several disposition possibilities. A judge can tend toward leniency, delivering only a stern reprimand or warning before releasing the juvenile into the custody of parents or other legal guardians. Otherwise, the choice is among incarceration in a juvenile correctional facility, probation, or community treatment. In most cases, the seriousness of the offense is the primary factor used in determining whether to incarcerate a juvenile, though history of delinquency, family situation, and the offender's attitude are all relevant.

Juvenile Corrections

In general, juvenile corrections are based on the concept of **graduated sanctions**—that is, the severity of the punishment should fit the crime. Consequently, status and first-time offenders are diverted or placed on probation, repeat offenders find themselves in intensive community supervision or treatment programs, and serious and violent offenders are

Adjudicatory Hearing The process through which a juvenile court determines whether there is sufficient evidence to support the initial petition.

Disposition Hearing A hearing in which the juvenile judge or officer decides the appropriate punishment for a youth found to be delinquent or a status offender; similar to the sentencing hearing for adults.

Predisposition Report A report prepared during the disposition process that provides the judge with relevant background material to aid in the disposition decision.

Graduated Sanctions A continuum of disposition options used in juvenile corrections with the goal of ensuring that the juvenile's punishment matches the wrongdoing in severity.

placed in correctional facilities. (See Figure 15.8 to get a better idea of how graduated sanctions apply to the juvenile justice system.)

Juvenile Probation

The majority of all adjudicated delinquents (64 percent) will never receive a disposition more severe than being placed on probation.[109] These statistics reflect a general understanding among juvenile court judges and other officials that a child should normally be removed from her or his home only as a last resort.

The organization of juvenile probation is very similar to adult probation (see Chapter 12), and juvenile probationers are increasingly subjected to electronic monitoring and other supervisory tactics. The main difference between the two programs lies in the attitude toward the offender. Adult probation officers have an overriding responsibility to protect the community from the probationer, while juvenile probation officers are expected to take the role of a mentor or a concerned relative in looking after the needs of the child.

Confining Juveniles

About 54,000 American youths (down from approximately 107,000 in 1995) are incarcerated in public and private juvenile correctional facilities in the United States.[110] Most of these juveniles have committed offenses against people or property, but a significant number (about 17 percent) have been incarcerated for technical violations of their probation or parole agreements.[111] After deciding that a juvenile needs to be confined, the judge has two sentencing options: nonsecure juvenile institutions and secure juvenile institutions.

Nonsecure Confinement Some juvenile delinquents do not require high levels of control and can be placed in **residential treatment programs.** These programs, run by either probation departments or social-services departments, allow their subjects freedom of movement in the community. Generally, the juveniles must follow certain rules, such as avoiding alcoholic beverages and returning to the facility for curfew.

Residential treatment programs can be divided into four categories:

1. *Foster care programs*, in which the juveniles live with couples who act as surrogate parents.
2. *Group homes*, which generally house between twelve and fifteen youths and provide treatment, counseling, and education services by a professional staff.

Residential Treatment Programs
A government-run facility for juveniles whose offenses are not deemed serious enough to warrant incarceration in a training school.

FIGURE 15.8 The Graduated Sanctions Model

In juvenile corrections, the severity of punishment is directly related to the seriousness of the delinquent behavior.

CAREERS IN CJ

Resident youth worker

Job description:

● Provide safety, security, custodial care, discipline, and guidance. Play a critical role in the rehabilitation of youth and, as a result, have a potentially great impact on a youth's success during and after his or her incarceration.

What kind of training is required?

● A bachelor's degree in human services, behavioral science, or a related field.

● Professional and respectful verbal communication skills.

Annual salary range?

● $30,000–$55,000

Carl McCullough, Sr. Resident Youth Worker

I had a shot in the NFL, playing for the Buffalo Bills and the Minnesota Vikings, but that lasted only a short time. Today, I work at the Hennepin County (Minnesota) Juvenile Detention Center, where I'm responsible for a group of twelve young men, aged thirteen to eighteen, who are awaiting trial, waiting for placements, or just being held in a secure place due to the high-profile nature of their cases. I'm with the kids every day and every other weekend from 6:30 A.M. to 2:30 P.M. I do everything from helping with homework to supervising their leisure time, running group programs, and just being a positive, caring adult with whom to talk.

Having the NFL experience is a huge icebreaker with the residents. "Why are you here?" they always ask me, and I tell them I am here because I care about them, because I want to see a change, and because I'd like to help them believe that something better is possible. To do this job well, you have to be good at building relationships. It helps to know how to work with different cultures as well. Then you have to have patience; without it you won't last long. You know they are going to test you, to see what they can and can't get away with. You also have to be willing to learn a few things from them. You have to be a good listener.

Courtesy of Carl McCullough, Sr.

SOCIAL MEDIA CAREER TIP Potential employers want information about you, but they do not want your life story. To capitalize on two primary benefits of social media, personalize your message and be concise.

---

3. *Family group homes*, which combine aspects of foster care and group homes, meaning that a single family, rather than a group of professionals, looks after the needs of the young offenders.

4. *Rural programs*, which include wilderness camps, farms, and ranches where between thirty and fifty children are placed in an environment that provides recreational activities and treatment programs.

Secure Confinement Secure facilities are comparable to the adult prisons and jails we discussed in Chapters 13 and 14. These institutions go by a confusing array of names depending on the state in which they are located, but the two best known are boot camps and training schools.

A **boot camp** is the juvenile version of shock probation. As we noted in Chapter 12, boot camps are modeled after military training for new recruits. Boot camp programs are based on the theory that giving wayward youths a taste of the "hard life" of military-like training for short periods of time, usually no longer than 180 days, will "shock" them out of a life of crime. At a typical youth boot camp, inmates are grouped in platoons and live in dormitories. They spend eight hours a day training, drilling, and doing hard labor, and also participate in programs such as basic adult education and job skills training.

No juvenile correctional facility is called a "prison." This does not mean that all such facilities lack any resemblance to prisons. The facilities that most closely mimic the atmosphere of an adult correctional facility are **training schools,** alternatively known

Boot Camp A variation on traditional shock incarceration in which juveniles (and some adults) are sent to secure confinement facilities modeled on military basic training camps.

Training School A correctional institution for juveniles found to be delinquent or status offenders.

as youth camps, youth development centers, industrial schools, and several other similar titles. Whatever the name, these institutions claim to differ from their adult countparts by offering a variety of programs to treat and rehabilitate the young offenders. In reality, training schools are plagued by many of the same problems as adult prisons and jails, including high levels of inmate-on-inmate violence, substance abuse, gang conflict, and overcrowding.

Aftercare Juveniles leave correctional facilities either through an early release program or because they have served their sentences. Juvenile corrections officials recognize that many of these children, like adults, need assistance in readjusting to the outside world. In addition, about two-thirds of youths who come in contact with the juvenile justice system have behavioral health problems, such as alcohol abuse, serious depression, trauma related to exposure to violence, risk for suicide, and disorders related to low self-control.[112]

▲ Juvenile inmates wait to go into the gym at the Juvenile Detention Center in Toledo, Ohio. **Why might young offenders who are transferred to adult correctional facilities have higher recidivism rates than those who remain in juvenile facilities?** Melanie Stetson Freeman/ *The Christian Science Monitor*/Getty Images

For all these reasons, released juveniles are often placed in **aftercare** programs. Based on the same philosophy that drives the prisoner reentry movement (discussed in the preceding chapter), aftercare programs are designed to offer services for the released juveniles, while at the same time supervising them to reduce the chances of recidivism.

The ideal aftercare program includes community support groups, education and employment aid, and continued monitoring to ensure that the juvenile is able to deal with the demands of freedom. Statistics suggest, however, that the aftercare needs of young offenders often go unmet. Nearly 60 percent of those who have been referred to juvenile court are "re-referred" before turning eighteen.[113]

More troubling is the notion that many juvenile offenders are likely, if not destined, to become adult offenders. Criminological research estimates that juvenile incarceration decreases the likelihood of high school graduation by 13 percent and increases the likelihood of adult incarceration by 22 percent.[114] A report on Illinois's juvenile justice system criticized it as "a 'feeder system' to the adult criminal justice system and a cycle of crime, victimization, and incarceration."[115]

Aftercare The variety of therapeutic, educational, and counseling programs made available to juvenile delinquents after they have been released from a correctional facility.

Policy Matters

Police in School

How Things Stand

In the 1970s, law enforcement officers were present in only about 1 percent of American schools. This percentage began to rise in the 1980s, when juvenile crime rates increased dramatically. Then, in 1999, two high school seniors killed twelve students and one teacher at Colorado's Columbine High School, leading to a wave of financing for school police. Today, 43 percent of all U.S. public schools—including 64 percent of high schools—are patrolled by about 46,000 full-time on-campus police officers known as School-Resource Officers (SROs).[116] The idea that schools need increased security has been strengthened by mass shootings such as the elementary school massacre in Newtown, Connecticut, in 2012 and a continuing desire to protect students from illegal drugs, gangs, and weapons.

As a Result...

The justification for having a police presence at American schools seems obvious: Trained law enforcement personnel increase the level of safety on campus, just as they would anywhere else. Indeed, SROs have helped prevent violent attacks in numerous locales, including Atlanta, Phoenix, and Plain City, Utah. At the same time, many educators and parents worry about the criminalization of commonplace teenage misbehavior. In Texas, for example, students have been arrested and charged with misdemeanors for throwing an eraser, chewing gum in class, and wearing too much perfume.[117] SROs arrest about 90,000 students a year, according to federal civil rights data.[118]

Concerns about the excessive use of force also enter this debate. In June 2015, for example, an SRO in Kissimmee, Florida, was charged with child abuse after he allegedly slammed a thirteen-year-old student to the ground. Later that same year, a federal judge ruled that SROs in Birmingham, Alabama, had used unconstitutional levels of force when they pepper-sprayed students for minor disciplinary infractions, including crying in the hallway.[119] Although the vast majority of school days pass without incident, when an SRO does use force as an instrument

David McNew/Getty Images News/Getty Images

of discipline, questions arise about the necessity of a police presence on campuses—particularly if the force is caught on video.

Up for Debate

"It's clear that as a nation, we are severely underestimating the traumatic impact of our children being subject to, or even just seeing or witnessing, unnecessary physical force and arrests in our schools and classrooms. Schools must be safe havens. They must be filled with compassion and love."[120]—*Former U.S. Education Secretary Arne Duncan*

"[Students are] doing badly, they don't want to learn, they just want to disrupt. They can be very threatening. The police get called because that way the teacher can go on with teaching instead of wasting half the class dealing with one child, and it sends a message to the other kids."[121]—*Anonymous high school teacher in Austin, Texas*

What's Your Take?

Review the discussion in this chapter on "School Violence and Bullying" and "Police Discretion and Juvenile Crime" before answering the following questions.

1. Suppose a math teacher calls an SRO for help with a student who is disrupting class by refusing to put away her cellphone. When the SRO arrives in the classroom, the student remains defiant and refuses to leave with the SRO. Is the SRO justified in using force to remove the student from class? Why or why not? (You can search the terms **South Carolina** and **student cellphone arrest** online to see how an actual SRO handled a similar situation.)

2. What are the benefits and drawbacks of having SROs involved in disciplining noncriminal behavior by students? Should they be prohibited from doing so? Explain your answers.

Digging Deeper...

Go online and research the **school-to-prison pipeline**. Explain what this term means. What are some of the consequences of the school-to-prison pipeline for students? What role do SROs play in facilitating this phenomenon? What policies, if any, should be put in place involving the discretion of SROs to lessen the impact that the school-to-prison pipeline has on juvenile and adult crime? Your written answer should be at least three paragraphs long.

For more information on these concepts, look back to the Learning Objective icons throughout the chapter.

 Describe the child-saving movement and its relationship to the doctrine of *parens patriae*. Under the doctrine of *parens patriae*, the state has a right and a duty to care for neglected, delinquent, and disadvantaged children. The child-saving movement, based on the doctrine of *parens patriae*, started in the 1800s. Its followers believed that juvenile offenders require treatment rather than punishment.

 List the four major differences between juvenile courts and adult courts. (a) No juries, (b) different terminology, (c) limited adversarial relationship, and (d) confidentiality.

 Identify and briefly describe the single most important U.S. Supreme Court case with respect to juvenile justice. The case was *In re Gault*, decided by the Supreme Court in 1967. In this case, a minor had been arrested for allegedly making an obscene phone call. His parents had not been notified and had not been present during the juvenile court judge's decision-making process. The Supreme Court held that juveniles are entitled to many of the same due process rights granted to adult offenders, including notice of charges, the right to counsel, the privilege against self-incrimination, and the right to confront and cross-examine witnesses.

 Describe the reasoning behind recent U.S. Supreme Court decisions that have lessened the harshness of sentencing outcomes for violent juvenile offenders. In banning capital punishment and limiting the availability of life sentences without parole for offenders who committed their crimes as juveniles, the Supreme Court has focused on the concept of "diminished culpability." This concept is based on the notion that violent juvenile offenders cannot fully comprehend the consequences of their actions and have a greater capacity for rehabilitation than adult violent offenders.

 Define *bullying*, and list the four components that are often present in this sort of behavior. Bullying is repeated, aggressive behavior that is characterized by (a) physical abuse, (b) verbal abuse, (c) social and emotional abuse, and/or (d) abuse that take place online or through the use of devices such as smartphones.

 Describe the one variable that always correlates highly with juvenile crime rates. The older a person is, the less likely he or she will exhibit criminal behavior. This process is known as aging out. Thus, persons in any at-risk group will commit fewer crimes as they get older.

 List the factors that normally determine what police do with juvenile offenders. The arresting police officers consider (a) the nature of the offense, (b) the youthful offender's past criminal history, (c) the setting in which the offense took place, (d) whether the parents can and will take disciplinary action, (e) the attitude of the offender, and (f) the offender's gender.

 Describe the four primary components of pretrial juvenile justice procedure. (a) Intake, in which an official of the juvenile court engages in a screening process to determine what to do with the youthful offender; (b) pretrial diversion, which may consist of probation, treatment and aid, and/or restitution; (c) jurisdictional waiver to an adult court, in which case the youth leaves the juvenile justice system; and (d) some type of detention, in which the youth is held until the disposition process begins.

 Explain the distinction between an adjudicatory hearing and a disposition hearing. An adjudicatory hearing is essentially a "trial." Defense attorneys may be present during the adjudicatory hearing in juvenile courts. In many states, once adjudication has occurred, there is a separate disposition hearing that is similar to the sentencing phase in an adult court. At this point, the court, often aided by a predisposition report, determines the sentence that serves the "needs" of the child.

1. What is the difference between a status offense and a crime? What punishments do you think should be imposed on juveniles who commit status offenses?

2. Do you agree with Supreme Court Justice Anthony Kennedy that all juveniles who commit murder "must be given the opportunity to show their crime did not reflect irreparable corruption; and, if it did not, their hope for some years of life outside prison walls must be restored." Or are mandatory life-without-parole sentences for juvenile killers justified? Explain your answer.

3. Do you think that bullying should be punishable as a felony along the same lines as assault? (For the definition of assault, go back to Chapter 1.) Why or why not?

4. Several years ago, eight Florida teenagers ranging in age from fourteen to eighteen beat a classmate so badly that she suffered a concussion. According to law enforcement officials, the teenagers recorded the assault so that they could post it on the Internet. If you were a prosecutor and could either waive these teenagers to adult court or refer them to the juvenile justice system, which option would you choose? What other information would you need to make your decision?

5. Why do juvenile court judges favor community service and probation, when appropriate, as sentencing options for juveniles?

KEY TERMS

adjudicatory hearing 514
aftercare 517
age of onset 504
aging out 504
automatic transfer 511
boot camp 516
bullying 502
child abuse 505
child neglect 505

detention 512
detention hearing 512
disposition hearing 514
graduated sanctions 514
intake 509
judicial waiver 511
juvenile delinquency 494
low-visibility decision making 508
parens patriae 493

petition 510
predisposition report 514
prosecutorial waiver 511
referral 508
residential treatment program 515
status offender 494
training school 516
youth gang 505

1. Jennifer M. O'Connor and Lucinda K. Treat, "Getting Smart about Getting Tough: Juvenile Justice and the Possibility of Progressive Reform," *American Criminal Law Review* 33 (Summer 1996), 1299.

2. *In re Gault*, 387 U.S. 1, 15 (1967).

3. Samuel Davis, *The Rights of Juveniles: The Juvenile Justice System*, 2d ed. (New York: C. Boardman Co., 1995), Section 1.2.

4. Quoted in Anthony Platt, *The Child Savers* (Chicago: University of Chicago Press, 1969), 119.

5. 383 U.S. 541 (1966).

6. *Ibid.*, 556.

7. 387 U.S. 1 (1967).

8. 397 U.S. 358 (1970).

9. 421 U.S. 519 (1975).

10. 403 U.S. 528 (1971).

11. Rebecca Santana, "At What Age an Adult? Many in Louisiana Say 17 Is Too Young," *www.bigstory.ap.org*. *Associated Press:* May 7, 2016, Web.

12. Research Network on Adolescent Development and Juvenile Justice, *Youth on Trial: A Developmental Perspective on Juvenile Justice* (Chicago: John D. & Catherine T. MacArthur Foundation, 2003), 1.

13. Richard E. Redding, "Juveniles Transferred to Criminal Court: Legal Reform Proposals Based on Social Science Research," *Utah Law Review* (1997), 709.

14. Kyle J. Thomas, "Delinquent Peer Influence on Offending Versatility: Can Peers Promote Specialized Delinquency?" *Criminology* (May 2015), 280–307.

15. Bureau of Justice Statistics, *Co-Offending among Adolescents in Violent Victimizations, 2004–13* (Washington, D.C.: U.S. Department of Justice, July 2016), 1.

16. Martha Grace Duncan, "'So Young and So Untender': Remorseless Children and the Expectations of the Law," *Columbia Law Review* (October 2002), 1469.

17. 543 U.S. 551 (2005).

18. *Ibid.*, 567.

19. 560 U.S. 48 (2010).

20. *Ibid.*, 50.

21. 132 S. Ct. 2455 (2012).

22. *Ibid.*, ar 2463.

23. *Montgomery v. Louisiana*, 577 U.S. _____ (2016).

24. Quoted in Adam Liptak, "Justices Expand Parole Rights for Juveniles Sentenced to Life for Murder," *New York Times* (January 26, 2016), A18.

25. *Surveillance Summaries: Youth Risk Behavior Surveillance—United States, 2015* (Washington, D.C.: Centers for Disease Control and Prevention, June 10, 2016).

26. Federal Bureau of Investigation, *Crime in the United States, 2015*, Table 38. *ucr.fbi.gov*. U.S. Department of Justice: 2016, Web.

27. Sarah Hockenberry and Charles Puzzanchera, *Juvenile Court Statistics 2013* (Washington, D.C.: National Center for Juvenile Justice, July 2015), 7.

28. "One Day Count of Juveniles in Residential Placement Facilities, 1997–2013." *www.ojjdp.gov*. Office of Juvenile Justice and Delinquency Prevention: visited March 22, 2017, Web.

29. David McDowell, "Juvenile Curfew Laws and Their Influence on Crime," *Federal Probation* (December 2006), 58.

30. *Crime in the United States, 2015, op. cit.*, Table 29.

31. Office of Juvenile Justice and Delinquency Prevention, "Community Prevention Grants Program." *www.ojjdp.gov*. Office of Juvenile Justice and Delinquency Prevention: visited March 24, 2017, Web.

32. *Juvenile Court Statistics, 2013, op. cit.*, 20.

33. Melissa Sickmund and Charles Puzzancherra, eds., *Juvenile Offenders and Victims: 2014 National Report* (Pittsburgh: National Center for Juvenile Justice, December 2014), 158, 196.

34. "Data Snapshot: School Discipline." *www.ocrdata.ed.gov*. U.S. Department of Education Office of Civil Rights: March 2014, Web.

35. *Juvenile Court Statistics, 2013, op. cit.*, 12.

36. Sara Goodkind, et al., "Are Girls Really Becoming More Delinquent? Testing the Gender Convergence Hypothesis by Race and Ethnicity, 1976–2005," *Children and Youth Services Review* (August 2009), 885–889.

37. "Girls and the Juvenile Justice System." *www.ojjdp.gov*. Office of Juvenile Justice and Delinquency Prevention: 2015, Web.

38. *Ibid.*

39. Meda Chesney-Lind, *The Female Offender: Girls, Women, and Crime* (Thousand Oaks, Calif.: Sage Publications, 1997).

40. Margaret A. Zahn, et al., "The Girls Study Group—Charting the Way to Delinquency Prevention for Girls," *Girls Study Group: Understanding and Responding to Girls' Delinquency* (Washington, D.C.: Office of Juvenile Justice and Delinquency Prevention, October 2008), 3.

41. *Crime in the United States, 2015, op. cit.*, Table 38 and Table 40.

42. Denise C. Gottfredson and David A. Soulé, "The Timing of Property Crime, Violent Crime, and Substance Abuse among Juveniles," *Journal of Research in Crime and Delinquency* (February 2005), 110–120.

43. National Center for Education Statistics and Bureau of Justice Statistics, *Indicators of School Crime and Safety: 2015* (Washington, D.C.: U.S. Department of Justice, May 2016), iv–v.

44. *Ibid.*, 42.

45. Heather L. Schwartz, et al, *The Role of Technology in Improving K-12 School Safety* (Santa Monica, Calif.: RAND Corporation, 2016), x.

46. *Juvenile Offenders and Victims: 2014 National Report, op. cit.*, 47.

47. *Indicators of School Crime and Safety, 2015, op. cit.*, 24.

48. *Ibid.*, 108.

49. Becky Lewis, "Virginia Evaluates Threat Assessment Processes," *TechBeat* (July/August 2015), 14–20.

50. Jacob Kang-Brown, et al., *A Generation Later: What We've Learned about Zero-Tolerance in Schools* (New York: Vera Institute of Justice, December 2013), 2.

51. *Indicators of School Crime and Safety: 2015, op. cit.*, 100.

52. "The Perils of Peanut Tossing," *The Economist* (December 21, 2013), 35.

53. Kathryn C. Monahan, et al., "From the School Yard to the Squad Car: School Discipline, Truancy, and Arrest," *Journal of Youth and Adolescence* (July 2014), 1110–1122.

54. Lana Shapiro and Andrew Adesman, "Exponential, Not Additive, Increase in Risk of Weapons Carrying by Adolescents Who Themselves Are Frequent and Recurrent Victims of Bullying," *Developmental & Behavioral Pediatrics* (May 2014), 165–171.

55. Young-Shin Kim and Bennett Leventhal, "Bullying and Suicide: A Review," *International Journal of Adolescent Medicine and Health* (April-June 2008), 133–154.

56. *Student Reports of Bullying: Results from the 2015 School Crimes Supplement to the National Crime Victimization Survey* (Washington, D.C.: National Center for Education Statistics, December 2016), Table 1.1.

57. Emily A. Greytak, et al., *From Teasing to Torment: School Climate Revisited* (New York: GLSEN, 2016), xiv.

58. Dewey G. Cornell and Susan P. Limber, "Do U.S. Laws Go Far Enough to Prevent Bullying at School?" *www.apa.org*. *Monitor on Psychology:* February 2016, Web.

59. "Jury Verdicts and Settlements in Bullying." *www.publicjustice.net*. Public Justice: January 2016, Web.

60. Marvin E. Wolfgang, *From Boy to Man, from Delinquency to Crime* (Chicago: University of Chicago Press, 1987).

61. Quoted in John H. Laub and Robert J. Sampson, "Understanding Desistance from Crime," in *Crime and Justice: A Review of Research* (Chicago: University of Chicago Press, 2001), 6.

62. Travis Hirschi and Michael Gottfredson, "Age and the Explanation of Crime," *American Journal of Sociology* 89 (1982), 552–584.

63. Robert J. Sampson and John H. Laub, "A Life-Course View on the Development of Crime,"

Annals of the American Academy of Political and Social Science (November 2005), 12.

64. David P. Farrington, "Offending from 10 to 25 Years of Age," in *Prospective Studies of Crime and Delinquency*, ed. Katherine Teilmann Van Dusen and Sarnoff A. Mednick (Boston: Kluwer-Nijhoff Publishers, 1983), 17.

65. Office of Juvenile Justice and Delinquency Prevention, *Juveniles in Court* (Washington, D.C.: U.S. Department of Justice, June 2003), 29.

66. Carl McCurley and Howard Snyder, *Cooccurrence of Substance Abuse Behaviors in Youth* (Washington, D.C.: Office of Juvenile Justice and Delinquency Prevention, 2008).

67. Gary McClelland, Linda Teplin, and Karen Abram, "Detection and Prevalence of Substance Abuse among Juvenile Detainees," *Juvenile Justice Bulletin* (Washington, D.C.: Office of Juvenile Justice and Delinquency Prevention, June 2004), 10.

68. Arrestee Drug Abuse Monitoring Program, *Preliminary Data on Drug Use and Related Matters among Adult Arrestees and Juvenile Detainees* (Washington, D.C.: National Institute of Justice, 2003).

69. Bonita M. Veysey, "Adolescent Girls with Mental Health Disorders Involved with the Juvenile Justice System." *www.ncmhjj.com*. National Center for Mental Health and Juvenile Justice: July 2003, Web.

70. Larry J. Siegel and Brandon C. Welsh, *Juvenile Delinquency: The Core*, 4th ed. (Belmont, Calif.: Wadsworth Cengage Learning, 2011), 268.

71. Edward P. Mulvey, *Highlights from Pathways to Desistance: A Longitudinal Study of Serious Adolescent Offenders* (Washington, D.C.: Office of Juvenile Justice and Delinquency Prevention, March 2011), 1–3.

72. David Finkelhor, et al., *Juvenile Justice Bulletin: Children's Exposure to Violence, Crime, and Abuse: An Update* (Washington, D.C.: Office of Juvenile Justice and Delinquency Prevention, September 2015), 7.

73. Kimberly A. Tyler and Katherine A. Johnson, "A Longitudinal Study of the Effects of Early Abuse on Later Victimization among High-Risk Adolescents," *Violence and Victims* (June 2006), 287–291.

74. Grover Trask, "Defusing the Teenage Time Bombs," *Prosecutor* (March/April 1997), 29.

75. Ashley Nellis, *The Lives of Juvenile Lifers: Findings from a National Survey* (Washington, D.C.: The Sentencing Project, March 2012), 2.

76. Cathy Spatz Widom, *The Cycle of Violence* (Washington, D.C.: National Institute of Justice, October 1992).

77. Janet Currie and Erdal Tekin, *Does Child Abuse Cause Crime?* (Atlanta: Andrew Young School of Policy Studies, April 2006), 27–28.

78. David C. Pyrooz and Gary Sweeten, "Gang Membership between Ages 5 and 17 Years in the United States," *Journal of Adolescent Health* (April 2015), 414.

79. Karl G. Hill, Christina Lui, and J. David Hawkins, *Early Precursors of Gang Membership: A Study of Seattle Youth* (Washington, D.C.: Office of Juvenile Justice and Delinquency Prevention, December 2001).

80. Amanda B. Gilman, Karl G. Hill, and J. David Hawkins, "Long-Term Consequences of Adolescent Gang Membership for Adult Functioning," *American Journal of Public Health* (May 2014), 938–945.

81. *Juvenile Offenders and Victims: 2014 National Report, op. cit.*, 69.

82. National Alliance of Gang Investigators Alliance, *2005 National Gang Threat Assessment* (Washington, D.C.: Bureau of Justice Assistance, 2005), 10–11.

83. *2013 National Gang Report*, (Washington, D.C.: National Gang Intelligence Center, 2014), 41–42.

84. Los Angeles Police Department, "Why Young People Join Gangs." *www.lapdonline.org*. Los Angeles Police Department: visited March 24, 2017, Web.

85. Michelle Arciaga Young and Victor Gonzalez, "Getting Out of Gangs, Staying Out of Gangs: Gang Intervention and Desistance Strategies," *National Gang Center Bulletin* (January 2013).

86. *Crime in the United States, 2015, op. cit.*, Table 32.

87. *Juvenile Court Statistics, 2013, op. cit.*, 31.

88. *Ibid.*, 20.

89. Carl E. Pope and Howard N. Snyder, *Race as a Factor in Juvenile Arrests* (Washington, D.C.: Office of Juvenile Justice and Delinquency Prevention, April 2003), 1.

90. *Ibid.*, 4.

91. National Institute of Justice, *The Code of the Street and African-American Adolescent Violence* (Washington, D.C.: U.S. Department of Justice, February 2009), 7, 10, 14.

92. George S. Bridges and Sara Steen, "Racial Disparities in Official Assessments of Juvenile Offenders," *American Sociological Review 63* (1998), 554.

93. *Juvenile Court Statistics, 2013, op. cit.*, 53.

94. 42 U.S.C. Sections 5601–5778 (1974).

95. S'Lee Arthur Hinshaw II, "Juvenile Diversion: An Alternative to Juvenile Court," *Journal of Dispute Resolution* (1993), 305.

96. *Juvenile Court Statistics, 2013, op. cit.*, 38.

97. Office of Juvenile Justice and Delinquency Prevention, *Delinquency Cases Waived to Criminal Court, 2011* (Washington, D.C.: U.S. Department of Justice, December 2014), 2.

98. Rhode Island General Laws Section 14-1-7.1 (1994 and Supp. 1996).

99. *State Trends: Legislative Victories from 2011–2013* (Washington, D.C.: Campaign for Youth & Justice, 2014), 5.

100. "Prison Rape Elimination Act: Prison and Jail Standards, Section 115.14." *www.prearesourcecenter.org*. National PREA Resource Center: visited March 23, 2017, Web.

101. Richard E. Redding, *Juvenile Transfer Laws: An Effective Deterrent to Delinquency?* (Washington, D.C.: Office of Juvenile Justice and Delinquency Prevention, June 2010), 4.

102. Richard E. Redding, "Juvenile Transfer Laws: An Effective Deterrent to Delinquency?" *Juvenile Justice Bulletin* (Washington, D.C.: Office of Juvenile Justice and Delinquency Prevention, August 2008), 7.

103. Quoted in Judi Villa, "Adult Prisons Harden Teens," *Arizona Republic* (November 14, 2004), A27.

104. Bureau of Justice Statistics, *Prisoners in 1997* (Washington, D.C.: U.S. Department of Justice, August 1998), 1, 10; and Bureau of Justice Statistics, *Prisoners in 2015* (Washington, D.C.: U.S. Department of Justice, December 2016), Appendix table 9, page 33.

105. 467 U.S. 253 (1984).

106. *Juvenile Court Statistics, 2013, op. cit.*, 32.

107. Julie Furdella and Charles Puzzanchera, *Delinquency Cases in Juvenile Court, 2013* (Washington, D.C.: Office of Juvenile Justice and Delinquency Prevention, October 2015), 3.

108. Barry C. Feld, "Criminalizing the American Juvenile Court," *Crime and Justice 17* (1993), 227–254.

109. *Delinquency Cases in Juvenile Court, 2013, op. cit.*, 3.

110. Sarah Hockenberry, *Juveniles in Residential Placement, 2013* (Washington, D.C.: Office of Juvenile Justice and Delinquency Prevention, May 2016), 1.

111. *Ibid.*, 4.

112. Thomas Grisso, *Double Jeopardy: Adolescent Offenders with Mental Disorders* (Chicago: University of Chicago Press, 2004), 2–3.

113. Howard N. Snyder and Melissa Sickmund, *Juvenile Offenders and Victims: 2006 National Report* (Washington, D.C.: National Center for Juvenile Justice, March 2006), 235.

114. Anna Aizer and Joseph J. Doyle, Jr., "Juvenile Incarceration, Human Capital and Future Crime: Evidence from Randomly-Assigned Judges." *www.nber.org*. The National Bureau of Economic Research, June 2013, Web.

115. *Youth Reentry Improvement Report* (Springfield, Ill.: Illinois Juvenile Justice Commission, November 2011), 9.

116. Anian Zhang, Lauren Musu-Gillette, and Barbara A. Oudekerk, *Indicators of School Crime and Safety: 2015* (Washington, D.C.: National Center for Education Statistics, May 2016), Table 20.3, page 183.

117. Gary Fields and John R. Emshwiller, "For More Teens, Arrests by Police Replace School Discipline," *www.wsj.com*. Wall Street Journal: October 20, 2014, Web.

118. Civil Rights Data Collection, *Snapshot: School Discipline* (Washington, D.C.: U.S. Department of Education Office for Civil Rights, March 2014), 6.

119. Emma Brown, "Police in Schools: Keeping Kids Safe, or Arresting Them for No Good Reason?" *www.washingtonpost.com*. *Washington Post:* November 8, 2015, Web.

120. Quoted in *ibid.*

121. Quoted in Chris McGreal, "The U.S. Schools with Their Own Police," *www.guardian.co.uk*. *The Guardian:* January 9, 2012, Web.

16

Today's Challenges:

Cyber Crime, Security vs. Liberty, and White-Collar Crime

To target your study and review, look for these numbered Learning Objective icons throughout the chapter.

Chapter Outline	Corresponding Learning Objectives
Cyber Crime	**1** Outline the three major reasons why the Internet is conducive to the dissemination of child pornography.
	2 Define *malware*, and identify the main way in which worms differ from viruses and Trojans.
	3 Explain how the Internet has contributed to piracy of intellectual property.
	4 Distinguish verbal threats that are protected by the Constitution from verbal threats that can be prosecuted as "true threats."
Security vs. Liberty	**5** Summarize the three federal laws that have been particularly influential on our nation's counterterrorism strategies.
	6 Explain why privacy expectations are so important to the federal government's metadata surveillance operations.
	7 Describe two factors that make it difficult for counterterrorism agents to predict and prevent acts of domestic terrorism.
White-Collar Crime	**8** Indicate some of the ways that white-collar crime is different from violent or property crime.
	9 Explain the concept of corporate violence.

"Revenge Porn"

▲ Former California Attorney General Kamala Harris discusses the case of Kevin Bollaert, who was recently sentenced to eighteen years in prison for operating the "revenge porn" site UGotPosted.com. Irfan Khan/*Los Angeles Times*/Getty Images

other states and Washington, D.C., also have laws that criminalize *nonconsensual pornography*, which can broadly be defined as the distribution of sexually graphic images of individuals without their consent. These laws cover many forms of wrongdoing, including stealing and selling nude images of celebrities and *sextortion*, in which the offender threatens to post explicit photographs online if the victim does not provide more such images, sexual favors, or money.

Victims of nonconsensual pornography suffer in numerous ways beyond the shame of exposure. They may find it difficult to find work, given that most employers now consult search engines to collect information on job applicants. Their personal relationships with family and friends who have viewed the images may be strained. And, crucially, they may be placed in physical danger. Several years ago, fifty men showed up at the home of a Maryland woman whose ex-husband posted fake ads using her image online, including one that said, "Rape Me and My Children."

A few months after Norma broke up with her boyfriend, she found out that he had posted sexually explicit selfies of her on an X-rated website called PornHub. Along with the photos, he included her first and last names, her phone number, her hometown, and a solicitation for oral sex. "I cannot get back my privacy that had been invaded when those pictures were online," Norma told a court in Newark, New Jersey. "I do not know how many people saw them, I do not know how many people saved them, and every single day I think about the fact that other people have seen me in my most private state."

Norma's ex-boyfriend was charged under New Jersey's so-called "revenge porn" law and sentenced to five years' probation. The legislation makes it a crime for one person to disclose online the image of another person in which her or his "intimate parts are exposed" without that person's approval. Thirty-three

FOR CRITICAL ANALYSIS

1. Why might the owner of a book or photography store that sells items online have a problem with nonconsensual pornography laws?

2. California's nonconsensual pornography law includes a provision that the images are shown "with the intent to cause emotional distress." What might be some of the unintended consequences of a "revenge porn" law that does not feature an intent requirement?

3. When someone finds unwanted explicit images of himself or herself online, the first impulse is to have the images removed or destroyed. Why might this be an unwise strategy in the context of criminal justice?

Cyber Crime

The Internet is teeming with *cyberdeviance*—behavior that, while not technically illegal, falls outside society's norms. By one measure, pornography websites receive more visitors than Amazon, Netflix, and Twitter combined.[1] Activities such as "sexting," or sharing sexually explicit photos online, are commonplace and generally are not illegal. Even filming sex acts and placing the videos on the Internet, if consensual, is beyond the reach of criminal law.

Without consent, the legal equation changes. In 2016, for example, Benjamin Barber, an Oregon resident, posted pornographic footage of himself engaging in sex with a former partner on multiple websites. Because the partner did not give her consent, Barber was charged with five counts of "unlawful dissemination of an intimate image" and sentenced to six months in jail. If Barber had posted the videos several years earlier, he probably would not have been arrested. In 2015, however, Oregon passed a nonconsensual pornography law, and Barber's behavior went from deviant to illegal.[2] In other words, he had committed a **cyber crime,** the broad term that we will use in this section to describe any criminal activity carried out by the use of a computer in the virtual community of the Internet.

Crime and the Internet

It is difficult, if not impossible, to determine how much cyber crime actually takes place. Often, people never know that they have been the victims of this type of criminal activity. Furthermore, businesses sometimes fail to report such crimes for fear of losing customer confidence.

Some estimates are, however, available. According to the cyber security firm Symantec, individuals worldwide are the targets of over one million Internet attacks every day.[3] Eight out of ten business executives recently surveyed indicated that their company had experienced a cyber security "incident" in the previous twelve months.[4] Juniper, a technology consulting firm, calculates that cyber crime will cost businesses $2.1 trillion globally each year by 2019.[5]

An Easier Path to Crime

As this textbook has made clear, committing a crime in the "real world" is difficult and full of uncertainty. A robber, for example, must plan out the logistics of the crime, determine a suitable victim with items worth taking, and accept the risk of law enforcement intervention. Technology makes cyber crime considerably easier. With relatively basic knowledge of how computers operate, a person can conduct a wide range of wrongdoing without leaving the relative safety of home.[6]

Technology also acts as a "force multiplier," allowing for the targeting of numerous victims. "Robbing one person at a time using a knife or a gun doesn't scale well," notes Marc

Peter C. Vey/The New Yorker Collection/Cartoonbank.com

"You know, you can do this just as easily online."

Goodman of the Future Crimes Institute. "But now one person can rob millions at the click of a button."[7]

Child Pornography Online

The example of *child pornography* shows how cyber crime has raised the stakes for the criminal justice system. (Child pornography is the illegal production and sale of material depicting sexually explicit conduct involving a child.) In the late 1970s, about 250 child pornography magazines were circulating in the United States, and it was relatively easy for law enforcement to confiscate hard copies of these publications.[8] With the advent of the Internet, however, child pornography became much easier to disseminate. The reasons for this include:

Learning Objective 1 Outline the three major reasons why the Internet is conducive to the dissemination of child pornography.

1. *Speed.* The Internet is a quick means of sending visual material over long distances. Child pornographers can deliver their material faster and more securely online than through regular mail.
2. *Security.* Any illegal material that passes through the hands of a mail carrier is inherently in danger of being discovered. This risk is significantly reduced with e-mail. Furthermore, Internet sites that offer child pornography can protect their customers with passwords, which keep random Web surfers (or law enforcement agents) from stumbling on the sites or chat rooms.
3. *Anonymity.* Obviously, anonymity is the most important protection offered by the Internet for sellers and buyers of child pornography, as it is for any person engaged in illegal behavior in cyberspace.[9]

Because of these factors, courts and lawmakers have had a difficult time controlling not only child pornography but also a wide variety of other online wrongdoing. In this section, we will focus on three general areas of online offending, as identified by cyber crime expert David Wall: (1) cyber trespass, (2) cyber deception and theft, and (3) cyber violence.[10]

Cyber Trespass

In early 2016, officials at the University of California, Berkeley sent notices to about 80,000 current and former students and faculty members. The notices warned that cybercriminals had breached a university account that stored Social Security and bank account numbers and that members of the UC Berkeley community should be alert to any signs that such data were being misused.[11]

This incident is an example of a *cyber trespass*, in which unauthorized persons illegally gain entry to computer systems. Although not all cyber trespass is carried out for financial gain, the costs of responding to such breaches are considerable. After one medium-sized retailer's credit-card database was broken into, the company was forced to spend about $2.5 million in investigation, crisis management, and legal expenses to remedy the situation.[12]

Hacking

The individuals who breached security at UC Berkeley are known as *hackers.* A **hack** is the act of using one computer system to gain illegal access to another computer system. In general, hackers take advantage of flaws in computer software or hardware, known as *vulnerabilities*, that allow them to enter the targeted system without permission.

Hacking is unnervingly frequent in the United States. Each hour, government agencies, businesses, and individuals are subjected to hundreds of hacking attempts. Over

Hack The illegal use of one computer system to gain access to another computer system and steal or manipulate the data in the targeted system.

the past several years, cybercriminals have successfully hacked the White House, the U.S. State Department, and the Pentagon, not to mention dozens of large companies such as Yahoo, Apple, and Verizon.

Malware Hackers rely on malicious software, or *malware*, to carry out their illegal activities. Over the past few decades, a dizzying array of malware has been developed, and more complex forms of this software are introduced each year. For our purposes, the four general categories of malware listed below provide a helpful introduction to the subject.

1. A **worm** is a software program that is capable of reproducing itself as it spreads from one computer to the next.
2. A **virus** is also able to reproduce itself, but must be attached to an "infested" host file to travel from one computer network to another.
3. **Trojans** are, at first glance, useful pieces of software that do damage when installed and activated on a computer.
4. **Botnets** allow a hacker to "take over" another computer without the knowledge of the targeted computer's owner. That computer is then used to spread malware, thus hiding the hacker's identity.

For the most part, viruses, Trojans, and botnets require a careless act, such as clicking on a file or attachment, to spread to targeted computers. Worms, in contrast, can move from computer to computer without further human action.

Ransomware Often, these basic forms of malware are combined into a *blended threat*. An example of a blended threat is *ransomware*, which is similar to a Trojan in that it must be activated by a computer user. Once this happens, the malware *encrypts* all the files on the targeted computer system. **Encryption** is the process of encoding information stored on computers in such a way that only authorized parties have access to it.

Generally, as you will see later in the section, encryption is used to protect information. When a computer system is infected with ransomware, however, its owners are unable to access their own files, and must pay hackers a fee to unlock the data. Over the past several years, a virulent strain of ransomware called CryptoWall has emerged, contaminating over 800,000 computers worldwide. According to the Cyber Threat Alliance, in 2015 businesses and individuals paid an estimated $325 million to free their files from CryptoWall encryption.[13]

Worm A computer program that can automatically replicate itself and interfere with the normal use of a computer. A worm does not need to be attached to an existing file to move from one network to another.

Virus A computer program that can replicate itself and interfere with the normal use of a computer. A virus cannot exist as a separate entity and must attach itself to another program to move through a network.

Trojan Malware that appears to be beneficial to a computer user, but causes damage to the computer when it is installed and activated. (Also known as a Trojan horse.)

Botnet A network of computers that have been appropriated without the knowledge of their owners and used to spread harmful programs via the Internet; short for robot network.

Encryption The translation of computer data into a secret code with the goal of protecting that data from unauthorized parties.

The Future of Hacking

Given that each year, (1) more individuals are connected to the Internet, (2) more businesses are operating on the Internet, and (3) malware continues to evolve, hacking will certainly continue to pose a significant challenge to those who operate online.[14] The growing use of mobile devices such as smartphones and tablets has added another sizable outlet for hacking. These devices generally do not have the same level of security software as desktop or laptop computers, and therefore provide an easier target for hackers.

For example, more than half of smartphone users with bank accounts take advantage of mobile banking apps to check their accounts or make balance transfers. Recently developed malware programs such as Acecard and GM bot are designed to infect these apps and steal the users' bank account information.[15] Undoubtedly, as the number of everyday items connected to the Internet grows, so will the opportunities to hack these items for illegal purposes.

Hacking the "Internet of Things"

The "Internet of things" (IoT) is set to dominate our daily lives in the near future. The term refers to objects that contain tiny computer chips that wirelessly connect them to the Internet. The roster of Web-connected items—including automobiles, refrigerators, televisions, pacemakers, light bulbs, and smoke detectors—is already extensive. It is estimated that the IoT will include fifty billion devices worldwide by 2020, up from twenty billion in 2017.

The tiny computers that form the basis of the IoT do not have as much processing power or memory as desktop computers or even smartphones. Consequently, the security software on these systems tends to be unsophisticated and easily bypassed by malware such as Mirai, which scours the Web for vulnerabilities. In October 2016, Mirai was able to gain access to hundreds of thousands of IoT devices with simple passwords such as "admin" or "12345." It used these captured devices to launch an attack on Dyn, a New Hampshire–based company that helps route Internet traffic. The result: temporary outages at popular websites such as Netflix, PayPal, Spotify, and Twitter. "When the Internet apocalypse comes, your smart thermostat may be to blame," remarked one observer after the attack.

Thinking about Hacking the "Internet of Things"

The dangers of a remotely controlled automobile or heart monitor are obvious. Experts warn that smart light bulbs are also susceptible to easy hacking. Using your imagination, describe the national security risks posed by a large number of malware-infected light bulbs.

Cyber Deception and Theft

Not all hacking is geared toward monetary gain, but it certainly can be used to that end. In 2016, for example, hackers managed to gain access to a computer network that arranges for transfers of funds between banks. With this access, they drained $81 million from accounts at the Bangladesh Bank before being discovered. Thus, *cyber deception and theft*, which involves the illegal acquisition of information or resources using computer networks, plays a significant role in cyber crime.

Cyber Consumer Fraud   The expanding world of e-commerce has created many benefits for consumers. It has also led to some challenging problems, including fraud conducted via the Internet. In general, fraud is any misrepresentation knowingly made with the intention of deceiving another person. Furthermore, the victim must reasonably rely on the fraudulent information to her or his detriment. **Cyber fraud,** then, is fraud committed over the Internet. Scams that were once conducted solely by mail or phone can now be found online, and new technology has led to increasingly more creative ways to commit fraud.

Online dating scams, for example, have increased dramatically in recent years, with fraudsters creating fake profiles to deceive unwitting romantic partners. According to the Internet Crime Complaint Center (IC3), operated as a partnership between the FBI and the National White Collar Crime Center, in 2015 online romance scam artists defrauded victims out of more than $200 million.[16] In one case, the FBI arrested a Houston resident for defrauding numerous older women he met on Internet dating websites out of millions of dollars. First, he would profess to fall in love with his victims. Then, he would offer to take over management of their personal finances, which he would steal as soon as the funds were naively placed in his control. (See Figure 16.1 to learn about the costs associated with other common forms of cyber fraud.)

Cyber Fraud Any misrepresentation knowingly made over the Internet with the intention of deceiving another and on which a reasonable person would and does rely to his or her detriment.

Cyber Theft A **data breach** is an incident in which unauthorized persons access and steal confidential or protected information. In cyberspace, those who carry out data breaches are not subject to the physical limitations of the "real" world. A thief with network access can steal data stored in a networked computer from anywhere on the globe. Only the speed of the connection and the thief's computer equipment limit the quantity of data that can be stolen.

Identity Theft This freedom from physical limitations has led to a marked increase in **identity theft,** which occurs when the wrongdoer steals a form of identification—such as a name, date of birth, or Social Security number—and uses the information to access the victim's financial resources. According to the federal government, about 7 percent of Americans aged sixteen and older are victims of identity theft each year.[17]

The vast majority of identity theft victims (86 percent) experience data breaches involving existing bank and credit card accounts.[18] Online, an identity thief can steal financial information by fooling websites into thinking that he or she is the true account holder. For example, important personal information such as one's birthday, hometown, or employer that is available on social media sites such as Facebook can be used to convince a third party to reveal the victim's Social Security or bank account number. Offenders are also installing undetectable devices in card terminals such as ATMs. The devices capture information from the magnetic strips on credit cards when the cards are inserted into the machines. This technique, called *skimming*, allows the wrongdoers to produce counterfeit credit cards that can be used to withdraw cash at ATMs or make a purchase at stores or online.

Password Protection The more personal information a cyber criminal obtains, the easier it is for him or her to find a victim's online user name. Once the online user name has been compromised, it is easier to steal a victim's password, which is often the last line of defense to financial information.

Numerous software programs aid identity thieves in illegally obtaining passwords. A technique called *keystroke logging*, for example, relies on software that embeds itself in a victim's computer and records every keystroke made on that computer. User names and passwords are then recorded and sold to the highest bidder. Internet users should also be wary of any links contained within e-mails sent from an unknown source, as these links can sometimes be used to illegally obtain personal information. (See Figure 16.2 for some hints on how to protect your online passwords.)

FIGURE 16.1 Fraudulent Activity on the Internet

In its most recent annual report on cyber crime, the Internet Crime Complaint Center highlighted five "frequently reported Internet crimes." These crimes, along with the annual total losses reported by their victims, are detailed below.

Business E-mail Compromise: Victims, mostly businesses, are instructed via e-mail to redirect invoice payments to nonexistent suppliers.

Non-payment/Non-delivery: Victims are scammed at e-commerce websites; either (1) goods and services are shipped, and payment is never rendered, or (2) payment is sent, and goods and services are never received.

Investment Fraud: Deceptive practices that convince victims to make investments or purchases (such as for real estate) on the basis of false information, usually promising a large return with minimal financial risk.

* Described in the text.

Source: Internet Crime Complaint Center, *IC3 2015 Internet Crime Report* (Glen Allen, Va.: National White Collar Crime Center, 2016), 16, 226–230.

Data Breach The illegal appropriation of protected or confidential information.

Identity Theft The theft of personal information, such as a person's name, driver's license number, or Social Security number.

FIGURE 16.2 Protecting Online Passwords

Once an online password has been compromised, the information on the protected website is fair game for identity thieves. By following these simple rules, you can strengthen the protection provided by your online passwords.

1. **Don't** use existing words such as your pet's name or your hometown. Such words are easy for computer identity theft programs to decode.

2. **Do** use at least eight characters in your passwords, with a nonsensical combination of upper- and lower-case letters, numbers, and symbols. A weak password is "scout1312." A strong password is "4X$dQ%3Z9j."

3. **Don't** use the same username and password for different Web accounts. If you do, then each account is in danger if one account is compromised.

4. **Do** use a different password for each Web account. If necessary, write down the various passwords and keep the list in a safe place.

5. **Don't** use information that can be easily found online or guessed at in choosing the questions that Web sites use to verify your password. That is, don't select questions such as "What is your birthday?" or "What is your city of birth?" Instead, choose questions with obscure answers that you are certain to remember or can easily look up.

6. **Don't** log on to any website if you are connected to the Internet via a wireless network (Wi-Fi) that is not itself password protected.

Phishing A distinct form of identity theft known as phishing adds a different wrinkle to this particular form of cyber crime. In a phishing attack, the perpetrators "fish" for financial data and passwords from consumers by posing as a legitimate business such as a bank or credit-card company. The "phisher" sends an e-mail asking the recipient to "update" or "confirm" vital information, often with the threat that an account or some other service will be discontinued if the information is not provided. Once the unsuspecting target enters the information, the phisher can use it to masquerade as the person or to extract funds from his or her bank or credit account.

The preferred method of phishing is through the use of spam, the unsolicited "junk e-mails" that flood virtual mailboxes with advertisements, solicitations, and other messages. Although 86 percent of the world's e-mail traffic still involves spam, filter systems are now able to block most unwanted e-mails.[19] To get around these filters, phishers are increasingly using tactics that target small groups of recipients rather than blasting fake e-mails to millions of people at a time. Phishing scams affect not only e-mail but also other areas, such as text messaging and social networking sites. According to the security firm Proofpoint, phishing on social media sites increased 150 percent from 2015 to 2016.[20]

Another form of phishing, called *spear phishing*, can be difficult to detect because the messages seem to have come from co-workers, friends, or family members. Several years ago, a cybergang infiltrated the security systems of a number of banks worldwide by sending bank employees e-mails containing links to news clips, apparently sent by colleagues. When the employees clicked on the links, they inadvertently downloaded software onto their computers that allowed the cyber thieves to drain hundreds of millions of dollars from accounts in the affected banks.[21]

Pirating Intellectual Property Online

Most people think of wealth in terms of houses, land, cars, stocks, and bonds. Wealth, however, also includes intellectual property, which consists of the products that result from intellectual, creative processes. The government provides various forms of protection for intellectual property, such as

Phishing Sending an unsolicited e-mail that falsely claims to be from a legitimate organization in an attempt to acquire sensitive information from the recipient.

Spam Bulk e-mails, particularly of commercial advertising, sent in large quantities without the consent of the recipient.

Intellectual Property Property resulting from intellectual, creative processes.

copyrights and patents. These protections ensure that a person who writes a book or a song or creates a software program is financially rewarded if that product is sold in the marketplace.

Learning 3 Objective — Explain how the Internet has contributed to piracy of intellectual property.

Intellectual property such as books, films, music, and software is vulnerable to "piracy"—the unauthorized copying and use of the property. In the past, copying intellectual products was time consuming, and the quality of the pirated copies was clearly inferior. In today's online world, however, things have changed. Simply clicking a mouse can now reproduce millions of unauthorized copies, and pirated duplicates of copyrighted works obtained via the Internet are often exactly the same as the original, or close to it. The Business Software Alliance estimates that 39 percent of all business software is pirated, costing software makers more than $52 billion in 2015.[22]

Cyber Violence

Cyber violence, our final category of cyber crime, focuses on the use of the Internet to cause harm. Although this form of cyber hostility may have financial consequences, those who engage in it are primarily interested in bringing about emotional harm, embarrassment, or shame.[23]

For example, several years ago, the collective Anonymous—made up of an unknown number of loosely affiliated so-called "hacktivists"—posted the online identities of hundreds of alleged members of the Ku Klux Klan. By exposing these adherents of white supremacy, the group claimed that it was trying to spark "a bit of constructive dialogue about race, racism, race terror, and freedom of expression."[24]

Cyberbullying   As texting and social networking sites such as Snapchat and Instagram have become an integral part of youth culture, so, it seems, has *cyberbullying*. A twenty-first century update on traditional bullying, which we discussed in the preceding chapter, cyberbullying uses electronic means to cause social embarrassment or emotional harm. The practice has become even more prevalent in recent years with the advent of social networking apps such as Yik Yak that allow users to make cruel, rude, and sexually suggestive comments about their peers anonymously.

To many, cyberbullying can be even more harmful than "old school" bullying. Not only does the anonymity of cyberspace seem to embolden offenders, causing them to be more vicious than they would be in person, but also the hurtful information spreads quickly to a large audience. "It's really horrifying the next day after the message has been sent around, and you're the laughingstock of the school," said one young victim. "You have no idea why or what's funny."[25] According to the Cyberbullying Research Center, about a quarter of American students aged twelve to seventeen had been the subject of "mean or hurtful comments online" in the thirty days before being surveyed.[26]

Cyberstalking   In the opening of this chapter, we discussed "revenge porn," a form of cyberbullying that involves the nonconsensual publication online of explicit sexual images. Revenge porn is often a component of cyberstalking, which occurs when one person uses e-mail, text messages, or some other form of electronic communication to cause a victim to reasonably fear for her or his safety or the safety of her or his immediate family. According to the most recent federal data on the subject, about 850,000 Americans are targets of cyberstalking each year.[27]

Nearly all the states, as well as the federal government, have passed laws to combat this form of criminal behavior. Most of these statutes require that the offender pose a true threat to his or her victim—that is, that the victim can be said to reasonably fear for his

Cyberbullying To bully electronically by sending repeated, hurtful messages via texting or the Internet, particularly on social media websites.

Cyberstalking The crime of stalking committed in cyberspace through the use of e-mail, text messages, or other forms of electronic communication.

True Threat An act of speech or expression that is not protected by the First Amendment because it is done with the intention of placing a specific victim or group of victims in fear of unlawful violence.

Cyberattack An attempt to damage or disrupt computer systems or electronic networks operated by computers.

or her safety.[28] In the absence of a true threat, the communication is protected by the First Amendment, discussed in Chapter 1.

A U.S. appeals court applied this test in a 1997 case involving a University of Michigan student. That student, Abraham Alkhabaz, posted a graphic story online in which a woman with the same name as one of his classmates was raped and murdered. Alkhabaz was eventually arrested by federal agents and charged with communicating threats across state lines to injure another person. The federal court overturned this arrest due to lack of evidence showing that the defendant would actually have carried out his violent fictional imaginings.[29] (See the feature *Discretion in Action—Facebook Fantasy?* to apply the true threat doctrine to a more recent case of possible online stalking and harassment.)

Cyberterrorism

In the spring of 2016, approximately eight hundred members of the Arkansas Library Association (ALA) were surprised to learn that they had become international news. Supporters of the extremist terrorist organization ISIS had hacked the ALA's computer system and published the members' names, addresses, and e-mail addresses on a "hit list" app. If the subjects of this action were concerned about being targeted by terrorists, it did not show. One library director called the hacking "vaguely amusing," adding, "Our credit card information didn't get stolen apparently, so we're glad for that."[30]

Cyberattacks Homeland security experts worry that such relatively harmless incidents are a precursor to a much more serious **cyberattack** by a terrorist organization. Cyberattacks are designed to damage a nation's infrastructure, which includes its power companies, water treatment plants, airports, chemical plants, and oil refineries. In a worst-case scenario, a cyberattack could allow a terrorist organization to seize control of

---

DISCRETION IN ACTION

Facebook Fantasy?

The Situation After Anthony's wife, Tara, leaves him, taking their children with her, Anthony's online behavior becomes increasingly erratic. He begins posting violent rap lyrics on Facebook aimed at Tara, including: "If I only knew then what I know now . . . I would have smothered your ass with a pillow. Dumped your body in the back seat. Dropped you off in Toad Creek and made it look like a rape and murder." He also writes that he would like to see a Halloween costume of his wife's "head on a stick." In due course, Anthony is arrested for breaking a federal law that makes it a crime to transmit "any communication containing . . . any threat to injure the person of another."

The Law According to the United States Supreme Court's interpretation of the First Amendment, Anthony's Facebook posts can be considered a "true threat," and therefore a criminal act, only if they represent "a serious expression of an intent to commit an act of unlawful violence to a particular individual or group of individuals."

What Would You Do? You are a juror at Anthony's trial. You hear him testify that his remarks were nothing more than a form of therapy to help "deal with the pain" of separation from his family. "I would never hurt my wife," he says. "I felt like I was being stalked," counters Tara during her testimony. "I felt extremely afraid for [my life] and my children's lives." This case poses a difficult question: If a person makes a statement that one might reasonably take as a threat, but that was not intended by the speaker as a threat, is it a true threat? Your answer will help determine whether you vote to convict Anthony of breaking federal law.

Learning Objective 4 Distinguish verbal threats that are protected by the Constitution from verbal threats that can be prosecuted as "true threats."

To see how the United States Supreme Court ruled in this case, see Example 16.1 in Appendix B.

the federal air traffic control system, or shut down national power grids. "This is a much bigger threat over time than losing some credit cards to cyber criminals," said one security expert.[31]

One of the potential methods of carrying out such a large-scale cyberattack is a *distributed denial of service (DDoS)*. As part of a DDoS, hackers flood a targeted system with malware, much of it meaningless electronic "traffic," causing the system to crash and become inaccessible. Hackers in Iran, for example, are suspected to have launched DDoS attacks at a number of targets in the United States, including several major banks, a small dam in New York State, and a Las Vegas casino whose owner had been critical of the country's rulers.[32]

Cyber-Recruiting The Internet has also proved instrumental as an arena for terrorist recruiting operations. ISIS and its sympathizers maintain thousands of active Twitter accounts in English to spread their anti-Western propaganda. According to the FBI, ISIS is putting out a "siren song" on social media that reads as follows:

> Troubled soul, come to the caliphate, you will live a life of glory, these are the apocalyptic end times, you will find a life of meaning here fighting for our caliphate, and if you can't come, kill somebody where you are.[33]

(The term *caliphate* refers to a new state under extremist Islamic rule that ISIS is trying to establish in parts of Syria and Iraq.)

A recent cyberterrorism tactic involves what homeland security experts refer to as "remote-controlled" attacks. As part of this approach, ISIS operatives in the Middle East control and guide domestic terrorists in their home countries. For example, Emanuel Lutchman had been communicating with an ISIS handler for five days before the FBI arrested him for planning a mass shooting at a Rochester, New York, restaurant on New Year's Eve, 2015. "I fear this is the future of ISIS," says one virtual security expert.[34]

Fighting Cyber Crime

During the 2013 holiday season, hackers used a malware program called Kaptoxa to steal credit- and debit-card data from at least 70 million customers of the retail giant Target. In response, the company hired private contractors to plug its security holes and erase the malware from its compromised systems. Ideally, of course, corporations should have software already in place to prevent hacking operations, and most do. Businesses spend billions of dollars a year to encrypt their vital information, and encryption is seen as the best strategy for protecting the "Internet of things," whose vulnerabilities were discussed in this chapter's *CJ & Technology* feature.

Companies also hire outside experts to act as hackers and attempt to gain access to their systems, a practice known as "penetration testing." In 2016, the passenger-referral company Uber launched a "bug bounty" program that pays as much as $10,000 to anybody who can find security weaknesses in its mobile app.[35] Even the most thorough private protection services often lag behind the ingenuity of the hacker community, however. In the Target attack, for example, the malware was programmed to constantly erase itself, making it practically impossible to detect. "The dynamics of the Internet and cyberspace are so fast that we have a hard time staying ahead of the adversary," admits former U.S. Secret Service agent Robert D. Rodriguez.[36]

The "Zero-Days" Problem The Internet was designed to promote connectivity, not security. As more and more online threats to companies such as Target have developed, those businesses have had to respond with increasingly novel defenses. Facebook, for example, has constructed ThreatData, a defense system that monitors new worms, viruses, and malicious websites to create a constantly updated "blacklist" of blocked malware. Still, it is virtually impossible to protect against "zero days," the industry term for new vulnerabilities that security software cannot detect and for which there are no existing defenses. The Internet security consulting firm Symantec uncovered an average of one new zero-day vulnerability per week in 2015.[37]

Clearly, private industry needs government help to fight off cyber criminals. With hundreds of millions of users in every corner of the globe transferring unimaginable amounts of information almost instantaneously, however, the Internet has proved resistant to government regulation. In addition, although a number of countries have tried to "control" the Internet (see the feature *Comparative Criminal Justice—The Great Firewall of China*), the U.S. government has generally adopted a hands-off attitude to better promote the free flow of ideas and encourage the growth of electronic commerce. Thus, in this country, cyberspace is largely unregulated, making efforts to fight cyber crime all the more difficult.

Federal Law Enforcement and Cyber Crime

Aside from investigating reports of online harassment and child pornography in their jurisdictions, local police do not play a large role in combatting cyber crime. Simply put, most police departments and sheriffs' departments do not have the training or the resources to effectively manage

COMPARATIVE CRIMINAL JUSTICE

Source: Central Intelligence Agency

The Great Firewall of China

With an estimated 650 million citizens online, China has the largest number of Internet users of any country in the world. China also has the global lead in another category: online repression. According to the Freedom House, an American pro-democracy group, no other developed country places as many restrictions on Internet use. This policy of "cyberspace sovereignty" starts at the source, with nine state-run operators controlling access to all text messaging services and Internet traffic. So, for example, after ethnic tensions erupted in the Xinjiang region in 2009, the Chinese government was able to essentially shut down all online communications in the region—home to 22 million people—for ten months.

A WEB OF RESTRICTIONS

On a daily basis, China exerts control over the Internet using human and technological means. Tens of thousands of government employees constantly monitor the country's online activity, reporting and censoring politically sensitive communications and illegal behavior such as pornography. At the same time, a system of constraints known as the Great Firewall automatically blocks access to websites disfavored by the government. In 2016, China's government temporarily blocked the websites of *The Economist* and *Time* after those Western magazines published articles critical of President Xi Jinping. Chinese citizens are permanently prohibited from using a number of U.S.-based websites, including Facebook, Google, Instagram, Twitter, and YouTube.

Finally, Chinese criminal law prohibits spreading "false information" or "inciting subversion of state power" online. Although relatively few "netizens" are imprisoned for Internet activity, the laws do have a strong deterrent impact on free expression in cyberspace. The only way the average Chinese citizen can avoid these myriad restrictions is by using an illegal virtual private network or hoping for a "crack in the wall." After an apparent glitch allowed brief access to Google and Instagram in March 2016, one user urged the Chinese to "remember this short period of happiness."

FOR CRITICAL ANALYSIS

There is very little anonymity in China's version of cyberspace. All users are required to use their real names when registering for any online service. What would be the drawbacks and benefits of a similar policy in the United States?

cyber crime investigations.[38] Consequently, the federal government has traditionally taken the lead in law enforcement efforts against cyber crime.

The FBI has the primary responsibility for enforcing federal criminal statutes involving computer crime and leads the federal government's law enforcement efforts to combat cyber criminals. Since 2002, the Bureau has operated a Cyber Division dedicated to investigating computer-based crimes. The Cyber Division and its administrators coordinate the FBI's efforts in cyberspace, specifically its investigations into cyber terrorism and intellectual property theft. The division also has jurisdiction over the Innocent Images National Initiative (IINI), the agency's online child-pornography subdivision.

Additionally, through its Financial Crimes division, the Secret Service is heavily involved in combatting cyber crime. The Secret Service has three primary investigatory responsibilities in this area: (1) cyber fraud against financial institutions such as banks and credit unions, (2) access-device fraud, or hacking operations that target credit and debit cards, and (3) acts of fraud that target the federal government or the interests of the federal government.[39]

Cyber Forensics

Law enforcement cannot put yellow tape around a computer screen or dust a website for fingerprints. The best, and often the only, way to fight cyber crime is with technology that gives law enforcement agencies the ability to "track" hackers and other cyber criminals through the Internet. For example, in the case that opened this chapter, Seth Yockel of the Essex County (New Jersey) prosecutor's office ordered Internet service providers (ISPs) to search for the IP address (a code that identifies individual computers on the Internet) from which Norma's photos were uploaded. With the help of a cooperative ISP, his office was able to trace the photos to a computer in the primary suspect's mother's house.[40]

In Chapter 6, we discussed forensics—the application of science to find evidence of criminal activity. Within the past two decades, a branch of this science known as cyber forensics has evolved to gather evidence of cyber crimes. The main goal of cyber forensics is to collect digital evidence, or information of value to a criminal investigation that is stored on, received by, or transmitted by an electronic device such as a computer. Generally speaking, there are three basic stages to gathering digital evidence:

1. The *survey/identification* stage, in which law enforcement and digital forensic technicians determine the physical crime scene (such as a home office) and digital crime scene (such as a website) that must be searched for evidence.
2. The *collection/acquisition* stage, which involves gathering all relevant evidence at these crime scenes and preserving it by making copies of any suspicious digital content.
3. The *report/presentation* stage, where the steps used in gathering the evidence are written in a report, and all relevant evidence is prepared for presentation in court.[41]

The latest challenge to cyber investigators is posed by *cloud computing*, in which data are stored not in a physical location but in a virtual, shared computing platform that is linked simultaneously to a number of different computers. Therefore, law enforcement officers investigating wrongdoing in the "cloud" may not have full control of the "crime scene." (The growing importance of cyber crime has led a number of universities to offer graduate certificates in cyber forensics. To learn about one of these programs, go to the website of the Marshall University Forensic Science Center.)

Jurisdictional Challenges

Regardless of what type of cyber crime is being investigated, law enforcement agencies are often frustrated by problems of jurisdiction (explained more fully in Chapter 8). Jurisdiction is primarily based on physical

Cyber Forensics The application of computer technology to finding and utilizing evidence of cyber crimes.

Digital Evidence Information or data of value to a criminal investigation that is either stored or transmitted by electronic means.

▲ In November 2015, U.S. authorities accused Gery Shalon of hacking into the computer systems of dozens of American businesses, including JPMorgan Chase & Co. and Dow Jones & Co. **Do you think that U.S. law enforcement should have the power to charge Shalon—an Israeli citizen shown here (in a white shirt) arriving at a Jerusalem courtroom—for crimes against American corporations? Why or why not?** REUTERS/Amir Cohen

geography—each country, state, and nation has jurisdiction, or authority, over crimes that occur within its boundaries. The Internet, however, destroys these traditional notions because geographic boundaries simply do not exist in cyberspace.

Determining Jurisdiction To see how jurisdictional issues can affect law enforcement, let's consider a hypothetical cyberstalking case. Phil, who lives in State A, has been sending e-mails containing graphic sexual threats to Stephanie, who lives in State B. Where has the crime taken place? Which police department has authority to arrest Phil, and which court system has authority to try him? To further complicate matters, what if State A has not yet added cyberstalking to its criminal code, while State B has? Does that mean that Phil has not committed a crime in his home state, but has committed one in Stephanie's?

The federal government has taken to answering this question by stating that Phil has committed a crime wherever it says he has. The Sixth Amendment to the U.S. Constitution states that federal criminal cases should be tried in the district in which the offense was committed.[42] Because the Internet is "everywhere," the federal government has a great deal of leeway in choosing the venue in which an alleged cyber criminal will face trial.

International Jurisdiction Even given the U.S. government's broad interpretation of its power over cyber crime, the rules of jurisdiction can make enforcing American law abroad difficult. For example, gambling online is, for the most part, illegal in this country. Nonetheless, hundreds of online gambling websites with customers in the United States have successfully evaded the reach of federal prosecutors by registering their headquarters in foreign countries.

Another problem concerns lack of international cooperation. Even if the U.S. government claims jurisdiction over a cyber criminal, such claims are meaningless if the suspect is able to avoid U.S. custody. Russia, in particular, has a reputation as a "safe haven" for hackers who attack targets in the United States. To give one example, in 2009, the Secret Service determined that Roman Seleznev, a Russian citizen, was stealing millions of credit card numbers from American e-businesses and selling them in the underground online marketplace. Secret Service agents traveled to Russia and asked their Russian counterparts for help in apprehending Seleznev. The suspect was apparently tipped off about American interest, and he vanished from the Internet.

Seleznev did not, however, vanish from the "real world." In 2014, Secret Service agents arrested him while he was on vacation in the Maldives, an island nation in the Indian Ocean. In 2016, he was finally tried in a Seattle courtroom and convicted of thirty-eight counts of hacking American businesses, causing damages of more than $169 million. While the Russian government decried Seleznev's unlawful "kidnapping," former U.S. deputy attorney general Sally Yates said, "Cybercriminals be forewarned: You cannot hide in the shadows of the Internet."[43]

Security vs. Liberty

How far should a government go in hacking its own citizens for purposes of national security? That question was at the forefront of the national political conversation in March 2017, when WikiLeaks—an international nonprofit organization that publishes secret information—released nine thousand pages of documents describing the inner workings of the Central Intelligence Agency (CIA).

The leaked documents described dozens of sophisticated hacking techniques that the CIA has developed to, for example, compromise Skype conversations, Wi-Fi networks, and personal passwords. One program, code-named Weeping Angel, purportedly allows CIA agents to use Samsung "smart" televisions as "bugs" to record nearby conversations, even when the television is turned off.[44]

The technological range of the CIA's spying capabilities may have come as a shock, but the agency's spying efforts should have been no surprise. Since the attacks of September 11, 2001, homeland security officials have placed paramount importance on tracking communications among suspected terrorists. To do so, the federal government has greatly enhanced the capabilities of law enforcement and intelligence agencies to collect and store information on these suspects. At the same time, the federal government has angered many Americans, who feel that their privacy rights have been ignored or discarded for the sake of national security. "We need a government that protects our civil liberties and privacy rights and protects our families from evil terrorists," says Washington, D.C., lawyer Lanny Davis, succinctly summarizing an ongoing balancing act that goes to the heart of American ideals of fairness and justice. "We must have both."[45]

National Security and Privacy

As has been noted several times in this textbook, our Constitution upholds the premise that Americans should not be subjected to the unreasonable use of government power. As we have also pointed out, reasonableness is a highly subjective concept, and Americans are often willing to give their government more leeway in times of national crisis.

When it comes to antiterrorism efforts and homeland security, this flexibility has manifested itself in the form of federal legislation

▼ A white rose is placed on the name of one of the victims of the September 11, 2001, terrorist attacks at a memorial in New York City. **Why does large-scale terrorist activity often make citizens of the targeted country more willing to trade certain freedoms for greater security against future attacks?** Jewel Samad/AFP/Getty Images

that expands the government's ability to locate, observe, prosecute, and punish suspected terrorists. The first legislative step in this direction, however, took place decades before September 11, 2001, and was designed primarily to weaken the office of the presidency.

Learning Objective 5 Summarize the three federal laws that have been particularly influential on our nation's counterterrorism strategies.

Foreign Surveillance

Until the 1970s, policies regarding governmental **surveillance**, or monitoring, of individuals or groups that posed national security threats to the United States were primarily the domain of the executive branch. That is, the president and his advisors decided who the federal government would target for its spy operations. Following President Richard Nixon's abuse of this discretion to eavesdrop on political opponents during the 1974 presidential campaign, in 1978 Congress passed the Foreign Intelligence Surveillance Act (FISA).[46] This legislation provided a legal framework for the government's electronic monitoring of suspected criminals or national security threats.

Under FISA, federal agents are able to eavesdrop on the communications of foreign persons or foreign entities, without a court order, for up to a year, as long as the purpose of the surveillance is national security and not law enforcement. If this surveillance uncovers wrongdoing by an American citizen, the government has seventy hours to gain judicial authorization to continue to monitor the suspect's activities.[47]

If the target is a "foreign agent" operating within the United States, FISA requires permission from a special court to engage in surveillance. This court, known as the Foreign Intelligence Surveillance Court, or FISA Court, is made up of eleven federal judges assigned by the chief justice of the Supreme Court. The FISA warrant application must identify the target of the surveillance, the nature of the information sought, and the monitoring method. The government agency must also certify that the goal of the surveillance is to "obtain foreign intelligence information."[48]

Material Support

Another crucial piece of counterterrorism legislation was passed in response to the 1995 truck bombing of the Alfred P. Murrah Federal Building in Oklahoma City, Oklahoma, which killed 168 people. The primary goal of this legislation, the Antiterrorism and Effective Death Penalty Act (AEDPA), is to hamper terrorist organizations by cutting off their funding. The law prohibits persons from "knowingly providing *material support* or resources" to any group that the United States has designated a "foreign terrorist organization."[49]

Material support is defined very broadly in the legislation, covering funding, financial services, lodging, training, expert advice or assistance, communications equipment, transportation, and other physical assets.[50] Because it covers such a wide range of activities, the material support statute has frequently been the basis for charges against domestic defendants linked with the terrorist group ISIS. The "support" does not have to be substantial. In 2016, Washington, D.C., Metro Transit Officer Nick Young was charged with providing material support to ISIS in the form of $245 worth of Google Play gift cards.

Furthermore, the statute does not require that a suspect *intend* to aid the terrorist organization in question.[51] About a decade ago, Javed Iqbal was successfully prosecuted in New York for providing a satellite television package that included a channel operated by Hezbollah, a government-designated terrorist organization based in Lebanon. Even though there was no evidence that Iqbal intended to further the goals of Hezbollah, the fact that his conduct provided material support to the organization was sufficient to allow his prosecution under the law.[52]

Surveillance The close observation of a person or group by government agents, in particular to uncover evidence of criminal or terrorist activities.

Material Support In the context of federal antiterrorism legislation, the act of helping a terrorist organization by engaging in any of a wide range of activities, including providing financial support, training, and expert advice or assistance.

The Patriot Act Enacted six weeks after the September 11, 2001, terrorist attacks, the **Patriot Act**[53] greatly strengthened the ability of federal law enforcement agents to investigate and incarcerate terrorist suspects. At 342 pages, the Patriot Act covered numerous areas related to homeland security, including immigration law and border protection, grants to local police departments, and compensation for the victims of the September 11 attacks. Here, we focus on the legislation's rules regarding surveillance, summarized in Figure 16.3. Critics of the Patriot Act have been especially concerned with Sections 213 and 215, which allow government agents to conduct searches and seizures without many of the Fourth Amendment protections discussed in Chapter 7.

Specifically, Section 215 provides the National Security Agency (NSA), a federal agency that focuses on foreign intelligence operations, with the authority to collect the telephone billing records of Americans who have made calls to other countries, as those records are considered reasonably "relevant" to the agency's counterterrorism investigations.[54] Furthermore, the Patriot Act requires third parties such as telephone companies and Internet providers to turn over records of stored electronic communications to the federal government without notice to the persons who made those communications. Government agents do not need judicial permission to issue **national security letters,** as such requests are called. The agents only need to show, after the fact, that the targeted communications are relevant to a terrorism investigation.[55] National security letters can be used to collect:

1. Credit information from banks and loan companies.
2. Telephone and Internet data, including names, call times, physical addresses, and e-mail addresses.
3. Financial records, such as money transfers and bank accounts.
4. Travel records held by "any commercial entity."[56]

As we will soon see, widespread use of such surveillance tactics has led to a great deal of controversy over the federal government's information-gathering practices.

Patriot Act Legislation passed in the wake of the September 11, 2001, terrorist attacks that greatly expanded the ability of government agents to monitor and apprehend suspected terrorists.

National Security Letters Legal notices that compel the disclosure of customer records held by banks, telephone companies, Internet service providers, and other companies to the federal government.

FIGURE 16.3 The Patriot Act and Electronic Surveillance

Under Title II of the Patriot Act, the following sections greatly expanded the ability of federal intelligence operatives and law enforcement agents to conduct electronic surveillance operations on suspected terrorists.

- **Section 201:** Enables government agents to wiretap the communications of any persons suspected of terrorism or the dissemination of chemical weapons.

- **Section 204:** Makes it easier for government agents to get a warrant to search stored e-mail communications held by Internet service providers (ISPs).

- **Section 206:** The "roving wiretap" provision removes the requirement that government agents specify the particular places or things to be searched when obtaining warrants for surveillance of suspected terrorists.

- **Section 210:** Gives government agents enhanced authority to access the duration and timing of phone calls, along with phone numbers and credit cards used to pay for cell phone service.

- **Section 213:** The "sneak and peek" provision removes the requirement that government agents give notice to a target when they have searched her or his property.*

- **Section 214:** Removes the requirement that government agents prove that the subject of a FISA search is actually the "agent of a foreign power."

- **Section 215:** The "business records" provision permits government agents to access "business records, medical records, educational records and library records" without showing probable cause of wrongdoing if the investigation is related to terrorist activities.

*In 2012, this rule was revised to require notice within thirty days of the search in most circumstances.

Protesting outside the Justice Department in Washington, D.C., this woman believes that the federal government should not be allowed to collect information about the telephone habits of U.S. citizens without first obtaining permission from a court. **Do you agree with her? Why or why not?** Win McNamee/Getty Images News/Getty Images

Mass Surveillance

Following a series of controversies concerning whether the NSA should be allowed to intercept telephone and e-mail communications of suspected terrorists, in 2008 Congress passed an amended version of FISA. This legislative action did not, however, place greater limits on the NSA, which had amassed a vast database by secretly keeping track of millions of phone calls made by Americans who were not under suspicion of any wrongdoing. Instead, it essentially legalized government surveillance tactics that had previously been illegal by giving the NSA more freedom to act without oversight by the FISA court.[57]

Fourth Amendment and Homeland Security   The problem with the original FISA, according to some observers, was that it required a lengthy review process before the FISA court would issue a warrant allowing government agents to monitor a terrorist suspect. In an environment where individuals can rapidly change their e-mail addresses and modes of Internet communication, or use multiple cell phone numbers, this procedure was, in the critics' view, too slow and cumbersome for effective intelligence gathering.[58] The NSA, FBI, and other government agencies argued that they needed more freedom to collect massive amounts of information quickly without judicial oversight.

This need, of course, must be tempered by the Fourth Amendment, which broadly requires that the government have probable cause of wrongdoing before intruding on a citizen's reasonable expectation of privacy. The amended FISA's authorization of large-scale warrantless electronic eavesdropping, in which hundreds of millions of phone and Internet records have been collected and stored in databases, created concerns that the federal government aimed to "write off the Fourth Amendment as technologically obsolete."[59]

Metadata Collection   In 2013, an NSA contractor named Edward Snowden revealed that, under the revised FISA, the NSA had monitored the cell phone and Internet activity of approximately 113 million Americans without probable cause or a warrant from the FISA court. Through a program known as Prism, the NSA gained access to the information by sending national security letters to several major telephone companies and ISPs, including Apple, Facebook, Google, Microsoft, Skype, Verizon, Yahoo, and YouTube.[60] The providers then allowed the NSA to access and store the information.

"Red Flagging"   Agents of the federal government had not been listening to actual phone conversations or reading hundreds of millions of e-mails. Rather, they had been collecting *metadata*, which reveals such things as the time and duration of the communication and the sender and recipient. The metadata collection—justified, according to the FISA court, under Section 215 of the Patriot Act (see Figure 16.3)[61]—had been designed to retroactively determine communications patterns that might raise a "red flag" of terrorist activity. If the NSA was able to uncover a pattern of communication that suggested

such activity, it would apply for a FISA warrant and undertake further investigations of the individuals involved. Using this process, the FISA court was issuing about 1,800 orders each year for domestic surveillance.[62]

Revising the Patriot Act   In 2015, following a firestorm of criticism in response to Snowden's revelations about "government spying," Congress ended the NSA's bulk collection of private phone data. Now, government agencies such as the NSA must petition the FISA Court for access to the metadata, which are stored by companies such as AT&T and Verizon.[63] In theory, a communications company could refuse to cooperate with an NSA request for metadata, subject to the court's review. In practice, it remains to be seen how this partnership will impact federal antiterrorism investigations.

Expectations of Privacy   According to a 2016 report by the news service *Reuters*, Yahoo, in compliance with a FISA Court order, recently created a special software program that scanned all incoming e-mail traffic for a particular digital signature provided by the FBI. Yahoo voluntarily agreed to turn over any e-mails containing this digital signature—presumably associated with a foreign terrorist organization—to U.S. intelligence officials.[64]

As Yahoo's cooperation with the FBI shows, in spite of revisions to the Patriot Act, the federal government still has access to large amounts of communications data. Thus, criticism of government metadata collection continues. Critics point out that while such tactics may contribute to a small number of homeland security investigations, there is no evidence that it has ever disrupted any major terrorist organizations or operations.[65] This limited impact, they argue, does not justify the significant *invasion of privacy* involved.

Learning Objective 6 Explain why privacy expectations are so important to the federal government's metadata surveillance operations.

Privacy Precedents   As you may recall from Chapter 7, an individual usually has no expectation of privacy with regard to information voluntarily disclosed to third parties. So, for example, a person does not have an expectation of privacy for something written on the outside of an envelope given to the U.S. Postal Service or garbage left on the curb for collection.[66] As a result, government agents can search and seize that information without a warrant.

Several federal appeals courts have held that defendants have no reasonable expectation of privacy over information "voluntarily" provided to a telephone company or an ISP. In 2013, a federal judge refused to grant a new trial to defendants convicted of providing material support in the form of funds to an African terrorist organization. Federal agents admitted that they had initially become interested in the defendants' behavior because of telephone records contained in the NSA database. The judge ruled that the agents did not need a warrant to obtain such information from the telephone company because individuals have "no legitimate expectation of privacy" in phone call data.[67]

In general, these judicial decisions rely on the precedent set by the United States Supreme Court in its *Smith v. Maryland* (1979)[68] decision. That case involved the police's warrantless seizure of phone numbers dialed from the home of a robbery suspect. The Court ruled that the defendant had voluntarily turned over the phone numbers to a third party—the phone company—for billing purposes and therefore had no reasonable expectation of privacy in the matter.

Privacy and Technology   One federal judge has gone against the tide with regard to metadata and expectations of privacy. In 2013, U.S. District Judge Richard Leon of the District of Columbia found that the NSA's phone-data collection program "almost certainly" violated the Fourth Amendment.[69] Judge Leon argued that the Supreme Court's *Maryland* case involved a "one-time" search of phone calls emanating from the home of a single criminal suspect. In contrast, the NSA metadata program was a "daily, all-encompassing indiscriminate dump" of information from "the phones of people who are not suspected of any wrongdoing."[70]

Judge Leon's opinion raises an interesting question: Have our reasonable expectations of privacy changed because of technological innovations? The judge referred to the Supreme Court's 2012 decision that it is unconstitutional for the police to use a GPS device to track a suspect's movement without a warrant, which we covered in Chapter 7, offering it as proof that such expectations have changed.[71] He noted that justices who made the *Maryland* ruling in 1979 could not "have ever imagined how the citizens of [today] would interact with their phones."[72] (A controversy involving smartphones, privacy, and government surveillance is the subject of the *Policy Matters* feature at the end of the chapter.)

Foreign Surveillance Targets

Foreign citizens do not enjoy the same protections under the Fourth Amendment as U.S. citizens. This distinction is important to the operation of a separate NSA data-collection program—mandated under the revised FISA of 2008—that allows the government to monitor non–U.S. citizens believed to be located in another country. Section 702 of the FISA Amendment Act permits eavesdropping (not merely metadata collection) without a warrant of foreign persons to obtain information related to the following:

1. National security matters, such as details of an "actual or potential attack" or "other grave hostile acts [by a] foreign power or agent of a foreign power."
2. Foreign "intelligence activities."
3. "The conduct of the foreign affairs of the United States."[73]

▼ In 2016, a federal appeals court upheld the conviction of U.S. citizen Mohamed Mohamud for, three years earlier, attempting to detonate a bomb at a Christmas tree lighting ceremony in Portland, Oregon. Mohamud's lawyers argued that evidence against their client gathered by federal agents conducting electronic surveillance of a foreign target was inadmissible as a warrantless search. **How were government lawyers able to counter this defense by pointing to the FISA Amendment Act?** Multnomah County Sheriff Office/Getty Images News/Getty Images

In the event that the target comes to the United States, surveillance without a warrant can continue for seventy-two hours if a lapse would pose a threat of death or bodily harm to U.S. citizens. After this time period, a warrant must be obtained to continue the surveillance on American soil.[74] The broad language of this amended law allowed the NSA to target nearly 90,000 foreign people and organizations for surveillance in 2013.[75]

The law also permits warrantless eavesdropping on any person who communicates with the target of foreign surveillance, even if that person is an American citizen. According to a detailed analysis of the NSA's global surveillance practices, the agency intercepts communications of nine incidental "bystanders" for every single "legally targeted" foreigner.[76]

This loophole has allowed the NSA to gather highly personal information, such as baby pictures, medical records, and flirtatious Webcam chats, involving innocent persons, including Americans.[77] At the same time, it provides a valuable tool to uncover terrorist operations on U.S. soil, a growing concern that we will examine in the following section.

National Security and Speech

In the context of homeland security, former FBI director James Comey was careful to distinguish the "mouth runners"—those who merely talk about their anti-American or violent beliefs—from potential terrorists. "This is a great country with lots of traditions of protecting mouth-running," said

Comey. "We should continue that. But those who are inclined to cross the line, I've got to focus on them."[78]

How do our federal intelligence and law enforcement agencies tell the "mouth runners," protected by the American tradition of free speech, from those who pose an actual threat? This question arises every time a "lone wolf," seemingly appearing out of nowhere and acting alone, carries out an act of violence on U.S. soil. Concern about such "small-scale attacks" by homegrown terrorists is "what keeps me up at night," says U.S. representative Michael McCaul, a Republican from Texas who chairs the House Homeland Security Committee.[79]

Hidden Threats   As a rule, individuals who intend to offer material support to terrorist organizations do not enjoy First Amendment protections. That is, they cannot claim to be harmless "mouth runners." Rather, by statute, many of the activities that constitute material support are considered true threats, as defined earlier in the chapter.[80] Sometimes, the true threat is legally obvious. Several years ago, for example, six Bosnian immigrants living in Illinois, Missouri, and New York were indicted for providing material support to terrorist organizations in Syria and Iraq after sending $8,000 worth of U.S. military uniforms, technical gear, and weapons to those countries. It would be difficult, if not impossible, to claim that such behavior was a protected form of free speech.

The vast majority of terrorist sympathizers online, however, behave like political supporters or sports fans, showing their enthusiasm by posting comments and videos to share with friends. Furthermore, being an ISIS advocate is not against the law. Neither is expressing hatred for the United States. Consequently, counterterrorism investigators are faced with the nearly impossible task of differentiating between those terrorism suspects who are fantasizing in public and those who are planning actual violence.

Following "Known Wolves"   In 2013, the FBI opened a preliminary investigation against Omar Mateen, who had been boasting of ties to the terrorist groups Hezbollah and Al Qaeda at his workplace in St. Lucie County, Florida. A year-long investigation followed, during which FBI agents monitored Mateen's movements and interviewed him twice. Finding no evidence to suggest that he was anything more than a "mouth runner," the FBI terminated the surveillance.

Two years later, early on the morning of June 12, 2016, Mateen fatally shot forty-nine people at the Pulse nightclub in Orlando before being killed by local police. (Recall that "lone wolves" are terrorists who are presumed to act alone, rather than as part of a terrorist group. Lone wolves like Mateen are sometimes called "known wolves," because authorities have reason to know that they post a threat.)

This example highlights two difficulties for America's homeland security efforts. First, "known wolves" such as Mateen are highly unpredictable. Second, thousands of people in the United States express support for ISIS and other terrorist groups, and law enforcement authorities do not have the resources to physically track each one. "We don't expect to eradicate crime, but we've made a political promise that we're going to stop every act of terrorism," said one observer. "It's ridiculous."[81]

Learning 7 Objective Describe two factors that make it difficult for counterterrorism agents to predict and prevent acts of domestic terrorism.

Limiting Internet Speech   Should the government take more drastic steps to crack down on terrorist sympathizers? Eric Posner, a professor of law at the University of Chicago, recently proposed legal limits on freedom of speech online to control "ideas that lead

Paul Morris Customs and Border Protection Agent

The most memorable day of my career was, without a doubt, September 11, 2001. That morning, as I watched the fall of the Twin Towers, I knew that things were going to be different. Personally, the attacks left me with a resolve to ensure, to the maximum extent possible, that nothing similar ever happens again. Professionally, that day marked a sea change with respect to how the federal border agencies viewed border security. Ever since, our antiterrorism mission has been elevated above our other responsibilities, such as controlling illegal immigration, protecting our agricultural interests, and stopping the flow of illegal narcotics into this country.

Courtesy of Paul Morris

To be sure, as each of these tasks is crucially important, the extra burdens of antiterrorism pose a significant challenge. With the volume of vehicles, cargo, and persons crossing our borders, there can be no guarantees that a potential terrorist or weapon of mass destruction cannot slip across the border. Nevertheless, with advanced identification technology, increased personnel, and a more efficient infrastructure, I am confident that the possibility of such a breach is low.

SOCIAL MEDIA CAREER TIP Consider setting up personal and career-oriented Facebook pages or Twitter accounts and keeping your posts on each separated. Remember, though, that even though material is on your "personal" page or account, it still may be seen by others outside your network.

directly to terrorist attacks." Specifically, Posner suggested that the mere act of visiting a website that supports ISIS or furthers its recruiting operations should be considered criminal. Under Posner's proposal, a first offense would result in a warning letter, with further offenses drawing gradually harsher punishments.[82]

Such a law would almost certainly be struck down by the courts as unconstitutional. Still, France has passed legislation that makes it illegal to use the Internet to disseminate terrorist propaganda, and legal experts can imagine circumstances under which something similar could occur in this country. If America were to be struck by a series of terrorist attacks inspired by Internet recruiting, says Geoffrey Stone, a colleague of Posner's at the University of Chicago, "You can imagine a scenario . . . in which you start watering down [online free speech] protections."[83]

ETHICS CHALLENGE

Several years ago, Jaelyn Young was arrested before boarding a flight from Columbus, Mississippi, to the Middle East, where she planned to join ISIS. Should taking concrete steps to travel abroad and join an anti-American terrorist organization be considered "material support," as defined earlier in this section? Why or why not? If you were Young's attorney, how could you argue that the act of boarding an airplane should never be a crime?

White-Collar Crime

Two New York men take $81 million from investors as part of a fraudulent scheme to buy and resell tickets for events such as the Broadway musical *Hamilton*. The scouting director for the St. Louis Cardinals illegally accesses the player personnel files of a rival professional baseball team. Operators at legitimate call centers in India pose as tax collectors from the Internal Revenue Service and other authority figures to extort $300 million from about 15,000 victims in the United States. A Santa Fe, New Mexico, luxury-home builder fails to complete projects for which he has already been paid.

These cases represent a variety of criminal behavior with different motives, different methods, and different victims. Yet they all fall into the category of *white-collar crime*, an umbrella term for wrongdoing marked by deceit and scandal rather than violence. As we mentioned in Chapter 1, white-collar crime has a broad impact on the global economy, causing American businesses alone hundreds of billions of dollars in losses each year. Despite its global and national importance, however, white-collar crime has consistently challenged a criminal justice system that has difficulty defining the problem, much less effectively combatting it.

What Is White-Collar Crime?

White-collar crime is not an official category of criminal behavior measured by the federal government in the Uniform Crime Report. Rather, the term covers a broad range of illegal acts involving "lying, cheating, and stealing," according to the FBI's website on the subject.[84] To give a more technical definition, white-collar crimes are financial activities characterized by deceit and concealment that do not involve physical force or violence. Figure 16.4 lists and describes some common types of white-collar crime.

Different Techniques   To differentiate white-collar crime from "regular" crime, criminologists Michael L. Benson of the University of Cincinnati and Sally S. Simpson of the University of Maryland focus on technique. For example, in an ordinary burglary, a criminal uses physical means, such as picking a lock, to get somewhere he or she should not be—someone else's home—to do something that is clearly illegal. Furthermore, the victim is a specific identifiable individual—the homeowner. In contrast, white-collar criminals usually (1) have legal access to the place where the crime occurs; (2) are spatially separated from the victim, who is often unknown; and (3) behave in a manner that is at least superficially legitimate.[85]

Benson and Simpson also identify three main techniques used by white-collar criminals to carry out their crimes:[86]

Learning Objective 8   Indicate some of the ways that white-collar crime is different from violent or property crime.

1. *Deception.* White-collar crime almost always involves a party who deceives and a party who is deceived. The nation's federal Medicare system, which provides health insurance for those sixty-five years of age and older, is a frequent target of deceptive practices. For example, over a period of fourteen years, the federal government allegedly paid $1 billion for unnecessary or even harmful treatments to Medicare patients at various health-care facilities in South Florida. The operator of those facilities, Philip Esformes, was charged with a host of crimes, including bribing state regulators to help cover up his schemes.[87]

2. *Abuse of trust.* A white-collar criminal often operates in a position of trust and misuses that trust for personal benefit. In 2017, for example, a Rhode Island financial advisor was sentenced to eighty-four months in prison for using $21 million of

FIGURE 16.4 **White-Collar Crimes**

Embezzlement

Embezzlement is a form of employee fraud in which an individual uses his or her position within an organization to *embezzle*, or steal, the employer's funds, property, or other assets. Pilferage is a less serious form of employee fraud in which the individual steals items from the workplace.

Tax Evasion

Tax evasion occurs when taxpayers underreport (or do not report) their taxable income or otherwise purposely attempt to evade a tax liability.

iStockPhoto.com/oztasbc

iStockPhoto.com/skodonnell

Credit-Card Fraud

Credit-card fraud involves obtaining credit-card numbers through a variety of schemes (such as stealing them from the Internet) and using the numbers for personal gain.

Mail and Wire Fraud

This umbrella term covers all schemes that involve the use of mail, radio, television, the Internet, or a telephone to intentionally deceive in a business environment.

Securities Fraud

Securities fraud covers illegal activity in the stock market.

Stockbrokers who steal funds from their clients are guilty of securities fraud, as are those who engage in *insider trading*, which involves buying or selling securities on the basis of information that has not been made available to the public.

Bribery

Also known as *influence peddling*, bribery occurs in the business world when somebody within a company or government sells influence, power, or information to a person outside the company or government who can benefit. A county official, for example, could give a construction company a lucrative county contract to build a new jail. In return, the construction company would give some of the proceeds, known as a *kickback*, to the official.

Consumer Fraud

This term covers a wide variety of activities designed to defraud consumers, from selling counterfeit art to offering "free" items, such as electronic devices or vacations, that include a number of hidden charges.

Insurance Fraud

Insurance fraud involves making false claims in order to collect insurance payments. Faking an injury in order to receive payments from a workers' compensation program, for example, is a form of insurance fraud.

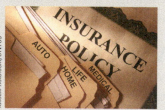
iStockPhoto.com/DNY59

his investors' funds to cover up his own business losses and stealing an additional $2.5 million to purchase a waterfront home.

3. *Concealment and conspiracy.* To continue their illegal activities, white-collar criminals need to conceal those activities. In *odometer fraud,* for example, an automobile dealership "rolls back" the odometers of used cars so that a higher price can be charged for the vehicles. As soon as the fraud is discovered, the scheme can no longer succeed.

Victims of White-Collar Crime   As the examples above show, sometimes the victim of a white-collar crime is obvious. A dishonest financial advisor is stealing directly from his or her clients, and odometer fraud denies consumers the actual value of their purchased automobiles. But who was victimized in the fraudulent Medicare scheme? In that instance, the "victims" were the U.S. taxpayers, who collectively had to cover the cost of the treatments. Such health-care scams defraud U.S. taxpayers out of at least $82 billion each year.[88] Often, white-collar crime does not target individuals but rather large groups or even abstract concepts such as "society" or "the environment."

Regulating and Policing White-Collar Crime

For legal purposes, a corporation can be treated as a person capable of forming the intent necessary to commit a crime. Thus, in March 2017, the German automobile company Volkswagen pleaded guilty to violating the Clean Air Act and and paid a $4.3 billion fine to the federal government. Volkswagen officials had knowingly equipped about 600,000 cars with software designed to evade American emissions tests.

Public health researchers at Harvard University and the Massachusetts Institute of Technology estimated that fifty-nine Americans will die prematurely because of the excess pollution caused by Volkswagen's deceitfulness.[89] The damage that resulted from Volkswagen's illegal activity is an example of *corporate violence*. In contrast to assaults committed by individual people, **corporate violence** results from policies or actions undertaken by a corporation. In the United States, parallel regulatory and criminal systems have evolved to prevent corporate violence and other forms of white-collar crime.

Learning

9

Objective

Explain the concept of corporate violence.

The Regulatory Justice System

Although most white-collar crimes cause harm, these harms are not necessarily covered by criminal statutes. Indeed, more often they are covered by *administrative* laws, which we first encountered in Chapter 4. Such laws make up the backbone of the U.S. regulatory system, through which the government attempts to control the actions of individuals, corporations, and other institutions. The goal of **regulation** is not prevention or punishment as much as **compliance**, or the following of regulatory guidelines.[90]

For example, in 2012, the appliance manufacturer Gree sold thousands of defective humidifiers that were prone to overheating and catching fire. Incidents involving this malfunction caused nearly $4.5 million in property damage, yet Gree did not recall the products until September 2013. Furthermore, the company failed to report the defect to the U.S. Consumer Product Safety Commission (CPSC) as required by federal law, and its employees lied to CPSC staff members during the investigation that followed. In 2016, Gree agreed to pay $15.45 million in penalties stemming from its lack of compliance with federal product safety regulations.

The CPSC—which protects the public from unreasonable risks of injury or death associated with consumer products—is one of the federal administrative agencies whose compliance oversight brings them into contact with white-collar crime. Other important federal regulatory agencies with regard to white-collar crime include:

1. The Environmental Protection Agency (EPA), which regulates air quality, water quality, and toxic waste. The EPA was involved in the federal government's response to Volkswagen's emissions-testing evasion scheme, described earlier.
2. The Food and Drug Administration (FDA), which protects public health by regulating food products and a wide variety of drugs and medical practices.
3. The Occupational Safety and Health Administration (OSHA), which enforces workplace health and safety standards.
4. The Securities and Exchange Commission (SEC), which ensures that financial markets such as the New York Stock Exchange operate in a fair manner.

In 2015, the Federal Communications Commission voted to regulate the Internet as a *public utility* (a company that provides a public service, such as electricity or telephone communications). This move may eventually impact federal law enforcement efforts to combat the various forms of cyber crime we discussed earlier in the chapter.

Law Enforcement and White-Collar Crime

In general, when officials at a regulatory agency find that criminal prosecution is needed to punish a particular violation, they will refer the matter to the U.S. Department of Justice. Either through such referrals or at their own discretion, federal officials prosecute white-collar crime using the investigatory powers of several different federal law enforcement agencies.

The FBI has become the lead agency when it comes to white-collar crime, particularly in response to financial scandals. The U.S. Postal Inspection Service is also active in such

Corporate Violence Physical harm to individuals or the environment that occurs as the result of corporate policies or decision making.

Regulation A governmental order or rule having the force of law that is usually implemented by an administrative agency.

Compliance The state of operating in accordance with governmental standards.

► Several years ago, the New York State attorney general's office began investigating claims that storebrand dietary supplements sold at "big-box" stores such as Walmart and Walgreens contained ingredients that cause allergies without listing such "allergens" on their labels. **If true, does this behavior fall into the category of white-collar crime? Why or why not?** Scott Olson/Getty Images News/ Getty Images

investigations, as fraudulent activities often involve the U.S. mail. In addition, the Internal Revenue Service's Criminal Investigative Division has jurisdiction over a wide variety of white-collar crimes, including tax fraud, and operates perhaps the most effective white-collar crime lab in the country.[91]

Local and state agencies also investigate white-collar crimes, but because of the complexity and costs of such investigations, most are handled by the federal government. Federal prosecutors are also in a unique position to enforce the federal Racketeer Influenced and Corrupt Organizations Act (RICO), which we discussed briefly in Chapter 12. Originally designed to combat organized crime, RICO makes it illegal to receive income through a pattern of *racketeering*.[92]

The definition of **racketeering** is so inclusive—basically covering any attempt to earn illegal income involving more than one person—that it can be used against a broad range of criminal activity, white-collar or otherwise. In 2016, for example, federal prosecutors used RICO to convict four members of the West Coast Crips street gang for working "together as a criminal enterprise to commit six murders, to use a 15-year-old girl and another female as prostitutes, and to commit robbery."[93]

Racketeering The criminal action of being involved in an organized effort to engage in illegal business transactions.

ETHICS CHALLENGE

Several years ago, General Motors Co. (GM) admitted criminal wrongdoing related to flawed ignition switches in its automobiles that have been linked to at least 124 deaths. GM employees were aware of the defect for nearly a decade before addressing the problem. Although the company paid a $900 million fine, no individual employees of GM were criminally charged in this matter. Do you think fines, civil lawsuits, and the financial ramifications of a damaged reputation are enough to ensure that corporations behave ethically? Or do you agree with the mother of one GM crash victim who said that "jail time" for executives is the only "serious deterrent" against corporate wrongdoing? Explain your answer.

Policy Matters

Encryption Battles

How Things Stand

Using encryption, a process described earlier in the chapter, companies such as Apple, Google, and Facebook insert complicated computer codes in their messaging services to protect users' communications from being read by third parties. In the words of one observer, "Without encryption, Internet traffic might as well be written on postcards."[94] The drawback, at least according to many law enforcement officials, is that a variety of wrongdoers—from drug dealers to international terrorists—can take advantage of these encrypted services to keep their electronic correspondence hidden from authorities.

As a Result...

The preferred method for evading password protections uses a computer program that enters an unlimited number of passwords until it arrives at the one that works. To counter this tactic, most Apple iPhones contain an encryption mechanism that erases all data on the phone after ten incorrect password attempts. This technology routinely hampers police efforts— New York law enforcement authorities estimated that they have been locked out of iPhones in 175 active criminal investigations.[95] The issue came to national prominence in late 2015 when the FBI discovered an iPhone left behind by Syed Rizwan Farook, a domestic terrorist who was killed after carrying out a mass shooting in San Bernardino, California.

The federal government ordered Apple to help agents gain access to data in the locked, encrypted iPhone, which may have held clues to Farook's movements prior to the attack and possible terrorist contacts. Apple refused, on the ground that doing so would undermine its customers' confidence that their data are safe not only from cybercriminals, but also from government surveillance. Although the standoff ended in April 2016 when the FBI hired a third party to unlock Farook's iPhone, the case provides a clear example of the difficulty in determining the proper balance between privacy and national security in an age of domestic terrorism.

Up for Debate

"Forcing Apple to extract data in this case, absent clear legal authority to do so, could threaten the trust between Apple and its customers and substantially tarnish the Apple brand."[96]
—*Marc Zwillinger, attorney for Apple*

"It is unfortunate that Apple continues to refuse to assist the department in obtaining access to the phone of one of the terrorists involved in a major terror attack on U.S. soil."[97]
—*Statement, United States Department of Justice*

What's Your Take?

Review the discussion in this chapter on "National Security and Privacy" and "Mass Surveillance" before answering the following questions.

1. Should Congress pass a law requiring any company that manufactures encrypted devices to create a way for the government to access those devices, if ordered to do so by a criminal court? Why or why not?

2. By refusing to aid the FBI's investigation of Syed Rizwan Farook, Apple essentially could be seen as placing the privacy rights of a domestic terrorist who helped kill fourteen people ahead of national security. Why, then, do you think that, according to opinion polls,[98] Americans seemed to approve of Apple's actions in this case?

Digging Deeper...

In 2016, **Facebook** launched a new service called **"Secret Conversations."** This form of **"end-to-end" encryption** has raised concerns that Facebook will become the "service of choice" for a wide range of criminals. Republican Senator Tom Cotton of Arkansas called it an "open invitation to terrorists, drug dealers, and sexual predators to . . . endanger the American people."[99] After researching this issue online, how would you describe end-to-end encryption? Do you agree that Facebook is "endangering" the American people with this service? Should the federal government take legislative action to ban end-to-end encryption? Your written answers to these questions should be at least three paragraphs long.

Justin Sullivan/Getty Images News/Getty Images

SUMMARY

For more information on these concepts, look back to the Learning Objective icons throughout the chapter.

 Outline the three major reasons why the Internet is conducive to the dissemination of child pornography. The Internet provides (a) a quick way to transmit child pornography from providers to consumers; (b) security, such as untraceable e-mails and password-protected websites and chat rooms; and (c) anonymity for buyers and sellers of child pornography.

 Define *malware*, and identify the main way in which worms differ from viruses and Trojans. Malware is a general term that describes any program or file that is harmful to a computer or a computer user. Worms can spread autonomously—that is, they do not require a human act to move from computer to computer. Viruses and Trojans require user intervention, such as a user's clicking on a corrupted file, to be installed on a target computer.

 Explain how the Internet has contributed to piracy of intellectual property. In the past, copying intellectual property such as films and music was time consuming, and the quality of the pirated copies was vastly inferior to that of the originals. On the Internet, however, millions of unauthorized copies of intellectual property can be reproduced with the click of a mouse, and the quality of these items is often the same as that of the original, or close to it.

 Distinguish verbal threats that are protected by the Constitution from verbal threats that can be prosecuted as "true threats." The First Amendment protects speech, including threats, so long as the threats do not constitute "true threats." A true threat expresses the serious intention to harm a specific person or group and has the effect of placing the person or group in reasonable fear of danger.

 Summarize the three federal laws that have been particularly influential on our nation's counterterrorism strategies. (a) The Foreign Intelligence Surveillance Act (FISA) laid the groundwork for electronically monitoring national security threats. (b) The Antiterrorism and Effective Death Penalty Act (AEDPA) prohibited the provision of material support to terrorist organizations. (c) The Patriot Act greatly strengthened the ability of law enforcement agents to investigate and prosecute suspected terrorists.

 Explain why privacy expectations are so important to the federal government's metadata surveillance operations. Under the Fourth Amendment, the government needs a warrant to eavesdrop on or record communications made by U.S. citizens, who have a reasonable expectation that those communications are private. Because a number of federal courts have ruled that there is no reasonable expectation of privacy with regard to communications involving phone calls and Internet use, the government has more leeway in "searching and seizing" information relating to that activity.

 Describe two factors that make it difficult for counterterrorism agents to predict and prevent acts of domestic terrorism. First, even when a suspected terrorist is under government surveillance, it is difficult, if not impossible, to predict when and where that person will engage in an act of violence. Second, many people actively support terrorist groups and criticize the U.S. government online, and federal agents do not have the resources to conduct effective surveillance on all of these people.

 Indicate some of the ways that white-collar crime is different from violent or property crime. A wrongdoer committing a "regular" crime usually uses physical means to get somewhere he or she should not be in order to do something clearly illegal. Also, the victims of violent and property crimes are usually easily identifiable. In contrast, a white-collar criminal generally has legal access to the crime scene, where he or she is doing something seemingly legitimate. Furthermore, victims of white-collar crimes are often unknown or unidentifiable.

 Explain the concept of corporate violence. Corporate violence occurs when a corporation implements policies that ultimately cause harm to individuals or the environment.

QUESTIONS FOR CRITICAL ANALYSIS

1. According to several studies, someone who is a victim of a cyber crime, such as identity theft, has a relatively high risk of being a victim of the same crime again. Why do you think this is the case?

2. Consider the following proposed state law: *It is unlawful for any person, with intent to terrify, intimidate, threaten, harass, annoy, or offend, to use ANY ELECTRONIC OR DIGITAL DEVICE and use any obscene, lewd, or profane language.* What is your opinion of this statute? What might be some of its unforeseen consequences?

3. Suppose a member of al Qaeda posts a video on YouTube that shows how to make an IED (improvised explosive device) out of common household cleaning detergents and a piece of pipe. Before YouTube can take down the video, a young man uses the instructions to carry out a terrorist attack during a high school basketball game. Do you think YouTube, as a corporate "person," could be charged with providing material support to al Qaeda, a terrorist organization? *Should* the company be so charged? Explain your answers.

4. Should the federal government make it a crime to publish bomb-making instructions online? Why or why not?

5. Using your own words, define *white-collar crime.*

KEY TERMS

botnet 529
compliance 549
corporate violence 549
cyberattack 534
cyberbullying 533
cyber crime 527
cyber forensics 537
cyber fraud 530
cyberstalking 533
data breach 531
digital evidence 537
encryption 529
hack 528
identity theft 531
intellectual property 532
material support 540
national security letters 541
Patriot Act 541
phishing 532
racketeering 550
regulation 549
spam 532
surveillance 540
Trojan 529
true threat 533
virus 529
worm 529

NOTES

1. "Porn Sites Get More Visitors Each Month Than Netflix, Amazon, and Twitter Combined," *www.huffingtonpost.com.* Huffington Post: May 4, 2013, Web.

2. "Senate Bill 188." *https://olis.leg.state.or.us.* 78th Oregon Legislative Assembly—2015 Regular Session: visited March 27, 2017, Web.

3. *2016 Internet Security Threat Report* (Mountain View, Calif.: Symantec, April 2016), 6.

4. *US Cybersecurity Progress Stalled: Key Findings from the 2015 US State of Cybercrime Survey* (New York: PwC United States, July 2015), 3.

5. "Cybercrime Will Cost Businesses over $2 Trillion by 2019." *www.juniperresearch.com.* Juniper Research: May 12, 2015, Web.

6. Thomas J. Holt, Adam M. Bossler, and Kathryn C. Seigfried-Spellar, *Cybercrime and Digital Forensics: An Introduction* (New York: Routledge, 2015), 11.

7. Quoted in "Special Report Cyber-Security: Hackers Inc.," *The Economist* (July 12, 2014), 5.

8. William R. Graham, Jr., "Uncovering and Eliminating Child Pornography Rings on the Internet," *Law Review of Michigan State University Detroit College of Law* (Summer 2000), 466.

9. Richard Wortley and Stephen Smallbone, "The Problem of Internet Child Pornography." *www.popcenter.org.* Center for Problem Oriented Policing: 2006, Web.

10. David Wall, "Cybercrimes and the Internet," in *Crime and the Internet,* ed. David Wall (New York: Routledge, 2001), 1–17.

11. Janet Gilmore, "Campus Alerting 80,000 Individuals to Cyberattack." *news.berkeley.edu.* Berkeley News: February 26, 2016, Web.

12. Rosalie L. Donlon, "Hacked! The Cost of a Cyber Breach, in 5 Different Industries." *www.propertycasualty360.com.* Property Casualty 360: October 16, 2015, Web.

13. Cyber Threat Alliance, "Lucrative Ransomware Attacks: Analysis of the CryptoWall Version 3 Threat." *www.cyberthreatalliance.org.* Cyber Threat Alliance: 2016, Web.

14. Holt, Bossler, and Seigfried-Spellar, *op. cit.,* 96.

15. Robin Sidel, "Mobile Bank Heist: Hackers Target Your Phone." *www.wsj.com. Wall Street Journal:* August 26, 2016, Web.

16. Internet Crime Complaint Center, *IC3 2015 Internet Crime Report* (Glen Allen, Va.: National White Collar Crime Center, 2016), 16.

17. Bureau of Justice Statistics, *Victims of Identity Theft, 2014* (Washington, D.C.: U.S. Department of Justice, September 2015), 1.

18. *Ibid.*

19. Jordan Robertson, "E-Mail Spam Goes Artisanal." *www.bloomberg.com. Bloomberg Technology:* January 19, 2016, Web.

20. *Social Media Brand Fraud Report* (Sunnyvale, Calif.: Proofpoint, 2016), 7.

21. David E. Sanger and Nicole Perloth, "Bank Hackers Steal Millions via Malware," *New York Times* (February 14, 2015), A1.

22. *Seizing Opportunity Through License Compliance: BSA Global Software Survey* (Washington, D.C.: Business Software Alliance, May 2016), 2, 5.

23. Holt, Bossler, and Seigfried-Spellar, *op. cit.,* 24.

24. Quoted in Jason Thomas, "Was It Right for Anonymous to Dox the KKK?" *www.bigthink.com. Big Think:* November 5, 2015, Web.

25. Quoted in Stephanie Chen, "In a Wired World, Children Unable to Escape Cyberbullying." *www.cnn.com. CNN:* October 5, 2010, Web.

26. Sameer Hinduja and Justin W. Patchin, "2016 Cyberbullying Data." *www.cyberbullying.org.* Cyberbullying Research Center: November 26, 2016, Web.

27. Bureau of Justice Statistics, *Stalking Victimization in the United States* (Washington, D.C.: U.S. Department of Justice, January 2009), 1.

28. Holt, Bossler, and Seigfried-Spellar, *op. cit.,* 229–230.

29. *United States v. Alkhabaz,* 104 F.3d 1492 (1997).

30. Quoted in Jack Moore, "ISIS Hit List of Arkansas Civilians Leaves Targets, Authorities Unmoved." *www.newsweek.com. Newsweek:* June 6, 2016, Web.

31. Derek Harp, quoted in Erin Kelly, "As Cyberthreats Rise, Push for Intelligence Heightened," *USA Today* (December 24, 2014), 3A.

32. Eduard Kovacs, "Cyberterrorist Attacks Unsophisticated but Effective: Former FBI Agent." *www.securityweek.com. Security Week:* March 14, 2016, Web.

33. Quoted in Marc Santora and Stephanie Clifford, "3 Brooklyn Men Accused of Plot to Aid ISIS's Fight," *New York Times* (February 26, 2015), A1.

34. Quoted in Rukmini Callimachi, "Not 'Lone Wolves' After All: How ISIS Guides World's Terror Plots from Afar," *New York Times* (February 5, 2017), A1.

35. "Welcome All Bug Bounty Hunters." *https://newsroom.uber.com.* Uber Newsroom: March 22, 2016, Web.

36. Quoted in Marc Santora, "In Hours, Thieves Took $45 Million in A.T.M. Scheme," *New York Times* (May 10, 2013), A1.

37. *2016 Internet Security Threat Report, op. cit.,* 5.

38. Holt, Bossler, and Seigfried-Spellar, *op. cit.,* 17–20.

39. *Ibid.,* 68.

40. Margaret Talbot, "Taking Trolls to Court," *New Yorker* (December 5, 2016), 61.

41. Holt, Bossler, and Seigfried-Spellar, *op. cit.,* 330–333.

42. Laurie P. Cohen, "Internet's Ubiquity Multiplies Venues to Try Web Crimes," *Wall Street Journal* (February 12, 2007), B1.

43. Both quoted in Adam Goldman and Matt Apuzzo, "Hurdles for U.S. in Bid to Thwart Russian Hackers," *New York Times* (December 16, 2016), A1.

44. Scott Shane, Matthew Rosenberg, and Andrew W. Lehren, "WikiLeaks Releases Trove of Alleged C.I.A. Hacking Documents," *New York Times* (March 8, 2017), A1.

45. Lanny J. Davis, "Protection from Terrorism and Intrusion on Privacy Rights—We Can, We Must Have Both." *www.thehill.com. The Hill:* June 7, 2013, Web.

46. 50 U.S.C. Sections 1801–1811.

47. 50 U.S.C. Sections 1801(a)(1)–(3).

48. 50 U.S.C. Section 1804(a)(6).

49. 18 U.S.C. Section 2339B(a)(1) (1996).

50. 18 U.S.C. Section 2339A(b) (Supp. I 2001).

51. 18 U.S.C. Section 2339B(a)(1) (2006).

52. William K. Rashbaum, "Law Put to Unusual Use in Hezbollah TV Case, Some Say," *New York Times* (August 26, 2006), B2.

53. Uniting and Strengthening America by Providing Appropriate Tools Required to Intercept and Obstruct Terrorism (USA PATRIOT) Act of 2001, Pub. L. No. 107-56, 115 Stat. 272 (2001).
54. 50 U.S.C. Section 1861(b)(2)(A) (2006).
55. 18 U.S.C. Section 2709 (2012).
56. John S. Dempsey and Linda S. Forst, *An Introduction to Policing*, 7th ed. (Clifton Park, N.Y.: Delmar Cengage Learning, 2014), 537.
57. FISA Amendment Act of 2008, Pub. L. No. 110-261, 122 Stat. 2436 (2008).
58. John Yoo, "The Legality of the National Security Agency's Bulk Data Surveillance Programs." *scholarship.law.berkeley.edu*. Berkeley Law Scholarship Repository: 2014, Web.
59. Jay Bookman, "Which Do You Value? Privacy, or the Illusion of Security." *www.ajc.com. AJC.com:* December 17, 2013, Web.
60. Timothy B. Lee, "Here's Everything We Know about PRISM to Date." *www.washingtonpost.com. Washington Post Wonkblog:* June 12, 2013, Web.
61. Steven G. Bradbury, "Understanding the NSA Programs: Bulk Acquisition of Telephone Metadata under Section 215 and Foreign-Targeted Collection under Section 702," *Lawfare Research Paper Series* (September 1, 2013), 2.
62. Charlie Savage and Matt Apuzzo, "U.S. Spied on 5 American Muslims, a Report Says," *New York Times* (July 10, 2014), A17.
63. Jennifer Steinhauer and Jonathan Weismanjune, "U.S. Surveillance in Place since 9/11 Is Sharply Limited," *New York Times* (June 2, 2015), A1.
64. Joseph Menn, "Yahoo Secretly Scanned Customer Emails for U.S. Intelligence Sources." *www.reuters.com. Reuters:* October 4, 2016, Web.
65. Jennifer Steinhauer and Jonathan Weisman, "U.S. Surveillance in Place since 9/11 Is Sharply Limited," *New York Times* (June 2, 2015), A1.
66. *Katz v. United States*, 389 U.S. 347, 351 (1967); and *California v. Greenwood*, 486 U.S. 35 (1988).
67. *United States v. Moalin et al.*, Case No. 10cr4246 JM (S.D. Cal. November 18, 2013).
68. 442 U.S. 735 (1979).
69. *Klayman v. Obama*, 957 F.Supp.2d 825 (D.D.C. December 16, 2013).
70. Quoted in "A Powerful Rebuke of Mass Surveillance," *New York Times* (December 17, 2013).
71. *United States v. Jones*, 565 U.S. _____ (2012).
72. Quoted in "A Powerful Rebuke of Mass Surveillance," *op. cit.*
73. 50 U.S.C. Section 1881a (2011).
74. Edward C. Liu, *Surveillance of Foreigners outside the United States under Section 702 of the Foreign Intelligence Surveillance Act (FISA)* (Washington, D.C.: Congressional Research Service, April 13, 2016), 1.
75. Ellen Nakashima, "Feds Report 90,000 Foreign Surveillance Targets," *Dallas Morning News* (June 28, 2014), 11A.
76. David E. Sanger and Matt Apuzzo, "Officials Defend N.S.A. after New Privacy Details Are Reported," *New York Times* (July 7, 2014), A9.
77. *Ibid.*
78. Quoted in "Colorado Teen Shannon Conley's Support of ISIS Raises Alarm about American *Jihadists*," *Associated Press* (September 10, 2014).
79. Quoted in Stephen Collinson, "Paris Attack: The New Terror." *www.cnn.com. CNN.com:* January 8, 2015, Web.
80. 18 U.S.C. Section 2339A(b)(1).
81. Quoted in Matt Apuzzo and Michael S. Schmidt, "F.B.I. Emphasizes Speed as ISIS Exhorts Individuals to Attack," *New York Times* (July 28, 2015), A11.
82. Eric Posner, "ISIS Gives Us No Choice but to Consider Limits on Speech." *www.slate.com. Slate:* December 15, 2016, Web.
83. Quoted in Erik Eckholm, "ISIS Influence on Web Prompts Second Thoughts on First Amendment," *New York Times* (December 28, 2015), A10.
84. The Federal Bureau of Investigation, "White-Collar Crime." *www.fbi.gov*. Federal Bureau of Investigation: visited March 31, 2017, Web.
85. Michael L. Benson and Sally S. Simpson, *White-Collar Crime: An Opportunity Perspective* (New York: Routledge, 2009), 79–80.
86. *Ibid.*, 81–87.
87. Jay Weaver, "Wealthy Miami Beach Executive Charged Anew with Bribing State Healthcare Regulators." *www.miamiherald.com. Miami Herald:* February 13, 2017, Web.
88. "That's Where the Money Is," *The Economist* (May 31, 2014), 13.
89. Steven R. H. Barrett, et al., "Impact of the Volkswagen Emissions Control Defeat Device on US Public Health." *http://iopscience.iop.org*. IOP Science: 2015, Web.
90. Benson and Simpson, *op. cit.*, 189.
91. David O. Friedrichs, *Trusted Criminals: White Collar Crime in Contemporary Society*, 4th ed. (Belmont, Calif.: Wadsworth Cengage Learning, 2010), 278–283.
92. Lawrence Salinger, *Encyclopedia of White-Collar and Corporate Crime*, 2nd ed. (Thousand Oaks, Calif.: Sage, 2004), 361.
93. "Federal Jury Convicts Four West Coast Crips Street Gang Members of Racketeering Conspiracy Involving Murders, Sex Trafficking and Robbery." *www.justice.gov*. United States Department of Justice: March 11, 2016, Web.
94. "When Back Doors Backfire." *www.economist.com. The Economist:* January 2, 2016, Web.
95. Matt Apuzzo, Joseph Goldstein, and Eric Lichtblau, "Line in the Sand over iPhones Was over a Year in the Making," *New York Times* (February 19, 2016), A1.
96. Quoted in *ibid.*
97. Quoted in Eric Lichtblau and Katie Benner, "As Apple Resists, Encryption Fray Erupts in Battle," *New York Times* (February 18, 2016), A1.
98. Jim Finkle, "Solid Support for Apple in iPhone Encryption Fight: Poll." *www.reuters.com. Reuters:* February 24, 2016, Web.
99. Quoted in "Encryption Row Spotlights Fears on Security, Privacy." *www.sg.finance.yahoo.com. AFP:* April 27, 2016, Web.

The Constitution of the United States

Preamble

We the People of the United States, in Order to form a more perfect Union, establish Justice, insure domestic Tranquility, provide for the common defence, promote the general Welfare, and secure the Blessings of Liberty to ourselves and our Posterity, do ordain and establish this Constitution for the United States of America.

Article I

Section 1. All legislative Powers herein granted shall be vested in a Congress of the United States, which shall consist of a Senate and House of Representatives.

Section 2. The House of Representatives shall be composed of Members chosen every second Year by the People of the several States, and the Electors in each State shall have the Qualifications requisite for Electors of the most numerous Branch of the State Legislature.

No Person shall be a Representative who shall not have attained to the Age of twenty five Years, and been seven Years a Citizen of the United States, and who shall not, when elected, be an Inhabitant of that State in which he shall be chosen.

Representatives and direct Taxes shall be apportioned among the several States which may be included within this Union, according to their respective Numbers, which shall be determined by adding to the whole Number of free Persons, including those bound to Service for a Term of Years, and excluding Indians not taxed, three fifths of all other Persons. The actual Enumeration shall be made within three Years after the first Meeting of the Congress of the United States, and within every subsequent Term of ten Years, in such Manner as they shall by Law direct. The Number of Representatives shall not exceed one for every thirty Thousand, but each State shall have at Least one Representative; and until such enumeration shall be made, the State of New Hampshire shall be entitled to chuse three, Massachusetts eight, Rhode Island and Providence Plantations one, Connecticut five, New York six, New Jersey four, Pennsylvania eight, Delaware one, Maryland six, Virginia ten, North Carolina five, South Carolina five, and Georgia three.

When vacancies happen in the Representation from any State, the Executive Authority thereof shall issue Writs of Election to fill such Vacancies.

The House of Representatives shall chuse their Speaker and other Officers; and shall have the sole Power of Impeachment.

Section 3. The Senate of the United States shall be composed of two Senators from each State, chosen by the Legislature thereof, for six Years; and each Senator shall have one Vote.

Immediately after they shall be assembled in Consequence of the first Election, they shall be divided as equally as may be into three Classes. The Seats of the Senators of the first Class shall be vacated at the Expiration of the second Year, of the second Class at the Expiration of the fourth Year, and of the third Class at the Expiration of the sixth Year, so that one third may be chosen every second Year; and if Vacancies happen by Resignation, or otherwise, during the Recess of the Legislature of any State, the Executive thereof may make temporary Appointments until the next Meeting of the Legislature, which shall then fill such Vacancies.

No Person shall be a Senator who shall not have attained to the Age of thirty Years, and been nine Years a Citizen of the United States, and who shall not, when elected, be an Inhabitant of that State for which he shall be chosen.

The Vice President of the United States shall be President of the Senate, but shall have no Vote, unless they be equally divided.

The Senate shall chuse their other Officers, and also a President pro tempore, in the Absence of the Vice President, or when he shall exercise the Office of President of the United States.

The Senate shall have the sole Power to try all Impeachments. When sitting for that Purpose, they shall be on Oath or Affirmation. When the President of the United States is tried, the Chief Justice shall preside: And no Person shall be convicted without the Concurrence of two thirds of the Members present.

Judgment in Cases of Impeachment shall not extend further than to removal from Office, and disqualification to hold and enjoy any Office of honor, Trust, or Profit under the United States: but the Party convicted shall nevertheless be liable and subject to Indictment, Trial, Judgment, and Punishment, according to Law.

Section 4. The Times, Places and Manner of holding Elections for Senators and Representatives, shall be prescribed in each State by the Legislature thereof; but the Congress may at any time by Law make or alter such Regulations, except as to the Places of chusing Senators.

The Congress shall assemble at least once in every Year, and such Meeting shall be on the first Monday in December, unless they shall by Law appoint a different Day.

Section 5. Each House shall be the Judge of the Elections, Returns, and Qualifications of its own Members, and a Majority of each shall constitute a Quorum to do Business; but a smaller Number may adjourn from day to day, and may be authorized to compel the Attendance of absent Members, in such Manner, and under such Penalties as each House may provide.

Each House may determine the Rules of its Proceedings, punish its Members for disorderly Behavior, and, with the Concurrence of two thirds, expel a Member.

Each House shall keep a Journal of its Proceedings, and from time to time publish the same, excepting such Parts as may in their Judgment require Secrecy; and the Yeas and Nays of the Members of either House on any question shall, at the Desire of one fifth of those Present, be entered on the Journal.

Neither House, during the Session of Congress, shall, without the Consent of the other, adjourn for more than three days, nor to any other Place than that in which the two Houses shall be sitting.

Section 6. The Senators and Representatives shall receive a Compensation for their Services, to be ascertained by Law, and paid out of the Treasury of the United States. They shall in all Cases, except Treason, Felony and Breach of the Peace, be privileged from Arrest during their Attendance at the Session of their respective Houses, and in going to and returning from the same; and for any Speech or Debate in either House, they shall not be questioned in any other Place.

No Senator or Representative shall, during the Time for which he was elected, be appointed to any civil Office under the Authority of the United States, which shall have been created, or the Emoluments whereof shall have been increased during such time; and no Person holding any Office under the United States, shall be a Member of either House during his Continuance in Office.

Section 7. All Bills for raising Revenue shall originate in the House of Representatives; but the Senate may propose or concur with Amendments as on other Bills.

Every Bill which shall have passed the House of Representatives and the Senate, shall, before it become a Law, be presented to the President of the United States; If he approve he shall sign it, but if not he shall return it, with his Objections to the House in which it shall have originated, who shall enter the Objections at large on their Journal, and proceed to reconsider it. If after such Reconsideration two thirds of that House shall agree to pass the Bill, it shall be sent together with the Objections, to the other House, by which it shall likewise be reconsidered, and if approved by two thirds of that House, it shall become a Law. But in all such Cases the Votes of both Houses shall be determined by Yeas and Nays, and the Names of the Persons voting for and against the Bill shall be entered on the Journal of each House respectively. If any Bill shall not be returned by the President within ten Days (Sundays excepted) after it shall have been presented to him, the Same shall be a Law, in like Manner as if he had signed it, unless the Congress by their Adjournment prevent its Return in which Case it shall not be a Law.

Every Order, Resolution, or Vote, to which the Concurrence of the Senate and House of Representatives may be necessary (except on a question of Adjournment) shall be presented to the President of the United States; and before the Same shall take Effect, shall be approved by him, or being disapproved by him, shall be repassed by two thirds of the Senate and House of Representatives, according to the Rules and Limitations prescribed in the Case of a Bill.

Section 8. The Congress shall have Power To lay and collect Taxes, Duties, Imposts and Excises, to pay the Debts and provide for the common Defence and general Welfare of the United States; but all Duties, Imposts and Excises shall be uniform throughout the United States;

To borrow Money on the credit of the United States;

To regulate Commerce with foreign Nations, and among the several States, and with the Indian Tribes;

To establish an uniform Rule of Naturalization, and uniform Laws on the subject of Bankruptcies throughout the United States;

To coin Money, regulate the Value thereof, and of foreign Coin, and fix the Standard of Weights and Measures;

To provide for the Punishment of counterfeiting the Securities and current Coin of the United States;

To establish Post Offices and post Roads;

To promote the Progress of Science and useful Arts, by securing for limited Times to Authors and Inventors the exclusive Right to their respective Writings and Discoveries;

To constitute Tribunals inferior to the supreme Court;

To define and punish Piracies and Felonies committed on the high Seas, and Offenses against the Law of Nations;

To declare War, grant Letters of Marque and Reprisal, and make Rules concerning Captures on Land and Water;

To raise and support Armies, but no Appropriation of Money to that Use shall be for a longer Term than two Years;

To provide and maintain a Navy;

To make Rules for the Government and Regulation of the land and naval Forces;

To provide for calling forth the Militia to execute the Laws of the Union, suppress Insurrections and repel Invasions;

To provide for organizing, arming, and disciplining, the Militia, and for governing such Part of them as may be employed in the Service of the United States, reserving to the States respectively, the Appointment of the Officers, and the Authority of training the Militia according to the discipline prescribed by Congress;

To exercise exclusive Legislation in all Cases whatsoever, over such District (not exceeding ten Miles square) as may, by Cession of particular States, and the Acceptance of Congress, become the Seat of the Government of the United States, and to exercise like Authority over all Places purchased by the Consent of the Legislature of the State in which the Same shall be, for the Erection of Forts, Magazines, Arsenals, dock-Yards, and other needful Buildings;—And

To make all Laws which shall be necessary and proper for carrying into Execution the foregoing Powers, and all other Powers vested by this Constitution in the Government of the United States, or in any Department or Officer thereof.

Section 9. The Migration or Importation of such Persons as any of the States now existing shall think proper to admit, shall not be prohibited by the Congress prior to the Year one thousand eight hundred and eight, but a Tax or duty may be imposed on such Importation, not exceeding ten dollars for each Person.

The privilege of the Writ of Habeas Corpus shall not be suspended, unless when in Cases of Rebellion or Invasion the public Safety may require it.

No Bill of Attainder or ex post facto Law shall be passed.

No Capitation, or other direct, Tax shall be laid, unless in Proportion to the Census or Enumeration herein before directed to be taken.

No Tax or Duty shall be laid on Articles exported from any State.

No Preference shall be given by any Regulation of Commerce or Revenue to the Ports of one State over those of another: nor shall Vessels bound to, or from, one State be obliged to enter, clear, or pay Duties in another.

No Money shall be drawn from the Treasury, but in Consequence of Appropriations made by Law; and a regular Statement and Account of the Receipts and Expenditures of all public Money shall be published from time to time.

No Title of Nobility shall be granted by the United States: And no Person holding any Office of Profit or Trust under them, shall, without the Consent of the Congress, accept of any present, Emolument, Office, or Title, of any kind whatever, from any King, Prince, or foreign State.

Section 10. No State shall enter into any Treaty, Alliance, or Confederation; grant Letters of Marque and Reprisal; coin Money; emit Bills of Credit; make any Thing but gold and silver Coin a Tender in Payment of Debts; pass any Bill of Attainder, ex post facto Law, or Law impairing the Obligation of Contracts, or grant any Title of Nobility.

No State shall, without the Consent of the Congress, lay any Imposts or Duties on Imports or Exports, except what may be absolutely necessary for executing its inspection Laws: and the net Produce of all Duties and Imposts, laid by any State on Imports or Exports, shall be for the Use of the Treasury of the United States; and all such Laws shall be subject to the Revision and Controul of the Congress.

No State shall, without the Consent of Congress, lay any Duty of Tonnage, keep Troops, or Ships of War in time of Peace, enter into any Agreement or Compact with another State, or with a foreign Power, or engage in War, unless actually invaded, or in such imminent Danger as will not admit of delay.

Article II

Section 1. The executive Power shall be vested in a President of the United States of America. He shall hold his Office during the Term of four Years, and, together with the Vice President, chosen for the same Term, be elected, as follows:

Each State shall appoint, in such Manner as the Legislature thereof may direct, a Number of Electors, equal to the whole Number of Senators and Representatives to which the State may be entitled in the Congress; but no Senator or Representative, or Person holding an Office of Trust or Profit under the United States, shall be appointed an Elector.

The Electors shall meet in their respective States, and vote by Ballot for two Persons, of whom one at least shall not be an Inhabitant of the same State with themselves. And they shall make a List of all the Persons voted for, and of the Number of Votes for each; which List they shall sign and certify, and transmit sealed to the Seat of the Government of the United States, directed to the President of the Senate. The President of the Senate shall, in the Presence of the Senate and House of Representatives, open all the Certificates, and the Votes shall then be counted.

The Person having the greatest Number of Votes shall be the President, if such Number be a Majority of the whole Number of Electors appointed; and if there be more than one who have such Majority, and have an equal Number of Votes, then the House of Representatives shall immediately chuse by Ballot one of them for President; and if no Person have a Majority, then from the five highest on the List the said House shall in like Manner chuse the President. But in chusing the President, the Votes shall be taken by States, the Representation from each State having one Vote; A quorum for this Purpose shall consist of a Member or Members from two thirds of the States, and a Majority of all the States shall be necessary to a Choice. In every Case, after the Choice of the President, the Person having the greater Number of Votes of the Electors shall be the Vice President. But if there should remain two or more who have equal Votes, the Senate shall chuse from them by Ballot the Vice President.

The Congress may determine the Time of chusing the Electors, and the Day on which they shall give their Votes; which Day shall be the same throughout the United States.

No person except a natural born Citizen, or a Citizen of the United States, at the time of the Adoption of this Constitution, shall be eligible to the Office of President; neither shall any Person be eligible to that Office who shall not have attained to the Age of thirty five Years, and been fourteen Years a Resident within the United States.

In Case of the Removal of the President from Office, or of his Death, Resignation or Inability to discharge the Powers and Duties of the said Office, the same shall devolve on the Vice President, and the Congress may by Law provide for the Case of Removal, Death, Resignation or Inability, both of the President and Vice President, declaring what Officer shall then act as President, and such Officer shall act accordingly, until the Disability be removed, or a President shall be elected.

The President shall, at stated Times, receive for his Services, a Compensation, which shall neither be increased nor diminished during the Period for which he shall have been elected, and he shall not receive within that Period any other Emolument from the United States, or any of them.

Before he enter on the Execution of his Office, he shall take the following Oath or Affirmation: "I do solemnly swear (or affirm) that I will faithfully execute the Office of President of the United States, and will to the best of my Ability, preserve, protect and defend the Constitution of the United States."

Section 2. The President shall be Commander in Chief of the Army and Navy of the United States, and of the Militia of the several States, when called into the actual Service of the United States; he may require the Opinion, in writing, of the principal Officer in each of the executive Departments, upon any Subject relating to the Duties of their respective Offices, and he shall have Power to grant Reprieves and Pardons for Offenses against the United States, except in Cases of Impeachment.

He shall have Power, by and with the Advice and Consent of the Senate to make Treaties, provided two thirds of the Senators present concur; and he shall nominate, and by and with the Advice and Consent of the Senate, shall appoint Ambassadors, other public Ministers and Consuls, Judges of the supreme Court, and all other Officers of the United States, whose Appointments are not herein otherwise provided for, and which shall be established by Law; but the Congress may by Law vest the Appointment of such inferior Officers, as they think proper, in the President alone, in the Courts of Law, or in the Heads of Departments.

The President shall have Power to fill up all Vacancies that may happen during the Recess of the Senate, by granting Commissions which shall expire at the End of their next Session.

Section 3. He shall from time to time give to the Congress Information of the State of the Union, and recommend to their Consideration such Measures as he shall judge necessary and expedient; he may, on extraordinary Occasions, convene both Houses, or either of them, and in Case of Disagreement between them, with Respect to the Time of Adjournment, he may adjourn them to such Time as he shall think proper; he shall receive Ambassadors and other public Ministers; he shall take Care that the Laws be faithfully executed, and shall Commission all the Officers of the United States.

Section 4. The President, Vice President and all civil Officers of the United States, shall be removed from Office on Impeachment for, and Conviction of, Treason, Bribery, or other high Crimes and Misdemeanors.

Article III

Section 1. The judicial Power of the United States, shall be vested in one supreme Court, and in such inferior Courts as the Congress may from time to time ordain and establish. The Judges, both of the supreme and inferior Courts, shall hold their Offices during good Behaviour, and shall, at stated Times, receive for their Services a Compensation, which shall not be diminished during their Continuance in Office.

Section 2. The judicial Power shall extend to all Cases, in Law and Equity, arising under this Constitution, the Laws of the United States, and Treaties made, or which shall be made, under their Authority;—to all Cases affecting Ambassadors, other public Ministers and Consuls;—to all Cases of admiralty and maritime Jurisdiction;—to Controversies to which the United States shall be a Party;—to Controversies between two or more States;—between a State and Citizens of another State;—between Citizens of different States;—between Citizens of the same State claiming Lands under Grants of different States, and between a State, or the Citizens thereof, and foreign States, Citizens or Subjects.

In all Cases affecting Ambassadors, other public Ministers and Consuls, and those in which a State shall be a Party, the supreme Court shall have original Jurisdiction. In all the other Cases before mentioned, the supreme Court shall have appellate Jurisdiction, both as to Law and Fact, with such Exceptions, and under such Regulations as the Congress shall make.

The Trial of all Crimes, except in Cases of Impeachment, shall be by Jury; and such Trial shall be held in the State where the said Crimes shall have been committed; but when not committed within any State, the Trial shall be at such Place or Places as the Congress may by Law have directed.

Section 3. Treason against the United States, shall consist only in levying War against them, or, in adhering to their Enemies, giving them Aid and Comfort. No Person shall be convicted of Treason unless on the Testimony of two Witnesses to the same overt Act, or on Confession in open Court.

The Congress shall have Power to declare the Punishment of Treason, but no Attainder of Treason shall work Corruption of Blood, or Forfeiture except during the Life of the Person attainted.

Article IV

Section 1. Full Faith and Credit shall be given in each State to the public Acts, Records, and judicial Proceedings of every other State. And the Congress may by general Laws prescribe the Manner in which such Acts, Records and Proceedings shall be proved, and the Effect thereof.

Section 2. The Citizens of each State shall be entitled to all Privileges and Immunities of Citizens in the several States.

A Person charged in any State with Treason, Felony, or other Crime, who shall flee from Justice, and be found in another State, shall on Demand of the executive Authority of the State from which he fled, be delivered up, to be removed to the State having Jurisdiction of the Crime.

No Person held to Service or Labour in one State, under the Laws thereof, escaping into another, shall, in Consequence of any Law or Regulation therein, be discharged from such Service or Labour, but shall be delivered up on Claim of the Party to whom such Service or Labour may be due.

Section 3. New States may be admitted by the Congress into this Union; but no new State shall be formed or erected within the Jurisdiction of any other State; nor any State be formed by the Junction of two or more States, or Parts of States, without the Consent of the Legislatures of the States concerned as well as of the Congress.

The Congress shall have Power to dispose of and make all needful Rules and Regulations respecting the Territory or other Property belonging to the United States; and nothing in this Constitution shall be so construed as to Prejudice any Claims of the United States, or of any particular State.

Section 4. The United States shall guarantee to every State in this Union a Republican Form of Government, and shall protect each of them against Invasion; and on Application of the Legislature, or of the Executive (when the Legislature cannot be convened) against domestic Violence.

Article V

The Congress, whenever two thirds of both Houses shall deem it necessary, shall propose Amendments to this Constitution, or, on the Application of the Legislatures of two thirds of the several States, shall call a Convention for proposing Amendments, which, in either Case, shall be valid to all Intents and Purposes, as part of this Constitution, when ratified by the Legislatures of three fourths of the several States, or by Conventions in three fourths thereof, as the one or the other Mode of Ratification may be proposed by the Congress; Provided that no Amendment which may be made prior to the Year One thousand eight hundred and eight shall in any Manner affect the first and fourth Clauses in the Ninth Section of the first Article; and that no State, without its Consent, shall be deprived of its equal Suffrage in the Senate.

Article VI

All Debts contracted and Engagements entered into, before the Adoption of this Constitution shall be as valid against the United States under this Constitution, as under the Confederation.

This Constitution, and the Laws of the United States which shall be made in Pursuance thereof; and all Treaties made, or which shall be made, under the Authority of the United States, shall be the supreme Law of the Land; and the Judges in every State shall be bound thereby, any Thing in the Constitution or Laws of any State to the Contrary notwithstanding.

The Senators and Representatives before mentioned, and the Members of the several State Legislatures, and all executive and judicial Officers, both of the United States and of the several States, shall be bound by Oath or Affirmation, to support this Constitution; but no religious Test shall ever be required as a Qualification to any Office or public Trust under the United States.

Article VII

The Ratification of the Conventions of nine States shall be sufficient for the Establishment of this Constitution between the States so ratifying the Same.

Amendment I [1791]

Congress shall make no law respecting an establishment of religion, or prohibiting the free exercise thereof; or abridging the freedom of speech, or of the press; or the right of the people peaceably to assembly, and to petition the Government for a redress of grievances.

Amendment II [1791]

A well regulated Militia, being necessary to the security of a free State, the right of the people to keep and bear Arms, shall not be infringed.

Amendment III [1791]

No Soldier shall, in time of peace be quartered in any house, without the consent of the Owner, nor in time of war, but in a manner to be prescribed by law.

Amendment IV [1791]

The right of the people to be secure in their persons, houses, papers, and effects, against unreasonable searches and seizures, shall not be violated, and no Warrants shall issue, but upon probable cause, supported by Oath or affirmation, and particularly describing the place to be searched, and the persons or things to be seized.

Amendment V [1791]

No person shall be held to answer for a capital, or otherwise infamous crime, unless on a presentment or indictment of a Grand Jury, except in cases arising in the land or naval forces, or in the Militia, when in actual service in time of War or public danger; nor shall any person be subject for the same offence to be twice put in jeopardy of life or limb; nor shall be compelled in any criminal case to be a witness against himself, nor be deprived of life, liberty, or property, without due process of law; nor shall private property be taken for public use, without just compensation.

Amendment VI [1791]

In all criminal prosecutions, the accused shall enjoy the right to a speedy and public trial, by an impartial jury of the State and district wherein the crime shall have been committed, which district shall have been previously ascertained by law, and to be informed of the nature and cause of the accusation; to be confronted with the witnesses against him; to have compulsory process for obtaining witnesses in his favor, and to have the Assistance of Counsel for his defence.

Amendment VII [1791]

In Suits at common law, where the value in controversy shall exceed twenty dollars, the right of trial by jury shall be preserved, and no fact tried by jury, shall be otherwise reexamined in any Court of the United States, than according to the rules of the common law.

Amendment VIII [1791]

Excessive bail shall not be required, nor excessive fines imposed, nor cruel and unusual punishments inflicted.

Amendment IX [1791]

The enumeration in the Constitution, of certain rights, shall not be construed to deny or disparage others retained by the people.

Amendment X [1791]

The powers not delegated to the United States by the Constitution, nor prohibited by it to the States, are reserved to the States respectively, or to the people.

Amendment XI [1798]

The Judicial power of the United States shall not be construed to extend to any suit in law or equity, commenced or prosecuted against one of the United States by Citizens of another State, or by Citizens or Subjects of any Foreign State.

Amendment XII [1804]

The Electors shall meet in their respective states, and vote by ballot for President and Vice-President, one of whom, at least, shall not be an inhabitant of the same state with themselves; they shall name in their ballots the person voted for as President, and in distinct ballots the person voted for as Vice-President, and they shall make distinct lists of all persons voted for as President, and of all persons voted for as Vice-President, and of the number of votes for each, which lists they shall sign and certify, and transmit sealed to the seat of the government of the United States, directed to the President of the Senate;—The President of the Senate shall, in the presence of the Senate and House of Representatives, open all the certificates and the votes shall then be counted;—The person having the greatest number of votes for President, shall be the President, if such number be a majority of the whole number of Electors appointed; and if no person have such majority, then from the persons having the highest numbers not exceeding three on the list of those voted for as President, the House of Representatives shall choose immediately, by ballot, the President. But in choosing the President, the votes shall be taken by states, the representation from each state having one vote; a quorum for this purpose shall consist of a member or members from two-thirds of the states, and a majority of all states shall be necessary to a choice. And if the House of Representatives shall not choose a President whenever the right of choice shall devolve upon them, before the fourth day of March next following, then the Vice-President shall act as President, as in the case of the death or other constitutional disability of the President.—The person having the greatest number of votes as Vice-President, shall be the Vice-President, if such number be a majority of the whole number of Electors appointed, and if no person have a majority, then from the two highest numbers on the list, the Senate shall choose the Vice-President; a quorum for the purpose shall consist of two-thirds of the whole number of Senators, and a majority of the whole number shall be necessary to a choice. But no person constitutionally ineligible to the office of President shall be eligible to that of Vice-President of the United States.

Amendment XIII [1865]

Section 1.   Neither slavery nor involuntary servitude, except as a punishment for crime whereof the party shall have been duly convicted, shall exist within the United States, or any place subject to their jurisdiction.

Section 2.   Congress shall have power to enforce this article by appropriate legislation.

Amendment XIV [1868]

Section 1.   All persons born or naturalized in the United States, and subject to the jurisdiction thereof, are citizens of the United States and of the State wherein they reside. No State shall make or enforce any law which shall abridge the privileges or immunities of citizens of the United States; nor shall any State deprive any person of life, liberty, or property, without due process of law; nor deny to any person within its jurisdiction the equal protection of the laws.

Section 2.   Representatives shall be apportioned among the several States according to their respective numbers, counting the whole number of persons in each State, excluding Indians not taxed. But when the right to vote at any election for the choice of electors for President and Vice President of the United States, Representatives in Congress, the Executive and Judicial officers of a State, or the members of the Legislature thereof, is denied to any of the male inhabitants of such State, being twenty-one years of age, and citizens of the United States, or in any way abridged, except for participation in rebellion, or other crime, the basis of representation therein shall be reduced in the proportion which the number of such male citizens shall bear to the whole number of male citizens twenty-one years of age in such State.

Section 3.   No person shall be a Senator or Representative in Congress, or elector of President and Vice President, or hold any office, civil or military, under the United States, or under any State, who having previously taken an oath, as a member of Congress, or as an officer of the United States, or as a member of any State legislature, or as an executive or judicial officer of any State, to support the Constitution of the United States, shall have engaged in insurrection or rebellion against the same, or given aid or comfort to the enemies thereof. But Congress may by a vote of two-thirds of each House, remove such disability.

Section 4.   The validity of the public debt of the United States, authorized by law, including debts incurred for payment of pensions and bounties for services in suppressing insurrection or rebellion, shall not be questioned. But neither the United States nor any State shall assume or pay any debt or obligation incurred in aid of insurrection or rebellion against the United States, or any claim for the loss or emancipation of any slave; but all such debts, obligations and claims shall be held illegal and void.

Section 5.   The Congress shall have power to enforce, by appropriate legislation, the provisions of this article.

Amendment XV [1870]

Section 1.   The right of citizens of the United States to vote shall not be denied or abridged by the United States or by any State on account of race, color, or previous condition of servitude.

Section 2.   The Congress shall have power to enforce this article by appropriate legislation.

Amendment XVI [1913]

The Congress shall have power to lay and collect taxes on incomes, from whatever source derived, without apportionment among the several States, and without regard to any census or enumeration.

Amendment XVII [1913]

Section 1. The Senate of the United States shall be composed of two Senators from each State, elected by the people thereof, for six years; and each Senator shall have one vote. The electors in each State shall have the qualifications requisite for electors of the most numerous branch of the State legislatures.

Section 2. When vacancies happen in the representation of any State in the Senate, the executive authority of such State shall issue writs of election to fill such vacancies: *Provided*, That the legislature of any State may empower the executive thereof to make temporary appointments until the people fill the vacancies by election as the legislature may direct.

Section 3. This amendment shall not be so construed as to affect the election or term of any Senator chosen before it becomes valid as part of the Constitution.

Amendment XVIII [1919]

Section 1. After one year from the ratification of this article the manufacture, sale, or transportation of intoxicating liquors within, the importation thereof into, or the exportation thereof from the United States and all territory subject to the jurisdiction thereof for beverage purposes is hereby prohibited.

Section 2. The Congress and the several States shall have concurrent power to enforce this article by appropriate legislation.

Section 3. This article shall be inoperative unless it shall have been ratified as an amendment to the Constitution by the legislatures of the several States, as provided in the Constitution, within seven years from the date of the submission hereof to the States by the Congress.

Amendment XIX [1920]

Section 1. The right of citizens of the United States to vote shall not be denied or abridged by the United States or by any State on account of sex.

Section 2. Congress shall have power to enforce this article by appropriate legislation.

Amendment XX [1933]

Section 1. The terms of the President and Vice President shall end at noon on the 20th day of January, and the terms of Senators and Representatives at noon on the 3d day of January, of the years in which such terms would have ended if this article had not been ratified; and the terms of their successors shall then begin.

Section 2. The Congress shall assemble at least once in every year, and such meeting shall begin at noon on the 3d day of January, unless they shall by law appoint a different day.

Section 3. If, at the time fixed for the beginning of the term of the President, the President elect shall have died, the Vice President elect shall become President. If the President shall not have been chosen before the time fixed for the beginning of his term, or if the President elect shall have failed to qualify, then the Vice President elect shall act as President until a President shall have qualified; and the Congress may by law provide for the case wherein neither a President elect nor a Vice President elect shall have qualified, declaring who shall then act as President, or the manner in which one who is to act shall be selected, and such person shall act accordingly until a President or Vice President shall have qualified.

Section 4. The Congress may by law provide for the case of the death of any of the persons from whom the House of Representatives may choose a President whenever the right of choice shall have devolved upon them, and for the case of the death of any of the persons from whom the Senate may choose a Vice President whenever the right of choice shall have devolved upon them.

Section 5. Sections 1 and 2 shall take effect on the 15th day of October following the ratification of this article.

Section 6. This article shall be inoperative unless it shall have been ratified as an amendment to the Constitution by the legislatures of three-fourths of the several States within seven years from the date of its submission.

Amendment XXI [1933]

Section 1. The eighteenth article of amendment to the Constitution of the United States is hereby repealed.

Section 2. The transportation or importation into any State, Territory, or possession of the United States for delivery or use therein of intoxicating liquors, in violation of the laws thereof, is hereby prohibited.

Section 3. This article shall be inoperative unless it shall have been ratified as an amendment to the Constitution by conventions in the several States, as provided in the Constitution, within seven years from the date of the submission hereof to the States by the Congress.

Amendment XXII [1951]

Section 1. No person shall be elected to the office of the President more than twice, and no person who has held the office of President, or acted as President, for more than two years of a term to which some other person was elected President shall be elected to the office of President more than once. But this Article shall not apply to any person holding the office of President when this Article was proposed by the Congress, and shall not prevent any person who may be holding the office of President, or acting as President, during the term within which this Article becomes operative from holding the office of President or acting as President during the remainder of such term.

Section 2. This article shall be inoperative unless it shall have been ratified as an amendment to the Constitution by the legislatures of three-fourths of the several States within seven years from the date of its submission to the States by the Congress.

Amendment XXIII [1961]

Section 1. The District constituting the seat of Government of the United States shall appoint in such manner as the Congress may direct:

A number of electors of President and Vice President equal to the whole number of Senators and Representatives in Congress to which the District would be entitled if it were a State, but in no event more than the least populous state; they shall be in addition to those appointed by the states, but they shall be considered, for the purposes of the election of President and Vice President, to be electors appointed by a state; and they shall meet in the District and perform such duties as provided by the twelfth article of amendment.

Section 2. The Congress shall have power to enforce this article by appropriate legislation.

Amendment XXIV [1964]

Section 1. The right of citizens of the United States to vote in any primary or other election for President or Vice President, for electors for President or Vice President, or for Senator or Representative in Congress, shall not be denied or abridged by the United States, or any State by reason of failure to pay any poll tax or other tax.

Section 2. The Congress shall have power to enforce this article by appropriate legislation.

Amendment XXV [1967]

Section 1. In case of the removal of the President from office or of his death or resignation, the Vice President shall become President.

Section 2. Whenever there is a vacancy in the office of the Vice President, the President shall nominate a Vice President who shall take office upon confirmation by a majority vote of both Houses of Congress.

Section 3. Whenever the President transmits to the President pro tempore of the Senate and the Speaker of the House of Representatives his written declaration that he is unable to discharge the powers and duties of his office, and until he transmits to them a written declaration to the contrary, such powers and duties shall be discharged by the Vice President as Acting President.

Section 4. Whenever the Vice President and a majority of either the principal officers of the executive departments or of such other body as Congress may by law provide, transmit to the President pro tempore of the Senate and the Speaker of the House of Representatives their written declaration that the President is unable to discharge the powers and duties of his office, the Vice President shall immediately assume the powers and duties of the office as Acting President.

Thereafter, when the President transmits to the President pro tempore of the Senate and the Speaker of the House of Representatives his written declaration that no inability exists, he shall resume the powers and duties of his office unless the Vice President and a majority of either the principal officers of the executive department or of such other body as Congress may by law provide, transmit within four days to the President pro tempore of the Senate and the Speaker of the House of Representatives their written declaration that the President is unable to discharge the powers and duties of his office. Thereupon Congress shall decide the issue, assembling within forty-eight hours for that purpose if not in session. If the Congress, within twenty-one days after receipt of the latter written declaration, or, if Congress is not in session, within twenty-one days after Congress is required to assemble, determines by two-thirds vote of both Houses that the President is unable to discharge the powers and duties of his office, the Vice President shall continue to discharge the same as Acting President; otherwise, the President shall resume the powers and duties of his office.

Amendment XXVI [1971]

Section 1. The right of citizens of the United States, who are eighteen years of age or older, to vote shall not be denied or abridged by the United States or by any State on account of age.

Section 2. The Congress shall have power to enforce this article by appropriate legislation.

Amendment XXVII [1992]

No law, varying the compensation for the services of the Senators and Representatives, shall take effect, until an election of Representatives shall have intervened.

Discretion in Action Case Studies

1.1 In 2015, prosecutor Thom LeDoux decided that no charges would be filed in a "sexting" scandal that involved about one hundred Cañon City High School students. Because nobody had been coerced to share or view the inappropriate images, LeDoux decided that the students were merely "doing stupid things" and did not deserve to be punished under Colorado criminal law.

On a practical level, it would be unreasonable for the criminal justice system to resolve the issue of sexting in the United States. According to one study, about 30 percent of American teenagers have shared a nude photo of themselves with another teenager. As one expert puts it, the child pornography laws under which this behavior often falls "are not meant to deal with a privacy violation but a really horrific form of abuse." Most prosecutors agree with Peter Weir, a district attorney in Jefferson County, Colorado, who believes that the goal in most teen sexting cases should be to "educate" rather than "prosecute."

Exceptions do, however, occur. Recently, two sixteen-year-old sweethearts who traded nude photos were charged with the felony of "exploiting a minor" by authorities in Fayetteville, North Carolina. The charges, which could have resulted in lengthy prison sentences, caused such a community outcry that the penalty was eventually reduced to a year's probation. Because of the possibility that prosecutors will use their discretion to severely punish young "sexters," approximately twenty states have passed laws mandating a softer approach to the problem in cases involving willing participants.

3.1 Several years ago, prosecutors in Mecklenburg County, North Carolina, dropped all domestic violence charges against professional football player Greg Hardy, citing lack of victim cooperation. The victim, despite assisting the police following Hardy's arrest, made it be known that she would not testify against Hardy in court, and in fact left North Carolina so that she could not be compelled to do so.

As noted in the text, faced with uncooperative victims, prosecutors will consistently "drop" domestic violence cases. To remedy this situation, many jurisdictions in the United States have implemented "no-drop" policies. Such policies require prosecutors to carry through with a domestic violence case once an arrest has been made, even if this goes against the wishes of the victim. There is little question that no-drop policies increase the prosecution and conviction rates of domestic violence offenders. Critics contend, however, that such policies are unethical because they ignore the wishes of domestic violence victims.

4.1 After University of Virginia senior George Huguely was arrested for the death of his twenty-two-year-old ex-girlfriend Yeardley Love in 2010, prosecutors charged him with first degree murder, punishable by life in prison. The prosecutors asserted that Huguely was enraged because Love was dating someone else, and that he intended to kill her in a premeditated act. Huguely's lawyers insisted that, at worst, their client was guilty of involuntary manslaughter. At the time of the crime, they pointed out, he was drunk and had no intent to harm Love, much less kill her. Furthermore, they argued, Love died from suffocation well after Huguely left her apartment.

In 2012, a Charlottesville, Virginia, jury found Huguely guilty of second degree murder, reasoning that although he did not intend to kill Love, he did act with malice aforethought and his violent behavior was the cause of her death. A judge later sentenced Huguely to twenty-three years in prison.

5.1 The two officers, Holder and Reynolds, believing that the matter required their "immediate attention," forced their way back into Teresa Sheehan's room. When Sheehan continued to wave the knife in a threatening manner, Officer Reynolds pepper-sprayed her in the face. Sheehan still refused to drop the knife. Then, Holder shot her twice.

Sheehan survived her gunshot injuries, and eventually brought a lawsuit against the city of San Francisco. In the suit, she alleged that the police officers, acting on behalf of the city government, had violated her rights under the Americans with Disability Act by subduing her in a way that did not take into account her mental illness. The case eventually made its way to the United States Supreme Court, where the justices ruled against Sheehan. The use of force by Officers Holder and Reynolds, the Court ruled, was reasonable under the circumstances, regardless of whether Sheehan suffered from a mental illness or not.

6.1 In December 2015, Cuyahoga County prosecutor Timothy J. McGinty recommended that the grand jury not bring any criminal charges against Cleveland police officer Timothy Loehmann for the death of twelve-year-old Tamir Rice. When the grand jury followed McGinty's recommendation, its decision was met with outrage, particularly in the city's African American community. Many of Cleveland's black residents believed that Loehmann, who is white, fired without hesitation on Rice because the boy was African American.

For his part, McGinty called the incident a "perfect storm of human error, mistakes, and miscommunications." He argued that Loehmann did not deserve to be charged because there was no way the officer could have known that Tamir was holding a pellet gun instead of a real one. Under those circumstances, McGinty felt, a police officer could reasonably have feared for his own life or the lives of those nearby.

7.1 In 1996, two Washington, D.C., police officers pulled over Michael J. Wren—a young African American male who was driving a truck with temporary plates in a high-crime neighborhood—for failing to signal while making a right turn. They found two large bags of crack cocaine in Wren's possession, and arrested him. The United States Supreme Court upheld Wren's conviction, ruling that as long as police officers have probable cause to believe that a traffic violation has occurred, the "real" reason for making the stop is irrelevant.

As Justice Antonin Scalia put it, "Subjective intentions play no role in ordinary, probable-cause, Fourth Amendment analysis." In practical terms, this ruling gives law enforcement agents the ability to confirm "hunches" about serious illegal behavior as long as the target of these hunches commits even the most minor traffic violation. Such violations could include failing to properly signal during a turn, making a rolling stop at a stop sign, or driving five miles over the posted speed limit.

8.1 In *United States v. Alvarez* (2012), by a vote of 6-3, the United States Supreme Court struck down the Stolen Valor Act. The Court found that the legislation was not necessary to protect the military's system of awarding honors, and therefore Xavier Alvarez's speech was protected by the Constitution. "The First Amendment requires that there be a direct causal link between the restriction imposed and the injury to be prevented," Justice Anthony M. Kennedy wrote in his opinion. "Here, that link has not been shown." The Court suggested, however, that if the legislation were rewritten to show that the false statement caused a particular harm, then a version of the Stolen Valor Act might pass constitutional muster. And, indeed, a year later, Congress did just that, making it a crime to lie about earning military honors "with the intent to obtain money, property, or some other tangible benefit."

In this case, those who favor the doctrine of judicial review would argue that the Supreme Court acted properly in overturning an overly broad law. Because Supreme Court justices are unelected and therefore insulated from the political process, they are in the best position to decide if legislation that may enjoy public support violates the Constitution. Certainly, in this instance, an elected official would think twice about opposing legislation to punish an individual who lies in public about being a war hero.

9.1 Gerard Marrone decided that his conscience prevented him from representing Levi Aron, and he withdrew from the case. His replacement, Jennifer McCann, criticized Marrone's actions. "To sit there and say, 'This is a hard case, I don't want to take it.'" McCann said. "That's for somebody else, that's not who I am." She added, "It's not about defending [Aron's] actions. It's about defending his rights." In 2012, Aron pleaded guilty to charges of second degree murder and kidnapping, and was sentenced to forty years to life in prison.

9.2 The North Carolina prosecutor in this case charged Judy Norman with first degree murder, reasoning that self-defense did not apply because Judy did not face any *imminent* danger from her husband, John. Despite his threats and the years of abuse, John was, at the time of his murder, asleep and thus incapable of harming her. A jury in the case, however, found Judy guilty of voluntary manslaughter only, and she was sentenced to six years in prison.

This case gained national attention because the trial court refused to allow evidence of *battered woman syndrome (BWS)* to be presented to the jury. The term describes the psychological state a person descends into following a lengthy period of physical abuse. In a courtroom, an expert might argue that anyone suffering from this syndrome is in a constant, and reasonable, fear for her or his life. Some states do allow evidence of BWS to support the defendant's claim of self-defense in these sorts of cases, and it has been effective. A New York woman who shot her abusive husband as he slept, for example, was acquitted after a jury accepted her self-defense claims, bolstered by expert testimony on BWS.

10.1 During a trial that was decided by a judge rather than a jury, defense attorney Norman Seigel insisted that the prosecution had failed to prove beyond a reasonable doubt that Oral "Nick" Hillary killed Garrett Phillips. "What evidence do they have?" Siegel asked during his opening statement. "Not one person will say, 'I saw Nick Hillary kill Garrett Phillips.' Why? Because it didn't happen."

Siegel also suggested that shoddy police work had let the real killer escape. Perhaps, he suggested, the culprit was the man in the hoodie, who could have fled the crime scene in the direction suggested by the police dog. In any event, Siegel created enough reasonable doubt that, on September 29, 2016, Judge Felix J. Catena acquitted the defendant, noting that the prosecution's entire case was circumstantial.

11.1 Pledge Chun "Michael" Deng died from injuries he suffered during a hazing ritual carried out by members of Baruch College's Pi Delta Psi fraternity in 2013. In all, thirty-eight members of the fraternity were charged in connection with Deng's death, including five who faced murder charges.

As of May 2017, only one of these defendants had gone to trial. In January 2017, twenty-five-year-old Ka-Wing Yuen pleaded guilty to conspiracy to hinder apprehension and conspiracy to haze for helping cover up Deng's death. A Monroe County, Pennsylvania, judge placed Yuen on five years' probation and ordered him to perform one hundred hours of community service and pay a $1,000 fine. "We have one down and thirty-seven to go," said assistant district attorney Kimberly Metzger after Yuen's plea bargain.

12.1 Susan Atkins was a disciple of cult leader Charles Manson and, in the summer of 1969, participated in one of the most sensationalized mass murders in American history. The woman Atkins stabbed sixteen times was Sharon Tate, an actress and the wife of film director Roman Polanski. On September 2, 2009, the California Board of Parole unanimously denied compassionate release for Atkins, marking the eighteenth time she had been refused parole. Three months later, Atkins died of brain cancer. Her case highlights the extent to which parole boards are often swayed by the nature of the crime above all other considerations.

14.1 The example given here is loosely taken from an online account of an inmate describing how he "downed a duck." After the correctional officer delivered the sympathy card with the funds, the inmate eventually turned the officer into a "golden goose" who helped with an escape attempt. Although this account is impossible to verify, there have been real-life examples of prison employees being duped into conspiring with inmates.

In the summer of 2015, for example, prisoners Richard Matt and David Sweat escaped the Clinton Correctional Facility in upstate New York with the help of correctional officer Gene Palmer and a civilian prison employee named Joyce Mitchell. Matt gave Palmer a series of paintings the inmate had finished while behind bars, and in return Palmer apparently smuggled tools into the prison that Matt and Sweat used to escape.

For her part, Mitchell told investigators that she talked with Matt "every day and he treated me with respect and was nice to me. He made me feel special." Mitchell eventually procured two pairs of spectacles equipped with lights for the inmates, so that they could work on their escape route at night. (After a three week manhunt, Matt was shot and killed and Sweat was shot and captured. Both Palmer and Mitchell received prison sentences for their misconduct.)

15.1 In 2008, a Denver, Colorado, prosecutor chose to charge seventeen-year-old James Stewart as an adult for vehicular homicide. After Stewart was moved to an adult jail, he tightened several bed sheets around his neck and hung himself. Stewart's suicide led to a change in state law that requires judges to review prosecutorial waivers in certain situations and makes it much less likely that a juvenile offender awaiting trial will be held in an adult jail.

In the first year after this law was passed, the number of juvenile offenders waived to state adult court dropped by nearly 85 percent. Nonetheless, Colorado prosecutors dislike the new law. One claims that he and his colleagues are in a better position than judges to decide whether a juvenile should be tried in adult court, due to a prosecutor's "experience" and "years and years of weighing one case against similarly situated cases."

16.1 After lower courts upheld the conviction of Anthony Elonis for threatening to commit an act of violence against his wife, he appealed to the U.S. Supreme Court. There, Elonis's attorneys argued that the prosecution should have been required to prove that their client intended to harm his wife, *not* that she reasonably feared he would do so. In other words, the Court was asked to decide which point of view matters most in such cases—the speaker's or the listener's.

In 2015, the justices decided in Elonis's favor by a 7-2 margin. Ordering a retrial, the Court ruled that the trial court had been wrong to convict Elonis without proving that he had intended for his violent online postings to be taken as threats by his wife. "Wrongdoing," explained Chief Justice John Roberts, Jr., "must be conscious to be criminal."

The decision in *Elonis v. United States* poses a difficult challenge for American courts—to establish the true motives of defendants such as Elonis who make online threats. "How does one prove what's in somebody else's mind?" asked Supreme Court Justice Ruth Bader Ginsberg. Along those same lines, Cindy Southworth of the National Network to End Domestic Violence points out that, "Every abuser says, 'I didn't mean for her to think I would kill her.'" On the other side, free speech advocates worry that "words are slippery things" and argue that laws disregarding the speaker's intent run the risk of punishing speech simply because it is "crudely" expressed.

Table of Cases

A

Adamson v. California (1947), 321–322
Alford, North Carolina v. (1970), 308
Allen v. United States (1896), 340
Argersinger v. Hamlin (1972), 289
Ash, United States v. (1973), 246
Atkins v. Virginia (2002), 378, 382

B

Ballew v. Georgia (1978), 321
Barker v. Wingo (1972), 319
Batson v. Kentucky (1986), 327–328
Baze v. Rees (2008), 376
Bell v. Wolfish (1979), 445
Bennis v. Michigan (1996), 411
Benton, New York v. (1981), 227
Benton v. Maryland (1969), 126
Berger v. United States (1935), 285
Berghuis v. Thompkins (2010), 242
Bowers v. Hardwick (1986), 104
Boykin v. Alabama (1969), 308
Brady v. United States (1970), 308
Breed v. Jones (1975), 495
Brewer v. Williams (1977), 220
Brigham City v. Stuart (2006), 224
Brown v. Entertainment Merchants Association (EMA) (2010), 53
Brown v. Plata (2011), 459, 460
Burger v. New York (1967), 229

C

Carroll v. United States (1925), 226
Chimel v. California (1969), 224
Cobb, Texas v. (2001), 243
Coolidge v. New Hampshire (1971), 228
County v. _____. See name of county

D

Davis v. United States (1994), 242
Duncan v. Louisiana (1968), 126, 320

E

Escobedo v. Illinois (1964), 126, 239
Estelle v. Gamble (1976), 472–473
Evans, Arizona v. (1995), 220

F

Fare v. Michael C. (1979), 512
Fulminante, Arizona v. (1991), 243
Furman v. Georgia (1972), 264, 377

G

Gagnon v. Scarpelli (1972), 400
Gant, Arizona v. (2009), 226–227
Gault, *In re* (1967), 126, 289, 495–496, 513
Georgia v. McCollum (1992), 327
Gideon v. Wainwright (1963), 126, 263, 289
Gonzales v. Oregon (2006), 11–12
Gonzales v. Raich (2005), 13
Graham v. Connor (1989), 199
Graham v. Florida (2010), 498
Greenholtz v. Inmates of the Nebraska Penal and
    Correctional Complex (1979), 406
Greenwood, California v. (1988), 221
Gregg v. Georgia (1976), 264

H

Hudson v. McMillan (1992), 471
Hudson v. Michigan (2006), 238

I

In re _____. See name of party

J

J.D.B. v. North Carolina (2011), 512
J.E.B. v. Alabama ex rel. T. B. (1994), 328
Jones, United States v. (2012), 221–222, 230

K

Katz v. United States (1967), 221, 229
Kent v. United States (1966), 495
King, Maryland v. (2013), 185
Klopfer v. North Carolina (1967), 126
Knights, United States v. (2001), 398

L

Lawrence v. Texas (2003), 104
Leon, United States v. (1984), 220
Lockyer v. Andrade (2003), 372

M

Malloy v. Hogan (1964), 126
Mapp v. Ohio (1952), 126
McCleskey v. Kemp (1987), 382
McKeiver v. Pennsylvania (1971), 496
Mempa v. Rhay (1967), 400
Mezzanatto, United States v. (1995), 308
Miller v. Alabama (2012), 498
Miranda v. Arizona (1966), 126, 240–241, 263, 342
Montana v. Egelhoff (1996), 118
Moran v. Burbine (1986), 243
Morrissey v. Brewer (1972), 400
Murphy, Minnesota v. (1984), 401

N

Nix v. Williams (1984), 220

O

Ohio v. Robinette (1996), 227
Oliver, *In re* (1948), 126

P

Parker v. Gladden (1966), 126
Pointer v. Texas (1965), 126
Powell, Florida v. (2010), 243
Powers v. Ohio (1991), 327

Q

Quirk, *In re* (1997), 397

R

Ricketts v. Adamson (1987), 308
Riley, California v. (2014), 231
Ring v. Arizona (2002), 378
Riverside, County of v. McLaughlin (1991), 219

R

Robinson, United States v. (1973), 224
Rochin v. California (1952), 126
Rodriguez v. United States (2015), 216, 217
Roper v. Simmons (2005), 379, 382, 498

S

Santobello v. New York (1971), 305, 308
Schall v. Martin (1984), 512
Schmerber v. California (1966), 246
Schneckcloth v. Bustamonte (1973), 225
Shatzer, Maryland v. (2010), 243
Smith v. Maryland (1979), 543
Sorrells v. United States (1932), 122
State v. _____. *See name of opposing party*
Strickland v. Washington (1984), 292
Strieff, Utah v. (2016), 238
Swain v. Alabama (1965), 327

T

Tennessee v. Garner (1985), 198–199
Terry v. Ohio (1968), 232–234

U

United States v. _____. *See name of opposing party*

W

Weems v. United States (1910), 376
Whitley v. Albers (1986), 470
Wilson v. Arkansas (1995), 236–237
Wilson v. Seiter (1991), 473
Winship, *In re* (1970), 322, 495

Z

Zolin, United States v. (1989), 294

Glossary

A

Acquittal A declaration following a trial that the individual accused of the crime is innocent in the eyes of the law and thus is absolved from the charges.

Actus Reus (pronounced *ak-tus ray*-uhs). A guilty (prohibited) act.

Adjudicatory Hearing The process through which a juvenile court determines whether there is sufficient evidence to support the initial petition.

Administrative Law The body of law created by administrative agencies (in the form of rules, regulations, orders, and decisions) in order to carry out their duties and responsibilities.

Admission A statement acknowledging that certain facts concerning a crime are true but falling short of a confession.

Adversary System A legal system in which the prosecution and defense are opponents, or adversaries, and strive to "defeat" each other in court.

Affidavit A written statement of facts, confirmed by the oath or affirmation of the party making it and made before a person having the authority to administer the oath or affirmation.

Affirmative Action A hiring or promotion policy favoring those groups, such as women, African Americans, and Latinos, who have suffered from discrimination in the past or continue to suffer from discrimination.

Aftercare The variety of therapeutic, educational, and counseling programs made available to juvenile delinquents after they have been released from a correctional facility.

Age of Onset The age at which a juvenile first exhibits delinquent behavior.

Aggravating Circumstances Any circumstances accompanying the commission of a crime that may justify a harsher sentence.

Aging Out A term used to explain the fact that criminal activity declines with age.

Alibi Proof that a suspect was somewhere other than the scene of the crime at the time of the crime, typically offered to demonstrate that the suspect was not guilty of the crime.

Allen **Charge** An instruction by a judge to a deadlocked jury with only a few dissenters that asks the jurors in the minority to reconsider the majority opinion.

Anomie A condition in which the individual feels a disconnect from society due to the breakdown or absence of social norms.

Appeal The process of seeking a higher court's review of a lower court's decision for the purpose of correcting or changing this decision.

Appellate Courts Courts that review decisions made by lower courts, such as trial courts; also known as *courts of appeals*.

Arraignment A court proceeding in which the suspect is formally charged with the criminal offense stated in the indictment.

Arrest To deprive a person suspected of criminal activity of his or her liberty.

Arrest Warrant A written order, based on probable cause and issued by a judge or magistrate, commanding that the person named on the warrant be arrested by the police.

Assault A threat or an attempt to do violence to another person that causes that person to fear immediate physical harm.

Attempt The act of taking substantial steps toward committing a crime while having the ability and the intent to commit the crime, even if the crime never takes place.

Attendant Circumstances The facts surrounding a criminal event that must be proved to convict the defendant of the underlying crime.

Attorney-Client Privilege A rule of evidence requiring that communications between a client and his or her attorney be kept confidential, unless the client consents to disclosure.

Attorney General The chief law officer of a state; also, the chief law officer of the nation.

Authority The power conferred on an agent of the law to enforce obedience.

Automatic Transfer The process by which a juvenile is transferred to adult court as a matter of state law.

B

Background Check An investigation of a person's history to determine whether that person should be, for example, allowed to legally purchase a firearm.

Bail The dollar amount or conditions set by the court to ensure that an individual accused of a crime will appear for further criminal proceedings.

Bail Bond Agent A businessperson who agrees, for a fee, to pay the bail amount if the accused fails to appear in court as ordered.

Ballistics The study of firearms, including the firing of the weapon and the flight of the bullet.

Ballot Initiative A procedure in which the citizens of a state, by collecting enough signatures, can force a public vote on a proposed change to state law.

Battery The act of physically contacting another person with the intent to do harm, even if the resulting injury is insubstantial.

Bench Trial A trial conducted without a jury, in which a judge makes the determination of the defendant's guilt or innocence.

Beyond a Reasonable Doubt The degree of proof required to find the defendant in a criminal trial guilty of committing the crime. The defendant's guilt must be the only reasonable explanation for the criminal act before the court.

Bill of Rights The first ten amendments to the U.S. Constitution.

Biology The science of living organisms, including their structure, function, growth, and origin.

Biometrics Methods to identify a person based on unique physical characteristics, such as fingerprints or facial configuration.

Blue Curtain A metaphorical term used to refer to the value placed on secrecy and the general mistrust of the outside world shared by many police officers.

Body Armor Protective covering that is worn under a police officer's clothing and designed to minimize injury from being hit by a fired bullet.

Booking The process of entering a suspect's name, offense, and arrival time into the police log following her or his arrest.

Boot Camp A variation on traditional shock incarceration in which juveniles (and some adults) are sent to secure confinement facilities modeled on military basic training camps.

Botnet A network of computers that have been appropriated without the knowledge of their owners and used to spread harmful programs via the Internet; short for robot network.

Boykin Form A form that must be completed by a defendant who pleads guilty. The defendant states that she or he has done so voluntarily and with full comprehension of the consequences.

Broken Windows Theory Wilson and Kelling's theory that a neighborhood in disrepair signals that criminal activity is tolerated in the area. By cracking down on quality-of-life crimes, police can reclaim the neighborhood and encourage law-abiding citizens to live and work there.

Bullying Overt acts taken by students with the goal of intimidating, harassing, or humiliating other students.

Bureaucracy A hierarchically-structured administrative organization that carries out specific functions.

Burglary The act of breaking into or entering a structure (such as a home or office) without permission for the purpose of committing a felony.

Burnout A mental state that occurs when a person suffers from exhaustion and has difficulty functioning normally as a result of overwork and stress.

C

Capital Crime A criminal act that makes the offender eligible to receive the death penalty.

Capital Punishment The use of the death penalty to punish wrongdoers for certain crimes.

Case Attrition The process through which prosecutors, by deciding whether to prosecute each person arrested, effect an overall reduction in the number of persons prosecuted.

Case Law The rules of law announced in court decisions.

Caseload The number of individual probationers or parolees under the supervision of a probation or parole officer.

Causation The relationship in which a change in one measurement or behavior creates a recognizable change in another measurement or behavior.

Challenge for Cause A *voir dire* challenge for which an attorney states the reason why a prospective juror should not be included on the jury.

Charge The judge's instructions to the jury following the attorneys' closing arguments.

Child Abuse Mistreatment of children involving physical, emotional, or sexual damage.

Child Neglect A form of child abuse in which the child is denied certain necessities such as shelter, food, care, and love.

Choice Theory A school of criminology based on the belief that individuals have free will to engage in any behavior, including criminal behavior.

Chronic Offender A delinquent or criminal who commits multiple offenses and is considered part of a small group of wrongdoers who are responsible for a majority of the antisocial activity in any given community.

Circumstantial Evidence Indirect evidence that is offered to establish, by inference, the likelihood of a fact that is in question.

Citizen Oversight The process by which citizens review complaints brought against individual police officers or police departments.

Civil Confinement The practice of confining individuals against their will if they present a danger to the community.

Civil Law The branch of law dealing with the definition and enforcement of all private or public rights, as opposed to criminal matters.

Civil Liability The potential responsibility of police officers, police departments, or municipalities to defend themselves against civil lawsuits.

Civil Liberties The basic rights and freedoms for American citizens guaranteed by the U.S. Constitution, particularly in the Bill of Rights.

Civil Rights Violation Any interference with a citizen's constitutional rights by a civil servant such as a police officer.

Classical Criminology A school of criminology that holds that wrongdoers act as if they weigh the possible benefits of criminal or delinquent activity against the expected costs of being apprehended.

Classification The process through which prison officials screen each incoming inmate to best determine that inmate's security and treatment needs.

Clearance Rates A comparison of the number of crimes cleared by arrest and prosecution with the number of crimes reported during any given time period.

Closing Arguments Arguments made by each side's attorney after the cases for the plaintiff and defendant have been presented.

Coercion The use of physical force or mental intimidation to compel a person to do something—such as confess to committing a crime—against her or his will.

Cold Case A criminal investigation that has not been solved after a certain amount of time.

Cold Hit The establishment of a connection between a suspect and a crime, often through the use of DNA evidence, in the absence of an ongoing criminal investigation.

Common Law The body of law developed from custom or judicial decisions in English and U.S. courts and not attributable to a legislature.

Community Corrections The correctional supervision of offenders in the community as an alternative to sending them to prison or jail.

Community Policing A policing philosophy that emphasizes community support for and cooperation with the police in preventing crime.

Competency Hearing A court proceeding to determine mental competence. In the context of criminal law, a hearing may be held before the trial, during the trial, or before sentencing.

Compliance The state of operating in accordance with governmental standards.

Computer-Aided Dispatch (CAD) A method of dispatching police patrol units to the site of 911 emergencies with the assistance of a computer program.

Concurrent Jurisdiction The situation that occurs when two or more courts have the authority to preside over the same criminal case.

Concurring Opinions Separate opinions prepared by judges who support the decision of the majority of the court but who want to make or clarify a particular point or to voice disapproval of the grounds on which the decision was made.

Conducted Energy Devices (CEDs) Less lethal weapons designed to disrupt a target's central nervous system by means of a charge of electrical energy.

Confession A statement acknowledging that the suspect participated in some aspect of a crime.

Confidential Informant (CI) A human source for police who provides information concerning illegal activity in which he or she is involved.

Conflict Model A criminal justice model in which the content of criminal law is determined by the groups that hold economic, political, and social power in a community.

Confrontation Clause The part of the Sixth Amendment that guarantees all defendants the right to confront witnesses testifying against them during the criminal trial.

Congregate System A nineteenth-century penitentiary system developed in New York in which inmates were kept in separate cells during the night but worked together in the daytime under a code of enforced silence.

Consensus Model A criminal justice model in which the majority of citizens in a society share the same values and beliefs. Criminal acts are acts that conflict with these values and beliefs and that are deemed harmful to society.

Consent Searches Searches by police that are made after the subject of the search has agreed to the action. In these situations, consent, if given of free will, validates a warrantless search.

Conspiracy A plot by two or more people to carry out an illegal or harmful act.

Constitutional Law Law based on the U.S. Constitution and the constitutions of the various states.

Control Theory A series of theories that assume that all individuals have the potential for criminal behavior, but are restrained by the damage that such actions would do to their relationships with family, friends, and members of the community.

Coroner The medical examiner of a county, usually elected by popular vote.

Corporate Violence Physical harm to individuals or the environment that occurs as the result of corporate policies or decision making.

Corpus Delicti The body of circumstances that must exist for a criminal act to have occurred.

Correlation The relationship between two measurements or behaviors that tend to move in the same direction.

Courtroom Work Group The social organization consisting of the judge, prosecutor, defense attorney, and other court workers.

Crime An act that violates criminal law and is punishable by criminal sanctions.

Crime Control Model A criminal justice model that places primary emphasis on the right of society to be protected from crime and violent criminals.

Crime Mapping Technology that allows crime analysts to identify trends and patterns of criminal behavior within a given area.

Criminal Justice System The interlocking network of law enforcement agencies, courts, and corrections institutions designed to enforce criminal laws and protect society from criminal behavior.

Criminal Model of Addiction An approach to drug abuse that holds that drug offenders harm society by their actions to the same extent as other criminals and should face the same punitive sanctions.

Criminology The scientific study of crime and the causes of criminal behavior.

Cross-Examination The questioning of an opposing witness during trial.

Cultural Deviance Theory A branch of social structure theory based on the assumption that members of certain subcultures reject the values of the dominant culture by exhibiting deviant behavior patterns.

Custodial Interrogation The questioning of a suspect after that person has been taken into custody. In this situation, the suspect must be read his or her *Miranda* rights before interrogation can begin.

Custody The forceful detention of a person or the person's perception that he or she is not free to leave the immediate vicinity.

Custody Level As a result of the classification process, the security designation given to new inmates, crucial in helping corrections officials determine which correctional facility is best suited to the individual offender.

Cyberattack An attempt to damage or disrupt computer systems or electronic networks operated by computers.

Cyberbullying To bully electronically by sending repeated, hurtful messages via texting or the Internet, particularly on social media websites.

Cyber Crime A crime that occurs online, in the virtual community of the Internet, as opposed to in the physical world.

Cyber Forensics The application of computer technology to finding and utilizing evidence of cyber crimes.

Cyber Fraud Any misrepresentation knowingly made over the Internet with the intention of deceiving another and on which a reasonable person would and does rely to his or her detriment.

Cyberstalking The crime of stalking committed in cyberspace through the use of e-mail, text messages, or other forms of electronic communication.

D

Dark Figure of Crime A term used to describe the actual amount of crime that takes place. The "figure" is "dark," or impossible to detect, because a great number of crimes are never reported to the police.

Data Breach The illegal appropriation of protected or confidential information.

Day Reporting Center (DRC) A community-based corrections center to which offenders report on a daily basis for treatment, education, and rehabilitation.

Deadly Force Force applied by a police officer that is likely or intended to cause death.

Defendant In a civil court, the person or institution against whom an action is brought. In a criminal court, the person or entity who has been formally accused of violating a criminal law.

Defense Attorney The lawyer representing the defendant.

Deferred Prosecution An alternative to prosecution in which the prosecutor agrees to delay criminal proceedings against a defendant as long as the defendant meets certain requirements for a predetermined amount of time.

Delegation of Authority The principles of command on which most police departments are based, in which personnel take orders from and are responsible to those in positions of power directly above them.

"Deliberate Indifference" The standard for establishing a violation of an inmate's Eighth Amendment rights, requiring that prison officials were aware of harmful conditions in a correctional institution and failed to take steps to remedy those conditions.

Departure A stipulation in many federal and state sentencing guidelines that allows a judge to adjust his or her sentencing decision based on the special circumstances of a particular case.

Deprivation Model A theory that inmate aggression is the result of

the frustration inmates feel at being deprived of freedom, consumer goods, sex, and other staples of life outside the institution.

Desistance The process through which criminal activity decreases and reintegration into society increases over a period of time.

Detective The primary police investigator of crimes.

Detention The temporary custody of a juvenile in a secure facility after a petition has been filed and before the adjudicatory process begins.

Detention Hearing A hearing to determine whether a juvenile should be detained, or remain detained, while waiting for the adjudicatory process to begin.

Determinate Sentencing Imposition of a sentence that is fixed by a sentencing authority and cannot be reduced by judges or other corrections officials.

Deterrence The strategy of preventing crime through the threat of punishment.

Deviance Behavior that is considered to go against the norms established by society.

Differential Response A strategy for answering calls for service in which response time is adapted to the seriousness of the call.

Digital Evidence Information or data of value to a criminal investigation that is either stored or transmitted by electronic means.

Directed Patrol A patrol strategy designed to focus on a specific type of criminal activity in a specific geographic area.

Direct Evidence Evidence that establishes the existence of a fact that is in question without relying on inference.

Direct Examination The examination of a witness by the attorney who calls the witness to the stand to testify.

Direct Supervision Approach A process of prison and jail administration in which correctional officers are in continuous visual contact with inmates during the day.

Discovery Formal investigation by each side prior to trial.

Discretion The ability of individuals in the criminal justice system to make operational decisions based on personal judgment instead of formal rules or official information.

Discretionary Release The release of an inmate into a community supervision program at the discretion of the parole board within limits set by state or federal law.

Discrimination The illegal use of characteristics such as gender or race by employers when making hiring or promotion decisions.

Disposition Hearing A hearing in which the juvenile judge or officer decides the appropriate punishment for a youth found to be delinquent or a status offender; similar to the sentencing hearing for adults.

Dissenting Opinions Separate opinions in which judges disagree with the conclusion reached by the majority of the court and expand on their own views about the case.

Diversion An effort to keep offenders out of prison or jail by diverting them into programs that promote treatment and rehabilitation rather than punishment.

DNA Fingerprinting The identification of a person based on a sample of her or his DNA, the genetic material found in the cells of all living things.

Docket The list of cases entered on a court's calendar and thus scheduled to be heard by the court.

Domestic Terrorism Acts of terrorism that take place on U.S. soil without direct foreign involvement.

Domestic Violence An act of willful neglect or physical violence that occurs within a familial or other intimate relationship.

Double Jeopardy To twice place at risk (jeopardize) a person's life or liberty. Constitutional law prohibits a second prosecution in the same court for the same criminal offense.

Double Marginality The situation in which minority law enforcement officers face suspicion both from their white colleagues and from members of the minority community to which they belong.

Drug Any substance that modifies biological, psychological, or social behavior. In particular, an illegal substance with those properties.

Drug Abuse The use of drugs that results in physical or psychological problems for the user, as well as disruption of personal relationships and employment.

Drug Enforcement Administration (DEA) The federal agency responsible for enforcing the nation's laws and regulations regarding narcotics and other controlled substances.

Dual Court System The separate but interrelated court system of the United States, made up of the courts on the national level and the courts on the state level.

Due Process Clause The provisions of the Fifth and Fourteenth Amendments to the Constitution that guarantee that no person shall be deprived of life, liberty, or property without due process of law.

Due Process Model A criminal justice model that places primacy on the right of the individual to be protected from the power of the government.

Duress Unlawful pressure brought to bear on a person, causing the person to perform an act that he or she would not otherwise perform.

Duty A police officer's moral sense that she or he should behave in a certain manner.

Duty to Retreat The requirement that a person claiming self-defense prove that she or he first took reasonable steps to avoid the conflict that resulted in the use of deadly force.

E

Electronic Monitoring A supervision technique in which the offender's whereabouts are kept under surveillance by an electronic device.

Electronic Surveillance The use of electronic equipment by law enforcement agents to record private conversations or observe conduct that is meant to be private.

Encryption The translation of computer data into a secret code with the goal of protecting that data from unauthorized parties.

Entrapment A defense in which the defendant claims that he or she was induced by a public official—usually an undercover agent or police officer—to commit a crime that he or she would otherwise not have committed.

Ethics The moral principles that govern a person's perception of right and wrong.

Evidence Anything that is used to prove the existence or nonexistence of a fact.

Evidence-Based Practices Approaches or strategies that have been extensively researched and shown consistently to produce the desired outcomes.

Exclusionary Rule A rule under which any evidence that is obtained in violation of the accused's rights, as well as any evidence derived from illegally obtained evidence, will not be admissible in criminal court.

Exigent Circumstances Situations that require extralegal or exceptional actions by the police.

Expert Witness A witness with professional training or substantial experience qualifying her or him to testify on a certain subject.

Expiration Release The release of an inmate from prison at the end of his or her sentence without any further correctional supervision.

Extradition The process by which one jurisdiction surrenders a person accused or convicted of violating another jurisdiction's criminal law to the second jurisdiction.

F

False Confession A confession of guilt when the confessor did not, in fact, commit the crime.

Federal Bureau of Investigation (FBI) The branch of the Department of Justice responsible for investigating violations of federal law.

Federalism A form of government in which a written constitution provides for a division of powers between a central government and several regional governments.

Fee System A system in which the sheriff's department is reimbursed by a government agency for the costs of housing jail inmates.

Felonies Serious crimes, usually punishable by death or imprisonment for a year or longer.

Felony-Murder An unlawful homicide that occurs during the attempted commission of a felony.

Field Training The segment of a police recruit's training in which he or she is removed from the classroom and placed on the beat, under the supervision of a senior officer.

Forensics The application of science to establish facts and evidence during the investigation of crimes.

Forfeiture The process by which the government seizes private property attached to criminal activity.

Formal Criminal Justice Process The model of the criminal justice process in which participants follow formal rules to create a smoothly functioning disposition of cases from arrest to punishment.

Frisk A pat-down or minimal search by police to discover weapons.

Fruit of the Poisoned Tree Evidence that is acquired through the use of illegally obtained evidence and is therefore inadmissible in court.

Furlough Temporary release from a prison for purposes of vocational or educational training, to ease the shock of release, or for personal reasons.

Fusion Center A collaborative effort between two or more agencies to prevent and respond to criminal and terrorist activities.

G

Genetics The study of how certain traits or qualities are transmitted from parents to their offspring.

"Good Faith" Exception The legal principle that evidence obtained with the use of a technically invalid search warrant is admissible during trial if the police acted in good faith.

"Good Time" A reduction in time served by prisoners based on good behavior, conformity to rules, and other positive behavior.

Graduated Sanctions A continuum of disposition options used in juvenile corrections with the goal of ensuring that the juvenile's punishment matches the wrongdoing in severity.

Graduated Sanctions A series of punishments that become more severe with each subsequent act of wrongdoing.

Grand Jury A group of citizens called to decide if there is probable cause to believe that the defendant committed the crime with which she or he is charged.

Gun Control Efforts by a government to regulate or control the sale of guns.

H

Habeas Corpus An order that requires corrections officials to bring an inmate before a court or a judge and explain why he or she is being held in prison.

Habitual Offender Laws Statutes that require lengthy prison sentences for those who are convicted of repeated felonies.

Hack The illegal use of one computer system to gain access to another computer system and steal or manipulate the data in the targeted system.

Halfway House A community-based form of early release that places inmates in residential centers and allows them to reintegrate with society.

"Hands-Off" Doctrine The unwritten judicial policy that favors noninterference by the courts in the administration of prisons and jails.

Hate Crime Laws Statutes that provide for greater sanctions against those who commit crimes motivated by bias against an individual or a group based on race, ethnicity, religion, gender, sexual orientation, disability, or age.

Hearsay An oral or written statement made by an out-of-court speaker that is later offered in court by a witness (not the speaker) concerning a matter before the court.

Home Confinement A community-based sanction in which offenders serve their terms of incarceration in their homes.

Homeland Security A concerted national effort to prevent terrorist attacks within the United States and reduce the country's vulnerability to terrorism.

Hormones A chemical substance, produced in tissue and conveyed in the bloodstream, that controls certain cellular and body functions, such as growth and reproduction.

Hot Spots Concentrated areas of high criminal activity that draw a directed police response.

Human Trafficking The practice of illegally transporting a person from one country to another for the purpose of forced labor or sexual exploitation.

Hung Jury A jury whose members are so irreconcilably divided in their opinions that they cannot reach a verdict.

Hypothesis A possible explanation for an observed occurrence that can be tested by further investigation.

I

"Identifiable Human Needs" The basic human necessities that correctional facilities are required by the Constitution to provide to inmates.

Identity Theft The theft of personal information, such as a person's name, driver's license number, or Social Security number.

Impeachment The formal process by which a public official is charged with misconduct that could lead to removal from office.

Incapacitation A strategy for preventing crime by detaining wrongdoers in prison, thereby separating them from the community and reducing criminal opportunities.

Inchoate Offenses Conduct deemed criminal without actual harm being done, provided that the harm that would have occurred is one the law tries to prevent.

Incident-Driven Policing A reactive approach to policing that emphasizes a speedy response to calls for service.

Indeterminate Sentencing Imposition of a sentence that prescribes a range of years rather than a specified number of years to be served.

Indictment A charge or written accusation, issued by a grand jury, that probable cause exists to believe that a named person has committed a crime.

"Inevitable Discovery" Exception The legal principle that illegally obtained evidence can be admissible in court if police using lawful means would inevitably have discovered it.

Infancy The status of a person who is below the legal age of majority. Under early American law, infancy excused young wrongdoers of criminal behavior because presumably they could not understand the consequences of their actions.

Informal Criminal Justice Process A model of the criminal justice system that recognizes the informal authority exercised by individuals at each step of the criminal justice process.

Information The formal charge against the accused issued by the prosecutor after a preliminary hearing has found probable cause.

Infraction In most jurisdictions, a noncriminal offense for which the penalty is a fine rather than incarceration.

Infrastructure The services and facilities that support the day-to-day needs of modern life, such as electricity, food, transportation, and water.

Initial Appearance An accused's first appearance before a judge or magistrate following arrest.

Insanity A defense for criminal liability that asserts a lack of criminal responsibility due to mental instability.

Intake The process by which an official of the court must decide whether to file a petition, release the juvenile, or place the juvenile under some other form of supervision.

Intellectual Property Property resulting from intellectual, creative processes.

Intelligence-Led Policing An approach that measures the risk of criminal behavior associated with certain individuals or locations so as to predict when and where such criminal behavior is most likely to occur in the future.

Intensive Supervision Probation (ISP) A punishment-oriented form of probation in which the offender is placed under stricter and more frequent surveillance and control than in conventional probation.

Intermediate Sanctions Sanctions that are more restrictive than probation and less restrictive than imprisonment.

Internal Affairs Unit (IAU) A division within a police department that receives and investigates complaints of wrongdoing by police officers.

Interrogation The direct questioning of a suspect to gather evidence of criminal activity and to try to gain a confession.

Intoxication A defense for criminal liability in which the defendant claims that the taking of intoxicants rendered him or her unable to form the requisite intent to commit a criminal act.

Involuntary Manslaughter A homicide in which the offender had no intent to kill the victim.

Irresistible-Impulse Test A test for the insanity defense under which a defendant who knew his or her action was wrong may still be found insane if he or she was unable, as a result of a mental deficiency, to control the urge to complete the act.

J

Jail A facility, usually operated by the county government, used to hold persons awaiting trial or those who have been found guilty of minor crimes (mostly misdemeanors).

Judicial Misconduct A general term describing behavior—such as accepting bribes or consorting with known felons—that diminishes public confidence in the judiciary.

Judicial Review The power of a court—particularly the United States Supreme Court—to review the actions of the executive and legislative branches and, if necessary, declare those actions unconstitutional.

Judicial Waiver The process in which the juvenile judge, based on the facts of the case at hand, decides that the alleged offender should be transferred to adult court.

Jurisdiction The authority of a court to hear and decide cases within an area of the law or a geographic territory.

Jury Trial A trial before a judge and a jury.

Just Deserts A sanctioning philosophy based on the assertion that criminal punishment should be proportionate to the severity of the crime.

Justice The quality of fairness that must exist in the processes designed to determine whether individuals are guilty of criminal wrongdoing.

Justice Reinvestment A corrections policy that promotes (a) a reduction in spending on prisons and jails and (b) reinvestment of the resulting savings in programs that decrease crime and reduce reoffending.

Juvenile Delinquency Illegal behavior committed by a person who is under an age limit specified by statute.

L

Labeling Theory The hypothesis that society creates crime and criminals by labeling certain behavior and certain people as deviant.

Larceny The act of taking property from another person without the use of force with the intent of keeping that property.

Lay Witness A witness who can truthfully and accurately testify on a fact in question without having specialized training or knowledge.

Learning Theory The theory that delinquents and criminals must be taught both the practical and the emotional skills necessary to participate in illegal activity.

Legalization To make a formerly illegal product or action lawful. In the context of marijuana, the process includes strict regulation, including a ban on sale to or use by minors.

Liable In a civil court, legal responsibility for one's own or another's actions.

Life Course Criminology The study of crime based on the belief that behavioral patterns developed in childhood can predict delinquent and criminal behavior later in life.

Lockdown A disciplinary action taken by prison officials in which all inmates are ordered to their quarters and nonessential prison activities are suspended.

Low-Visibility Decision Making A term used to describe the discretionary power police have in determining what to do with misbehaving juveniles.

M

Magistrate A public civil officer or official with limited judicial authority within a particular geographic area, such as the authority to issue an arrest warrant.

Mala in Se A descriptive term for acts that are inherently wrong, regardless of whether they are prohibited by law.

Mala Prohibita A descriptive term for acts that are made illegal by criminal statute and are not necessarily wrong in and of themselves.

Mandatory Release Release from prison that occurs when an offender has served the full length of his or her sentence, minus any adjustments for good time.

Mandatory Sentencing Guidelines Statutorily determined punishments that must be applied to those who are convicted of specific crimes.

Master Jury List The list of citizens in a court's district from which a jury can be selected; compiled from voter-registration lists, driver's license lists, and other sources.

Material Support In the context of federal antiterrorism legislation, the act of helping a terrorist organization by engaging in any of a wide range of activities, including providing financial support, training, and expert advice or assistance.

Maximum-Security Prisons A correctional institution designed and organized to control and discipline dangerous felons, as well as prevent escape.

Medical Model A model of corrections in which the psychological and biological roots of an inmate's criminal behavior are identified and treated.

Medical Model of Addiction An approach to drug addiction that treats drug abuse as a mental illness and focuses on treating and rehabilitating offenders rather than punishing them.

Medium-Security Prisons A correctional institution that houses less dangerous inmates and therefore uses less restrictive measures to prevent violence and escapes.

Mens Rea (pronounced mehns *ray*-uh). Mental state, or intent. A wrongful mental state is usually as necessary as a wrongful act to establish criminal liability.

Militarism The use of military training, tactics, and weaponry in policing.

Minimum-Security Prison A correctional institution designed to allow inmates, most of whom pose low security risks, a great deal of freedom of movement and contact with the outside world.

Miranda **Rights** The constitutional rights of accused persons taken into custody by law enforcement officials, including the right to remain silent and the right to counsel.

Misdemeanor A criminal offense that is not a felony; usually punishable by a fine and/or a jail term of less than one year.

Missouri Plan A method of selecting judges that combines appointment and election.

Mitigating Circumstances Any circumstances accompanying the commission of a crime that may justify a lighter sentence.

M'Naghten **Rule** A common law test of criminal responsibility, derived from *M'Naghten's* Case in 1843, that relies on the defendant's inability to distinguish right from wrong.

Morals Principles of right and wrong behavior, as practiced by individuals or by society.

Motion for a Directed Verdict A motion requesting that the court grant judgment in favor of the defense on the ground that the prosecution has not produced sufficient evidence to support the state's claim.

Murder The unlawful killing of one human being by another.

N

National Security Letters Legal notices that compel the disclosure of customer records held by banks, telephone companies, Internet service providers, and other companies to the agents of the federal government.

Necessity A defense against criminal liability in which the defendant asserts that circumstances required her or him to commit an illegal act.

Negligence A failure to exercise the standard of care that a reasonable person would exercise in similar circumstances.

New-Generation Jail A type of jail that is distinguished architecturally from its predecessors by a design that encourages interaction between inmates and jailers and that offers greater opportunities for treatment.

Night Watch System An early form of American law enforcement in which volunteers patrolled their community from dusk to dawn to keep the peace.

Noble Cause Corruption Knowing misconduct by a police officer with the goal of attaining what the officer believes is a "just" result.

Nolo Contendere Latin for "I will not contest it." A plea in which a criminal defendant chooses not to challenge, or contest, the charges brought by the government.

Nonpartisan Elections Elections in which candidates are presented on the ballot without any party affiliation.

O

Opening Statements The attorneys' statements to the jury at the beginning of the trial.

Opinions Written statements by appellate judges expressing the reasons for the court's decision in a case.

Oral Arguments The verbal arguments presented in person by attorneys to an appellate court. Each attorney offers reasons why the court should rule in his or her client's favor.

P

Pardon An act of executive clemency that overturns a conviction and erases mention of the crime from the person's criminal record.

Parens Patriae A doctrine that holds that the state has a responsibility to look after the well-being of children and to assume the role of parent if necessary.

Parole The conditional release of an inmate before his or her sentence has expired.

Parole Board A body of appointed civilians that decides whether a convict should be granted conditional release before the end of his or her sentence.

Parole Contract An agreement between the state and the offender that establishes the conditions of parole.

Parole Grant Hearing A hearing in which the entire parole board or a subcommittee reviews information, meets the offender, and hears testimony from relevant witnesses to determine whether to grant parole.

Parole Guidelines Standards that are used in the parole process to measure the risk that a potential parolee will recidivate.

Part I Offenses The most serious crimes recorded by the FBI in its Uniform Crime Report. Part I offenses include murder, rape, robbery, aggravated assault, burglary, larceny, and motor vehicle theft.

Part II Offenses All crimes recorded by the FBI that do not fall into the category of Part I offenses. These crimes include both misdemeanors and felonies.

Partisan Elections Elections in which candidates are affiliated with and receive support from political parties.

Patriot Act Legislation passed in the wake of the September 11, 2001, terrorist attacks that greatly expanded the ability of government agents to monitor and apprehend suspected terrorists.

Patronage System A form of corruption in which the political party in power hires and promotes police officers and receives job-related "favors" in return.

Penitentiary An early form of correctional facility that emphasized separating inmates from society and from each other.

Peremptory Challenges *Voir dire* challenges to exclude potential jurors from serving on the jury without any supporting reason or cause.

Petition The document filed with a juvenile court alleging that the juvenile is a delinquent or a status offender and requesting that the court either hear the case or transfer it to an adult court.

Phishing Sending an unsolicited e-mail that falsely claims to be from a legitimate organization in an attempt to acquire sensitive information from the recipient.

Plaintiff The person or institution that initiates a lawsuit in civil court proceedings by filing a complaint.

Plain View Doctrine The legal principle that objects in plain view of a law enforcement agent who has the right to be in a position to have that view may be seized without a warrant and introduced as evidence.

Plea Bargaining The process by which the accused and the prosecutor work out a mutually satisfactory conclusion to the case, subject to court approval.

Police Corruption The abuse of authority by a law enforcement officer for personal gain.

Police Subculture The values and perceptions that are shared by members of a police department and, to a certain extent, by all law enforcement agents.

Policy A set of guiding principles designed to influence the behavior and decision making of police officers.

Positivism A school of the social sciences that sees criminal and delinquent behavior as the result of biological, psychological, and social forces.

Precedent A court decision that furnishes an example or authority for deciding subsequent cases involving similar facts.

Predisposition Report A report prepared during the disposition process that provides the judge with relevant background material to aid in the disposition decision.

Preliminary Hearing An initial hearing in which a magistrate decides if there is probable cause to believe that the defendant committed the crime with which he or she is charged.

Preponderance of the Evidence The degree of proof required in a civil case. In general, this requirement is met when a plaintiff proves that a fact more likely than not is true.

Prescription Drugs Medical drugs that require a physician's permission for purchase.

Presentence Investigative Report An investigative report on an offender's background that assists a judge in determining the proper sentence.

Pretrial Detainees Individuals who cannot post bail after arrest and are therefore forced to spend the time prior to their trial incarcerated in jail.

Pretrial Diversion Program An alternative to trial offered by a judge or prosecutor, in which the offender agrees to participate in a specified counseling or treatment program in return for withdrawal of the charges.

Preventive Detention The retention of an accused person in custody due to fears that she or he will commit a crime if released before trial.

Prisoner Reentry A corrections strategy designed to prepare inmates for a successful return to the community and to reduce their criminal activity after release.

Prison Gang A group of inmates who band together within the corrections system to engage in social and criminal activities.

Prisonization The socialization process through which a new inmate learns the accepted norms and values of the prison culture.

Prison Programs Organized activities for inmates that are designed to improve their physical and mental health, provide them with vocational skills, or simply keep them busy while incarcerated.

Prison Segregation The practice of separating inmates based on a certain characteristic, such as race or ethnicity.

Private Prisons Correctional facilities operated by private corporations instead of the government and, therefore, reliant on profits for survival.

Private Search Doctrine The legal principle that a private search eliminates an owner's reasonable expectation of privacy regarding the object searched.

Private Security The provision of policing services by private companies or individuals.

Proactive Arrests Arrests that occur because of concerted efforts by law enforcement agencies to respond to a particular type of criminal or criminal behavior.

Probable Cause Reasonable grounds to believe the existence of facts warranting certain actions, such as the search or arrest of a person.

Probation A criminal sanction in which a convict is allowed to remain in the community rather than be imprisoned.

Probationary Period A period of time at the beginning of a police officer's career during which she or he may be fired without cause.

Problem-Oriented Policing A policing philosophy that requires police to identify potential criminal activity and develop strategies to prevent or respond to that activity.

Problem-Solving Courts Lower courts that have jurisdiction over one specific area of criminal activity, such as illegal drugs or domestic violence.

Procedural Criminal Law Law that governs procedures for investigating and prosecuting crimes.

Procedural Due Process A provision in the Constitution that states that the law must be carried out in a fair and orderly manner.

Professionalism Adherence to a set of values that show a police officer to be of the highest moral character.

Professional Model A style of policing advocated by August Vollmer and O. W. Wilson that emphasizes centralized police organizations, increased use of technology, and the use of regulations and guidelines to limit police discretion.

Property Bonds An alternative to posting bail in cash, in which the defendant gains pretrial release by providing the court with property as assurance that he or she will return for trial.

Prosecutorial Waiver A procedure used in situations where the prosecutor has discretion to decide whether a case will be heard by a juvenile court or an adult court.

Psychoanalytic Theory Sigmund Freud's theory that attributes our thoughts and actions to unconscious motives.

Psychology The scientific study of mental processes and behavior.

Public Defenders Court-appointed attorneys who are paid by the state to represent defendants who cannot afford private counsel.

Public Order Crime Behavior that has been labeled criminal because it is contrary to shared social values, customs, and norms.

Public Prosecutors Individuals, acting as trial lawyers, who initiate and conduct cases in the government's name and on behalf of the people.

Q

Qualified Immunity A doctrine that shields law enforcement officers from damages for civil liability so long as they have not violated an individual's statutory or constitutional rights.

R

Racial Profiling The practice of targeting people for police action based solely on their race, ethnicity, or national origin.

Racketeering The criminal action of being involved in an organized effort to engage in illegal business transactions.

Random Patrol A patrol strategy that relies on police officers monitoring a certain area with the goal of detecting crimes in progress or preventing crime due to their presence. Also known as *general* or *preventive patrol*.

Reactive Arrests Arrests that come about as part of the ordinary routine of police patrol and responses to calls for service.

Real Evidence Evidence that is brought into court and seen by the jury, as opposed to evidence that is described for a jury.

"Real Offense" The actual offense committed, as opposed to the charge levied by a prosecutor as the result of a plea bargain.

Reasonable Force The degree of force that is appropriate to protect the police officer or other citizens and is not excessive.

Rebuttal Evidence given to counteract or disprove evidence presented by the opposing party.

Recidivism The act of committing a new crime after having been punished for a previous crime by being convicted and sent to jail or prison.

Recklessness The state of being aware that a risk does or will exist and nevertheless acting in a way that consciously disregards this risk.

Recruitment The process by which law enforcement agencies develop a pool of qualified applicants from which to select new employees.

Referral The notification process through which a law enforcement officer or other concerned citizen makes the juvenile court aware of a juvenile's unlawful or unruly conduct.

Regulation A governmental order or rule having the force of law that is usually implemented by an administrative agency.

Rehabilitation The philosophy that society is best served when wrongdoers are provided the resources needed to eliminate their criminal behavior.

Reintegration A goal of corrections that focuses on preparing the offender for a return to the community unmarred by further criminal behavior.

Relative Deprivation The theory that inmate aggression is caused when freedoms and services that the inmate has come to accept as normal are decreased or eliminated.

Release on Recognizance (ROR) A judge's order that releases an accused person from jail with the understanding that he or she will return of his or her own will for further proceedings.

Relevant Evidence Evidence tending to make a fact in question more or less probable than it would be without the evidence. Only relevant evidence is admissible in court.

Repeat Victimization The theory that certain people and places are more likely to be subject to repeated criminal activity and that past victimization is a strong indicator of future victimization.

Residential Treatment Programs A government-run facility for juveniles whose offenses are not deemed serious enough to warrant incarceration in a training school.

Response Time The speed with which calls for service are answered.

Restitution Monetary compensation for damages done to the victim by the offender's criminal act.

Restorative Justice An approach to punishment designed to repair the harm done to the victim and the community by the offender's criminal act.

Retribution The philosophy that those who commit criminal acts should be punished for breaking society's rules to the extent required by just deserts.

Revocation The formal process that follows the failure of a probationer or parolee to comply with the terms of his or her probation or parole, often resulting in the offender's incarceration.

Risk Assessment A method for determining the likelihood that an offender will be involved in future wrongdoing.

Robbery The act of taking property from another person through force, threat of force, or intimidation.

Rule of Four A rule of the United States Supreme Court that the Court will not issue a writ of *certiorari* unless at least four justices approve of the decision to hear the case.

Rule of Law The principle that the rules of a legal system apply equally to all persons, institutions, and entities— public or private—that make up a society.

S

Search The process by which police examine a person or property to find evidence that will be used to prove guilt in a criminal trial.

Searches and Seizures A legal term, as found in the Fourth Amendment to the U.S. Constitution, that generally refers to the search for and confiscation of evidence by law enforcement agents.

Searches Incidental to Arrests Searches for weapons and evidence that are conducted on persons who have just been arrested.

Search Warrant A written order, based on probable cause and issued by a judge or magistrate, commanding that police officers or criminal investigators search a specific person, place, or property to obtain evidence.

Secondary Policing The situation in which a police officer accepts off-duty employment from a private company or government agency.

Security Threat Group (STG) A group of three or more inmates who engage in activity that poses a threat to the safety of other inmates or the prison staff.

Seizure The forcible taking of a person or property in response to a violation of the law.

Self-Defense The legally recognized privilege to protect one's self or property from injury by another.

Self-Reported Surveys Methods of gathering crime data that rely on participants to reveal and detail their own criminal or delinquent behavior.

Sentencing Discrimination A situation in which the length of a sentence appears to be influenced by a defendant's race, gender, economic status, or other factor not directly related to the crime he or she committed.

Sentencing Disparity A situation in which those convicted of similar crimes do not receive similar sentences.

Sentencing Guidelines Legislatively determined guidelines that judges are required to follow when sentencing those convicted of specific crimes.

Separate Confinement A nineteenth-century penitentiary system developed in Pennsylvania in which inmates were kept separate from each other at all times, with daily activities taking place in individual cells.

Sequestration The isolation of jury members during a trial to ensure that their judgment is not tainted by information other than what is provided in the courtroom.

Sex Offender Notification Law Legislation that requires law enforcement authorities to notify people when convicted sex offenders are released into their neighborhood or community.

Sexual Assault Forced or coerced sexual intercourse (or other sexual acts).

Sexual Harassment A repeated pattern of unwelcome sexual advances and/or obscene remarks. Under certain circumstances, sexual harassment is illegal and can be the basis for a civil lawsuit.

Sheriff The primary law enforcement officer in a county, usually elected to the post by a popular vote.

Shock Incarceration A short period of incarceration that is designed to deter further criminal activity by "shocking" the offender with the hardships of imprisonment.

Social Conflict Theories Theories that view criminal behavior as the result of class conflict.

Social Disorganization Theory The theory that deviant behavior is more likely in communities where social institutions such as the family, schools, and the criminal justice system fail to exert control over the population.

Socialization The process through which a police officer is taught the values and expected behavior of the police subculture.

Social Process Theories Theories that consider criminal behavior to be the predictable result of a person's interaction with his or her environment.

Social Reality of Crime The theory that criminal laws are designed by those in power to help them keep power at the expense of those who do not have power.

Sociology The study of the development and functioning of groups of people who live together within a society.

Spam Bulk e-mails, particularly of commercial advertising, sent in large quantities without the consent of the recipient.

Split Sentence Probation A sentence that consists of incarceration in a prison or jail, followed by a probationary period in the community.

Stalking The criminal act of causing fear in a person by repeatedly subjecting that person to unwanted or threatening attention.

Stare Decisis (pronounced ster-ay dih-*si-ses*). A legal doctrine under which judges are obligated to follow the precedents established in prior decisions.

Status Offender A juvenile who has engaged in behavior deemed unacceptable for those under a certain statutorily determined age.

Statutes of Limitations Laws limiting the amount of time prosecutors have to bring criminal charges against a suspect after the crime has occurred.

Statutory Law The body of law enacted by legislative bodies.

Statutory Rape A strict liability crime in which an adult engages in a sexual act with a minor.

Stop A brief detention of a person by law enforcement agents for questioning.

Strain Theory The assumption that crime is the result of frustration felt by individuals who cannot reach their financial and personal goals through legitimate means.

Street Gang A group of people, usually three or more, who share a common identity and engage in illegal activities.

Stressors The aspects of police work and life that lead to feelings of stress.

Strict Liability Crimes Certain crimes, such as traffic violations, in which the defendant is guilty regardless of her or his state of mind at the time of the act.

Subculture A group exhibiting certain values and behavior patterns that distinguish it from the dominant culture.

Substantial-Capacity Test (ALI/MPC) Test A test for the insanity defense that states that a person is not responsible for criminal behavior when he or she "lacks substantial capacity" to understand that the behavior is wrong or to know how to behave properly.

Substantive Criminal Law Law that defines crimes and punishments.

Substantive Due Process The constitutional requirement that laws must be fair and reasonable in content and must further a legitimate governmental objective.

Supermax Prison A highly secure, freestanding correctional facility—or such a unit within a correctional facility—that manages offenders who would pose a threat to the security and safety of other inmates and staff members if housed in the general inmate population.

Supremacy Clause A clause in the U.S. Constitution establishing that federal law is the "supreme law of the land" and shall prevail when in conflict with state constitutions or statutes.

Surveillance The close observation of a person or group by government agents, in particular to uncover evidence of criminal or terrorist activities.

Suspended Sentence A judicially imposed condition in which an offender is sentenced after being convicted of a crime, but is not required to begin serving the sentence immediately.

System A set of interacting parts that, when functioning properly, achieve a desired result.

T

Technical Violation An action taken by a probationer or parolee that, although not criminal, breaks the terms of probation or parole as designated by the court.

Terrorism The use or threat of violence to achieve political objectives.

Testimony Verbal evidence given by witnesses under oath.

Testosterone The hormone primarily responsible for the production of sperm and the development of male secondary sex characteristics, such as the growth of facial and pubic hair and the change of voice pitch.

Theory An explanation of a happening or circumstance that is based on observation, experimentation, and reasoning.

Therapeutic Community (TC) A group-based form of substance abuse treatment that focuses on identifying the underlying social and psychological problems of abusers to help change negative behaviors linked to drug and alcohol addiction.

Time Served The period of time a person denied bail (or unable to pay it) has spent in jail prior to his or her trial.

Total Institution An institution, such as a prison, that provides all of the necessities for existence to those who live within its boundaries.

Trace Evidence Evidence such as a fingerprint, blood, or hair found in small amounts at a crime scene.

Training School A correctional institution for juveniles found to be delinquent or status offenders.

Trial Courts Courts in which most cases begin and in which questions of fact are examined.

Trojan Malware that appears to be beneficial to a computer user, but causes damage to the computer when it is installed and activated. (Also known as a Trojan horse.)

True Threat An act of speech or expression that is not protected by the First Amendment because it is done with the intention placing a specific victim or group of victims in fear of unlawful violence.

Truth-in-Sentencing Law Legislative attempts to ensure that convicts will serve approximately the terms to which they were initially sentenced.

 U

Uniform Crime Reports (UCR) An annual report compiled by the FBI to give an indication of criminal activity in the United States.

U.S. Customs and Border Protection (CBP) The federal agency responsible for protecting U.S. borders and facilitating legal trade and travel across those borders.

U.S. Immigration and Customs Enforcement (ICE) The federal agency that enforces the nation's immigration and customs laws.

U.S. Secret Service A federal law enforcement organization with the primary responsibility of protecting the president, the president's family, the vice president, and other important political figures.

 V

Venire The group of citizens from which the jury is selected.

Verdict A formal decision made by the jury.

Victim Any person who suffers physical, emotional, or financial harm as the result of a criminal act.

Victim Impact Statement (VIS) A statement to the sentencing body (judge, jury, or parole board) in which the victim is given the opportunity to describe how the crime has affected her or him.

Victim Survey A method of gathering crime data that directly surveys participants to determine their experiences as victims of crime.

Virus A computer program that can replicate itself and interfere with the normal use of a computer. A virus cannot exist as a separate entity and must attach itself to another program to move through a network.

Visa Official authorization allowing a person to travel to and within the issuing country.

Voir Dire The preliminary questions that the trial attorneys ask prospective jurors to determine whether they are biased or have any connection with the defendant or a witness.

Voluntary Manslaughter A homicide in which the intent to kill was present in the mind of the offender, but malice was lacking.

 W

Warden The prison official who is ultimately responsible for the organization and performance of a correctional facility.

Warrantless Arrest An arrest made without a warrant for the action.

White-Collar Crimes Nonviolent crimes committed by business entities or individuals to gain a personal or business advantage.

Widen the Net The increase in the number of citizens who are under the control and surveillance of the American corrections system.

Work Release Program Temporary release of convicts from prison for purposes of employment. The offenders may spend their days on the job, but must return to the correctional facility at night and during the weekend.

Worm A computer program that can automatically replicate itself and interfere with the normal use of a computer. A worm does not need to be attached to an existing file to move from one network to another.

Writ of Certiorari A request from a higher court asking a lower court for the record of a case. In essence, the request signals the higher court's willingness to review the case.

Wrongful Convictions The conviction, either by verdict or by guilty plea, of a person who is factually innocent of the charges.

Y

Youth Gang A self-formed group of youths with several identifiable characteristics, including a gang name and other recognizable symbols, a geographic territory, and participation in illegal activities.

Name Index

A

Abbott, Jack Henry, 467
Aborn, Richard, 25
Abraham, Henry J., 124
Abram, Karen, 504
Adams, Sharyn, 397
Adesman, Andrew, 502
Adler, Freda, 89
Agnew, Robert, 48
Aizer, Anna, 517
al-Adanani, Abu Mohammed, 26
Alito, Samuel, 377
Allen, Josh, 358
Allenbaugh, Mark H., 408
Alpert, Geoffrey P., 139
Alschuler, Albert W., 306, 307
Alvarez, W., 197
Amendola, Karen L., 176
Andenaes, Johannes, 74
Anderson, Brian P., 270
Anderson, Dale, 227
Anderson, Elijah, 47–48
Anderson, James M., 291
Anderson, Jami L., 353
Anderson, Michelle J., 333
Anglin, Deirdre, 198
Appelbaum, Binyamin, 481
Apuzzo, Matt, 26, 144, 153, 538, 543, 544, 545, 551
Arbuthnot, Jack, 373
Aristotle, 101
Armstrong, Martin, 417
Arter, Michael L., 196

B

Bachman, Ronet, 476
Bacon, John, 257
Baldus, David C., 367, 382
Ball, Jeremy, 298
Bandyopadhyay, Siddhartha, 286
Barbee, Andy, 416
Barchenger, Stacey, 326
Barnes, J. C., 137
Barnes, Roger C., 380
Barrett, Devlin, 27
Barrett, Steven R. H., 548
Barry, Ellen, 5

Barthe, Emmanuel P., 140, 141
Bartollas, Clemens, 151, 459, 471, 476
Barua, Vidisha, 378
Baskin, Deborah, 181
Basu, G., 43
Battles, Lindsey, 468
Bauerlein, Valerie, 25
Baumer, Eric P., 77
Bayens, Gerald, 395
Beattie, James M., 425
Beccaria, Cesare, 40–41
Beck, Allen J., 437, 475
Becker, Howard S., 52, 57
Becker, Ronald F., 206
Bedard, Kelly, 475
Beh, Hazel Glenn, 203
Behrens, Angela, 449
Beitsch, Rebecca, 358
Belkin, Douglas, 25
Belluck, Pam, 43
Benner, Katie, 551
Benner, Laurence, 289, 309
Bennett, Brian, 443
Benoit, Carl A., 225
Ben-Porath, Yossef S., 146
Benson, Michael L., 547, 549
Bentham, Jeremy, 354
Berdejo, Carlos, 270
Bergeron, Claire, 50
Bergeron, Mark, 62
Berkson, Larry C., 375
Berman, Mark, 200, 383
Berner, David, 60
Bernstein, David, 78
Berry-Jester, Anna Maria, 62
Best, Arthur, 335
Bhati, Avinash Singh, 355
Bianchi, Herman, 5
Bidgood, Jess, 287
Bieler, Sam, 46
Biggs, David C., 107
Bilby, Charlotte, 481
Bittner, Egon, 135
Black, Julia L., 371
Blackstone, Erwin A., 442
Blakely, Curtis R., 442
Blinder, Alan, 17

Blitz, Cynthia, 476
Bloom, Barbara, 475, 476
Bloomberg, Michael, 121
Blount, Roy, 4
Blumberg, Abraham S., 277, 278
Blumberg, Mark, 79
Blumstein, Alfred, 428, 481
Bogard, David, 448
Bolton, Kathy A., 372
Bookman, Jay, 542
Boots, Denise Paquette, 380
Bopp, William J., 139
Borelli, Frank, 196
Bossler, Adam M., 529, 533, 534, 537
Bostaph, Lisa, 298
Bostock, Mike, 247
Bostwick, Lindsay, 397
Bouie, Jamelle, 247
Bouza, Anthony V., 201
Bowker, Lee H., 463
Bowley, Graham, 345
Bowling, Julia, 189, 380
Bowman, Frank O., III, 354
Boyd, Dan, 383
Boyle, Douglas J., 412
Bozelko, Chandra, 461
Bozeman, William P., 200
Braccialarghe, Randolph, 293
Bradbury, Steven G., 542
Braiden, Chris, 140
Brandl, Steven G., 195
Bratton, William, 137
Breyer, Stephen, 383
Brezina, Timothy, 48
Bridges, George S., 509
Brockway, Zebulon, 427
Broeder, David W., 339
Bronner, Ethan, 242
Brooke-Eisen, Lauren, 189
Brooks, David, 437
Brown, Charles, 188
Brown, Delores, 149
Brown, Elizabeth Nolan, 473
Brown, Emma, 518
Brown, Jasmine, 362
Brown, Robert A., 151
Bruck, David, 374

Brunner, Hans G., 42
Bulman, Philip, 184, 412
Bumphus, Vic W., 442
Burchfield, Keri B., 56
Burgess, Ernest, 46
Burke, Kimberly S., 357
Burruel, Armand R., 472
Burt, Callie H., 42
Burton, Derwyn, 291
Busch, Jason, 136
Butler, Paul, 25
Buzawa, Eve S., 89
Bynum, Ross, 322
Byrne, James M., 416

C

Cabranes, José A., 363
Cadoret, Remi J., 42
Cain, Calli M., 462
Caldwell, H. Mitchell, 309
Call, Corey, 332
Callimachi, Rukmini, 535
Calvert, Scott, 85
Campbell, Rebecca, 397
Campoy, Ana, 25
Canada, Kelli E., 91
Canterbury, Chuck, 175
Cantor, David, 71, 75
Caplan, Joel M., 409
Carlson, Joseph R., 475
Carlson, Peter M., 431, 432, 468
Carr, Craig L., 119
Carroll, Leo, 464
Carter, Steven, 192
Casey, Pamela M., 402
Casper, Jonathan D., 293
Caspi, Avshalom, 43
Cassell, Paul G., 124, 373
Castor, Jane, 151
Catalano, Shannan, 89
Cataldo, Joseph, 254
Cathey, Dan, 186
Cerchiai, Brian, 181
Cevallos, Danny, 117
Chaiken, Jan, 356
Chaiken, Marcia, 356
Chambers, Jennifer, 126
Chang, Cindy, 164
Chase, Monique, 272, 273
Cheeseman, Kelly A., 472
Chen, Edward M., 273
Chen, Stephanie, 533
Chenoweth, James H., 145
Chesney-Lind, Meda, 89, 476, 500
Chishti, Muzaffar, 50
Chuan-Yun, Li, 58

Chyn, Eric, 46
Clair, Matthew, 367
Clark, Daniel W., 197
Clark, John W., III, 327
Clark, Patricia M., 356
Clark, Valerie, 83, 475
Clear, Todd R., 356, 372, 399, 404, 405, 407, 413, 428, 432, 447, 460, 468
Clegg, Roger, 449
Clemmer, Donald, 458
Clifford, Mary, 416
Clifford, Stephanie, 344, 535
Coffee, John C., 369
Cohen, Larry, 82, 83
Cohen, Laurie P., 538
Cohen, Neil P., 398
Cohen, Richard, 113
Cohen, Sarah, 59, 153
Cohen, Thomas H., 270
Colangelo, Anthony J., 259
Cole, Dave, 227
Cole, George F., 372, 399, 404, 407, 413, 428, 432, 447, 460, 468
Cole, Simon A., 182
Collier, Linda J., 237
Collinson, Stephen, 545
Comino, Stefano, 83
Connor, Tracy, 333, 384
Contardo, Jeanne B., 462
Cooper, Jonathan J., 407
Coppola, Michele, 143, 182
Cordner, Gary W., 179
Cornell, Dewey G., 503
Corsaro, Nicholas, 193
Cottrell, Leonard S., 47
Covington, Stephanie, 475, 476
Cox, Steven M., 150
Cramer, Maria, 332
Crip, Clair A., 469
Cronin, James M., 181
Crowe, Raymond R., 42
Crump, Catherine, 230
Cullen, Francis T., 48
Cuniff, Mark, 447
Cunningham, John P., 376
Cunningham, Terrence, 175
Currie, Janet, 505

D

Dale, Maryclaire, 473
D'Alessio, Stewart J., 201
Darley, John M., 354
Davey, Monica, 83
David, Kenneth Culp, 173
Davis, Julie H., 368
Davis, Kenneth C., 301

Davis, Lois M., 461
Davis, Richard, 269
Davis, Samuel, 493
Dawson, Jim, 184
Deja, Daniel R., 269
del Carmen, Rolando V., 218, 223, 235, 236, 241
DeLisi, Matt, 465
DelValle, Lauren, 292
DeMichele, Matthew, 415
Dempsey, John S., 149, 153, 176, 186, 195, 202, 206, 541
Dennis, Cindy-Lee, 43
deVuono-Powell, Saneta, 478
Dewan, Shaila, 297, 328, 394, 417
Diamond, John L., 105
Dieckman, Duane, 188
Dienst, Jonathan, 201
DiIulio, John J., 84, 431, 432, 443, 467
Dolan, Maura, 384
Dollar, Cindy Brooks, 50
Donavan, Pat, 197
Donger, Rand D., 87
Donlon, Rosalie L., 528
Donner, Christopher, 202
Doob, Anthony N., 439
Dorn, Tom Van, 238
Douglas-Gabriel, Danielle, 462
Downing, Michael, 143
Downs, Ray, 122
Doyle, Joseph J., Jr., 517
Dressler, Joshua, 117
Drury, Alan J., 465
Duff, H. Wayne, 207
Duncan, Martha Grace, 498
Dunham, Roger G., 139
Durkheim, Emile, 48
Durose, Matthew, 234
Duwe, Grant, 44, 475

E

Eckholm, Erik, 103, 309, 343, 384
Egan, Timothy, 61
Ehrenfreund, Max, 247
Ehrlich, Isaac, 355
Eisen, Lauren-Brooke, 380
Eisenstein, James, 277
Eitle, David, 201
Elek, Jennifer K., 402
Elinson, Zusha, 86, 184, 204
Ellis, Reggie, 271
Ember, Sydney, 345
Emshwiller, John R., 518
Engel, Robin S., 193
Enker, Arnold N., 119
Enright, Shellie, 62

Epperson, Matthew W., 91
Epstein, Richard A., 331
Erez, Edna, 373
Erisman, Wendy, 462
Erosheva, Elena A., 54
Evans, Tim, 345

F

Fachner, George, 192
Fagan, Jeffrey, 247
Fahim, Kareem, 369
Fahy, Stephanie, 413
Fairbanks, Phil, 180
Farrington, David P., 504
Fazel, Seena, 90
Feeley, Malcolm, 277
Feinberg, Joel, 104
Feinman, Clarice, 368
Felson, Marcus, 77, 82, 83
Felson, Richard B., 56
Fernandez, Manny, 197
Fessenden, Ford, 247
Fessler, Pam, 92
Fields, Carlton, 408
Fields, Gary, 400, 518
Fifield, Jen, 149
Figlio, Robert, 61
Finkelhor, David, 505
Finkle, Jim, 551
Fins, Deborah, 382
Flemming, Roy, 297
Fletcher, Connie, 177, 179
Fletcher, George P., 17
Foderaro, Lisa W., 299
Forst, Brian, 354
Forst, Linda S., 149, 153, 176, 186, 195, 202,
        206, 541
Foucault, Michel, 467
Fox, James Alan, 61, 84
Frana, John F., 54
Frandsen, Ronald J., 23
Frank, James, 151
Frederick, Bruce, 302
Freud, Sigmund, 45
Friedman, Lawrence M., 105, 319
Friedman, Richard, 59
Friedrichs, David O., 550
Frohmann, Lisa, 303
Frosch, Dan, 204
Fryer, Ronald G., Jr., 205
Fuller, Thomas, 63
Furdella, Julie, 86, 513

G

Gabrielli, William F., 42
Gaes, Gerald G., 442

Gardiner, John, 271
Gartner, Rosemary, 439
Gastwirth, Joseph L., 341
Gathman, Dave, 77
Gay, William, 178
Gehrke, Robert, 273
Geisler, Gregory, 442
Gelman, Andrew, 247
Gendreau, Paul, 427
George, Tracey E., 272
Gerard, Daniel W., 191
Gerber, Marisa, 396
Gershman, Bennett L., 288
Gershman, Jacob, 417
Gill, Charlotte, 51
Gilman, Amanda B., 506
Gilmore, Janet, 528
Ginsberg, Ruth Bader, 216, 383
Ginther, Andrew, 135
Giordano, Peggy C., 54
Givelber, Daniel, 17, 19
Glawe, Justin, 86
Glaze, Lauren E., 90, 446
Gobert, James J., 398
Goel, Vindu, 8
Goff, Phillip Atiba, 205
Goffard, Christopher, 276
Goffman, Erving, 457, 469
Goldberg, Rose Carmen, 376
Goldkamp, John S., 298
Goldman, Adam, 25, 538
Goldstein, Herman, 192
Goldstein, Joseph, 247, 551
Gonzales, Jessica, 416
Gonzalez, Victor, 507
Goode, Erica, 28, 484
Goodkind, Sara, 500
Goodman, Marc, 527–528
Goodnough, Abby, 483
Goolsakian, Gail A., 196
Gordon, Belinda Brooks, 481
Gordon, Stanford C., 270
Gorner, Jeremy, 203
Gottfredson, Denise C., 501
Gottfredson, Michael R., 54, 298, 504
Gottschalk, Marie, 406
Grace, Anthony A., 58
Graham, William R., Jr., 528
Grann, Martin, 90
Graves, Wallace, 194
Greene, Edith, 373
Greene, Jack R., 135
Greene, Judith A., 164
Greenman, Emma, 272, 273
Greenwood, Peter W., 179
Greytak, Emily A., 503

Grinberg, Emanuella, 292
Grisso, Thomas, 517
Guerin, Paul, 186
Guirguis, Michael, 198

H

Haarr, Robin N., 151
Haber, Lyn, 331
Haber, Ralph Norman, 331
Haberman, Cory P., 189
Haddad, Ron, 145
Hagan, Frank A., 79
Hahn, Paul H., 394
Hakin, Simon, 442
Haller, Mark H., 139
Hamilton, Alexander, 263
Hammel, Paul, 29
Hancox, Robert J., 52
Haney, Craig, 382, 465
Hannah, Larry, 368
Hanson, R. Karl, 481–482
Hanssen, Andrew F., 270
Harlan, John, Jr., 221
Harp, Derek, 535
Harrell, Erika, 89
Harress, Christopher, 463
Harrington, Lois H., 80
Harris, Gardiner, 368
Hart, Henry M., Jr., 105
Hart, Kevin, 273
Hartley, Carolyn C., 303
Hartley, Richard, 291
Harvell, Samantha, 439
Hassine, Victor, 478
Hastie, Reid, 330
Hawken, Angela, 403
Hawkins, J. David, 506
Healey, Jack, 92
Heath, Brad, 145, 231
Heaton, Paul, 291
Heinz, John, 15
Heinzmann, David, 203
Helland, Eric, 475
Herman, Susan, 81, 82
Hernstein, Richard J., 41
Hess, Karen M., 176, 181
Heumann, Milton, 306
Higham, Scott, 25
Hill, Karl G., 506
Hill, Lauretta, 146
Hinduja, Sameer, 533
Hinkel, Dan, 203
Hinkle, D. P., 146
Hinshaw, S'Lee Arthur, II, 510
Hipp, John R., 51
Hipple, Natalie Kroovand, 188

Hirschi, Travis, 52, 54, 504
Hirsh, Milton, 219
Hockenberry, Sarah, 499, 515
Hoffman, Jan, 71
Hofschneider, Anita, 103
Hogan, John, 268
Holcomb, Jayme W., 225
Holland, Jesse J., 243
Holleran, David, 366, 367, 428
Holley, Peter, 407
Holloway, Colin, 62
Holmes, Oliver Wendell, Jr., 101
Holt, Lucinda, 150
Holt, Thomas J., 529, 533, 534, 537
Horowitz, Ben, 299
Horowitz, Michael E., 459
Horowitz, M. J., 197
Horujko, Alan, 134
Huber, Gregory A., 270
Hudson, John, 160
Hullinghorst, Dickey Lee, 63
Humburg, Connie, 127
Humphreys, Keith, 86
Hundley, Kris, 127
Hundsdorfer, Beth, 337
Husak, Douglas N., 75
Hussain, Murtaza, 145
Hutchings, Barry, 42
Hutchinson, Virginia A., 448
Hutson, H. Range, 198

I

Ifill, Sherrilyn A., 273
Inciardi, James A., 59, 461
Ingold, John, 13
Ingraham, Christopher, 22
Irwin, John, 446, 458, 464
Isackson, Noah, 78
Izadi, Elahe, 60

J

Jacob, Herbert, 173, 277
Jaime, Michael H., 472
James, Doris J., 90, 446
Jany, Libor, 136, 152
Jennings, Wesley G., 202
Johnson, Brian, 367
Johnson, Donald, 181
Johnson, Eddie, 25
Johnson, Katherine A., 505
Johnson, Kevin, 83, 150, 479
Johnson, Richard R., 173
Johnson, Robert, 462
Johnston, Lloyd D., 60
Jonas, Steven, 75
Jones, Michael R., 298
Jordan, Miriam, 25

Jouvenal, Justin, 143
Joy, Peter A., 291

K

Kaltreider, N. B., 197
Kalven, Harry, 329
Kamp, Jon, 25
Kanapaux, William, 459
Kane, Robert J., 202
Kang-Brown, Jacob, 502
Kant, Immanuel, 353
Kaplan, John, 294, 326
Kappeler, Victor E., 79
Kappelman, Kristen, 174
Karberg, Jennifer C., 23, 446
Kassin, Saul M., 244
Katz, Charles M., 192, 203
Katz, Jack, 41
Kauder, Neal B., 371
Kelling, George L., 52, 137, 139, 176, 188,
       190, 191
Kennedy, Anthony, 104, 378, 498–499
Kennedy, David, 83
Kennedy, Randall L., 205
Kennedy, Robert F., 311
Kerman, Piper, 476
Keve, Paul W., 360, 395, 416
Khatiwada, Ishwar, 87
Kim, Young-Shin, 503
Kimball, Peter, 431
Kindy, Kimberly, 143, 144
King, Nancy J., 363
Kiss, Alex, 247
Kix, Paul, 344
Kleck, Gary, 137
Kleinfield, N. R., 39, 44
Kleinig, John, 19
Kling, Ryan, 458
Klinger, David, 205
Klockars, Carl B., 135, 137, 188, 398
Knox, George W., 465, 466
Kohfeld, C., 297
Kolata, Gina, 59
Konda, Srinivas, 462
Koniceck, Paul, 413
Kovacs, Eduard, 535
Kovandzic, Tomislav V., 380
Kowalyk, Apollo, 184
Kramer, John, 368
Kratcoski, Peter C., 463
Kreager, Derek A., 54
Kreig, Andrew, 272
Kreuz, L. E., 43
Kubrin, Chris E., 82, 83
Kubu, Bruce, 196
Kuppers, Terry, 436
Kurlychek, Megan, 10

Kurtz, Josh, 414
Kurzman, Charles, 26
Kuznia, Rob, 372, 440
Kwolek, Stephanie, 195
Kyriacou, Demetrious N., 198

L

Labrecque, Ryan M., 484
Labrecque, Stephen, 266
LaFave, Wayne R., 257
LaFond, John Q., 111
Lahman, Sean, 150
Laird, Lorelei, 278, 291
Lammers, Marre, 83
Land, Kenneth C., 380
Langton, Lynn, 77, 82, 234
Lanier, Mark M., 363
Larson, Matthew, 40
Latessa, Edward, 405
Laub, John H., 54, 504
Lauritsen, Janet L., 52, 77
La Vigne, Nancy, 438
Lawler, Joseph, 174
Leach, Molly Rowan, 358
Lee, Jacqueline, 363
Lee, Jason Vaughn, 141
Lee, Timothy B., 542
Lehren, Andrew W., 394, 539
Leo, Richard A., 243
Leventhal, Bennett, 503
Levine, James P., 324
Lewis, Becky, 501
Lewter, Judith E., 183
Lichtblau, Eric, 26, 144, 180, 551
Light, Miles, 63
Light, Stephen C., 463
Limber, Susan P., 503
Liping, Wei, 58
Liptak, Adam, 227, 298, 309,
       328, 499
Lisak, David, 80
Liu, Edward C., 544
Logan, Charles H., 428, 430
Lombardo, Lucien X., 468
Lombroso, Cesare, 41
Longan, Patrick Emery, 270
Longmore, Monica A., 54
Lonsway, Kim, 149, 151
Lord, Kenneth M., 122
Lord, Vivian B., 178
Louwagie, Pam, 204
Love, Hanna, 439
Lozano, Juan A., 472
Lozier, James E., 270
Luallen, Jeremy, 458
Ludwig, Edmund V., 269
Lui, Christina, 506

Lurigio, Arthur, 91, 416
Lynch, Mary, 415
Lynn, Teresa, 151

M

MacDonald, Heather, 193
MacDonald, John H., 51
MacLeish, Kenneth T., 45
Malega, Ro, 270
Manchak, Sarah, 402
Maniglio, Roberto, 91
Manikas, Peter, 15
Manning, Peter K., 138, 140
Manza, Jeff, 449
Marenin, Otwin, 194
Markowitz, Eric, 415
Marks, Alexandra, 474
Markus, David Oscar, 219
Marquart, James W., 472
Martin, Randy, 463
Martin, Susan Taylor, 127
Martinelli, Thomas J., 206
Martinson, Robert, 427, 428
Maruschak, Laura M., 475
Marx, Karl, 49
Mastrobuoni, Giovanni, 83
Mastrofski, Stephen D., 188
Mather, Kate, 208
Matsueda, Ross L., 54
Mauer, Marc, 475
Mayhew, Stephen, 183
McAnally, Helena M., 52
McBride, Duane C., 461
McCamey, William P., 150
McCannon, Bryan C., 286
McCarthy, Duncan J., 331
McCarthy, Justin, 356
McClellan, Chandler B., 127
McClelland, Gary, 504
McCrary, Gregg, 244
McCrary, Justin, 149
McCurley, Carl, 504
McDowell, David, 499
McGloin, Jean Marie, 45
McKay, Dan, 191
McKay, Henry D., 47
McKenzie, Roderic, 46
McKibben, Diana, 358
McKinley, James C., Jr., 322
McKirdy, Euan, 292
McLaughlin, Jenna, 145
McLaughlin, Joseph, 87
McMunigal, Kevin C., 291
Mears, Daniel P., 435, 462
Medina, Jennifer, 384
Mednick, Sarnoff A., 42
Meier, Robert, 88

Ménard, Kim S., 196
Menn, Joseph, 543
Meranze, Michael, 425
Merton, Robert K., 48
Metzl, Jonathan M., 45
Midgette, Greg, 403
Miller, Charles E., 173
Miller, Claud H., III, 363
Miller, Holly V., 291
Miller, Paul M., 80
Miller, R. L., 101, 448
Mitchell, Renée J., 189
Mnookin, Jennifer L., 244
Moffitt, Terrie, 54, 504
Mohler, Henry Calvin, 426
Monahan, Kathryn C., 502
Mooallem, Jon, 478
Moore, Jack, 534
Moore, Mark H., 139, 176, 191
Moore, Solomon, 368
Moran, Michael, 162
Morash, Merry, 151
Morato, Michelle, 441
Morin, Rich, 194
Morris, John Charles, 428
Morton-Bourgon, Kelly, 481–482
Moses, Marilyn C., 461
Mukherjee, Elora, 417
Mullen, Thomas A., 105
Muller, Eric L., 327
Mullings, Janet L., 472
Mullins, Harry J., 194
Mulvey, Edward P., 505
Mumford, Elizabeth A., 196
Murphy, Christopher K., 229
Murphy, Gerard R., 181
Murray, Jon, 92
Musu-Gillette, Lauren, 518
Myers, Bryan, 373
Myers, David G., 45, 57

N

Nagyk, Pamela S., 376
Nakaruma, Kiminori, 481
Nakashima, Ellen, 544
Nalla, M. K., 138
Natapoff, Alexandra, 319
Neilson, Susie, 484
Neilson, William S., 340
Nellis, Ashley, 355, 475, 505
Nelson, Janai S., 449
Neubauer, David W., 275, 296, 342
Newman, G. R., 138
Nicolo, Antonio, 83
Nijboer, Johannes F., 276
Nixon, Ron, 158
Noble, Rosevelt L., 363

Novak, Kenneth J., 151
Novogrod, James, 333

O

O'Connor, Jennifer M., 493
O'Connor, Patrick, 27
O'Connor, Sandra Day, 372
O'Keefe, Maureen L., 484
Ollove, Michael, 459
Olson, David E., 360
O'Reilly, Gregory W., 359
Orthmann, Christine Hess, 181
Ostrom, Brian J., 371
O'Sullivan, Julie R., 364
Oudekerk, Barbara A., 518
Owen, Barbara, 475, 476

P

Pacheco, Igor, 181
Packer, Herbert, 15, 16, 19, 287, 353
Page, Douglas, 435
Pager, Devah, 461
Palmer, Jennifer, 442
Palmer, Ted, 427
Palumbo, Dennis, 416
Park, Robert, 46
Parker, William, 406
Parks, Erika, 28
Parsons, Jim, 373
Patchin, Justin W., 533
Pate, Anthony M., 188
Pate, Tony, 188
Patrice, Joe, 345
Peak, Ken, 140, 141
Pearce, Matt, 341
Peel, Robert, 138, 141
Penko, Phil, 358
Pennington, Nancy, 330
Percival, Robert V., 319
Pérez-Peña, Richard, 25
Perkinson, Robert, 436
Perlroth, Nicole, 8, 9, 532
Perrin, L. Timothy, 331
Persky, H., 43
Persons, Vicci, 448
Peters, Heather L., 447
Petersilia, Joan, 179, 396, 412, 416, 438, 477
Peterson, Joseph, 181
Peterson, Ruth D., 87
Pfaff, John, 437, 439
Phillips, Dave, 30
Phillips, Mary T., 311
Pickett, Justin T., 354
Pinedo, Aris, 362
Pinizzotto, Anthony J., 173
Planty, Michael, 86
Pletcher, Mark J., 61

Pogrebin, Mark, 293
Pollock, Jocelyn M., 206
Pope, Carl E., 509
Porter, Nicole D., 404
Posner, Eric, 545–546
Potter, Gary W., 79
Pound, Roscoe, 255
Powell, Lewis F., 378
Pratt, C. E., 173
Preston, Julia, 235
Price, Byron Eugene, 428
Pridemore, William Alex, 87
Pryal, Katie Rose Guest, 345
Pulaski, Charles A., 382
Puzzanchera, Charles, 86, 499, 500, 513
Pyrooz, David C., 39, 505

Q

Queally, James, 5, 208
Quinney, Richard, 50
Quinsey, Vernon, 479

R

Rabin, Charles, 127
Rafter, Nicole Hahn, 50
Raghavanjan, Anita, 414
Rankin, Bill, 341
Rankin, Mark P., 408
Rashbaum, William K., 540
Ratcliffe, Jerry H., 188
Rathbone, Cristina, 471, 475
Redding, Richard E., 498, 512
Reed, Thomas J., 332, 333
Rehnquist, William, 219, 233
Reisig, Michael D., 372, 399, 404, 407, 413, 432, 447, 460, 468
Reiter, Keramet, 435
Resendez, MaryEllen, 481
Reyes, Jessica M., 383
Reyes, Jessica Wolpaw, 43–44
Rhode, Deborah L., 17
Rhodes, William, 356, 371
Rice, Phillip, 198
Riley, Kristine, 89
Ritter, Nancy, 137, 184, 403
Rivers, James E., 461
Roberts, John G., 231, 266
Robertson, Campbell, 24, 449
Robertson, James E., 464
Robertson, Jordan, 532
Robertson, Lindsay A., 52
Robinson, Paul H., 116, 354
Robles, Frances, 197
Roche, Sean Patrick, 354
Rodriguez, Robert D., 535
Roeder, Oliver, 189, 380
Roettger, Michael E., 51

Roman, John K., 46, 127
Rookey, Bryan D., 89
Rosario, Rubén, 304
Rosay, André B., 88, 278
Rose, R. M., 43
Rosenberg, Eli, 482
Rosenberg, Matthew, 539
Rosenbloom, Deborah D., 237
Rosenfeld, Richard, 191
Ross, Bob, 427
Ross, Janell, 247
Roth, Mitchell P., 138
Rowe, David C., 42
Ruback, R. Barry, 83
Rubin, Joel, 143
Ruddell, Rick, 466
Ruger, Todd, 231
Rule, Nicholas O., 365

S

St. John, Paige, 465, 473
Salinger, Lawrence, 550
Sampson, Robert J., 54, 504
Samuels, Julie, 438
Sanger, David E., 9, 532, 544
Santana, Rebecca, 497
Santora, Marc, 535
Saul, Josh, 247
Savage, Charlie, 543
Scalia, Antonin, 18, 238
Scaramella, Gene L., 150
Schack, Stephen, 178
Schaller, Barry R., 268
Schanzer, David, 26
Schell, Theodore, 178
Schirmer, Sarah, 475
Schmidt, Michael S., 242, 545
Schmitt, Eric, 26
Schnacke, Timothy R., 311
Schoenberg, Shira, 164
Schouten, Fredreka, 443
Schriever, Theresa Hsu, 344
Schroeder, Ryan D., 54
Schulhofer, Stephen J., 306
Schwaller, Kevin, 127
Schwartz, Heather L., 501
Schwartz, Jennifer, 89
Schwartz, John, 384
Schwirtz, Michael, 25, 447
Scott, David K., 270
Scott, Eric J., 177
Scullin, Sara, 447
Seagrave, Jayne, 141
Sedelmaier, Christopher M., 188
Seelye, Katharine Q., 59
Seffrin, Patrick M., 54
Seidler, Kelsey, 163

Seigfried-Spellar, Kathryn C., 529, 533, 534, 537
Seligman, Dan, 439
Sellin, Thorsten, 61
Serra, Joseph, 208
Shackford, Scott, 373
Shallwani, Pervaiz, 25, 27, 77
Shane, Scott, 26, 539
Shapiro, Lana, 502
Shapiro, Nina, 372
Shaw, Clifford R., 47
Shearer, John D., 426
Shelor, Ben, 416
Sheppard, Howard, 136
Sherman, Lawrence W., 62, 189, 190
Shi, Jing, 476
Shibani, Pervaiz, 85, 86
Shishkin, Philip, 27
Shornack, Lawrence L., 49
Shultz, Donald O., 139
Sibilla, Nick, 417
Sickmund, Melissa, 500, 517
Sidel, Robin, 529
Siegel, David, 254, 443
Siegel, Jane, 476
Siegel, Larry, 256, 289, 505
Sikes, Bryan L., 441
Silber, Rebecca, 411
Silberman, Lawrence H., 22
Simmons, David, 127
Simons, Ronald L., 42, 48, 87
Simpson, Sally S., 547, 549
Sinclair, Michael D., 341
Singer, Richard G., 111
Siprut, Joseph, 230
Skeem, Jennifer L., 402
Sklansky, David Alan, 152
Skogan, Wesley, 189
Skolnick, Jerome, 137, 277
Skolnick, Sam, 301
Slade, John, 75
Smallbone, Stephen, 528
Smith, Alison, 12, 103
Smith, Christopher R., 471
Smith, Cindy J., 461
Smith, K., 43
Smith, Mitch, 143, 203
Smykla, John Ortiz, 395
Snowden, Edward, 542, 543
Snyder, Howard, 504, 509, 517
Snyder-Joy, Zoann K., 416
Sommers, Ira, 181
Sontag, Deborah, 464
Sotomayor, Sonia, 238
Soulé, David A., 501
Soury, Lonnie, 201
Sousa, William, 191

Spahr, Lisa L., 181
Spinelli, Margaret, 43
Spohn, Cassia, 291, 366, 367, 428
Spotts, David J., 197
Spotts, Maia, 411
Spriggs, James F., II, 266
Stack, Liam, 208
Staff, Jeremy, 54
Stageberg, Paul, 413
Starr, Douglas, 244
Starr, Sonja B., 368
Steblay, Nancy K., 344
Steen, Sara, 509
Steffensmeier, Darrell, 368
Steinbach, Michael B., 26, 180
Steiner, Benjamin, 462
Steinhauer, Jennifer, 543
Stemen, Don, 302
Stempel, Jonathan, 125
Stetzer, William T., 288
Stevens, John Paul, 153
Stevenson, Bryan, 380
Stewart, Eric A., 48, 87
Stewart, Potter, 377
Stith, Kate, 363
Stoiloff, Stephanie, 181
Stolberg, Sheryl Gay, 287
Stolzenberg, Lisa, 201
Stoughton, Seth, 144
Stras, David R., 266
Streifel, Cathy, 368
Strom, Kevin, 163
Stroshine, Meghan S., 195
Strote, Jared, 198
Subramanian, Ram, 89, 411
Sullivan, Jennifer, 442
Sullivan, S. P., 477
Sullum, Jacob, 417
Sum, Andrew, 87
Sutherland, Edwin H., 51
Sutton, Randy, 202
Swanson, Jeffrey W., 39, 44, 90
Swatt, Marc L., 142
Swavola, Elizabeth, 89
Sweeten, Gary, 40, 505
Swift, Art, 60
Swisher, Raymond, 51

T

Taibbi, Matt, 372
Talbot, Margaret, 537
Tanger, Jason M., 331
Tannenbaum, Frank, 463
Taxy, Samuel, 438
Taylor, Bruce G., 196
Taylor, Ralph B., 191
Teachman, Ronald, 439

Teeters, Negley K., 425, 426
Tekin, Erdal, 127, 505
Telep, Cody W., 187
Teplin, Linda, 504
Teske, Raymond H. C., Jr., 380
Thomas, Clarence, 238
Thomas, Jason, 533
Thomas, Kyle J., 45, 498
Thompson, Cheryl W., 200
Thompson, Matthew B., 331
Thompson, Richard M., 12, 103
Tierney, John, 440
Tiffany, Lawrence P., 118
Tiffany, Mary, 118
Tiihonen, Jari, 43
Tittle, Charles, 88
Toliver, Jessica I., 181
Tonry, Michael, 393, 415, 438
Torres-Spelliscy, Ciara,
        272, 273
Torrey, E. Fuller, 178
Trask, Grover, 505
Treat, Lucinda K., 493
Truman, Jennifer L., 86
Trusock, Mark A., 268
Tsiaperas, Tasha, 195
Turner, George, 150
Turner, Susan, 396, 412
Tyler, Kimberly A., 505
Tyler, Tom, 200

U

Uchida, Craig D., 142
Uggen, Christopher, 449
Uhlman, Thomas, 297
Ulery, Bradford T., 331
Useem, Bert, 431, 463
Uviller, H. Richard, 240

V

Valencia, Milton J., 397
Valiente, Alexa, 362
Valiquette, Joe, 201
van den Haag, Ernest, 380
Van Kessel, Gordon, 276
van Wormer, Katherine Stuart, 151, 459,
        471, 476
Velman, Gerald F., 256
Veysey, Bonita M., 505
Vicini, James, 222
Vick, Kark, 185
Vieraitis, Lynne M., 380, 401
Vigod, Simone N., 43
Villa, Judi, 512
Violanti, John, 196, 197
Vitiello, Michael, 459
Vollmer, August, 146

W

Walker, Jeffrey T., 235
Walker, Mark, 291
Walker, Samuel, 139, 143, 175, 177, 425
Wall, David, 528
Wallenstein, Arthur, 444
Walsh, Paul, 118
Waltz, Jon R., 326
Wan, William, 258
Wang, Xia, 367
Ward, Cynthia, 127
Warner, Cody, 83
Warren, Patricia Y., 87
Warren, Roger K., 402
Weaver, Jay, 547
Weger, Richard E., 181
Weisburd, David, 187, 189, 247
Weisman, Jonathan, 543
Weismanjune, Jonathan, 543
Weiss, Debra C., 397
Weiss, Susan, 63
Welsh, Brandon C., 505
Welsh-Huggins, Andrew, 135
Welsh-Loveman, Jeremy, 439
Wertsch, Teresa Lynn, 151
Western, Bruce, 461, 478
Westly, William, 194
Wetzel, Dan, 333
Wheeler, Russell, 255
Whitcomb, Howard, 255
White, Byron, 289
White, Elizabeth K., 197
White, Michael D., 176, 192, 200, 202
White, Steven, 311
Widom, Cathy Spatz, 505
Williams, Keith, 366
Williams, Timothy, 22, 24, 25, 85, 143, 208,
        442, 484
Wilner, N., 197
Wilson, Bonnie, 413
Wilson, James Q., 15, 41, 52, 84, 137, 190,
        191, 355, 403
Wilson, John Paul, 365
Wilson, Michael, 25
Wilson, Reid, 85
Winsten, Jay, 10
Winter, Alix S., 367
Winter, Harold, 340
Winter, Tom, 333
Winterdyk, John, 466
Wolf, Robert V., 356
Wolfe, Scott E., 39
Wolff, Nancy, 476
Wolfgang, Marvin, 61, 503
Wood, Graeme, 403
Wood, Harlington, Jr., 269

Woodworth, George, 367, 382
Worden, Alissa P., 275
Wortley, Richard, 528
Wright, Emily M., 474, 475
Wright, John Paul, 48
Wright, Robin, 26
Wrightsman, Lawrence S., 244
Wrobleski, Henry M., 176
Wyllie, Doug, 63

X

Xizeng, Mao, 58

Y

Yager, Sarah, 475
Yoeman, Barry, 89
Yoffe, Emily, 125
Yoo, John, 542
Yoon, Albert H., 272
Young, Michelle Arciaga, 507
Yutchman, Noam, 270

Z

Zacharias, Fred C., 306
Zahn, Margaret A., 501

Zalman, Marvin, 360
Zamble, Edward, 479
Zamora, Ana, 384
Zapotosky, Matt, 25
Zeisel, Hans, 329
Zhang, Anian, 518
Zimbardo, Philip G., 45, 51
Zimmerman, Sherwood, 463
Zimring, Franklin, 444
Zimring, Franklin E., 84, 439, 444
Zraick, Karen, 369
Zuidema, Brandon V., 207

Subject Index

A

Abuse, child, 504–505
Accomplice liability, 111
Accountability, police
  administrative accountability, 202
  citizen oversight, 203
  citizen surveillance, 203
  internal disciplinary measures, 202
  liability, 203–204
  self-accountability, 202
  self-surveillance, 202–203
  supervisory accountability, 202
Acecard, 529
Acquittal, 321
Actus reus (guilty act), 107–108, 111
Adam Walsh Child Protection and Safety
  Act, 483
Addiction
  basics of, 57–58
  criminal model of, 59
  drug-crime relationship, 58–59
  enslavement theory of, 59
  medical model of, 59
Adjudicatory hearing, 514
Administrative accountability, 202
Administrative building assignment, 469
Administrative duties, of patrol officer,
  176–179
Administrative law, 103–104
Administrative leave, 175
Administrative sentencing
  authority, 360
Admission, 239
Adoption studies, 42–43
Adultery, 5–6
Adversary system, 276–277
  plea bargaining and, 307–309
Affidavit, 222
Affirmative action, hiring by law
  enforcement agencies, 148–149
Affirmative consent policies, 91
Affirmative defense, 336–337
African Americans
  biases in policing and, 204–206
  consequences of high incarceration
    rate and, 440–441
  crime and, 86–88
  death penalty and, 382

  gang membership, 506
  incarceration rate of, 29
  as judges, 272–273
  jury selection, 327–328
  juvenile arrests and, 508–509
  as law enforcement officers, 148–150,
    152–153
  murder rate and, 86
  poor relations with police, 141
  prison violence and, 464
  on probation, 396
  racial threat theory, 50–51
  risk of victimization, 83
  sentencing discrimination,
    366–368
  social conflict theory and, 50–51
  stops and, 234
Aftercare, 517
Age
  crime and, 84, 85, 504
  juveniles tried as adults and, 497
  of prison population, 458, 459
  risk of victimization and, 83
Age of onset, 504
Aggravated assault
  defined, 76
  by juveniles, 500
Aggravating circumstances, 364–365
Aggression, hormones and, 43
Aging out, 504
Albuquerque Police Department, 172, 173,
  174, 191, 203
Alcohol
  abuse by police officers, 196
  crime victimization and use of, 56
  deaths from misuse of, 74
  juvenile delinquency and, 504–505
Alcohol beverage control commission
  (ABC), 156
Alibi, 115
Alibi defense, 336–337
ALI/MPC test, 117
Allen Charge, 340
al Queda, crowdsourcing
  terrorism, 26
Alternate jurors, 329
Alternative sanctions, as form of
  punishment, 361

American Bar Association (ABA)
  defending the guilty, 289
  public defender caseload, 291
American Law Institute (ALI), 117
Ankle bracelet, 414
Anomie, 48
Anonymous, 533
Anti-Drug Abuse Act, 371
Antiterrorism and Effective Death Penalty
  Act (AEDPA), 540
Apologies, in restorative justice, 362
Appeals
  double jeopardy, 341–342
  habeas corpus, 344
  reasons for, 342
  steps in, 343
Appellate courts
  jurisdiction of, 259
  opinions of, 259
  state court system, 262–263
  U. S., 263, 264
Apple, encryption and national security
  issues, 551
Arraignment, 295, 305
Arrestee Drug Abuse Monitoring
  Program, 504
Arrests, 235–239
  authority to, 236
  compared to stop, 235, 236
  elements of, 235–236
  exigent circumstances, 237–238
  intent and, 235–236
  knock and announce rule, 238
  minority youths and, 508–509
  proactive, 189
  reactive, 189
  seizure or detention, 236
  understanding of, 236
  with a warrant, 236–238
  without a warrant, 238–239
Arrest warrant, 236–238
Arson, 8, 76
Aryan Brotherhood, 465, 466
Asian Americans
  crime and, 88
  as judges, 272–273
  as law enforcement officers, 148–150,
    152–153

Ask, tell, make (ATM) strategy, 144
Assault
    defined, 7
    gangs and, 506
    sentencing disparity, 367
    simple, 77
Assistant prosecutors, 286
Association, probable cause based on, 218
Association of American Universities
        (AAU), 70
Atlanta Police Department, 149–150
Attempt, 108
Attendant circumstances, 112–113
Attitude test, 509
Attorney-client privilege
    defense attorneys, 293–294
    defined, 293
    exceptions to, 294
Attorney general, 285
Attorneys. *See* Defense attorneys;
        Prosecutors
Auburn Prison, 426
Auburn system, 426
Authority
    delegation of, 176
    as element of arrest, 236
    of probation officer, 399–400
    use of force and, 197–200
Automatic License Plate Recognition
        (ALPR), 230
Automatic transfer, 511
Automobiles
    Automatic License Plate Recognition
        (ALPR) technology, 230
    containers within vehicle, 227–228
    high-tech cop cars, 140
    officers killed in automobile accidents,
        195–196
    patrol cars and reform era, 140
    pretextual stops, 227
    protective searches, 227
    searches of, 226–228
    warrantless searches of, 226–227

B

Background checks, 23
Bail
    average amounts, 296
    community safety and, 297
    defined, 296
    for-profit bail debate, 311
    guidelines, 296–297
    overcrowded jails and, 297
    posting, 297
    purpose of, 296
    reasonable, 296
    risk and, 296–297

    setting, 296–297
    ten percent cash bail, 298
    uncertainty and, 296
Bail bond agent, 297–298, 311
Bailiff, 274, 275
Bail Reform Act, 298–299
Bail tariffs, 296
Ballistics, 181
Ballot initiatives, 103
Baltimore Police Department, 139
Ban the box laws, 481
Battery, 7
Beats, 176
Bench trial, 320
Berkeley Police Department, 139
Beware program, 143
Beyond a reasonable doubt, 72
Bifurcated death penalty process, 377–378
Bigamy, 105
Big data, crime-fighting strategies and,
        142–143
Bill of attainder, 122
Bill of Rights. *See also* individual
        amendments
    defined, 123
    procedural safeguards and, 123–124
Biological theories of crime, 42–46
Biology, 42
Biometrics, 21
Black Guerrilla Family, 466
Blended threat, 529
Block officers, 468–469
Bloods, 466
Blue curtain, 194
Body armor, 195
Booking, 295
    Fifth Amendment and, 246
Boot camps, 413, 515, 516
Border Patrol, 158
    totality of circumstances test, 233
Boston Police Department, 138–139
    SARA Model of problem-oriented
        policing, 193
Botnets, 529
Boykin form, 308
Brady Handgun Violence Prevention Act, 23
Brady rule, 285
Brain, crime and, 43–44
Bribery, 201, 548
    during political era of policing, 139
Bridewell Place, 425
Broken window effect, 52
Bullying
    anti-bullying legislation, 503
    changing perspectives, 502–503
    cyberbullying, 502, 533
    defined, 502

Burden of proof, 72
Bureaucracy, 175
    courts as, 256
Bureau of Alcohol, Tobacco, Firearms and
        Explosives (ATF), responsibilities
        of, 14, 157, 161–162
Burglary
    defined, 8, 76
    sentencing disparity, 367
Burnout, 196–197
Business Software Alliance, 533

C

Calls for service, 177, 178
    cold calls for, 186
    hot calls for, 186
    911 technology, 187
    response time and efficiency, 186
Cameras, body-worn, 172–173
    accountability and, 202–203
    increased pressure from, 25
    releasing videos, 208
    use of, 25
Campus Sexual Violence Elimination
        Act, 71
Campus style, 434
Canada
    InSite heroin program, 60
    Ontario Domestic Assault Risk
        Assessment (ODARA), 62
Capital crime, 28
Capitalism, vs. Marxism, 49–50
Capital offenses, 72
Capital punishment. *See also* Death
        penalty
    defined, 374
    as form of punishment, 360
Case attrition, 301–304
Case citations, 35
Case law, 104
Caseload, probation officers, 400
Causation
    as element of crime, 112
    theory of criminology, 39
Cell block, 434
Cell phones
    search warrants and, 231
    tracking, 230–231
Center for Policing Equity, 204–205
Central Intelligence Agency (CIA), spying
        capabilities of, 539
Chain of command, police departments
        and, 175–176
Challenges for cause, 326
Charge to jury, 339
Charging conference, 339
Chastity requirement, 333

Chicago, murder rate in, 22
Chicago Police Department,
        139, 149
    crime reporting by, 77–78
Chicago school, 46
Child abuse, 505
Child neglect, 505
Children. *See also* Juveniles
    abuse of, 505
    infancy defense, 115
    life course theories of crime and
        childhood, 53–56
    neglect of, 505
    online child pornography, 9
    parens patriae, 493
Child savers, 493
China, Internet firewall, 536
Choice theory, 40–42
    death penalty and, 42
    public policy and, 42
Chronic 6 percent, 62, 503
Chronic offender, 61–62
Cincinnati Police Department, 139,
        150–151
Circuit judges, 101
Circumstantial evidence, 332
Citizen oversight, 203
City attorney, 285
Civil confinement, 483
Civil forfeiture, 417
Civil law
    burden of proof, 72
    compared to criminal law,
        71, 73
    defined, 71
    police liability and, 203–204
    preponderance of evidence, 72
    responsibility and, 71
Civil liability, 204
Civil liberties
    defined, 27
    homeland security and, 27
Civil Rights Act, 148
Civil rights violation, 205–206
Civil suits, double jeopardy, 342
Class, crime and, 86–88
Classical criminology, 40–41
Classification, of prisoners, 432
Clean Air Act, 548–549
Clearance rates
    cold cases and, 180–181
    declining, 180–181
Clerk of the court, 275
Closed-circuit television (CCTV)
        cameras, 230
Closing arguments, 338
Cloud computing, 537

Cocaine
    crack, 84
    crime trends and, 84
    use of, in United States, 56
CODIS, 183
Coercion
    confession and, 239
    false confessions and, 243–244
    inherent, 240
    Reid Technique, 244
Cold cases
    databases and cold hit, 183
    defined, 180–181
Cold hit, 183
Collaborative reform, 192
Collective incapacitation, 356
Columbine school shooting, 518
Commission on Law Observance and
        Enforcement, 139
Common law, 101
Community-based corrections, 15
Community corrections, 392–417
    cost of, 394
    defined, 393
    diversion, 393–394
    intermediate sanctions, 409–416
    justification for, 393–394
    low-cost alternative, 394
    number of people in, 393
    paradox of, 416
    probation, 395–403
    reintegration, 393
Community courts, 411
Community dispute resolution centers, 411
Community policing, 136
    collaborative reform, 192
    defined, 191
    historical perspective on, 141
    return to community, 191
Community service
    as form of punishment, 362
    provided by police, 177–178
Competency hearing, 117
Compliance, 549
Compressed workweek, 176
CompStat, 189
Computer-aided dispatch (CAD)
        systems, 187
Computer crime. *See* Cyber crimes
ConAgra Grocery Products, 104
Concealment, white-collar crime and, 548
Concurrence, 112
Concurrent jurisdiction, 257
Concurring opinions, 266
Conducted energy devices (CEDs), 200
Confessions
    attorney-client privilege and, 293–294

    coercion and, 239
    defined, 239
    false, 243–244
    recording, 244
    Reid Technique, 244
    as self-incrimination, 239
Confidential informant, 179
Conflict model, 6
Confrontation clause, 334
Congregate system, 426
Consensus model, 5–6
Consent
    electronic surveillance and, 229–230
    searches with, 225
Consent decree, 149
Consent searches, 225
Conspiracy, 114
    white-collar crime and, 548
Constitutional law, 102
Constitution of United States. *See also*
        specific amendments
    amending, 123–124
    arrests, 235–239
    Bill of Rights, 123–124
    choice of defense attorney, 289
    cruel and unusual punishment, 124
    double jeopardy, 124
    due process, 124–126
    excessive bail and fines, 124
    exclusionary rule, 219–220
    expanding, 124
    identification process and, 246
    interrogation process, 239–245
    juveniles and, 495–496
    Miranda warning, 239–243
    prisoners' rights, 472–473
    probable cause, 217–219
    public trial, 124
    reasonableness, 217
    right to lawyer, 124
    search and seizure, 220–231
    as source of American criminal law, 102
    speedy trial, 124
    stops and frisks, 232–235
    supremacy clause, 103
    Supreme Court as interpreter of,
        264–265
    unreasonable searches and seizures, 123
    warrants for searches, 123
    witness incrimination, 124
Constitutions, state, 102
Consumer fraud, 548
    as cyber crime, 530
Consumer Product Safety Commission
        (CPSC), 549
Continuity theory of crime, 54
Controlled Substances Act (CSA), 161

Control theory, 52
drug use and, 57
Coroner, 155
Corporate violence, 549
Corpus delicti (body of crime), 106–107, 112, 333
Correctional Offender Management Profiling for Alternative Sanctions (COMPAS), 62
Correctional officers, 467–473
becoming, 468
as dangerous job, 462
discipline, 467–468, 469–471
diversity and, 468
duties of, 468–469
female, 471–472
legitimate security interests, 471
malicious and sadistic standard, 471
rank of, 468
salary of, 468
sanctioning prisoners, 469–470
use of force, 470–471
Corrections
federalism and, 14–15
juvenile, 516–517
role in criminal justice system, 14–15
Corrections Corporation of America (CCA), 441, 442
Correlation, theory of criminology, 39
Corruption. *See* Police corruption
Cosby effect, 345
Counterterrorism
Antiterrorism and Effective Death Penalty Act (AEDPA), 540
civil liberties and, 27
Foreign Intelligence Surveillance Act (FISA), 540
foreign surveillance, 540, 544
fusion centers, 144
known wolves, 545
mass surveillance, 542–544
metadata collection, 542–544
Patriot Act, 541
public relations and, 145
Shared Responsibility Committees, 145
County attorney, 285
County sheriff, 12
Court martial, 259
Court reporters, 275
Courtroom work group, 274–277
adversary system, 276–277
docket, 269
formation of, 275
ritualized aggression vs. negotiators, 276
Courts
bureaucratic function, 256
community dispute resolution, 411

crime control function, 255–256
drug courts, 411
dual system of, 14
due process function, 255–256
federal court system, 259–260, 263–267
federalism and, 14
functions of, 255–256
jurisdiction of, 257–259
legitimacy of, 255
lie detection in, 268
problem-solving courts, 410–411
rehabilitation function, 256
specialty, 262
state court system, 260–263
Supreme Court, 263–267
work group in, 274–277
Courtyard style, 434
Crack cocaine, 84
sentencing and, 368
Credit-card fraud, 531, 535, 548
Crime(s). *See also* Crime theories; specific types of crimes
age and, 84, 85
attendant circumstances, 112–113
brain and, 43–44
causation, 112
class and, 86–88
classification of, 71–75
concurrence, 112
conflict model of, 6
consensus model of, 5–6
criminal act of, 107–108
cyber crime, 8–9
decline, 84–85
defined, 5, 6–7
degree of, 7, 72, 109–110
vs. deviance, 6
drop in crime rate, 20
drug-crime relationship, 58–59
drugs and, 22, 56–61
economy and, 84
elements of, 106–114
ethnicity and, 88
gangs and, 22
genetics and, 42–43
guns and, 22–23
harm, 113–114
homelessness and, 92
imprisonment and, 84, 85
income and, 87–88
mala in se, 73–75
mala prohibita, 73–75
measuring, 75–80
mental illness and, 44, 90–91
mental state and, 108–111
organized crime, 8

prevention of, 137
property crime, 7
psychology and, 45
public order crime, 8
race and, 86–88
seduction of, 41
seriousness of, and sentencing, 364
strict liability, 110–111
theories of (*See* Crime theories)
trends in, 84–92
types of, 7–9
victimless, 8
violent crime, 7
white-collar crime, 8
women and, 88–89
Crime control model, 19
compared to due process model, 20
courts and, 255–256
defined, 19
homeland security and, 19
overview of main concepts, 20
Crime in the United States, 76
Crime mapping, 189
Crime rate, 75
Crime registries, 483
Crime scene, forensics and, 181
Crime scene photographer, 121
Crime statistics
gangs and, 506
juveniles and, 499–500
Crime theories, 39–62
biological, 42–46
choice, 40–42
classical criminology, 40–41
life course, 53–56
positivism, 41
psychological, 42–46
rational choice, 41
role of, 39–40
social conflict, 49–51
social process, 51–53
sociological, 46–49
Crime Victims Fund, 358
Crime Victims' Rights Act (CVRA), 81, 307, 373, 409
Criminal court
defined, 14
dual court system, 259–260
Criminal harm, 104–105
Criminal justice
today, 19–28
wedding cake model of, 319
Criminal Justice Information Services Division, 173
Criminal justice process
as assembly line, 15–16
formal, 15–16

informal, 17
as system, 15–16
Criminal Justice Reform Act, 191
Criminal justice system, 9–16
compared to juvenile justice system, 513
courtroom work group, 274–277
crime control model, 19–20
defined, 9
discretion in, 17–18
due process model, 19–20
ethics and, 18–19
federal court system, 263–267
federalism and, 11–15
goals of, 10
judges in court system, 267–273
jurisdiction of, 257–259
maintaining justice, 9
medical model of, 256
process in, 15–16
protecting society, 10
purpose of, 9–10
state court system, 260–263
structure of, 11–16
trial and appellate courts, 259
Criminal law, 100–127
beyond a reasonable doubt, 72
burden of proof, 72
compared to civil law, 71, 73
defenses under, 115–122
development of American, 101–104
due process, 124–126
elements of crime, 106–114
goals of, 71
guilt and, 71
procedural, 122–126
purposes of, 104–106
substantive, 122
written sources of, 101–104
Criminal model of addiction, 59
Criminal trials. *See also* Trials
presumption of innocence, 322
privilege against self-incrimination,
321–322
role of jury, 320–321
special features of, 319–323
strict standard of proof, 322–323
Criminologists, 39, 49
Criminology
chronic offender and, 61–62
classical, 40–41
defined, 39
father of, 41
Crips, 466
Crisis intervention centers, 82
Crisis intervention teams, 178
Critical Response Command, 144
Cross-examination, 334–335

Cruel and unusual punishment
death penalty and, 378
defined, 376
method of execution and, 375
Supreme Court on, 376–377
three-strikes laws, 372
CryptoWall, 529
CSI effect, 332
Cultural deviance theory, 48
Curfew, home confinement and, 413
Custodial interrogation, 241
Custodial model for prisons, 428
Custody, defined, 240
Customs and Border Protection (CBP),
156–158
agent for, 546
Border Patrol, 158
under Homeland Security Department,
156–158
responsibilities of, 156–157
Visa issues, 157–158
Cyberattack
defined, 534
distributed denial of service, 535
Cyberbullying, 502, 533
Cyberbullying Research Center, 533
Cyber crimes, 527–538
child pornography and, 528
cloud computing and, 537
computer crime and Internet, 527–528
consumer fraud, 530
costs of, 527, 528
credit card crime, 531, 535
cyberbullying, 533
cyber deception and theft, 530–533
cyber-recruiting of terrorist, 535
cyberstalking, 533–534
cyber theft, 531–532
cyber trespass, 528–530
cyber violence, 533–535
defined, 8, 527
as easier path to crime, 527–528
fighting, 535–538
challenges for law enforcement,
536–537
cyber forensics, 537–538
encryption, 529
FBI and, 537
jurisdictional challenges, 537–538
zero-day vulnerability, 535–536
hackers, 528–529
hacktivism, 533
identity theft, 531
incidence of, 527
keystroke logging, 531
malware, 529
online dating scams, 530

phishing, 532
pirating intellectual property online,
532–533
protecting online passwords, 531–532
ransomware, 529
remote-controlled attacks, 535
revenge porn, 526
terrorist cyberattacks, 534–535
types of, 9
Cyber forensics, 537–538
Cyber fraud, 9, 530
Cyberstalking, 9, 533–534
Cyber terror, 9
Cyber Threat Alliance, 529
Cyber violence, 533–535

D

Dark figure of crime, 79, 80
Day-fines, 410
Day reporting centers, 412
Deadly force
defined, 198
in self-defense, 120
Death by dealer laws, 100, 111
Death penalty, 374–384
arbitrariness of, 381
bifurcated process, 377–378
choice theory and, 42
in colonies, 425
cost of, 383, 384
as cruel and unusual punishment,
376–377, 378
debate over, 380–382
decline in executions, 382–383
declining use of, 28–29
deterrence argument, 380
discriminatory effect, 382
Eighth Amendment and, 375, 377, 378
executions by state, 381
fallibility and, 380–381
as form of punishment, 360
future of, 382–383
historical perspective on, 375
insanity and, 378
intellectually disabled, 374
jury and, 363, 378
juveniles and, 379, 498
methods of execution, 375
mitigating circumstances, 378–379
number of executions 1976 to 2007,
374–375
number of prisoners on death row, 374
persons sentenced and later found to
be innocent, 380
public opinion and, 383
race and, 382
reform in California, 384

Death penalty (*Continued*)
  Sixth Amendment and, 378
  Supreme Court rulings on, 375–383
  victim impact statement and, 373
Death Penalty Information Center, 380
Death row, number of prisoners on, 374
Decarceration, 438–440
Deception, white-collar crime and, 547
De-escalation, 174
Defendants
  affirmative defenses, 336–337
  appeals, 341–342
  attorney-client privilege and, 293–294
  in civil case, 71
  creating reasonable doubt, 336
  Fifth amendment and, 321–322
  placing on stand, 336
  plea bargaining, 306
  presumption of innocence, 322
  protecting, and plea bargaining,
    308–309
  self-incrimination, 321–322
Defense(s)
  affirmative defense, 336–337
  alibi, 336–337
  creating reasonable doubt, 336
  under criminal law, 115–122
  duress, 337
  entrapment, 337
  excuse defenses, 115–119
  insanity, 337
  justification and, 119–122
  responsibility and, 115–119
  self-defense, 337
Defense attorneys, 288–292
  attorney-client privilege, 293–294
  attorney-client relationship, 292–293
  charging conference, 339
  closing arguments, 338
  constitutional right to, 124
  creating reasonable doubt, 336
  cross-examination and, 334–335
  defending the guilty, 289, 293–294
  defense strategies, 336–337
  evidence and, 330–333
  hearsay, 335
  jury selection, 324–329
  opening statements, 330
  placing defendants on stand, 336
  plea bargaining, 306
  preliminary hearing, 299–300
  pretrial motions, 304–305
  private attorneys, 289
  prosecutorial screening process,
    301–305
  public defenders, 289–292
  responsibilities of, 289

ritualized aggression, 276
  in sentencing process, 363
  surrebuttal, 337
Deferred prosecution, 301–303
Delegation of authority, 176
Deliberate indifference, 473–474
Deliberation, degree of crime and, 109
Delinquency in a Birth Cohort (Wolfgang,
    Figlio & Sellin), 61–62
Department of Homeland Security
    (DHS). *See* Homeland Security,
    Department of (DHS)
Departure, 371
De-policing movement, 25
Deprivation model, 463
Desistance, 504
  promoting, 479–481
Detectives, 179, 218
  activities of, 179
  function of, 179
Detention
  as element of arrest, 236
  pretrial, 294–299
  preventive, 297, 512
Detention hearing, 512
Determinate sentencing, 359
Deterrence
  death penalty as, 380
  general, 354
  low probability of punishment, 354
  by patrol officers, 177
  as purpose of sentencing, 353–354
  specific, 354
Deviance, 6
  labeling theory and, 52
DHS. *See* Homeland Security, Department
    of (DHS)
Differential association, theory of, 51–52
Differential response strategy, 186
Digital evidence, 537
Directed patrol, 188
Direct evidence, 331–332
Direct examination, 334
Direct supervision approach, 448
Discipline, by correctional officers,
    467–471
Discovery, 300
Discretion
  advantages and disadvantages of, 17–18
  crime reporting and, 77–78
  in criminal justice system, 17–18
  defined, 17
  elements of, 173–174
  ethics and, 206
  factors in, 173–174
  force and, 175
  high-speed pursuits, 174

judicial, 360, 369, 397, 514
  justification for, 173
  juveniles and police, 507–508
  limiting, 174
  policy and, 174–175
  prosecutorial, 285, 301–304
  role of, in policing, 173–175
  sixth sense, 173
Discretionary release, 406–407
Discrimination
  hiring by law enforcement agencies, 148
  in sentencing, 366–369
Disorder, crimes of, 135
Disorderly conduct, 77
Disorganized zones, 47
Disposition hearing, 514
Dispositions, 360
Dissenting opinions, 266–267
Distracted driving, 10
Distributed denial of service, 535
District, 176
District attorney, 285
District Courts, U.S., 263
Diversion
  community corrections as, 393–394
  pretrial programs, 410, 510
  probation as, 510
  treatment and aid, 510
Diversion programs, 28, 510
DNA data/profiling
  CODIS and cold hits, 183
  collection policies, 184
  defined, 21
  DNA fingerprinting, 182–183
  efficiency improvements from, 21
  familial searches, 183
  genetic witness, 184
  touch DNA, 183
  wrongful convictions and, 342–343
Docket, 269
Domestic terrorism
  defined, 26
  entrapment issue and, 180
  preventive policing and, 180
Domestic violence
  defined, 89
  risk assessment and, 62
  uncooperative victims and, 303
  women as victims of, 89
Domestic violence courts, 262
Donald W. Reynolds Crisis Intervention
    Center, 82
Dopamine, drug addiction and, 57–58
Double jeopardy, 124, 341–342
  civil suits, 342
  hung jury, 342
  juveniles, 495

Double marginality, 152–153
Driving under the influence, 77
Drug abuse
    addiction basics, 57–58
    defined, 57
    jail population and, 446
    juvenile delinquency and, 504–505
    naloxone for reversing opioid
        overdose, 136
    prisons and substance abuse
        treatment, 461
Drug abuse violations, 77
Drug courts, 259, 262, 411
Drug Enforcement Administration (DEA), 14
    classification of marijuana as Schedule
        I drug, 12
    responsibilities of, 157, 161
Drug offenses
    average length of sentence, 396
    death by dealer laws, 100, 111
    increases in prison population and,
        437–438
    sentencing disparity, 367
Drugs
    crack cocaine sentencing, 368
    crime and, 22, 56–61
    defined, 22
    drug-crime relationship, 58–59
    drug use theories, 57
    learning process and, 57
    legalizing marijuana, 60–61, 63
    mandatory sentencing guidelines,
        371–372
    Mexican drug cartels, 159
    national health and, 59
    opioid and heroin epidemic, 22
    social disorganization theory and, 57
    society and legality of, 74–75
    use of, in United States, 56
Drug-sniffing dogs, probable cause and,
    216, 217
Drug trafficking, sentencing disparity, 367
Drug Use Forecasting Program, 79–80
Drunkenness, 8
Dual court system, 14, 259–260
Dual intent, 111
Due process
    arraignment and, 305
    constitutional guarantee of, 124
    in the courts, 255–256
    judicial system's role in, 125
    juveniles and, 495–496
    national security and, 126
    parole revocation hearing, 405
    predator drones and, 126
    procedural, 124–125
    revocation process, 400–401

substantive, 125
    Supreme Court's role in, 125
    terrorist watch list and, 126
Due process clause, 124
Due process model
    compared to crime control model, 20
    defined, 19
    overview of main concepts, 20
Duress
    as defense, 119, 337
    defined, 119
Duty
    defined, 207
    ethical dilemmas of, 207
Duty to aid statutes, 108
Duty to retreat, 120–121

E

Early release for nonviolent offenders, 28
Eastern Penitentiary, 426, 433
Economy, crime and, 84
Educational programs, for prisoners,
    461–462
Ego, 45
Eighth Amendment, 124
    death penalty and, 375, 377, 378
    deliberate indifference and, 472
    identifiable human needs and, 473
    reasonable bail and, 296
    use of force by prison officials and,
        470–471
Electric chair, 375
Electronic monitoring
    ankle bracelet, 414
    continuously signaling device, 414
    defined, 413
    programmed contact programs, 414
    technology advances in, 414
    types of, 414
Electronic surveillance
    Automatic License Plate Recognition
        (ALPR) technology, 230
    consent and probable cause, 229–230
    constitutional concerns, 230
    defined, 229
    as force multiplier, 230
    privacy concerns, 230
    video and digital surveillance, 230
Elmira Reformatory, 427, 433
Embezzlement, 548
Encryption, 529, 551
Ending Federal Marijuana Prohibition
    Act, 63
England
    common law in, 101
    early police experience, 138–139
Enslavement theory of addiction, 59

Entrapment defense, 122, 337
Entrapment issues, preventing terrorism
    and, 180
Environmental Protection Agency (EPA),
    104, 549
Equal Employment Opportunity
    Commission (EEOC), 148
Essays on Crime and Punishment
    (Beccaria), 40–41
Ethics
    critical thinking and, 19
    defined, 18
    discretion and, 206
    duty, 207
    elements of, 206–207
    ethical dilemmas, 206
    honesty, 207
    law and, 18–19
    loyalty, 207
    noble cause corruption, 206
    police corruption, 200–202
    professionalism, 200
    racial and ethnic biases in policing,
        204–206
Ethnicity
    bias in policing, 204–206
    crime and, 88
European Court of Human Rights
    (ECHR), 355
Evansville (Indiana) Police Department, 175
Evidence
    circumstantial, 332
    defined, 330
    digital, 537
    direct, 331–332
    evil character, 332–333
    exclusionary rule and, 219–220
    fruit of the poisoned tree, 219
    good faith exception, 220
    hearsay, 335
    inevitable discovery exception, 219–220
    prejudicial, 332–333
    preponderance of, 72
    probable cause based on, 218
    real evidence, 330
    relevant, 332
    role in trial, 330–333
    testimonial, 331
    of victim's behavior, 333
Evidence-based practices, 20–21
Evil character, 332–333
Exclusionary rule, 301
    defined, 219
    exceptions to, 220
    good faith exception, 220
    inevitable discovery exception, 219–220
Excuse defenses, 115–119

Exigent circumstances, arrests and, 237–238
Expert witness, 331
Expiration release, 477
Ex post facto law, 122
Expungement laws, 481
Extradition, 258

F

Facebook, 146, 534, 535–536
Facial recognition software, 21
Fairness, duty of, prosecutors, 285
False confessions, 243–244
    coercion and, 243–244
Familial DNA searches, 183
Family
    child abuse and juvenile delinquency, 505
    street and decent, 48
Family group homes, 516
Federal Bureau of Investigation (FBI), 14
    careers in, 160
    counterterrorism efforts, 144
    creation of, 159
    cyber crime and, 537
    fighting white collar crime, 549
    Next Generation Identification (NGI) program, 161
    responsibilities of, 157, 159–160
    Uniform Crime Report (UCR) and, 75–77
Federal Bureau of Prisons (BOP), 429, 435
Federal Circuit, 263, 264
Federal Communications Commission, 549
Federal court system, 14
    in dual court system, 259–260
    federal prisons for, 429
    judges for, 263
    selection of judges, 269–270
    sentencing disparity, 366
    Supreme Court, 263–267
    U.S. Courts of Appeal, 263, 264
    U.S. District Court, 263, 264
Federal Emergency Management Agency, 159
Federalism, 11–15
    corrections and, 14–15
    courts and, 14
    defined, 11
    importance of, 11–13
    law enforcement and, 13–14
Federalist Papers, 263
Federal law enforcement agencies, 14, 156–162
    Bureau of Alcohol, Tobacco, Firearms and Explosives (ATF), 157, 161–162
    Customs and Border Protection (CBP), 156–158

Drug Enforcement Administration (DEA), 157, 161
    Federal Bureau of Investigation (FBI), 159–161
    Homeland Security, 156–159
    Immigration and Customs Enforcement (ICE), 158–159
    Justice Department, 157, 159–162
    Secret Service, 159
    Treasury Department, 157, 162
    U.S. Marshals Service, 157, 162
Federal Reporter, 35
Federal Rules of Evidence, 333
Federal statutes, as source of criminal law, 102–103
Federal Supplement, 35
Fee system, of jails, 446
Felonies
    average outcome of felony arrest, 301, 302
    case attrition, 301–304
    defined, 72
    degrees of, 72
    fleeing felon rule, 198–199
    initial appearance, 295
    three-strikes laws, 372
Felony-murder law, 111
Field services, 176–179
    clearance rates and cold cases, 180–181
    defined, 176
    forensic investigations and DNA, 181–184
    investigations, 179–184
    patrol, 177–179
Field training, 148
Field training officer (FTO), 148
Fifth Amendment, 124, 126
    arraignment, 305
    booking procedure and, 246
    double jeopardy, 341
    due process clause of, 124
    juveniles and, 495
    Miranda warning and, 239
    pretrial detention and, 294
    privilege against self-incrimination and, 321–322
    probation officer meeting with probationer and, 401
    witnesses and, 321–322
Fines
    day-fines in Sweden, 410
    as form of punishment, 361
Fingerprint readers, 21
Fingerprints
    challenging evidence of, 331
    DNA fingerprinting, 182–183
    human fingerprinting, 181–182

Firearms. *See* Guns
Fire marshal, 14
First Amendment
    prisoners' rights and, 473
    true threat exception, 5, 533–534
Fish, game and watercraft wardens, 14
Flag burning, 103
Fleeing felon rule, 198–199
Folsom, 433
Food and Drug Administration (FDA), 104, 549
Force
    amount of, in self-defense, 120
    authority and, 197–200
    deadly, 120, 198
    discretion and, 175
    incidence of use of, 197–198
    less lethal weapons, 199–200
    nondeadly, 120, 198
    by prison officials, 470–471
    reasonable, 198
    Supreme Court decisions on, 198–199
    tasers and, 200
    use of force matrix, 198
    use of force policies, 174–175
Force multiplier, electronic surveillance as, 230
Foreign Intelligence Surveillance Act (FISA), 540, 542
Foreign Intelligence Surveillance Court (FISA) Court, 540
Forensics, 181–184
    ballistics, 181
    crime scene, 181–182
    cyber crimes and, 537–538
    DNA fingerprinting, 182–183
    human fingerprinting, 181–182
    trace evidence, 181
Forensic scientist, 182
Forfeiture, 411–412
    civil, 417
Formal criminal justice process, 15–16
Fort Worth (Texas) Police Department, 186
Foster care programs, 515
Fourteenth Amendment, 124
Fourth Amendment, 123, 126, 217–220
    automobile searches, 226
    exclusionary rule, 219–220
    garbage and, 220–221
    good faith exception, 220
    inevitable discovery exception, 219–220
    NSA and surveillance, 542, 544
    prisons and right to privacy, 472
    probable cause, 217–219
    reasonableness, 217

search warrants, 222
thermal imagers and, 228–229
wording of, 217
France, training for judges, 272
Fraternal Order of Police, 175
Fraud
cyber consumer, 530
types of, 548
white-collar crime and, 548
Free Alabama Movement, 456, 461
Fresno Police Department, real-time
crime centers (RTCCs), 143
Frisk
defined, 233
reasonable suspicion, 234
Fruit of the poisoned tree, 219
Furlough, 477
Fusion centers, 144

G

Gambling, 8
online, 9
Gang investigator, 11
Gangs
defined, 505
girls in, 506
guns and, 22
in prison, 465–466
reasons for joining, 507
as risk factor for juvenile delinquency,
505–507
street, 22
Garbage, privacy and, 220–221
GED programs, 461
Gender
jury selection, 328
juvenile delinquency and, 500–501
sentencing discrimination, 368–369
social conflict theory and, 50
General deterrence, 354
General (unlimited) jurisdiction,
259, 262
General Motors (GM), 550
General strain theory, 48
General Theory of Crime, A (Gottfredson &
Hirschi), 54
Genetically modified organisms, ballot
initiatives and, 103
Genetics
crime and, 42–43
defined, 42
MAOA gene, 42–43
Genetic witness, 184
GEO Group, Inc., 441
GM bot, 529
Good faith exception, 220
Good time, 359–360

GPS
electronic monitoring and, 415
privacy and electronically following
automobiles, 222, 230
Graduated sanction, 514–515
Graduated sanctions, 401–402
Grand Forks (North Dakota) Police
Department, 175
Grand jury, 295, 300–301
as rubber stamp, 301
special features of, 300
Great Law, 425
Gross misdemeanor, 72
Group A offenses, 77
Group homes, 515
Guardian mentality, 143–144
Guilt
factual, 287–288
legal, 287–288
Guilty/guilty plea, 295
beyond a reasonable doubt, 322–323
criminal law and, 71
defense attorneys defending, 289, 293–294
guilty but mentally ill statutes, 118
misdemeanor cases at initial
appearance, 295
plea bargaining, 305–309
pleading, 305–310
Gun control
background checks, 23
defined, 22
drug abuse and, 91
mental health issues, 23, 44, 91
nullification laws, 106
recent legislative efforts, 23–24
Gun Control Act, 161
Guns
AFT responsibilities and, 161–162
concealed carry on campuses, 30
crime and, 22–23
gangs and, 22
gunshot detectors in schools, 502
increase prison population and weapon
crimes, 437
ownership in Germany, 24
ownership rate, 22

H

Habeas corpus
petition, 344
writ of, 122
Habitual Criminal Sterilization Act, 125
Habitual offender laws, 372
Hacking/cracking, 9
future of, 529
Internet of things, 530
types of, 528–529

Hacktivists, 533
Halfway house program manager, 480
Halfway houses, 15, 480
Hallucinogens, use of, in United States, 56
Hand geometry scanners, 21
Hands-off doctrine, 472
Harm, 113–114
Hate crime laws, 113
Hate speech laws, 114
Hawaii's Opportunity Probation with
Enforcement (HOPE), 403
Hearsay, 335
Heroin
Canadian program for addicts, 60
crime and, 22
deaths from overdose, 59
use of, in United States, 6, 22, 56
High-speed pursuits, discretion and, 174
High-tech crimes. *See* Cyber crimes
Highway patrol, 14
number of agencies, 155
purpose of, 155
vs. state police, 155–156
Hispanics. *See* Latinos.
Hollister (California) Police Department
(HPD), 230
Holman Correctional Facility, 456, 463
Home confinement, 413–415
defined, 413
effectiveness of, 414–415
levels of, 413–414
number of offenders under, 413
Home detention, 413
Home incarceration, 414
Homeland security. *See also* National security
civil liberties and, 27
cyberattacks, 534–535
defined, 26
infrastructure security, 534–535
Homeland Security, Department
of (DHS)
creation of, 156
Customs and Border Protection (CBP),
156–158
Immigration and Customs Enforcement
(ICE), 158–159
purpose of, 14
Secret Service, 157, 159
Homelessness, criminalizing, 92
Homicide. *See also* Murder
justifiable, 120–121, 127
mens rea, 109–110
race and, 86
by relative or acquaintance, 76–77
Honesty, ethical dilemmas of, 207
Honor killings, 74
Horizontal overcharging, 308

Hormones
   aggression and, 43
   postpartum psychosis, 43
Hot spots, 85, 188–189
   policing, 20
   technology for, 142
House of Refuge, 493
Houston Police Department, real-time
      crime centers (RTCCs), 143
Human trafficking, 158
Hung jury, 321, 336, 340
   double jeopardy and, 342
Hypothesis, defined, 39

I

Id, 45
Identifiable human needs, 473
Identification process, 245–246
   lineups, 246
   nontestimonial evidence, 246
   photo arrays, 246
   showups, 245
Identity theft, 9, 531
Illinois Disproportionate Justice Impact
      Study Commission, 367
Illinois Juvenile Court Act, 493–494
Immigration
   Arizona law on, 235
   increase in prison population and
         violations of, 438
   local police and immigration law, 164
   racial profiling and, 234–235
Immigration and Customs Enforcement (ICE)
      under Homeland Security Department,
         158–159
   investigating human trafficking, 158
   Operation Diablo Express, 159
   responsibilities of, 157, 158
   Secure Communities (S-COMM)
         program, 164
Impeachment, of federal judges,
      271–272
Imprisonment, as form of punishment, 361
Incapacitation
   collective, 356
   impact of, 255–256
   as purpose of sentencing, 355
   selective, 356
Incarceration
   consequences for high rate of, 440–441
   crime rate and, 84, 85
   decrease in rate of, 27
   economics of, 27–28
   effectiveness of reducing crime, 439, 440
   as form of punishment, 361
   high rate of, in U.S., 424, 425, 428,
         440–441

increased probability of, 437
of juveniles, 516–517
race and, 29
recent drop in rate, 424
shock, 395
Inchoate offenses, 114
Incident-driven policing, 185–186
Income, crime and, 87–88
Indeterminate sentencing
   defined, 358
   discretionary release, 406–407
   individualized justice, 360
   rehabilitation and, 360
India, national anthem requirement, 5
Indictment, 295
   defined, 300
   grand jury and, 300
Individualized justice, 360
Industrial schools, 517
Industrial shop and school officers, 469
Inevitable discovery exception, 219–220
Infancy defense, 115, 497
Informal criminal justice process, 17
Informants, probable cause based on, 218
Information
   defined, 300
   issued by prosecutor, 300
   probable cause based on, 218
Infraction, 73
Infrastructure, 159
   cyberattacks on, 534–535
Inherent coercion, 240
Initial appearance, 294–295
In loco parentis, 507
Inmates. *See* Prisoners
Innocence, presumption of, 322
Innocence Project, 343
Innocent Images National Initiative
      (IINI), 537
Insanity
   death penalty and, 378
   as defense under criminal law,
         115–118, 337
   determining competency, 117
   guilty but mentally ill, 118
   measuring sanity, 116–117
   myth and reality of, 117
Insanity defense, 115–118, 337
InSite program, 60
Insurance fraud, 548
Intake, 509–510
Intellectually disabled, death penalty
      and, 378
Intellectual property theft, 9, 532–533
Intelligence-led policing, 20, 141–142
   counterterrorism and, 144–145
Intensive supervision probation, 412

Intent, 108
   attendant circumstances, 112
   dual intent, 111
   as element of arrest, 235–236
Intermediate sanctions, 409–416
   boot camp, 413
   community service, 409
   day-fines, 410
   day reporting centers, 412
   defined, 409
   drug courts, 411
   electronic monitoring, 413–415
   fines, 409, 410
   forfeiture, 409, 411–412
   home confinement, 413–415
   intensive supervision probation, 412
   judicially administered, 409–412
   pretrial diversion programs, 409, 410
   restitution, 409
   restorative justice, 411
   shock incarceration, 412–413
   in Sweden, 410
   widen the net, 415–416
Intermittent incarceration, 395
Internal affairs unit (IAU), 202
Internal Revenue Service (IRS), 157,
      162, 550
International Association of Chiefs of
      Police, 175
Internet. *See also* Cyber crimes
   child pornography, 528
   China and firewall, 536
   counterterrorism efforts, 545–546
   evidence of criminal behavior on, 145
   incidence of cyber crime, 527
   online crime, 527–528
   as public utility, 549
   terrorist recruiting operations, 545–546
Internet Crime Complaint Center (IC3), 530
Internet of Things, 8–9
   hacking, 530
Interrogation process, 239–245
   custodial interrogation, 241
   defined, 239
   false confessions, 243–244
   inherent coercion and, 240
   Miranda rights and, 239–243
   PEACE method, 245
   recording, 244
   Reid Technique, 244
Intimate partner violence, 89
Intoxication
   as defense under criminal law, 118
   involuntary, 118
   voluntary, 118
Intuitive policing, 173
Investigating officers, probation, 398

Investigations, 179–184
  clearance rates and cold cases, 180–181
  confidential informant, 179
  detective division, 179
  entrapment issues, 180
  forensic investigations and DNA,
      181–184
  presentence, 398
  preventive policing and domestic
      terrorism, 180
  undercover operations, 179
Involuntary manslaughter, 109–110
Irresistible-impulse test, 117
Islamic State (ISIS)
  crowdsourcing terrorism, 26
  cyber attacks by, 534
  cyber-recruiting, 535

J

Jails, 444–448
  administration, 446–448
  characteristics of population, 444–445
  compared to prisons, 444
  defined, 14–15
  direct supervision approach, 448
  fee system, 446
  function of, 444
  new generation of, 448
  number of inmates in, 15, 27, 444
  overcrowding, 297, 447–448
  podular design, 448
  population of, 444–445
  pretrail detainees, 444–445
  sentenced jail inmates, 445
  sociology of, 446
  time served and, 445
  traditional design of, 448
  video visits for, 443
Japan
  election of judges, 272
  prosecutorial discretion and, 302
Jim Crow laws, 50
Judges
  appointment of, 269
  bail setting and, 296–297
  charge to jury, 339
  discretion and, 18, 360, 362, 369, 397
  diversity and, 272–273
  election of, 269–270
  federal, 263
  independence and accountability of, 270
  intermediate sanctions, 409–412
  merit selection and, 270
  misconduct, 270–271
  Missouri Plan, 270
  removal of, 270
  roles

  in courtroom work group, 275–276
  of trial judges, 267–268
  selection of, 269–270
  sentencing
    authority, 360–362
    departures, 371
    factors in, 364–365
    individualized justice, 360–362
    role in process, 360, 362
    sentencing disparity, 366
  Supreme Court, 263–267
Judicial conduct commission, 271
Judicial discretion, 360, 362, 369, 514
Judicial misconduct, 270–271
Judicial review, 264
Judicial system
  courtroom work group, 274–277
  dual court system, 259–260
  federal court system, 263–267
  judges in court system, 267–273
  state court system, 260–263
  trial and appellate courts, 259
Judicial waiver, 511
Jurisdiction, 257–259
  appellate, 259
  concurrent, 257
  cyber crime and, 537–538
  defined, 257
  extradition and, 258
  general (unlimited), 259, 262
  geographic, 257–258
  on Indian reservations, 258, 278
  international, 258–259
  limited, 259, 261–262
  original, 259
  subject-matter, 259
  of Supreme Court, 265
  tribal, 258, 278
  universal, 259
Jury
  Allen Charge, 340
  alternate jurors, 329
  charge to, 339
  death penalty and, 363, 378
  deliberations, 339–340
  hung, 321, 336, 340
  impartial, 320
  instructions for, 339
  requirements for, 323
  role of, 320–321
  selection
    challenges for cause, 326
    goal of, 323
    master jury list, 324–325
    of peers, 323
    peremptory challenges, 326
    race and, 327–328

  venire, 325
  voir dire, 325–327
  women, 328
  sentencing process and, 363
  sequestered, 339–340
  size of, 320–321
  unanimity of, 321
  wireless devices in courtroom, 340
Jury instructions, 339
Jury nullification, 340–341
Jury pool, 325
Jury selection, 323–329
Jury selection consultant, 326–327
Jury trials, 320. *See also* Trials
  juveniles and, 494
Just deserts, 353
Justice
  defined, 10
  ethics and, 18–19
  maintaining, 10
Justice court, 261
Justice Department, 157, 159–162
Justice of the peace, 261–262
Justice reinvestment, 28
Justifiable homicides, 120–121, 127
Justification defenses, 119–122
Juveniles. *See also* Juvenile delinquency;
      Juvenile justice system
  age tried as adults, 497
  constitutional protections, 495–496
  crimes committed by, 499–500
  culpability and, 497–499
  curfew, 499
  death penalty and, 379, 498
  detention, 512
  incarceration
    boot camps, 515, 516
    nonsecure confinement, 515–516
    recidivism, 517
    residential treatment programs,
        515–516
    secure confinement, 515–516,
        516–517
    training schools, 516–517
  infancy defense, 115, 497
  juvenile justice process, 508
  life-without-parole sentences, 498–499
  parens patriae, 493
  police and, 507–509
    arrests and minority youth, 508–509
    culture-gap, 509
    discretion and, 507–509
    failing attitude test, 509
    low-visibility decision making, 508
  probation for, 515
  resentencing issues, 498–499
  status offender, 494

Juveniles. *See also* Juvenile delinquency;
 Juvenile justice system (*Continued*)
 on trial, 513–517
 tried as an adult, 510–512
Juvenile corrections, 516–517
Juvenile courts, 262
 age tried as an adult, 497
 constitutional protections, 495–496
 double jeopardy, 495
 due process, 495–496
 establishment of, 493–494
 Fifth Amendment, 495
 Illinois Juvenile Court Act, 493–494
 jury trial, 494
 juvenile justice process, 508
 reasonable doubt standard, 495
 tried as an adult, 494–495, 510–512
Juvenile curfews, 499
Juvenile delinquency
 chronic 6 percent, 503
 chronic offenders, 62
 curfews, 499
 defined, 494
 family-based delinquency, 500–501
 girls and, 500–501
 risk factors, 503–507
  age, 504
  child abuse and neglect, 505
  gang involvement, 505–507
  overview, 504
  substance abuse, 504–505
 school violence, 501–502
 trends in
  crime statistics, 499–501
  girls in juvenile justice system,
   500–501
  rise and fall of juvenile crime, 499–500
  school violence and bullying, 501–503
 UCR data on, 499–500
Juvenile Justice and Delinquency
 Prevention Act, 504, 510
Juvenile justice process, 508
Juvenile justice system
 compared to criminal justice system, 513
 evolution of
  child-saving movement, 493
  constitutional protections, 495–496
  Illinois Juvenile Court, 493–494
  juvenile delinquency, 494–495
 girls in, 500–501
 pretrial procedures, 507–512
  detention, 512
  intake, 509–510
  petition, 510
  pretrial diversion, 510
  transfer to adult court, 510–512

on trial, 513–517
 adjudication, 514
 disposition hearing, 514
 sentencing, 514

K

Kansas City Preventive Patrol
 Experiment, 188
Keystroke logging, 531
Knapp Commission, 200–201
Knock and announce rule, 238
Knock and talk strategy, 225
Knoxville (Tennessee) Police
 Department, 154

L

Labeling theory, 52
Laguna Beach (California) Police
 Department, 220–221
La Nuestra Familia, 465, 466
Larceny, 8, 76
Latinos
 biases in policing and, 204–206
 crime and, 88
 as fastest-growing minority group in
  prisons, 88
 gang membership, 506
 incarceration rate of, 29
 increasing prison population and
  immigration offenses, 438
 as judges, 272–273
 juvenile arrests and, 508–509
 as law enforcement officers, 148–150,
  152–153
 prison violence and, 464
 on probation, 397
 racial profiling and S.B. 1070, 235
 racial threat theory, 50–51
 risk of victimization, 83
 sentencing discrimination and, 366–368
 stops and, 234–235
Law(s)
 administrative, 103–104
 ballot initiatives, 103
 case, 104
 civil, 71–72
 common, 101
 constitutional, 102
 criminal (*See* Criminal law)
 definition of, 101
 hate crime, 113
 legal function of, 104–105
 police enforcing, 135
 social function of, 105–106
 stand your ground law, 121, 127
 stare decisis, 104

statutory, 102–103
 supremacy clause, 103
 Supreme Court's interpretation of,
  266–267
 written sources of, 101–104
Law enforcement
 changing landscape of, 24–25
 continuing challenges for, 22
 de-policing movement, 25
 evidence-based practices, 20–21
 federal, 14
 federalism and, 13–14
 identifying criminals, 21
 local, 13
 race issues and public trust, 25
 racial and ethnic bias, 204–206
 secondary policing, 163
 smarter policing, 20–21
 state, 13–14
Law enforcement agencies, 153–162
 benefit of cultural diversity, 153
 cyber crime and, 536–537
 effective police strategies, 184–193
 federal agencies, 156–162
 limited-purpose law enforcement
  agencies, 156
 municipal agencies, 154
 private security and, 162–163
 sheriffs and county, 154–155
 state police and highway patrol,
  155–156
 use of social media by, 145
Law Enforcement Code of Ethics, 136
Law enforcement officers. *See also* Police
 academy training, 147
 accountability, 202–204
 authority and use of force, 197–200
 background checks and tests, 146
 broken window effect, 190–191
 community policing, 191–193
 community services provided by, 136
 corruption by, 200–202
 crime prevention, 137
 cultural diversity and, 153
 differential response strategy, 186
 discretion and, 17, 173–175, 507–509
 educational requirements, 146–147
 effective police strategies, 184–193
 enforcing laws, 135
 ethics and, 206–207
 field services, 176–179
 field training, 148
 incident-driven policing, 185–186
 intuitive policing, 173
 investigations, 179–184
 juveniles and, 507–509

killed in the line of duty, 195
local, state and federal officers, 12–13
minorities as, 148–152
patrol, 177–179
peacekeeping role, 137
physical dangers of police work, 195–196
police liability, 203–204
police subculture, 194
predictive policing and crime mapping, 188–189
probationary period, 147
problem-oriented policing, 192–193
racial and ethnic biases in policing, 204–206
reactive and proactive arrest strategies, 189–191
recruitment for, 145–147
requirements for, 146–147
services provided by police, 177–178
sixth sense, 173
stress and mental dangers of work, 196–197
training, 147–148
undercover officers, 179
Lawyers' Edition of the Supreme Court Reports, 35
Lay witness, 331
Lead damage, crime rates and, 44
Leading questions, 334
Learning theory, 51–52
Legal guilt, 287–288
Legalization of drugs, 60–61
Legislative sentencing authority, 358–360
Legislative waiver, 511
Legitimate security interests of prison, 471
Less lethal weapons, 196–197, 199–200
Lethal injection, 375
Liability
accomplice, 111
defined, 71
police, 203–204
strict, 110–111
Lie detectors, 268
Life course criminology, 53–56
Life-without-parole sentence, 406
as alternative to death penalty, 382
juveniles and, 498–499
number of, 355
Limited jurisdiction, 259
Limited-purpose law enforcement agencies, 156
Linear jail design, 448
Line officers, probation, 398
Line services, 176
Lineups, 246

Local law enforcement, 12
Local police department. *See* Municipal law enforcement agencies
Lockdown, 435
London Metropolitan Police, 138, 139
Los Angeles County Jail, 446
Los Angeles County Sheriff's Department, 154
Los Angeles Police Department (LAPD)
Operation LASER, 142
SWAT units, 143
Low-visibility decision making, 508
Loyalty, ethical dilemmas of, 207
Lubbock (Texas) Police Department, 149, 150

M

Magistrate, 262
Magnetic resonance imaging technology, 44
Mail and wire fraud, 548
Mala in se crimes, 73–75
Mala prohibita crimes, 73–75
Malicious and sadistic standard, 471
Malware, 9, 529
Mandatory release, 408
Mandatory sentencing guidelines, 371–373
Manslaughter
compared to murder, 109–110
types of, 109–110
MAOA gene, 42–43
Mara Salvatrucha 13 (MS-13), 466
Marijuana
African American arrest rate for, 18
crime rate and legalization, 85
debate over legalization, 60–61, 63
diversion, 61
federal and state laws of, 12–13, 14
legalization, 60–61, 63
medical use, 103
use of, in United States, 56
"Marsy's Law," 81
Marxism, vs. capitalism, 49–50
Mass shooting, 22
Master jury list, 324–325
Material support, 540, 545
Maximum-security prison, 433–435
Media, violence in, and crime, 52
Medical model, 427
of addiction, 59
of criminal justice system, 256
Medium-security prison, 436
Megan's Law, 482
Mens rea (guilty mental state)
accomplice liability, 111
attendant circumstances and, 112–113
defined, 108

duress and, 119
as element of crime, 107
elements of, 108–109
homicide and, 109–110
intoxication and, 118
strict liability, 110–111
Mental health courts, 262
Mental illness. *See also* Insanity
crime and, 44, 90–91
guilty but mentally ill, 118
gun control and, 23, 44, 91
inmates in prisons and jail, 459
jail inmates and, 446
jail population and, 446, 447
Miami-Dade County's Criminal Mental Health Project, 447
patrol activities and, 177–178
police providing services and, 136
as risk factor for victimization, 91
risk factors for violent crime, 90–91
Metadata collection, 542–543
Metadata surveillance, 27
Metropolitan Police Act, 138
Metropolitan Police Department of Washington, D.C., 175
Mexican Mafia (EMC), 465, 466
Mexico
drug cartels, 159
inquisitorial trial model, 323
Miami-Dade County's Criminal Mental Health Project, 447
Miami Police Department, 186
Militarism, 143
Milwaukee Police Department, high-speed chases policy, 174
Minimum-security prison, 436
Minorities
consequences of high incarceration rate and, 440–441
death penalty and, 382
jury selection and, 327–328
juvenile arrests and, 508–509
as law enforcement officers, 148–152
sentencing discrimination and, 366–368
Miranda rights, 240
Miranda warning, 239–243
clear intent and, 242
legal basis for, 239–241
public-safety exception, 242
setting the stage for, 239
waiving rights, 242
weakening of, 243
when not required, 241–242
when required, 241
wording of, 238

Misdemeanors
  defined, 72
  gross, 72
  initial appearance, 295
  petty, 72
Missouri Plan, 270
Mistake
  as defense under criminal law, 118–119
  of fact, 119
  of law, 119
Mistrial, 340
Mitigating circumstances
  death penalty, 378–379
  defined, 365
  as factor in sentencing, 378–379
M'Naghten rule, 116
Model Penal Code, 117
Mooching, 201
Morals, 5
Mothers Against Drunk Driving (MADD), 80
Motion for a directed verdict, 336
Motor vehicle compliance (MVC)
    agencies, 156
Motor vehicle theft, 8
  defined, 76
  sentencing disparity, 367
Municipal court judge, 262
Municipal law enforcement agencies
  authority of, 154
  local police and immigration law, 164
  population served by, 154
  vs. sheriff's department, 154
Murder. *See also* Homicide
  African Americans and, 86
  compared to manslaughter, 109–110
  defined, 7, 76
  degrees of, 109
  deliberation, 109
  felony-murder law, 111
  increase in rate of, 20, 22, 85
  by juveniles, 500
  as *mala in se* crime, 74
  premeditated, 109
  sentencing disparity, 367
  willful, 109

N

Naloxone, 136
National Advisory Commission on Civil
    Disorder, 141
National Association of Women Law
    Enforcement Executives, 150
National Center on Addiction and
    Substance Abuse (CASA), 461
National Combined DNA Index System
    (CODIS), 183

National Crime Victimization Survey, 79,
    83, 89, 354
  advantages and disadvantages of, 79
  compared to UCR, 79
  sample questions from, 79
National Gang Crime Research Center, 465
National government
  express powers of, 12
  federalism and, 12
National Incident-Based Reporting
    System (NIBS), 77–78
  compared to UCR, 78
National Institute of Justice, 184
National Law Center on Homelessness
    and Poverty, 92
National Law Enforcement Memorial, 152
National Police Misconduct Statistics and
    Reporting Project, 151
National Reporter System, 35
National security. *See also* Homeland
    security
  Antiterrorism and Effective Death
    Penalty Act (AEDPA), 540
  cyberattacks, 534–535
  due process and, 126
  Foreign Intelligence Surveillance Act
    (FISA), 540
  foreign surveillance, 540, 544
  Fourth Amendment and homeland
    security, 542
  known wolves, 545
  vs. liberty, 539–546
  metadata collection, 542–544
  national security letters, 541
  Patriot Act, 541
  privacy and, 539–544
  terrorist Internet recruiting operations,
    545–546
National Security Agency (NSA)
  Fourth Amendment, 542
  metadata collection by, 542–543
  Patriot Act and, 541
National security letters, 541
National victim advocate, 87
National White Collar Crime Center, 530
Native Americans
  crime and, 88
  jurisdiction on Indian reservations,
    258, 278
  peacemaking approach to criminal
    justice, 356
  as victims of crime, 278
Necessity, as defense under criminal law,
    121–122
Negative emotionality, 48
Negligence, criminal, 108

Netherlands, life imprisonment and ECHR
    rules, 355
Neurocriminology, 43–44
Newgate Prison, 426
New-generation jails, 448
New Haven (Connecticut) Police
    Department (NHPD), 188
New Orleans Police Department (NOPD),
    139, 193
New York Police Department (NYPD)
  corruption and, 200–201
  crime-mapping system, 189
  crime reporting by, 77
  Critical Response Command, 144
  establishment of, 139
  homeland security and, 144
  internal affairs unit, 202
  size of department, 154
  stops, 247
New York system, 426
New Zealand, legalization of prostitution, 74
Next Generation 911, 187
Next Generation Identification (NGI)
    program, 21, 161
Nicotine, addiction and, 75
Night watch system, 138
911 app, 187
911 technology
  differential response strategy, 187
  next generation 911, 187
  911 app, 187
Noble cause corruption, 206
Nolle prosequi, 301–302
Nolo contendere plea, 305
Nonconsensual pornography, 526, 527
Nondeadly force, 120, 198
Nonpartisan elections, 270
Nontestimonial evidence, 246
Nonviolent offenders, reducing rates of
    imprisonment of, 439
Norway, prison system, 436–437
Not guilty plea, 310
Notification laws, sex offenders, 482–483

O

Observation, probable cause based on,
    218
Occupational Safety and Health
    Administration (OSHA), 104, 549
OC pepper spray, 200
Odometer fraud, 548
Officer Down Memorial Page, 195
Officer-initiated activities, 178
Officers. *See* Law enforcement officers
Ohio State University Police
    Department, 134

Omission, act of, 107
Omnibus Crime Control and Safe Streets
      Act, 141
Online crimes. *See also* Cyber crimes
    child pornography, 9
    gambling, 9
Online dating scams, 530
Ontario Domestic Assault Risk
      Assessment (ODARA), 62
Opening statement, 330
Operation Diablo Express, 159
Operation LASER, 142
Operations, 176
Opinions, 259
Opioid drug use, 22, 59
Oral arguments, 266
Ordinances, 103
Organized crime, 8
Original jurisdiction, 259
Overcharging, 308

P

Pardon, 477
Parens patriae, 493
Parole
    administrative sentencing authority
        and, 360
    authority, 405
    characteristics of offenders, 405
    compared to probation,
        404–405
    concepts based on, 404
    conditions of, 404
    decarceration and, 439
    defined, 15, 403, 405
    denial of, 407
    discretionary release, 406–407
    eligibility for, 359, 406
    guidelines for, 408
    halfway houses, 480
    life sentence without 406
    mandatory release, 408
    number of prisoners on, 403
    parole contract, 404
    parole grant hearing, 407
    parole officer and, 405
    preparation for reentry behind bars,
        479–480
    promoting desistance, 479–481
    rehabilitation and, 360
    revocation of, 404–405
    technical violation, 404–405
    timing of, 405
    truth in sentencing and, 408
    victims' rights and, 408–409
    work release programs, 480

Parole board, 359
    defined, 406
    good time and, 359
    historical perspective on, 360
    indeterminate sentencing and, 359
    parole hearing, 407
    roles of, 406
Parole Commission, U.S., 360
Parole contract, 404
Parole officers
    presentence investigation report, 398
    role of, 405
Parole revocation, 404–405
Part I offenses, 75, 76–77
Part II offenses, 77
Particularity requirement of search
      warrants, 222–223
Partisan elections, 270
Password protection, 531–532
Patriot Act
    national security letters, 541
    NSA metadata program, 542–543
    passage of, 541
    surveillance and, 541
Patrol, 177–179
    activities of, 178–179
    administrative duties, 178
    calls for service, 177, 178
    community concerns, 177
    directed, 188
    mental illness interventions, 177–178
    officer-initiated duties, 178
    predictive policing and crime mapping,
        188–189
    preventive patrol, 178
    purpose of, 177
    random patrol, 187–188
    strategies for, 187–188
Patrol cars, technology and, 140
Patronage system, 139
    appointment of judges and, 269
Paul's Law, 492
Payday lenders, routine activities theory
      and, 83
Payoffs, 201
Peacekeeping role, 137
PEACE method, 245
Pell Grant program, 462
Penalty enhancements, 113
Penitentiary, 425. *See also* Prisons
Pennsylvania System, 426
Pepper spray, 200
Peremptory challenges, 326
Petition, 510
Petty misdemeanor, 72
Petty offense, 73

Philadelphia Adult Probation and Parole
      Department (APPD), 403
Philadelphia Police Department, 138, 139,
      185, 188, 193
Phishing, 532
Phoenix Police Department, 203
Photo arrays, 246
Physician-assisted suicide, 11–12
Piracy, 533
Pittsburgh Police Department, 149
Plaintiff, 71
Plain view doctrine, 228–229
Platoons, 176
Plea bargain/plea bargaining
    adversary system and, 307–309
    Boykin form, 308
    defendants, 306
    defense attorneys, 306
    defined, 305
    motivations for, 306–307
    prosecutors, 306, 364
    protecting defendant, 308–309
    in steps of trial, 295
    strategies to induce, 307–308
    victims and, 306–307
Podular jail design, 448
Police. *See also* Law enforcement officers
    accountability, 202–204
    citizen oversight, 203
    corruption, 200–202
    ethics, 206–207
    historical perspective
      administrative reforms, 139–140
      anti-terrorism challenges, 144–145
      community era, 141
      English roots, 138–139
      first police department, 138–139
      intelligence-led policing, 141–142
      political era and corruption, 139
      professionalism, 139–140
      real-time crime centers (RTCCs),
        142–143
      spoils system, 139
      technology and, 140
      turmoil in 1960s, 140–141
      warrior-guardian mentalities,
        143–144
    police-prosecutor conflict, 287–288
    responsibilities of
      community services provided by, 136
      crime prevention, 137
      enforcing laws, 135
      peacekeeping, 137
Police academy, 147
Police brutality, reform era in reaction
      to, 139

Police corruption, 200–202
    bribery, 201
    defined, 200
    mooching, 201
    noble cause corruption, 206
    patronage system and, 139
    during political era of policing, 139
    shakedowns, 201
    theories of, 201–202
    types of, 201
Police culture. *See* Police subculture
Police cynicism, 194
Police departments
    administrative reforms, 139–140
    American, earliest, 138–139
    bureaucratic model for, 175
    chain of command and, 175–176
    compared to prison management
        structure, 430
    delegation of authority, 176
    effective strategies for, 184–193
    field services, 176–179
    as generalists, 176
    organizing by area and time, 176
    span of control, 176
    structure of, 175–176
    use of social media and, 145
Police detective. *See* Detectives
Police ethics. *See* Ethics
Police officers. *See* Law enforcement
        officers; Police
Police power, state governments and, 12
Police Services Study, 177
Police strategies, 184–193
    broken window effect, 190–191
    community policing, 191–193
    differential response strategy, 186
    evidence-based practices, 20–21
    hot-spot policing, 20
    incident-driven policing, 185–186
    911 technology, 187
    predictive policing and crime mapping,
        188–189
    proactive policing, 21
    problem-oriented policing, 192–193
    random and directed patrol, 187–188
    reactive and proactive arrest strategies,
        189–191
Police subculture
    authority and use of force, 197–200
    blue curtain, 194
    core values of, 194
    cynicism, 194
    defined, 194
    physical dangers of police work and,
        195–196
    socialization and, 194

Policy, 174–175
Political era of policing, 139
Polygraph tests, 268
Pornography
    child, 528
    cyber crime and, 9
    online, 528
    revenge porn, 526, 527
Positivism, 41
Postal inspectors, 156, 549–550
Postpartum psychosis, 43
Post-traumatic stress disorder (PTSD),
        196–197
    victims of crimes and, 81–82
Power, social conflict theory and, 50
Precedent, 101
Precincts, 176
Predator drones, due process and, 126
Predictive policing, 20, 142, 188–189
Predisposition report, 514
Prejudicial evidence, 332–333
Preliminary hearing, 295
    to establish probable cause, 299–301
    pretrial diversion programs, 410
    revocation of probation, 400
    waiving right to, 300
Preponderance of evidence, 72
Prescription drugs
    deaths from overdose, 59
    use of, in United States, 56
Presentence investigation report,
        363, 398
President's Commission on Law
        Enforcement and Administration
        of Justice, 15
Pretrial detainees, 444–445
Pretrial detention, 294–299
    bail bond agent, 297–298
    initial appearance, 294–295
    in jails, 444–445
    posting bail, 297
    preventive detention, 297
    release on recognizance, 298
Pretrial diversion programs, 409, 410
Pretrial motions, 304–305
Pretrial procedures
    arraignment, 305
    plea bargaining, 305–309
    prosecutorial screening process,
        301–305
Preventive detention, 297
Preventive patrol, 178
Preventive policing
    defined, 180
    domestic terrorism and, 180
Prima facie case, 327
Prison Community, The (Clemmer), 458

Prison crowding, 361
Prisoner reentry, 476–481
Prisoners, 456–484. *See also* Prisons
    adapting to prison society, 458
    age of, 458, 459
    classification, 432
    contraband cell phones, 467
    culture of, 457–462, 462–463
    decarceration, 438–440
    discipline, 467–468, 469–471
    employment in prison, 456
    gangs, 465–466
    health and health care for, 459
    recidivism rate, 481–482
    rehabilitation and prison programs,
        460–462
    release of, 477
        barriers to reentry, 478
        challenges of, 477–481
        community-based reentry
            programs, 480
        conditional, 403
        discretionary, 406–407
        expiration release, 477
        furlough, 477
        mandatory release, 408
        pardon, 477
        parole, 403–405
        probationary release, 477
        promoting desistance, 479–481
        reentry programs, 28
        sex offenders, 481–483
        temporary release, 477
        threat of relapse, 479
    rights of, 472–473
        deliberate indifference, 472–473
        First Amendment, 473
        hands-off doctrine, 472
        identifiable human needs, 473
        iron curtain and, 472
    tattoos, 457
    video visits for, 443
    violence
        deprivation model, 463
        incidence of, 462
        in prison culture, 462–463
        race and ethnicity, 464
        rape, 463–464
        relative deprivation model, 463
        riots, 463
        security threat group (STG),
            465–466
        women, 476
    vocational and educational programs
        for, 461–462
    voting rights, 449
    women, 473–476

Prison guard. *See* Correctional officers
Prisonization, 458
Prison programs, 460–462
Prison Rape Elimination Act, 464
Prisons, 424–449. *See also* Prisoners
  administration
    formal management of, 430
    goals of, 430
    governing prisons, 431–432
    order, amenities and services,
      431–432
  admissions and release rates, 28, 29
  average length of sentence, 396
    vs. time served, 359
  classification process, 432
  community corrections as low-cost
    alternative to, 394
  compared to jails, 444
  congregate system, 426
  consequences of high incarceration
    rate, 440–441
  correctional officers, 467–473
  cost of, 27–28, 394, 424
  crime rate and imprisonment, 84, 85
  culture of, 457–462
  custodial model of, 428
  decarceration, 438–440
  declining use of death penalty, 28–29
  defined, 15
  deincarceration movement, 27–28
  designs of, 433–435
  diversion programs, 28
  early release for nonviolent
    offenders, 28
  effectiveness of reducing crime,
    439, 440
  as form of punishment, 361
  gangs, 465–466
  good time, 359
  growth in population of, 372, 428
  history of
    in colonies, 425
    first penitentiary, 425–426
    high rate of incarceration, 424, 425
    Pennsylvania vs. New York
      system, 426
    reassertion of punishment, 427–428
    reformers and progressives, 427
    role in modern society, 428
  justice reinvestment, 28
  legitimate security interests, 471
  malicious and sadistic standard, 471
  medical model, 427
  organization of, 429–436
  population
    aging, 458, 459
    ailing, 459

    decline in, 438–440
    decrease in, 27
    federal prison growth, 438
    growth in, 428, 437–438
    high rate of incarceration and, 424,
      425, 428, 440–441
    increased probability of
      incarceration, 437
    number of inmates in, 15, 27
    recent drop in, 424
  private, 441–443
    arguments against, 442–443
    cost efficiency of, 441–442
    future of, 443
    outsourcing inmates, 442
    overcrowding, 442
    philosophical concerns, 443
    reasons for, 441–442
    safety concerns, 442
  rape, 463–464
  reducing recidivism rate, 28
  rehabilitation and prison programs,
    460–462
  rehabilitation model of, 428
  reintegration model of, 428
  riots, 463
  role in modern society, 428
  security measures in, 435
  separate confinement, 426
  solitary confinement, 484
  substance abuse treatment in, 460–462
  as total institution, 457
  truth-in-sentencing laws, 359–360
  types of
    classification process, 432
    maximum-security, 433–435
    medium-security, 436
    minimum-security, 436
    supermax, 435–436
  video visits for, 443
  violence in, 462–466
  vocational and educational programs
    in, 461–462
  warden of, 430–431
  women in, 89, 473–476
Prison segregation, 464
Privacy
  in automobile, 226
  closed-circuit television (CCTV)
    cameras and, 230
  counterterrorism strategies and, 27
  electronic surveillance, 230
  garbage and, 220–221
  metadata collection and, 543–544
  national security and, 539–544
  private search doctrine, 221
  reasonable expectation of, 221

  role in searches, 221–222
  satellite monitoring and, 221–222
  thermal imagers and, 228–229
Private prisons, 441–443
  arguments against, 442–443
  future of, 443
  outsourcing inmates, 442
  overcrowding, 442
  philosophical concerns, 443
  safety concerns, 442
Private search doctrine, 221
Private security, 162–163
  growth in, 163
  privatizing law enforcement, 162–163
  secondary policing, 163
Proactive arrests, 189
Proactive policing, 21
Probable cause, 217–219
  drug-sniffing dogs and, 216, 217
  electronic surveillance and, 229–230
  establishing, 299–301
  framework, 219
  meaning of, 217
  preliminary hearing, 299–300
  search warrant and, 222
  sources of, 217–218
Probation, 392–417
  advantages/disadvantages of, 395
  authority, 405
  average length of, 396
  caseload and, 400
  characteristics of offenders, 405
  compared to parole, 404–405
  conditions for, 397–398
  decarceration and, 439
  defined, 14, 395, 405
  demographics of, 396–397
  diversion, 393–394
  in diversion programs, 510
  effectiveness of, 402–403
  eligibility for, 396
  as form of punishment, 361
  graduated sanctions, 401–402
  intensive supervision probation, 412
  intermittent incarceration, 395
  juveniles, 515
  as low-cost alternative, 394
  new models of, 402–403
  number of people under, 393, 395
  principles of, 397–398
  probation officer's supervisory role in,
    398–400
  recidivism and, 402–403
  revocation of, 397, 400–402
  sentencing and, 395–397
  shock probation, 395
  split sentence, 395

Probation (*Continued*)
  successful completion of, 400
  suspended sentence, 395
  timing of, 405
Probationary period, 147
Probationary release, 477
Probation officers
  authority of, 399–400
  career in, 399
  caseload and, 400
  investigating officers, 398
  line officers, 398
  presentence investigative report, 363
  role of, 398–400, 405
  supervisory role, 398–400
Problem-oriented policing
  focused deterrence, 193
  long-term solutions, 192
  SARA Model of, 193
Problem-solving courts, 262, 410–411
Procedural criminal law, 122–126
Procedural due process, 124–125
Product test, 116
Professionalism, 200
Professional model of policing, 139–140
Progressive era of policing, 139
Progressive movement, 427
Property bonds, 297
Property crime
  average length of sentence, 396
  defined, 8
Proposition 47, 440
Prosecuting attorney, 285
Prosecutorial waiver, 511
Prosecutors, 285–288
  assistant prosecutors, 286
  attorney general and, 285
  Brady rule, 285
  burden of proving guilt, 322–323
  case attrition, 301–304
  charging and, 304–305
  charging conference, 339
  closing arguments of, 338
  community pressures on, 287
  as crime fighter, 287–288
  deferred prosecution, 301–303
  direct examination of witnesses, 334
  discretion and, 285, 301–304
  double jeopardy, 341–342
  duties of, 285
  as elected official, 286
  establishing probable cause pretrial,
    299–300
  evidence and, 330
  fairness duty and, 285
  grand jury and, 300–301

hearsay, 335
information issued by, 300
jury selection, 324–329
office of, 285–286
opening statements, 330
organization of, 285
overcharging, 308
plea bargaining, 306, 364
police-prosecutor conflict, 287–288
power of, 285
preliminary hearing, 299–300
rebuttal, 337
redirect examination, 335
ritualized aggression, 276
screening process, 301–305
in sentencing process, 363
strict standard of proof, 322–323
victims and, 288
Prostitution, 8, 50, 74
Prostitution Reform Act, 74
Psychoanalytic theory, 45
Psychological theories of crime, 42–46
Psychology
  crime and, 45
  defined, 42
Psychotherapeutics, use of, in United
    States, 56
Public defenders
  attorney-client relationship, 292–293
  caseload of, 291
  defense counsel programs, 290–291
  defined, 289
  effectiveness of, 291–292
  eligibility issues, 290
  role of, 289
  Strickland standard, 291–292
Public order crime, 7
  average length of sentence, 396
Public policy
  choice theory and, 42
  life course theories and, 54, 56
  social conflict theory and, 51
  social process theory and, 52–53
  social structure theory and, 49
  trait theory and, 46
Public prosecutors, 285–288. *See also*
    Prosecutors
Public relations, counterterrorism
    strategies and, 145
Public trust, of police and racial issues, 25
Public utility, Internet as, 549
Punishment
  cruel and unusual punishment, 376–377
  death penalty, 374–384
  forms of, 360–362
  goals of, 40, 41

intermediate sanctions, 409–416
probation as, 395

Q
Qualified immunity, 204
Questions of fact, 259
Questions of law, 259
Quotas, 149

R
Race
  bias in policing, 204–206
  consequences of high incarceration
    rate and, 440–441
  crime trends and, 86–88
  death penalty and, 382
  homicide and, 86
  incarceration and, 29
  issues of, and public trust, 25
  jury selection and, 327–328
  prison violence and, 464
  racial threat theory, 50–51
  reasonable suspicion and, 234–235
  risk of victimization and, 83
  sentencing and, 366–368
  social conflict theory and, 50–51
Racial profiling, 18
  defined, 234
  immigration and, 234–235
  S.B. 1070 and, 235
Racial threat theory, 50–51
Racketeer Influenced and Corrupt
    Organizations Act (RICO), 411, 550
Racketeering, 550
Radial design, 433, 434
Random patrol, 187–188
Ransomware, 529
Rape, 7
  affirmative consent policies, 91
  chastity requirement, 333
  as common crime against women, 89
  crime statistics and, 80
  defined, 76
  by juveniles, 500
  pressure cycling and untested rape
    kits, 288
  prisons and, 463–464
  rape shield laws, 334
  rate of in UCR compared to NCVS, 80
  statutes of limitations for, 345
  statutory rape, 111
  in women's prisons, 476
Rape shield laws, 334
Rational choice theory, 41
Reactive arrests, 189
Real evidence, 330

Real offense, 364
Real-time crime centers (RTCCs), 142–143
Reasonable bail, 296
Reasonable doubt, 322–323
    creating, in defendant's case, 336
    juveniles and, 495
Reasonable force, 198
Reasonable suspicion
    frisk, 234
    race and, 234–235
    Terry case and, 232
    totality of the circumstances, 232–233
Rebuttal, 337
Recidivism, 28
    educational programs and, 461
    juveniles and, 517
Recidivism, probation, 402–403
Recklessness, 108–109
Recruitment, of police officers, 145–148,
    149–150
Red flagging, 542–543
Redirect examination, 335
Reentry programs, 28
Referral, 508
Reform era of policing, 139–140, 175
Regulation
    defined, 549
    as source of criminal law, 103–104
    white-collar crime, 548–550
Regulatory agencies, 103–104
Rehabilitation
    boot camp and, 413
    courts and, 256
    criticism of, by Martinson, 427–428
    day reporting centers, 412
    indeterminate sentencing and,
        358–359, 360
    parole and, 360
    Pennsylvania and first penitentiary,
        425–426
    prison programs and, 460–462
    Progressives and, 427
    as purpose of sentencing, 356
    reintegration through community
        corrections, 393
    trait theory and, 46
Rehabilitation model for prisons, 428
Reid Technique, 244
Reintegration, community
    corrections, 393
Reintegration model for prisons, 428
Relapse process, 479
Relative deprivation, 463
Release on recognizance, 298
Relevant evidence, 332
Remote-controlled attacks, 535

Research Network on Adolescent
    Development and Juvenile
    Justice, 498
Residency laws, 482
Residential centers, 15
Residential treatment programs, 515–516
Resident youth worker, 516
Response times
    to 911 calls, 186
    defined, 186
    differential response strategy, 186
    efficiency and, 186
Responsibility
    civil law and, 71
    criminal, 115–119
Restitution
    defined, 357
    as form of punishment, 361–362
    goal of restorative justice, 357
    in pretrial diversion program, 510
    victims and, 81
Restorative justice
    apologies and, 362
    compensating victims, 356, 358
    components of, 357
    as form of punishment, 356–358, 361–362
    intermediate sanctions and diversion, 411
    listening to victim, 357, 358
    restitution and, 361–362
    victim-offender dialogue (VOD), 358
Retribution, as purpose of sentencing, 353
Revenge, 353
Revenge porn, 526
Reverse discrimination, 149
Reverse transfer, 511
Reviewing court, 262
Revocation, of probation, 397, 400–402
Revocation hearing, 401
Revocation sentencing, 401
Riots, prison, 463
Risk assessment
    defined, 62
    domestic violence and, 62
    sentencing and, 62
Robbery
    defined, 7, 76
    gangs and, 506
    by juveniles, 500
    sentencing disparity, 367
Rochester (New York) Police Department
    (RPD), 150
Role models, value of, 47–48
Routine activities theory, 82–83
Rule of four, 266
Rule of law, 101
Rural programs, 516

S
Sacramento Police Department, 189
San Diego Police Department, 175
San Quentin, 433
SARA Model of problem-oriented
    policing, 193
Satellite monitoring, privacy and, 221–222
S.B. 1070, 235
Schizophrenia, crime and, 44
School-Resource Officers (SROs), 518
Schools
    bullying, 502–503
    gunshot detectors in schools, 502
    police in, 518
    safe schools, 501
    school shooting, 518
    violence in, 501–502
    zero tolerance policies, 501–502
Scientific method, 39–40
Scotland, conflict avoidance, 199
Screening process, 302–304
Search(es). *See also* Search and seizure
    automobiles, 226–228
    cell phones, 230–231
    with consent, 225
    defined, 221
    incidental to arrest, 224
    knock and talk strategy, 225
    private search doctrine, 221
Search and seizure, 220–231
    automobiles, 226–228
    blood used in drunk driving cases, 225
    cell phones, 230–231
    with consent, 225
    digital devices on border, 225
    drug-sniffing dog searches, 216, 217
    electronic surveillance, 229–230
    exclusionary rule, 219–220
    good faith exception, 220
    of home over absent resident
        objection, 225
    incidental to arrest, 224
    inevitable discovery exception, 219–220
    knock and talk strategy, 225
    plain view doctrine, 228–229
    reasonableness during, 223–224
    role of privacy in, 221–222
    thermal imagers and, 228–229
    unreasonable, 123, 216, 217
    without warrant, 224–226
Search warrants
    cell phones, 231
    defined, 222
    electronic surveillance, 229
    example of, 223
    exceptions to requirements for, 226

Search warrants (*Continued*)
    particularity requirements, 222–223
    probable cause and, 222
    purpose of, 222
    search and seizure without, 224–226
Second Amendment, 23
Secondary policing, 163
Second Chance Pell Pilot program, 462
Secret Service, 14
    fighting cyber crime, 537
    under Homeland Security, 157, 159
    responsibilities of, 157, 159
Secure Communities (S-COMM)
        program, 164
Securities and Exchange Commission
        (SEC), 549
Securities fraud, 548
Security. *See* National security; Private
        security
Security Housing Unit, 435
Security threat group (STG), 465–466
Securus Technologies, 443
Seizure. *See also* Search and seizure
    categories of items for, 222–223
    defined, 222
    as element of arrest, 236
    plain view doctrine, 228–229
Selective incapacitation, 356
Self-accountability, 202
Self-control theory, 54
Self-defense
    as defense, 120–121, 337
    defined, 120
    duty to retreat, 120–121
    stand your ground law, 121, 127
Self-incrimination
    booking and, 246
    confession as, 239
    privilege against, 321–322
    witnesses, 321–322
Self-reported surveys, 79–80
Sentences/sentencing, 352–384
    average length of, 396
        vs. time served, 359
    community service and, 409
    crack cocaine sentencing, 368
    determinate, 359
    discrimination in, 366–369
    disparity in, 366
    factors in
        judicial philosophy, 364
        mitigating and aggravating
            circumstances, 364–365
        real offense, 364
        seriousness of crime, 364
    fines, 409, 410

forfeiture, 409
forms of punishment, 360–362
good time, 359–360
growth in prison population and,
        437–438
guidelines, 369–371
indeterminate, 358–359
individualized justice and judge,
        360–362
intermediate sanctions, 409
juveniles, 514
philosophies of
    deterrence, 353–354
    incapacitation, 355–356
    rehabilitation, 356
    restorative justice, 356–358
    retribution, 353
plea bargaining and, 307–309
presentence investigative report, 363
pretrial diversion programs, 409, 410
probation and, 395–397
process of, 363
reform, 369–374
restitution, 409
revocation, 401
risk assessment and, 62
split sentence, 395
structure of
    administrative authority, 360
    judicial authority, 360–362
    legislative authority, 358–360
suspended sentence, 395
truth-in-sentencing laws, 359–360,
        437–438
Sentencing discrimination, 366–369
Sentencing disparity, 366
    defined, 366
    federal vs. state courts, 366
    geographic disparities, 366
Sentencing guidelines
    federal, 371
    grid for, 369–370
    habitual offender laws, 372
    judicial departures from, 371
    mandatory, 371–373
    state, 369–371
    three-strikes laws, 372
Sentencing reform, 369–374
    departure, 371
    mandatory sentencing guidelines,
        372–373
    sentencing guidelines, 369–371
    victim impact evidence, 373
Sentencing Reform Act (SRA), 368,
        371, 438
Separate confinement, 426

September 11, 2001 terrorist attacks
    homeland security movement and, 25–27
    local police department and
        anti-terrorism efforts, 144
Sequestration, 339–340
Service provided by police, 136
Seventh Amendment, trial by jury, 323
Sex offender notification law, 482–483
Sex offenders
    civil confinement, 483
    conditions of release, 482
    fear of, 481–482
    Megan's Law, 482
    recidivism rate, 481–482
    release of, 481–483
    residency laws, 482
    sex offender notification law, 482–483
Sextortion, 526
Sexual assault. *See also* Rape
    affirmative consent policies, 91
    college students and, 70–71, 91
    Cosby effect, 345
    defined, 7
    pressure cycling and untested rape
        kits, 288
    sentencing disparity, 367
    statistical measurement of, 70–71
    statutes of limitations for, 345
Sexual harassment, of female police
        officers, 151–152
Shakedowns, 201
Shared Responsibility Committees, 145
Sheriffs
    county law enforcement and, 12
    defined, 154
    jail administration by, 446–448
    vs. local police departments, 154
    number of departments, 154
    political aspect of, 154
    size and responsibility of departments,
        154–155
Shifts, 176
Shock incarceration, 395
    boot camp programs, 413
    defined, 412
    value of, 413
Shock probation, 395, 515
Showups, 245
SHU (security housing unit) syndrome,
        435, 436
Signal app, 9
Simple assault, 77
Sing Sing, 433
Sixth Amendment, 124, 126
    cross-examination and, 334
    death penalty, 378

defense attorneys and, 289
impartial jury, 320
interrogation, 240
jurisdiction and cyber crime, 538
pretrial detention and, 294
showups and photo arrays, 246
speedy trial and, 319–320
trial by jury, 323
Sixth sense, 173
Skimming, 531
Smoking, deaths from, 74
Social conflict theories, 49–51
Social disorganization theory, 46–48
disorganized zones, 47
drug use and, 57
stages of, 47
value of role models, 47–48
Socialization, 194
Social media
background check using, 146
crowdsourcing terrorism, 26
police department's use of, 145
Social process theories, 51–53
control theory, 52–53
labeling theory, 52
learning theory, 51–52
public policy and, 52–53
Social psychology, 45
Social reality of crime, 50
Sociological theories of crime, 46–49
Soledad Prison, 464
Solitary confinement, 484
South Dakota's 24/7 Sobriety Project, 403
Spam, 532
Span of control, 176
Spear phishing, 532
Special prosecution, 286
Specialty courts, 262
Specific deterrence, 354
Speech, freedom of
national security and, 544–546
true threat exception, 5, 533–534
Speedy trial, 319–320
Speedy Trial Act, 320
Split sentence probation, 395
Spoils system, 139
Stalking
as common crime against women, 89
cyberstalking, 533–534
Stand your ground law, 121, 127
Stare decisis, 104
State attorney, 285
State court system, 14
court of appeal, 262–263
courts of limited jurisdiction, 261–262
in dual court system, 259–260

jurisdiction and, 257–258
magistrate courts, 261–262
organization of, 260–261
selection of judges, 269–270
sentencing disparity, 366
specialty courts, 262
state prisons for, 429
trial courts of general jurisdiction, 262
State government
federalism and, 12
police power and, 12
State law enforcement, 13–14
State police, 14
vs. highway patrol, 155–156
number of departments, 155
purpose of, 155
State statues, as source of criminal law, 103
Statewide Automated Victim Information
and Notification System (SAVIN), 82
Station, 176
Status offenders, 494
low-visibility decision making and, 508
treatment of girls, 500
Statute of limitations, 320, 321
for sex crimes, 345
Statutes, as source of criminal law, 102–103
Statutory law, 102–103
Statutory rape, 111
StingRay, 230–231
Stolen Valor Act, 265
Stop and frisk, 232–235
NYPD strategy, 247
Stop-and-identify laws, 233
Stops, 232–235
compared to arrest, 235, 236
defined, 233
length of time and, 233
pretextual, 227
reasonable suspicion, 232–233
Terry case and, 232
totality of the circumstances, 232–233
Strain theory, 48
Street gangs, 22
Stress, on-the-job pressures and, 196–197
Stressors, 196
Strickland standard, 291–292
Strict liability crimes, 110–111
Subculture. See Police subculture
Subculture theory, 48
Subject-matter jurisdiction, 259
Substance abuse
jail population and, 446
juvenile delinquency and, 504–505
treatment for, in prisons, 460–462
Substantial-capacity test (ALI/MPC)
test, 117

Substantive criminal law, 122
Substantive due process, 125
Suicide, physician-assisted, 11–12
Superego, 45
Supermax prison, 435–436
Supermax syndrome, 435–436
Supervisory accountability, 202
Supremacy clause, 103
Supreme Court, state, jurisdiction of, 257,
262–263
Supreme Court justices, 263–265
appointment and terms of, 269
Supreme Court of United States
cases heard by, 265–266
concurring opinions, 266
conference, 266
dissenting opinions, 266–267
in dual court system, 259–260
impact of, 263–264
as interpreter of law, 264–265
judicial review, 264
jurisdiction of, 257, 260, 265
oral arguments before, 266
process of reaching a decision, 266–267
rulings of
Allen Charge, 340
arrests, 236–238
attorney-client privilege exceptions, 294
automobile searches, 226–228
cell phone searches, 231
choice of defense attorney, 289
civil confinement law, 483
conspiracy, 114
cruel and unusual punishment,
376–377
death penalty, 375–383
deliberate indifference, 472–473
double jeopardy, 342
drug-sniffing dogs and probable
cause, 216, 217
due process and, 125
electronic surveillance, 229–230
entrapment, 122
exclusionary rule, 220
forfeiture, 411
frisks, 234
good faith exception, 220
guns and right to bear arms, 23
hands-off approach, 472
hate crime laws and, 113
identifiable human needs, 473
inevitable discovery exception,
219–220
initial appearance, 294
jury selection, 327–328
jury size, 320–321

Supreme Court of United States (*Continued*)
jury unanimity, 321
juveniles and, 495–496, 498
knock and announce rule, 238
Miranda warning, 239–241, 240–241
"papers, please" provision, 235
parole, 406
physician-assisted suicide, 11–12
plain view doctrine, 228–229
plea bargaining and, 305, 308
pretrial detainees, 445
preventive detention, 512
prisoners' rights, 472–473
prison segregation, 464
privacy, 221–222
probable cause, 217, 219
probation, 400–401
public defenders and, 289, 292
reasonable doubt standard, 322–323
reasonable search, 216, 217
rule of four, 266
satellite monitoring, 221–222
searches incidental to arrest, 224
searches with consent, 225
self-incrimination, 321–322
showups and photo arrays, 246
speedy trial, 319–320
stop-and-identify, 233
stops, 232–233
three-strikes laws, 372
totality of the circumstances, 232–233
use of force, 198–199
use of force by prison officials, 470–471
victim impact statements, 373
voluntary intoxication defense, 118
warrantless arrest, 238–239
writ of *certiorari*, 265–266
stare decisis and, 104
Supreme Court Reporter, 35
Surrebuttal, 337
Surveillance
defined, 540
Foreign Intelligence Surveillance Act (FISA), 540
foreign surveillance, 540, 544
mass surveillance, 542–544
Patriot Act, 541
Suspended sentence, 395
SWAT units, 143
Sweden, day-fines, 410
Switzerland, election of judges, 272
Sworn officers, 177
Symantec, 527, 536

T

Tactical camera spheres, 229
Target, 535
Tasers, 200
Tattoos, prison, 457
Tax evasion, 548
Technical violation, 400, 404–405
video visits for inmates, 443
Technology
Automatic License Plate Recognition (ALPR) technology, 230
biometrics, 21
body-worn cameras for officers, 172–173, 202–203
contraband cell phones in prison, 467
crime mapping, 189
crime registries, 483
CSI effect, 332
cyberbullying, 502
decrease in crime rate and use of, 85
DNA profiling, 21, 182–183
electronic monitoring, 414–415
facial recognition software, 21
GPS, 415
gunshot detectors in schools, 502
hacking the Internet of Things, 529
high-tech cop cars, 140
hot spot technologies, 142
intelligence-led policing and, 142
lie detectors, 268
mapping brain irregularities, 44
911 app, 187
polygraph tests in court, 268
pressure cycling and untested rape kits, 288
real-time crime centers (RTCCs), 142–143
reform era of policing and, 140
Statewide Automated Victim Information and Notification System (SAVIN), 82
tactical camera spheres, 229
thermal imagers, 228–229
unmanned aerial vehicles (UAVs), 105
wireless devices in courtroom, 340
Telegram app, 9
Telephone-pole design, 434
Television, violence on, and crime, 52
Temporary release, 477
Ten percent cash bail, 298
Tenth Amendment, 102
Terrorism
counterterrorism strategies
Antiterrorism and Effective Death Penalty Act (AEDPA), 540
encryption battles, 551
foreign surveillance, 540, 544
fusion centers, 144
intelligence-led policing, 144–145
local police department and anti-terrorism efforts, 144
mass surveillance, 542–544
metadata surveillance, 27
Patriot Act, 541
public relations and, 145
security vs. privacy, 27
Shared Responsibility Committees, 145
undercover operations, 26–27
crowdsourcing, 26
cyber-recruiting, 535
cyber terror, 9
defined, 26
domestic, 26
entrapment issues, 180
known wolves, 545
material support for, 540, 545
preventive policing and domestic terrorism, 180
remote-controlled attacks, 535
terrorist Internet recruiting operations, 545–546
terrorist watch list and due process, 126
Testimony
defined, 330
as evidence, 331
Testosterone, aggression and, 43
Theft
cyber, 531–532
defined, 76
gangs and, 506
identity, 531
as misdemeanor or felony, 112
motor vehicle, 8
as property crime, 8
Theory. *See* Crime theories
Thermal imagers, 228–229
Thirteenth Amendment, prisoners' rights, 472
ThreatData, 536
Three-strikes laws, 372
Thrill offenders, 41
Time served, 445
Tokenism, 150–151
Topeka Correctional Facility, 434
Tort, 71
Total institution, 457
Totality of the circumstances, 232–233
Touch DNA, 183
Tours, 176
Tower guards, 469
Trace evidence, 181
Traditional jail design, 448

Traffic laws, 106
Training schools, 516–517
Trait theory, 42, 46
Transportation Security Administration (TSA), 159
Treasury Department, 157, 162
Trial court administrator, 328
Trial courts
    defined, 259
    jurisdiction and, 259
Trial judges
    administrative role of, 269
    roles and responsibilities of, 267–268
    before trial, 267–268
    during trial, 268
Trials
    bench, 320
    change of venue, 322
    elements of
        appeals, 341–343
        closing arguments, 338
        cross-examination, 334–335
        defendant's case, 336–337
        jury deliberation, 339–340
        jury instructions, 339
        motion for a directed verdict, 336
        opening statements, 330
        overview of steps in, 329
        prosecution's case, 333–334
        rebuttal and surrebuttal, 337
        role of evidence, 330–333
        verdict, 340–341
    jury selection, 323–329
    pleading guilty, 305–310
    pretrial procedures
        establishing probable cause, 299–300
        grand jury, 300–301
        pleading guilty, 305–309
        preliminary hearing, 299–300
        pretrial detention, 294–299
        prosecutorial screening process, 301–305
    special features of criminal trials, 319–323
        presumption of innocence, 322
        privilege against self-incrimination, 321–322
        role of jury, 320–321
        speedy trial, 319–320
        strict standard of proof, 322–323
    speedy, 319–320
    statute of limitations, 320, 321
    steps leading to, 295, 329
Tribal jurisdiction, 258, 278
Trojans, 529
Trolling, 4

True threat exception, 5, 533–534
Truth-in-sentencing laws, 359–360
    increased length of prison terms, 437–438
    mandatory release and, 408
Twin studies, 42
Two Rivers Correctional Institution, 434–435

U
UCR. *See* Uniform Crime Report (UCR)
Unconscious, 45
Undercover officers, 179
Uniform Code of Military Justice, 259
Uniform Crime Report (UCR), 75–77, 135
    compared to NCVS, 79
    compared to NIBRS, 78
    defined, 75
    discretionary distortions in, 77–78
    information based on, 75
    juvenile delinquency and, 499–500
    Part I offenses, 75, 76–77
    Part II offenses, 77
    underreporting crime, 77
United States Reports, 35
Universal jurisdiction, 259
Unmanned aerial vehicles (UAVs), 105
USA Freedom Act, 27
USA Patriot Act. *See* Patriot Act
Use of force. *See* Force
Use of force matrix, 198
U.S. Coast Guard, 156, 159
U.S. Marshals Service
    creation of, 162
    responsibilities of, 157, 162

V
Vehicles, searches of, 226–228
Venire, 325
Verdict, 340–341
    motion for a directed verdict, 336
Vertical overcharging, 308
Veterans courts, 262
Victim advocates, 82
Victim impact statement, 373
Victimization
    mental illness as risk factor for, 91
    repeat, 83
    risks of, 82–83
Victimless crimes, 8
Victim-offender dialogue (VOD), 358
Victims of crime, 80–83
    chastity requirement, 333
    civil lawsuits brought by, 342
    compensating, 356, 358
    creating reasonable doubt about credibility, 336

evidence of victim's behavior, 333
    impact evidence and sentencing, 373
    listening to, 357, 358
    Native Americans as, 278
    parole and rights of, 408–409
    plea bargaining and, 306–307
    prosecutors and, 288
    repeat victimization, 83
    restorative justice, 356–358
    rights of
        enforceability of, 81
        informed, present and heard rights, 80–81
        legal rights of, 80–81
        political strength of, 29
        prosecutors and, 288
        restitution, 81
    risks of victimization, 82–83
    routine activities theory, 82–83
    services for, 81–82
    Statewide Automated Victim Information and Notification System (SAVIN), 82
    surveys of, 78–79
    uncooperative, 303
    unreliable, 303
    victim-offender connection, 82
    victim-offender dialogue (VOD), 358
    of white-collar crime, 548
    women as, 89
Victims of Crime Act, 358
Victims' Rights Amendment, 124
Victim surveys, 78–79
Video games, violence in, and crime, 52, 53
Video surveillance, 230
Violence
    corporate violence, 549
    in prisons, 462–466
    in schools, 501–502
    on television and crime, 52
Violent crimes
    average length of sentence, 396
    categories of, 7
    decline in rate of, 84–85
    defined, 7
    increase in rate of, 85
    juveniles, 500
    mental illness and risk factors for, 90–91
Virus, 529
Visa, 157–158
Vocational training, for prisoners, 461
Voir dire, 325–327
Volkswagen, 548–549
Voluntary manslaughter, 109–110
Voting rights, felons and, 449

W

Waiver
    automatic, 511
    judicial, 511
    legislative, 511
    prosecutorial, 511
Walnut Street Jail, 425–426
Warden, 430–431
War on crime, 137
Warrantless arrest, 238–239
Warrants
    arrests with, 236–238
    arrests without, 238–239
    defined, 217
Warrior gene, 42–43
Warrior mentality, 143–144
Washington, D.C. Police Department, 154
Weapons crimes, increase in prison
    population, 437
Wedding cake model of criminal
    justice, 319
Western House of Refuge, 50
Western Penitentiary, 426
White-collar crime, 547–550
    characteristics of, 547
    corporate violence, 549
    by corporations, 548–549
    defined, 8, 547
    examples of, 547
    law enforcement and, 549–550
    regulating and policing, 548–550
    techniques used in, 547–548
    victims of, 548

Wickersham Commission, 139
Wickr app, 9
Widen the net, 415–416
Wikileaks, 539
Willful wrongdoing, 353
Wilmington (Delaware) Police
    Department, 135
Witnesses
    competence and reliability of, 334
    cross-examination of, 334–335
    direct examination of, 334
    expert, 331
    Fifth amendment, 321–322
    genetic witness, 184
    granted immunity, 322
    hearsay, 335
    lay, 331
    redirect examination, 335
    self-incrimination, 321–322
Women
    chivalry effect, 368–369
    common crimes against, 89
    as correctional officers, 471–472
    crime and, 88–89
    as crime victims, 89
    girls in gangs, 506
    girls in juvenile justice system, 500–501
    increasing number incarcerated, 438
    as judges, 272–273
    jury selection, 328
    as law enforcement officers, 148–152
    in prison, 474–476
    on probation, 397

    rise in arrest rate, 88–89
    sentencing discrimination,
        368–369
Women's prisons
    characteristics of inmates, 474–475
    health problems and, 475
    history of abuse, 474
    motherhood problems, 475
    pseudo-family, 476
    rape in, 476
    violence in, 476
Work detail supervisors, 469
Work release programs, 15, 480
Worm, 529
Writ of *certiorari*, 265–266
Writ of *habeas corpus*, 344
Wrongful convictions, 201
    causes of, 343–344
    defined, 342
    DNA evidence and, 343

Y

Yahoo, 8
Yard officers, 469
Youth camps, 517
Youth development centers, 517
Youth gangs, 505–507

Z

Zero-day vulnerability, 535–536
Zero-tolerance arrest policy, 191
    crime rate decline and, 84
Zero-tolerance theory, 137